CHRISTMAS IN THE KORAN

CHRISTMAS IN THE KORAN

Luxenberg, Syriac, and the Near Eastern and Judeo-Christian Background of Islam

Edited by Ibn Warraq

Prometheus Books
59 John Glenn Drive
Amherst, New York 14228

Cover design by Nicole Sommer-Lecht

Inquiries should be addressed to
Prometheus Books
59 John Glenn Drive
Amherst, New York 14228
VOICE: 716-691-0133
FAX: 716-691-0137
WWW.PROMETHEUSBOOKS.COM

18 17 16 15 14 5 4 3 2 1

Library of Congress Cataloging-in-Publication Data

Christmas in the Koran: Luxenberg, Syriac, and the Near Eastern and Judeo-Christian background of Islam / edited by Ibn Warraq.
pages cm
Includes bibliographical references.
ISBN 978-1-61614-937-6 (hardback)
1. Jesus Christ—Nativity. 2. Jesus Christ—In the Qur'an. 3. Luxenberg, Christoph. 4. Islam—Sources. I. Ibn Warraq
BP134.J37C47 2014
297.2'465—dc23

2014007264

Printed in the United States of America

For

Elisabeth, Gerd, and Markus

Contents

Appendixes

Preface and Acknowledgements

The present volume would surely not have been possible without the help of two friends, Markus Gross and Dr. Elisabeth Puin. Markus Gross was able to proofread and format the entire book of over eight hundred pages to meet the house style requirements of Prometheus Books so that it could be ready to be sent to the printers in just a few weeks. To say that I am truly beholden to Dr. Markus Gross is an understatement.

Dr. Elisabeth Puin has translated six intimidating articles by Anton Baumstark for the present volume. Anyone at all familiar with Baumstark's German literary style will know immediately what a harrowing task it is to simply understand it. Even a native German speaker struggles with it. Dr. Puin has provided us with analytical, lucid, and elegant translations into English, even though it is not her mother tongue. Baumstark was an original scholar of immense learning, and the contents, arguments, and conclusions of his articles, I believe, will come as a revelation for many Islamologists.

I should like to thank Robert Kerr for his help in all matters linguistic. I also thank Christoph Luxenberg for his forbearance, and tolerance for my ignorance, during the long hours spent painstakingly correcting and revising the translations from the German of his articles. His additions to the essays mean that the latter contain new arguments, analyses, and examples not to be found anywhere else.

I also wish to thank the in-house editor at Prometheus Books for his patience and professionalism.

Finally, it remains for me to stress that the opinions expressed, and any errors that persist, especially in the introduction, are entirely my responsibility.

Transliteration and Other Technical Matters

There is no universally accepted system of transliteration (transcription) of the Semitic scripts. The authors in this anthology use two different systems for the Arabic alphabet. As some editors in whose journals the articles first appeared insisted that we not change one single letter as a precondition for allowing us to reproduce them, I was unable to standardize all the articles and adopt just one system. However, the two systems are not that difficult to come to grips with. For Arabic they are:

(1) ʾ, b, t, th, j, ḥ, kh, d, dh, r, z, s, sh, ṣ, ḍ, ṭ, ẓ, ʿ, gh, f, q, k, l, m, n, h,w, y. *Short vowels*: a, u, i. *Long vowels*: ā, ū, ī

(2) ʾ, b, t, ṯ, ǧ, ḥ, ḫ, d, ḏ, r, z, s, š, ṣ, ḍ, ṭ, ẓ, ʿ, ġ, f, q, k, l, m, n, h, w, y. *Short vowels*: a, u, i. *Long vowels*: ā, ū, ī

The journal *Studia Islamica* uses and recommends system (1), the journal *Arabica* and most publications in German use system (2). On the whole I have used the latter system. Readers are also likely to encounter, though not often in this anthology, the following variations: dj for j, and ḳ for q, for example, in *EI*[2] [the second edition of *The Encyclopedia of Islam*].

For the Hebrew and Syriac, I use the following:

ʾ, b, g, d, h, w, z, ḥ, ṭ, y, k, l, m, n, s, ʿ, p, ṣ, q, r, ś/š, t, ḇ, ḏ, ḡ, p̄, ṯ, ḵ, ə, a, e, i, o, u, ā, ē, ī, o, ū, ᵃ, ᵉ, ⁱ, ᵒ, ᵘ

All long vowels are overlined. The small raised ᵉ stands for a hurried or neutral vowel. Underlined letters (as in bēṯ) are pronounced as fricatives, thus ṯ = English "th" as in "thin"; p̄ = "f" as in "five."

Right up to the 1930s, Western scholars used the edition of the Koran by Gustav Flügel (sometimes spelled Fluegel), *Corani Textus Arabicus* (1834), whose numbering of verses differs from what has now become the "official" or Standard Egyptian edition, first published in 1924. Again, not only was it obviously much easier for me to leave the original Flügel numbering in the pre-1924 article included in this anthology, but in some cases it was even essential not to interfere with the original numbering, since some pieces only referred to Flügel's edition. As one scholar reminded me, attempting to change the numbering would only have increased the possibility of further errors.

Transcription/Transliteration

Consonants

ا	alif	ʾ	ض	ḍād	ḍ
ب	bāʾ	b	ط	ṭāʾ	ṭ
ت	tāʾ	t	ظ	ẓāʾ	ẓ
ث	ṯāʾ	ṯ, th	ع	ʿayn	ʿ
ج	ǧīm	ǧ, j, dj	غ	ġayn	ġ, gh
ح	ḥāʾ	ḥ	ف	fāʾ	f
خ	ḫā	ḫ, kh, x	ق	qāf	q
د	dāl	d	ك	kāf	k
ذ	ḏāl	ḏ, dh	ل	lām	l
ر	rāʾ	r	م	mīm	m
ز	zāʾ	z	ن	nūn	n
س	sīn	s	ه	hāʾ	h
ش	šīn	š, sh	و	wāw	w
ص	ṣād	ṣ	ي	yāʾ	y

ء (hamza) – ʾ

Vowels

ا	ā, â	َ	fatḥa	a
و	ū	ُ	ḍamma	u
ى	ī	ِ	kasra	i

Dipthongs: aw, ay

آ	alif-madda	ʾā	لا	lām-alif lā
ة	tāʾ marbūṭa	-at-	ّ	shadda (doubling consonant)
ى	alif maqṣūra (pronounced like lenghtening alif) ā			

Part 1

Introduction

In Search of Avocado

IBN WARRAQ

For Classical Arabic there has long been a need for a new etymological dictionary in which Arabists would recognize, possibly for the first time, that there were other Semitic languages; this lacuna is being filled by a glacially slow appearance of the Wörterbuch der klassischen arabischen Sprache,[1] *which started with the letter k in 1970 and is already halfway through l.*

John Huehnergard[2]

Wa-qad daḫala fī ʿarabīyati ʾahli š-šaʾmi kaṯīrun mina s-suryānīyati kamā staʿmala ʿarabu l-ʿirāqi ʾašyāʾa mina l-fārisīya.
[A great deal of Syriac has pervaded the Arabic of the population of Syria, just as the Arabs of Iraq make use of Persian borrowings.]

Abū Bakr ibn Durayd (died 933)

1. Introduction

1.1. Background to Luxenberg's Thesis of a *Mischsprache*

When Christoph Luxenberg's *Die Syro-Aramäische Lesart des Koran* first came out in 2000, one of his theses that inspired incomprehension and even derision was his conclusion that the language of the Koran must have been a "*aramäisch-arabische Mischsprache,*"[3] that is an Aramaic-Arabic mixed or hybrid language. If we get away from the ideas imposed upon us by Islamic tradition, and instead heed the pleas of scholars such as John Wansbrough by placing the theatre of the rise of Islam and the compilation of the Koran in the Near East rather than the Arabian peninsula, then the importance of Syriac, and more generally, the Aramaic substratum not only in the formation of the Koran, but also of the Arabic language, can no longer be denied, since Syro-Aramaic or Syriac, in one form or another, was the language, in the words of Claude Gilliot and Pierre Larcher, "of written communication in the Near East from the second to the seventh centuries CE."[4]

Scholars in the field of New Testament Studies have been vigorously defending the idea that that the original language of the New Testament may well have been Syriac ever since at least[5] the seventeenth century, when that incomparable philosopher, Baruch Spinoza, put forward such a thesis, in

1670, in his extraordinarily influential work *Tractatus Theologico-Politicus* (*Theological-Political Treatise*),[6] which is seen by many as the beginning of Biblical Criticism. Spinoza wrote that "the native language of the Apostles is none other than Syriac" and then suggested, as Steven Nadler reminds us in his superb study of the *Tractatus,* that "what we have in the Gospels is a Greek translation of the Syriac original."

Nadler continues, "Spinoza also insists, earlier in the Treatise, that the language that is essential for making sense of the Christian Gospels is Hebrew, not Greek."[7] He then quotes Spinoza's observation:

> Because all the authors, both of the Old and the New, were Hebrews, it is certain that the History of the Hebrew language is necessary above all others, not only for understanding the books of the Old Testament, which were written in this language, but also for understanding those of the New Testament. For although they have been made common to all in other languages, nevertheless they express themselves in a Hebrew manner.[8]

In other words, even the New Testament contains Hebraisms. In which case, it is not such a stretch to conjecture that the Koran may also contain, if not Hebraisms, at least Syriacisms. Before I come back to the Koran I wish to explore further the work of Biblical Scholars on Syriac and the New Testament, since their work, I believe, can teach us much about the Syriac background to the Koran, and their methodology can perhaps be fruitful for Koranic Studies.

1.2. New Testament Studies

Matthew Black (1908–1994), who was Professor of Divinity and Biblical Criticism at the University of St. Andrews, and the first editor of the journal *New Testament Studies*, published in 1946 his work that is now considered a classic,[9] *An Aramaic Approach to the Gospels and Acts.*[10] Black calls his approach "linguistic," and he begins by surveying the linguistic situation in first-century Palestine, when four languages were to be found flourishing:

> Greek was the speech of the educated "hellenized" classes and the medium of cultural and commercial intercourse between Jew and foreigner; Latin was the language of the army of occupation and, to judge from Latin borrowings in Aramaic, appears also to some extent to have served the purposes of commerce, as it no doubt also did of Roman law; Hebrew, the sacred tongue of the Jewish Scriptures, continued to provide the lettered Jew with an important means of literary expression and was cultivated as a spoken tongue in the learned coteries of the Rabbis; Aramaic was the language of the people of the land and, together with Hebrew, provided the chief literary medium of the Palestinian Jew of the first century; Josephus wrote his *Jewish War* in Aramaic and later translated it into Greek.

"If," continues Black,

> Jesus was a Galilean Rabbi, it is not unlikely that He made use of Hebrew as well as Aramaic, especially . . . in His formal disputations with the Pharisees. . . . In the Palestinian Talmud Aramaic and Hebrew are found together, sometimes in the form of a kind of *Mischsprache*, sentences half Hebrew, half Aramaic, are familiar to the reader of the Talmud, and this artificial language, rabbinical in origin, may well have been in use before as after the Fall of Jerusalem. [My emphasis, I.W.]

Here we have the use of the term *Mischsprache*, fifty-four years before Luxenberg's own usage.[11] Black further argues,

> The Gospels were written in a predominantly hellenistic environment, and they were written in Greek. But Greek was was not the native language of their central Figure, nor of the earlier apostles, if it was not unfamiliar to them. Jesus must have conversed in the Galilean dialect of Aramaic, and His teaching was probably almost entirely in Aramaic. At the basis of the Greek Gospels, therefore, there must lie a Palestinian Aramaic tradition, at any rate of the sayings and teaching of Jesus, and this tradition must at one time have been translated from Aramaic into Greek. Some have thought that the Evangelists themselves were the translators of these Aramaic sources of the Gospels; they certainly must have utilized, if they did not themselves translate, early translation sources. The "Aramaic problem" of the Gospels is to determine, by internal evidence, to what extent the Greek Gospels are written in or embody "translation Greek" or how much Aramaic influence can be detected in them.[12]

At this stage, Black adds Syriac into the mix,

> but Aramaic, other than Jewish Palestinian, may have influenced the Evangelists' work and the early transmission of the Gospels in Greek. Syriac was widely spoken and written, especially in Antioch, the first great Christian centre, and there is a respectable tradition that St. Luke was a native of that city. If the third Evangelist was a "Syrian of Antioch," he was probably bilingual, with Syriac as his second language. Moreover, Palestinian Jewish Aramaic was a dialect little known outside of Palestine: much of the Palestinian Aramaic Gospel tradition may have passed through the more familiar medium of Syriac before it was finally written down in Greek. The influence of Syriac, therefore, as well as of Jewish Palestinian Aramaic, may have contributed to the shaping of the Gospel Greek.[13]

Taking both a linguistic and textual approach, Black examines the grammar, syntax, and vocabulary of the Gospels to ferret out what may be Aramaisms, Syriacisms, or, more generally Semitisms. More precisely, he looks at the style and structure of the sentence: order of words, Casus Hyperbaton, and the distribution of Asyndeton; then at the Aramaic subordinate clause. In chapter 6 he examines the Aramaic influence on grammar and vocabulary: the definite article, the pronoun, preposition, verb, and vocabulary. In part 3 Black looks at Semitic poetic form: that is, the formal element of Semitic poetry in the Gospels: for example, parallelism of lines and clauses, alliteration, assonance, and paronomasia. In part 4, Black addresses the question of translation of Aramaic, surveying synoptic variants from Aramaic, and also mistranslation and interpretation of Aramaic, and finally Aramaic as a cause of textual variants. Matthew Black's survey of the results has much to teach us; it

> yields one conclusion only which can be regarded as in any degree established, that an Aramaic sayings-source or tradition lies behind the Synoptic Gospels [i.e., Matthew, Mark, and Luke]. Where any one Semitic or Aramaic construction could be observed recurring, its distribution showed that it tended to be found most frequently, and sometimes exclusively, in the Words of Jesus. The same conclusion emerged from a study of the translation and mistranslation of Aramaic in the Gospels. . . . [The main impression remains] that we have to do with a translation-tradition, sometimes literal, mostly, however, literary and interpretative, but generally bearing the stamp upon it, in one feature or another, of its Aramaic origin. Whether that source was written or oral, it is not possible from the evidence to decide. . . .
>
> In [Luke], apart from the sayings of Jesus, there are far fewer indications of Aramaic influence, The asyndeton openings, λέγει, λέγουσι, [says, they say], characteristic of the first Gospel, though Aramaic in origin, are more likely to be a feature of Matthew's Jewish Greek style than an indication of source. Similarly, Luke's temporal conjunction, ἐν αὐτῇ τῇ ὥρᾳ [Luke 10:21; 12:12; 13:31; 20:19: *en autē té hóra* : *In the same hour*, or *at that very time*], need not imply the use of sources; it may be a Lucan Aramaism or Syriacism. The hymns embodied in the Infancy narrative are thoroughly Semitic, but not necessarily translations, though the observation of word-play when we render them in Aramaic strongly supports the translation hypothesis. In the narrative peculiar to Luke of the Emmaus Appearance it is very probable that the Greek text of Luke in WH [editor's note: Edition of New Testament by Westcott & Hort, 1881] mistranslates an Aramaic adjective in XXIV:32.[14]

Black further asks,

> What of the Fourth Gospel? Is it a translation of an Aramaic document, as Burney maintained?[15] How far is the linguistic evidence adduced by Burney, which certainly proves a strong Aramaic element, capable of proving more than that St. John is written in "Aramaized" Greek, the work perhaps of an Aramaic-speaking writer with Greek as his second language? The evidence by which translation can be most convincingly demonstrated is that of

> mistranslation. When all other explanations are considered and evidence weighed, there remains a residuum of such evidence where, if the element of conjecture cannot be eliminated altogether, it may nevertheless be said that alternative suggestions are inferior as explanations.

Noted Semitist and Assyriologist, G. R. Driver (1892–1975), quoted by Black, puts forward a theory for the Fourth Gospel which is the corresponding theory concerning the Koran put forward by Luxenberg. Here is Black again:

> Nevertheless, it is possible that an Aramaic sayings-tradition may have been utilized by John, most probably in early Greek translation sources. A not dissimilar conclusion was reached by G. R. Driver, who, while rejecting the theory of an Aramaic documentary source, thought that the evidence supported the hypothesis that John "was mentally translating, as he wrote, logia handed down by tradition and current in Christian circles in Aramaic, from that language into Greek in which he was actually composing his Gospel."[16]

Again, Black's observations concerning what he calls "Translation Greek" seem to me to be of the greatest interest and relevance for Islamology and Koranic Studies. If we take seriously the notion of the Gospels being "translated" into Greek, in some sense, where Aramaic sources were employed, then we must look at the character of the Greek "translation." Black concludes,

> The Greek Evangelists or the first Greek translators of the Gospels have not simply transmitted a tradition unaltered: they have interpreted a tradition originally circulating in one language, Aramaic, and composed in more or less literary Greek the results of their interpretation. All translation involves interpretation, but the Gospels are not just the interpretation of translators; they are also Targum[17] of the Evangelists. The consequence is that, in the transmission of the Teaching of Jesus, the end-product in Greek is often less the mind of Jesus than the ideas and interpretation of the Greek Evangelists.[18]

Black then draws attention to a feature that has taken on greater significance since the work of Günter Lüling, as we shall see in a moment: Semitic poetic form to be found in the Gospels.

> That the sayings of Jesus were cast originally in poetic form has for long been well-known, In *his Poetry of Our Lord*, Burney[19] drew attention to such features as parallelism, rhythmic structure, and even rhyme which could be detected in the underlying Aramaic of the Words of Jesus. But such characteristic features of Semitic poetry are also to be found in the hymns of Luke, in the sayings of the Baptist, and perhaps even in several non-dominical sayings in the Gospels. The most striking and one of the most characteristic features of all Semitic poetry is paronomasia,[20] together with its associated alliteration

> and assonance. When the sayings of Jesus and especially the longer connected passages are turned into simple Aramaic many examples of paronomasia, alliteration and assonance come to light. Paronomasia in particular appears to have been a regular feature of the style and teaching of our Lord in His native Aramaic. It has for the most part disappeared in the Greek Gospels.[21]

Günter Lüling put forward, first in 1974 and then in greater detail in 2003,[22] the thesis that

> considerable parts of the Koran text itself were pre-Islamic Christian strophic hymns, most probably predating by about 200 years the emergence of Islam, and quite obviously originally a real pre-Islamic Christian Koran, written in a vernacular Arabic, were reworked and reinterpreted by the earliest Islamic collectors and editors of the Koran text. The original strophic structure, with what were once regular rhymes, was intentionally destroyed and turned into continuous classical Arabic prose, the original content often being reversed into its diametrical opposite.[23]

Lüling acknowledged that his thesis was but the development of the work of such scholars as David Heinrich Müller, Rudolf Geyer, and Karl Vollers.[24]

Discussing the issue of texts and textual criticism, Black, making an explicit reference to the Koran, points out that

> in the earliest periods these writings in use in Church and Synagogue were subject to the most radical changes and alterations in both their subject-matter and text, with little regard for the author's original work. As far as the substance and contents of the Gospels are concerned, we have no reason to believe that they have suffered in any material way. . . . But while the tradition in this respect remained constant, its form in text and language went through the same stages of historical development as the Hebrew and Greek Old Testaments, the Aramaic Targums, or the *Qoran* [my emphasis, I.W.]. An early period of a "fluid text" with different "editions" varying in form and language, if substantially the same message and import, circulated in different localities. It was not till some degree of ecclesiastical unity was achieved over sufficiently wide areas that standard or Vulgate texts took place of the local Gospels and finally superseded them.[25]

The Koran text, in other words, like the Old and New Testament texts, has a history. For that matter, any text must be explicated by what Maxime Rodinson once called "the normal mechanisms of human history".

2. Precursors of Matthew Black

2.1. Fifth Century to Eighteenth Century

Matthew Black was of course not the first scholar to talk of the Aramaic substrate in the Greek Gospels, for even before Spinoza there were the works, published in 1650, of Kaspar Wyss, professor of Greek in Zurich until his death in 1659, as well as those published in 1658 of Johann Vorst (1623–1658), a German philologist and rector of a college in Berlin.[26]

Elliott C. Maloney reminds us that as early as the fifth century Christian writers found the Greek of the New Testament strange, and certainly "different from that of the Classical Greek authors, and even from the literary Hellenistic Greek used by Polybius, Epictetus, and Plutarch."[27] Isidore of Pelusium (died before 449 or 436), for instance, wrote that

> the Greeks . . . despise the divine Scripture [i.e., the New Testament] as barbarous language, and composed of foreign-sounding words, abandoning necessary conjunctions, and confusing the mind with the addition of extraordinary words.[28]

During the rediscovery of Antiquity of the Renaissance,

> scholars studying the biblical languages found that New Testament Greek was full of problems caused by the influence of a Semitic language they considered to be Hebrew.[29]

For instance, Sebastien Castellion (1515–1563), French preacher of tolerance and liberty of conscience, wrote in the preface to *Biblia Sacra* (Basel, 1551), that

> one should know that the New Testament was written in such a way that its diction be Hebraic . . . [for] the Apostles were Hebrews by birth, and they hebraized when writing a foreign, that is, the Greek language.

Erasmus (1466–1536) made a similar point, noting that "although the Apostles write in Greek, nevertheless they convey much from the peculiarity of their own language [Hebrew]."[30]

Theodore Beza (1519–1605), important French Protestant theologian, in his notes on the New Testament demonstrated that its books are filled with Hebraisms.[31] Joachim Camerarius (1500–1574), German Classical scholar, came to the same conclusion.[32] Isaac Casaubon (1559–1614), in

> his notes on the New Testament, written while he was only in his twenties, paid close attention to what he took as "Hebraisms": Greek words and phrases used in senses that derived from the Hebrew Old Testament.[33]

Edward Lively (died 1605), a professor of Hebrew at Cambridge, wrote several learned works on the Old Testament, indicating "an execellent grasp of Hebrew and uncommon familiarity with rabbinic writings."[34]

However, as Grafton and Weinberg point out,

> when Lively read the Greek of the Gospels—especially when he encountered expressions of time—he heard undertones that his predecessors had missed. He vividly sensed the presence of Hebrew and Aramaic beneath the Greek, and he used Jewish texts to identify the words and phrases in question.[35]

2.2. Nineteenth Century

Black himself refers to the work of Arnold Meyer and Gustaf Dalman.[36] Dalman (1855–1941), a German Lutheran theologian, and author of an important grammar of Jewish Palestinian Aramaic,[37] whose observations are relevant for Koranic Studies, brings forward incontestable evidence for the argument that Aramaic was the language of the Jews of Palestine. He summarized the evidence in the following manner:

(1) "The custom, represented in the second century after Christ as very ancient, of translating into Aramaic the text of the Hebrew Pentateuch in the synagogues of the Hebraists of Palestine."[38] (By "Hebraists," Dalman meant the putatively "Hebrew"-speaking Jews of Palestine, who formed a class distinct from the "Hellenists"; and according to Dalman, the Hebraists did not in reality speak Hebrew, but rather Aramaic, for a custom had grown up over the years whereby the Bible text and Targum were inseparable, and this custom arose at a time when the Hebrew text was no longer understood by those who frequented the synagogues. At least in public worship the Holy Scripture was not read without the translation into Aramaic. We can notice similar developments in the history of early Islam: it was clear from the beginning that large parts of the Koran were not understood, and the Hadith (Ḥadīṯ), the Traditions, were invented to explain obscure passages in the Holy Text. To translate the Koran without the Hadith still remains an impossible task, as the two are inseparable.)

(2) The Aramaic titles for classes of the people and for feasts attested by Josephus and the New Testament.

(3) The use of Aramaic language in the Temple.

(4) Old Official documents in the Aramaic language.

(5) The language of the public documents relating to purchases, debts, marriages and so forth.

(6) The unquestioned adoption in the time of Jesus of the Aramaic characters in place of the Old Hebrew in copies of the Bible Text.
(7) The Syntax and the vocabulary of the Hebrew of the Mishna, which prove themselves to be the creation of Jews who thought in Aramaic.
(8) The custom of calling the Aramaic "Hebrew."[39]

From all this evidence, Dalman draws the conclusion that Jesus must have grown up speaking Aramaic, and that he spoke in Aramaic to his disciples and to the people in order to be understood. What is of primordial importance is to establish the linguistic situation in Palestine at the time of Jesus, and the way Aramaic permeated and influenced the other languages in the area. Dalman argues that

> the Greek of the Jewish Hellenists must have been affected by Semitic tongues in several ways. In the first place, it must be assumed that the Greek spoken from Syria to Egypt was in many particulars influenced in no small degree, by the Aramaic language of the country; and further, it holds true for that portion of the Jewish people that adopted Greek in place of its Semitic mother-tongue, that this mother-tongue had been Aramaic, and that the world of thought peculiar to the Jews, which had then to be apprehended in a Greek mould, had already been fashioned in Aramaic and no longer in Hebrew. The spiritual intercourse also which Jewish Hellenists continuously had with Hebraists in Palestine implied constant interchange between Greek and Aramaic (but not Hebrew) modes of expression. Hebrew influence was active only indirectly: first, in so far as a Hebrew past underlay the Aramaic present of the Jewish people; secondly and in particular, because the Greek translation of the Old Testament had necessarily a powerful influence on the religious dialect.[40]

Many Islamologists are not familiar with dialects, and they tend to see Arabic in isolation, and subscribe to the myth of the purity of the Arabic language. As I wrote many years ago, no civilization is pure; there are no more pure civilizations than there are pure races. As a character in Nabokov's *Lolita* says, we are all a salad of racial genes; this is even more true of civilizations: civilizations are a salad of cultural genes, different interpenetrating, inter-influencing strands. Most civilizations have not developed in isolation. Let us add languages to the mix. Languages have not everywhere developed in isolation. As Dalman wrote,

> He who knows the East is aware that familiarity with several languages is not necessarily proof of higher education, but is rather a state of things arising out of the conditions of intercourse between the different populations.[41]

Growing up in Karachi in newly created Pakistan in the early 1950s, I can vouch that out in the streets I used a *Mischsprache* made up of my mother tongue, *Kutchi*, a form of Sindhi; *Urdu*, adopted as the national language, and *English*, the language of higher education. There was yet some influence from another language: *Gujarati*, the dominant language of the region where my father and I were born.

Kutchi was only used within the family for everyday purposes, so new words, for example, those for technical innovations, would have to be inserted from one of the other languages. English was taught in schools, but the pronunciation was heavily influenced by the phoneme systems of local languages. Moreover, the style was not what an English native speaker would accept as genuine colloquial English, whether British or American. Urdu, the national language of Pakistan, is a very special case: It is one of the two varieties of *Hindustani*, the most important *Modern Indo-Aryan* language. Indo-Aryan languages are all offsprings of Sanskrit (also called "Old Indo-Aryan"), an Indo-European language closely related to Old Persian and Avestan, but as such also to Greek, Latin and—of course—English. Modern Indo-Aryan languages[42] comprise most of the languages spoken in Northern India, Bangladesh, most of Nepal and large parts of Pakistan, some of them (Bengali, Gujarati, Punjabi, Nepali, Assamese, Oriya, Sindhi) with many million speakers. Sanskrit is the "genealogical mother" of Modern Indo-Aryan languages, from which Gujarati, Punjabi, and so on derived. So words that go back to the "normal" linguistic development like *Hindustani/Urdu* "hāth" from *Sanskrit* "hasta" (meaning "hand") are not borrowings. However, just like French adopted learned Latin words (e.g., "légal" from Lat. "legalis") in addition to Latin words that had undergone the normal linguistic development (e.g., "loyal" from Lat. "legalis"), Hindustani, especially its Indian variety *Hindi,* often did the same.

Hindustani and the other Modern Indo-Aryan languages are about as closely related as Italian, Spanish, and French, the case of Hindustani being special insofar as there are two written standards in use with next-to identical grammar and phoneme system: *Urdu* (written in a slightly modified Arabic alphabet), and the already-mentioned *Hindi* (written in the Devanagari alphabet, which is also used for Sanskrit). Hindustani, named after "Hindustan" (Persian: "land of the Indus," an old designation of "India"). It had adopted many Persian words, and—due to the fact that the ruling Moghul dynasty was Muslim—many Arabic words from the religious vocabulary, albeit in Persian guise, much like English adopted thousands of French words after the battle of Hastings in 1066. The new language had an early standard called *Khari Bholi,* based on the dialect of Delhi, but its colloquial form was mainly spoken in the *army*, in the Turkic language of the Moghuls (often referred to as *Chagatay* or *Old Uzbek*) called *urdu.* This word has independently been adopted into European languages as *hord* (German:

Horde)—think of the empire of the "Golden Horde"—and it etymologically corresponds to the modern Turkish word *ordu* or *army*. So this "language of the army"—*Urdu*—written in Arabic letters, was to become the new national language of India. The Hindus, however, did not want all of the Persian and Arabic words, especially those that stemmed from the religious terminology. So they replaced them by Sanskrit and pseudo-Sanskrit forms and wrote this variety of the language in the alphabet normally used for Sanskrit at that time. The language was called *Hindi*, which, in fact, is also an Arabic form (*hind* = India + adjective ending *-ī*). Moreover, concerning Modern Indo-Aryan languages in general, one should not forget the English influence.

A good example of the mixed character of Hindustani/Urdu is the words for "love": *mohabbat* (from Arabic *muḥabbat*, the *o* in the first syllable showing that it first went through Persian), *prem*, *pyār*, *išk*; and for "physical love" there is also the semantic unit (morpheme) *kām(a)* (Sanskrit) that we all know from the "*Kama*-sutra." So what the author was exposed to during his childhood was more than just a "*mischsprache*," to use a German play on words, it was a "*Misch-masch*-Sprache (*Mischmasch*—'mingle-mangle' [compare the vowels!]; 'jumble' [think of 'mumbo-jumbo'!])."

Coming back to the holy land: The problem for all scholars, whether of the Old or New Testament, or the Koran, is to ascertain the linguistic situation in Palestine at various moments of history. Dalman argues that at

> the time of Christ there was prevalent over all Palestine, from the extreme north to the south, a single literary language in Aramaic, varying but slightly in the different parts of the country. In this literary Aramaic are written the Aramaic sections in Daniel and in Ezra, the Targum of Onkelos,[43] and the other documents assigned to the Judaen dialect, as well as the Palmyrene and Nabataean inscriptions. Concurrently (with this literary dialect) there existed a whole series of popular dialects: a Middle Palestinian, which we can recognise in a later phase as Samaritan Aramaic, and a North Palestinian, which is known to us in a Jewish and Christian form—both belonging to a subsequent period. It is highly probable that after the final overthrow of the Judaean centre of Jewish-Aramaic culture, which was the result of the Bar Kochba revolution, the North Palestinian popular dialect got the upper hand over nearly all Palestine.[44]

2.3. Developments in the Twentieth Century

Dalman was writing at the end of the nineteenth century, but since then, in the words of Joseph A. Fitzmyer, the scholar who has done the most to examine their import, "the number of texts written in some form of Aramaic that have come to light during the last seventy-five to a hundred years has been extraordinary."[45] Fitzmyer, now Professor Emeritus of Biblical Studies at the Catholic University of America, writing in the late 1970s, gives us a brief picture of the situation:

> By and large, they [editor's note: these newly discovered texts] have given us a good idea of earlier forms of the language and some of its intermediate stages. Most of the texts have come from Egypt, Palestine, or Syria, even though it is now apparent that during the period of its heyday, when it served as a sort of *lingua franca* for vast areas of the eastern Mediterranean world, it was used in many other countries as well. These new acquisitions have shed light on all sorts of older texts, biblical, ancient Near Eastern, and otherwise.

Fitzmyer suggests that the Aramaic preserved in the Greek of the Gospels points to the phenomenon of Semitic interference in that language, and in particular to Aramaic interference. I shall come back to the whole notion of "interference," an important area of research in the fairly new discipline of translation studies. Fitzmyer was the first, perhaps, to bring some methodological rigor to discussions of the Aramaic background of the New Testament, and the presence, prevalence and use of Aramaic in Palestine, which is attested from the ninth century onward.

> The earliest text is a short inscription on a jar from 'Ein Gev, dated to the middle of the ninth century by B. Mazar; and likewise from that century comes an inscribed bowl from Tell Dan, published by N. Avigad.[46] From these (currently) earliest attestations of the language right down to roughly A.D. 500 one can trace a line of evidence showing a continuous use of Aramaic in Palestine, which includes the numerous fragments from the Qumran caves, and not a few from various synagogue inscriptions dating from the third to the sixth centuries. Moreover, the invasion of Aramaisms, Aramaic vocabulary, and Aramaic syntax into the Hebrew of the later books of the Bible and into Post-Biblical Hebrew suggests its predominant use.[47]

Not only was cultural and linguistic exchange and influence the norm, but translation activity began early also. Fitzmyer writes:

> Furthermore, the existence of Aramaic targums in written form from Qumran (4Qtg.Job, 11Qtg.Job, 4QtgLev) indicates that the practice of translating the Hebrew Scriptures into Aramaic was well under way, and presumably for the usually stated reason, because the original Hebrew text read in synagogues was no longer so readily and widely understood. . . . Lastly, the use of Aramaic on tombstones and ossuaries of the first century in and around Jerusalem clearly shows that the language was in popular use, not to mention an Aramaic I.O.U. dated to the second year of Nero Caesar, A.D. 56 (Murabba'at texts 18).

While he remains skeptical about the alleged differences between the literary and spoken forms of Aramaic of this period, Fitzmyer, nonethess, makes an important observation:

> Everyone knows that the distinction [between literary and spoken forms] is valid and that it is precisely the *spoken form* [my emphasis, I. W.] of a language that eventually invades the literary and brings about the development of one dialect or phase of it from another.[48]

And yet, as we shall see, in the field of Koranic Studies there are eminent scholars who maintain that the Arabic vernaculars developed out of Classical Arabic!

3. Fitzmyer: The Languages of Palestine, and Phases of Aramaic

3.1. The Linguistic Situation in Palestine in the First Century CE

In an article first published in 1970,[49] Fitzmyer in a brilliant examination of all the extant evidence comes to the following conclusion about the linguistic situation in Palestine in the first century CE :

> I should maintain that the most commonly used language of Palestine in the first century A.D. was Aramaic, but that many Palestinian Jews, not only those in Hellenized towns, but farmers and craftsmen of less obviously Hellenized areas used Greek, at least as a second language. The data collected from Greek inscriptions and literary sources indicate that Greek was widely used. In fact, there is indication, despite Josephus' testimony, that some Palestinians spoke only Greek, the 'Ελληνισταί [Hellēnistaí]. But pockets of Palestinian Jews also used Hebrew, even though its use was not widespread. The emergence of the targums supports this. The real problem is the influence of these languages on one another. Grecized Aramaic is still to be attested in the first century. It begins to be attested in the early second century and becomes abundant in the third and fourth centuries. Is it legitimate to appeal to this evidence to postulate the same situation earlier? Latin was really a negligible factor in the language-situation of first-century Palestine, since it was confined for the most part to the Roman occupiers. If Aramaic did go into an eclipse in the Seleucid period[50], as some maintain, it did not remain there. The first-century evidence points, indeed, to its use as the most common language in Palestine.[51]

3.2. The Phases of Aramaic

In chapter three of his essay collection *A Wandering Aramean*, Fitzmyer proposed a reclassification of the phases of Aramaic into five periods:

1. Old Aramaic, from roughly 925 BCE to 700 BCE

Evidence: inscriptions on stone and other materials written in borrowed Phoenician alphabet.

Geography: northern Syria, Upper Mesopotamia, northern Palestine.
Examples: Tell Halaf inscription, Hazor sherd, Tell Dan Bowl, etc.

2. Imperial Aramaic, from roughly 700 BCE to 200 BCE

Also called "Reichsaramäisch," Official, or Standard Aramaic. Widespread and standardized.
Evidence: Vast corpus of Official Aramaic texts: letters on papyrus, skin, literary texts, graffiti, ostraca messages, clay tablets, etc.
Geography: Egypt (chiefly in Upper Egypt at Elephantine and Aswan, but also in Lower Egypt at Saqqarah and Hermopolis West), in Arabia and Palestine, Syria, and in scattered areas of Asia Minor, Assyria, Babylonia, Armenia, Ancient Indus Valley.

3. Middle Aramaic, from roughly 200 BCE to 200 CE

Emergence of real local dialects. To this phase belong the dialects of
(a) Palestine and Arabia: Nabatean, Qumran, Murabba'at, that of the inscriptions on Palestinian ossuaries and tombstones, of the Aramaic words preserved in the Greek texts of Josephus and the New Testament, and some of the texts of early Palestinian rabbinic literature;
(b) Syria and Mesopotamia: those of Palmyra, Edessa, and Hatra, and perhaps also the beginnings of early Babylonian rabbinic literature.

4. Late Aramaic, roughly 200 CE to 700 CE

(a) Western: dialects of Jewish-Palestinian Aramaic, Samaritan Aramaic, Christian Syro-Palestinian Aramaic;
(b) Eastern: the dialects of Syriac (further distinguished into a western [Jacobite] form and an eastern [Nestorian] form), Babylonian Talmudic Aramaic, and Mandaic.

Fitzmyer writes of this fourth phase, which is, perhaps, the most important phase for those looking at the history of Arabic, and the origin and rise of Islam:

> The closing limit of this phase of the language is not easily set. 700 is taken merely as a round number close to the Muhammadan Conquest and the consequent spread of Arabic which put an end to the active use of Aramaic in many areas of the Near East. But it is obvious that neither Aramaic nor Syriac died out at this time. There are, indeed, all sorts of reasons for extending the lower limit of the phase to the end of the 11th century (i.e., to the end of the Gaonic period in Palestine and Babylonia)[52] and even to the end of the 13th century among Syriac writers (Bar Hebraeus, or Abu 'l-Faraj Gregory (1226–

> 1286), and his contemporaries). The extent of the areas in which Aramaic or Syriac was still spoken was greatly reduced; and the position that it assumed vis-à-vis Arabic even in those areas is problematic. Was it being used only in closed circles (domestic, scholastic, synagogal)? In any case, it is obvious that the language did not die out completely, as the following fifth phase shows, even though it is not easy to trace the line of connection between the Late and the Modern phases.

Fitzmyer continues,

> What is striking in the Late Phase of Aramaic is not only the elements that set off its various dialects (such as the imperfect in *neqtol* or *liqtul*, the waning of the absolute and construct states of the noun, the piling up of pronominal forms, the widespread use of the possessive pronoun *dīl-*, etc.), but also the mounting influx of Greek words and constructions into almost all dialects of the language. Though the Hellenization of the eastern Mediterranean areas, such as Palestine and Syria, began much earlier, the sparse incidence of Greek words in Aramaic texts of the Middle phase stands in contrast to that of this phase.[53]

5. Modern Aramaic

Still spoken in various parts of northern Syria, Iran, Iraq and related regions. Examples include the closely related dialects of *Maʿlūla*, *Jubbʿadin*, *Baḫʿa*, all spoken in the mountains near Damascus and the only survivor of West Aramaic, *Ṭurōyō*, the modern language most closely related to Classical Syriac, originally spoken in Ṭūr ʿAbdīn in modern Turkey—most speakers meanwhile having emigrated—and a language often referred to as *Assyrian Neo-Aramaic*, the modern Aramaic language with most speakers, spoken in different dialects in Iraq, Iran, and some parts of the former Soviet Union. All of them have been heavily influenced by modern local languages such as Arabic, Kurdish, or Turkish.

4. Language Contact, Language Interference—*Mischsprache*, *Langue Mixte*, and *Langue Mélangée*

Es gibt keine völlig ungemischte Sprache
[There is no entirely unmixed language]
Hugo Schuchardt, 1884

4.1. Languages in General

Before coming back to Classical Arabic, and the language of the Koran, I should like to further explore the nature of mixed languages and the curious reluctance of Islamologists in particular to consider the history of the Arabic language in its linguistic and cultural milieu.

In his preface to Uriel Weinreich's classic *Languages in Contact*,[54] Professor André Martinet, head of the Department of Linguistics at Columbia University in the 1950s, makes a number of pertinent observations about research and researchers in the field of linguistics:

> There was a time when the progress of research required that each community should be considered linguistically self-contained and homogeneous. Whether this autarchic situation was believed to be a fact or was conceived of as a working hypothesis need not detain us here. It certainly was a useful assumption. By making investigators blind to a large number of actual complexities, it has enabled scholars, from the founding fathers of our science down to the functionalists and structuralists of today, to abstract a number of fundamental problems, to present for them solutions perfectly valid in the frame of the hypothesis, and generally to achieve, perhaps for the first time, some rigor in a research involving man's psychic activity.
>
> Linguists will always have to revert at times to this pragmatic assumption. But we shall now have to stress the fact that a linguistic community is *never* [emphasis in the original] homogeneous and hardly ever self-contained. Dialectologists have pointed to the permeability of linguistic cells, and liguistic changes have been shown to spread like waves through space. But it remains to be emphasized that linguistic diversity begins next door, nay, at home and within one and the same man. It is not enough to point out that each individual is a battlefield for conflicting linguistic types and habits, and, at the same time, a permanent source of linguistic interference. What we heedlessly and somewhat rashly call "a language" is the aggregate of millions of such microcosms many of which evince such aberrant linguistic comportment that the question arises whether they should not be grouped into other "languages." What further complicates the picture, and may, at the same time, contribute to clarify it, is the feeling of linguistic allegiance which will largely determine the responses of every individual. This, even more than sheer intercourse, is the cement that holds each one of our "languages" together: It is different allegiance which makes two separate languages of Czech and Slovak more than the actual material differences between the two literary languages. . . . We leave aside one totally homogeneous system and shunt off to another totally homogeneous one. This is at least what we assume would take place in an ideal bilingual situation. But to what extent is this situation actually realized? By the side of a few linguistic virtuosos who, by dint of constant cultivation, manage to keep their two, or more, linguistic mediums neatly distinct, wouldn't careful observation reveal in the overwhelming majority of cases some traces at least of structural merger? On the other hand couldn't we imagine all sorts of intermediate cases between every successive two among the

> following ones; a unilingual who shifts from style to style; a substandard speaker who can, if need be, trim his speech into something close to standard; a patois speaker who can gradually improve his language from homely and slipshod to what we might call his best linguistic behavior, for all practical purposes the standard language; another patois speaker who will treat his vernacular and the standard as two clearly different registers with largely deviating structures. Contact breeds imitation and imitation breeds linguistic convergence. Linguistic divergence results from secession, estrangement, loosening of contact. In spite of the efforts of a few great scholars, like Hugo Schuchardt, linguistic research has so far favored the study of divergence at the expense of convergence.[55]

In the words of Hugo Schuchardt: *Es gibt keine völlig ungemischte Sprache* [There is no entirely unmixed language].[56]

Historical linguists have tended to concentrate on system-internal motivations and mechanisms in studying language change, dismissing external influence as insignificant. Heine and Kutieva[57] summarize the resistance among historical linguists to the idea of language contact and interference as external agents of change, and point to studies that challenge this conservative viewpoint:

> That language structure is fairly resistant to change in situations of language contact has been widely held among students of linguistics for a long time, presumably rooted in Ferdinand de Saussure's distinction between "internal" and "external" linguistics. In this tradition, Edward Sapir managed to persuade a generation of American linguists that there were no really convincing cases of profound morphological influence by diffusion.[58] While it was conceded that certain parts of language, such as phonology and the lexicon, tend to be affected by pressure from other languages, grammar was considered to be immune to major restructuring. More recent studies have shown that this view is incorrect. As some of these studies have demonstrated, essentially *any part of language structure* [emphasis added by I.W.] can be transferred from one language to another.[59] In fact, there is substantial evidence to support this general claim. . . .

Sapir did not really claim that grammar is not influenced by language contact at all, but he saw its effect as rather negligeable if compared to internal reasons, although he should have known better: Especially in Indo-European studies there are numerous well-known examples of grammatical influence between languages, e.g. of Latin on European languages, a good example being the *ablativus absolutus* or the *consecutio temporum.*

A conditional sentence in English like "If I had known (*past perfect*), I would not have done it (*past conditional*)" is exactly congruent with its

French counterpart "si j'avais su (*past perfect*), je ne l'aurais pas fait (*past conditional*)." What Sapir actually did claim, however, is that language contact does not change the phonetics/phonology of a language very much and that sound changes normally go back to internal reasons and not to language contact—a view which is probably true, at least in most cases; examples to the contrary are cases of "areal phonetics": e.g., *Sorbian* (also called *Lusatian*, a Slavonic language) is phonetically influenced by German, which can easily be heard: the Slavic rolled *r* was replaced by the French "r grasseyé"; but these influences are rather on the level of phonetic *realization*, less on the *phonemic* level.

Sapir's view can be explained by a misconception which had survived among linguists for a long time: Generations of them had grown up with the notion that *every* linguistic change process was explained by either *subtratum* (i.e., influence of the former language like Gaulish for French), *superstratum* (i.e., influence of an imposed language, like English on Welsh) or *adstratum* (i.e., influence of a neighboring language like German on Hungarian). Sapir tried to put the importance of these phenomena into perspective. As Heine and Kuteva continue,

> The main purpose of [our] book is to demonstrate that the transfer of grammatical meanings and structures across languages is regular, and that it is shaped by universal processes of grammatical change.

Frans van Coetsem (1919–2002), distinguished American linguist of Flemish origin, made many contributions to the study of language contact, to which he was led by his initial research into linguistic variation. Van Coetsem begins his article *Topics in Contact Linguistics*[60] with a quote from the Polish linguist Jan N. I. Baudouin de Courtenay (1845–1929), known for his pioneering work on phonemes. De Courtenay wrote in 1897,

> All existing and extinct languages arose by way of mixture. Even individual speech, which originates and is formed in contact with fully developed individuals, is the product of mixture and interaction.[61]

Van Coetsem then makes these invaluable observations based on fifty years of reflection,

> The study of language contact is an important, integral part of linguistics, but it is still very much in the process of being proven so. In spite of the commendable efforts of such consummate linguists as Weinreich (1953) and Haugen (1969 [1953]),[62] who brought the language contact phenomenon to the forefront, it has traditionally been seen as a marginal topic in linguistics. Where in textbooks the aspect of interaction between languages is brought up at all, it is often handled in a casual manner under the notion of *borrowing* and without much further differentiation. The language system has been seen too much in

> itself rather than in its language-interactive function. . . . A directly related and strongly resistant bias has produced the glorification of the "purity" of language, with all this implies. However, a "pure" language does not exist, since all languages are mixed, albeit in different ways and to different degrees, as already Baudouin de Courtenay forcefully argued. Language contact and mixing language is the rule, not the exception. And Burney[63] mentioned [Albert] Dauzat[64] as viewing language mixing as a boon, and as having stated that: "Les plus grandes langues sont les plus métissées." Dauzat is not the only one to think that way.

Thus for van Coetsem "contact and interaction between languages is an intrinsic part of language itself."[65] Van Coetsem points to the example given by Baudouin de Courtenay of

> a type of language mixing in the which the lexicon originates from one language and the morphology from another. [Baudouin de Courtenay] described this mixed pattern, which must have been considered very remarkable at the time, as follows: "One . . . typically mixed language is the Russian-Chinese language of Kjaxta and Majmačina on the Siberian-Chinese border. . . . Its lexicon . . . is almost exclusively Russian, but its structure, its morphology bear a clear imprint of Chinese."[66]

A good example is the linguistic situation in Paraguay, where in everyday situations the Native American language Guaraní and Spanish are constantly mixed, although written standards of both languages exist, but also the case of "Spanglish" in the United States or intermediate forms of Spanish and Portuguese in the border regions of Uruguay and Brazil; another often-cited example is *Michif*, an intermediate form of the Algonquian language *Cree* and French.

However, it was undoubtedly the work of Thomason and Kaufman that made the academic study of language contact and language change respectable, and methodologically rigorous. Thomason and Kaufman, along with Schuchardt, Bailey, and Mühlhäusler, believe

> that foreign interference in grammar as well as in lexicon is likely to have occurred in the histories of most languages. . . that the history of a language is a function of the history of its speakers, and not an independent phenomenon that can be thoroughly studied without reference to the social context in which it is embedded.[67]

Clearly, many historical linguists deny the possibility of mixed languages, since that would negate the entire Comparative Method: no language could be proven to be the descendant of an earlier stage of a single other language.

In other words, mixed languages challenge the universality of the tidy family tree.[68] In the words of Thomason and Kaufman,

> For over a hundred years, mainstream historical linguists have concentrated heavily on system-internal motivations and mechanisms in studying language change. The methodological principles embodied in the powerful Comparative Method include an assumption that virtually all language change arises through intrasystemic causes. Most historical linguists, therefore would probably still agree with Welmers' view that, in phonology and morphosyntax, external influences "are insignificant when compared with internal change . . . the established principles of comparative and historical linguistics, and *all we know about language history and language change*, demand that . . . we seek explanations first on the basis of recognized processes of internal change"[69] [Emphasis added by Thomason and Kaufman]. Max Müller's claim that mixed languages do not exist reflects this prejudice, both because a mixed language could not arise without extensive foreign influence and because the existence of mixed languages would constitute a potential threat to the integrity of the family tree model of genetic relationship (and hence to the Comparative Method itself).[70]

In Germany, already in the nineteenth century there was an alternative theory that tried to replace the notion of a tree structure of linguistic development, called the "Wellentheorie" ("wave theory"). According to this view, linguistic change is like throwing a stone into a pond: around the epicenter the ripples are biggest; moreover several stones might be thrown into the pond in different places.

Moreover, the comparative method can hardly be applied to a *dialect continuum* (like German and Arabic dialects), that is to say a situation where many dialects are spoken in a country, with neighboring dialects still being more or less mutually intelligible, but where intelligibility sinks dramatically with growing distance. *Dialect continua* seem to be the "normal case" of language split, except if there is a clear geographical boundary, as in the case of German, Icelandic, and Swedish.

In the above quotation, the famous German Indologist Max Müller and his opinion that "mixed languages do not exist" was mentioned. Especially he should have known better: Classical Sanskrit, the language he investigated so thoroughly that he is revered for it up to this day in India, is a kind of mixed language: the phonology, "*Lautstand*" (phonemic status) of the words and the morphology of the language is 98 percent Old Indo-Aryan (like in the Rigveda, composed more than three thousand years ago), but the syntax with its conspicuuous nominal style is clearly *Middle Indian*. Therefore, the Middle Indian passages in *Kalidāsas* dramas (e.g., the famous drama *Śakuntalā*) can easily be rendered into Sanskrit by replacing corresponding forms word by word. Isn't this a mixed language par excellence?

To adduce a hypothetical example: If our scholars had done the same with medieval Latin, there would be forms like "Egomeindefutuismus" ("j'm'enfoutisme"—an attitude of "not giving a damn") < ego + me + inde + futu[ere] + ismus. Still, this does not mean that the family tree should be totally dismissed: once languages have ceased to be mutually intelligible, they are on different branches.

As Thomason and Kaufman point out, it is surely no accident that it was the great creolist, Hugo Schuchardt, who argued robustly against those scholars such as Max Müller who denied the very possibility of mixed languages. Pidgins and creoles were obviously the prime candidates for mixed-language status. But Schuchardt's interests were by no means confined to pidgins and creoles, and his research on contact-induced language changes of all sorts confirmed his belief in the universality of language mixture.

Thomason and Kaufman lay down certain important principles that seem to have been denied or neglected by Arabists when discussing the Arabic language in general.

> First, *all languages change through time.* The main stimuli for change are *drift*, i.e. tendencies within language to change in certain ways as a result of structural imbalances; *dialect interference*, between stable, strongly differentiated dialects and between weakly differentiated dialects through the differential spread (in "waves") of particular changes; and *foreign interference.* Just as it is often difficult to tell whether two speech forms are dialects of one language or separate languages, so the borderline between dialect interference and foreign interference is often fuzzy. Nevertheless, many clear cases attest to the basic difference between these two types of interference. A language's geographical area may become fragmented, through the physical and/ or social factors, from the point of view of regular intercommunication. In such cases, change over time can result in dialect diversity and even language splits. Metaphorically, then, *a language can have multiple offspring.*[71]

Thomason and Kaufman further remark that "as far as the strictly linguistic possibilites go, any linguistic feature can be transferred from any language to any other language."[72]

There can be diffusion between unrelated languages that did not originally have similar grammars. Phonological rules, grammatical rules of all sorts can be transferred from one language to another.[73]

> It is the sociolinguistic history of the speakers, and not the structure of their language, that is the primary determinant of the linguistic outcome of language contact. . . . Linguistic interference is conditioned in the first instance by social factors, not linguistic ones.[74]

Thomason and Kaufman make a distinction between borrowing and substratum interference. In the latter kind of interference a group of speakers shifting to a target language (TL) fails to learn the TL perfectly.

> The errors made by members of the shifting group in speaking the TL then spread to the TL as a whole when they are imitated by original speakers of that language. . . . Interference through imperfect learning does *not* begin with vocabulary: it begins instead with sounds and syntax, and sometimes includes morphology as well before words from the shifting group's original language appear in the TL.[75]

Extensive structural borrowing is more common than has been acknowledged.[76]

A. Rosetti [77] makes a distinction between "langue mixte" and "langue mélangée." The former is applicable where there has been an interpenetration of the two morphologies, as in Norwegian, and the latter where there has been borrowing but the morphology has been left intact. Perhaps the best translation of the term "langue mélangée" would be "infused language." Rosetti attributes the existence of mixed languages and "langue mélangée" to bilingualism. He believes the bilingualism of a speaker is reflected in linguistic calques; that is, in the reproduction of the internal form of a foreign word; in German, for instance, *Eindruck* and *Ausdruck* are calqued on *im-pression* and *ex-pression.* No language is entirely exempt from infusions; that is, most languages are "langues mélangées."

4.2. Language Contact in Semitic Languages

Where Thomason and Kaufman discuss principles applicable to *all* languages, John Huehnergard, professor at the University of Texas at Austin, writing in 1996, focuses on Semitic ones. He is very critical of Arabists who refuse to recognize the existence of other Semitic languages:

> For Classical Arabic there has long been a need for a new etymological dictionary in which Arabists would *recognize, possibly for the first time, that there were other Semitic languages*; this lacuna is being filled by a glacially slow appearance of the *Wörterbuch der klassischen arabischen Sprache*,[78] which started with the letter *k* in 1970 and is already halfway through *l*.[79] [Emphasis added, I.W.]

Huehnergard also feels more work needs to be done on the very large number of Aramaic dialects,

> many of which are still not readily accessible in the form of good descriptive grammars. We need comprehensive studies, for example, of Imperial Aramaic,

> of the Aramaic of *Targum Onqelos*, of Jewish Palestinian Aramaic, and other dialects.[80]

John Huehnergard makes a similar point to the one made by Thomason and Kaufman when he notes and regrets the tendency to treat the "big five" Semitic languages (Akkadian, Classical Arabic, Aramaic (usually Syriac), Classical Ethiopic, and Biblical Hebrew)

> as discrete and coordinate branches of the family, so that, frequently, equal weight is given to each in reconstructions. In other words, if a feature has the same manifestation in Arabic, Aramaic, and Hebrew but differs in Akkadian and Ethiopic, reconstruction may favor the former simply by weight of numbers. But such procedures are methodologically unsound. We should not be comparing all attested languages directly with one another as though they all descended directly from Proto-Semitic without any intermediate steps. The picture of the family tree is not a simple fan, with Proto-Semitic at the apex and a series of rays going directly to each of the attested languages. Rather, it has two primary rays, which lead to East and West Semitic. West Semitic in turn has two rays, which lead to South and Central Semitic, and so on. For the purposes of reconstruction, therefore, one should first compare not all attested languages, but rather only those that share an immediate common ancestor; then that intermediate ancestral language may be compared with a language or branching with which it shares an immediate ancestor still farther back. Ideally, then, what should be compared in attempts to reconstruct language history are coordinate points, or nodes, in the family tree. To return to the example I used above: a feature attested jointly in Arabic, Aramaic, and Hebrew may reflect a development in *their* common ancestor, Central Semitic, rather than a Proto-Semitic feature; its presence in three of the attested Semitic languages should not outweigh its absence in two languages if the three are all members of the same subbranch.[81]

In the middle of a lengthy footnote,[82] Huehnergard makes an important reflection,

> Further attested languages exist as a part of a continuum of related dialects and are constantly affected by neighbouring dialects (related or not), and these facts naturally obtain equally for the real historical ancestors of attested languages.

This point is further developed, and it leads naturally to the phenomenon I have been at pains to emphasize, namely, language contact:

> Another fruitful area of sociolinguistics, as significant for the ancient Near East as for any other time and place, is the study of language contact, that is, what happens when groups speaking different languages or dialects come into

> contact with one another.[83] Several aspects of the study of languages in contact are of interest. There is, first of all, the phenomenon of linguistic interference, where part of the grammar of one language is influenced by that of the other. The most celebrated cases of large-scale interference among the Semitic languages are Akkadian and Amharic. Cushitic influence on Amharic was already discussed several decades ago by Wolf Leslau, and others have written about it . . . .[84] Linguistic interference is also seen in Ugaritic prose texts, which exhibit the same word order as the Akkadian models on which they were based,[85] in Persian or Akkadian influence on some Aramaic dialects,[86] and elsewhere.[87]

Huehnergard points to the importance of bilingualism,

> a phenomenon that is documented directly for the first time in history in third-millennium Mesopotamian lexical texts. References to bilingualism also crop up frequently in texts. At Ugarit, as is well-known, no fewer than eight languages are attested.

The linguistic processes at work in the phenomena of pidginization and creolization are also present in the ancient Near East, as for example in the Late Bronze Age Akkadian texts:

> These Akkadian texts, written by nonnative speakers in Anatolia, the Levant, and Egypt, exhibit certain simplifications and reductions in their grammar vis-à-vis the Akkadian of native Mesopotamian scribes, but also frequently exhibit other processes that suggest that they were real, spoken languages.[88]

Diglossia, an aspect of language contact, is well-attested among the Semitic languages. But not only the phenomenon of the influence of a prestige language on the spoken language, but the reverse process, vernacularization, are asseverated in Semitic languages. Huehnergard notes that

> influence of the spoken language on the learned or literary is also assumed by Assyriologists when, for example, they come across "late" features in otherwise "good" Old Babylonian, or when they consider the grammar of Standard Babylonian literary texts, in which first-millennium scribes attempted to write the classical Babylonian of the early second millennium.[89]

Finally, Edward Lipiński in his monumental study *Semitic Languages: Outline of a Comparative Grammar*,[90] devotes nearly nine pages to "Language Contact," and confirms the findings of Thomason and Kaufman, Huehnergard, and others mentioned above. He begins:

> Living languages never hold still and one way languages change is through the influence of other languages. This problem was already discussed by Sībawayh (d. 793 A.D.) in his *Kitāb*, where he deals with Persian loanwords in Arabic, and Abū Manṣūr al-Ǧawālīqī (1072–1145 A.D.) handled the subjects in his treatise *Kitāb 'al-Mu'arrab min 'al-kalām 'al-'a'ǧamī.*

Lipiński then underlines the thesis proposed by Thomason and Kafman,

> We must accept at once that interference does not occur merely at lexical level. It can be reflected in sound substitution in the borrowing language (e.g. Old Syriac *'dryṭ'* for Greek ἀνδριάς, "statue"), in the adoption of its own patterns to replace the patterns of the source language (e.g. Old Syriac *'rkwnwt'*, "governorship," from Greek ἄρχων). It can be intrusion in morphology, as shown by the verbal plural morpheme *-ūni* in the Syrian Middle Babylonian, e.g. in *i-gám-me-ru-ni*, "they will annihilate," comparable with Aramaic *yəkattəbūn* and Arabic *katabūna*. There can be intrusion in syntactical patterns as well, e.g. in the Aramaic syntagm *'ăbīd lī*, "I have done," borrowed from Old Persian.

Lipiński expresses an important thought, almost a statement of principle, which I have been at pains to bring out throughout this introduction, namely that "language contact, leading to language interference and transference, has left its mark on *all* the Semitic languages." [Emphasis added, I. W.]

There is evidence of lexical borrowing, both between a Semitic and a non-Semitic language. Changes in the syntax or phonology of a language may result from borrowing. As for bilingualism, "there can be little doubt that there was in Mesopotamia a Sumero-Semitic bilingualism from the mid-third millennium B.C. on," a fact that explains the large number of Sumerian loanwords in East Semitic.[91] However, Lipiński feels that

> in the consideration of the extent of linguistic interference in Mesopotamia too little attention is sometimes paid to the influence on Old Akkadian and Assyro-Babylonian in spheres other than that of lexicon. Phonemic and grammatical interference should receive equal attention. The impact of the Sumerian language was felt, no doubt, also in phonology and syntax.

Lipiński, during a historical survey of the linguistic complexities of Syro-Phoenicia and Palestine, quotes from the Arab lexicographer Abū Bakr ibn Durayd (died 933), evidence that is of the utmost importance for Luxenberg's thesis:

> *Wa- qad daḫala fī 'arabīyati 'ahli š-ša'mi kaṯīrun mina s-suryānīyati kamā sta'mala 'arabu l-'irāqi 'ašyā'a mina l-fārisīya.*
> "A great deal of Syriac has pervaded the Arabic of the population of Syria, just as the Arabs of Iraq make use of Persian borrowings."

4.3. Hebrew as Mischsprache, or Langue Mélangée

As early as 1910,[92] Hans Bauer adumbrated a thesis, which he later developed fully with Pontus Leander,[93] wherein he suggested that

> Hebrew is not a homogeneous linguistic system but a "*Mischsprache*," in which it is possible to distinguish an early Canaanite layer, very close to Akkadian, and another more recent layer, closer to Aramaic and Southern Semitic.[94]

Though rejected by many, this thesis seems to be accepted in some form by certain scholars such as G.R. Driver, who wrote, "Clearly the two main strands of which Hebrew is woven are Accadian and Aramaean."[95]

More recently, Professor E. Y. Kutscher has argued that while Mishnaic Hebrew has been influenced on the level of vocabulary by many languages, it is Aramaic that has had the greatest influence at all linguistic levels:

> Aramaic had a far-reaching impact and left its mark on all facets of the language, namely, orthography, phonetics and phonology, morphology including inflection, syntax, and vocabulary. There is room for investigation as to whether Mishnaic Hebrew was a *Hebrew-Aramaic mixed language* [emphasis added]. This question may be posed owing to the fact that Aramaic had a pervading influence in all spheres of the language, including inflection, which is generally considered to be impenetrable to foreign influence. It is possible, however, that because of the symbiosis of Aramaic and Hebrew-Canaanite the two exerted a mutual influence.[96]

Jack Fellman disagrees with Kutscher and, instead, considers Mishnaic Hebrew as, borrowing the term from A. Rosetti discussed above, a "langue mélange," which he translates as "composite language." [97]

4.4. Aramaic—Arabic Language Contact

Stefan Weninger, in the comprehensive handbook on Semitic languages he edited,[98] usefully summarizes the history of Arabic-Aramaic language contact and the ways Aramaic has influenced Arabic phonology, morphology, syntax, and lexicon, and vice versa. He writes,

> When the name of "Gindibu, the Arab" was set in stone in the mid-9th century B.C. in an inscription commemorating the Assyrian king Šalmanassar's victories in Syria, he became the first Arab to be mentioned in the historical record, in an environment in which Aramaeans had been present for at least two centuries.[99] In much later periods, when Arabian dynasties founded polities such as Hatra, Edessa, Palmyra or Petra, they frequently ruled over mixed populations which included Aramaic-speaking communities. Aramaic was also the medium of written communication.[100]

As for morphology, in Classical Arabic one finds, for instance, the derivational suffix *-ūt* which was imported from Aramaic via loanwords such as *malakūt* < *malkūṯā*, "kingdom,"[101] while Aramaic syntactical influence on

Arabic dialects is also evident. But it is in the area of lexicon we have the greatest amount of testimony of Aramaic-Arabic contact:

> Aramaic loanwords had already penetrated Arabic and its Ancient North Arabian predecessors in Pre-Islamic times in large numbers. . . .In late Antiquity, monotheism spread in the Arabian peninsula and with it Jewish and Christian concepts and terms, e.g. *'umma*, "people, religious community" (< Aramaic *'ummā*, *'ummṯā* "people" < Hebrew *'ummā* "people, tribe") or *ṣalāh*, "prayer" (< *ṣlōṯā* "id.") were imported. Many Aramaic lexemes in this category are attested in the Koran[102] and in the Life of the Prophet by Ibn Hišām.[103]

On the whole, however, Weninger's account is disappointing and inadequate, and one has the feeling that he is reluctant to say anything that may smack of "controversy" or may be considered politically incorrect. While he does list Fraenkel and Jeffery's classics in his bibliography, Weninger leaves out Rudolf Dvořák's *Über die Fremdwörter im Koran* (Wien, 1885), Alphonse Mingana's *Syriac Influence on the Style of the Koran*, and, of course, Luxenberg.[104]

However, Weninger does refer to Jan Retsö's entry from the *Encyclopedia of Arabic Language and Linguistics*,[105] and it is to that article we now turn. Retsö points out that by the sixth century BCE most areas of Syria-Palestine and Mesopotamia were Aramaic speaking.

> In the Arabo-Nabatean kingdom there was interaction between the users of late Imperial Aramaic as a written language and large groups of speakers of Arabic dialects. The interference between Aramaic and different forms of Arabic is thus most likely to have existed more than one millennium before the Islamic conquest. During the first two centuries of Islam, Aramaic continued to be spoken in Syria and Mesopotamia by the peasantry.

Retsö also underlines the importance of the phenomenon of bilingualism,

> In the cities, a bilingual situtation arose soon after the conquest when Arabic increasingly became the language from the time of the Crusades onwards, Aramaic came to be limited to Christian and Jewish quarters. The religious minorities were more prone to guard bilingualism.

Retsö concludes that "a bilingual Arabic-Aramaic situation has probably existed in many areas for a very long time but unfortunately this is poorly documented."

As for the Koran, Retsö argues that

> many of the most important and frequent words in the *Qur'ān* are clear Aramaic borrowings, which can be shown by a comparison with Syriac:
> *'aslam-* "to submit [to the new religion]" < *ašlem*;
> *bāb* "door," "gate" < *bāḇā*;

bīʿa "church" < *biʿṯā*;
rabb "lord," *raḥmān* "merciful" (most likely via South Arabian);
sabīl "way," "path" < *šḇīlā*;
sabt "Sabbath" < *šabṯā*;
sağad- "prostrate" < *sgeḏ*; -
safīna "ship" < *sfi(n)tā*;
tāb -/yatūb- "repent" < *tāḇ/yṯūḇ* or *nṯūḇ*;
tatbīr "destruction," from Aramaic *tḇar* "break," cf. Arabic *ṯabar-* "destroy";
'asbāṭ, pl. of *sibṭ* < *šiḇṯā* "tribes";
ʿālam "world" < *ʿālmā*;
ṣalāt "religious service, ceremony" < *ṣlūṯā*;
zakāt "alms" < *zḵūṯā*;
ʿīd "festival" < *ʿīḏā*;
qurbān "offering" < *qurbānā*;
furqān "salvation," "redemption" < *purqānā*;
madīna "town" < *mḏi(n)tā*
malakūt "kingship," < *malkūṯā*;
masīḥ "Christ" < *mšīḥā* (Jeffery 1938).

Retsö continues,

> The Aramaic origin of these words and many others is made likely by the fact that they have no semantic cognates in Arabic from which they can be derived. Thus, for instance, jannat- "garden" has no direct cognate in Arabic where the verb *janna* means "to cover." Aramaic *gi(n)tā*, on the other hand, is clearly formed from the root GNN "to surround, to protect."

But borrowings can be of several kinds. As Retsö explains,

> In the *ʿarabiyya* of the *Qur'ān* we also find several semantic borrowings which give homonyms[106] like daras- "to study" (from Aramaic draš) or "to wipe out" (original Arabic).

We also have examples of Aramaic loanwords in the earliest poetry and in Ibn 'Isḥāq's *Sīra* of the Prophet, and these loans "seem to reflect an archaic form of Aramaic." Retsö includes Luxenberg in his bibliography, and refers to him in his article, but only to dismiss his thesis without any arguments:

> In the approach taken here the Aramaic congnates in the ʿarabiyya are regarded as borrowings from Aramaic. The much further reaching claim that the ʿarabiyya of the Qur'ān is in fact a transformation of a text originally written in Aramaic or even Syriac, as claimed by Luxenberg (2000), is most difficult to verify and remains highly unlikely.

Why it is "highly unlikely" we are not told.

5. Taking Translation Seriously: In Search of a Syriac *Vorlage* or *Vorlagen* for the Koran

5.1. Prolegomena

The Koran is a text—a human product, and hence must be explicable, to quote Maxime Rodinson once again, by "the normal mechanisms of human history."[107] In other words, like all texts, the Koran has a history. The Koran shows considerable signs of the later editing, and arrangement of Surahs, and verses within the Surahs, of an already existing text. Both Karl Vollers (1857–1909) librarian at Vice-Royal library at Cairo, and later professor of Semitic languages at Jena, and Paul Casanova (1861–1926) professor of Arabic at Collège de France, developed theories to account for what they believed were obvious signs of extensive reworking of an already existing text that eventually came to be known as the Koran. The difficulty is to establish exactly how this pre-existent text came into being. The sources of several stories found in the Koran have been located, and many of these sources are literary, occasionally in the Hebrew language, and occasionally in Aramaic or even Syriac. But how were these stories derived from these written sources? How did the stories end up in the Arabic of the Koran? Was there a conscious translation into Arabic of a Syriac or Hebrew text? Some of the Biblical narratives may, of course, have been picked up from a certain cultural milieu, from storytellers in the marketplace, from daily social intercourse with people from already deeply entrenched religious traditions. And yet, as has already been suggested, some narratives seem to have been acquired from already existing literary texts, or as Gerd Puin once put it, "The Koran is made up of a cocktail of different texts"; or, is it a composition, parts of which, at least, are, in the words of John Wansbrough,[108] "made up of originally unrelated periscopes"?[109] Does a pericope suggest a written text, albeit of a liturgical kind? Was there at some stage a series of translations, even if only in the mind of the person transmitting the narrative orally?

5.2. Methodological Principles

Scholars in recent years have paid much attention to the problem of Greek translations of Semitic originals. Professor Davila, professor of Early Jewish Studies at St Mary's College, University of St Andrews, summarizes the areas of research,[110]

> First, there are studies of the translation technique of the LXX [The Septuagint], and attempts to work out principles for retroverting the original Hebrew or Aramaic. . . . Second, there is research on the question of the original languages of the traditions preserved in Greek in the New Testament Gospels

> and, attempts to establish the existence of or even retrovert the alleged Semitic (generally Aramaic) traditions or documents behind the Greek. . . . Third are studies of the translation technique of Greek Jewish Apocrypha and pseudepigrapha whose Hebrew or Aramaic originals survive at least in part. . . . Fourth and last are studies attempting to recover or at least establish the existence of the lost Semitic originals of specific Apocrypha or pseudepigrapha.[111]

Professor Davila lays out with exemplary lucidity the methodological principles that are necessary to establish whether Semitisms in the Greek translation are due to the influence of a written text in Hebrew or Aramaic; in other words, whether a Hebrew or Aramaic *vorlage* may have existed. Often one only needs to substitute Syriac for Hebrew or Aramaic, and Arabic for Greek, to see that his principles are highly relevant for Koranic Studies in the light of the work by Christoph Luxenberg. And in the light of the work of Günter Lüling, we see that we do not even need to change "Hebrew," the only substitution required is "Arabic" for "Greek."

Our task is of course made that much more difficult by the fact that both Syriac and Arabic belong to the Semitic branch of the Afro-Asiatic phylum, whereas Greek and Hebrew (and Aramaic), belong to two different phyla, the Indo-European and Afro-Asiatic respectively. But, as we shall see in what follows, a similar difficulty besets Biblical Studies—how to establish whether the Semitisms in a Greek translation are from Hebrew or Aramaic? We know that

> the LXX is a Greek translation of Hebrew and Aramaic works that still survive and which became canonical for all Jews and Christians. Some of the Old Testament Apocrypha are Greek compositions, whereas others are certainly translations from Hebrew or Aramaic (because fragments of the originals survive, mostly in the Qumran library) or else have been argued to be such translations.

Equally,

> A number of pseudepigrapha existed in Greek versions (although often these versions do not survive in full today) but were undoubtedly translated from Hebrew or Aramaic.

For example, the Book of Jubilees is preserved in full only in Ethiopic,

> but the Greek version is quoted by Byzantine writers, and Hebrew fragments of it were found at Qumran. . . . In short, the translation into Greek of books whose canonicity would later be debated began as early as the late second century BCE and was under way by the end of the first century CE still further along by the end of the second.[112]

As Davila argues, the study of the Semitic linguistic background of Greek Apocrypha and pseudepigrapha has two possible agendas, both of which are worth pondering to see if they could also be agendas for scholars of the Koran convinced of the importance of Luxenberg's work.

> One may aim either for "retroversion," an attempt to work backwards from the surviving Greek to reconstruct the actual wording of the original Hebrew or Aramaic document or, less ambitiously, for establishing "Semitic interference"; showing that the Greek text must have been translated from a Semitic original, but not attempting a global reconstruction of that original.[113]

In the present state of Koranic Studies, even with the efforts of Lüling and Luxenberg, all such agendas are far too ambitious. All one can hope for, at the moment, is to discover Syriacisms, building up to the search for Syriac syntactic structures and morphology in the Koran.

Davila then carefully develops his preliminary methodological principles: when searching for Semitic interference or attempting retroversion first

> look for signs of improper or unusual Greek in the text. Ideally, one would find transliterations of Semitic words, nonsensical Greek that suddenly makes sense when successful retroversion shows the Greek to be an obvious mistranslation, or dual translations of a Semitic original in different Greek manuscripts.

Here, scholars like Luxenberg who are skeptical of the entire Islamic tradition, of not just the compilation of the Koran, but of the meaning of the text, would be able to show Davila many examples of "improper or unusual" Arabic, and "nonsensical" Arabic that suddenly makes sense when successful retroversion shows the Arabic to be an obvious mistranslation.

How do New Testament scholars establish that the Greek shows non-Greek, Semitic syntax? One possibility is to show that the Greek contains a high level of parataxis; that is,

> connection of clauses with the word "and" rather than subordination, use of participles, or use of other particles. Other arguments are also advanced, such as use of Semitic poetic parallelism and the alleged recovery of wordplays and puns in the retroverted original.[114]

But we are still far from establishing Semitic interference by these means.

Davila goes through some of the translation techniques used for scriptural and quasi-scriptural literature in anitiquity, contrasting "literal" translation with "dynamic equivalence." The former

> implies a one-to-one correspondence between all the grammatical and lexical elements in the original language and the target language rather than a translation that expresses the equivalent sense naturally in the target language.

Whereas the latter is freer but "dynamic," capturing "the meaning of the original on a thought-by-thought basis." Thus the crassly literal will render metaphors and idioms with word-for-word exactness often resulting in gibberish in the target language, while

> a dynamically equivalent translation seeks to translate the sense of the expression into the target language, even if this means altering the wording substantially.[115]

Discussing the whole notion of consistency of translation, Davila leans on the study of Staffan Olofsson,[116] who proposes a number of methodological principles. The three most relevant for us are the following,

> [First], more weight should be given to words in the source language which have a wide semantic range and thus would be difficult to render sensibly with a single word in the target language. [Second], the resources of the target language, the degree to which its lexicon and grammar match the source language, should be taken into account, as should, [third], the translator's knowledge of the source language, insofar as we can deduce it.

5.3. Avocados

Luxenberg has argued very persuasively for precisely what the first principle posited above has asked us to consider, namely, the polysemic nature of the words of the source language, in this case, Syriac, and the difficulties encountered in finding the right word in the target language, Arabic. Before giving evidence from Luxenberg's work, I should like to give the following example from personal experience. For several years in the late 1980s, I taught American Constitution and Institutions to first-year students at the University of Toulouse (France). All the students were French-speaking, with French as their mother tongue, but they were asked to write their class essays in English. One student writing about American attitudes and behavior wrote the following sentence:

> Americans are a litigious people, they are frequently consulting their *avocados*.

Those who know French will recognize immediately what happened. But let us, nonetheless, go through the steps that led to this error. The word "avocado" makes no sense here. We know the student is French, and therefore thinks in French. Let us translate backward, and look up "avocado" in an English-French dictionary, which gives the meaning, "avocat." Now we can look up "avocat" in a French-English dictionary, which gives the following *meanings*:

1. Lawyer, solicitor, attorney (at law), barrister, counsel.
2. Advocate (of); champion of (a cause, person).
3. Avocado (botanical).

The word "avocat" in the source language, French, had several meanings (polysemic), but our student not knowing English, the target language, chose the wrong word from a dictionary.

Similarly, Luxenberg looks at the word *baqīya*, which is used three times, in various forms, in the Koran, at Surah 2:248; 11:86, and 11:116.

> Surah 11:116: *fa-law-lā kāna mina l-qurūni min qablikum 'ulū baqiyyatin yanhawna 'ani l-fasādi fī l-'arḍi 'illā qalīlan mimman 'anğaynā minhum wa-ttaba'a llaḏīna ẓalamū mā 'utrifū fīhi wa-kānū muğrimīna.*

T1. Bell's translation:

> If only there had been of the generations before you men of perseverance restraining from corruption in the land—except a few of those whom We rescued from amongst them; but those who have done wrong have followed that in which they luxuriated, and have become sinners.

T2. Pickthall's translation:

> If only there had been among the generations before you men possessing a remnant (of good sense) to warn (their people) from corruption in the earth, as did a few of those whom We saved from them! The wrong-doers followed that by which they were made sapless, and were guilty.

T.3. Blachère's translation :

> Parmi les générations qui furent avant vous, pourquoi les gens de piété qui interdirent le scandale sur la terre et que Nous sauvâmes, ne furent-ils que peu nombreux, alors que les Injustes suivirent le luxe où ils vivaient et furent coupables?

T.4. Paret's translation :

> Warum gab es denn unter den Generationen vor euch nicht Leute (begabt) mit (moralischer) Stärke (?), (oder: mit einem trefflichen Charakter?), die dem Unheil auf der Erde Einhalt geboten—abgesehen von (einigen) wenigen von ihnen, die wir erretteten? Diejenigen, die frevelten (– und das war die überwiegende Mehrzahl –) folgten dem Wohlleben, das ihnen zugefallen war, und waren sündig.

C.1. Bell's Commentary:

> *'ūlū baqiyyatin* is of uncertain meaning; it is usually taken as "possessors of a remnant" of good sense or piety, but this is not very satisfactory. The exhortation to endurance in the previous verse suggests that *baqiyyah* should here be taken in the sense of "persistence." The sense will then be that if only in past times there had been men of persistence to dissuade people from corruption, the evil which necessitated the punishment of the towns would not have arisen, but unfortunately there were only a few—the messenger and those who believed him—who in each case had been rescued when the punishment fell.

If we take the Arabic word *baqīya*, which, in the phrase *'ūlū baqīyatin*, is, as Bell says, of uncertain meaning, and look it up in an Arabic-Syriac dictionary, we arrive at the Syriac verbal root *iṯar*. If we then look up the word *iṯar* in a Syriac-Arabic dictionary, such as the one by Mannā,[117] we can verify immediately that this verbal root has several meanings. The translator, an Aramaic native speaker, picked, from the many possibilities, the wrong word for this context. Among the meanings possible, Mannā gives, under (4), *faḍula* and *kāna fāḍilan*, meaning "virtuous, to be excellent." Luxenberg explains,

> And corresponding to these Mannā gives us further under (2) the Arabic meaning of the Syro-Aramaic nominal forms *m-yattartā* and *m-yattrūṯā*: *faḍīla, ḥasana* (virtue, excellence). In Arabic, the expression *faḍīla*, a lexical borrowing from the Syro-Aramaic, has been taken up into the language in the figurative sense of "virtue, excellence," but not the synonymous expression *baqīya*, which is only understood in its concrete sense of "rest." It is clear from the Koranic context, however, that with *baqīya* ("rest") the Koran, following the Syro-Aramaic semantics, really means *faḍīla*, virtue. As a result, our Koranic expression *'ūlū baqīya* (=*'ūlū faḍīla*) would be expalined as "[people] with virtue. That is to say, virtuous [people]."[118]

Astonishingly enough, John Penrice in his *A Dictionary and Glossary of the Koran*,[119] first published in 1873, under the word *baqīya*, gives, without any philological explanation, the correct, Luxenbergian translation for *'ūlū baqīyatin*; namely, "Endued with prudence or virtue."

The meanings of *baqīya* at Surahs 2:248 and 11:86 can also be explicated in a similar fashion under the root *iṯar* as "relics" and "rewards," respectively.

We can present the steps schematically in this way (SL=Source Language; TL=Target Language):

First example: "Avocado"

Previous Reading:
"Americans are a litigious people, they are frequently consulting their ***avocados***."

(the following scheme has been modified a bit)
SL [French] → TL [English]
TL "avocado" (no sense in this context)

First step: "translate the unclear word back into the SL"
English: "avocado" → French: "avocat"
Second step: "look for different meanings of the word in the SL"
SL "avocat" → TL_1 "lawyer"
→ TL_2 "champion, advocate (of a cause)"
→ TL_3 "avocado"
Third step: "pick the alternative meaning that fits the context in the TL"

Correct Reading:
"Americans are a litigious people, they are frequently consulting their ***lawyers***."

Second example: "baqīya"

Previous Reading: (Surah 11:116)
"'ulū baqīyatin"—"those ***of a remnant***":
Pickthall: "If only there had been among the generations before you ***men possessing a remnant*** (of good sense) to warn (their people) from corruption in the earth."

SL: Syriac; TL: Arabic
First step: "translate the unclear word back into the SL"
Arabic: "baqīya" → Syriac: "iṯar"
Second step: "look for different meanings of the word in the SL"
SL "iṯar" → TL_1 / TL_2 / TL_3
→ TL_3 "*faḍula / kāna fāḍilan*"—"virtuous / to be excellent"
Third step: "pick the alternative meaning that fits the context in the TL"

Correct Reading:
"'ulū baqīyatin" —"***the virtuous ones***":
"If only there had been among the generations before ***you men with virtue (virtuous people)*** to warn (their people) from corruption in the earth."

Third example: "yassara"

Previous Reading:
"fa-'innamā ***yassarnā***-hu bi-lisānika"—

"We have ***made*** it ***easy*** in thy tongue (in order that thou mayest thereby give good tidings to those who show piety)." *(Surah 19:97)*
SL: Syriac; TL: Arabic

First step: "translate the unclear word back into the SL"
Arabic: "yassara (3rd sg.)" → Syriac: "paššeq"
Second step: "look for different meanings of the word in the SL"
SL "paššeq" → TL_1 "to make easy, facilitate"
→ TL_2 "to explain, annotate"
→ TL_3 "to transfer, translate"
Third step: "pick the alternative meaning that fits the context in the TL"

Correct Reading:
"We ***have translated*** it (the Koran or the Scripture) into your language so that you may proclaim it (the Koran or the Scripture) to the (god-)fearing."

For the above example, Luxenberg provides a quote from Payne Smith's celebrated dictionary, *Thesaurus Syriacus*,[120] which renders the Syriac *paššeq* as "translated," and then refers us to Surah 54:17, 22, 32, and 40, where the following phrase is repeated:

> wa-la-qad yassarnā l-qur'āna li-ḏ-ḏikri fa-hal min muddakirin.

This verse is normally translated as:

> We have the Qur'ān available for the Reminder, but is there any one who takes heed? (Bell).

But Luxenberg renders it as:

> We have translated the Koran (that is, the Lectionary) as a reminder; are there then those that may (also) allow themselves to be reminded?

Luxenberg argues that

> in these passages, as a technical term, *yassara*, cannot be paraphrased in such a way as to say that God has "*made it easy*" for the Prophet insofar as He has "*revealed*" the Koran to him "*specifically in his own language,*" as Paret, for example, says. Instead, the term clearly states that this occurs indirectly by way of a *translation* from the *Scriptures*.[121]

5.4. Methodological Principles Continued

Let us come back to Davila's discussion of the methodological principles necessary to establish the *Vorlage* of a translation. He shows

> how difficult retroversion of the original text of a lost *Vorlage* is in principle. The slippage of structure and meaning between *Vorlage* and translation makes a perfect or even fairly good retroversion somewhere between difficult and impossible, and it creates many difficulties even for establishing Semitic interference.

Davila points to the added problem of distinguishing Semitic and Greek morphology and syntax:

> The basis of attempts to retrovert a Semitic original or to establish bilingual interference for Greek texts is to make distinctions between Semitic and Greek morphology and syntax, but much of their syntax is the same, and it is often difficult to be sure if a particular construction is Semitic rather than Greek.[122]

Of course, the problem is aggravated in our case, the search for a Syriac *Vorlage* of the Arabic Koran, for self-evident reasons.

For New Testament scholars, there is an urgent need to distinguish Greek from Semitic grammar. Davila refers to the work of Elliot C. Maloney[123] and Raymond Martin.[124] Martin, in particular, has proposed seventeen syntactical criteria for isolating Greek that has been translated from Hebrew or Aramaic.

Criteria 1–8 are derived from the relative frequency of eight prepositional constructions in relationship to the preposition ἐν: διά with genitive; διά in all its occurrences; εἰς ; κατά with accusative; κατά in all its occurrences; περί in all its occurrences; πρός with dative; ὑπό with genitive;

(9) the comparative frequencies of kaí and δέ in coordinating independent clauses;
(10) the separation of the Greek definite article from its substantive;
(11) a tendency to place genitives after the substantive on which they depend;
(12) a greater frequency of dependent genitive personal pronouns;
(13) a tendency to omit the article on a substantive with a dependent genitive personal pronoun;
(14) a tendency to place attributive adjectives after the word they qualify:
(15) less frequent use of attributive adjectives;
(16) less frequent use of adverbial participles; and
(17) less frequent use of the dative case without a preposition.[125]

According to Davila, "these features appear frequently in the verifiably translated Greek of the Septuagint (LXX) but are rare in in works composed in Hellenistic Greek."

I shall come back to what lessons we can learn from the translations in the Septuagint later. Maloney in a favorable review of the Martin's book suggests "that the criterion of the preposition πρός plus the dative as an indicator of Semitic origin be dropped, "because it is also very infrequent in nontranslated

Hellenistic Greek." Maloney would prefer to add four additional criteria namely,

> (1) verb-subject word order in independent clauses, (2) direct or indirect object pronouns placed immediately after their verb, (3) the frequency of third person pronouns in the oblique cases, and (4) the frequency of the remote demonstrative (eikeinos)—all of which I have shown to be more frequent in Semitic than in nontranslated Hellenistic Greek.[126]

Davila concludes that despite certain problems with Martin's criteria, his work is an important contribution to the discussion of ways to distinguish Greek morphology and syntax from that of Hebrew and Aramaic.[127]

5.5. The Problem of Interference from LXX, the Septuagint

5.5.1. Introductory Remarks

The Septuagint (or LXX) is the name given to the translation of the OT from Hebrew into Greek. According to the legendary Letter of Aristeas the LXX owes its origins to Ptolemy Philadelphus II (285–246 BCE), King of Egypt, who desired a translation for his Library at Alexandria, and commissioned seventy two (or perhaps seventy) Jerusalem elders for the onerous task; or the translation was made to meet the needs of the Jewish community who had forgotten their Hebrew. Only the Pentateuch or the Five Books of Moses were translated at first. Other books of the OT, and books of the Jewish and Protestant canon, and the Apocrypha, were translated in later centuries, and other locations, and the entire anthology came to be called the Septuagint. Thus, far from being a unitary work,

> there is wide-ranging diversity and heterogeneity within the collection—to the point that some scholars now question the continued use of the term "Septuagint," which to the unwary might suggest a greater degree of uniformity than can be demonstrated.[128]

Thus, many scholars prefer the term "Old Greek" to refer, "in the case of each individual book or unit of translations, to the earliest rendition into Greek."[129]

The importance of the LXX in the present context lies in the fact that it

> had a literary influence on Jewish literature, most of which contained a significant religious element. This is most obvious in the realm of vocabulary: many religious terms originating in the Greek Bible, especially the Pentateuch, were absorbed into the Greek written by Jews and then into New Testament and Christian Greek.[130]

Thus, the Semitic influence evident in the Greek of some of the Gospels (and the Acts) may be due to the deliberate imitation of the language of the LXX. The Semitic influence in Luke (1:5–2:52), for example,

> may (or may not) be due in part to the absorption of translated Semitic sources (especially poetic compositions), but it is difficult to escape the impression that Luke, having written the prologue (1:1–4) in good Greek style, deliberately varied his style in the infancy narrative to imitate the language of the LXX. This impression is reinforced by the high level of Septuagintalisms in the language of the Gospel of Luke overall.[131]

Another example would be the beginning of the Acts, when Moses is told to take off his sandals as he is standing on holy ground. The passage in the NT seems to be almost a direct quotation from the Septuagint (bold forms are identical):

> **εἶπεν** μὴ ἐγγίσῃς ὧδε **λῦσαι τὸ ὑπόδημα** ἐκ **τῶν ποδῶν σου ὁ γὰρ τόπος ἐν ᾧ σὺ ἕστηκας γῆ ἁγία ἐστίν**—Then He said, "Do not come near here; remove your sandals from your feet, for the place on which you are standing is holy ground." (Ex 3:5)
> **εἶπεν** δὲ αὐτῷ ὁ κύριος **λῦσον τὸ ὑπόδημα τῶν ποδῶν σου ὁ γὰρ τόπος ἐν ᾧ σὺ ἕστηκας γῆ ἁγία ἐστίν**—But the Lord said to him, "take off the sandals from your feet, for the place on which you are standing is holy ground." (Acts 7:33)

Hence, apparent Semitisms in Greek works could simply be imitations of the style of the LXX.

> The logical conclusion . . . is that Septuagintalisms—expressions found frequently in LXX Greek as well as direct allusions to specific LXX passages—cannot be advanced as decisive proof of Semitic interference due to translation from a Semitic *Vorlage*.

5.5.2. Translation Techniques and the Septuagint

Here, I think, it would be appropriate to discuss the work of Theo A.W. van der Louw on the translation techniques used in the Septuagint. His study *Transformations in the Septuagint* bears the subtitle *Towards an Interaction of Septuagint Studies and Translation Studies.* Thus his work bears the explicit duty of promoting interaction between Translation Studies and the study of the LXX. Since Translation Studies became a respected academic discipline in the 1970s, there has been a boom in publications, both monographs and journals devoted entirely to aspects of translation.[132] Van der Louw clearly believes that this research can be applied to Septuagint Studies fruitfully since the Septuagint is a translation.

If we think that parts of the Koran are dependent on some source text, perhaps, in Syriac, we need to reconstruct the source text. And we cannot achieve this without knowledge of the translation techniques, hence the importance of works like van der Louw's study on the Septuagint. The following discussions and examples are taken from his work *Transformations in the Septuagint.*

Chaim Rabin describes the characteristics of the Septuagint that he believes are a result of a certain type of translation technique:

(1) non-appreciation of poetic diction,
(2) the tendency to replace metaphors by plain statements,
(3) omission of parts of text,
(4) mechanical renderings,
(5) lack of consistency, and
(6) translating word for word without regard for the order or the syntax of the target language.[133]

Free translations, on the other hand, result in additions for the sake of clarity, omissions of elements considered superfluous, and exegetical substitutions, mostly for theological reasons.

Louw throughout his study makes it clear that in some cases in the Septuagint the "Greek words do not make sense in the translated text unless we take recourse to the Hebrew original,"[134] which is also a methodological principle of Luxenberg. On occasions it is clear that by his literal translation the translator has preserved the exegetical difficulty of the Masoretic Text.[135]

Finally ven der Louw gives us a comprehensive inventory of different kinds of translations, or as he prefers to call them, transformations: graphological and phonological translation, transcription or borrowing (loanword), calque, literal translation, modulations or lexcical changes, transpositions or grammatical changes, addition, omission, redistribution of semantic features, situational translation, idiomatic translation of idiom, non-idiomatic translation, explicitation, implicitation, anaphoric translation, stylistic translation and compensation, and morphematic translation.[136]

5.6. The Problem of Bilingual Interference

I have already referred, above, to the works of several Semiticists who discuss the phenomenon of bilingualism and its consequences for the study of translations. Davila reminds us of its import for Biblical Studies. I believe it is equally important for Christoph Luxenberg's thesis. Davila writes,

> If a native speaker of Hebrew or Aramaic were to compose a text in Greek, it is entirely possible—likely, even—that the writer would produce a text containing elements of Semitic interference purely because he or she thought in a

> Semitic language. This simple observation raises new difficulties for establishing that a Greek text was translated from Hebrew or Aramaic. If a Greek word displays a high density of Semitisms and many of these are not characteristic of the LXX, they could still mean that the writer was composing in Greek but thinking in Hebrew or Aramaic. There need not be a Semitic *Vorlage*.[137]

However, some linguists would be a bit more cautious here. To adduce an example from German: Even people who do not know English well will nowadays use English phrases like "am Ende des Tages," which goes back to the English expression "at the end of the day" and is more and more replacing the "real German" idiom "letzten Endes." How did this come about: the fact is that some writers or speakers—often well-known journalists—who used English every day and had to translate from it into German started to literally render these phrases into German instead of using the "semantically" corresponding form. Then other Germans inadvertently started to use them as well—they were just copying role models after all.

In the case of Greek and Aramaic this might mean the following: if "Semitic" phrases are used in a text, this might go back to linguistic interference, but it might also go back to *older stages* of influencing. Thus, Luke was maybe not *thinking in Aramaic*, but he used *the variant of Greek spoken by descendants of people who had spoken both languages, which had at that time influenced each other*.

There is yet another reason to doubt that Luke knew Hebrew or Aramaic: He tells us that St. Paul spoke "in the Hebrew" language to the Jews, probably meaning Aramaic. Could such a blunder have happened to somebody who "thought in Aramaic"?

In the book of Daniel (written in Hebrew, Aramaic, and Greek) the change of language is indicated with the words: *aramīt* and *ʿiḇrīt*. So the Jews of this era were well aware that Hebrew and Aramaic were not the same.

To adduce another example: as already mentioned, modern Hindi has replaced many Persian words common in Hindustani by Sanskrit etyma. But if a modern speaker uses these words we cannot conclude that he or she knows Sanskrit, or even that Sanskrit is his or her mother tongue; but we can conclude that at least some people *in the past* who had an impact on the linguistic development of Hindi knew Sanskrit! So the question remains: How can we detect Semitic bilingual interference in a Greek text that contains Semitisms?

> A translation written in otherwise good Greek but showing numerous Semitisms would be unlikely to be by a writer who did not know Greek well and who was displaying Semitic bilingual interference. But the other side of this coin is that a writer who could write in good Greek and who was translating a

> work into otherwise good Greek would not be likely to leave many Semitisms in the translation. So in this hypothetical case, if we found blocks of text containing a high density of Semitisms alongside blocks of good Greek we could conclude that the writer was either incorporating translated Greek passages into the work or translating passages from a Semitic source in some places while writing in his or her normal style in others.[138]

One can also conjecture that bilingual interference is not the source of Semitisms if we find clear cases of mistranslations of a Semitic original in a Greek text.

> If it can be established that the composer of the Greek text did not understand a Hebrew or Aramaic term, it shows that this writer was thinking in Greek, not a Semitic language, and therefore the Semitisms in the text are not the result of the writer mentally translating from Semitic into Greek.

Of course, in the absence of the *Vorlage* it is almost impossible to show such misunderstandings.[139]

Davila cites the work of Zipora Talshir on double translations, whose appearance in the Greek would be a possible indicator of translation. Talshir defines a double translation as follows:

> To sum up, we argued that a "double translation" comprises alternate renderings which are not free exegetical additions and do not serve another purpose than the rendering of the *Vorlage* word. We also implied that there should be a difference between the components of the "double translation" in order to justify the use of the term. It is not enough that a *Vorlage*-item is represented twice. The duplicity should be the result of two different solutions provided to one and the same problem presented by the *Vorlage*-item.[140]

Davila explains the importance of double translations:

> Thus a double translation consists of two different attempts to translate the same word or phrase of the *Vorlage*, each based on different exegetical solution to the problem. Talshir also distinguishes between double translations of single words and double translations of larger units. A double translation of a single word might arise from two attempts by the original translator to translate a word whose meaning was in doubt, or another mechanism could explain it, such as the attraction of a marginal gloss from another translation of the same work into the text or the introduction of a different rendering by a bilingual scribe who accesses to the original. . . . A double translation of a larger unit, such as a long clause or a sentence, is mush less likely to have been the work of the original translator. . . . The appearance of double translations of single words in a Greek text suspected of being a translation would not be very significant, since a possible explanation would be that the writer, whose knowledge of Greek may have been imperfect anyway, was unsure which Greek

> word was the more appropriate and so included both. But if the double translation is of a larger unit, it is much more likely that either it comes from a translator attempting to make sense of an imperfectly grasped Semitic phrase or it is a gloss from another, now lost, translation of the Semitic work. Presumably an author who was a native speaker of the Semitic language would know what the phrase meant and would not need to include two different exegeses of it in the translation. Thus the appearance of a double translation of a unit greater than a single word and based on different understandings of that unit would be a persuasive indicator that the Semitisms in the Greek work were not the result of bilingual interference.[141]

Davila ends by laying out ten steps one must take to establish Semitic interference due to translation from a Semitic *Vorlage*:

1. Look at all possible linguistic and stylistics features—morphology, vocabulary, syntax, word order, and poetic elements—for apparent Semitisms.
2. Distinguish Hebrew from Aramaic Semitisms.
3. Use Hebrew and Aramaic of the right time and place.
4. Eliminate those features also characteristic of Greek.
5. Do not eliminate apparent Semitisms found only in the non-literary Greek papyri if these Semitisms are also found in Coptic, since they may be due to Egyptian interference in the Greek of the papyri.
6. "All Semitisms that are used commonly in the LXX ('Septuagintalisms') should be set apart as a special category."
7. "Likewise, Semitisms that appear in only one or a few LXX passages, but passages frequently quoted because of their use in liturgical and apologetic contexts, should be set apart with the Septuagintalisms."
8. "Some control has to be introduced to factor out interference from the language of the LXX."
9. "Controls also have to be introduced to factor out bilingual interference."
10. "Allegedly Semitic poetic and stylistic features should be advanced—if at all—only as ancillary evidence."

6. Arabic and the Koran

Many modern non-Muslim scholars step gingerly when discussing Arabic, its history, and especially its relationship to the Koran. One wonders, for example, if Herbjørn Jenssen in his article "Arabic Language" in *Encyclopaedia of the Qur'ān*,[142] is not trying to have it both ways even if he perhaps avoids contradicting himself formally by his use of imprecise and ambiguous language. We are first informed that there are twenty modern states that use Arabic as an official language, Then, at the beginning, he tells us that

> the language used in all these states and taught in their schools, is said to be structurally identical to the claasical langauge and the language of the Qur'ān (*al-fuṣḥā* or "classical Arabic"). It is, however, freely admitted that both its vocabulary and idiomatic usage have developed *considerably* [I. W.'s emphasis]. One, therefore, frequently finds a distinction being made between classical Arabic, on the one hand, and contemporary Arabic (*al-lugha al-ʿarabiyya al-ḥadītha* or *al-muʿāṣira*), on the other.

Then, at the end of the article, Jenssen insists that

> Arabic is more than the language of Islam, it is a part of Islam. It is, as indeed are all languages, a phenomenon of culture, not one of nature, and changes as does the culture for which it is a medium but at the core it is *unchanging* [emphasis added by I.W.], just as the document which is at the core of the culture of Islam, the Qur'ān, is unchanging.

Has Arabic changed and developed, or has it remained unchanging? Does he mean Classical Arabic? Or Arabic in general? But what is "Arabic" in general? Furthermore, Jenssen's attitude is clearly Islamic—not scientific—since he equates the language of the Koran with Classical Arabic (CA, henceforth). As we shall see the language of the Koran is not CA despite the insistence of Muslim theologians.

As Jenssen points out, CA is not the first langauge of anyone. But he then takes an entirely apologetic stance, trying not to offend the tender sensibilities of the Arabs, when he adds,

> this may, unless due care is taken, lead to a view of classical Arabic as somehow "artificial" or "congealed" or as a "dead language" artificially kept alive by the conservatism of certain elites. The feeling that the "real" or "living" Arabic language is represented by the colloquials is widespread. This has the laudatory effect of drawing attention to the actual colloquial usage in which most communication within the Arab world takes place, a field which is seriously understudied. It is, however, also an attitude which an Arab may regard as offensive. Not only is this person denied the status of a "native speaker" of his own language, he is also being told that he may not really master it (Parkinson),[143] and that it is a foreign language, or at least a strange dialect, even to great linguists from whom he inherited its rules (Owens).[144] One cannot help but feel that this is quite unnecessary and certainly counterproductive.[145]

The above account is hopelessly confused, begs too many questions to be taken seriously, and has as its sole justification the blazoning of the author's Islamically and politically correct sentiments. Who is responsible for this "counterproductive" attitude? The Western scholars named, D. B. Parkinson and Jonathan Owens, or, perhaps, foreign experts on Arabic linguistics in general? But if the "Arab" who may be offended does *not* speak Classical Arabic as his first language how can he be described as a "native speaker" of classical Arabic. He is *not* being denied the status of a "native speaker" of his own language, since Classical Arabic is not his language. On the contrary, one could argue, that the ordinary Arab is being told that he should not despise his own colloquial language; he should not feel inadequate if he does not speak Classical Arabic—no one has ever spoken Classical Arabic. Arab intellectuals themselves have lamented the way Classical Arabic and its modern avatar, Modern Standard Arabic, have been foisted upon them as a label and artificial indentity. In 1929, Tawfiq Awan had argued that the vernaculars of the Middle East were languages in their own right, not mere dialects of Arabic. He wrote,

> Egypt has an Egyptian language; Lebanon has a Lebanese language; the Hijaz has a Hijazi language; and so forth—and all of these languages are by no means Arabic languages. Each of our countries has a language, which is its own possession: So why do we not write [our language] as we converse in it? For, the language in which the people speak is the language in which they also write.[146]

No less a figure than Ṭāhā Ḥusayn, (often spelled Taha Hussein, 1889–1973), the greatest modern man of letters of Egypt and the Arab world,

> made a sharp distinction between what he viewed to be Arabic *tout court*—that is, the classical and modern standard form of the language—and the sundry vernaculars in use in his contemporary native Egypt and elsewhere in the Near East. For Egyptians, Arabic is virtually a foreign language, wrote Ḥusayn: "Nobody speaks it at home, [in] school, [on] the streets, or in clubs; it is not even used in [the] Al-Azhar [Islamic University] itself. People everywhere speak a language that is definitely not Arabic, despite the partial resemblance to it."[147]

Ṭāhā Ḥusayn also wrote in 1956 that Modern Standard Arabic is

> difficult and grim, and the pupil who goes to school in order to study Arabic acquires only revulsion for his teacher and for the language, and employs his time in pursuit of any other occupations that would divert and soothe his thoughts away from this arduous effort. . . . Pupils hate nothing more than they hate studying Arabic.[148]

E. Shouby, a trained clinical and social psychologist, and a native speaker of Arabic, wrote an essay in 1951 titled, "The Influence of the Arabic Language on the Psychology of the Arabs"[149] that examined the anguished, complex, tortured relationship of Arabs to their language. Shouby wrote that

> In spite of the numerous cries for reform in both the language and the style of Arabic literature, it is still impossible for any Arab to write with no consideration for such grammatical, idiomatic, or stylistic requirements as are exemplified in the Qur'an without running the risk of being denounced as an ignorant or a stupid person, if not as an impudent abuser of the integrity of Arabic as well as of the sacredness of the revealed word of God. But whereas an Arab must write in "literary Arabic," he is not expected to use the same language in his everyday conversations; for that purpose he has to use the colloquial Arabic, which differs from one country to another, even from one city to the next. Should he try to write with the declared intention of using the colloquial—which is usually done for "humorous" purposes or to quote the spoken word—he will have to face the difficulty of spelling, and in all probability very few people outside the area in which this brand of spoken Arabic is used will fully understand him. Should he, on the other hand, try to speak the literary Arabic he writes, our writer will find himself misunderstood by the illiterate and ridiculed by all, as has been the misfortune of many purists who try to make the literary language of the books the language of everyday life. Educated Arabs themselves make fun of anybody who uses it for practical everyday life purposes, but they require any public speaker to use it rather than the colloquial. . . . The gap between the literary language and any one of the colloquials is so great that an educated Egyptian who knows the literary language as well as the colloquial Egyptian finds it difficult to understand correctly the Iraqi colloquial; and so may the educated Syrian fail to understand the spoken Arabic of Morocco or Tunis. This situation is a strong reminder of medieval Europe, when educated people wrote and read Latin but spoke the different dialects which later developed into what are now the various European languages. The medieval scholar, however, could speak Latin correctly and without the risk of being ridiculed whenever he met other scholars from other countries; the contemporary educated Arab has difficulty in mastering all the endless intricacies of literary Arabic, and even after a lifetime of study he usually has to be very alert if he wants to use it correctly.

Here is what I wrote in 2002[150]:

> Even for contemporary Arabic-speaking peoples, reading the Koran is far from being a straightforward matter. The Koran is putatively (as we shall see, it is very difficult to decide exactly what the language of the Koran is) written in what we call Classical Arabic (CA), but modern Arab populations, leaving aside the problem of illiteracy in Arab countries,[151] do not speak, read, or write, let alone think, in CA. We are confronted with the phenomenon of *diglossia*,[152] that is to say, a situation where two varieties of the same language live side by side. The two variations are high and low. High Arabic is sometimes called Modern Literary Arabic or Modern Standard Arabic; is learned through formal education in school, like Latin or Sanskrit; and would be used

> in sermons, university lectures, news broadcasts, and for mass media purposes. Low Arabic, or Colloquial Arabic, is a dialect native speakers acquire as a mother tongue, and is used at home conversing with family and friends, and also in radio or television soap operas. But, as Kaye points out, "the differences between many colloquials and the classical language are so great that a *fallāḥ* who had never been to school could hardly understand more than a few scattered words and expressions in it without great difficulty. One could assemble dozens of so-called Arabs (*fallāḥīn*) in a room, who have never been exposed to the classical language, so that not one could properly understand the other."[153]

In the introduction to his grammar of Koranic and Classical Arabic, Wheeler M. Thackston writes,

> The Koran established an unchanging norm for the Arabic language. There are, of course, certain lexical and syntactic features of Koranic Arabic that became obsolete in time, and the standardization of the language at the hands of the philologians of the eighth and ninth centuries emphasized certain extra-Koranic features of the Arabic poetic *koine* while downplaying other, Koranic usages; yet by and large not only the grammar but even the vocabulary of a modern newspaper article display only slight variation from the established norm of classicized Koranic Arabic.[154]

Though he does allow for some change and decay, Thackston it seems to me, paints a totally misleading picture of the actual linguistic situation in modern Arabic-speaking societies. He implies that anyone able to read a modern Arabic newspaper should have no difficulties with the Koran or any Classical Arabic text. Thackston seems totally insensitive "to the evolution of the language, to changes in the usage and meaning of terms over the very long period and in the very broad area in which Classical Arabic has been used."[155] Anyone who has lived in the Middle East in recent years will know that the language of the press is at best semiliterary,[156] and it's certainly simplified as far as structure and vocabulary are concerned. We can discern what would be called grammatical errors from a Classical Arabic point of view in daily newspapers or on television news. This semiliterary language is highly artificial, and certainly no one thinks in it. For an average middle-class Arab it would take considerable effort to construct even the simplest sentence, let alone talk, in Classical Arabic. The linguist Pierre Larcher has written of the

> considerable gap between Medieval Classical Arabic and Modern Classical Arabic [or what I have been calling Modern Literary Arabic], certain texts written in the former are today the object of explanatory texts in the latter.

He then adds in a footnote that he has in his library, based on this model, an edition of the *Risāla* of Shāfiʿī (died 204/820) that appeared in a collection with the significant title *Getting Closer to the Patrimony*.[157] As Kaye puts it,

> In support of the hypothesis that modern standard Arabic is ill-defined is the so-called "mixed" language or "Inter-Arabic" being used in the speeches of, say, President Bourguiba of Tunisia, noting that very few native speakers of Arabic from any Arab country can really ever master the intricacies of Classical Arabic grammar in such a way as to extemporaneously give a formal speech in it.[158]

Pierre Larcher[159] has pointed out that wherever you have a linguistic situation where two varieties of the same language coexist, you are also likely to get all sorts of linguistic mixtures, leading some linguists to talk of *triglossia*. Gustav Meiseles[160] even talks of *quadriglossia*: between Literary Arabic and Vernacular Arabic, he distinguishes a Substandard Arabic and an Educated Spoken Arabic. Still others speak of *pluri-* or *multi-* or *polyglossia*, viewed as a continuum.[161]

Given Wheeler Thackston's views quoted above it was a surprise to me to learn from Franck Salameh's article already cited that

> Harvard linguist Wheeler Thackston—and before him Taha Hussein, Ahmad Lutfi al-Sayyed, Abdelaziz Fehmi Pasha, and many others—have shown that the Middle East's demotic languages are not Arabic at all, and consequently, that one can hardly speak of 280 million native Arabophones—or even of a paltry one million such Arabic speakers—without oversimplifying and pervertting an infinitely complex linguistic situation. The languages or dialects often perfunctorily labeled Arabic might indeed not be Arabic at all.[162]

However, I have been unable to procure Thackston's book referred to by Salameh, *The Vernacular Arabic of the Lebanon;*[163] thus I am forced to rely on Salameh's interpretation of Thackston's findings.

> Thackston has identified five dialectal clusters that he classified as follows: "(1) Greater Syria, including Lebabon and Palestine; (2) Mesopotamia, including the Euphrates region of Syria, Iraq, and the Persian Gulf; (3) the Arabian Peninsula, including most of what is Saudi Arabia and much of Jordan; (4) the Nile Valley, including Egypt and the Sudan; and (5) North Africa and [parts of] the . . . regions of sub-Saharan Africa."

There is substantial comprehension within each cluster, but, writes Thackston,

> When one crosses one or major boundaries, as is the case with a Baghdadi and a Damascene for instance, one begins to encounter difficulty in comprehension; and the farther one goes, the less one understands until mutual com-

> prehension disappears entirely. To take an extreme example, a Moroccan and an Iraqi can no more understand each other's dialects than can a Portuguese a Rumanian.[164]

The United Nations Arab Human Development Report of 2003, written by Arabs, such as Laila Abdel Majid, Fowziyah Abdullah Abu-Khalid, Muhammad Hassan Al-Amin, Aziz Al-Azmeh, and Sami Al-Banna, for Arabs, noted the difficulties of the Arabic language when confronted with the problems of the twenty-first century:

> Today, at the gates of the knowledge society and the future, the Arabic language is, however, facing severe challenges and a real crisis in theorization, grammar, vocabulary, usage, documentation, creativity and criticism. . . . The teaching of Arabic is also undergoing a severe crisis in terms of both methodology and curricula. The most apparent aspect of this crisis is the growing neglect of the functional aspects of (Arabic) language use. Arabic language skills in everyday life have deteriorated and Arabic language classes are often restricted to writing at the expense of reading.
>
> The situation of Arabic language teaching cannot be separated from that of classical Arabic in general, which has in effect ceased to be a spoken language. It is only the language of reading and writing; the formal language of intellectuals and academics, often used to display knowledge in lectures. Classical Arabic is not the language of cordial, spontaneous expression, emotions, daily encounters and ordinary communication. It is not a vehicle for discovering one's inner self or outer surroundings.[165]

The report ended by underlining the importance of teaching foreign languages at an early age in government schools.[166]

Kees Versteegh's much-lauded book *The Arabic Language*[167] correctly observes that

> since the Second World War, Arabic studies have become somewhat isolated from the developments in Semitic languages. Whereas before this time Arabic was usually studied within the framework of the Semitic languages, there has been a growing tendency to emphasise its character as an Islamic language and study its connection with other Islamic languages, such as Persian and Turkish. The knowledge of Arabic remains important for comparisons between Semitic languages, but increasingly these comparisons are no longer initiated from within the circle of Arabic studies.[168]

Given this promising start, one expected something more robust, scientific, and skeptical from Versteegh's study of the Arabic language, with, at least, an attempt to rectify the above-cited inadequacies. Instead we have Versteegh's uncritical acceptance of the entire Islamic tradition about the history of Arabic, despite his occasional token skepticism. He refers to the Koran as "revealed" or a "revelational document" or a "revelation,"[169] which is a theological position, and hardly a scientific attitude. To treat the Koran as "revealed" assumes Versteegh knows how the Koran came into being. All our putative knowledge of the entire history of the the Prophet, the compilation of the Koran, and the rise of Islam is derived from very late tendentious and contradictory material, so we must treat with skepticism all we are told about the dialects in Pre-Islamic Arabia, the very existence of Pre-Islamic poetry, and the Koran, and so on. Therefore, Versteegh's account of the history of the Arabic language, in other words as a diachronic study, is highly unsatisfactory.

The fascinating study, by Michael Zwettler,[170] on the language of pre-Islamic poetry, the Koran, and the relationship of Arabic to the vernaculars, and also the linguistic situation in seventh century Arabia, is equally uncritical of the sources, likewise treating the Koran as a "revealed"[171] text. Zwettler's conclusions are also unsatisfactory, but along the way he provides useful summaries of the debates surrounding the vexed subject of the language of Pre-Islamic poetry and the language of the Koran. Both Zwettler and Versteegh seem to think that one can leave to one side the question of "How the Koran Came to Us," and still discuss the history of the Arabic language, pre-Islamic poetry, and so on. But until we take John Wansbrough's work seriously and work out the implications of his conclusions we cannot possibly make any progress. Wansbrough's *Quranic Studies* came out in 1977, Zwettler's thesis in 1978, and Versteegh's monograph in 1997. Neither Zwettler nor Versteegh refer to *Quranic Studies*. It was probably too late for Zwettler to take it into account, but it is scandalous that Versteegh ignores Wansbrough's *Quranic Studies* and *The Sectarian Milieu* (1978) totally.

If the Koran grew out of the polemical arenas of Palestine and the Near East, then it is possible that the answers to our questions regarding the rise of Islam lie not in the Hijaz, or the mythical cities of Mecca and Medina, but much farther north. We need to examine the linguistic and religious situation of Palestine in the seventh century; we need to examine the linguistic promiscuity of the traditional Holy Land, for which some seventh-century sources are extant, and not at the fictive dialects of the heavily romanticized Bedouins, for which, in any case, there are no seventh-century records.

Zwettler takes for granted that Pre-Islamic poetry is authentic, and he dismisses out of hand the views of skeptics such as David S. Margoliouth[172] and Ṭāhā Ḥusayn,[173] who, he believes, have been definitively refuted by scholars such as A. J. Arberry.[174] But they have not. John Wansbrough was one of the first to point out that so-called Pre-Islamic poetry often served a polemical purpose:

> Whatever may have been the original motives for collecting and recording the ancient poetry of the Arabs,[175] the earliest evidence of such activity belongs, not unexpectedly, to the third/ninth century and the work of the classical philologists. The manner in which this material was manipulated by its collectors to support almost any argument appears never to have been very successfully concealed. The procedure, moreover, was common to all fields of scholarly activity: e.g. the early dating of a verse ascribed to the *mukhaḍramī*[176] poet Nābigha Ja'dī in order to provide a pre-Islamic proof text for a common Quranic construction (finite verb form preceded by direct object),[177] Mubarrad's admitted invention of a *Jāhilī* [Pre-Islamic] verse as a gloss to a lexical item in the *ḥadīth*,[178] and Abū 'Amr b. 'Alā's candid admission that save for a single verse of 'Amr b. Kulthūm, knowledge of Yawm Khazāz would have been lost to posterity.[179] The three examples share at least one common motive: recognition of pre-Islamic poetry as authority in linguistic matters, even where such contained non-linguistic implications. Also common to all three is another, perhaps equally significant feature: Ibn Qutayba, who adduced the verse of Nābigha to explain/justify Quranic syntax, lived at the end of the third/ninth century, as did Mubarrad; Abū 'Amr, of whom no written works were preserved, lived in the second half of the second/eighth century, but this particular dictum was alluded to only in Jāḥiẓ (third/ninth century) and explicitly in Ibn 'Abd Rabbih (fourth/tenth century). Now, that pre-Islamic poetry should have achieved a kind of status as linguistic canon some time in the third/ninth century may provoke no quarrel. That it had achieved any such status earlier must, I think, be demonstrated. The fact that it had not, in one field at least, can be shown: the absence of poetic *shawāhid* in the earliest form of scriptural exegesis might be thought to indicate that appeal to the authority of *Jāhilī* (and other) poetry was not standard practice before the third/ninth century. Assertions to the contrary may be understood as witness to the extraordinary influence exercised by the concept of *faṣāḥat al-jāhiliyya* [that is, the purity of the Arabic language of Pre-Islamic, pagan times].[180]

In other words, the putative eloquence of pre-Islamic poetry became commonplace only in the third/ninth century; there are no references to pre-Islamic poetry in the early, pre-third century, works of Koranic exegesis.

What was the nature of Arabic before and after the rise of Islam, particularly between the third and sixth centuries, and then between the seventh and ninth centuries? When did the break between the spoken and written language (the phenomenon of diglossia) take place? Out of what and when did Classical Arabic develop? In what language was the Koran written?

As I wrote in 2002,[181]

> Let us begin with the last two questions. According to Muslims, the Koran was written in the dialect of the Quraysh of Mecca, and CA was born out of the

> Meccan dialect, which was considered the linguistic norm. The language of the Koran, which is identical to the poetical *koine*, is one of the two bases of CA; Muhammad, being from Mecca, could only have received the revelation in his original dialect, that of the Quraysh. Nöldeke seems to accept the tradetional Muslim view that the Koran and pre-Islamic poetry (poetical *koine*) were the two sources of CA, and that the Koran was written in the Meccan dialect: "For me it is highly unlikely that Muhammad in the Koran had used a form of language absolutely different from the usual one in Mecca, that he would have used case and mood inflexions if his compatriots had not used them."[182]

Even if we take the traditional accounts of the rise of Islam and the compilation of the Koran as historically sound, (which they are not), there still remain a certain number of objections to the Muslim view. First, it is unlikely that there existed a linguistic norm. If Mecca were an important commercial town and center of pilgrimage, it must have been open to the linguistic influence brought by travelers from Yemen, Syria, and Najd. Second, Muhammad's preaching had at least Pan-Arab pretensions, but these pretensions would seem hardly realizable if he was using only his local dialect. Surely Muhammad's preaching in the urban language of Mecca would have had no meaning for the nomads, whose language, according to the account of Muslim scholars themselves, was considered more prestigious.

Most Western Islamologists buy this story at face value without becoming aware of the fact that this latter point is highly questionable: it will be difficult to find a language with *urban* and *rural* varieties, where the rural varieties are more prestigious! Who wants to sound like a hillbilly? In their fifth Inârah anthology, Markus Gross[183] compares the allegedly romantic attitude of Arabs (old and modern) toward Bedouin life to the romantic attitude of the Romans up to Shakespeare toward "shepherd life": consider the *bucolic* and *pastoral* poetic tradition (e.g., Theocritus, Ovid) and the idealization of "Arcadia." In the 1960s many French would have claimed to dream of being a "shepherd in the Vosges mountains," although they had never seen or touched a living sheep in their whole life. Had these Romans and French had to castrate or slaughter sheep or to stave off a pack of wolves with their shepherd's staff—this is what the crook is meant for—they would certainly not have dreamt of being shepherds! Bedouin and Shepherd life is extremely boring! Real shepherds, Bedouins and Prairie Indians ("eternal hunting-grounds") have as much tendency to romanticize their life as steel workers are prone to dream of an "eternal steel mill."

For some Western scholars, like Blachère,[184] CA was derived from pre-Islamic poetry and the language of the Koran. But for Blachère, the language of the Koran has nothing to do with the dialect of Mecca; rather it is the language of pre-Islamic poetry (the so-called poetical *koine*). As Schaade put it,

> The earliest specimens of classical Arabic known to us are found in the pre-Islamic poems. The problem arises how the poets (who for the most part must have been ignorant of writing) came to possess a common poetical language,—either (perhaps with the object of securing for their works a wider field of circulation?) they used for their purposes a language composed of elements from all the different dialects, such as may have been created by the necessities of trade, and which it only remained for them to ennoble, or the dialect of any particular tribe (perhaps owing to political circumstances?) achieved in pre-historic times special pre-eminence as a language of poetry.[185]

Blachère certainly accepts the idea that *diglossia* is an old phenomenon going back to pre-Islamic times. That is to say, scholars like Blachère, Vollers,[186] Wehr,[187] and Diem,[188] believe that the poetical *koine*, the language of pre-Islamic poetry, was a purely literary dialect, distinct from all spoken idioms and supertribal. Other scholars, like Nöldeke,[189] Fück,[190] and Blau,[191] agree with the traditional Arab view that diglossia developed as late as the first Islamic century as a result of the Arab conquests, when non-Arabs began to speak Arabic.

Karl Vollers upset many people when he argued at the beginning of the twentieth century that the Koran was written, without *iʿrāb*, inflection, or case endings, in a dialect of Nağd, and was a result of editing and emendation carried out long after Muhammad with a view to harmonizing the sacred text with the language of so-called pre-Islamic poetry, which is that of Nağd. Vollers is certain that the Koran as we have it today is not linguistically the revelation as it was received by Muhammad. One must take into account the numerous phonetic variants preserved in the commentaries and special treatises. These variants of a dialectal origin attest to the contrast between the speech of the Ḥiğāz and that of Nağd. The Koran preserves everywhere certain linguistic features maintained in Nağd and on the way to disappearance in the Ḥiğāz, according to Muslim grammarians; thus, the Koran represents the speech of Nağd. The Koran is the result of adaptation, and it issues from the emendations of the text by readers of Nağdian atavism or influenced by the nomadic dialects of this region. As to the linguistic identity of the Koran and pre-Islamic poetry, it is explained by the fact that Muslim scholars unified them one by the other during the course of the establishment of the grammar. Vollers concludes that the Koran and pre-Islamic poetry are truly the two sources of CA, but with this reservation that the Koran is an adaptation of the Ḥiğāzi dialect to the norms of the poetical language.

Blachère contended that Vollers made too much of the putative contrast between the western dialect and eastern dialect. The contrast between the Ḥiğāz and Nağd is not as clear-cut as Vollers makes out. Vollers also seems to accept certain linguistic features as true of the time of Muhammad, but which, in reality, were the creations of much later Muslim philologists. If there had been harmonization of the Koranic text with the dialects of Naǧd, one would expect to find the essential character of these dialects, the *taltala*. One would find traces of this adaptation in the vocabulary and syntax.

Wansbrough has his own reasons for rejecting Vollers's theory:

> The basic error lay in Vollers' adherence to an arbitrary and fictive chronology, though that may have been less important than his contention that the refashioned language of scripture could be identified as the CA of the Arabic grammarians. Neither from the point of view of lexicon nor from that of syntax could the claim be justified.[192]

In other words, the language of the Koran is not Classical Arabic.

However, Vollers's theory was revived in 1948 by Paul Kahle, who sees in a saying of al-Farrā' promising reward to those reciting the Koran with *iʿrāb* support for Vollers's view that the original Koran had no *iʿrāb*.[193]

Corriente also makes the point in his classic paper[194] that the language of the Koran is not CA. For Corriente, CA was standardized by the grammarians in the eighth and ninth centuries CE, on the whole depending on a central core of Old Arabic dialects as koineized in pre-Islamic poetry and rhetoric, and the speech of contemporary Bedouins. Grammarians did not invent the *iʿrāb* system, which must have existed in the texts they edited. (*Iʿrāb* is usually translated as "inflexion," indicating case and mood, but the Arab grammarians define it as "the difference that occurs, in fact or virtually, at the end of a word, because of the various antecedents that govern it.")[195] They did come with their preconceptions about what constituted good Arabic, but they nonetheless respected what they learned from their Bedouin informants in order to standardize the language, and thus fix what came to be CA. However, some did reject certain utterances of the Bedouins as being incorrect.

Koranic Arabic is structurally intermediate between OA *koine* and Eastern Bedouin Arabic and Middle Arabic, and, of course, the Koran cannot have been written in CA since this was only finally standardized over a period of time during the eighth and ninth centuries.

Native tradition identifies two groups of dialects, Ancient West and East Arabian, neither of them identical to the OA *koine*. Corriente adds a third kind of Arabic, Nabataean, the immediate forerunner of the Middle Arabic of Islamic cities. It was very widespread indeed.

Finally, Corriente calls attention to the fact that Bedouin vernaculars themselves must also have been undergoing change under various sociolinguistic pressures, a point perhaps overlooked by the romanticization of Bedouin speech by overeager Muslim grammarians.

All the above accounts rest on a number of assumptions that are not always either spelled out or subjected to rigorous questioning. For example, all our knowledge about the early dialects of Naǧd, the Ḥiǧāz, and the highland area of the southwest seems to have been gathered during the second and third Islamic centuries, when these dialects were already declining. Much of our data are preserved only in late works whose sources we cannot check.[196] Second, these accounts also accept without hesitation the traditional Muslim chronology and the accounts of the compilation of the Koran. The first scholar in modern times to radically question these accounts is, of course, John Wansbrough, who wrote:

> To draw from the same data conclusions about the origins and evolution of CA involves implicit acceptance of considerable non-linguisitic material often and erroneously supposed to be "historical fact." I refer to such assumptions as that of the isolation of speakers/writers of Arabic within the Arabian peninsula up to the seventh century, or that of the existence of *ne varietur* text of the Islamic revelation not later than the middle of the same century.[197]

Wansbrough points out that the Muslim accounts of the origins of CA have as their aim the establishment of the Ḥiǧāz as the cradle of Islam, in particular Mecca, and in the polemical milieu of the eighth-century CE Near East, to establish an independent Arab religious identity, with a specifically Arabic Holy Scripture.

> Suppression of claims made on behalf of other tribal groups to the title *afṣaḥ al-ʿarab* [the most eloquent of the Arabs] is symbolized in the account ascribed to Farrā' of how the inhabitants of cosmopolitan (!) Mecca (i.e. Quraysh) were in a position to recognize and adopt the best ingredients from each of the bedouin dialects in Arabia.[198] Besides drawing attention to the role of Mecca as cultic and commercial center, this tradition, like the ones it eventually replaced, served to identify the northern regions of the Arabian peninsula as the cradle of CA at a date prior to the proclamation of Islam.[199]

Nor can we uncritically accept Muslim claims that the language spoken by Bedouins must be identical with that of the poetry called pre-Islamic. The Bedouins were hardly disinterested referees. But more important,

> for our purposes it is well to remember that the written record of transactions between bedouin and philologist dates only from the third/ ninth century, and is thus coincident with the literary stabilization of both Quranic exegesis and Muslim historiography.[200]

There are even a number of scholars, such as Alphonse Mingana[201] and D. S. Margoliouth,[202] who think that all pre-Islamic poetry is forged, inspired by Koranic preoccupations. The Egyptian Ṭāhā Ḥusayn, in *Of Pre-Islamic Lite-*

rature,[203] the second of his two famous books, concludes that most of what we call pre-Islamic literature was forged, though he seems to accept the authenticity of some poems, albeit a tiny number.

This cautious acceptance of some pre-Islamic poetry as authentic seems to have been shared by several Western scholars, such as Goldziher, Tor Andrae, W. Marçais, and Tritton, who reject the total skepticism of Margoliouth, but shy away from the too-generous credulity of Nöldeke and Ahlwardt.[204] Of course, if all pre-Islamic poetry is forged, then there was no such thing as a poetical *koine*, and the language of the Koran obviously could not owe anything to this fictive poetical language. We would have to look elsewhere for the origins of the language of the Koran.

If the Koran did not originally have *iʿrāb*, then the present rhyme scheme[205] to be found in the Koran must be a later addition, since rhyme depends on *iʿrāb*, and the changes required in the Koranic text must have been considerable. The lack of original *iʿrāb* in the Koran, if true, also suggests that there is less of a relationship between poetry and the Koran than previously thought, and that the text of the Koran is primary.

In a comparatively recent study, Jonathan Owens makes a number of very important points, taking into account the work of Rabin, Corriente, Zwettler, and Vollers. He begins with the observation that,

> after over one hundred and fifty years of Western research on the language, there is no meaningful comparative linguistic history of Arabic. . . . Arabic is better conceptualized not as a simple linear dichotomous development, the Old vs. Neo split, but rather as a multi-branching bush, whose stem represents the language 1300 years ago.[206]

Owens applauds the work of Diem (1973)[207] which examined

> the case endings in the Arabic words found in the Aramaic inscriptions of the Arabs of Nabataea in southern Jordan, dating from about 100 BC.[208] Diem shows that Arabic personal names found in the inscriptions did not show traces of a living case system. If Diem's interpretation of the data is correct, it would mean that the *oldest* written evidence of Arabic is characterized by a linguistic trait, the lack of functional case endings, which is otherwise said to be characteristic par excellence of *Neo*-Arabic.[209]

Owens agrees with Corriente who insisted "on the need to recognize a caseless form of Arabic existing contemporaneously with case varieties." However, Owens is far more cautious than Corriente about postulating "a simple link between one variety of Old Arabic (Nabataean Arabic) and the modern dialects."[210] Instead Owens argues that the Arabic dialects descend from a variety that never did have case endings. This claim "implies that the relevant forms are so distributed that they could not have descended from the Classsical Arabic as described by Sibawaih." [211] On his own admission,

Owens's idea that modern Arabic dialects are the descendent of a caseless variety is not entirely new—Vollers had proposed in 1906

> that pre-diasporic caseless varieties of Arabic existed, and that these represent the ancestor(s) of the modern dialects (see Spitaler 1953; Diem 1973. 1991; Retsö 1994; and Corriente 1975, 1976).

However, Owens points out where his interpretation differs:

> All these scholars, however, assume that some point in the pre-history of Arabic a unique case-variety ancestor existed. The present proposal [Owens's proposal] is a qualitatively different interpretation of the development of Arabic, however, in arguing that there was a variety of proto-Arabic which never had morphological case in its history. Lately Zaborski (1995) and Retsö (1995) have argued, convincingly in my opinion, that there are various traits in the modern Arabic dialects, notably pronominal forms and the "pseudo-dual," which preserve old Semitic or proto-Afroasiatic forms which are lacking in the Classical language. This latter work is important, for it creates a geometric figure out of what in comparative Semitics has too often been defined as one-dimensional structure beginning with Akkadian and ending with Classical Arabic. Adding the modern Arabic dialects creates a geometric structure with at least two dimensions in the sense that developments and/or archaisms from proto-Semitic may move directly from the proto-language to the modern dialects, bypassing Classical Arabic completely.[212]

Combining the insights of Corriente and Diem, Owens comes to the conclusion

> that at least between 100 BC and AD 800, a period of almost a millennium, there coexisted case and caseless varieties of the language. Clearly, one cannot put an absolute duration on how long the coexistence occurred, though if it lasted for 900 years it must have been of an extremely stable sort.[213]

Owens believes that, in general, linguists need to take into account the evidence from modern Arabic dialects to further research on comparative Arabic language history, and on the larger Semitic and Afroasiatic families.

Owens accords Karl Vollers a richly deserved homage. As I have already indicated above, Vollers argued that the Koran was originally composed in a variety of Arabic without case endings. Vollers's insights were lost since his arguments were

> embedded in a larger one in which he claimed that the *Qur'ān* was revealed in a west Arabian dialect differing in many respects from Classical Arabic. In what he regarded as the official version of the *Qur'ān*, this variety was later

> replaced by a more prestigious variety, associated basically with an eastern Arabian dialect.[214]

Owens continues with a robust defense of Vollers against such distinguished scholars as Nöldeke:

> Despite any shortcomings, however, [Vollers's] linguistic interpretation of the state of Arabic in the early seventh century was remarkably prescient. Moreover, . . . his assumption that there was a Koranic variant without case ending receives partial support from the Koranic reading tradition itself. . . . The present chapter may be read in conjunction with Kahle's (1948) summary of a manuscript written perhaps by a fifth-century scholar named al-Maliki, in which various *ḥadith* are cited, pointing directly and indirectly to the practice of reading the *Qur'ān* without case endings.[215]

The tradition of a caseless variety of Koranic reading is associated with a Basran Koranic reader Abū 'Amr ibn 'Alā' (died 770), and if this tradition is true then a tradition with a caseless variety is as old as traditions with case endings.[216] But, as Owens underlines, this conclusion has grave implications:

> To accept Vollers's position would require a fundamental rethinking, *inter alia*, of the status of caseless vs. case forms of Arabic. Indeed, already in 1906 in the preface to his book, Vollers decried the intolerant scepticism to which he was subjected when he presented his thesis to Arab scholars in Algiers. For Arabicists, the criticisms of the distinguished Theodor Nöldeke (1910) were probably of greater importance.

Owens concludes his chapter with this summary:

> With Vollers, it is argued that case and caseless forms coexisted in the eighth century, but against Vollers, there is no decisive linguistic evidence to assume that the case forms are historically primary, even if the argument for a prestige differential is compelling. It follows from this that there is no contradiction in having coexisting Koranic variants, about which no conclusions can be drawn as to historical anteriority. Indeed, assuming that the reading traditions developed before a standardizing grammatical model became prevalent, it is quite natural to expect that reading traditions should develop simultaneously around any varieties prevalent in the community.[217]

In an important footnote, Owens explains how present-day Arabic linguistics is divided into two interpretive approaches:

> The two general, opposing positions which I define here are, in the contemporary state of Arabic linguistics, relatively poorly profiled. In fact, only the first has much currency. This is unfortunate, as I believe it may be associated with a highly scholarly, but at the same time highly orthodox and restrictive interpretation of Arabic linguistic history. Among its best-known representa-

> tives are Brockelmann, Nöldeke, and Fück. What today is little appreciated is that contemporaries of Brockelmann and Nöldeke such as Vollers, de Landberg, and later Kahle argued for a broader reading of what the ʿArabiyya was. Even if I would not agree in all detailed interpretations with this latter group, I would see my position as reviving their perspectives.[218]

Pierre Larcher has argued that it was time to overthrow the theological, ideological and mythological model that has dominated the field of Koranic Studies for so long. There are two grand myths: first, that the Arabic of the Koran is Classical Arabic—in fact there is, at the least, Pre-Classical Arabic, with phonological, morphological and syntactical features that one does not find in Classical Arabic. The second myth is that the dialects were simply a "corruption" of Classical Arabic—in fact, no classical language is a point of departure, but always a point of arrival. [219] Lutz Edzard suggests that

> the fact that Classical Arabic was viewed for a long time as the "Ur-ancestor" of all the later dialects is clearly motivated by religious considerations, inasmuch as Classical Arabic is considered in the Muslim tradition to be of divine origin.[220]

Classical Arabic is not the source of the Arabic dialects. Edzard even suggests "that scholars generally no longer view Classical Arabic as the ancestor of all Arabic dialects."[221] The dialects did not emerge from a degradation of Classical Arabic. On the contrary, the opposite is true, namely Classical Arabic emerged out of the dialects. Classical Arabic is a carefully considered construction wrought from the dialects. It is worth underlining that at the center of this construction was placed the *iʿrāb,* on whose otiosity Larcher has remarked upon, and which continues to terrorize all learners of the language. The most likely hypothesis, even if it is not the only one, that remains is that the iʿrāb is a feature of great antiquity. It was retained in poetry for metrical and prosodical reasons, not because it served a syntactical purpose. It was subsequently adopted in Classical Arabic because of the prestige attached to poetry, both written and recited.[222]

7. Arabic and Syriac, Syriac and Arabic

There are a number of confused, contradictory and, not to be too coy about it, totally mythical accounts in Islamic literature and tradition on the origin of languages, though they all seem to end by proclaiming the superiority of Arabic. For ʿAbd al-Malik b. Ḥabīb (died 238 AH/ 852 CE), a Cordoban jurist and historian,

> the languages of the "prophets" were Arabic, Syriac and Hebrew: All the sons of Israel spoke Hebrew; the first whom God allowed to speak it was Isaac. Sy-

> riac was the language of five prophets: Idrīs, Noah, Abraham, Lot and Jonah. Twelve of them spoke Arabic: Adam, Seth, Hūd, Ṣāliḥ, Ishmael, Shu'ayb, al-Khiḍr, "the three in Sūrat Yā Sīn" (Q. 36:14), Jonah, Khālid b. Sinān al-'Absī, and Muḥammad. According to 'Abd al-Malik b. Ḥabīb, Adam first spoke Arabic, but later his language was distorted and changed into Syriac.[223]

According to Ibn 'Abbās, Adam's

> language in paradise was Arabic, but when he disobeyed his lord, God deprived him of Arabic, and he spoke Syriac. God, however, restored him to his grace, and he gave him back Arabic.[224]

It has been said that Adam "spoke 700,000 languages, of which the best was Arabic." [225]

The Muslims were, in fact, imitating the corresponding attitudes of the Jews and Syrian Christians, who advocated the superiority of their own languages. And these natural assumptions of the Jews and Christians had rather surprising results among the Muslims, as we shall see in a moment.

As David H. Aaron points out,[226] at first, during the Biblical era, there was no notion of Hebrew as a Holy Tongue:

> In the *Tanakh* [Hebrew Bible, or Old Testament], Hebrew served as a marker of tribal allegiance but lacked the religious connotation that typifies post-biblical documents. One is particularly struck by the lack of language consciousness in the books of Ruth and Esther, both of which focus on the relationship between Jews and indigenous populations *outside* of the land of Israel. We thus find a remarkable degree of uniformity even among radically different genres and eras. Throughout the early literature, there is no discrete notion that Hebrew had a unique value or purpose. Hebrew during the biblical era is not yet a language of Judaism, let alone, a holy tongue.

It is only during the post-Biblical era that Hebrew first achieves religious significance, especially in the period following the conquest of the Middle East by Alexander the Great at the end of the fourth century BCE.[227] Contacts with Greek culture and language led to social and religious tensions, and attempts at self-definition. In texts deriving from the two centuries prior to the destruction of the Second Temple by the Romans in 70 CE,

> five distinct, but surely related attitudes toward Hebrew are discernable. Each notion of the Hebrew language represents a concrete response to overt political and social conflicts with Greek pagans. But, at a more subtle level, each constitutes an attempt to confront the pressures of syncretistic tendencies within the Jewish community as well. The five notions are: (1) allegiance to language as a form of allegiance to one's ancestors; (2) language as a unifying factor in the people's politic; (3) Hebrew as the original language of all human

> beings; (4) Hebrew as the forgotten language of civilization, retaught to Abram by God; (5) Hebrew as a holy language [לשון הקודש].[228]

David H. Aaron explains notion (1):

> Confronted by the prospect of a strong cultural challenge to their national identity—perhaps in a way never previously encountered—those responding to the pressures of cultural assimilation under the Seleucids (312 BCE–63 BCE) augmented the biblical notion of ancestral inheritance (as Torah) with the notion of language.[229]

In the *Testament of the Twelve Patriarchs* (second century BCE), "the concept of the End of Days includes the notion that the tribes of Jacob will become "one people of the Lord, with one language."[230] In the *Book of Jubilees*, probably dating from between 161 and140 BCE,[231] God sends an angel to dictate the Torah to Moses. The angel, talking of Abraham, says:

> Then the Lord God said to me: "Open his mouth and his ears, to hear and speak with his tongue in the revealed language." For from the day of the collapse it had disappeared from the mouth(s) of all mankind. I opened his mouth, ears and lips, and began to speak Hebrew with him—in the language of the creation. He took his fathers' books (they were written in Hebrew), and copied them. From that time he began to study them while I was telling him everything that he was unable (to understand).[232]

Milka Rubin comments on this passage,

> Three things are stated in these passages. The first is that the language of revelation and the language of creation are one and the same. The second is that this language is undoubtedly Hebrew, the language in which the books of the fathers were written. The third is that there was a period, between the confusion of languages and this revelation to Abraham, when the Hebrew language was dormant and forgotten. Another idea which appears in Jubilees is that all living creatures were familiar with the language of creation, and in fact spoke this language until the confusion (Jub. 3:28).[233]

In the Hebrew version of the *Testament of Naphtali* we are told that seventy angels divided the seventy languages among the families of the earth.

> But the holy language, the Hebrew language, remained only in the house of Shem and Eber, and in the house of Abraham our father, who is one of their descendents.[234]

In a fragment from Qumran, two new elements are introduced: Hebrew is called "the holy language," and it is asseverated that it was the original language of mankind at the moment of creation, and will once again be spoken at the end of days.[235] Thus this fragment contains the earliest known use of the idiom, holy tongue, לשון הקודש, *lešōn ha-qōḏeš*. But as Aaron explains,

> the phrase in the Qumran fragment occurs one line above an idiom derived from Zephaniah 3:9 that is clearly represented; "For then I will change the speech of the peoples to a *pure speech*." If *pure speech* and *holy tongue* are parallel in this context (which is a safe bet), then we may surmise that the author used the Zephaniah verse as proof-text for the destiny of the *holy tongue*. Esther Eshel and Michael Stone speculate that the Qumran writer was leaning upon the Zephaniah verse to convey that the End of Days involved the restoration of Hebrew to its once primal status, ubiquity among the civilizations. Thus the Qumran fragment represents the earliest known use of this phrase with the connotations (1) Hebrew is the holy tongue, and, perhaps, (2) Hebrew would be the universal language in the End of Days. Eshel and Stone also contend that Hebrew was the choice of the Qumran writers specifically because, "they believed that they lived on the eve of the End of Days," when Hebrew would again become the only linguistic option.[236]

As Milka Rubin summarizes,[237]

> These traditions, which originated in Jewish circles in the second and first century BCE apparently, echoed and resonated again and again both in time and in space among all partakers in this discussion. In Jewish literature, they are prevalent in Midrashic literature which formed in the third and fourth centuries CE Thus the *Tanhuma Yelamdenu* (Gen. 11), which preserves early traditions some of which go back to the fourth century CE,[238] says that the language spoken before the confusion of languages was "*Leshon Haqodesh* the holy language through which the world had been created."[239] According to Zephaniah 3:9, says Tanhuma, this will also be the language which will be spoken by all nations in the world to come.[240] The same idea is found in the different versions of *Yerushalmi Targum* referring to Genesis 11:1.[241]

From the second century BCE onward, Hebrew was considered the language of revelation, and the primordial language in which God created the world, and in which God spoke to Adam. Hebrew was spoken by all creatures until the fall, and the onset of the confusion of tongues.[242]

The above notions about Hebrew should be seen against the background, especially of the Hasmonaean period (162–43 BCE), of the Jewish people's search for national identity. The Hebrew language became a symbol of a unique cultural identity—a national symbol, and was thus being used for ideological reasons.[243]

> The view which became prevalent in the second century BCE, that Hebrew, being God's language, was superior to all other languages, was, it seems, part of the cultural and political reaction to the hellenistic rule and culture which

> prevailed among segments of Jewish society and culture at the time, a reaction which culminated in the Hasmonaean revolt. . . . The superiority of the "people and language" of Israel appear in the Festival prayers, both in the central benediction of the Amidah and in the blessing on the wine—the *qiddush*—said at the beginning of the holiday: "Blessed art thou God . . . who has chosen us from all people and exalted us above all languages."[244]

However, given the prevalence of Aramaic in Palestine and Syria, and the fact that Hebrew was no longer understood by large parts of the population, there developed a more universal cultural trend. *Exodus Rabba* 28,[245] for example, quotes Rabbi Yochanan as saying, "One voice was divided into seven voices and these divided themselves into seventy languages."

As Van der Louw comments,[246]

> In [the latter] Midrash, dating back to the 1st century AD,[247] there is no hint at the superiority of Hebrew. The divine speech is equally communicable into all languages, a universalist thought indeed. In a later, different tradition it is said that the promulgation of the written Torah took place in four languages simultaneously: Hebrew, Latin, Arabic and Aramaic. This is tantamount to saying no language is divine. Indeed, rabbi Yishmael (2nd century AD) stated squarely that the Torah speaks human language.

Despite the fact that the *Exodus Rabbah II* was only compiled in the ninth century CE, it contains earlier material, in which case, one is tempted to ask whether the Islamic doctrine of the Koran being revealed in seven different ways[248] is not derived from the sayings of Rabbi Yochanan, one of which, as noted, reads, "One voice was divided into seven voices and these divided themselves into seventy languages."

We now turn to the Christians. Initially, the Greek and Latin church fathers, and later Byzantine sources were almost unanimous that Hebrew was the language of creation. A passage in the *Pseudo-Clementine Recognitiones* [249] (book 1, chapter 30) tells us that Hebrew was the sole language in the world until the fifteenth generation "when, for the first time, men set up an idol and worshipped it."

For St.Augustine (354–430) the Hebrew language was the primordial tongue, which God had bequeathed to the Hebrew people because they had not sinned.[250]

However, in general, Christianity did not identify itself in terms of language, and though Hellenized Christianity preferred Greek, it strove to be a universal religion transcending linguistic and cultural barriers. The Christian liturgy was translated into Syriac, Armenian and Ethiopian, early on. For the Greek church father Gregory of Nyssa (ca. 330–ca. 395)

> human language is the invention of the human mind or understanding. . . . God, willing that men should speak different languages, gave human nature full liberty to formulate arbitrary sounds, so as to render their meaning more intelligible.[251]

Greek rationalism led Gregory and Eusebius of Caesarea (ca. 260–ca. 340) to refute the mystical idea of the language of creation in general.

On the other hand, Theodoret of Cyrrhus (ca. 393–ca. 460) was the first Greek church father to advocate Syriac as a primordial language.

> He bases his proof upon the etymology of the names of the primordial people: Adam is attributed to Syriac *'odamtho* (earth), Qain to Syriac *qenyono* (property), Noa to Syriac *nawho* (rest), and Abel to Syriac *'eblo* (mourning). On the other hand, he does not reject the Hebrew altogether, and ascribes to it a special status. Hebrew, according to Theodoret, is a holy language, which was given to Moses by God as an acquired language rather than as a natural language. In support of his claim, he says, children of the "Hebrews" do not speak Hebrew naturally; rather, they speak the language of their native country. Only later are they taught Hebrew letters and are able to read the Hebrew Scriptures. To assist his claim, Theodoret, too, uses Psalms 81:5: "I understood a language I did not know." He then proceeds to undermine the common and accepted proof among the Greek fathers, that Hebrew comes from "Heber," who alone was granted the privilege to hold on to the primordial language. If indeed, he says, Heber spoke Hebrew, then all his progeny, and many nations beside the Jewish people, should have spoken Hebrew. The Hebrew language is called so, in his opinion, because Abraham, on his way to Palestine, crossed the Euphrates. Hebra, he notes, in Syriac, means crossing.[252]

However, among Syriac writers Theodoret's position is encountered frequently: they are adamant that Syriac was the primordial language. They seemed to have been inspired by the views, or perhaps the putative views, of Ephraem the Syrian (ca. 306–373) and Theodore of Mopsuestia (ca. 350–428). In the Syriac work known as *The Cave of Treasures*, probably written in the sixth century CE, we are told that the sole language spoken from Adam until the confusion of languages was Syriac, and that "Syriac is the queen of all languages."[253]

As its translator, E. A. Wallis Budge, explains,

> In the title it is attributed to Ephraim the Syrian, and this indicates that the Syrians themselves were prepared to believe that it was written early in the IVth century, for this great writer died A.D. 373. Even if this attribution be wrong, it is important as suggesting that, if not written by Ephrem himself, one of his disciples, or some member of his school, may have been the author of the book.[254]

The Cave of Treasures elaborates further,

> The ancient writers have commited an error in writing that the Hebrew language was prior, and they admitted this [bad] error herein into their writings. All languages upon the earth derive from Syriac and are tempered with it.[255]

There are four Syriac commentaries that refer to this question: the anonymous commentary of *Diyarbakir 22* (first half of the eighth century); Theodore Bar Koni, *The Book of Scholia* (ca. 791/792); Isho'dad of Merv (ca. 850); and *The Anonymous Commentary* from the Mingana collection (ninth to tenth century).[256] Though aware of the tradition that recognized Hebrew as the primordial language, the four commentaries still insist that it was in pure and uncontaminated Syriac language that God talked to Adam—an attitude indicative of the desire to promote a Syriac cultural and historical identity, and to prove its superiority. Thus, for example, Tatian (fl. 170–180), though writing in Greek, felt that Greek civilization was a mass of evil incompatible with Christianity, and he set out to prove the superiority of Syriac culture.

Against this background of Judeo-Christian polemics, one would expect Muslim tradition to promote Arabic as the language of God, as the most pure and beautiful of all languages. Therefore, it will come as a surprise to many to learn that

> the concept that Hebrew and Aramaic (or Syriac) were both ancient languages which contested over the title of the primordial language was so deeply embedded that it found its way into Muslim tradition as well. Not surprisingly, it was Syriac—the ancestral language of the Christians living in the important Muslim centres, which was still being spoken by them and was held in high esteem as the primordial language—which gained primacy among the Muslims. Ibn al-Nadim (end of tenth century), who was well acquainted with Christian literature, cites in *Kitab al-Fihrist*[257] Theodore "the Interpreter" (i.e. Theodore of Mopsuestia) as saying that God spoke to Adam in the Nabati dialect, which is purer than the Syriac dialect. Ibn al-Nadim goes on to explain that "Nabati is the dialect spoken by villagers, it is a broken (dialect of) Syriac, and its pronounciation is not right." There are others, he continues, who say that it is the written classical Syriac which is the pure dialect, while still others believe that it was the contemporary spoken Syriac of his day that was used by God when he spoke to Adam. When writing about the Hebrew language, Ibn al-Nadim exhibits his wide knowledge of the sources. He says[258] that he "read in some of the old books that the first who wrote Hebrew was 'Abir b. Shalikh (i.e. 'Eber), and he placed it (this writing) among his people." Yet, he immediately goes on to quote Theodore's opinion saying that the Hebrew language is derived from the Syriac, and it was only called Hebrew after Abraham had crossed the Euphrates. Ibn al-Nadim is therefore acquainted with both tradi-

> tions, and is well versed in the prominent opinion among Syriac Christians of his day that Syriac was the primordial language, and that Hebrew was a language which derived from the Syriac and was formed only in Abraham's day. What is especially interesting is that he is aware of the internal argument amongst Syriac Christians themselves concerning the exact Syriac dialect which served as the primordial language, and was thus the pure dialect. Ibn al-Nadim does not contest the special status of the Syriac, nor does he bring any contradicting traditions on behalf of the Arabic language.

Historian and exegete, al-Ṭabarī[259] (839–923), equally faithful to the Syriac tradition, wrote,

> In that era 'Ād was called "'Ād of Iram," and when 'Ād was destroyed, Thamūd in turn was destroyed, the remaining sons of Iram were called Armān—they are Nabateans. All of them were of Islam while they lived in Babylon, until Nimrod b. Cush b. Canaan b. Ham b. Noah ruled over them and called on them to worship idols, which they did. Whereas one evening their speech was Syriac, the next morning God had confused their tongues, and thus they became unable to understand each other. As a result, the descendants of Shem came to have eighteen languages. The descendants of Ham also came to have eighteen languages, while the descendants of Japheth had thirty-six languages.[260]

A little later, al-Ṭabarī tells us that God destroyed the Tower of Babel, and

> on that day the languages of mankind became confused from fright, and mankind came to speak seventy-three languages. Before that the *only* language had been Syriac [emphasis added].[261]

Finally, Al-Ṭabarī cites a tradition going back to the suspiciously prolific Ibn 'Abbās:

> When Abraham fled from Kūthā and came out of the fire, his language was Syriac. But when he crossed the Euphrates from Ḥarrān, God changed his language and it was called Hebrew (*'Ibrānī*) because he had crossed (*'abara*) the Euphrates. Nimrod sent men to look for him, telling them, "If you find anyone who speaks Syriac, do not leave him, but bring him to me." They met Abraham, but left him because he spoke Hebrew and they did not understand his language.[262]

Al-Mas'ūdī (ca. 896–ca. 956) in his *Murūǧ al-Ḏahab*, *Meadows of Gold*,[263] tells us that

> in his [Nimrod's] time God divided the languages; so that the descendants of Sam spoke nineteen different tongues, the descendants of Ham seventeen, and the children of Yafeth thirty-six. Later the languages broke up into a great number of dialects.

But no particular language is specified.

The traditions of Syriac as the original language were so well-entrenched in the social milieu of the Near East that even Islamic ḥadīṯ-traditions bear witness to the fact. For instance, M. J. Kister records the following tradition,

> According to another tradition God sent down to Adam 21 books *(ṣaḥīfa)* and enjoined him to perform 50 *rak'as.* He forbade him to eat pork, carrion and blood (of animals); God also forbade him to lie, to behave treacherously and to fornicate. God's injunctions were dictated by Gibril and written down by Adam in Syriac. In Paradise Adam spoke Arabic; after his disobedience and expulsion he spoke Syriac.[264]

Kister privides us with further examples of Adam's linguistic abilities,

> *wa-'allama ādama l-asmā'a kullahā,* "and He taught Adam the names, all of them" [Koran 2:31] is interpreted in several different ways in the commentaries of the Qur'ān. God taught him, according to the commentators, one of the following things: the names of all the creatures, the names of events which happened in the past or which will happen in the future, all the languages (so that he could speak with each of his sons in a special language), the names of all the stars, the names of the angels, the names of his progeny, or the names of the various species of His creatures; or He taught him everything, including even the grammar of Sibawayh.[265]

Kister continues,

> Some traditions say that the secret language which God taught Adam was Syriac.[266] An early report states that God taught Adam the names in Syriac in order to hide from the angels the knowledge thus acquired. Al-Suyuti records a tradition saying that Adam spoke Arabic in Paradise; when he committed the sin he began to speak Aramaic, but after God accepted his repentance he reverted to Arabic.[267] The early 'Abd al-Malik b. Ḥabīb has a more detailed account of the language of Adam; Adam is included in the list of prophets whose language was Arabic. He descended from Paradise speaking Arabic because Arabic was the language of God, of the angels, and the people of Paradise. This is supported by the words spoken by the Prophet to Salman al-Farisi: "You should love the Arabs because of three things: your Quran and your Prophet are Arab and your language in Paradise will be Arabic." 'Abd al-Malik b. Ḥabīb explains the position of Arabic in comparison with Aramaic: Adam and his progeny spoke Arabic. In a later period Arabic degenerated *(ḥurrifa)* into Syriac, which is akin to Arabic.[268]

Thus we can see that the Muslim exegetes felt the force of the Syriac traditions regarding the primordial language, and they were forced to reply to them: Adam had spoken Arabic in Paradise; after the expulsion he spoke

Syriac (which was, according to some of the exegetes, deteriorated Arabic). But the significance of the above claims and counterclaims for Hebrew, Syriac, and Arabic are of wider import. They give credence to those theories that emphasize the slow emergence of Islam and the Koran against a background of monotheistic polemics.

As Wansbrough has stressed over and over again, all the claims of the Koran that it is "clear" Arabic only make sense in this sectarian milieu of contending cultures, prophets, and, of course, languages. The Arabic of the Koran is only clear if we assume that the target group of these texts knew other languages like Syriac as well and understood the allusions to the religious debates of the time. At least some of the so-called pre-Islamic poetry was composed after the Koran, and many of the verses adduced by lexicographers of Classical Arabic were ad hoc forgeries to prove that a certain word in the Koran was indeed Arabic, had this or that specific meaning and was of great antiquity.

Notes

1 Manfred Ullmann, ed., *Wörterbuch der klassischen arabischen Sprache,* [Dictionary of the Classical Arabic Language] (Wiesbaden: Harrossowitz, 1970–).

2 John Huehnergard, "New Directions in the Study of Semitic Languages" in Jerrold S. Cooper and Glenn M. Schwartz, eds., *The Study of the Ancient Near East in the Twenty-First Century* (Winona Lake, IN: Eisenbrauns, 1996), p. 254.

3 Christoph Luxenberg, *Die Syro-Aramäische Lesart des Koran* (Berlin: Das Arabische Buch Verlag, 2000), p. 299; also *The Syro-Aramaic Reading of the Koran* (Berlin: Verlag Hans Schiler, 2007), p. 327.

4 Claude Gilliot and Pierre Larcher, "Language and Style of the Qur'ān," in *Encyclopaedia of the Qur'ān*, vol. 3 (J–O), ed. Jane Dammen McAuliffe (Leiden/Boston: Brill, 2003), p. 129.

5 As we shall see below, as early as the fifth century scholars wondered at the strangeness of the Greek of the New Testament.

6 Baruch Spinoza, *Theological-Political Treatise* [Tractatus Theologico-Politicus], trans. Samuel Shirley (Indianapolis: Hackett, 1998), p. 247.

7 Steven Nadler, *A Book Forged in Hell: Spinoza's Scandalous Treatise and the Birth of the Secular Age* (Princeton, NJ: Princeton University Press, 2011), p. 171.

8 Steven Nadler, op. cit., p. 171, quoting Spinoza's *Tractatus*, chapter 7, "On the Interpretation of Scripture," p. 90 in Samuel Shirley translation (see note 6 above.)

9 Sebastian Brock, review of Matthew Black's *An Aramaic Approach to the Gospels and Acts, Journal of Theological Studies 20* (1969): pp. 274–78.

10 Matthew Black, *An Aramaic Approach to the Gospels and Acts, 3rd ed.* (Oxford: Clarendon Press, 1967.

11 Luxenberg had never heard of Matthew Black until I brought Black's work to his attention about three years ago, i.e., 2010.

12 Black, op. cit., pp.15–17.

13 Ibid., p. 17
14 Black, op. cit., pp. 271–72.
15 C. F. Burney (1868–1925), *The Aramaic Original of the Fourth Gospel* (Oxford: Clarendon Press, 1922).
16 Black, op. cit., p. 273, quoting G. R. Driver, "The Original Language of the Fourth Gospel," *Jewish Guardian*, January 5 and 12, 1923.
17 *Targum* (Hebrew plural : *targumim*): translations of the books of the Hebrew Bible into Aramaic, made when Aramaic was the common spoken language in Judea, and for the benefit of Jews who longer understood Hebrew (produced between ca. 250 BCE and 300 CE and read in the synagogues).
18 Black, op. cit., p. 275.
19 Charles Fox Burney, *Poetry of Our Lord* (Oxford: Clarendon Press, 1925).
20 The *Oxford English Dictionary* defines paronomasia as follows: "A playing on words which sound alike; a word-play; a pun from L., a. Gr. παρονομασία, f. παρ(α- PARA[1] 1) + ὀνομασία naming, after παρονομάζειν to alter slightly in naming."
21 Black, op. cit., pp. 276–77.
22 Günter Lüling, *Über den Ur-Qur'ān* (Erlangen, 1974); idem., *A Challenge to Islam for Reformation* (Delhi, 2003).
23 Lüling, *Challenge to Islam*, pp. XII–XIII.
24 D. H. Müller, *Die Propheten in ihrer ursprünglichen Form: Die Grundgesetze der ursemitischen Poesie, erschlossen und nachgewiesen in Bibel, Keilinschriften und Koran und ihren Wirkungen erkannt in den Chören der griechischen Tragödie*, 2 vols. (Wien, 1896). [The Prophets in their Primordial Form: The Basic Laws of Ur-Semitic Poetry Developed and Demonstrated in the Bible, Koran and Cuneiform Inscriptions and Their Effects Identified in the Choruses of Greek tragedy]; Rudolf Geyer, "Zur Strophik des Qurāns," *WZKM 22* (1908): 265–86; [English translation in Ibn Warraq, ed., *What the Koran Really Says* (Amherst, NY: Prometheus Books, 2002), pp. 625–46); idem., Review of Karl Vollers, *Volkssprache und Schriftsprache im alten Arabien* (Strassburg, 1906), *Göttinger Gelehrter Anzeiger* 171 (1909): 10–56; Karl Vollers, *Volkssprache und Schriftsprache im alten Arabien* (Strassburg, 1906).
25 Black, op. cit., p. 280.
26 Kaspar Wyss, *Dialectologia Sacra* (Zurich, 1650); Johann Vorst, *Philologia Sacra, seu de Hebraismis Novi Testament II* (Leyden, 1658); vol. I appeared in Amsterdam in 1665 with the general title *De Hebraismis Novi Testamenti Commentarius* (Amsterdam, 1665).
27 Elliott C. Maloney, *Semitic Interference in Marcan Syntax* (Chico, CA: Scholars Press, 1981), SBL Dissertation Series 51: PhD 1979, Fordham University, p. 1.
28 Isidore of Pelusium, Epist. 4.28, in J-P. Migne, *Patrologia Graeca,* vol. 78, pp. 1080–81, quoted by Maloney, *Semitic Interference*, p. 5.
29 Maloney, op. cit., p. 1.
30 Erasmus, *Paraphrases in Novum Testamentum* (Basel, 1516), on Acts 10:33, quoted by Maloney, op. cit., p. 5.
31 Theodore Beza, "Digressio de dono linguarum et apostolico sermone," in *Annotationes maiores in Novum Testamentum* (Geneva, 1556) on Acts 10:46.

32 Referred to by Morus, "On the Style of the New Testament," in Charles Hodge, *A Collection of Tracts in Biblical Literature*, vol. 1 (Princeton, 1825), pp. 411–13, where he gives a further list of eleven scholars, writing between the fifteenth and eighteenth century, who came to similar conclusions.

33 Anthony Grafton and Joanna Weinberg, *I have Always Loved the Holy Tongue: Issac Casaubon, the Jews, and a Forgotten Chapter in Renaissance Scholarship* (Cambridge, MA: Harvard University Press, 2011), p. 68.

34 G. Lloyd-Jones, *The Discovery of Hebrew in Tudor England: A Third Language* (Manchester: Manchester University Press, 1983), p. 194.

35 Grafton and Weinberg, op. cit., p. 228.

36 Arnold Meyer, *Jesu Muttersprache* [Jesus's Mother Tongue] (Leipzig, 1896); Gustaf Dalman, *Die Worte Jesu* (Leipzig, 1898; 2nd ed., 1930), English translation, *The Words of Jesus*, trans. D. M. Kay (Edinburgh, 1902).

37 Gustaf Dalman, *Grammatik des jüdisch-palästinischen Aramäisch* (Leipzig, 1905).

38 Dalman, *Die Worte Jesu*, op. cit., p. 1.

39 Ibid., pp. 1–6.

40 Ibid., p. 17

41 Gustaf Dalman, *Jesus-Jeshua: Studies in the Gospels*, trans. by Paul P. Levertoff (New York: Macmillan, 1929), p. 5.

42 A good survey of this important group of languages can be found in Colin P. Masica, *The Indo-Aryan Languages* (Cambridge MA: Cambridge Language Surveys, 1991).

43 Onkelos Targum: "the best known of the targumim, and the one with the greatest authority. A literal translation of the complete text of the Pentateuch, following the plain sense of scripture with many exegetical elements, especially in the poetic passages." See Alec Gilmore, *A Dictionary of the English Bible and Its Origins* (Sheffield: Sheffield Academic Press, 2000), s. v. Onkelos Targum.

44 Dalman, *Die Worte Jesu*, p. 80.

45 Joseph A. Fitzmyer, *A Wandering Aramean: Collected Aramaic Essays* (Missoula, MT: Scholars Press, 1979), p. xv.

46 B. Mazar et al., "'Ein Gev: Excavations in 1961," *Israel Exploration Journal* 14 (1964): 1–49; N. Avigad (In Hebrew), "An Aramaic Inscription on the Tell Dan Bowl," *Yediot* 30 (1966): 209–12; "An Inscribed Bowl from Dan," *Palestine Exploration Quarterly* 100 (1968): 42–44 (+pl. XVIII).

47 Fitzmyer's footnote: Cf. M. Wagner, *Die lexikalischen und grammatikalischen Aramaismen im alttestamentalischen Hebräisch* (Beihefte zur Zeitschrifte für die alttestamentalische Wiseenschaft, 96; Berlin: de Gruyter, 1966); E. F. Kautzsch, *Die Aramaismen in Alten Testament* (Halle a. d. S.: M. Niemeyer, 1902); A. Hurvitz, "The Chronological Significance of 'Aramaisms' in Biblical Hebrew," *IEJ* 18 (1968), pp. 234–40.

48 Fitzmyer, op. cit., p. 9.

49 Originally published as the "Presidential Address of the Catholic Biblical Association" (21 August 1970) in the *Catholic Biblical Quarterly* 32 (1970): 501–31, but also chapter 2 in Fitzmyer, *Wandering Aramean*, pp. 29–56.

50 The Seleucids (312–64 BCE), a dynasty of Hellenistic Kings, founded by Seleucus (ca. 358–281 BCE), ruled a vast realm stretching from Anatolia via Syria and Babylonia to Iran and thence to central Asia.

51 Fitzmyer, *A Wandering Aramean*, p. 46.
52 The Gaonic or Geonic period lasted from approximately 600 CE to 1040 CE.
53 Fitzmyer, *A Wandering Aramean*, p. 62.
54 Uriel Weinreich, *Languages in Contact: Findings and Problems.* Preface by André Martinet (New York: Publications of the Linguistic Circle of New York, no. 1, 1953).
55 André Martinet, "Preface," in Weinreich, *Languages in Contact*, pp. vii–viii.
56 Hugo Schuchardt, *Dem Herrn Franz von Miklosich zum 20. November 1883: Slawo-deutsches und Slawo-italienisches* (Graz, 1884), p. 5.
57 Bernd Heine and Tania Kutieva, *Language Contact and Grammatical Change* (Cambridge, MA: Cambridge University Press, 2005), p. 1.
58 Heine and Kutieva's footnote: Andrei Danchev, "Language Contact and Language Change" *Folia Linguistica* 22 (1988), pp. 37–53; p. 38; "Language Change Typology and Adjectival Comparison in Contact Situations" in *Folia Linguistica Historica* 9, no. 2 (1989), pp. 161–74.
59 Heine and Kutieva's footnote: Sarah G. Thomason and Terrence Kaufman, *Language Contact, Creolization, and Genetic Linguistics* (Berkeley: University of California Press, 1988), p. 14; Alice C. Harris and Lyle Campbell, *Historical Syntax in Cross-Linguistic Prespective* (Cambridge: Cambridge University Press, 1995), pp. 149–50; Alexandra Aikhenvald, *Language Contact in Amazonia*, 2002: pp. 11–13.
60 Frans van Coetsem, "Topics in Contact Linguistics," *Leuvense Bijdragen* 92 (2003), p. 30 (Published posthumously).
61 Jan N. I. Baudouin de Courtenay in E. Stankiewicz, ed., *A Baudouin de Courtenay Anthology: The Beginnings of Structural Linguistics* (Bloomington and London: Indiana University Press, 1972), p. 213.
62 E. Haugen, *The Norwegian Language in America*, vol. 1, *The Bilingual Community*, vol. 2, *The American Dialects of Norwegian* (Bloomington: Indiana University Press, 1969 [1953]).
63 P. Burney, *Les Langues internationales* (Paris: Presses universitaires de France, 1962), p. 108.
64 Albert Dauzat (1877–1955), French linguist, known for his work on onomastics.
65 van Coetsem, op. cit., pp. 30–31.
66 Idem., p. 31.
67 Thomason and Kaufman, *Language Contact*, pp. 3, 4; Charles-James N. Bailey, *Variation and Linguistic Theory* (Arlington, VA: Center for Applied Linguistics, 1973); "Linguistic Change, Naturalness, Mixture, and Structural Principles," *Papiere zur Linguistik* 16 (1977): 6–73; Peter Mühlhäusler, "Structural Expansion and the Process of Creolization," in Albert Valdman and Arnold Highfield, eds., *Theoretical Orinetations in Creole Studies* (New York: Academic Press, 1980).
68 Thomason and Kaufman, op. cit., pp. 2, 8, quoting the work of Regna Darnell and Joel Sherzer, "Areal Linguistic Studies in North America: A Historical Perspective," *International Journal of American Linguistics* 37 (1971): 25, 26.
69 William E. Welmers, "Language Change and Language Relationships in Africa," *Language Sciences* 12: 4–5.
70 Thomason and Kaufman, op. cit., pp. 1–2.
71 Thomason and Kaufman, op. cit., p. 9; emphases (bold letters) in original.

72 Ibid., p.14
73 Ibid., pp. 16–17.
74 Ibid., p. 35.
75 Ibid., p. 39
76 Ibid., p. 65
77 A. Rosetti, "Langue Mixte et Mélanges de Langues," *Acta Linguistica* 5 (1945–49): 73–79.
78 Ullmann, *Wörterbuch der klassischen arabischen Sprache.*
79 Huehnergard, "New Directions in the Study of Semitic Languages," p. 254.
80 Ibid.
81 Ibid., p. 260.
82 Ibid., p. 261 n. 40.
83 Huehnergard's note 72: The classic study is Uriel Weinreich, *Languages in Contact: Findings and Problems* (The Hague: Mouton, 1953); more recent works are René Appel and Pieter Muysken, *Language Contact and Bilingualism* (London: Arnold, 1987); Ilse Lehiste, *Lectures on Language Contact* (Cambridge, MA: MIT Press, 1988).
84 Huehnergard's note 73: Wolf Leslau, "The Influence of Cushitic on the Semitic Languages of Ethiopia: A Problem of Substratum," *Word* 1 (1945), pp. 59–82; Greta D. Little, "Syntactic Evidence of Language Contact: Cushitic Influence in Amharic," in Roger W. Shuy and Charles-James N. Bailey, eds., *Towards Tomorrow's Linguistics* (Washington: Georgetown University Press, 1974), pp. 267–75.
85 Huehnergard's note 76: Anson F. Rainey, "The Scribe at Ugarit: His Position and Influence," *Proceedings of the Israel Academy of Sciences and Humanities* 3 (1969), pp. 126–47; Sally W. Ahl, "Epistolary Texts from Ugarit: Structural and Lexical Correspondences in Epistles in Akkadian and Ugaritic" (Ph.D. diss., Brandeis University, 1973), p. 177; Burkhart Kienast, "Rechtsurkunden in ugaritischer Sprache," *Ugarit-Forschungen* 11 (1979), pp. 431–44; John Huehnergard, *The Akkadian of Ugarit* (*HSS* 34; Atlanta: Scholars Press, 1989), pp. 212, 224.
86 Huehnergard's note 77: See E. Y. Kutscher, "Two Passive Constructions in Aramaic in the Light of Persian," *Proceedings of the International Conference on Semitic Studies, Jerusalem, 19–23 July 1965* (Jerusalem: Israel Academy of Sciences and Humanities, 1969), pp. 132–51; Stephen A. Kaufman, *The Akkadian Influences on Aramaic* (*Assyriological Studies* 16; Chicago: The Oriental Institute, 1974).
87 Huehnergard, op. cit., pp. 268–270.
88 Huehnergard, p. 270.
89 Idem., pp. 270–271.
90 Edward Lipiński, *Semitic Languages: Outline of a Comparative Grammar* (Leuven: Peeters Publishers and Department of Oriental Studies, 2001), pp. 569–577.
91 See also Françoise Briquel-Chatonnet, *Mosaïque de Langues, Mosaïques Culturelle. Le Bilinguisme dans le Proche-Orient Ancien. Actes de la Table-Ronde du 18 novembre 1995 organisée par l'URA 1062 "Etudes Sémitiques"* (Paris: Jean Maisonneuve, 1996).

92 Hans Bauer, *Die Tempora in Semitischen: ihre Entstehung und ihre Ausgestaltung in den Einzelsprachen* (Berlin, 1910).

93 Hans Bauer and Pontus Leander, *Historische Grammatik der hebraischen Sprache des Alten Testamentes* (Halle, 1922).

94 Angel Sáenz-Badillos, *A History of the Hebrew Language*, trans. by John Elwolde (Cambridge: Cambridge University Press, 1993; first published in Spanish, 1988), p. 54.

95 G. R. Driver, *Problems of the Hebrew Verbal System* (Edinburgh, 1936), p. 15, cited by Angel Sáenz-Badillos, op. cit., p. 55.

96 *Encyclopaedia Judaica*, vol. 8, Mishnaic Hebrew in article "Hebrew Language," p. 648.

97 Jack Fellman, "The Linguistic Status of Mishnaic Hebrew," in F. Charles Fensham, ed., *Journal of Northwest Semitic Language* 5 (1977): p. 22.

98 Stefan Weninger, ed., in collaboration with Geoffrey Khan, Michael P. Streck, Janet CE Watson, *Semitic Languages: An International Handbook* (Berlin/Boston: Walter de Gruyter, 2011), pp. 747–55.

99 Jan Retsö, *The Arabs in Antiquity: From Assyrians to the Umayyads* (Oxford: Routledge, 2003), p. 126.

100 Weninger, op. cit., p. 747.

101 William Wright, *A Grammar of the Arabic Language*, 3rd ed., 1896–1898 (Cambridge: Cambridge University Press, 1967), p. 166 A.

102 Arthur Jeffery, *The Foreign Vocabulary of the Qur'ān* (Gaekwad's Oriental Series 79; Baroda Oriental Institute, 1938).

103 A. Hebbo, *Die Fremdwörter in der arabischen Prophetenbiographie des Ibn Hischām* (gest. 218/834) (*Heidelberger orientalistische Studien* 7) (Frankfurt: Lang, 1984), cited in Weninger, op. cit., p. 751.

104 S. Fraenkel, *Die aramäischen Fremdwörter im Arabischen* (Leiden, 1886); Arthur Jeffery, *The Foreign Vocabulary of the Qur'ān* (Baroda: 1938); Alphonse Mingana, "Syriac Influence on the Style of the Koran," *Bulletin of the John Rylands Library* 11 (1927): 77–98, reprinted in Warraq, *What the Koran Really Says*, pp. 171–92.

105 Jan Retsö, "Aramaic/Syriac Loanwords," in K. Versteegh et al., eds., *Encyclopedia of Arabic Language and Linguistics* (Leiden: E. J. Brill, 2006), pp. 178–82.

106 Oxford English Dictionary: "Philol. Applied to words having the same sound, but differing in meaning: opp. to heteronym and synonym."

107 Maxime Rodinson, "The Western Image and Western Studies of Islam," in J. Schacht and C. E. Bosworth, eds., *The Legacy of Islam* (Oxford, 1974), p. 59.

108 John Wansbrough, *Quranic Studies: Sources and Methods of Scriptural Interpretation* (Amherst, NY: Prometheus Books, 2004; 1st ed., 1977), p. 12.

109 Pericope: according to the *Oxford English Dictionary*: "A portion of Scripture appointed for reading in public worship.

1695 J. Edwards Perfect. Script. i. xiii. 566: 'Jerome speaks of a Pericope of Jeremiah.'

1869 Ginsburg in L'pool Lit. & Phil. Soc. Proc. XXIII. 313: 'Next in point of antiquity is the division of the Pentateuch into 175 Pericopes.'

1884 D. Hunter tr. Reuss's Hist. Canon i. 3: 'These passages . . . were disconnected fragments, . . . simply pericopes or lessons, as they were called afterwards in the Christian Church.'"

110 James R. Davila, "How Can We Tell If a Greek Apocryphon or Pseudepigraphon Has Been Translated from Hebrew or Aramaic?" *Journal for the Study of the Pseudepigrapha* 15 (2005): 3–61.

111 Davila, op. cit., pp. 11–16.

112 Ibid., pp. 4–11.

113 Ibid., p. 12.

114 Ibid., pp. 16–17.

115 Ibid., pp. 17, 22.

116 Staffan Olofsson, "Consistency as a Translation Technique," *Scandinavian Journal of the Old Testament*, no. 1 (1992): 14–30.

117 Jacques Eugène Manna, *Vocabulaire Chaldéen-Arabe* (Mosul, 1900); reprinted with a new appendix by Bidawid (Beirut, 1975).

118 C. Luxenberg, *The Syro-Aramaic Reading of the Koran: A Contribution to the Decoding of the Language of the Koran* (Berlin: Schiler, 2007), pp. 204–206.

119 John Penrice, *A Dictionary and Glossary of the Koran*, with Copious Grammatical References and Explanations of the Text (1873) (Delhi, India: Low Price Publications, 1990), p. 19.

120 R. Payne Smith, ed., *Thesaurus Syriacus*, vol. 1 (Oxford, 1879); vol. 2 (1901), p. 3326.

121 Luxenberg, op. cit., pp. 123–24.

122 Davila, op. cit., p. 27.

123 Maloney, *Semitic Interference in Marcan Syntax.*

124 Raymond A. Martin, *Syntactical Evidence of Semitic Sources in Greek Documents* (Eugene, OR: Wipf and Stock, 2004), first published 1974 by the Society of Biblical Literature.

125 Ibid., pp. 5–43, summarized in Davila, op. cit., p. 28 n. 68.

126 Elliot C. Maloney, "Review of Martin, *Syntax Criticism of the Synoptic Gospels*," *Catholic Biblical Quarterly* 51(1989): 378–80, quoted in Davila, op. cit., p. 29.

127 Davila, op. cit., p. 31.

128 Albert Pietersma and Benjamin G. Wright, eds., *A New Translation of the Septuagint* (Oxford/ New York: Oxford University Press, 2007), p. xiii.

129 Ibid.

130 Davila, op. cit., p. 33.

131 Ibid., p. 33.

132 See Susan Bassnett, *Translation Studies* (London: Routledge, 2002; first edition 1980), which has a useful bibliography of eighteen pages.

133 Theo A. W. van der Louw, *Transformations in the Septuagint: Towards an Interaction of Septuagint Studies and Translation Studies* (Leuven: Peeters, 2007), p. 13, citing C. Rabin, "The Translation Process and the Character of the Septuagint," Textus 6 (1968): 22 ff.

134 Van der Louw, op. cit., p. 90.

135 Ibid., p. 108

136 Ibid., pp. 61–62.

137 Davila, op. cit., p. 37.

138 Ibid., p. 38

139 Ibid., p. 39.

140 Zipora Talshir, "Double Translations in the Septuagint," in Claude E. Cox, ed., *Proceedings of the Sixth Congress of the International Organization for Septuagint and Cognate Studies*, Jerusalem, 1986 (Atlanta, GA: Scholars Press, 1987), pp. 21–63, quoted in Davila, op. cit., p. 40.

141 Davila, op. cit., p. 41.

142 Herbjørn Jenssen, "Arabic Language," in *Encyclopaedia of the Qur'ān* (Leiden: E. J. Brill).

143 D. B. Parkinson, "Variability in Standard Arabic Grammar skills," in Alaa Elgibali, ed., *Understanding Arabic: Essays in contemporary Arabic linguistics in honor of of El-Said Badawi* (Cairo, 1996).

144 J. Owens, *The Foundations of Grammar: An Introduction to Medieval Arabic Grammatical Theory* (Amsterdam, 1988).

145 Herbjørn Jenssen, op. cit.

146 Israel Gershoni and James Jankowski, *Egypt, Islam, and the Arabs: The Search for Egyptian Nationalism, 1900–1930* (New York: Oxford University Press, 1986), p. 220, quoted in Franck Salameh, "Does Anyone Speak Arabic?" *Middle East Quarterly* 18, no. 4 (Fall 2011): 51.

147 Taha Hussein, *The Future of Culture in Egypt* (Washington, DC: American Council of Learned Societies, 1954), pp. 86–87, quoted in Salameh, op. cit., p. 51.

148 Taha Hussein [Ṭāhā Ḥusayn], *Yasiru am-Nahw wa-l-Kitaba* no. 11 (Beirut: al-Adab, 1956), pp. 2, 3, 6, quoted by Salameh, op. cit., p. 53.

149 E. Souby, "The Influence of the Arabic Language on the Psychology of the Arabs," *Middle East Journal* 5, no. 3 (Summer 1951): 284–302.

150 Warraq, *What the Koran Really Says*, pp. 24–26.

151 In Saudi Arabia, a rich country for many decades, the adult literacy rate for both sexes (percent aged fifteen and above) is not higher than 86.6 percent (for comparison: Cuba 99.8 percent; China 94.3 percent; Thailand 93.5 percent; Egypt: 72 percent); see the 2013 Human Development Report of the UNDP athttp://hdr.undp.org/en/countries/profiles/EGY.html. This figure, however, is misleading, as the definition of this skill is as follows: "Percentage of the population ages 15 and older who can, with understanding, both read and write a short simple statement on their everyday life." If the fact is taken into consideration that the mother tongue of virtually all native speakers of Arabic are their often very divergent dialects, not the written Classical language, it becomes clear that only a minority is able to read and understand newspapers and books. In the UNESCO report "Adult and Youth Literacy 1990–2015: Analysis of Data for 41 selected Countries" another problem can be seen: the disparity in the literacy rates of men and women, although there has been some progress in the past few decades: "In Egypt, the female adult literacy rate was 31% in 1990, 44% in 2000, and 64% in 2010, and is projected to reach 66% in 2015." The respective figures for men were: 1990: 57 percent, 2000: 67.2 percent, 2010: 80.3 percent, and 2015: 82.1 percent. The report is downloadble as a pdf athttp://www.uis.unesco.org/Education/Documents/UIS-literacy-statistics-1990-2015-en.pdf

152 Charles Ferguson, "Diglossia," *Word* 15, no. 2 (1959): 325–40; William Marçais, "La diglossie arabe," *L'Enseignement public—Revue Pédagogique* 104, no. 12

(1930): 401–409; Alan S. Kaye, "Arabic," in Bernard Comrie, ed., *The Major Languages of South Asia, the Middle East and Africa* (London: Routledge, 1990), p. 181.

153 Kaye, op. cit., "Arabic," p. 173.

154 Wheeler M. Thackston, *An Introduction to Koranic and Classical Arabic* (Bethesda, MD: Iranbooks, 1994), p. xii.

155 B. Lewis, *Islam and the West* (Oxford: Oxford University Press, 1993), p. 65.

156 It is in fact becoming more and more Westernized (i.e., de-Semitized) under the influence of the international news agencies.

157 P. Larcher, "Les Incertitudes de la Poesie Arabe Archaique," *La Revue des Deux Rives,* no. 1 (1999): 129.

158 Kaye, "Arabic," op. cit., p. 183.

159 P. Larcher, "La Linguistique Arabe d'Hier a Demain: Tendances Nouvelles de la Recherche," *Arabica* 45 (1998): 409–29.

160 Gustav Meiseles, "Educated Spoken Arabic and the Arabic Language Continuum," *Archivum Linguisticum* 11, no. 2 (1980): 118–42; quoted in Larcher, "Les Incertitudes de la Poesie Arabe Archaique."

161 A. S. Kaye, "Formal vs. Informal in Arabic: Diglossia, Triglossia, Tetraglossia, etc., Polyglossia—Multiglossia Viewed as a Continuum," *ZAL* 27 (1994): 47–66.

162 Franck Salameh, "Does Anyone Speak Arabic?" *Middle East Quarterly* 18, no. 4 (Fall 2011): 50.

163 Wheeler M. Thackston Jr., *The Vernacular Arabic of the Lebanon* (Cambridge, MA: Dept. of Near Eastern Languages and Civilizations, Harvard University, 2003). It is neither in the New York Public Library nor in the Columbia University Library, and is untraceable via BookFinder, AbeBooks or Amazon.com. According to World Catalogue there is one copy in the Harvard Library—no other library in the world is mentioned.

164 Thackston Jr., *The Vernacular Arabic of the Lebanon*, p.vii, quoted in Salameh, "Does Anyone Speak Arabic?" p. 51.

165 The United Nations Arab Human Development Report (UNAHDR) 2003, available online in English at http://hdr.undp.org/en/reports/regionalreports/arabstates/RBAS_ahdr2003_EN.pdf.; also quoted by Salameh, op. cit., p. 54.

166 Ibid., pp. 69, 135.

167 Kees Versteegh, *The Arabic Language* (Edinburgh: Edinburgh University Press, 2001). This book, first published in 1997, carries on its back cover impressive blurbs from Clive Holes, Lutz Edzard, M. G. Carter, and others.

168 Ibid., p. 6.

169 Ibid., pp. 37, 40, 41, respectively.

170 Michael Zwettler, *The Oral Tradition of Classical Arabic Poetry* (Columbus: Ohio State University Press, 1978).

171 Ibid., p. 101.

172 D. S. Margoliouth, "The Origins of Arabic Poetry," *Journal of the Royal Asiatic Society* (1925): 417–49, also in Ibn Warraq, ed., *Koranic Allusions* (Amherst, NY: Prometheus Books, 2013), pp. 165–93.

173 Ṭāhā Ḥusayn, *Fī š-ši'r al-Ǧāhīli* (Cairo, 1926).

174 A. J. Arberry, *The Seven Odes: The First Chapter in Arabic Literature* (London: Allen and Unwin, 1957), pp. 228–45.

175 J. Wansbrough's note: A not very convincing enumeration in Blachère, *Histoire de la littérature arabe*, Paris i–iii, 1952–66, pp. 94–95.
176 Constituting the class of pagan poets who died after the proclamation of Islam, e.g., al-Aʿshā Maymūn, Labīd, Abū Dhu'ayb, and al-Ḥuṭayʾa.
177 Wansbrough's note: A. Spitaler, "Review of Bloch, Vers und Sprache" *Oriens* ii (1949), 317–22, p. 320.
178 Wansbrough's note: D. S. Margoliouth, "The Origins of Arabic Poetry," *JRAS* (1925): 417–49, p. 431; also in Warraq, *Koranic Allusions*, p. 175.
179 Wansbrough's note: Ibn ʿAbd Rabbih, *Al-ʿIqd al-farīd Bulaq*, 1293, iii, 106–7; the problematic character of this particular one of the *ayyām al-ʿarab* may be guessed from its inclusion in Ǧāḥiẓ, "Kitāb al-Tarbiʿ wal-tadwīr'" in *Tria Opuscula* (Leiden, 1903), 86–107, p. 10.
180 John Wansbrough, *Quranic Studies: Sources and Methods of Scriptural Interpretation* (Oxford: Oxford University Press, 1977); reprinted with foreword by Andrew Rippin (Amherst: Prometheus Books, 2004), p. 97.
181 Warraq, *What the Koran Really Says*, pp. 32 ff.
182 T. Nöldeke, *Beiträge zur Kenntniss der Poesie der alten Araber* (Hanover, 1864), p. 2.
183 Markus Gross, "Die erfundenen Relativpronomen," in M. Gross and K.-H. Ohlig, *eds., Die Entstehung einer Weltreligion*, vol. 2 (Berlin, 2013), pp. 441–552, at 551.
184 R. Blachère, *Histoire de la Littérature Arabe: Des Origines à la fin du XVe siècle de J.-C.*, vol. 1 (Paris, 1952), p. 79.
185 A. Schaade, "Arabia(e). Arabic Language. Classical Arabic," in Martijn Theodoor Houtsma et al., eds., *Encyclopedia of Islam: A Dictionary of the Geography, Ethnography and Biography of the Muhammadan Peoples*, 1st ed., 4 vols. (Leiden: E. J. Brill/London: Luzak, 1913–38), 1: 393.
186 Karl Vollers, *Volkssprache und Schriftsprache im alten Arabien* (Strassburg, 1906).
187 Hans Wehr, "Review of Fück (1950)," *ZDMG* 102 (1952): 179–84.
188 Werner Diem, "Die nabatäischen Inschriften und die Frage der Kasusflexion im Altarabischen," *ZDMG* 123 (1973): 227–37.
189 Theodor Nöldeke, "Zur Sprache des Korāns," in Theodor Nöldeke, ed., *Neue Beiträge zur semitischen Sprachwissenschaft* (Strassburg: Verlag von Karl J. Trübner, 1910), pp. 1–30, also translated as "Language of the Koran," in Warraq, *Which Koran?* pp. 83–129; the original article in German can be downloaded at http://www.menadoc.bibliothek.unihalle.de/inhouse/content/titleinfo/214615.
190 Johann Fück, Arabiya: "Untersuchungen zur arabischen Sprach- und Stilgeschichte" *Abhandlungen der Sächsischen Akademie der Wissenschaften zu Leipzig, Philologisch-historische Klasse 45/1* (Berlin, 1950).
191 J. Blau, "The Jahiliyya and the Emergence of the Neo-Arabic Lingual Type," *JSAI* 7 (1986): 35–43.
192 Wansbrough, *Quranic Studies*, p. 102.
193 Rabin, "ʿArabiyya," in P. J. Bearman et al., *Encyclopedia of Islam*, 2nd ed., 12 vols. (Leiden: E. J. Brill, 1960–2005), 1: 566a; see also Paul Kahle in Warraq, *What the Koran Really Says.*

194 F. Corriente, "From Old Arabic to Classical Arabic, the Pre-Islamic Koine: Some Notes on the Native Grammarians' Sources, Attitudes and Goals," *JSS* 21 (1976): 62–98.
195 "Iʿrāb," in Bearman, et al., *Encyclopedia of Islam*, quoting al-Ǧurǧānī.
196 Rabin, "ʿArabiyya," p. 565.
197 Wansbrough, op. cit., p. 85.
198 Ibid., p. 94; J. Wansbrough's note: "Suyūṭī, Muzhir i, 221; cf. Kahle, 'Readers,' pp. 70–71: the story was pressed into the service of a number of distinct but related causes; for the literary effect of similar traditions see also above," pp. 42–3, 69–70.
199 Wansbrough, *Quranic Studies,* p. 94.
200 Ibid., p. 95.
201 J. R. Harris and A. Mingana, *Odes and Psalms of Solomon*, vol. 2 (London: Longmans, Green and Company, 1920), p. 125.
202 D. S. Margoliouth, "The Origins of Arabic Poetry."
203 Ṭāḥa Ḥusayn, *Fī l-adab al-ǧāhili* (Cairo, 1927).
204 For full bibliography, see Blachère, *Histoire de la Littérature Arabe*, vol. 1, pp. xviii–xxxiii.
205 The rhyme may have been there originally to aid memorization; the recording of rhyme depends on iʿrāb, but the use of rhyme does not.
206 Jonathan Owens, *A Linguistic History of Arabic* (Oxford: Oxford University Press, 2006), pp. 77–78.
207 Werner Diem, "Die nabatäischen Inscriften und die Frage der Kasusflexion im Altarabischen," *ZDMG* 123: 227–37.
208 Owens's footnote: "The Nabataean Arabs used Aramaic as their literary variety. Diem (1973, p. 237) writes: 'Es wurde zu zeigen versucht, dass das Nabatäisch-Arabische schon im ersten Jahrhundert v. Chr. das Kasussystem des Semitischen aufgegeben hat.' Whether this variety of Arabic ever had case becomes a question of historical reconstruction."
209 Owens, *Linguistic History of Arabic*, p. 86.
210 Ibid., p. 87.
211 Ibid., pp. 101–102
212 Ibid., p. 114.
213 Ibid., p. 117.
214 Ibid., p. 119.
215 Ibid., p. 120
216 Ibid., p. 120
217 Ibid., p. 136.
218 Ibid., p. 167 n. 20.
219 Pierre Larcher: personal communication, June 5, 2013.
220 Lutz Edzard, *Polygenesis, Convergence, and Entropy: an Alternative Model of Linguistic Evolution Applied to Semitic Linguistics* (Wiesbaden, 1998), p. 42 n. 38.
221 Ibid., p. 32.
222 Pierre Larcher, "Qu'est-ce que l'Arabe du Coran? Réflexions d'un Linguiste," *Cahiers Linguistique de L'Inalco* 5 (2003–2005): 27–47, 42–43.
223 Claude Gilliot and Pierre Larcher, "Language and Style of the Qur'ān," in *Encyclopaedia of the Qur'ān*, vol. 3 (Leiden: Brill, 2003), p. 118. Gilliot and Larcher give the following references: ʿAbd al-Malik b. Ḥabīb, Abū Marwān al-

Qurṭubī, *Kitāb al-Ta'rīḫ*: La Historia, ed., J. Aguadé (Madrid, 1991), pp. 27–28; Ǧalāl al-Dīn Suyūṭī, *al-Muzhir fī 'ulūm al-luġa wa-anwā'ihā*, ed. A. Jādd al-Mawlā et al., 2 vols. (Cairo, 1958), vol. 1, pp. 30–31/English translation, A. Czapkiewicz, *The Views of the Medieval Arab philologists on language and Its Origin in the Light of as-Suyūṭī's "al-Muzhir"* (Cracow, 1988), pp. 66–67; Ignaz Goldziher, *On the History of Grammar among the Arabs*, trans. and ed. K. Dévényi and T. Iványi (Amsterdam/Philadelphia, 1994), pp. 44–45; H. Loucel, "L'Origine du langage d'après les grammairiens arabes Arabica," *Arabica* 11, no. 2 (May 1964), IV, pp. 167–68.

224 Gilliot and Larcher, idem., citing Ibn 'Asakir, *Ta'rīḫ*, ed. al-'Amrawī, 80 vols. (Beirut, 1995–2000), vol. 7, p. 407; Suyūṭī, *Muzhir*, 1:30, H. Loucel, "L'Origine du langage d'après les grammairiens arabes," p. 167.

225 Gilliot and Larcher, idem., citing "Ṯa'labī, Abū Isḥāq Aḥmad b. Muḥammad, *al-Kašf wa-l-bayān 'an tafsīr al-Qur'ān*, ms. Istanbul, Ahmet III 76, *From Sūra 5 to the End of the Qur'ān*, part 4 (ad Q 41:44) ad Q 55:4, from an anonymous source; Goldziher, *Grammar*, 45, quoting Baġawī, *Ma'ālim*, presently still only in manuscript form; but the figure '700' in Baġawī, *Ma'ālim* 4, 266 has to be corrected!"

226 David H. Aaron, "The Doctrine of Hebrew Language Usage," in Jacob Neusner and Alan J. Avery-Peck, eds., *The Blackwell Companion to Judaism* (Oxford: Blackwell, 2003; first published 2000), p. 270.

227 Ibid., p. 272.

228 Ibid., p. 272, 273.

229 Ibid., p. 273.

230 David H. Aaron's footnote in ibid., p. 273: "See 25:3, in James H. Charlesworth, *Old Testament Pseudepigrapha* (Garden City, 1983), vol. 1, pp. 801–02."

231 O. S. Wintermute, "Jubilees," in James H. Charlesworth, ed., *The Old Testament Pseudepigrapha*, vol. 2 (New York: Doubleday, 1985), p. 44.

232 J. C. Vanderkam, ed., *The Book of Jubilees*, 12:25–27, transl. J. C. Vanderkam, Corpus Scriptorum Christianorum Orientalium (hereafter CSCO) vol. 115 (Louvain, 1989), pp. 73–74, quoted in Milka Rubin, "The Language of Creation or the Primordial Language: A Case of Cultural Polemics in Antiquity," *Journal of Jewish Studies* 49 (1998): 310.

233 Milka Rubin, "Language of Creation," p. 310.

234 See H. W. Hollander and M. de Jonge, *The Testaments of the Twelve Patriarchs* (Leiden, 1985), Appendix I, p. 449; see also L. Ginzberg, *The Legends of the Jews*, vol. 2 (Philadelphia, 1947), p. 214, quoted by Rubin, op. cit., p. 310.

235 E. Eshel and M. E. Stone, "The Holy Language at the End of the Days in Light of a New Fragment Found at Qumran," *Tarbiz* 62 (1992/1993): 169–78 (in Hebrew), quoted by Rubin , op. cit., pp. 310–11.

236 Aaron, *Doctrine of Hebrew Language Usage*, p. 275, citing E. Eshel and M. E. Stone, "The Holy Language at the End of the Days in Light of a New Fragment Found at Qumran."

237 Rubin, op. cit., p. 311.

238 See M. Bregman, "Early Sources and Traditions in the Tanhuma-Yelammedenu Midrashim," *Tarbiz* 60 (1990/1991): 269–74, who cites S. Liebermann, D. Sperber, and others, quoted by Rubin, op. cit.

239 Shelmo Buber, ed. (New York, 1946), p. 58 (in Hebrew); transl. by J. T. Townsend, *Midrash Tanhuma*, vol. 1, *Genesis* (Hoboken, NJ: Ktav, 1989), p. 60; quoted in Rubin, op. cit.

240 This idea is preserved also in Karaite tradition. See Y. Erder, "Yefet Ben Eli's Attitude towards Islam," *Mikhael* 14 (1997): 46 n. 99 (in Hebrew), quoted in Rubin, op. cit.

241 Pseudo Jonathan, Gen. 1:1: A similar version appears in Neofiti I: see A. Diez Macho, *Neophiti I, vol. I: Genesis* (Madrid, 1968), p. 57. On the tradition of the Yerushalmi Targum, see A. Shinan, *The Embroidered Targum* (Jerusalem, 1992), pp. 113–15 (in Hebrew), quoted in Rubin, op. cit.

242 Rubin, "Language of Creation," p. 312.

243 Ibid., p. 313

244 Ibid., pp. 313–14.

245 Exodus Rabba—the second part (12–40) is a homiletical Midrash, which, according to the *Encyclopaedia Judaica*, "makes use of tannaitic literature, the Jerusalem Talmud, and early amoraic Midrashim, but not entire themes from the Babylonian Talmud. Many of its homilies also occur in the known editions of the Tanḥuma. It contains several halakhic expositions, numerous parables, and some aggadot of a comparatively late type. For the most part, however, it exhibits features which place it earlier than Exodus Rabbah I, and it was apparently compiled in the ninth century CE."

246 Theo A. W. van der Louw, *Transformations in the Septuagint: Towards an Interaction of Septuagint Studies and Translation Studies* (Leuven: Peeters, 2007), p. 52.

247 Van der Louw's note in ibid.: "The Midrash is attributed to Rabbi Jochanan (3rd century AD), but it underlies the famous NT passage of Acts 2 and must hence be older. There a multiplication of languages takes place on the Feast of Weeks (Pentecost), at which the giving of the Torah (!) was celebrated (חג מתן תורה)."

248 For example in al-Bukhārī, *al-Ṣaḥīḥ*, trans. M. M. Khan, 9 vols. (Riyadh, Saudi Arabia, 1997), vol. 6, book LXVI, ch. 5 Hadith, 4991, pp. 427–28.

249 *Pseudo-Clementine Recognitions*: according to Georg Strecker, "the Recognitions came into being independently of the Homilies—probably about 350 A.D.—in Syria or Palestine," in Wilhelm Schneemelcher, ed., *New Testament Apocrypha*, vol. 2 (Louisville, KY: John Knox Press, 1991), p. 485.

250 St. Augustine, *The City of God* (originally, *De Civitate Dei contra Paganos*, trans. Marcus Dods (1871) (Peabody, MA: Hendrickson Publishers Marketing, LLC, 2013), book 16, pp. 481–483.

251 Gregory of Nyssa, *Contra Eunomium*, 2 vols., ed. W. Jaeger (Leiden, 1960), vol. 1, p. 300 (par. 254); trans. in *Answer to Eunomius' Second Book*, transl. by M. Day in *Nicene and Post-Nicene Fathers*, vol. 5 (Edinburgh; repr. 1988), p. 276; quoted by Rubin, op. cit., p. 320.

252 Rubin, op. cit. pp. 321–22.

253 Su-Min Ri, "Le Caverne des tresors-les deux recensions syriaques," *CSCO*, vol. 486 (text), vol. 487 (transl.) (Louvain, 1987), ch. 24, text pp. 186–88, translation pp. 70–72, quoted in Rubin, op. cit., p. 323.

254 E. A. Wallis Budge, *The Book of the Cave of Treasures* (London: Religious Tract Society, 1927), Introduction.

255 Su-Min, op. cit., vol. 486, p. 186, quoted in Rubin, op. cit., p. 323.

256 L. Van Rompay, ed., *Le Commentaire sur la Genese Exode 9, 32 du manuscrit (olim) Diyarbakir 22* (Louvain, 1986), CSCO, vol. 483, pp. 68–69 (text); vol. 484, pp. 88–89 (transl.) (=Van Rompay); Theodorus Bar Koni, *Livre des scolies* (recension de Séert), transl. R. Hespel and R. Draguet (Louvain, 1981, 1982), CSCO, vol. 431, pp. 112–13 (text); 432, pp. 126–27 (transl.) (=Theodore Bar Koni); J. M. Voste and C. Van Den Eynde, eds., *Commentaire d'Isho'dad de Merv sur l'Ancien Testament, 1: Genese* (Louvain, 1950, 1955), CSCO, vol. 126, pp. 134–36 (text); vol. 156, pp. 146–48 (trans].) (=Isho'dad); A. Levene, *The Early Syrian Fathers on Genesis: From a Syriac MS on the Pentateuch* (London, 1951), pp. 7–8 (text); p. 86 (transl.) (=Levene).

257 Ibn al-Nadīm, *Kitāb al-Fihrist*, ed. G. Flugel (Leipzig, 1872), p. 12.

258 Ibid., p. 14.

259 See Ṭabarī, *Annales* I, ed. M. J. De Goeje (Leiden, 1879), pp. 220, 322, transl. William M. Brinner in *The History of al-Tabari*, vol. 2 (Albany: State University of New York Press, 1987), pp. 18, 108.

260 Brinner, trans., *The History of al-Ṭabarī*, vol. 2, p. 18, notes: "Thus yielding 72, the supposed number of languages spoken in the world."

261 Ibid., p. 108.

262 Ibid., p. 128.

263 Abul-l-Hasan 'Ali al-Mas'ūdī, *Les Prairies d'Or*, trans. C. Barbier de Meynard et Pavet de Courteille, vol. 1 (Paris, 1861), pp. 78–79.

264 M. J. Kister, "Adam: A Study of Some Legends of Tafsir and Hadith Literature," in J. L. Kraemer, ed., *Israel Oriental Studies*, vol. 13 (Brill, 1993), pp. 118–19. Kister gives the following reference: "Anonymous, Siyar al-anbiyd', MS Br. Mus. Or. 1510, fol. 19b."

265 Ibid., pp. 140–41. Kister gives the following references: "Abū Ḥayyān, op. cit., I, 145–146; and comp. al-Faḍl al-Ṭabarī, *Mağma' al-Bayān fī tafsīr al-qur'ān*, Beirut 1380/1961, I, 168–196; and see al-Mağlisī, op. cit., XI, 146. *Knowledge of language ('ilm al-luġa)* follows in importance the perception of the unity of God; God showed the angels the superiority of Adam by his knowledge of language (see al-Samarqandī, Tafsīr, MS, fol.13b.)."

266 Kister's note: "Al-Ṣāliḥī, *al-Sīra al-šāmiyya* (= Subul al-hudā wa-l-rašād), I, 364."

267 Kister's note: "Al-Suyūṭī, *al-Durr al-manṯūr*, 1, 58; and see a similar report in al-Mas'ūdī's *Aḫbār al-zamān*, p. 49."

268 Kister's note: "'Abd al-Malik b. Ḥabīb. *Ta'rīḫ*, MS, p. 19. And see René Dagom, *La Geste d' Ismaēl* (Paris 1981), pp. 289 penult. - 290."

Part 2

Aramaic and Syriac

On Some Insights Gained through an Arabic Reading of Epigraphic Tadmuraean Aramaic

Albert F. H. Naccache

Originally published in Proceedings of the Seminar for Arabian Studies *26 (1996): 97–113.*

We all know that the prevailing paradigm of the history of the Mashriqian languages[1] lies on its death bed, exhausted, overwhelmed by the constant flow of data that the archaeologists have uncovered, and still uncover, from all over the Mashriq of the Arab World. We process the data at our disposal with all the theoretical ingenuity we can muster, but the field is so vast, and our habit of dealing piecemeal with it so deeply entrenched, that the understanding in gestation is slow to take shape, even its outline yet unclear. In this predicament, any heuristic help we can get should be welcome.

In this paper I would like to share a perspective that sheds some new light upon part of the field. It is the perspective provided by teaching, in Arabic and to Arabic speaking students, the Ancient Mashriqian languages, and more particularly, the corpus of the Palmyrene Aramaic inscriptions.

Looking at Aramaic through Arabic, and, as a corollary, reflecting upon Arabic in the light of Aramaic, provides a perspective that cannot fail to elicit, even if by serendipity, some insights and reflections into the variegated and complex relationship linking the two overarching linguistic realities that we refer to as Aramaic and Arabic. For instance, what should we make of the feeling of "recognition" that a native speaker of the modern Lebanese vernacular often has when dealing, in Arabic, with the Aramaic of the inscriptions found at Tadmur/Palmyra, or of his/her impression, acquired with increased familiarity with the material, that her/his vernacular is as strikingly akin to Tadmuraean Aramaic as it is to Classical Arabic, and closer to the former than to the latter?

Such observations do not square well with some of the main tenets of our old paradigm for the reconstruction of the history of Arabic and of the so-called "NeoArabic" dialects. Attempting to account for these observations within a coherent historical framework provides us with some interesting leads for further research.

Let us try to flesh up this claim. We will start by a description of the *Diwān Nuṣūṣ Tadmur*, the tool developed to teach, in Arabic, and to Arabic speaking Lebanese students, Epigraphic Tadmuraean Aramaic, and whose elaboration, as well as use, provided the above-mentioned heuristic change in perspective. The *Diwān Nuṣūṣ Tadmur* is a chrestomathy of just over 200 of the complete, near-complete and/or satisfactorily restored Aramaic inscriptions from Tadmur/Palmyra and its vicinity. It was completed in 1990, and, since then, used in conjunction with a dictionary (Jean et Hoftijzer, 1965) and a grammar (Cantineau, 1935), in a third year undergraduate course at the archaeology department of the Lebanese University.[2]

Since the linguistic methodology followed in the *Diwān Nuṣūṣ Tadmur* has been presented elsewhere (Naccache, *forth. a)*, we can concentrate here upon highlighting those elements of the configuration of this collection, and of its use as a teaching tool, that proved instrumental in providing a new point of view upon the subject. All these elements have one thing in common, they are all derived from the constant linguistic switching between Epigraphic Tadmuraean Aramaic (ETA), modern Standard Arabic (MSA, the version of literary Arabic with which the students are familiar) and modern Lebanese vernacular (MLV, an abstraction from the various local speech forms current in Lebanon today, and an instance of the *Bilād aš-šām* vernacular, or modern Arabic dialect), that is both embodied in the *Diwān* and enforced by its use as a teaching aid.

When used by Arabic-speaking Lebanese students, the *Diwān* taps into the "competence in interglossic transfer" (Dicky, 1994), which the students have long-since acquired through daily and repeatedly switching between the MLV and MSA instances of the Arabic continuum. While reading, in parallel, vocalised ETA texts and their Arabic rendering, the students are automatically and unavoidably required to call upon their acquired mechanism of interglossic transfer. The teaching approach that is followed takes advantage of this ability the students have to subliminally perceive the lexical, morphological and syntactical patterns of correspondence between MLV and MSA, and to act automatically upon these patterns to switch from one instance to the other. For these students, the attentive reading of vocalised Aramaic in this familiar context helps them progressively to extend their "field of switching" to embrace ETA. This easy propaedeutic is then bolstered and methodologically grounded through the recourse to dictionaries and grammar books.

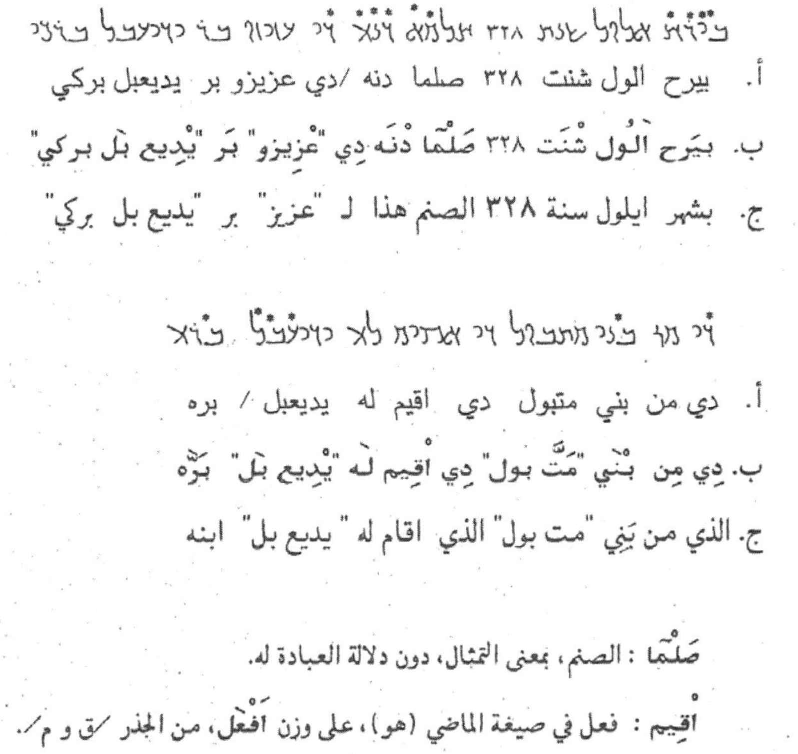
أ. بيرح الول شنت ٣٢٨ صلما دنه /دي عزيزو بر يديعبل بركي
ب. بيَرح اَلُول شْنَت ٣٢٨ صَلْمَا دْنَه دِي "عْزِيزو" بَر "يْدِيع بَل بركي"
ج. بشهر ايلول سنة ٣٢٨ الصنم هذا لـ "عزيز" بر "يديع بل بركي"
أ. دي من بني متبول دي اقيم له يديعبل / بره
ب. دِي مِن بْنَي "مَتّ بول" دِي اقْيم لَه "يْدِيع بَل" بَرّه
ج. الذي من بَنِي "مت بول" الذي اقام له "يديع بل" ابنه
صَلْمَا : الصنم، بمعنى التمثال، دون دلالة العبادة له.
اقِيم : فعل في صيغة الماضي (هو)، على وزن اَفْعَل، من الجذر /ق و م/.

Figure 1: A sample from *Diwān Nuṣūṣ Tadmur*

To give a clearer idea of how this approach is implemented, we will examine a sample of the material as it appears in the *Diwān* (fig. 1). Each inscription is presented in four formats or lines, the first being a copy of the inscription in Tadmuraean script, the second its transliteration in Arabic letters, the third its transcription in Arabic script, and the fourth its "isomorphic transform" into the morphologically congruent Arabic words. These four lines are followed by notes providing the grammatical analysis of verbs and deverbal nouns, and, when appropriate, commentaries.

Line 1 is a copy, in a Tadmuraean script, of the original inscription.[3] Its intended function is not to familiarise the students with the ETA script, though it does that, but, for reasons that will be made clear in what follows, to serve as a constant reminder to the students that these are ancient texts that should not be read as Arabic. In conjunction with line 2, it also helps the students overcome their deeply ingrained confusion between script and language. This confusion is illustrated by the efforts most students have to expend in order to overcome their first impression that line 1 is in Aramaic and line 2 in Arabic. Explaining that line 1 is simply computer-generated from line 2 by copying it in a changed font is not, by itself, enough to have them accept that both are transliterations differing only in the fonts used to produce them. Although they have already spent a year with Ezra and Daniel in the Kittel Bible's format, it is only after the students have become familiar with the *Diwān* that they finally internalise the fact that script and language are not to be confused.

The transliteration in line 2 is neutral in the matter of the phonetic realisation of the letters. The mapping of the 22 Aramaic letters into 22 of the 28 Arabic letters is straightforward. Since we are dealing with epigraphic Aramaic, Aramaic *s* has been transliterated as Arabic *s*, and Aramaic *š* as Arabic *š* (no *hamza* is used in the transliteration, only *aleph* s). This option is supported by comparing the Eastern *abǧad* arrangement of the letters of the Arabic alphabet with the Aramaic alphabet (Churchyard, 1993, p 318).

Using the *Diwān* in the classroom has convinced me that Lebanese students need specific guidance on how to use ETA texts in Arabic transliteration properly. This is because the consonantal skeleton of ETA, stripped of its vocalisation, shares so much with the consonantal skeleton of the Arabic continuum that it is confusing to the learner, whose first and overwhelming tendency is to read ETA texts transliterated in Arabic script as if they were Arabic texts, written in the Arabic language! This is why beginners should not read the transliteration, but use it solely as a base from which to work out their analysis of the inscription. This analysis is then embodied in the transcription in line 3.

The transcription proposed in line 3 represents, expressed within the conventions of the Arabic script, the proposal made by the epigraphist for how the original graphemes were realised in speech,[4] i.e., it represents a reading of the text. Because the *Diwān* is intended for teaching purpose, the readings found in it are rarely original, and in an overwhelming majority of cases simply transcribe in Arabic the readings adopted by the primary editors.[5] The only originality claimed here is that transcriptions are used in the *Diwān* for whole inscriptions, while in the field of Aramaic studies they are usually limited to one-word commentaries. This means that the Arab readers are provided with a vocalised ETA text in the script with which they are familiar, and in whose medium all their acquired mechanisms of "interglossic transfer" are grounded.

Given the repetitive nature of most of the inscriptions and the ease with which the inscriptions transcribed in Arabic can be read, the students grasp the language of ETA very quickly. After reading a score of inscriptions, they are encouraged to use the transliterations to work transcriptions out for themselves. Observing the results of these efforts has led me to the following remarks about the students' performance in switching between ETA, MLV and MSA:

The students do pay special attention to what, from their point of view, are the most exotic parts of speech, such as the verbs and derived nouns.

After just a few weeks of using the *Diwān* the root, stem and form of the great majority of these words would be quickly identified, and the word therefore correctly vocalised. However the same is not true of the most common parts of speech. It is thus a long battle to get even the most perceptive student to vocalise consistently the ubiquitous *lh* as *leh* (Aramaic) and not as *lahu* (Arabic).

The students take very easily to the "Aramaic characteristic" of starting a word with an unvocalised consonant, a characteristic that MLV shares with Aramaic. However, a rather frequent observation was that, while trying to vocalize in Aramaic a word shared by ETA, MLV and MSA, the student would come up with an MSA vocalisation and not with "their" MLV vocalisation, even though that last might be a better approximation. It is as if, since the students' switching mechanism between ETA and MLV is not yet well established, they fall back on the much used MLV to MSA switch.

Finally there are two related problems that the Arab-speaking Lebanese students have to face while dealing with the transcription of ETA texts. The first is the difference in spelling conventions between ETA and MSA. The second is that in the case of shared roots there is an ever-present possibility of a semantic shift between ETA and MLV or MSA. The students are helped to confront these problems by having to produce the "isomorphic transform" represented in line 4.

Line 4, or, as I propose to call it, the "isomorphic transform" is a step justified and made possible by the congruence that exists between "Aramaic" and "Arabic" morphology. Having noticed my own reliance on an "interglossic transfer" mechanism while learning "Semitic" at LT.C.B., the "isomorphic transform" is a step I started implementing since 1987, both in teaching and for Arabic editions of ancient Mashriqian texts. Its foundation, in the present case, is that all the morphological set of ETA is mappable in a one-to-one, unambiguous and reciprocal relationship onto the MSA morphological set,[6] the only two non-essential deviations being that the verbal stem *ʾitfʿel / ʾiftʿel* of ETA maps onto both the *ʾiftaʿala* and the *ʾinfaʿala* stems of MSA, and that ETA's *dī* has a dozen MSA correspondents.

The production of the "isomorphic transform" is straightforward and does not entail the investment of any new effort in analysis, since all the information required to perform it has already been specified while producing the transcription, that is at the point when all the words of the inscription were analysed. Based on this analysis all that the operation of transformation requires is to produce, the MSA word equivalent to the ETA word. Interestingly it is possible, in a large number of cases, to produce the word in MSA garb from the very same root as was used in ETA.

It is worth noting that from a linguistic point of view, the "isomorphic transform" could have targeted MLV rather than MSA, i.e., produced words in their vernacular form, both options being methodologically equivalent.

The choice of MSA is political, not linguistic. It does not prevent the students, while practising in the classroom or alone, from performing this operation in two steps, first from ETA to their congenial MLV, and then, "automatically," from MLV to MSA when writing down the result.

The result of the "isomorphic transform" is a text which is comprehensible with minimal effort by the students, even though—and this is important—the syntactic structure of this text is still that of its epigraphic original. This text is comprehensible because all of its words are in correct MSA (or MLV), and because the difference in syntax between ETA and MLV is not qualitatively different from that prevailing today between the ideal (the syntax of Classical Arabic, CA) and the practice (the various syntaxes of MLV, or even of one of the levels of MSA with which one is confronted daily).

This comprehensibility is one of the most useful aspects of the "isomorphic transform," which is that it results in an instantaneous understanding of the original inscription in an easily recognisable form. This is because line 4 represents, in a familiar form, one's comprehension of the original text, which can be tested against the criteria of coherence and meaning. If line 4 does not make sense, it means something is wrong in line 3, the transcription, which means that we have to re-analyse line 2, the transliteration, and come up with a different analysis of the words in ETA, repeating the process till a satisfactory reading is achieved.

This constant and active interglossic switching forces the student constantly to compare ETA, MLV and MSA. It is this compulsory process of comparison that we referred to as the perspective opened to the user of the *Diwān*. Now, as a matter of course, such comparisons lead to evaluation of the similarities or dissimilarities between the things compared. Table 1 presents an overview of the result of such an evaluation, which would be reached by any Arabic speaking Lebanese student working on the ETA corpus as presented in the *Diwān*. It is clear from Table 1 that, by most terms of comparison, MLV would be perceived to be closer to ETA than MSA is.

It needs to be stressed that, when they approach it via the *Diwān*. modem inhabitants of the region consider the Aramaic of the Tadmuraean inscriptions to be a strange variant of their dialect.

Although this impression is of course anachronistic, it is worth examining in the context of our prevailing theories about the history of Arabic, for two reasons. First, because it can help us evaluate the various theories about the origin of the modem Arabic vernaculars, and secondly, because it has some heuristic value that can lead to promising venues for further research. In the remainder of this paper, we will briefly consider each in turn.

The study of the origin of the Arabic vernaculars, has stagnated despite the fact that when, and from what, the dialects developed is a crucial question in the field (see Abboud, 1970; Miller, 1986). We have seen that the similarities across all linguistic categories between MLV and ETA, are greater than those between MSA and ETA. This observation is relevant in the context of the study of the origin of the Arabic vernaculars because none of the theoretical explanations that have been used, be it "family tree," substrate influences, parallel developments, "wave theory," diglossic situations or any combinations thereof, could account for an across the board similarity between MLV and ETA if MLV had developed from CA, the urform of MSA.

Yet, the assumption that the modern sedentary dialects, or vernaculars have developed from CA has dominated the nearly ninety years old debate, a debate which is sometimes traced back to two opposing hypothesis advanced by Nöldeke (1904) and Vollers (1906, notwithstanding his hypothesis about the Koran).

The former hypothesis, propounding the development, after the Islamic conquest, of the vernaculars from CA or from a *Koinè* has held sway. It has as many variations as it has advocates (Rick, 1955; Ferguson, 1959a; Blau, 1965; Blau, 1977, Blau, 1981), and now attracts arguments from sociolinguistics (Versteegh, 1984; Ferguson 1989; Hary, 1989; Eksell, 1995). Still, it can be epitomised in the statement that NeoArabic, or the modern vernaculars and with it Arabic diglossia, developed from CA as late as the first Islamic century as a result of the great Arab conquest (Blau, I 977), a statement still commonly found in the literature (Kaye, 1994, 54).

The latter hypothesis, most recently propounded by Corriente, derives the vernaculars from the pre-Islamic languages of "the populations of Syria and Iraq, who were speakers of Nabaṭī Arabic or had just been obliged to learn it. . ." (1976, 72). This position is bolstered by an analysis of the linguistic nature of the poetic and Koranic *Koinè* which concludes that CA "can never have served any group as their standard speech" (Zwettler, 1978, 148 and n.115–6).

The literature is however replete with equivocations, such as Ferguson's statements that

> it may even be true that a few of the features of the *Koiné* (from which the dialects are derived) continued an original state while the corresponding forms of Classical were the innovations (3959a, 618),

or that

> Arabic diglossia seems to reach as far back as our knowledge of Arabic goes (1959b, 327),

or Blau's statement that

> if one wants to continue the metaphor of kinship, one will rather consider pre-Islamic standard Arabic and Proto-Neo-Arabic to be "sister" languages, close-

> ly related and mutually intelligible. (1981–2, 223; on Blau's terminological inconsistencies, see Hary, 1989, 23–6).

It is also often stated that it is an "*assumption* (my italics) that all Arabic dialects have developed from the Arabic *Koinè* of the first centuries of the Islamic era" (Garbell, 1959), and there are many cautionary notes about the geographical and substratic diversity of the vernaculars and about the postulated identity of the poetic and Koranic *Koinè* with the postulated spoken "Arabic *Koinè*" (Cohen, 1962, 143, 119).

		MODERN STANDARD ARABIC	EPIGRAPHIC TADMURAEAN ARAMAIC (ETA)	MODERN LEBANESE VERNACULAR (MLV)
MORPHOLOGY				
VERBS	State / tense		shared between the three	*b*-imperfect (6/12th c. Yemenite influence?)
	Stems / form	15 forms, 11 actives	6 forms; 3, plus 3 with *t*-infix	midway between MSA and ETA
NOUNS	Formation	full range of forms	limited range of forms (NP excluded)	medium range (neologisms)
	Numbers	*’iṯnayn*	one attestation of dual (similar to MLV) *trēn*	dual use for nouns (not verbs) *tnēn*
	Inflection	yes	no	no
SYNTAX		CA and MSA syntax restricted to a few standardised types. Should not be followed when reading an ETA text in "isomorphic transform" (line 4)	not well known, varies with type and date of text, apparently relative fluidity of constructions	ETA texts in "isomorphic transform" more readily understood in MLV due to the latter choice of syntactical constructions
LEXICAL		Many word survival due to the antiquarian approach of CA lexicography: *ziqq; ḥāyr; ḥafāwa; ḥassaka; ẓa‘ūn; mākis; nāmūs; ‘ansus; farnas* etc	A majority of roots used in ETA are shared with MSA and MLV such as: *ftḥ* or *’ḥd / ’ḫd / ’ḫḏ* etc. even some derived nouns such as: *maǧǧān* etc	A number of diagnostic isoglosses link ETA specifically with MLV: *dabbar; balā; barra; ǧuwwa; ǧins; hēyk; zġīr; kīs; šarǧab* etc

Table 1: An a-historical linguistic comparison between ETA, MLV and MSA from the perspective of the *Diwān Nuṣūṣ Tadmur*

Even if the two major hypotheses are not mutually exclusive, our observation would best be explained if both Classical Arabic (with or without a *Koinè)* and the vernaculars developed from the same original continuum, that is, within the context of the second hypothesis. That this conclusion could not be framed in a more robust way is a reflection of the weakness of the hypotheses currently dominating the field.

In his introduction to an issue devoted to the methodological and thematic renewal of the field of Arabic studies P. Larcher (1991) noted that, in spite of "the remarkably complex sociolinguistic situation" of the Arabic language, its study has lagged behind the general field of linguistics. The same can be said about the remarkably complex historical situation of Arabic and the dearth of historical studies devoted to it relative to those of Indo-European linguistics. It is in this context that the perspective offered by the *Diwān* could have some heuristic value, not only in helping to define the field of study, but also in suggesting ways of approaching it.

One tenet of the dominant paradigm is that CA is of great antiquity.[7] This led to the assumption that the modem vernaculars were derived from CA. In the sixties, a more realistic historical appreciation of the innovative nature of CA morphology developed (Petráček, 1981), and also, through a re-evaluation of the classical Arabic sources (Blachère, 1958; Baalbaki, 1983; Fleisch, 1984; Langhade, 1994), of the genesis of CA (Zwettler, 1978). In spite of this, Arabic still often "passes implicitly or explicitly for the starting point of diachronic speculations" (Petráček, 1981, 162, my translation), if not CA, then "the large number of regional dialects or subdialects (that) existed prior to the written evidence of the establishment of Old Arabic in its pseudo-classical form" (Eksell, 1995, 65). The feeling of familiarity experienced by Lebanese students while reading ETA texts should warn us against such restrictive tendencies, and invite us to widen the horizon of our search.

Even though we are only concerned here with the history of the vernaculars of *Bilād aš-Šām,* we should widen the horizon of our search and consider all the available Mashriqian linguistic evidence that has come down to us from this region. Some of this material has been used in the study of the history of Old Arabic and Proto-Arabic, as well as for the study of the development of Arabic writing (Rabin, 1984; Milik, 1985a; Greenfield, 1992; Healey, 1991; Healey, 1993; Robin, 1993a; Robin,1993b; Gruendler, 1993). From such studies we can now say with Rabin that

> geographically, through its earlier appearance in the Syrian Desert, and grammatically, as well as lexico-statistically, Arabic is closer to the North-West Semitic languages, especially to Aramaic, but the relation has not yet been fully worked out. (1984, 131)

We now also classify Proto-Arabic together with Canaanite in the *ha(n)*-dialects category in opposition to the Aramaic dialects that make up the *-ā* category (Milik, 1985b), but observe the gradual transition from Nabataean Aramaic to Arabic (Healey and Smith, 1989; Greenfield, 1992), within the historical framework of a spectrum of Aramaic dialects (Cook, 1992). And we should not forget Syriac sources, which, in their earliest attestation (Maricq, 1962) display the same relations with MLV as does ETA, and which provide us with rich palaeographic (Desreumaux, 1987), sociological (Lavenant, 1983; Segal, 1984; Troupeau, 1991) and linguistic sources (Bar-Asher, 1988).

It is evidence from all these linguistic sources and not simply from Old-Arabic that should form the "continuum of dialects with its fluctuations and shifts (which) we should courageously admit to be the origin of Old Arabic, instead of looking for the miraculous missing dialect or *Koiné* form" (Eksell, 1995, 65), and we would add, not only the origin of Old Arabic, but of Neo-Arabic too. It is only a derivation from such a dialect continuum, of which ETA was part, that could explain MLV's relationship with ETA.

But how are we to organise and deal with such a tremendous mass of disparate data? Here again the perspective offered by the *Diwān* suggests ways of approaching the problem. The disjunction that is apparent between the historical situation implied by our observation and the one derived from the hypotheses of the prevailing paradigm has some interesting implications. To reconstruct a coherent representation of the historical and sociological linguistic situation that lead to the present outcome, it will not be enough to import models and theories developed to account for the Indo-European languages, however rich these are (Parker, 1983; Kahane, 1986; Tarrier, 1991; Chambers, 1992). This is illustrated by contrasting the shortcomings of the application of the pidginization creolization decreolization model to the Arabic domain (Versteegh, 1984; Ferguson, 1989) with the amazingly rich and complex picture of the present day sociolinguistic situation of the speakers of Arabic that emerges from a methodologically aware attempt to account directly for the specificity of the subject (Dichy, 1994).

Unfortunately, when we turn to historical situations, we are not offered this opportunity to generate new data "at will," but have to squeeze whatever we can from the material that has come to us through tradition or archaeology. To do so we should be ready to deconstruct the traditionally accepted histories. This rewarding process, illustrated in a connected field by M. Sharon's (1988) iconoclastic but highly stimulating reappraisal of the birth of Islam as a historical and sociological phenomenon, should equally embrace the standing representations and their epistemological grounding.

Here again, and this will be our concluding point, the fact that the modern Lebanese vernacular has so much affinity with the language written at Tadmur nearly two millennia ago can be exploited to some heuristic end. This fact is very hard to account for from within the traditional classification of the "Semitic" languages, which is predicated upon a common, punctual origin and a cladistic model of linguistic development, as illustrated by this archetype of "cladograms," or branching diagrams, the "family tree." Within such a model the modern Arabic vernaculars could be derived either from Arabic or from Aramaic, both choices being mutually exclusive, because "the logic of cladism, and the graphics derived from that logic, demand that each entity must have one and only one parent" (Moore, 1994, 929). Such a restriction in the spectrum of possibilities has no justifications in the field of human social history, which is replete with all kind of combinations and alternations, all kind of separation and recombination. Therefore, to account for our finding and be able to represent its historical development in a coherent context, we have to abandon the cladistic genealogies—and look for alternatives, such as the

> rhyzotic theories (which) emphasise the extent to which each human language, culture, or population is considered to be derived from or rooted in several different antecedent groups (ib., 925).

Two examples of rhyzotic diagrams are illustrated in figure 2, the first a model of the channels of a river separating and recombining in a complex fashion, the second a schematic of the brachial plexus of the nerves of the upper limb.

This is the kind of diagram we would need in order to represent the historical path followed by the vernaculars of *Bilād aš-Šām*, whose roots can be traced back to Canaanite, Proto-Arabic and Aramaic, with other influences not to be excluded, who went back and forth through many linguistic levels and had many social carriers, and who had been in prolonged contact with Classical Arabic, with all what that contact implies of dominance, resistance and adaptation. This and more we should include in our representation if we want it to do justice to the genius of a language nearly two thousand years old.

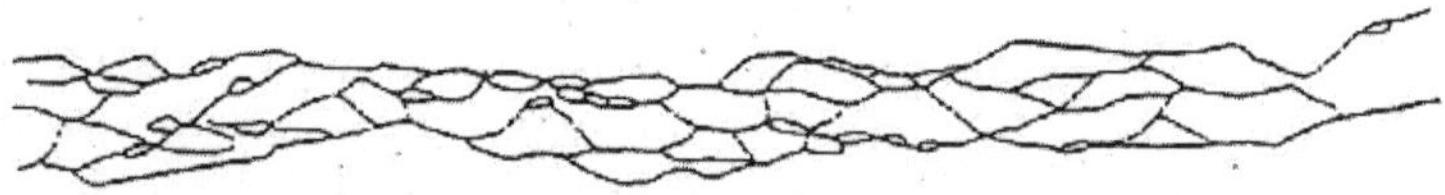

a) Channels of a river separating and recombining
(adapted from Moore, 1994)

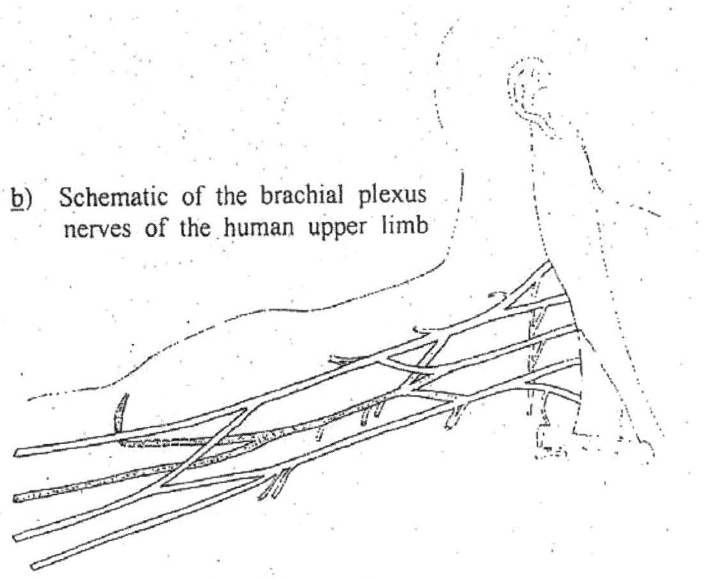

Figure 2: Two examples of rhyzotic diagrams

Bibliography

Abboud, P. F. 1970. "Spoken Arabic," in Ferguson C. A. et al. (eds.) *Linguistics in South West Asia and North Africa*, The Hague-Paris. *Current Trends in Linguistics* 6.

Baalbaki, R. 1983. "Early Arab lexicographers and the use of Semitic languages," *Berytus* 31: pp. 117– 27.

Bar-Asher, M. 1988. "Le Syro-Palestinien: Études grammaticales," *Journal Asiatique* 276: pp. 28–59.

Beeston, A. F. L. 1981. "Languages of pre-Islamic Arabia," *Arabica* 28:178–86.

Blachère, R. 1958. "Regards sur la littérature narrative en arabe au ler siècle de l'hégire," *Semitica VI*: pp. 75–86.

Blau, J. 1965. *The emergence and linguistic background of Judaeo-Arabic: A study in the origins of Middle Arabic*. London.

Blau, J. 1969. "Some problems of the formation of the Old Semitic Languages in the light of Arabic dialects," in *Proceedings of the International Conference of Semitic Studies held in Jerusalem* (Jerusalem, 1965), publications of the Israel Academy of Sciences and Humanities.

Blau, J. 1977. "The beginnings of the Arabic diglossia. A study of the origins of NeoArabic," *Afroasiatic linguistics* 4/3: pp. 175–202.

Blau, J. 1981. "The state of research in the field of the linguistic study of Middle Arabic," *Arabica* 28: pp. 187–203.

Blau, J. 1981–82. "On some Proto-Neo-Arabic and early Neo-Arabic features differing from Classical Arabic," *JSAI* 3: pp. 223–35.

Cantineau, J. 1935. *Grammaire du palmyrénien épigraphique.* Le Caire. Chambers, J. K. 1992. "Dialect acquisition," *Language* 68: pp. 673–705.

Churchyard, H. 1993. "Early Arabic siin and šiin in light of the Proto-Semitic fricative-lateral hypothesis," In Eid, M and Holes C. (ed.) *Perspectives on Arabic Linguistics* V. Amsterdam: *Amsterdam Studies in the Theory and History of Linguistic Science*, vol. 101. pp. 313–42.

Cohen, D. 1962. "Koiné, langues communes et dialectes arabes," *Arabica* 9: pp. 119–44.

Cook, E. M. 1992. "Qumran Aramaic and Aramaic dialectology," *Abr-Nahrain Sup.* 3: pp. 1–21.

Corriente, F. 1976. "From Old Arabic to Classical Arabic through the Pre-Islamic Koine: Some notes on the native grammarians sources, attitudes and goals," *JSS* 21: pp. 62–98.

Desreumaux, A. 1987. "La naissance d'une nouvelle écriture araméenne à l'époque byzantine," *Semitica* 37: pp. 95–107

Dichy, J. 1994. "La pluriglossie de l'Arabe," *Bulletin d'études orientales* XLVI: pp. 19–42.

Eksell, K. 1995. "Complexity of linguistic change as reflected in Arabic dialects," *SO* 75: pp. 63–73.

Ferguson, C. A. 1959a. "The Arabic Koiné," *Language* 25 : pp. 616–30.

Ferguson, C. A. 1959b. "Diglossia," *Word* 15: pp. 325–40.

Ferguson, C. A. 1989. "Grammatical agreement in Classical Arabic and the Modern Dialects. A response to Versteegh's pidginization hypothesis," *Al-ʿArabiyya* 22: pp. 5–17.

Fleisch, H. 1984. "Les grammairiens arabes et la grammaire," *Rocznik Orientaliysticzny* 43: pp. 71–79.

Fück, J. 1955. *ʿArabīya. Recherches sur l'histoire de la langue et du style arabes* (trad. de Pallemand par C. Denizeau). Paris.

Garbell, I. 1958. "Remarks on the historical phonology of an East Mediterranean Arabic Dialect," *Word* 14: pp. 303–37.

Greenfield, J. C. 1992. "Some Arabic loanwords in the Aramaic and Nabatean texts from Naḥal Ḥever," *JSAI* 15: pp. 10–21

Gruendler, B. 1993. *The development of the Arabic scripts. From the Nabatean Era to the First Islamic Centwy according to dated texts.* Atlanta.

Gruber-Miller, A. M. 1990. "Loss of nominal case endings in the modern Arabic sedentary dialects: Evidence from southern Palestinian Christian middle Arabic texts," In Eid, M. (ed.) *Perspectives on Arabic Linguistics 1. Amsterdam: Amsterdam Studies in the Theory and History of Linguistic Science*, vol. 63. pp. 235–53.

Hary, B. 1989. "Middle Arabic. Proposals for new terminology," *Al-ʿArabiyya* 22: pp. 19–36.

Healey, J. F. 1991. "Nabataean to Arabic: Calligraphy and script development among the pre-Islamic Arabs," in Bartlet J. et al. (eds), *The role of the book in the civilisations of the Near East.* Manuscripts of the Middle East 5. Leiden. pp. 41–52.

Healey, J. F. 1993. "The Nabataean tomb inscriptions of Mada'in Salih," *JSS supplement* 1. Oxford.

Healey, J. F. and Smith G. R. 1989. "Jaussen-Savignac 17: The earliest dated Arabic document (A.D. 267)," *Atlal* 12: pp. 77–84.

Jean, C.-F. and Hoftijzer, J. 1965. *Dictionnaire des inscriptions sémitiques de l'ouest.* Leiden.

Kahane, H. 1986. "A typology of the prestige language," *Language* 62: 495–508.

Kaye, A. S. 1994. "Formal vs. Informal in Arabic: Diglossia, triglossia, tetraglossia, etc., polyglossia multiglossia viewed as a continuum," *Journal of Arabic Linguistics* 27: pp. 47–66.

Langhade, J. 1994. "Études linguistiques au moyen-age, un regard interculturel: Le silence des sources sur la science lexicographique arabe," *Bulletin d'Études Orientales* 46: pp. 99–110.

Larcher, P. 1991. "Preface," *Bulletin d'Études Orientales* 43: XIII–XVI.

Lavenant, R. (ed.) 1983. "Les contacts du monde syriaque avec les autres cultures. Proceedings of the IIIrd Symposium Syriacum," *Orientalia Christiania Analecta* 221. Rome.

Maricq, A. 1962. "Classica et Orientalia. Notes posthumes," *Syria* 39: 83–101.

Milik, J. T. 1985a. "Epigraphie Safaftique," in Dentzer J.-M. (ed.) Hauran I. *Recherches archéologiques sur la Syrie du Sud à l'époque hellénistique et romaine,* Première partie. Paris. pp. 180–88.

Milik, J. T. 1985b. "Origine des Nabatéens," in Hadidi A. (ed.) *Studies in the history and archaeology of Jordan.* I. Amman. pp. 261–65.

Miller, A. M. 1986. "The Origin of the modern Arabic sedentary dialects: An evaluation of several theories," *Al-ʿArabiyya* 19: pp. 47–74.

Moore, J. H. 1994. "Putting anthropology back together again: the ethnogenetic critique of cladistic theory," *American Anthropologist* 96: 925–48.

Naccache, A. F. 1985. *The representation of the long-time-span structures of human history: The case of the Mashriq.* University Microfilms International. Ann Arbor.

Naccache, A. F. forth. a. "On some implications of the Tadmuraean Aramaic/Arabic diglossia," in the forthcomming *Proceedings of the International Conference "Palmyra and the Silk Road,"* Palmyra, April 1992.

Naccache, A. F. forth, b. "A brief description of a curriculum for teaching in Arabic the Ancient Mashriqian Languages," in the forthcomming *Proceedings of "The first regional conference on the writings of Bilād aš-šām before Islam,"* Yarmuk University, April 1994.

Nöldeke, T. 1904. *Beiträge zur semitischen Sprachwissenschaft.* Strassburg.

Parker, 1. 1983. "The rise of the vernacular in early modern Europe: An essay in the political economy of language," in Bain B. (ed), *The sociogenesis of language and human conduct.* New York. pp. 323–51.

Petráček, K. 1981. "Le système de l'arabe dans une perspective diachronique," *Arabica* 28: pp. 162–77.

Rabin, C. 1984. "On the probability of South-Arabian influence on the Arabic vocabulary," *JSA1* 4: pp. 125–34.

Robin, Ch. 1993. "Les plus anciens monuments de la langue arabe," *Revue du Monde Musulman et de la Méditerranée* 61: pp. 113–26.

Robin. Ch. 1993. "Les écritures de l'Arabie avant l'Islam," *Revue du Monde Musulman et de la Méditerranée* 61: pp. 127–38.

Segal. J. B. 1984. "Arabs in Syriac literature before the rise of Islam," *JSAI* 4: pp. 89–123.

Sharon, M. 1988. "The birth of Islam in the Holy Land," in Sharon M. (ed) *The Holy Land in history and thought.* Leiden. pp. 225–35.

Tarrier, J.-M. 1991. "A propos de sociolinguistique de l'arabe: Présentation de quelques difficultés," *Bulletin d'Études Orientates* 43: pp. 1–15.

Troupeau, G. 1991. "Le rôle des syriaques dans la transmission et l'exploitation du patrimoine philosophique et scientifique grec," *Arabica* 38: pp. 1–10.

Versteegh, K. 1984. "Pidginization and creolization: The case of Arabic," Amsterdam: *Amsterdam Studies in the theory and history of Linguistic Science* 4.

Vollers, K. 1906. *Volkssprache and Schriftsprache im alten Arabien.* Strassburg.

Zwettler, M. 1978. *The oral tradition of Classical Arabic poetry. Its character and implications.* Columbus.

Notes

---

1 The proposal to replace "Semitic" by "Mashriqian" was advanced in order to avoid an ethnic reference in the naming of language families, and to fit in with the general linguistic practice that uses a geographic and not an ethnic referent to name language families (Naccache, 1985). The name "Mashriq" was chosen because it is the name used by the local inhabitants to refer to the large area comprising the Arabian Peninsula and the Fertile Crescent—the Mashriq of the Arab World. Such a practice, followed when naming as "Sayhadic" the languages "virtually confined to the areas west, south and east of the Sayhad sand desert" (Beeston, 1981, 179), would furthermore fit very well with the higher and lower level terms in current use, such as AfroAsiatic or North-West or Central.

2 Since joining, in September 1986, the faculty of the Archaeology department of the Lebanese University, and although I consider myself a historian, I have been teaching, in Arabic, five courses:—a general introduction to the Ancient Mashriqian Languages,—an introduction to Biblical Aramaic,—an Aramaic follow-

up,—an Introduction to Akkadian,—and an Akkadian follow-up. This curriculum has been described elsewhere (Naccache, forth. b). The Tadmuraean Aramaic course has served till now as the Aramaic follow-up.

3 The Tadmuraean script that has been scanned to generate the computer font used in line 1 was taken from the column "AD 232" of Cantineau's table of Palmyrene scripts. There is no overriding justification for this choice, apart from the fact that any choice would have been equally arbitrary.

4 Contrary to a widespread misconception, there is no problem in representing the Ancient Mashriqian Languages in the Arabic script. This script has a convenient and well established way of representing the three vowels /a/, /u/ and /i/ in both short and full length. As for the *imēleh* /e/, known to grammarians at least since Sibawaih, and routinely written down in editions of the Koran, I have simply chosen a graphic implementation that reflects more its phonetic nature than the one used in the Koran (in differentiating between /e/ and /ē/ the same convention is used as that between /a/ and /ā/). And finally, it is interesting to note that the realisation of /ā/ as /ō/, which, in any case, is non-morphological and non-binding, though not indicated in this transcription scheme, is heard when the texts are read by students from specific areas of Lebanon.

5 Where the reading of a word differs from the one offered by the primary editors, the adopted reading is explained in the accompanying notes.

6 The reverse is not true, and the MSA set is much larger that the ETA one.

7 Thus we read in a paper presented in 1965, "Until the appearance of Mohammed, the Arabs lived to a great extent in almost complete isolation from the outer world ... This accounts for the *prima facie* astonishing fact that Classical Arabic, though appearing on the stage of history hundreds of years after Canaanite and Aramaic, nevertheless in many respects has a more archaic structure than these Old Semitic languages. The Arabs, being almost completely insulated front external influences and living under the same primitive conditions as their ancestors, preserved the ancient form of their speech..." (Blau, 1969, 38).

Syriacisms in the "Arabic Qur'ān": Who Were Those who Said "Allāh Is Third of Three" According to al-Mā'ida 73?

Sidney H. Griffith

Originally published in Meir M. Bar Asher et al., eds., A Word Fitly Spoken: Studies in Mediaeval Exegesis of the Hebrew Bible and the Qur'ān Presented to Haggai Ben-Shammai *(Jerusalem, 2007), pp. 83 ff.; with kind permission of the Ben Zvi Institute for the Study of Jewish Communities in the East.*

1. The Aramaean context of early Islam

Modern Western scholars, for the most part operating outside the hermeneutical horizons of the Islamic communities, have long searched for the intercultural, interreligious and multilingual historical circumstances that the "Arabic Qur'ān's" (Q 12 *Yūsuf* 2) own narratives seem to demand for a fuller understanding of the context in which the Islamic scripture first appeared. The high profile that the Aramaic expression of Christianity can be seen to have, against the background of the "Arabic Qur'ān" in its canonical recension, is a special case. Of course, the Christian Aramaean context is only one of several that may be profitably examined; the Qur'ān certainly has more than one context, and even more than one Christian horizon, For example, to name just a few of them, there are Manichean affinities to be explored, along with Ethiopian and Egyptian Christian frames of reference, not to mention the numerous interactions with Samaritan, Jewish and Rabbinic law and lore.[1]

Here it is not a question of alleging that Aramaic-speaking Christians actively influenced the composition of the "Arabic Qur'ān." Rather, it is a matter of perceiving in the Qur'ān's Arabic diction, particularly in passages that evoke biblical narratives or other accounts of Christian lore or Christian teaching, wording or phrasing that reveals the Aramaic cast of many of the Christian topics the Qur'ān addresses. Historically speaking, this is only to be expected; the Arabic-speaking Christians in the milieu in which Islam was born, be they from Sinai, Palestine, Trans-Jordan, Syria, lower Mesopotamia or even southern Arabia, all belonged to communities whose liturgies, doctrines and ecclesiastical associations were of primarily Aramaic expression.[2]

In the case of Christians living in Sinai, Palestine or Trans-Jordan, where "Byzantine" Orthodoxy held sway from the mid-fifth century and Greek was the dominant ecclesiastical language in the numerous international monastic communities, the Aramaic dialect of the local churches was Christian Palestinian Aramaic.[3] In Syria and Mesopotamia, where the local Christian communities straddled the frontiers of the Roman and Persian empires, and where "Byzantine" imperial Orthodoxy was often rejected, Syriac was the Aramaic dialect that served as the dominant ecclesiastical language. Most Syriac-speaking Christians accepted Christological formulae articulated the most effectively either by Severus of Antioch (c. 465–538) and Philoxenus of Mabbug (c. 440–523),[4] echoing the theology of St. Cyril of Alexandria (d. 444), or by Babai the Great (551/2–628), reflecting the positions of Theodore of Mopsuestia (c. 350–428).[5] Popularly, the three Christian denominations represented in the Syriac-speaking milieu of the world in which Islam was born were the three called "Melkites," "Jacobites" and "Nestorians,"[6] usually initially by their theological adversaries.

But it is worth noting in the present context that these appellations, all common in Syriac and Arabic texts, gained currency for the most part only in early Islamic times.[7]

Presumably, the Christians whom the "Arabic Qur'ān" had in mind when speaking of "those who say 'We are *al-* Naṣārā (Q 5 *al-Mā'ida* 14, 82)" were Arabic-speaking Christians. And given the probability that the Qur'ān's Arabic term here reflects the cognate Syriac term *Naṣrāyē* in the sense of "Nazoreans" or "Nazarenes,"[8] a term also sometimes used to designate "Christians" in Syriac works by east Syrian writers living in the Persian empire, particularly when reporting the references of non-Christian speakers to "Christians,"[9] it is reasonable to suppose that the Arabic/Qur'ānic usage followed suit.[10] While the Qur'ān itself makes no further specification, it also seems reasonable to presume that by means of the term *Naṣārā* the Qur'ān intends to refer to Christians actually present in its own Arabic-speaking milieu of the early seventh century, and not to any earlier group who may have been designated by the Greek form of this name in the works of Christian heresiographers who wrote in Greek with reference to a much earlier time and a different place. In the present study, I hope to show that the most likely case is that the Christians whose doctrines and practices are subject to critique in the "Arabic Qur'ān" are Arabic-speaking Christians associated with the largely Aramaic-speaking denominations, the existence of whom to Arab tribesmen in the early seventh century is a matter of historical record. They are the "Melkites," "Jacobites" and "Nestorians" of whom the later Syriac and Arabic sources, both Muslim and Christian, regularly speak.[11] But this presumption requires further discussion because neither Muslim nor Western non-Muslim commentators on the Qur'ān have in fact always assumed it.

While most writers in the Arabic-speaking world, both Christians and Muslims, have in fact used the term *Naṣārā* to designate "Christians" in general, some Muslim commentators over the centuries have argued that the term

Naṣārā should be considered to refer only to a now unknown community of "Christians" in Arabia at the time of Muḥammad, of whom the Qur'ān had some good things to say (e.g. Q 5 *al-Mā'ida* 82), and who were therefore commendable. They say that the "Melkites," "Jacobites," and "Nestorians," whom Muslim scholars in the early Islamic period knew well by name,[12] were different groups of "Christians," of whom there is little positive to say from an Islamic point of view and much to which to object.[13] But there is little or no historical evidence to support this contention; it seems to have been motivated solely by the requirements of interreligious polemics.[14]

Western commentators have also often sought to identify the Christians whose views they assume are reflected in the Qur'ān. Most often, researchers have looked for Christian influences on Qur'ānic and other early Islamic doctrinal formulae that seem to them to reflect Christian teachings at variance with the main-line Christian views of the Qur'ān's own day, but that seem to accord well with the Qur'ān's own judgements. This endeavour has led many scholars to postulate the influence of such earlier groups as those vaguely classified as "Jewish Christians,"[15] the heretical "Nazarenes,"[16] the "Ebionites," the "Elchasaites" and even the "Collyridians."[17] From the present writer's point of view, there are at least two problems with most of these suggestions. First, there is little or no historical or linguistic evidence for the presence of any of these groups in the world into which Islam was born and in which the Qur'ān first appeared.[18] As both Tor Andrae and M. Fiey have pointed out, all the available historical evidence points to the conclusion that the Arabic-speaking Christians actually present in the Qur'ān's milieu were associated with the well-known "Melkites," "Jacobites," and "Nestorians" pressing into the Arabic-speaking heartlands from the peripheries, whose scriptural, liturgical and patristic heritage was largely Aramaean.[19] Second, and perhaps more important, the search for "influences" or "borrowings," or for pre-existing Christian templates for the Qur'ān's Christological or theological judgements, seems to be methodologically flawed.[20] Those who have engaged in this search seem to have paid insufficient attention to the Qur'ān's own rhetorical purposes and to have overlooked the Qur'ān's manifest intention not to report but to critique the religion of the "People of the Book:"

> Do not exceed the proper bounds in your religion (Q 4 *al-Nisā'* 71; Q 5 *al-Māi'da* 77).

As many scholars of the past and the present have suggested, it seems not unlikely that Arabic-speaking Jews and Christians in Arabia at the time of Muḥammad and the Qur'ān, in addition to winning converts to their own creeds, will have also come into conversation with persons who as a consequence will have elaborated distinctive religious views of their own. In addition to Muḥammad himself, and his associates—the most notable cases in point[21] one thinks most readily in this connection of those whom Islamic tradition calls *ḥanīf*[22] and of others who are often presented as non-Jewish and non-Christian Arabic-speaking monotheists.[23] It may well have been the case that from the point of view of the theologies of the mainline Aramaean churches, not all of the Christian interlocutors of the Arab monotheists were well tutored. But when all is said and done, in most instances the most plausible suggestions about Christian confessional identity seem to flow from the assumption that in the first third of the seventh century the Qur'ān's *Naṣārā* were in fact Arabic-speaking Christians with connections to the "Melkites," "Jacobites" and "Nestorians," historically and archaeologically actually discoverable in the region.[24]

The proposal advanced in the present essay is that one should read the Qur'ān as a scripture in its own right, in dialogue with previous scriptures through the oral reports of them that circulated among the Arabic-speaking Jews and Christians in the Qur'ān's own milieu. There is so far no completely convincing evidence that there were any pre-Islamic written translations of the Torah or the Gospel into Arabic,[25] nor that among the Arabs in pre-Islamic times there was an Arabic, Christian, strophic hymnody that can still be discerned in the deep structures of the Qur'ān.[26] As for the evocations of Christianity in the text, the assumption here is that the Qur'ān's announcer became aware of the Bible and of the lore of the Christians through their oral expression among the Arabic-speaking Christians of the day, whose Christianity was largely what was preached and taught by Aramaic-speaking monks, missionaries and traders who brought Christianity to the Arabs from the world of the Aramaeans during the fifth and sixth centuries. Furthermore, it is assumed that the mind behind the Qur'ān was well aware of the Christian doctrinal formulae in regular use among the Arabic-speaking Christians and that the Qur'ān's rhetorical purpose was to critique and often to reject the doctrines expressed in these formulae. On the basis of these assumptions it seems that a more likely account can be given of the Qur'ān's interactions with Christians, one that in the end will ring historically and literarily truer than any account given on the basis of other assumptions, such as those that presume "influences," "borrowings" or repetitions of pre-existing Christian doctrinal paradigms on the Qur'ān's part. This approach offers the possibility for a fuller account of the Aramaean context of the Qur'ān, as might be detected in the "Syriacisms" in its diction—a term to be defined below, especially in those passages of the Qur'ān that deal expressly with Christian doctrines and practices.

2. Syriac and the "Arabic Qur'ān"

Muslim commentators after the time of Jalāl ad-Dīn as-Suyūṭī (1445–1505) seem to have concentrated almost exclusively on Arabic philology and lexicography to aid their reading and understanding of the Qur'ān. Non-Muslim, mostly Western scholars have in modern times given renewed attention to the Arabic scripture's "foreign vocabulary." The Aramaic, and specifically the Syriac background for a significant portion of the Qur'ān's wording has assumed a significant place in their work.[27] Alphonse Mingana, writing in 1927, estimated that 70 percent of the "foreign influences on the style and terminology" of the Qur'ān could be traced to "Syriac (including Aramaic and Palestinian Syriac)."[28] Noting this high incidence of Syriac etymologies for a significant portion of the Qur'ān's "foreign vocabulary," Arthur Jeffery said in 1938 that

> one fact seems certain, namely that such Christianity as was known among the Arabs in pre-Islamic times was largely of the Syrian type, whether Jacobite or Nestorian.[29]

He noted further that numerous early Islamic texts mention Muḥammad's contacts with both Syrian and Arabian Christians, and this observation prompted Jeffery to conclude that these texts

> at least show that there was an early recognition of the fact that Muḥammad was at one time in more or less close contact with Christians associated with the Syrian Church.[30]

Looking beyond the Syriac etymologies for much of the "foreign vocabulary" of the Qur'ān, a more recent commentator, writing under the pseudonym Christoph Luxenberg, has been exploring what he calls the "Syro-Aramaic" reading of the Qur'ān.[31] This is a much broader enterprise than Mingana's or Jeffery's inquiries, involving the use of the Syriac lexicon and the consultation of Syriac grammatical usages to help in the reading of some early passages in the Qur'ān. Alleging that traditional Muslim *mufassirūn* and modern scholars alike have neglected what he calls the "Syro-Aramaic" roots of Qur'ānic Arabic in favour of an overly exclusive reliance on Bedouin language for data to substantiate their researches,[32] Luxenberg's method is to examine selected *cruces interpretum* in the text from his own "Syro-Aramaic" perspective. He changes the vowels and diacritical points as necessary, to explore the possibility that with the Syriac lexicon in hand a more intelligible reading of hitherto obscure passages may be attained, often found to be congruent with earlier, Aramaean Christian ideas and formulations. In the ensemble, the overall impression is given that when it is read from Luxenberg's "Syro-Aramaic" perspective, the Qur'ān can be thought to have once been a very different scripture from the one it has become in the hands of its Muslim and Western commentators. Luxenberg's enterprise seems, under the guise of a philological quest, to be a modern-day analogue of the efforts of some earlier Arabic-speaking Christian apologists in the early Islamic period to argue that before it was "corrupted" by early Muslims and Jewish converts to Islam, the Qur'ān was actually a book of Christian meaning and sensibility.[33] Luxenberg's work once again calls attention to how much Syriac one can be tempted to try to read into the "Arabic Qur'ān," but that may be precisely the problem with many of the alternate readings he proposes. We will return to Luxenberg's suggestions below. For now, let us note in passing only what seems to be the fundamental conundrum of his enterprise—namely, the effort to read the indisputably "Arabic Qur'ān" as if much of it were written instead in "Syro-Aramaic," i.e. Syriac.

Tor Andrae undoubtedly remains the modern scholar who has most systematically investigated what he considered to be Muḥammad's and the Qur'ān's indebtedness to the Syriac expression of Christianity.[34] In his study *The Origins of Islam and Christianity,* Andrae readily speaks of "influences" and "borrowings" from Syriac in the Qur'ān, but his emphasis is on religious ideas and their characteristic formulae rather than on grammar or lexicography. He first calls attention to the Christianity in Arabia at the time of Muḥammad, mentioning in particular its flourishing in Nağrān and al-Ḥira and among the Ghassanids; he highlights the Syriac cast of the Christianity flourishing in these milieux. Then, having dismissed the pre-Islamic Arabic poets and the so-called *ḥanīfs* as sufficient sources for the Christian ideas and expressions he finds in the Qur'ān, Andrae in fact devotes most of his study to what he calls "the eschatological piety *(Frömmigkeit)* of Muḥammad." He means the Muslim prophet's systematic thinking about the "last things," final judgement and the hereafter, resurrection, reward and punishment. According to Andrae, this piety of Muḥammad's was

> a coherent, well-defined conception *(Anschauung)* that provided the most important expression of his religious personality.[35]

What is more, according to Andrae, this eschatological conception, articulated in finished formulae, reflected a precise homiletic programme (*prédication précise* < *bestimmte Verkündigung*) with which he thought Muḥammad must have been thoroughly familiar.[36] In the sequel, following his detailed analyses and comparisons of passages in the Qur'ān and in selected Syriac texts, Andrae argues that this "precise homiletic programme" was that of the Syriac-speaking Christian community, which, in his view, served as the model for Muḥammad's own eschatological preaching.[37] According to Andrae, "whatever Muḥammad received from Christianity he only learned it by way of oral preaching and personal contacts."[38]

Presumably, although he does not say so explicitly, Andrae supposed that Arabic was the language of the oral preaching and personal contacts. He does say that he thinks the "Church of the East," the so-called "Nestorian" church, was the source of the influences and borrowings from the Syrian Christians that went into the make-up of Muḥammad's "eschatological piety."[39] More specifically, Andrae proposed that the missionary preaching of the "Nestorians" came to Muḥammad's attention from Yemen, where a "Nestorian" mission had been established in the late sixth century.[40]

But Andrae was also alive to what he called the "Monophysite" influence on Muḥammad and the Qur'ān. He found it in the Qur'ān's reflection of the Christology it rejected. According to Andrae, the Qur'ān's surprising idea that the Trinity consists of God, Jesus and Mary,[41] its polemic against the allegation that God is the Messiah,[42] and its reflection of an interest in the apocryphal narratives of Jesus' infancy all suggest a polemical response to "Monophysite" interlocutors. He supposed that they were to be found in the Abyssinian associations of the early Islamic community.[43] But later Western commentators would posit as close a connection between Muḥammad and the originally Syriac-speaking "Jacobites" as Andrae had posited between Muḥammad and the "Nestorians." For example, John Bowman, pointing to the presence of the so-called "Monophysites" in Nağrān and among Arab confederations such as the Ghassānids, argued that the Qur'ān's prophetology and its biblical awareness are best explained on the hypothesis that Muḥammad was in conversation with "Jacobites" among whom the *Diatessaron* circulated. According to Bowman, Muḥammad gained even his knowledge of the Old Testament from the harmonised Gospel; he noted that the only Old Testament personages named in the Qur'ān are those that also appear in the *Diatessaron.*[44]

Tor Andrae singled out the works of St. Ephraem the Syrian (c. 306–373), the early Syriac writer beloved by "Melkites," "Jacobites" and "Nestorians" alike, as texts in which he could most readily find vocabulary, turns of phrase and religious conceptions cognate with those to be found in the Qur'ān.[45] One of his suggestions in particular instigated a minor scholarly storm. Andrae proposed that the *houris* of Paradise as depicted in the Qur'ān (Q 44 *al-Duḫān* 54; Q 52 *al-Ṭūr* 20; Q 55 *al-Raḥmān* 72; Q 56 *al-Wāqi'a* 22) could be found prefigured in one of St. Ephraem's hymns, *De Paradiso* (7:18).[46] Andrae wrote:

> One may recognize a veiled reference to the virgins of Paradise in Afrem's saying: "Whoever has abstained from wine on earth, for him do the vines of Paradise yearn. Each one of them holds out to him a bunch of grapes. And if a man has lived in chastity, they (feminine) receive him in a pure bosom, be-

> cause he as a monk did not fall into the bosom and bed of earthly love."[47] . . . Popular piety certainly interpreted this daring imagery in a crass and literal sense, and under such circumstances one cannot blame a citizen of pagan Mecca for doing the same thing.[48]

In 1948 Dom Edmund Beck, OSB, the modern editor of the critical editions of most of the Syriac works of Ephraem the Syrian, wrote a response to what he took to be Andrae's claim about St. Ephraem's meaning.[49] Beck took it that Andrae was proposing that St. Ephraem's words suggested a heavenly reward for the celibate monk comparable to that provided by the *houris* of the Qur'ān for the faithfully departed Muslim. So he went to some trouble to show that such could not have been St. Ephraem's meaning. Beck called attention to the faulty text of the *Editio Romana* of Ephraem's hymn that Andrae had used, and then set about explaining the imagery and symbolism of the passage in its context. by a somewhat complicated word-study of several key terms. In sum, Beck argued that St. Ephraem's imagery of the grape-vine, its stocks and shoots, evoked a vision of Paradise and a line of thinking that he thought definitively excluded any concept of the kind of delights provided by the *houris.* While Beck's exposition of St. Ephraem's own thought is convincing, it seems that he did not in fact completely grasp Andrae's point. Andrae did not actually say that Ephraem envisioned *houris* in Paradise. Rather, he suggested that "popular piety," not to mention "a citizen of pagan Mecca," might have been inspired by such lines as Ephraem wrote to conjure up the *houris.* It was Andrae's major point that homiletic descriptions such as those by Ephraem, envisioning the blessings of Paradise in terms of a garden of delights, could reasonably be supposed somehow to lie behind the similar descriptions of Paradise in the Qur'ān, especially if one were prepared to concede that Ephraem's descriptions could well have been reflected in the discourse of Arabic-speaking Christians.

In his recent, aforementioned book on the "Syro-Aramaic" reading of the Qur'ān,[50] Christoph Luxenberg also addresses the subject of the *houris.* He examines all the passages that concern both the *houris* and the "immortal boys" (Q 52 *al-Ṭūr* 24; Q 56 *al-Wāqiʿa* 17; Q 76 *al-Insān)* who are said to be in attendance on the believers in Paradise. To begin with, Luxenberg calls the reader's attention to how much, in his opinion, the very idea of the *houris* departs from the Qur'ān's principle to confirm the teachings of the Bible (e.g. in Q 40 *al-Aḥqāf* 12), in which, he says, no such notion can be found. He recalls the efforts of Western commentators to explain the *houris* by reference to Persian lore and practice.[51] He highlights the lexical, grammatical and syntactical difficulties that one might have with the traditional, Islamic understanding of the Arabic text, and how he thinks it puts the contexts askew. He proposes that the conventional idea of the *houris* stands in contrast and even contradiction to other passages in the Qur'ān that have to do with life in the hereafter. Then he turns his attention to the key phrase in Q 44 *al-Duḫān* 54 and Q 52 *al-Ṭūr* 20:

وزوجنهم بحور عين

Luxenberg proposes that the first word in this phrase be re-pointed to وروحنهم and that it be read as *rawwaḥ-nā-hum* in the sense of "We give them rest or comfort." With this change in the reading of the consonants, and with the "Syro-Aramaic" lexicon in hand, the phrase can now be contrived to say "We will make it comfortable for them under white, crystal-clear [grape clusters]."[52] The adjectives are made to yield their sense when read through the lens of Syriac usage. The context of the "garden of delights," both Qur'ānic and Syrian, is invoked to supply the "grape clusters." With this reading achieved, Luxenberg moves on to the other passages in the Qur'ān that have customarily been interpreted in light of their supposed reference to the *houris*. He proposes that the imagery of the "grape clusters" can, with the help of the "Syro-Aramaic" lexicon, be read into all of them. The resulting interpretation he offers is an understanding of the descriptions of Paradise that is not only much more consistent with what Luxenberg takes to be their own Qur'ānic contexts, but they are also consistent with what Luxenberg and Tor Andrae posit as their eschatological background in Syriac eschatological homiletics, such as are to be found, for example, in St. Ephraem the Syrian's hymns *De Paradiso*.

The assumption behind both what one might call the "history of religions" approach of Tor Andrae and the lexical, philological approach of Christoph Luxenberg is much the same. It seems to be that in the Arabic-speaking world in which Islam was born and the Qur'ān came down, the Arabic-speaking Christians of whom the Qur'ān speaks would have acquired their religious phraseology and biblical lore from the originally Syriac-speaking Christians from whom they presumably first learned Christianity. Against this background, the "Arabic Qur'ān" would then be thought to have addressed its own distinctive message to the Arabs and to have criticised the Christian teachings that ran counter to its central tenets. On Luxenberg's assumption, Qur'ānic Arabic would itself be seen as emerging from a "Syro-Aramaic" linguistic matrix. It would be thought to have become an independent language only after the "collection" of the Qur'ān and the inception of its function as a text in a society whose lexicographers and grammarians systematised it by reference to Persian and Bedouin sources, ignoring its "Syro-Aramaic" origins.

This is not the place to undertake a systematic critique of the work of Luxenberg, a task that would call for a closer analysis of the details of his arguments than can be undertaken in the present essay. Suffice it now to say only that from the point of view of the present writer, a major problem with the approach he adopts is that it ignores the integrity of the Qur'ān's Arabic text almost completely, along with the distinctly Islamic hermeneutical horizon within which one would expect to find the text's fundamental meaning. The methodology allows for the reconstruction of the text's orthography, words and phrases, and grammar and syntax solely on the basis of a reference to comparable features of the Syriac language in any period. In the process, Luxenberg readily appeals to the hermeneutic control of the Qur'ān's own principle to confirm the teachings of the Bible, but he leaves out of account any control that might be supplied by the Qur'ān's equally evident purpose to critique, from its own distinctive point of view, the interpretations of the Bible's teachings as articulated by the earlier "People of the Book." Consequently, the only criterion of verisimilitude for Luxenberg's own *Lesart des Koran* seems to be the congruity of the new readings he proposes with a single, Syro-Aramaic and Christian frame of reference, limited only by the possibilities of reading the bare Arabic script as if it were being used to express religious ideas already current in Syriac. Nowhere does he seem to leave any room for the hermeneutical difference that the Islamic inspiration of the Qur'ān might be expected to have contributed to the sense of the narrative in the first place. And he leaves out of his hook any satisfactory account of how the text in fact became an "Arabic Qur'ān." Nevertheless, as in the case of Tor Andrae's earlier work, Luxenberg's proposed readings of a number of the Qur'ān's verses do forcefully call attention to the unavoidable Syriac resonance of much of the Qur'ān's Arabic diction, especially when it is read in the interreligious context of its origins.[53] So how can one reasonably take account of it?

3. Syriacisms in the "Arabic Qur'ān"

While the theories so far mentioned about the high level of Syriac influence on the Qur'ān are far-reaching and controversial, they do serve the purpose of linguistically and thematically calling attention to the already historically plausible suggestion of an Aramaic, and specifically Syriac frame of reference for much of the intertextual and interreligious material in the Qur'ān. This material consists, on the one hand, of the allusions to and interactions with the biblical narratives, the evocations of the apocryphal stories and legends about biblical figures and hagiographical lore such as the Christian legend of the "Seven Sleepers" in *Sūrat al-Kahf* (Q 18).[54] On the other hand, there are also the passages in the Qur'ān that speak explicitly about the Christians and criticise their doctrines and practices. Without going all the way with either Tor Andrae or Christoph Luxenberg, one can at the very least accept that their suggestions have called attention to an important dimension of the Qur'ān's interaction with Christians. Specifically, their work gives one every encouragement to be on the watch for what I have called "Syriacisms" in the Christian-oriented passages in the Qur'ān and in other early Islamic literature.

For the present purpose, one may define Syriacisms as words or phrases in the Arabic diction of the Qur'ān that betray an underlying Syriac locution. That is to say, they are calques, or "loan translations" from Syriac into Arabic; they are not simply Syriac words used in place of Arabic words and phrases. Syriacisms may be thematic, lexical or even grammatical. The recognition of Syriacisms implies prior recognition of the integrity of the Arabic syntax and vocabulary of the Qur'ān. One may then expect that these Syriacisms could supply a new dimension to the search for the *asbāb al-nuzūl* of any number of the *āyāt* in the scripture. The Syriacisms should help the interpreter to identify more exactly the Christian motif addressed in a given passage, as well as to gauge more correctly the Qur'ān's response to it. In short, the identification of Syriacisms has the potential to allow the commentator to identify with more confidence Arab Christian locutions with which the Qur'ān itself would already have been familiar.

The discernment of Syriacisms in the Qur'ān requires commentators on the Islamic scripture to make a certain attitudinal adjustment in their customary approach to the text. On the one hand, the admission of Syriacisms implies the presence of actual Christian dialogue partners in the Qur'ān's own world of discourse; on the other hand, the fact that the Syriacisms are part of the Qur'ān's Arabic discourse means that they should find their interpretation primarily within the parameters of meaning of the Arabic language, and not solely by reference to the Syriac or any other non-Arabic lexicon. While consultation of the Syriac lexicon may significantly enhance understanding of the Syriacisms, the Qur'ān's Arabic should not be read as if it were simply Syriac in a different script.

Historically, as far as the Syriacisms are concerned, the Qur'ān's dialogue partners would hypothetically be presumed to have been Arabic-speaking Christians who learned their Christianity directly or indirectly from its earlier, Syriac expression. Furthermore, the hypothesis requires one to presume that these Arabic-speaking Christians were in association with the contemporary "Melkites," "Jacobites" or "Nestorians," virtually the only Christian communities known to have been in the original ambience of the Qur'ān. One can find no real historical traces of primitive "Jewish Christians," Elchasaites, Ebionites or heretical "Nazarenes" in the Qur'ān's Arabia. As mentioned above, the suggestions of their presence there by many scholars, both early and late, are all based on perceived doctrinal parallels between passages in the Qur'ān and the reported teachings of one or another of these groups.

Intentionally, the hypothesis of the presence of Syriacisms in the Qurʾān, interpreted in the context of the Qurʾān's own Arabic diction, supports a presumption of familiarity on the part of the Qurʾān's audience with the biblical narratives, apocryphal and hagiographical legends to which the Qurʾān alludes or makes reference, as they could be reasonably supposed to have actually circulated among Arabic-speaking Christians. The Qurʾān makes comments about them, makes its own points in reference to them, and some times "inter-textually" adds elements to their stories.[55] Similarly, the hypothetical presence of Syriacisms suggests that the Qurʾān's critique of Christian doctrines and practices, from the perspective of Islam's distinctive point of view, expresses a judgement about the veracity or propriety of the doctrines and practices actually current among contemporary Arabic-speaking Christians. This recognition then entails the further assumption that the Qurʾān's rhetoric of critique should not be mistakenly read as a somehow faulty report of what Christians believed or did in the time and place of its origins. Rather, the hypothetical assumption should be that the Qurʾān expresses itself in reaction to what its contemporary Christians believed and in reaction to the formulae in which they confessed their beliefs, the Qurʾān's own intention being to highlight what is wrong with them from an Islamic perspective, to critique and even correct them.

The method of recognising Syriacisms in the Qurʾān's diction and using them to help discern its fuller meaning in passages with an immediate Christian relevance does not in the first instance involve a presumption of influences or borrowings. Neither does it rely on reading Arabic as if it were Syriac. Rather, it is a method of understanding more concretely the Qurʾān's own references to the Christian language, lore or practice it evokes. So at this point it would be better to consider a concrete example rather than to continue talking about Syriacisms in the abstract. Ideally it would be more enlightening to study an example of the Qurʾān's involvement with an extended Christian narrative. But space will not allow that here. Suffice it for now to be content with consideration of the Qurʾān's evocation of a hitherto not often recognised Syriac title of Christ in the context of the Qurʾān's rejection of the Christian belief in the Christ's divinity.

4. Who were "those who said '*Allah is third of three*'"?

The Qurʾān says

> They have disbelieved who say that God is third of three (*ṯāliṯu ṯalāṯatin*) and there is no god except one God (Q 5 *al-Māʾida* 73).

In the immediate context the concern is to reject the divinity of Jesus, son of Mary, whom both the Christians and the Qurʾān call "the Messiah." The preceding verse says

> They have disbelieved who say that God is the Messiah. son of Mary (Q 5 *al-Māʾida* 72).

It is clear that the intention is to reject what the Christians say about Jesus the Messiah. Yet no Christian of that time customarily said "God is the Messiah" in so many words. Rather, Christians in the world of the Qurʾān would more readily have said "Jesus, the Messiah, is God." Similarly, while Christians in that same world would not object to calling Jesus "Son of Mary," as the Qurʾān does, they nevertheless did not normally do so; they regularly spoke of him as "Son of God." It seems most reasonable, then, to suppose that in both instances the Qurʾān's adoption of a different phraseology was for the purpose of rhetorically more forcefully expressing its negative judgement of a Christian teaching. It would not likely have been the case that the Qurʾān was unaware of the actual Christian parlance. In fact some commentators have seen in these very phrases the Qurʾān's rejection of its understanding of the theological position of the "Jacobites," because of their stress on the divinity of Christ and their seeming de-emphasis of his humanity, and therefore of his status as a creature.[5656]

The phrase "They have disbelieved who say that God is. . ."—used three times in this *Sūrah* (Q 5 *al-Māiʾda* 17, 72, 73), twice reproving those who say "God is the Messiah" (vv. 17, 72)—obviously intends to emphasise the incompatibility of the Christian belief in the divinity of Christ with the main premise of Qurʾānic monotheism—indeed, the more forcefully to stress rhetorically the absurdity of the Christian confession from the Qurʾān's perspective. The conundrum is in the third utterance of the formula, where the text reproves those who say "God is third of three" (v. 73), using the curious phrase *ṯāliṯu ṯalāṯatin.* Readers ancient and modern, Muslim and Christian have thought immediately in this connection of the doctrine of the Trinity. They often recall that in another place where the Qurʾān critiques and corrects what the Christians say about the Messiah, the text admonishes them "Do not say 'Three'; stop it; it is better for you" (Q 4 *al-Nisāʾ* 171). Here is the evidence of the realization in the Qurʾān that from the Islamic perspective, the Christian doctrine of the divinity of Christ leads to the equally objectionable doctrine of the Trinity. This too reflects a rudimentary Christian consciousness—namely, that the doctrine of the divinity of Christ entails the doctrine of the Trinity. But what exactly does the enigmatic Arabic phrase "third of three" actually mean, and who were the Arabic-speaking Christians in the Qurʾān's milieu who might be thought to have said it?

The classical Muslim commentators reached something of a consensus that the Arabic phrase *ṯāliṯu ṯalāṯatin* grammatically means "one of three"[57] and that it is Christ who is so described. While some of them took the Qurʾān verse then to be a rejection of what they perceived to be Christian "tritheism," others rejected this idea as inaccurate, rightly pointing out that the Christians did not in fact profess a belief in three gods.[58] Rather, these latter commentators offered two alternate explanations.[59] Some said that the phrase refers to one of the three *aqānīm* (i.e. "hypostases") that the Christians postulate in the one God.[60] Others proposed that as applied to Christ, the epithet named him the third member of the Trinity: *Allah, Mary* and *Christ*. They cited as confirmation, the passage in Q 5 *al-Māʾida* 116, where God said "O Jesus, son of Mary, did you say to the people 'Take me and my mother as two gods, apart from Allah?'"

The first explanation reflects the Muslim commentators' knowledge of contemporary Christian theology in Arabic and its technical vocabulary, originally derived from Syriac.[61] The second explanation interprets the phrase in question by reference to another passage in the Qur'ān. In the process, this second explanation has given currency to an erroneous idea of the Qur'ān's presentation of the Christian Trinity, supposed by mistaken commentators actually to be in the Qur'ān, one that has often been repeated, even by later Western scholarly commentators.[62] There is no indication here that the Qur'ān itself really entertained any such idea of the Christian Trinity. Rather, the Muslim commentator sought to explain the phrase *ṯāliṯu ṯalāṯatin* in Q 5 *al-Māʾida* 73, which he recognised as an epithet modifying the Messiah, by reference to the passage in Q 5 *al-Māʾida* 116, where no triad is named, but where the Messiah may be thought of as "third" in the triad, Allah, Mary, Jesus. But in fact the rhetoric of the passage suggests the absurdity, from the Islamic point of view, of the Christian designation of the Messiah as "Son of God" by intimating that such an appellation would logically imply the obviously unacceptable conclusion that the Messiah and his mother must then be reckoned as "two gods, apart from Allah." It is one more instance of the suppositions of the commentators wrongly attributing a mistaken idea to the Qur'ān, which is then cited as evidence that the Christians in the Qur'ān are other than those historically known to have been present in its milieu.

Some further light may be shed on the sense of the phrase *ṯāliṯu ṯalāṯatin* by recognising it as a Syriacism. That is to say, it may be understood to be an Arabic calque on an originally Syriac expression, presumably used by Arabic-speaking Christians in the world in which the Qur'ān was revealed. The Syriac term is *tlīṯāyā*, approximately congruent in meaning with the Arabic term *ṯāliṯ* and usually defined in English as meaning "third, threefold, triple, treble, trine."[63] In Syriac texts it not uncommonly occurs in Trinitarian contexts, where it is used to characterise a noun in terms of the divine triad. For example, a text may speak of God as *tlīṯāy qnōmē*, i.e. "treble of hypostases/persons," "three-personed;"[64] or, in the plural, one may speak of the divine names Father, Son and the Holy Spirit as *šmāhē tlīṯāyē wa-mšabbḥē*, i.e. "the threefold and glorious names."[65] In these instances the adjective is not just an ordinal "third," but it describes its referent as "treble" or "threefold," in the sense of being somehow characterised by reference to a triad. This sense of the word is perhaps clearer when Christ himself is described as *tlīṯāyā*.

In a number of instances in his religious poetry St. Ephraem the Syrian, who was by far the most often quoted of the early Syriac writers, spoke of Christ as *tlīṯāyā* within several frames of reference. Several times he spoke of Christ as "the treble One" in reference to his three-day stay in the grave prior to his resurrection,[66] once, probably in this same context, calling him "God's own treble one" (*tlīṯāyā d-Alāhā*).[67] In another passage Ephraem spoke of Christ as "the treble one" (*tlīṯāyā*) in reference to his threefold role in God's dispensation as priest, prophet and king.[68] In all of these contexts, of course, given Ephraem's typological hermeneutic and Nicene orthodoxy, there would have been for him and his readers an evocation of Christ as one of the divine Trinity. All of the other "triads" or "threesomes" in the biblical accounts of Christ, either in the Gospel or prophetically in the Torah, Ephraem would also have read as types, and interpreted proleptically, in reference to the persons of the Trinity.[69]

A further instance of the typological echo of the term *tlīṯāyā* in Syriac exegetical discourse about Christ may be seen in the works of another popular writer, Jacob of Sarug (c. 451–521), whose compositions often made their way into the liturgy and hence into the popular religious consciousness. In Genesis 22:4 the text speaks of Abraham's journey with his son Isaac to the place where Abraham intended to sacrifice his son at God's command. The text says "And on the third (*tlīṯāyā*) day Abraham raised his eyes and saw the place from afar." In his homily on this verse in Genesis, Jacob of Sarug wrote that while, according to the narrative, father and son on the first day of their journey saw nothing special, nor on the second day was there any typology to be discerned by the Christian interpreter, it was another matter with the "third" day, which Moses mentioned explicitly. Jacob says:

a) The burial of the Son [Christ] was depicted by the righteous one [Moses]; on "the third" [day] he overcame murder and escaped from it.
b) Three days Isaac was without care in his father's company; so that he might hold up the image of the Son's death, after which he would be resurrected.
c) On the third [day] he overcame murder and escaped from it; this is the fact: it was the Son, who on the third [day] rose from the grave.[70]

Already long before the time of the Syriac writers Ephraem and Jacob of Sarug, the Greek writers Origen (c. 185– c. 254) and Clement (c. 150– c. 215), both of Alexandria, had called attention to what they thought of as the mystical, typological significance of the phrase "on the third day" in Genesis 22:4, within the broader context of what they considered to be the Christological cast of the whole narrative in Genesis 22:1 18, where they saw Isaac as a type of Christ.[71] As for their thoughts on "the third day," Origen developed the theme most helpfully when he wrote:

> The third day, however, is always applied to the mysteries. For also when the people had departed from Egypt they offered sacrifice to God on the third day and they were purified on the third day (Exodus 19:11, 15, 16; 24:5). And the third day is the day of the Lord's resurrection (Mt. 27:63; Mk. 8:31). Many other mysteries also are included within this day.[72]

It was in the tradition of scriptural exegeses along these lines that Syriac writers like Ephraem, Jacob of Sarug and others could find the matrix for carrying the mystical significance of the term "third" beyond its immediate reference to "the third day" and to associate it with other triads in their discourse about the Messiah. They came eventually to employ the term *tlīṯāyā* as a personal epithet of Christ. For them in this context Christ was the one whose truth was to be discerned in terms of the several mystical triads in reference to which, from their typological viewpoint, Jesus, the Messiah, can be accurately characterised.

The recognition of this use of the Syriac epithet *tlīṯāyā* as a title of Christ should now add depth to the understanding of the Qur'ān's rejection of "those who say God is *ṯāliṯu ṯalāṯatin*" (Q 5 *al-Māʾida* 73), if the phrase is seen to be a Syriacism. In context, the Qur'ān is surely rejecting the divinity of Christ, as we have seen. And Christians in the Qur'ān's audience, whose patristic, liturgical and theological heritage was Aramaic, and specifically Syriac, would undoubtedly have been the ones prepared to describe Christ as *tlīṯāyā*, thereby alluding to the full range of typological reminiscences we have described above.[73] But in the Qur'ān's world the Christians would surely have been speaking in Arabic. In Arabic the cognate word *ṯāliṯ*, being the equivalent ordinal number, would definitely have recommended itself as a translation term for the Syriac ordinal *tlīṯāyā*. But *ṯāliṯ* would not by itself have carried the full nuance of the Syriac term in this context. And this circumstance most likely explains the choice of the ordinal *ṯāliṯ*, somewhat awkwardly in construct with the cardinal number *ṯalāṯatin*, to heighten its intended sense of describing its referent as one of three, or as characterised by his relationship to a set of typological "triads," which only the Christians could have had firmly in mind. While one must inevitably seek an explanation for the terms the text actually provides, one may nevertheless wonder why Arabic-speaking Christians would not have chosen the Arabic word *ṯulāṯī* to render the Syriac *tlīṯāyā* in this context. But this choice—suggesting that its referent is tripartite, made up of or somehow related to three things[74]—though perhaps serviceable from an abstract point of view, would ultimately have been misleading. Suggesting, as it does, something of three component parts, it lacks the full lexical redolence of the Syriac epithet as the classical writers actually used it, and it also removes the immediate echo of the "third day" *(yawmā tlīṯāyā)*, the underlying Syriac scriptural phrase from Genesis 22:4 (Peshiṭta) which lies behind the derived typologies.

The range of meanings inherent in the expression *ṯāliṯu ṯalāṯatin*, as a Syriacism, translating a typologically inspired epithet of Christ, would perhaps have been fully understood only by the Christians; but on the reading proposed here the Qur'ān can nevertheless be seen to have correctly reported, critiqued and rejected a genuine Christian locution. One has only to recognise it as a Syriacism to understand its authenticity. The recognition of its authenticity in turn frees the commentator from the temptation to impugn the Qur'ān's veracity as a reporter in this instance, or to use the expression as a basis to postulate an impossible Christian Trinity. The phrase could easily be imagined to have been on the lips of any "Melkite," "Jacobite" or "Nestorian" of the sixth or seventh century; St. Ephraem's legacy lived among them all.[75]

It is interesting to observe in passing, and by way of a *suasio* for the interpretation of *ṯāliṯu ṯalāṯatin* proposed here, that an Arab Christian apologetic writer of the tenth or eleventh century still understood Q 5 *al-Māi'da* 73 in this "Syrian" way. He spoke of God,

> the *ṯāliṯu ṯalāṯatin*in person *(bi-l- 'ayn)*, according to the saying of the Qur'ān[76]

as the one who had once enjoyed a meal with Abraham. In context, the author was citing biblical passages that stand in the background of the doctrine of the Trinity. His reference was to the passage in Genesis 18:1–21, where the Lord is said to have appeared to Abraham, as the Christians understood it typologically, in the guise of three men. In the history of Christian biblical interpretation, this passage, with its divine/human triad, has early and late been cited both as a type of the three persons of the one God, as confessed by the Christians, and as a type of Christ, "the threefold one." For the Arab Christian apologetic writer of the tenth or eleventh century the phrase *ṯāliṯu ṯalāṯatin* in the Qur'ān clearly still evoked this same understanding.

5. Islam and Syrian Christianity

The study of Syriacisms in early Islamic diction takes one beyond the range of the search for foreign vocabulary in the Qur'ān. As Arabic expressions of underlying Syriac words and concepts, Syriacisms open the path for the researcher into the very terms of the dialogue between the Qur'ān and Syrian

Christianity. They also mark the probable point of entry for much of the biblical, hagiographical and apocryphal lore of the Christians into the religious discourse of the Arabs who first articulated the Islamic critique of Christianity. It is clear that the Qur'ān already presumes in its audience a ready familiarity with these matters. The presence of Syriacisms in its diction suggests that the familiarity came about by way of the oral circulation of Christian ideas and practices among Arabic-speaking Christians who learned their Christianity from originally Aramaic sources. Furthermore, the recognition of Syriacisms as genuine Arabic locutions rather than borrowed words or phrases enables the interpreter to discern how the Qur'ān uses them for its own rhetorical purposes, often to critique and not just to report alleged Christian views. In other words, by the evidence of the Syriacisms the "Arabic Qur'ān" came to participate in an already ongoing interreligious conversation in Arabic. It made its intervention and in the process called a new religious community into being. That new community, in the felicitous phrase of Garth Fowden, would, through further dialogue and interchange, evolve into the Islamic Commonwealth,[77] the fruit of the religiously productive encounter between the cultures of Roman and Persian Late Antiquity and the world of the Arabs.

The discernment of Syriacisms in early Islamic diction could go a long way toward taking the guesswork out of the effort to identify the Qur'ān's Christian dialogue partners. Attempts in this enterprise have often relied on the search for Christian groups that espoused theological positions comparable to those perceived to be espoused in the Qur'ān. Without overlooking the homology evident in a number of these instances, the fact remains that most often there is little or no evidence for the presence of these groups in the cultural or linguistic milieu of the Qur'ān. Put concretely, the Syriacisms could help the researcher recognise the "Melkite," "Jacobite" or "Nestorian" in the world in which the Qur'ān was revealed and warn him away from "Nazarenes," "Elchasaites," "Ebionites" and other ill-defined "Jewish Christian" groups who otherwise have left no trace now discernible in Arabia.

The recognition of Syriacisms and their function in the burgeoning Arabic religious vocabulary in the era of the emergence of Classical Arabic from the welter of pre-existent Arabic and Bedouin dialects could help the scholar avoid the traps of reductionism in the study of early Islam. The presumptions of the comparative religionist, such as Tor Andrae, prompt him to speak of influences and borrowings, without any suggestion of how the common themes he perceives in both the Syriac and the Arabic discourses can otherwise be at home in both of them. One is left with the impression that in his judgement the Qur'ān simply took over the whole eschatological framework of the Syriac-speaking Christians. Rather, from the point of view of the discernment of Syriacisms, one may think of the Qur'ān as participating in an ongoing Arabic conversation in which the eschatological framework had already been translated into Arabic, at least orally, and become part of the hermeneutical horizon within which new ideas were being suggested. Similarly, Luxenberg's "Syro-Aramaic" reading of the Qur'ān often seems to ignore the fact that while it owes much to its Aramaic heritage, not least in the realm of its religious lexicon, Arabic is after all a different language. The Qur'ān, as read by its early interpreters, is arguably Classical Arabic's first real textual expression. The recognition of Syriacisms in its diction may enable the interpreter to engage it on its own terms and avoid reading it as if it were simply Syriac transposed, thereby creating a *tertium quid,* neither Syriac Christian nor Arabic Islamic, in its message.

This concentration on discerning possible Syriacisms in early Arabic diction draws attention away from many other interpretive temptations. The purpose has been to propose a way to gain entry to the Christianity in the world in which Islam was born. Even here they cannot provide a complete guide; the Christianity of that time and place also had other linguistic expressions, albeit that those in Syriac seem to have been the dominant ones in Arabia. Early Islam obviously interacted with Jewish thought and practice in a determinative way, and other scholars than those named here have been and are exploring the historical and thematic evidence for this interaction in Islam's origins. There are intimations of a Manichaean presence as well, not to mention the indigenous religious traditions of the Arabic-speaking peoples. All of these are strains in the religious discourse in Arabic that flourished in the world in which Islam was born. Islam itself cannot be reduced to any of them, nor is it an amalgam of all of them, although it can be seen to have been conversant with all the religious ideas of the world in which it was born. The recognition of Syriacisms in early Islamic Arabic diction merely affords the researcher a glimpse into one corner of the foreground of the Qur'ān and other early Islamic documents. They help reveal the largely Aramaean context of the Christianity that was one of the important religious strains in that milieu.

Notes

1 The several contexts of the Qur'ān most readily appear in the "foreign vocabulary" of the text. See Arthur Jeffery, *The Foreign Vocabulary of the Qur'ān* (Baroda: Oriental Institute, 1938), esp. pp. 1–41.

2 For a quick survey of Christians in Arabia prior to Islam see J. M. Fiey, "Naṣārā," *EI*², vol. 7, pp. 970–73. See also René Tardy, Najrān: *Chrétiens d'Arabie avant l'Islam* (Beyrouth: Dar el-Machreq Éditeurs, 1999).

3 See Sidney H. Griffith, "From Aramaic to Arabic: the languages of the monasteries of Palestine in the Byzantine and Early Islamic Periods," *Dumbarton Oaks Papers* 51 (1997), pp. 11–31.

4 Severus of Antioch's works were originally in Greek; his very influential Cathedral Homilies survive only in Syriac. Philoxenus wrote in Syriac. For further bibliographic guidance see Joseph Lebon, "La christologie du monophysisme syrien," in *Das Konzil von Chalkedon; Geschichte und Gegenwart*, ed. Aloys Grillmeier and Heinrich Bacht, 3 vols. (Würzburg: Echter-Verlag, 1951–1954), vol. 1, pp. 425–586; André de Halleux, *Philoxène de Mabbog; sa vie, ses écrits, so théologie* (Louvain: Imprimerie Orientaliste, 1963); Roberta Chesnut, *Three Monophysite Christologies* (Oxford: Oxford University Press, 1976).

5 On Babai and the theology of the "Church of the East" see Geevarghese Chediath, *The Christology of Mar Babai the Great* (KMttayam: Oriental Institute of Religious Studies; Paderborn: Ostkirchendienst, 1982); Sebastian Brock, "The Christology of the Church of the East in the synods of the fifth to early seventh centuries: preliminary considerations and materials," in Sebastian Brock, *Studies in Syriac Christianity,* No. 2: *History Literature and Theology* (Hampshire: Variorum/Ashgate, 1992), no. XII.

6 See Sebastian P. Brock; "The 'Nestorian' Church, a lamentable misnomer," *BJRL* 78 (1996), pp. 23–35.

7 See Sidney H. Griffith, "'Melkites,' 'Jacobites' and the Christological controversies in Arabic in third/ninth-century Syria," in *Syrian Christians under Islam; the First Thousand Years,* ed. David Thomas (Leiden: Brill, 2001), pp. 9–55

8 See Jeffery, *The Foreign Vocabulary,* pp. 280–81.

9 See Sebastian Brock, "Christians in the Sasanid Empire: a case of divided loyalties," in *Religion and National Identity,* ed, Stuart Mews, Studies in Church History 18 (Oxford: Oxford University Press, 1982), pp. 1–19, esp. 3–6. See also Sebastian Brock, "Some aspects of Greek words in Syriac," in *Synkretismus im syrisch-persischen Kulturgebiet,* ed. A. Dietrich (Symposion, Reinhausen bei Göttingen, 1971), *Abhandlungen der Akademie der Wissenschaften in Göttingen, Philologisch-historische Klasse,* Dritte Folge, 96; Göttingen: Vandenhoeck and Ruprecht, 1975), pp. 91–95; Christelle Jullien and Florence Jullien, "Aux frontiers de l'lranité: 'Naṣrāyē' et 'Krīstyonē' des inscriptions du Mobad Kirdīr; enquête littéraire et historique," *Numen* 49 (2002), pp. 282–335.

10 See Fiey, "Naṣārā," p. 970. The most recent study of this term as it appears in the Qur'ān is by François De Blois, "Naṣrānī (Ναζωραιος) and ḥanīf (ἐθνικος): studies on the religious vocabulary of Christianity and of Islam," *Bulletin of the School of Oriental and African Studies* 65 (2002), pp. 1–30. For reasons that will appear below, the present writer does not accept De Blois' final conclusions regarding the ecclesial identity of the Arabic-speaking Christians whose religious idiom is reflected in the Qur'ān.

11 See Fiey, "Naṣārā," p. 970—notwithstanding De Blois, "Naṣrānī and ḥanīf," who seems to posit the presence of Judeo-Christian "Nazarenes," known from a much earlier era and a different milieu, in the Qur'ān's Arabic-speaking ambience of the early seventh century.

12 The most astute Muslim observer of Christian denominations in the early Islamic period was undoubtedly Abū 'Īsā al-Warrāq (fl. c, 850). See esp. David Thomas, Anti-Christian Polemic in Early Islam: Abū 'Īsā al-Warrāq's "Against the Trinity," *University of Cambridge Oriental Publications* 45 (Cambridge: Cambridge University Press. 1992); idem, Early Muslim Polemic against Christianity; Abū 'Īsā al-

Warrāq's "Against the Incarnation," *University of Cambridge Oriental Publications* 59 (Cambridge: Cambridge University Press, 2002).

13 Paul of Antioch, the "Melkite" bishop of Sidon in the 12th century, addressed this issue in his famous "Letter to a Muslim Friend." See Paul Khoury, *Paul d'Antioche; évèque melkite de Sidon (XIIe s.)* (Beyrouth: Imprimerie Catholique, 1964), pp. 169–87 (French), 59–83 (Arabic).

14 See e.g. the case of Ibn Taymiyya (1263–1328) in Thomas F. Michel, ed. and trans., *A Muslim Theologian's Response to Christianity: Ibn Taymiyya's al-Jawāb al-ṣaḥīḥ* (Delmar, NY: Caravan Books, 1984).

15 In this connection see especially H. J. Schoeps, *Theologie und Geschichte des Judenchristentums* (Tübingen: J. C. B. Mohr, 1949), esp. pp. 334–42. See also the studies on Judeo-Christians by Shlomo Pines, now collected in Shlomo Pines, *Studies in the History of Religion, The Collected Works of Shlomo Pines*, vol. 4: Jerusalem (Jerusalem: Magnes Press. 1996), pp. 211–486.

16 See Ray A. Pritz, *Nazarene Jewish Christianity: From the End of the New Testament Period until its Disappearance in the Fourth Century* (Jerusalem/Leiden: Magnes Press/ Brill, 1988); Simoun C. Mimouni, "Les Nazoréens: recherche étymologique et historique," *Revue Biblique* 105 (1998), pp. 208–62. See also De Blois, "Naṣrānī and ḥanīf" for arguments in support of the thesis that the ancient "Nazarenes" were the Christians to whose views the Qur'ān refers.

17 See e.g. Joseph Azzi, *Le prêtre et le prophète: aux sources du coran* (Paris: Maisonneuve et Larose, 2001); Joseph Dorra-Haddad, "Coran, prédication nazaréenne," *Proche Orient Chrétien* 23 (1973), pp. 148–55; Geoffrey Parrinder, *Jesus in the Qur'ān* (New York: Oxford University Press, 1977); J. M. Magnin, "Notes sur l'ebionisme," *Proche Orient Chrétien* 23 (1973), pp. 233–65, 24 (1974), pp. 225–50, 25 (1975), pp. 245–73, 26 (1976), pp. 293–315. 27 (1977), pp. 250–73, 28 (1978), pp. 220–48; M. P. Roncaglia, "Éléments ébionites et elkésaïtes dans le coran: notes et hypotheses," *Proche Orient Chrétien* 21 (1971), pp. 101–26.

18 As François De Blois has written, "It is one thing to notice similarities between the teachings of two religious traditions, and another to construct a plausible historical model to account for the influence of one upon the other." De Blois, "Naṣrānī and ḥanīf" pp. 25–26. De Blois is convinced he has met this criterion in the instance of the Qur'ānic *naṣārā*. He concludes (p. 16) that it is "likely that there was a community of Nazoraean Christians in central Arabia in the seventh century, unnoticed by the outside world." But the likelihood seems to rest (ibid.) ultimately on the assumption that "if *naṣārā* means 'catholic Christians,' then it is very difficult to see how their food should be 'permitted to you.'" Here the reference is to Q 5 *al-Mā'ida* 5, where the Qur'ān speaks of the "food of the People of the Book" as "permitted to you," i.e. to the Muslims, not the food of the *Naṣārā* specifically. Arguably, the Qur'ān no more has the *Naṣārā* in mind here than it has the Jews in mind when it speaks of the "People of the Book" who "say three" in Q 4 al-Nisā' 171. So it is difficult in the end to see how De Blois' argument really depends on more than the old perception of doctrinal or practical similarities, without the historical plausibility.

19 See Tor Andrae, *Les origines de l'!slam et le christianisme*, trans. Jules Roche (Paris: Adrien-Maisonneuve. 1955), esp. pp. 201–11; Fiey, "Naṣārā," p. 970.

20 Seemingly prompted by the assumption that the Qur'ān must have borrowed or inherited its doctrinal positions from some earlier religious community, rather than have elaborated them from its own religious principles and assumptions, scholars have often looked for earlier groups with parallel or comparable views, and then designated them as "sources" for the Qur'ān's similar teachings, without paying much attention to the socio-historical plausibility of the designated group's presence in the actual Arabian milieu in which Islam was born. What is more, the designated influences have then often been used to explain only one or two Qur'ānic usages, without any discussion of how they might fit into the larger framework of the critique of the Christians and their doctrines in the Qur'ān.

21 See Claude Gilliot, "Les 'informateurs' juifs et chrétiens de Muḥammad: reprise d'un problème traité par Aloys Sprenger et Theodor Nöldeke," *Jerusalem Studies in Arabic and Islam* 22 (1998), pp. 84–126,

22 The most recent, thorough study of the significance of the term *ḥanīf* in its several senses, along with bibliographical references to earlier studies, is in De Blois, "Naṣrānī and ḥanīf," pp. 16–25.

23 See the sometimes intriguing ideas presented in Yehuda D. Nevo and Judith Koren, *Crossroads to Islam: The Origins of the Arab Religion and the Arab State* (Amherst, NY: Prometheus Books, 2003).

24 See Barbara Finster,"Arabian in der Spätantike: ein Überblick über die kulturelle Situation der Hatbinsel in der Zeit von Muḥammad," *Archäologischer Anzeiger* (1996), pp. 288–319: René Tardy, Najrān. For more bibliography on this subject see Sidney H. Griffith. "Christians and Christianity," in *Encyclopaedia of the Qur'ān*, ed. Jane D, McAuliffe (Leiden: Brill. 2001), vol. I, pp. 307–16.

25 See Sidney H. Griffith, "The Gospel in Arabic: an inquiry into its appearance in the first Abbasid century," *Oriens Christianus* 69 (1985), pp. 126–67

26 Günter Lüling has argued in support of the proposal that about a third of the Qur'ān as we now have it is built on the foundation of an earlier Christian, strophic hymnody that was concealed under successive layers of the Qur'ān's text after a number of revisions, about which Islamic tradition itself furnishes some evidence. According to him, this early Arabic, Christian hymnody, which celebrated an angel-Christology, was at home among the pre-Islamic Arabs of the Hiğāz and had a place in Christian liturgy in the then-Christian Ka'bah in Mecca. Lüling discerns this pre-existing hymnody on the basis of his analysis and reconstruction of the unvowelled, consonantal text of selected passages from the Qur'ān. See Günter Lüling, *Über den Ur-Qur'ān: Ansätze zur Rekonstruktion vorislamischer christlicher Strophenlieder im Qur'ān* (Erlangen: H. Lüling, 1974); idem. Der christliche Kult an der vorislamischen Kaaba als Problem der Islamwissenschaft und christlichen Theologie (Erlangen: H. Lüling. 1977); idem, *Die Wiederentdeckung des Propheten Muḥammad: eine Kritik am "christlichen" Abendland* (Erlangen: Hannelore Lüling. 1981). For a more personal discussion of his idea and its reception among scholars see Günter Lüling, "Preconditions for the scholarly criticism of the Koran and Islam, with some autobiographical remarks," *Journal of Higher Criticism* 3 (1996), pp. 73–109.

27 See the review, in a broader context, in Martin R. Zammit, *A Comparative Lexical Study of Qur'ānic Arabic (Leiden: Brill, 2002), esp.* pp. 51–63.

28 A. Mingana, "Syriac influence on the style of the Ḳur'ān," *BJRL* 11 (1927), pp. 77–98.
29 A. Jeffery, *The Foreign Vocabulary*, pp. 20–21
30 Ibid., p. 22.
31 See Christoph Luxenberg, *Die syro-aramäische Lesart des Koran: ein Beitrag zur Entschlüsselung der Koransprache* (Berlin: Das Arabische Buch, 2000; 2nd rev. ed.; Berlin: Verlag Hans Schiler, 2004).
32 In this connection see also Joshua Blau, "The role of the Bedouins as arbiters in linguistic questions and the mas'ala az-zunburiyya," *JSS* 8 (1963), pp. 42–51
33 In this connection see Sidney H. Griffith, "The Qur'ān in Arab Christian texts; the development of an apological argument: Abū Qurrah in the mağlis of al-Ma'mūn," *Parole de l'Orient* 24 (1999), pp. 203–33.
34 See Andrae, *Les origines de l'Islam et le christianisme.* This work was originally published as a series of articles under the title "Der Ursprung des Islams und das Christentum" in three successive issues of the periodical Kyrkohistorisk Årsskrift 23 (1923), pp. 149–206; 24 (1924), pp. 213–92; 25 (1925), pp. 45–112. It was subsequently published in monograph form in Tor Andrae, *Der Ursprung des Islams und das Christentum* (Uppsala: Almqvist and Wiksells, 1926). References to this work in the present essay are to the French translation by Jules Roche. See also the later works of Tor Andrae, *Mohammed, sein Leben und sein Glaube* (Göttingen: Vandenhoeck and Ruprecht, 1932), English trans. Theophil Menzel, *Mohammed: the Man and His Faith* (New York: Charles Scribner's Sons, 1936); and I Myrtenträdgården: *Soldier i Tidig Islamisk Mystik* (Lund: Albert Bonniers Forlag, 1947), English trans. Birgitta Shame, *In the Garden of Myrtles: Studies in Early Islamic Mysticism* (Albany: State University of New York Press, 1987).
35 Andrae, *Les origines de l'Islam*, p. 68
36 See ibid.
37 See ibid., pp. 145, 160, 203
38 Ibid., p. 146.
39 See ibid., pp. 192, 199, 202.
40 See ibid., p. 206, with a reference back to p. 24.
41 Presumably a reference to Q 5 *al-Mā'ida* 116. More on this verse below
42 Presumably a reference to the Qur'ān's dictum "They have disbelieved who say God is the Messiah, son of Mary" (Q 5 *al-Mā'ida* 72).
43 See Andrae, *Les origines de l'Islam*, p. 68, pp. 209–10. See also Andrae, *Mohammed: The Man and his Faith*, p. 91.
44 See John Bowman, "The debt of Islam to monophysite Syrian Christianity," *Nederlands Theologisch Tijdschrift* 19 (1964/65), pp. 177–201; also published in E. C. B. MacLaurin (ed.), *Essays in Honour of Griffithes Wheeler Thatcher* (1863–1950) (Sydney: Sydney University Press, 1967), pp. 191–216, part 6, chapter 5 in the present volume. In connection with the "Jacobite" Ghassanids, see esp. Irfan Shahid, *Byzantium and the Arabs in the Sixth Century*, 2 vols. (Washington: Dumbarton Oaks. 2002).
45 See esp. Andrae, *Les origines de l'Islam*, p. 68 pp. 145–61. Andrae used the old, uncritical Editio Romano of the works of Ephraem; see J. S. Assemani (ed.), *Sancti*

Patris Nostri Ephraem Syri Opera Omnia quae exstant Graece, Syriace, Latine, 6 vols. (Rome, 1732–1746). He was apparently unaware of the problems of distinction and authenticity between the works of the so-called "Ephraem Syrus" and "Ephraem Graecus"; he refers to them indiscriminately. In this connection see Sebastian Brock, "A brief guide to the main editions and translations of the works of St. Ephrem," *The Harp* 3 (1990), pp. 7–29.

46 See Andrae, *Les origines de l'Islam*, pp. 151–54, where, on p. 151 n. 4, he attributes the original insight to Hubert Grimme, *Muḥammad*, 3 vols. (Munster im W.: Aschendorff, 1892–1895), vol. 2, p. 160 n. 9. See also Andrae, *Mohammed: The Man and his Faith*, pp. 87–88

47 This is Andrae's version of a strophe from St. Ephraem's Syriac, *Hymni de Paradiso*, VII:18, based on the text in the Editio Romano of his works, Assemani, Opera Omnia, vol. 3, pp. 563ff.

48 Andrae, *Mohammed: The Man and his Faith*, p. 88.

49 See Edmund Beck, "Eine christliche Parallele zu den Paradiesesjungfrauen des Korans?," *Orientalia Christiana Periodica* 14 (1948), pp. 398–405. Beck returned to the issue with some further observations in a later communication; see idem, "Les Houris du Coran et Ephrem le syrien," *MIDEO* 6 (1959–1961), pp. 405–8. For Beck's own understanding of Ephraem's hymn see idem, "Ephraems Hymnen über das Paradies," *Studia Anselmiana* 26 (Rome: Herder, 1951), pp. 63–76, See also Edmund Beck, "Des heiligen Ephraem des Syrers Hymnen de Paradiso und Contra Julianum," *CSCO*, 174 and 175 (Louvain: Peeters, 1957).

50 See Luxenberg, *Die Syro-Aramäische Lesart*, pp. 221–61.

51 Luxenberg quotes in extenso from A. J. Wensinck, "Ḥūr," *EI*[2], vol. 3, pp. 581ff.; Luxenberg, *Die Syro-aramäische Lesart*, pp. 222–24.

52 Luxenberg, *Die Syro-Aramäische Lesart*, p. 226: "Wir werden es ihnen unter weißen, kristall(klaren) (Weintrauben) behaglich machen."

53 The reviews and discussions of Christoph Luxenberg's work that have appeared by now are too numerous to be listed here. For an account of the ongoing controversy see Christoph Burgmer, *Die Luxenberg-Debatte: Eine Koran-Exegese und ihre Folgen* (Berlin: Hans Schiler Verlag, 2004).

54 For a summary, with rich bibliography, of this material sec François Jourdan, *La tradition des sept dormants: une rencontre entre chrétiens et musulmans* (Paris: Maisonneuve and Larose, 2001).

55 In this connection see the studies included in John C. Reeves (ed.), "Bible and Qur'ān: Essays in Scriptural Intertextuality," *Symposium Series* 24 (Atlanta: Society of Biblical Literature, 2003).

56 See e.g. the remarks of Neal Robinson, *Christ in Islam and Christianity* (Albany, NY: State University of New York Press, 1991), pp. 15–22. See also the comments of Taqī al-Dīn Ibn Taymiyyah, *al-Tafsīr al-kabīr*, 7 vols. (Beirut: Dār al-kutub al-'ilmiyya, n.d.), vol. 4, esp. pp. 53–58, where he also reports the views of earlier Muslim commentators regarding these verses.

57 See W. Wright, *A Grammar of the Arabic Language*, 3rd ed.. 2 vols. (Cambridge: Cambridge University Press, 1896–1898), vol. 2, par. 109, p. 246; H. Reckendorf, *Arabische Syntax* (Heidelberg: Carl Winter's Universitätsbuchhandlung, 1921), par. 117, pp. 210–11; idem, *Über Paronomasie in den semitischen Sprachen; ein Beitrag zur allgemeinen Sprachwissenschaft* (Giessen: Alfred Töpelmann, 1909), p. 127.

58 See e.g. the discussion in Ibn al-Ǧawzī, *Zādu al-masīr fī 'ilm al-tafsīr*, vol. 4 (Beirut/Damascus: al-Maktab al-islāmī, 1974), pp. 402–3

59 See the summary in Ibn Taymiyyah, *al-Tafsīr al-kabīr*, vol. 4, pp. 53–58. See also Abū Ǧa'far Muḥammad ibn Jarīr aṭ-Ṭabarī, *Ǧāmi' al-bayān 'an ta'wīl āy al-Qur'ān*, 24 vols. (Cairo: Dār al-ma'ārif, n.d.), vol. 10, pp. 481–83; vol. II, pp. 233–37; Fakhr al-Dīn al-Rāzī, *Tafsīr al-Faḫr al-Rāzī: al-mašhūr bi-l-tafsīr al-kabīr* sea (*mafātīḥ al-ġayb*, 16 vols. (Beirut: Dār al-fikr, 1981), vol. 4, pp. 63–65.

60 Arabic-speaking Christians regularly used the Arabic word *uqnūm* (pl. *aqānīm*), a loan from the Syriac term *qnōmā* (pl. *qnōmē*), to designate what Greek-speaking Christians called the hypostases of the one God. On the *aqānīm* in post-Islamic Christian Arabic literature, see Sidney H. Griffith, "The concept of *al-uqnūm* in 'Ammār al-Baṣrī's Apology for the Doctrine of the Trinity," *Orientalia Christiana Analecta* 218 (1982), pp. 169–91; Rachid Haddad, *La trinité divine chez les théologiens arabes (750–1050)* (Paris: Beauchesne, 1985).

61 The Christian Arabic term *uqnūm* (pl. *aqānīm*) is a loan from the Syriac term *qnōmā* (pl. *qnōmē*), as explained in n. 60 above.

62 See e.g. Ludwig Hagemann and Ernst Pulsfort, "Maria, die Mutter Jesu, in Bibel und Koran," *Religionswissenschaftliche Studien* 19 (Würzburg: Echter Verlag/ Altenherge: Oros Verlag. 1992), pp. 119–21

63 See J. Payne Smith (ed.), *A Compendious Syriac Dictionary. Based upon the Thesaurus Syriacus by R. Payne Smith* (Oxford: Oxford University Press, 1903). p. 614.

64 See R. Payne Smith, *Thesaurus Syriacus* (Oxford: Clarendon Press, 1879–1901), col. 4453.

65 See e.g. George Howard (trans.), *The Teaching of Addai, Texts and Translations* 16, Early Christian Literature Series 4 (Chico, CA: Scholars Press, 1981), p. 60.

66 See Edmund Beck, "Des heiligen Ephraem des Syrers Carmina Nisibena (Erster Teil)," *CSCO* 218 and 219 (Louvain: Secrétariat du Corpus SCO, 1961), 1:11, 2:5; Edmund Beck, "Des heiligen Ephraeni des Syrers Cartnina Nisibena (Zweiter Teil)," *CSCO* 24 and 241 (Louvain: Secretariat du Corpus SCO, 1963), 41:16.

67 See Edmund Beck, "Des heiligen Ephraem, des Syrers Hymnen de Nativitate (Epiphania)," *CSCO* 186 and 187 (Louvain: Secretariat du Corpus SCO, 1959), de Epiphania 8:6. See also Beck's explanatory note, ibid., vol. 187, pp. 157–58 n. 9.

68 See Edmund Beck, "Des heiligen Ephraem des Syrers Hymnen de Virginitate," *CSCO* 223 and 224 (Louvain: Secrétariat du Corpus SCO, 1962), 17:5.

69 See Sidney H. Griffith, "'Faith Adoring the Mystery': Reading the Bible with St. Ephraem the Syrian," *The Père Marquette Lecture in Theology*, 1997 (Milwaukee, WI: Marquette University Press, 1997).

70 Jacob of Sarug's *mēmrā*, "On Abraham and His Types," in P. Bedjan. *Homiliae Selectae Mar-Jacobi Sarugensis*, 5 vols. (Paris: Via Dicta/ Leipzig: Harrassowitz, 1905–1910), vol. 4, pp. 77–78. Lines b and c are repeated in Jacob's mēmrā "On the Mystery-Symbols, Types and Images of the Messiah," in Bedjan, *Homiliae Selectae*, vol. 3, p. 312.

71 See Clement of Alexandria, "Les Stromates; Stromate V," *Sources Chrétiennes* 278, ed. A. Le Boulluec, trans. P. Voulet (Paris: Éditions du Cerf, 1981), pp. 146–47;

Origen, *Homilies on Genesis and Exodus*, trans. Ronald E. Heine: *The Fathers of the Church* (Washington: Catholic University of America Press, 1982), pp. 136–41.

72 Origen, *Homilies on Genesis*, p. 140.

73 In Q 5 *al-Māi'da* 73 the Qur'ān actually says "They disbelieve who say Allah is ṯālitu ṯalāṯatin." The phrase. is parallel to the immediately preceding statement in Q 5 *al-Māi'da* 72: "They disbelieve who say Allah is the Messiah." One recognises the Qur'ān's rhetorical strategy in its reversal of the customary Christian usage, which would be to confess that the Messiah is God. The reversal accents the Qur'ān's critique of the Christian usage by pointedly highlighting its logical import.

74 See Edward William Lane, *An Arabic-English Lexicon* (London: Williams and Norgate, 1863 ff.), vol. I, p. 348.

75 See Sidney H. Griffith, "Christianity in Edessa and the Syriac-speaking world: Mani, Bar Daysan and Ephraem; the struggle for allegiance on the Aramean frontier," *Journal of the Canadian Society for Syriac Studies* 2 (2002), pp. 5–20.

76 Sinai Arabic MS 434, f.176v. For more information on this text by an anonymous writer preserved in a text copied in the year 1138, see Haddad, *La Trinité divine chez les théologiens arabes*, p. 38; Robert G. Hoyland, *Seeing Islam as Others Saw It: A Survey and Evaluation of Christian, Jewish and Zoroastrian Writings on Early Islam* (Princeton: Darwin Press. 1997) pp. 504–5, esp. n. 178

77 See Garth Fowden, *Empire to Commonwealth: Consequences of Monotheism in Late Antiquity* (Princeton: Princeton University Press, 1993).

Aramaisms in the Qur'ān and their Significance

Robert M. Kerr*

Originally published in M. Gross and K.-H. Ohlig, eds., Die Entstehung einer Weltreligion II: Von der koranischen Bewegung zum Frühislam *(Berlin: Schiler, 2012), pp. 553–614 under the title "Von der aramäischen Lesekultur zur aramäischen Schreibkultur II: Der aramäische Wortschatz des Koran," revised by the author and translated by Kira McLean.*

Priusquam nostris temporibus memoria rerum antiquarum adhiberetur ad oeognidis reliquias recte intelligendas, fieri non potuit quin docti homines perverse de oeognide judicarent: quamquam non tam perverse, quam eis judicandum esset, nisi pudor restitisset et nimia quædam antiquitatis æstimatio quominus clarissimo Græcorum pœtæ obtrectarent.

– Friedrich Nietzsche, *De Theognide Megarensi* 1864

Prologue[1]

When we look at Late Antique Syro-Palestine and Arabia in the early seventh century, the time when Islam is said to have become a religion, an interesting yet complex mosaic of cultures and languages can be observed. Linguistically, various languages were spoken and written. Here we confront a common long-persisting misconception, namely that the Arabs were largely illiterate before Islam. Nothing could be farther from the truth. Roughly speaking, Arabia in Antiquity was divided into three geographical regions: *Arabia Felix*, *Deserta* and *Petraea.*

In the South-western corner (approximately modern Yemen), *Arabia Felix*, or "Happy Arabia," various South Arabian Semitic languages were spoken, the most important of which is Sabaean, written in a Semitic script which split off from the Syro-Palestinian alphabetic tradition during the Bronze Age. Ancient Yemen was heavily involved in the spice and incense (later also the silk) trade from which it garnered considerable wealth.

To the North, in what is now more or less Saudi Arabia was the Classical *Arabia Deserta*, or "Abandoned Arabia," home to Mecca and Medina, a region sparsely inhabited by nomadic tribes and various oasis settlements, often caravanserais for the long-distance trade. The contemporary local languages are nowadays designated as Ancient North Arabian: they are interrelated Semitic (oasis) dialects that, however, are not direct ancestors of

Classical Arabic. Inscriptions in these languages or dialects are attested roughly from the sixth century BC to the sixth century AD throughout the region into the modern Hashemite Kingdom of Jordan. The writing culture of *Arabia Deserta* was thus borrowed from the South – i.e., they used variants of the Ancient (epigraphic) South Arabian script.

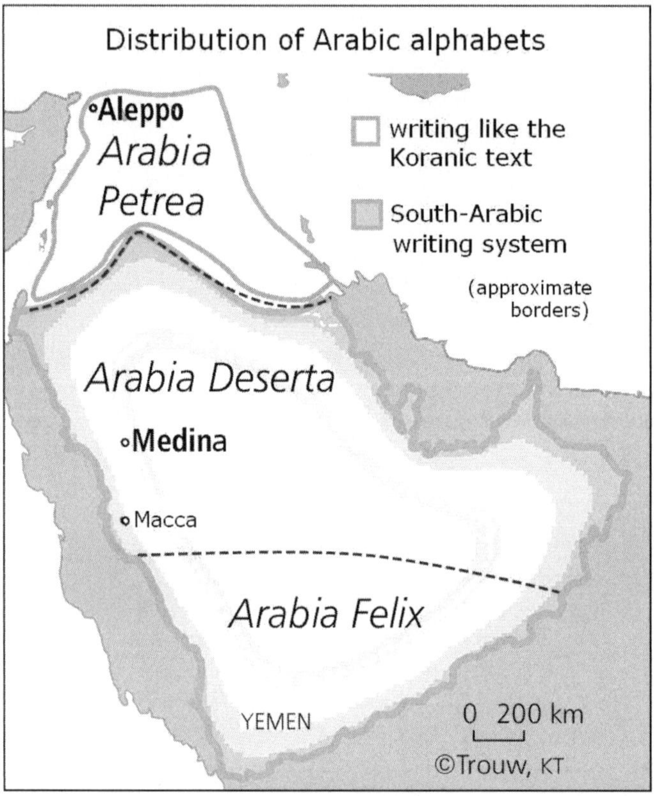

Figure 1: Distribution of Arabic Alphabets; with kind permission of *Trouw* (Dutch daily newspaper).

Further to the North, in the geographical area of Syro-Palestine (which includes the Egyptian Sinai, Israel, Jordan, Lebanon, Syria and South-eastern Turkey and North-western Iraq) was *Arabia Petraea*, or the *Provincia Arabia*, the Roman border province whose capital was Petra. This region had been exposed to Greco-Roman culture for close to a millennium. The major written languages here were Greek and various Aramaic dialects, the most important of which was Syriac. Furthermore, much of the population of this region (unlike in *Arabia Deserta*) had converted to one form or another of Christianity (which was anything but an homogenous, monolithic entity).

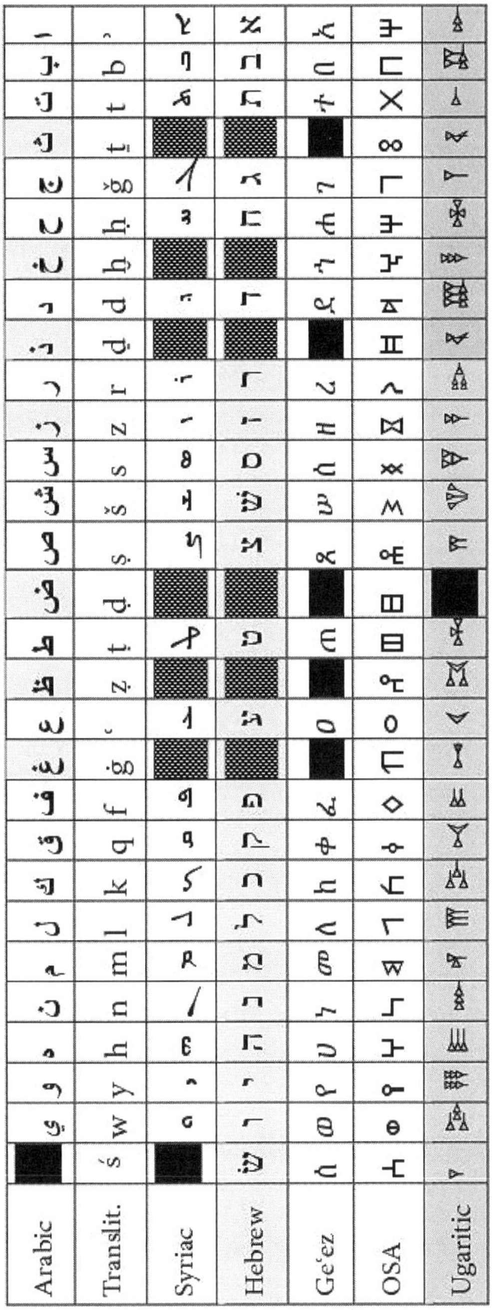
Arabic
Translit.
Syriac
Hebrew
Geʿez
OSA
Ugaritic
ʾ b t ṯ ǧ ḥ ḫ d ḏ r z s š ṣ ḍ ṭ ẓ ʿ ġ f q k l m n h w y ś

OSA = Old South Arabic

Hatched boxes (in the lines with Syriac and Hebrew letters): Phonemes lost in Aramaic, in Arabic replaced by the nearest phonetic equivalent

Black boxes: equivalent missing

The Arabic letters for ǧ, *f*, *q*, and *n* and the Syriac letters for *d* and *r* merged due to cursive writing.

Figure 2: Alphabets of the Ancient Middle East.

The important point that must be noted is that although in *Arabia Petraea* Aramaic and Greek texts are often attributed to the Nabataeans, Palmyrenians and others who were actually neither Aramaic nor Greek, their names and occasional stray words in inscriptions show that they were ethnically Arabs. We are dealing with a situation similar to that of medieval Western Europe in which Latin was the written language, while the spoken languages (vernaculars) were the precursors of the languages spoken today.

Briefly summarised, the Arabic language (especially with regard to the primary diagnostic feature, the definite article ال – *al-*) and script of *Arabia Petraea* are the precursors of the classical Arabic script and language. Before Islam, texts in the Aramaic script are hardly attested south of the modern state of Jordan and then only in the extreme North-west corner of modern Saudi Arabia. In *Arabia Felix* and *Deserta*, other scripts and languages were current. It is in *Arabia Petraea* that we find occasional Arabic texts in an Aramaic script and even Arabic written in Greek characters. A sixth/seventh century fragment of Psalm 78 found in the Umayyad "Mosque" at Damascus shows just how close this Arabic is to what would later morph into Classical Arabic (e.g., إمالة – *imāla*). The precursor to Classical Arabic was thus spoken in Syria, not in the Hijaz.

We now have two independent sources of *prima facie* contemporary evidence—aerial linguistics and script distribution—to show that the language of the Qur'ān must be based on a Syro-Palestinian Arabo-Semitic dialect and that the script employed was not that used in Mecca and Medina of the period, but the one used in *Arabia Petraea*. If the Qur'ān is actually a product of the Hijaz, then we would expect it to be in a different (Ancient North Arabian) Semitic language and written in a different script. That is not the case. The traditional account of the Qur'ān's origins is not supported by the evidence.

The peculiar thing about the Arabic script we are familiar with today is its polyvalence—i.e., it needs diacritical dots (اعجام – *iʿǧām*) to distinguish between otherwise identical consonantal characters (رسم – *rasm*). For example, the Arabic glyph ں can be read as *b* (ب), *t* (ت), *ṯ* (ث), *n* (ن) and medially as *y* (ي). Thus the Arabic script distinguishes eighteen glyphs that are made distinct by diacritics to render twenty-eight phonemes. A part of this polyvalence is not phonetically conditioned; it is due to the cursive erosion of distinct forms (e.g., *b*, *n*, medial *y*). In other cases, it is due to the fact that a twenty-two letter Aramaic alphabet was later supplemented to render additional Arabic phonemes (i.e., sounds that Aramaic had lost, but which survived in Arabic) by adding diacritical dots, a practice already found e.g. in Palmyrenian Aramaic, to the nearest phonetic approximant. This, along with borrowed Aramaic orthographic customs (such as ة, the *tā' marbūṭa* to mark the feminine ending, the *alif otiosum*, etc.) and the method of adding vowel marks (حركات – *ḥarakāt*) shows unmistakably that Arabic writing evolved from a long tradition of writing Aramaic and can, therefore, only have occurred in a region where the Arabs had had a long exposure to Aramaic writing culture: that is Aramaic writing was *arabicised*—note that the perhaps anachronistic notation of suffixed case vowels which had been lost in Aramaic at least a millennium and a half previously is known in Arabic grammar as such (إعراب - *i'rāb*). The only place where this could have happened is *Arabia Petraea*. If the Qur'ān were actually a product of Mecca and Medina, then (besides it being written in a different Semitic language) it would have had to have been composed in the South Arabian script which unambiguously differentiates each of the twenty-eight phonemes of Arabic and which, by this time, had a twelve hundred year tradition in the Hijaz. That this ideally suited script was not used means that it was unknown to the writers of the Qur'ān (the only attestation hitherto of pre-Classical Arabic being written in the Ancient South Arabian script is by an apparent resident alien at Qaryat al-Fāw on the North-Western edge of the Empty Quarter, situated on a major trade route from the Yemen to Eastern Arabia and the Gulf - see M. C. A. Macdonald, "Ancient Arabia and the Written Word," in idem (ed.), *The development of Arabic as a written language* (Supplement to the PSAS 40; Oxford, 2010, 17).

The fact that both the script and language of the Qur'ān point to the Classical *Arabia Petraea* of Syro-Palestine, and not *Arabia Deserta*, is further supported by the fact that the Qur'ān's vocabulary is largely borrowed from Aramaic, especially Syriac, the liturgical language of the local churches. Needless to say, the semantics of the technical religious vocabulary of the Qur'ān, the spelling of the names of biblical figures, and the often subtle biblical allusions presuppose an intimate knowledge of biblical literature in its Syro-Aramaic tradition. Syro-Palestine was heavily Christianised by the seventh century. Although there is some evidence of Christianity and Judaism in "happy" and "deserted" Arabia during this period, it just does not appear to have had the critical mass necessary to launch a new religion. Furthermore, the theological, doctrinal controversies that gave rise to the "heresies" that permeated Late Antique society were largely absent, or rather were not so significant outside of the Roman Empire. Thus, all of the contemporary epigraphical, literary, and linguistic evidence points to Islam being a product of Arabs living in Syro-Palestine.

This claim stands in stark contrast to the traditional narrative of a *blitzkrieg* from the Hijaz into Syro-Palestine. This event has vexed modern archaeologists. There is simply no archaeological support for a quick, violent and destructive invasion of Syro-Palestine as reported by traditional Islamic sources. Instead, excavations reveal a continuity of occupation and culture: the period in question is, archaeologically speaking, quite uneventful and conservative. The major cultural changes in ceramics and the like (such as the introduction of glazed wares) only occur in the eighth century. There is an uninterrupted settlement continuum through the Umayyad period (in which the mosaic as an art-form reached its peak) into Abbasid times. Even then the change is gradual rather than sudden. Where there was change, it consisted of a tendency towards smaller settlements in the countryside, which became favoured over towns. Archaeologically speaking, then, an Arab or Muslim conquest of Syro-Palestine is invisible. And the reason for this was that the Arabs were already living in the region as evidenced by their language.[2] In the end, archaeology, epigraphy and linguistics mitigate against a Hijazi origin of the Qur'ān. The latter can only be a product of Hellenistic Syro-Palestine.

1. Introduction

We have now seen that, based on archaeology, script geography and areal linguistics in the Late Antique Roman-Byzantine Middle East (including Arabia), the Qur'ān could not have originated in the Arabic script or language in the Mecca/Medina region. Current epigraphic and linguistic knowledge decisively contradicts the traditional narrative; one must instead look more closely at greater Syria, toward the Ghassanids and in particular the Lakhmids or the descendants of deported Arabs from in and around Merv. This is where the precursor of the Arabic language we know today was spoken, and where the transition from *Aramaic* to *Arabic* script was completed. If these arguments for how and where the Qur'ān was written down are examined, then much of its content will be easier to understand.

The following article will proffer a discussion on the theological and technical loan-words in the Qur'ān. By taking these into consideration, it becomes clear that Syria must be considered as the most likely place of origin of the holy book of Islam.

A reader of the Qur'ān will quickly notice its biblical legacy. What also stands out, however, is how the Qur'ān understands the Bible. This supposedly revealed book asserts the biblical lore it conveys as historical fact. The Qur'ān is guilty of the same mistake that many Christians and Jews still make today, specifically, confusing revelatory truth, or biblical historiography, with actual history. As the Qur'ān largely recognises the historical validity of Judaeo-Christian salvation history, as would be expected based on the period of its writing, which can be seen for example in 2:136 (also 3:84):

قُولُوا آمَنَّا بِاللَّهِ وَمَا أُنزِلَ إِلَيْنَا وَمَا أُنزِلَ إِلَىٰ إِبْرَاهِيمَ وَإِسْمَاعِيلَ وَإِسْحَاقَ وَيَعْقُوبَ وَالْأَسْبَاطِ وَمَا أُوتِيَ مُوسَىٰ وَعِيسَىٰ وَمَا أُوتِيَ النَّبِيُّونَ مِن رَّبِّهِمْ لَا نُفَرِّقُ بَيْنَ أَحَدٍ مِّنْهُمْ وَنَحْنُ لَهُ مُسْلِمُونَ

qūlū āmannā bil-lāhi wa-mā unzila ilaynā wa-mā unzila ilā 'ibrāhīma wa-'ismā'īla wa-'isḥāqa wa-ya'qūba wal-asbāṭi wa-mā 'ūtiya mūsā wa-'īsā wa-mā 'ūtiya l-nabiyyūna min rabbihim lā nufarriqu bayna 'aḥadin min-hum wanaḥnu lahu muslimūna

Say (O Muslims): We believe in Allāh and that which is revealed unto us and that which was revealed unto Abraham, and Ishmael, and Isaac, and Jacob, and the tribes, and that which Moses and Jesus received, and that which the prophets received from their Lord. We make no distinction between any of them, and unto Him we have surrendered. (Pickthall)

Thus the Qur'ān cannot claim any historical authenticity for itself. Historical and critical biblical research over roughly the past two-hundred years has uncovered the complex origins and history of the Hebrew Bible and the Christian New Testament, granting some aspects remain to be clarified in detail. Nonetheless, while academic Bible research can show that hardly any story in the Bible is historically true in the modern sense of the word, this must also apply to the versions of these biblical stories which appear in the Qur'ān.[3] This subject would best be clarified elsewhere, but in passing we merely want to note, for instance, that the narrative of the Deluge clearly must have originated from a similar *topos* out of Mesopotamia, where floods were very frequent and where a very early literary model of the (Sumero-)Babylonian *Epic of Gilgamesh* came from. Another example is the question of whether Abraham/Ibrahim was the first monotheist. This can be ruled out. Today we know that the blessing of Abraham by Melchizedek (Genesis 14:19) does not refer to a single God as the translation based on an understanding of the Epistle to the Hebrews might suggest ("Blessed be Abram by God Most High, Creator of heaven and earth"). Rather, this verse refers to three deities (a more correct translation would be: "Blessed be Abraham by *Elyon*, *El*, [and *El*], *the Creator of heaven and earth.*") The same goes for Moses. There is no way he could have been the founder of Israelite Monotheism (and it must be explicitly noted that the monotheism attributed to Moses has nothing to do with the Amarna period in Egypt). For one, the narratives concerning him have a complex history of composition which only began centuries after the events were allegedly narrated. Similar remarks could be made in regard to the doctrine of angels or prophecy. Hence, the Qur'ānic understanding of the Bible rather represents the preliminary end of a long history of development. The Qur'ān therefore largely follows in the traditions of the Judaeo-Christian divine revelations.[4]

But where does this monotheistic, biblical, influence on the Qur'ān come from? In the past, also based on Islamic traditional literature, it has been reported that local Jewish and Christian Arabic tribes exerted varying degrees of influence on "Muḥammad." Some epigraphical evidence also suggests a history of Judaism in Arabia, as well as Christian missions in the region.[5] Of course, there were also various tribes with diverse traditional Semitic religions other than Judaism and Christianity, and the Qur'ān pursues a polemic against these as well, although surprisingly enough quite imprecisely. Some evidence for these religions has been found in the form of inscriptions, although these, as we have noted, are not particularly helpful or informative and are mostly related to the kingdom of Sheba in present day Yemen. North Arabian inscriptions are for the most part simply graffiti and mostly inconsequential, except perhaps for possible theophoric elements in the individual names. Although it is entirely possible that an originally pagan "Muḥammad" could have had Jewish and Christian teachers from whom he would have been taught about both Judaism and Christianity, as well as about the Old and New Testaments from which he created a new, autonomous, religion, I have my doubts about this interpretation.

Although there is still a lot of work to be done in the archaeological exploration of Arabia, so far this research has simply not produced sufficient evidence for mass conversion to Judaism and Christianity in the region to make a plausible case supporting the idea of a direct transfer of these religions to Islam. This applies especially to Christianity, which in my opinion is presupposed by the Qur'ān. On the other hand, there is nothing in the holy book of Islam which could be exclusively interpreted as Jewish, or at least no traditions which could be evaluated and attributed uniquely to (rabbinic) Judaism. The Qur'ānic stories originating from the Hebrew Bible certainly could have come from a Christian source, for example from an Aramaic translation of the Bible.

To thoroughly investigate the possible origins of the Qur'ān, it is essential to analyse the text itself.

One particularly notable problem with trying to do this is that a critical edition of the Qur'ānic text does not exist. That is, no raw consonantal text (رسم – *rasm*) without diacritical marks (إعجام – *iʿǧām*) with variant readings of relevant early manuscripts exists. There is also no diachronic etymological dictionary of Arabic. The current stage of text-critical research into the Qur'ānic text takes the Cairo edition of the Qur'ān as the standard, which essentially means that Qur'ānic textual criticism is at the same stage of development as were biblical studies in the seventeenth-century. This was a time when a conflict was raging over whether or not the Masoretic vowel-pointing was revealed together with the text itself to Moses on Mount Sinai. Some Jewish scholars, such as Ibn Ezra, had previously pointed out that the addition of vowels must have originated with the Tiberian Masoretes only in the Middle Ages. This thesis gained notoriety among Christian scholars in the sixteenth century through Elias Levita, although it was highly contested, especially by the Buxdorfs. It was Louis Cappel who first scientifically proved this theory in his anonymous work *Arcanum Punctationis Revelatum*, which was published by the Leyden professor Thomas Erpenius in 1624. Since then, and in fact even before then, the text of the Hebrew Bible, as well as that of the New Testament, was understood in a context of ongoing change. Thus the Old and New Testaments should not historically be considered "canons." This term must be understood here as an anachronism, in part thanks to many recent discoveries such as the Dead Sea Scrolls in 1947. The development of comparative linguistics has also helped to transform our understanding of these texts. No respectable Old Testament Bible scholar today would still rely on works like מחברת מנחם – *Maḥbärät̲ Mənaḥēm* by the tenth century Menahem ben Jakob ibn Saruq of Cordoba, or שרשות כסף – *Šaršōt̲ Käsäp̄* ("Chains of Silver") of the thirteenth/fourteenth centuries by Joseph ibn Kaspi from the Provence region. Similarly, no scholar would rely on early scientific dictionaries, which in some respects are based on the work of mediaeval Jewish scholars. One such example would be the *Lexicon hebraicum et chaldaicum complectens omnes voces, tam primas quàm derivatas, quœ in Sacris Bibliis, Hebrœâ, and ex parte Chaldœâ linguâ scriptis extant* ... (Basel, 1631[1]), by the Buxdorfs (père et fils). It was very well known in its time, as was the *Lexicon et commentarius sermonis hebraici et chaldaici veteris testamenti* ... (Amsterdam, [1]1669; [2]Frankfurt, 1689) of Johannes Coccejus from Bremen. Regardless, it is likely that many theologians today–to their own detriment–would not understand enough Latin to use these resources anyway!

These works were ground-breaking in some respects at the time of their writing, but for modern academic Bible study they have become obsolete. The advancement of academic Hebrew and biblical Aramaic lexicography over the course of the last two centuries can be seen by the various editions of Wilhelm Gesenius' lexicons.[6] The eighteenth edition of this publication has recently been completed by the Old Testament scholar and Egyptologist Herbert Donner from Kiel, and is now regarded as the "state of the art" tool for serious Bible scholars. The older works, especially those compiled by mediaeval Rabbis, are of course still valuable. They are important in their own right for research into the rabbinical, or classical Jewish understanding of biblical writings–I even used the first edition of Gesenius on occasion during my studies of rabbinical texts. However, they are now essentially useless for understanding the conceptual meaning of biblical words and texts at the time of their supposed writing. This makes it all the more surprising that Qur'ānic exegesis is still based on pre-scientific works, such as the deservedly famous لسان العرب – *Lisān al-ʿarab* of Ibn Manzur, living in the thirteenth/fourteenth century, or القاموس المحيط – *Al-qāmūs al-muḥīṭ* by al-Firuzabadi, who lived in fourteenth/fifteenth century Iran.

These dictionaries, as well as those produced by Western scholars, offer profound support for the reading of classical Arabic texts, but are only of limited use in the philological work related to the "first Arabic book," since they assume the later Islamic interpretation of it. Here would be the place to mention the *Lexicon Arabico-Latinum* of Jacob Golius, a Leyden scholar and Erpenius' student (Leyden, 1653), as well as the revised edition by Georg Wilhelm Freytag (*Lexicon Arabico Latinum*, 4 Vols.; Hallc, 1830–1837). Also worth mentioning are Al-Zabidi's تاج العروس – *Tāğ al-ʿarūs* and the subsequent extended *Arab-English Lexicon* (incomplete; London, 1863–1893) by the English scholar Edward William Lane as well as the *Supplément aux dictionnaires arabes* (Leyden, 1881) by the Dutch Orientalist Reinhart Dozy and the *Wörterbuch der klassischen arabischen Sprache* by the Tübingen arabist Manfred Ullmann (Wiesbaden, 1970–). Despite Fück's conclusion that a philological-etymological dictionary would be required for any translation of the Qur'ān, as for study of the Bible, such a resource does not actually exist for the former. The most recent Qur'ānic dictionary is the *Arabic-English Dictionary of Qur'ānic Usage* by the scholars Elsaid M. Badawi and Muhammad Abdel Haleem, published (twice!) by the renowned Leyden publishing house E.J. Brill in 2010. This dictionary is far from reaching the same scientific level as the new edition of the "Koehler-Baumgartner" biblical Hebrew lexicon,[7] also published by E.J. Brill, which includes epigraphical findings and results of comparative Semitic linguistics, among other things. The older works certainly drew from the most current knowledge of their time, but the newer Qur'ānic works have yet to reach a state of the art academic level, thus scientific philological study of the Qur'ān is still for the most part impossible.

The problems with interpreting the Qur'ān are essentially the same as with Bible exegesis. Religions are human creations and are thus constantly evolving; they are not fixed programmes, despite what fundamentalists say. Without critical analysis, any reading of for example the *Germania* by Tacitus, Roman Law, the Bible, the Qur'ān, *Don Quixote* by Cervantes, or any other literary work, will only ever be understood in terms of the present views and circumstances of the reader. For example, every Christian today knows at least roughly what is supposedly meant by the religious terms "Son," "Trinity," and "Last Supper." However, the current meaning(s) of these words simply represent the provisional end of a long semantic evolution, and in no way have the same meaning they did during the time when Jesus is said to have lived. Historical linguistic research into the meanings of Hebrew and Greek words is well established, but with Arabic this work has hardly yet begun. With this method, we can see that the *Donatio Constantini* is a forgery and that the surviving copies of the *Karelsprivilege* have nothing to do with Charlemagne. The Greek of the New Testament is not the Greek of the Homeric epics; the language of the Hebrew Bible is not the same rabbinic language of the *Mishna* and the *Tosefta*. Likewise, the Arabic of the commentators (مفسرون – *mufassirūn*) is not the Arabic of the Qur'ān.

Here, it must be pointed out that the philological method is universally applicable; it can be applied to any text. Although the traditional commentary literature (تفسير – *tafsīr*) on the Qur'ān is important for understanding this book in the context of Islamic traditions, it is not really useful for research into its origins and original meaning. This problem has been previously mentioned on occasion, even by Old Testament scholars who regularly draw on Arabic vocabulary for their research. The remarks of L. Kopf are important to note here:

> A large portion of the vocabulary that Arabic philologists have recorded and interpreted was not previously known to them either from everyday usage or from comprehensive reading. Their main task, then, was not to find a clear and definitive meaning for words that were already known to every scholar, but rather to find meanings for rare and lesser-known words, which they very well may have encountered for the first time in their professional endeavours. There were two essential foundations for this type of research which were missing, specifically knowledge of other Semitic languages and the availability of large and systematically structured sets of linguistic data. As a result, many imprecise and even completely absurd definitions arose. The numerous varying meanings which have been assigned to many seldom-used Arabic words should be seen as the result of efforts undertaken without adequate resources by philologists attempting to explain difficult expressions using the resources available to them … Since the knowledge of other Semitic languages was missing and parallel passages were often not available for comparison, the floodgates were opened to this type of guesswork. Especially often, the use of different methods led to varying results. Along with the erroneous definitions provided by philologists themselves were others which were motivated by either religious considerations … or old linguistic traditions of the "pre-scientific" times.[8]

An example of this can be seen in the oldest monument of the Arabic language, the كتاب العين – *Kitāb al-ʿayn* by Al-Ḫalil ibn Aḥmad al-Farahid,[9] which does not even discuss commonplace words like كلب – *kalb* "dog," كثير – *kaṯīr* "many," or even the very common adverb كل – *kull* "all." Kopf provides a good example of the workings of traditional Arabic philology (*art. cit.* 298) from the above mentioned القاموس المحيط – *Al-qāmūs al-muḥīṭ*, specifically the common word كرسي – *kursī* "chair." This lexeme is obviously related to the Hebrew lexeme כִּסֵּא – *kissēʾ* "throne" (but must be borrowed from a later Aramaic form such as Syriac ܟܘܪܣܝܐ – *kursyā*), but in this work it surprisingly takes on the meaning "knowledge," alongside its primary meaning. This is due to the "Throne Verse" (2:255) of the Qur'ān:

وَسِعَ كُرْسِيُّهُ السَّمَاوَاتِ وَالأَرْضَ

wasiʿa kursiyyuhu l-samāwāti wal-arḍa

"His Throne comprehends[10] Heaven and Earth."

There are many such examples from traditional Arabic lexicography.[11] However, the previous example makes the problem sufficiently obvious: the traditional dictionaries are not helpful in determining the Qur'ānic meaning of Arabic words. They are more comparable to unrealistic thesauri. Imagine what would happen if *Beowulf* or Chaucer's *Canterbury Tales* were read using a dictionary of modern English usage. Goethe's "Seek only to confuse people, it is too difficult to please them" surely applies, then, to research on Arabic words of the Qur'ān.

2. Foreign Words as a Feature of Cultural Exchange

Thus, there is no academic critical edition of the Qur'ān and no scientific study of its lexicon. Anyone who reads the Qur'ān in Arabic (or is even perplexed by the varying renditions of the translations), will quickly become confused. Each word can seemingly be assigned an unexpected meaning according to the preferences of each researcher, thanks to the legacy of the older traditions. A student of comparative Semitic linguistics will also be confused, as the necessity of such leaps often remains a mystery.

What also stands out to Semiticists is the high frequency of foreign words in Qur'ānic Arabic. Foreign words are an interesting linguistic phenomenon; they can reveal something about the history of the speakers of a language and their past encounters.[12] We can see this in German, for example. The vocabulary relating to wine production is of Latin origin, suggesting that this aspect of Germanic culture was introduced by the Romans (for example, "Wein" ("wine") <*vinum*, "Kelter" ("wine-press") <*calcatura* etc.). This becomes especially clear when we also consider the fact that the regions in Germany where traditionally the most wine is produced previously belonged to the Roman Empire – beer was the traditional beverage of the Germanic peoples.[13]

It is also not surprising that the English Christian vocabulary has largely Latin origins as well: *advent*, *accident* (*accidens* <συμβεβηκός), *confession*, *confirmation, Eucharist, host, liturgy, mass, mission, oblate, passion, pastor, real presence, sacrament, substance* etc., leaving no doubt as to how and from where Christianity spread to the English (vis-à-vis the Greek derivation of such words in Slavic languages and even in Arabic). It is important to note here that these words have a specific theological meaning in English, regardless of what their definitions are in classical Latin (or their respective etymologies).[14] In addition to these loan-words, there are also so-called loan-translations. These are verbatim *(verbum pro verbo)* translations from Latin to English which (etymologically) make no sense in the latter. The meanings of the terms are thus derived from the donor language, like "holy spirit" *(<spiritus sanctus)*, "holy" (<*sanctus*), "shepherd" (<*pastor*), "body" (*corpus* <σῶμα), "baptism" (<*baptismus*[15] <βαπτισμός) or even "God," in the sense of a single and specific entity (<*deus*), etc. Most of these words have long since been adopted into English (as well as other European languages) and are no longer even perceived as foreign.

Thus it should come as no surprise that there are also foreign words and loan-translations in the Bible. For example, the Old Testament contains lexemes derived from Akkadian (and Sumerian),[16] Egyptian,[17] Greek,[18] Aramaic[19] etc. The Greek New Testament further reflects its origin in the Semitic world through its usage of many borrowed terms, like *Mammon* (Matthew 16:24; Luke 6:9,11,13) or the last words of Jesus: "*Eloi, Eloi, lama sabachtani*?" (Mark 15:34; Matthew 27:46 <Psalm 22:2).[20] The use of these words, especially in the field of theology or in other scientific areas, is not a coincidence, but rather has a lot to do with the introduction of previously unknown novel concepts or terms into the intellectual realm of a particular language. One example of an old (pre-Hebrew) loan word in the Old Testament must suffice here to briefly illustrate this process: The Hebrew loan-word הֵיכָל – *hēḵāl* "temple" (actually found in all Northwest Semitic languages) is derived from Akkadian *ekallum*, which itself goes back to Sumerian é.gal "big house." This indicates that the construction of an architecturally specific building, imagined as the house of a deity, is a custom that has its origins in Mesopotamia. Confirmation of this can also be found in the archaeology of the Early Dynastic Period (early Bronze Age). Similarly, there are many loan words in the tale of the construction of the Tower of Babel (Genesis 11:1–9), which describes the construction of a ziggurat (namely, inspired by the famous one commenced by the neo-Babylonian king Nebuchadnezzar II). In this case, the loan words come from a later language stratum, like for example לְבֵנָה – *ləḇēnā*^{h} "a sun-dried mud brick"– in Akkadian *libittu*^{m}. The fabrication and use of mud bricks was also a Mesopotamian practice–in Palestine one built with stone.

3. The loan-vocabulary of the Qur'ān

Returning to the main topic of this paper—the foreign words (including the loan-translations) in the text of the Qur'ān—it should have been made clear above that these must relate to the texts and faiths with which the authors of the Qur'ān were in contact. In this section I deal primarily with the work of the Australian scholar Arthur Jeffery, *The Foreign Vocabulary of the Qur'ān,* which thankfully has been re-published by the Brill publishing house (2007).[21] In this compilation, he deals with three hundred and eighteen different words (without inflected forms; in the following, I add a few more). The Qur'ān contains three to seven thousand words, depending on how the different word-forms are counted. Bearing this in mind, between six and ten percent of the vocabulary is of foreign origin. This in itself is not surprising, considering that approximately eighty percent of English words have foreign roots (from an etymological point of view), without this completely obscuring its Germanic origins. With respect to the Qur'ān it is important to note, however, that all of the important theological terms stem from Aramaic and in fact largely from Syriac. A few are potentially of Ethiopian or Persian origin, but many Iranian words were in all likelihood borrowed into Arabic through Syriac. I will also show that a few key terms demonstrate prior knowledge of the classical Syriac translation of the Bible, the *Peshitta.* An interesting example of this situation is the word خردل – *ḫardal* "mustard seed" in the Qur'ānic verses 21:47:

وَنَضَعُ الْمَوَازِينَ الْقِسْطَ لِيَوْمِ الْقِيَامَةِ فَلَا تُظْلَمُ نَفْسٌ شَيْئًا ۖ وَإِن كَانَ مِثْقَالَ حَبَّةٍ مِّنْ
خَرْدَلٍ أَتَيْنَا بِهَا ۗ وَكَفَىٰ بِنَا حَاسِبِينَ

wa-naḍa'u l-mawāzīna l-qisṭa li-yawmi l-qiyāmati fa-lā tuẓlamu nafsun šay'an wa-'in kāna miṯqāla ḥabbatin min ḫardalin 'ātaynā bi-hā wa-kafā binā ḥāsibīn^{a}

"And We shall set up balances of justice on the Day of Resurrection, then none will be dealt with unjustly in anything. And if there be the weight of a mustard seed, We will bring it. And Sufficient are We to take account."

And Qur'ān 31:16

يَا بُنَيَّ إِنَّهَا إِن تَكُ مِثْقَالَ حَبَّةٍ مِّنْ خَرْدَلٍ فَتَكُن فِي صَخْرَةٍ أَوْ فِي السَّمَاوَاتِ أَوْ فِي الْأَرْضِ
يَأْتِ بِهَا اللَّهُ ۚ إِنَّ اللَّهَ لَطِيفٌ خَبِيرٌ

yā-bunayya 'inna-hā 'in taku miṯqāla ḥabbatin min ḫardalin fa-takun fī ṣaḫratin 'aw fi s-samāwāti 'aw fī l-'arḍi ya'ti bi-hā llāhu 'inna llāha laṭīfun ḫabīr^{un}

"O my son! If it be (anything) equal to the weight of a grain of mustard seed, and though it be in a rock, or in the heavens or in the earth, Allāh will bring it

> forth. Verily, Allāh is subtle (in bringing out that grain), well-aware (of its place)."

It will be obvious to a knowledgeable reader that these verses bear a certain resemblance to the "Parable of the Mustard Seed" in Matthew 13:31–32 and to the "Healing of a Demon-Possessed Boy" in Matthew 17:20 (Mark 4:31, Luke 13:19 and 17:6 have less bearing here). The Peshitta actually translated the Greek ὡς κόκκον σινάπεως with ܦܪܕܬܐ ܕܚܪܕܠܐ – *perdtā d-ḥardlā*. The Arabic word is also found in allegedly "pre-Islamic" poetry (*Divan Hudhail* 97:11), suggesting at least the possibility that the word was adopted even earlier. Although this may be the case, the fact is that the Aramaic[22] loanword *ḥardlā* is not a common lexeme (and has more common synonyms), and also that it is used in the specific context of the same parable by all accounts, make it extremely likely that we are dealing with the influence of an Aramaic source.

The example given above is striking. However, it could be argued that this was a migrant word which was acquired along with the product it describes, as is the Greek word cited in the Gospels τό σίναπι (comp. German "Senf") which seems to come ultimately from Akkadian. There are certainly examples of such as well. Consider خمر – *ḫamr* "wine" (2:219; 5:90f; 12:36,41; 47:5), which undoubtedly stems from the Aramaic ܚܡܪܐ – *ḥamrā* (compare this to the word used in Old Testament poetry חֶמֶר – *ḥämär* <**ḥamr*), since the wine trade in the Syro-Arabian world at that time was firmly in Christian hands (and the Arabic root means "to cover, to hide.")[23] The word خبز – *ḫubz* "bread"– not a customary food item among the ancient Arabs–is only found in the dream of the baker in Sura *Yusuf* (12:36). It stems from the Old Ethiopian ኅብስት – *ḫəbəst* (with the retroactive assimilation < ኅብዝት – *ḫəbəz(ə)t*, compare to Tigré ሕብዝት – *ḥəbəzat* "thick, round bread.")[24] Also consider زجاجة – *zuǧāǧa* "glass," a commodity most likely imported from the Aramaic world <ܙܓܘܓܝܬܐ – *zəgugīṯā* (cf. Revelations 21:21) or زيت – *zayt* "olive," a tree not native to Arabia <ܙܝܬܐ – *zaytā* (this word for this fruit was also lent to Africa, for example ϫⲉⲉⲓⲧ/ϫⲟⲉⲓⲧ – *djeit/djoit*, ዘይት – *zayət*, and to the East, e.g. classical Armenian ձէթ – *jêt'* and Georgian ზეთი – *zeti* with the meaning "oil"– the primary exported product made from the olive), because the tree was originally only native to the eastern Mediterranean coast. These loan words are interesting because they point toward Syria as the source of the main cultural contact of the Arabs, and much less toward Ethiopia. There are also isolated (Middle-) Persian loan words, mostly for imported luxury goods, such as إستبرق – *istabraq* "silk brocade" (i.e. from the same source which the English word is ultimately derived from). In such exceptional cases, the words must have been borrowed from Persian and not through Syro-Aramaic due to their morpho-phonetic features. Old South-Arabic loan words are surprisingly rare, especially since according to the traditional narrative, the Qur'ān emerged in the "back-yard" of this linguistic and cultural entity.

Although these examples are very interesting and warrant further study in their own right, they shed but little light on the linguistic origins of the Qur'ān–they all could have been borrowed at any given time: the relevant trade routes are ancient. We are interested in focussing on the technical theological vocabulary, as it was described above for English. When we find Syro-Aramaic vocabulary in the Arabic of the Qur'ān whose specific religious and liturgical meanings depend on the donor language, we can draw conclusions about the intellectual environment and the sphere of influence which led to its emergence. However, in the following analysis some philological exceptions are taken into account. They are already apparent from the examples given above. As Jeffery has already noted (*op. cit.* 39f.), foreign words in the Qur'ān belong to three basic groups:

1. Words that cannot be Arabic (or even Semitic) at all, like for example إستبرق – *istabraq* "silk brocade." This could be compared in English to the word "schnitzel."
2. Words which have attested Arabic roots, but with a different meaning, like for example خمر – *ḫamr* "wine" (most of the infamous homonymous roots in Arabic belong in this category). This is roughly comparable to the English word "cool" in German; although it is etymologically related to *kühl*, in German it takes on only a specific meaning derived from modern colloquial English.
3. Homonyms, words which are genuinely Arabic but have a nuanced technical meaning alongside their Arabic meaning and must be borrowed. An English example would be "gill"– which usually refers to the breathing organs of fish and is of Germanic origin; the measure mostly used for alcohol, derives from French as indicated by its pronunciation, and ultimately from a Late Latin term for a jar. Loan translations ("calques") also belong in this category (see e.g., "Holy Spirit" *supra*).

I would also like to add a fourth category, which is:

4. Lexemes with a seemingly Semitic root which must be borrowed due to their morpho-phonetic forms. These include the names of biblical figures, such as the Patriarchs, as I will show in the following sections. Compare in English "vessel" (vs "vat").

4. The Vocabulary of Writing in Arabic

Without getting into the specifics of word formation and other morphological details of Semitic languages, I would like to briefly discuss one of their main characteristics: the interaction between consonants and vowels. The consonants provide a rough indication of the meaning; for instance the root √*ktb* usually has something to do semantically with writing. Through the addition of vowels (but also consonants)–mostly according to a particular modification sequence–the specific meaning can emerge, as we see with the given root:

كتب	/kataba/	"he wrote"
كتبنا	/katabnā/	"we wrote"
يكتب	/yaktubu/	"he writes/will write"
نكتب	/naktubu/	"we (will) write"
أكتب	/aktaba/	"he dictated"
يكتب	/yuktibu/	"he dictates/will dictate"
استكتب	/istaktaba/	"he had (something) written/copied"
يستكتب	/yastaktibu/	"he orders/will order (something) written/copied"
كاتب	/kātib/	"writer" (actually "writing" -active participle)
مكتوب	/maktūb/	"letter, something written" (passive participle)
مكتب	/maktab/	"office, desk"
مكتبة	/maktaba/	"library, bookshop"

As this root is widespread throughout Semitic languages, the problem is obvious. In the North-West Semitic branch of Semitic languages, both the Canaanite branch (e.g. Phoenician-Punic and Hebrew) and Aramaic, as well as Ugaritic of the Late Bronze Age, attest this root in this meaning in various derivations. However, writing is a relatively new phenomenon in human history. Its first beginnings hearken back to southern Mesopotamia of the fourth millennium bc, and then somewhat later in Egypt. Our own alphabet developed under Egyptian influence and its origins are to be found among Semitic miners in the Sinai during the first half of the second millennium bc. Consequently, the original meaning of this root cannot logically have been "to write." Further proof of this lies in the fact that this root is found neither in Akkadian (Assyro-Babylonian), nor in South-Semitic.[25] We can thus establish that the root √*ktb* only came to describe the action of writing at some later time, and only in the North-West Semitic languages. Other branches of the Semitic language family used other roots, since different and certainly older writing traditions than what we today call Arabic existed there, as we have briefly seen (*supra* §0).

In addition to semantically describing "writing," this root in Arabic also carries a second, independent meaning, namely "to bring together, to bind, to close, to stitch."[26] This is an example of an homonymous root, whereby one meaning is from Arabic itself and the other was necessarily borrowed and adopted into the language. The meaning "to write" must have been taken over from Aramaic when the Arabs of Syro-Palestine adopted and adapted Aramaic writing culture. Jeffery (*op. cit.* 249) suggests that the borrowing may have happened at al-Ḥīrah (الحيرة)[27]–the seat of the Lakhmids–as I have discussed elsewhere. Regardless, the use of the root √*ktb* in its borrowed sense of "to write" further indicates the influence of the Syro-Aramaic writing culture on the Arabs resident in Syro-Palestine.

If we look at the semantic domain of literacy in Arabic, interestingly enough we find only loan-words. Take, for example, the root √*ṣḥf* mentioned above. This root is attested in the Arabic of the Qur'ān as the noun صحف – *ṣuḥuf* (the plural of صحيفة – *ṣaḥīfa* "sheet, page;" Modern Standard Arabic: "newspaper"), always in the sense of something previously revealed: 20:133 (بينة ما في الصحف الأولى – *bayyinatu mā fī ṣ-ṣuḥufi l-'ulā*), as well as 53:36 (صحف موسى – *ṣuḥufi mūsā*); 74, 52; 80:13; 81:10; 87:18f. (إن هذالفي الصحف الأولى صحف إبراهيم وموسى – *'inna hāḏā la-fī ṣuḥufi l-'ulā ṣuḥufi 'ibrahīma wa-mūsā*)[28] and with an indication of the new revelation 98:2 (رسول من الله يتلو صحفا مطهرة – *rasūlun mina llāhi yatlū ṣuḥufan muṭahharatan*). There is no doubt that we are dealing with a loan-word from South Semitic (linguistically, not necessarily geographically speaking). It is already well-documented in "pre-Islamic" poetry for one, and it also appears in Sabaean and Qatabanian as TfAS – *ṣḥft* (pl. fAS – *ṣḥf*)[29] "document." This root was borrowed once again later on into Arabic, however, this time from Classical Ethiopian as مصحف – *muṣḥaf* "book" (actually, a bound volume of the Qur'ān)–in Gəᶜəz this is the customary word for "book," but also "holy writing" (i.e. the Bible), i.e., መጽሐፍ – *maṣəḥaf* (also pl. መጽሐፍት – *maṣəḥafət* [scil. ቅዱሳት – *qəddusāt*]).[30] The Arabic verbal derivation with the meaning "to misread, to falsely place diacritical marks" is in Form II (D-Stem), which here is an indication of its secondary, nominal derivation (which in turn produced the noun تصحف – *taṣaḥḥuf* "mistake in writing, distortion").[31] Here we can see the Qur'ān in the context of Late Antiquity: the vocabulary of writing is borrowed from the neighbouring cultures from which the Arabs took their writing traditions. Since the (Syro-Palestinian) Arabs were for the most part in contact with the Syro-Aramaic writing culture, as is evident from the visual resemblance which both writing systems display, it is not surprising that most of the roots describing this action were borrowed from that culture. Other terms come from more distant regions such as southern Arabia and Ethiopia.

There are other Qur'ānic expressions with reference to the written word that are also borrowed. For example, سجل – *siğill*, a *hapax legomenon*, is documented in the Qur'ān only in 21:104. The classic commentators had great difficulty with this word and translated it in different ways, such as "angel" *as-Sijill* (i.e., "engel" in Keyser's Dutch translation), "the secretary of *Muḥammad*" (Pickthall), or as "sheet" ("Blatt" Paret). In post-Qur'ānic Arabic, it is defined as "an anthology of judiciary rulings" (>"archive, land registry," etc.) and forms a denominal verb the D-stem "to record, to note." Although the relevant passage يوم نطوي السماء كطي السجل للكتب – *yawma naṭwī s-samā'a kaṭayyi s-siǧilli li-l-kutubi* (21:104) is still difficult (at least for me), this word originates from Latin, specifically from *sigillium* (<*signum*)–also the origin of the word "seal" in English. This word was also borrowed by Greek as σιγίλλον and often had the meaning "imperial edict" or "decree" in the Byzantine Empire. Whether the word was borrowed into Arabic directly from Greek or through a derivation of the Syriac ܣܝܓܝܠܝܘܢ – *sigiliyōn* "diploma (spec. quo chalifa patriarcham confirmat)" (Brockelmann, 459a; compare, for instance ܡܣܓܠܣܢܝܬܐ – *msglsnyt'* "libellus, scriptum accusatorium") remains uncertain. In my opinion the latter is more likely.

Furthermore, the word *Qur'ān* itself is an Aramaic loan-word, as Chr. Luxenberg convincingly shows (*Die syro-aramäische Lesart des Koran*, 2nd edition 2004: 81ff.; cf. Jeffery *op. cit.* 233f). This word is derived from the root √*qr'* (*pace* al-Jawhari *aṣ-Ṣaḥāḥ* s.v. <*qarana*!), which primarily means "to read (aloud)" in modern Arabic. Of course this cannot be the original meaning, for the same reasons discussed above regarding the √*ktb*–"writing" must exist before anything can be *read*. In Akkadian (*qerû*^{m}) and in Ugaritic we come across this root in the meaning "to call; to invite." In South Semitic, this root has nothing to do with the semantic domain of reading. In Sabaic it means "to command" and exists in Old Ethiopian, possibly as a relic, as ቈርቈረ – *q*^{w}*erəq*^{w}*era* "to cry out, to knock, to be confused."[32] But then again, the semantic development of "to call" > "to read out" >"to read aloud" (> "to read") was only carried out in the North-West Semitic languages (Hebrew, Phoenician-Punic, Aramaic, etc.) during the Iron Age and then further in a particular theological sense, like the Hebrew מִקְרָא – *miqrā'* "reading" (Nehemiah 8:8, which the German *Revidierte Eberfelder* renders literally with "das Vorgelesene," i.e., ". . . and caused them to understand the *reading*"– most other translations render the Hebrew with "book, scroll"), which subsequently became the common designation for the Hebrew Bible in later Hebrew. Following the path set out by Jeffery and Luxenberg, I would also suggest that the Arabic term *Qur'ān* derives from a Syriac usage such as ܩܪܝܢܐ – *qrīnā (ḏ-ktāḇā)* which can also have the meaning "scriptura sacra" (Brockelmann 690b).[33]

The same holds true for أسفار – *asfār*, the plural of سفر – *sifr* "book," only found in the Qur'ān in 62:5:

مَثَلُ الَّذِينَ حُمِّلُوا التَّوْرَاةَ ثُمَّ لَمْ يَحْمِلُوهَا كَمَثَلِ الْحِمَارِ يَحْمِلُ أَسْفَارًا

> *maṯalu llaḏīna ḥummilū t-tawrāta ṯumma lam yaḥmilu-hā ka-maṯali l-ḥimāri yaḥmilu ʾasfāran*
>
> "The likeness of those who are entrusted with the Law of Moses, yet apply it not, is as the likeness of the ass carrying *books*." (Pickthall)

As well as in سفرة – *safara* (sing. سافر – *sāfir*) in 80:15, actually "writer (transcriber)" and not angel, or messenger, as it is often translated. The root √*sfr* in Arabic has many meanings, for instance: "to remove a woman's veil," and "to send (someone) away, to expel," "to travel, to go on a journey" etc. In any case, nothing that could be interpreted as "book," as was even acknowledged by the early commentators,[34] which makes a borrowing from Syriac quite certain. The quote from 62:5 just cited in which the *Torah* (تورة – *tawrāt*) is cited in conjunction with "books" (أسفار – *asfār*) makes it clear that (some component of) the Bible was being referred to here, the same way it still is in modern Arabic, e.g. سفر التكوين – *Sifr al-takwīn* "the Book of Genesis."

Words derived from this root and with this meaning have a long history in the Syro-Aramaic donor and ܣܦܪܐ – *sāp̄rā* "scriba."[35] The Aramaic meaning of this root itself ultimately stems from Akkadian: *šapāru*^{m} "to send (a message), to write (to)" with derivations like *šapru*^{m} "envoy, messenger," *šipāru*^{m} "regulations, instructions," *šipirtu*^{m} "message, letter, instruction" etc.[36]

Another Arabic root denoting things written is again certainly borrowed from Syro-Aramaic and of Akkadian origin, namely √*sṭr*.[37] In the Qur'ān this verb always appears in relation to the "well-preserved tablets" (في لوح محفوظ – *fī lawḥin maḥfūẓin* 85:22), at least in the conventional interpretation[38] (17:58; 33:6; 52:2, 37; 54:53; 68:1; 88:22). The verb *šaṭāru*^{m} is commonly used in Akkadian to indicate the activity of writing (originally thus "to incise," much like Greek γράφω) and has nominal derivations like *šaṭāru*^{m} (infinitive) "(trans)script, document" and with similar meaning *šiṭru*^{m}, *šiṭirtu*^{m}, *mašṭaru*^{m} "inscription, prescription." This root is used only as a participle in Hebrew and Imperial Aramaic in the sense of "clerk" or "scribe." In Syriac, as well as some other Aramaic dialects, there are substantives such as ܫܛܪܐ – *šṭārā* "syngraphum" (*melior* "syngraphus"), by which the Peshitta translates סֵפֶר - *sēp̄ār* "book" in Jeremiah 32:10, and renders χειρόγραφον, "debt certificate" in Tobit 5:3 and Colossians 2:14. The Aramaic word appears to be derived from Akkadian *šaṭāru*^{m}, mentioned above. It appears to be a morphologically unproductive root in the former language. Here it must be noted: rts – *s*^{1}*ṭr* is the predominant verb in the Old South Arabian languages for "to write." However, I think it is unlikely that this root is directly borrowed from Akkadian, meaning there may be an Aramaic connexion. The causative forms rtsh – *hs*^{1}*ṭr* and rts – *s*^{1}*ṭr* with the meaning "scribe" must also be noted; they have only been documented in the last, monotheistic, period of Sabaean,[39] but a Qatabanian or Sabaean source cannot be ruled out entirely. In any case, we have another term describing writing borrowed from a neighbouring language.

The well-preserved planks, or rather the "guarded planks" (Pickthall), mentioned above, is the last term related to writing to be discussed here. It is interesting in terms of the third category mentioned earlier–it is a true Arabic word with a borrowed technical meaning. The root √*lwḥ* with the meaning "plank, board" is well-attested throughout the Semitic languages,[40] e.g. Akkadian (nominal) *le'u*^{m}. In Arabic, as well as in "pre-Islamic" poetry, it is used as in Qur'ān 54:13 for the wooden planks of Noah's Ark: وحملناه على ذات ألواح ودسر – *wa-ḥamalnāhu ʿalā ḏāti 'alwāḥin wa-dusurin*, similar to the አልዋሕ – *'aləwāḥ* (sg. ሌውሕ – *lawəḥ*)[41] in Acts 27:44 of the Ethiopian version of the New Testament where it specifically refers to the planks used by those who couldn't swim to save themselves when the boat taking St. Paul to Rome struck a reef before Malta. In Hebrew, it (לוּחַ – *lūaḥ*) is mentioned in connexion with the construction of the altar of burnt-offering in Exodus 27:8 (*et passim*). The archetype of the Qur'ān is what is being referred to in Sura 85:32, mentioned above, and in 7:145ff. The term refers to the "stone tablets," which the Lord delivered to Moses on Mt Sinai – the same word we find used in Hebrew in Exodus 24:12 (*et passim*) which is also used here by the Targums (לוחי אבנא – *lūḥē 'aḇnā*) and, significantly, the Peshitta (ܠܘܚܐ ܕܟܐܦܐ – *lūḥē d-kēpā*). The semantic development of "board" > "writing tablet" appears to have first occurred in Akkadian, also in the theological sense similar to the *le'u ša balāṭi* "tablet of life" (that is, on which destinies are written). Wax tablets are apparently being described here, i.e. similar to the *tabula cerata* or perhaps more appropriately the mediaeval *diptycha ecclesiastica*.[42] The word had already been recorded in Amarna-Canaanite with this meaning (358:9), also in Ugaritic, Hebrew (e.g. Proverbs 3:3; 7:3; Song of Songs 8:9; Isaiah 30:8; Jeremiah 17:1), and in some forms of Aramaic. So, we have here a technical loan word from Akkadian which spread throughout neighbouring languages. There is no possibility, however, that the Arabic word is directly borrowed from Hebrew–here we must once again look into Aramaic, specifically Syriac. As we noted, in the Peshitta ܠܘܚܐ – *lawḥā* is used in Exodus 24:12 and elsewhere, as well as for the *INRI*-inscription (τίτλος) of Pilate on Jesus' cross in John 19:19,[43] for example, and is therefore certainly the source of the Arabic word.

5. Borrowed Terms in the Qur'ān

5.1 Introduction

So far it has been shown that the literary culture from which the Qur'ān emerged was in close contact with both the Syro-Aramaic region and its local manifestations of Christianity. This has been made clear by the borrowings from Aramaic already discussed.[44] Many of the words discussed here have undergone a long evolution—even the Hebrew word that everyone knows: "Torah"—until they eventually acquired the meanings they now have (or are given) in the Qur'ān. The fact that the Arabic vocabulary with regard to reading and writing stems from the language of the culture(s) from which the writing culture was adopted is not surprising. It can be compared to German *lesen* (< Latin *legere*– "to read") and *schreiben* (< *scribere* – "to write"). If we dig a little bit deeper, though, we find a surprising abundance of key theological terms borrowed from Aramaic in the vocabulary of the Qur'ān. Here I will mention just a few from Jeffery's work with a few additional comments of my own.

5.2 Adam: آدم – *'ādam*

The Hebrew word אָדָם – *'āḏām*, as in Ugaritic, Phoenician etc. means "human(ity)" (in Sabaean, "vassal, subject"). In the Qur'ān however, it appears only in the sense of the name of the first human (compare to ابن آدم – *ibn ādam* lit. "son of Adam"="human," as in 7:35, for example). This interpretation can already be found in the Septuagint. In the Hebrew story of creation, אָדָם – *'āḏām* was translated as ἄνθρωπος "human" until Genesis 2:15; however, in the next verse, when God places humans in the Garden of Eden, the Hebrew word was understood as a name and was transcribed as Αδαμ. The interpretation of this word as a proper noun "Adam," can already be found in later books of the Hebrew Bible such as I Chronicles 1:1 and Hosea 6:7. This is also the understanding of this lexeme in the New Testament (for instance Romans 5:14 *et passim*) and in fact Christianity in general until the early modern period. Although the root √*'dm* retains its Aramaic meaning in Syriac, ܐܳܕܳܡ – *'āḏām* is always used as the name of the first human, just as in Classical Ethiopian አዳም – *'ādām*. Although this root is well attested in Arabic, for example اديم – *'adīm* "skin," its interpretation as the name of the original human assumes a prior knowledge of Christianity or Judaism. Verses like Qur'ān 3:59, 7:172 (تقولوا يوم القيامة – *taqūlū yawma l-qiyāmati*) and 124:20ff. make it obvious that we are dealing with a Christian influence. Because *Adam* is only used in the Qur'ān to describe the first human, whereas in Hebrew it was originally used as a term for humans in general, Arabic presupposes a certain exegetical evolution. Thus, this word falls into the third category listed above.

5.3 Islam: الإسلام – *al-'islām*

The root √*šlm* (>Arab. *s-l-m*) is well-attested with the meaning "to be complete, finished" in most Semitic languages. Another meaning emerged from this one: "to be healthy, well," as can be seen in Akkadian. The meaning "peace" as in Hebrew *shalom*, in the sense of a greeting is a logical development. In Arabic, the IInd form has undergone the development "to make healthy, unharmed" > "to protect from damage" >"to deliver safely" > "to deliver" (compare to the French *sur-rendre*), in the sense of *dedito*. The original semantics can certainly be found in the Qur'ān, for example in 31:22 ومن سلم وجهه إلى الله – *wa-man yuslim wağha-hu 'ila-llāhi* "And whosoever submits his face (himself) to Allāh," as well as in 2:112 and 131. The verbal root from which the noun الإسلام – *'al-'islām* (causative!) is a nominal derivation, is used here as a religious *terminus technicus*, once again certainly presupposing a Syriac semantic development. The causative conjugation ܐܫܠܡ – *'ašlem* is also found in Syriac in the sense of "to commit" (Luke 1:2, John 18:35, 19:30 (the Spirit), Acts 8:3 (to a prison); > "to betray" >Matthew 10:4 etc.) but also as a specifically Christian term: "*to commit* to the faith," so in the sense of "to be devoted to" or "to be dedicated to" (i.e. *devotio*). Therefore, *Islam* does not mean "peace" in the sense of a *pacificatio* or *debellatio*, but rather it means to commit oneself to the will of God, i.e. "surrender," "dedication," *dedicatio*. This is another example of a genuine Arabic root which took on a secondary Christian-technical meaning–this belongs in the third category as well.

5.4 God: الله – Allāh

Although there can be no doubt that the root of this word is a good and genuine Arabic lexeme, its morpho-phonetics point rather to Syro-Palestine than to the Hijaz; I have discussed the problems associated with it elsewhere.[45] Briefly, the form *'il* as a noun to denote a deity is well-attested in Semitic. The word *'il* can in Semitic refer to a god but is also the name of the chief divinity of the Semitic pantheon 'Il (>'El).[46] The singular *'lh* (already attested, though rarely in Ugaritic), however, seems to be a back-formation of the plural *'ilhm* (which is a strategy sometimes employed in Semitic to make a tri-radical root out of a bi-radical one in the plural) that is only found in North-West Semitic and Ancient North Arabian. *'lh* is especially common as the generic term for a(n unnamed) god in Aramaic where this form largely replaces *'l*[47] and which also seems to be the source of this form in Ancient North Arabian. The usage in Arabic, however, in which *'ilāh* is appended with the article *al-* (see *supra* §0) to denote "*The* God" (i.e. the one and only) and not *a* god or the chief deity of a pantheon, presumes the invention and evolution of monotheism. The roots of this term can be found in later passages of the Hebrew Bible that refer to the God of Israel as הָאֵל – *hā-'ēl* "the God" (instead of using the plural אֱלֹהִם – *ᵉlōhīm*; as in Phoenician) which becomes the norm in later Jewish and Christian dialects of Aramaic: e.g. Official Aramaic מאת לי ביהו אלהא "you have sworn to me by *Yahu*, the God" (*TAD* B2.2,r.4); Syriac ܐܠܗܐ – *'ălāhā* "(the) God" (both *status emphaticus*, i.e. determined). Thus, the base form *'lh*, the usage of the definite article (أداة التعريف – *'adāt at-ta'rīf*), and that this form, despite the availability of other lexemes (see *infra* §7.2.2) was used to denote "God" and not just "God," but "God" in a "Judaeo-Christian" understanding shows that this lexeme with this specific meaning was borrowed, also because it starkly contrasts with traditional Semitic forms of divine address. This is further supported by the fact that Arab Christians also use this word when referring to God.[48]

Further support for the adoption of this term can be found in the usage of epithets for this monotheistic deity. Besides ربّ – *rabb* (§7.2.2), one also finds e.g. السكينة – *as-sakīna* (2:248; 9:26,40; 48:4,18,26) which is variously rendered, e.g. Pickthall "peace of reassurance," Yusuf Ali "assurance," Shakir "tranquility;" the officialesque Muhsin Khan translation has "Sakinah (peace and reassurance)." The ultimately Jewish origin of this term was recognised by Keyzer in his Dutch rendition (9:28) "dat de arke waarin de Godheid woont." In later Rabbinic Judaism, שְׁכִינָה – *šəḵīnāʰ* (not in the Hebrew Bible, but cf. e.g. Exodus 25:8 וְעָשׂוּ לִי מִקְדָּשׁ וְשָׁכַנְתִּי בְּתוֹכָם – *wə-'āśū lī miqdāš wəšāḵạntī bəṯōḵām* "And have them make me a sanctuary, so that I may *dwell* among them"; Deuteronomy 33:16 וּרְצוֹן שֹׁכְנִי סְנֶה – *u-rəṣōn šoḵnī sənäh* "and for the good will of him that *dwelt* in the bush"; in later tradition, such as with Saadia Gaon in the tenth century, the term came to mean the فشرف الله "honour of God" i.e. כָּבוֹד – cf. idem, كتاب الأمانات والإعتقادات – *Kitāb ul-'amānāt wal-i'tiqādāt* ed. Landauer p. ٩٩) became a term used to indicate that the "Divine Presence" was *residing* (שָׁכַן – *šāḵan*) when e.g. "ten are gathered for prayer" (*Sanh.* 39a), "three sit as judges" (*Ber.* 6a), "one goes into exile" (*Meg.* 29a) from whence derived meanings such as "peace," "tranquility," "holiness" etc., attributed to the presence of the divinity, arose (cf. Greek σκηνή/ σκῆνος – lxx "tabernacle" Exodus 26:1 Καὶ τὴν σκηνὴν ποιήσεις δέκα αὐλαίας ἐκ βύσσου κεκλωσμένης; also Euripides, *Ion* 806 σκηνὰς ἐς ἱεράς). This term, as ܫܟܝܢܬܐ – *šḵīntā*, also entered Christian Syriac with the meaning "divine presence," e.g. Peshitta II Chronicles 5:14 (ܘܠܐ ܐܫܟܚܘ ܟܗ̈ܢܐ ܠܡܩܡ ܘܠܡܫܡܫܘ ܡܢ ܩܕܡ ܥܢܢܐ܇ ܡܛܠ ܕܐܬܡܠܝ ܒܝܬܗ ܕܡܪܝܐ ܡܢ ܗܘܐ ܕܫܟܝܢܬܗ), Aphrahat ܢܦܩ ܓܪܒܐ ܡܢ ܩܕܡ ܫܟܝܢܬܗ ܕܩܘܕܫܐ – "leprosy went out from the presence of the Holy One" (D. Ioannes Parisot, "Aphraatis sapientis persae demonstrationes," in R. Graffin (ed.), *Patrologia Syriaca*, (Paris, 1894–1907); note also N. Séd, "Les Hymnes sur le Paradis de Saint Ephrem et les traditions juives" *Muséon* 81 (1968): 455–501). This loan-word presupposes theological developments in Judaism and their borrowing into Oriental Christianity.

5.5 Hell: جهنم – *ğahannam*

This word is clearly borrowed and presupposes a complex development, namely the differentiation between heaven and hell, in other words a final judgement for humanity. This notion, introduced through apocalyptic ideas, is by no means an originally Semitic one. In fact it is not even found in the Hebrew Bible; the dead all descended to *Sheol*, regardless of their deeds in this life. *Sheol* in the Hebrew Bible is in many ways quite similar to the archaic Greek notion of Hades. *Gehenna* was originally the name of a place, גֵּי־(בֶן־)הִנֹּם – *gē-(bän-) hīnnōm*, the "Valley of (the son of) Hinnom," in other words where the Jerusalemite Moloch (not a divinity!) cult was practiced (see for example, 2 Kings 23:10, Jeremiah 7:31f, where children were burned alive for the Lord). As for the word-form, there are translations in the Septuagint, along with transcriptions, such as γαιβενενομ, γαι-βαναι-εννομ as well as the contracted phonetic form γαιεννα(μ), which is then attested in the New Testament as γέεννα. With regards to the meaning, we find it in the apocryphal literature, e.g. in 1 Enoch[49], 4 Ezra, and later in the Sibylline Oracles as a place of future punishment for sinners and evildoers. The word appears in the New Testament with this meaning, e.g. Matthew 5, Mark 9 etc. The doctrine of hellfire and the eternal suffering of non-believers, still widespread today, has a long (unhistorical!) history of development–it testifies to a combination of an ancient sacrificial cult, Zoroastrian beliefs, together with a good dose of Hellenistic influence. The Qur'ānic-Islamic doctrine of after-life, similar to and derived from the Christian one, is thus a later development, and therefore presumes the development(s) described. The Arabic form with the preserved final {-m} could indicate a borrowing from *Hebrew*, however, the Old Ethiopian ገሀ/ሃነም – *gaha/ hānam* could just as easily be the source of this loan word (possibly through Hebrew or from now lost Greek spelling). Syriac ܓܗܢܐ – *gihannā* scarcely applies here. Thus the lexeme along with the associated beliefs were necessarily derived from Christianity.[50]

5.6 The Satan: الشيطان – aš-šayṭān

Obviously the notion of a master of hell presupposes the concept of hell itself. The Arabic word, like ours, has its origins in Hebrew. The etymology is still unclear; however, the details do not need to be worked out here.[51] In the Hebrew Bible, we find שָׂטָן – *śāṭān* in the earlier books with the meaning "adversary," such as 1 Samuel 29:4 where David is identified as a (possible) *satan* of the Philistines (lxx: μὴ γινέσθω ἐπίβουλος τῆς παρεμβολῆς), as we also see in 1 Kings 11:14, 23:25 and Numbers 22:22–32. Only the Chronicler uses this word as the name of a particular person, the (proto-)Devil, 21:1 (compare to the lxx: Καὶ ἔστη διάβολος ἐν τῷ Ισραηλ καὶ ἐπέσεισεν τὸν Δαυιδ τοῦ ἀριθμῆσαι τὸν Ισραηλ), which was most likely also meant in Zachariah 2:1f. (an intermediate stage might be the Book of Job). The origin of this term could stem from legal terminology, where it refers to a "prosecutor," such as in Psalms 109:6. In the New Testament, we find this form, the Σατανᾶ (= διάβολος, lit. "the confuser"), also found in the Rabbinic literature (although entirely absent in later Judaism), which developed into the personification of evil–in contrast to Jesus, who is portrayed as an advocate, the παράκλητος. This meaning is also found in the Peshitta, ܣܛܢܐ – *sāṭānā* (this form could stem from Hebrew, just as well as from Greek). The Arabic form *šayṭān* may have previously been borrowed by pre-Islamic Arabic in the sense of "evil spirits," for example 6:71:

كَٱلَّذِي ٱسْتَهْوَتْهُ ٱلشَّيَاطِينُ فِي ٱلْأَرْضِ حَيْرَانَ لَهُۥٓ أَصْحَٰبٌ يَدْعُونَهُۥٓ إِلَى ٱلْهُدَى ٱئْتِنَا

ka-llaḏī stahwat-hu š-šayāṭīnu fī l-'arḍi ḥayrāna la-hū 'aṣḥābun yad'ūna-hū 'ilā l-hudā 'tinā

"... like one bewildered whom the devils have infatuated in the earth, who hath companions who invite him to the guidance ..." (Pickthall)

Which is roughly a synonym to the جن – *ǧinn* "genies." Although this could be the case, the word is probably borrowed from the Ethiopian ሰይጣን – *sayṭān* (<Aramaic), a lexeme that can also possess this nuanced meaning (pl. ሰያጥን – *sayāṭən*, pl. ሰያጥናት – *sayāṭənāt* "demons"). In any case, the connexion between the incarnation and this word makes the semantic development clear and shows that it culminated in Christianity, as found e.g. in 58:19.

5.7 Forgiveness: حطة – *ḥiṭṭa*

In this context I will also discuss حطة – *ḥiṭṭat*^{un} "forgive" (2:58; 7:161) and the common verb خطى – *ḫaṭṭā* "to sin" (خطيئة – *ḫaṭī'a* "sin"), all of which presume the semantic evolution of this root which took place in Hebrew. The root √*ḥṭ'* originally had the meaning "to fall short of, to miss," similar to Arabic "to miss the mark (shooting)" in the causative IVth stem. In this sense, the word is used, for example, in Isaiah 65:20 ". . . for one who dies at a hundred years will be thought a mere youth, and one who falls short of (החוטא – *haḥōṭä'*, literally "misses") a hundred years will be considered accursed." The beginning of the development "to miss" > "to displease" (as a result of misconduct) can be seen, for instance, in Proverbs 8:36 "But those who miss (חטאי – *ḥoṭə'ī*) me injure themselves. All who hate me love death." From here, the developmental path to indicate a misdemeanour is easily understandable–a development that was also completed in Akkadian *ḫaṭû*^{m}, Ugaritic *ḫṭ'*, as well as in Sabaean, Qatabanian, etc. However, there is a large difference between *offence* (with or without intention) and *sin*, in the sense of a moral offence against a deity. This understanding is not found in the older parts of the Hebrew Bible, but rather is the result of a later, complicated, theological evolution of the term, which cannot be examined in any detail here. Nonetheless, the New Testament notion of sin is not a self-evident development. In this specific theological-technical sense we find the Syriac ܚܛܐ – *ḥṭā* "peccavit" (with nominal derivations, such as ܚܛܐ – *ḥṭā*, ܚܛܝܬܐ – *ḥṭīṯā*, ܚܛܝܬܢܝܐ – *ḥṭīṯānāyā*, ܚܛܝܢܐ[52] – *ḥeṭyānā*, ܚܛܝܐ – *ḥṭāyā* etc.). In Arabic as well as in Old Ethiopian, this root with the semantic domain briefly touched upon here can only have been borrowed from Syriac. In fact, its use in these languages presupposes hamartiology.

The meaning of the word حطة – *ḥiṭṭa* "forgive" is clear to all commentators; however, their work has not yet produced a satisfactory derivation. Based on their suggestions, I suspect a possible borrowing of the meaning from Hebrew *Pi'el* (D-Stem), חִטֵּא – *ḥiṭṭē'* "to cleanse (of sin)."

5.8 Angel: ملائكة – *malā'ika*

Finally, one other important term for Islam should be mentioned. Once again, this term underwent a long semantic development before it came to have its Qur'ānic meaning.[53] The word ملائكة – *malā'ika* "angel" obviously assumes a prior conception of the existence of such spiritual beings. Indeed, this word stems from the Hebrew מַלְאָךְ – *mal'āḵ* (from the root √*l'k* "to send a message").[54] This nominal derivation means "messenger," or the bearer of a message in the older parts of the Hebrew Bible, as in Ugaritic, for example. In this sense it is even attested in Ezekiel 23:40:

> "And furthermore, that you have sent for men to come from afar, unto whom a messenger (מַלְאָךְ – *mal'āḵ*) was sent"

That this word came to mean a divine being sent by God to bring a message to humans is the result of an inner-"Israelite" development mitigated by external influences. The later traditions that we find in the New Testament, as well as elsewhere, depicted Gabriel (גַּבְרִיאֵל – *gaḇrī'ēl* "Man" or "Hero of God," Daniel 8:15ff; 9:20ff.) and Michael (מִיכָאֵל – *mīḵā'ēl* "Who is like God?"; Daniel 10, 13ff.) as "angels"[55]—it cannot be a coincidence that these just happen to be the only two angels referenced by name in the Qur'ān, as in 2:98:

مَن كَانَ عَدُوًّا لِّلَّهِ وَمَلَائِكَتِهِ وَرُسُلِهِ وَجِبْرِيلَ وَمِيكَالَ فَإِنَّ اللَّهَ عَدُوٌّ لِّلْكَافِرِينَ

man kāna 'aduwwan li-llāhi wa-malā'ikati-hi wa-rusuli-hi wa-ğibrīla wa-mīkāla wa-'inna llāha 'aduwwun li-lkāfirīna

"Whoever is an enemy to Allāh, His Angels, His Messengers, *Jibrīl* (Gabriel) and *Mīkā'īl* (Michael), then verily, Allāh is an enemy to the disbelievers."

The use of both the terminus technicus ملائكة – *malā'ika* and the proper nouns جبريل – *ğibrīl* and ميخائيل – *mīḫā'īl* must have been borrowed, in terms of both the words themselves and the underlying concept. These words were borrowed by Syriac from Hebrew. In the Peshitta, ܡܠܐܟܐ – *malāḵā* is expressed in the sense of the Hebrew term (e.g. Genesis 16:7); the same is true of the Greek term ἄγγελος as we see in this verse in both the Septuagint and in the New Testament. The Syriac lexeme was in turn borrowed by Old Ethiopian መልአክ – *mal'ak*. Whether these words were adopted into Arabic directly from Syriac or possibly through Gəʻəz is difficult to determine.

Incidentally, it should also be noted that the early commentators surprisingly considered Gabriel foreign and there are countless different spellings such as جبرائيل – *ğibrā'īl* besides جبريل. The Arabic spelling of Gabriel جبريل is a phonetic rendition of /ğibrīl/. This must be derived from a Syro-Aramaic form such as ܓܒܪܝܐܝܠ – *gaḇri'el*, compare to Γαβριήλ, thus /găbri'əl/ > /găbrîl/ > /gĭbrīl/ (vowel harmony!). The vocalisation of Michael مِيكَال – /mika'al/ can by no means be genuine–the theophoric element /'el/ (*supra* §5.4) would never have been understood as such. Furthermore, the alternate form ميخائيل – *mīḫā'īl* is a transcription of a North-West Semitic spelling, most likely a Syriac transcription (< Hebrew, *supra*) ܡܝܟܐܝܠ – *miḵā'īl* (i.e. Syriac post-vocalic ܟ – {k} is pronounced as /x/ which can be rendered in Arabic with خ – {ḫ}).[56] The orthography and vocalisation of these forms contradict the possibility that an indigenous Arabic tradition is the source of these names. Because of their Semitic etymology, these can only be phonetic transcriptions whose origins are to be found in another language, namely *in casu* Syriac.

This is also incidentally the case with many names of biblical figures in the Qur'ān. With an authentic Arabic revelation, we would expect to see etymological spelling and not a transcription of Aramaic (or Ethiopic) forms, which themselves were often borrowed from Greek. This applies for example to Isaac إسحاق – *isḥāq*; based on the Hebrew form, יִצְחָק – *yiṣḥāq*, in Arabic something like يصحق* – *yaṣḥaqu* or even يضحك* – *yaḍḥaku* ("he laughs") would be expected, that is if there had been a genuine tradition of the traditional folk etymology of Genesis 17:17; 18:12. In this sense, this form can only be a phonetic transcription of the Syriac form ܐܝܣܚܩ – *isḥāq*; in other words, this form would not have been understood as a conjugated verb + a theophoric element (<**yisḥāq-'el*). We find a similar situation with the name Israel إسرائيل – *isrā'īl* ultimately from the Hebrew יִשְׂרָאֵל – *yiśrā'ēl*. Although the etymology of the first (verbal) element remains unclear,[57] it is a (short) prefix conjugation with the theophoric element /'l/ (compare to the discussion above §5.4 on "Allāh"). The Arabic orthography recognised neither the verb nor the name of God as such and is certainly to be understood as a transcription of a Syriac form ܐܝܣܪܐܝܠ – *isrā'el* or similar (var. ܝܣܪܐܝܠ – *(y)isrā'el*,

ܐܝܣܪܐܝܠ – *isrā'el*; or less likely < Ethiopic እስራኤል – *əsrā'il*). Surprisingly, the same phenomenon also applies to the orthography of Ishmael: إسماعيل – *ismā'īl* does not express the Hebrew יִשְׁמָעֵאל – *yišmāᶜēl* "God heard (scil. the request for a child, i.e. son)," so <√*šmᶜ* "to hear" + *'l* "God"–in fact it can only be a transcription of a form ܐܫܡܥܝܠ – *išma'īl*.[58] Concerning the name Jacob, يعقو – *ya'qū* and يعقوب – *ya'qūb* are indeed etymological renditions of the Hebrew יַעֲקֹב – *yăᶜᵃqōḇ* >Syriac ܝܰܥܩܽܘܒ – *ya'quḇ*; however, the disagreement among the early Qur'ānic commentators regarding the etymology of this name (cf. Jeffery, *op. cit.* 291) makes it clear that the name was borrowed, especially since the verbal root عقب – *'aqaba* can have a similar meaning to Hebrew עָקֵב – *'āqaḇ*, cf. Genesis 25:26; 27:36.[59] Furthermore, the fact that the verbal prefix in Arabic is written here without any knowledge of its derivation must certainly indicate a borrowing from Syriac. A similar situation occurs with Arabic يوسف – *yūsuf* <Syriac ܝܰܘܣܶܦ – *yawsep̄* (with vowel harmony in Arabic) <Hebrew יוֹסֵף – *yōsēp̄*. It cannot simply be a coincidence that the Arabic spelling of biblical names always transcribes Syriac orthography rather than following Semitic etymology. This alone makes it quite clear that the Qur'ān is not so much entirely new revelation to an illiterate prophet, but rather it must be viewed as a continuation, or rather an evolution, of a literary tradition that had already been long established.

Further evidence of this can be seen in cases where the diacritical marks were apparently incorrectly placed on the consonantal skeleton, such as يحيى – *y-ḥ-y-y* for "John (the Baptist)" /yaḥyà/. Of course what is meant here is the Hebrew יוֹחָנָן – *yoḥānān* >Syriac ܝܘܼܚܲܢܵܢ – *yuḥanān*–only a *rasm* ىحىى can form the basis of this, which by mistake was not pointed يحنن – *y-ḥ-n-n* (see above §0 on the phonetic polyvalence of the Arabic archigrapheme ٮ)–the issue is made clear by the Christian Arabic realisation of this name as يُوحَنَّا – *yuḥan-na*. An interesting case of this phenomenon in the extra-Qur'ānic tradition is the exegetical fate of the Egyptian bureaucrat *Potiphar*, in Hebrew פּוֹטִיפַר – *pōṭīpār* (Genesis 37:36 and elsewhere; Syriac ܦܘܛܝܦܪ). In Sura *Yusuf* (12), he is not mentioned by name and in v. 21 is merely called الذي اشتراه من مصر – *allaḏī štarā-hū min miṣra* "The man from Egypt who bought him" (in vv30 and 51 العزيز – *al-'azīz* "the powerful one"). In the commentary literature, we though find for instance وهو قطفير – *wa-huwa qiṭfīr* "and he is *Qiṭfīr*" (*Tafsir Jalalayn* a.l.; also for example Al-Baizawi, Djami, قصص الأنبياء – *Qiṣaṣ al-'anbiyā'* [my edition: Cairo, n.d., pp. 94ff.] etc.). Here it is important to establish that *qiṭfīr* is by all accounts meaningless gibberish, however *pōṭīpār* is an Egyptian personal name <*p3-dj-p3-rᶜ*, "given by Ra."[60] Clearly فطفر was written (i.e. the Arabic archigrapheme ٯ can render either ف – {f} or ق – {q}) reminiscent of the Syriac ܦܘܛܝܦܪ – a form perceived as foreign, where there was likely very little guidance and a(n incorrect) guess was ventured.

6. On the Five Pillars of Islam

6.1 Introduction

The influence of Syro-Aramaic on the theological vocabulary of the Qur'ān should by now be evident. The examples given above may appear to have been selected at random, but they were chosen pars pro toto to make a point. To complete this picture, I will discuss a few key terms, namely the "Five Pillars of Islam" (أركان الإسلام – *'Arkān al-'Islām*):

1. The profession of faith: الشهادة – *aš-šahāda*
2. Prayer: صلاة – *ṣalāṭ*
3. Charitable giving: زكاة – *zakāt* or صدقة – *ṣadaqa*
4. Fasting: صوم – *ṣawm*
5. Pilgrimage: حج – *ḥağğ*.

Although these terms could all be genuinely Arabic lexemes based on their morpho-phonetic structure, their technical meanings, as they relate to faith, clearly suggest Syriac as their origin in most cases.

6.2 The profession of faith: الشهادة – *aš-šahāda*

The Arabic root √*šhd* "to testify," here in the specific sense of "to bear witness to one's faith," presupposes Syriac ܣܗܕ – *sheḏ* with a similar meaning,[61] for example in Deuteronomy (5:20): ܠܐ ܬܣܗܕ ܥܠ ܚܒܪܝܢ ܣܗܕܘܬܐ ܕܕܓܠܬܐ – *lā tsaheḏ ʿal ḥḇarīn sāhdūṯā d-daggāltā* "Neither shall you bear false witness against your neighbour." In the New Testament, this root is used (compare to the noun ܣܗܕܐ – *sāhdā*) to express the Greek root μάρτυρ-: μάρτυρ "witness," μαρτυρίαν "testimony," μαρτυρέω "to testify" etc., for example in John 3:11:

> ἀμὴν ἀμὴν λέγω σοι ὅτι ὃ οἴδαμεν λαλοῦμεν καὶ ὃ ἑωράκαμεν μαρτυροῦμεν, καὶ τὴν μαρτυρίαν ἡμῶν οὐ λαμβάνετε –
> "Verily, verily, I say unto thee, We speak that we do know, and testify that we have seen; and ye receive not our witness."
>
> ܐܡܝܢ ܐܡܝܢ ܐܡܪ ܐܢܐ ܠܟ: ܕܡܕܡ ܕܝܕܥܝܢ ܚܢܢ ܡܡܠܠܝܢ ܚܢܢ. ܘܡܕܡ ܕܚܙܝܢ ܡܣܗܕܝܢ ܐܢܚܢܢ. ܘܣܗܕܘܬܢ ܠܐ ܡܩܒܠܝܢ ܐܢܬܘܢ.
>
> *'amīn 'amīn 'āmar-nā lāḵ: d-meddem d-yāḏʿīn ḥnan məmalləlīn ḥnan. wə-meddem da-ḥzayn mashəḏīn 'anaḥnan. wə-sāhduṭan lāk mqabbəlīn 'antun*

The nuanced meaning of *martyrs* (شهيد – *šahīḏ* ~ ܣܗܕܐ – *sahdā*), used to describe a person who dies for their beliefs in both languages, is also noticeable. A borrowing from Syriac is the only feasible possibility here.[62]

6.3 Prayer: صلاة – *ṣalāṭ*

The root √*ṣlw* in Arabic is only used in the second (factitive) conjugation and would seem to be denominal. A look at Aramaic shows the meaning of ܨܠܐ – *ṣlā* in the Peal to be "inclinavit, flexit" etc.–the physical act of bowing (compare to 2:43 واركعوا مع الراكعين – *wa-ārka'ū ma'a r-rāki'īn*). In the second form, the D-stem (Syriac: *Pael*), however, it is used in the sense of "to pray,"[63] for example Matthew 6:6:

> ܬܪܥܟ: ܘܨܠܐ ܠܐܒܘܟ ܕܒܟܣܝܐ. ܘܐܒܘܟ ܕܚܙܐ ܒܟܣܝܐ ܢܦܪܥܟ ܒܓܠܝܐ
>
> *tar'āḵ: wə-ṣalā la'ḇuḵ daḇ-ḵesyā. wa-'ḇuḵ d-ḥāzeh bə-ḵesyā nepr̄'āḵ bə-ḡelyā*
>
> "...pray to your Father who is in secret; and your Father who sees in secret shall reward you openly."

Here once again the semantics of Syriac are determining–the Arabic term can have its origins only in Syriac, based on the specific use of this root in the sense of bowing to ask something of God, and which displays the long semantic evolution that led to this meaning. Indicative of such a conclusion is also 48:29:

> تَرَاهُمْ رُكَّعًا سُجَّدًا يَبْتَغُونَ فَضْلًا مِّنَ اللَّهِ وَرِضْوَانًا ۖ سِيمَاهُمْ فِي وُجُوهِهِم مِّنْ أَثَرِ السُّجُودِ ۚ
>
> ذَٰلِكَ مَثَلُهُمْ فِي التَّوْرَاةِ ۚ وَمَثَلُهُمْ فِي الْإِنجِيلِ كَزَرْعٍ أَخْرَجَ شَطْأَهُ فَآزَرَهُ فَاسْتَغْلَظَ فَاسْتَوَىٰ
>
> عَلَىٰ سُوقِهِ يُعْجِبُ الزُّرَّاعَ
>
> *tarāhum rukka'an suǧǧadan yabtaġūna faḍlan mina l-lāhi wariḍwānan sīmāhum fī wuǧūhihim min aṯari l-suǧūdi ḏālika maṯaluhum fī l-tawrāti wa-maṯaluhum fī l-inǧīli kazar'in 'aḫraǧa šaṭ'ahu fāzarahu fa-istaġlaẓa 'alā sūqihi yu'ǧibu l-zurā'a*
>
> "... You see them bowing and prostrating [in prayer], seeking bounty from Allāh and [His] pleasure. Their mark is on their faces from the trace of prostration. That is their description in the Torah. And their description in the Gospel is as a plant which produces its offshoots and strengthens them so they grow firm and stand upon their stalks, delighting the sowers ..."

Here, it is clear that Qur'ānic prayer, by its own account, is based on biblical practice. This is supported by the fact that this root was also borrowed from Syriac into Late Sabaic (Period E; cf. n39) 𐩮𐩡𐩩 – *ṣlt* "prayer," along with monotheism, e.g. Ha11:3–5 (Ash 1952.499; cf. I Gajda, *Ḥimyar gagné par le monothéisme (IVe-VIe siècle de l'ère chrétienne). Ambitions et ruine d'un royaume de l'Arabie méridionale antique* (Université d'Aix-en-Provence, 1997):

> *l-ys¹mʿn Rḥmnn ṣlt-s¹m*
> "may Rḥmnn listen to his prayer" (cf. §7.2.4 on Rḥmnn);

Gar Bayt al-Ashwal 1:2–3 (Gajda, op. cit.)

> *b-rdʾ w-b-zkt mrʾ-hw ḏ-brʾ nfs¹-hw mrʾ ḥyn w-mwtn mrʾ s¹myn w-ʾrḍn ḏ-brʾ klm w-b-ṣlt s²ʿb-hw Ys³rʾl*
> "avec l'aide et grâce de son Seigneur qui s'est créé lui-même, seigneur de la vie et de la mort, seigneur du ciel et de la terre qui a créé tout et avec les prières de son peuple Israël."

Of further significance here is that the adjectival noun سجدا – *suǧǧadan* "prostrating" in the Qur'ānic quotation just given, must also be of Syro-Aramaic origin.[64] The common Aramaic root √*sgd* (Syriac ܣܓܶܕ – *sged*) "to bow down" has a long history in this language of being used to denote "prostration" as in "The Words of Aḥiqar" (*TAD* 3 C1.1:13): א]חר גהנת וסגדת̇ לם אחיקר קדם אסרח[אד]ן מלך [ ]אתור... "...[T]hen, I bowed and prostrated myself, verily <I> Aḥiqar, before Esarh[addo]n, [King of] Assyria" (note Late Sabaic 𐩯𐩴𐩵 – *s³gd* "to submit," e.g., *w-s³gd l-hmw l-ys³ḫln* "he submitted himself to be subject to" – Wellcome A 103664, Gajda, *op. cit.*), but then evolved to "worship, prayer, adore, venerate"[65] as in the Old Syriac gospels, Matthew 2:2 where the Magi tell Herod ܚܙܝܢ ܓܝܪ ܚܙܝܢ ܟܘܟܒܗ ܒܡܕܢܚܐ. ܘܐܬܝܢ ܠܡܣܓܕ ܠܗ – "For we have seen his star in the east and have come to *worship* (*l-masgad*) him." From this root, the unsurprisingly nominal derivatives in the meaning "worship, adoration, veneration" (cf. in Bar Hebraeus, *Menerat Qudshe* ܣܓܕܬ ܦܬܟܖ̈ܐ i.e. "idolatry"), so ܣܓܕܬܢܝ – *segdtānāy* "pertaining to veneration," ܣܳܓܽܘܕܳܐ – *sāgōḏā* "worshipper," ܣܓܕܬܗ ܕܨܠܝܒܐ – *segdte d-ṣlībā* "veneration of the Cross," ܒܝܬ ܣܓܕܬܐ – *bēṯ segdtā*, lit. "house of worship, prostration," but also the term for the lection John 14:15–31 (read on Whitsun and the eve of Good Friday) etc. The word in the meaning "submisse venerari, precibus venerari (homines, Deum)" also seems to have been borrowed by Old Ethiopic from Syriac as ሰገደ – *sagada*.[66]

It should thus be no surprise then that a nominal derivation of this root then is also found which denotes the *place* of worship. So for example in Samaritan Aramaic to denote a pagan temple (*Tibat Marqé* 1.856): ושרו תפוכה בבתי סגדתון "and they began overturning some of their shrines." Frequently in Nabataean, a place of worship is denoted as a *mšgd*. This word–already attested at the Persian-era Jewish military colony at Elephantine (Egypt; *TAD* B7.3:3): בח[רם אלה]א במסגדא ובענתיהו "{Oath to be sworn} ... by Ḥ[erem the go]d at the "place of prostration" (i.e. shrine) and by Anat-Yahu"[67]–is from whence the Arabic word مسجد – *masǧid* is derived, i.e. literally "place of prostration." Thus the Islamic manifestation of prayer and its location have Aramaic predecessors in Syro-Palestine and not in the far distant Hijaz. Finally, with regard to the act of prayer (صلاة – *ṣalāh*) itself in

Islam, as a recent study has shown, all of its major features are pre-Islamic with many interesting parallels to be found in Mesopotamian and Ancient Egyptian depictions.[68]

6.4 Charitable giving: زكاة – *zakāt* or صدقة – *ṣadaqa*

The giving of alms, which is the obligation to provide a particular portion of one's wealth (نِصاب – *niṣāb*) to the destitute and needy as well as other defined social groups. زكاة – *zakāt* can hardly be derived from زكى – *zakā* "to clean" as some traditions claim. The nearest cognate meaning of this root is found in Jewish Palestinian/Galilean Aramaic זכי – "to give to charity." The precursors of this semantic development can probably still be seen in Syriac ܙܳܟ݂ܽܘܬ݂ܳܐ – *zāḵūṯā* "acquittal, innocence" (also "grave of a martyr")—or possibly in Jewish-Babylonian-Aramaic, Palestinian Targum-Aramaic and Galilean Aramaic זְכוּתָא – *zəḵūṯā* "reward, commendable deed." The latter seems more likely to me.

The "voluntary donation" صدقة – *ṣadaqa* has a specific meaning and thus is certainly of foreign origin. In Amorite, Ugaritic, (older) Hebrew, Sabaean, Gəʿəz, etc. this semantic domain encompasses "justice, to be righteous, to be documented as true" (compare *the Tzaddik*; Sadducee) – from which the classical commentators derived the Arabic term.[69] The development of "to be righteous" > "that which is right(eous) > "that which is proper (to give)" > "to give charitably" > "to give a portion, toll" was completed in Aramaic. Syriac, which renders here the /ṣ/ with {z} is less relevant here. However, here we do find a similar semantic development: ܙܕܘܬܐ – *zadūṯā* (<√*zdq*!) "beneficium, eleemosyne," for example, as in Matthew 6:2, where this word expresses the Greek ἐλεημοσύνη:

ܐܡܬܝ ܗܟܝܠ ܕܥܒܕ ܐܢܬ ܙܕܘܬܐ ܠܐ ܬܩܪܐ ܩܪܢܐ ܩܕܡܝܟ܆ ܐܝܟ ܕܥܒܕܝܢ ܢܣܒ̈ܝ ܒ̈ܐܦܐ
ܒܟܢܘܫܬ̈ܐ ܘܒܫܘܩ̈ܐ܆ ܐܝܟ ܕܢܫܬܒܚܘܢ ܡܢ ܒܢ̈ܝ ܐܢܫܐ܂ ܘܐܡܝܢ ܐܡܪ ܐܢܐ ܠܟܘܢ܆ ܕܩܒܠܘ
ܐܓܪܗܘܢ

ʾimmattī hāḵēl d-ʿāḇed ʾatt zadūṯā lā teqrā qarnā qadmayḵ ʾayḵ d-ʿāḇdīn nāsbar baʾpe ba-ḵnušāṯā wa-ḇ-šuqe: ʾayḵ d-nešbḥun men bnay (ʾ)nāšā wa-ʾmīn ʾāmar (ʾ)nā lḵun d-qabbel[u] *ʾağrhun*

"So when you give alms do not sound a horn before you as the hypocrites do in the synagogues and in the streets, that they may have glory of men. Verily I say unto you, they have their reward."

This usage is also found elsewhere: ܡܕܡ ܕܡܢ ܕܐܬܝܗܒ ܠܕܝܪ̈ܬܐ ܘܠܐܟܣܢܕܘ̈ܟܝܢ ܘܠܙܕܘ̈ܬܐ "… whatever has been donated to monasteries, guest-houses, and alms" (E. Sachau, *Syrische Rechtsbücher* Vol. 3, 176:2).

The unaltered root √*ṣdq* found in Western Aramaic is, however, in all likelihood the source of the Arabic borrowing. So for example Christian-

Palestinian ܨܕܩܐ – *ṣdqʾ* as well as the Hebrew word borrowed by Jewish dialectsצְדָקָה – *ṣəḏāqā*^{h} "liberality, especially almsgiving."[70] Although the exact Aramaic source of this word is not clear, it is most likely the same one which lent this word into Classical Ethiopian ጸደቃት – *ṣadəqāt* (pl.; sing. ጸደቅ – *ṣadəq*). In any case, the particular semantic development of the root √*ṣdq* here, from "righteousness" to "alms(giving)" is somewhat convoluted so as to preclude the same semantic development having occurred twice independently. The precedence of this development in Aramaic certainly shows that it was borrowed by Arabic. The fact that it, unlike most of the borrowed Aramaic lexemes hitherto discussed, seems to have been borrowed from a Jewish Western Aramaic dialect could indicate that it is an Islamic continuation of an originally Jewish custom, possibly a relic of Islam's Judaeo-Christian origins (see §7.2.9).

6.5 Fasting: صوم – *ṣawm*

In Arabic, the root √*ṣwm,* in the limited religious sense of forgoing food, drink, sexual intercourse etc., can only have been borrowed–its phonology disqualifies it being Arabic. In Ugaritic the word is attested as *ẓm* with this meaning. Were صوم – *ṣawm* a genuine Arabic lexeme, we would then expect to see something resembling ظوم* – **ẓawm*. The origin of this word is most likely the Hebrew צום – *ṣôm* "to fast"[71] (verb Qal "to fast, a self-depreciation rite, generally performed during the day"; Gesenius[18] s.v.), since Aramaic ܨܘܡ – *ṣwm* must itself also be a loan-word: proto-Semitic /*ẓ*/ evolved into /*ṭ*/ in Aramaic, which would here have resulted in ܛܘܡ* – **ṭwm*. In Judaism, rites of fasting were not uncommon, e.g. צומא רבא – *ṣō/awmā rabbā* "the great fast" (i.e., *Yom Ha-Kippurim*; *PTMeg*70.b: 25[2]). Fasting was also widespread in early Christianity, particularly in its Oriental varieties, something which requires no further explanation in light of its Jewish roots. We merely note here the month-long fast during Advent (ܨܘܡܐ ܕܝܠܕܐ/ܕܣܘܒܪܐ – *ṣawāmā ḏ-suḇrā/ḏ-yaldā*). Both the word and the religious concept were likewise borrowed by Old Ethiopian, i.e. ጾም – *ṣom* from Aramaic, certainly with the introduction of Christianity.[72] Thus, this lexeme demonstrates in a striking manner the Judaeo-Christian roots of Islam.

6.6 Pilgrimage: حج – *ḥağğ*

This word, specifically referring to the Meccan pilgrimage appears also to have been borrowed. Again, the semantic development of the root betrays its Syro-Aramaic origins. In Biblical Hebrew, the root √*ḥgg* is defined as a religious festival in general and is commonly derived from the verbal root √*ḥwg* "to draw a circle, to measure precisely" (compare to طواف – *ṭawāf*), so originally "to dance in a circle" >"to take part in a procession." In Arabic though, besides the by all accounts quite specific verbal meaning "to undertake the *Ḥağğ*," this root furthermore encompasses a second, judicial semantic domain, e.g. حجة – *ḥuğğa* "argument, proof, plea etc." (probably related to a secondary form حق – *ḥaqq* "truth"; note Sabaic 𐩢𐩗 – *ḥg* "to command" etc., Classical Ethiopic ሐገገ – *ḥagaga* "to legislate" ሕግ – *ḥəgg* "law"). As this Arabic root is very productive in the semantic domain of law and displays no other obvious connexions to (the) pilgrimage, it seems certain that it is a loan. This premise is supported by the fact that the meaning "to celebrate" in a specifically religious context is wide-spread throughout Aramaic,[73] and is an Hebraism—cf. the Jewish wish *Chag sameach* "happy holiday." Especially in Syriac though, this root in a religious sense becomes quite productive: ܚܓܐ – *ḥaggā* "feast," ܚܓܝܘܬܐ – *ḥaggāyūṯā* "festivity" ܡܚܓܝܢܐ – *mḥaggəyānā*, ܡܚܓܝܢܘܬܐ – *mḥaggəyānūṯā* "festivity," ܡܚܓܝܢܐܝܬ – *mḥaggyānā'īṯ* "in a joyous or festal manner," also in conjunction with "worship" (*sgd* see sub §5.2) with Jacob of Sarug:[74]

ܠܝܫܘܥ ܣܓܕܝܢ ܚܓܐ ܘܟܢܫܐ ܘܐܬܪܘܬܐ܀

... *l-yēšūʿ sagdīn ḥaggā wə-kenšā wə-'aṯrūṯā*

"... groups and assemblies and regions worship Jesus."

It is also in this language that we see the further, less obvious semantic development to *pilgrimage*, e.g. ܚܓܝܐ – *ḥaggāyā* "solemnis; peregrinans ad festum agendum."[75] In Sabaean we find 𐩢𐩗 – *ḥg* most often with the meaning something along the lines of "divine destiny, claim, authority; order," although in late Sabaean it can also mean "pilgrimage" (e.g. seemingly in Ha 11; cf. ad §6.3). This must constitute a borrowing from Aramaic and may possibly be attested in Old Northern Arabic (Thamudic) as well.

In the German version of this article, I left some possibility open that this word might be the product of an inner-Arabic development. The fact, however, is that the semantics of religious festivity culminating in a pilgrimage derive ultimately from Hebrew, from whence these semantics entered Aramaic, preclude such. Furthermore, since then, I have become increasingly convinced that the association of Islam with Mecca first came about during the Abbasid period, when Mecca seemingly emerges out of nowhere – the بكة – *bakkah* of the Qur'ān simply cannot be convincingly associated with this city as I intend to demonstrate in a forthcoming publication. Therefore, the pilgrimage to Mecca is not so much the Islamic reinterpretation of an indigenous Hijazi rite, but rather the later transposition of a Syro-Palestinian Judaeo-Christian one to the Hijaz. In passing, it should be noted that the lesser, voluntary Meccan pilgrimage, the عمرة – *ʿumrah* also has Syro-Aramaic roots: <√*ʿmr* ("to dwell") "habitavit specialiter in coenobio," i.e. to lead a monastic life ܥܘܡܪܝܐ – *ʿumrāy* "monk." So too إحرام – *iḥrām*, the sacred state in which one enters to perform these pilgrimages has Syro-Aramaic origins, scil. the causative conjugation of the root √*ḥrm*, i.e. ܐܚܪܡ – *aḥrem* "to devote, to consecrate"[76] whose specific semantics were in turn borrowed from Hebrew as can be seen by comparing the Peshitta with the Masoretic Text of Leviticus 27:29:

> ܘܟܠ ܚܪܡܐ ܕܡܚܪܡ ܡܢ ܐܢܫܐ ܠܐ ܢܬܦܪܩ. ܐܠܐ ܡܬܩܛܠܘ ܢܬܩܛܠ.
>
> *we-kul ḥermā d-maḥram min (ʾĕ)nāšā lā neṯpreq ʾellā meṯqāṭlū neṯqṭel*
>
> כָּל־חֵרֶם אֲשֶׁר יָחֳרַם מִן־הָאָדָם לֹא יִפָּדֶה מוֹת יוּמָת׃
>
> *kol-ḥäräm ʾăšär y*^{o}*ḥŏram min-hā-ʾāḏām lō(ʾ) yippaḏe*^{h} *mōṯ yūmāṯ*
>
> "None *devoted*, that may be *devoted* of men, shall be ransomed; he shall surely be put to death." (JPS)

Here again, it is the specific religious semantics of this root that reveal its Syro-Aramaic heritage in Arabic.

7. سورة الفاتحة – The First Surah of the Qur'ān

7.1 Variations of the Fātiḥa

In the previous sections, I have discussed some of the theological vocabulary of the Qur'ān and of Islam. It is has been shown that the words discussed (as well as many others) are largely borrowed from Aramaic, especially Syriac–the language of a large portion of Eastern Semitic Christianity during the time of "Muḥammad." In conclusion then, it is perhaps fitting to provide an example of a Qur'ānic text, in order to demonstrate the role of Aramaic in context. For simplicity's sake, I will take the opening Sura, the *Surat Al-Fātiḥah* (سورة الفاتحة), the "Exordium." Here I provide a literal Anglicisation and a table of notes where the borrowed words are briefly explained.

بِسْمِ ٱللَّهِ ٱلرَّحْمَٰنِ ٱلرَّحِيمِ ﴿١﴾

D C B A

ٱلْحَمْدُ لِلَّهِ رَبِّ ٱلْعَٰلَمِينَ ﴿٢﴾ ٱلرَّحْمَٰنِ ٱلرَّحِيمِ ﴿٣﴾

G F E

مَٰلِكِ يَوْمِ ٱلدِّينِ ﴿٤﴾ إِيَّاكَ نَعْبُدُ وَإِيَّاكَ

I H

نَسْتَعِينُ ﴿٥﴾ ٱهْدِنَا ٱلصِّرَٰطَ ٱلْمُسْتَقِيمَ ﴿٦﴾

صِرَٰطَ ٱلَّذِينَ أَنْعَمْتَ عَلَيْهِمْ غَيْرِ ٱلْمَغْضُوبِ

عَلَيْهِمْ وَلَا ٱلضَّآلِّينَ ﴿٧﴾

1. *bi-smi llāhi r-raḥmāni r-raḥīm*	In the name of God the merciful Merciful
2. *al-ḥamdu li-llāhi*[A] *rabbi*[B] *l-ʿālamīn*[C]	Praise be to God, the Lord of the eternities
3. *ar-raḥmāni*[D] *r-raḥīm*	The merciful Merciful
4. *māliki yawmi*[E] *d-dīn*[F]	Who will reign on the day of judgement[77]
5. *iyyāka naʿbudu*[G] *wa-iyyāka nastaʿīn*	You alone we worship and you alone we ask assistance
6. *ihdinā ṣ-ṣirāṭ*[H] *al-mustaqīm*[I]	Guide us on the straight path (=faith)
7. *ṣirāṭa l-laḏīna anʿamta ʿalayhim ġayri l-maġḍūbi ʿalayhim wa-lā ḍ-ḍāllīn*	The way of those upon whom you have bestowed your mercy, not (the way) of those who have fallen to (your) anger and who go astray

Although the Qur'ān claims to be unique and singular, its textual transmission is no more unique than that of its predecessors (scil. the Hebrew Bible and the New Testament). The notion that only one version of the text exists is an anachronistic myth and other interesting versions of the text, *in casu* Sura 1, are attested, such as the two published by Jeffery.[78] Here I give them, including his translations:

1. nuḥammidu llāha rabba l-ʿālamīn	نُحَمِّدُ ٱللهَ رَبَّ ٱلْعَالَمِينَ
2. ar-raḥmāna r-raḥīma	ٱلرَّحْمَٰنَ ٱلرَّحِيمَ
3. mal'aka yawm ad-dīn	مَلأَكَ يَوْمِ ٱلدِّينِ
4. hayyāka naʿbudu wa-yyāka nastaʿīn	هَيَّاكَ نَعْبُدُ وِيَاكَ نَسْتَعِينُ
5. turšidu sabīla l-mustaqīm	تُرْشِدُ سَبِيلَ ٱلْمُسْتَقِيمِ
6. sabīl l-laḏīna naʿʿamta ʿalayhim	سَبِيلَ ٱلَّذِينَ نَعَّمْتَ عَلَيْهِمْ
siwā l-maġḍūbi ʿalayhim wa-lā ḍ-ḍāllīna	سِوَى ٱلْمَغْضُوبِ عَلَيْهِمْ وَلَا ٱلضَّالِّينَ

We greatly praise Allāh, Lord of the worlds,
The Merciful, the Compassionate,
He who has possession of the Day of Judgment.
Thee do we worship, and on Thee do we call for help.

Thou dost direct to the path of the Upright One,
The path of those to whom Thou hast shown favor,
Not that of those with whom Thou are angered, or those who go astray.

1. bi-smi llāhi r-raḥmāni r-raḥīm	بِسْمِ ٱللَّهِ ٱلرَّحْمَٰنِ ٱلرَّحِيمِ
2. al-ḥamdu li-llāhi sayyidi l-ʿālamīna	ٱلْحَمْدُ لِلَّهِ سَيِّدِ ٱلْعَالَمِينَ
3. ar-razzāqi r-raḥīm	ٱلرَّزَّاقِ ٱلرَّحِيمِ
4. malʾaki yawm ad-dīn	مَلاَّكِ يَوْمِ ٱلدِّينِ
5. inna laka naʿbudu wa-inna laka nastaʿīnu	إِنَّ لَكَ نَعْبُدُ وَإِنَّ لَكَ نَسْتَعِينُ
6. ʾaršid-nā sabīla l-mustaqīm	أَرْشِدْنَا سَبِيلَ ٱلْمُسْتَقِيمِ
7. sabīla l-laḏīna mananta ʿalayhim	سَبِيلَ ٱلَّذِينَ مَنَنْتَ عَلَيْهِمْ
siwā l-maġḍūb ʿalayhim wa-ġayra	سِوَى ٱلْمَغْضُوبِ عَلَيْهِمْ وَغَيْرَ
ḍ-ḍāllīna	ٱلضَّالِّينَ

In the Name of Allāh, the Merciful, the Compassionate.
Raise be to Allāh, Lord of the worlds,
The Bountiful, the Compassionate,
He who has possession of the Day of Judgment,
As for us, to Thee do we worship, and to Thee we turn for help,
Direct us to the path of the Upright One,
The path of those on whom Thou hast bestowed favors,
Not that of those with whom Thou art angered,
Nor that of those who go astray.

These two versions present very interesting variations, although I will not elaborate on them here – I hope to have the chance to deal with this elsewhere. Most of the variants reflect the use of synonyms. These reveal that the textual tradition is not nearly as consistent as is suggested by believers.

Before the borrowed vocabulary of this Sura is discussed in detail, it should be pointed out that due to these loan-words and the theological concepts that underlie them, the Sura contains many *cruces interpretationis* and hence the meaning of many verses (آيات – *āyāt*) was unclear to the traditional commentators.[79]

7.2 Discussion of the individual forms

7.2.1 (=A) الله – Allāh

Allāh الله <*al-ilāhu*, "God"–see above §5.4.

7.2.2 (=B) رب – *rabb*

This lexeme from the root √*rbb* in the sense of *Rabbi* ("master, teacher") is a technical term, cf. NT ῥαββί. Without wanting to go into excessive detail here, I merely note that the semantic development of this specific meaning was completed in Aramaic. In Late Sabaean of the monotheistic period, this is attested as 𐩧𐩨 𐩺𐩠𐩵 – *rb yhd* "Lord of the Jews," as well as in Old Ethiopian as ረባን – *rabbān*, also borrowed from Aramaic. Thus, it is no surprise that we find this usage well-attested in Syriac as e.g.: ܪܒܢ – *rabbān* and ܪܒܘܠܝ – *rabbūlī* (diminutive) etc. and which are obviously loan words in Arabic (as well as their derivations, such as "to own, to control" etc.).

In passing, it should be noted that the usage of رب – *rabb* here displays the undoubtedly Christian origins of the Qur'ān and precludes an ancient Arabic monotheistic tradition that hearkens back to the mythical figure of Abraham:[80] behind the epithet "Lord" lies the name of the Hebrew deity *Yahweh* (Hebrew יהוה, the Tetragrammaton). In an earlier stage of what became Judaism, reflected by the consonantal Hebrew text of the Masoretic tradition, there was no prohibition in pronouncing the name of the deity (which is confirmed by Hebrew names such as יְשַׁעְיָהוּ – *yəšạ'yāhū* "Y. is salvation," i.e. *Isaiah* and e.g. the texts from Elephantine). In later Jewish and Samaritan tradition, this name was considered to be too holy which is reflected in the vocalisation tradition of the Masoretic text which points this word (a *Qrê pepetuum*) as יְהֹוָה, that is with the vowels of אֲדֹנָי – *ʾădōnāy* "my Lord" (which was misunderstood by the early Bible translators who thus falsely read the word as *Jehovah*).[81] Whether it was Jews or Christians who first rendered the name of the deity with Κύριος "Lord" in Greek texts such as the translation of the Hebrew Bible, the Septuagint, is not entirely clear although there was a tendency in some Greek Jewish texts to write the Tetragrammaton in Hebrew/Aramaic letters.[82] That is Judaism always remembered that the name of their God was yhwh. Although some later Christian writers were still aware if this,[83] in Christian tradition already attested by the New Testament, "Lord" (Κύριος, Syriac ܡܪܐ, ܡܪܝܐ – *mārē, māryā, mārā*) has become an epithet (and not the given name) of the Deity.[84] The fact that the Qur'ān shows no knowledge of the Jewish tradition[85] and follows Christian usage is a certain indication of this book's Semitic Christian origins (see below §7.2.9). Thus the Islamic conception of God as "Lord" and not being named *Yahweh* precludes any notion of an old Hijazi tradition or direct Jewish influence.[86]

7.2.3 (=C) علامين -*ʿālamīn*

The root √*ʿlm* in Arabic has the basic meaning "to know" > "science," cf. modern calqued forms of similar compounds ending in *-logy*: علم الاحياء – *ʿilm al-ʾāḥyāʾ* "biology," علم الإجتماع – *ʿilm al-ʾiǧtimāʿ* "sociology," علم الحساب – *ʿilm al-ḥisāb* "mathematics" etc.[87] The meaning "eternity" (sg.), "eternities" (pl.) is a borrowing from Aramaic. For the original sense of the word here, compare Ugaritic "duration" > "eternal," such as *lht wʿlmh* "now and forever," as well as the title of a deified dead King *mlk ʿlm* "eternal King" (cf. *ḥq3 ḏt* as a title of Osiris!)–very similar to the usage dealt with here, also in Hebrew וַיהוָה אֱלֹהִים אֱמֶת הוּא־אֱלֹהִים חַיִּים וּמֶלֶךְ עוֹלָם – *wạ-yhwh ʾᵉlōhīm ʾᵃmäṯ hûʾ-ʾᵉlōhīm ḥạyyīm ū-mäläḵ ʿolām* "But the Lord is the true God, he is the living God, the eternal king" (Jeremiah 10:10) andוַיִּקְרָא־שָׁם בְּשֵׁם יְהוָה אֵל עוֹלָם – *wạy-yiqrāʾ-šām bə-šēm yhwh ʾēl ʿōlām* "and there he called on the name of the Lord, the Eternal God" (Genesis 21:33; cf. also in Syriac ܒܬܘܠܬ ܥܠܡܝܢ – *bəṯūlaṯ ʿālāmīn* "Mary ever virgin," ἀειπάϱθενος). From this original sense, under influence of ***apocalypticism***, the meaning "future, or coming time" > "end time" > "eternity" developed, which also exists in the plural in Hebrew (for emphasis), for example Psalms 77:8 הַלְעוֹלָמִים יִזְנַח | אֲדֹנָי וְלֹא־יֹסִיף לִרְצוֹת עוֹד – *hạ-lə-ʿōlāmīm yiznạḥ* | *ʾᵃḏonāy wə-lōʾ-yōsīp̄ li-rəṣôṯ ʿōḏ* Has his unfailing love vanished forever? Has his promise failed for all time?" (*Statenvertaling:* "in eeuwigheden," so also lxx αἰῶνας). This semantic domain is also attested in Aramaic with this meaning, e.g. Daniel 2:20 שְׁמֵהּ דִּי־אֱלָהָא מְבָרַךְ מִן־עָלְמָא וְעַד־עָלְמָא – *šmēh dī-ʾᵉlāhāʾ məḇārạḵ min-ʿālmāʾ wə-ʿạḏ ʿālmāʾ* "Blessed be the name of God forever and ever," and is also attested in the plural. This word is used in Syriac with this meaning, however also in the further semantic development >"land" such as Matthew 4:8:

> ܬܘܒ ܕܒܪܗ ܐܟܠܩܪܨܐ ܠܛܘܪܐ ܕܛܒ ܪܡ. ܘܚܘܝܗ ܟܠܗܝܢ ܡܠܟܘܬܐ ܕܥܠܡܐ[88] ܘܫܘܒܚܗܝܢ
> *tūḇ daḇreh ʾaḵelqarṣā lə-turā də-ṭāḇ dām. wə-ḥawyeh kul-heyn-malkwāṯā d-ʿālmā wə-šuḇḥ-heyn*
> "Again, the devil taketh him up into an exceeding high mountain, and sheweth him all the kingdoms of the world and their splendour."

In the Syriac New Testament, as well as in other sources, the singular often has the meaning "world" and the plural is frequently used in the expression ܠܥܠܡ ܥܠܡܝܢ – *lə-ʿālam ʿālmīn*, lit. "eternity of eternities," such as for example in the Lord's Prayer (Matthew 6:13: εἰς τοὺς αἰῶνας) or even in the sense of "eternal life" (ܥܘܠܡܐ – *ʿullāmā*).[89] This meaning of the word has been borrowed by Late Sabaean[90] and by Old Ethiopian.[91] In the interest of brevity: God as the Lord of eternity is well attested in Syriac which presupposes the apocalyptical notion of eternity and this is the product of late Jewish/early Christian theological developments; the Arabic equivalent can only have been borrowed–whereby the customary translation "Lord of the Worlds"[92] should in light of the preceding be more properly rendered by "Lord of Eternity."[93]

7.2.4 (=D) رحمن – *raḥmān*

The term الرحمن – *ar-raḥmān* "the merciful" as an epithet of God has long been recognised as a borrowing. The noun *rḥm* in Semitic originally means "womb," also in Ugaritic, for example (with the derived connotation "woman").[94] From this, the term "motherly love" >"mercy" developed in Hebrew and Aramaic, and it also came to be used to describe a divinity, for example already at Tal Faḫariye l. 5 (*KAI*[5] 309), where it is said of the god Ḥadad: *ʾlh rḥmn zy tṣlwth ṭbh* "merciful God, to whom prayer is good."[95] It is also often used in this sense in the Hebrew Bible. In post-biblical Judaism, however, this term becomes a description of God, such as in the Tosefta (סדר נזיקין מסכת בבא קמא פרק ט,יא[96]) where it says: כל זמן שאתה רחמן הרחמן מרחם עליך – *kōl zəmān šeʾāttāh raḥmān hā-raḥmān məraḥēm ʿēleḵā* "Whenever you are merciful, the Merciful will show you mercy."[97] This term was also used to describe gods at pagan Palmyra, where it was also used as an epithet for an otherwise unnamed deity which was often worshipped together with *Allat* and *Shamash*,[98] such as *lbryk šmh lʿlmʾ ṭbʾ rḥmnʾ wtyrʾ* "May his name be blessed forever, the Good, the Merciful, and the Compassionate." In Syriac, a derived form was used–Greenfield[99] wonders whether Christian Syriac avoids this expression in reaction to the pagan use of *rḥmnʾ* and uses ܡܪܚܡܢ – *mraḥmān* instead, for example in James 5:11: ܡܛܠ ܕܡܪܚܡܢ ܗܘ ܡܪܝܐ ܘܡܪܚܦܢ – *meṭṭūl da-mraḥmān hu māryā wa-mraḥpān* (from Greek: ὅτι πολύσπλαγχνός ἐστιν ὁ Κύριος καὶ οἰκτίρμων) "for the Lord is full of compassion and mercy."[100]

In Sabaic of the late monotheistic period (cf. also Ha11 *supra* §6.3), we find forms of this root used as both an epithet and as a name for a God, which has already been shown by an inscription. Some of these are clearly Jewish, such as *CIH* 543 (note also Gar Bayt al-Ashwal 1, *supra* §6.3):

1 *[b]rk w-tbrk s^1m Rḥmnn*[101] *ḏ-b-s^1myn w-Ys^3rʾl w-*	Bless and be blessed the name of Raḥmān who is in heaven, and Israel and
2 *ʾlh-hmw rb-yhd ḏ-hrd(ʾ)ʿbd-hmw pn_1 w-*	Its God, the Lord of the Jews who helped his servant pn_1 and
3 *ʾm-hw bdm w-ḥs^2kt-hw s^2ms^1m w-ʾl-*	his mother pn_2, and his wife pn_3 and their

4 wd-hmy ḏmm w-ʾbs^{2}ʿr (w-)mṣr-	children pn_4 and pn_5 (and) pn_6
5 m w-kl bhṯ-h [...]	And all of their kin ...
6 [.]w[...]	... and ...

And other (later?) ones are apparently Christian, like the long inscription commemorating the building of the dam at Marib by Abraha, *CIH* 541 (only the relevant opening passage is cited here):

1 b-ḫyl w-[r]dʾ w-rḥ-	With the power, support and mer-
2 mt rḥmnn w-ms^{1}-	cy of the Raḥmān and his Mes-
3 ḥ-hw[102] *w-rḥ [q]ds^{1} s^{1}ṭrw*	siah and the Holy Spirit, wrote
4 n ms^{3}ndn ʾn ʾbrh ...	this inscription, I Abraha ...

As can also be seen for example in another inscription, *Ry* 508 (the ending, l. 11):

11. ... w-b-]ḫfr rḥmnn (ḏ)n ms^{1}ndn bn kl ḫs^{1}s^{1}{s^{1}}m w-mḫdʿm w-trḥm ʿly kl ʿlm rḥmnn rḥmk mrʾ ʾt	... and with the protection of Raḥmān for this inscription against harm and robbers. Because you Raḥmān are merciful for the entire world, you are the merciful Lord.

In this last inscription, we see the use of the three loan termini discussed here: *rb*, *ʿlm* and *Raḥmān*. In some inscriptions, a pagan deity might be referred to instead of or alongside the Judeo-Christian God. It is also important to note that in Sabaic inscriptions which refer to Judaism and Christianity, an originally Aramaic term was used to describe God (note too the middle Sabaic text,+/- 3rd cent. ad, *CIH* 40:5 where reference is made to a deity *rḥm s^{1}gḥ bʿl s^{3}ydm*). As I have argued previously, I do not believe that Sabaic culture had any significant influence on Islam; rather we are dealing with a borrowed term for "God." الرحمـنِ الرحِيم – *ar-raḥmān ar-raḥīm* then, should be translated as either "the most gracious Merciful One" or "the merciful Raḥmān" (كرياليسون ? – *kryʾlyswn*). The usage described here thus has a long history and its Qurʾānic meaning must derive from (Judaeo-)Christian Aramaic divine nomenclature.

7.2.5 (=E) يوم- *yawm*

The lexeme يوم – *yawm* "day" is doubtlessly a genuine Arabic word. Its eschatological semantics, here, in the sense of "day of judgement" (يوم الدين – *yawm ad-dīn*), "day of the resurrection" (يوم القيامة – *yawm al-qiyāma*; cf. Syriac *qyāmtā*, *qayyāmtā* "Resurrection," e.g. Matthew 27:53 [... μετὰ τὴν ἔγερσιν αὐτοῦ...], Peshitta: ܘܢܦܩܘ. ܘܒܬܪ ܩܝܡܬܗ ܥܠܘ ܠܡܕܝܢܬܐ ܩܕܝܫܬܐ. ܘܐܬܚܙܝܘ ܠܣܓܝܐܐ; cf. also §7.2.10 *infra*), or "the last days," must be a borrowed term, as such presuppose the notion apocalyptic prophecy which was especially prevalent in early forms of Christianity (re. the Second Coming of Jesus).[103]

7.2.6 (=F) الدين – *ad-dīn*

The word الدين – *ad-dīn* used here meaning "the (final) judgement," but also in the sense of God as "judge." Although the semantics of judgement as they relate to this root are indeed very old, as can be seen e.g. from Ugaritic *dn* and Akkadian *diānu/dânu*, the usage of the term to indicate the *final judgement*, or of God as the *judge* on the last days, is a product of the developments touched upon above in 7.2.5. The understanding of God as a "judge" (ܕܝܳܢܳܐ/דיין – *dayān(ā)*) as well as the expectation of a "day of judgement" (Hebrew: יום הדין – *yōm had-dīn* /Aramaic יום דינא – *yōm dīnā*) was quite common among contemporary Jewish and Christian circles and was thus unsurprisingly also borrowed by Old Ethiopian as ደይን – *dayən* "damnation." It is indicative of borrowing that the Arabic term with the meaning "judge" is only used as an epithet of God on the Last Day–in Syro-Aramaic[104] it is the general term for judge, analogous to the generic Arabic lexeme القاضي – *al-qāḍī*. The restricted eschatological usage of this term to describe God at the Final Judgement illustrates that this (late Christian) concept was borrowed along with its vocabulary.

Here it should be noted that in Arabic الدين – *ad-dīn* can also mean "religion" (even if not yet in the modern sense as a terminus technicus; not only with regard to Islam as "the Religion," but also used significantly in Arabic Christianity). The restrictive semantics here also indicate a borrowing from Syriac ܕܝܢ – *dīn* / ܕܐܝܢ – *dayn* "religio" (cf. Brockelmann, *Lexicon* 151 s.v.) which in turn was borrowed from Iranian,[105] cf. Avestan *daēnā* "insight," "revelation" > "conscience" > "religion" (> Farsi دين – *dīn*; also Classical Armenian դէն – *den*). Thus while the root √*dyn* may well be Arabic, the technical theological meanings of God as the "Judge" at the "Final Judgement" and its use to denote (the revealed) 'Religion' are clearly borrowings from Syriac where the former meanings had their theological semantic evolution and the latter meaning was borrowed from Persian.

7.2.7 (=G) عبد – *'abd*

The root √*'bd* "to serve," from which the lexeme عبد – *'abd* "slave" comes, is once again a true Arabic word. The semantics of slavery, also attested in e.g. Hebrew עבד – *'ābäd* (the verb is expressed in the Peshitta as ܦܠܚ – *plaḥ*), are well-attested in Semitic, but are not directly relevant here. In Aramaic, this root normally forms the general verb for "to do, to make" (Hebr. עָשָׂה – *'āśā^h*,

Arab. فعل – *faʿala*), though in Syriac[106] we also see an expanded meaning for this root in the semantic domain of religion. Here, in this technical sense, it can mean "to celebrate" and "to worship, to adore," such as in Acts 20:16: ܕܐܢ ܡܫܟܚܐ: ܝܘܡܐ ܕܦܢܛܝܩܘܣܛܝ ܒܐܘܪܫܠܡ ܢܥܒܕܝܘܗܝ. – *d-'en meškḥā: yawmā d-penṭiqāwsṭī b-'urišlem neʿbdīwhy* "… if it were possible for him, to be at Jerusalem the day of Pentecost," and which can also have the meaning "ordination, consecration."[107] It would thus seem that here and in similar cases the cultic activity of human adoration of the Deity is intended, i.e. "to worship" and not "to serve (as a slave)."

7.2.8 (=H) صراط – *ṣirāt*

The lexeme صراط – *ṣirāṭ* "path" is certainly a loan-word from Latin *strata* >στϱάτα >(ܐܣܛܪܛܐ – *esṭrāṭā)* > صراط- *ṣirāṭ*,[108] a word that entered the region with the Roman road-building occupiers, cf. also the English word "street," with the same origins. The word is common in the Qur'ān and often appears with the adjective مستقيم – *mustaqīm*. It can also be used in the figurative sense to mean a teaching, such as those of Moses (Qur'ān 37:118) وهديناهما الصراط المستقيم – *wa-hadaynā-humā ṣ-ṣirāṭa l-mustaqīma*, or significantly Jesus (3:51) إن الله ربي وربكم فاعبدوه هذا صراط مستقيم - *'inna llāha rabbī wa-rabbukum fa-ʿbudūhu hāḏā ṣirāṭun mustaqīmun,* as well as in the general sense (7: 16) قال فبما أغويتني لأقعدن لهم صراطك المستقيم – *qāla fa-bi-mā 'aġwaytanī la-'aqʿudanna lahum ṣirāṭaka l-mustaqīma*. What is actually meant by the "straight path" is not mentioned here; in this sense it is similar in meaning to شريعة – *šarīʿa* (e.g. 45:18) >"legislation." Typically the *path* is taken to mean the *path of Islam*, but this is practically impossible from a historical perspective[109]– and would in any case be an anachronism–a reference here to Islam is just as inconceivable as Qur'ān 2:2 ذلك الكتاب لا ريب فيه هدى للمتقين – *ḏālika l-kitābu lā rayba fīhi hudan li-l-muttaqīna* referring to the Qur'ān we have today.

Since a critical edition of the Qur'ān still does not exist, as I mentioned earlier, we can neither assess nor rely on *variae lectiones*. Of interest here though are the texts with significant variant readings published by Jeffery and cited above.

Both of these texts use a common synonym for صراط – *ṣirāṭ*, namely سبيل – *sabīl*, a word which too is borrowed from Aramaic. In Syriac, ܫܒܝܠܐ – *šḇīlā* renders the Greek κανών ("rule, standard, principle;" > قانون) in Galatians 6:16 and Philippians 3:16, but also τϱίβος in Matthew 3:3 "Prepare the *Way* for the Lord," and τϱοχιά in Hebrews 12:13—so "path" here is meant in the figurative sense of "path" or "way of life," i.e., "route of salvation." The Greek terms are synonyms for ὁδός, a lexeme which can also describe Christian beliefs and the Christian *Way* of life in the New Testament, such as in John

14:6.[110] The latter Greek word is typically translated by ܐܘܪܚܐ – *'ūrḥā* in the Peshitta, which is a synonym in Syriac for ܫܒܝܠܐ – *šḇīlā*.
This latter Greek word, however, is also used to describe the new faith, cf. Acts 9:2: Saul wants to apprehend those who "belonged to the Way" (ὅπως ἐάν τινας εὕϱῃ τῆς ὁδοῦ ὄντας, ἄνδϱας τε καὶ γυναῖκας = ܕܪܕܢ ܒܣܗܕܐ ܐܘܪܚܐ ܓܒܪ̈ܐ ܐܘ ܢܫ̈ܐ – *d-rāḏen b-sāhḏē 'ūrḥā gaḇrē 'aw neše'* – "so that if he found any there who belonged to the Way, whether men or women ..."), to take them as captives to Jerusalem, cf. also 19:23 (Ἐγένετο δὲ κατὰ τὸν καιϱὸν ἐκεῖνον τάϱαχος οὐκ ὀλίγος πεϱὶ τῆς ὁδοῦ), and also the alleged statement made by Paul in 22:4: ὅς ταύτην τὴν ὁδὸν ἐδίωξα ἄχϱι θανάτου θανάτου δεσμεύων καὶ παϱαδιδοὺς εἰς φυλακὰς ἄνδϱας τε καὶ γυναικὰς (ܘܠܗܕܐ ܐܘܪܚܐ ܪܕܦܬ ܥܕܡܐ ܠܡܘܬܐ܆ ܟܕ ܐܣܪ ܗܘܝܬ ܘܡܫܠܡ ܗܘܝܬ ܠܒܝܬ ܐܣܝܪ̈ܐ ܓܒܪ̈ܐ ܘܢܫ̈ܐ – *wa-l-hāḏē 'ūrḥā reḏpeṯ 'ḏammā l-mawtā: kaḏ 'āsar ʰwīṯ wə-mašlemʰwīṯ l-beyṯ 'asīrē gaḇrē wə-nešē* "And I persecuted this way unto the death, binding and delivering into prisons both men and women"). It is important to note here that at Paul's trial in chapter 24, Tertullus describes him as the πϱωτοστάτην τε τῆς τῶν Ναζωϱα ίων αἱϱέσεως in v. 5, to which Paul replies in v. 14 ὁμολογῶ δὲ τοῦτό σοι, ὅτι κατὰ τὴν ὁδὸν [Peshitta: ܝܘܠܦܢ̈ܐ – *yūlpānē* "doctrine"] ἣν λέγουσιν αἵϱεσιν οὕτω λατϱεύω τῷ πατϱῴῳ Θεῷ, πιστεύων πᾶσι τ οἷς κατὰ τὸν νόμον καὶ τοῖς ἐν τοῖς πϱοφήταις γεγϱαμμένοις. Here we see the "Way" as an early self-description for Semitic Christians. Their opponents though, first the Jews, and later Greco-Romans, described them as Nazarenes.[111] Seeming confirmation for this proposal is given by 19:36:

وَإِنَّ ٱللَّهَ رَبِّي وَرَبُّكُمْ فَٱعْبُدُوهُ هَٰذَا صِرَٰطٌ مُّسْتَقِيمٌ

wa-inna l-laha rabbī warabbukum fa'budūhu hāḏā ṣirāṭun mustaqīmun
[Jesus said] "And lo! Allāh is my Lord and your Lord. So serve Him. That is the right path." (Pickthall)

It is of course obvious that the Qur'ān was revealed spontaneously from heaven above just as much as was the Hebrew Bible or the New Testament. The holy book of Islam presumes a prior knowledge of oriental Christianity, as the discussion in the previous sections should have made clear, especially in as much as that the Qur'ān shows a definite familiarity with the Peshitta. Thus if the roots of the Qur'ān are to be found in a (heterodox) current of Semitic Christianity–something which I am only briefly able to touch upon in this article–then the mysterious "Path" is self explanatory: it is a religious self-description.

7.2.9 Excursus النصراني "Nazarene" and الأنصار "Anṣar"

At this juncture, it is worthwhile to briefly discuss the term "Nazarene." As Pritz[112] has already explained, an inhabitant of Nazareth would not have been described as Ναζωϱαῖος,[113] rather the term stems from Isaiah 11:1: "And there shall come forth a rod out of the stem of Jesse (יִשָׁי – *yišāy*), and a branch (וְנֵצֶר – *wə-nēṣär*) shall grow out of his roots."[114] This term, along with Ἰεσσαῖοι (> Isais, Jesse),[115] were terms used to denote indigenous Christianity before it became Graecised and the name Χϱιστιανός became common.[116] However, Ναζωϱαῖος was preserved in the Semitic languages as the word for Christianity, such as Arabic النصراني – *al-naṣrānī* and Hebrew נוצרי – *nōṣrī*.[117] Although the root √*nṣr* in Arabic has the well-attested meaning "to help, to support" alongside its "Christian" meanings and derivations, I have long wondered whether the الأنصار – *al-'anṣār*, the Medinan helpers/supporters of "Muḥammad" in the Qur'ān, were actually Christians–perhaps they were about as Muslim as Jesus was from Nazareth?[118]

Although interpreting الأنصار – *al-'anṣār* as "Christian" might at first seem outrageous; a second look in light of the context of its *Sitz im Leben* in Late Antiquity could make this hypothesis entirely plausible. Both attestations of this word in the Qur'ān (9:100,117), are found together with المهاجرون – *al-muhāğirūn* "émigrés,"[119] and taken in their own right offer no bearing at all for their interpretation in later Islamic exegetical traditions. Sura 9:100:

وَالسَّابِقُونَ الْأَوَّلُونَ مِنَ الْمُهَاجِرِينَ وَالْأَنصَارِ وَالَّذِينَ اتَّبَعُوهُم بِإِحْسَانٍ رَّضِيَ اللَّهُ
عَنْهُمْ وَرَضُوا عَنْهُ وَأَعَدَّ لَهُمْ جَنَّاتٍ تَجْرِي تَحْتَهَا الْأَنْهَارُ خَالِدِينَ فِيهَا أَبَدًا ذَٰلِكَ الْفَوْزُ
الْعَظِيمُ

> *wa-s-sābiqūna l-'awwalūna mina l-muhāğirīna wa-l-'anṣāri wa-llaḏīna taba-ʿūhum bi-'iḥsānin raḍiya llāhu ʿanhum wa-raḍū ʿanhu wa-'aʿadda lahum ğannātin tağrī taḥtahā l-'anhāru ḫālidīna fīhā 'abadan ḏālika l-fawzu l-ʿaẓīmu*
>
> "And the first forerunners [in the faith] among the Muhajireen and the Ansar and those who followed them with good conduct–Allāh is pleased with them and they are pleased with Him, and He has prepared for them gardens beneath which rivers flow, where they will abide forever. That is the great attainment."

Sura 9:117:

لَّقَد تَّابَ اللَّهُ عَلَى النَّبِيِّ وَالْمُهَاجِرِينَ وَالْأَنصَارِ الَّذِينَ اتَّبَعُوهُ فِي سَاعَةِ الْعُسْرَةِ مِن بَعْدِ
مَا كَادَ يَزِيغُ قُلُوبُ فَرِيقٍ مِّنْهُمْ ثُمَّ تَابَ عَلَيْهِمْ إِنَّهُ بِهِمْ رَءُوفٌ رَّحِيمٌ

> *la-qad tāba llāhu ʿalā n-nabiyyi wa-l-muhāğirīna wa-l-ʾanṣāri lladīna ttabaʿūhu fī sāʿati l-ʿusrati min baʿdi mā kāda yazīġu qulūbu farīqin minhum ṯumma tāba ʿalayhim ʾinnahū bihim raʾʾūfun raḥīmun*
>
> "Allāh has already forgiven the Prophet and the *Muhajireen* and the *Ansar* who followed him in the hour of difficulty after the hearts of a party of them had almost inclined [to doubt], and then He forgave them. Indeed, He was to them Kind and Merciful."

We can only conclude from these verses that both were pious, God-fearing groups of people. There is no further information provided by the Qur'ān itself. The later traditions referring to a possible flight of the prophet "Muḥammad," along with faithful followers (المهاجرون - *al-muhāğirūn*) to "Medina" (المدينة), a city *sui generis*, are just as irrelevant here as is for example the *Liber de infantia* for research on the historical Jesus. Examining the morpho-phonology of the Arabic root √*nṣr* discussed here, it can only be concluded that it is a borrowing. The semantics "to help, to support" would seem to be a secondary denominal derivation from الأنصار - *al-ʾanṣār* and thus presuppose later Islamic tradition. It is not the customary Arabic word for "to aid, to help" and usually only means such in a theological context (especially the *ʾAnṣār* which always only refers to the supposed Medinan *helpers* of "Muḥammad"). The original meaning of this root in Arabic was certainly "to Christianise, to convert to Christianity." Unsurprisingly then, in the Qur'ān this root is also frequently used to describe Christians, such as 2:111:

> لَن يَدۡخُلَ ٱلۡجَنَّةَ إِلَّا مَن كَانَ هُودًا أَوۡ نَصَٰرَىٰ
>
> *lan yadḫula l-ğannata ʾillā man kāna hūdan ʾaw naṣārā*
>
> "None will enter Paradise except one who is a Jew or a Christian."

2:113:

> وَقَالَتِ ٱلۡيَهُودُ لَيۡسَتِ ٱلنَّصَٰرَىٰ عَلَىٰ شَيۡءٖ وَقَالَتِ ٱلنَّصَٰرَىٰ لَيۡسَتِ ٱلۡيَهُودُ عَلَىٰ شَيۡءٖ وَهُمۡ يَتۡلُونَ ٱلۡكِتَٰبَۗ كَذَٰلِكَ قَالَ ٱلَّذِينَ لَا يَعۡلَمُونَ مِثۡلَ قَوۡلِهِمۡۚ فَٱللَّهُ يَحۡكُمُ بَيۡنَهُمۡ يَوۡمَ ٱلۡقِيَٰمَةِ فِيمَا كَانُواْ فِيهِ يَخۡتَلِفُونَ
>
> *wa-qālati l-yahūdu laysati n-naṣārā ʿalā šayʾin wa-qālati n-naṣārā laysati l-yahūdu ʿalā šayʾin wa-hum yatlūna l-kitāba ka-ḏālika qāla lladīna lā yaʿlamūna miṯla qawlihim fa-llāhu yaḥkumu baynahum yawma l-qiyāmati fī-mā kānū fīhi yaḫtalifūna*

> "The Jews say 'The Christians have nothing [true] to stand on,' and the Christians say, 'The Jews have nothing to stand on,' although they [both] recite the Scripture. Thus the polytheists speak the same as their words. But Allāh will judge between them on the Day of Resurrection concerning that over which they used to differ."

My own rendition:

> "The Jews say: 'The Christians don't have [anything/a leg] to stand on.' The Christians say: 'The Jews don't have [anything/a leg] to stand on." Though they (both) are based on (the Holy) Scripture. Even the ignorant [~ pagans?] express themselves in a similar way. On the Day of Resurrection, God will judge among them regarding their controversy."

Or 3:67:

مَا كَانَ إِبْرَاهِيمُ يَهُودِيًّا وَلَا نَصْرَانِيًّا

> *mā kāna ʾibrāhīmu yahūdiyyan wa-lā naṣrāniyyan*
> "Abraham was neither a Jew nor a Christian."

The first meaning, "to help," might also be found in Late Sabaean 𐩬𐩮𐩧 – *nṣr*,[120] where 𐩮 /ṣ/ can be confused with 𐩼 /ẓ/. However, this is a lexeme that is only attested in late texts, and which was mostly used in a fixed expression to describe a god, often the above mentioned *Raḥmān*, such as in *CIH* 540:81f:

> *b-nṣr w-rdʾ ʾlhn b-ʿl* s^{1}*myn w-ʾrḍn*
> "With the help and support of God (Allāh!), who is above heaven and earth."

Here though, the meaning "protection," or verbally "to preserve, to guard, to protect" is conceivable and in light of the comparative evidence from Hebrew, Akkadian, etc. would be seemingly more appropriate. Since the later Aramaic realisation of this root is √*nṭr*[121] and it is attested in Ugaritic as *n-ǵ-r*,[122] the proto-Semitic root can be presumed to have been *√*nẓr*. This then would also be the expected form of the root in Classical Arabic. And in fact, such a form is well-attested, namely نظر "to behold" etc.; note also correspondingly Gəʿəz ነጸረ - *naṣṣara* "to view" (መነጽር – *manaṣər* "spectacles"). The semantic development then appears to have been "to look, to see, to behold" >"to protect" (cf. *(re)garder* in French and *to watch* in English). Hence the Arabic root √*nṣr*, on account of its phonetic shape, must be a borrowing.

Arabic must therefore have borrowed this root as a designation for Christianity, as did other Semitic languages, and then later reinterpreted it in the sense of "to help." As mentioned above, and already noted by Eusebius, the origins of this root are the Hebrew noun נֵצֶר – *näṣär*.[123] "Judaeo-Christians"[124] called *Nazarenes* as well as a sub-sect of them, the *Ebionites*, are well-known in Church History as Christians, who to some extent still felt bound by the Jewish ("Mosaic"—also an anachronism) Law.[125] Often, they are mentioned in connexion with the so-called "Hebrew" Gospel, τὸ καθ' Ἑβραίους εὐαγγέλιον. According to the preserved testimonies,[126] this document was supposedly similar to the canonical Gospel of Matthew, apparently a collection of Jesus' logia written in Hebrew. This gospel, only preserved in fragmentary quotations of some Church Fathers,[127] is by all accounts originally identical to what later became known as the "Gospel of the Nazarenes"[128] and the "Gospel of the Ebionites,"[129] although no witnesses from these groups themselves have survived, but only (hostile) views and quotes as preserved by Church Fathers. It is important to remember in this regard that there were many manifestations of Christianity during the first few centuries ad, before that what became orthopraxis could establish itself. It is probably more appropriate to speak of "Christianities," as is evident from the work of heresiologists, such as Epiphanius of Salamis, a contemporary of SS Augustine and of Jerome, who wrote the *Panarion*. According to these few, pejorative, and often secondary accounts, the Nazarenes, among others, were Jewish Christians. The main difference between their sect and the emerging (Greek-influenced) orthodoxy was their continuing adherence to Jewish customs.

This is not the place to deal with the native Christianities of the Syro-Palestinian world during Byzantine Late Antiquity–a field of study that is in any case beyond the expertise of this author.[130] The evidence is in any case by all accounts scarce and often confusing. In the citation from Epiphanius given above, it is said that originally "all Christians were called Nazarenes" (πάντες δὲ Χριστιανοὶ Ναζωραῖοι τότε ὡσαύτως ἐκαλοῦντο). However, here he lists them as one of sixty Christian heresies, between the Cerinthians (Κήρινθιανοὶ)[131] and the Ebionites (Ἐβιωναῖοι), in accordance with his assessment of when they came into existence. One of course must exercise due caution when employing such sources besides their depreciatory nature, we can no longer ascertain and assess the sources used.[132] Although Epiphanius undoubtedly saw and read "heretical" scriptures himself, which will be discussed in due course, he appears in most cases to give preference to Nicaeophile informants, usually not because of any greater reliability of their reports, but because of their orthodox views. Furthermore, using these accounts, it is also difficult to assess the extent of the alleged heresies numerically and chronologically.

The three heretical traditions just mentioned have in common using the said "Gospel according to the Hebrews," an adherence to Jewish customs, such as circumcision. The Cerinthians (*Pan.* i.29) in addition distinguished between "Jesus" and the "Christ" ("Adoptionism")—Jesus was a common man, the child of Mary and Joseph, whereas Christ (i.e. the Messiah, the "anointed one") came into him at the former's baptism and departed from him at his crucifixion, without thole. The most orthodox group of the three were seemingly the Nazarenes. In terms of their Christology, they were in fact Jews (ὄντες μὲν κατὰ τὸ γένος Ἰουδαῖοι καὶ τῷ νόμῳ προσανέχοντες καὶ περιτομὴν κεκτημένοι–28.5), who believed in Christ.[133] The Ebionites, a branch of the Nazarenes, according to Epiphanius, were similar to them; however, they lived according to stricter purity requirements (they were supposedly also vegetarian) and one group by this name believed in the virgin birth of Jesus.[134] Furthermore, they supposedly also rejected consuming wine.[135] There were supposedly also other similar sects, such as those of the Assyrian Tatians (Τατιανός; idem, sub i.46).

The rejection of Paul[136] among these groups (re. Baur's "Petrine" Christianity) and in Epiphanius' "refutation" 5:2–4 is a common recurring element in such descriptions. In this account, a certain inaccuracy is also noticeable, for example things that are ascribed to the *Nazarenes* by Epiphanius are attributed to the Ebionites by Irenaeus in his work *Adversus Hæreses*,[137] a source used by both Epiphanius and Eusebius. In all likelihood, this has to do with Epiphanius' classification and not actual contemporary self-descriptions – all of these groups could have described themselves as Nazarenes, which Epiphanius was aware of.[138] Also common among these groups, as mentioned, is the use of a supposedly Hebrew *original version* (which is likely better understood as Aramaic in this time[139]) of the Gospel of Matthew *Hebraice*.[140] The Ebionites are said to have used nothing else but this text.[141] At least some of the Nazarenes also made use of only *one* Gospel, which is always described as a Semitic composition.

Although an attempt to precisely define the respective doctrine(s) of this/these sect(s) based on surviving testimonies, the previous observations are of seemingly unanimous and of considerable significance. We see that these Judaeo-Christians adhered to some extent to Jewish laws, including circumcision and the rejection of unclean meat, along with some particular views concerning the nature of Jesus Christ. When we consider the Qur'ānic view of these issues, which cannot have originated *ex nihilo* and show signs of having a long and accepted tradition, it is clear that these must have originated among such milieux. A case in point is the Docetic or perhaps Gnostic Christology found in 4:157–158 (on which see G. Said Reynolds, "The Muslim Jesus: Dead or alive?" *BSOAS* 72 (2009): 237–258) in which Christ is depicted as one who shewed the "Way of God" rather than being the Redeemer:

لوَقَوْلِهِمْ إِنَّا قَتَلْنَا الْمَسِيحَ عِيسَى ابْنَ مَرْيَمَ رَسُولَ اللَّهِ وَمَا قَتَلُوهُ وَمَا صَلَبُوهُ وَلَٰكِن
شُبِّهَ لَهُمْ ۚ وَإِنَّ الَّذِينَ اخْتَلَفُوا فِيهِ لَفِي شَكٍّ مِّنْهُ ۚ مَا لَهُم بِهِ مِنْ عِلْمٍ إِلَّا اتِّبَاعَ الظَّنِّ ۚ وَمَا قَتَلُوهُ
يَقِينًا بَل رَّفَعَهُ اللَّهُ إِلَيْهِ ۚ وَكَانَ اللَّهُ عَزِيزًا حَكِيمًا

"And because of their saying: We slew the Messiah, Jesus son of Mary, Allāh's messenger–they slew him not nor crucified him, but it appeared so unto them; and lo! Those who disagree concerning it are in doubt thereof; they have no knowledge thereof save pursuit of a conjecture; they slew him not for certain. But Allāh took him up to Himself. Allāh was ever Mighty, Wise." (Pickthall)

We must though bear in mind that we don't know of every such sect and their doctrines, nor are testimonies by these groups themselves preserved, and the accounts of heresiologists on the Nazarenes stop *grosso modo* in the fifth century. This, however, does not mean that such "heresies" ceased to exist, but only that combating other ones which posed more serious threats to the by then established Orthodoxy became more urgent. Besides the fact that both the Qur'ān and Islamic tradition preserve Jewish tradition and a non-divine Christology, especially the former's usage of the loan-word mentioned above, الإنجيل – *al-'inǧīl* is notable in light of the preceding especially since in the Qur'ān it is only ever used in the singular (although Arabic has a perfectly sound broken plural, namely الأناجيل – *al-'anāǧīl*). This word is naturally frequent in the Qur'ān, for example, in Sura 5:46:

وَقَفَّيْنَا عَلَىٰ آثَارِهِم بِعِيسَى ابْنِ مَرْيَمَ مُصَدِّقًا لِّمَا بَيْنَ يَدَيْهِ مِنَ التَّوْرَاةِ وَآتَيْنَاهُ الْإِنجِيلَ
فِيهِ هُدًى وَنُورٌ وَمُصَدِّقًا لِّمَا بَيْنَ يَدَيْهِ مِنَ التَّوْرَاةِ وَهُدًى وَمَوْعِظَةً لِّلْمُتَّقِي

wa-qaffaynā ʿalā 'āṯārihim bi-ʿīsā bni maryama muṣaddiqan limā bayna yadayhi mina t-tawrāti wa-'ātaynāhu l-'inǧīla fīhi hudan wa-nūrun wa-muṣaddiqan li-mā bayna yadayhi mina t-tawrāti wa-hudan wa-mawiẓatan lil-muttaqīna

"And We sent, following in their footsteps [scil. The Hebrew prophets], Jesus, the son of Mary, confirming that which came before him in the Torah; and We gave him the Gospel, in which was guidance and light and confirming that which preceded it of the Torah as guidance and instruction for the righteous."

The exclusive usage of the singular form strongly indicates that only one Gospel was used by the writers of the Qur'ān and not the four "canonical" (an anachronism here) Ευαγγέλια, something that cannot be attributed to coincidence—although this could at least theoretically also be explained by the use of Tatian's *Diatessaron*.[142]

Another point of interest regarding this connexion is the geographical placement of these groups. Epiphanius places both the Nazarenes[143] and the Ebionites[144] in the Transjordan (cf. §0 *supra*) at Pella (*Taqabat Fahl*), in the Decapolis (after a flight from Jerusalem), Paraea (Abila in Moab, today *Abil ez-Zeit*), Kokabe in Qarnaim, specifically Ashtaroth (cf. Genesis 14:5), as well as in Coele-Syria[145] around the Beroea (today Aleppo) and in Arabia (scil. Petraea) in general. This brings us, as was noted at the beginning of this article, to the region of the Nabataeans, also that of the Ghassanids and Lakhmids, the area in which Qur'ānic Arabic and Arabic script emerged. A further remark of Epiphanius is also of importance in this respect. In his polemic against the persistence of circumcision after the death of Christ (30:26ff.), he notes that this custom was also prevalent among other sects (30:33–cf. already Herodotus, ii.104; Josephus, *Contra Apionem* i.22): ἀλλὰ καὶ οἱ Σαρακηνοὶ οἱ καὶ Ἰσμαηλῖται περιτομὴν ἔχουσι καὶ Σαμαρεῖται [καὶ Ἰουδαῖοι] καὶ Ἰδουμαῖοι καὶ Ὁμηρῖται "The Saracens, too, also called Ishmaelites …" From this, we can establish that the *Saracens* (not Ἄραβες!) at this time did not yet belong to these groups, but on the other hand, the association with Ishmael already existed.

The Arabic usage of theologically loaded terms dealt with here, صراط – *ṣirāṭ* ~ Syriac ܫܒܝܠܐ – *šḇīlā* ~ Greek τροχιά or ὁδός "path," i.e. "Christianity," الأنصار – *al-'anṣār* <Greek Ναζωραῖοι "Nazarenes," i.e. "Christians," الإنجيل – *al-'inǧīl* <Greek (τὸ κατὰ Ματθαῖον) εὐαγγέλιον "Gospel (of Matthew)" taken together, including their placement in Arabia Petraea, where the language and script used in the Qur'ān must have also emerged, form a strong body of evidence, or as Tor Andrae noted:

> L'idée de révélation chez Mahomet témoigne donc d'une parente avec la doctrine ébionite-manichéenne, qui ne peut être fortuite.[146]

Indeed, some memory of this tradition may be preserved in Islamic literature, in the *ḥadīṯ* (*Ṣaḥīḥ al-Bukhārī* i.1.3) relating to the commencement of "Muḥammad's" prophecy, when it is related that Kahdijah took her husband to her cousin Waraqah ibn Nawfal ibn Asad ibn 'Abd al-'Uzza (ورقه بن نوفل بن أسد بن عبد العزّى بن قصي القرشي) who confirms the prophethood of the Messenger of God: هذا الناموس الذي نزل الله على موسى "This is the law[147] which God had sent down to Moses …" Previously, he is introduced:

بِهِ خَدِيجَةُ حَتَّى أَتَتْ بِهِ وَرَقَةَ بْنَ نَوْفَلِ بْنِ أَسَدِ بْنِ عَبْدِ الْعُزَّى ابْنَ عَمِّ خَدِيجَةَ ـ وَكَانَ
امْرَأً تَنَصَّرَ فِي الْجَاهِلِيَّةِ، وَكَانَ يَكْتُبُ الْكِتَابَ الْعِبْرَانِيَّ، فَيَكْتُبُ مِنَ الإِنْجِيلِ
بِالْعِبْرَانِيَّةِ مَا شَاءَ اللَّهُ أَنْ يَكْتُبَ، وَكَانَ شَيْخًا كَبِيرًا قَدْ عَمِيَ

"Khadija then accompanied him (scil. "Muḥammad") to her cousin Waraqah bin Naufal bin ʾAsad bin ʿAbdul ʿUzza, who, during the "Days of Ignorance" (*ǧāhiliyyah*) converted to Christianity (*tanaṣṣara*) and used to write the book with Hebrew letters. He would write from the Gospel in Hebrew as much as Allāh wished him to write. He was an old man and had lost his eyesight."

Although this tradition is not unanimous, as elsewhere the Gospel he read is described as being in Arabic (iv.55.605, cf. nearly identical ix.87. 111):

وَكَانَ رَجُلاً تَنَصَّرَ يَقْرَأُ الإِنْجِيلَ بِالْعَرَبِيَّةِ

"He was a Christian convert and used to read the Gospel in Arabic."

This is also found in *Ṣaḥīḥ Muslim* (I.301/160a):

وَكَانَ امْرَأً تَنَصَّرَ فِي الْجَاهِلِيَّةِ وَكَانَ يَكْتُبُ الْكِتَابَ الْعَرَبِيَّ وَيَكْتُبُ مِنَ الإِنْجِيلِ
بِالْعَرَبِيَّةِ مَا شَاءَ اللَّهُ أَنْ يَكْتُبَ وَكَانَ شَيْخًا كَبِيرًا قَدْ عَمِيَ

"And he was the man who had converted Christianity in the "Days of Ignorance" and he used to write books in Arabic and, therefore, wrote the Gospel in Arabic as God willed that he should write."

Whatever the historicity of these accounts are,[148] they offer some confirmation for what has been set out in the preceding, including the revelations to the رسول الله being thought of as being in the Judaeo-Christian tradition along with the use of one Gospel.

Why then did later, a new cult, namely Islam emerge? The answer is relatively simple. Concrete accounts by the Church Fathers regarding the Nazarenes *cum suis* largely cease during the course of the fifth century ad, i.e. after Theodoret Cyrensis; later references such as by Eugippus Abbas Africanus, Isidore of Seville, Paschasius Radbertus (who coined the term "evangelium Nazarenorum") were largely copied from the older authors quoted in the preceding.[149] In most cases, it is assumed that these by all accounts relatively small Judaeo-Christian sects experienced a quiet and well-deserved death and thence disappeared from history entirely. However, if one considers the vehemence with which John Chrysostom, Bishop of Antioch in the fourth century, combated these groups in his surviving homilies, it would indeed be surprising if they had actually disappeared so suddenly, nigh spontaneously.[150] The small number of Nazarene Jewish Christians mentioned by the Church Fathers (Justin and Origen use the symbolic figure[151] of 144,000 for the entire Roman Empire), are clearly programmatic and secondary. If we look at the flourishing of Christian communities of different types in Coele-Syria however during the first few centuries (von Harnack, *op. cit.* 660–682) as well as the movement toward Arabia (idem, *op. cit.* 699–705; Briquel-Chatonnet *art. cit.*), we can only be puzzled, as was von Harnack (p. 72). He ascribes the surviving image of the circumstances of the time, handed down through the church history, to the fact that "in gewisser Weise … ja das Christentum bis auf den heutigen Tag griechisch geblieben <ist>" ("In a certain way … Christianity has indeed remained Greek until today").[152]

In my opinion, the stress on Hellenism and its influence is understandable for von Harnack's time, but nonetheless still too strongly emphasised. From a historical perspective, it would seem that the later success of Islam in this region was because for a large part the inhabitants of Coele-Syria had no affinity for Greek-influenced (Orthodox) Christianity. Inland, however, in the Transjordan, on the borders of the Arabian Desert, there where the Greek influence was not as prominent as it was in regions closer to the Mediterranean coast, there was no reason why a Jewish-Semitic Christianity could not have survived and even flourished in this area until the seventh century, much as did other regional "heresies" such as Arianism in Germania or Donatism in Africa.

Even after the fifth century, especially after the Council of Chalcedon in 451, Theodoret's (393–457) "*Arabia hæresium ferax,*" Wansbrough's *Sectarian Milieu*, continued to apply. The struggle between pro- and anti-Chalcedonian elements continued to be fought out at many levels in the East. Various attempts were made to re-unite the Church. There were meetings with anti-Chalcedonians in Constantinople in 532 (the "Conversations with Syriac Orthodoxy"), Justinian's efforts in the next decade to have the "Three Chapters" condemned and then the Second (Fifth Ecumenical) Council of Constantinople in 553 (which recognised the hypostatic union of Christ as two natures, one divine and one human, united in one person with neither confusion nor division) by which Justinian hoped to reunite Chalcedonians and Monophysites in the East, but which really only gave rise to yet another group, the so-called "neo-Chalcedonians" (which emphasised the synthesis of natures in Christ). Increasingly the matter became more and more confused as various parties denied or shared communion with others and competing bishops were ordained. Justin ii and the empress Sophia also attempted to bridge the theological differences unsuccessfully at Callinicium. Heraclius twice promoted a compromise: firstly advocating Sergius' doctrine of *Monoenergetism*[153] discussed first at the Synod of Garin in 622. Although this proposal initially seemed to gain wide acceptance, it was officially denounced by staunchly Chalcedonian Sophronius after he became Patriarch of Jerusalem in 634. He saw this compromise as a threat to Chalcedonian Orthodoxy and as promoting Dyothelitism–the doctrine of the two wills of Christ.

Sergius and Heraclius too abandoned Monoenergetism. In 638, they released a slightly amended formula, called the Ἔκθεσις. In this revision, the question of the energy of Christ was not relevant; instead, it promoted the belief that while Christ possessed two natures, he had only a single will, the teaching of *Monotheletism*. The "Doctrine of the Single Will" as proscribed in the *Ecthesis* was sent as an edict to all four eastern metropolitan sees and when Sergius died in December 638, it looked as if Heraclius might actually achieve his goal of ecclesiastical unity. However, in the same year Pope Honorius I, who had seemed to support the new formulation, also died. His successor Pope Severinus condemned the *Ecthesis* outright (and was thus denied his seat until 640). His successor Pope John IV also rejected the doctrine completely, leading to a major schism between the eastern and western halves of the Catholic Church at the moment Heraclius was dying.

Subsequently, Heraclius' grandson Constans II, who rejected the doctrine of Monotheletism was determined to end the dispute with the West. Consequently, he ordered that all discussion about the Monothelite doctrine was to cease and that all theological positions were to reflect the *status quo ante* of Chalcedon, issuing his Τύπος in 648 to this effect. Ignored in the West, the *Ecthesis* was condemned by the Lateran Council of 649. This infuriated emperor Constans who ordered the abduction and trials of Pope Martin I and Maximus the Confessor. In 668 Constans died, and Monothelitism was condemned once and for all at the Third Council of Constantinople (the Sixth Ecumenical Council, 680–681) in favour of Dyothelitism.

The events which I have attempted to relate in an oversimplified form in the preceding largely coincide with what is traditionally seen as the "Arabic Invasions," the enigmatic human tsunami from deserted Arabia which, as we saw, was entirely apocryphal. While we often read that the new conquerors permitted the non-Chalcedonians to practice their faith in peace, there actually was no need to bend their beliefs to the Byzantine hierarchy; or rather official orthodoxy disappeared with the Byzantine overlords. As the areas that remained to the empire were largely Chalcedonian, the need to reach a theological compromise soon disappeared. Even today, the Council of Chalcedon–which made official the dogma of the Trinity–is still rejected by the Armenian, Syrian, Coptic, and Ethiopian churches, collectively known as "Oriental Orthodoxy." In light of this, it is no surprise that in the homeland of Christianity most people have rejected Hellenistic Christianity. They either cling to a non-Chalcedonian branch or have converted to Islam.

However, Heraclius' failed attempts to unite Christendom under one acceptable Christological formulation might be an explanation as to why Heraclius is the only Roman Emperor whose memory is preserved in Islamic literature, and quite positively too. Some traditions claim that he recognised "Muḥammad" as the Prophet of God whilst others claim that he was a Muslim and tried to convert his Court to the new religion.

Jewish Christianity however, unlike these other "heresies," was rejected by more than just the Nicene main church. As their name suggests, they felt simultaneously Jewish *and* Christian–and this at a time when both religions were distinctly differentiating themselves from each other and were thus consciously carving out their own independent identities. They were denounced as Christians by the Jews[154] and accused of heresy by the Christians.[155] Independence was probably the only way out of this balancing act. It is nonetheless clear that Islamic theology must have emerged from a Judaeo-Christian antithesis to Byzantine orthodoxy.

7.2.10 (=I) مستقيم – *mustaqīm*

The word *mustaqīm* "straight" e.g. in the phrase الصراط المستقيم – *aṣ-ṣirāt al-mustaqīm* is of course reminiscent of the "straight paths of the Lord" (ἂς ὁδοὺς Κυϱίου τὰς εὐϑείας) in Acts 13:10. This derivation of the root √*qwm* here is by all accounts Arabic. Other meanings, however, are likely borrowed from Aramaic, such as يوم القيامة – *yawm al-qiyāma*, discussed above in (§7.2.5), in the sense of "resurrection" (ανάστασις)–cf. i.a. Syriac ܩܝܡܐ – *qyāmā* in the NT with this meaning:[156] ܘܛܘܒܝܟ܂ ܕܠܝܬ ܠܗܘܢ ܕܢܦܪܥܘܢܟ ܢܗܘܐ ܓܝܪ ܦܘܪܥܢܟ ܒܩܝܡܐ ܕܙܕܝܩܐ܂ – *wə-ṭūḇayk d-layt l-hūn d-nefrʿūnāḵ nehweʾ gēr pūrʿānāḵ ba-qyāmā də-zaḏīqē*. Here, once again, the concept of resurrection of the dead is borrowed together with the term that accompanies it–the semantic development "to get up" >"to revive" was first completed in Syriac. The term الحي القيوم – *al-ḥayyu l-qayyūmu* "the eternally existent and the eternal preserver of creation (2:255; 3:2; 20:111) is also borrowed. ܚܝܐ – *ḥayyā* "life" also means "salvation" in Syriac, such as in Luke 3:6:܂ ܘܢܚܙܐ ܟܠ ܒܣܪ ܚܝܐ ܕܐܠܗܐ – *wə-neḥzē kul bsar ḥayyē ḏalāhā* "…and all flesh shall see the salvation of God," however also in the sense of the (eternally) living God, such as in John 6:69:

ܚܢܢ ܗܝܡܢܢ ܘܝܕܥܢ: ܕܐܢܬܘ ܡܫܝܚܐ܂ ܒܪܗ ܕܐܠܗܐ ܚܝܐ

ḥnan haymenən w-īḏaʿn: d-ʾaⁿṯ-ʰū mšīḥā brēh d-ʾalāhā ḥayyā

"And we believe and are sure that you are that Christ, Son of the living God."

Or 1 Peter 1:3:

ܡܒܪܟ ܗܘ ܐܠܗܐ ܐܒܘܗܝ ܕܡܪܢ ܝܫܘܥ ܡܫܝܚܐ: ܗܘ ܕܒܪܚܡܘܗܝ ܣܓܝܐܐ ܐܘܠܕܢ ܡܢ
ܕܪܝܫ: ܒܩܝܡܬܗ ܕܝܫܘܥ ܡܫܝܚܐ: ܠܣܒܪܐ ܕܚܝܐ܂

> *mḇarak ^{h}ū 'alāhā 'abū ^{h}y d-māran yešūʿ mšīḥā: haw d-ba-ḥnānēh sagī'ā 'aw-lədan men drīš: ba-qyāmtēh d-yešūʿ mšīḥā: l-saḇrā d-ḥayyē*
>
> "Blessed be the God and Father of our Lord Jesus Christ, who according to His great mercy has caused us to be born again to a living hope through the resurrection of Jesus Christ from the dead ..."

In each case, however, the Syriac word ܩܝܡܐ – *qyāmā* can also be understood in the sense of "to preserve, to exist eternally" (1 Peter 1:25):

> ܘܡܠܬܗ ܕܐܠܗܐ ܩܝܡܐ ܠܥܠܡܝܢ. ܘܗܕܐ ܗܝ ܡܠܬܐ ܗܝ ܕܐܣܬܒܪܬܘܢ
>
> *wə-melṯēh dalāhā qayāma lə-ʿālmīn wə-hāḏēh ^{h}y melṯā hāy d-'estaḇartūn*
>
> "But the word of the Lord endureth for ever. And this is the word which by the gospel is preached unto you."

Outside of the Bible it is used with a different meaning, roughly with the semantics of ὑπόστασις. The use of this root in the theological context to denote a characteristic of God, specifically the resurrection, can only be a semantic borrowing from Aramaic.

8. Conclusion

In the preceding, an argument has been made that points to Syro-Palestine as the Qur'ān's likely place of origin. In the Prologue (§0), it was briefly argued that both script-distribution and language (areal linguistics) point to this region. After discussing the significance of loan-words (§§1-2), especially in relation to the Qur'ān (§3), some loan-words in various semantic spheres were discussed: in relation to the vocabulary of writing (§4)–which supports the argument made in §0; some key theological terms (§5); the "Five Pillars of Islam" (§6); and, finally, the loan vocabulary found in the First Sura of the Qur'ān was discussed (§7). Briefly, we can note here that the loan vocabulary of the "first" Arabic book, the holy book of Islam, largely employs words of Syro-Aramaic origin for key terms with isolated and sporadic *Wörter und Sachen* also deriving from Southern Arabia and Ethiopia; Persian loans usually entered Arabic via Syriac.

It is important to note here, that the focus of this exercise was not on Semitic cognates, or proto-Semitic etymologisation. Rather, an attempt was made to show the borrowed semantic load of especially theological termini technici.[157] Both the quantity as well as the nature of the borrowed terms discussed here clearly shows that the authors of the Qur'ān possessed an intimate knowledge of the Syriac Bible, probably the common version of the time, the Peshitta (=*Vulgata*). Although some of the terms discussed also found their way into Old South and especially Old North Arabic languages after their transfer to monotheism (cf. n39), the concentration of Syro-Aramaic terms, as well as the writing system is indicative of a transfer from Syriac.

The vocabulary of a language can tell the story of its speakers (cf. n12), and to what extent they came into contact with other peoples. Thus English has borrowed but a few lexemes from the Celtic languages (as opposed to many Anglicisms in Celtic languages)[158] which says something about the nature of the contact. The Viking Age left its traces in the vocabulary Old English,[159] and even more so the Norman Conquest with a myriad of French and Latinate loans; Dutch maritime technology, thanks to which Britannia once ruled the waves, left its linguistic traces too,[160] as did the Dutch colonial presence in New York on *Americanese.*[161] The Raj continues to live on in the vocabulary of English.[162] Vocabulary and semantics are a powerful tool, that, when properly applied, can tell us something about the past of the respective speakers. As with the inner-Semitic loans in Arabic, in English the North Germanic, Old Norse and West Germanic Dutch loans at first glance seem to be quite English even as do many Old French loans from the Norman period. Nonetheless their semantics and morpho-phonology betray their foreign origins.

As has been shown, the roots of what we now know as "Arabic" are to be found in Syro-Palestine, especially in the *Jazirah* (cf. note 2). This area has a left a long written record and the linguistic history of the region can be traced to at least the third millennium since the finds from Ebla (Tal Mardikh) have come to light. It should then come as no surprise that the Arabic language spoken here displays to some extent in its vocabulary this past. Some words, such as that for an alcoholic beverage discussed in note 23 are old words that have stuck to the product denoted by it (cf. "mead" in English), but whose morpho-phonetic forms betray the path(s) taken. This product even reached Ethiopia, where its realisation indicates that it, like the Arabic form, must have been borrowed from Syro-Aramaic with its introduction.

In the case of theological vocabulary, we are not dealing with a word describing a product, rather with a lexeme denoting an idea. Naturally, in both cases, the existence of the product or idea is a pre-requisite. As was discussed in §1, the theological evolution of Judaeo-Christian monotheism was a long, drawn-out and intricate process. Philology can help us to understand when words took on certain meanings and help us date texts by identifying anachronisms both in the vocabulary and contents of texts. The vocabulary of the Qur'ān betrays its place and time of origin.[163] Here, Classical Ethiopic serves as an interesting comparative case. As was seen in the examples given in the preceding, Gəʿəz loans are infrequent in Arabic (and some of them suggested here were in all likelihood borrowed by Arabic from a lost Syro-Aramaic source). However, it was also shown that, like Arabic, it borrowed much of its Christian theological vocabulary from Syriac.[164] That is, a similar process of conversion to Christianity led to the adaption of Aramaic vocabulary by Arabic speakers in Syro-Palestine as by Gəʿəz speakers in Ethiopia – much like the borrowing of Latin terms in English and other Western European languages discussed above.

Islam, as a "religion of the book," and its consequent development of such a belief system of course presupposes the presence of a literate and literary culture. The present article sheds some light on the evolution of this culture over the course of Semitic and Semito-Hellenistic religious history, as well as the formation and development of monotheism. Since both the Qur'ān and Islamic tradition view biblical historiography as history that actually occurred – an anachronism – they constitute a part of this continually evolving revelatory truth. Understood in this way, the religion that emerged from the Qur'ān is one of many on a continuum that began in the Syro-Palestinian region: the local cults of the Bronze and Early Iron Ages gave rise to the religions of Judah, which later brought about manifestations of Jewish religion when the former came into contact with Hellenism. This later gave rise to Judaisms[165] and Christianities, from which Islam would later arise. The latter as a religion which originated "in the full light of history" only makes sense in the context of Church History.

There is no historical basis for asserting that these religions and their traditions enjoyed one uninterrupted and continuous course of development. If we look at the various interpretations of scripture in Judaism, such as those found in the orders of the Mishna, the Tosefta, and the Talmuds, or, for example, the confusion with regard to the nature of Jesus Christ[166] and his Death in early Christianity,[167] we can only conclude that we are dealing with the invention of traditions and not with the preservation of ancient ones. The remarks of Adolf von Harnack on nascent Christianity in the introduction (p. iv) of his previously mentioned *Mission und Ausbreitung*, are also relevant for Islam:

> The oldest missionary-history is buried under legends, or rather replaced by a tendentious history which supposedly played out in just a few decades in all the countries of the world. This story has been worked over for more than a thousand years–because the creation of the legend about the apostolic missions started in the first century and continued on until the Middle Ages, and even continues to flourish into modern times; its uselessness is now generally recognised.[168]

The use of the word "uselessness" (*Wertlosigkeit*) here applies to the value of traditions and tradition literature (including sacred texts) as historical sources. While for the scientific historical-critical study of Judaism and Christianity such is generally accepted, Islamic Studies today still often uncritically accepts the primacy of traditional literature. Whilst such retain relevance for homiletics, they have but little value for hermeneutic investigations such as scientific exegesis. The question with which Nietzsche commenced his historical-critical study on the life of the sixth century bc Greek poet Theognis:

> "illos enim aetati ejus propiores nescio an verisimilius sit de eo rectius judicasse, quam nos recentiores viros" applies here as does his own answer: "neque illis neque his omnibus in partibus suffragandum esse mihi persuasi."

Indeed, the ancient sources had potentially more information at their disposal than we will ever have. However, this information was used selectively and uncritically and (cf. ad n132) we must understand how ancient historiography worked[169] – Herodotus did not set out to become the "Father of History," but rather to tell a good story. We must learn not to read more into sources than they can properly render. Furthermore, in the case of religious history, textual documentation is usually not contemporary to the events related: for Islam, the relevant sources only commence at the end of the eighth/early ninth century, i.e. a century and half after the events which they purport to narrate. At best, they then can only tell us what their authors thought happened elsewhere in the early seventh century. While these texts undoubtedly contain some historical information, they do not qualify as scientific historical sources; they interpret the past in light of an orthodoxy fashioned post factum as von Harnack noted. Texts that are viewed as sacred by faith groups relate *Heilsgeschichte* and not history.

The religions known today popularly as the "Abrahamic" faiths, Judaism, Christianity and Islam, traditionally justify at least part of their veracity on the fact that their respective scriptures relate to the intervention of their deity in history with his human creations in a past, normally formative period of these respective faiths. Hierophany in these religions usually commences with a narrative of origins placed in a mythical past, to demonstrate that the deity is eternal having existed before time and is the creator thereof, and which then continues displaying the close relationship of the deity with those whom he has chosen, his elect. The revelation of the deity to his elect was then written down in a canonical form that has validity for all time. Whether or not these texts actually contain the *ipsissima verba dei* is not a question that science can ask or is able to answer, this is a religious question that must be asked and answered by the believers and theologians of the respective faiths. The question though whether sacred time and historical time are or were once congruent, however, is one which concerns the essence of science, since if sacred time is historical time then the latter should also be provable by factual evidence. We know that the religious scriptures in question, the Hebrew Bible, the New Testament and the Qur'ān, like much of the literatures contemporary to them, largely contain allegory, a pre-modern, pre-scientific manner of illustrating complex ideas and concepts in a digestible, concrete way and indeed for much of the history of these faiths their scriptures were interpreted in such a fashion. One must remember that kerugma is a theological and not an historical concept.

Hence it is clear that if we wish to seriously understand the origins of such religious traditions, we must transcend traditions and traditional literature–as they are not evidence driven – but rather employ historical and textual criticism.[170] Here, it must be noted that the only evidence for the Islamic narrative of its beginnings is the said narrative. As such it is no different from the Hebrew Bible or the New Testament. What would later become Islam only enters the light of history in Syro-Palestine with the caliphate rise of the Umayyad Caliphate under Muʿāwiyah I (cf. n119)–who in inscriptions and contemporary accounts saw himself as a Christian–an independent confirmation of the arguments proposed here. Historically speaking, the Hijazi origins of Islam in Mecca and Medina and the rule of the "Rightly Guided Caliphs" (الخلفاء الراشدون) are entirely apocryphal, and indeed the sagas which narrate this period are riddled with anachronisms–much like the David saga in the Hebrew Bible or the biography of Jesus in the Gospels. As was briefly seen in the preceding, and which is also evident from the anti-Chalcedonian Christology expressed by the later Umayyad Caliph ʿAbd al-Malik ibn Marwān in his inscriptions found in the "Dome of the Rock" (مسجد قبة الصخرة), the religious sentiments which would later crystallise as Islam were a reaction to Byzantine orthodoxy. As such, their *Sitz im Leben* must be the Syro-Palestinian hotbed of theological controversy and not the far-off Hijaz, where such debate would have been largely irrelevant. As has been shown, the classical Islamic interpreters of the Qur'ān, such as Ṭabarī, often had no idea as to the meaning of Qur'ānic verses. They were often not Arabs, or even native speakers of Arabic, and lived during the Abbasid period. Unsurprisingly, in distant Baghdad, the Aramaic heritage stored in the Qur'ān went unnoticed. It is in this period when the origins of Islam were retroprojected to the Hijaz for theological reasons (cf. Galatians 14:22-26), but the discussion of such must be the subject of its own study.

In the preceding (§7.2.8), we have noted that two Arabic words found in the Qur'ān and which were borrowed from Aramaic, namely صراط – *ṣirāṭ* and سبيل – *sabīl* have by all account the semantic load of the New Testament terminus technicus ἡ ὁδός "the Way" and denote the religion adhered to. Furthermore (§7.2.9), the apocryphal helpers of "Muḥammad" at Medina, the الأنصار – *anṣar* were seen to be Ναζωραῖοι which does not refer to Nazareth, but rather is another old term for Christianity deriving from the Messianic interpretation of the Hebrew word נֵצֶר – *näṣär* "branch" in Isaiah 11:1. In the works of the Church Fathers, written after Constantine's toleration of

Christianity which facilitated the later emergence of an imperial orthopraxis, it was seen that *Nazarene* was a term loosely employed to describe what might be anachronistically called "Judaeo-Christians," i.e. Jewish followers of Jesus, who rejected the teaching of Paul and continued in some manner to adhere to the Jewish Law (including circumcision). Although the sources are polemical and somewhat imprecise, it was seen that some of these groups believed, as does the Qur'ān, in the virgin birth of Jesus while rejecting his divinity. They are also said to have used but one Gospel (written in a Semitic language, probably Aramaic), corresponding to Qur'ānic usage (الإنجيل – *al-'ingīl*) and additionally rejected the consumption of alcohol. We thus see in the convergence of vocabulary, creed and practice the roots of what would later evolve into Islam. Here we have a convincing explanation for the curious phenomenon of Islam's retaining Jewish custom while believing in a psilanthropic, parthenogenetic Jesus Christ. Indeed the use of رب – *rabb* "Lord" as an epithet of God (§7.2.2) certainly confirms Christian rather than Jewish origins.

Here we see the historical background from which Islam would emerge. I have, however, only been able to portray a landscape in broad outlines here: much still remains to be investigated. As long as what is customarily known as "Islamic Studies" (or for that matter "Biblical Studies") merely continues to paraphrase tradition, ignorance will prevail. The fashionable ideology of the post-colonial age to ascribe ahistorical unicity to peoples once colonised by Europe only serves to promote ignorance and prejudice and the nonsensical division between the "East" and the "West." Worthwhile contributions to science and fundamental research desiderata *in casu* would be a critical edition of the Qur'ān and a diachronic lexicon of its vocabulary.

This being said, the preceding should have made clear the value of philological investigation of the Qur'ān. In contrast with the cluelessness or perplexity of early commentators such as Ṭabarī in mind, as well as the legendary hagiographic narratives of Ibn Isḥāq, Ibn Sa'd, Wāqidī etc. (who must have used *aḥādīṯ* as sources, as Goldziher has already noted), the only conclusion is that Islam, like Judaism and Christianity, unsurprisingly preserved no historical memory of its origins: traditions can only surface after the completion of a formative period and the creation of an hierophantic revelatory history. It should by now be clear that the emergence of Islam belongs to the discipline of Church History, just as early Christianity is a part of Jewish history. Thus the actual historicity of Muḥammad is just as irrelevant as that of Moses, David or Jesus–their respective fates in later traditions lead lives of their own. Ultimately all manifestations of "Abrahamic Faiths" are by definition each other's heresy.

9. References

Unless otherwise stated, the definitions provided in these dictionaries have been used:

Akkadian:

W. Frhr. von Soden, *Akkadisches Handwörterbuch* 3 Vols. (Wiesbaden, 1965–1981).

Amharic:

J. Baetman, *Dictionnaire amharigna-français suivi d'un vocabulaire français-amharigna* (Dire Daoua, 1929).

Arabic :

R. P. A. Dozy, *Supplément aux dictionnaires arabes* 2 Vols. (Reprint; Beirut, 1991).

E. W. Lane, *Arabic–English Lexicon* 8 vols. (Reprint; Beirut, 1997).

Aramaic:

J. Hoftijzer and K. Jongeling, *A Dictionary of the North-West Semitic Inscriptions* 2 Vols. (Leyden, 1995).

M. Jastrow, *Dictionary of the Targumim*, the Talmud Babli and Yerushalmi and the Midrashic Literature (Reprint; Peabody MA, 2005).

Gəʿəz:

Chr. Fr. Dillmann, *Lexicon Linguæ Æthiopicæ* (Leipzig, 1865).

W. Leslau, *An Etymological Dictionary of Geʿez* (Wiesbaden, 1991).

Hebrew:

L. Koehler and W. Baumgartner, *The Hebrew and Aramaic Lexicon of the Old Testament* 2 Vols. (Leyden, 2002).

Qatabanian:

S. D. Ricks, *Lexicon of Inscriptional Qatabanian* (Rome, 1989).

Syriac:

C. Brockelmann, *Lexicon Syriacum* (Halle, 21928).

Sabaean:

A. F. L. Beeston, M. A. Ghul, W. W. Müller, J. Ryckmans, *Sabaic Dictionary (English-French-Arabic)* (Louvain–Beirut, 1982).

Ugaritic:

G. del Olmo Lete and J. Sanmartín, *A Dictionary of the Ugaritic Language in the Alphabetic Tradition* 2 Vols. (Leyden, 2003).

---

* *I would like to take this opportunity to thank the English translator for her dedicated hard work. My thanks also go to Prof. K.-H. Ohlig (Saarbrücken) for his patience and revision of the German version of this paper; to Mr Th. Milo (Amsterdam) for his typographic help; and to Prof. M. Gross (Saarbrücken) for his*

correction of the oriental citations and formatting. Prof. M. Schub (Hartford) was kind enough to provide additional corrections and suggestions. In order to improve readability, transcriptions of most of the examples (except those in Greek) have been included. They are meant to facilitate reading and are not intended as exact phonetic renditions.

Notes

1 This section is a summary of the arguments presented in another article: R. M. Kerr, "Von der aramäischen Lesekultur zur arabischen Schreibkultur: Kann die semitische Epigraphik etwas über die Entstehung des Korans erzählen?" in M. Gross and K.-H. Ohlig (eds.), *Die Entstehung einer Weltreligion I: Von der koranischen Bewegung zum Frühislam* (Berlin/Tübingen, 2010), pp. 354–376.

2 This area, roughly the Jazira (roughly the former province known as the Djézireh) encompassing the Chabur, Euphrates and Tigris basins in NE Syria, SE Turkey and NW Iraq is what was usually meant by "Arabia" in Antiquity. Here e.g., is found an Ἀραβάρχης at Dura-Europos (cf. C. B. Welles et al., *The Excavations at Dura-Europos.* Final Report V, Part I [New Haven, 1959], 115 Nr. 20, 5); at Sumatar Harabesi in modern Turkey, five inscriptions were found at the ancient cemetery bearing the Syriac pendant ܫܠܛܢܐ ܕܥܪܒ – *šulṭānā d-ʿarab* "Governor of Arab(ia)" (cf. H. J. W. Drijvers and J. F. Healey, *The Old Syriac Inscriptions of Edessa and Osrhoene* [Leyden, 1999], 104f. et passim); at Hatra, a mlk' dy 'rb(y) "King of Arabia" is attested (cf. B. Aggoula, *Inventaire des inscriptions hatréenes* [Paris, 1991], 92 Nr. 193, 2; 135f. Nr. 287, 3–4)–note also e.g. Pliny, *Nat. Hist.* V.xxi.86 "Arabia supra dicta habet oppida Edessam, quæ quondam Antiochia dicebatur, Callirhœm, a fonte nominatam, Carrhas, Crassi clade nobile. Iungitur præfectura Mesopotamiæ, ab Assyriis originem trahens, in qua Anthemusia et Nicephorium oppida. . . . [87] ita fertur [scil. Euphrates] usque Suram locum, in quo conversus ad orientem relinquit Syriæ Palmyrenas solitudines, quæ usque ad Petram urbem et regionem Arabiæ Felicis appellatæ pertinent." This is the "Arabia" which St Paul must have visited (Galatians 1:17). Noteworthy in this regard is that Fredegar (Chronicon lxvi) even localises the Hagarenes somewhat more to the North: "Agareni, qui et Sarraceni, sicut Orosii [Boh. Eorosii] liber testatur, gens circumcisa a latere montis Caucasi, super mare Caspium, terram ..."

3 For example, see Sh. Sand, *The Invention of the Jewish People* (London, 2009), p. 64–189 and the references it cites as well as the now classical work by Th. L. Thompson, *The Bible in History. How Writers Create a Past* (London, 1999).

4 This is not the place to deal with this question in detail. However, I will refer to the discussion in M. S. Smith, *God in Translation* (Tübingen, 2008), as well as the references it cites.

5 Cf. F. Briquel Chatonnet "L'expansion du christianisme en Arabie: l'apport des sources syriaques," *Semitica et Classica* 3 (2010). Note also the comments of François Villeneuve "Jamais le christianisme n'arrive à prendre pied bien loin au sud en Arabie," and that beyond a line passing approximately the latitude Aqaba, "il n'y a tout simplement presque aucune trace chrétienne" (F. Villeneuve, "La résistance des cultes béthyliques d'Arabie face au monothéisme: de Paul à Barsauma et à Muhammad," in H. Inglebert, S. Destephen and B. Dumézil (eds.), *Le problème de la christianisation du monde antique* (Paris, 2010), pp. 219–231, here 228).

6 W. Gesenius, *Hebräisch-deutsches Handwörterbuch über die Schriften des Alten Testaments...* (Leipzig, 1810–1812), 2 vols. 18th edition, H. Donner et al. (eds.), Wilhelm Gesenius, *Hebräisches und Aramäisches Handwörterbuch über das Alte Testament* (Berlin etc., 1987–2010), 6 fasc.

7 Compare the remarks of J. Fück, *Die arabischen Studien in Europa bis in den Anfang des 20. Jahrhunderts* (Leipzig, 1955), 166ff. L. Koehler and W. Baumgartner et al. (eds.), *Hebrew and Aramaic Lexicon of the Old Testament* (2 vols.; trans. M. E. J. Richardson; Leyden, 2002).

8 "Ein großer Teil des Wortschatzes, den die arabischen Philologen aufzeichneten und erklärten, war ihnen weder aus dem alltäglichen Gebrauch noch von ausgedehnter Lektüre her bekannt. Ihre Hauptaufgabe bestand deshalb nicht in der Festlegung genauer und treffender Erklärungen für Wörter, die jedem Gebildeten geläufig waren, sondern im Auffinden der Bedeutungen seltener und unbekannter Wörter, denen sie wohl zum ersten Male im Zuge ihrer professionellen Tätigkeit begegneten. Da ihrer Forschungsarbeit auf diesem Gebiet zwei notwendige Grundlagen fehlten, nämlich die Kenntnis anderer semitischer Sprachen und das Vorhandensein von ausgedehntem und übersichtlichem sprachlichen Rohmaterial, entstand eine Menge von ungenauen und sogar völlig abwegigen Worterklärungen. Die vielen verschiedenen Bedeutungen, die einer großen Anzahl seltener arabischer Wörter zugeschrieben wurden, sind grundsätzlich als Ergebnisse von Versuchen verschiedener Philologen aufzufassen, schwierige Ausdrücke mit Hilfe der unzulänglichen Mittel, die ihnen zur Verfügung standen, zu erklären ... Da die Kenntnis anderer semitischen Sprachen fehlte und Parallelstellen gewöhnlich nicht herangezogen werden konnten, wurde auf diese Weise mannigfaltigen Vermutungen Tür und Tor geöffnet. Besonders oft führte die Anwendung verschiedener Methoden zu abweichenden Ergebnissen. Zu den irrigen Wörterklärungen, die von den Philologen selbst stammten, gesellten sich noch andere hinzu, die entweder auf religiösen Erwägungen beruhten, ... oder in alten sprachlichen Traditionen aus der 'vorwissenschaftlichen' Zeit ihren Ursprung hatten." L. Kopf, "Das arabische Wörterbuch als Hilfsmittel für die hebräische Lexikographie," *Vetus Testamentum* 6 (1956): pp. 286–302; quote from p. 297.

9 S. W. Wild, "Neues zur ältesten arabischen Lexikographie," *Zeitschrift der deutschen morgenländischen Gesellschaft* 112 (1962): pp. 292–300. Here I cite the edition published in 1967 in eight volumes in Baghdad.

10 R. Paret "His throne comprises the heavens and the earth." Here the problem is also obvious: the Arabic verb وسع – *w-s-ʿ* can mean "wide, to be spacious, to house" >"to have understanding," depending on the context. I must confess that I do not think I have ever come across the latter meaning.

11 Cf. Wild, art. cit. 50 with extreme examples, like ضحك – √ḍḥk "laughter" as "menstruation" in 11:71 وامرأته قائمة فضحكت – wa-mra'atu-hu qā'imatun fa-ḍaḥikat "His wife (Sara) who was standing there, laughed," cf. Genesis 18:11–15.

12 This is how we can determine the path of Gypsies from India to Europe, for example; see L. Campbell, *Historical Linguistics* (Edinburgh, 1998), 363f.

13 The Latin word for beer, cerevisia, is itself a loan-word from Gaulish, compare Welsh *cwrw*.

14 See for example to W. Stroh, *Latein ist tot, es lebe Latein!* (Berlin, 2007), 121–135.
15 The first major Latin Christian author Tertullian uses "tinctio."
16 P. V. Mankowski, *Akkadian Loanwords in Biblical Hebrew* (Winona Lake, 2000).
17 T. O. Lambdin, "Egyptian Loanwords in the Old Testament," *JAOS* 73 (1953): 144–155.
18 As for example in the book of Daniel which therefore could not have originated in the time of Nebuchadnezzar II.
19 Cf. M. Wagner, *Die lexikalischen und grammatikalischen Aramäismen in alt Hebräisch* (Berlin, 1966)–now somewhat outdated.
20 Matthew: Ηλι ηλι, λεμα σαβαχθανι; Peshitta: ܐܝܠ ܐܝܠ ܠܡܢܐ ܫܒܩܬܢܝ Western Syriac ʾīl ʾīl ləmānā šḇaqtāny, Eastern Syriac: ʾēl ʾēl ləmānāh šḇaqtāny; OT: אֵלִי אֵלִי לָמָה עֲזַבְתָּנִי – ʾēlī ʾēliīlāmā ʿăzạḇtānī "My God, my God, why have you forsaken me?"
21 Although early Islamic commentators also dealt with this topic, their work was deficient because they generally did not know the donor languages which were mentioned. Cf. Jeffery, op. cit. 12–35 and Kopf, art. cit.
22 Cf. S. Fraenkel, *Die aramäischen Lehnwörter im Arabischen* (Leyden, 1881), 141.
23 The other Qur'ānic root for an intoxicating alcoholic beverage √skr (سكر – sakar 16:67; سكرى – sukārā 4:42, 22:2; verbal سكرت – sukkirat 15:15) is also of Aramaic derivation: Syriac ܫܟܪܐ; JBA שכרא/ שיכרא – šḵar, ša/iḵrā etc. In Aramaic, the root √ḥmr is used for grape-based intoxicants whilst √skr denotes such made from dates or grain (i.e. beer) –cf. e.g. Numeri Rabbah 10:8 (ad Num. 6:3): למה כפל הכתוב יין ושכר והלא יין הוא שכר ושכר הוא יין "… are not yáyin ("wine") and šēḵār the same thing?" … יין זה חי ושכר זה מזוג "yáyin ("wine") is unmixed and šēḵār mixed wine"–is of Akkadian origin (wine did not grow in Southern Mesopotamia!): šikarum "beer" >Hebrew שֵׁכָר – šēḵār >τό σίκερα "strong drink" vs οἶνος "wine" e.g. Luke 1:15 καὶ οἶνον καὶ σίκερα οὐ μὴ πίῃ "and he shall drink neither wine nor strong drink"~ܘܚܡܪܐ ܘܫܟܪܐ ܠܐ ܢܫܬܐ – wə-ḥamrā wə-šiḵrā lā nešte (; >Ethiopic ሰከረ – sakara, cf. e.g. Psalm 106(107):27: ደንገፁ፡ወተሀውኩ፡ከመ፡ሰኩር፤ወተሰጥመ፡ከሉ፡ጥበቦሙ። We must be dealing with an Aramaic borrowing: were the form Ethiopic or borrowed from Akkadian, a realisation with ሠ /ś/, i.e. *ሠከረ would be expected)–a root of which is still found e.g. in the Amharic version: የወይን፡ጠጅና፡የሚያሰክር፡መጠጥ፡አይጠጣም፤
24 E. Littmann and M. Höfner, *Wörterbuch der Tigrē-Sprache* (Wiesbaden, 1962), 80.
25 For example, it is not documented in Sabaean and Qatabanian. Gəʿəz ከተበ – kataba in this sense with derivations like ክታብ "book" (/kətāb/ <*/kitāb/!) etc. as well as the phonetic variants ከተፐ – *kətəp* are borrowed from Arabic. The actual word in Classical Ethiopian for writing, such as 𐩮𐩢𐩰 – ṣḥf in Sabaean and Qatabanian, is ጸሐፈ – ṣaḥafa–which was in turn borrowed into Arabic, and will be picked up on later in this article. Akkadian ṣêpum "to write down," ṣê̂'pum "a sealed letter (Old Babylonian)" (von Soden, AHw 1091) is related to the South Semitic term.
26 See for example in Lane's *Dictionary*, Vol. VII, p. 2589f. This meaning is also productive in modern Arabic, cf. e.g. كتيبة – katība "regiment, conscription" etc.
27 Here I would suggest that حراء – Ḥirā' the cave in which according to later tradition "Muḥammad" received his first revelation, and whose precise location is contested, actually refers to this Christian Arab city.
28 The reference here must be to a pseudo-epigraphical work such as "The Testament of Abraham." I am of the opinion that some version of this text must be the

source for much of the Qur'ānic information on this Patriarch. On the history of this figure see the classic works J. Van Seters, *Abraham in History and Tradition* (New Haven, 1975); Th. L. Thompson, *The Historicity of the Patriarchal Narratives* (Berlin, 1974).

29 These forms could very well have been pronounced like resp. Arabic ṣaḥīfa (sg.), ṣuḥuf (pl.).

30 This root is also active in the modern Semitic languages of Ethiopia, for instance Amharic ጸሐፊ – ṣəḥafi "writer," የጽሕፈት፡መኪና – yaṣəḥəfit makinā (<Italian macchina da scrivere) "typewriter" and as the verb ጻፈ – ṣāfi.

31 This root is used in Modern Standard Arabic with reference to news reporting. It is possible that the original meaning of the Arabic root can be seen in nouns such as صحفة – ṣaḥfa "bowl," صحيفة – ṣaḥīfa "sheet."

32 "Reading" is normally formed with the causative (IV) stem of the root √nbb: አንበበ – 'anbaba in Gəʿəz as well as other modern Ethio-Semitic languages like Amharic and Tigré. This root is well attested in Semitic languages, as for example in Arabic "bleat in sexual excitement (billy goat)" (Lane, s.v.). This weak root is possibly related to the root √nb' in Semitic. The Arabic word نبى – nabī "prophet" <ܢܒܝܐ – nəbiyā, originated from this root, which itself stems from < נָבִיא – nābī'. The precondition is of course the concept of the prophecy as a means of communication. For the origins of this phenomenon see D. Flemming, "Nabu and munabbiatu: Two new Syrian religious personnel," *JAOS* 113 (1993): 175–183.

33 ܩܪܝܢܐ – qrinā translates מִקְרָא – miqrā' in the Peshitta in Nehemiah 8:8, interestingly enough.

34 Cf. the authorities cited by as-Suyūṭī (الإتقان في علوم القرآن – *Al-itqān fī ʿulūm al-qur'ān* 319–321), and the sources given in Jeffery, op. cit. 170ff.

35 Also in the description of the scribes (γραμματεύς) in Matthew 9:3 of the Peshitta! This lexeme was also borrowed by Armenian: սովեր – sover; but pace Jeffery, op. cit. 171, Ethiopian ሰፈረ – safira shows no Aramaic influence.

36 From the sense of "teaching, instruction," Syriac ܣܦܪܐ – seprā doubt took on the meaning of "Holy Scripture." The Akkadian root also has another semantic domain with reference to "work," e.g. šiprum, probably in turn borrowed from Sabaean 𐩧𐩰𐩦 – s²fr "labour-force, corvée" (partly because they had to provide forced labour for the Mesopotamia?). Hebrew forms, like סֵפֶר – sēp̄ār "book," סֹפֵר – sōp̄ēr "scribe" etc., are deliberately disregarded here.

37 Here שְׂטַר – śəṭar "side" is disregarded (e.g. Daniel 7:5 "And behold, another beast, a second one, like a bear. It was raised up on one side (ולשׂטר־חד). It had three ribs in its mouth between its teeth; and it was told, 'Arise, devour much flesh.'"), = šṭr3 in J. Hoftijzer and K. Jongeling, *Dictionary of the North-West Semitic Inscriptions* (Leyden, 1995), 1124f.

38 With reference to 57:22 ما أصاب من مصيبة في الأرض ولا في أنفسكم إلا في كتاب من قبل أن نبرأها إن ذلك على الله يسير – *mā 'aṣāba min muṣībatin fī l-'arḍi wa-lā fī 'anfusikum 'illā fī kitābin min qabli' 'an nabra'ahā 'inna ḏālika ʿalā llāhi yasīrun.*

39 Period E. "During the second half of the fourth century the pagan formulas disappear from the texts (one single pagan text is later). Taking their place appear monotheistic formulas invoking the 'Lord of Heaven' (or … 'of Heaven and

Earth') and the 'Merciful' (Raḥmānān). Christianity and Judaism using the same terminology had supplanted paganism"— J. Ryckmans, "The Old South Arabian Religion," in W. Daum (ed.), *Yemen: 3000 Years of Art and Civilization in Arabia Felix* (1987), 110; cf. as well Chr. Robin, "Le judaïsme de Himyar," *Arabia* 1 (2003): 97–172, and idem, "Himyar au IVème siècle de l'ère chrétienne. Analyse des données chronologiques et essai de mise en ordre," *ABADY* 10 (2005):133–151.

40 From the same root as Akkadian lētum (<*laḫtum), Ugaritic lḥ "jaw, cheek."

41 The verb ለቀሀ – leha "writing" is found in Amharic as well as ሉክ – luk (with the variation ሉሀ – luh) "blank sheet of paper" which must have come from ለወሐ – lawaḥa, although an Arabic source cannot be ruled out. This root is not attested in Old Northern Arabian or Old South Arabian, to the best of my knowledge.

42 I.e. the "folding tablets" (πίναξ πτυκτός) used to write the Bellerophontic letter in the Iliad 6:169.

43 Other versions use the transcription ܛܛܠܘܣ – ṭiṭlos as a loan-word.

44 Here I do not deal in great detail with توراة – tawrāt "Torah" and إنجيل – inǧīl "Gospel" (yet cf. §7.2.9) as both clearly must have been borrowed. The first term was likely adopted from the Jews, though not from Hebrew per se (the Hebrew word was probably borrowed from the Akkadian *tî/êrtum* [from older *tā'ertum* "instruction"]). The Syriac lexeme ܐܘܪܝܬܐ – *oraytā* "Pentateuch, Old Testament" (>Gəʿəz ኦሪት – *'orit* "Octateuch") is formed from the same root. The latter of course ultimately stems from the Greek εὐαγγέλιον. Whether it was borrowed from the Aramaic ܐܘܢܓܠܝܘܢ – *ewangeliyon* or Old Ethiopian ወንጌል – *wangel* (because of the long vowels and missing Greek ending), is not important for the purposes of this article. In Syriac, the Greek loan word is roughly as common as its indigenous Aramaic synonym ܣܒܪܬܐ – *sbarṭā*, a form originating by way of metathesis. The root b-š-r can mean "to bring a message" >"to praise a deity" among other things, like Akkadian bussurum (D-stem; >bussurtum, mubassirum [Mari], tabsertum etc.), Ugaritic bšr (D-stem), and Hebrew בִּשֵּׂר – biśśêr "to exhibit." Here the semantic development appears to have been "to communicate a message" >"to communicate a good message," such as >Sabaean rGb – bs2r, Old Ethiopian አብሠረ – abśara "to announce good news." The Arabic root بشر – b-š-r with the meaning "to be glad" must have been derived from this. Aramaic appears to have followed its own semantic path, for example ܣܒܪ – sbar "putavit, speravit, expectavit." I suspect this was borrowed by Arabic possibly from Gəʿəz (perhaps also ܣܒܪܬܐ – sbarṯā), because this root was already common in this language in an "evangelical" sense, such as ብሥራት – bəśrāt "good news, Gospel," ብሥራታዊ – bəśrātāwi "bearer of good news, evangelist," በዓለ፡ብሥራት – baʿāla bəśrāt the "Annunciation of Mary" etc., which we also find in non-Qur'ānic (i.e. Christian) Arabic: بشارة – bišāra "good news, Gospel," بشير – bašīr "bearer of good news, evangelist," تبشير – tabšīr, literally "the Spreading of Good News"–Christian missionary work, مبشر – mubaššir "missionary," عيد البشارة – ʿīd al-bišāra etc.

45 R. M. Kerr, *Latino-Punic Epigraphy. A descriptive Study of the Inscriptions* (Tübingen, 2010), 81f.

46 Interestingly enough, this is also the situation in Indo-European. The head of the Greek pantheon Ζεύς, (genitive Διός; <*di̯ēus) seemingly the only Olympian deity with an Indo-European name, is cognate with Latin deus "god" and Jupiter (<*dyeu[s]-ph$_2$tēr "Sky-Father"~Ζεύς πατὴϱ [ἀνδϱῶν τε θεῶν τε]). The latter is of

course the archaic Vedic sky god द्यौष्पितृ – *dyauṣpitṛ* attested a handful of times in the Rig-Veda.

47 See already Tell Fakhariyeh 5: *'lh rḥmn zy tṣlwth ṭbh* "merciful god whose prayer is beneficial."

48 On the Syriac origins of *Allāh* see also M. Gross, "Neue Wege der Koranforschung aus vergleichender sprach- und kulturwissenschaftlicher Sicht" in K.-H. Ohlig (ed.), *Der frühe Islam* (Berlin, 2007), 457–640, esp. 597 ff.

49 For example 90:24ff.: ወኰነኔ፡ኮነ፡ቅድመ፡እምከዋክብት፡ወተኰነኑ፡ወኮኑ፡ኀጥኣነ፡ወሖሩ፡መካነ፡ኰነኔ፡ወወደይዎሙ፡ውስተ፡ዕሙቅ፡ወምሉእ፡እሳተ፡ወይልህብ፡ወምሉእ፡ዐምደ፡እሳት።ወእልኩ፡፸ኖላውያን፡ተኰነኑ፡ወኮኑ፡ኃጥኣነ፡ወተወድዩ፡እሙንቱ፡ ውስተ፡ዝኩ፡ማዕምቀ፡እሳት።ወርኢኩ፡በውእቱ፡ጊዜ፡ከመ፡ተርኅው፡፩ማዕምቅ፡ከማሁ፡በማእከለ፡ምድር፡ዘምሉዕ፡እሳተ፡ወአምጽእዎሙ፡ለእልኩ፡አባግዕ፡ጽሉላን፡ወተኰነኑ፡ኵሎሙ፡ወኮኑ፡ኃጥኣነ፡ወተወድዩ፡ውስተ፡ዝኩ፡ዕመቀ፡እሳት፡ወውዕዩ፡ወዝንቱ፡ማዕምቅ፡ኮነ፡በየማኑ፡ለዝኩ፡ቤት።ወርኢክዎሙ፡ለእልኩ፡አባግዕ፡እንዘ፡ይውዕዩ፡ወአዕፅምቲሆሙ፡ይውዒ። "And the judgement was held first over the stars, and they were judged and found guilty, and went to the place of condemnation, and they were cast into an abyss, full of fire and flaming, and full of pillars of fire. And those seventy shepherds were judged and found guilty, and they were cast into that fiery abyss. And I saw at that time how a like abyss was opened in the midst of the earth, full of fire, and they brought those blinded sheep, and they were all judged and found guilty and cast into this fiery abyss, and they burned; now this abyss was to the right of that house."

50 A possible relict of the older view of the after-life in the Qur'ān may be مالك – mālik the angel who guards hell in 43:77. This could be equated with the Bronze Age deified royal ancestors attested in texts from Syro-Palestinian Ugarit.

51 It is unclear whether the verbal forms of this root in Hebrew and Aramaic are original or later denominal derivations.

52 In the Peshitta, ܣܛܝܢܐ – ḥeṭyānā renders Hebrew שִׂטְנָה – śiṭnāh "accusation" in Ezra 4:6.

53 For a relevant discussion on this matter see now E. Muehlberger, *Angels in Late Ancient Christianity* (Oxford, 2013).

54 The verbal root is not attested in Hebrew, but compare this to Ugaritic l'k, Gəʿəz ለአከ – la'aka etc. For this word see also Luxenberg, op. cit. 59ff.

55 The angel Raphael, who plays a role in the biblical book of Tobit and in the Book of Enoch, seems to find no continuation here.

56 Such transcripted loans are not uncommon in Arabic. So for example تاريخ – tāriḫ "date, time; history; annals" (and the denominal factitive verb أرخ -'arraḫa "to date, to write the date") would seem to come from a root √'rk.

57 The name is in any case pre-Hebrew and already documented in the Bronze Age, e.g. Egyptian  – /ysAr/, cf. K. A. Kitchen, *Ramesside Inscriptions, Historical and Biographical*, IV, (Oxford, 1969), 19.7.

58 As we shall see (§7.2.9), the identification of the Arabs as Ishmaelites predates Islam. It is an ideological term used by Christian historiography and is not originally an ethnonym or a self-designation.

59 The name is pre-Hebrew and documented with theophoric elements in the Bronze Age, for instance at Ugarit. The actual meaning of the root √ʿqb here must have

been similar to the Gəʿəz ዐቀበ – aqaba "to guard, to protect"– cf. Amharic ጠባቂ – ṭabāqi "minder."

60 The fact that this name is of Egyptian origin is, however, not a confirmation of the historicity of the story of Joseph. This name is only attested in the Late Period (664–332bc) and not during the Bronze Age, when Joseph supposedly lived, if one were to take the chronological data of the Bible literally.

61 Vs the secular legal usage of this root e.g. in Official Aramaic and at Palymra: šhd, verb "to testify" (scil. "on someone's behalf" + lh); noun "witness."

62 In Jewish Aramaic "to be sure, to be present, to testify" etc., although not in the sense of martyrdom. The Arabic usage matches Syriac more closely. Late Sabaic 𐩦𐩠𐩵 – šhd "testimony" is borrowed from Aramaic.

63 Cf. neo-Assyrian and Late Babylonian ṣullûm "to pray," an Aramaic borrowing, similar to Sabaic 𐩮𐩡𐩩 – ṣlt and Gəʿəz ጸለየ – ṣalaya "to pray" (ጸሎት – ṣalot "prayer").

64 ركعا – rukkaʿan from the root ركع – rakaʿa "to bow" has an Aramaic cognate in Christian Palestinian Aramaic: ܠܐ ܡܪܟܥܝܢ (see A. Smith Lewis, "Apostolic Myth and Homily Fragments" in idem (ed.), *Codex Climaci Rescriptus [Horae Semiticae VIII]* (Cambridge, 1909), 190ff.). We will, however, due to constraints of space, not further discuss this lexeme here.

65 Note ܣܓܕ ܠܫܡܫܐ – sāgeḏ l-šemšā lit. "sun worshipper," the genus Heliotropium.

66 See for example Genesis 18:2 ወሶበ፡አልዐለ፡አዕይንቲሁ፡ወነጸረ፡ወናሁ፡ሠለስቱ፡ ዕደው፡ይቀውሙ፡ መልዕልቴሁ፡[ወርእየ፡ወሮጸ፡ለተቀብሎቶም፡እምኆኅተ፡ይመት፡]ወሰገደ (wa-sagada)፡ውስተ፡ምድር ። wa-sagada rendering Greek προσκυνέω "to fall down and worship (at someone's feet)."

67 I.e the God of Israel together with one his female consorts, which shows that "Judaism" in Achaemenid Egypt was considerably different than today.

68 See H. and M. Weippert, "Der betende Mensch. Eine Außenansicht" in A. Grund et al. (eds.) *Ich will Dir danken unter den Völkern. Studien zur israelitischen und altorientalischen Gebetsliteratur: Festschrift für Bernd Janowski zum 70. Geburtstag* (Gütersloh, 2013), 435–490. See esp. 437f.: "Besonders auffallend ist freilich eine teilweise Parallelität zwischen den muslimischen und den ägyptischen Gruß- bzw. Gebetsgebärden, wie sie auf Bildwerkenseit dem Neuen Reich dargestellt sind."

69 Note 2 Samuel 15:4 "Absalom said moreover, 'Oh that I were made judge in the land, that every man which hath any suit or cause might come unto me, and I would do him justice!'"(AV) the final clause "and I would do him justice" וְהִצְדַּקְתִּיו – wi-hiṣiddạqittiw is rendered with forms of the root √zky, just discussed, in the Targum (ואיזכיניה) and the Peshitta (ܘܐܙܟܝܘܗܝ ܒܕܝܢܐ).

70 Jastrow, *Dictionary* 1263. Note in addition the Targum of Esther 1 9:22 לשדרא דורון איניש לחבריה ומעין דצדקתא מתנן לחשוכי "each person to send a gift to his comrade and charitable coins as gifts to the needy" (B. Grossfeld, *The First Targum to Esther According to the MS Paris Hebrew 110 of the Bibliothèque Nationale* [New York, 1983]).

71 See T. Podella, *Ṣôm-Fasten: kollektive Trauer um den verborgenen Gott im Alten Testament* (Kevelaer, 1989).

72 In Old Ethiopic, the word came to mean hardship in a more general sense, e.g. Leviticus 25: 43 ወኢ[ታ]ጠውቆ ፡በጸማ (ba-ṣoma) ፡ወፍራሁ፡እግዚአብሔር፡አምላክከ። rendering Greek μόχθος "labour, hardship." The original Ethiopic form of the root seems to have been ፀመመ – ṭamama.

73 So for example in the Talmud (BT Hag 10b(9)) אכלו ושתו וחוגו חגא קמאי "eat, drink, and celebrate the holiday before me"; Lamentations Rabbah (EchR[1]54 (9)) דמטי חגא ולא הוה ליה לההוא גברא כלום "for the holiday is coming, and I (lit. that man) have nothing." In *Galilaean Aramaic, in the Pesikta de Rav Kahana* (ed. B. Mandelbaum; New York, 1962) 68.8 it refers to Succoth: מן פסחה לחגא "from Passover to Succoth."

74 M. Albert (ed.), *Jacques de Saroug. Homélies contre les Juifs* [*Patrologia Orientalis* 38/1 No 174] (Turnhout, 1976), 112–35.

75 ܚܰܓ – ḥagg "peregrinatio Moslemorum" is of course a later term re-borrowed from Arabic. Possibly the meaning "pilgrimage" for ḥg is already attested in Nabataean, although this is uncertain. It certainly could be used in pagan contexts as is clear from ܚܶܓܬܳܐ – *ḥeggṯā* "the shrine or fans of an idol," i.e. ܟܰܕ ܥܳܒܕܺܝܢ ܚܶܓܶܐ ܒܚܶܓܶܐ – *kaḏ ʿiḇdīn ḥeggē b-ḥeggē* "when they make feasts in the temples of idols" (J. Payne Smith, *A Compendious Syriac Dictionary*, 126).

76 The fact that the Arabic root has dual the meanings "to devote, consecrate" (in the ivth, causative stem) and the nuance of "forbidden," i.e. حرام – ḥarām (i.e. one of the الأحكام الخمسة – al-aḥkām al-ḫāmsah) unequivocally shows that the Islamic semantics of this root were borrowed from Syro-Aramaic, in which the verb can also mean "to excommunicate, anathematise," e.g. ܟܕ ܚܙܝ ܕܡܫܝܚܐ ܠܐ ܗܘܐ ܠܗ. ܘܐܚܪܡܢ ܗܟܝܠ ܕܠܐ ܕܝܠܝܬܐ "we anathematise, then–not those who confess the characteristics of the natures ... but rather ..." (W. Wright, *The Homilies of Aphrates, The Persian Sage*. Vol. 1: *The Syriac Text* (London–Edinburgh, 1869), 7.143:17). Furthermore, the notion something ḥrm being a sanctuary or a holy site, e.g. the Mosque at Mecca, the مسجِد الحرام – masǧid al-ḥarām the "sacred mosque" (not necessarily the structure mentioned e.g. in 17:1, 2:144), or the Kaaba, the بيت الحرام – *bayt al-ḥarām* "the sacred house" is also Aramaic and most definitely pre-Islamic as the usage of ḥrm in Nabataean with the meaning "sanctuary" clearly demonstrates.

77 Literally, "He who owns the Day of Judgement."

78 A. Jeffery, "A variant text of the Fātiḥa," *The Muslim World* 29 (1939): 158–162.

79 This can be seen by viewing the tafsīr literature. For example, in 2 الحمد لله رب العالمين – *Al-ḥamdu li-llāhi rabbi l-ʿālamīn* the definite article appended to the first word was correctly seen as problematic by aṭ-Ṭabarī (a.l. instead of *حَمْدًا لِلّٰهِ رَبِّ الْعَالَمِينَ), and received a somewhat forced explanation. Similarly Tafsīr Jalalayn a.l. جملة خبرية قصد بها الثناء على الله بمضمونها من أنه تعالى : مالك لجميع الحمد من الخلق أو مستحق لأن يحمدوه، والله علم على المعبود بحق "... is a predicate of a nominal clause, the content of which is intended to extol God [by stating that]: He possesses the praise of all creatures, or that He [alone] deserves their praise. God is a proper noun for the One truly worthy of worship."

80 The biblical tradition is not unanimous as to when the God of Israel reveals himself by name to his elect. The account of the Jahwist in the Hexateuch presumes that it is known that the Deity's name is Yahweh from its beginning (Genesis 2:4b). According to the Priestly source, a critic of J, the Lord only reveals himself as Yahweh to Moses in the burning bush (Exodus 3:4ff.). Nonetheless, it should be noted that the notion of Abraham as the patriarch of the Israelites is a

late (post-)exilic literary production that presumes events originally related to Nabonidus.

81 For the later Jewish tradition cf. e.g. in the Talmud Qiddushin 71a: זה זכרי אמר ר"ת ת"ף דל"י ונקרא באל"ד ה"ה לא כשאני נכתב אני נקרא נכתב אני ביו"הקב "I am not referred to as it [scil. my name] is written. My name is written yod-hé-vav-hé and it is pronounced 'Adonai.'" Already in the Mishna (Seder Nezikin, tractate Sanhedrin 10.1), according to Rabbi Shaul those who pronounce the proper name of God will have no place in the world to come: אבא שאול אומר אף ההוגה את השם באותותיו.

82 See e.g. St Jerome, *Epistola* xxv "De decem nominibus dei" to Marcella (d.d. 384; *Migne, PL* Vol. 22, p. 428f.): "Septimum adonai, quem nos Dominum generaliter appellamus. Octavum ia, quod in Deo tantum ponitur : et in alleluia extrema quoque syllaba sonat. Nonum τετϱάγϱαμμον, quod ἀνεκφώνητον, id est ineffabile putaverunt, quod his litteris scribitur, jod, he, vav, he. Quod quidam non intelligentes propter elementorum similitudinem, cum in Graecis libris repererint, πιπι legere consueverunt."

83 See B. D. Eerdmans, "The Name Jahu," *OTS* 5 (1948): 1–29.

84 See for example in the Decalogue (Exodus 20:2): אָנֹכִי יְהוָה אֱלֹהֶיךָ אֲשֶׁר הוֹצֵאתִיךָ מֵאֶרֶץ מִצְרַיִם מִבֵּית עֲבָדִים – 'ānōḵī yhwh 'ĕlōhăḵā … "I am Y. your God, who brought you out of the land of Egypt, out of the house of bondage" in e.g. the Septuagint ἐγώ εἰμι κύϱιος ὁ θεός …, the Syriac Peshitta: ܐܢܐ ܐܢܐ ܡܪܝܐ ܐܠܗܟ – *'ănā 'ănā māryā ălāhāk* … and in the Classical Ethiopic Bible አነ፡ውእቱ፡እግዚእ፡ እግዚአብሔር፡ – 'ana wə'ətu 'əgzi' 'əgzi'abḫer … This is of course what is also found in Arabic translations of this passage: … انَا الرَّبُّ الَهُكَ

85 While the pointing of the Tetragrammaton as 'ăḏōnay is certainly of Jewish origin–based on an ancient Canaanite custom of using an epithet to avoid using the proper name of the deity, re. 'Adūn for Eshmun at Sidon, Melqart for an unknown deity at Tyre etc.–although in Jewish tradition this was later restricted to usage in prayer and God was then addressed by other terms such as הַשֵּׁם – *haš-šēm* "the Name" (cf. already Leviticus 24:11) or הַקָּדוֹשׁ בָּרוּךְ הוּא – *haq-qādōš bārūḵ hū'* "The Holy One, blessed be He" (abbrev. HKBH). Thus the Qur'ān follows Christian tradition and seems entirely ignorant of Jewish custom here.

86 While the mufassirūn such as aṭ-Ṭabari understood the meaning of the word (فَإِنَّ الرَّبَّ فِي كَلَام الْعَرَب مُتَصَرِّف عَلَى مَعَانٍ : فَالسَّيِّد الْمُطَاع فِيهَا يُدْعَى رَبًّا), he did not understand the roots of the term as discussed here.

87 From which is derived عالم – 'ālim "scholar," pl. علماء – *'ulamā'* – experts in Islamic law.

88 I.e. τὰς βασιλείας τοῦ κόσμου.

89 And note e.g. bēṯ 'ālmā as a term for "sepulcher, grave, tomb" in later Aramaic dialects: Palmyra (PAT 24:1.1) 'ksdr' dnh bt 'lm' dy bgw m'rt' m'lyk mn bb' 'l ymyn' "this arcade, the sepulcher within the burial cave on the right of the doorway as you enter"; Qumran (4Q549 1.6) פטר לבית עלמה. Cf. also Syriac 'ālmāyūṯā "this world" e.g. Ephesians 2:2 ܒܗܝܢ ܕܡܢ ܩܕܝܡ ܗܠܟܬܘܢ ܗܘܝܬܘܢ ܒܗܝܢ ܐܝܟ ܥܠܡܝܘܬܗ ܕܥܠܡܐ ܗܢܐ – "wherein in time past ye walked according to the course of this world …"

90 Such as e.g. the prayer fragment CIH 538:

1 *[…]' ykfrn ḥb-hmw w-yqbln qrbn-hm[w …]*
[…]may (the God) forgive their sins and may He accept their offering […]

2 *[…]ʿ w-b-ʿlmn bʿdn w-qrbn w-s^{2}ym ʿl[…]*
[…] and in the future and present world the patron of […]
3 *[…]n w-bs^{2}rn w-bn s^{2}rk l-mrʾm […](s1)m[…]*
[…]and the people and due to the wicked arrangement with the Lord(?)
4 *[…] w-mrḍym l-s1m Rḥmnn ḏ-Klʿn[…]*
[…] and the gratification in the name of Rḥmnn of Klʿn (?) […]
5 *[…]Rḥmnn rḍw ʾmrʾ-hmw ʾmlkn […]*
[…] Rḥmnn goodwill of their Lord, the kings of […]
6 *[…]w-ʿw(s1m) w-ḍllm w-mḥlm w-tm[…]*
[…] and epidemic, disease, drought, and […]

In older Sabaean 𐩲𐩴𐩣 – ʿgm has judicial semantics, such as "signature, document."

91 In Classical Ethiopic, which also borrowed this term from Aramaic, we find the same semantic development as in Arabic including the usage of the plural and plural i.a. in the sense of "tempus remotissimum, sive præteritum sive futurum; tempus perpetuum, sæcula, æternitas" (Dillmann, *Lexicon* 951), e.g. ንጉሠ፡ዓለም፡ – nəguśa ʿālam (Vulgate:) "rex sæculorum" (Tobit 13:6), and similar to the plural Qurʾānic usage discussed here Enoch 81:10 ወቦእኩ፡ኀበ፡ሰብእየ፡እንዘ፡እባርኮ፡ለእግዚአ፡ዓለማት፡ "And I returned to my fellow men, blessing the Lord of Eternity" (la-ʾəgziʾa ʿālamāt).

92 Or is this a reference to the Jewish terms העולם הזה – hā-ʿōlām hạz-zäh "this world" and העולם הבא – hā-ʿōlām hạb-bāʾ "the coming world"?

93 The usage of the lexeme in the plural perplexed the mufassirūn who clearly had no idea what was meant. Ṭabarī took the word here to mean "generation":

وَالْعَالَم اِسْم لِأَصْنَافِ الْأُمَم , وَكُلّ صِنْف مِنْهَا عَالَم , وَأَهْل كُلّ قَرْن مِنْ كُلّ صِنْف مِنْهَا عَالَم ذَلِكَ الْقَرْن وَذَلِكَ الزَّمَان , فَالْإِنْس عَالَم وَكُلّ أَهْل زَمَان مِنْهُمْ عَالَم ذَلِكَ الزَّمَان . وَالْجِنّ عَالَم وَكَذَلِكَ سَائِر أَجْنَاس الْخَلْق , كُلّ جِنْس مِنْهَا عَالَم زَمَانه . وَلِذَلِكَ جُمِعَ فَقِيلَ " عَالَمُونَ وَوَاحِده جَمْع لِكَوْنِ عَالَم كُلّ زَمَان مِنْ ذَلِكَ عَالَم ذَلِكَ الزَّمَان . وَمِنْ ذَلِكَ قَوْل الْعَجَّاج فَخِنْدِفُ هَامَةُ هَذَا الْعَالَم فَجَعَلَهُمْ عَالَم زَمَانه

"ʿalām is the name for various groups–each type is an ʿalām. The members of each generation of each kind are the ʿalām of that generation and that time: humanity is an ʿalām and all the people of a given time are the ʿalām of that time. The genies are also an ʿalām etc. with other created beings. Each species is the ʿalām of its own time."

Aṭ-Ṭabarī then quotes Ibn ʿAbbās رَبّ الْعَالَمِينَ : الْجِنّ وَالْإِنْس – *rabb l-ʿālamīn: al-ǧinn wal-ʾnās* "rabb l-ʿālamīn means genies and people" (although one would then expect a dual!); similarly Tafsīr al-Ǧalālayn:

أي مالك جميع الخلق من الإنس والجن والملائكة والدواب وغيرهم، وكل منها يُطلق عليه عالم، يقال عالم الإنس وعالم الجن إلى غير ذلك، وغلب في جمعه بالياء والنون أولي العلم على غيرهم، وهو من العلامة لأنه علامة على موجده

> "That is the One Who owns all of creation: humans, genies, angels, animals and others as well, each of which may be referred to as a 'world'; one says 'the world of men,' or 'world of the jinn' etc. This plural form with the yā' and the nūn [scil. 'ālamīn] is used to denote, predominantly, cognizant beings (ūlū 'ilm). The expression ['ālamīn] relates to [the term] 'sign' ('alāma), since it is an indication of the One that created it."

Here, aṭ-Ṭabarī implicitly presumes an additional meaning of 'ālam that took place in Syriac, namely the meaning "nation, people" (Brockelmann 527b "homines"), e.g. Acts 17:26: ܘܡܢ ܚܕ ܕܡ ܥܒܕ ܥܠܡܐ ܟܠܗ ܕܒܪܢܫܐ܇ ܕܢܗܘܘܢ ܥܡܪܝܢ ܥܠ ܐܦܝ ܐܪܥܐ ܟܠܗ. – *wə-men ḥaḏ dem 'ḇaḏ 'ālmā kulleh d-barnāšā d-nehwūn 'amrīn 'al 'appayyé 'ar'ā kulleh* "And he hath made of one blood all nations of men (πᾶν ἔθνος ἀνθρώπων) for to dwell on all the face of the earth." The problems with the translation "worlds" becomes clear e.g. in 45:16:

وَلَقَدْ آتَيْنَا بَنِي إِسْرَائِيلَ الْكِتَابَ وَالْحُكْمَ وَالنُّبُوَّةَ وَرَزَقْنَاهُم مِّنَ الطَّيِّبَاتِ وَفَضَّلْنَاهُمْ عَلَى الْعَالَمِينَ

> *walaqad ātaynā banī isrā'īla l-kitāba wal-ḥukma wal-nubuwata wa-razaqnā-hum mina l-ṭayibāti wafaḍḍalnā-hum 'alā l-'ālamīna*
>
> "And verily we gave the Children of Israel the Scripture and the Command and the Prophethood, and provided them with good things and favoured them above (all) peoples" (Pickthall)

In the various translations, we find, following the commentators, the last lexeme also rendered as "worlds." The translation "eternity" would of course make the most sense here as elsewhere (e.g. 2:131).

94 As the title of a goddess. For the profane use cf. Judges 5:30 "They must be dividing the captured plunder–with a woman or two (רַחַם רַחֲמָתַיִם לְרֹאשׁ גֶּבֶר – *rạḥạm rạḥămāṯạyīm lə-rō'š gāḇär*) for every man. There will be colourful robes for Sisera, and colourful, on both sides." In Akkadian, the verbal realisation of this root, rêmum, means "to love," a meaning also found for this root in Aramaic (cf. e.g. in Official Aramaic TAD D.1 2.13 אנֹהֿ אשכב עמה רחם אנה להי שגיא "I shall lie with her; I love her greatly") with numerous derivations (cf. in Syriac, often for calques of Greek terms, e.g. ܪܚܡܬ ܐܢܫܘܬܐ, ܪܚܡܬܐܢܫܐ "philanthropy").

95 Akkadian version 6f.: ilu rēmēnû šá si-pu-šú ṭābu ...

96 Reference to Deuteronomy 13:18. For more instances, cf. Jastrow, Dict. 1468.

97 See also J. Naveh, *On Stone and Mosaic* (Jerusalem, 1978) 42.4: עמלֹהֿ מן דרחמנה ומן "from his from the Merciful One and from his own acquisitions."

98 Cf. J. Texidor, *The Pantheon of Palmyra* (Leyden, 1979), 62ff. Also found as a feminine epithet for a goddess, rḥmnyt'.

99 J. C. Greenfield, "From 'lh rḥmn to al-raḥmān: The source of a divine epithet," in B. H. Hary, J. L. Hayes and F. Astren (eds.), *Judaism and Islam: Boundaries, Communication and Interaction—Essays in Honor of William M. Brinner* (Leyden, 2000), 381–292, here 385f. Note also A. Rippin, "RḤMNN and the Ḥanīfs" in W. B. Hallaq and D. P. Little (eds.), *Islamic Studies Presented to Charles J. Adams* (Leyden, 1991), 153–168.

100 Cf. ܡܪܚܡܢܘܬܐ – *mraḥmānuṯā* as a title of Byzantine kings, ܡܪܚܡܢܘܬܟ – *mraḥmānuṯāḵ* "Your mercy." Whether or not the Christian-Syriac usage stems originally from Judaism, which could well be the case, is irrelevant here.

101 Although the Bismillah (بسم الله – bismi-llāhi) is certainly also a borrowed term, in my opinion it is used in a general sense here, but it would be well worthwhile to study it diachronically in detail, especially in the collocation بسم الله الرحمن الرحيم – *bismi-llāhi r-raḥmāni r-raḥīm*. Note also the Christian Trinitarian variant بِاسْمِ الآبِ وَالاِبْنِ وَالرُّوحِ الْقُدُسِ – *bismi l-ābi wa-l-ibni wa-r-rūḥi l-qudus* "In the name of the Father, the Son and the Holy Spirit." In passing, it is worth noting that after Odo of Châteauroux' arrival in the Holy Land in 1250, when he prohibited Crusader coin issues with Islamic inscriptions and Innocent IV's confirmation and explication of this prohibition ("nomen Machometi atque annorum a nativitate ipsius (sic) numerus sculpebantur"; cf. E. Berger, *Les registres d'Innocent IV*, vol. 3 (Paris, 1897), n° 6336) after 1253, the Shahada is replaced with the Bismillah (Damascus imitative types v and vi)—besides a "Christianised" Shahada لااله الا الله مخايل رسول الله "There is no God but God and Michael is the Messenger of God" or a stress on the oneness of the Trinity, e.g. الاب والبن والروخ القدس الله واحد – *al-'āb wal-ibn war-rūḥ al-qudus ilāh wāhid* "The Father, and the Son and the Holy Spirit: One God" (see M. Bates and I. F. Preston in: A. G. Malloy, I. F. Preston, A. J. Seltman et al., *Coins of the Crusader States 1098–1291* [New York, 1994], 129–140).

102 This expression is important for understanding the manifestations of Christianity that would later lead to Islam. The "Anointed One" (i.e. the Messiah, or the Christ) is not described as the Son of God here, cf. 5:75: ما المسيح ابن مريم إلا رسول قد خلت من قبله الرسل وأمه صديقة كانا يأكلان الطعام انظر كيف نبين لهم الآيات ثم انظر أنى يؤفكون – *mā l-masīḥu bnu maryama 'illā rasūlun qad ḫalat min qablihi r-rusulu wa-'ummuhū ṣiddīqatun kānā ya'kulāni ṭ-ṭa'āma nẓur kayfa nubayyinu lahumu l-'āyāti ṯumma nẓur 'annā yu'fakūna* as well as 3:45; 4:157, 172; 5: 17, 72; 9: 31, but rather as "his anointed one!"

103 A discussion of the Christian roots of Qur'ānic apocalyptic thinking would exceed the limits of the current discussion and the capabilities of the author. For a general of the subject see i.a. F. Hahn, *Frühjüdische und urchristliche Apokalyptik. Eine Einführung* (Neukirchen-Vluyn, 1998); and especially the various articles found in D. Hellholm (ed.), *Apocalypticism in the Mediterranean World and the Near East. Proceedings of the International Colloquium on Apocalypticism.* Uppsala, August 12–17, 1979 (Tübingen 1983); also H. Gese, "Anfang und Ende der Apokalyptik, dargestellt am Sacharjabuch," in idem, *Vom Sinai zum Zion* (Munich, 1974), 202–230. In passing, it should be noted that Islamic eschatological views presuppose Christianity (and not Judaism or indigenous ideas), for example the "False

Messiah" (المسيح الدجّال – al-masīḥ ad-daǧǧāl) who will pretend to be the Messiah on the Day of Resurrection (يوم لقيامة – yawm al-qiyāma) was borrowed from Syriac ܡܫܝ̈ܚܐ ܕܕܓܠܘܬܐ – mšīḥe d-daggālūṯā "pseudo-Christs, false Messiahs" along with the notions conveyed (cf. also e.g. Bar Hebraeus, *Menaret Qudshe* 7.1.3.1 ܢܒܝ̈ܐ ܕܕܓ̈ܠܐ "the false prophets").

104 Cf. e.g. Hebrews 12:23 ܘܠܐܠܗܐ ܕܝܢܐ ܕܟܠ (<καὶ κριτῇ θεῷ πάντων) "and to God the judge of all."

105 Cf. C. A. Ciancaglini, *Iranian Loanwords in Syriac* (Wiesbaden, 2008), 152. The term would seem to be an Indo-European cognate with **ध्यान** – dhyāna, a technical term for forms of meditation in Hinduism and Buddhism (in the latter, a state of **समाधि**; cf. 禪 vulgo "Zen").

106 Cf. also in the Talmud עבד דנורא – ʿabd d-nūrā "fire worshipper, servant of fire" (מסכת נדרים פרק ט), i.e. belonging to the personnel of a Zoroastrian fire temple; see for this term M. Macuch, *JSAI* 26 (2002): 109ff. Note also ʿbdn, ʿbdnʾ "ritual practitioner" used on Babylonian magic bowls. In Syriac, this root can also be used in the technical theological sense for the "Creator," "Creation," e.g. ܡܫܘܬܦܬܐ ܗܘܬ ܘܡܢ ܕܐܡܪ ܕܠܥܒܕܘܬܐ "one who says that it took part in the Creation" (R. M. Tonneau (ed.), *Sancti Ephraem Syri in Genesim et in Exodum* [CSCO 152, Scriptores Syri 71] (Louvain, 1955) ad Ex 11:24).

107 Note also the Syriac expression ܝܗܘܕܝܘܬܐ ܥܒܕ (Brockelmann, *Lexicon*, 299b) <ἰουδαίσαι "to judaise."

108 Also spelt سِراط – sirāṭ in the text of Ibn ʿAbbās (cf. A. Jeffery, *Materials for the History of the Text of the Qurʾān* [Leyden, 1937], 195), which corresponds to the Aramaic form (the uncertainty between /ṣ/ and /s/ is also a certain indicator of a loan-word here). Note also M. Cook, *The Koran: A Very Short Introduction* (Oxford, 2000), 40. Another, albeit impossible, derivation is given by Chr. Luxenberg, op. cit. 18.

109 The mufassirūn are quite perplexed as to what this expression might have meant. Aṭ-Ṭabarī a.l.:

وَذٰلِكَ هُوَ الصِّرَاط الْمُسْتَقِيم , لِأَنَّ مَنْ وُفِّقَ لِمَا وُفِّقَ لَهُ مَنْ أَنْعَمَ اللَّه عَلَيْهِ مِنْ النَّبِيِّينَ وَالصِّدِّيقِينَ وَالشُّهَدَاء , فَقَدْ وُفِّقَ لِلْإِسْلَامِ , وَتَصْدِيق الرُّسُل , وَالتَّمَسُّك بِالْكِتَابِ , وَالْعَمَل بِمَا أَمَرَ اللَّه بِهِ , وَالِانْزِجَار عَمَّا زَجَرَهُ عَنْهُ , وَاتِّبَاع مَنْهَج النَّبِيّ صَلَّى اللَّه عَلَيْهِ وَسَلَّمَ , وَمِنْهَاج أَبِي بَكْر وَعُمَر وَعُثْمَان وَعَلِيّ , وَكُلّ عَبْد لِلَّهِ صَالِح . وَكُلّ ذَلِكَ مِنْ الصِّرَاط الْمُسْتَقِيم. وَقَدْ اِخْتَلَفَتْ تَرَاجِمَة الْقُرْآن فِي الْمَعْنِيّ بِالصِّرَاطِ الْمُسْتَقِيم , يَشْمَل مَعَانِي جَمِيعهمْ فِي ذَلِكَ مَا اِخْتَرْنَا مِنْ التَّأْوِيل فِيهِ

"This is the 'straight path,' because he who succeeds the prophets, the righteous and the martyrs, upon whom God has bestowed favour, have succeeded, succeeds in Islam, in believing in the prophets, in adhering to the Book, in doing what God commands, and in restraining himself from what He abhors, in following the course the Prophet took, the way of Abū Bakr,

'Umar, 'Uthmān and 'Alī, and of every devout servant of God. All this is the 'straight path.' The interpreters differed about the meaning of the 'straight path,' but all their interpretations are contained in the interpretation we have proffered here" …

And citing 'Abd Allāh b. 'Abbās:

وَالصِّرَاط الْمُسْتَقِيم كِتَاب اللَّه

"The 'straight path' is the Book of God" … citing Jābir b. 'Abd Allāh:

اِهْدِنَا الصِّرَاط الْمُسْتَقِيم قَالَ : الْإِسْلَام , قَالَ : هُوَ أَوْسَع مِمَّا بَيْن السَّمَاء وَالْأَرْض

"Guide us in the 'straight path' [means] Islam, which is wider than heaven and earth" … citing Abū-'l-'Āliya [and al-Ḥasan al-Baṣrī]:

هُوَ رَسُول اللَّه صَلَّى اللَّه عَلَيْهِ وَسَلَّمَ وَصَاحِبَاهُ مِنْ بَعْده : أَبُو بَكْر وَعُمَر

the 'straight path' "is the messenger of God, and his two Companions after him Abū Bakr and 'Umar." It is clear that aṭ-Ṭabarī c.s. have no idea what is meant here, nor of the relevant historical details.

110 Cf. E. Repo, *'Der Weg' als Selbstbezeichnung des Urchristentums* (Helsinki, 1964).

111 Cf. Tertullian, *Adversus Marcionem* iv.8: "Nazaræus vocari habebat secundum prophetiam Christus creatoris. Unde et ipso nomine nos Iudæi Nazarenos appellant per eum. Nam et sumus de quibus scriptum est: Nazaræi exalbati sunt super nivem, qui scilicet retro luridati delinquentiæ maculis et nigrati ignorantiæ tenebris. Christo autem appellatio Nazaræi in extraneum Iesu post tibi transtulit, sed addidit Junius quæro an scribendum fuerit eum se confirmavit competitura erat ex infantiæ latebris, ad quasi apud Nazareth descendit, vitando Archelaum filium Herodis"; also Pliny, *Naturalis Historia* v.81: "Cœle habet Apameam Marsya amme divisam a Nazerinorum tetrarchia."

112 R. A. Pritz, *Nazarene Jewish Christianity* (Leyden-Jerusalem, 1988), 11–47. See also J. Gnilka, *Die Nazarener und der Koran: Eine Spurensuche* (Freiburg, 2007). Gnilka notes striking parallels between Sura 19 and the Protoevangelium of James (sive Liber Iacobi de nativitate Mariæ). Note also S. C. Mimouni, "Les Nazoréens: recherche étymologique et historique," *Revue Biblique* 105 (1998): 208–262; idem, *Le judéo-christianisme ancien: essais historiques* (Paris, 1998). For a somewhat different view see F. C. de Blois, "Naṣrānī (Ναζωραῖος) and *ḥanīf* (ἐθνικός): Studies on the Religious Vocabulary of Christianity and of Islam," *BSOAS* 65 (2002): 1–30.

113 As every reader of the New Testament knows, Jesus was not from Nazareth, but from the Galilee. In Antiquity, he and his teaching were known as Galilean—cf. e.g. Julian's famous last words according to Theodoret Γαλιλαῖενε νενίκηκας! A similar usage is also found in his refutation of Christianity Contra Galilæos (e.g. Bk. 1: Καλῶς ἔχειν ἔμοιγε φαίνεται τὰς αἰτίας ἐκθέσθαι πᾶσιν ἀνθώποις, ὑφ' ὧν ἐπείσθην ὅτι τῶν Γαλιλαίων ἡ σκευωϱία πλάσμα ἐστὶν ἀνθϱώπων ὑπὸ κακουϱγίας

συντεθέν; yet in his letter to Phontinus "Diodorus autem Nazaræi magus" … "et ilium novum eius deum Galilæum").

114 Isaiah 11:1–10 has a long story of messianic exegesis, also in early Judaism. The rendition of the Targum makes this clear: וְיִפּוֹק מַלְכָּא מִבְּנוֹהִי דְיִשַׁי וּמְשִׁיחָא מִבְּנֵי בְנוֹהִי יִתְרַבֵּי – *wə-yippōq malkā mi-bənōhī d-yišā' ū-mšīḥā mi-bənēy bnōhī yiṯraḇēy* "A king will arise from the sons of Jesse, and a Messiah from the sons of his sons." Cf. in the NT Acts 13:22–23, Romans 15:12, Revelation 5:5, and possibly 1 Corinthians 1:23, 2:2. This verse by Isaiah is probably what Matthew 2:22–23 alludes to: καὶ ἐλθὼν κατῴκησεν εἰς πόλιν λεγομένην Ναζαρὲτ, ὅπως πληρωθῇ τὸ ῥηθὲν διὰ τῶν προφητῶν, ὅτι Ναζωραῖος κληθήσεται. The Coptic Gospel of the Egyptians iii.64:9ff. may preserve some memory of such, as well as similarly Zostrianos 47:5: ϩⲉⲛ]ⲡⲛⲁ [ⲛ]ⲉ ⲛ̄ⲛⲁⲧⲙⲟⲩ · ⲓⲉⲥⲥⲉⲩⲥ [ⲙ]ⲁⲍⲁⲣⲉⲩ[ⲥ] ⲓⲉ[ⲥ]ⲥⲉⲇⲉⲕⲉⲩⲥ [Ce sont des] esprits immortels, Yessée [M]azar[ée] Yé[s]sédékée" (see C. Barry, W.-P. Funk, P.-H. Poirier and J. D. Turner, Zostrien (NH viii, 1) [Bibliothèque copte de Nag Hammadi, Section « Textes » 24] (Québec–Louvain, 2000), 328f.; A. Böhlig, F. Wisse and P. Labib (eds.), *Nag Hammadi Codices iii,2 and iv,2. The Gospel of the Egyptians (The Holy Book of the Great Invisible Spirit)* (Leyden, 1975), 148). On נֵצֶר – nēṣär "shoot"cf. e.g. Syriac ܢܨܪܬܐ – nāṣartā "surculus."

115 Cf. Epiphanius, *Panarion* 28:1: Ναζωραῖοι καθεξῆς τούτοις ἕπονται, ἅμα τε αὐτοῖς ὄντες ἢ καὶ πρὸ αὐτῶν ἢ σὺν αὐτοῖς ἢ μετ' αὐτούς, ὅμως σύγχρονοι· οὐ γὰρ ἀκριβέστερον δύναμαι ἐξειπεῖν τίνες τίνας διεδέξαντο. Καθὰ γὰρ ἔφην, σύγχρονοι ἦσαν ἀλλήλοις καὶ ὅμοια ἀλλήλοις κέκτηνται τὰ φρονήματα. Οὗτοι γὰρ ἑαυτοῖς ὄνομα ἐπέθεντο οὐχὶ Χριστοῦ οὔτε αὐτὸ τὸ ὄνομα τοῦ Ἰησοῦ, ἀλλὰ Ναζωραίων. Πάντες δὲ Χριστιανοὶ Ναζωραῖοι τότε ὡσαύτως ἐκαλοῦντο· γέγονε δὲ ἐπ' ὀλίγῳ χρόνῳ καλεῖσθαι αὐτοὺς καὶ Ἰεσσαίους, πρὶν ἢ ἐπὶ τῆς Ἀντιοχείας ἀρχὴν λάβωσιν οἱ μαθηταὶ καλεῖσθαι Χριστιανοί. Ἐκαλοῦντο δὲ Ἰεσσαῖοι διὰ τὸν Ἰεσσαί, οἶμαι, ἐπειδήπερ ὁ Δαυὶδ ἐξ Ἰεσσαί, ἐκ δὲ τοῦ Δαυὶδ κατὰ διαδοχὴν σπέρματος ἡ Μαρία, πληρουμένης τῆς θείας γραφῆς, κατὰ τὴν παλαιὰν διαθήκην τοῦ κυρίου λέγοντος πρὸς τὸν Δαυίδ, ἐκ καρποῦ τῆς κοιλίας σου θήσομαι ἐπὶ τὸν θρόνον σου'. Further idem, 3–9.

116 Cf. Acts 11:26: χρηματίσαι τε πρώτως ἐν Ἀντιοχείᾳ τοὺς μαθητὰς Χριστιανούς. The historicity of this passage is not at issue here. The relevance is the awareness that "Christianity" was not the original lexeme used to describe what later became the new religion.

117 Cf. also Syriac ܢܨܪܝܘܬܐ – nāṣrāyūṯā; Gəʿəz ነዘራዊ – *nazarāwi* (probably from Greek) along with ክርስቲያን – *kərəsətiyān* as in Amharic etc. Something which Tertullian was well aware of op. cit. (n111) "nomine nos Iudæi Nazarenos appellant."

118 According to John (19:19), citing the previously mentioned INRI-inscription, the only NT attestation which renders Pilate's supposed text as ἰησοῦς ὁ ναζωραῖος ὁ βασιλεὺς τῶν ἰουδαίων, it cannot be translated as "Jesus of Nazareth," as this would be Ναζαρηνός or Ναζαρέτ (re. the Greek spelling in Matthew 2:23). The Greek word is morphologically the same here as in the expression used by Tertullus in Acts 24:5 (τῶν Ναζωραίων), "Jesus the Nazarene, the King of the Jews." Although the rendition of the Semitic phoneme /ṣ/ with ζ in Greek might appear odd, and could cast doubt on the derivation proposed here, e.g. the rendition ܕܢܨܪܝܐ – d-nāṣrāyā etc. in the Syriac NT make it clear that this etymology is correct and it should not be derived from an alleged root <*√nzr (this spelling, ܢܘܙܪܘܝ – nzrwy "Nazarene" found in Christian Palestinian Aramaic is

probably calqued from Greek; cf. also Gəʿəz 𝑛𝑎𝑧𝑒̄ in the previous note). In Modern Hebrew (Ivrit), the term נוֹצרי – *nōṣrī* (sg.) is the common word for Christian (whereas another group uses מְשִׁיחִי – *mašīḥī* "Messianic Jews" as a self-description; cf. Arabic مسيحي – *masīḥī*, المسيحية – *al-masīḥiyyah* "Christianity"); note also Mandaic naṣuraia. The root √nṣr is unsurprisingly productive for things Christian in Arabic, e.g. منصر – *munaṣṣir* "missionary," تنصير – *tanṣīr* "to become Christian," "to be baptised." A derivation of this root, borrowed ultimately from Syriac, is used in Malayalam to denote the St Thomas Christians of Kerala, the മാർ തോമാ നസ്രാണികൾ – *mar toma nasrani*.

119 I have discussed this term at length in a forthcoming essay ("Annus Hegiræ vel Annus (H)Agarorum? Etymologische und vergleichende Anmerkungen zum Anfang der islamischen Jahreszählung" in: K.-H. Ohlig and M. Gross (eds.), *Inârah 7* [Berlin–Tübingen, 2014]). Briefly, the traditional account of "Muḥam-mad's" life tells us that in June of 622, upon getting wind of an assassination plot against him at Mecca, he escaped with some of his loyal followers and eventually made his way to Yathrib/Medina. The traditionally accepted reference for this event is in Sura 9: 100 (cited above). In Islam, this event is viewed as so significant a turning-point that the Islamic calendar commences with the "year of the exile" (sanat or ʿam al-hiǧra, not referred to in the Qur'ān). Traditionally, the مهاجرون – *muhāǧirūn* (from a supposed root √hǧr "to emigrate, go into exile") are interpreted as the "émigrés" who left with "Muḥammad." However, several problems arise from this traditional interpretation. First, the Qur'ānic quotation is vague at best. Second, as the Qur'ān is by all accounts the first book in Arabic, we lack internal comparative evidence for the meanings of key words as this essay demonstrates. The root *haǧara* is only attested in South Semitic in the meaning of "city(-dweller)" and in Hebrew and Aramaic as the name of Abraham's concubine, Hagar. This datum, the lack of comparative Semitic support, is cause for suspicion. We know about the Islamic dating system, which begins with the "year of the exile," from contemporary evidence in Arabic, Syriac, Greek and even Chinese sources. The Syriac and Greek sources usually refer to a "year of the Arabs." We further know that in Late Antique literatures, one of the many synonyms for Arabs is "Hagarite" (along with Ishmaelite and Saracen, for example), and that in Syriac we find a derivation ܡܗܓܪ̈ܝܐ – *mhaggrāyā* (also borrowed into Greek as μαγαροί). An Greek inscription of the Caliph Muʿawiyah from Hammat Gader, dated in Classical fashion, includes the year of the colony, the indiction years for taxation (indicating that there still was some association with Constantinople, imagined or real) and the year of the local Metropolitan. In addition, it is dated "year 42 κατὰ Ἀραβας" which, based on the other dating systems, denotes the year 664. Arabic sources, such as an inscription of Muʿawiyah from Taif (modern Saudi Arabia), as well as Chinese sources, mention only the year, without reference to the dating system employed. Indeed, Muʿawiyah's inscriptions have no Islamic content whatsoever, posing additional serious questions about the traditional narrative. From the comparative evidence we have briefly touched upon here, it seems clear that the المهاجرون – *al-muhāǧirūn* are Arabs (ܡܗܓܪ̈ܝܐ – *mhaggrāyā*) and not otherwise unknown 'émigrés.'

What then are the origins of the Islamic year (هجرة – *hiǧra*)? For one answer, we know that Easter 622 was when the Romano-Byzantine Emperor Heraclius initiated a “Holy War.” Led by an icon of Christ said to have come into existence miraculously (ἀχειροποίητα), that is, as if led by Christ himself, Heraclius’ goal was to re-conquer lost Syro-Palestinian possessions and then ultimately destroy the Sassanid Empire. These are the events that led to the formation of the Umayyad Caliphate, a Byzantine shadow-empire in which the Arabs and not the Romans were to rule the region. They marked the birth of an Arab dynasty – not an Islamic one – that would rule much of the former Roman and Sassanid Empires. This is what was meant by “the year of the Arabs.” The hiǧra from Mecca to Medina described in Islamic sources has no historical underpinnings.

120 Cf. in the Sabaean dictionary by Beeston et al., op. cit. p. 100 “aide, appui, soutien, secours.”

121 Well-attested in Aramaic dialects, in Syriac also with the further semantic development >“observance,” for example nāṭōrūṯā cf. e.g. JECan 3:8 ܢܛܘܪܘܬܐ ܝܗܘܕܝܬܐ “Jewish observances.”

122 Cf. J. Tropper, *Ugaritische Grammatik* (Münster, 2000), 94f. et passim.

123 Note e.g. the etymology of the (Gnostic) Gospel of Philip: ⲛⲁⲡⲟⲥⲧⲟⲗⲟⲥ ⲉⲧϩⲓ ⲧⲛ̄ⲛⲉϩⲏ ⲧⲉⲉⲓϩⲉ ⲛⲉⲩⲙⲟⲩ ⲧⲉ ϫⲉ ⲓ̅ⲏ̅ⲥ̅ ⲡⲛⲁⲍⲱⲣⲁⲓⲟⲥ ⲙⲉⲥⲥⲓⲁⲥ ⲉⲧⲉ ⲙⲉⲥⲥⲓⲁⲥ ⲉⲧⲉ ⲡⲁⲉⲓ ⲡⲉ ⲓ̅ⲏ̅ⲥ̅ ⲡⲛⲁⲍⲁⲣⲁⲓⲟⲥ ⲡⲉⲭ̅ⲥ̅ … ⲛⲁⲍⲁⲣⲁ ⲧⲉ ⲧⲁⲗⲏⲑⲉⲓⲁ ⲡⲛⲁ ⲍⲁⲣⲏⲛⲟⲥ ϭⲉ ⲧⲉ ⲧⲁⲗⲏⲑⲉⲓⲁ “The apostles who have gone before us called [him] Jesus the Nazarene, the Messiah, that is Jesus the Nazarene Christ (“the Anointed One”) . . . Nazara means “truth,” thus the (Nazarene) is the “true one” (Text according to W. Till (ed.), *Das Evangelium nach Philippos* (Berlin, 1963), 62; translation by the author); cf. however also 114.12f.: ⲡⲛⲁⲍⲁⲣⲏⲛⲟⲥ ⲡⲉⲧⲟⲩⲟⲛϩ ⲉⲃⲟⲗ ⲡⲉ ⲙ̄ⲡⲡⲉⲑⲏⲡ “the revealed Nazarene is the secret,” interpreted as Jesus’ second name, without any linguistic basis. Nevertheless, such exegesis points out the problems regarding the interpretation of Ναζωραῖος already in Antiquity.

124 The usage of this term, currently in vogue in anti-Islamic religious cultural polemics in the West, has its origins with the Irish freethinker John Toland (1670–1722), who coined it in his work on the Jewish origins of Christianity: Nazarenus: or Jewish, Gentile and Mahometan Christianity, containing the history of the ancient gospel of Barnabas... Also the Original Plan of Christianity explained in the history of the Nazarens.... with... a summary of ancient Irish Christianity... (London, 1718). He formulated in detail, largely basing himself on the ‘Gospel of Barnabas,’ the Jewish Christian origins of Islam, presupposing by over a century and a half Nöldeke’s view of Islam being an Arab manifestation of Christianity; from his conclusion: “You perceive by this time … that what the Mahometans believe concerning Christ and his doctrine, were neither the inventions of Mahomet, nor yet of those Monks who are said to have assisted him in the framing of his Alcoran; but that they are as old as the time of the Apostles, having been the sentiments of whole Sects or Churches: and that tho the Gospel of the Hebrews be in all probability lost, yet some of those things are founded on another Gospel anciently known, and still in some manner existing, attributed to Barnabas. If in the history of this Gospel I have satisfy’d your curiosity, I shall think my time well spent; but infinitely better, if you agree, that, on this occasion, I have set The Original Plan of Christianity in its due light, as far as I propos’d to do” (84f.). Toland’s book gained notoriety, especially on the Continent through

Johann Lorenz von Mosheim's (1693–1755) rebuttal, *Vindiciæ antiquæ christianiorum disciplinæ adversus . . . Johannis Tolandi, . . . Nazarenum* (Kiel, 11722; Hamburg, ²1722) – which went to great lengths to rebut Toland's views on Christian origins. Ferdinand Christian Baur (1792–1860) of the Tübingen School would later pursue the former's line of thought in a Hegelian fashion of second century Christianity being the synthesis of two opposing theses: Jewish (Petrine) Christianity vs Gentile (Pauline) Christianity. Baur assumed, indirectly following Toland, that the Christianity represented by the Ebionites (apud Epiphanius), which as has been mentioned saw Paul (=Simon Magus, cf. Acts 8:9–24, according to Baur) as a heretic, represented 'original' Christianity, i.e. that of the Twelve Disciples.

125 On their name, cf. e.g. Eusebius, *Hist. eccl.* iii.27.6 … ὅθεν παρὰ τὴν τοιαύτην ἐγχείρησιν τῆς τοιᾶσδε λελόγχασι προσηγορίας, τοῦ Ἐβιωναίων [i.e. אביונים – 'eḇyōnīm ~ πτωχοί] ὀνόματος τὴν τῆς διανοίας πτωχείαν αὐτῶν ὑποφαίνοντος· ταύτῃ γὰρ ἐπίκλην ὁ πτωχὸς παρ' Ἑβραίοις ὀνομάζεται; cf. 1: Ἐβιωναίους τούτους οἰκείως ἐπεφήμιζον οἱ πρῶτοι, πτωχῶς. On their Judaicising teaching, e.g. … καὶ τὸ μὲν σάββατον καὶ τὴν ἄλλην Ἰουδαϊκὴν ἀγωγὴν ὁμοίως ἐκείνοις παρεφύλαττον, ταῖς δ' αὖ κυριακαῖς ἡμέραις ἡμῖν τὰ παραπλήσια εἰς μνήμην τῆς σωτηρίου ἀναστάσεως ἐπετέλουν· ὅθεν παρὰ τὴν τοιαύτην ἐγχείρησιν τῆς τοιᾶσδε λελόγχασι προσηγορίας. That the name is derived from Hebrew אביון meaning 'poor' and was used by Jewish Christians is also noted by Origen, Contra Celsum ii.1: Ἐβίων τε γὰρ ὁ πτωχὸς παρὰ Ἰουδαίοις καλεῖται, καὶ Ἐβιωναῖοι χρηματίζουσιν οἱ ἀπὸ Ἰουδαίων τὸν Ἰησοῦν ὡς Χριστὸν παραδεξάμενοι.

126 Cf. e.g. St Jerome who presumes that the document was well-known and kept e.g. in the library at Caesarea, Dialogus Adversus Pelagianos 3.2 (*Migne, PL* Vol. 23, 597): "In evangelio juxta Hebræos, quaod Chaldaico quidem Syrioque sermone, sed Hebraicis litteris scriptum est, quo utuntur usque hodie Nazareni, secundum Apostolos, sive, ut plerique autumant, juxta Mathæum, quod et in Cæsariensi habetur bibliotheca …"; idem, De viris illustribus liber ad dextrum Book 3 (op. cit. 643–644): "Mattæus, qui et Levi, ex publicano apostolus (Matth. ix, 9 ; Marc. ii, 14 ; Luc. v, 27), primus in Judæa propter eos qui ex circumcisione crediderant, Evangelium Christi Hebraicis litteris verbisque composuit : quod quis postea in Græcum transtulerit, non satis certum est. Porro ipsum Hebraicum habetur usque hodie in Cæsariensi bibliotheca, quam Pamphilus martyr studiosissime confecit. Mihi quoque a Nazaræis, qui in Berœ urbe Syriæ hoc volumine utuntur, describendi facultas fuit. In quo animadvertendum, quod ubicunque evangelista, sive ex persona sua, sive ex persona Domini Salvatoris, veteris Scricptu ræ testiminiis abutitur, non sequatur Septuaginta translatorum auctoritatem, sed Hebraicam, …"; and idem, In Michæam 7 "… credideritque Evangelio, quod secundum Hebræos editum nuper transtulimus (in quo ex persona Salvatoris dicitur: Modo tulit me mater mea, sanctus Spiritus in uno capillorum meorum (Matth. x)." Eusebius, *Historia ecclesiastica* iii.24.6: Ματθαῖός τε γὰρ πρότερον Ἑβραίοις κηρύξας, ὡς ἤμελλεν καὶ ἐφ' ἑτέρους ἰέναι, πατρίῳ γλώττῃ γραφῇ παραδοὺς τὸ κατ' αὐτὸν εὐαγγέλιον, τὸ λεῖπον τῇ αὐτοῦ παρουσίᾳ τούτοις ἀφ' ὧν ἐστέλλετο; iii.25.5: ἤδη δ' ἐν τούτοις τινὲς καὶ τὸ καθ' Ἑβραίους εὐαγγέλιον

κατέλεξαν, ᾧ μάλιστα Ἑβραίων οἱ τὸν Χριστὸν παραδεξάμενοι χαίρουσιν, i.e. ταῦτα δὲ πάντα τῶν ἀντιλεγομένων ἂν εἴη; citing Papias (14: Καὶ ἄλλας δὲ τῇ ἰδίᾳ γραφῇ παραδίδωσιν Ἀριστίωνος τοῦ πρόσθεν δεδηλωμένου τῶν τοῦ κυρίου λόγων διηγήσεις καὶ τοῦ πρεσβυτέρου Ἰωάννου παραδόσεις) iii.39.16: περὶ δὲ τοῦ Ματθαίου ταῦτ' εἴρηται: 'Ματθαῖος μὲν οὖν Ἑβραΐδι διαλέκτῳ τὰ λόγια συνετάξατο, ἡρμήνευσεν δ' αὐτὰ ὡς ἦν δυνατὸς ἕκαστος'; v.8.2: ὁ μὲν δὴ Ματθαῖος ἐν τοῖς Ἑβραίοις τῇ ἰδίᾳ αὐτῶν διαλέκτῳ καὶ γραφὴν ἐξήνεγκεν εὐαγγελίου; found in 'India' by Pantænus, v.10.3: ὧν εἷς γενόμενος καὶ ὁ Πάνταινος, καὶ εἰς Ἰνδοὺς ἐλθεῖν λέγεται, ἔνθα λόγος εὑρεῖν αὐτὸν προφθάσαν τὴν αὐτοῦ παρουσίαν τὸ κατὰ Ματθαῖον εὐαγγέλιον παρά τισιν αὐτόθι τὸν Χριστὸν ἐπεγνωκόσιν, οἷς Βαρθολομαῖον τῶν ἀποστόλων ἕνα κηρῦξαι αὐτοῖς τε Ἑβραίων γράμμασι τὴν τοῦ Ματθαίου καταλεῖψαι γραφήν, ἣν καὶ σῴζεσθαι εἰς τὸν δηλούμενον χρόνον; vi.25.2: ἐν παραδόσει μαθὼν περὶ τῶν τεσσάρων εὐαγγελίων, ἃ καὶ μόνα ἀναντίρρητά ἐστιν ἐν τῇ ὑπὸ τὸν οὐρανὸν ἐκκλησίᾳ τοῦ θεοῦ, ὅτι πρῶτον μὲν γέγραπται τὸ κατὰ τόν ποτε τελώνην, ὕστερον δὲ ἀπόστολον Ἰησοῦ Χριστοῦ Ματθαῖον, ἐκδεδωκότα αὐτὸ τοῖς ἀπὸ Ἰουδαϊσμοῦ πιστεύσασιν, γράμμασιν Ἑβραϊκοῖς συντεταγμένον; cf. also Clement, *Stromateis* ii.9.

127 See e.g. J. Frey, "Die Fragmente des Hebräerevangeliums" in: Ch. Markschies and J. Schröter (eds.), *Antike christliche Apokryphen in deutscher Übersetzung: I. Band - Evangelien und Verwandtes* (Tübingen, 72012), 593–606. In English see for example W. C. Allen, *A Critical and Exegetical Commentary on the Gospel According to S. Matthew* (Edinburgh, ^{3}1965), lxxix–lxxxv; M. R. James, *The Apocryphal New Testament* (Oxford, 1955), 1–10; B. Ehrman and Z. Pleše, *The Apocryphal Gospels: Texts and Translations* (Oxford, 2011), 216–221. We deliberately avoid here taking a stance on the nature of these works as discussed in recent literature on Early Christianity. For an overview of the debate see D. Lührmann, *Die apokryph gewordenen Evangelien: Studien zu neuen Texten und zu neuen Fragen* (Leyden, 2004); in English e.g., F. Lapham, *An Introduction to the New Testament Apocrypha* (London, 2003); B. D. Ehrman, *Lost Christianities* (Oxford, 2005); O. Skarsaune and R. Hvalvik (eds.), *Jewish Believers in Jesus: the Early Centuries* (Peabody, 2007); M. Jackson-McCabe (ed.), *Jewish-Christianity Reconsidered: Rethinking Ancient Groups and Texts* (Minneapolis, 2007).

128 See e.g. J. Frey, op. cit. (prev. note) 623–648 and his "Synopse zur Zuordnung der Fragmente zum Hebräer- und Nazoräerevangelium," 649–654.

129 Frey, op. cit. 607–622. Eusebius, *Historia Ecclesiastica* iii.27.4 … εὐαγγελίῳ δὲ μόνῳ τῷ καθ' Ἑβραίους λεγομένῳ χρώμενοι, τῶν λοιπῶν σμικρὸν ἐποιοῦντο λόγον.

130 For a detailed discussion of this subject see, Th. Hainthaler, *Christliche Araber vor dem Islam. Verbreitung und konfessionelle Zugehörigkeit: eine Hinführung* (Louvain, 2007).

131 Named after Cerinthus, cf. Ch. Markschies, Kerinth: "Wer war er und was lehrte er?" *Jahrbuch für Antike und Christentum* 41 (1998): 48–76. St Augustine, *De hæresibus VIII:* "mundum ab angelis factum esse dicentes, et carne circumcidi oportere, atque alia hujusmodi legis præcepta servari. Iesum hominem tantummodo fuisse, nec resurrexisse, sed resurrecturum asseverantes."

132 In his proem 2:4 he says about his working methods: τῶν δὲ ὑφ' ἡμῶν μελλόντων εἰς γνῶσιν τῶν ἐντυγχανόντων ἥκειν <περὶ> αἱρέσεών τε καὶ σχισμάτων τὰ μὲν ἐκ φιλομαθίας ἴσμεν, τὰ δὲ ἐξ ἀκοῆς κατειλήφαμεν, τοῖς δέ τισιν ἰδίοις ὠσὶ καὶ ὀφθαλ-

μοῖς παρετύχομεν· καὶ τῶν μὲν τὰς ῥίζας καὶ τὰ διδάγματα ἐξ ἀκριβοῦς ἀπαγγελίας ἀποδοῦναι πεπιστεύκαμεν, τῶν δὲ μέρος τι τῶν παρ' αὐτοῖς γινομένων. Ἐξ ὧν τοῦτο μὲν διὰ συνταγμάτων παλαιῶν συγγραφέων, τοῦτο δὲ δι' ἀκοῆς ἀνθρώπων ἀκριβῶς πιστωσαμένων τὴν ἡμῶν ἔννοιαν ἔγνωμεν.

133 Τὰ πάντα δέ εἰσιν Ἰουδαῖοι καὶ οὐδὲν ἕτερον. χρῶνται δὲ οὗτοι οὐ μόνον νέᾳ διαθήκῃ, ἀλλὰ καὶ παλαιᾷ διαθήκῃ, καθάπερ καὶ οἱ Ἰουδαῖοι. Οὐ γὰρ ἀπηγόρευται παρ' αὐτοῖς νομοθεσία καὶ προφῆται καὶ γραφεῖα τὰ καλούμενα παρὰ Ἰουδαίοις βιβλία, ὥσπερ παρὰ τοῖς προειρημένοις· οὐδέ τι ἕτερον οὗτοι φρονοῦσιν, ἀλλὰ κατὰ τὸ κήρυγμα τοῦ νόμου καὶ ὡς οἱ Ἰουδαῖοι πάντα καλῶς ὁμολογοῦσι χωρὶς τοῦ εἰς Χριστὸν δῆθεν πεπιστευκέναι. Παρ' αὐτοῖς γὰρ καὶ νεκρῶν ἀνάστασις ὁμολογεῖται καὶ ἐκ θεοῦ τὰ πάντα γεγενῆσθαι, ἕνα δὲ θεὸν καταγγέλλουσι καὶ τὸν τούτου παῖδα Ἰησοῦν Χριστόν–28:6. See also St Augustine, *De Hæresibus IX*: "Nazoræi, cum Dei Filium confiteantur esse Christum, omnia tamen veteris legis observant, quæ Christiani per apostolicam traditionem non observare carnaliter, sed spiritaliter intellegere didicerunt."

134 Τουτέστιν τοῦ Ἰωσήφ, τὸν Χριστὸν γεγεννῆσθαι ἔλεγεν· ὡς καὶ ἤδη ἡμῖν προείρηται ὅτι τὰ ἴσα τοῖς ἄλλοις ἐν ἅπασι φρονῶν ἐν τούτῳ μόνῳ διεφέρετο, ἐν τῷ τῷ νόμῳ τοῦ Ἰουδαϊσμοῦ προσανέχειν κατὰ σαββατισμὸν καὶ κατὰ τὴν περιτομὴν καὶ κατὰ τὰ ἄλλα πάντα, ὅσαπερ παρὰ Ἰουδαίοι καὶ Σαμαρείταις ἐπιτελεῖται. Ἔτι δὲ πλείω οὗτος παρὰ τοὺς Ἰουδαίους ὁμοίως τοῖς Σαμαρείταις διαπράττεται. Προσέθετο γὰρ τὸ παρατηρεῖσθαι ἅπτεσθαί τινος τῶν ἀλλοεθνῶν, καθ' ἑκάστην δὲ ἡμέραν, εἴ ποτε γυναικὶ συναφθείη καὶ ᾖ ἀπ' αὐτῆς, βαπτίζεσθαι ἐν τοῖς ὕδασιν, εἴ που δὰν εὐποροίη ἢ θαλάσσης ἢ ἄλλων ὑδάτων. Ἀλλὰ καὶ εἰ συναντήσειέν τινι ἀνιὼν ἀπὸ τῆς τῶν ὑδάτων καταδύσεως καὶ βαπτισμοῦ, ὡσαύτως πάλιν ἀνατρέχει βαπτίζεσθαι, πολλάκις καὶ σὺν τοῖς ἱματίοις. Τὰ νῦν δὲ ἀπηγόρευται παντάπασι παρ' αὐτοῖς παρθενία τε καὶ ἐγκράτεια, ὡς καὶ παρὰ ταῖς ἄλλαις ταῖς ὁμοίαις ταύτῃ αἱρέσεσι. Ποτὲ γὰρ παρθενίαν ἐσεμνύνοντο, δῆθεν διὰ τὸν Ἰάκωβον τὸν ἀδελφὸν τοῦ κυρίου· <διὸ> καὶ τὰ αὐτῶν συγγράμματα πρεσβυτέροις καὶ παρθένοις γράφουσι. As noted by Eusebius, Hist. eccl. iii.27.2: καὶ ταπεινῶς τὰ περὶ τοῦ Χριστοῦ δοξάζοντας. Λιτὸν μὲν γὰρ αὐτὸν καὶ κοινὸν ἡγοῦντο, κατὰ προκοπὴν ἤθους αὐτὸ μόνον ἄνθρωπον δεδικαιωμένον ἐξ ἀνδρός τε κοινωνίας καὶ τῆς Μαρίας γεγεννημένον; whilst according to him (3): ἄλλοι δὲ παρὰ τούτους τῆς αὐτῆς ὄντες προσηγορίας, τὴν μὲν τῶν εἰρημένων ἔκτοπον διεδίδρασκον ἀτοπίαν who adhered to an archaic pre-Nicene Christology, roughly compatible with that of Islam: ἐκ παρθένου καὶ ἁγίου πνεύματος μὴ ἀρνούμενοι γεγονέναι τὸν κύριον, οὐ μὴν ἔθ' ὁμοίως καὶ οὗτοι προϋπάρχειν αὐτὸν θεὸν λόγον ὄντα καὶ σοφίαν ὁμολογοῦντες, τῇ τῶν προτέρων περιετρέποντο δυσσεβείᾳ, μάλιστα ὅτε καὶ τὴν σωματικὴν περὶ τὸν νόμον λατρείαν ὁμοίως ἐκείνοις περιέπειν ἐσπούδαζον. Origen, Contra Celsum v.61 also refers to the two differing views of Jesus' nature among the Ebionites: … ἔτι δὲ καὶ κατὰ τὸν Ἰουδαίων νόμον ὡς τὰ Ἰουδαίων πλήθη βιοῦν ἐθέλοντες οὗτοι δ' εἰσὶν οἱ διττοὶ Ἐβιωναῖοι, ἤτοι ἐκ παρθένου ὁμολογοῦντες ὁμοίως ἡμῖν τὸν Ἰησοῦν ἢ οὐχ οὕτω γεγεννῆσθαι ἀλλὰ ὡς τοὺς λοιποὺς ἀνθρώπους … In both cases, the heresy consists of denying the divinity of Jesus Christ, whereby the former view, in which parthenogenesis is

advocated, corresponds with the Islamic view as for example found in Surah 4:171–172 (also quoted on 'Abd el-Malik's inscription on the Dome of the Rock):

يا أهل الكتاب لا تغلوا في دينكم ولا تقولوا على الله إلا الحق إنما المسيح
عيسى ابن مريم رسول الله وكلمته ألقاها إلى مريم وروح منه فآمنوا بالله
ورسله ولا تقولوا ثلاثة انتهوا خيرا لكم إنما الله إله واحد سبحانه أن يكون
له ولد له ما في السماوات وما في الأرض وكفى بالله وكيلا لن يستنكف
المسيح أن يكون عبدا لله ولا الملائكة المقربون ومن يستنكف عن عبادته
ويستكبر فسيحشرهم إليه جميعا

yā ahla l-kitābi lā taġlū fī dīni-kum wa-lā taqūlū ʿalā llāhi illā l-ḥaqqa inna-mā l-masīḥu ʿĪsā bnu Maryama rasūlu llāhi wa-kalimatu-hu alqā-hā ilā Maryama wa-rūhun min-hu fa-āminū bi-llāhi wa-rusuli-hi wa-lā taqūlū ṯalāṯatun ʾintahū ḫairan la-kum innamā llāhu ilāhun wāḥidun subḥāna-hu an yakūna la-hu waladun la-hu mā fī s-samawāti wa-mā fī l-arḍi wa-kafā bi-llāhi wakīlan lan yastankifa l-masīhū an yakūna ʿabdan li-llāhi wa-lā l-malāʾikatu l-muqarrabūn wa-man yastankif ʿan ʿibādati-hi wa-yastakbir fa-sa-yaḥšuru-hum ilai-hi ǧamīʿan

"O People of the Scripture! Do not exaggerate in your religion nor utter aught concerning Allāh save the truth. The Messiah, Jesus son of Mary, was only a messenger of Allāh, and His word which He conveyed unto Mary, and a spirit from Him. So believe in Allāh and His messengers, and say not 'Three'–Cease! (it is) better for you! – Allāh is only One Allāh. Far is it removed from His Transcendent Majesty that He should have a son. His is all that is in the heavens and all that is in the earth. And Allāh is sufficient as Defender. The Messiah will never scorn to be a slave unto Allāh, nor will the favoured angels. Whoso scorns His service and is proud, all such will He assemble unto Him." (Pickthall)

19:34–35.

ذلك عيسى ابن مريم قول الحق الذي فيه يمترون ما كان لله أن يتخذ من ولد
سبحانه إذا قضى أمرا فإنما يقول له كن فيكون

ḏālika ʿĪsā bnu Maryama qaulu l-ḥaqqi llaḏī fī-hi yamtarūna[82] mā kāna li-llāhi an yattaḫiḏa min waladin subḥāna-hu iḏā qaḍā amran fa-inna-mā yaqūlu la-hu kun fa-yakūn

"Such was Jesus, son of Mary: (this is) a statement of the truth concerning which they doubt. It befits not (the Majesty of) Allāh that He should take unto Himself a son. Glory be to Him! When He decrees a thing, He saith unto it only: Be! and it is." (Pickthall)

Note also St Augustine, *De Hær. X*: "Hebionitæi Christum etiam ipsi tantummodo hominem dicunt. Mandata carnalia legis observant, circumcisionem scilicet carnis, et cætera, a quorum oneribus per Novum Testamentum liberati sumus."

135 See note 137 and note A. McGowan, *Ascetic Eucharists: Food and Drink in Early Christian Ritual Meals* (Oxford, 1999).

136 Cf. also Eusebius, Hist. eccl. iii.27.4: οὗτοι δὲ τοῦ μὲν ἀποστόλου πάμπαν τὰς ἐπιστολὰς ἀρνητέας ἡγοῦντο εἶναι δεῖν, ἀποστάτην ἀποκαλοῦντες αὐτὸν τοῦ νόμου .... Cf. also the following note iii.15 "Ebionæos perstringit, qui Pauli auctoritatem elevabant."

137 Described using only the Gospel of Matthew, rejecting Paul, following Jewish custom and venerating Jerusalem as the House of God i.26.2: "Qui autem dicuntur Ebionæi, consentiunt quidum mundum a Deo factum; ea autem quæ sunt erga Dominum, son similiter, ut Cerinthus et Caprocrates opinantur. Solo autem eo quod est secundum Matthæum, Evangelio utuntur, et apostolum Paulum recusant, apostatum cum legis dicentes. Quæ autem sunt prophetica, curiosus exponere nituntur ; et circumciduntur, ac perseverant in his consuetudinibus, quæ sunt secundum legem, et Judaico charactere vitæ, uti et Hierosolyman adorent, quasi domus sit Dei" (cf. also idem In Is. Ad 8:14). On only using the Gospel of Matthew iii.7: "Ebioneitenim eo Evangelio, quod es secundum Matthæum, solo utentes." On rejecting Paul iii.15: "Ebionæos perstringit, qui Pauli auctoritatem elevabant, hancque confirmat ex Lucæ scriptis ..." "Eadem autem dicimus iterum et his, qui Paulum apostolum non cognoscunt, quoniam aut reliquis verbis Evangelii, quæ per solum Lucam in nostram venerunt agnitionem, renuntiare debent, et non uti eis ..."; The Ebionites following Theodotian the Ephesian and Aquila of Pontus, both of whom were Jewish proselytes, reject the virgin birth of Jesus iii.21.1: "Deus igitur homo factus est, et ipse Dominus salvabit nos, ipsi dans Virginis signum. Non ergo vera est quorumdam interpretatio, qui ita ardent interpretari Scripturam: 'Ecce adolescentia in ventre habebit, et pariet filium' ; quemadmodum Theodotion Ephesius est interpretatus, et Aquila Ponticus, utrique Judæi proselyti ; quos sectati, ex Joseph generatum eum dicunt ..."; Ebionites rejecting the divinity of Christ iv.33.4: "Judicabit autem et Ebionitas : quomodo possunt salvari, nisi Deus est qui salutem illorum super terram operatus est ? Et quomodo homo transiet in Deum, si non Deus in hominem ? Quemadmodum autem relinquet mortis generationem, si non in novam generationem mire et inopinate a Deo, in signum autem salutis, datam, quæ est ex virgine per fidem, regenerationem ?"; Further rejection of the divinity of Christ and seemingly also abstaining from alcohol (cf. also cf. Epiphanius, Pan. 30.16, Acts of Peter and Simon, Clement, Strom. i) 96,v.1.3: "Vani autem ei Ebionæi, unitionem Dei et hominis per fidem non recipientes in suam animam, sed in veteri generationis perseverantes fermento ; neque intelligere volentes, quoniam Spiritus sanctus advenit in Mariam, et virtus Altissimi obumbravit eam ; quapropter et quod generatum est, sanctum est, et filius Altissimi Dei Patris omnium, qui operatus est incarnationem eius, et novam ostendit generationem ; uti quemadmodum per priorem generationem mortem hæreditavimus, sic per generationem hanc hæreditaremus vitam."

138 Πάντων καλούντων τοὺς Χριστιανοὺς τότε τούτῳ τῷ ὀνόματι διὰ Ναζαρὲτ τὴν πόλιν, ἄλλης μὴ οὔσης χρήσεως τῷ ὀνόματι πρὸς τὸν καιρόν, ὥστε τοὺς ἀνθρώπους <Ναζωραίους> καλεῖν τοὺς τῷ Χριστῷ πεπιστευκότας, περὶ οὗ καὶ

γέγραπται «ὅτι Ναζωραῖος κληθήσεται». Καὶ γὰρ καὶ νῦν ὁμωνύμως οἱ ἄνθρωποι πάσας τὰς αἱρέσεις, Μανιχαίους τέ φημι καὶ Μαρκιωνιστὰς Γνωστικούς τε καὶ ἄλλους, Χριστιανοὺς τοὺς μὴ ὄντας Χριστιανοὺς καλοῦσι καὶ ὅμως ἑκάστη αἵρεσις, καίπερ ἄλλως λεγομένη, καταδέχεται τοῦτο χαίρουσα, ὅτι διὰ τοῦ ὀνόματος κοσμεῖται· δοκοῦσι γὰρ ἐπὶ τῷ τοῦ Χριστοῦ σεμνύνεσθαι ὀνόματι, οὐ μὴν τῇ πίστει καὶ τοῖς ἔργοις–28.6. Also 30:2, where he refers to a certain overlap or exchangeability: συναφθεὶς γὰρ οὗτος ἐκείνοις καὶ ἐκεῖνοι τούτῳ, ἑκάτερος ἀπὸ τῆς ἑαυτοῦ μοχθηρίας τῷ ἑτέρῳ μετέδωκε. Καὶ διαφέρονται μὲν ἕτερος πρὸς τὸν ἕτερον κατά τι, ἐν δὲ τῇ κακονοίᾳ ἀλλήλους ἀπεμάξαντο. Note also Eusebius, Hist. eccl. iii.27.2: ἄλλοι δὲ παρὰ τούτους τῆς αὐτῆς ὄντες προσηγορίας, τὴν μὲν τῶν εἰρημένων ἔκτοπον διεδίδρασκον ἀτοπίαν.

139 In 29:9 the emphasis appears to be on "Hebrew letters," which here probably refers to the square script: ἔχουσι δὲ τὸ κατὰ Ματθαῖον εὐαγγέλιον πληρέστατον Ἑβραϊστί. παρ' αὐτοῖς γὰρ σαφῶς τοῦτο, καθὼς ἐξ ἀρχῆς ἐγράφη, Ἑβραϊκοῖς γράμμασιν ἔτι σῴζεται. In 30:13, he appears somehow not to be impressed by the Hebrew: ἐν τῷ γοῦν παρ' αὐτοῖς εὐαγγελίῳ κατὰ Ματθαῖον ὀνομαζομένῳ, οὐχ ὅλῳ δὲ πληρεστάτῳ, ἀλλὰ νενοθευμένῳ καὶ ἠκρωτηριασμένῳ (Ἑβραϊκὸν δὲ τοῦτο καλοῦσιν). It was common for Greek writers of this period to use "Hebrew" (Ἑβραίος, Ἑβραιστί) pars pro toto for any Semitic language, which in most cases was probably Aramaic; "Hebrew" here appears to be used in the sense of "Jewish."

140 Quoting Tatian (46), mention is made in this regard of the (Syriac) Diatessaron ὅπερ κατὰ Ἑβραίους τινὲς καλοῦσι. Here, Epiphanius follows an established tradition, which is also attested by Eusebius and Theodoret, among others. *Panarion* 30:3 speaks of other Semitic translations such as the Gospel of John and Acts: ἤδη δέ που καί τινες πάλιν ἔφασαν καὶ ἀπὸ τῆς Ἑλληνικῆς διαλέκτου τὸ κατὰ Ἰωάννην μεταληφθὲν εἰς Ἑβραΐδα ἐμφέρεσθαι ἐν τοῖς τῶν Ἰουδαίων γαζοφυλακίοις, φημὶ δὲ τοῖς ἐν Τιβεριάδι, καὶ ἐναποκεῖσθαι ἐν ἀποκρύφοις, ὥς τινες τῶν ἀπὸ Ἰουδαίων πεπιστευκότων ὑφηγήσαντο ἡμῖν κατὰ λεπτότητα· οὐ μὴν ἀλλὰ καὶ τῶν Πράξεων τῶν ἀποστόλων τὴν βίβλον ὡσαύτως ἀπὸ Ἑλλάδος γλώσσης εἰς Ἑβραΐδα μεταληφθεῖσαν λόγος ἔχει ἐκεῖσε κεῖσθαι ἐν τοῖς γαζοφυλακίοις, ὡς καὶ ἀπὸ τούτου τοὺς ἀναγνόντας Ἰουδαίους τοὺς ἡμῖν ὑφηγησαμένους εἰς Χριστὸν πεπιστευκέναι; Eusebius, *Hist. eccl.* iii.38.2 (also vi.14.2 f.) on Paul allegedly writing the Epistle to the Hebrews "in his native tongue" which was supposedly translated by Luke: Ἑβραίοις γὰρ διὰ τῆς πατρίου γλώττης ἐγγράφως ὡμιληκότος τοῦ Παύλου, οἳ μὲν τὸν εὐαγγελιστὴν Λουκᾶν, οἳ δὲ τὸν Κλήμεντα τοῦτον αὐτὸν ἑρμηνεῦσαι λέγουσι τὴν γραφήν.

141 Καὶ δέχονται μὲν καὶ αὐτοὶ τὸ κατὰ Ματθαῖον εὐαγγέλιον. Τούτῳ γὰρ καὶ αὐτοί, ὡς καὶ οἱ κατὰ Κήρινθον καὶ Μήρινθον χρῶνται μόνῳ. Καλοῦσι δὲ αὐτὸ κατὰ Ἑβραίους, ὡς τὰ ἀληθῆ ἔστιν εἰπεῖν, ὅτι Ματθαῖος μόνος Ἑβραϊστὶ καὶ Ἑβραϊκοῖς γράμμασιν ἐν τῇ καινῇ διαθήκῃ ἐποιήσατο τὴν τοῦ εὐαγγελίου ἔκθεσίν τε καὶ κήρυγμα–30:3.

142 As suggested e.g. by C. Gilliot, "Zur Herkunft der Gewährsmänner des Propheten," in K.-H. Ohlig and G.-R. Puin (eds.), *Die dunklen Anfänge* (Berlin/ Tübingen, 2005), p. 165. I have my doubts about the validity of this suggestion in light of the testimonies for a Hebrew Gospel discussed in the preceding. The Diatessaron (<διὰ τεσσάρων ~ secunda quarta, scil. Evangelia) is usually well distinguished in literature, although it had been the standard Gospel text for some divisions of the Syriac Church for several centuries previously–but by the period

in question was seemingly already out of circulation–and where it is known variously as the ܐܘܢܓܠܝܘܢ ܕܡܚܠܛܐ - *ʾewangeliyōn d-mhalltē* "Gospel of the mixed" or ܐܘܢܓܠܝܘܢ ܕܡܦܪܫܐ - *ʾewangeliyōn d-mep̄arrešē* "Gospel of the separated," but translated literally into Arabic, الإنجيل الرباعي.

143 E.g. 29:7: ἔστιν δὲ αὕτη ἡ αἵρεσις ἡ Ναζωραίων ἐν τῇ Βεροιαίων περὶ τὴν Κοίλην Συρίαν καὶ ἐν τῇ Δεκαπόλει περὶ τὰ τῆς Πέλλης μέρη καὶ ἐν τῇ Βασανίτιδι ἐν τῇ λεγομένῃ Κωκάβῃ, Χωχάβῃ δὲ Ἑβραϊστὶ λεγομένῃ. Ἐκεῖθεν γὰρ ἡ ἀρχὴ γέγονε, μετὰ τὴν ἀπὸ τῶν Ἱεροσολύμων μετάστασιν πάντων τῶν μαθητῶν ἐν Πέλλῃ ᾠκηκότων, Χριστοῦ φήσαντος καταλεῖψαι τὰ Ἱεροσόλυμα καὶ ἀναχωρῆσαι δι' ἣν ἤμελλε πάσχειν πολιορκίαν. Καὶ ἐκ τῆς τοιαύτης ὑποθέσεως τὴν Περαίαν οἰκήσαντες ἐκεῖσε, ὡς ἔφην, διέτριβον. Ἐντεῦθεν ἡ κατὰ τοὺς Ναζωραίους αἵρεσις ἔσχεν τὴν ἀρχήν.

144 E.g. 30:2: γέγονε δὲ ἡ ἀρχὴ τούτων μετὰ τὴν τῶν Ἱεροσολύμων ἅλωσιν. Ἐπειδὴ γὰρ πάντες οἱ εἰς Χριστὸν πεπιστευκότες τὴν Περαίαν κατ' ἐκεῖνο καιροῦ κατῴκησαν τὸ πλεῖστον, ἐν Πέλλῃ τινὶ πόλει καλουμένῃ τῆς Δεκαπόλεως τῆς ἐν τῷ εὐαγγελίῳ γεγραμ ένης πλησίον τῆς Βαταναίας καὶ Βασανίτιδος χώρας, τὸ τηνικαῦτα ἐκεῖ μεταναστάντων καὶ ἐκεῖσε διατριβόντων αὐτῶν, γέγονεν ἐκ τούτου πρόφασις τῷ Ἐβίωνι. Καὶ ἄρχεται μὲν τὴν κατοίκησιν ἔχειν ἐν Κωκάβῃ τινὶ κώμῃ ἐπὶ τὰ μέρη τῆς Καρναῒμ τῆς καὶ Ἀσταρὼς ἐν τῇ Βασανίτιδι χώρᾳ, ὡς ἡ ἐλθοῦσα εἰς ἡμᾶς γνῶσις περιέχει. Ἔνθεν ἄρχεται τῆς κακῆς αὐτοῦ διδασκαλίας, ὅθεν δῆθεν καὶ οἱ Ναζωραῖοι, οἳ ἄνω μοι προδεδήλωνται … ἤδη δέ μοι καὶ ἐν ἄλλοις λόγοις καὶ κατὰ τὰς ἄλλας αἱρέσεις περὶ τῆς τοποθεσίας Κωκάβων καὶ τῆς Ἀραβίας διὰ πλάτους εἴρηται.

145 Cf. the chapter "Christian Judaizing Syria. Barnabas, the Didache, and Pseudo-Clementine Literature" in M. Murray, *Playing a Jewish Game. Gentile Christian Judaizing in the First and Second Centuries CE* (Waterloo, 2004), 29–42.

146 T. Andrae, *Mahomet, sa vie et sa doctrine* (Paris, 1945), 99.

147 ناموس – namūs <Syriac ܢܡܘܣܐ – nāmōsā (also נימוס – nīmos) <Greek νόμος "law, custom." Cf. e.g. Peshitta ad Genesis 26.5 ܚܠܦ ܕܫܡܥ ܐܒܪܗܡ ܒܩܠܝ ܘܢܛܪ ܢܛܘܪܬܝ ܘܦܘܩܕܢܝ ܘܩܝܡܝ ܘܢܡܘܣܝ – *ḥūlap̄ d- šmaʿ ʾab̲rāhām bə-qāli wə-nṭar nṭūrāṯi wə-puqdāni wə-qyāmi wə-nāmōsi* "because that Abraham obeyed my voice, and kept my charge, my commandments, my statutes, and my laws." Note in casu ܬܢܝܢܢܡܘܣܐ – tenyānnāmōsā <Hebrew משנה תורה – "Mishne Torah," i.e. Deuteronomy; cf. Ishodad of Merv: ܣܦܪܐ ܗܢܐ ܕܬܢܝܢܢܡܘܣܐ ܩܕܡ ܥܡܐ ܒܟܠ ܫܢܐ ܥܐܕܥܐܕܐ ܕܡܛܠܠܬܐ – *sep̄rā hānā d-tenyānnāmōsā qd̲ām ʿammā bə-k̲ul šnā ʿad̲ʿēd̲ā d-mṭallət̲ā* "this book of the Second Law should be read before the people every year on the Festival [> عيد – ʿīd] of Booths" (C. van den Eynde, (ed.), *Commentaire d'Išoʿdad de Merv sur l'Ancien Testament: V. Jérémie, Ézéchiel, Daniel* [CSCO 328; Scriptores Syri 146] Louvain, 1972, 44).

148 See in detail i.a. on this matter, especially whether Waraqah might have been an Ebionite, the work of E.-M. Gallez, *Le messie et son prophète: aux origines de l'Islam*, Vol. I: *De Qumran à Muhammad*, Vol. II: *Du Muhammad des Califes au Muhammad de l'histoire* (Paris, 2005), and Vol. III: *Histoire et légendologie* (Versailles, 22010). Note also J. Azzi, *Le prêtre et le prophète: aux sources du Coran* (Paris, 2001), 85f.

149 Cf. Pritz, op. cit. 71–82. Some contemporary authors, such as St Augustine writing in distant North Africa, necessarily also relied on secondary information (in De hær. X – cf. n134 supra – he cites Epiphanius; note also Jerome's Letter 79 to Augustine). See also the following note ad finem.

150 For further discussion see A. Schlatter, "Die Entwicklung des jüdischen Christentums zum Islam," *Evangelisches Missions-Magazin*, n.F. 62 (1918): 251–264; H.-J. Schoeps, *Theologie und Geschichte des Judenchristentums* (Tübingen, 1949). The classic explanation of their disappearance cf. A. von Harnack, *Die Mission und Ausbreitung des Christentums in den ersten drei Jahrhunderten* (Leipzig, [4]1924), 48–79 et passim: "Der größere Teil derselben [scil. the Jewish Christians] ist im folgenden Jahrhundert gräzisiert worden und in die große Christenheit übergegangen" 633, Jewish Christianity due to its Hellenisation "hob sich damit selbst auf" 69. For a modern reflection on von Harnack and his relationship with Judaism and Judaeo-Christianity cf. Murray, op.cit. 129–133. This view is still current among some, e.g. G. Stemberger, *Jews and Christians in the Holy Land: Palestine in the Fourth Century* (Edinburgh, 1999), 80: "no significant Jewish-Christians communities were left in Palestine itself" [scil. by the fourth century]. In a forthcoming study, Peter von Sivers convincingly argues for active Monarchian/Adoptionist congregations in the region of the northern Fertile Crescent after 325 and into the 600s, decisively contradicting the prevailing view that the clerical establishments of the Chalcedonian, Monophysite, and Nestorian Churches had succeeded by the mid-400s in eradicating Judeo-Christianity from the Middle East (P. von Sivers, "Christology and Prophetology in the Umayyad Arab Empire" in K.-H. Ohlig and M. Gross (eds.), *Inârah 7* [Berlin–Tübingen, 2014]). It should be noted in passing that Jewish-Christian sects such as the Passagians (or Circumcisi) are attested in the Lombardy—also mentioned by Bonacursus and Gregorius of Bergamo; note also the "Nazarenes" mentioned by Humbert de Moyenmoutier and in Constantine ix's bull of excommunication (1054).

151 A reference to Revelation 7:3ff., 14:1ff.

152 Note, however, in von Harnack's *Lehrbuch der Dogmengeschichte* ([Tübingen, [4]1909], Vol. II, 529–538) he notes the importance of Judaeo-Christian theology for nascent Islam. Schoeps, *Theologie*, would later pursue this aspect.

153 Not ενέϱγεια in the Aristotelian sense but rather in the sense of actus, i.e. that Christ had but one active force (i.e. God's energeia is one, as he has but one nature of the three Persons). Supposedly, this was a formulation which the Chalcedonians could interpret to mean all are the actions of one subject though either divine or human according to the nature from which they are elicited whilst the Monophysites could read their theandric interpretation into this, i.e. all actions, human and divine, of the incarnate Son are to be referred to one agent, who is the God-man and that consequently His actions, both the human and the Divine must proceed from a single theandric energeia. That is the nature of Christ's humanity and divinity and their interrelationship was avoided in favour of agreeing that whatever the latter, the Godhead had only one active force.

154 E.g. the phrase וכל הנוצרים כרגע יאבדו – *wə-ḵōl hạn-noṣrīm kə-rägạʿ yăʾăḇdū* "And may all the Noṣrim pass in a moment." Cf. for this the discussion and the works cited in Pritz, op. cit. 95–107.

155 E.g. *Panarion* 29:9: πάνυ δὲ οὗτοι ἐχθροὶ τοῖς Ἰουδαίοις ὑπάρχουσιν. Οὐ μόνον γὰρ οἱ τῶν Ἰουδαίων παῖδες πρὸς τούτους κέκτηνται μῖσος, ἀλλὰ καὶ ἀνιστάμενοι ἕωθεν καὶ μέσης ἡμέρας καὶ περὶ τὴν ἑσπέραν, τρὶς τῆς ἡμέρας ὅτε εὐχὰς ἐπιτελοῦσιν ἑαυτοῖς ἐν ταῖς συναγωγαῖς ἐπαρῶνται αὐτοῖς καὶ ἀναθεματίζουσι, τρὶς τῆς ἡμέρας φάσκοντες ὅτι «ἐπικαταράσαι ὁ θεὸς τοὺς Ναζωραίους». Δῆθεν γὰρ τούτοις περισσότερον ἐνέχουσι, διὰ τὸ ἀπὸ Ἰουδαίων αὐτοὺς ὄντας Ἰησοῦν κηρύσσειν εἶναι <τὸν> Χριστόν, ὅπερ ἐστὶν ἐναντίον πρὸς τοὺς ἔτι Ἰουδαίους, τοὺς τὸν Ἰησοῦν μὴ δεξαμένους.

156 Also ܢܘܚܡܐ – nūḥāmā, e.g. John 11:25.

157 James Barr's criticism of the difference between etymology and semantics, especially with regard to biblical philology are also especially relevant for Qur'ānic philology (James Barr, *The Semantics of Biblical Language* [Oxford, 1961]). Etymology "is not, and does not profess to be, a guide to the semantic value of words in their current usage, and such value has to be determined from the current usage and not from derivation" (107), and that "… there is a normative strain in the thought of many people about language, and they feel that in some sense the 'original,' the 'etymological meaning,' should be a guide to the usage of words, that the words are used 'properly' when they coincide in sense with the sense of the earliest known form which their derivation can be traced; and that when a word becomes in some way difficult or ambiguous an appeal to etymology will lead to a 'proper meaning' from which at any rate to begin" (109). To use an example of Barr's, it is indeed irrelevant for English semantics that the adjective 'nice' <Latin nescio "I don't know." Such criticism does indeed apply to much of the past research on alleged loan-words in the Qur'ān.

158 One of the few English words with a Welsh etymology is probably "Dad," "father" <tad (pl. tadau).

159 So for example *bylaw* < bylög "village law"; "dirt" <drit "merda"; "husband" < husbondi "master of the house"; "slaughter" < slahtr "butchering"; "thrift" < þrift "prosperity" etc.

160 Such as "bow" <boeg; "buoy" <boei; "deck" <dek; "freight" <vracht; "keel"<kiel; "mast"<mast; "skipper" <schipper; "yacht" <jacht etc.

161 Which is why Americans eat 'cookies' (<koekje, diminutive) with their coffee and not biscuits with their tea. With the Dutch colonial presence in the New World are also the roots of 'Santa Claus' <Sinterklaas "Saint Nicholas."

162 For example 'avatar' < **अवतार** avatāra "descent"; 'Blighty' < **विलायती** – vilāyatī "foreign" (ولايتى "provincial, regional," cf. French Wilaya); 'bottle' < بوتل – botul "rigid container"; 'bungalow' < **बंगला** – baṅglā "Bengali"(-style) (<Gujarati બંગલો – baṅgalo); 'candy' < **கண்டு** – kaṇṭu; 'cash' < **காசு** – kācu; 'cot' < **खाट** – khāṭ (Urdu كهاٹ); 'pyjamas' < **पैजामा** – paijāmā (<جامه + پاى); 'shampoo' < **चाँपो** – chāmpo (Sanskrit **चपयति** – capayati "kneading"?); 'thug' < **ठग** – thag (<Sanskrit **स्थग** – sthaga "scoundrel"?) etc.

163 It is beyond the scope of this article to discuss Arabic as a Semitic language. It should be noted, that its morphology indicates that it is most closely related to the North-West Semitic phylum of Semitic languages—aerially it may be best plotted in the Syro-Palestinian dialect continuum somewhere between Phoenician and

Hebrew on the one axis and Ancient North Arabic on the other; it displays no close affinities with the South Semitic branch. Furthermore, Arabic is by no means archaic–this thesis, often found in older works on Semitic languages, is no longer valid. With the decipherment of third millennium Semitic languages such as Eblaite and Old Akkadian, we now have a much better idea of ancient Semitic (cf. e.g. R. Hasselbach, *Sargonic Akkadian: A Historical and Comparative Study of the Syllabic Texts* [Wiesbaden, 2005]). Breviter, that Classical Arabic seemingly preserves more of the original Semitic consonantal inventory makes it no more archaic than English, one of the few Germanic languages which preserves the sound þ, i.e. /ṯ/. Arabic is far removed from proto-Semitic, as one would logically expect.

164 This can be seen especially in pivotal loans such as ሃይማኖት – *hāymānot* < ܗܝܡܢܘܬܐ – *haymānūṯā* "faith, religion" (i.e. Christianity); Dillmann, *Lexicon* 14: "perigrinæ formationis, ab Aramæis petitum, ab Æthiopibus frequentissime usisatum…" According to tradition, Ethiopia became Christian with the conversion of King Ezānā (ዔዛና) by the Syriac monk St Frumentius (ፍሬምናጦስ; †383) in the fourth century; cf. G. Lusini, 'Naufragio e conservazione di testi cristiani antichi: il contributo della tradizione etiopica,' Università degli Studi di Napoli "L'Orientale" annali 69 (2009): 69–84 with literature.

165 Indeed the origins of rabbinic Judaism are largely the result of the polemic with Christianity in the fourth century, cf. e.g. D. Boyarin, "Rethinking Jewish-Christianity: An Argument for Dismantling a Dubious Category," *Jewish Quarterly Review* 99 (2009): 7–36.

166 The doctrine of the parthenogenesis of Jesus Christ, also found in the Qur'ān (cf. supra n134), presupposes the Greek Bible translation and in no way the Hebrew understanding from Isaiah 7:14! Indeed all of the alleged 'prophecies' of Jesus Christ in the Hebrew Bible are exegetical anachronisms.

167 See above n134.

168 "Die älteste Missionsgeschichte ist unter Legenden begraben oder vielmehr durch eine tendenziöse Geschichte ersetzt worden, die sich in wenigen Jahrzehnten in allen Länder des Erdkreises abgespielt haben soll. In dieser Geschichte ist mehr als tausend Jahre hindurch gearbeitet worden–denn die Legendenbildung in bezug auf die apostolische Mission beginnt schon im ersten Jahrhundert und hat noch im Mittelalter, ja bis in die Neuzeit hinein geblüht; ihre Wertlosigkeit ist jetzt allgemein anerkannt."

169 See the comprehensive study: J. Van Seters, *In Search of History: Historiography in the Ancient World and the Origins of Biblical History* (Winona Lake, 1997).

170 Interestingly, historical criticism of the Bible has been noticed in the Islamic world. For example, the impressive synthesis by the Indian scholar Rahmatullah Kairanawi (1818–1891) إظهار الحق – *Al-'iẓhār al-ḥaqq* "Testimony of Truth" (6 Vols., 1864), uses the first fruits of critical biblical scholarship to demonstrate the 'corruption' of the Bible and Christianity—in contrast to Islam—(cf. C. Schirrmacher, "The Influence of German Biblical Criticism on Muslim Apologetics in the 19th Century" in A. Sanlin (ed.), *A Comprehensive Faith: An International Festschrift for Rousas John Rushdoony* [1997]).

Part 3

Apocrypha, Jewish Christianity, and the Koran

Islam

Adolf von Harnack

Excerpt translated by Markus Gross, from Lehrbuch der Dogmengeschichte *[Textbook of the History of Dogma], reprint of the revised and augmented 4th ed., Tubingen, 1909 (Wissenschaftliche Buchgesellschaft: Darmstadt, 1964), vol. 2,* Die Entwicklung des kirchlichen Dogmas I *[The Development of Ecclesiastical Dogma I], ch. 3, pp. 529–38.*

When dealing with the history of church and dogma it seems more justified to enlarge upon Islam than upon Manichaeism. I already expounded this thesis of mine in a more paradoxical form on the occasion of my senior doctorate defence in 1874 ("Muhamedanismum rectius quam Manichaeismum sectam Christianam esse dixeris" ["You would rather say/ It is more justified to say that Mohammedanism is a Christian sect than Manichaeism."]). As the relationship between Islam and Christianity (and Judaism respectively) has aroused more and more interest in the past few years, I allow myself to publish the explanations given thirty-two years ago at the Lecturers' Society in Leipzig, hitherto only extant as a manuscript (see also a reference to them in vol. 1, p. 331 no. 2). With the exception of two lines I have not altered anything, as on a whole I profess as much to them today as I did then. At the end of the chapter I will add a few future perspectives required by the study of Islam within the framework of the History of Dogma.

The nature of the relationship between Islam and Christianity is a question often discussed. Especially in recent times there have been studies about how much the founder of Islam was influenced by Christian thought, how much he knew about the Christian faith, how the amazing analogies between the two religions can be explained and whether Islam, in any way possible, can be understood from the perspective of the history of the Christian Church, even if only indirectly or partially. Direct and reliable historical reports are almost completely missing; so in order to answer these questions we have no recourse except a comparison of the two religions based exclusively on *internal* criteria. The very nature of the matter makes their interpretation uncertain and subjective, yet this procedure promises to yield more—and more relevant—results than we have come by so far. If one does not want to go astray in such an undertaking, the crucial point is the method to be applied. It is enormously difficult to judge the interdependence and the value of two religions, as the features that allow a complete and reliable assessment of their relationship can hardly ever be identified with a reasonable degree of certainty. External similarities in cultic, ceremonial and dogmatic forms may as well have emerged spontaneously, or they can have a totally different purpose in the two religions, which requires a different interpretation. On the other hand parallelisms and analogies of purpose may be hidden behind divergent forms, so that the truly similar elements cannot immediately be detected as such. And finally the degree of impact of one religion upon the development of another is an issue on all levels of interaction, from the most external and superficial influence of one religion upon another up to the actual triggering of the emergence of a new religion.

Above all, one has to beware of assessing the nature of the relationship between two religions based on their theology, the religious metaphysics they have generated. Academic theology is almost always a bad witness and interpreter of the faith it represents. First, it usually has an apologetic motivation, therefore the faith it purports to define and present is regarded from a forced and unfitting perspective, thereby distorting the original order and purpose of its simplest expressions; moreover, the development of doctrine and theology takes place a long time after the emergence of the religion itself, therefore a pure and unbiased understanding of one's own religion cannot be expected anymore. And finally, theology in the state of emergence has to operate with a terminology which it often only partially creates itself, the main elements of which it therefore has to adopt from other and different religious and ethical mindsets. Therefore it comes as no surprise that the theology of the Christian Fathers—and this does not only apply to its *forms*—is heavily influenced by Plato, Aristotle, Stoicism and the dogmatic and ethical theorems of the philosophy and science of antiquity. The same influence, however, has had an impact on the formation of Muhammedan theology and doctrine. It is therefore quite easy to identify major parallels and congruencies between the two. But these similarities do not refer to the religions themselves, but only their systematic adaptations. The academic exchange between professional representatives of religions has not necessarily anything to do with their internal relationship and attitude to each other. This, of course, does not mean that the academic adaptations of religions do not have an impact on the further historical development of the religion itself, and especially that ties between a certain religion with the one or other philosophical way of thinking could not be one of its very characteristics, but the comparison of theologies should not claim more than secondary importance and its results have to be cross-checked with more reliable findings.

The same applies to the comparison of ethical maxims and public morals imposed by religions on their believers. Such an investigation will not allow more than just preliminary and limited judgment, as the moral state of a religious community is only partially dependent on the intended or actually exerted impulses of the founder of the respective religion. The number of true adherents of a religion is always very small, the lives they lead often not less hidden than the motives they are driven by, while at the same time innumerable factors determine the activities of those who publicly profess their adherence to the founder of a religion.

In contrast, the comparison of peculiar views on history typical for specific religious communities will lead to much safer results, as much as the investigation of the position in the world or the state that a religious group ascribes to itself or its attitude towards the goods and purposes of life. History teaches us that the self-awareness of a religious community visible in these matters is much more long-lived and displays less propensity to change than is usually the case in other respects; moreover, modifications of the original consciousness are much easier to detect as such here and can subsequently be eliminated from our considerations. The public policy of a religious community is fundamentally dependant on these historico-philosophical and meta-political concepts, and the bigger the conflicts between a religious community and the reigning power and political order, the more likely it is that these antagonisms reveal their original interest and thus their original nature and essence. Nevertheless, however, even the field of religious constitution and law is not immune to outside influence. Therefore, it is not advisable to take the comparison of the attitudes of religions toward the world as a basis for an investigation about their relationship toward each other.

If a religion is to be judged from its current state, then its *cult* is the comparatively best point of departure; for it is beyond doubt that of all religious functions it is the cult which resists outside influences most vigorously and for the longest time, thus representing the typical traits of a religion most conspicuously. But the most reliable method will always start with or limit itself to a comparison of the *original* shape of the religions to be investigated. When assessing the relationship between two religions, the situation is different if one of them is centuries older, like in the case of Islam and Christianity. Here it does not suffice to ascertain the *classical* shape of the older of the two. It is rather necessary to find out which varieties of the older religion existed at the time the younger religion emerged. What has to be compared to the younger religion are these later varieties, which, however, cannot be understood without knowledge of the oldest stage of the religion of which they might not be more than a very distorted copy.

It would seem that the most authentic traits of religion can be inferred from the authentic words and actions of its founder. Nevertheless, a second source may be or rather has to be used as well, and for a good reason: the characteristic feature of moral and universal religions is that they were *founded* in a specific era, that they have *founders*. Within the context of the divine revelation they proclaimed, these founders of religions attributed a specific and religious dignity to themselves, which they linked so inseparably and in such a peculiar way with their preaching about God, that the one cannot be illustrated without the other. The nature and extent of this dignity, however, cannot be inferred from the words of these founders alone. Their effect on others and their personal way of finding faith must inevitably be taken into consideration. A number of relations and claims must be taken account of that can only be measured and clarified from their effects. Therefore, the statements of the religious community as collected by the founder himself must be considered in order to reconstruct the authentic shape of a religion.

A common trait in both original Christianity and Islam is their emphasis on pure monotheism, in contrast to all deification of creatures and to polytheism, as well as against all national and particular limitations of faith, their partial adoption of Jewish traditions from the Old Testament, a doctrine of general retribution in the hereafter, in this context the commitment to pure veneration of God and moral conduct, and finally the propagation of faith over the whole world. Nevertheless, these parallels appear in a different light if the differences between the two religions are considered. The decisive notions by which Christianity summarized these doctrines were the *complete revelation from God*, the *redemption of mankind* and the *realm of God*. Nobody can deny that they represent the typical features of Christianity as a religion. God has been revealed to the human race, his being and will has become known. The Christian community has been redeemed from sin and death and through this community mankind, which had been separated from God, is lead back to him. Finally a realm of God on earth has been founded, which is a realm of good, comprising the highest goods and purposes, in which the law of love alone is valid and the children of God meet their destiny guided by the providence of God. These three sentences are central ideas of the Christian religion, and the estimation of the founder of the religion within his community, based on his own words, was determined according to these notions. For it is in these three regards that he shall be known and believed as the personal and everlasting mediator and representative of God. Therefore, the community attributed characteristics to him described by the predicates of unique prophet, priest and king—and summarized under the notion son of God. The same predicates designate the religious and moral perfection of the members of the realm of God, as these are dependant of the founder. They shall recognize God and proclaim him on the ground that God has been revealed to them; they shall come to God, pray to him and have him forgive their sins, because, as redeemed ones, they are priests of God and are allowed to approach him; and they shall imitate God's love in their lives and in their actions as citizens and children of the realm.

In Islam these notions of redemption and of the realm of God are missing completely. Instead, the notion of the right view of God, which only now has become accessible, dominates the whole religion. Therefore the dignity of the founder is secured only under the predicate of prophet, as it is also limited to his temporal existence. As the notion of redemption is missing, Islam has not developed a particular view of sin; as a consequence, the notions of God's love and grace became secondary. And as the idea of the realm of God remained widely misunderstood, Islam never demanded the moral dominance of the world due to religious faith; as a consequence of this attitude, Islam is indifferent to all ethical relations, which cannot be linked to the notion of God's absolute power and his punishing and rewarding justice. Thus, the religious and moral moods Islam strives to evoke are limited to a certain belief in God and his prophet, to the unconditional submission to the divine will, which can be inferred empirically from the course of events, and to the exact fulfillment of those duties that God imposes. One of the first and foremost of them is the propagation of the right view of God. The indifference as to the means to be applied when achieving this propagation—and from the start Islam has explicitly mentioned them—is evidence that Islam connects religious faith only very loosely with higher moral motives.

Muhammedan theology has not only commented and executed these chains of ideas in many ways, but has undoubtedly added a number of regulations and thoughts, which make Islam seem to be a religion of higher value. It will, however, be hard to prove that it filled real gaps and that its additions easily fit into the original circle of views. The latter is a closed system and as such without gaps. Now the question arises, what the relation between Islam and Christianity is and whether the above-mentioned sketches allow to state a true dependance of the former on the latter. This question has to be answered in the negative. The extent of congruence between Judaism and Islam is at least equal to that between the basic notions of Christianity and the latter. In the age Islam emerged from, the ideas represented by this religion may have been taken over and merged from so many different sources that only the most conclusive evidence seems acceptable here. Moreover, the sketch given of Christianity above must be considered a very idealized one when dealing with the Christianity of the seventh century CE. Oriental Christianity was then represented by the Byzantine Imperial Church as the official church of the State on the one hand and a varied number of sects on the other, the origins of which go back to the the period of time between the second or even first century CE and the fifth. Regarding the characteristics of the form of Christianity within the Byzantine Church it is true that the original views concerning revelation, redemption and realm of God had not been completely dismissed; yet, they had been distorted and garbled to the extent that it would have been difficult to see a connection between what had been the Christian religion in the first and in the sixth century. However, after an only cursory glance at the changes the Catholic Church had gone through since the second century, it becomes clear that in no respect can they be regarded as preconditions for or primary stages of the emergence of Islam, unless we assume that the Muhammadan movement did not only possess the ability to rapid expansion, but also had its origins in an *antithesis* against the Catholic Christianity of Byzantium, Alexandria and Antioch. This latter hypothesis, however, is totally unfounded, as much as the former is justified: therefore the Byzantine shape of Christianity can be left out of our considerations. That Muhammad was in no respect influenced by it, that formulae of faith, cult, politics and the discipline of the Oriental patriarchies have less in common with Islam's religious program than any other religious or ecclesiastical movement of the era is beyond doubt. But if we may not compare Islam to the original shape of Christianity in order to find out more about the origins of this religion or its dependance on its Christian predecessor, and if furthermore a comparison with the Byzantine form of the Christian religion will lead us astray, then what would remain is the investigation of Catholic Christian sects with the aim of ascertaining their relationship with Islam.

In fact there is evidence for the formation of [yet another] Christian sect which is to a much greater extent worthy of a close comparative inspection.

Regarding many core tenets, Islam is congruent with [original] Christianity, regarding others with Judaism. With Christianity in its peculiar Catholic shape no major parallel can be drawn. So the religious group to be considered in our comparative study is the one which in church history is known as *Judeo-Christianity*. The origin of this movement goes back to the first century CE and its later development can be observed until the fifth century and later.

Judeo-Christianity itself can be subdivided into a number of rather independant sects, which are distinguished by doctrine as well as discipline and cult. Most of these sects share the following traits:

(1) a view of the notion of God which dismisses all speculation about several personae merged in the godhead.
(2) the unimportance of the notion of redemption.
(3) an understanding of the realm of God as a visible, particular and future one—or in this context the indifference toward the notion of a moral and invisible realm of God.
(4) an energetic fanaticism in the propagation of faith.

Judeo-Christianity started to spread in the first century CE from Palestine, was brought by emissaries to the whole Roman Empire in the form of small colonies, but, like Gnostic sects, gradually withdrew to the East. From the fourth century on, the only traces of Judeo-Christianity are to be found at the Eastern border of the Byzantine Empire and beyond. Organized in small communities living in villages and some specific areas, Judeo-Christian congregations are attested in Palestine, Syria, Arabia, probably even in the East.

The above-mentioned characteristic traits of Judeo-Christianity as opposed to the Catholic religion undoubtedly let it seem much more akin to Islam than the latter, and its geographical distribution is highly remarkable. Nevertheless, one branch of Judeo-Christianity, in fact its strongest variety, must be excluded from further consideration. The so-called *vulgar* Judeo-Christianity or *Ebionism* is characterized by its staunch adherence to the everlasting validity of the Old Testament laws and its limitation of the Christian religion to the sons of Abraham, the Jewish nation. In this sect Christianity is kept small as a particular, national and ceremonial-statutory religion. Islam no longer accepts these limitations. Therefore, if the distinctive feature of vulgar Judeo-Christianity was its claim that such limitations existed, then it seems highly improbable that this religious group had any influence on the formation of Islam.

So the only religion apt for a comparison is Gnostic Judeo-Christianity, or those varieties of general Judeo-Christianity which were under strong influence of Gnostic speculations in the second century CE. Gnostic Judeo-Christianity can to a certain extent already be detected in the New Testament (*Epistle to the Colossians*, *Pastoral Epistles*), later in the accounts of the Church Fathers (Hippolytus, *Philosophumena* IX, 13-17. X, 29; Origen as mentioned in Eusebius' *Ecclesiastical History* VI, 38; Epiphanius, *Panarion* h. XIX, XXX, LIII; Theodoret, haeret. fab. II, 7), and finally in a literary monument which goes back to it—the source of the so-called *Pseudo-Clementine Writings*. The first thing we can state about this form of Judeo-Christianity is that it shared all its above-mentioned general characteristics. Apart from that, however, it displayed a number of specific traits *which demonstrate that it was a religious variety congenial and on a par with Islam*. It will suffice to summarize these traits in the following. The parallels to be found in Islam are assumed to be so well-known that further explanations have been considered unnecessary.

(1) Gnostic Judeo-Christianity can be distinguished from its vulgar counterpart by its tendency to strip Judaism, which is still the basis of the latter, from its specific legal and national regulations and thereby elevating it to the status of a universal religion.
(2) For this purpose Gnostic Judeo-Christianity criticizes the Old Testament, above all its regulations concerning sacrifice and its ceremonial-legal instructions. The latter are dismissed as later and falsified

elements, instead the veneration of God shall take place in an unadulterated and spiritual form.

(3) Gnostic Judeo-Christianity (at least this is true of some of its variants) ceases to consider circumcision as a precondition for salvation, and where it is retained, it is only seen as a venial ritual.

(4) Gnostic Judeo-Christianity emphasizes *one* thought: pure monotheism. In all its varieties it opposed the notions of hypostases and the doctrine of Jesus as the son of God propagated by the church.

(5) Gnostic Judeo-Christianity proclaims itself to be a form of pure Mosaism restored with prophetic vigor. It did not aspire to be a totally new religion, but a re-establishment and pure representation of an old one.

(6) Gnostic Judeo-Christianity therefore acknowledges Jesus only as a great, or better *the* great prophet and dismisses any view that goes beyond the notion of him being a true prophet. If occasionally the designation ὁ μέγας βασιλεύς ["the Great King"] for Jesus is used, then the notion connected with this title does not imply any consequence. But as Christianity only guarantees the restoration of the old religion of the patriarchs and of true Mosaism, thus not displaying any kind of absolutely new revelation, it is assumed that the true prophet, who is or was Jesus, had appeared already *in* the patriarchs and *in* Moses, according to others had appeared *to* the patriarchs and *to* Moses. Especially the line Adam, Abraham, Moses, Elijah, Jesus is emphasized.

(7) A characteristic of Gnostic Judeo-Christianity is its unbreakable drive and fanaticism to propagate its faith to a much greater extent than to its vulgar counterpart. The literature it left to us is totally dedicated to propaganda; in order to promote it, the history of the Apostolic era was radically and brazenly rewritten and falsified by the Judeo-Christians. Until the beginning of the third century, starting from Syria and Palestine, their emissaries went as far as Rome.

As we have seen, Gnostic Judeo-Christianity in general, especially regarding some striking details, displays profound parallels with Islam. This is even more the case with one of its specific varieties: the *Elkesaites*. The group called Elkesaites by the Church Fathers are one sect within Gnostic Judeo-Christianity which probably did not appear before the end of the second century CE, although their book of revelation is dated at the third year of the emperor Trajan (the designation Elkesai/Chelkesai = δύναμις ἀπόρρητος [*transl.:* dýnamis apórrētos – "unspeakable, secret force"] probably refers to this book, the Church Fathers erroneously using this name for the founder of the sect). They were originally domiciled in Syria and Palestine. An emissary of this sect, Alcibiades, came to Rome at the time of the Roman bishop Calixtus (about 220 CE). Hippolytus and perhaps Origen met him there and tried to refute him. The account of Epiphanius (end of the fourth century) goes back to contemporary, direct reports, which, however, were arranged in a confusing way by the bishop. Theodoret, according to his own words, is dependant on Hippolytus. The Fihrist confirms the existence of these Elkesaites as late as the tenth century, but does not offer more than very obscure information about them, calling them Mogtalisah [Muġtasilah] and their founder el-Hasai'h [al-Ḥasīḥ].

The characteristic traits of Elkesaism, apart from the general Gnostic Judeo-Christian and some astrological and magic peculiarities, are the following:

(1) The founder mitigated the strict asceticism in his religious group and judges cases of denial under prosecution in a very moderate way. He does not only allow marriage, but even calls for it. The consumption of wine, however, remains forbidden.

(2) Instead of a unique act of baptism, the founder established repeated ablutions of baptism and purification, which were strongly emphasized.

(3) The founder claims to possess a new revelation, which is congruent with the old ones sent down [to prophets] beginning with Adam up to Christ, but surpasses them. He exhibits a new, sacred book of revelation, which according to one source is said to have fallen from heaven, according to another one was handed over to him by a third person from an angel. The angel is portrayed as 96 miles long and 24 miles wide.

(4) The founder proclaims that after Jesus, the true prophet, which had appeared in the patriarchs and so forth, would also reveal himself in other persons.

(5) Among the Elkesaites the founder and his family, up to his grandchildren and great-grandchildren, were revered very highly. In general, the extended family of the new prophet is central to the religion. Thus, Epiphanius gives the following account: "Up to the age of Constantine, two sisters, Marthus and Marthana, were venerated like gods in their country, because they were descendants of Elkesai. Marthus died some time ago, but Marthana is still among the living. Their saliva and other things were used by these sectarians for healing purposes and so forth."

(6) The Elkesaites teach that one should not pray toward the East, but toward Jerusalem.

The parallels with Islam are immediately obvious. The most interesting point, however, is the fact that early religious movements emerged from this Gnostic Judeo-Christian background and stayed alive, yet they cannot be called

Christian anymore, as the claim of the founder of Elkesaism that he has received a revelation superior to that given to Christ annihilates the originally Christian character of his creation and turns his work into the founding of a new religion, albeit with the means of a predecessor religion. It cannot be denied that Gnostic Judeo-Christianity, in its developed Elkesaite form, in many and decisive regards appears as congenial and on a par with Islam. Moreover, it is certain that at the time of Muhammad it existed in areas not far from those where he sojourned. I see myself unable to decide whether he knew it or was influenced by it. In any case, at his time there were religious groups in existence that had emerged in Christianity, in relation to which his creation was nothing new.

This is what I wrote in the year 1877 [so we can conclude that:] *Islam is a transformation of the Jewish religion, which itself had already been transformed by Gnostic Christianity, on an Arabic foundation by a great prophet.* Islam's strength is its strict monotheism with the pronounced claim of God as the sole source of power and mercy and the struggle against any kind of idolatry, a view of faith as unconditional submission to the will of God, the doctrine of the last and highest prophet, the absolute trust in his revealed word, the simple and certain conviction of the reward for good and punishment for evil deeds, and the performance of divine service in the form of prayer. These are great yet simple elements, which, contrasted with the pre-Islamic Arabian religion, are tantamount to a full-fledged revelation, and proved their power even against monophysite and Byzantine Christianity, whereever these were encountered. Due to the strong emphasis on the oneness of God and the rejection of imagery, in fact due to its general simplicity, which let a spiritual religion reappear, Islam was certainly superior to the Christianity then common with its doctrine of trinity, which was only comprehensible as a form of monotheism to sophisticated scholars, together with all its magic cult and paraphernalia. The liberating reduction of monotheism to some decisive issues led a considerable number of Christian to put up with the new prophet, the more so as they were allowed to continue in their veneration of Abraham, Moses and Christ. Those, however, who refused to give up Jesus, were, as a rule, tolerated by victorious Islam as fellow monotheists and the practice of their religion was consequently permitted. It did not take long until Islamic scholars from Alexandria to Buḫāra would merge the creation of their founder, the great semi-barbarian Muhammad, with the spiritual, philosophical and theological culture of the Greeks, and lead the latter onto the soil of Arabian culture (the mediators being Persians, thus not *Semites*). Thus, Islam developed in a way similar to that of Christianity in the days of the apologists of the second century: it absorbed the philosophical tradition of the Greeks.

If all these facts are taken together, what surprises is not how quickly Islam spread over the Christian orient, but rather how staunchly Christianity still survived in many places, and that Islam hardly had an impact on the development of Byzantine Christianity, and no effect on European Christianity, while Manichaeism led the latter to react with such vigorous propaganda. The following reasons might have to be considered:

(1) Due to its nature, Islamic propaganda was unable to tread any secret paths and never tried to; compromises like those accepted by Manichaeism were never made by Islam. "Allāh and his prophet"—this simple slogan could not be reduced or tampered with. This is at the same time the strength of Islam and its weakness. It is always sincere and straightforward, there is only an "either—or". Whereever it intrudes, it will stick; but there is only *one* direct way of expansion. That it failed to *penetrate* ecclesiastical Christianity has hampered its propaganda.

(2) Islam did not manage to lose its warlike character, much as it became saturated with other elements. Because of this and some other, inferior traits it remained alien to the Greek and Christian spirit. The latter, taught by the Gospels on the one hand and Plato together with Greek philosophy of religion on the other, always perceived Islam as somehow semi-barbaric and itself as superior. Therefore it is understandable that Arabic scholars showed so much interest in adopting Greek philosophy and culture, which, however, failed to be truly imbibed by Islam. In contrast, the Church and its dogmatic theology is itself a product of Greek culture and simply belongs to Greek history as much as it belongs to the history of Judaism. Therefore it is comprehensible that even in those days when Arabic culture in some places reached its peak, the representatives of Greek culture never ceased to look down on it.

(3) When Islam met the Oriental churches, these had already merged ecclesiastical dogmatics with their folklore, customs and patriotism, so that it did not only deal with the religion of these peoples, but with their whole identity and being. This is the reason why Islam could not simply roll over the previous religion in these areas, above all as it had to tolerate it according to its own principles, and that its simple religiousness and even the common origin it shared with at least some of the Christian nations did not prove strong enough. To a much greater extent this applies to the Byzantine church.

(4) One might try to emphasize those elements which make contemporary Christianity look inferior to Islam (it must be mentioned that concerning most of these points Islam gradually had to adapt to the inevitable, e.g., in the case of the veneration of saints), but one should not forget that Christianity had assets unreachable by the Koran and

> Islamic morals in the form of the New Testament, its faith in redemption and in its sublime and profound ethics.

From these sources, in spite of baroque Church doctrine, time and again forces of higher life emerged and with them personalities appeared that Islam was unable to produce. Moreover—Islam has a very limited ability to develop. Whatever attempts are made to higher development, from a certain point on they stumble upon the Koran as an unsurmountable obstacle, even if allegoric interpretations are taken refuge to. Muhammedanism is an inflexible system which emcompasses all aspects of life and forces them into a fixed mould. The Bible, on the other hand, has survived the terrible blow received by historical criticism, because relativism as such is inherent in the relation between Old and New Testament, and because the latter already contains the difference between the Lord's and his disciples' words. Islam is unfit to take a similar blow, at least it does not look like there is a way it could. It is not only centered on Allah, but also on the figure of Muhammad—the Muhammad who represents "the book", i.e., the Koran, a scripture full of fables and inferior sayings. This fact was once very welcome, and for the propagation of a faith among semi-barbarian and barbaric peoples the idea of the identification of a founder personality with his book seems very fortunate. But the situation becomes hopeless as soon as the target group are representative of higher culture, true historical insight and finally enlightened piousness, unless Islam should be imaginable with only limited dignity of its founder and of the Koran.

Ebionite Elements in Islam

Hans Joachim Schoeps

Translated by Markus Gross from Theologie und Gesschicte des Judenchristentums *[Theology and History of Judeo-Christianity], section 10, "Ebionitische Elemente im Islam" (Tübingen: Mohr, 1949), pp. 334–42.*

Despite numerous attempts at solving the problem of ascertaining in how far Islam is dependent on Judaism and Christianity, this question remains open. Due to our insufficient knowledge of the peculiarities of the pre-islamic variety of Judaism and Christianity of Arabia, compelling evidence cannot be expected. *Harnack*, who calls Islam "a transformation of the Jewish religion, which itself had already been transformed by Gnostic Christianity, on an Arabic foundation,"[1] has bridged the gap between the Elkesaite sect and Islam with his bold hypotheses. According to him the specific dependence can be seen in seven points.[2] Carl *Clemen* contested a closer dependence, favoring one with Manichaean Gnosticism, but conceded that such a relationship, "although certainly there, is probably not as significant as Harnack wants it to be."[3]

However, there are some aspects hitherto never summarized for this purpose, which go beyond the limitations of mere speculation and ought to be seriously considered. They refer to the *history of tradition* and they partially confirm Harnack's view.

First of all the occurence of a name should make us think: Aṣ-Ṣābiyūn, derived from Hebrew באצ (*ṣb'*) or Mandaic *ṣəḇa* = to baptize. As a third entity between Jews and Christians, the Ṣābiyūn are classified in the Qur'ān as *ahl al-kitāb*, "possessores of the (heavenly) book," who believe in Allah and Judgment Day and who act justly (Surahs 2:59; 5:73; 22:17). Muḥammad seems to consider them to be "the entirety of all Baptist sects."[4] One explanation in the Ḥadīṯ concerning this matter is very revealing; it can be found in the annals of Ḥamza al-Iṣfahānī:[5]

> The true Sabians (i.e. those referred to in the Koran) are a Christian sect, that lives between the desert and the marshlands, they dissent from most of the Christians and are considered by the latter as heretics.

There are several old reports of pagan opponents of Muḥammad, who call him and his adherents "Sabians."[6] This would make it the oldest name of the

Muslim community, probably because of the strict ablutions to be performed before prayer by Muḥammad. Therefore it seems justified to consider the doctrine of Muḥammad as a

> modification of the Sabian [doctrine], which must have shared many a common trait with the oldest form of Islam as e.g. the ablutions, maybe even full immersion without taking off one's clothes (74,4 Horovitz),

traits which must have characterized the early Muslims in the eyes of their Arabian environment. This might be an argument in favor of *Harnack*'s view of the closer relationship between Islam and especially the Elkesaites, the more so as they were named Σοβίαι [*transl.: Sobíai—cf. Sabians*].[7]

Regarding tradition history, however, they have even more essential characteristics in common: the notion of a ἀληθὴς προφήτης [*transl.: alēthēs prophḗtēs—true prophet*] common in Ebionitism reappears as the doctrine of reincarnation with the Mandaeans[8] and Manichaeans, as well as in Islam—in the latter case in the form of a typical sequence of seven (ἑπτὰ στῦλοι—Hom. 18,14) [*transl.: heptà stŷloi—seven pillars*], which already Mani had taken over, albeit with a different cast (Adam, Seth, Noah, Jesus, Buddha, Zarathustra, Mani). Muḥammad's order of messengers (messenger = rasūl) deviates as well from his predecessors: Noah, Lot, Moses, three Arabian messengers (Hūd, Ṣāliḥ, Šuʿayb) and Abraham. *Horovitz* therefore concludes that he only took over the number.[9] But that would mean that the most important feature of the list is overlooked: the fact that it is precisely those names that we would first and foremost expect in such a list of prophets which are missing: Elijah, Isaiah, Jeremiah, Ezekiel etc., while others are mentioned instead, whom we would not even consider prophets.[10] That Adam is not mentioned is probably coincidental, considering the fact that in Surah 3:52 he is—in the normal Ebionite way—put on a level with Jesus—with special regard to his having been created:

> Lo! the likeness of Jesus with Allah is as the likeness of Adam. He created him of dust, then He said unto him: Be! and he is.[11] *(transl.: the translation of Qur'ānic verses is Pickthall's; the verse in his version is 3:59; Schoeps might have used a different verse numbering).*

Henoch however, who is also missing in Hom. 2:52—like Isaak—is totally unknown to the Qur'ān. In exchange the linkage between Judeo-Christianity and Islam is present in *Abraham* the *Imam* of all believers (2:118), neither Jew nor Christian, but in the Medinan Surahs called a *Ḥanif* (synonym and predecessor type of Muslim—3:60 and others). The *millat Ibrāhīm* (2:129 ff.) unites all believers on the same level even before the *tawrat* (Torah) and the *inǧīl* (gospel); Muḥammad considers the restauration of this *millat Ibrāhīm* his task.[12]—This pre-Mosaic revelation is identical with the doctrine of Islam. Muḥammad's share of the revelation of the *kitāb* (heavenly book) only confirms those parts of the heavenly book that had been revealed earlier and thus make him a sort of prophet of religious tolerance. Moreover, as the 5th Surah, 5:48–53, is nothing but the expansion of Judeo-Christian theology of Covenants by Muḥammad, the new messenger sent by God to the population of Arabia.

What now is hidden behind this notion of a prophetic line of Islam, which is also emphasized in the *Ḥadīṯ* (e.g. ʿAbdullāh ibn Saba)?—A similar, totally universalist thought we find in Ebionitism: the prophets (*nabī* probably a term with a narrower meaning than *rasūl*) are representants of mankind, with whom God makes a covenant (*miṯāq*). In a strict sense, Noah, Abraham, Moses, Jesus and Muḥammad are contractors of a divine covenant. Every *nabī* opens a new epoch of salvation history, "a very common notion in the Near East."[13] In the Qurʾān it is explicitly stated that God sent a *rasūl* to every people (*umma*), who delivers the divine messenge (6:42, 48, 16, 38 et al.). Muḥammad himself, who as *Ḫatam/seal* is at the end of the prophetic line—according to Ahrens (p. 155) a Manichaean term—has been sent to his people, which had not had a prophet before (28:46; 32:2; 34:43). The rasūl Allāh is a commissioned messenger, but neither son of God nor an angel (6:50).[14]

"Qurʾān" is the name given by Muḥammad to the holy book (56:76 f.; 85:21), a scripture preexistent like the Jewish Torah—this again an Elkesaite notion[15]—from which all revelations of all former prophets stem. The contents of the revelations, which go back to a primal scripture kept on well-preserved tables in heaven, was the same; there messengers were sent in different ages to different people.[16] The truth conveyed by each former messenger has been taken over into the revelation of his successor, so that Muḥammad combines the truth of all of them. (5:48–52). In Medinan times, Muḥammad called himself *an-nabī l-ummī* (7:156; 158), which, as *Horovitz*[17] conclusively demonstrated, means that he had adopted a Jewish term:[18] *nəbiʾe ʿummoṯ haʿolam*. Thus the tractate Baḇa Baṯra from the Talmud enumerates seven prophets from the peoples of the earth—the number seven referring to the line of prophets here being elucidated—and, according to *Horovitz*, Muḥammad had in mind to present himself to the Jews as such a prophet. Of course, this would also apply to the Judeo-Christian successor groups!

Especially the Ebionite faith in a *novus Moses*, i.e. the expectation of a coming prophet, inspired the emerging religion Islam. According to the tradition of *Ibn Isḥāq* Muḥammad had been predicted by Abraham, Moses and Jesus as the coming prophet, thus he had to be believed. It could be concluded from Surah 7:156 that Moses had promised his coming. Whether this has to be regarded as an allusion to Deut. 18:15 is at best a guess.[19] And Jesus, son of Mary, whom he—in best Judeo-Christian manner considers as a purely *human* prophet[20]—"al-masīḥ 'Īsā b. Maryam,"[21] is said to have predicted, according to Surah 61:6:

> O Children of Israel! Lo! I am the messenger of Allah unto you, confirming that which was (revealed) before me in the Torah, and bringing good tidings of a messenger who cometh after me, whose name is the Praised One (*Aḥmad*).

Pautz[22] thinks that he is referring to the gospel of John (14:16, 26; 15:26; 16:7), that the promised one would be the παράκλητος (paráklētos), a word translated into Arabic as *Aḥmad* (Surah 61:6; in the middle),[23] the elative form of his name *Muḥammad*. In fact, Mani and Montanus had claimed this title before him. This is not contradicted by the fact that Muḥammad, in other places, refers to old Arabian prophets, whom he acknowledges according to the line of seven prophets, just like Moses and Jesus. For him, the latter was always only a *rasūl*, never the son of God, something the Jesus of the Qur'ān decidedly refuses to be called. (2:130; 4:169; 5:76–79, 116–117); [according to the Qur'ān] it was the misinterpretation of scripture which led to the notion of the divine nature of Jesus. (3:72–74, 57–59). This matches Judeo-Christian views very well. Other than that, Muḥammad's image of Jesus (esp. in 4:156) displays traces of a post-Ebionite docetic christology.

The notion of an ἀληθὴς προφήτης [*transl.: alēthēs prophētēs*—true prophet] of the heavenly book is—apart from the designation Sabians—the clearest piece of evidence of a connection between Muḥammad and the old Judeo-Christians based on tradition history. *Andrae* calls the connection "not coincidental"[24] and, following *Schaeder*'s opinion, it can easily be attributed to "oral tradition of proselytes from Christian and Jewish sectarian circles."[25] The absolute unity of God, his μοναρχία [monarchía], is as much an intrinsical element of Muḥammad's view as it is characteristic for both Ebionism and Judeo-Christianity.[26] The definition of religion in the Clementina (7:8):

> Θρησκεία ἐστὶν αὕτη. τὸ μόνον αὐτὸν σεβεῖν καὶ τῷ τῆς ἀληθείας μόνῳ πιστέυων προφήτῃ [*transl.*: Religion is the following: to venerate the only one, believing in the only prophet of truth].

seems downright construed in a way to enable Islam to find a suitable creed for itself in it. According to its view, Muḥammad is the legitimate successor of Moses and Jesus in their mission to enlighten the world.[27] The concept of God we find in Islam is entirely congruent with the heretical christology prevalent among the Ebionites and up to the monarchianists of the 5th century, which is represented by the monarchy of God, the μοναρχικῇ θρησκείᾳ (Hom. 7:12). Moreover, the fact that the population of countries in the neighborhood of Arabia, which had formerly been primarily Monophysite and Nestorian, so quickly adopted Islam, can only be explained by a largely similar structure of Judeo-Christianity and Islam.

Those elements in Islam which go back to Jewish religious laws, in some parts clearly in an Ebionite guise, and especially the Judeo-Christian rites of baptism and purification (e.g. ablutions before the five daily prayers) would deserve a more detailed investigation than possible in the present article. It is, however, evident, that a great deal of the Jewish Torah was passed on to Islam through Ebionite and Elchesaite tradition and modification: the daily ablutions (also after sexual intercourse),[28] the original Qibla to the north, facing Jerusalem,[29] maybe even the ban on wine,[30] or the Jewish assessment of marriage as a religious duty especially attested for Elchesai (Epiph. 19:1) and many more. The idea that Jews had an anthropomorphic image of God and that they have falsified their scriptures (especially ʿUzayr-Ezra) very probably also goes back to Judeo-Christian origins:[31]

> 2:70 (*transl.: Kairo edition: 2:75*): ... when a party of them used to listen to the Word of Allah, then used to change it, after they had understood it knowingly?

(In 2:154, 169, 207; 3:72; 5:16, 45 and others the Pharisees are alluded to as falsifiers of scriptures). In any case, the notion of "false pericopes" plays a major role in Muḥammad's sense of mission to restore the old law.[32] Muḥammad's claim—elaborated in the Ḥadiṯ—that the Jewish dietary laws had been imposed on them as a punishment for their sins (3:87; 4:158; 6:147; 16:119) reminds us of the train of thoughts of the Didascalia and certainly belongs here![33] It has to be mentioned that there is a certain interdependence with the [Qurʾān's] own deitary laws, which itself is dependent on the regulations in the Acts (prohibition of "what is strangled," blood and meat [things] contaminated by idols [*transl.:* in the Qurʾān: "(only eat) over which the name of Allah hath been mentioned."] In addition [in the Qurʾān], pork is explicitly forbidden (6:118, 121, 146; 16:116 and others).[34]—The Mohammedan form of asceticism, however, has got another intention as well.[35]—Last but not least the fact that later Islamic theologians like Isfarayni and Šahrastānī (cf. Exk. V, 3) know about a vehemently anti-Pauline tradition much in the sense of Judeo-Christianity,[36] should encourage further research about the history of tradition.

It can be stated that Muḥammad referred to the old law and Schlatter was certainly right when he surmised that the point of reference could not have been Judaism, but can only have been Judeo-Christianity, which, after all, was convinced that Jesus himself had only *confirmed* the Torah and that he, through his new word—the gospel—had only *reinterpreted* [the old scriptures] in a more profound sense. And if in Judeo-Christianity a *New* Law could be added to the *Old* Law, then "it was certainly no problem for the *Newest* Law to find room after the New one."[37] For the *nova lex*, from the perspective of Judeo-Christianity, is identical with the Oldest Law. "Ebion," as much as Muḥammad, wanted nothing but wrong developments in the law to be corrected and the restoration of the original state.

We have come to the end of our presentation. Even if conclusive evidence for the connection cannot be provided, it stills seems beyond doubt that there was an indirect dependence of Muḥammad on sectarian Judeo-Christianity.

And thus, as a paradox of a veritably cosmopolitan scope the fact emerges that although Judeo-Christianity ceased to exist within the Christian Church, it has still been preserved within Islam, and still exerts the influence of some of its most vigorous impulses.

The Ebionite combination of Moses and Jesus has found its fulfillment in Muḥammad and the main characteristics of both of them has—in the sense of Hegel's philosophy—been elevated in [the synthesis of] Islam.*

* *Translator's note:*
Hegel stated that in the interaction between thesis and antithesis what will emerge is a synthesis, in which the characteristics of thesis and antithesis will be "aufgehoben," i.e.—due to the three meanings of this German verb (its infinitive being "aufheben") in German—they will be 1) "elevated" 2) "canceled/suspended" and 3) "preserved."

Notes
In Schoeps' article the numbering of footnotes starts anew on each page; as with all other articles in this anthology, footnotes have been numbered throughout and turned into endnotes.

1 See *Dogmengschichte* II 4, p. 537.
2 Ibid. p. 534 ff.
3 "Muhammads Abhängigkeit von der Gnosis" ("Muhammad's dependence on the Gnosis" in *Harnack-Ehrung* ["liber amicorum for Harnack"] (1922)—In my opinion, Harnack's 7 theses, after Clemen's criticism with a few modifications, can still be considered valid.
4 See Jos. Horovitz, *Qoranische Untersuchungen* ["Qoranic Studies"] (Berlin, 1926), p. 131; B. Carra de Vaux, in *EI* (1), vol. IV, 22; according to him, however, the name only refers to the Mandaeans. After Sprenger it was especially J. Pedersen (op. cit., p. 389), who equated them with the ḥanifs. However, he also explains the term *Ṣābiyūn* as "Gnostics."—The last scholar to write about them was W. Hirschenberg, *Jüdische und christliche Lehren im vor- und frühislamischen Arabien* ["Jewish and Christian Doctrines in Pre- and Early-Islamic Arabia"] (Krakau, 1939), p. 32 ff. About the Sabians in the Islamic Heresiologist literature cf. J. Thomas, *Le mouvement baptiste en Palestine et Syrie* (Gembloux, 1935), p. 197 ff.
5 Quoted according to Chwolson, op. cit. II, p. 205.—More information about the Sabians can be found in the "Chronologie d'Albérouni" and "Al-Masoudi," see J. Thomas, op. cit., p. 197 ff.

6 For attestations see J. Wellhausen, *Reste* etc. (op. cit.), p. 236 ff.; F. Buhl, op. cit. p. 238.

7 Cf. Waitz 1922, pp. 103 f.; K. Ahrens, *Muhammad als Religionsstifter* (Leipzig, 1935), p. 10.—Ahrens ibid. p. 59 points to a second linguistic analogy between Elkesaites and Islam: Muhammad's term for Judgment Day: *yawmu d-dīn* is also found in a prayer formula of Elkesai (cf. above p. 324).

8 Cf. The doctoral thesis of H. Meyer, *Die Mandäische Lehre vom Göttlichen Gesandten* (Kiel, 1929).

9 Op. cit., p. 28.—If Muhammad himself is added to the list, the number is eight, exactly as with the Ebionites (cf. chapter II, § 4), where seven predecessor-prophets and a prophet-messiah are counted.

10 About this question also cf. Wensinck, "Muhammad und die Prophetie" *Acta Orientalia* II [Oslo, 1924], pp. 170 f. Wensinck opposes Rudolph's view (*Die Abhängigkeit des Qorans vom Judentum und Christentum* (Stuttgart, 1922), pp. 45 ff.), that this conspicuous fact is due to the ignorance of the Jews of Medina, but does not come up with a satisfying explanation himself—because he did not know the Ebionite dogma.

11 The creation of Adam through blowing the Divine spirit into him (15, 29; 32, 8; 38, 72) also goes back to a Judeo-Christian Adam-Christ-Haggada; cf. Epiph. 30, 3, 3. Moreover, it was taken over and elaborated by Syrian theology.

12 Concerning the significance of Abraham as patriarch of the whole human race see H. Speyer, *Die biblischen Erzählungen im Koran* (Gräfenhainichen, no year indicated [1932?]), pp. 120 ff., 487 f.—Through Ishmael, the ancestor of the Northern Arabs according both Jewish and Islamic tradition, Muhammad traces his ancestry back to Abraham.

13 Wensinck, op. cit. p. 175; cf. also his article "rasul" in *Enz. d. Isl.* (Encyclopedia of Islam [in German]) III, p. 1217.

14 I. Goldziher, in "Neuplatonische und Gnostische Elemente im Ḥadith" *Zeitschr. f. Assyriol* 19009, pp. 337 ff.) thinks that this goes back to the Clementine notion of ἀνάπαυσις [anápausis]. According to him, Muhammad claimed that the reappearances of the true propet had come to an end with him. The orthodoxy of the Arabs certainly asserted this; on page 340, Goldziher quotes a saying by Muhammad as transmitted by Ibn Sa'd: "I have been sent [by God] again and again, from age to age, from the best generations of men, until I was finally been sent in the period in which we now live."

15 Cf. Tor Andrae, *Die Person Muhammeds in Lehre und Glauben seiner Gemeinde* (Stockholm, 1917), p. 293.

16 Cf. Wellhausen, *Reste arabischen Heidentums* (Stud. u. Vorarb. III [1888], p. 210 f.) and Rudolph, op. cit. p. 38.

17 [*transl.: the footnote number is missing in the main text, the footnote itself, however, makes it clear that it belongs here*] Horovitz, *Qoran in Islam XIII* (1923), p. 68; cf. also the instructive article "'umma' and 'ummī'" by Paret in: *Enz. d. Isl.* IV, 1099 ff.

18 *Qoranische Untersuchungen*, op. cit., p. 52.

19 That the Ebionite tendency to see parallels between Moses and Jesus has had an effect up to the time of Muhammad has been demonstrated by G. Rösch, *Die*

Jesusmythen des Islams, Theol. Stud. U. Krit., 1876, based on the Haggada of Miriam being the mother of Jesus, a notion later adopted in Islam (which means the adoption of the idealized image of the Messiah).

20 Muḥammad's polemic against Jesus cannot go back to Jewish notions, especially as Jesus is repeatedly called *al-Masīḥ* in Medinan Surahs, as Ahrens ("Christl. im Qoran" *ZMDG* (1930), p. 153) convincingly demonstrated. The way he tried to persuade points to a "brusque Nestorian Christianity," which I also consider the missing link between Ebionism and Islam.

21 Ahrens, *Muhammed als Religionsstifter* (Leipzig, 1935), pp. 197 f., thinks that the model for this designation is the Nestorian-East-Syriac name form *Išō'm'šīḥa.*

22 *Muhammeds Lehre von der Offenbarung quellenmäßig dargestellt* (Leipzig, 1898), p. 128 f.

23 According to Ahrens p. 154 f. Muhammad and his sources of information had the form παράκλυτος [paráklytos] instead of παράκλητος [paráklētos] in mind; Christian doctrine equates the Paraclete with the Holy Spirit.

24 Cf. *Kyrkohistorisk Årsskrift* 1923, p. 153; *Der Ursprung des Islams und des Christentums* (1926), S. 204; *Muhammed* (1932), S. 87.—It should be noted that the doctrine of the true prophet came to Jewish *kalamists* [*transl.:* "theologians"] like Sa'adia Gaon (cf. M. Ventura, *La Philosophie de Saadia Gaon* (Paris, 1934), pp. 199f.) or J^ehuḏa hal-levi (cf. Schoeps, "Weiteres zur Auserwählung Israels" *Judaica* 1946, S. 195f.).

25 "Die islamische Lehre vom vollkommenen Menschen, ihre Herkunft und ihre dichterische Gestaltung" ("The Islamic doctrine of a perfect human being, its origin and poetic elaboration") *ZDMG*, 1925, p. 231; similarly *Carra de Vaux* in the article "Indjil" of the *Enc. of Isl.* II, p. 535.

26 Siouville (op. cit. 200) does not consider this a common trait connecting the Qur'ān with the K.Π.

27 Cf. Siouville, *Introduction zur französischen Homilienausgabe*, p. 60.

28 Cf. especially A. J. Wensinck, "Die Entstehung der islamischen Reinheitsgesetzgebung," *Der Islam V* (1914), p. 68 f.—The ablutions before prayer are seen by *Wellhausen* (op. cit., p. 237) in connection with Jewish customs of the Sabians.

29 Due to its attestation for Ebionites and Elchesaites, Schwally, in *Geschichte des Qorans I* (Leipzig 1909), p. 175, thought that Muhammad's original direction to be faced during prayer was a Jewish institution and that he only established the new qibla in the direction of the Ka'ba while in Medina, with the aim of a spiritual split [with the Jews] (Surah 2:136–145). Also cf. the article "Qibla" in the *Enc. of Islam* II, 1059 ff.—Moreover, the Islamic *'Āšūrā'*, a day of fasting, seems to be modeled after the Day of Atonement of both the Jews and Judeo-Christians, as far as both the name and the meaning of the day is concerned (see עָשׂוֹר ['āśūr]– Lev. 16:29; 23:27).

30 Elaborated in Surah 2:116; 5:92 f. and the Ḥadīt. Cf. the article "khamr" in the *Enc. of Islam* II, 959 ff. The Ebionite chalice of water and their aversion against wine has to be remembered here.

31 A similar idea, however, can also be found with the Mandaeans; cf. V. S. Pedersen, *Bidrag till en Analyse af de Mandeiske Skrifter* (Århus, 1940), p. 172 f.

32 Cf. Nöldeke-Schwally, *Geschichte des Qorans* II (Leipzig, 1919), p. 121.—The claim that scriptures have been falsified often appears in the Ḥadīṯ especially in anti-Jewish polemics. Ibn Ḥazm (died 456 = 1064) counted 57 cases off so-called

Jewish text modifications in the Torah. Cf. also the article "Tawrat" by Horovitz in the *Enc. of Islam* IV, 765f.; Pautz, op. cit. p. 129, and especially Steinschneider, *Polemische und apologetische Literatur in arabischer Sprache* (Leipzig, 1877), p. 320 ff.—Qaraites and Samaritans casted the same reproaches.

33 Cf. Horovitz, *Qoranische Studien*, op. cit., p. 38; Ahrens, *ZDMG*, 1930, p. 158; Less probable is the idea of J. Rivlin, *Gesetz im Koran* (Jerusalem, 1934), 75, who thinks that the idea that the law was given as a punishment goes back to Jewish traditions.

34 Cf. Rudolph, op. cit., p. 86 f.—Concerning the pig as the only animal forbidden by the Qur'ān I would like to point to the statements of the Didaskalia about heretics, which seem to refer especially to a Judeo-Christian group: "And others say, that one should *only* refrain from eating pork, and that one should eat whatever the Law declares lawful." (121:27 ff.)

35 Tor Andrae, *Der Ursprung des Islam* etc., op. cit., p. 151, sums up: "Ebionite asceticism is ritualistic and consists of the observation of certain commandments, while Muhammad's asceticism is of a ethical-moral nature: to become inwardly free of the world, this is the view propagated by the piety of the East Syrian Church, a view influenced by monasticism."

36 About this point cf. G. Klinge, "Die Beziehungen zwischen christlicher und islamischer Theologie im Anfang des Mittelalters," *ZKG*, 1937, p. 52f.—It is also important to note that Muhammad never refers to St. Paul, who seems a figure totally out of the question.

37 Schlatter, *Die Entwicklung des jüdischen Christentums zum Islam*, op. cit., p. 252.

Part 4

Baumstark on the Christian Background of the Koran

The Life and Works of Anton Baumstark[1]

Ibn Warraq

Karl Anton Joseph Dominikus Baumstark, born in Konstanz in May 1872 to an intellectual German family newly converted to Catholicism, was a philologist, liturgist, and orientalist. He is seen as the founder of the study of the Christian Orient and of comparative liturgy.

After receiving training in classical and oriental philology, in Leipzig, Baumstark completed a doctorate with a thesis on Greek-Syriac translation literature, which was followed by a habilitation thesis on the Syriac-Arabic biographies of Aristotle at the University of Heidelberg. He spent five years (1899–1904) in Rome, where he devoted his time to early Christian history, in particular the literature, liturgy, and art of the Christian East. He was able to obtain the necessary support in 1901 to found the journal *Oriens Christianus*, which Baumstark edited, save for a brief break in 1906–1908, until 1941, when World War II caused its publication to be interrupted. During 1904–1905 Baumstark also traveled to the Near East, studying monuments and collecting documents.

In the period 1906–1921, Baumstark taught at a private Roman Catholic secondary school, and he married Frieda Anna Trondle (1891–1979). He did not, however, neglect his studies of the Eastern Church. By the end of the First World War, Baumstark had made the liturgy of the Western Church also a focus of his work.

Just as he was completing his book *Geschichte der syrischen Literatur* [History of Syriac Literature], Baumstark was offered a position as professor honorarius for the History and Culture of the Christian Orient and Oriental Liturgy at the University of Bonn; in 1925 that institution granted him an honorary doctorate in theology. For a time during the 1920s, Baumstark lectured in Comparative Liturgy and Semitic Languages at the University of Nijmegen in the Netherlands. From 1926 he served as professor for Islamic Studies and Arabic at the University of Utrecht.

After a spell of five years in the department of Oriental Studies at the University of Münster, Baumstark held a part-time position at the University of Utrecht, which ended when in 1940 the German government withdrew his permission to teach abroad. In the last years of his life, he turned his attention toward the Bible, with a particular focus on the textual traditions of Near Eastern Biblical texts and harmonizations of the Bible, notably the Diatesseron. He delivered a series of lectures on comparative liturgy for the monks at the Priory of Amay-sur-Meuse, Belgium, who transcribed and published them, first as articles in their journal *Irenikon* and then in book form as *Liturgie comparée*. Baumstark died of heart failure in 1948 at the age of seventy-six.

Baumstark was particularly known for his work on the rites of the Eastern Church and the history of Oriental liturgy in all its facets, including its effects on cult, art, and literature. He pointed to the roots of the Koran in the Christian and Jewish liturgy. It is the latter pioneering work that is translated here into English for the first time. But the translations proved extremely arduous because of Baumstark's difficult German style, described by Otto Spies (1901–1981), a colleague at the University of Bonn, in this manner:

> To be sure his articles are not easy to read because of his elaborate style. One gets the clear impression that one has before one here Latin constructions in German dress. Substantives and substantive abstractions preponderate as well as elaborately pretentious and exaggerated participial constructions in whose place we would simply use a straightforward relative or causal clause. His sentences are too long, too elaborate with one thought packed inside another, so that one no longer knows at the end of a sentence what one read at its beginning. For this reason his popular essays were not able to be effective. A typical example is his letter written for the soldiers on January 1944 about "Die Orthodoxe Kirche:" the first printed page consists of two complete sentences. It is also often difficult to find one's way through the scholarly articles. At least in my experience each sentence must be read three times in order to understand and grasp what it was meant to say.[2]

However, despite the difficulties, Dr. Elisabeth Puin has made a distinguished attempt to translate Baumstark into English. The results are readable but without sacrificing Baumstark's precision, terseness, and style, and they thus still require one's utmost attention. Readers are urged to persist, and to read, if necesssary, the intricate sentences several times. At times, it is advisable to read some of the endnotes at the same time as the main text where indicated by Dr. Puin in square brackets. For greater comprehension, we have provided transliterations, and translations of the Syriac, Hebrew, Greek, and Arabic not present in the original articles. For technical reasons in writing Syriac it was necessary to use Estranagelo rather than the Serto used by Baumstark himself. Baumstark's use of Flügel numbering for the Koranic verses has been retained, but the verse numbering of the Cairo edition has been added in square brackets immediately afterward. Baumstark firmly accepted Muhammad as the author of the Koran, a fact that must be constantly borne in mind when trying to understand some of his complex formulations. I should like to thank Dr. Walter Burnikel for translations of all the Greek passages.

WORKS BY ANTON BAUMSTARK

"Lucubrationes Syro-Graecae," *Jahrbücher für classische Philologie*, supplementary vol. 21 (1894), pp. 353–524 (doctoral thesis).

Syrisch-arabische Biographieen des Aristoteles: *Syrische Kommentare zur Eisagoge des Porphyrios* (Leipzig: Teubner, 1900),

Aristoteles bei den Syrern vom 5. bis 8. Jahrhundert: *Syrische Texte*, edited, translated, and analyzed (Leipzig, 1900).

Die Messe im Morgendland (Kempten/München, 1906).

"Das Gesetz der Erhaltung des Alten in liturgisch hochwertiger Zeit," *Jahrbuch für Liturgiewissenschaft* 7 (1927): 1–23.

Festbrevier und Kirchenjahr der syrischen Jakobiten (Paderborn, 1910).

Die christlichen Literaturen des Orients (Leipzig: Göschen, 1911), 2 vols., *Das christlich-aramäische und das koptische Schrifttum*, vol. 1, and *Das christlich-arabische und das äthiopische Schrifttum*; *Das christliche Schrifttum der Armenier und Georgier*, vol. 2.

Geschichte der syrischen Literatur mit Ausschluß der christlich-palästinischen Texte (Bonn: Markus und Weber, 1922; reprinted Berlin: deGruyter, 1968).

Vom geschichtlichen Werden der Liturgie (Freiburg im Breisgau, 1922); Polish transl. by M. Wolicki, "O historycznym rozwoju liturgii," *Vetera et nova* 6 (Kraków: Wydawn. UNUM, 2001).

Liturgie comparée: Conférences faites au Prieuré d'Amay, revised ed. (Chevetogne, 1939); 3rd ed., revised by Bernard Botte (Chevetogne, 1953).

Comparative Liturgy, revised by B. Botte, English ed. by F. L. Cross, A. R. Morsbray, et al. (London, 1958).

SELECTED ARTICLES BY ANTON BAUMSTARK

"Eine arabische Palästinabeschreibung spätestens des 16 Jahrhundert," *Oriens Christianus* 6 (1906): 238–99.

"Jüdischer und christlicher Gebettypus im Koran," *Islam* 16 (1927): 229–48.

"Das Problem eines vorislamischen christlichkirchlichen Schrifttums in arabischer Sprache," *Islamica* 4 (1931): 562–75.

"Eine altarabische Evangelienübersetzung aus dem Christlich-Palästinensischen," *Zeitschrift für Semitistik und verwandte Gebiete* 8 (1932): 201–209.

"Arabische Übersetzung eines altsyrischen Evangelientextes und die in Sure 21, 105 zitierte Psalmenübersetzung [Arabic Translation of an Old-Syriac

Gospel and the Psalm Translation Quoted in Surah 21:105]," *Oriens Christianus* 9 (1934): 165–88.

"Erbe christlicher Antike im Bildschmuck eines arabischen Evangelienbuches des XIV. Jahrhunderts," *Oriens Christianus* 35 (1938): 1–38.

"Eine frühislamische und eine vorislamische arabische Evangelienübersetzung aus dem Syrischen [An Early Islamic and a Pre-Islamic Arabic Gospel Translation from the Syriac]" in *Atti del XIX Congresso Internazionale degli Orientalisti 1935* (Rome: G. Bardi, 1938), pp. 682–84.

"Zur Herkunft der monotheistischen Bekenntnisformeln im Koran," *Oriens Christianus* 37 (1953): 6–22.

Notes

1 For Baumstark's biography I have leaned heavily on Fritz West's superb introduction to his translation of Baumstark's *Vom geschichtlichen Werden der Liturgie*, *On the Historical Development of the Liturgy* (Collegeville, MN: Liturgical Press, 2011), pp. 7–9.

2 Otto Spies, "Anton Baumstark (1872–1948)," in Bonner Gelehrte, *Beiträge zur Geschichte der Wissenschaften in Bonn: Sprachwissenschaften* (Bonn: Ludwig Rohrschied Verlag, 1970), p. 349; translated by Fritz West in *op. cit.*, p. 34.

Jewish and Christian Prayer Type in the Koran

Anton Baumstark

Originally published as "Jüdischer und christlicher Gebetstypus im Koran," Der Islam *16 (1927), pp. 229–48; translated by Elisabeth Puin.*

Recently, research on the historical connections between the *Ur*-Islam and the two older great monotheistic religions that emerged from the Semitic world has been significantly furthered by Tor Andrae's profound studies.[1] However, one aspect that, to me, seems of particular value for the exact solution of the problems with which the said research is confronted has, so far, been left unexploited: the formal structure of the *Ur*-Islamic prayer. And yet, prayer is the true pulse and breath of life of any religion, so that the dependence of one religion on another must almost necessarily be very clearly reflected in it. Within that field, observations on the purely formal side of the phrasing of the prayers are the least affected by subjective feelings and therefore the most reliable ones. So far, the only model for the method of such a purely formal treatment of man's word addressed to the Divine is the one by Ed. Norden.[2]

Reliable evidence of the form of *Ur*-Islamic prayer can only be gained from the Koran. At first sight, however, the only direct prayer contained in the Koran is the opening Fātiḥa. But besides it we also find, introduced simply by the word قُل [*qul* "say"], the creed formulated by surah 112 and the two appeals for help of the surahs 113 and 114 which seem to have some connection to the circle of magic formulas and prayers; in numerous places we find other prayer formulas which, as the Prophet [as the author of the Koran] put it, God commands him to recite by means of the same introducing قُل ; we find, put in the form of prayers of praise, words that introduce and conclude whole surahs as well as individual text passages mostly of a more or less clear hymnic character; and finally, we find words of prayer coming from the mouths of protagonists in the narrative passages of the holy book, and in its eschatological promises of paradisical bliss we find, on the lips of the blessed, the sounds of the praise of God that immediately remind us, at least with regard to their function, of the celestial chants of the Apocalypse of John.

Thus it is, after all, a very rich material, which was already once before, in the Frankfurt dissertation by Fr. Goitein[3]—which the difficult times unfortunately did not allow to print—the subject of a summarizing treatise. But this thesis, too, neither aims at gathering knowledge about the relationship of Islam to Judaism and Christianity from that material, nor does it, although it refers to Norden, essentially and with methodological soundness aim at formal aspects.[4] Indeed, it leaves the shortest stereotyped expressions of diverse kinds of predication, and thereby a section of the material that is crucial for the purely formal approach, entirely unregarded.

What gives us the right, in the first place, to submit the Koranic prayer elements to formal examination and to compare them, from this point of view, with Jewish and Christian prayer types, is the stereotyped nature that a great many—albeit by no means all—of them display. It is only this stereotyped nature that guarantees that we are dealing not with occasional, isolated phenomena which owe the form of their phrasing more or less to sheer chance but, instead, with manifestations of fixed prayer types which played a dominant role in the prayer life of the Prophet and his earliest community; we can even quantify to what extent the individual Koranic elements are moulded according to such types. This stereotyped nature is incomparably more distinct in predications as well as in preachings and confessions resembling creed formulas than it is in prayers of supplication. Thus, for a comparison of Koranic, Jewish and Christian prayer formulation we must not, like Goitein, focus on prayers of supplication, but we will have to take the types of predication as our starting point.

Had Muhammad, in creating his new religious texts, mostly or at least originally been under Jewish influence, then this would mean that we would find a particular form of predication prevailing in those texts, namely: that of the *Bərāḵāh,* the gradual development of which becomes apparent in the Old Testament and the final form of which we encounter as the predominant prayer form of Rabbinic Judaism. In it, the fixed introducory words בָּרוּךְ אַתָּה יהוה אֱלֹהֵינוּ מֶלֶךְ הָעוֹלָם [*bārūḵ attāh YHWH ēlohēnū meleḵ hā-ʿōlām*] "Blessed be you, Lord our God, king of the universe"] are, in the fully developed form of the prayer, followed by either a participle or a relative clause which expresses, more or less broadly, the specific reason of the praise of God. A second בָּרוּךְ אַתָּה יהוה [*bārūḵ attāh YHWH* "Blessed be you, Lord"], expanded by an apposition or a participial attribute, very briefly summarizes the content of the prayer and closes it. We must, however, be aware that besides this final, common version of the *Bərāḵāh* in the second person there is also an older version put in the third person. And indeed, we do encounter the opening as well as the concluding words of this older version of the Jewish prayer type in the Koran. The equivalent of the Hebrew nominal clause introduced by בָּרוּךְ [*Bārūḵ* "Blessed be"] is an Arabic verbal clause, introduced regularly by تَبَارَكَ ["blessed be"] and in the exceptional case of Q 27:8 by بُورِكَ ["blessed be"], instead, which latter is probably supposed to express the optative meaning of the formula more clearly. However, the phenomenon is restricted to a very limited circle of a few particular surahs.

The one surah 25, in the verses 1, 11 [25:10] and 62f. [25:61f], displays as many as three instances commencing with تَبَارَكَ ٱلَّذِى ["Blessed be who"] followed by a relative clause.[5] We also meet with the same opening words in Q 43:85 as well as at the beginning of a longer, hymn-like passage, in Q 67:1[6], joined by the بُورِكَ مَن ["Blessed be who"] of Q 27:8[7] which differs only at the surface. As a concluding formula, the combination of تَبَارَكَ ["blessed be"] or فَتَبَارَكَ ٱللَّهُ ["blessed be God"] with a following apposition is, on the other hand, in Q 7:52 [7:54] attached to a dogmatic kerygma, and in 23:14 and in 40:66 [40:64] it follows a hymnic depiction of the creational works of God; it is certainly no coincidence that, in two out of those only three instances,[8] the apposition reads رَبُّ ٱلْعَالَمِينَ [*rabbu l-ʿālamīn*, "Lord of the worlds"] which is the equivalent of the stereotype מלך העולם [*melek̲ hā-ʿōlām*] – "king of the universe"] of the full *Bərāk̲āh*. In all those instances we are dealing with texts from the later middle-Meccan or late-Meccan period.

Only in one instance, in Q 55:78, an at least related conclusion of a surah leads us back to early-Meccan times: تَبَـٰرَكَ ٱسْمُ رَبِّكَ ذِى ٱلْجَلَـٰلِ وَٱلْإِكْرَامِ ["Blessed be the name of your Lord, owner of majesty and glory"]. But there is, to say the least, no proof that this wording, too, should be connected to the standardized Jewish prayer form of the *Bərāk̲āh*. One might feel reminded of a specific, and probably even particularly time-honoured, formula of the liturgy of the synagogue, namely the words בָּרוּךְ שֵׁם כְּבוֹד מַלְכוּתוֹ לְעוֹלָם וָעֶד [*Bārūk̲ šēm keb̲ōd̲ malk̲ūt̲ō lə-ʿōlām wā-ʿäd̲* – "Blessed be the name of His glorious kingdom for ever and ever" which follow, spoken in a low voice, the recitation of Dt. 6,4 in the text of the *Šĕmaʿ*. But it is much more natural to think of Psalm 113 (112),2: יְהִי שֵׁם יְהוָה מְבֹרָךְ [*yehī šēm YHWH məb̲ōrāk̲*] = Εἴη τὸ ὄνομα Κυρίου εὐλογημένον ["Blessed be the name of the Lord"]. This would mean that not only the Psalter in general (which is the only Biblical book explicitely quoted in the Koran, in 21:105) but also this particular wording was conveyed to Muhammad through liturgy; and here, already, we should think of the liturgy of a Christian ritual rather than of that of the synagogue. For one thing, the Psalter as a cohesive book plays a decidedly more vital role in the Christian liturgy than in that of the synagogue.[9] And for another thing, already Old Arabic poetry speaks of the Psalter as in the hands of Christian monks.[10] Thus, although the particular Psalm passage in question is indeed not insignificant already in the ritual of the synagogue,[11] it is of incomparably greater importance within all kinds of Christian rituals of the East and the West.[12]

Even for the type of the *Bərāḵāh* itself, the fact of the matter is that, on the one hand, if Muhammad had been decidedly dependent on Judaism, the *Bərāḵāh* necessarily would have been of crucial importance for the formulation of the *Ur*-Islamic prayer; but on the other hand, the fact that the *Bərāḵāh* left some—not very significant—traces in the Koran, this would, if not for the noticeable restriction of those traces to a few surahs from a particular period, not at all necessarily mean that this must be due to Jewish influence—because that same type had also been adopted by Christianity. The earliest Christian communities used it in worship, which is echoed by the expressions of the New Testament: Εὐλογητὸς ὁ Θεὸς καὶ πατὴρ τοῦ Κυρίου ἡμῶν Ἰησοῦ Χριστοῦ ["Blessed be God and the father of our Lord Jesus Christ"], and: Εὐλογητὸς εἰς τοὺς αἰῶνας. Αμήν. ["He be blessed in eternity. Amen"][13] In the older texts of the Greek Euchologion, prayers beginning with the words Εὐλογητὸς ὁ Θεὸς or Εὐλογητὸς εἶ Κύριε ["Blessed be God," "Blessed be you, Lord"] are no rarities and even occupy, in some instances, an outstanding position.[14] Also, in the non-Greek rites of the Christian east there are corresponding formulations;[15] they occur especially frequently in the rite of Armenia.[16] With particular tenacity the ancient form seems to have been retained in the liturgical table prayer. In accordance with that of the Greek church,[17] even in the Roman West of today a section of the Canon begins, in true *Bərāḵāh* style, with the words: "Benedictus Dominus" ["Blessed be the Lord"].[18]

The prevailing form on Christian soil, however, has become, instead of such eulogies, the doxology: a form of predication which originally belongs to the sphere of acclamations and which I should like to call possessive; it declares splendour, glory, praise, honour, or with what other term one may render the ambivalent Greek δόξα, something that is the Deity's or is due to the Deity.[19]

Already in the oldest non-canonical literary document of the Christian religion, namely in the *Didache* that was written in the corn-growing Palestinian-Syrian highlands, two of the eucharistic prayers that are known to be closely connected to texts of the Jewish *birkaṯ ham-māzōn* do not have the *Bərāḵāh* conclusion but are, instead, ending with the shortest doxological formula: Σοὶ ἡ δόξα εἰς τοὺς αἰῶνας ["Thine is the glory, in eternity"].[20] Like an interesting sepulchral inscription of the Catacomb of Priscilla in Rome ending with COI ΔΟΞΑ ΕΝ ΧΡ(ιστῷ) ["Thine is the glory, in Jesus Christ"],[21] an early Christian building inscription of central Syria is concluded by ΔΟΞΑ ΑΥΤω ΠΑΝΤΟΤΕ ["His is the glory, always"].[22] Similarly short formulas became the nucleus of the whole multifarious development of doxological conclusions of prayers and sermons of, above all, the Christian Orient. Unconnected doxological short formulas had been, in Syriac, preferably used by Ephrem as refrain,[23] and even today the liturgy of both the East and the West is full of them, in the form of phrases like Δόξα σοὶ ὁ Θεὸς δόξα σοί

["Thine is the glory, God, thine is the glory], "Gloria tibi Domine" ["Thine is the glory, Lord"], "Laus tibi Christe" [Thine is the praise, Christ"]. The example of a hymnic prayer construed as a long row of shorter textual elements beginning with Δόξα σοι ["Thine is the glory"] followed by an address as an apposition to σοι ["thine"], has, according to the apocryphal Acts of John, been given to us by Christ himself after the Last Supper.[24] In an old Coptic Easter liturgy we find another prayer displaying the same structure, composed of alternating eulogies and doxologies of this kind.[25] In other texts, too, the transition from the type of the *Bərāḵāh* into the doxocological type is directly evident, when the datival δόξα formula is followed by a participial apposition or address, like, e. g., in the words of an early Christian sepulchral inscription in Bosra:[26] ΔΟΞΑ ΤΩ ΑΩΝΙΩ ΧΡΙΣΤΩ ΤΩ ΣΥΓΧΩΡΟΥΝΤΙ ΤΑΣ ΑΜΑΡΓΙΑΣ ["Glory to the eternal Christ, to him who forgives the sins"]; another example is the exclamation of the people conveyed to us by a Palestinian biography of a saint[27] of the 6th century: Δόξα σοι, Κύριε, ὁ ποιῶν θαυμάσια ["Thine is the glory, Lord, who do wonderful things"]. Examples of long prayer texts beginning with Δόξα σοι or ܫܘܒܚܐ ܠ [*šūḇḥā lə-* "Glory be to"], respectively, are a popular table prayer conveyed to us by Chrysostomos of Antioch [John Chrysostom, ca. 347–407],[28] and also pieces of prose like some hymns of the Nestorian daily prayer.[29] In the Liturgy of St. James[30] which is indigenous in Jerusalem, the deacon says, after Communion, a prayer which is remarkable because it, entirely in the style of the full *Bərāḵāh*, begins with Δόξα σοι, Χριστὲ βασιλεῦ ["Thine is the glory, Christ, king"] etc., and then, after a sentence with ὅτι ["because"] that gives the reason for the praise of God, concludes with another δόξα σοι ["thine is the glory"].

How strongly all those formulations have to be understood as specifically Christian is clearly indicated by the attitude of Judaism. In times past, Judaism, too, must have been familiar with the possessive form of predication of, at first, the simple doxology; this is evident by the occurrence of the simple doxology in the liturgy of the Samaritans[31] which, in its main prayers, proves to be an older sister of the liturgy of the synagogue. Rabbinical Judaism, however, does not know this prayer type anymore. It is obvious that we are dealing with one of those phenomena of anti-Christian opposition in the shaping of the ritual of the synagogue to which Joachim Jeremias, referring to a general development, just recently pointed;[32] already quite some time ago, L. Venetianer[33] explained specifically the development of the reading of the Prophets in the ritual of the synagogue as being the consequence of a deliberate break with an older practise that had been adopted from Christianity.

I purposefully chose the individual texts that illustrate the role played by doxology in early Christian prayer life so as to demonstrate, at the same time, how widespread this form of predication was in the Syrian areas neighbouring Arabia, specifically. Because, now, as for the formal structure of Islamic prayer, the decisive point is that it is not the *Bərāḵāh* but the doxology which proves to be the normal form of predication in the Koranic prayer elements. In the Koran, doxology occurs in two different wordings: that of the exclamation in the accusative سُبْحَانَ ["glory be to"] combined with a pronominal suffix or followed by a noun in the genitive, and that of a nominal clause with أَلْحَمْدُ ["praise"]. All in all, we encounter over fifty instances with either the one or the other of those wordings in the Koran—whereas the *Bərāḵāh* type only occurs nine times. And what may matter even more than the fact of the much higher frequency of this material is the fact that it also occurs in texts of all periods, from early Middle-Meccan up to Medinan surahs. Moreover, we may also ascribe some significance to the fact that, in a number of cases, a doxological formula is introduced by قُلْ ["say"] and thus, directly sanctioned by God, is given a, so to speak, official character, which was not the case with any of the formulas of the *Bərāḵāh* type in the Koran.

Closer examination tells us that all sorts of variants that we encountered in the early Christian use of the doxology also occur in the Koranic texts. The acclamatory use of unconnected doxological short formulas which has, to this day, been so frequent in Christian liturgy has a Koranic equivalent in the simple سُبْحَانَكَ ["Glory be to you!"] uttered by Moses in Q 7:140 [7:143] when he recovers his senses after God's appearance had made him fall down unconcious; Moses then adds that he, as "the first of the believers," will "turn to (God) in repentance."[34] To the same category belongs the سُبْحَانَ رَبِّنَا ["Glory be to our Lord!"] of Q 17:108 which is followed by the similarly concise confession that God's promise is fulfilled.[35] No less concise is the short أَلْحَمْدُ لِلَّهِ ["Praise be to God!"] that, in Q 31:24 [31:25], is explicitly quoted as a complete formula which to recite God commands by the usual قُلْ ["say"]. Q 27:60 [27:59] begins with the same formula, combined with the wish that there be سَلَامٌ ["peace"] upon the servants chosen by God; it is the opening of a polemical speech with which, according to Muhammad [as the author of the Koran], God charges him. In several instances we come across the formula in the function of the simplest possible doxological prayer close. This can be the case either at the end of surahs, like in Q 27:95 [27:93] and, in combination with the apposition رَبُّ ٱلْعَالَمِينَ ["Lord of the worlds"], in 37:182 and 39:75; or, like in 40:67 [40:65], as the conclusion of a confession of God's one-ness; or, like in 6:45, as the ending of a passage of a teaching nature. Where to the early Christian doxology a participial apposition is added, the equivalent following after أَلْحَمْدُ لِلَّهِ is almost always a relative clause. Such a combination opens the surahs 6, 18, 34 and 35;[36] we also encounter it in Q 14:41 [14:39] coming from Abraham's lips,[37] in 23:29 [23:28] uttered by Noah and his family,[38] in 27:15 in the mouth of David and Salomo,[39] and in 7:41 [7:43], 35:31 [35:34] and 39:74 in the mouth of the blessed in paradise.[40]

A predication put as a relative clause that is, instead, opened by سُبْحَانَ ٱلَّذِى can be found in Q 36:36, embedded, for a change, in a polemical dispute;[41] in 43:12 [43:13] it appears in a sentence in which people thank God for having let them use (ship and?) riding animal;[42] in surah 17 such a formula with سُبْحَانَ ٱلَّذِى is used as the opening of the surah;[43] and in 36:83 a similar formula is used as the conclusion of the surah, just like, in 17:111, a formula composed of ٱلْحَمْدُ لِلَّهِ and an added relative clause.[44] That, in 27:8, the *Bərāḵāh* formula [بُورِكَ مَن فِى ٱلنَّارِ وَمَنْ حَوْلَهَا "Blessed be who is in the fire and who is around it"] is followed by the doxology سُبْحَانَ ٱللَّهِ رَبِّ ٱلْعَٰلَمِينَ ["Glory be to God, the Lord of the worlds"] reminds us of the Coptic Easter prayer which is formed of alternating eulogies and doxologies. And the fact that the *Bərāḵāh* has taken here, of all places, the unusual form of بُورِكَ مَن [instead of the usual تَبَارَكَ] gains, in connection with this addition, a very specific significance. It becomes apparent that the *Bərāḵāh,* too, is, in this instance, not due to Jewish influence. Instead, we are dealing, not only in the following formula with سُبْحَانَ but also in this formula, with the consistent influence of a Christian prayer style which mixes eulogies and doxologies.

In another Koranic passage we find an example of a shorter doxological text, complete in itself, which might directly be connected to the Christian daily prayer [for examples see endnote 45].[45] It is the predication in surah 30:16f. [30:17f.] that unites سُبْحَانَ ["glory be"]and ٱلْحَمْدُ ["praise be"]:

فَسُبْحَٰنَ ٱللَّهِ حِينَ تُمْسُونَ وَحِينَ تُصْبِحُونَ

وَلَهُ ٱلْحَمْدُ فِى ٱلسَّمَٰوَٰتِ وَٱلْأَرْضِ وَعَشِيًّا وَحِينَ تُظْهِرُونَ

["Glory be to God when you enter te night and when you enter the morning, // and praise be to Him in the heavens and the earth, and at the sun's decline and at noon"].

In Q 3:189–192 [3:191–194], a passage from the Medinan period, we have the case of a doxological introduction by سُبْحَانَكَ ["Glory be to you!"] to a long prayer which then even in its contents maintains a petitionary charakter.

Q 10:10f. describes the prayer of the Blessed in paradise:

دَعْوَاهُمْ فِيهَا سُبْحَانَكَ اللَّهُمَّ وَتَحِيَّتُهُمْ فِيهَا سَلَامٌ وَآخِرُ دَعْوَاهُمْ أَنِ الْحَمْدُ لِلَّهِ رَبِّ الْعَالَمِينَ

["Their prayer therein will be: Glory be to you, God!; ... and the close of their prayer will be: Praise be to God, the Lord of the worlds!"];

this text presupposes the style of the words of the deacon in the Liturgy of St. James [cf. above], which, strictly transforming the type of the canonical, full *Bərāḵāh* into doxology, opens and concludes the prayer with doxologies.

In contrast to all of this, there is only one Koranic usage of simple doxology for which I do not know, at least for the time being, a direct early Christian model. It is a peculiar, more or less directly adversative usage of, quite frequently, سُبْحَانَ , and sometimes also of أَلْحَمْدُ لِلَّهِ ; the fact that it is, in Q 21:87 and 68:29, a confession of sin that is introduced by سُبْحَانَكَ and سُبْحَانَ رَبِّنَا respectively, is probably related to this aspect.[46] To this category belongs the سُبْحَانَكَ uttered by the angels in Q 2:30 [2:32] when they refuse to do what then Adam is able to do: to call all creatures by their names.[47] It belongs to this category when, beginning with this word, the angels (in 34:40 [34:41]),[48] or Jesus (in 5:116),[49] or the infidels (in 25:19 [25:18])[50] give the expected negative answer to a rhetorical question. To this belong the many other cases concerned, above all sharply formulated passages with polemics against polytheism or the Christian doctrine of the Trinity, harshly rejecting the adversary's view.[51] In all those instances the erupting indignation about thoughts that are felt to be blasphemous is uniformly expressed in a positive way, as a doxological praise of God.

Still, in my view we can, for this usage of the formula, too, at least imagine how it may have evolved from the specific language use of Jewish and Christian prayers. From a grammatical point of view, this asyndetically inserted exclamation has a parallel in the use of a shortest *Bərāḵāh* formula on Jewish soil, when quite frequently and equally asyndetically a בָּרוּךְ הוּא [*bāruḵ hū* – "he be blessed"] or an equivalent בָּרוּךְ שְׁמוֹ [*bāruḵ šəmo* – "blessed be his name"] is inserted after a mention of God. A translation of this Hebrew expression into Greek, with the doxological diction of Greek-speaking Christians, would result in Αὐτῷ ἡ δόξα ["Glory to him!"], or something like it; and it would be only natural to add such a pious insertion after having spoken God's name, if not always, at least in cases when it had to be spoken in a more or less awkward context. Perhaps further examination of, above all, the popular strata of early Christian literature will unearth textual evidence of such a language use—evidence which, then, would differ from the Koranic expressions in nothing else but language.

In this case *Ur*-Islam would be, here, too, as is essentially the case throughout, in line with a just completed transformation of the *Bərāḵāh* type into doxology, as we found it in the eucharistic prayers of the *Didache* [cf. above; for an excursus related to the question see endnote 52].[52] Those eucharistic prayer formulas, however, already clearly go beyond the simplest form of doxological prayer close, since in two instances[53] we find δόξα in combination with δύναμις ["power"]. We are dealing there with a richer, less stereotyped elaboration of the possessive form of predication, in which, besides or instead the δόξα, other features to do with glory or power are introduced as being owned by the Deity or due to him. This richer form of possessive predication, too, used to be well-known on Jewish soil, since we find it in the Old Testament in David's last song (1 Chronicles 29:10–13), broadly elaborated following an introducing *Bərāḵāh* formula. From the liturgy of the synagogue, however, it, too, has practically completely vanished. Instead, it became as widespread as one can imagine on the Christian side, starting already with the heavenly songs of praise of the Apocalypse (which are, of course, echoing real existing congregational worship) and the liturgical concluding formula of the Lord's prayer of Mt. 6:13: ὅτι σοῦ ἐστιν ἡ βασιλεία καὶ ἡ δύναμις καὶ ἡ δόξα εἰς τοὺς αἰῶνας. Ἀμήν. ["For thine is the kingdom, and the power, and the glory, in eternity. Amen"]. The term βασιλεία ["kingdom"], especially, which here is the first in the series, has kept an outstanding position in this context also in later times; already in the just mentioned instance in the Book of Chronicles, however, the מַמְלָכָה [*mamlāḵā* "kingdom"] appeared besides the כֹּל בַּשָּׁמַיִם וּבָאָרֶץ [*kol ba-š-šāmayyim u-ḇā-ʾāräṣ* "all that is in heaven and on earth"].

Now, again, we find that the picture of *Ur*-Islamic prayer that we can infer from the Koran has its parallels in the language use of Christian liturgy, whereas it is in contrast to that of rabbinical Judaism. There are about 25 more instances in the Koran, in surahs from various periods, where we encounter a richer form, or at least a form differing from simple doxology, of possessive predication. For example, Q 64:1 reads, with the equivalent of βασιλεία ["kingdom," i. e. ٱلْمُلْك] preceding one of the two regular equivalents of δόξα [i. e. ٱلْحَمْد]: لَهُ ٱلْمُلْكُ وَلَهُ ٱلْحَمْدُ وَهُوَ عَلَىٰ كُلِّ شَيْءٍ قَدِيرٌ ["His is the kingdom, and his is the praise, and he is able to do all things"]. Or we read, in 28:70, after a proclamation of God's one-ness: لَهُ الْحَمْدُ فِي الْأُولَىٰ وَالْآخِرَةِ وَلَهُ الْحُكْمُ ["His is the praise, in the first (or: in this world) and in the last (or: in the hereafter), and his is the decision"]. Or, especially elaborate, at the end of surah 45, in 45:35f. [45:36f.]: فَلِلَّهِ ٱلْحَمْدُ رَبِّ السَّمَاوَاتِ وَرَبِّ ٱلْأَرْضِ رَبِّ الْعَالَمِينَ وَلَهُ الْكِبْرِيَاءُ فِي السَّمَاوَاتِ وَالْأَرْضِ ["God's is the praise, Lord of the heavens and Lord of the earth, Lord of the worlds, and his is the majesty in the heavens and the earth"].—Tellingly enough, it is especially the expressions مَا فِي ٱلسَّمَٰوَٰتِ وَٱلْأَرْضِ ["what is in the heavens and on earth"] and مُلْكُ ٱلسَّمَٰوَٰتِ وَٱلْأَرْضِ ["the kingdom of the heavens and earth"] that, in this context, come to the fore with their striking, strictly stereotyped character.[54]

So far I have deliberately left the Fātiḥa unreferred to; but finally, I may not refrain to place the Fatiḥa, too, into the circle of the phenomena just discussed. In Nöldeke-Schwally, *Geschichte des Korans* [History of the Koran] I, pp. 112ff., a rich material of parallels to the individual expressions has been compiled in a long annotation. Perhaps, in a certain sense, less would have been even more. At least one would, in many instances, have to sift the material more rigorously and to more clearly emphasize the relationships between the unique *prayer* text and the *liturgical* texts of Judaism and Christianity. However, what is crucial here is probably not the details at all, but rather the fact that the Islamic "Lord's prayer," in its whole structure, is most strongly connected to one specific Christian doxological prayer text. I am referring to one of the Greek daily prayers, the one that is quite simply called Δοξολογία and that also exists, translated into the respective language, in all non-Greek rites of the East, the one that already the Codex Alexandrinus shows to be equal to the Biblical Odes [Canticles], the one that is, in the Roman-Western Mass, the "Gloria in excelsis" [or "Greater Doxology"].[55]

Both prayers begin with the simple doxology which is slightly expanded only at the surface:

Δοξα ἐν ὑψίστοις Θεῷ,
"Gloria in excelsis Deo,"
["Glory to God in the highest"],
ٱلْحَمْدُ لِلَّهِ رَبِّ ٱلْعَٰلَمِينَ ٱلرَّحْمَٰنِ ٱلرَّحِيمِ
["Praise be to God, Lord of the worlds, the beneficient, the merciful"].

Both prayers emphasize God's royal power:

Βασιλεῦ ἐπουράνιε Θεέ,
"Rex coelestis Deus"
["King, heavenly God"],
مَٰلِكِ يَوْمِ ٱلدِّينِ ["King of the Day of Doom"]

In both prayers, the possessive predication of the doxology is followed by a predication that may best called subjective, since it introduces those who are praying, in the first person plural:

Ὑμνοῦμέν σε, εὐλογοῦμέν σε, προσκυνοῦμέν σε, δοξολογοῦμέν σε, εὐχαριστοῦμέν σοι,
"Laudamus te, benedicimus te, adoramus te, glorificamus te, gratias agimus tibi"
["We praise you, we bless you, we worship you, we glorify you, we give thanks to you"]
إِيَّاكَ نَعْبُدُ وَإِيَّاكَ نَسْتَعِينُ ["Thee only we serve; to thee we pray for succour"].

In this passage the Koranic prayer is even less verbose, simpler than the Christian prayer. But on the other hand, [in its إِيَّاكَ ... وَإِيَّاكَ] it uses the typical Hellenistic anaphora of the pronoun of the second person that was treated in detail by Norden;[56] thereby it shows iself even more strictly opposed to the idiomatic Semitic language use of the liturgy of the synagogue, and more closely connected to yet another early Christian prose hymn: the Ambrosian Hymn [or "Te Deum"]: "*Te* Deum laudamus, *te* dominum confitemur, *te* aeternum Patrem omnis terra veneratur, *tibi* omnes angeli ..." [*Thee* we praise, o God; *thee* we acknowledge to be the Lord. *Thee*, the Father everlasting, all the earth doth worship. *To thee* all Angels ..."] etc.

And in both prayers the predication finally turns into a prayer of supplication:

ἐλέησον ἡμᾶς ... πρόσδεξαι τὴν δέησιν ἡμῶν ... ἐλέησον ἡμᾶς,
"miserere nobis ... suscipe deprecationem nostram ... miserere nobis,"
["Have mercy on us ... Receive our prayer ... have mercy on us"]
ٱهْدِنَا ٱلصِّرَٰطَ ٱلْمُسْتَقِيمَ.. ["Guide us in the straight path"] etc.

In other instances, we may be inclined to really suppose a direct relationship of dependence of Koranic prayer elements from the Greater Doxology. Thus, in 27:60 [27:59] the ٱلْحَمْدُ لِلَّهِ ["Praise be to God"],is followed by وَسَلَامٌ عَلَىٰ عِبَادِهِ الَّذِينَ اصْطَفَى, ["and peace be on his servants whom he has chosen"] for which we will hardly find a more natural explanation than that it was taken from the model of Lk. 2,14: Δόξα ἐν ὑψίστοις θεῷ καὶ ἐπὶ γῆς εἰρήνη ἐν ἀνθρώποις εὐδοκίας, "Gloria in excelsis Deo et in terra pax hominibus bonae voluntatis" ["Glory to God in the highest, and on earth peace among men in whom he is well pleased"]. Hardly less striking is the parallel between the sequence of the Greater Doxology πρόσδεξαι τὴν δέησιν ἡμῶν, ... ἐλέησον ἡμᾶς, "suscipe deprecationem nostram, ... miserere nobis" ["Receive our prayer, ... have mercy on us"] and the twofold plea in Abraham's prayer in Q 14:42 [14:40–41]: رَبَّنَا وَتَقَبَّلْ دُعَآءِ رَبَّنَا ٱغْفِرْ لِى ["Our Lord! And accept my prayer. Our Lord! Forgive me"]. Of course, I am far from suggesting such a relationship of dependence for the Fātiḥa. Only that much is evident: that the main prayer of the Koran is structured in strict accordance with the formal pattern on which the ancient Christian prose hymn is based but which cannot be discerned, in equal completeness, anywhere in the liturgy of the synagogue.

I already mentioned the Te Deum in the context of the discussion of the twofold إِيَّاكَ . At the same time, the Te Deum is one of the classic examples of a last form of predication in Christian prayers to which I should like to point, since we encounter it in the Koran as well. I should like to refer to it as "indirect predication." It is characterized by the fact that it introduces not the praying persons themselves but some other circles of God's creations as those who perform the praise of God. Those are, in the western text, the "whole earth," the various choirs of the heavenly host, several classes of saints, and the "sancta ecclesia" which has spread "per orbem terrarum."[57] In the east, there is a passage in the eucharistic prayer of Jerusalem according to the Liturgy of St. James, apparently already known to Origen [184/5–253/4], where, in the corresponding context, the classes of saints and the angelic choirs are preceded by a long list of all visible elements of God's creation.[58] Also, we can point to the corresponding passage in the Egyptian Liturgy of Gregory [Gregory of Nazianus, 330–389/390] which is partly preserved already in a papyrus of the collection of archduke Rainer [today part of the

Austrian National Library in Vienna]; in it, to the list of individual angelic choires singing the Trisagion the more general phrase is added: σέ ὑμνεῖ τὰ ἀόρατα, σέ προςκυνεῖ τὰ φαινόμενα ["Thee praises what is invisible, thee praises, prostratingly, what is visible"].[59] This kind of indirect predication can be observed in the religious speech of, above all, old Egypt where it goes way back, and we could also easily add further Christian examples from both the east and the west. To the liturgy of the synagogue, however, it is alien; also, in the latest passages of the Old Testament, like in Psalm 148 or in the song of the three young men in the Greek additions [of the Septuagint] to the Book of Daniel, we find similar ideas expressed differently: all things are *called upon to* praise God. In fact, the Koran, too, seems to contain a reminiscence of Psalm 148, when, in 38:17 [38:18], Muhammad [as the author of the Koran] lets God speak of how he made the mountains sing, together with David, the praises of the creator at evening and sunrise.[60] But the notion in the Koran is that the mountains did indeed carry out what they were told, whereby this passage, strictly speaking, already goes beyond the Biblical model where the psalmist only *summons* the "mountains and all hills" to praise God. In quite a number of other Koranic passages, however, we are dealing with an obvious application of the style of indirect predication known from Christian prayers, although the subject is never elaborated as broadly as it is in the Te Deum or the Liturgy of St. James. Specifically mentioned as praising or worshipping God we find, at any rate, the birds (in Q 24:41), the angels (42:3 [42:5]), and the stars and trees (55:5 [55:6]).[61] The first of those three instances (24:41) additionally gives the general expression مَن فِي ٱلسَّمَـٰوَٰتِ وَٱلْأَرْضِ ["whatsoever is in the heavens and the earth"] as the subject of the worship of God; the same subject of worship also occurs, on its own and as a strictly stereotyped formula, in Q 13:16 [13:15] as well as, with the variant of مَا instead of مَن , in 57:1, 59:1, 59: 24, 61:1, 62:1 and 64:1.[62]

There could be more observations added to the picture resulting from all this. For example, it is certainly no coincidence that the frequently occuring expression رَبُّ ٱلْعَالَمِينَ ["Lord of the worlds"], always in the plural, corresponds well to the Christian βασιλεὺς τῶν αἰώνων ["King of the Eternities"] but contrasts with the מֶלֶךְ הָעוֹלָם [*mäläḵ hā-ʿōlām* – "king of the universe," part of the *Bərāḵāh*] of the synagogue [the root ʿ-l-m in Syriac has mainly the meaning "age, eternity," whereas "world" is only the second meaning; the plural also means "ages, eternity." See Louis Costaz, S. J. Dictionnaire Syriaque-Français, Syriac-English Dicionary, Beyrouth: Dar El-Machreq, 1994, p. 254. Baumstark seems to presuppose this to be well-known, the Arabic *rabb al-ʿālamīn* could indeed mean: Lord of Eternities], both formulas being no less fixed in the sphere of their respective *liturgy*.

And when, in Q 3:25f. [3:26f.], in a prayer which is commanded to recite by قُلْ ["say"], the address ٱللَّهُمَّ مَـٰلِكَ ٱلْمُلْكِ ["O God, master of the kingdom"] is followed by the declaration:

تُؤْتِى ٱلْمُلْكَ مَن تَشَآءُ

وَتَنزِعُ ٱلْمُلْكَ مِمَّن تَشَآءُ ,

["You give the kingdom to whom you will, // and you take the kingdom away from whom you will"; but many translations have "sovereignty" for *mulk*], then it would be difficult not to understand the ٱلْمُلْك in the specifically Christian sense of βασιλεία ["kingdom"] ("of God" or "of the heaven"), as the comprising term for the "last things" of eschatology.

Also, when in 3:191 [3:193] a prayer of supplication opened by سُبْحَانَكَ attaches to the plea for forgiveness of sins a second plea: وَتَوَفَّنَا مَعَ ٱلْأَبْرَارِ ["make us die with the righteous"], then this has a most close parallel in a formula that is so common in the litanies of the deacons in the Christian-Oriental liturgies: the wish, formulated in the prayer, that Χριστιανὰ τὰ τέλη τῆς ζωῆς ἡμῶν ἀνώδυνα, ἀνεπαίσχυντα ["Christian be the end of our life, without pain and (reason for) shame"].[63]

However, to digress in such details would hardly be an essential contribution to the deepening of the overall picture that we received by comparing the structure of *Ur*-Islamic prayers with that of Jewish and Christian prayers.

It has become perfectly clear that Muhammad, from early on until the last period of his work, was, with regard to the formal structure of the prayer formulas coined by him, under Christian influence. Jewish influence, which is additionally discernible, was restricted to the time from around the middle until the end of the Meccan period; it should probably be seen as a—and perhaps the oldest—phenomenon that was part of the general turn towards Judaism which culminated in the temporary introduction of the Yom Kippur Lent and the direction of prayer towards Jerusalem, as well as in the fiction of a restoration of an Old-Arab religion of Abraham, but which then, after the hopes that had been built on the Jews of Jathrib were dashed, changed completely into the blazing anti-Judaism of the Medinan period. The examination of the prayer type of the *Ur*-Islam, too, shows that it was, from the beginning, decidedly determined by Christianity, and not by Judaism.

Finally, we should at least touch upon a side issue. How can it be explained that the Prophet was influenced by prayer forms of the Christian liturgy? The fact that, in Q 27:8, the echo of a Christian eulogy has a wording that differs from the usual reverberation of the Jewish *Bərāḵāh* type [cf. above] seems to indicate that the Christian liturgical prayer which influenced Muhammad was already put in Arabic when he encountered it. Tor Andrae's studies that I mentioned at the beginning point to a particular importance of Nestorian influence on Muhammad's religious thought world, which naturally brings the Nestorian Christianity of the Laḫmid kingdom into focus. And the Nestorian church displayed, in advancing onto new missionary territory, again and again a remarkable inclination to give up its traditional liturgical language, the Syriac, and to adopt the vernacular of the new area, instead. The significance of Persian as liturgical language of the metropolitan diocese of Persis is well-known to us.[64] Manuscript tradition shows that fragments of Persian song texts were even embedded into the normal Syriac office of the feast of Epiphany.[65] The monument of Sin-gan-fu has told us about translations of liturgical books into Chinese already a long time ago. Evidence of a liturgical use of Soghdian by Nestorian Christians is given by the fragments found in Turfan;[66] evidence of the use of Turkish as the language of Nestorian liturgy has, in the last years, passed through my hands. In the light of all this it does not seem too daring to assume that, in the Laḫmid kingdom or by Nestorian missionaries who tried, coming from there, to advance into the heart of the Arabian Peninsula, Christian worship may have been celebrated in Arabic. This assumption would only agree with thoughts that have already been uttered by Wellhausen.[67]

Notes

---

1 Tor Andrae, *Der Ursprung des Islams und das Christentum* [Christianity and the Origin of Islam] (Uppsala-Stockholm 1926) (reprint from: Kyrkohistorisk Årsskrift 1923–1925).

2 Eduard Norden, *Agnostos Theos. Untersuchungen zur Formengeschichte religiöser Rede* [Studies on the history of forms of religious speech] (Berlin-Leipzig 1913 and 1923 resp.); pp. 141–276: "Untersuchungen zur Stilgeschichte der Gebets- und Prädikationsformeln" [Studies on the history of the style of prayer and predication formulas].

3 Fritz [/Schlomo Dov] Goitein, *Das Gebet im Qoran* [Prayer in the Koran]. [defended 1923, not published]—The thesis was available to me in a typewritten copy that had been sent on loan to the Oriental Seminar of the University of Bonn.

4 How much it lacks precision in grasping the real formal problems can be deduced, e. g., from the fact that a clear doxology is referred to as a eulogy [i. e. blessing]—probably because a German-Greek school dicionary gives both εὔλογεῖν [eulogein] and δοξολογεῖν [doxologein] as translations for "preisen – to praise"!

5 The rest of the sentence reads:
in Q 25:1: نَزَّلَ الْفُرْقَانَ عَلَى عَبْدِهِ لِيَكُونَ لِلْعَالَمِينَ نَذِيرًا ["who sent down the Criterion upon his servant that he may be to the worlds a warner"];
in Q 25:11 [25:10]: إِن شَاءَ جَعَلَ لَكَ خَيْرًا مِّن ذَٰلِكَ جَنَّاتٍ ["who, if he willed, could have made for you something better than that: gardens ..."];
in Q 25:62f. [25:61f], like a hymn:
جَعَلَ فِي السَّمَاءِ بُرُوجًا وَجَعَلَ فِيهَا سِرَاجًا وَقَمَرًا مُّنِيرًا وَهُوَ الَّذِي جَعَلَ اللَّيْلَ وَالنَّهَارَ خِلْفَةً
["who has placed in the sky great stars and placed therein a lamp and a luminous moon. He is who has appointed night and day in succession ..."].

6 The sentence continues, in Q 43:85, with a wording that is, in turn, itself highly stereotyped: لَهُ مُلْكُ السَّمَاوَاتِ وَالْأَرْضِ وَمَا بَيْنَهُمَا ["to whom belongs the kingdom of the heavens and the earth and whatever is between them"]. In Q 67:1 the sentence

continues بِيَدِهِ ٱلْمُلْكُ وَهُوَ عَلَىٰ كُلِّ شَيْءٍ قَدِيرٌ ["in whose hand is the kingdom, and he is able to do all things"], followed by further predications put as relative clauses.

7 The sentence continues فِي ٱلنَّارِ وَمَنْ حَوْلَهَا ["is in the fire and who is around it"], referring to God's appearance in the burning bush.

8 In Q 7:52 [7:54] and 40:66 [40:64]. In 23:14 it reads differently: أَحْسَنُ ٱلْخَالِقِينَ ["the best of creators"].

9 Consider, e. g., that the entire Psalter was recited, in the church's daily prayer, within a specific timeframe (which could be two weeks, one week or half a week, one day, sometimes even one single night).

10 Cf., e.g., Imra' al-Qays LX 2: كَخَطِّ زَبُورٍ فِي مَصَاحِفِ رُهْبَانِ ["like the script of a Psalter in the books of the monks"].

11 The formula is the basis of the old Aramaic יְהֵא שְׁמֵהּ רַבָּא מְבָרַךְ לְעָלַם וּלְעָלְמֵי עָלְמַיָּא *yəhē' šᵊmēh rabbā' məḇārak̠ ləʿālam ūlə-ʿālᵊmē* of the Qaddīš prayer.

12 Thus, in the rite of Rome, *Psalm* 113 (112:2) is the first of the two versicles that open every solemn blessing bestowed by bishops. In the Greek rite, the verse is sung by the choir at the end of every celebration of the Eucharist, and the same used to be the custom in the orthodox local rite of Alexandria. Cf. F. E. Brightman, *Liturgies Eastern and Western*, Oxford 1896, p. 143.

13 II. Cor. 1:3; *Eph.* 1,3; I *Peter* 1:3 resp. Romans 1:25; Romans 9:5.

14 Cf., e. g., Brightman, op. cit. [cf. note 12], p. 355 lines 5f., 24, 29ff., 33f., and p. 356, lines 25f. Also cf. A. Dmitriewskij, *Beschreibung der liturgischen Handschriften in den Bibliotheken des orthodoxen Orients* [Description of the liturgical manuscripts in the libraries of the Orthodox East] (Russian), vol. II Εὐχολόγια, Kiew 1901, pp. 46f., 58f., 80, 94, 111f., 116, 151, 153, 210f., etc.

15 Cf., e. g., some instances in the baptismal liturgy of the Copts, in H. Denzinger, *Ritus Orientalium, Coptorum, Syrorum et Armenorum, in administrandis sacramentis* [The rites of the Orientals, Copts, Syrians and Armenians, in administering the sacraments] (Würzburg, 1863), pp. 195, 203, 207f., 211, 219, 223, 227, 244f.

16 Cf. F. C. Conybeare, *Rituale Armenorum* (Oxford; 1905), pp. 30, 36, 44f., 49f., 57f., 61, 63f., 93, 110f., 115, 127, 132, 166, 221, 250f., 263, 284, 285, 468, 483.

17 Ὡρολόγιον τὸ Μέγα [The great book of Hours], Rome 1876, pp. 88f.

18 The text of the prayer is to be found in every edition of the Breviarium Romanum, in the context of the "Benedictio Mensae."

19 On the doxology and its original acclamatory character cf. the book, which just came out and is rich in substance, by E. Peterson, *ΕΙΣ ΘΕΟΣ. Epigraphische, formgeschichtliche und religionsgeschichtliche Untersuchungen* [One God: Studies on epigraphy and the history of forms and religion]. Göttingen 1926 (= *Forschungen zur Religion und Literatur des Alten und Neuen Testaments.* Neue Folge, 24. Heft), pp. 224–227.

20 Didache, 9:2f.; 10:2; 10:4.

21 C. M. Kaufmann, *Handbuch der altchristlichen Epigraphik* [Handbook of early Christian epigraphy] (Freiburg im Breisgau, 1917), p. 166.

22 Waddington no. 2666 [William Henry Waddington, *Inscriptions grecques et latines de la Syrie (Greek and Latin inscriptions of Syria)* (Paris, 1870)].

23 Cf. E. Peterson, *ΕΙΣ ΘΕΟΣ*, op. cit., p. 225.

24 ([Richardus Adelbertus] Lipsius-) [Maximilianus] Bonnet, *Acta Apostolorum apocrypha II 1* [Leipzig, 1898], p. 197. According to Augustinus' Epistula 237 (ad Ceretium) the text was, at his time, in use among the Priscillianists. Its home, like that of the old Gnostic Acts of John that were used, among others, by the Manichaeans, probably lies in the border area of Hellenistic Christianity and the Iranian religion.

25 Translated into Latin by H[enri] Hyvernat ["Fragmente der altcoptischen Liturgie: Fragments of the Old-Coptic liturgy"], in *Römische Quartalschrift für christliche Altertumskunde und für Kirchengeschichte* II [1888, pp. 20–27], pp. 23f. [available online: https://archive.org/details/rmischequartals02instgoog].

26 Waddington [cf. note 22] no. 1936 = *CIG* [*Corpus Inscriptiorum Graecarum*] no. 9144.

27 The Biography of Theognios of Betilia (d. 522) [Theognios, bishop of Bethelia, Cappadocian monk in Palestine] by Paulos of Elusa [Paulos, Hesychast of Elousa], edited by P. J. van den Gheyn, *Analecta Bollandiana X* [Brussels 1882][pp. 73–118], p. 93 [available online:
https://archive.org/details/analectabolland00unkngoog].

28 Homilia 55 in Matth.: PG [J. P. Migne, *Patrologia Graeca*, vol. 1–161 (Paris, 1857–1866), LVIII column 561. Even today, the prayer is still used by the Greek church: *Ὡρολόγιον τὸ Μέγα* [The great book of Hours] (Rome, 1876), p. 88.

29 Prose prayers of the Night Office: cf. *Breviarium Chaldaicum* pp. 27 and 41f. of every edition. Metrical Ḥuttāmā for the Vesper on Sundays and feast days; and Tešboḥtā for the Night Office on Fridays ascribed to Narsai [Narsai of Nisibis, d. ca. 500] or his relative Jôḥannān: cf. ibid., pp. 17 and 28.

30 Brightman, *Liturgies Eastern and Western* [cf. note 12], p. 65, lines 14–22.

31 At the beginning of a long prayer after the Qĕdîšās: cf. A[rthur Ernest] Cowley, *The Samaritan Liturgy* (Oxford, 1909), I, p. 12: בנצירו ובקשט וברחתו נימר כהלן תשבחתה לך *b-nṣyrw w-bqšṭ w-brḥtw nymr khln* [available online:
https://archive.org/details/samaritanliturgy01cowluoft].

32 In the excellent article by Joachim Jeremias, "Das Gebetsleben Jesu," in *Zeitschrift für die neutestamentliche Wissenschaft und die Kunde der älteren Kirche* XXV, p. 128.

33 L[udwig] Venetianer, *Ursprung und Bedeutung der Propheten-Lektionen*, in *ZDMG* 63 [1909], p. 103–170.

34 تُبْتُ إِلَيْكَ وَأَنَا أَوَّلُ ٱلْمُؤْمِنِينَ.

35 إِن كَانَ وَعْدُ رَبِّنَا لَمَفْعُولًا.

36 The additions after the doxology read, in the sense of the Christian daily prayer,
in Q 6:1: الَّذِي خَلَقَ السَّمَاوَاتِ وَالْأَرْضَ وَجَعَلَ الظُّلُمَاتِ وَالنُّورَ ["who has created the heavens and the earth and has appointed darkness and light"],
and in 18:1: الَّذِي أَنزَلَ عَلَى عَبْدِهِ الْكِتَابَ ["who has sent down upon his servant the book"].
In 34:1 the addition is itself a doxology:
الَّذِي لَهُ مَا فِي السَّمَاوَاتِ وَمَا فِي الْأَرْضِ وَلَهُ الْحَمْدُ فِي الْآخِرَةِ ["to whom belongs whatever is in the heavens and whatever is in the earth, and to him belongs all praise in the hereafter, and he is the wise, the aware"];
and in 35:1 it is, for once in Arabic, too, a participial addition:
فَاطِرِ السَّمَاوَاتِ وَالْأَرْضِ جَاعِلِ الْمَلَائِكَةِ رُسُلًا ["creator of the heavens and the earth, who appoints the angels as messengers"] etc.

37 The addition reads: الَّذِي وَهَبَ لِي عَلَى الْكِبَرِ إِسْمَاعِيلَ وَإِسْحَاقَ ["who has granted to me in my old age Ishmael and Isaac"].
38 The addition reads: الَّذِي نَجَّانَا مِنَ الْقَوْمِ الظَّالِمِينَ ["who has saved us from the wrongdoing people"].
39 The addition reads: الَّذِي فَضَّلَنَا عَلَى كَثِيرٍ مِّنْ عِبَادِهِ الْمُؤْمِنِينَ ["who has favoured us over many of his believing servants"].
40 The additions read: in 7:43 الَّذِي هَدَانَا لِهَٰذَا ["who has guided us to this"]; in 35:34: ٱلَّذِىٓ أَذۡهَبَ عَنَّا ٱلۡحَزَنَ ["who has removed from us all sorrow"]; and in 39:74: ٱلَّذِى صَدَقَنَا وَعۡدَهُۥ وَأَوۡرَثَنَا ٱلۡأَرۡضَ نَتَبَوَّأُ مِنَ ٱلۡجَنَّةِ حَيۡثُ نَشَآءُ ["who has fulfilled for us his promise and has made us inherit the earth so we may settle in paradise wherever we will."
41 The addition reads: خَلَقَ ٱلۡأَزۡوَٰجَ كُلَّهَا مِمَّا تُنۢبِتُ ٱلۡأَرۡضُ وَمِنۡ أَنفُسِهِمۡ وَمِمَّا لَا يَعۡلَمُونَ ["who created all the sexual pairs, of that which the earth grows, and of themselves, and of that which they know not"].
42 The addition reads: سَخَّرَ لَنَا هَٰذَا وَمَا كُنَّا لَهُۥ مُقۡرِنِينَ ["who has subdued these to us, and we were not capable"].
43 The addition reads: أَسۡرَىٰ بِعَبۡدِهِۦ لَيۡلٗا مِّنَ ٱلۡمَسۡجِدِ ٱلۡحَرَامِ إِلَى ٱلۡمَسۡجِدِ ٱلۡأَقۡصَا ["who took his servant by night from the Inviolable Plave of Worship to the Far distant place of worship"].
44 The additions read: in 36:83: بِيَدِهِۦ مَلَكُوتُ كُلِّ شَيۡءٖ وَإِلَيۡهِ تُرۡجَعُونَ ["in whose hands is the realm of all things, and to him you will be returned"], and in 17:111: ٱلَّذِى لَمۡ يَتَّخِذۡ وَلَدٗا وَلَمۡ يَكُن لَّهُۥ شَرِيكٞ فِي ٱلۡمُلۡكِ وَلَمۡ يَكُن لَّهُۥ وَلِيّٞ مِّنَ ٱلذُّلِّ ["who has not taken to himself a son and has no partner in his kingdom and has no protecting friend through dependence"].
45 Cf., e. g., the εὐχὴ τῆς εἰσόδου [introit prayer] of the *Greek Vesper (Εὐχολόγιον τὸ Μέγα [Great collection of prayers]* (Rome, 1873), pp. 14f.) with its first words: Ἑσπέρας καὶ πρωῒ καὶ μεσημβρίας αἰνοῦμεν, εὐλογοῦμεν, εὐχαριστοῦμεν καὶ δεόμεθά σου, Δέσποτα τῶν ἁπάντων ["In the evening and in the morning and at the height of noon we laud, praise, thank, and plead you, Lord of everything"], or the combination of all hours in a stanza of the Ambrosian morning hymn (H. Lietzmann, *Lateinische altkirchliche Poesie* [Early Christian Latin poetry] (Bonn, 1910), p. 10):

"Laetus dies hic transeat,
pudor sit ut diluculum,
fides velut meridies,
crepusculum mens nesciat."

["May this day pass gaily // may shame be like dawn // faith be like the height of noon // may mind not know dusk"].
46 The سُبۡحَٰنَكَ and confession of sins are uttered by Jonas, the سُبۡحَانَ رَبِّنَا and confession of sins by the infidels that become converted.—In both instances we already seem to be dealing with fixed formulas, since the wording of the respective confession, too—إِنِّي كُنتُ مِنَ ٱلظَّٰلِمِينَ ["I have been of the wrongdoers"] and إِنَّا كُنَّا ظَٰلِمِينَ ["we were wrongdoers"]—is almost identical.

47 سُبْحَانَكَ لَا عِلْمَ لَنَا إِلَّا مَا عَلَّمْتَنَا إِنَّكَ أَنتَ الْعَلِيمُ الْحَكِيمُ ["Glory be to you! We have no knowledge except what you have taught us. It is you who is the knower, the wise."].

48 سُبْحَانَكَ أَنتَ وَلِيُّنَا مِن دُونِهِم بَلْ كَانُوا۟ يَعْبُدُونَ ٱلْجِنَّ أَكْثَرُهُم بِهِم مُّؤْمِنُونَ ["Glory be to you! You alone are our guardian, not them. Rather, they used to worship the ğinn; most of them were believers in them."].

49 سُبْحَانَكَ مَا يَكُونُ لِي أَنْ أَقُولَ مَا لَيْسَ لِي بِحَقٍّ ["Glory be to you! It was not for me to say that to which I have no right."].

50 سُبْحَانَكَ مَا كَانَ يَنۢبَغِى لَنَآ أَن نَّتَّخِذَ مِن دُونِكَ مِنْ أَوْلِيَآءَ ["Glory be to you! It was not for us to take besides you any protecting friends"]. الله أكبر

51 سُبْحَانَهُ ["Glory be to him"] in 2:110 [2:116], 4:169 [4:171], 6:100, 9:31, 10:19 [10:18], 10:69 [10:68], 16:1, 16:59 [16:57], 17:45 [17:43], 19:36 [19:35], 21:26, 30:39 [30:40], 39:6 [39:4], 39:67. سُبْحَانَ الله ["Glory be to God"] in 12:108, 23:93 [23:91], 28:68, 52:43, 59:23. سُبْحَانَ رَبِّي ["Glory be to my Lord"] in 17:95 [17:93]. سُبْحَانَ رَبِّكَ ["Glory be to your Lord"] in 37:180. Particularly broadly elaborated, with the original doxological meaning behind it clearly perceptible, as سُبْحَانَ رَبِّ ٱلسَّمَٰوَٰتِ وَٱلْأَرْضِ رَبِّ ٱلْعَرْشِ ["Glory be to the Lord of heavens and earth, the Lord of the throne"], in 43:82; similar but shorter, as فَسُبْحَٰنَ ٱللَّهِ رَبِّ ٱلْعَرْشِ ["Glory be to God, the Lord of the throne"], in 21:22. In 24:15 [24:16] we find a simple سُبْحَانَكَ without there being any real address to God; the word seems to have turned into a sheer negation—unless the whole adversative expression has been erroneously placed here, which is possible. Rather frequent are additions like عَمَّا يُشْرِكُونَ ["above what they associate with him"] or عَمَّا يَصِفُونَ ["above what they ascribe to him"] or the like, with or without preceding وتعالى ["high exalted"].

52 In this context it may be allowed to at least put the question whether there is not yet another, even much more literal parallel between liturgical texts of the early Christian church order and the world of Ur-Islamic prayer. In two Koranic instances the wording of which varies not too profoundly, Muhammad is, by قُل ["say"], commanded to utter a formula which contrasts the word حَقٌّ ["truth, rightness"] with بَاطِل [usually tranlated as "untrue, falsehood," but it mainly means "nugatory, vain, worthless"]. In the first instance (Q 17:83 [17:81]) it is expressed positively: جَآءَ ٱلْحَقُّ وَزَهَقَ ٱلْبَٰطِلُ [usually translated as: "truth has come and falsehood has vanished"], whereas in the second instance (34:48 [34:49]) the second constituent is negatively put: جَآءَ ٱلْحَقُّ وَمَا يُبْدِئُ ٱلْبَٰطِلُ وَمَا يُعِيدُ [usually understood as: "The truth has come, and falsehood shows not its face and will not return"]. If we are allowed to understand the grammatical perfect of the verbs in an optative sense instead of, as is always done in these instances, in the perfective sense, then we are getting a surprisingly striking parallel to the eschatological prayer call of the Didache that is directly connected to the administration of the Eucharist: Ἐλθέτω χάρις καὶ παρελθέτω ὁ κόσμος οὗτος ["May come the grace, and may pass away this world"].

53 Chapter 9, § 4: σοῦ ἐστιν ἡ δόξα καὶ ἡ δύναμις διὰ Ἰησοῦ Χριστοῦ εἰς τοὺς αἰῶνας ["thine is the glory, and the power, through Jesus Christ, in eternity"]; chapter 10, § 5: ὅτι σοῦ ἐστιν ἡ δύναμις καὶ ἡ δόξα εἰς τοὺς αἰῶνας ["for thine is the power, and the glory, in eternity"].

54 مَا فِي ٱلسَّمَٰوَٰتِ وَٱلْأَرْضِ ["what is in the heavens and on earth"]: in Q 2:110 [2:116], 4:168 [4:170], 14:2, 24:64, 31:25 [31:26], 42:2 [42:4]; with the variant مَن ["who"] instead of مَا ["what"] in 30:25 [30:26], and with وَمَا فِي instead of وَ فِي in 22:63

[22:64] and 53:32 [53:31]. مُلْكُ ٱلسَّمَـٰوَٰتِ وَٱلْأَرْضِ ["the kingdom of the heavens and earth"]: in Q 3:186 [3:189], 24:42, 25:2, 39:45 [39:44], and 57:2. Instead of the simple مَا ["what"], 30:26 [30:27] has أَلْمَثَلُ الأعلى ["the highest attribute"]; instead of مُلْكُ ["kingdom"], 11:123 has غَيْبُ ["unseen"], and 48:7 has جُنُودُ ["hosts"]. In 39:8 [39:6] we have only لَهُ ٱلْمُلْكُ ["his is the kingdom"], and in 53:25 we read فَلِلَّهِ ٱلْآخِرَةُ وَٱلْأُولَىٰ ["God's is the last (or: hereafter) and the first (or: world)"].

55 For my comparison, I am using the normal and, as I think, original Greek-Latin form of the text. On the various recencions of this version cf. A. Baumstark, "Die Textüberlieferung des Hymnus angelicus" [The textual transmission of the "Hymnus evangelicus"], in the Festschrift: *Hundert Jahre*, A. Marcus und E. Webers Verlag 1818–1918 (Bonn 1919), pp. 83–87.

56 E. Norden, *Agnostos Theos*, op. cit. [cf. note 2], pp. 150–160.

57 "Te aeternum Patrem omnis terra veneratur, Tibi omnes angeli, tibi Coeli et universae Potestates, Tibi Cherubim et Seraphim incessabili voce proclamant: Sanctus (etc.). Te gloriosum Apostolorum chorus, Te Prophetorum laudabilis numerus, Te Martyrum candidatus laudat exercitus, Te per orbem terrarum sancta confitetur Ecclesia" ["Thee, the Father everlasting, all the earth doth worship. To thee all Angels cry aloud, the Heavens, and all the Powers therein. To thee Cherubim and Seraphim continually do cry: Holy (etc.). Thee the glorious company of the Apostles, the goodly fellowship of the Prophets praise. Thee the noble army of Martyrs praise. Thee the holy Church throughout all the world doth acknowledge."].

58 Brightman (op. cit.) [cf. note 12], p. 50: Τῷ πάντων θεῷ καὶ δεσπότῃ, ὃν ὑμνοῦσιν οὐρανοὶ καὶ οὐρανοὶ οὐρανῶν καὶ πᾶσα ἡ δύναμις αὐτῶν, ἥλιός τε καὶ σελήνη καὶ πᾶς ὁ τῶν ἄστρων χορός, γῆ, θάλασσα καὶ πάντα τὰ ἐν αὐτοῖς, Ἱερουσαλὴμ ἡ ἐπουράνιος πανήγυρις, ἐκκλησία πρωτότοκων ἀπογεγραμμένων ἐν τοῖς οὐρανοῖς, πνεύματα δικαίων καὶ προφητῶν, ψυχαὶ μαρτύρων καὶ ἀποστόλων, ἄγγελοι, ἀρχάγγελοι, θρόνοι, κυριότητες, ἀρχαί τε καὶ ἐξουσίαι, καὶ δυνάμεις φοβεραί, χερουβὶμ τὰ πολυόμματα καὶ τὰ ἑξαπτέρυγα σεραφίμ. ["To God, Lord of everything, goes the praise of the heavens and the heavens of the heavens and of all their power; of the sun and the moon and the whole choir of the stars, the earth, the sea and everything that is in them; of those who are assembled in the heavenly Jerusalem, of the assembly of the 'firstborn' that are written down in heaven, of the ghosts of the righteous people and the prophets, the souls of the martyrs and apostles, and of the angels: the archangels, 'thrones,' 'reigns,' 'powers,' 'forces' and 'terrifying forces,' the 'cherubim' with the many eyes and the 'seraphim' with the six wings"].

Cf. Origen *Κατὰ Κέλσου* VII 67: ὑμνοῦμέν γε θεὸν καὶ τὸν μονογενῆ αὐτοῦ ὡς καὶ ἥλιος καὶ σελήνη καὶ πᾶσα ἡ οὐρανία στρατιά. Ὑμνοῦσι γὰρ πάντες οὗτοι θεῖος ὄντες χορὸς μετὰ τῶν ἐν ἀνθρώποις δικαίων τὸν ἐπὶ πᾶσι θεὸν καὶ τὸν μονογενῆ αὐτοῦ ["Praising God and his only begotten son are the sun, the moon and the whole heavenly host. Praise him do they all, a divine choir, with the righteous among men, him, God of everything, and his only begotten son"].

59 Eusèbe Renaudot, *Liturgiarum orientalium collectio* (Frankfurt [reprint], 1847, vol. I, p. 93. Cf. also *Dictionnaire d'Archéologie chrétienne et de Liturgie* I, column 1905: It gives the text of that Vienna papyrus, as well as the concerning literature.

60 إِنَّا سَخَّرْنَا ٱلْجِبَالَ مَعَهُۥ يُسَبِّحْنَ بِٱلْعَشِيِّ وَٱلْإِشْرَاقِ ["We subdued the mountains to hymn the praises with him (=David) at nightfall and sunrise"].

61 24:41 أَلَمْ تَرَ أَنَّ ٱللَّهَ يُسَبِّحُ لَهُۥ مَن فِي ٱلسَّمَاوَاتِ وَٱلْأَرْضِ وَٱلطَّيْرُ صَافَّاتٍ كُلٌّ قَدْ عَلِمَ صَلَاتَهُۥ وَتَسْبِيحَهُۥ ["Have you not seen that it is God, whom all that are in the heavens and the earth praise, and the birds in their flight? Of each he knows verily the worship and the praise"]; 42:5: وَٱلْمَلَٰٓئِكَةُ يُسَبِّحُونَ بِحَمْدِ رَبِّهِمْ ... أَلَآ إِنَّ ٱللَّهَ هُوَ ٱلْغَفُورُ ٱلرَّحِيمُ ["while the angels hymn the praise of their Lord ... God, he is the forgiver, the merciful"]; 55:6: وَٱلنَّجْمُ وَٱلشَّجَرُ يَسْجُدَانِ ["The stars and the trees adore"].

62 The verb used in this context is سَجَدَ in 13:15; in all other instances it is سَبَّحَ .

63 Brightman op. cit. [cf. note 12], p. 39, line 29; 382, l. 1ff.; 496, l. 17. One could also compare the passage with the Liturgy of St. Basil: ἵνα εὕρωμεν ἔλεον καὶ χάριν μετὰ πάντων τῶν ἁγίων τῶν ἀπ᾽ αἰῶνός σοι εὐαρεστησάντων ["so that we find mercy and grace with all saints with whom you have been well pleased from eternity"], or with a passage in the Liturgy of St. Mark that combines both thoughts: ἡμῶν δὲ τὰ τέλη τῆς ζωῆς χριστιανὰ καὶ εὐάρεστα καὶ ἀναμάρτητα δώρησαι καὶ δὸς ἡμῖν μερίδα καὶ κλῆρον ἔχειν μετὰ πάντων τῶν ἁγίων σου ["The end of our life be Christian, complacent and without sins; let us have a share (in the heavenly reward), together with the communion of all your saints"] (op. cit., p. 330, l. 21–24 and p. 129, l. 27ff.), or the expression of the second thought in the Roman Canon of the Mass: "Nobis quoque ... partem aliquam et societatem donare digneris cum tuis sanctis" etc. ["do condescend to give us a share and community with your saints" etc.].

64 On the work of Maʿnā as a liturgical poet writing in Persian cf. A. Baumstark, *Geschichte der syrischen Literatur* (Bonn, 192), p. 105. Or cf. the fragments of a Syriac-Neo-Persian psalter from Chinese-Turkestan, edited by F. K. Müller ["Ein syrisch-neupersisches Psalmenbruchstück aus Chinesisch-Turkestan"] in: Festschrift Eduard Sachau zum siebzigsten Geburtstage gewidmet [Festschrift for Eduard Sachau on his Seventieth Birthday], Berlin 1915, pp. 214–222.

65 Cf. the translation of this festive Office by A. J. Maclean in Conybeare, *Rituale Armenorum*, op. cit. [cf. note 16], p. 367f.

66 Edited by F. W. K. Müller, "Neutestamentliche Bruchstücke in soghdischer Sprache" [Fragments of the New Testament in Soghdian], in *Sitzungsberichte der Preußischen Akademie der Wissenschaften* 1907, Berlin, pp. 260–270.

67 Julius Wellhausen, *Reste arabischen Heidentums* [Remnants of Arabic Paganism], 2nd edition (Berlin, 1897), p. 232: "Christians were surely the first to use Arabic as a written language. Specifically, the Ibâdis of Hira and Anbâr seem to have rendered a great service in this regard."

The Problem of Pre-Islamic Ecclesiastical Christian Literature in Arabic

Anton Baumstark

Originally published as "Das Problem eines vorislamischen christlich-kirchlichen Schrifttums in arabischer Sprache," Islamica *4 (1929–1931), pp. 562–75.*

Translated by Elisabeth Puin.

The assumption that the beginnings of a literary life in Arabic are to be found in Christian circles of pre-Islamic times has been, with great confidence, uttered already by no less a figure than Julius Wellhausen.

> Christians were surely the first to use Arabic as a written language. Specifically, the Ibâdis of Hira and Anbar seem to have rendered a great service in this regard.

That is what we read in his classic work, *Reste arabischen Heidentums* [Remnants of Arabic Paganism] (2nd edition) on page 222. He then points to those writings of profane content, created by some poets of the *Ǧāhilīya* who personally professed Christianity, that were, because of their deviations "from the classical language," not transmitted by "the rhapsodists:" the drinking songs of ʿĀdī ibn Zaid as well as the *Qasīds* of Abū Duād that were renowned for the virtuosity of their descriptions of horses. But, why, of all people, it should have been worshippers of the triune God who wove the golden threads of an artful song through Bedouin life, or preserved such a song in written language, before worshippers of Hubal, or Ḏū-š-Šarā, of al-Lāt or al-ʿUzzā did, is not at all clear. Thus, if the Christian faith is at all relevant for the elevation of Arabic to a literary language, then its relevance lies in a different direction. Above all, the oldest *book* in Arabic was not the Koran, for the Koran was preceded by liturgical books of a Christian ritual celebrated in Arabic. First of all, we should consider Gospel books and Psalters in Arabic.

In order to approach the problem correctly from the start, we must be aware that the attitude of the Christian mission of the East towards the vernacular of every newly tackled field of work was utterly different from the attitude of the Latin West. To translate into the vernacular, if not instantly the whole Bible, at least those Bible passages that are most important in the liturgy, and then naturally also the liturgical prayer texts themselves, would, in the East, always be the first step in founding a new national church. With regularity, the national missionaries become the founders of *the*—or at least of a new Christian—national literature.

In the case of Ulfilas the Goth, as with Sahak the Armenian and those around him, things are in the clear light of attested history. Since their Bible translations are similarly old, we can be certain that the procedures were no different in the founding of the East Aramaic, Georgian ad Abyssinian Christianity and the spreading of the Christian faith on the plains of Egypt. And not only the beginnings of the principal literatures of the Christian Orient should be mentioned here. There are also reports on an ecclesiastical-Christian literature of the Persians written in their Iranian language,[1] and Persian hymn fragments that are embedded in Syriac texts of the Nestorian Epiphany Office,[2] as well as the extensive remnants of a liturgical Psalter in Pehlevi[3] and the fragment of a Syriac-Neo-Persian Psalter from Chinese-Turkestan which was brought to light by F. W. K. Müller.[4] Of the same origin are documents of a liturgical use of Sogdian by central Asian Nestorians.[5] A number of liturgical and other ecclesiastical books in Chinese is at least named by the monument of Singanfu. Really preserved, on the other hand, are remnants of a Nubian Christian literature, among which the fragment of a lectionary and a litany-like Hymn of the Cross are primary.[6] The Christian Palestinian language owes its existence to the liturgical use that was made of the West Aramaic dialect, in local churches of the Patriarchate of Jerusalem. Also, Turkish texts of Christian prayers and cantos[7] turn up in manuscripts, and there is an island in Lake Egerdir in Asia Minor where from time immemorial the Byzantine mass has been celebrated in the Ottoman tongue[8]. In the light of such a body of facts we must ask ourselves how likely it is that, just—or we ought to say: exclusively—in the Arabic language area until the days of the Meccan prophet, a Christianity that was centuries older would have dispensed with a liturgy, and with the Biblical and non-Bibilical books serving it, in their vernacular. This would concern the Christianity of Ḥīra, which sent an episcopal representative to the Persian imperial synod of Seleukeia-Ktesiphon as early as the year 410 (as is attested in its records)[9], and it would concern the Christianity of the παρεμβολαί, the Bedouin camps on the Palestinian border, which was founded in 420 by Euthymios and whose first bishop, Petros, in the year 431 signed the decrees of the council of Ephesos.[10] That among those Christians, up until the 7th century, exclusively Syriac or Greek liturgical books should have been in use, would be so unlike everything we know about the development of these things in the Orient that we have the right to say: The burden of proof lies not with those who assume the existence of a pre-Islamic ecclesiastical-Christian literature in Arabic but with those who deny its existence.

Thus, the *Sīra* seems to presuppose that existence as something that is commonly known. In Ibn Hišām,[11] we hear of Waraqa ibn Naufal, the cousin of Ḫadīğa, that he تنصّر وقرأ الكتب ("had become a Christian and was reading the books"), and not a word is said to indicate that this reading of those obviously specifically Christian "books" had first required learning Greek or Syriac. Also, the tradition about the conversation between Ḫadīǧa and Waraqa on the occasion of the vision that was the basis of Mohammed's self-awareness as a prophet is, in two respects, of importance. Waraqa's exclamation قدّوس قدّوس ("Holy! Holy") directly touches on Christian liturgy. Furthermore, his other utterance: جاءه النموس الاكبر الذى كان يأتى موسى ("to him had come the great *Nāmūs* that used to visit Moses") reflects a most unusual concept. It is the notion of *nāmūs* as an angel incarnate. How are we to understand this idea?

I should like to refer here to the typical expression of a thought which, at a very specific point of the eucharistic prayer of thanksgiving in the Oriental liturgy, is almost a *locus communis* [commonplace] of it. It is about the shepherding actions of God toward fallen humanity: ἐκάλεσας αὐτὸν διὰ νόμου ἐπαιδαγώγησας διὰ τῶν προφητῶν ["you called him through the Law, you educated him through the prophets"] says the Jerusalem Liturgy of St. James,[12] which is authoritative for the Christianity of the παρεμβολαί; ἀνεκαλέσω διὰ νόμου, ἐπαιδαγώγησας διὰ προφητῶν ["you called him up through the Law, you educated him through the prophets"] are the almost identical words of the Alexandria Liturgy of St. Mark[13] which may have exerted its influence via Abyssinia through to South Arabia. When something of the sort, in an Arabic translation that retained the foreign word *nāmūs*, reached Bedouin ears, nothing seemed more natural than to regard the *nāmūs* of the first clause, in analogy to the prophets of the second clause, as a person, a powerful heavenly being. This could particularly easily happen if the relevant liturgical wording spoke, in the same breath, of "angels," as is in fact the case in the liturgy of the VIIIth Book of the Apostolic Constitutions, whose ideal text is based on the actual liturgical situation in Antiochia: μετὰ νομικὴν παραίνεσιν, μετὰ προφητικοὺς ἐλέγχους καὶ τὰς τῶν ἀγγέλων ἐπιστάσεις ["after the admonition through the Law, after the prophetic instruction, and after the angels' appearance"].[14]

Beside the *Sīra*, also the Koran itself contains evidence for a pre-Islamic Arabic literature. As is well known, we find an explicit quotation of Psalm 37 (36):29 , δίκαιοι κληρονομήσονται γῆν ["the righteous will inherit the earth"], in Surah 21:105, as:

> وَلَقَدْ كَتَبْنَا فِي الزَّبُورِ مِن بَعْدِ الذِّكْرِ أَنَّ الْأَرْضَ يَرِثُهَا عِبَادِيَ الصَّالِحُونَ ("in the *Zabūr* [i. e., the Psalter], we have written that my servants—the righteous ones—will inherit the earth").

Such an almost *verbatim* exactness in quotation only seems conceivable if we assume that the Prophet had at his disposal an Arabic Psalter text for which the rendering of δίκαιος ["just, righteous"] as صالح , unheard of in all extant Arabic Psalter texts, would have been a distinctive feature. In this context it is noteworthy enough that we come across a corresponding rendering of δικαιοσύνη ["justice"] as صلاح in the highly remarkable Psalm quotations of Ibn Ḥazm,[15] the great Spaniard who died in 1064 and whose quotations of the Old Testament I hope soon to see subjected to well-deserved closer examination by a student. The text used by Ibn Ḥazm, at least, indubitably traces back to Christian, not Jewish tradition, which is proven by the fact that Ibn Ḥazm, in a precise accounting of the origin of his individual quotations, does not follow the numbering of the Masoretic text but that of the Septuagint.

Moreover, as I noted in my study on the relationship of the Qur'ān to Jewish and Christian prayer types,[16] Muḥammad knows two renderings of the doxological formula of the latter as Δόξα with the dative: الحمد لله and سبحان الله. The second rendering, as well as the denominative سَبَّحَ [second verbal stem: "to praise"] which derives from it and has nothing to do with the original-Arabic meaning of سَبَحَ , [first verbal stem: "to swim"] is a linguistic loan; it does not originate in the Aramaic North but in the Abyssinian-South-Arabian area, as is indicated by the س where otherwise we would have a ش . But if a foreign-word formula was adopted here, why did not the same thing happen in the first rendering which seems to trace back to the Northern area? It would be difficult to offer any explanation other than that the الحمد لله was inherited from the world of a Christian ritual whose language had already been Northern Arabic,[17] and that it was such a ritual—and not one the language of which was Greek or Aramaic—that advanced into the Arabic Peninsula from the north.

In the question of a literary use of Arabic by Christians in pre-Islamic times we have, however, by no means to rely on just such conclusions alone. Of crucial importance are, rather, the oldest preserved documents of a Christian-Arabic literature themselves.

Concerning these documents, too, a first, general consideration is necessary. On the one hand, they are, or at least most of them are, texts that were—to put it very cautiously: at some stage—intended for use in worship. This is confirmed by the pericopic notations that were, by the original scribe, added to the pertinent Gospel texts, like Paul's Epistles in a Sinai manuscript edited by M. D. Gibson.[18] On the other hand, those documents had been written in the scriptoria of the Palestinian Sabas-Lawra and the monastery of St. Catherine in the Sinai. If it were true—as has, heretofore, been the prevalent assumption—that the Arabic translations handed down by them really owe their origin to the advance of Arabic into a previously Greek language territory in the course of the triumph of Islam, then this would mean that Christian worship was subsequently, during the first centuries of Islamic rule, in both monasteries practised in Arabic, to which the said translations would have served. We can, however, declare with certainty that this was not the case. A. Dmitriewskij, in the first volume of his Τυπικά,[19] made known two recensions of the Sinai Canonarion originating from the 9th to 10th and the 10th to 11th century respectively; in the second volume he presented the widely ramified transmissions of the Sabas Typicon.[20] Here as well as there, the documents belonging to the Islamic era unfold the picture of a ritual that was, with regard to its language, purely and exclusively Greek. In contrast it was, in the world of Palestinian monasteries of pre-Islamic times, specifically, customary for the different ethnic groups within the monastic community to perform the church's daily prayer separately in their own small sanctuaries and in their respective mother tongue, and to also celebrate the pre-anaphoric part of the mass, which contained the Scripture readings, in the same way. It was only the celebration of the eucharistic sacrifice that united the whole community of the monks in the monastery's main church and that was performed in Greek exclusively. For the Sabas-Lawra, however, this old practice is not attested until the fragment of a monastic rule dating from the 12th or 13th century.[21] But for another stronghold of Palestinian monasticism, the cenobium of St. Theodosios, attestation lies in the much earlier eulogy in praise of its founder, made by bishop Theodorus of Petra on the first anniversary of the founder's death, on January 11 of the year 530.[22] Only in these liturgical conditions of pre-Islamic times—and not in those of early Islamic times—is there room for a use of the old Arabic books containing the text of the New Testament with added pericopic notations. Not the formation of a Christian liturgical life in Arabic language, but the extinction of such a life which had previously existed, was the natural consequence of the Islamic conquest, inasmuch as the previously Christian Arab population on the border of Palestine now embraced Islam; and if the old Bible texts are preserved in manuscripts dating from later times, then this is due to the monks' industrious hands that would reproduce texts which had ceased being used in liturgical practise, along with the long-obsolete rubrics of those texts, as purely literary documents.

A second consideration leads directly to a particular, individual text, this time one of the Psalter. It is the Arabic Psalter manuscript which is, as no. 39, described in the Hiersemann catalogue 500 and presently located in Zurich, and which, judging from its old script style, appears to belong to the most venerable items of preserved Christian-Arabic literature. If it were true that the oldest texts of such a literature had originated in the context of the spread of Qur'ānic Arabic as a new universal language impelled by the Islamic conquest, then this would mean that, consequently, the language of those oldest texts could only be that of the Qur'ān. The language of our Psalter, however, is so different from the linguistic usage of the Qur'ān that for Greek φῶς ["the light"] we consistently find ضوء instead of the Qur'ānic نور , and as comparative particle we find مِثْل instead of كَ .

And finally: Besides the Zurich Psalter, there is also evidence in a Gospel translation which seems to have been very widespread since three copies of it are still extant; that it originates from pre-Islamic times can be—I daresay: mathematically—proven from a liturgical perspective. The oldest and only complete copy—the one used by Guidi[23] for his analysis of the Gospel translation—namely *Borg. arab. 95*, previously *K II* 31 of the Vatican, seems to date from the 9th century. Part of an apparently somewhat younger copy were two folios in Leipzig, designated Cod. Tischendorf XXXI, which had previously been described by Fleischer.[24] The third copy which was acquired in Egypt for the present Berlin State Library by P. Kahle and is defective only at the beginning, was written as late as 1046/7.

Recently, in my article for the Festschrift[25] dedicated to A. Heisenberg for his 60th birthday, I studied the third copy's pericopic notation which matches the corresponding rubrics of the Leipzig pages. Like the pericopic notation of the Sinai Pauline text, it exemplifies the pre-Byzantine liturgical Scripture reading of Jerusalem and therewith belongs, with regard to liturgical history, to the same category as the Old Armenian lectionary published by F. C. Conybeare[26], as well as the relevant Christian-Palestinian writings—such as, above all, the lectionary with texts from the Old Testament and the Praxapostolos, published by A. Smith Lewis,[27] and also certain parts of her *Codex Climaci rescriptus*,[28]—and also K. Kekelidze's Georgian canonarion.[29] With regard to the delimitation of the individual pericopes, as well as to certain elements in the underlying form of the rite of the city of Jerusalem, the Arabic document is by far much closer to the Armenian document which reflects the situation around the middle of the 5th century, than it is to the Georgian document which reflects the situation in the time soon after the Islamic conquest of Jerusalem.[30] To offer at least one example: Like the Armenian, the Arabic document assumes two celebrations of the mass on Pentecost Saturday and two on Easter night, whereas the Georgian canonarion requires but one.[31] A quite decisive indication of age lies in the fact that the Arabic order does not yet know the κυριακὴ τῆς Ἀπόκρεω ["Sunday of the Leave-taking from Meat"] and the τυροφάγος ἑβδομάς ["Cheese Week"] that follows it,[32] for this pre-Lent week which already prohibits the consumption of meat while the consumption of dairy products is still allowed was—as A. Rahlfs[33] has convincingly shown—created by Emperor Heraclius subsequent to the victorious Persian campaign of the years 622–629. This new liturgical creation was very closely connected to older traditions that had prevailed in Jerusalem in particular, demanding an eight-week duration of pre-Easter fasting; this means that the new liturgical creation, in the Palestinian area the old Arabic documents are pointing to, without doubt must have found acceptance as swiftly as anywhere. The liturgical reading cycle that we find in the Berlin manuscript and the Leipzig folios can, therefore, be placed with absolute certainty before the epoch mentioned.

To exercise all possible caution, I had, however, to leave open the question whether the said rubrics were later additions to a preexisting Arabic Gospel text, or whether the translator already took them from the Greek model he was copying from. Only in the first case does the epoch of Heraclius mark a *terminus ante quem* for the origin of our Arabic Gospel translation, whereas in the latter case it could be a *terminus ante quem* only for the age of the Greek text on which the translator based his work. I had to finish my observations in my contribution to the *Heisenberg Festschrift* with this question unanswered. Since then, I have been able to look at the Roman manuscript, and as a result it became quite evident that indeed the former was the case.

If the rubrics of the Berlin copy and the Leipzig folios had really been taken from the Greek vorlage and were part of the translated text, then this would necessarily imply that the rubrics should also already be present in the Rome manuscript, the oldest branch of transmission. But this is not the case; it does *not* have that complete and strictly standardized notation complying with an early Christian-Palestinian reading cycle. Instead, we find now instances where there is, in the text, space left open for a reference to liturgical use; now in the text, now in the margin we find annotations concerning such liturgical use, some in Arabic, some—still in majuscule script!—in Greek. And what is most important: With regard to the liturgical geography, these annotations point somewhere else than to the patriarchate of Jerusalem.

First of all, the underlying structure of the liturgical year and the nomenclature of at least two of its most prominent high points are not the same as in the Arabic notation that goes back to Jerusalem. The word for "Epiphany" is not the specifically Palestinian القلند = Καλάνδαι, by which the solemnity of January 6 as the beginning of the civic year is designated,[34] but عيد المعمودية ("Feast of the Baptism"); or TA ΦΩΤ', Pentecost, is not called العنصرة but, in direct connection with the Greek Πεντηκοστή, الخمسين or (ἡ) N'. Also, the feast of the Cross of the 13th and 14th of September which is characteristic for Palestine because it evolved from the annual commemoration of the consecration of the magnificent Constantinian buildings on Golgotha is not mentioned at all. And instead of giving two distinct series of Sundays after Pentecost and after the feast of the Cross, as do the notations of the Berlin manuscript, the Sundays between Pentecost and Christmas time are enumerated in one go.

No less considerable are the discrepancies concerning the text passages the pericopes begin with on the respective days; in this respect, the notations of the Rome manuscript are different even from the Palestinian notations of the Berlin (and Leipzig) manuscripts. For example, the pericopes of the 6th,

7th, 11th and 14th Sunday after Pentecost begin [in the Rome manuscript], one after the other, with Mt. 6:16; 7:9; (apparently) 7:12 and 8:1 instead of Mt. 9:9; 9:27; 14:22 and 17:14. And the lesson of the Gospel of John, which is read during Eastertide until Pentecost, already begins on Easter Sunday and not, as was the practise of Jerusalem, a week later, on the so-called New or Thomas Sunday.[35] This latter feature, however, characteristicly agrees with the common Byzantine practise which, starting from Constantinople, finally gained sole dominance in the orthodox Oriental church. But still, the Roman notations are, on the whole, certainly not yet based on this Byzantine practise; this becomes unequivocally clear if we look at the text passages with which, in the common Byzantine practise, the pericopes begin on the four mentioned Sundays after Pentecost, which are Mt. 9:1; 9:27; 18:23 and 22:2. The common denominator, so to speak, for Constantinople and the non-Palestinian Syria with regard to liturgical history was, however, Antioch;[36] and to the Patriarchate of Antioch belonged the Ghassanid Empire with Rusapha-Sergiopolis, whose ritual of St. Sergius casts its shadow far into the Bedouin world of Arabia.[37] It is to this sphere, and not that of the Palestinian παρεμβολαί and its Euthymius' mission, that the pericopic notations of the Roman manuscript point. The manuscript itself, however, by dint of the character of its script, points directly to that Palestinian sphere with the scriptoria of Mar Saba and the Sinai.

Thus, it would be wrong to suppose that the Palestinian notation of Berlin and Leipzig is the original one and that, accordingly, the Palestinian South is the home of the Arabic Gospel translation which is everywhere present there; it would be wrong to suppose that this "original" Palestinian notation was only later, during the northward spread of the text, replaced by one that was in harmony with the practise of a church of the Antiochene patriarchate. Instead, the development must have been the other way round. Home of the translation must have been the soil of the Ghassanid Empire, since this was the home of that pericopic notation which shared characteristics with Antioch and the *disiecta membra* (scattered fragments) of which are preserved in the Vatican manuscript. The notation agreeing with the rite of Jerusalem that is almost completely preserved in the Berlin copy is a secondary insertion related to the southward spread of the text.

The purpose of this insertion was, of course, to enable a comfortable liturgical use of the text on new soil; this means that it can, in all its particulars, only have been made on the basis of the rite that was valid *at that period.* Thus, it is this *insertion* that can, because of the lacking "cheese week," be dated to the time before ca. 630. *How* much further back it is to be dated is impossible to even vaguely estimate. In contrast, it is obvious that the Arabic Gospel text itself, into which the insertion was placed as it was spreading from the Antiochian patriarchate into the hierosolymitanic [city of Jerusalem] patriarchate, must have been considerably older. We may confidently consider it to be, at least, of the same age as the songs of Imra'a-l-Qais,[38] who died in 540 in Angora [Ankara] on the return trip from Justinian's imperial court. Dating from the year 512 is the well-known building inscription of a Christian church of Zebed, which, besides Greek and Syriac, uses Arabic; dating from the year 568 is the one of Ḥarrān in Trachonitis, which besides Greek has only Arabic. That, in churches like these or in the monastery church of Hind near Ḥīra whose apparently exclusively Arabic dedicatory inscription has been preserved in literature,[39] service was celebrated in Arabic, is really so self-evident that it should never have been doubted.[40] That something from the Biblical texts used in such service should have even survived does, at least, not come as a surprise.

Notes

1 The relevant evidence in A. Baumstark, *Geschichte der syrischen Literatur mit Ausschluß der christlich-palästinischen Texte* (Bonn: Markus und Weber, 1922), p. 105, notes 5 and 6.

2 Cf. their translation by A. Maclean in F. C. Conybeare, *Rituale Armenorum* (Oxford: Clarendon Press, 1905), pp, 367 f.

3 Cf. F. C. Andreas, "Bruchstücke einer Pehlewi-Übersetzung der Psalmen aus der Sassanidenzeit" *Sitzungsberichte der Preußischen Akademie der Wissenschaften* (1910), pp. 869–872 and then A. Baumstark's comments in *Oriens Christianus*, New Series III, pp. 328.

4 F. W. K. Müller: "Ein syrisch-neupersisches Psalmenbruchstück aus Chinesisch-Turkestan" in: *Festschrift Eduard Sachau zum siebzigsten Geburtstage gewidmet* [Festschrift for Eduard Sachau on his Seventieth Birthday] (Berlin, 1915), pp. 214–222.

5 Published by F. W. K. Müller: "Neutestamentliche Bruchstücke in soghdischer Sprache" in: *Sitzungsberichte der Preußischen Akademie der Wissenschaften (*Berlin, 1907), pp. 260–270 and "*Soghdische Texte* I" [Sogdian Texts I], in *Abhandlungen der Preußischen Akademie der Wissenschaften* 1912 (Berlin 1913). Cf A. Baumstark *loc. cit.*, p. 329; IV, pp. 123–128.

6 On these remnants cf. the informative report by H. Junker, "Die neuentdeckten christlichen Handschriften in mittelnubischer Sprache," in *Oriens Christianus* VI, 1906, *Oriens Christianus*, VI, pp. 437–442.

7 Such texts have, in manuscript fragments presented to me for examination by the K. Hiersemann company, passed through my hands. In addition, the older Christian-Turkish Turfan texts from a martyrdom of St. George and about the adoration of the magi, which were translated into German by W. Bang, "Türkische Bruchstücke einer nestorianischen Georgpassion," in *Le Muséon* 39, (1926), 41–75.

8 Cf. A. Baumstark, *Die Messe im Morgenland* [The Mass in the Orient] (Kempten-Munich, 1906), p. 61.

9 His signature on those records in K. Chabot, *Synodicon Orientale* (Paris, 1902), p. 36 (=translation p. 275).

10 J. D. Mansi, *Sacrorum Conciliorum Nova et Amplissima Collectio* IV, 1759–1798, (Florence) col. 1366 D. – Best treatise on the παρεμβολαί mission: R. Génier, *Vie de saint Euthyme le Grand* [Life of Saint Eurhymius the Great] (Paris, 1909), pp. 94–117.

11 Ibn Hišām, *Sīrat Rasūl Allāh*, ed. F. Wüstenfeld. 2 vols. Göttingen, 1858–1860, p. 153. Cf. Buḫārī, *Ṣaḥīḥ* at the beginning.

12 F. E. Brightman, *Liturgies Eastern and Western* (Oxford, 1896), p. 51, l. 16 f.

13 F. E. Brightman, *Liturgies* (loc. cit.), p. 125, l. 31

14 Ed. F. H. Funk, *Didascalia et constitutiones Apostolorum*, 2 vols. (Paderborn, 1905 I, p. 506, l. 13 f. = Brightman, p. 19, l. 10 f.

15 Ibn Ḥazm: *K. al-milal wan-niḥal*, Ed. Cairo 1347. part I, p. 153: Ps. 44 (45) احببت اصلاح وابغضت المكروه = ἠγάπησας δικαιοσύνην καὶ ἐμίσησας ἀνομίαν.

16 A. Baumstark: *Jüdischer u. christlicher Gebetstypus im Koran* [Jewish and Christian Prayer Type in the Koran] in: *Der Islam* XVI, pp. 229–248. [Now translated into English in the present volume].

17 In fact, the formula is already present in a song fragment of Imra'a-l-Qais (number 15 in Ahlwardt, *Six Divans*, p. 124) أرى إبلى والحمد لله أصبحت. Therefore, it is at least certain that it is independent from the Qur'ān and that it already existed in pre-Islamic times. Thus, the use of the formula in Qais ibn al-Ḥaṭīm, number 13, verse 12 can also be independent of the Qur'ān: الحمد لله ذى البَنِيّة. Its quite frequent occurrence in Umayya ibn Abī-ṣ-Ṣalt must be judged in the context of the overall problem which the alleged poet-*Ḥanīf* poses.

18 M. D. Gibson: *An Arabic Version of the Epistles of St. Paul to the Romans, Corinthians, Galatians with part of the Epistle to the Ephesians*. Studia Sinaitica II. (London, 1894).

19 A. Dmitrievskij: *Описание литургических рукописей, хранящихся в библиотеках православнаго Востока* I (Kiev, 1895), pp. 172–221. On the two liturgical documents cf. A. Baumstark, "*Denkmäler d. Entstehungsgschichte d. byzantin. Ritus*" [Monuments of the History of the Origin of Byzantine Rites] in *Oriens Christianus*, 3rd series II, pp. 16 ff.

20 A. Dmitrievskij: *Описание* (loc. cit.) III (Kiev, 1917). Cf. *Oriens Christianus*, loc. cit., pp. 26–31

21 In A. Dmitrievskij: *Описание* (loc. cit.) I, pp. 222 f.

22 In H. Usener, *Der heilige Theodosios, Schriften d. Theodoros u. Kyrillos* [Saint Theodorius, Writings of Theodorus and Kyrillos] (Leipzig, 1890) pp. 45 f.

23 I. Guidi: *Le traduzioni degli evangelii in arabo e in etiopo* (Rome, 1888) pp. 8 f.

24 H. L. Fleischer: "*Beschreibungen der von Prof. Dr. Tischendorf im J. 1853 aus dem Morgenlande zurückgebrachten christlich-arabischen Handschriften*" *ZDMG* VIII [1854], p. 584.

25 A. Baumstark: "Die sonntägliche Evangelienlesung in vorbyzantinischen Jerusalem" [The Sunday Gospel Lection in Pre-Byzantine Jerusalem], *Byzantinische Zeitschrift* XXX (Leipzig, 1929/30), pp. 350–359:.

26 F. C. Conybeare, *Rituale Armenorum* (Oxford, 1905) pp. 516–527.

27 A. Smith Lewis, *A Palestinian Syriac Lectionary*, Studia Sinaitica VI. (London, 1897).

28 A. Smith Lewis, *Codex Climaci rescriptus*, Horae Semiticae VIII (Cambridge, 1909).

29 Iерусалимскiў каиоиаръ, VII Вюка (Tiflis [Tbilisi], 1912). German translations,

annotated by me, of the paragraphs on the Quadragesima, Passion Week and Easter time until Pentecost Monday, by Th. Kluge, *Oriens Christianus*, New Series V, pp. 201–233; VI, pp. 223–239, and on the Christmas celebration, by G. Peradze, ibid. 3rd series I, pp. 310–318.

30 Cf. A. Baumstark *Nichtevangelische syrische Perikopenordnungen des ersten Jahrtausends* [Nongospel Syrian pericopic cycles of the First Millenium] (Münster i. W., 1921), pp. 138–141, and *Oriens Christianus*, 3rd series II, pp. 5–10, respectively.

31 For more cf. A. Baumstark *Die sonntägliche Evangelienlesung*, loc. cit., p. 356 f., note I.

32 Cf. A. Baumstark *Die sonntägliche Evangelienlesung*, loc. cit., pp. 357 ff. There also proof that the mention of the κυριακὴ τῆς Ὀρθοδοξίας, which would indeed lead beyond the year 843, doubtlessly is not part of the original text of the rubric concerned.

33 In the treatise by A. Rahlfs, *Die alttestamentlichen Lektionen der griechischen Kirche: Nachrichten der Königlichen Gesellschaft der Wissenschaften zu Göttingen*, Philol.-histor. Klasse [The Old Testament Lections of the Greek Church: Reports of the Royal Society for Sciences in Göttingen, Philological-Historical Class] 1905 (pp. 28–136), pp. 107–111.

34 On this subject, see A. Baumstark, "Zur Arabischen Archelideslegende" [On the Arabic Legend of Archelides], *ZDMG* LXVII, pp. 126 ff.

35 On the latter, see in the study by Th. Kluge and A. Baumstark on "Ostern- und Pfingstfeier Jerusalems im siebten Jahrhundert" [Easter and Pentecostal Celebrations in Jerusalem in the Seventh Century] in *Oriens Christianus*, New Series VI, p. 232. It is related to the more general phenomenon, observable on the Syrian-Jacobite soil, of the beginning of the entire year cycle of liturgical Scipture reading with this day. Cf. A. Baumstark, *Nichtevangel. syr. Perikopenordnungen,* loc. cit., pp. 117 f.

36 Cf A. Baumstark, *Nichtevangel. syr. Perikopenordnungen*, loc. cit., p. 182.

37 As late as the Umayyad period, the Banū Taġlib still carried, besides the cross, the picture of St. Sergius on military campaigns. Cf. al-Aḫṭal *Dīwān*, ed. by Ṣalḥānī, p.309: لمّا رأوناوالصليب طالعا *ومار سرجيس وسمّا ناقعا* وابصروا راياتنا and L. Cheikho, *Machriq* XVIII, p. 541, respectively.

38 Already, Wellhausen has pointed to something like an echo of the Christian Κύριε ἐλέησον in Imra'a-l-Qais; cf. *Reste arab. Heidentums* [Remains of Arab Paganism] (2nd edition), p. 234. Cf. also what was said above in note 17.

39 In Bakrī p. 364, Jāqūt II, p. 709. Cf. also Rothstein, *D. Dynastie d. Laḫmiden* [The Dynasty of the Lakhmids], pp. 23 f.

40 To this circle also belongs the inscription of Umm-iğ-Ğimāl, recently published by E. Littman [Die vorislamisch-arabische Inschrift aus Umm-ig-Gimāl], in *ZfS* [*Zeitschrift für Semitistik und verwandte Gebiete*] VIII [1929], pp. 197–204. But, even aside from the lack of an exact date, it is of lesser significance also because it is not an official dedicatory inscription for the church building in question.

An Old Arabic Gospel Translation from the Christian-Palestinian

Anton Baumstark

Originally published as "Eine altarabische Evangelienübersetzung aus dem Christlich-Palästinensischen," Zeitschrift für Semitistik und verwandte Gebiete *8 (1932), pp. 201–209; translated by Elisabeth Puin.*

In my talk on the "Problem of a Pre-Islamic Christian-Eccelsiastical Literature in Arabic"[1] that I gave at the 6th Orientalistentag [Conference of Oriental Studies] in Vienna I was able to demonstrate that, preserved in several manuscripts, an Arabic Gospel translation survived which had been made in the patriarchate of Antioch and then, even before the epoch of the Emperor Heraclius' victorious Persian campaign [622–629], spread into the neighbouring patriarchate of Jerusalem. This result may have come as a surprise. But the question that has to be put next is whether that translation was the only one or whether there were more which were similarly old. An attempt to answer it should take into specific consideration the Gospel quotations of—especially older—Islamic authors. We will have to try to account, as precisely as possible, for the *vorlage* of every respective Arabic text; after that we will have to determine the time frame within which a *vorlage* of such a nature seems conceivable.

First I should like to point to a quotation the significance of which becomes evident on closer examination. It is the quotation of John 15:23–16:2 which was preserved in Ibn Hišām's *Sīra* (ed. Wüstenfeld I, pp. 149f.) from the older work of Ibn Isḥāq; since the latter author died in 768 [probably 767] AD, the quotation leads us back to the time around the middle of the 8th century. Ibn Isḥāq was told that John the Evangelist had preserved a saying of Jesus referring to the prophet, the wording of which read as follows:

من ابغَضَنى فقد ابغض الربَّ ولولا انى صنعت بحضرتهم صنايعَ لم يَصْنَعْها احدٌ قبلى ما كانت لهم خطيئَةٌ ولكن من الآن بَطِرُوا و ظَنُّوا انهم يَعِزُّوننى و ايضا للربّ ولكن لا بُدَّ من ان تَتِمَّ الكلمة التى فى النموس انهم ابغَضُونى مَجَّانا اى باطلاً فلو قد جاءَ المَنْحَمَنَّا (or المُنْحَمَنَّا) هذا الذى يُرْسله الله اليكم من عند الربّ وروح القِسْطِ هذا الذى من

عند الرب خرج فهو شهيدٌ عليّ وانتم ايضا لانّكم قديما كنتم معى هذا قلت لكم لكى ما لا تشَكّوا

A closing remark explains:

فالمَنْحَمَنَّا بالسُّريانية محمّد وهو بالرُّوميَّةِ البرقليطس

["He that hateth me hateth the Lord. And if I had not done in their presence works which none other before me did they had not had sin: but from now they are puffed up with pride and think that they will overcome me and also the Lord. But there can be no doubt that the word that concerns the Nāmūs [Law] must be fulfilled 'They hated me without a cause,' i. e. without a reason. But when the مَنْحَمَنَّا [according to the Greek original: "comforter"] has come whom God will send to you from the Lord's, and the Spirit of Truth which will have gone forth from the Lord's presence, he (shall bear) witness of me, and ye also because ye have been with me from the beginning. I have spoken to you about this that ye should not be in doubt."—Closing remark: "The مَنْحَمَنَّا in Syriac is Muḥammad. In Greek he is 'the Paraclete'"].
[The English translation follows, slightly modifiying, Alfred Guillaume's translation of the passage; cf. his article in the present volume.].

The Aramaic status emphaticus ܡܢܚܡܢܐ [mənaḥḥəmānā] makes it perfectly clear that the text is not dependent on a Greek *vorlage* but on an Aramaic one. With equal certainty we can conclude from the closing remark that Ibn Isḥāq, or his informant, did not take the quotation directly from that *vorlage* but, instead, from a full text of John's Gospel that was written in Arabic and had retained the Aramaic word as a proper name. The text equates both the "Syriac" مَنْحَمَنَّا [manḥamannā] and the Greek برقليطس [paraqlīṭis, "the Paraclete"] with محمّد, which is correct for the برقليطس if the Arabic consonantal writing of the word is understood as a transcription of the Greek περίκλυτος ["the praised one"] and not παράκλητος ["comforter, helper, intercessor, advocate"]; but it can never apply to مَنْحَمَنَّا . Had the Arab writer directly used the Aramaic text, and had he been able to understand the Aramaic and to do the translation of only this passage into Arabic himself, then this problem would certainly not have escaped him.

And yet a third conclusion can be drawn with certainty from this one Aramaic word: that the Aramaic *vorlage* of the Arabic Gospel translation that is discernible behind Ibn Isḥāq's quotation was not a Syriac one, in the narrow sense of the word, but a Christian-Palestinian one. Since, in Syriac the meaning of ܢܚܡ [naḥem] has become narrower and specialised in the sense of "resurrection of the dead," and accordingly the word ܡܢܚܡܢܐ [mənaḥḥəmānā] as the "raiser of the dead" has become a, so to speak, technical term for Jesus Christ; therefore it has become impossible to use this word for the Holy Ghost.[2] Thus, the Greek word παράκλητος is, in John 15,26, as in general, not translated at all but retained in transcription—by the Syriac Sinaiticus (= S^{Sin}), which is the only representative of the Old-Syriac text form for this passage since the Curetonian Gospels are defective here, as well as by the Pešitta (=P). In Christian-Palestinian, in contrast, the original, more general meaning "to comfort" of ܢܚܡ [n-ḥ-m] has survived. Thus, at least the Evangeliarum Hierosolymitanum (= EvH) renders, in general and also in John 15,23 specifically, the Greek παράκλητος as ܡܢܚܚܡܢܐ [mənaḥḥəmānā]; another, secondary witness of the Syro-Palestinian Gospel text (= Sp), however, namely the "Codex Climaci rescriptus" (= CCl)[3] [today known as Uncial 0250] in which the passage of John 15:19–16:9, specifically, is extant, again only gives the transcription—doubtlessly due to the influence of P.

The Arabic quotation also agrees with Sp—against S^{Sin} and P—in three other, very characteristic textual elements. Those are:

[The symbol = means: The Arabic text is identical with the version in the other language; the symbol > means: the Arabic text differs from it.]

(1) John 15,26: τὸ πνεῦμα τῆς ἀληθείας ["the spirit of the truth"]:
Arabic روح القِسْطِ
= Sp: ܪܘܚܐ ܕܩܘܫܛܐ [rūḥā ḏ-qūsṭā]
> S^{Sin}, P: ܪܘܚܐ ܕܫܪܪܐ [rūḥā ḏ-šarrərā].
Attention should also be paid to the orthographical contrast, typical for Christian-Palestinian Western Aramaic, to what would read ܩܘܫܬܐ [qūštā] in Syriac Aramaic.

(2) John 15,26: μαρτυρήσει ["he will bear witness"]:
Arabic: شهيدٌ
= Sp: ܡܣܗܕ [masīḏ]
> S^{Sin}, P: ܢܣܗܕ [nəshaḏ].
The version of S^{Sin} and P is in accordance with the frequently apparent tendency of the Christian-Palestinian to render a Greek future tense as the present tense.

(3) John 16,1: ὑμῖν ["to you"]
لكم
= Sp: ܠܟܘܢ [lekōn]
> S^{Sin}, P: ܥܡܟܘܢ [ʿimmakōn];
The version of S^{Sin} and P keeps closer to the Greek original.

Finally, when Ibn Isḥāq introduces the name of the Evangelist as يُحَنِّس,[4] then this is equally different from the Greek Ἰωάννης as it is from the Syriac ܝܘܚܢܢ [yuḥannan]; it is in accordance only with the Christian-Palestinian ܝܘܚܢܝܣ [yuḥannis].

However, the text of Sp to which the textual fragment of the Arabic version leads us differed considerably from the wording preserved in EvH and CCl; this can be concluded, above all, from several instances where the said fragment, with regard to its wording, completely goes its own way, ending, in at least two instances, in rather wild results. This is anything but surprising. After all, an examination of directly surviving Biblical texts in the Christian-Palestinian dialect shows that generally the same passages are very frequently rendered differently by the different witnesses of transmission. As for John 15:23–16:2, specifically, EvH and CCl, not least, differ from each other, although their discrepancies are never as wide as the differences which seemingly exist between EvH and CCl on the one side and the *vorlage* of the Arabic version on the other. But it is remarkable that the peculiarities of the Arabic quotation, or at least most of them, lead us to a form of the *vorlage* which is either still closer to the one of EvH and CCl than it is to that of S^{Sin} and P, or which is, by its specifically Christian-Palestinian character, linguistically in contrast to the Syriac tradition.

It should be noted, however, that the fact that the Greek πατήρ ["father"] is consistently replaced by الربّ ["the Lord"] must not be included in our argumentation. This is clearly an alteration of the text by a Muslim hand, due to the wish to eliminate one of the alleged Christian corruptions of the Gospel by deleting from Jesus' mouth the offensive notion of God being a father, and accordingly of himself being God's son. Also, the و ["and"] preceding روح ["the spirit"] probably owes its existence to the interest of Islam which wanted to make a distinction between the prophet who was thought to be referred to by the term مَنْحَمَنَّا , and the "spirit" which was known from the Koran as the transmitter of the revelation.

But the explanation of the other, even the strangest, peculiarities of the Arabic text seems to lie in a Christian-Palestinian *vorlage*—which is, however, itself not entirely free from textual distortions.

15:24: οὐδεὶς ἄλλος ["none other"] ܐܢܫ ܚܘܪܢ ܠܐ = [ʾnāš ḥūren lā];
S^{Sin}: ܐܚܪܝܢ ܠܐ [aḥārīn lā];
P: ܐܢܫ ܐܚܪܝܢ ܠܐ [ʾnāš aḥārīn lā].
Arabic: لم ... احدٌ قبلى . Unless this is itself a free rendering of the transmitted text of the Sp, it leads back to a more free Aramaic wording ܐܢܫ ܩܘܕܡܝ ܠܐ [anaš qūdemī lā] which would agree with it—and which would, at least in its first element, for once also agree with P, against S^{Sin}.

15:24: νῦν ["now"]
= Sp: ܟܕܘ [kadō "enough, thus far, now"],
S^{Sin}, P: ܗܫܐ [hašā "now"]
Arabic: من الآن = ܡܢ ܟܕܘ [min kadō "at that very time; even now; already"]. This is a frequently occurring, expanding variant of Sp; a correxsponding expansion of ܗܫܐ [hašā "now"], however, is out of the question.

15:24: καὶ ἑωράκασιν καὶ μεμισήκασιν καὶ ἐμέ ["and they have seen, and they have hated me"]

= EvH: ܚܡܘ ܘܣܢܘ ܐܘܦ ܠܝ [ḥamū wə-snū awp̄ lī], CCl: ܐܘܦ ܕܚܡܘ ܣܢܘ ܝܬܝ [awp̄ ḏ-ḥamū snū yāṯʸ], S^Sin: ܚܙܘ ܥܒܕܝ ܘܠܝ ܣܢܝܢ [ḥazū ʿaḇḏʸ w-lī senīn], P: ܘܚܙܘ ܘܣܢܘ ܐܦ ܠܝ [wə-ḥazū w-šenū ap̄ lī].

Arabic: بَطِرُوا و ظَنُّوا انهم يَعِزُّوننى . First of all, we can disregard بَطِرُوا since it is simply a corruption, purely internal to Arabic, of نظروا = ܚܡܘ [ḥamū] (ἑωράκασιν) ["they have seen"].

Apart from that, the Arabic version seems to be based on an expanding and paraphrasing translation which was itself corrupted in two instances: ܘܡܬܚܫܒܝܢ ܕܝܚܣܢܘܢ ܠܝ [*w-maṯḥašḇīn ḏ-yəḥsinōn lī* "they think that they overcome me"] instead of ܘܡܬܚܝܒܝܢ ܕܝܣܢܘܢ ܠܝ [*w-maṯḥīḇīn ḏ-yəsnūn lī* "and they find me guilty and they hate me"]. An expansion saying that the Jews, by hating Jesus and his father even after they had seen Jesus' "works," had "committed a sin" or "deserved condemnation," was only natural since the Gospel itself mentions what would otherwise be the case: ἁμαρτίαν οὐκ εἴχοσαν ["they had not had sin"]. The Semitic version(s) render the Greek perfect tense μεμισήκασιν ["they have hated"] by a grammatical imperfect which has the meaning of the present tense; this is in complete accordance with a liberty in the use of tenses which is characteristic for the techniques of translation evident, above all, in the Psalm texts of a hitherto unedited Horologion [Book of Hours] in Berlin, the publication of which is currently being prepared by P. Kahle and myself[5]. The verbal stem ܚܣܢ [ḥ-s-n "to overcome"] has been attested for Syriac but not yet for the Christian-Palestinian; but since it does occur in Jewish Western-Aramaic we may safely assume it for the Christian-Palestinian, too. As for the erroneous insertion of the letter ܚ [ḥ], this could, without any doubt, much more easily happen with a Christian-Palestinian ܝܣܢܘܢ [yesnūn] "they hate" than it would have been with a Syriac ܢܣܢܘܢ [nesnūn] "they hate" [prefix 3rd person plural "nə" instead of "yə"].

15,25: ἀλλ' ἵνα ["but so that"]

= Sp: ܐܠܐ ܕ [ellā ḏə "but (so) that"]; S^Sin: ܐܠܐ ܡܛܠܐ ܕ [ellā miṭlā ḏə "but because/ in order to"]

> P: ܕ [ḏə "that"], only, on the basis of an omission of ἀλλά ["but"].

Arabic: ولكن لا بُدَّ من ان ["But there can be no doubt that"], again, unmistakeably, on the basis of an expanding and paraphrasing translation which takes the ܕ [ḏə "that"] as a conjunction depending on an expression of knowing. In the Arabic version this expression is so strong that it points to a ܦܢܛܘܣ [panṭōs "altogether, by all means"], which would be the assumed Christian-Palestinian word, much rather than to a ܙܕܩ [zeḏaq “to be seemly”?] or ܘܠܐ [wa-lō “to be seemly”?] which we would have to assume if it were Syriac.

15,25: ἐν τῷ νόμῳ αὐτῶν [“in their law”]

= Sp: ܒܢܡܘܣܗܘܢ [bə-nīmūshōn “in their law”]; S^{Sin}: ܒܐܘܪܝܬܗܘܢ [bə-ʾōrīṯhōn “in their law”]; P: ܒܢܡܘܣܗܘܢ [be-nāmūshōn “in their law”].

Arabic: في النموس [“in the law”]. This ultimately leads us back to a variant of the Greek text which omitted the word αὐτῶν [“their”]. This kind of omission is very common in the *vorlagen* of, specifically, Christian-Palestinian Bible texts, as can be easily seen on the annotations on variants in the text editions. The text of the Sp, as it has been transmitted, should, in this light, be seen as the result of a correction in accordance with P—corrections of that kind are recognized to have been a rather common thing.

15,26: ὃν ἐγὼ πέμψω [“whom I will send”] (with the variant: πέμπω [“I send”] in D)

= Sp: ܕܐܢܐ ܡܫܠܚ [*ḏ-anā mašlaḥ* “whom I send”]; S^{Sin}: ܕܡܫܕܪܢܐ [ḏ-mašaddar ªnā “that I send”]; P: ܕܐܢܐ ܡܫܕܪ ܐܢܐ [ḏ-anā mšaddar ªnā “that I send”].

Arabic: الذى يُرْسله الله [“whom God will send”] = ܕܐܠܗܐ ܡܫܠܚ [ḏ-alahā mašlaḥ “whom God sends”]. This Aramaic version should be seen as a corruption of ܕܐܢܐ ܗܐ ܡܫܠܚ [*ḏ-anā hā mašlaḥ* “whom I send”], which is only possible if the postposed ܐܢܐ [*ªnā* “I”] of the Syriac transmission is omitted, which is characteristic of Sp.

As for the use of ܗܐ [hā “behold, here, this”] within the subordinate clause assumed by me, cf., e. g., in a homily, in *Anecdota Oxoniensia*. Vol. 1, part 9 (Oxford 1896), p. 65: ܕܗܐ ܡܪܐ ܕܢ ܕܐܬܥܝܪ ܡܢ ܫܦܘܠܐ ܕܐܠܦܐ ܘܫܕܟ ܝܬܗ ܠܝܡܐ ܘܠܡܚܫܝܠܘܝ ✣ ܗܐ ܗܘ ܩܡ ܡܢ ܒܝܢ ܡܝܬܐ [*d-hʾ mrʾ dn d-ʾtʿyr mn špwlʾ d-ʾlpʾ w-šdk ytʾ lymʾ wlmhšylwy. hā hū qām men bayn maytā* “(transl. of the last sentence ed.: “It is he who rose from death.”].

It is clear that we are not dealing with a deliberate Islamic textual correction, although such a correction of an original انا ارسل would have been absolutely natural; but that this is not the case can be concluded with certainty from the following من عند الربّ which is, in combination with the الذى يُرْسله الله , utterly needless and otiose. Had there been a deliberate correction, then the من عند part would have been deleted, too; and instead of الله a corrector would very probably have used الربّ as the designation of God, just like it is used throughout the whole passage.

Now that we have established that the *vorlage* of the quotation in Ibn Isḥāq, as far as we managed to reconstruct it, is not identical with the text of

Sp handed down to us—in which direction do the discrepancies between the *vorlage* and Sp, all in all, point?

Crucial here are, obviously, the expanding and more or less paraphrasing elements: ܩܘܕܡܝ [qūḏmʸ "before me"] and ܐܬܚܝܒܘ ܕ [eṯḥībū ḏ- "were found guilty because of"] in 15,24, ܦܢܛܘܣ [panṭōs "altogether, by all means"], in 15:25 and ܗܐ [hā "here; behold; this"] in 15:26. They are all features of one consistent picture, and although none of the expansions is, in itself, very long, their number in so short a passage is strikingly large. The relation between the Christian-Palestinian *vorlage* of the Arabic Gospel translation quoted by Ibn Isḥāq and the text of EvH and CCl was essentially the same as the relation between the Palestinian Targum and the Babylonian Targum Onkelos. This comparison is deeply justified. The Christian-Palestinian Bible text is, by its nature, nothing else but a Christian "Targum." Just like the Jewish Targum, it too has its roots in the improvised, oral interpretation of the reading of Scripture during worship. That much is attested, by the end of the 4th century, by the Western pilgrim to Palestine, "Aetheria"[6]: "*Lectiones etiam, quaecumque in ecclesia leguntur, quia necesse est graece legi, semper stat, qui siriste interpretatur propter populum, ut semper discant*" ["Since it is necessary that all lections read in church should be read in Greek, there is always some-one standing by, translating it into Syriac on behalf of the people, so that they can always understand"]. Having similar starting points, the development on the Jewish and on the Christian side was, as is natural, basically parallel.

Now that our knowledge of the Palestinian Targum has been broadened so considerably by the Geniza treasures and especially by the pertinent publications of Paul Kahle[7], there can be no doubt that the development of Jewish Bible translation, like the development of early Bible translation in general, is essentially characterised by an increasing literality. The Palestinian Targum is not overly anxious about giving a literal translation (although we should be aware that the very broad Aggadic expansions were probably not initially a part of it), and it is older than the Targum Onkelos which strives most for literality. The Targum Pseudo-Jonathan is not a later version of the Targum Onkelos from a further stage when it was allowed to take more paraphrasing liberties, but it is the other way round: The Pseudo-Jonathan is the result of a profound revision of the Old Palestinian Targum, which had had a tendency to paraphrase, in order to adapt it to the much more literal Onkelos[8]. It seems clear that, in the light of this parallel, the Christian-Palestinian Gospel text that we can distinguish through the Arabic quotation in Ibn Isḥāq should be seen as a version that is essentially older than EvH and CCl[9].

I would find it hard to believe that such an old version of the text should have been used for a translation into Arabic as late as in the eighth or seventh century, which would naturally mean that this would have been the prevailing version at that time. Instead, the fact alone that a Christian-Palestinian *vorlage* had been used rather indicates that the Arabic Gospel text quoted by Ibn Isḥāq was written in pre-Islamic times. Why else should the translator have chosen a text written in Christian-Palestinian Aramaic, of all languages, as his *vorlage*, if not because this was, at his time, *the* language of those parts of Palestine that neighboured his own surroundings, and because this was the language in which the Bible texts that were the most directly available to him were written? After the Islamic conquest, however, it was Arabic that became, very quickly, the Semitic vernacular of Palestine. The only other language that went on playing a role was Greek—mainly as the language of the Orthodox ritual; the only place with a literature still being written in Christian-Palestinian was now ʿĀbūd in northern Judea.

There had been times when, in rural areas, a Christianity that was speaking the old Palestinian-Aramaic dialect and an Arabic-speaking Christianity were closely connected; but in the centuries to come that brought forth the main documents of Christian-Palestinian literature preserved to us, those times had already been long gone. The said close connections of the two Christianities and languages existed in the border area between the world of the Transjordanian rural towns and the world of the Bedouin camps which had become Christian through the missionary works of Euthymius; their first bishop, Petros, in the year 431 signed the decrees of the council of Ephesos, which indicates that the Christianity of those Bedouin camps, the παρεμβολαί, had a full hierarchic structure. Thus, in my view it is most likely the παρεμβολαί for whom that Arabic Gospel text had been made (although not necessarily already in the period when that Christianity was being founded), a text whose only extant textual fragment, so far, has been preserved by Ibn Hišām.

Notes

1 Published in *Islamica* 4 (1931), pp. 562-572; also in the present volume.

2 Cf., e. g., the old chant of the (Nestorian) Eastern Syriac liturgy that is called ܠܟܘܡܪܐ [lə-ḵūmrā] after its first words: ܠܟܘܡܪܐ ܕܒܠܐ ܡܘܪܝܢܢ ܘܠܟ ܝܫܘܥ ܡܫܝܚܐ. ܕܐܢܬܘ ܡܢܚܡܢܐ ܕܦܓܪܝܢ. ܘܐܢܬܘ ܦܪܘܩܐ ܕܢܦܫܬܢ l-kmr' d-bl' mwrynn w-lk yšwʿ mšyḥ'. d-antw mnḥmn' d-pgryn. w-'ntw prwq' d-npštn. *Breviarium Chaldaicum*, p. 4 of every edition.

3 Edited by Agnes Smith Lewis, *Codex Climaci rescriptus* (= Horae Semiticae 8) (Cambridge, 1909), p. 82.

4 About this form of the name see Wüstenfeld, ed., p. 972. The name form is after all attested in a strange note about the areas of the missionary work of Jesus' disciples, which belongs to a corpus of apocryphal Acts.

5 Cf. in this context, e. g., in the first three Psalms of the so-called ἑξάψαλμος alone: Ps. 3,8: ἐπάταξας ... συνέτριψας ["you have stamped on . . . you have crushed"] = ܐܝܬ ܫܚܩ . . . ܐܝܬ ܫܩܦ 'yt šḥq . . . 'yt šqp; Ps. 37,14: οὐκ ἤκουον ["I/they did not

hear"] = ܠܐ ܫܡܥ lā šmaʿ!; Ps. 62,2: ἐδίψησεν ["he was thursty"] = ܨܗܝܐ ṣahyā 62,3: ὤφθην ["I appeared/was seen"] = ܝܬܚܡܐ ytḥm'; 62,12: ἐνεγράφη ["he was written in"] = ܝܣܬܒܪ ystbr

6 *Itinera Hierosolymitana saeculi III–VIII rec.* P. Geyer, (Prag-Wien-Leipzig, 1898), p. 99, lines 19ff.

7 Paul Kahle, *Masoreten des Westens. II. Das palästinensische Pentateuchtargum. Die palästinensische Punktation. Der Bibeltext des Ben Naftali* (Stuttgart, 1930) [reprint: Hildesheim 2005].
Cf., e. g., the Targum text of Gn 4,7: p. 6. It is remarkable—and would be worth a closer examination—how an echo of this paraphrasing style of the Palestinian Targum occasionally travelled even as far as into the liturgy of Rome.

8 Cf. my remarks in Anton Baumstark, "Wege zum Judentum des neutestamentlichen Zeitalters" [Ways to Judaism in the age of the New Testament], *Bonner Zeitschrift für Theologie und Seelsorge*, 1928, p. 50.

9 A relation which resembles that between the Old Palestinian Gospel translation and EvH and CCl is discernible when we compare the Christian-Palestinian fragment—comprising the verses 19,1–10 of the once complete text of Genesis – published by Friedrich Schulthess, *Christlich-Palästinensische Fragmente aus der Omajjaden-Moschee zu Damaskus* [Christian-Palestinian fragments from the Umayyad Mosque in Damascus], (Berlin, 1905), pp. 19f., with the corresponding lectionary text published by Agnes Smith Lewis, *A Palestinian Syriac Lectionary.* (Studia Sinaitica No. VI), (London, 1897), pp. 100ff.

The Arabic Translation of an Old-Syriac Gospel Text and the Psalm Translation Quoted in Surah 21:105

Anton Baumstark

Originally published as "Arabische Übersetzung eines altsyrischen Evangelientextes und die in Sure 21:105 zitierte Psalmenübersetzung," dedicated to Paul Kahle on his 60th birthday on January 21st, 1935, Oriens Christianus *31 (1934): 165–88; translated by Elisabeth Puin.*

In pre-Islamic times Christianity, in all its various denominational manifestations, had advanced into the heart of the Arabian Peninsula from four directions.[1] Orthodox—it could not yet be called Chalcedonian—Christianity had spread, in the first third of the 5th century, through the mission of Saint Euthymios[2] from Palestine into the neighboring Bedouin camps from whence a bishop of those παρεμβολαί, Petros, as early as 431, participated in the Council of Ephesus. Monophysite Christianity was, in the South in 523, the victim of the bloody persecution unleashed on it by the Jewish usurper on the Ḥimyarī throne, Ḏū Nuwās; this happened in Neǧrān which in the South had been the place where it had been flourishing most. And yet Monophysite Christianity was in the North, in 542, at the hands of its great patron Ḥāriṯ the Ġassānid (529–569) and helped by the Empress Theodora, able to wrest from Justinian the restoration of a Syrian hierarchy of this confession. Nestorianism had—as of the entire official church of the Sassanid empire—become the denomination of the Christianity of al-Ḥīra which even had sent an episcopal representative to an imperial synod of that church as early as 410 (although the first of the Laḫmid rulers of al-Ḥīra to personally profess the religion of the cross was only ʿAmr ibn Munḏir (ru. 554–569)); and to frequently visit the royal city of the Laḫmids was, by the bedouins of inner Arabia, considered a thing that seemed to almost inevitably end in the acceptance of the Christian faith.[3]

Judging from the inviolable practice of the missionary work of Early Christianity in the East we must assume that on all those fronts of Christian advance at least the Gospels and the Psalter, as those parts of the Bible that were most important for liturgy, were immediately translated into the Arabic vernacular of the new missionary territory. This cannot be emphasized often and strongly enough, in the face of all doubts coming from a way of looking at things which only reflects the point of view imposed by Islamic Studies. Today the (although, unfortunately, presently still sparse) remnants of Christian-Nubian literature attest that the aforementioned general missionary activity of eastern Christianity had an effect even under the blazing sun of the Sudan, where the general cultural level was certainly no higher than in the Christianized fringe areas of Arabia; thus, one should finally stop doubting that in Lord's houses which even contain monumental dedicatory inscriptions in Arabic, like the one in a cloister founded by Hind, mother of ʿAmr ibn Munḏir, which Yāqūt reported to us,[4] also the mass was celebrated, i.e. the Gospels were read and the Psalms sung, in Arabic.

Only in the northwest missionary area of Monophysite Christianity the specific situation at first probably made the translation of the gospel book and the Psalter into Arabic unnecessary. Here, Arab customs and traditions had for centuries been inexorably advancing into an Aramaic language area in which, already since the days of a Bardayṣān, Christianity had created its ritual and a rich theological literature, using the old Aramaic language of the country. The instreaming Arab part of the population itself had adopted Aramaic as the language of communication. Consider Edessa with her Abgarid dynasty that was—judging from its name-giving—doubtlessly of Arab ethnicity. And we can assume that even at the time of Justinian and Ḥāriṯ, the aforementioned, ever-growing Arab part of the population still had a knowledge of the language of their new home that was thorough enough to allow them to participate in a service conducted in that language. Linguistically it was a thoroughly Syrian churchdom, which the Arab phylarch endeavoured to renew by gaining the Emperor's approval to the ordination of two Monophysite missionary bishops for the seats of Buṣrā and Edessa.

Gospel book and Psalter of the Monophysite Christianity in the South were certainly couched in the native South-Arabian language and, therefore, naturally perished together with all the other, doubtlessly not insignificant literature in that same language—a literature whose existence besides the rich world of South-Arabic inscriptions we deduce conclusively from the said inscriptions and from the high cultural level reflected by them. Even still ʿAbīd ibn Šarya and Wahb ibn Munabbih,[5] South Arabians from Sanʿāʾ and vicinity, would certainly not have written their works in North Arabic, had the new "book of God" not appeared, couched in the Meccan dialect, and had Muʿāwiya not called them to the court of the successors of the North Arab prophet in Syrian Damascus.

That highly significant material from pre-Islamic times, from the sphere of the orthodox Arab mission which had spread from Palestine, has indeed survived, should, however, no longer be doubted. First of all, only that sphere can have been the home of the Arabic Gospel translation after an evidently ancient Christian-Palestinian *vorlage*, a quotation from which we find, as I have shown,[6] in Ibn Hišām's Sīra. Also, we have the Arabic Gospel translation from the Greek of the manuscripts *Borg. arab.* 95 (previously *K II* 31) in Rome and *Or. 1108* in Berlin and of the two Leipzig folios *Cod. Tischendorf XXXI* respectively, which, by the original system of pericopic orders noted in it, no less conclusively points to the ecclesiastical territory of Jerusalem; the nature of that pericopic system confirms, from the point of view of liturgical history, that the Gospel translation originated in pre-Islamic times.[7] Furthermore, the Psalter No 39 of catalogue 500 of the Hiersemann firm (now preserved in Zürich), the antiquity of which is confirmed by the nature of the Greek vorlage rendered by the translation,[8] seems to be so closely connected to the Jerusalem territory that we probably have to class it, too, as belonging to the Arab Christianity that had grown out of the παρεμβολαί mission of the early 5th century.

Whereas in that sphere the translation of Gospels and Psalter was—be it directly or through a Christian-Palestinian intermediate link—always based on a Greek text as vorlage, in the Nestorian East the vorlage can only have been a Syriac text. The Arabic translation of such a Syriac text—namely of a Syriac Gospel text which to ascribe to Islamic times is, judging from its nature, just as unthinkable as is the case with the Greek vorlage of the Zürich Psalter—is very clearly evident in a number of scattered fragments of textual evidence.

My starting point is the remarkable Arabic quotation of a Gospel passage in which Tatian's *Diatessaron*, the ultimate basis of all Old-Syriac representation of the Gospel text, particularly strongly deviates—as is ascertained by a plethora of evidence material—from the Greek text the wording of which is almost completely rendered also by the P(ĕšittā). It is the quotation of Mt. 1:18–21 in the *Kitāb al-Maʿārif* (ed. Wüstenfeld, p. 22; ed. Cairo 1300 AH, p. 18) by Ibn Qutayba (d. 276 AH = 889 AD). For those four verses a complete rendering of the said material and also the text of the P shall be given below the Greek text.

In this comparison, as in general, I am using the same scribal abbreviations as in my earlier publications on the *Diatessaron* problem: P = Pĕšīttā; S^S and S^C, respectively, for the old Syriac Sinaïticus and Curetonianus; T^K for the commentary of Ephrem, preserved in Armenian, on the *Diatessaron*; T^A for the Arabic "translation" of the *Diatessaron*; T^N, if necessary with notation of the relevant manuscript of the same, for the Middle Dutch *Leven van Jezus*; T^{Ahd} for the Old High German "Tatian," and finally Vel. for the Gospel translation by the Mozarab Isaac Velasquez from the year 946, the vorlage of which must have been a text that was still essentially Old-Latin, teeming with the most obvious Tatianisms[9]. [The symbol = means: The Greek text is identical with the version in the other language; the symbol > means: the Greek text differs from it].

18. μνηστευθείσης γὰρ τῆς μητρὸς αὐτοῦ Μαρίας τῷ Ἰωσήφ (1),
πρὶν ἢ συνελθεῖν αὐτοὺς (2),
εὑρέθη ἐν γαστρὶ ἔχουσα (3)
ἐκ Πνεύματος Ἁγίου (4).
19. Ἰωσὴφ δὲ ὁ ἀνὴρ αὐτῆς (5),
δίκαιος ὢν (6),
καὶ μὴ θέλων αὐτὴν παραδειγματίσαι (7),
ἐβουλήθη (8) λάθρᾳ ἀπολῦσαι αὐτήν (9).
20. ταῦτα δὲ αὐτοῦ ἐνθυμηθέντος ἰδοὺ ἄγγελος Κυρίου κατ' ὄναρ ἐφάνη αὐτῷ λέγων· Ἰωσὴφ υἱὸς Δαυίδ, μὴ φοβηθῇς παραλαβεῖν Μαρίαν τὴν γυναῖκά σου· τὸ γὰρ ἐν αὐτῇ γεννηθὲν ἐκ πνεύματός ἐστιν ἁγίου.
21. τέξεται δὲ υἱόν, καὶ καλέσεις τὸ ὄνομα αὐτοῦ Ἰησοῦν · αὐτὸς γὰρ σώσει τὸν λαὸν αὐτοῦ ἀπὸ τῶν ἁμαρτιῶν αὐτῶν.

(1) = P: ܟܕ ܡܟܝܪܐ ܗܘܬ ܡܪܝܡ ܐܡܗ ܠܝܘܣܦ (When <u>Mary</u>, his mother, was betrothed to Joseph)
> T$^{\text{N Lütt}}$: *In den tide dat Joseph hadde ghesekeret Marien Jhesuss moeder* (At that time, when <u>Joseph</u> had become betrothed to Mary, mother of Jesus).
(2) = P: ܥܕܠܐ ܢܫܬܘܬܦܘܢ (before <u>they</u> had had intercourse)
> Vel.: من غير ان يباشرها (without <u>him</u> having lain with her).
(3) = P: ܐܫܬܟܚܬ ܒܛܢܐ (<u>she</u> was found to be pregnant),
> T$^{\text{N Lütt}}$: *so wart Joseph geware dat si ene vrocht hadde ontfaen* (thus <u>Joseph</u> became aware that she had conceived a "fruit"), T$^{\text{N Stuttg.}}$: *so van hise hebbende in den licham* (thus he found her having [a child] in her womb).
(4) = P: ܡܢ ܪܘܚܐ ܕܩܘܕܫܐ (of the Holy Ghost)
> T$^{\text{N Lütt}}$: omitted; correspondingly also omitted in Margery Goates, ed., *The Pepysian Gospel Harmony*, (London, 1922).
(5) = P: ܒܥܠܗ (her husband)
> S^{C}; T^{K}; Vel.: omitted
(6) = P: ܟܐܢܐ ܗܘܐ (was righteous)
> S^{C}: ܕܓܒܪܐ ܗܘܐ ܟܐܢܐ (who was a righteous man); the Old-Latin versions: *cum esset homo* (or *vir*) *iustus*; T^{K}: քանզի այր արդար էր (because he was a righteous man); T$^{\text{N Lütt}}$: *wan hi en gherecht mensche was* (since he was a righteous man); T^{Ahd}: *mit thiu recht man uuas* (since he was a righteous man).
(7) = P; S^{SC}: ܕܢܦܪܣܝܗ (+ܗܘܐ) ܨܒܐ ܘܠܐ (and did not want to defame her)
> T$^{\text{N Lütt}}$: *so ne woude hise nit in sijne gheselscap ontfaen* (did he not wish to receive her in his company); Petrus Comestor: *Qui nolens eam traducere in coniugem.*
cf. Zacharias Chrysopolitanus: *traducitur sponsa cum de domo sua in*

domum sponsi ducitur, ut sibi coniugem recipiat.

(8) > P: ܐܬܪܥܝ; S^SC^: ܐܬܪܥܝ ܗܘܐ (he thought to himself); T^N Lütt^: *mar pinsde* (but he thought); Arm: խորհեցաւ (he thought) and correspondingly also Georg., as well as the Pepysian Harmony.
Vel.: أسرّ بمفارقتها (he made a secret of separating from her) does not allow a reliable conclusion regarding its Latin model, but appears rather to incline in the direction of the Syriac version.

(9) = P: ܕܒܛܠܝܘܬܐ ܢܫܪܝܗ̇ (that he release her secretly); S^SC^: ܕܒܗܠܡܐܝܬ ܢܫܕܝܗ̇ (that he release her privily)
> T^N Lütt^: *dat hi al verholenlec hare soude ontflin* (that he should quite secretly flee from her).

In both cases (7) and (9), the Tatian text did not really substantially deviate from the Greek text. (7) is, instead, a case of a misunderstanding purely internal to Latin, by virtue of which the verb *traducere* which was meant in the sense of Greek παραδειγματίσαι ["to pillory, to expose to scorn"], was misinterpreted as a technical term for the marriage ceremony. In (9) we are faced with a classic piece of evidence for the fact that the ultimate basis of the European-Old-Latin Gospel text is a Syriac one. An *effugere eam* that is behind the wording of T^N Lütt.^ points to a vorlage which could have both meanings: this one [="to flee"] and the meaning of the Greek ἀπολῦσαι ["to release"]. Such a vorlage was present in the Syriac ܕܢܥܪܘܩܝܗ̇, which comprised the meaning "to release her" as well as "to flee from her."

Leaving these two cases aside, there remain in the other one-and-a-half verses of Biblical text no less than seven characteristic deviations of the wording of the *Diatessaron* transmission from the Greek, all of which, except for one, are at the same time deviations from the P as well: The three-fold introduction of Joseph as grammatical subject of the sentences in v. 18 [whereas, in the Greek and in the P version, he is not the subject in any of them, see (1), (2), (3)]; the omission of ἐκ Πνεύματος Ἁγίου ["of the Holy Ghost" which is there, in v. 18 (see (4)), in the Greek and P versions]; the omission of the ὁ ἀνὴρ αὐτῆς ["her husband" which is there in the Greek and P versions, in v. 19, see (5)] and the appearance of the word ἀνήρ ["man"] in combination with δίκαιος ["righteous"], instead [see (6)]; and finally [see (8)] the replacement—which alone is also retained in P—of "to want" by "to think by himself" concerning the secret separation. Most, namely the first four, of those phenomena are not once attested in all of the hitherto known sphere of Syriac writing based on or influenced by the *Diatessaron* but occur only in the Western branch of tradition. Should those phenomena be found in Old-Syriac tradition, too, then we would have to rate this as a sign of the closest proximity to the *Diatessaron* and therefore of the greatest antiquity.

Bearing this in mind, let us now approach the text of Ibn Qutayba:

وكان يوسف هذا خطب مريم
وتزوجها فيما يذكر الانجيل فلمّا
صارت اليه وجدها حبلى قبل ان
يباشرها وكان رجلا صالحا فكره ان
يفشي عيلها وايتمر ان يسرّحها
خفية فترآى له ملك في النوم فقال
يا يوسف بن داود ان امراتك مريم
تلد ابنًا يسمّى عيسى وهو ينجي
امّته من خطاياهم

And this Joseph had courted and married Mary, as the Gospel mentions. Now when she was with him, he found that she was pregnant before he had lain with her, and he was a righteous man. Thus, he did not want to defame her, and considered by himself to release her secretly. At that time, an angel appeared to him in a dream and spoke to him: "Oh, Joseph, son of David, your wife, Mary, will bear a son who shall be named Jesus and he will free his people from their sins."

It is clear that this is an intrinsically literal quotation from the Gospel. Nothing could be a stronger argument for this than the fact that even the characteristic plural of the Greek τῶν ἁμαρτιῶν αὐτῶν ["their sins"], which is construed *ad sensum* since it refers to the grammatical singular τὸν λαὸν ["the people"], finds its exact echo [in the Arabic version: امّته .... خطاياهم]. On the other hand, it is just as clear that at the beginning of this passage the transition from the style of continuous narration into this citation could only be done gradually so that we, in our comparison, must not be too severe on the wording of the beginning; and it is also clear that concerning verses 20 and 21 the Muslim author decidedly condensed the text—the remaining words, though, displaying the strongest literality. The very unique يسمّى ("who shall be named"), finally, is nothing else than a corruption of تسمى ("whom you shall name"), which can very easily occur in Arabic. Having taken all of this into account, it remains to state that we find precisely six of the seven phenomena which are characteristic of the *Diatessaron* text in Ibn Qutayba, too. One *might*, of course, call it a sheer coincidence that six liberties of quotation taken by the Muḥammadan Arab of the 9th century AD textually coincide with just as many distinctive features of the early Christian Syriac Gospel harmony from the 2nd century AD. But if we, with respect to such evidence as we have here, were to seriously contemplate merely theoretical possibilities of this kind, then this would render it impossible for any research in the humanities to come to solid results. That the quotation of Ibn Qutayba is ultimately based on an Old-Syriac gospel text, and that this Old-Syriac Gospel text was even richer in ancient material [and hence was more ancient and closer to the *Diatessaron*] than the two surviving Old-Syriac manuscripts Syriac Sinaiticus and Syriac Curetonianus, must be accepted as a solid result—if such research is to remain meaningful at all.

Another matter is the question whether the Muḥammadan author of the

Abbasid period had access to a complete Arabic Gospel translation based on such an Old-Syriac text. It might, after all, be possible to surmise that he owed the quote—possibly even at second-, third-, or fourth-hand—to a source the author of which had translated directly from the Syriac text. But this assumption, too, would have to be regarded as highly unlikely, thanks to the traits of strong literality which, in that case, the text would probably have lost. However, it would probably not be justified to reject this assumption as categorically as we have to reject the idea that the correspondence between Ibn Qutayba and the tradition of the *Diatessaron* could be purely accidental.

That much more significant is, therefore, a second quote where there is no doubt that it comes from an Arabic Gospel translation based on an Old Syriac text of exactly the same extremely ancient structure—so ancient that it even leads beyond Syriac Sinaiticus and Curetonianus—that we just worked out. We find that quotation in the *Risāla fī r-radd ʿalā n-Naṣārā* of ʿAmr ibn Baḥr al-Ǧāḥiẓ[10] (edition of J. Finkel, *Three Essays of Abu ʿUṯmān ʿAmr ibn Baḥr al-Ǧāḥiẓ*, (Cairo, 1926), p. 27) who died in 255 AH. = 869 AD. Explicitly mentioning the Gospel of Mark (فى انجيل مرقس), Ǧāḥiẓ quotes the words of Mark 3,32 مازاذ أمك وأخوتك على الباب (مازاذ your mother and your brothers <are> at the door) and then gives an explanation for the group of letters at the beginning which is, such as we have it in front of us, evidently corrupted: وتفسير مازاذ معلم ("and the explanation of مازاذ is: teacher"). Thus, he was aware that the group of letters in question contained, in any case, a salutation addressed to Jesus, which he thought must be understood in the said sense [as "teacher"]. There can be no doubt that the group of letters must, really, read مار (= ܡܪܐ) اذ [*mār (=mār-ā) iḏ*] (my Lord, behold), مار being a loan-word from the Syriac.

And thus three things are established.

1. The quotation really does come from a Gospel text in Arabic, for only from such a text could an isolated, residual Syriac textual element stand out as one that required an explanation.
2. The basis of the Arabic text was a Syriac text, for only from such a text could the said textual element be left over.
3. And finally, that Syriac basis was not the P but an Old-Syriac text which differed even more from P than S^S does (the respecting passage in S^C is not preserved), for neither in the P nor in S^S do we find the salutation that entered the Arabic translation as a loan word, and in the Greek tradition the salutation has no equivalent either.

As a consequence, we find ourselves, through such an "apocryphal" expansion, once again directed towards the *Diatessaron*. The expansion—the Syriac loan word—however, is not the only element in the quotation of Ǧāḥiẓ which points in that direction. The Greek text of that passage [Mk. 3:32] reads: ἰδοὺ ἡ μήτηρ σου καὶ οἱ ἀδελφοί σου καὶ αἱ ἀδελφαί σου ἔξω ζητοῦσίν σε, ["Behold, your mother, your brothers and your sisters outside are looking for you"]; there are also widespread variants of it which, harmonising the text with the parallel passages in Mt. 12:47 and Lk. 8:20, omit the καὶ αἱ ἀδελφαί σου ["and your sisters"] and—very rarely—the ἰδοὺ ["behold"], too. Further adaptations—especially to Matthew 12:47—occur at the end of the verse, in the Old-Latin tradition and in the D[iatessaron] which is, as usual, dependent on the Old-Latin tradition. P strictly renders the version of the Greek text with the sisters omitted. In S^S we read, instead of ἔξω ζητοῦσίν σε [". . .outside are looking for you"], the words ܩܝܡܝܢ ܠܒܪ ܘܒܥܝܢ ܠܟ (are standing outside, looking for you) which correspond exactly to the ἔξω στήκουσι ζητοῦντές σε of D. Naturally, in the—however largely—expanded text versions a legacy of the *Diatessaron* does, in one way or another, live on. Now we have to ask whether, in the *Diatessaron*, it were really the words of the crowd addressed to Jesus that displayed the greatest possible richness of expression, or whether such richness was, rather, to be found only in the narrative, reporting verse Mt. 12:46 which is lacking in Mk and Lk but which had, according to the available sources on the structure of Tatian's work, of course been included in the *Diatessaron*. If we had no further testimony, it would be impossible to answer that question. But, in fact, one of the most important textual witnesses containing more specific evidence about the wording of the text of the *Diatessaron*, namely Vel., gives the words addressed to Jesus within Mk., in a version which is, compared to the Greek standard text, shortened even at the end [since the "looking for you" is omitted]: هذه امك واقاربك بالباب ("Behold, your mother and your relatives at the door!"). Since in all of Syriac tradition the mention of the sisters, too, is omitted—evidently on the basis of the *Diatessaron*—, one even gets the strong impression that Tatian put the words adressed to Jesus in the briefest possible form. And now the text read by Ǧāḥiẓ [مازاذ أمك وأخوتك على الباب] agrees, in the briefness of its phrasing, exactly with Vel., since there is no reason at all why Ǧāḥiẓ should, in quoting, have withheld any verbal expansion to the nominal clause he is citing—had there, in the text he was quoting from, been such an extension.

Now that we have established that Ǧāḥiẓ was directly using an actual Arabic Gospel translation made on the basis of an Old-Syriac model, we have no choice whatsoever but to assume the same situation for Ibn Qutayba and, consequently, also to assume that the two authors—who were, both as to time and to place, so close to each other[11]—should naturally have used the same translation. This is all the more so since in the same 9th century AD in yet a third work at least clear outlines of the same phenomenon of an Arabic Gospel translation are recognizable—an Arabic Gospel translation whose Old-Syriac vorlage betrayed the ultimate dependence of all development of the Syriac Gospel text from the *Diatessaron* even more clearly than this is done by the surviving Syr. Sinaiticus and Curetonianus. The said work is the

Kitāb ad-dīn wa-d-dawla by ʿAli ibn Sahl Ibn Rabban aṭ-Ṭabarī,[12] written about 855 AD,[13] the authenticity of which was, with almost passionate vehemence, disputed by M. Bouyges[14] but is corroborated, not least, by means of its quotes from the Old and New Testament.[15]

The Gospel quotations, especially, of the *K. ad-dīn wad-dawla* are not consistent. The majority is introduced with an explicit mention of not only the respective Evangelist, but also the respective chapter. As opposed to those we see, however, a smaller number of quotations which have no such introduction, and there is even a quotation (ed. Mingana, p. 128) whose source is, most sharply contrasting with the majority, indicated most vaguely as الانجيل الذى هو فى ايدى النصارى ("the Gospel that is in the hands of the Christians"). Here as well as, probably, in all cases where the otherwise almost stereotypical introductory formula with the name of the Evangelist and the identification of the chapter is lacking, Ibn Rabban aṭ-Ṭabarī is apparently dependent on some source from which he took the quotations without verifying them. The others, introduced by him with such precision, he had probably taken directly from a Gospel text. That this Gospel text must have been an Arabic one based on the Syriac, and was not the P itself—which would, after all, have been a theoretical possibility since Ibn Rabban had a Christian background—we can conclude with absolute certainty from a quotation of Lk. 22:35f. Because there, a ترمال (=ܬܪܡܠܐ) for πήρα is expressly explained: يعنى به المزود ("by this, he means the bag"). This means that the word ترمال , like the مار ("my Lord") of the Ǧāḥiẓ quote, must have had entered, from the Syriac vorlage, the text from which Ibn Rabban took it—which text must, in this case too, definitely have been written in Arabic.

Despite the precision of their introduction, though, even this main section of the *Kitāb ad-dīn wa-d-dawla*'s quotations from the Gospels is far from being quoted stricly literally. First of all, they are regularly attached by ان ("that") to قال ("he says") followed by the evangelist's name; thus, they are *a priori* given the character of indirect speech which does not encourage such literality. Also, very often a text is condensed and shortened, just like we saw it in Ibn Qutayba on Mt. 1,20, and sometimes even more severely. And finally, we also have the opposite phenomenon of textual expansions, for instance when, in a quote from Mt. 4:18 ff., the Arabic الذى لقّبه الصفا ("whom he gave the epithet 'rock'"), which corresponds to the Greek τὸν λεγόμενον Πέτρον, is extended by a reminiscence of Jo. 21,7 and Mt. 16,18: الذى استرعاه أمرامته وجعل اساس ملّته ("to whom he gave his people's sheep to pasture and made him the foundation of his community"). And yet, despite those discrepancies, in quite a number of Gospel quotations we find enough and strong enough evidence of a connection not only to Old-Syriac texts as they are still preserved today but also to the whole sphere of the tradition of the *Diatessaron*—

enough evidence for us to receive a very specific impression of the quality of the relationship between the Arabic Gospel text on which the quotations are based and the said sphere.

In light of the indicated result, it would not make sense to give, in this article, the full text of all Gospel quotations, since the text is easily available in Mingana's inexpensive edition. Therefore it may, instead, suffice to give a list of the relevant passages that contain evidence for the connection of the quotations to the Old-Syriac text form, in the order of their occurence in the Biblical text, and to compare them to the Greek standard text and the P.

[The symbol = means: the text of the versions coincide; the symbol > means: the texts of the versions differ.]

(1) Matthew 4:3 f. (ed. Mingana, pp. 128 f.):

(1a) فقل لهذه الصّخور تصر طعامًا ("Thus speak to these stones: <u>Become bread</u>")

= S^S: ܐܡܪ ܠܗܠܝܢ ܟܐܦܐ ܕܢܗܘܘܢ ܠܚܡܐ ("Speak to these stones <u>that they shall become bread</u>")

> εἰπὲ ἵνα οἱ λίθοι οὗτοι ἄρτοι γένωνται ["Speak <u>that these stones shall become bread</u>"].

Cf. P: ܐܡܪ ܕܗܠܝܢ ܟܐܦܐ ܢܗܘܝܢ ܠܚܡܐ ("Speak <u>that these stones shall become bread</u>")

We are, in the Arabic version and S^S, dealing with a harmonisation of the text with Luke 4,3: εἰπὲ τῷ λίθῳ τούτῳ ἵνα γένηται ἄρτος ["Speak to this stone that is shall become bread"].

(1b) حياة الناس ليست بالخبز فقط ("The <u>life of men</u> is not by bread alone")

> οὐκ ἐπ' ἄρτῳ μόνῳ ζήσεται ὁ ἄνθρωπος = P: ܕܠܐ ܗܘܐ ܒܠܚܡܐ ܒܠܚܘܕܘܗܝ ܚܝܐ ܒܪܢܫܐ ("that in no wise by bread alone <u>lives man</u>").

T^N Lütt differs from the Arabic version only by the number of the subject: *Nit allene in den broden es des menschen leven* ("Not only in bread consists <u>man's life</u>").

(2) Matthew 4:18 ff. (ed. Mingana, p. 125):

(2a) فى ساحل بحر ("<u>on the shore</u> of the sea")

literally = Arm. ընդ եզր ծովուն and Georg.

> παρὰ τὴν θάλασσαν = P: ܥܠ ܝܕ ܝܡܐ ("<u>along</u> the sea").

Cf. S^S: ܥܠ ܓܢܒ ܣܦܬܗ ܕܝܡܐ ("<u>at the side of the coast</u> of the sea").

Whereas the second half of the Old-Syriac [cf. S^S] textual expansion ["the coast"] left traces only in the Armenian and Georgian versions, its first half ["the side"] was preserved by T^A: على شاطى البحر ("<u>at the side</u> of the sea").

(2b) وهما يصيدان السمك ("while they <u>caught fish</u>"),

a shortened version of βάλλοντας ἀμφίβληστρον εἰς τὴν θάλασσαν· ἦσαν γὰρ ἁλιεῖς ["they flung their nets into the sea, because they <u>were fishermen</u>"], the latter part = P: ܗܘܘ ܓܝܪ ܨܝܕܐ ("because they were fishermen").

Cf. S^S: ܡܛܠ ܕܨܝܕܐ ܗܘܘ ܕܢܘܢܐ ("because they were catchers of fish").

(2c) اجعلكم بعد يومكما هذا تصيدان الناس ("I will make you, after this present day, catch men")

The passage [from Mt. 4,19] is expanded in harmonisation with Luke 5,10: ἀπὸ τοῦ νῦν ἀνθρώπους ἔσῃ ζωγρῶν ["From now on you will be a catcher of men"].

> ποιήσω ὑμᾶς ἁλιεῖς ἀνθρώπων = P: ܐܥܒܕܟܘܢ ܕܬܗܘܘܢ ܨܝܕܐ ܕܒܢܝ ܐܢܫܐ ("I will make you fishers of men").

(3) Matthew 4:21 ff. (ed. Mingana, p. 125)

(3a) omitted [in the Arabic version:] τὸν ἀδελφὸν αὐτοῦ = P: ܐܚܘܗܝ ("his brother")

also [omitted in] S^S; T^N.

(3b) omitted [in the Arabic version:] εὐθέως = P ܡܚܕܐ ["instantly"]

also [omitted in] S^S.

(3c) اباهما فى السفينة ("their father in the ship")

= S^S: ܠܐܒܘܗܘܢ ܒܣܦܝܢܬܐ

> τὸ πλοῖον καὶ τὸν πατέρα , in essence = P: ܠܐܠܦܐ ܘܠܐܒܘܗܘܢ ("the ship and their father").

(4) Matthew 5:31 f. (ed. Mingana, p. 136)

(4a) سمعتم التوراة تقول ("You have heard the Torah say")

>'Ερρέθη = P: ܐܬܐܡܪ. ["it was said"]

Cf. $T^{N\ Lütt.}$: *ghi hebt wel gehoert dat man wilen leerde* ("you have well heard that it was formerly taught").

(4b) فانه قد فجر ("behold, he has whored")

= T^N: *heft hi doet overhoer* ("he has practiced whoring")

> μοιχᾶται = P: ܓܐܪ ("he whores").

(5) Matthew 5:38 ff. (ed. Mingana, p.136)

(5a) omitted [in the Arabic version:] δεξιὰν (preceding σιαγόνα) = P: ܕܝܡܝܢܐ ("right-hand"),

also [omitted in] Syr^S, Syr^C, T^K, Ap(h)rahat, D and the Old-Latin versions d, k.

(5b) فلا تمنعه [v. 42]("do not fend him off")

= S^C, P: ܠܐ ܬܟܠܘܢ

> μὴ ἀποστραφῇς ["do not turn away"]

(6) Matthew 9:9 (ed. Mingana, p. 126)

رجلا عشّارا ("a man, a tax collector")

> ἄνθρωπον καθήμενον ἐπὶ τὸ τελώνιον = P: ܓܒܪܐ ܕܝܬܒ ܗܘܐ ܒܝܬ ܡܟܣܐ ("a man who was sitting in the tax house").

Cf. $T^{N\ Lütt}$: *enen tollnere sitten in syn tollhus* ("a tax collector sitting in his tax-house").

(7) Matthew 21:23–37 (ed. Mingana, p. 127 f.)

(7a) عن مسألة ("a <u>question</u>") = T^N Lütt. *ene questie* ("a <u>question</u>")

> λόγον ἕνα = P: ܡܠܬܐ ܚܕܐ ("*<u>one</u>* question").

(7b) ان أجبتمونى عنها أجبتكم من مسألتكم ("if you <u>answer to it</u> [my question], I will <u>answer to your question</u>")

> ὃν ἐὰν εἴπητέ μοι, κἀγὼ ὑμῖν ἐρῶ , essentially = P: ܘܐܢ ܬܐܡܪܘܢ ܠܝ܆ ܐܦ ܐܢܐ ܐܡܪ ܐܢܐ ܠܟܘܢ. ("and if you <u>tell</u> <u>me</u>, I too will <u>tell</u> <u>you</u>")

Cf. T^N Lütt: *ende berichtti mi dis ic u vrage so salic u oc berechte* ("and if you <u>report</u> to me <u>what I ask you about</u>, I too will <u>report</u> to you").

(8) Luke 22:35 (ed. Mingana, p. 121)

(8a) وليس معكم كيس ولاترمال ..... ولاخفّ ("and you did not have with you a purse <u>and not</u> a bag ...... <u>and not a shoe</u>")

= T^N Lütt: *sonder sac en sonder scherpe en sonder geschoite* ("<u>without</u> sack <u>and without</u> bag <u>and without</u> shoe"); the singular "shoe" is due to the absence of dots indicating the plural in the Syriac.

Cf. S^S: ܕܠܐ ܟܝܣܐ ܘܕܠܐ ܬܪܡܠܐ ܘܕܠܐ ܡܣܢܐ: ("without purse and <u>without</u> bag and <u>without</u> shoes"), literally = Vel. بلا عرارة ولا مخلاة ولاخفاف

> ἄτερ βαλλαντίου καὶ πήρας καὶ ὑποδημάτων ["without purse and bag and shoes"]

P with a ܘܕܠܐ ("and <u>without</u>") only in the second element, has at least in that instance likewise preserved the Old-Syriac text form.

(8b) من لم يكن له سيف ("he to whom there is no sword")

literally = S^C, P: ܡܢ ܕܠܝܬ ܠܗ ܣܝܦܐ.

Cf. T^K: որ ոչն ունիցի իւր սուսեր ("he who does not possess his sword")

> ὁ μὴ ἔχων ["he who does not have"]

(9) John 14:16 (ed. Mingana, p. 119)

ان يرسل اليكم ("<u>that he send</u> to you")

literally = S^S: ܕܢܫܕܪ ܠܟܘܢ

> καὶ ... δώσει ὑμῖν = P: ܘ ... ܢܬܠ ܠܟܘܢ ("and ... he will give you").

S^C: ܕܢܬܠ ܠܟܘܢ ("<u>that</u> he <u>give</u> you") has at least the characteristic hypotaxis of the clause; T^A: فينفذ اليكم ("and he will <u>send to you</u>") has retained only the verb of the old text form.

I am certain that, concerning this material, too, no one will seriously dare speak of a play of mischievous coincidence. Now that we found three texts containing evidence for it, we are certainly justified in saying that indeed there existed, around the middle of the 9th century AD in the heart of the Eastern Islamic world, an Arabic Gospel translation which was, being the current one of the time, available to those Muḥammadan scholars who were willing to go to the trouble of dealing with Christian matters and sources.

And the quotations in the *Kitāb ad-dīn wa-d-dawla* in particular, although not very literal, are valuable indicators as to how large an extent the said Arabic Gospel translation was characterised by features of the Old-Syriac representation of the text originating from the *Diatessaron*. Now: Does it make sense to suppose that such an Arabic Gospel text came into existence only shortly before it was used by the three learned Muslims of the 9th century, perhaps at the beginning of the 9th or toward the end of the 8th century or, at any rate, during the time between the rise of the political rule of Islam and the flowering of the Abbasid caliphate?

An attempt to answer this question may begin with a very general consideration. In contrast to the Palestinian West where, according to the manuscript from that region, broad circles of the Melkite population must, in the 9th century, already have completely gone over to full use of the language of the new Arab ruling class, the situation of the Christianity of ʿIrāq was by no means the same. Although, here too, individual scholars and princes of the Church began to make use of Arabic besides or instead of Syriac, the traditional Aramaic language of the forefathers was, certainly above all under the influence of the liturgy, still commonly known.

Within the church there was, therefore, no need for an Arabic Gospel translation. Thus, in the time and region in question [i. e. the ʿIrāq of the 9th century or slightly earlier], such a translation is only conceivable as being aimed at impinging on Muḥammadan circles by making the sacred text accessible to them.

But whether done for such ultimately apologetic reasons or really on behalf of circles of the Christian population that had, already, no longer a sufficient knowledge of Syriac—a translation of the Gospels from Syriac into Arabic, made in the 8th or 9th century, would naturally have been based on the Syriac text version that was current at that time. And this text version was, and had already been for a long time, at least on the soil of the Nestorian Christianity that prevailed in the Mesopotamian East, exclusively the text of the P. It is utterly implausible to assume that besides the P even only a few stray manuscripts of an Old-Syriac text should have been still available—of an Old-Syriac text from a stage of development that would have been even earlier than the text forms of Sinaiticus and Curetonianus. As can be concluded from its relationship to T^{N} and to Velasquez' Spanish-Arabic translation [= Vel.], this Old-Syriac text would essentially have been from the stage of the Old-Latin tradition which we know only indirectly through the said two witnesses [i. e. T^{N} and Vel] and which is earlier than that of all surviving manuscripts.

S^{S} is a palimpsest the original script of which, drawn up at the end of the 4th or beginning of the 5th century, was sacrificed as early as 778 to a re-use of the writing material. S^C which originated in the 5th century probably was a rarity when seemingly abbot Mōšē [Moses] of Nisibis [today Nusaybin in Turkey] discovered it in 932, on a trip to his native East in some monastic library, and purchased it for the library of his Monastery of the Holy Virgin in the Nitrian Desert [in Lower Egypt]. A representation of Old-Syriac Gospel text which is, compared to both said manuscripts [i. e. S^S and S^C], intrinsically even more ancient, is extant not only in the Messalian "Book of Steps"[16] but also in the quotations that we find in the Syriac translations of [the work of] Titus of Bostra [d. 378] and of the Theophany of Eusebius[17] [of Caesarea, 260/265–339/340], which [Syriac translations] are preserved in a manuscript written as early as 411.

How very strongly even the text of the *Diatessaron* itself was in the 9th century, in those manuscripts in which it was still extant at that time, modified according to P can be seen in the translation made in Baghdad in 1043 by Abū l-Farağ ʿAbdallāh ibn aṭ-Ṭayyib. The vorlage on which this translation was based stood, with regard to modification, in an approximately similar relation to the P as, in the West, already the Latin "*unum ex quattuor*" (from which bishop Victor of Capua had, between 541 and 546, a copy made: the harmonistic Gospel text of the Codex Fuldensis) did to the Vulgate. Ibn aṭ-Ṭayyib's vorlage was, as we learn from the invaluable Subscriptio to the Borgiana manuscript, written by the hand of the excellent Christian physician ʿIsā ibn ʿAlī [court physician of the Caliph al-Mutawakkil], a pupil of Ḥunayn ibn Isḥāq (d. 876 AD).[18]

It is necessary to realize all this in order to become aware of the untenability of the idea that the Arabic translation of an Old-Syriac Gospel text of the highest ancientness known to us should have been made as late as the 9th century, or even the 8th century or the late 7th century. An Arabic rendering of such a text seems unthinkable after the 5th or at most the 6th century; instead, it only seems imaginable on the soil of the Old-Arab Christianity of al-Ḥīra.

We come to the same result as by examining the wording of the text of the vorlage from which the Arabic Gospel version was translated, as we have done above, by determining the formal side of the Arabic Gospel translation itself that had been used by Ibn Rabban aṭ-Ṭabarī, Ğāḥiẓ and Ibn Qutayba. Cases of preservation of lexical elements from the Syriac vorlage, like the ماار of Mark 3:32 that we found in Ğāḥiẓ, and the ترملال of Luke 22:5 in the *Kitāb ad-dīn wa-d-dawla,* can hardly have been rarities within that translation, judging from that fact that even the comparatively very sparse corpus of scattered fragments [of textual evidence] contained as many as two examples. Such a situation seems typical for a time and region in which Arabic and Syriac naturally coexisted, without an imbalance caused by literary pretensions, and were equally actively used—as was the case within the Christianity of the Laḫmid kingdom. But it would be imcomprehensible at the peak of the cultural and, above all, literary life to which the ʿIrāqī Christians of the 9th century adapted themselves by using Arabic for their literary works. Furthermore, a new translation of the Gospels undertaken with an eye to Muslim circles—and as we saw, only a new translation makes sense when it comes to Muslim circles—would, in order not to forfeit any chance of success from the start, have had to at least make a great effort to choose the correct Arabic words, if not to aspire to higher literary qualities. That such an aspiration did, indeed, prevail in the creation of Arabic Gospel texts in that period, can, to cap it all, be learnt very clearly from two texts which are kept in the form of artistic, even rhymed prose, and one of which may have been written by a member of the famous Boḫtīšōʿ family. One text became the source of the ample body of quotations in the *Kitāb ar-radd ʿalā n-naṣārā*[19] by the Zaydī imām al-Qāsim ibn Ibrāhīm al-Ḥasanī (d. 246 AH = 860 AD) in remote Yemen. The other one—which was demonstrably not identical with the just mentioned text[20]—is completely preserved in the manuscripts *Vat. Arab. 17, 18* and *Leid. 2348*, the middle one of which was written in the year 993 AD;[21] how old the work copied in it was at the time cannot even approximately be determined.

The authors of such higher literature, however, had certainly not taken the trouble to make a completely new translation, whether from the Greek or from the Syriac, but may, instead, have chosen as a source for their work some older, literarily unambitious Arabic Gospel text which then in their hands underwent formal restructuring and, in instances where it was not in agreement with what their denomination considered the canonical "original" text, also textual correction. Instructive in this regard is the relationship of a certain stylistically honed Gospel text, present in the three mss. *Bodl. 15, 19* and *Ambr. E95,* to a literarily less sophisticated Gospel text which is present in two manuscripts preserved in Rome and two others preserved in Leyden, and, through this text, to an even older text whose pre-Islamic origin can be discerned from its pericopic references to the pre-Byzantine Palestinian ritual.[22] Further, a similar relationship can be established for one of the two above mentioned Gospel texts in artistic prose which is completely preserved [in the mss. *Vat. Arab. 17, 18* and *Leid. 2348*] to just the translation of an Old-Syriac vorlage that was used by the three erudite Muslims of the 9th century.

Compare for Matthew 1:18 and 19 the textual form offered by the quotation in Ibn Qutayba [see above] with the textual form of the literary piece of art [see here]:[23]

اذ يوسف لمريم خطيب وما ان كان بينهما قراب [ما] وجدت مثقلا من روح القدس وان يوسف لمن الصالحين وما كان لإبارتها من المبتغين فاعتقد لما التسريح فى السرّ الكتيم.	When Joseph was engaged to Mary, and it was not as though there had been any intercourse between them, she was found pregnant of the Holy Ghost. And behold, Joseph was one of the righteous and not one of those who would have wished to ruin her. So he resolved upon releasing her in the greatest secrecy.

The text in artistic prose still brings, with the first of the three introductions of Joseph as grammatical subject [cf. above v. 18, discrepancies (1)–(3)], and with the omission of ὁ ἀνὴρ αὐτῆς ["her husband," cf. above v. 19, discrepancy (5)], definitely two of the characteristic features of an Old-Syriac text form which is close to the *Diatessaron*—much as the text was otherwise adapted to the textual features of the Greek tradition and the P. And what is even more important: The literary text agrees with Ibn Qutayba's quotation in a purely formal feature of the greatest significance, one that lies in the lexical field. It is the use of صالح ("righteous") as the equivalent of the Syriac ܙܕܝܩܐ ("just") or, ultimately, of the Greek δίκαιος ["just"], which is of *crucial* importance, and this not only with regard to the dependence of the [literary] text of the mss. V*at. Arab. 17,18* and *Leid. 2348* on the text quoted by Ibn Qutayba.

Thanks to the fact that Ign. Guidi, in his classic treatise on the Arabic and Ethiopic Gospel translations, has chosen, of all passages, Matthew 1:18–25 as the random sample for his comparison of the texts, we are excellently informed on the Arabic wording of Matthew 1:19, and we can determine that within all of the broad, extensive corpus examined by Guidi this same word usage does not recur even once in any of the other texts. And there is more! This usage is otherwise even unknown within the entire Christian-Arabic translation literature of the East, as far as it is directly preserved. The fact that both versions [i. e. the literary one and the one by Ibn Qutayba] coincide in the usage of this word, specifically, as well as in the two said textual features, should therefore for now be sufficient to confirm that there is a relationship of dependence between them.

This word usage is—apart from the remnant of a translation of an Old-Syriac Gospel text that we just discussed—unheard-of in later times, so far as we can tell; but we have evidence of it in the world of still pre-Islamic Bible translation, namely in the instance where this world, without the slightest doubt, comes into our view. As is well known, sura 21:105 quotes God's word explicitly as being written فى الزبور ("in the Psalter"): أَنَّ الْأَرْضَ يَرِثُهَا عِبَادِيَ الصَّالِحُونَ ("that my servants, the righteous ones, will inherit the earth"). The quotation goes back to Psalm 37 (36),29 which reads: δίκαιοι δὲ κληρονομήσουσι γῆν according to the Septuagint, and [identically] ܢܪܬܘܢ ܐܪܥܐ ܙܕ̈ܝܩܐ ("the just inherit the earth") according to P. In its almost strict literality, the passage can only be understood as a quotation from an Psalter text that was already put in Arabic. Whether this Arabic Psalter had been translated from a Greek or from a Syriac vorlage can, at first, not be decided, because the Arabic imperfect can stand for the Greek future tense as well as for the Syriac present participle. It might lead us to the Psalter text of the P as the vorlage of the Arabic text that became known to the Meccan prophet, but this could only be easily and with certainty established if it were possible to interpret عِبَادِىَ ("my servants") as alluding to a connection of the Arabic text to al-Ḥīra; since the Christians of al-Ḥīra referred to themselves, equivalently to the early Christian δοῦλος τοῦ Θεοῦ, quite simply as عِبَاد ("servants") of God, and this was so technical a term that عبادى became a Nisba, which in the 9th century, e. g. in Ḥunayn ibn Isḥāq, still designated the origin from the former royal city of the Laḫmids. But be that as is may, we find in the quotation in any case the same use of صالح that, otherwise, only occurs in the translation of the Old-Syriac Gospel text (and the said remnant of it). And this alone would, again, be sufficient as a further very substantial indication that the origin of this text [= the said Arabic translation of the Old-Syriac Gospel text], too, goes back to pre-Islamic times.

But there is more to add. We meet with our word usage again in another Bible quotation by Ibn Qutayba, and this time we are dealing with a quotation from the Psalter itself. Among the Bible quotations in an as yet unknown work by Ibn Qutayba that were preserved by Ibn Ğawzī in his *Kitāb al-wafā fī faḍā'il al-muṣṭafā*[24] we find the citation of the greater part of Psalm 149.[25] Missing are only v.1^{B}, the end of v. 2 and all of v. 3, and also, together with v. 9, the last word of v. 8, all of which seems due to corruption within the Arabic text, namely a corruption of the quotation proper.[26] The rendering is in almost every instance strictly literal. In v. 4^{B} and 5^{A}, where this is seemingly not the case, the rendering is really that of an already corrupt form of the vorlage text; cf. the relevant comments in the comparison with P following below. This time, we can discern with absolute certainty that the vorlage was the Syriac text of the P. A survey of instances where the Septuagint and the P disagree and the position that the Arabic text takes shall corroborate this.

v.1. ῍Ασατε τῷ κυρίῳ ᾆσμα καινόν ["Sing the Lord a new song"]
> ܫܒܚܘ ܠܡܪܝܐ ܬܫܒܘܚܬܐ ܚܕܬܐ ("Praise the Lord with a new <song of> praise") = سبّحوا الربّ تسبيحا حديثا ("Praise the Lord with new praise")

v.4 ὑψώσει πραεῖς ἐν σωτηρίᾳ ["He will raise the humble to salvation"]

> ܘܝܗܒ ܠܡܣ̈ܟܢܐ ܦܘܪܩܢܗ ("and he gave to the poor his salvation").

In the Arabic rendering واعطاه النظر ("and he gave him the insight"), the pronominal suffix of the 3rd person singular masculine is, in the syntactical context, incomprehensible, which shows that we are dealing with a slavish rendering of a corrupt vorlage The correspondence of the Arabic verb to the P, however, in any case corroborates the derivation of the quotation from the P. In the vorlage used by the translator, the ܦܘܪܩܢܗ appears to have been missing, and instead of ܠܡܣ̈ܟܢܐ, it seems to have had something like ܠܗ ܣܘܟܠܐ.

v. 5. καυχήσονται ὅσιοι ["Let the saints be joyful"]

> ܢܬܥܫܢܘܢ ܙܕ̈ܝܩܐ ("let the righteous strengthen themselves").

Again, the Arabic version شدّد الصالحين منهم ("he strengthened the righteous among them") is a rendering of a corruption: ܥܫܢ ܡܢܗܘܢ, or else of a defective ܥܫܢܘܢ understood in this sense.

v. 6. αἱ ὑψώσεις τοῦ θεοῦ ἐν τῷ λάρυγγι αὐτῶν ["Let the high praises of God be in their throats"]

> ܢܪܘܡܘܢ ܠܐܠܗܐ ܒܓܓܪ̈ܬܗܘܢ ("They may exalt God with their throats").

For this, the Arabic reads مرتفعة يكبّرون الله باصوات ("They may praise God highly with raised voices"), which is probably due to a deficient understanding of the last Syriac word.

About the age either of directly the quoted Arabic Psalter translation proper, or of its Syriac vorlage—and by that at least indirectly of the quoted translation, too—we can gain very clear knowledge from the perspective of liturgical history. Within the qotation, v. 1^A is followed by another imperative sentence: سبحوا الذى هيكله الصالحون ("Praise the one whose temple are the righteous ones"). This is to be explained neither as an unexpectedly and arbitrarily free rendering of 1^B: ܬܫܒܘܚܬܗ ܒܥܕܬܐ ܕܙܕ̈ܝܩܐ ("His praise <is> in the community of the just"), nor by some corruption of this hemistich. Rather, we are dealing with one of the antiphon-like formulas called ܩܢ̈ܘܢܐ (canons) which, according to the Nestorian ritual, would formulate the sense of every psalm in the shortest possible way and would be placed after the first verse of every psalm for the liturgical reading [of that psalm].[27] Verse 1^B itself, however, was displaced by this element. The final text of those Nestorian Psalm-"canons" is a work of the Catholicos Mār(j) Āḇā [Mar Aba] I. (540–552),[28] and his "canon" for Psalm 149 runs, differently: ܬܫܒܘܚܬܐ ܫܒܚܘ ܥܡܡܐ ܠܐܠܗܐ ܕܦܪܩ ܐܢܘܢ ("With a praise<song> praise, you people, the Lord who has saved them").[29] Two things are possible here. Either the differing, ergo older "canon" was translated into Arabic together with the Psalm text. Or—this seems, because of its grammatical structure, more likely—it is an originally Arabic creation that was made for liturgical use on Arabic soil as an addition following v. 1^B especially; and the Syriac text originally rendered by the Arabic translator did not yet have any "canonic" notations. If the latter case is true, then this clearly means that the Arabic Psalter translation quoted by Ibn Qutayba was, on Arabic soil, already used in liturgy at a time before the pontificate of Mār(j) Āḇā—which also means that the translation itself must have been drawn up before his time. If the former case is true, then this means that at least the Syriac Psalter copy [that already contained the "canon" with the differing wording] must have been derived from a time before Mār(j) Āβā. Since it would not have made sense for a translation of a liturgical book, which the Psalter first and foremost is, to use a vorlage that had already been outdated for quite some time by the liturgical development, we should, however, be fairly safe in assuming that even in this case the Arabic text cannot have been drawn up very long after the middle of the 6th century, at the latest.

At any rate, an Arabic text of a liturgical Psalter of Nestorian ritual, stemming from pre-Islamic times, is the one from which Ibn Qutayba took his quotation of Psalm 149 which was preserved by Ibn Ğawzī. And in this quotation, the same use of صالح that we saw in the quotation from the Psalter in Surah 21:105 of the Qurʾān now returns directly in v. 5 and can, by medium of the liturgical "canon," also be corroborated for v. 1. Unless we are willing to again call this just one of those coincidences which cannot, by any research in the field of humanities even remotely related to ours, be assumed without negating itself, we will have to draw the conclusion that it was the Psalter text itself, the one which was quoted in the Qurʾānic passage, that was still available to the 9th century scholar in Baghdad. Now, the Syriac of the P is, on the one hand, definitely proven to be the basis of the said Psalter text. And, on the other hand, only al-Ḥīra can have been the home of the Psalter text, since it was meant for the use in the liturgy of Nestorian ritual.

And so it becomes imperative to assume that the Gospel text which is, by the characteristic peculiarity of word usage discussed above, closely connected to this Psalter text, also originated from, in terms of region as well as time, the same sphere as the latter; the more so, since already textual evidence from its deducible vorlage and also another element of a formal nature pointed to that sphere. It will hardly be ever possible to achieve anything like mathematical conclusiveness of reasoning in the solution of problems like those of the oldest Christian-ecclesiastical literature in Arabic. But there is the highest degree of probability allowed by the nature of things—this much at least may be said with all certainty!—that, around the middle of the 9th century, a Syriac-Arabic Psalter translation, and the Arabic rendering of an Old-Syriac Gospel text connected to that translation, still existed—a Syriac-Arabic Psalter translation which had already been known to Muḥammad and the home of which was al-Ḥīra. And it is equally certain that we can still discern them both, even today: The Arabic Psalter translation from the Syriac becomes visible in Ibn Qutayba's quotation of Psalm 149; and the Arabic rendering of the Old-Syriac Gospel text becomes visible in Ibn Qutayba's quotation of Mt. 1:18–21, in the quotation of Mk. 3:22 in Ğaḥiẓ, and also as the basis of the greater part of the Gospel quotations of the *Kitāb ad-dīn wa-d-dawla* as well as, more remotely, in the background of the "elegant" Gospel text, for the origin of which the year 993 forms the uttermost *terminus ante quem*.

Notes

---

1 On the spread of Christianity in pre-Islamic Arabia, cf. best R. Bell *The Origin of Islam in its Christian Environment* (London, 1926), pp. 1–63. De Lacy O'Leary *Arabia before Muhammad* (London, 1927), pp. 125–152 and the last literary gift of the deceased F. Nau, *Les Arabes chrétiens de Mésopotamie et de Syrie du VIIe au VIIIe siècle* [The Christian Arabs of Mesopotamia and Syria in the 7th and 8th Century] (Paris 1933) which, however, leads us into the first centuries of Islam.

2 On this, cf. especially R. Génier *Vie de saint Euthyme le Grand.* [The life of St. Euthymius the Great] (Paris, 1909) pp. 94–117.

3 Cf. the word of Ḥātim Ṭaj XLIX, v. 6, of his time in al-Ḥīra مَتَى خُفْتُ أَن أَتَنَصَّرَا (until I was afraid I would become a Christian).

4 II, p. 709. Similarly in Bakrī, p. 364.—Recently, The first probes for excavation on the soil of al-Ḥīra have immediately unearthed the remains of two 6th century churches decorated with frescoes. Cf. D. T. Rice, *Oxford Excavations of Hira, 1931* in *Antiquity* VI, pp. 276–291. We shall have to await the further course of this monumental research to see whether similar material will be brought to light.

5 Cf. C. Brockelmann, *Geschichte der Arabischen Litteratur* [History of Arabic Literature] (Weimar, 1898) I, pp. 64f. and the older literature cited there. Especially Wahb ibn Munabbih seems to be a main source of the beginning of Ibn Qutayba's *Kitāb al-ma'ārif.*

6 A. Baumstark, "Eine altarabische Evangelienübersetzung aus dem Christlich-Palästinensischen" [An Old-Arabic Gospel Translation from the Christian-Palestinian], *Zeitschrift für Semitistik* IIX (1932), pp. 201–209.

7 Cf. A. Baumstark, "Die sonntägliche Evangelienlesung im vorbyzantinischen Jerusalem" [The Sunday Gospel Reading in Pre-Byzantine Jerusalem], *Byzantinische Zeitschrift* XXX (1930) pp. 350–359. Cf. Also A. Baumstark, *Das Problem eines vorislamischen christlich-kirchlichen Schrifttums in arabischer Sprache* [The Problem of a Pre-Islamic Christian-Ecclecsiastical Literature in Arabic], *Islamica* IV (1931), pp. 562–575, particularly pp. 570–575 [in: present volume].

8 Cf. A. Baumstark, "Der älteste erhaltene griechisch-arabische Text von Ps. 110 (109)" [The Oldest Preserved Greek-Arabic Text of Psalm 110 (109)] in the previous volume of this periodical [= *Oriens Christianus* ser. 3, vol. 9 (1934)], pp. 55–66.

9 Cf. the previous volume of this periodical [A. Baumstark, "Zur Geschichte des Tatianstextes vor Aphrem," *Oriens Christianus* ser. 3, vol. 8 (1933), pp. 1–12], p. 12, Ak. 1.

10 Cf. Brockelmann, loc. cit., I, pp. 152f. and E. Fritsch, *Islam und Christentum im Mittelalter. Beiträge zur Geschichte der muslimischen Polemik gegen das Christentum in arabischer Sprache* [Islam and Christianity in the Middle Ages. Essays on the History of Muslim Polemics against Christianity in Arabic Language], (Breslau, 1930), pp. 13f.

11 At least, both of them pursued their scholarly and literary work in the 9th century AD. As for Ibn Qutayba, Baghdad was his permanent place of activity, and the older Ǧāḥiẓ, too, was repeatedly drawn there by his varying ties to the court of the caliph and the governmental circles.

12 Cf. Fritsch, loc. cit. pp. 6–12 and the literature cited there on p. 6. Also cf. M. Meyerhof, "'Alī ibn Rabban aṭ-Ṭabarī, ein persischer Arzt des 9. Jahrhunderts" ['Alī ibn Rabban aṭ-Ṭabarī, a Persian Physician of the 9th Century], *ZDMG* LXXXV (N. F. X) [see http://menadoc.bibliothek.uni-halle.de/dmg/periodical/pageview/69941] [1931] pp. 38–68.

13 According to a comment of the author on Dan. 12:12. Cf. Fritsch, loc. cit., p. 7.

14 M. Bouyges, *Le kitab addin wad-daulat récemment édité et traduit par Mingana est-il authentique?* [The kitab addin wad-daulat recently translated and edited by Mingana—is it authentic?], (Beirut, 1924). Cf. also *Le kitab addin wad-dawlat n'est pas authentique.* (The kitab addin wad-daulat is not authentic), (Beirut, 1925).

15 Cf. the article by F. Taeschner, "Die alttestamentlichen Bibelzitate, vor allem aus dem Pentateuch, in Aṭ-Ṭabari's Kitāb ad-dīn wad-daula und ihre Bedeutung für die Frage nach der Echtheit dieser Schrift" [The Old Testament Bible quotations, especially from the Pentateuch, in aṭ-Ṭabarī's *Kitāb ad-dīn wad-dawla* and their significance for the question of the genuineness of this document] in the previous volume of this periodical [= *Oriens Christianus* ser. 3, vol. 9 (1934)], pp. 23–39.

16 Cf. Ad. Rücker, "Die Zitate aus dem Matthäusevangelium im syrischen ‚Buche der Stufen" [The Quotations from the Gospel of Matthew in the Syrian "Book of Steps"], *Biblische Zeitschrift* XX, pp. 342–354.

17 Cf. A. Baumstark, "Das Problem der Bibelzitate in der syrischen Übersetzungsliteratur" [The Problem of the Bible Quotations in Syriac Translation Literature] in VIII, pp. 208–225 of this journal [= *Oriens Christianus* ser. 3, vol 8 (1933)], especially page 219, lines 22 f. The study mentioned there on p. 219, on the relevant material of the Syriac Titos translation, is to appear soon in *Biblica.*

18 On Ḥunayn ibn Isḥāq cf. Ibn Abī Uṣaybi'a, I, p. 203; on the history of the transmission of the Arabic *Diatessaron* cf. S. Euringer, *Die Überlieferung der arabischen Übersetzung des Diatessarons* (*Biblische Studien* XVII, 2), (Freiburg i. Br., 1912).

19 Edited and translated by I. di Matteo, *Confutazione controi Cristiani dello Zaydita al-Qāsim b. Ibrāhīm*, RStO. IX, pp. 301–364. Cf.Fritsch, loc. cit., pp. 12 f.

20 Compare the quotation from Matthew, 1,20 f. in al-Qasim, p. 322 (translation p. 354) with the text of the other translation *"di ricercata eleganza"* presented by I. Guidi, *Le traduzioni degli Evangelii in Arabo e in Etiopico*, Rome 1888, p. 26.

21 Cf. Guidi, loc. cit. [cf. previous note], pp. 25f.

22 Cf. ibid., pp. 27f.

23 Rendered according to *Vat. Arab. 17* and the Leiden ms., loc. cit. [= Guidi *Le traduzioni ...*] p. 26.

24 Cf. C. Brockelmann, "Ibn Ǧauzî's Kitâb al-Wafâ fî fadâ'il al-Muṣṭafâ nach der Leidener Handschrift untersucht" [Ibn Ǧauzî's Kitâb al-Wafâ fî fadâ'il al-Muṣṭafâ, examined in the version of the Leyden Manuscript], *Beiträge zur Assyriologie und semitischen Spachwissenschaft* III, pp. 1–59.

25 Ibid. p. 49.

26 This is the only explanation for the completely random scope of the textual defects. Beside them there are two more corruptions which were corrected by Brockelmann in a wrong way and obviously also belong to the textual history of only the Arabic quotation: in v.2, سوب from بنو, not تنوب; and in v. 5, سدد from شدد, not سرر.

27 On them [= the canons] and their connection with the Greek notion of the ὑπόψαλμα or the ὑπακοή, cf. A. Baumstark, *Festbrevier und Kirchenjahr der syrischen Jakobiten* [Festal Breviary and Church Year of the Syrian Jacobites], (Paderborn, 1910), p. 70.

28 According to the testimony of ʿAḇdīšōʿ of Sōḇā in the *Mēmrā* on the documents of Syriac literature (Assemani, *Bibl. Ar.* [probably *Bibliotheca Orientalis*] III, p. 76) and according to the "Arabic Chronicle of Seert," II, p. 66 (*Patrologia Orientalis* [Paris 1908–19], VII 2, p.158). Cf. A. Baumstark, *Festbrevier und Kirchenjahr,* loc. cit. [cf. previous note] and A. Baumstark, *Geschichte der syrischen Literatur* [History of Syriac Literature] (Bonn, 1922), p. 118.

29 Paul Bedjan (ed.), *Breviarum Chaldaicum* (1886–1887; reprint Rome 1938), p. 330* in each of the three volumes.—A *Qānōnā* to psalm 99 differing from the one by Mār(j) Āḇā is also found in the fragment of a Pahlevi Psalter which was edited posthumously from F. C. Andreas' unpublished works by K. Barr in *SbPAW* 1933, pp. 91–152 [F. C. Andreas, "Bruchstücke einer Pehlevi-Übersetzung der Psalmen," ed. by K. Barr, in: *Sitzungsberichte der Preußischen Akademie der Wissenschaften*, (Berlin, 1933), whereas in the Syriac-Neo-Persian Psalter fragment that was published by F. W. K. Müller in *Festschrift Eduard Sachau zum siebzigsten Geburtstag gewidmet* [Festschrift dedicated to Eduard Sachau on his 70th Birthday], (Berlin, 1915), pp. 215–222, *Qānōnē* are altogether lacking.

An Early Islamic and Pre-Islamic Arabic Gospel Translation from the Syriac

Anton Baumstark

Originally published as "Eine frühislamische und eine vorislamische arabische Evangelienübersetzung aus dem Syrischen," Atti del XIX Congresso Internazionale degli Orientalisti *(1935) (Rome: G. Bardi, 1938), pp. 682–84; translated by Elisabeth Puin.*

For the research into the documents and the history of Arabic Gospel translation, a classic treatise by Ignazio Guidi[1] laid the first foundation. If a continuation of that research is to lead beyond what was already accomplished by Guido, it would have to focus, above all, on explicit relevant reports and on the quotations from the Arabic Gospel text by Muslim authors.

Such quotations, found in Ibn Qutayba, al-Ǧāḥiẓ and Ibn Rabban aṭ-Ṭabarī, seem to go back to one and the same translation from the Syriac, which [Syriac] vorlage maintained a closer dependence on Tatian's Diatessaron than did the text of the two Old-Syriac manuscripts, Sinaiticus and Curetonianus; that an early Arabic Gospel text should be connected to Tatian's Diatessaron is, however, something that we can, judging from the results of recent research on the Diatessaron, always expect.

Of two reports on Arabic Gospel translations from the Syriac, a first one—in a shorter form presented by Bar ʿEḇrāyā—was already known to Guidi. Today it is also present in a longer form, namely in the Syriac World Chronicle of Michael the Great [1126–1199] and in the anonymous parallel work which originally reported on events up to the year 1203/1204. Giving account of a translation that had (allegedly) been made by the Jacobite patriarch Yōḥannān I (died December 14, 648) for a certain Muslim potentate called ʿAmr b. Saʿd, this report is admittedly burdened by not insignificant difficulties. And yet, the highly remarkable details given by it compel us to assume that it does have a historical nucleus at its base. Thus, we can either assume that the information on the said dignitary of the Syrian church is correct, and consequently surmise that the translation was made, about the middle of the 7th century, really for the great ʿAmr b. al-ʿĀṣ [d. ca. 663]. Or we can rather assume—and this is probably much more likely—that the said Muslim potentate was really the Umayyad ʿAmr b. Saʿīd al-Ašdaq [d. 689/690], which means that we have to give up on the name of the Jacobite patriarch so as to be able to place the origin of the translation into the next-to-last decade of the 7th century.

The second report is given by al-Bīrūnī, in his invaluable reports on the calendar of the Melkite Christians of Ḫuārizm [Khwarezm]. According to his report, a characteristic of the Arabic Gospel translation (which had, naturally, been drawn up on the basis of a Syriac vorlage) by Dāḏīšōʿ,[2] whose name points toward the Iranian East, was the use of the short form Šaʿyā as the name of the prophet Isaiah. This peculiarity also occurs in the Arabic Gospel text of of the Karšūnī manuscript *Vat. Syr. 197*, which [Gospel text], being surprisingly rich in Tatianisms, at the same time proves to be still dependent on an Old-Syriac vorlage. Thus we have, on the one hand, no choice but to recognize in the Karšūnī manuscript the work of Dāḏīšōʿ, although in a certainly much younger and revised version. On the other hand, Dāḏīšōʿ's work itself, rendering an Old-Syriac text of the greatest closeness to the Diatessaron, is not conceivable as being written in Islamic times, any more than is the Arabic Gospel translation quoted by Ibn Qutayba, al-Ǧāḥiẓ and Ibn Rabban.

That this Gospel translation should be identified with the work of the said East Syrian Christian of probably Iranian blood, seems at least highly probable. This being so, the same is true of the Arabic rendering of an Old-Syriac vorlage which is behind two—clearly distinct, despite their kinship—representations of the Arabic Gospel text. Guidi, however, still attributed those two versions to a Greek vorlage, but they were really only given their final form by a very far-reaching revision in accordance with the Greek. On closer examination, there even seem to have been two different revisions of this kind to which the original Syriac-Arabic translation was subjected, and whose results are present in those two versions. Guidi, even without knowing the ms. *D 226* of the Asiatic Museum in Leningrad which is the most valuable witness of the manuscript tradition of the said translation, correctly identified one of the two versions as the earlier one. This version maintains to a greater extent than the other traces of the original connection with the Old-Syriac Gospel text and, ultimately, with the Diatessaron.

Furthermore, another representative of the older version which also only recently appeared—namely the Arabic ms. *1108* of the Prussian State Library in Berlin [today: Staatsbibliothek zu Berlin]—gains the highest significance as evidence for the still pre-Islamic origin of what seems to be the only Arabic translation of a still Old-Syriac Gospel text, since, in the case of at least this older version, even the revision towards the Greek had already taken place in pre-Islamic times. This can be concluded from the liturgical rubrics which, in the said Berlin manuscript, give account of the use of certain passages of the Gospel text as pericopes for the liturgical year. For, at an important point, they require a specific form of the liturgical year which was, at the point in question, in the Byzantine rite which alone is possible here, then changed in the immediate wake of the Emperor Heraclius' victory over the Persians [in 629/30].

Notes

---

1 Ignazio Guidi, *Le traduzioni degli evangelii in arabo e in etiopo* (Rome, 1888).

2 [Professor Sebastian Brock noted in a letter to Ibn Warraq (April 24, 2014) that "it is unclear which Dadisho is meant. The source, al-Biruni on the Melkite calendar, in *Patrologia Orientalis* 10, simply gives the name as the translator of the Gospel into Arabic; curiously, Sidney Griffith in his good recent book on the Bible in Arabic (*The Bible in Arabic: The Scriptures of the "People of the Book" in the Language of Islam*, Princeton, NJ: Princeton University Press, 2013) does not seem to mention Dadisho anywhere (at least not in the index!). Since the name is not uncommon in the Church of the East, it is probably not possible to specify which Dadisho is meant."]

On the Origin of the Monotheistic Creed Formulas in the Qur'ān

Anton Baumstark

Originally published [posthumously] as "Zur Herkunft der monotheistischen Bekenntnisformeln im Koran," Oriens Christianus *37 (1953): 1–17; translated by Elisabeth Puin.*

Not the confession of the absolute oneness of God, but the notion of the Last Judgement was the point of departure of Muḥammad's prophecy; Snouck Hurgronje was the first to memorably point this out to us. However, in struggling against the rejection that the notion of the Last Judgement, and of the resurrection of the dead which is inextricably connected to it, encountered among Muḥammad's polytheist fellow citizens in Mecca, the confession of the one-ness of God became (in contrast to the Christian doctrine of the Trinity which was strangely misunderstood)[1] more and more important. In Muḥammad's time in Medina it had already completely gained centre stage and thus it became, finally, the fundamental dogma of Islam. In the Koran, it finds its expression in three different formulas, two of which are positively put whereas the third, which is the most frequent one and was to become authoritative, expresses in a uniquely negative way that besides "*the God,*" *Allāhu,* there is no other [God].

One of the two positive formulations uses the simple numeral ["aḥad – one"] and is represented only by the initial words of Surah 112, the Creed Surah, which is chronologically difficult to place[2] and is, by the introducing *qul,* "speak," characterised as something like a formula intended for ritual use.[3] I will, In another context, have to show in more detail that this Surah 112 both in content and in form is in antithetical dependence on the type of Trinitarian Christian Creed formulas spoken during Baptism, and that, accordingly, the words of the Surah *huwa Allāhu aḥadun,* "He, God, is one," correspond to their words εἰς ἕνα θεόν[4] ["in one God"] which are, in the Orient, an inviolable element of the Creed. At this point it may suffice to have just mentioned both facts.

Distinctive for the other positive formulation is the attributive connection of the stronger *wāḥidun* with the article-less *ilāhun,* i.e., that it talks of *one sole* God. Only in one of those instances, namely in Q 4:169 [4:171] from the Medinan period, this predicate is combined with the preceding subject *Allā-hu*, giving the sentence [*Allāhu ilāhun wāḥidun*] "God is one sole God." The sentence is emphasised by a preceding *innamā*, and the same is true for the instances in the verses from late-Meccan times 6:19, 16:53 [16:51], and 14:52, in which latter case the preceding word is *annamā*. Emphasized in this way is in those instances the statement *huwa ilāhun wāḥidun* ["He is one sole God"], and the word "God" [Allāh] is mentioned earlier in the text; thus, the sentence says that "God is *only* one sole God," i.e., "He is *the* one sole God," or "there is *only* one sole God." On the other hand, there is a series of examples of the address *ilāhukum ilāhun wāḥidun* "Your God is one sole God" which is evidently used as a stereotyped formula; the series ends with the verses 16:23 [16:22] and 41:5 [41,6], which are also from late-Meccan times, and verse 22:35 [22:34] from Medinan times, but begins already with the middle-Meccan verses 2:158 [2:163], 18:110 and 21:108. Judging from the age and extent of the material concerned, it is unmistakable that this is the original and normal form of the statement of [God's] one-ness, in other words, the statement of one-ness was first put in the form of an address. Thus, this form is what we have to refer to when we attempt to answer the question whether Muḥammad may have been completely independent in coining that statement or rather here, too, dependent on some—and if so, which—older monotheistic Creed formula. I cannot at the moment determine whether and, if so, by whom the thought to be uttered here might have been already expressed.[5] I must therefore run the risk of repeating something already said by someone else, if I now point out the surprisingly close formal relationship in which the Qur'ānic addressing formula stands to the decisive introductory words of the Jewish-Palestinian *Šěma'* prayer, from Deuteronomy 6:4 [wording cf. below]. That the *Šěma'* was recited in the morning and evening is, if at all, only imprecisely testified in Flavius Josephus' *Antiquities* [*of the Jews*] IV, 8, 19, as a μαρτυρεῖν τῷ θεῷ ["to profess God"] for the benefactions bestowed upon Israel during and after the exodus from Egypt; but it is evidently presupposed in Jesus' question in Lk. 10:26: ἐν τῷ νόμῳ τί γέγραπται; πῶς ἀναγιγνώσκεις ["What is written in the Law? How do you read it?"], which is to be understood not so much as "How do you read?" but rather "How do you recite?," and to which the person addressed replies by quoting Dt. 6:5.[6]

Naturally, there is anything but an exact congruence between the Arabic formulation [in the Qur'ān] and the Hebrew wording of the Biblical text [Dt. 6:4]:

> שְׁמַע יִשְׂרָאֵל יהוה אֱלֹהֵינוּ יהוה אֶחָד [*šəma' yiśrā'ēl; YHWH 'ělōhnū YHWH 'eḥāḏ*]
> "Hear, Israel, Yahweh, our God Yahweh, is one."[7]

Aside from the omission of the address to Israel and of the imperative following it, three discrepancies can be discerned at first glance. In the Hebrew formula, the place of the Qur'ānic predicate nominative *ilāhun* is taken, still within the framework of a tripartite subject, by the repeated name of God. Instead of the Arabic suffix of the second person, which establishes the addressing character of the sentence, the Hebrew formula has the suffix of the first person plural; the [Hebrew] numeral is used predicatively instead of attributively [like the Arabic numeral]. However, on closer examination, all those discrepancies become considerably less significant. First of all, even in the case that Muḥammad, in coining his formula the succinctness of which takes some beating, followed the Jewish Creed formula, this does not necessarily mean that he had to slavishly copy it. The first of the three parts of the *Šĕmaʿ* already comprises as much as the verses Dt. 6:4–9; Muḥammad could well summarise and condense elements from different instances within that part. In this context, it is significant that immediately afterwards [i.e., after the above mentioned formula of Dt. 6:4,], in Deuteronomy 6:5, the וְאָהַבְתָּ אֵת יְהוָה אֱלֹהֶיךָ [*wəʾāhaḇtā ʾēṯ YHWH ʾĕlōheḵā*] "and thou shalt love Yahweh, *thy* God" not only brings the connection of אֱלֹהִים [*ʾĕlōhīm*] "God" with a suffix now likewise of the second person, albeit formally in the singular; moreover, the Targum Jonathan, in its strongly paraphrasing version of this passage which seems, in contrast to the literal rendering of the Babylonian Targum Onkelos, to be based—as is so often the case—on the Old-Palestinian Targum tradition,[8] even gives us a אלהכון [*ʾĕlāhăḵōn*] "your [plural!] God" which is construed *ad sensum* and directly corresponds to the Arabic *ilāhukum*. Furthermore, as for God's name, Yahweh, it was, in the oral recitation of the Bible passage within the *Šĕmaʿ*, in any case not spoken. On the other hand it was, as the Mishna tells us,[9] allowed to perform that recitation in any language, and the Jews of Arabia certainly did it in Arabic. That the link between this Arabic version and the Hebrew original was an Aramaic version is not only a possibility but can even be stated with certainty, unless we assume that the close similarity between the Qur'ānic formula and the Targum Jonathan is due to sheer coincidence. And it is, again, no pure assumption that, in this Aramaic version, instead of God's name [Yahweh] a אלהא [*ʾĕlāhā*] "God" was spoken. Indeed, there is a phenomenon definitely pointing in this direction. In quite a number of quotations there is evidence for a connection between Tatian's Diatessaron and the Aramaic[10] Targum tradition; and in this context we rather frequently find, in Dutch-German and Italian Diatessaron texts, and sometimes also in the Persian Diatessaron text which was only recently (and still insufficiently) made accessible,[11] traces hinting at a Syriac ܐܠܗܐ [*ʾălāhā*] "God" instead of a Greek κύριος ["Lord"][12] Such a אלהא [*ʾĕlāhā*] "God" [—always provided that this was the word of the Aramaic version—]

could, then, easily itself be understood as a part of the predicate, and the numeral at the same time understood as an attribute, just like, in fact, the Greek κύριος ὁ θεὸς ἡμῶν κύριος εἷς ἐστιν of the Septuagint and the Syriac ܡܪܝܐ ܐܠܗܢ ܡܪܝܐ ܚܕ ܗܘ [*mry' 'lhn mry' ḥd hw*] of the Peshitta are subjected to the same (necessarily double) misunderstanding, [since both can be translated either as "The Lord, our God, the Lord is One," the predicate being "is One" or as "The Lord, our God, is one sole Lord," the predicate being "is one sole Lord," like in the Aramaic version assumed by Baumstark] Therewith we have found the immediate vorlage of the earliest, addressing version of the Qur'ānic monotheistic Creed which is characterised by the use of *wāḥidun*; now we know not only the vorlage of its subject, which lies in the אלהכון [*'ĕlāhăḵōn*] from the Targum Jonathan of Deuteronomy 6:5, but also the vorlage of its predicate. Thus, there can hardly be any longer any doubt that this form of the Qur'ānic formula is, indeed, to be traced back to the first words of the *Šĕma'*.

It may be rated as a not entirely insubstantial corroboration of this result that the *wāḥidun* formula, in its addressing form, is followed in 22:35 [22:34] by *fa-lahu aslimū* "and with him make the covenant," in 41:5 [41:6] by *fa-staqīmū ilayhi wa-'staġfirūhu* "and turn to him straightly and ask his forgiveness;" and in 16:53 [16:51], where the formula is introduced by *innamā huwa* and put in God's mouth, by *fa-iyyāya fa-rhabūna* "and me you must fear." Although all these additions, in accordance with the Qur'ānic concept of God, differ from Dt. 6:4 ff. in content, they immediately remind us in form of the way in which, in Dt. 6:4 ff., the solemn proclamation of God's one-ness is followed by the *commandment* to love God—too immediately for us to be, after what we discerned about the Creed formula itself, inclined to believe in a sheer accidental similarity.

The second of the two positive formulations of the monotheistic Creed of the Qur'ān [i.e., *ilāhukum ilāhun wāḥidun* "your God is one sole God"] is, in the instance of perhaps its earliest occurrence,[13] again put in its original addressing form, but is already followed by the negative formulation which has, in this case, the wording *wa-lā ilāha illā huwa* "and not is there a God except him" and is concluded by *ar-raḥmānu r-raḥīmu* "the beneficent, the merciful." That this negative formula—in its more complete version *lā ilāha illā Allāhu* "not is there a God except God," which subseqently became authoritative—derives "from a Jewish formula" was already stated in Nöldeke-Schwally;[14] the reason given there was that in the Psalm 18 (17), verse 32, which also recurs in II Sam 22,32, the question מִי-אֵל מִבַּלְעֲדֵי יהוה [*mī-'ēl mibbal'ăḏê YHWH*] "Who is God except Yahweh?" of the Hebrew original is rendered, in the Targum as well as in the Peshitta, by the negative declarative sentence לית אלהא אלא יהוה [*lēt Alāhā illā YHWH*] [in the Targum] and ܠܝܬ ܐܠܗܐ ܠܒܪ ܡܢ ܡܪܝܐ [*lēt Alāhā lə-bar men māryā*] [in the Peshitta]: "not is there a God except Yahweh" resp. "Not is there a God except the Lord." I must confess that this fact alone would hardly seem to me to offer sufficient, substantial reason for the conclusion drawn from it. And the conclusion—namely that the Arabic formula which had, expanded by the confession of belief in Muḥammad's being God's messenger, become *the* Creed of Islam, should derive from some Jewish formula neither the use nor even the exact wording of which can be determined—could only be called rather vague. But we will indeed be able to find more, and more reliable, evidence for this by considering and sifting all of the material available on both sides.

As for the Arabic side, it can be stated that the wording of the Islamic formula with the concluding *illā Allāhu* "except God," which has achieved canonical validity, occurs only twice in the Qur'ān itself. Its second occurrence takes place apparently not before the Medinan period and, more exactly, probably shortly after the battle at Badr, in Q 47:21 [47:19], dependent on *fa-ʿlam annahu* "know then, that;" but it appears for the first time in 37:34 [37:35], as early as in the middle-Meccan time, and is here already understood as *the* missionary kerygma of the new revealed religion. And the form with merely *illā huwa* "except him" [instead of *illā Allāh*] first occurs even still much earlier, namely in 73:9, i.e., in a probably particularly old text from the early Meccan period.[15] Here, it is the predicate of a compound nominal clause with the subject *rabbu l-mašriqi wa-l-maġribi* "the Lord of the East and the West" which [subject] could, perhaps, be interpreted as a substitute of the Yahweh name that might possibly have been common in Arab Judaism.[16] The same form [with *illā huwa*] occurs again, but probably only in the Medinan period, in the same syntactical function in 64:13, as a predicate following the simple subject *Allāhu* "God," and also [cf. above] in 2:158 [2:163] where it is connected to the second positive formulation of the monotheistic Creed.

Besides those instances we find—especially in relatively early passages—several freer variations of the negative formula. Thus, it appears as *lā ilāha illā anā* "not is there a God except me" in the verses 20:14 and 21:25 from the middle-Meccan period and in verse 16:2 from the late-Meccan period, put in the first person and spoken directly by God himself. In Q 21:87 from the middle-Meccan period the addressing version *lā ilāha illā anta* "not is there a God except you" is put into the mouth of the prophet Jonah; and even in the anti-Christian polemics of the Medinan period we still find, in 5:77 [5:73], a long version *wa-mā min ilāhin illā ilāhun wāḥidun* "not is there anything of divine nature except one sole God" which differs from the wording that subsequently became canonical.

The predominant version within the Qur'ānic language, however, is the wording of the negative formula in which it first appeared. We encounter it in a variety of formal functions. Thus, in verse 13:29 [13:30] from the middle-Meccan period it is an independent sentence, following the brief *huwa rabbī*

"He is my Lord" as the second part of a statement of faith by which Muḥammad is to turn away from his idol-worshipping fellow citizens. In the late-Meccan period, in 35:3, it is the answer to the rhetorical question *hal min ḫāliqin ġairu Allāhi yarzuqukum min as-samā'i wa-l-arḍi* "Is there of a creator any except God to provide you from the heaven and from the earth?" In 11:17 [11:14] it is, introduced by *wa-'an* "and that," the second part of a subordinate clause dependent on *fa-'lamū* "then know," As a relative clause dependent on an indeterminate antecedent, it completes, in 9:31 from the Medinan period, a *wa-mā umirū illā li-ya'budū ilāhan wāḥidan* "and they were commanded nothing but to serve one sole God;" the whole sentence is an example of late-Medinan polemics against Jews and Christians. In some instances it is an insertion that interrupts the syntactical coherence, mostly after *Allāhu* "God" as the subject of a simple or compound nominative clause; it is used just in the same way as, in later times, the expressions *ta'ālā* "He is the Highest," *'azza wa-ğalla* "He is strong and glorious" or the eulogy of the prophet *ṣallā Allāhu 'alayhi wa-sallam*, or, like ultimately all of those expressions, as the Hebrew בָּרוּךְ הוּא [*bārūk̲ hū'*] "Praised be (or is) he" of Jewish texts. We find such instances already in the middle-Meccan period in 20:7 [20:8] and 27:26, and also in the late-Meccan period in 6:106 as well as in the Medinan period in 3:1; 9:130 [9:128] and 4:89 [4:87].

The just described variety of formal functions corresponds to a likewise relatively great diversity of contexts, into which the formula is fitted. Contrasting to it, however, is a last phenomenon which shall be shown to be particularly noteworthy and to which the fact that the formula itself is quasi-used as a eulogy is probably not unrelated. That phenomenon is the striking frequency with which the Qur'ānic formula, in its (as we may now call it with all certainty) original and normal form, joins—itself being a motif of the praise of God—short textual constructs that are doxological in the narrow as well as the broader sense of the word. This occurs within passages of a more or less hymnic tone: e. g. already in 44:7 [44:8] from the middle-Meccan period, in 6:102, 7:158, 28:70, 28:88 and 40:2 [40:3] from the late-Meccan period, and in 3:4 [3:6] from the Medinan period. In one instance (3:16 [3:18]) the formula is, apparently in reference to the old variant where it was a statement coming directly from God's mouth and put in the first person [cf. above: 20:14, 21:25, 16:29], embedded in an alleged self-statement of God: "God has witnessed that there is no God except him."[17] The formula can be written at the beginning of a larger hymnic passage, as in 39:8 [39:6] from the late-Meccan time, or at the end of such a passage, as in 2:256 [2:255; B. erroneously has 2:156] and 59:22f. from the Medinan time, or it can appear at the beginning and then again in the middle of such a passage, as in 40:64 and 67 [40:62 and 65].

However, *verbatim* congruence on the Jewish side (apart from God's name [Yahweh] and its Syriac substitute ܡܪܝܐ [*māryā*] "Lord" [discussed above]) we find, of all those variants of the negative formula, only for that version of the Islamic Creed which later became canonical but is so scarce in the Qur'ān [*lā ilāha illā Allāh*]. As we saw above, we do not find it in the original Hebrew text where it is put in the form of a question ["Who is God except Yahweh?"], but in the Targumic rendering of Ps. 18 (17):32 (and, identically, of II. Sam. 22:32); that the same rendering recurs in the Peshitta corresponds to the general relationship of the Peshitta and the tradition of the Targum.[18] In this context we should also consider it significant that, indeed, Muḥammad appears to have known an Arabic Psalter translation, as can be concluded from the Qur'ānic quotation from Ps. 37 (35):29 in Surah 21:105; I have been able to show[19] that this Arabic Psalter translation was connected to the Arabic translation of an Old-Syriac Gospel text, which means that it was of Christian origin and had flowed from the Syriac text of the Peshitta.

As for a parallel to the above mentioned, addressing variant of the negative form of the monotheistic Creed uttered by the prophet Jonah in Q 21:87 [*lā ilāha illā anta* "not is there a God except you"], it may, in the light of this, become less important that the Targum gives us for Psalm 18 (17):32 an ample paraphrase likewise put as an address, in which the negative declarative clause in the third person, identical with the Targumic rendering of II. Sam. 22:32 ["Not is there a God except the Lord," cf. above], is inserted as a quotation, but which also contains, behind that quotation, a negative declarative sentence in the second person: ארום לית בר מנך [*'ārūm lēt bar minnāḵ*] "because there is not (a God) except you."—The said Qur'ānic passage has, on the other hand, an—at first glance—striking parallel in the ὅτι οὐκ ἔστιν θεὸς πλὴν σοῦ, κύριε ["that there is no God except you, o Lord"] of Sirach 36(33):5; but certainly nobody will be inclined to consider a direct connection.

Above all, however, a clear inclination of the wording of the monotheistic Creed towards stereotyped fixity is anything but foreign to the Hebrew urtext of the Old Testament; rather, it is practically a characteristic of a specific, Deuteronomistic-prophetic style. In this context, we will have to come back later to the two neighboring passages Deuteronomy 4:35 and 4:39. Besides them, we first have to refer to I (III) Kings 8:60:

> לְמַעַן דַּעַת כָּל-עַמֵּי הָאָרֶץ כִּי יהוה הוּא הָאֱלֹהִים אֵין עוֹד [*ləma'an da'aṯ kōl-'ammê hā'āreṣ kî Yahweh hū' hā'ĕlōhîm'ên 'ōḏ*] "So that all the peoples of the earth know that Yahweh is God and there is not another (one)."

Apart from those instances, it is particularly the Qur'ānic examples of God's self-statement, put in the first person, which have parallels in the Old Testament. The oldest Biblical example is Deuteronomy 32:39:

> רְאוּ עַתָּה כִּי אֲנִי אֲנִי הוּא וְאֵין אֱלֹהִים עִמָּדִי
> [*rəʾū ʿattāh kī ʾănī ʾănī hūʾ wə-ʾên ʾĕlōhīm ʿimmāḏī*]
> "See now that I am I and there is not a God besides me."

Then we find pertinent material, cumulated closely next to each other, in Deutero-Isaiah 45:5:

> אֲנִי יְהוָה וְאֵין עוֹד, זוּלָתִי אֵין אֱלֹהִים [*ʾănī Yahweh wə-ʾēn ʿōḏ, zūlāṯī ʾên ʾĕlōhīm*] "I am Yahweh, and not is there another (one), and except me there is no God;" after 45,14: אַךְ בָּךְ אֵל וְאֵין עוֹד אֶפֶס אֱלֹהִים [*ʾak bāḵ ʾēl wə-ʾēn ʿōḏ ʾepēs ʾĕlōhīm*] "Only in you is God and not is there another God" almost immediately follow 45:18 אֲנִי יהוה וְאֵין עוֹד [*ʾănī Yahweh wə-ʾên-ʿōḏ*] "I am Yahweh and there is not another (one)," 45:21: הֲלוֹא אֲנִי יהוה וְאֵין-עוֹד אֱלֹהִים מִבַּלְעָדַי [*hălō ʾănī Yahweh wə-ʾên-ʿōḏ ʾĕlōhīm mibbalʿāḏay*] "Am I not Yahweh and there is not a God apart from me?," 45:22: כִּי אֲנִי-אֵל וְאֵין עוֹד [*kī ʾănī ʾēl wə-ʾēn ʿōḏ*] "For I am God and not is there another (one)" and 46:9: כִּי אָנֹכִי אֵל וְאֵין עוֹד אֱלֹהִים [*kī ʾānōḵī ʾēl wə-ên ʿōḏ ʾĕlōhīm*] "That I am God and another God there is not."

It is certainly at least very possible that, by whatever path and in whatever way transmitted, this linguistic usage which is, in its uniform use of the negatively expressed monotheistic statement put in the first person, such a strong feature in the Old Testament, could have exerted influence on Muḥammad, too; and in his coining of the final form of that Creed, he was—we may be safe to state—very probably influenced by the Targum version of the Psalm passage 18 (17):32, by way of the Arabic translation of the Peshitta Psalter.

However, for the question where the first wording of the [negatively put] Creed, which Muḥammad never entirely dismissed, comes from, this decides nothing. So far, we have not encountered a parallel for its ending with *illā huwa* "except him" which is the characteristic of this version. Curiously, we first find such a parallel in a variant of Tobias 13:4 [which is a passage within the prayer written by Tobias] which seems to be conveyed only through the Latin text of Hieronymus and not through the older Aramaic version that was known to that Church Father:

> quoniam ideo dispersit vos inter gentes, quae ignorant eum, ut vos enarretis mirabilia eius et faciatis scire eos, quia non est alius deus omnipotens praeter eum.[20] ["For he therefore scattered you among the Gentiles, who do not know him, that you may declare his wonderful works and let make them know that *there is no other almighty God except him*"].

After having stated this, we must, however, now turn to the passages Deuteronomy 4:35 and 4:39. With the greatest emphasis, already the first of them [i.e. Dt. 4:35] says

> כִּי יהוה הוּא הָאֱלֹהִים אֵין עוֹד מִלְּבַדּוֹ [*kī Yahweh hūʾ hāʾĕlōhīm ʾên ʿōḏ milləḇaddō*]
> "that Yahweh is *the* God. There is not another (one) except him alone."

Even more solemn is the tone of the second one [i.e., Dt. 4:39]:

> וְיָדַעְתָּ הַיּוֹם וַהֲשֵׁבֹתָ אֶל-לְבָבֶךָ כִּי יהוה הוּא הָאֱלֹהִים בַּשָּׁמַיִם מִמַּעַל וְעַל-הָאָרֶץ מִתָּחַת אֵין עוֹד [*wə-yāḏaʿtā hayyōm wa-hăšēḇōṯā ʾel-ləḇāḇeḵā kī Yahweh hūʾ hāʾĕlōhīm baššāmayim mimmaʿal wəʿal-hāʾāreṣ mittāḥaṯ ʾēn ʿōḏ*] "and you shall know and you shall take it to your heart that Yahweh is *the* God. In heaven above and on earth below there is not another (one)."

Here appears in this Hebrew urtext, at least in the first instance, the equivalent of the Arabic *illā huwa* "except him" that we were looking for, albeit in indissoluble connection with an emphasized expression of God's one-ness that is is not there in the Arabic version.

The fact that the Greek of the Septuagint has, in both instances, the identical ἔτι πλὴν αὐτοῦ ["another (one) except him"] also [i.e., like the Arabic] without an expression of one-ness, would, in and of itself, hardly be worth consideration, since it seems highly unlikely that Muḥammad should have depended, from the early-Meccan period onward, on an Arabic translation of the Torah based on a Greek, i.e., Christian, version. Of greater importance, however, seems the fact that the said Greek rendering corresponds to a [Jewish!] Targum tradition that is extant in Aramaic, too. The wording ܘܠܝܬ ܛܘܒ ܠܒܪ ܡܢܗ [*w-lēt tōḇ le-bar minneh*] "and not is there another (one) except him" of the Peshitta corresponds, in both instances, exactly to the Greek version but can, within the Pentateuch, hardly be suspected of being due to the influence of the Septuagint. And the wording appears again, always with the characteristic lack of an emphasizing expression for God's one-ness, at least in the first instance [i.e., Dt. 4:35] as לית תוב בר מנה [*lēṯ tūḇ bar minneh*] in the Targum Jonathan and, retaining the Hebrew עוֹד [*ʿōḏ*] instead of תוב [*tūḇ*], in the Targum Onkelos; in the second instance [i.e., Dt. 4:39], it is, in the Targum Jonathan, just slightly expanded to a לית חורן בר מנה [*lêṯ ḥōran bar minnêh*] "Not is there *any other* except him."

In none of those cases, however, exists a direct connection to an element corresponding exactly to the Arabic *lā ilāha* "not is there a *God*," as we found it in the "*non est alius deus*" in the Tobias variant. And yet, it is really striking that two peculiar features of the said Targum tradition correspond with the Septuagint, namely that [on the one hand] both use the same simple "except him" without rendering the additional element that is given in the [Dt. 4:35] Hebrew מִלְּבַדּוֹ [*milləḇaddō*] "except him alone," and that [on the other hand] both expand the simple Hebrew עוֹד [*ʿōḏ*] "another" by an additional element [i.e., "but him," which is not there in the Hebrew Deuteronomy 4:39]; the correspondence is striking, indeed, and it demands some attempt at explanation.

In fact, Deuteronomy 4:39 is a very special and interesting case. In chapters 33–38 of the 7th book of the Apostolic Constitutions, we find, under a very thin Christian veneer, prayer texts of Hellenistic Judaism. I indicated this already four decades ago in my booklet "Die Messe im Morgenland"[21] which, despite the desperate need for a new, revised edition, was repeatedly reprinted by the publisher without any changes; W. Bousset[22] then exhaustively substantiated this observation. To be more precise, it is essentially an *ordo officiorum*, a manual of guidance for Sabbath morning services, in which the closest parallels to the nucleus of the "Eighteen" prayer [i.e., the Eighteen Blessings, the Shmoneh Esreh], and to the benedictions framing the recitation of the *Šĕmaʿ* in the later liturgy of the synagogue are almost palpable.[23] A recitation of the *Šĕmaʿ* itself, however, was not a part of it. Instead of a quotation of Deuteronomy 6:4 or 6:4–9 as the Creed, we encounter, solemnly introduced by the words μὴ γὰρ ἡμέτερόν ἐστι τοῦτο, δέσποτα τοῦ θεράποντός σου λόγιόν ἐστι φάσκοντος the quotation of essentially[24] Deuteronomy 4:39 in the version of the Septuagint, which differs from the Masoretic text in other distinctive traits[25] as well: καὶ γνώσῃ τῇ καρδίᾳ σου καὶ συνήσεις, ὅτι κύριος ὁ θεός σου ἐν οὐρανῷ ἄνω καὶ ἐπὶ γῆς κάτω καὶ οὐκ ἔστιν ἔτι πλὴν αὐτοῦ ["and you will understand in your heart and know that the Lord your God (is God) in heaven above and on earth beneath and there is not another (one) except him."—The standard text reads slightly different, cf. fn. 24].

The liturgical use of this passage, which at a first glance appears to be a peculiarity of the Hellenistic-Jewish prayer order contrasting to the Palestinian order that uses Dt. 6:4, is, really, very old. It is certainly rather Dt. 4:39, quoted probably together with some preceding verses, than Dt. 6:4, to which Flavius Josephus refers when he qualifies the two daily obligatory confession prayers as a grateful reminiscing of the benefactions bestowed upon Israel during and after the exodus from Egypt [cf. above], since a reference to the exodus immediately precedes, from Dt. 4:34 on, this first of the two instances of the negative wording of the monotheistic Creed, whereas we find no mention of the exodus anywhere in the closer or further vicinity of Dt. 6:4.

Various arguments offer decisive support even for the assumption that, like the unique Targum version of Deuteronomy 4:35 and 4:39 in general, also specifically already the version of the Septuagint is—albeit not in all its special features not found anywhere on Aramaic soil[26]—determined by the liberties which could naturally be taken concerning its wording in the liturgical use of the Biblical text. In this direction points, for one thing, the Greek ὅτι οὐκ ἔστιν ἄλλος θεὸς παντοκράτωρ πλὴν αὐτου ["that not is there any other almighty God except him"] which can be reconstrued as the direct[27] vorlage of the variant of Tobias 13:4 given by Hieronymus [cf. quotation above]. This Greek passage shared the "except him" at the end with the general Targum tradition and displayed in its παντοκράτωρ the new liberty of a specifically Greek element, but also coincided, in its ἄλλος, with the חורן [*ḥŏrān*] "another" in the Targum Jonathan of Deuteronomy 4:39.

If we assume that individual features even of already the prayer text that, in the Jewish urtext of VII 33–38 of the Apostolic Constitutions, directly framed the quotation from Deuteronomy, could also be very old, we can now, for another thing, explain the fact that the Targum tradition in both Greek and Aramaic ignores the emphasizing expression of [God's] one-ness found in the Hebrew מִלְּבַדּוֹ [*milləḇaddō*] "except him alone." Because, in the Greek text [of the Apostolic Constitutions, VII 35], the prayer continues, after the said quotation of Dt. 4:39, with the sentence οὐδὲ γὰρ ἔστι θεὸς πλὴν σοῦ μόνου ["and not is there a God except you alone"]; and this is, except for the conjunction ["and"] at the beginning, nothing else but the second half of Dt. 4:35, transformed into an address and expanded by the θεὸς which corresponds to the *deus omnipotens* in Hieronymus' text of Tobias 13:4, and here [with μόνου "alone"] also including the emphasized expression of the oneness that we encountered in the Hebrew version. If it is now allowed to surmise something similar for that version of a liturgical text which determined the wording of Dt. 4:35 and 4:39 in the Septuagint and in the parallel Aramaic texts, then we can easily understand how even an individual feature of the quotation that, [in the Hebrew original,] directly followed the quoted sentence and was there strongly emphasized, could be omitted in the liturgical text.

And finally, an old liturgical usage of Deuteronomy 4:39 and its neighbouring passages cannot, since it has left traces in the Aramaic text form as well, originally have been restricted to the Greek language area of the Hellenic diaspora. That it was indeed not restricted to that area can be deduced, with all certainty, in another way which, at the same time, also gives valuable confirmation of the old age of such usage. It is the liturgy of the Samaritans at which we have to take a final look.

Negative ways of expressing the monotheistic Creed are, first of all, current in that liturgy; and, since a great variety of exact wording on the one side [i.e., the Qurʾān] is opposed by only two unvarying formulations on the other side [i.e., the Samaritan liturgy], nobody will suspect that this phenomenon could be due to Islamic influence. In the Samaritan liturgy, there is, on the one hand, the less frequent Hebrew אין כיהוה אלהינו [*ʾēn kə-Yahweh ʾĕlōhēnū*] "not is there (a second one) like Yahweh, our God,"[28] which was, as an independent formula, reserved to the special liturgies of some specific days. And there is, on the other hand, the Aramaic לית אלה אלא אחד [*lēṯ ʾĕlāh ʾellā ʾeḥāḏ*] "not is there a God except one," which is predominant, above all, within the unchangeable basic texts and was, also as an independent formula, added after hymns,[29] or combined with related elements of various type giving short, doxological formulas,[30] or, at the end of prayers, mostly used as doxological addition,[31] and sometimes also repeated like a litany.[32]

One single time, however, in one of the basic texts which is called "Prayer of Joshua, son of Nun"[33] and is an outstanding and certainly also very old text of the Samaritan area, we find a formulation which is composed of the Hebrew יהוה הוא האלהים [*Yahweh hū' hā'ĕlōhīm*] "Yahweh is *the* God" from the beginning of Dt. 4:35 and 4:39, and the Aramaic ולית אלה לבר מנה [*wə-lēṯ 'ĕlāh lə-bar minneh*] "and not is there a God except him." To a very special significance of this formula points the fact that its first part[34] is, in the special liturgy of a particular day, repeated like a litany, and that its second part[35] has a parallel in the relative clause דלית אלא הוא [*də-lēṯ 'ellā hū*] "apart from whom there is none" [which is also recited in that special liturgy]. Despite the *verbatim* congruence which here, indeed, exists, we cannot assume this last version to be an Aramaic translation of the normal [i.e., most frequent] wording of the Qur'ānic formula, since, if Islamic influence really were involved, the choice would have naturally fallen on the final, standard version with *illā Allāhu* "except God" at the end. Instead, like the expansion that we found in the *alius deus omnipotens praeter eum* of the Vulgate version of Tobias 13:3 in the and in the θεὸς πλὴν σοῦ μόνου of the Apostolic Constitutions, it is another example, this time on Samaritan soil, of the ending of both Biblical verses in the wording of the Jewish Targum tradition which is determined by liturgical use [i.e., "except him"].

This correspondence is all the more significant, first because the *Samaritan* Targum, at least in the version available to date (most readily accessible is the edition by Ad. Brüll),[36] sticks more closely to the Hebrew original text,[37] and, therefore, does not help towards an explanation [of the simple "except him" which is not there in the Hebrew original]. Second, the regular [i.e., most frequent] Aramaic Creed formula of the Samaritan liturgy [i.e., לית אלה אלא אחד (*lēṯ 'ĕlāh 'ellā 'eḥāḏ*) "not is there a God except one," cf. above] displays a modification of the wording apparently under the influence of Dt. 6:4[38]. And third, both verses Dt. 4:35 and 4:39 seem to have played a very important part within the Samaritan liturgy, as can be clearly deduced from an Aramaic prayer[39] that was to be spoken upon entering the Church; since this prayer contains a quotation of 4:39 which begins with כִּי אָתָּה יהוה [*kī 'āttāʰ Yahweh*] "that you, Yahweh"—by which it is, compared to the original Hebrew version [which, instead, begins with כִּי יהוה [*kī Yahweh*] "that Yahweh"], transformed into an address—and to which is added the ending אֵין עוֹד מִלְּבַדּוֹ [*'ēn 'ōḏ milləbaddō*] "except him *alone*" of 4:35.

Thus, we find ourselves thrown back into a time before the final hardening of the Jewish-Samaritan polarity[40], when the Creed formula was not yet taken from Dt. 6:4–9 but from Dt. 4. And we learn that also the element "(there is no) *God*" (the Biblical sources of which are Dt. 32:39 and Isaiah 45:5–21 and 46:9 [cf. above]) which is part of the variant rendered in

Hieronymus' Tobias 13:3 [*quia non est alius* deus *omnipotens praeter eum*] and and is also part of the Hellenistic-Jewish *ordo officiorum* as the basis of the 7th book of the Apostolic Consitutions [οὐδὲ γὰρ ἔστι θεὸς πλὴν σοῦ μόνου "and not is there a God except you alone"], but which does not exist in the Septuagint and in the Jewish Targum texts, goes back to the older form of the Creed.

We have now established that the first element of the Islamic Creed, the *lā ilāha* "there is not a God," has no parallel anywhere in the Jewish Targum texts, and that the second element of the Islamic Creed (in its oldest and most frequent form in the Qurʾān), the *illā huwa* "except him," has no equivalent in the Hebrew original version of Dt. 4:35 and 4:39. We have established that the complete negative Creed formula of the Qurʾān, in its earliest and most frequent form [i.e., *lā ilāha illā huwa*], practically *verbatim* agrees, instead, with such a negative formula used in ancient Jewish liturgical prayer, and agrees *only* with this formula. From this, we must necessarily conclude that Muḥammad did not—as one could have assumed—coin his Creed formula on the basis of the passages in Deuteronomy that he may have found in an Arabic translation of the Pentateuch (that such a translation, of Jewish origin and written in pre-Islamic times, really did exist, is attested in the *Sifre*[41] for Dt. 33:2; and even as late as around the year 1000 AD, namely in quotations by the Spanish author Ibn Ḥazm, we seem to find traces of such an Arabic translation, as is revealed by the meticulous examination of those quotations by E. Algermissen).[42] Instead, Muḥammad seems to have taken the formula from the said, ancient liturgical prayer—which, accordingly, must have been still in use in certain circles of Arab Judaism of his time.

This also explains (which can, in turn, be rated as a first, not worthless confirmation of our conclusion) the frequency with which the Qurʾānic formula occurs in contexts of hymnic elevation—if we take into consideration how very much the Jewish prayer concerned, judging by its Hellenistic version that lives on in the Apostolic Constitutions, was such a hymnic praise of God. A second confirmation seems to arise from the one instance [in the Qurʾān] in which the negatively put profession that there is only one God is formulated as an address. It is clear that the passage in the book of maxims of Jesus Sirach that we quoted above as a parallel cannot have been the archetype. Instead, it is possible to surmise as the model of that formulation of the Qurʾān, and perhaps even of the passage in Jesus Sirach, a wording within a liturgical text—maybe originally still put in Hebrew—that corresponds to the Greek οὐδὲ γὰρ ἔστι θεὸς πλὴν σοῦ μόνου.

The apparent contradiction between this new result and the conclusion reached earlier, namely that Muhammad, when he first coined the positively put, addressing formula of the monotheistic Creed, was, rather, inspired by the Jewish model of a final liturgical usage already of Deuteronomy 6:4, is not irreconcilable. As was the case with Christianity,[43] so could also Judaism of a great variety in form and origin have penetrated Arabia,[44] and accordingly it is possible that religious Jewish circles of differing observance could have used prayer texts that were greatly differing in age.

Notes

1 According to Surah 5:116, the other "two Gods" worshipped "besides God" by the Christians are Jesus and his mother. Already W. Rudolph, *Die Abhängigkeit des Qorans von Judentum und Christentum* [The Dependence of the Koran on Judaism and Christianity] (Stuttgart, 1922) 87, has, as an explanation of the strange misunderstanding, in addition to the designation Θεοτόκος, which *alone* would not suffice as an explanation, pointed out that—"corresponding to the grammatical gender of the Semitic word which could, at least, fluctuate—the Holy Ghost was in Oriental sects considered the feminine principle next to the male Christ," which (allegedly) allowed for the confusion of the Holy Ghost with the human mother of Jesus. We may, however, ask ourselves whether we should not, in this connection, rather bring to mind the peculiar sentence, Ἄρτι ἔλαβέ με ἡ μήτηρ μου τὸ ἅγιον πνεῦμα ["Now has seized me my mother, the Holy Ghost"], *Tom.* II,6 and *Hom. in Jerem* [Homiliae in Ieremiam] XV,4, and in the Latin translation of his Aramaic original text by Hieronymus *in Mich.* [Commentarius in Micham], VIII,6 and *in Jes.* [Commentarius in Jesaiam] XL,12—as a saying of Jesus, from the Gospel of the Hebrews which was used not far from the Palestinian-Arabic border area by the "Nazarenes." On the other hand, it is no less likely that we should think of the women's sect of the Collyridians who, according to reports by Epiphanios [of Salamis] *Panar.* [Panarion] *LXXVII,* 25f; *LXXVIII,* 1f, LXXIX, 1f., exactly on the soil of "Arabia," actually worshipped Mary as a goddess.

2 Cf. Th. Nöldeke, *Geschichte des Qorāns* [History of the Qoran], 2nd ed. revised by Friedrich Schwally. *Part I: Über den Ursprung des Qorans* (Leipzig, 1909) 107f. The datings vary from the assumption of its origin from the earliest period of Muhammad's appearence as a prophet, as alleged by Muir and Hirschfeld, to the assumption of an origin not until the Medinan period, which is uttered by the Islamic authorities mentioned in Nöldeke-Schwally, ibid. 107, note 4. Personally, I am inclined to connect the unusual piece with a deepening of the relationships of Muḥammad to Christianity, which probably took place during the time of the use of the designation of God as *ar-raḥmān.*

3 The meaning of this *qul*—for which a sufficient explanation is usually not sought—can be either the one that is considered here, or a command issued personally to Muḥammad in a specific situation or for a specific situation that is to come. It will not be all too difficult to decide which is right in the respective individual case.

4 On this formulation with the numeral which is, at least since the middle of the 3rd century, characteristic for the East, in contrast to the Western simple θεόν or *deum,* cf. H. Lietzmann, "Symbolstudien" LVII, *ZntW* [Zeitschrift für die neutestamentliche Wissenschaft] 19 (1920), I/14, particularly p. 7.

5 E. Diez, *Glaube und Welt des Islam* [The Belief and World of Islam] (Stuttgart, 1941) 49, does not do more than to casually note an essentially purely contentual

congruence when he, talking, oddly enough, about the negatively put Qurʾānic formula, instead, says that it begins "quite similarly" like the Jewish "Shema," so as to attest by it the truism that the "content of the first commandment of Moses' Tablets of the Law" is also "main principle of Islam."

6 Only if we assume that ἀναγιγνώσκεις was used in this sense, and that it was referring to a specific, commonly known formula taken from the "Law," we get to understand the absolute certitude of the answer; i.e., it had *a priori* been clear what the answer would be.

7 At least I believe that this is how he have to, strictly grammatically, understand the sentence; it may differ from the understanding of the old versions like Luther's "der Herr, unser Gott, ist ein einziger Herr"—"the Lord, our God, *is one sole God*" which is still under the influence of the Vulgate and its common punctuation "Deus noster, *dominus unus est,*" but it agrees with the English translation "The Lord, our God, *the Lord is One*" in I. H. Hertz, *The Pentateuch and Haftorahs*. Hebrew text. English Translation and Commentary (London 5698—1938), 769. It would also be possible to assume two nominative sentences: "Yahweh is our God, Yahweh is One," for which understanding the commentary of the English translation wrongly refers, along with *Sifra* and "most Jewish translators and commentators" also to the Septuagint with its ὁ θεὸς ἡμῶν κύριος εἷς ἐστιν.

At any rate, it is absolutely unthinkable to assume that it is a plurality of divine beings named Yahweh being rejected by the Bible verse [i.e., "Yahweh our God is (but) one Yahweh"], which would mean that the second יהוה [YHWH] were to be understood as a predicate complement, with the numeral as its attribute. From the point of view of philology, It is similarly irrelevant when, on the other hand, on the Christian side, the Catholic translations like the one by Allioli, infelicitously and with the obvious intention to differ, at least in *one* word, from Luther, render [instead of the Hebrew original] the Latin of the Vulgate, then naturally in accordance with its official punctuation, namely as "ist *ein einiger Gott*" [which can be misunderstood as "is a *unanimous* (or *united*) God"]. And it is, philologically, likewise negligible when the liberal Protestant theology of recent times is less interested in a clear grammatical understanding of the passage than in stating—as does, tellingly enough, K. Martini in the third edition of E. Kautsch, *Die Heilige Schrift des Alten Testaments* I [The Holy Scripture of the Old Testament] (Tübingen, 1909), 251—with placid acceptance of the fact that it is "disputable how the words should be construed," an "indubitable" agreement of the passage "according to its context" with some theory on religious history or critique of the Pentateuch or other.

8 Cf. A. Baumstark, "Peschitta und palästeninensches Targum" [The Peshitta and the Palestinian Targum], *BiblZ* [Biblische Zeitschrift] 19 (1931), 257–70 and my lecture, published in the *ZDMG* New Series 14 (1935) 89–128: *Neue orientalische Probleme biblischer Textgeschichte* [New Oriental Problems of Biblical Textual History], especially p. 90f. Cf. as well the excellent dissertation: "Peschitta und Targum" Mus [Peschitta und Targumim des Pentateuchs: Ihre Beziehungen untersucht im Rahmen ihrer Abweichungen vom massoretischen Text], *Muséon*

48 (1935), 1–48, by C. Peters who was executed during the war in accordance with the verdict of a German occupation court in Holland.

9 Sota VII, 1. On the *Šĕma'* and questions concerning it in general, especially E. Schürer, *Geschichte des jüdischen Volkes im Zeitalter Jesu* I [History of the Jewish People in the time of Jesus] (Leipzig, 1898) 459f.

10 Cf. A. Baumstark, the article cited in Fn. 8, *ZDMG*, N.F. 14, pp. 114ff.

11 By G. Messina, "Notizia su un Diatessaron Persiano tradotto del Siriaco," Bibilica et Orientalia, number 19 (Rome, 1943). Of course, Baumstark could not make allowance for the publication of the text and of its translation which only appeared three years after his death: Giuseppe Messina, "Diatessaron Persiano. I. Introduzione. II. Testo e traduzione," *Biblica et Orientalia* 14 (Rome, 1951). Note of the [German] Editor.

12 The first [i.e., the Syriac ܐܠܗܐ (*'ălāhā*)] is, in some cases, also preserved directly like, for example, in Lk I,58 (in agreement with the Arabic and Persian Diatessaron text) in the Peshitta, besides the Old-Tuscan *Dio*.

13 On the origin of the verses II,158–62 [2:163–167] still from Meccan times in general, cf. Nöldeke-Schwally I, 178. More precisely, these verses too derive from the middle Meccan period, from the time of the use of the designation of God as *ar-raḥmān*. The designation appears here, perhaps for the first time, like in the prayer Surah I in the alliterative combination *ar-raḥmān ar-raḥīm* which is later used in canonical setness and unmistakably originates from the sphere of South Arabian Judaism. Cf. in A. Moberg, *The Book of the Himyarites. Fragments of a hitherto unknown Syrian work.* (Lund, 1924) 10b, lines 1ff. (= CVII of the translation) the Jewish oath by ܐܠܗܐ ܪܒܐ ܪܚܡܢܐ ܘܒܢܡܘܣܐ ܕܡܘܫܐ [*'alāhā rb' raḥmānā w-bnmws' d-mwš'*]—"the great God, the Compassionate (*raḥmānā*) and the Law of Moses"; cf. ibid. p. 13a, lines 14ff. (= CIX) the Jewish claim that Jesus falsely called himself ܒܪܗ ܕܐܠܗܐ ܪܚܡܢܐ [*bareh d-'alāhā raḥmānā*] "Son of God, the Compassionate" and, p. 28e, line 21f. (= CXIX), that he was worshipped by Christians as the ܒܪܗ ܕܪܚܡܢܐ [*bareh ḏ-raḥmānā*] "Son of the Compassionate." The "Book of the Ḥimyarites" also contains quite some other things that are interesting and new with regard to the question of Muḥammad's dependence on Judaism. E. g. Muḥammad's designation of Jesus as *'Īsā ibn Maryam* "Jesus, son of Mary," which occurs in the Qur'ān (2:81, 254 [2:87, 253]; 3:40 [3:45]; 4:169 [4:171]; 5:50, 82, 109, 112, 116 [5:46, 78, 110, 112,116]; 19:35 [19:34]; 33:7; 57:27; 61:6) with formulaic invariability, finds here, in p. 26a, line 14 (= 16) and 27a, line 28f. (= 18), its verbatim model, namely in a Jewish report that talks about ܝܫܘܥ ܒܪ ܡܪܝܡ *(Yesū' bar Maryam)* whom the Christians designated as ܡܫܝܚܐ [*masīḥā*] "the Christ" and whom they worshipped as God. Moreover, when, in p. 13a, line 12f., a Jewish statement, this time itself, abbreviatingly, referring to Jesus as "Christ," speaks of ܝܫܘܥ ܡܫܝܚܐ ܒܪ ܡܪܝܡ [*Yesū' masīḥā bar Maryam*] "Jesus Christ, son of Mary," then this has its parallel, no less strikingly pointing in the same direction, in the statement in the verse Q 4:156 [4:157] that the Jews boast of having killed *al-masīḥa 'Īsā bna Maryama* "the Christ, 'Īsā, son of Maryam." When, on p. 13a, l. 12f. ; 22b, l. 17 (= XIV); 27a, l. 20ff. (= CXVII), the Jewish persecutor asks the Christian believers to admit that Jesus ܒܪܢܫܐ ܡܝܘܬܐ ܐܝܟ ܟܠܢܫ [*barnāšā mywt' ayḵ klnš*] is "a mortal human being like everyone," then this corresponds with the—almost *verbatim* identically expressed—notion uttered in the verse Q 3:52 [3:59] that *maṯala 'Īsā inda Allāhi maṯli Ādama* "'Īsa is, before

God, exactly like Adam," that is, 'Īsā is man (= like any human being). Also, it can hardly be denied that there seems to be a, at least a formal, connection between the formulation of the Jewish repudiation of the doctrine of the divinity of Christ quoted above and and the assurance of Muḥammad concerning his own person which occurs twice, identically put, in the Qur'ān (18:110 and 41:5 [41:6]): *innamā anā bašarun miṯlakum*, "Behold, I am only a human being, like you" or the (in 3:138 [3:144] and 39:31f. [39:30f.]) expressed prediction of his death, and other Qur'ānic passages which declare that Muḥammad is nothing but a man. And when, in 5:116, Jesus is said to be asked by God whether he has taught the—misunderstood—doctrine of the Trinity and thus claimed to be God, then this sounds as though the text refutes the allegation, uttered by Jews in the "Book of the Ḥimyarites" (cf. the third passage quoted above in this footnote), that Jesus did indeed make that claim.

14 Nöldeke-Schwally I, 7, as a piece of evidence of the statement which, put so generally, hardly puts things in their proper light, "that also principal clauses that are common to both Islam and Christianity, have a 'Jewish tinge.'"

15 The possibility of a very great antiquity of 73:1–11 is naturally not at all compromised by the most obviously, even certainly quite late, Medinan origin of the peculiar, long, unrhymed concluding passage of the Surah (= Q 73:20). Whereas the early, principal part of the Surah is characterized by the strictest, most uniform rhyme on *ilā* and the address to Muḥammad, the verses 12–19 also seem to be younger, if still from the early-Meccan or, at the latest, middle-Meccan period. They are rather impurely rhymed and address, in the verses 15–17, a crowd that refuses to believe in the announcement of the Last Judgement; it is not even clear whether this passage is consistent in itself or, rather, combined of several smaller elements of, in the verses 12 ff. and 17 ff, parallel content.

16 On the one hand, the expression vaguely reminds one (which points, should this interpretation be correct, to a certain intentionality [from the part of Muḥammad]) of the god of the morning star עתתר שרקן [sic! Read rather *ʿṯtr s*^{2}*rqn* "Athtar Shāriqān'], the "oriental" *Attar* of numerous South Arabian inscriptions, and his occidental counterpart; this counterpart would be the god of the evening star, as we can conclude with some certainty from the model of the Sun cultists of Edessa who, according to Iamblichus Chalkidensis quoted in Julian [ruled 361–363] (*Oratio* IV 150c), worshipped the couple Ἄζιζος (='Aziz) and Μόνιμος (=Mun'im) [i.e., the morning star and the evening star] as attendants of Helios.

On the other hand, the expression also very strongly reminds one of the מִמִּזְרַח-שֶׁמֶשׁ (וְ)עַד-מְבוֹאוֹ [*mimmizraḥ-šemeš [wə-]ʿaḏ-məḇō'ô*] "from the place of the rising of the sun (and) unto the place of its setting" from Ps. 113 (112):3 and its parallel, Is. 59:19. The Arabic expression seems like a circumlocution for the "God of heaven" which appears, judging from the records of the Book of Ezra (1:2; 5:12; 6:10; 7:12; 7:23) and the beginning of the memoirs of Nehemiah (1:4f.; 2:4) as well as the Elephantine Papyri, to have been the official denotation for Yahweh in the Persian era; on the tendentious relation of this name to Ahura Mazda, or to the general non-Jewish notion of the God of heaven, cf. Ed. Meyer, *Geschichte des Altertums* IV [History of Antiquity] (Stuttgart, 1944) 161; pp. 205 f.

17 *Šahida Allāhu annahu lā ilāha illā huwa* "God bears witness that there is no God except him." The formula is repeated directly afterward, apparently conceived as in the mouths of the "angels and possessors of knowledge."

18 Cf. A. Baumstark, the article cited in Fn. 8, *ZDMG*, N. F. 14, especially pp. 91–96; also cf. the dissertation of C. Peters.

19 A. Baumstark, "Arabische Übersetzung eines altsyrischen Evangelientextes und die Sure 21,105 zitierte Psalmübersetzung," *Oriens Christianus 3, 9* (1934), 165–188 [Arabic Translation of an Old-Syriac Gospel Text and the Psalm Translation quoted in Surah 21,105, in: present volume].

20 An, at least indirect, Greek vorlage of this variant must have been involved, as is indicated by the Latin *omnipotens* that must render a Greek παντοκράτωρ. In the younger Aramaic text, brought to light by Ad. Neubauer in *The Book of Tobit. A Chaldee text from a unique Ms. in the Bodleian Library with other rabbinical texts, English translations and the Itala* (Oxford, 1878), 3–16, chapter 13 is missing. The Old Latin text which is also involved in Hieronymus' translation renders, in this passage (Neubauer, p. LXXXVII), the normal Greek text, which latter is probably also the basis of the greatly abbreviated wording in the 1542 Hebrew revision edited by Seb. Münster (ibid. p. 349. 17 f.—LXIII).

21 A. Baumstark, *Die Messe im Morgenland* (Kempten and Munich, 1906) 33. More particularized now in: A. Baumstark, *Liturgie comparée. Conférences faite au prieuré d'Amay.* Édition refondue. (Chevetogne, 1939) 12, [There is also a later version: 3ème édition revue par Bernard Botte. Ed. de Chevetogne, Chevetogne 1953, and the English edition: F. L. Cross, A. R. Morsbray and Co., eds., *Comparative Liturgy*, revised by B. Botte (London, 1958), where I also already pointed out the connection to Samaritan liturgy, to be dealt with further

22 W. Bousset, "Eine jüdische Gebetssammlung im 7. Buch der Apostol. Konstutionen" [A Jewish Prayer Collection in the 7th Book of the Apostolic Constitutions], *Nachrichten von der Königlichen Gesellschaft der Wissenschaften zu Göttingen. Philologisch-historische Klasse aus dem Jahre 1915* (Berlin, 1916), pp. 435–489.

23 Besides the normal text of the Jewish-Hellenistic synagogal morning prayer and, written behind 36,4, the special text for the sabbath morning prayer, the Jewish document on which those chapters of the 7th book are based seems to have contained, written behind 37:24 and 38:2 respectively, inserts for fast days, for Purim and for Hanukkah. This, like the closer connections to post-Mishnaic Jewish liturgy in general, was not yet recognized by Bousset. To the connections to post-Mishnaic Jewish liturgy—of which I became clearly aware during the first years of World War I and independently of Kahle,—refer also the pencil notations from the hand of P. Kahle in a copy of Lagarde's edition of the Constitutions in possession of the Oriental Seminar of the University of Bonn.

24 Lacking here, compared to the text of the Septuagint, are—apart from a second θεός which is extant in some Septuagint manuscripts but is perhaps nothing but a dittography—after ὁ θεός σου the words οὗτος θεός (in 4,39) or οὗτος θεός ἔστιν respectively (in 4,35). [The text of the Saptuagint reads: καὶ γνώσῃ σήμερον καὶ ἐπιστραφήσῃ τῇ διανοίᾳ ὅτι Κύριος ὁ Θεός σου οὗτος Θεὸς ἐν τῷ οὐρανῷ ἄνω καὶ ἐπὶ τῆς γῆς κάτω, καὶ οὐκ ἔστιν ἔτι πλὴν αὐτοῦ].

25 Apart from the οὗτος θεός (ἔστιν) just mentioned [cf. previous footnote], the difference concerns mainly the personal pronoun of the preceding ὁ θεός σου.

26 The σου οὗτος θεός (ἔστιν) probably traces back to the Hebrew variant of a אֱלֹהֶיךָ הוּא [*'ĕlōhek̲ā hū'*] "your God (is) he," inserted before הָאֱלֹהִים [*hā'ĕlōhīm*] "the God" (so that the passage read "in heaven etc. is your God). In this, possibly original, wording, the two passages [Dt. 4:35 and 4:39]—and, if we assume that it is to be read as two nominal clauses, also Deuteronomy 6:4—would make a declaration on two things: on the special relationship of Yahweh to Israel as to his being *Israel's* God, and on his absolute one-ness. To take, in either case, nothing but a "monolatric" meaning from the text would have to remain restricted to an "unbiased science" thoroughly committed to very clear premises.

27 It is, of course, still possible that the Greek version itself was, in turn, based on an Aramaic or Hebrew text.

28 A. E. Cowley, *The Samaritan Legacy* (Oxford, 1909) pp. 136, 188, 185, 253, 292, 396, 452–457, 462, 504, 511, 519, 532, 534, 552.

29 Ibid. pp. 18–35, 38 f., 83, 95, 127, 201, 272, 461f.

30 Ibid. pp. 267, 396, 435, 483.

31 Ibid. pp. 3, 7, 39–48, 77, 82, 105, 124, 126, 315 f., twice: p. 87.

32 Ibid. pp. 83f., in a "prayer" of Marqa. Also [repeated] on its own, in the middle of a prayer within an, again, specifically doxological passage, p. 5.

33 Ibid. p. 4.

34 Ibid. p. 101, in a prayer of the liturgy of the Sabbath that opens Eastertide, p. 354 in a prayer of the Pentecostal liturgy.

35 Ibid. p. 101, at the beginning of the same prayer for the above-mentioned [cf. previous footnote] sabbath.

36 Ad. Brüll, *Das samaritanische Targum zum Pentateuch. Zum erstenmale in hebräischer Quadratschrift nebst einem Anhange textkritischen Inhaltes herausgegeben.* [The Samaritan Targum to the Pentateuch. Edited for the first time in Hebrew Square Script with an Appendix of Text-Critical Content] (Frankfurt am Main, 1875).

37 In Dt. 4:35, the Samaritan Targum emphatically expresses God's one-ness in *verbatim* congruence with the Hebrew urtext; at the end of 4,39, the עוֹד ['ōd̲] "yet another" of the Hebrew urtext is extant but is not expanded by an additional element.

38 The said Samaritan Aramaic Creed formula is apparently composed of the first three words of the second half of the extensive formulation extant in the "Prayer of Joshua" [i.e., *lēt̲ 'ĕlāh 'ellā*—not is there a God except], and of the last word of the profession of faith taken from Deuteronomy 6:4 [i.e., *'eḥād̲*—one]. That the Creed formula taken from Dt. 6:4, in this function, was not unknown to the Samaritans can be deduced from the ending of a "Prayer of Moses" (see Cowley, loc. cit. 3) where the Hebrew text of the Creed (from the first "Yahweh" on [i.e., without the "Hear, Israel]) is written behind the normal Aramaic formula ["Not is there a God except one"] which, in this case, is composed of the Hebrew word אֵין [*'ēn*] "There is not" and the other words in Aramaic.

39 Cowley, loc. cit. 3, and also in J. Rosenberg, *Lehrbuch der samaritanischen Sprache und Literatur* [Primer of Samaritan Language and Literature] (Vienna-Leipzig, no date), 109.

40 It is not certain when exactly this took place. The determination depends on whether one abides by the historical dependability of the report in [Flavius] Josephus' *Antiquities* [*of the Jews*] XI, 7, 2ff.—as does, e. g., K. F. Lehmann-Haupt, *Israel: Seine Entwicklung im Rahmen der Weltgeschichte* [Israel: Its Development in the Context of World History] (Tübingen, 1911), 173 f.—or whether one believes with Ed. Meyer, loc. cit., 201, that we have to shift the assumed time of that process from the time of Nehemiah to, rather, the time of Alexander the Great [356–324 BC].

41 Since among the four languages in which the Torah, according to the *Sifre*, had been given to Israel—i.e., obviously the languages which its author knew—Arabic is mentioned next to Hebrew, Greek and Aramaic, as the third element of the list even before Aramaic.

42 E. Algermissen, *Die Penteuchzitate Ibn Hazms: Ein Beitrag zur Geschichte der arabischen Bibelübersetzung* [The Pentateuch quotations of Ibn Hazm. An Essay on the History of Arabic Bible Translation.] (Münster [Westphalia], 1933).

43 Several different Christian denominations from different regions tried, later, to clear their path to the cradle of Islam: From the North it was, from the Lakhmid empire, the Nestorian denomination, and from the Ghassanid empire the Monophysites; from the South, perhaps both; and from Palestine, it was Chalcedonian orthodoxy.—Scholars used, in addition to that, to (possibly too generously) assume older Jewish-Christian and Gnostic sects of all kinds which, spread all across Arabia, could have played a role in Islam's rise. Be that as it may, it is indeed highly remarkable that the "Arab" Μονοΐμος, whose Gnostic teaching is thoroughly treated in Hippolytus' *Philosophumena* VII 12/5; X 17 around the middle of the 3rd century, seems in fact to have been bearer of the good Arabic name *Mun'aimu*.

44 How deeply Judaism may have had penetrated into Arabia already in Early Christian times can be deduced neither from the mention of the Ἄραβες ["Arabs"] in the report on the Pentecostal miracle in Acts 2,11 which is the oldest evidence of Arab Judaism or proselytism, nor from the assertion of the Apostle Paul in Galatians 1:17 that he had gone to "Arabia" immediately after his Damascus experience. However, considering the Jewish capacity "to reconcile themselves to all situations and to draw some advantage from them" so as to "get on in the world," which Ed. Meyer (loc. cit. 203), certainly rightly, assumes already for the early postexilic time, it would not be surprising if there had been, even relatively very early, among others, also a Jewish trading colony—for instance in Taima where a heathen, Aramaic speaking population is attested as early as the 5th century BC by the well-known inscription CIS II, 113 (= G. A. Cooke, *A Text-Book of North Semitic Inscriptions* (Oxford, 1903) # 69).

Part 5

Christoph Luxenberg

An Introduction to, and a Bibliography of, Works by and about Christoph Luxenberg

Ibn Warraq

Fa-mā minkum aḥadin ʿanhu ḥāǧizīna
Surah 69:47, is also odd; such constructions occur quite often in Syriac, however.

Theodor Nöldeke, *Zur Sprache des Korāns*[1]

1. Christoph Luxenberg's Theory and Its Reactions

Christoph Luxenberg is a scholar who has been engaged in research and teaching in Germany for many years, specializing in Semitic philology. He taught not only Classical Arabic, but also several vernaculars or dialects, and Syriac in German universities. His years of teaching, when he adopted what could be called a comparative study of the two languages, gave him a deeper understanding of Arabic and Syriac, an understanding that went beyond grammars and dictionaries. Luxenberg's doctoral thesis concerned a Syriac manuscript of the eight and ninth century CE that refers to earlier texts of the fifth and sixth centuries. He discussed homilies, among them the homily of Jacob of Sarug. He was able to give a fuller description, than hitherto, of the manuscript, having identifed the texts of the Syriac with the help of the original Greek. Luxenberg realised that often the translation of the Greek into Syriac was very literal, and difficult to comprehend. He had to constantly compare the Syriac to the original Greek, when extant, to understand or clarify the Syriac translation, thereby acquiring important insights that led him to develop a method that he was able to apply, with spectacular results, to the understanding of the opaque parts of the Koran. In the Syriac manuscript, his task was to identify the fragments and their authors, hitherto unknown, for which he needed to order an unedited Greek manucript from Cambridge, England. One of the original Greek texts was lost, but Luxenberg was able to identify the fragments in the Syriac manuscript as the work of Severus of Antioch, on the basis of their theological subject matter. A later discovery in Damascus, by a Jesuit scholar from Rome, of a manuscript confirmed Luxenberg's conjecture of the authorship of the fragments in the Syriac manuscript.

Luxenberg also taught several other subjects, such as medieval history (the Crusades) and German literature and language to foreigners, and he often provided translation services (Arabic to German and vice versa). Indeed it was his experience in these translations that further opened his eyes to the difficulties that any serious translator between languages encounters.

The revolutionary works of Günter Lüling[2] and John Wansbrough[3] were met with, not just incomprehension, incredulity, and polite, intellectual disagreement but astonishing hostility, and ad hominem attacks that were a disgrace to the profession, and which, in the case of Lüling, destroyed a career. Unfortunately, the profession continues to disgrace itself, particularly in its initial reaction to the iconoclastic book, and the handful of essays, of Christoph Luxenberg. Two distinguished researchers in the field of Koranic Studies, Claude Gilliot and Jan van Reeth, very courageously called attention to the scandalous review that François de Blois wrote of Luxenberg's book. Gilliot referred to de Blois' critique in a footnote:

> Outre le fait que ce compte rendu déforme souvent la pensée de Luxenberg, il contient des allégations sur l'origine ethnico-religieuse de l'auteur qui sont à la limite du supportable (p. 96–7), et pour lesquelles le proverbe vaut qui dit: "si tu veux tuer ton chien, dis qu'il a la gale!"[4] [Apart from the fact that this article often distorts the thoughts of Luxenberg, it also contains allegations about the ethnic and religious background of the author (i.e., Luxenberg) which are hardly bearable (p. 96–7), and to which the proverb applies: "If you want to kill your dog, say he's got scabies"!]

Indeed, when seeking to harm someone, you can often do so with calumny, that is, false and malicious misrepresentation of the words of others calculated to injure their reputation, in brief, slander. Whereas Van Reeth wrote,

> Pendant de longues années, depuis la deuxième Guerre Mondiale, les études coraniques ont stagné, répétant avec une lueur de critique historique la tradition musulmane (la *Sīrat al-Nabī* et les *ḥadīṯ*-s) qui décrit la révélation de l'islam d'une façon légendaire. Cette présentation des faits est maintenant mise au défi, ce qui explique sans doute certaines réactions. Une des plus virulentes recensions du livre de Luxenberg est celle de François de Blois. À la fin, sa critique devient même malveillante et personelle; en outre, certaines de ses remarques nous paraissent dénuées de fondement. Ainsi, pour ne donner qu'un exemple, concernant le terme خليفه , *ḫalīfah* que Luxenberg met en rapport avec le mot syriaque ܚܠܝܦܐ, de Blois remarque: *no reason is given why, in this "phonetic transcription," the Aramaic laryngeal h̲ is not "transcribed" by the phonetically identical Arabic laryngeal h̲ but by x.* Or, l'emprunt de mots à une langue étrangère ne suit pas nécessairement les lois phonétiques; on rend les sons tels qu'on les entend, indépendamment de la dérivation étymologique correcte; aussi, dans sa nouvelle édition, Luxenberg met le doigt sur un *Sprachhistorischer Irrtum* de certains de ses critiques, qui considèrent l'arabe comme plus ancien que que l'araméen.[5] [For many years, since WW II, Koranic Studies had been stagnating, repeating with a glimpse of

historical criticism the tenets of Islamic tradition (the *Sīrat al-Nabī* and the *ḥadīṯ*-s), which describes the revelation of Islam in a legendary manner. This presentation of facts has now been challenged, which undoubtedly explains certain reactions. One of the fiercest reviews of Luxenberg's book is the one written by François de Blois. At the end, his criticism becomes wicked and personal; moreoever, some of his remarks show an apparent lack of foundation. Thus, to adduce an example, Luxenberg connects the term خليفه *ḫalīfah* with the Syriac word ܚܠܝܦܐ [translator's note: *ḥlīp̄ā*], which is commented as follows by de Blois: *no reason is given why, in this "phonetic transcription," the Aramaic laryngeal h̲ is not "transcribed" by the phonetically identical Arabic laryngeal h̲ but by x.* Well, the borrowing of words from a foreign language does not necessarily follow phonetic rules; one renders words as one hears them, irrespective of their correct etymological derivation; furthermore, in the new edition [of his book], Luxenberg points out the *Sprachhistorischer Irrtum* [translator's note: historical linguistic mistake] of some of his critiques [brought forward against him], which consider the Arabic language as older than Aramaic.]

Now, it is true that borrowings do not always follow phonetic rules, the English word ***hubris*** going back to Greek *hybris* (as which it was adopted into German), whereas the Greek prefix *hyper-* does not appear in English as ***huper-***, but as *hyper-*. So why were the English not able to adopt the first example as "hybris"?

Regarding Arabic *ḫalīfa* and its Syriac equivalent *ḥlīp̄-ā*, the case is more complicated: First of all, the Arabic word designates a male, but has a feminine ending *-a*, which is unique among the Semitic languages. Luxenberg's explanation is that the only *seeming* feminine ending *-a* is in fact the Syriac definite article *-ā*, the root of the word being *ḥlīp̄-*. So the problem remains why the Syriac *ḥ* was adopted as an Arabic *ḫ*.

At this point we have to consider not only the sounds of the languages involved, but also the *phoneme systems*, phonemes being abstract units of distinctive elements of a pronunciation system. In modern English, for example, we can distinguish words with the consonants *n* and *ng*, their phonetic symbols being [n] and [ŋ], as, for example, in the words t*hing* and *thin*. Such a pair of words is called a *minimal pair*. To establish the phoneme system of a language, we have to find minimal pairs.

In Italian, however, the situation is different. The two sounds [n] and [ŋ] do appear, pronounced exactly as in English, as, for example, in the word *mano* and the name *Franco* [fraŋko], but you cannot find a minimal pair distinguished only by these two sounds. Instead, there is a rule: whenever the letter *n* is followed by a *c* [k] or a *g* [g], it is pronounced [ŋ]. Therefore, we can state that in Italian we have one phoneme /n/ (a linguist's way to write phonemes) with two allophones (=variants) [n] and [ŋ], *depending on their position*. In English, the sounds [n] and [ŋ] belong to two different phonemes /n/ and /ŋ/. An English native speaker might now assume that such a merely "theoretical" difference is negligeable and that it should not be too difficult for an Italian to pronounce an English word with *ng*, but this is not the case: "swing" is an English designation for a musical style that is used in Italian as well, but most Italians do not pronounce the *ng* correctly. As the sound [ŋ] in their mother tongue only appears before a *g* or a *c*, they will tend to insert a *g* after the [ŋ], which automatically leads to another problem: In Italian, words do not end in consonant clusters. Therefore, many speakers will add a vowel, at least a short one, their pronunciation resulting in something like [swiŋgᵊ].

In the relationship between Arabic and Aramaic, the situation is very similar: In Arabic we have three phonemes usually transliterated as *ḫ*, *ḥ*, and *k*, in phonetic script: *ḫ* – /x/, *ḥ* – /ħ/, and *k* – /k/. The same sounds appear in Aramaic, but here they belong to only two phonemes: *k* – /k/ and *ḥ* – /ħ/. The phoneme /k/ in Aramaic, as in the Masoretic pronunciation of Hebrew, was pronounced as a [k], for example, in initial position, and as a [x] (i.e., the sound of "ch" in *Lo<u>ch</u> Ness*) in most other positions, for example, between vowels. Moreover, in many cases the etymological equivalent of words that in Arabic have a *ḫ* have a *ḥ* in Aramaic, for example, the word for *brother*: Arabic *aḫ*, Aramaic *aḥ(-ā)*.

Luxenberg in one of his publications pointed out that in the Eastern Aramaic dialect the "*ḥ* is pronouned *ḫ* (often transliterated as 'kh' or 'x')."[6] Phonetically, this is not very surprising, as the sound [x] is already there in the language (albeit belonging to another phoneme), and the articulation of [ħ] and [x] is not very different—both are voiceless fricatives, [ħ] is pharyngeal and [x] velar. Moreover, at least in initial position (e.g., in the word *ḥlīp̄ā*), this sound shift does not affect the phoneme structure of the language and does not lead to misunderstandings, as their are no words distinguished by the sounds [ħ] and [x]; that is, even if *ḥlīp̄ā* is pronounced [xliːfaː] instead of [ħliːfaː] in the East, the form remains unambiguous.

For Arabic ears, however, the pronunciation [xliːfaː] instead of [ħliːfaː] will lead to a different phonemic interpretation of the word: it will be adopted with a *ḫ* [x] as its first consonant, and—as Arabic words never start with a consonant cluster—a vowel ("a") will be inserted. Moreover, the definite article *-ā* will be interpreted as the (normally feminine ending) *-a*, thus the resulting form is: *ḫalīfa* – خليفة.

Taking the phonological and etymological background of Arabic and Aramaic into consideration, no unbiased phonetician or general linguist would be surprised by an Arabic form *ḫalīfa* going back to a Syriac form *ḥlīp̄ā*. But the standards and achievements of other disciplines, be they historical, linguistic, or philological, have hardly ever bothered scholars from the field of Koranic Studies!

Given that thirteen years after its publication Luxenberg's work forges on, and continues to bear fruit in the form of articles by an ever-growing group of scholars inspired by his methodology, perhaps another fitting proverb would be one from the Middle East: "The Caravan passes, and a few mangy dogs bark."

Jan van Reeth, who teaches the History of Religions, Ancient Philosophy, and Islamic Theology at the Faculty for Comparative Study of Religions (Antwerp), has written several articles that touch on Luxenberg's work.[7] In the article cited above, Van Reeth finds much of value in Luxenberg's study, which he calls "groundbreaking," though he would not necessarily endorse all of Luxenberg's new Syro-Aramaic readings. Van Reeth, with his unequaled knowledge of the history of Christianity, in general, and Syriac Christianity, in particular, builds on Luxenberg's thesis concerning the Koranic descriptions of Paradise to produce a totally convincing account of the sources of the entire tradition. Where Luxenberg goes back to St. Ephrem, Van Reeth's starting point is two Biblical passages in Genesis and Psalms that were then "combined, and glossed, giving rise to an apocalyptic vision in the book of Enoch 10:19."

Then comes the second Book of Baruch 29:5–6, the vision reaching its climax in the ecstatic words of Papias, Bishop of Hierapolis, with the *Hymns of Paradise* of St. Ephrem filling in the gaps and closing the story. Finally, Van Reeth describes Luxenberg's analysis of the Koranic *immortal ephebes* as brilliant. Van Reeth concludes that

> Luxenberg's method thus proves to be productive, provided that we compare the restored Qur'ānic text with its Christian sources. Only then may we hope to arrive at the true meaning of the prophetic text.[8]

In another article,[9] Van Reeth refers to Luxenberg's new reading of the inscriptions in the Dome of the Rock, Jerusalem, and agrees with him that

> the name Muḥammad may very well be a title, given to the Prophet by his already *ḥanafī* family, pointing to a prophetic function, similar to that of the "first" Paraclete Jesus, without saying however that the Prophet Muḥammad would be an entirely fictitious, invented personality. There is no doubt in my mind, indeed, that he has been an actual living, historical person. All the elaboration in that sense, such as those of Ohlig, K.-H., "Vom Muḥammad Jesus zum Propheten der Araber: Die Historisierung eines christologischen Prädikats," in idem, ed., *Der frühe Islam: Eine historisch-kritische Rekonstruktion anhand zeitgenössischer Quellen*, pp. 327–76 (Berlin, 2007), are to be totally

> rejected: they are not a "historisch-kritische Rekonstruktion," but unfortunately only a mere *construction* of historical phanstasy. It is to be deplored that Luxenberg has been led astray by all this.

Though he does *hint* that Muhammad, the Prophet of Islam, *may* only be a symbolic figure, Luxenberg is far from being dogmatic on this issue, pointing out that the historicity of Muhammad is "a task for the historians."[10] Luxenberg does not claim to be a historian, and he is very careful in his choice of words:

> The first name of his father, "ʿAbd Allāh," which may in fact be similarly symbolic, reflecting the expression "servant of God" from the Dome of the Rock, helps to suggest this latter possibility.[11]

"*May*," "helps to *suggest*," "*possibility*" are not the words of a dogmatist or an absolutist. More decisively, in an interview with Christoph Burgmer, Luxenberg admits, "I would not go so far as to say that Muḥammad and the Qurʾān never existed."[12] And, of course, Luxenberg is never "led" by anyone, astray or otherwise. The conclusions that he has arrived at are a result of his own revolutionary research—he is very much his own man. That was Luxenberg's position in approximately 2005.

By contrast, what should we make of the absolute certainty of Van Reeth himself, that Muḥammad did exist: "There is no doubt in my mind, indeed, that he has been an actual living, historical person." Where does the burden of proof lie?

And yet, Luxenberg's subsequent philological enquiries, conducted and reported on after his new reading of the inscriptions at the Dome of the Rock, have *indeed* led him to a far more skeptical position on the question of the historicity of Muhammad and all the traditional accounts of the redaction of the Koran. For Luxenberg, philology helps or can help to recover the historical truth, in the same way that archeology does. Thus, his skepticism is hardly surprising for a scholar who feels he has managed to destroy the conventional historical interpretation of various "terms" in the Koran: *Muhammad* is a title, and it does not refer to a Prophet of the Arabs; *ʿAbd Allah* is not the putative name of the father of the Prophet, but also a title derived from the inscriptions at the Dome of the Rock; *Bakka* is not the alternative name for the City of Mecca;[13] the so-called Battle of *Badr* never took place, and the term *badr* has been misread;[14] the term *quraysh* in the Koran has nothing whatsoever to do with a tribe called the *Quraysh*; "the year of the elephant" has nothing to do with the year of the Prophet's birth, or with elephants; *ʿArafāt* (Surah 2:198) is not a place name but means "benefaction;"[15] and the *kaʿba* is not the *Kaʿba* of Islamic tradition.[16] Just what is left of Islam after this scholarly hurricane?

Since his important book *Exégèse, langue et théologie: L'exégèse coranique de Ṭabarī* appeared in 1990, Claude Gilliot, professor emeritus at the University of Provence, Aix-en-Provence, France, has established himself as one of the foremost authorities on the Koran in the West. Gilliot has written appreciatively of Luxenberg's work in a number of articles,[17] including one, cowritten with his colleague Pierre Larcher, for the *Encyclopaedia of the Qur'ān*,[18] of which he was associate editor. Gilliot and Larcher wrote,

> Of course, Luxenberg's work must be discussed by Semitists and Islamicists, and poses other complicated problems, e.g., on the history of the redaction of the Qur'ān. But some of his theses do appear convincing, at least to the present writers. For instance, Q 108 (Sūrat al-Kawthar), a text which has little meaning for a normal reader, and which is also a *crux interpretum* for the Islamic exegetes, has been convincingly deciphered by Luxenberg. . . . The method of Luxenberg applied to passages of the Qur'ān which are particularly obscure cannot be brushed aside by mere repetition of the Nöldeke/Spitaler thesis, or, as some would say, dogma. . . . It must be examined seriously. From a linguistic point of view the undertaking of Luxenberg is one of the most interesting. It will provoke in some Islamic circles the same emotion as did the hypothesis of Vollers formerly, because it amounts to seeing in the Qur'ān a kind of palimpsest. Such hypotheses, and the reactions they generate, push scholarship on the language and style of the Qur'ān continually to examine and question its acknowledged (and implicit) premises.[19]

Of course, Gilliot would not necessarily accept all of Luxenberg's new readings. Luxenberg's fecundity inspires skepticism, and leaves Gilliot wondering if there is something mechanical in his later productions:

> It should be clear to the reader that it is not necessary to follow either Lüling (pre-Islamic Arabic Christian hymns), or Luxenberg (entire passages of the Meccan Qur'ān being mere palimpsests of Syriac primitive text) in their systematic, sometimes probably too automatic ways of proceeding, if we consider that a part of their point of departure and some of their ideas have some *fundamentum in re*, or rather a certain basis in the Qur'ānic text itself, in the Islamic tradition, and in the cultural environment in which the Qur'ān was born.[20]

Federico Corriente, a Semitist and lecturer in Arabic literature at the University of Zaragoza, has written a number of highly regarded and discussed articles on Arabic linguistics and the Arabic of the Koran.[21] In his review of Luxenberg,[22] Corriente lauds Luxenberg's grasp of Syriac and Classical Arabic, writing,

> We must say here and now that [Luxenberg] appears to be an undoubtedly seasoned scholar, well at home in Syriac language and literature, also endowed with a remarkable command of Classical Arabic and versed in the Qur'anic sciences.

Corriente also finds much to praise in Luxenberg's study, accepting a certain number of the latter's new readings,

> among the cases in which Luxenberg's proposals may be considered as positive contributions to the interpretation of the Qur'anic text and to the present levels of knowledge of the Arabic language are some terms of Aramaic origin to be added to those listed by Jeffery, such as *qayyūm* "everlasting" (p. 44) in 2:255, 3:2 and 20:111, *musaḫḫarāt* (pp. 211–213), to be understood as Syriac *mšawḥrāt* "held") in 16:79, *šarrikhum* in 17:64 (pp. 219–220, "entrap them," better than *šārikhum* "share with them"), *kawṯar* in 108:1 (p. 273, plausibly interpreted as Syriac *kūṯārā* "steadiness"; cf. also calques like *baqiyyah* "gain" in 11:86, pp. 200–201, where the uncommon meaning in Arabic reflects the semantics of Syriac *yutrānā*), as well as other instances in which his surmise of misreading of the consonantal skeleton provides an alternative interpretation which may be preferable to the traditional one (e.g., p. 60–61, *iḏḏāka* "they said then," vs. *āḏannāka* "we protest to Thee" in 41:47, pp. 138–139, *bāraknā ʿalayhimā* "We blessed them," better as *taraknā* in 37:78–9, pp. 170–171, *arattu an uġayyibahā* "I wanted to hide it," better than *uʿayyibahā* "to damage it" in 18:79, p. 220, *ġayra nāẓirīna ināṭahu* "not looking to his wives." better than *ināhu* "his time" in 33:53), plus a host of other cases where each scholar may be more or less prone to accept the presence of Syrianisms, depending on his position regarding the rather complex issues of interference between Semitic languages and degree of authenticity of the received Qur'anic text.

However, Corriente terminates his review on a negative note (to which I shall return), but even then he manages to squeeze in something positive:

> This rather negative judgment on his enterprise does not detract a bit from his merit as a very knowledgeable scholar endowed with an active and provocative mind, who has devoted considerable time and effort in an interesting attempt to cast light on an abstruse subject, surrounded by scientific and other perils. As stated above, he appears to have hit the mark at times, although his personal convictions and professional preferences have not contributed to keep him in the middle of the road or let him avail himself of all the extant data, even those which he probably knows well.[23]

Corriente's negative conclusion is that

> Luxenberg's plea for an interpretation of dark passages of the Qur'ān based upon the hypothesis of a misread or misinterpreted Syriac *vorlage* of its texts is not convincing in most cases, because the philological arguments wielded by

> him in order to prove his case do not have the necessary weight to counteract the previous more traditional views on this topic, grounded as they are on solid historical and socio-linguistic data.

Here we have Corriente's deficiencies as a reviewer—an astonishingly naïve faith in "traditional views," and his absolute certainty in the "solid historical and socio-linguistic data." Credulity, as P. R. Davis once said, does not become a historian. That is why, like many philologists, Corriente is not a historian, and lacks the necessary skepticism of the sources that is the hallmark of the true historian, and is, in fact, a basic methodological requirement. In his discussion of Luxenberg's proposal concerning Mecca, Corriente refers to "Ptolemy's famous report, the original name of that town was Macoraba, i.e., South Arabian *mkrb* 'shrine.'" Corriente's seems unaware of Patricia Crone's decisive refutation of the notion that *Macoraba* was Mecca:

> The plain truth is that the name of Macoraba has nothing to do with that of Mecca, and that location indicated by Ptolemy for Macoraba in no way dictates identification of the two.[24]

In note 2, Corriente tells us with supreme confidence that Vollers has been refuted:

> As purported by K. Vollers, *Volkssprache und Schriftsprache im alten Arabien* (Strassburg, 1906), whose theory has been repeatedly refuted by scholars since Th. Nöldeke, *Neue Beiträge zur semitischen Sprachwissenschaft* (Strassburg, 1910) on account of both internal and historical grounds, as reported by Luxenberg himself (p. 4) who, nevertheless, appears to accept it.

He has not been refuted. On the contrary, as Jonathan Owens has argued recently, Nöldeke's arguments against Vollers are

> surprisingly weak for a scholar of his stature. . . . Rather than assume an air of caution, however, Nöldeke displayed a zealousness in rejecting Vollers's thesis which carried him beyond the bounds of measured academic judgment.[25]

Owens goes on to point out some of Vollers's insights that are still relevant.

Corriente evidently accepts without a murmur of doubt the entire traditional Islamic account of the rise of Islam, including the unexamined tales of the dialects of the Hijaz, pre-Islamic poetry, the language of the Quraysh, the oral transmission of the Koran, the role of Muhammad in the creation of the Koran, and even the mythic memories of the ancient Arabs. All our sources are dated two hundred years after the putative events, and *cannot*, I repeat, *cannot be the basis of a sound historical reconstruction.* Scholars such as John Wansbrough, Andrew Rippin, Patricia Crone, Michael Cook, Martin Hinds,

Yehuda Nevo, and Judy Koren, among others, have been chipping away at this traditional picture. Skepticism of the oral tradition has been expressed by Fritz Krenkow, Gerd-R. Puin, Günter Lüling, and more recently Fred Donner. His criticisms of Luxenberg rely solely on what Corriente naively takes to be "trustworthy," "undeniable fact[s]," or "facts generally accepted as historical and recorded in the works of unimpeachable authors that cannot be contradicted without a heavy burden of proof," or "solid historical and socio-linguistic data" and not on philological arguments. Corriente innocently, once again, refers to Arabic grammars and dictionaries as though that should settle the matter. But these dictionaries and grammars are all eighth century or later productions, and they are precisely the problem, since they reflect and are solidly based on the erroneous readings that Luxenberg is trying to correct. Corriente does not realize that even if a small percentage of Luxenberg's new readings is correct, then we have to revise the traditional accounts of the redaction of the Koran. We cannot start with traditional Islamic account as the major premise, and then proceed, rather we should look at the philological arguments and then revise the traditional account. Let us stick with the philology, wherever it may lead.

Another Semitist, Martin F. J. Baasten of Leiden describes many of Luxenberg's new readings of the Koran as "stunning,"[26] and like Gilliot, he considers Luxenberg's rereading of *Sūrat al-Kawṯar* particularly convincing:

> It must be said that many of L.'s findings are stunning indeed. In some cases he even manages to reread entire sūrahs, which, when read against their Syriac background, suddenly turn out to be coherent texts. A convincing example is L.'s treatment (pp. 269–276) of *Sūrat al-Kawṯar* (108).

Baasten also feels Luxenberg's reading of *Sūrah* 96 (*al-ʿalaq*, "the blood-clot") is the correct one, though he does take issue with some of the details:

> The same can be said for L.'s reinterpretation of *Sūrah* 96 (*al-ʿalaq*, "the blood-clot"), another challenge to both traditional and modern exegetes. The word علق *'alaq*, according to L., does not refer to a blood-clot from which God is supposed to have created man. It should rather be connected with Syriac ܥܠܘܩܐ *ʿālōqā* "sticky clay." The fact that corroborating evidence for this idea is found in the Qur'ān itself simply clinches the matter: إنا خلقنهم من طين لازب *'innā ḫalaqnāhum min ṭīn lāzib* "We created them of sticky clay" (Q 37:11). Even though L. is at his most convincing here, one is inclined to disagree with some of his conclusions, such as his interpretation of the last word of this sūrah, واقترب *wa-qtarib*, which he translates as "and celebrate the Eucharist!" But the verb اقترب *iqtaraba* "to draw near" cannot simply be identified, as L. does, with the form تقرّب *taqarraba*, which is actually the Christian Arabic term for celebrating the Eucharist.

Baasten is critical of some other aspects of Luxenberg's work:

> Sometimes it seems that when L. has found a pair of cognates in Syriac and Arabic, he simply declares the Arabic word to be a loan from Syriac, even when from a historical-linguistic point of view this is not plausible. Such is the case, for instance, with the root طغى *ṭaġā* and its Syriac cognate ܛܥܐ *ṭʿā*. In making such claims, however, one implicitly takes issue with major themes in historical phonology of Semitic: L. presupposes that we do not have merger of /ġ/ and /ʿ/ in Aramaic, but rather *split* of these phonemes in Arabic. While L. is entitled to such a view, a critical reader is justified in expecting an exposition on the matter.

However, Baasten's conclusion is positive:

> All in all, Luxenberg's *Syro-aramäische Lesart des Koran* contains a wealth of original ideas and interesting observations, which might indeed have major implications for our understanding of the emergence of Islam. In many instances he makes a convincing case for what he calls a "Syriac reading of the Qur'ān." His proposals often do lead to a better understanding of impenetrable Qur'ānic passages, which in itself is a major achievement and a challenge for historians of early Islam. Whether one should go along with his more far-reaching statements, on the Syriac-Arabic mixed language of Mecca or an Aramaic Urkoran, is something that further research will make clear.

The most hostile review from a recognized scholar came from Angelika Neuwirth, who concluded her joint review of Lüling and Luxenberg with these comments on the latter:

> It is striking that the alleged extent of hybridity in Qur'anic language as such does not interest Luxenberg seriously—he nowhere reflects about the actual use of that language, as limited to cultic purposes or as vernacular—hybridity merely serves as a means to de-construct the Qur'an as genuine scripture, or, phenomenologically speaking, to de-construct Islamic scripture as the transmitter's faithful rendering of what he felt to have received from a supernatural source. The Qur'an thus is presented as the translation of a Syriac text. This is an extremely pretentious hypothesis which is unfortunately relying on rather modest foundations. Luxenberg does not consider previous work in the diverse disciplines of Qur'anic studies—neither concerning the pagan heritage, nor the poetical Arabian background, nor the Jewish contacts. He takes interest neither in religio-historical nor in literary approaches to the Qur'an although his assumptions touch substantially on all these discourses. Luxenberg limits himself to a very mechanistic, positivist linguistic method without caring for theoretical considerations developed in modem linguistics. Luxenberg has the merit to have raised anew the old question of the Syriac stratum of Qur'anic textual history that had—since Mingana—been marginalised. But

> the task of a profound and reliable study of the Syriac elements of the Qur'an is still waiting to be fulfilled.

Though she does concede that "Luxenberg has the merit to have raised anew the old question of the Syriac stratum of Qur'anic textual history that had—since Mingana—been marginalised,"Neuwirth does not really engage with any of Luxenberg's detailed philological arguments. Perhaps she does not have the necessary competence in Syriac to do so. In any case, surely his work needs to be assessed on a case-by-case basis, and this is what is precisely lacking. Luxenberg is not a historian, though his findings have enormous implications for our knowledge of the rise of Islam and the redaction of the Koran.

Simon Hopkins is another reviewer who does not engage with Luxenberg's arguments. Instead, Hopkins, a distinguished Semitist, seems to think that by presenting two or three of those arguments with little or no comment or analysis, he has accomplished his duty. He does not think it is even worth going into particulars, and abdicates his scholarly obligation by telling us that "there seems little point in going into further detail."

The closest Hopkins comes to voicing an opinion is when he finds Luxenberg's explanations of the presence of *tā' marbūṭa* on masculine words "ad hoc and mechanical." Elsewhere, Hopkins describes Luxenberg's methodology as "reckless," and his philology "wayward," and accuses him of "exegetical caprice." Nowhere does he tell us where and how Luxenberg is wrong philologically.

Hopkins pretends not to understand what Luxenberg was trying to accomplish when the latter embarked on an analysis of the expression *hal yastawiyāni maṯalan* found in Surah 11:24 and 39:29. But Luxenberg is making an important point about the puzzling presence of a final *alif* in a word following an Arabic dual verb. Arab grammarians see *maṯalan* as an accusative singular. But this is problematic since one would expect an Arabic dual noun after an Arabic dual verb. Second, why is *maṯalan* in the accusative? It should be in the nominative. Third, the definite article, *al*, is missing; the *al* is necessary since two determined examples have been given. However, in Syriac a final *alif* could also designate a plural (since, apart from a few exceptions, the dual in Syriac is not usual). The interpretation of this *alif* as *tamyīz* (accusative of specification) of Arabic grammar was a later ad hoc creation precisely to explain this puzzling *alif*, the Arab grammarians being evidently unaware of the function of the final *alif* as designating a plural in Syriac. The final *alif* can also designate the definite article in Syriac. Surely, Luxenberg's new reading yields a far more coherent sentence, "Are the two examples somehow equal?" (instead of: "Are the two somehow equal as example?"). As Luxenberg explains:

> According to this, when translated into modern-day Arabic (and taking into account the Qur'ānic dual), the sentence would then read: *hal yastawiyāni l-maṯalān* (in Classical Arabic: *hal yastawī l-maṯalān*).[27]

Ironically, it is precisely this explanation of *maṯalan* that Professor Y. Tzvi Langermann finds convincing in his brief review, to which we now turn.

Perhaps the most surprising review appeared in the *American Journal of Islamic Social Sciences*—surprising for two reasons: first it was a positive review, and in an Islamic journal, whose editors are committed Muslims; and second, it was written by an Israeli professor, Y. Tzvi Langermann, Professor of Arabic at Bar Ilan University. So, we have an Israeli scholar writing a positive review in an Islamic journal! Langermann wrote:

> However tenuous, even preposterous, Luxenberg's sweeping thesis may seem, the myriad examples he adduces of problematic passages, the meaning of which is clarified when their Syro-Aramaic roots are exposed, cannot be dismissed out of hand.[28]

He then goes on to endorse Luxenberg's new reading of *al-raqim* from Surah 18:9, albeit with circumspection, since Langermann suddenly feels obliged to make allowances for his Muslim audience. Furthermore, Langermann writes:

> On the strong side, Luxenberg suggests that the final alif, which has, with great difficulty, been interpreted as an accusative in words such as *mathalan* (11:24) or *al-ḥawāyā* (6:146), can be better explained on the basis of corresponding Aramaic forms.[29]

Professor Johannes J. G. Jansen of the University of Leiden urges the scientific community in the West to take Luxenberg's work seriously without constantly worrying about the tender sensibilities of Muslims, "Christoph Luxenberg offers a startling number of repunctuations that need to be considered seriously."

Luxenberg's methodology seems to give us convincing results, and could be a fruitful approach for the analysis of the difficult passages in the Koran.

> It is not difficult to see why pious traditional Muslims might have great difficulty with Luxenberg's work. But why would non-Muslim scholars hesistate to debate his views and to applaud him for his original approach—even if he might be wrong some of the time? Are they afraid of the Elders of Mecca and their Protocols? . . . It cannot be doubted that Luxenberg's book will cause distress to many pious Muslims. That is a sad thing. But, on the other hand, it is not the duty of Western scholarship to protect the Muslim masses from spiritual distress. Moreover, nobody will dare to accuse the Ulema of not being able to protect the Muslim masses adequately against such distress. It is, then,

> to be hoped for that Christoph Luxenberg will take a look at the whole text of the Qur'ān, apply his unique method, and will soon publish his findings, that will consequently become the subject of a wide debate.[30]

Jansen discovered confirmation of one of Luxenberg's readings in some inscriptions. He wrote[31]:

> Enno Littmann, in a publication from 1940,[32] mentions three inscriptions in which Safaitic רוח *rwḥ* is used about the dead, after a vocative, "O God!" The meaning is obviously: "O God, give [them] rest." A version of Dona eis requiem?
>
> Luxenberg has suggested that Quranic *zawwağnāhum* (Q 44:54 and Q 52:20) might be a misreading for *rawwaḥnāhum*. These three Safaitic inscriptions may convince someone who has doubts about this suggestion that the reading *rawwaḥnāhum* (زَوَّجْنٰهُم > روحىهم > رَوَّحْنٰهُم) at least deserves serious consideration.
>
> Also *an-nufūsu zuwwiğat* in Q 81:7 looks improbable. Here too, a form of "to rest" seems to be much more plausible: *ruwwiḥat (زُوِّجَت > روحٮ > رُوِّحَت).*
>
> William G. Oxtoby (1968)[33] mentions Safaitic ארח *'rḥ* which, according to him, means "to give rest," a hiph'il/aph'el or form IV, Standard Arabic أراح. The context of the inscription in which *'rḥ* occurs, Oxtoby 79, is, however, different from that of the three Littmann inscriptions. Oxtoby 79 is a short inscription of ten words. It does not refer to the dead. It must refer to a herd since *r'y*, "to pasture," cf. Hebrew רעה, is used.
>
> Oxtoby also refers to C 4956[34] where Allāt is asked to grant rest to the dead. Here too we meet with an imperative, of form IV of *rwḥ*, not a form II.
>
> C 2718, on the other hand, again may show a form II of *rwH*: פהבעלסמן רוח *f-h-b'l-smn rwḥ*, "O Lord of the Heavens, give rest." It is difficult to put a precise date to Safaitic inscriptions. They are written in a form of early Arabic. They are assumed to date back to the third/fourth century AD.

Daniel King of Cardiff University has argued from the perspective of a Syriacist that though Luxenberg's "method is severely lacking in many areas, . . . he may on occasion have hit upon a useful emendation. Thus, although the hypothesis as a whole is faulty, the individual textual suggestions ought to be treated on a case-by-case basis."[35] King criticizes Luxenberg's frequent recourse to metathesis. However, even al-Manẓūr in his *Lisān al-'Arab,* tells us that the "Arabs are exceedingly fond of metathesis," and Luxenberg's examples must be judged on a case-by-case basis. Also, King, like many others, deplores Luxenberg's use of Ya'qob Awgen (Jacques-Eugène) Manna's *Chaldean-Arabic Dictionary*, which first appeared in 1900. But in fact Manna (1867–1928) frequently refers to the earliest Syriac literature, and he depends, for instance, on Bar Bahlul's tenth-century dictionary. Finally, here is how the prestigious Dumbarton Oaks Library of Georgetown, Washington, DC, describes Manna:

> Y. A. Manna, *Qāmūs kaldānī-ʿarabī / Vocabulaire chaldeen-arabe / Chaldean Arabic Dictionary*, 2nd ed., with suppl. by R. Bidawid (Beirut, 1975).
> This is an outstanding dictionary. Its main defect is that Manna does not provide citations to let one know what texts he is deriving his words and definitions from, but Syriac scholars have often made recourse to this dictionary and always with profit. For instance, Brockelmann's second edition (still under copyright) is extraordinary in its coverage of rare words—it is a not uncommon experience to be reading an off-the-beaten-track text, come across an unknown or unfamiliar word, not find it in Mrs. Margoliouth's Dictionary or the Thesaurus, and then to find its meaning in Brockelmann, with a citation from precisely (and sometimes, only) the passage being read. Brockelmann also has meanings which you cannot find in Payne Smith (but, it should be noted, the opposite is sometimes true), and reading an author like Jacob of Sarugh is much easier when done with Brockelmann at one's side. With all this said, however, we have, on a number of occasions, found meanings in Manna that are in neither Brockelmann nor in Payne Smith. This can be especially true when reading unpublished texts in manuscript. Manna is definitely a lexical resource that is worth keeping ready to hand. It is Syriac-Arabic, but even a person with a basic grasp of the Arabic alphabet and a lexicon like Steingass's *Arabic-English Dictionary* nearby (which lists words alphabetically rather than by root) can profit from using Manna. It is a real gem and an underappreciated resource in the world of Syriac dictionaries. This is a re-typing of Manna, in modern Arabic and Syriac fonts.[36]

One may note that King does not accept Luxenberg's arguments concerning the *waw* of apodosis in Koranic Arabic (King, pp. 55–61). However, in a forth-coming article, Guillaume Dye makes a convincing case for its plausibility.[37]

Luxenberg's revolutionary study has given us not only new readings and interpretations of the difficult and problematic passages of the Koran, but he has also provided us with a methodology. Several scholars have taken up the challenge and applied his methods to make discoveries for themselves. Munther Younes, in an article included in the present volume, proceeds in an exemplary fashion, reconstructing

> the first five verses of Koran 100 (*wa-l-ʿādiyāt*) by changing the dotting scheme of four words. Informed by a close examination of the syntactic structure and vocabulary of these verses and a comparison with cognates in Syriac and Hebrew, two languages with a clear influence on the Qur'ān, this recon-

> struction results in a narrative that is more coherent semantically and syntactically than the traditional interpretation. Whereas in the traditional interpretation these verses describe steeds charging into battle, in my reconstruction they refer to maidens bringing light to the world.

Munther Younes's study is one of two paths to follow in order to build on the work of Luxenberg. The second path is also very rewarding, especially in the hands of gifted scholars such as Jan Van Reeth and Guillaume Dye, who bring to bear on Koranic problems their immense knowledge of the history of Christianity, the Old and New Testaments, the Apocrypha, Targumim, and the Greek, Hebrew, and Syriac writings. Dye, in a superb essay,[38] builds on Luxenberg's insights on Surah 97 (*sūrat al-qadr*), submitting it, with patience and analytical brilliance, to the most thorough examination imaginable, suggesting every possible objection to Luxenberg's thesis, and then answering those objections. Dye thereby strengthens Luxenberg's position. Finally, he clinches the argument by proposing a Syriac text as the direct inspiration for Surah 97, namely *Hymns on the Nativity* by Ephrem the Syrian. Luxenberg provides the restored text of the Koran, while Van Reeth and Dye refine the new readings and provide the Christian sources.

Thus Luxenberg's work has truly opened up a new era in Koranic Studies. He has provided the philology. His colleagues and coresearchers must now provide the historical context, and furnish the Judaeo-Christian and other Near Eastern and Babylonian sources.

2. Precursors of Luxenberg: Anticipations and Contrasts

Luxenberg, concentrating on philology, had left the historical context of his new readings of the Koran to the historians. By the mid-nineteenth century, Western historians of religion had already begun writing on the influence of Christianity on the religious ideas to be found in the Koran. More specifically, for a few scholars this Christianity was felt to be some form of Ebionism. It is also remarkable that many of these scholars came to the study of Islam with a solid grounding in Christian theology, hence their perspective was firmly theological, not philological.

In a tantalizing introduction to his *Der Ursrpung des Islams und das Cristentum,*[39] Swedish scholar Tor Andrae (1885–1947), historian of comparative religion and bishop of Linköping, indicates some of the scholars of the late-nineteenth century who had anticipated some of his own conclusions on the influence of Syrian Christianity on the Koran:

> Since Sprenger [1813–1893] established his important thesis of the similarity between the Qur'ānic doctrine of revelation and Elchaism, one finds, among all the scholars who consecrate some time on the influence of Christianity on

> the world of religious ideas of Muḥammad, the conviction that this Christianity must have been some sort of Ebionism.[40]

Thus Harnack (1851–1930), the German Lutheran theologian, suggested in 1874 that Islam should be viewed as a branch or descendant of a Jewish-Christian heretical sect, very probably the Elkesaites. Harnack wrote,

> Islam is the transformation of Jewish religion, which itself had already been transformed by Gnostic Jewish Christianity on an Arabic base and by a great prophet.

This idea is bolstered by the remarks of the Syrian exegete Theodor bar Koni, who, toward the end of the eighth century, without mentioning Islam, confirms the presence of Elkesaites in northwest Arabia.

In a decisive manner, the Judaeo-Christian sects, particularly Elchaism, are taken to have provided the models to Muhammad as much as Christianity in the writings of Gerhard Uhlhorn (1826–1901),[41] also a Lutheran theologian; Hugo J. Bestmann (1854–1925)[42]; Henry Preserved Smith (1847–1926)[43]; and Édouard Sayous (1842–1898).[44]

Sayous, for instance, wrote:

> L'influence capitale sur la naissance de l'Islam a été celle de trois dérivés de l'Essénisme, à savoir le Nazaréisme, l'Elkésaïsme, et le Hanyfisme. . . . Le judéo-christianisme nazaréen, qui se distinguait de l'ébionitisme proprement dit par une tendance judaïque plus modérée, et par la reconnaissance de la naissance miraculeuse du Christ, a été certainement la provenance principale des notions de Mahomet sur la vie de Jésus. . . . L'elkésaïsme, secte de même origine, et qui a développé avec des allures mystérieuses, au Sud de la Mer Morte, les doctrines des Homélies clémentines; l'elkésaïsme, avec sa négligence systématique des épitres de Saint-Paul, avec son livre secret venu du ciel, avec son incorporation de l'Esprit de Dieu dans une série de prophètes depuis Adam jusqu'à Jésus, a dû être la provenance principale des opinions de Mahomet sur lui-même, sur l'Écriture et sur son Coran.[45] [Of paramount influence for the emergence of Islam were three offshoots of Essenism, i.e., Nazareism, Elchesaism and Hanifism. . . . Nazarene Judeo-Christianity, which was distinguished from Ebionism proper by a more moderate Jewish tendency and by the recognition of the miraculous birth of Christ, was certainly the primary source for Mohammed's notions about Jesus' life . . . Elchesaism, a sect of the same origin, which, on mysterious ways in the south of the Dead Sea, developed the doctrines of the Clementine Homilies; Elchesaism, with its systematic negligence of the epistles of St. Paul, with its secret book, which had come down from heaven, with its incorporation of the Holy Spirit in a series of prophets starting with Adam and ending with Jesus, must have been the

main source of Mohammed's opinions about himself and the scripture of the Koran!]

For Tor Andrae, it was Julius Wellhausen (1844–1918) who gave the most penetrating account of the depth and extent of the influence of Christianity on nascent Islam deriving the Christian elements from Christian asceticism. The strands in the Koran that seem to depend on Jewish teachings were, according to Wellhausen, mediated through apocryphal and pseudepigraphal Christian sources.[46] For Wellhausen, the Christianity in question must have been Monophysite, Nestorian, or Judeo-Christian.

Andrae does not believe we can attribute everything in the Koran to Ebionism. Instead he turns to the history of Christianity in the Arabian Peninsula. Persuaded by Nöldeke, Andrae believes that it was Syrian Christianity that predominated in the Yemen, and that "the liturgical language, very likely, must have been Syriac."[47]

The Church in southern Arabia had lost touch with Western Christianity and was unable to fight Nestorian missionary zeal. Andrae wrote[48]:

> The similarity between Mohammed's religion and Syrian Christianity appears not only in the general agreement of the content of ideas, but also in expression, form, and style of preaching. In this connection a study of Afrem (Ephraim the Syrian) [i.e., Ephrem the Syrian or St. Ephrem the Syrian, Syriac: ܡܪܝ ܐܦܪܝܡ ܣܘܪܝܝܐ, *Mār Efrêm Sûryāyâ*; Greek: Ἐφραίμ ὁ Σῦρος; Latin: *Ephraem Syrus*; *ca.* 306–373, Ephrem, henceforth], the greatest preacher of the Syrian church is instructive. This church father, who was held in the highest esteem both by Monophysites and Nestorians, discussed no other subjects with such partiality and such rhetorical power as the eschatological themes: death, the judgment, and eternal rewards. We find many points of similarity between his sermons on the judgment and the well-known descriptions of the Qur'ān, even expressions and images being often in striking agreement. A glance at Ephrem's *Hymns of Paradise* is of special interest. . . . [It is an] irrefutable fact that the Qur'ān's descriptions of Paradise were inspired by the ideas of this Christian Syrian preacher. Ephrem's *Hymns of Paradise* depict the joys of the blessed in very mundane colours.
>
>> I saw the dwelling-places of the just, and they themselves, dripping with ointments, giving forth pleasant odours, wreathed in flowers and decked with fruits. . . . When they lie at the table the trees offer their shade in the clear air. Flowers grow beneath them and fruits above. Their roof is composed of fruits and their carpets are of flowers. . . . Swift winds stand before the blessed, ready to do their will. One of them wafts appeasement, another causes drinks to flow. One wind is filled with oil, another with ointment. Who among you has ever seen the winds act as servants! or breezes which one may eat and drink! In

> Paradise the winds give nourishment in a spiritual fashion to spiritual beings. It is a feast without effort, and the hands do not become tired. . . . Think, O aged one, of Paradise! When its aroma refreshes you and its pleasant odours renew your youth, your blemishes will vanish in the beauty which surrounds you. Let Moses be an example to you. His cheeks, which were covered with wrinkles, became beautiful and radiant. This is a mystical symbol, showing how age shall be rejuvenated in Paradise.

> The wine which the redeemed enjoy is likewise not lacking in the Christian Paradise, and one may recognize a veiled reference to the virgins of Paradise in Ephrem's saying:
>
>> Whoever has abstained from wine on earth, for him do the vines of Paradise yearn. Each one of them holds out to him a bunch of grapes. And if a man has lived in chastity, they (feminine) receive him in a pure bosom, because he as a monk did not fall into the bosom and bed of earthly love.
>
> To be sure, Ephrem occasionally points out that this is only an attempt to give some idea of a joy which no earthly mind is able to grasp. But most of his listeners and readers no doubt remained quite oblivious to his feeble attempts to spiritualize his sensual images. Popular piety certainly interpreted this daring imagery in a crass and literal sense, and under such circumstances one cannot blame a citizen of pagan Mecca for doing the same thing.[49]

Where did Muhammad acquire the notion that the soul sinks into complete unconsciousness after death, so that the Day of Judgment seems to follow immediately after death? Tor Andrae believes the Koranic doctrine is derived from the Nestorian Church in Persia, and its most prominent theologian, Babai the Great. As Andrae argues:

> Besides quoting scriptural passages to prove his theory, Babai also cites the legend of the seven sleepers, which Mohammed likewise used for the same purpose (18, 8–24). . . . In my opinion this, along with other reasons, proves that Mohammed received from the Nestorians of Persia the impressions which decisively influenced his personal message. The Christian Arabs of Hira, on the border of Mesopotamia, with whom the Meccans were in especially vital contact, belonged to the Nestorian Church.[50]

Tor Andrae's approach is theological, but he is not entirely insensitive to linguistic matters. Just before Alphonse Mingana, and several years before Arthur Jeffery, Andrae is confident of the origin of the word *qur'ān*: "The word used in the Syrian Church for the scripture reading in Divine Service, *qeryānā*, Mohammed took and applied as a title to his revelation."[51] Andrae also believes that the Arabic *ḥanīf* comes from the Syriac *hanp̄a*.[52]

Edmund Beck famously attacked Tor Andrae for the above analysis. But as Sidney Griffith shows, in an article reproduced in the present volume, Beck simply missed Andrae's point altogether:

> Andrae did not actually say that Ephraem envisioned houris in Paradise. Rather, he suggested that "popular piety," not to mention "a citizen of pagan Mecca," might have been inspired by such lines as Ephraem wrote to conjure up the houris.[53]

Ephrem the Syrian is invoked once again to support another reading of Luxenberg's. Guillaume Dye, in the article referred to above, argues persuasively that Luxenberg's interpretation of Surah 97 (*al-Qadr*) is prefigured in Ephrem's *Hymns on the Nativity* or *Madrāšē ḏ-bēṯ yaldā*. Hymn 21: 2, 1–2 sings: "Let us not take our vigil (*šahrā*) as an ordinary vigil; It is a celebration whose reward passes beyond one hundred for one."

Though hymn 21 was not accepted, at first, as authentic by some scholars, but, for no less a figure than Edmund Beck, the editor of Ephrem's poems in the *Corpus Scriptorum Christianorum Orientalium*,

> who had a great sense of what is genuine and what is not, this hymn is pretty certainly genuine, even if it is not one of those preserved in 6th-century manuscripts.[54]

Sebastian Brock, one of the greatest contemporary scholars of Syriac literature, "would certainly agree with him."[55]

There is another scholar who arrives at a smilar conclusion to Luxenberg's concerning Surah 97. Padre Giulio Basetti-Sani (1912–2001), Tuscan nobleman and Franciscan, O. F. M (*Order of Friars Minor*, or *Ordo Fratrum Minorum*), firm believer, and active in Muslim-Christian dialogues, studied at the Pontifical Institute of Oriental Studies in Rome, and taught at various universities in Europe and the United States. Basetti-Sani began his Koranic research with the assumption that the Koran was of divine origin, a fact that, he feels, Catholic scholars can verify by applying to it the rules of hermeneutics used in Biblical research. He is convinced that the mystery of Christ may also be found in the Koran, whose mysteries can be revealed with a Christian key. Basetti-Sani wrote:

> The story of Christ, his apostles, and Christian origins is absent from the Qur'ān. Those for whom the Qur'ān is intended are just barely at the first glimmerings of some knowledge of Christ. It is reserved to Christians to supply what the Qur'ān did not proclaim.

In the section of his book *The Koran in the Light of Christ*,[56] titled "A Christian Reading of the Qur'ān Discovers Christ in the Full Meaning of the Texts," Basetti-Sani writes:

> It has been regarded as legitimate for Muslim exegetes to give full rein to their imaginations, which has resulted in fantastic interpretations of a text. This being so, I feel justified in attempting, in the light of Christ, and basing myself upon the hypothetically sacred origin of the Qur'ān, to bring out all that there may be in the Koran about Christ, reading the text in its "fuller sense."
>
> In truth we revealed it [made it come down]
> on the Night of Destiny.
> Whatever may be the Night of Destiny?
> The Night of Destiny is more beautiful than a thousand months.
> There descend Angels and the Spirit
> with the permission of God,
> to settle every thing.
> Night of Peace even to the coming of the dawn. (Sura 97:1–5)
>
> The usual interpretation of Muslims and Orientalists sees this sura as describing the "night" in which the Koran was communicated, all at once, to Mohammed. But this descent of the complete Koran in one night contains a contradiction, which exegetes get around by saying that God took it back again into Heaven and then revealed it anew, but this time in sections, one at a time. Because this "explanation" is based upon the theory that the Koran was an actual, physical book, written in Heaven, I cannot accept it. This is one more place where we have to "dematerialize."
>
> The night of *Qadr* is Christmas night, when Christ made his visible appearance upon earth. This is the night of "power," during which the divine decree was carried out: "the mystery which was hidden from ages and generations" (Colossians 1:26, Ephesians 1:4–14). The Semite's mind—and this includes the Bible, of course—sees night as the time of darkness, or ignorance and unbelief (Romans 13:12; 1 Thessalonians 5:5). It is also the time of affliction and sorrow (Isaiah 21:12). It is the time of death: "Night comes, when no one can work" (John 9:4). But *this* night is the only one of its kind; it is the night of destiny, and more beautiful than a thousand months. During it the angels descend, which immediately calls to mind the angels at Bethlehem (Luke 2:13). The Koran calls Jesus "a Spirit from the Lord" (sura 4:171). Jesus is witnessed to by the "Spirit of Holiness" (sura 2:87, 253; sura 5: 110). Hence the phrase makes sense if we read it as referring to the descent of the Spirit of Holiness with Jesus on Christmas night. The phrase "with God's permission," which is found in other texts of the Koran where the subject is Jesus' activity (sura 3:49), must be seen as the full adherence of the human will of Christ to

the divine will (John 4:34, 5:30, 6:38), as that perfect obedience to the Father which earned the exaltation of the Son's name (Philippians 2:7–11).

min kulli 'amrin, which some translate "to establish everything," granted its wide range of meanings *('Amr* = "command," "order," "divine plan or decree"), can be understood in the Pauline sense that the whole plan of creation is fixed and founded upon Christ. And the "night of peace" is that night when peace was heralded by the angels to all men with whom God is pleased (Luke 2:14).

The Koran recites the story of the birth of Jesus in another passage (sura 19:22–35); but here we have a personal vision or revelation to Mohammed which calls up the tremendous mystery of God's goodness to men. Other passages of the Koran also refer to this night of destiny, or rather night of the birth, and Muslim exegetes and Orientalists explain them as the night of the Koran's descent. But this reinterpretation in the light of Christ allows me to refer them to Christ's birth:

> H. M.
> [By means of] the Most Clear Book
> In truth we have revealed it
> in a BLESSED NIGHT that men might be warned
> In that night every wise order was decreed. (sura 44:1–4)

The "most clear book" is not the Koran. When we dematerialize this passage, as we do for the vision of Ezekiel (2:9), the book is a symbol of the gospel revelation: of God's Word, who on Christmas night manifested himself to mankind. Christ enters the world to alert men and to witness to the truth. Nor is the plural *We* merely the majestic plural; it is the *We* of the three divine Persons. The sura goes on, and becomes an argument with the Jews of Mecca. It runs thus: If now, at this time, the preaching of the prophet Mohammed is a new call of God to his people, the fact that the Jews rejected the message of Christ in times past gives reason to think that they are about to do the same thing this time.

> But how can the Warning aid them,
> when a clear Messenger already came to them!
> And still they disdainfully turned their
> shoulders and said:
> "Crazy Imposter." (sura 44:13–14)

Cf. John 10:19–21:

> 19: There was a divison therefore among the Jews for these sayings.
> 20: And many of them said, "He hath a devil, and is mad; why hear ye him?"
> 21: Others said, These are not the words of him that hath a devil. Can a devil open the eyes of the blind.

The works of Luxenberg and Hartwig Hirschfeld (1854–1934)[57] intersect at a number of interesting points.

In his analysis of Surah 96:1–19, Luxenberg dicusses the correct interpretation of the expression *iqra'* (actually *iqrā*) *bi-smi rabbika*:

> Hartwig Hirschfeld, who in pointing to the frequent occurrence in the Bible of the Hebrew expression *qrā ḇ-šem Yahwē*, had translated the Qur'ānic expression correctly with "proclaim the name of thy Lord!"[58]

Hirschfeld[59] himself had written:

> [I translated the word *iqra'*] by "proclaim," my object being to call attention to the early misunderstanding of the word by traditionists and interpreters of the Qur'ān as well as by modern translators and biographers of the Prophet. For the sentence in question is nothing but an Arabic version of the phrase in the Pentateuch (Gen. XII.8 in connection with IV.26), "He proclaimed the name of the Lord."

Hirschfeld then discusses the various aspects of the legend of *Baḥīrā*, the putative mentor of Muhammad, mentioned in Ibn Ishaq's *Sīra* and in Ibn Sa'd's biography of the prophet. Hirschfeld concludes that the elements from which the legends have been developed "represent homilies on several Biblical passages which have become mixed up," passages such as 1 Sam. 16:2–13.

> The boy David who is left in the field to tend the sheep, while his brothers are brought before the Prophet, but who is fetched at the request of the latter, corresponds to the boy Muḥammad left behind with the luggage. . . . It may not be superfluous to remark that the term *bāḥar* ("has chosen") occurs three times (1 Sam. 16, verses 9, 10, 11) in the report of the proceedings. With this we must connect Ps. 78:10; 84:4, 20, where the word *b'ḥirī*, whilst referring to David, gives a clue to the meaning of the name *Baḥīrā* . . . [which] is thus nothing but the personification of the (New) Hebrew term *bḥīrā* ("Election") which is quite common. Now Muḥammad was acquainted with several verses in the Old Testament in which the form *b'ḥīr* ("chosen") is used in reference to Israel (Isaiah 45:4: "For Jacob my servant's sake, and Israel mine elect. . . ."); Isaiah 44:1: "Yet now hear, O Jacob my servant; and Israel, whom I have chosen;" to Moses (Psalms, 104:23: "Therefore he said that he would destroy them, had not Moses his chosen stood before him. . . .") as can be seen from Qur'ān Sura 7:141: "He said: O Moses! I have preferred thee above mankind. . . ."; Sura 27:59: "Say: Praise be to Allah, and peace be on His slaves whom he hath chosen! . . ." (cf. Sura 35:32: "Then We gave the Scripture as inheritance unto those whom We elected of our bondmen. . . ."; Sura 44:32: "And We

> chose them purposely, above (all) creatures."). The Arabic translation of *b'ḥīr* is *almuṣṭafā*, one of Muḥammad's names. He is himself the Baḥirā. . . . As we now see the Baḥīrā legend represents a profusion of Biblical ideas blended together in a manner similar to the Jewish Agāda. There is, however, another point which occurs in various versions of the legend, viz., the tree casting its shadow wherever Muḥammad sat. This situation is described, Song of Solomon 2:3, where we find the apple tree, the sitting under its shadow, and the word *himmadti* in which it should not be difficult now to recognize the embryo of the name Muḥammad, the roots ḤMD and BḤR being in some degree synonymous in Hebrew (see Ezek. 23:6, 12, 23) the former makes an appropriate rendition in Arabic for the latter which has quite a different meaning. From this we may conclude that the time when the Prophet assumed the name Muḥammad coincides with that when the first elements of the Baḥīrā legend were produced, which can only have been very shortly before his death. The name Muḥammad, it is true, occurs several times in the Qur'ān, but there are grave doubts as to the genuineness of the verses in question.[60]

Both Gerd Puin and Luxenberg, in forthcoming articles, argue, in their different ways, that the four terms in Surah 5, verse 103—*baḥīrāh*, *sā'ibah*, *waṣilah*, and *hami*—have nothing whatsoever to do with "sacrificial camels," rather they point to certain classes of people who, in other religions, may play a role as individuals who intercede with God for man but who are forbidden in Islam; ancient priests or notables; and finally, the elects. Luxenberg interprets *Baḥīrāh* in the same way as Hirschfeld above; that is, as a term meaning "chosen," "elect." Frère Bruno Bonnet-Eymard[61] also translates *Baḥīrāh* as "the chosen," "elect" ("élu"), referring to Isaiah 42:1 ("Behold my servant, whom I uphold; mine elect, in whom my soul delighteth"), and he cites from that passage in Isaiah the Hebrew word *bāḥīr*, meaning "elect."

Let us come back to Hirschfeld, who makes a series of observations that seem to me pertinent to Luxenberg's arguments concerning the term *muḥammad*, which Luxenberg takes to mean the "praised one," referring to Jesus. Silvestre de Sacy suggested in 1832 that Surah 3:144 (Flügel number= 3:138) was inauthentic; that is, a later interpolation. The verse concerned reads:

> Muḥammad is but a messenger, messengers (the like of whom) have passed away before him. Will it be that, when he dieth or is slain, ye will turn back on your heels? He who turneth back doth no hurt to Allah, and Allah will reward the thankful. (3:144)

Needless to say, the Islamic tradition has fabricated another specimen of those innumerable *asbāb al-nuzūl* ("occasions/reasons of sending down" [of Koranic verses]). For this verse, as Hirschfeld tells us,

> the Moslims, relates Al Tabari, seeing the Prophet on the ground, called: "If he be dead, [remember that] all Messengers before him have died." When Muḥammad recovered consciousness, he revealed Sura 3:144.

Hirschfeld continues:

> I believe neither in the authenticity of this exclamation, nor of the verse in question. . . . The verse contains yet another element which speaks against its authenticity, *viz.*, the name Muḥammad. I even go further and assert that all verses in the *Qur'ān* in which this name, or Aḥmad, occurs are spurious. The reasons on which I base my suggestions are the following.
>
> In Chapter II. I have endeavoured to shew that the fabrication of the name *Muḥammad* stands in close connection with the elements of the Baḥīrā legend. If this be so, that name could not have come into practical use until a period of the Prophet's life, when the material of the *Qur'ān* was all but complete. Now it might be objected that the texts of the missionary letters which Muḥammad commenced to send in the seventh year of the Hijra to unconverted Arab chiefs, as well as to foreign potentates, were headed by the phrase: "From Muḥammad, the Messenger of Allah, to, *etc.*"—The authenticity of the majority of these letters, one of which will occupy our attention presently, is very doubtful, and besides, even if the genuineness of the texts of the documents be admitted, the superscription may have been added by the traditionists who took it for granted. At any rate I do not believe that *Muḥammad* was an official name till after the conversion of Abd Allāh b. Salām, or a year or two before his death. At the period of the battle of Uḥud (A. H. 3) there was certainly no trace of the name, and it is too superfluous to demonstrate how unlikely it was that Muḥammad's friends, seeing him prostrate, should have uttered the words quoted above. If they had really thought him dead, they would have run away, as all would then have been lost. If, on the other hand, we assume that the name *Muḥammad* was meant to signify something similar to *Messiah,* the verse in question is nothing but an imitation of the chief portion of another which was revealed *before* the battle of Badr *(Sura* 5:75) and runs thus: "The Messiah the son of Maryam, is nothing but a Messenger, the messengers before him have passed away. . . ." The authors of 3:144 simply replaced *almasīḥ 'bnu Maryama* by *Muḥammad,* and the verse was ready.
>
> This is, however, not the only *Muḥammad-verse* which stands in connection with the Baḥīrā legend, as in *Sura.* 33:40 we find another reference to it. This revelation is appended to one of the paragraphs which deal with the affairs of Muḥammad's wives, though it does not belong to it, the preceding sermon ending with verse 39. As each of these paragraphs commences with the words: "O thou Prophet!" we have seen that they refer to matters prior to

the adoption of the name *Muḥammad.* The verse in question runs thus: "Muḥammad is no father of any of your men, but [he is] the Messenger of Allah and the Seal of the Prophets, Allah knows everything." From its very place we can gather that the verse's only function is the condonation of the Prophet's marriage with the divorced wife of his adopted son, which event took place in the year *four.* As to the "Seal of the Prophets," this is surely nothing but a skilful alteration of the "Seal of prophecy" in the Baḥīrā legend.

3. Bibliography

3.1. Books by Christoph Luxenberg

1. *Die syro-aramäische Lesart des Koran: Ein Beitrag zur Entschlüsselung der Koransprache* [The Syro-Aramaic Reading of the Koran: a Contribution to the Decoding of the Koranic Language], 1st ed. (Berlin, 2000); 2nd ed., corrected and augmented (Berlin, 2004).
2. *The Syro-Aramaic Reading of the Koran: A Contribution to the Decoding of the Language of the Koran* (Berlin: Verlag Hans Schiler, 2007), English translation of previous entry, with additions (new findings) not in the German edition.

3.2. Articles by Christoph Luxenberg

1. "Weihnachten im Koran," *Imprimatur* 1 (Trier, Germany) (2003).
2. "Der Koran zum islamischen Kopftuch," *Imprimatur* 2 (Trier, Germany) (2003).
3. "Zur Morphologie und Etymologie von syro-aramäische *sāṭānā*=Satan und koranisch-arabisch *šayṭān,*" in C. Burgmer, ed., *Streit um den Koran* (Berlin: Schiler, 2004), pp. 46–66.
4. "Weinachten im Koran," in C. Burgmer, ed., *Streit um den Koran* (Berlin: Schiler), 2004, pp. 35–41.
5. "Der Koran und das "islamische Kopftuch," in C. Burgmer, ed., *Streit um den Koran* (Berlin: Schiler, 2004), pp. 83–89.
6. "Noël dans le Coran," in A.-M. Delcambre et al. eds., *Enquêtes sur l'Islam* (Paris: Éditions Desclée de Brouwer, 2004), pp. 117–38.
7. "Quel est la langue du coran?" in Yves-Charles Zarka, ed., *Islam en France,* Cités. Hors-Série (special issue not part of the normal series) (Paris: PUF, 2004), pp. 661–68.
8. "Neudeutung der arabischen Inschrift im Felsendom zu Jerusalem," in Karl-Heinz Ohlig and Gerd-R. Puin, eds., *Die dunklen Anfänge, Neue Forschungen zur Entstehung und frühen Geschichte des Islam* (Berlin:

Schiler, 2005), 3rd ed., 2007; Inârah: Schriften zur frühen Islamgeschichte und zum Koran, vol. 1, pp. 124–47.

9. "A New Interpretation of the Arabic Inscription in Jerusalem's Dome of the Rock" (translation of the preciding article), in Karl-Heinz Ohlig and Gerd-R. Puin, eds., *The Hidden Origins of Islam* (Amherst, NY: Prometheus Books, 2010), pp. 125–51.
10. "Zum Ursprung des Namens 'Mohammed' (Muḥammad = Der Gelobte). Eine in der Arabistik und Semitistik bisher nicht geklärte Etymologie" *Imprimatur* 7 (2007).
11. "Relikte syro-aramäische Buchstaben in frühen Korankodizes im ḥiǧāzī und kūfī-Duktus," in Karl-Heinz Ohlig, ed., *Der frühe Islam, Eine historische-kritische Rekonstruktion anhand zeitgenössischer Quellen* (Berlin: Schiler, 2007), Inârah: Schriften zur frühen Islamgeschichte und zum Koran, vol. 2, pp. 377–414.
12. "Relics of Syro-Aramaic Letters in Early Qur'ān Codices in Ḥiǧāzī and Kūfī Ductus" (translation of the preceding article), in Karl-Heinz Ohlig, ed., *Early Islam: A Critical Reconstruction Based on Contemporary Sources* (Amherst, NY: Prometheus Books, 2013), pp. 308–338.
13. "Die syrische Liturgie und die 'geheimnisvollen Buchstaben' im Koran. Eine liturgievergleichende Studie," in Markus Gross and Karl-Heinz Ohlig, eds., *Schlaglichter. Die beiden ersten islamischen Jahrhunderte*, Inârah: Schriften zur frühen Islamgeschichte und zum Koran, vol. 3 (Berlin: Schiler, 2008), pp. 411–56.
14. "Keine Schlacht von Badr: Zu syrischen Buchstaben in frühen Koranmanuskripten," in Markus Gross and Karl-Heinz Ohlig, eds., *Vom Koran zum Islam*, Inârah: Schriften zur frühen Islamgeschichte und zum Koran Berlin, vol. 4 (Berlin: Schiler, 2008), pp. 642–76.
15. "'Inārah' im Koran: Zu einem bisher übersehenen Hapax Legomenon (Sure 46)," in Markus Gross and Karl-Heinz Ohlig, eds., *Die Entstehung einer Weltreligion I: Von der koranischen Bewegung zum Frühislam*, Inârah: Schriften zur frühen Islamgeschichte und zum Koran, vol. 5 (Berlin: Schiler, 2008), pp. 377–81.
16. "Keine Polygamie und kein Konkubinat im Koran (Sure 4:3)," in Markus Gross and Karl-Heinz Ohlig, eds., *Die Entstehung einer Weltreligion II: Von der koranischen Bewegung zum Frühislam*, Inârah: Schriften zur frühen Islamgeschichte und zum Koran, vol. 6 (Berlin: Schiler, 2008), pp. 615–45.
17. "Al-Najm. Chapter of the Stars: A New Syro-Aramaic Reading of Verses 1–18," in Gabriel Said Reynolds, ed., *New Perspectives on the Qur'an: The Qur'an in Its Historical Context 2*, Routledge Studies in the Qur'an (London: Routledge, 2011), pp. 279–98.

18. "Kein 'Mekka' (Makka) und kein 'Bakka' im Koran: Zu Sure 48:24 und 3:96: Eine philologische Analyse," *Imprimatur* 7 (2012).

3.3. Interviews with Luxenberg

1. *L'actualité* (Canada) 28, no. 14, dated September 15, 2003.
2. *Die Tageszeitung (taz)*, no. 7331 (Berlin, Germany), conducted by Edith Kresta, "Eine andere Form der Bibel," dated April 10, 2004, p. 21.
3. *Süddeutsche Zeitung* (Munich, Germany), conducted by Alfred Hackensberger, February 24, 2004, p. 15.
4. ITI, *Bulletin of the Institute of Translation and Interpreting* (Milton Keynes, UK), conducted by Rebecca Fiederer, "The radical," November-December 2008, pp. 11–13.
5. *The Qur'ān*, television documentary by filmmaker Antony Thomas, Channel 4 (UK), 2008.

3.4. Reviews of, and Articles Discussing, Christoph Luxenberg's Work

Academic Journals:

1. *Caelestis Eichenseer in Vox Latina* (Journal of Societas Latina, University of the Saarland, Saarbrücken, Germany) 36, no. 142 (2000).
2. Rainer Nabielek, *Inamo: Informationsprojekt Naher und Mittlerer Osten* (Berlin, Germany), *Journal on the Middle East*, no. 23/24, 6th year, (Fall/Winter 2000): 66–72.
3. Piet Horsten, *islamochristiana* 28 (2002): 310 ff. (published by the Pontifical Institute for Arabic and Islamic Studies [PISAI], Rome, Italy).
4. Claude Gilliot and Pierre Larcher, "Language and Style of the Qur'ān," in *Encyclopaedia of the Qur'ān*, vol. 3 (Brill: Leiden, 2003), pp. 113–39.
5. Robert R. Phenix Jr. and Cornelia B. Horn, *Hugoye: Journal of Syriac Studies* 6, no. 1 (January 2003).
6. Federico Corriente, "On a proposal for a 'Syro-Aramaic' Reading of the Qur'ān," *Collectanea Christiana Orientalia* 1 (2003): 305–314.
7. Rémi Brague, "Le Coran: sortir du cercle?" *Critique*, no. 671 (April 2003): 232–51.
8. Michael Marx, "Ein neuer Impuls für die Erforschung des Korans," *Inamo: Informationsprojekt Naher und Mittlerer Osten*, no. 33, 6th year (Spring 2003): 45–47.
9. Johannes J. G. Jansen, *Bibliotheca Orientalis* 60, nos. 3–4 (May–August 2003), columns 477–80.
10. François de Blois, *Journal of Qur'anic Studies* 5, no. 1 (2003): 92–97.
11. Angelika Neuwirth, *Journal of Qur'anic Studies* 5, no. 1 (2003): 1–18.

12. Wilhelm Maria Maas, "Der Koran: ein christliches Lektionar?" *Novalis, Zeitschrift für spirituelle Entwicklung* (November/December 2003): 18–22.
13. Claude Gilliot (Aix-en-Provence), "Langue et Coran: Une lecture syro-araméenne du Coran," *Arabica* 50, no. 3 (2003): 381–93.
14. Simon Hopkins (Jerusalem), *Jerusalem Studies in Arabic and Islam* 28 (2003): 377–80.
15. Manfred Kropp, "Viele fremde Tische, und noch einer im Koran: Zur Etymologie von äthiopisch *maʾəd(d)ə* und arabisch *māʾida/mayda*," *Oriens Christianus* 87 (2003): 140–43.
16. Martin F. J. Baasten, *Aramaic Studies* 2, no. 2 (2004): 268–72.
17. Richard Kroes "Zendeling, Dilettant or Visionair? Een recensie van Ch. Luxenberg: Die Syro-Aramäische Lesart des Qurʾan," *Dialoog, tijdschrift voor Oudheidstudies*, no. 4 (June 2004).
18. Michael Marx, Was ist eigentlich der Koran?" *inamo* 37 (2004).
19. Angelika Neuwirth, Nicolai Sinai, Michael Marx, eds., *The Qurʾan in Context: Literary and Historical Investigations into the Qurʾanic Milieu* (Leiden, 2010).
20. Manfred Kropp, "Der äthiopische Satan = šayṭān und seine koranischen Ausläufer; mit einer Bemerkung über verbales Steinigen" *Oriens Christianus* 89 (2005): 93–102
21. J. van Reeth, "Le vignoble du paradis et le chemin qui y mène: La thèse de C. Luxenberg et les sources du Coran," *Arabica* 53 (2006): 511–24.
22. Jean-Michel Lavoie, *La revue Laval théologique et philosophique* 62, no.1 (2006): 151 ff.
23. Jan Retsö, "Aramaic/Syriac Loanwords," in K. Versteegh et al., eds., *Encyclopedia of Arabic Language and Linguistics*, vol. 1 (Leiden: E. J. Brill, 2006), pp. 178–82.
24. Manfred Kropp, "The Ethiopic Satan = Šayṭān and Its Quranic Successor, with a Note on Verbal Stoning," *Christianisme Oriental: Kerygme et Histoire*, Mélanges offerts au père Michel Hayek, Coordination Charles Chartouni (Paris, 2007), pp. 331–341.
25. Dr. Ahmad Muḥammad Ali al-Gamal, "al-Qurʾān wa-luġat al-Suryān" [The Koran and the Language of the Syrians = Syriac language], *Maǧallāt Kulliyyat al-Luġāt wa-l-Tarǧama* [Bulletin of Faculty of Languages and Translation] (Ǧāmiʿat al-Azhar [al-Azhar University]), no. 42 (2007): 62–107.
26. Manuela Galizia, "Il Corano e la tradizione cristiana siriaca," in Davide Righi, ed., *Patrimonio Culturale Arabo Cristiano: La letteratura arabo-cristiana e le scienze nel periodo abbaside (750–1250 d.C.)*, proceedings of

the 2nd conference of Arab-Christian Studies, Rome, March 9–10, 2007 (Turin : Silvio Zamorani, 2008).

27. V. Comerro, *Bulletin Critique des Annales Islamologiques*, no. 24 (2008) : 63–65.
28. Solomon I. Sara (Georgetown University), *Theological Studies* (March 2008).
29. Stefan de Warsage, "Het ontstaan van de koran," *Katholiek Nieuwsblad*, April 4, 2008.
30. Y. Tzvi Langermann (Professor of Arabic at Bar Ilan University, Ramat Gan, Israel), *American Journal of Islamic Social Sciences* 25, no. 3 (Summer 2008): 121–23.
31. Daniel King, "A Christian Qur'ān? A Study in the Syriac Background to the Language of the Qur'ān as Presented in the Work of Christoph Luxenberg," *Journal for Late Antique Religion and Culture* 3 (2009): 44–71.
32. Manfred Kropp, "'People of powerful South Arabian kings' or Just 'people of their kind we annihilated before?': Proper Noun or Common Noun in Qur'ān 44:37 and 50:14," *Proceedings of the Seminar for Arabian Studies* 39 (2009): 237–44.
33. Peter Bruns, "Der Islam: eine (juden-)christliche Sekte? Eine kurze dogmengeschichtliche Betrachtung," *Forum Katholische Theologie* 26, no. 1 (2010).
34. Stefan Weninger, ed., in collaboration with Geoffrey Khan, Michael P. Streck, Janet CE Watson, *Semitic Languages: An International Handbook* (Berlin/Boston: Walter de Gruyter, 2011), pp. 747–55.

Popular Accounts in Newspapers or Magazines:

1. Mona Naggar, *Neue Zürcher Zeitung* (Zurich, Switzerland) (February 3, 2001).
2. Ibn Warraq, "Virgins? What Virgins?" *Guardian* (London, UK) (January 12, 2002).
3. Alexander Stille, "Scholars Are Quietly Offering New Theories of the Koran," *New York Times* (March 2, 2002).
4. Roger-Pol Droit, "Et si les vierges célestes du Coran n'étaient que fruits blancs?" *Le Monde* (May 5, 2003).
5. Jörg Lau, "Keine Huris im Paradies" *Zeit Online* (May 15, 2003).
6. Claude Gilliot, "L'origine syro-araméenne du Coran," *Le Nouvelle Observateur*, Hors-Série (with France Culture) "Les nouveaux penseur de l'islam" (April/May 2004), p. 64 ff., also "Les sources du Coran," *Le Monde des religions* 19 (September–October 2006), pp. 30–33.

3.5. Books Discussing Luxenberg's Work

1. Christoph Burgmer, ed., *Streit um den Koran* (Berlin: Verlag Hans Schiler, 2004).
2. Alfred-Louis de Prémare, *Aux origines du Coran: Questions d'hier, Approches d'aujourd'hui* (Paris: Téraèdre, 2004).
2. Gabriel Said Reynolds, ed., *The Qur'ān in its Historical Context* (London: Routledge, 2007).
3. Manfred Kropp, ed., *Results of Contemporary Research on the Qur'ān: The Question of a Historical-Critical Text of the Qur'ān* (Beirut, 2007).
4. Joachim Gnilka, *Die Nazerener und der Koran: Eine Spurensuche* (Freiburg im Breisgau: Herder, 2007).
5. Joachim Gnilka, *Qui sont les chrétiens du Coran ?* (translation of the previous entry) (Paris: Cerf, 2008).
6. J. J. G. Jansen, *Mohammed: Eine Biographie*, trans. M. Müller-Haas (Munich: C. H. Beck), pp. 191–93.
7. Norbert G. Pressburg, *Goodbye Mohammed: Wie der Islam wirklich entstand* (Norderstedt: Books on Demand, 2009).
8. Eildert Mulder and Thomas Milo, *De omstreden Bronnen van de Islam*, (Zoetermeer, NL: Meinema, 2009).
9. Barbara Köster, *Der missverstandene Koran* (Berlin: Schiler Verlag, 2010).
10. Édouard-Marie Gallez, *Le Messie et son Prophète: Aux origines de l'Islam, vol. 2, Du Muḥammad des Califes au Muḥammad de l'Histoire* (Versailles: Éditions de Paris, 2010).
11. Gabriel Said Reynolds, ed., *The Qur'ān and its Biblical Subtext* (London: Routledge, 2010).
12. Gabriel Said Reynolds, ed., *New Perspectives on the Qur'an: The Qur'an in Its Historical Context 2*, Routledge Studies in the Qurʾan (London: Routledge, 2011).
13. Guillaume Dye and Fabien Nobilio, *Figures Bibliques en Islam* (Brussels: EME and InterCommunications, 2011).
14. Carlos A. Segovia and Basil Lourié, *The Coming of the Comforter: When, Where, and to Whom? Studies on the Rise of Islam and Various Other Topics in Memory of John Wansbrough* (Piscataway, NJ: Gorgias Press, 2012).
15. Nicolai Sinai, *Die heilige Schrift des Islams: Die wichtigsten Fakten zum Koran* (Freiburg: Herder, 2012).
16. Karl-Friedrich Pohlmann, *Die Entstehung des Korans: Neue Erkenntnisse aus Sicht der historisch-kritischen Biblewissenschaft* (Darmstadt: WBG, 2012).

Notes

1 Theodor Nöldeke, "Zur Sprache des Korāns," in *Beiträge Zur Semitischen Sprachwissenschaft* (Strassburg: Verlag Von Karl J. Trübner, 1904), p. 13.
2 See Günter Lüling's own account of the unscholarly reception of his book, "Preconditions for the Scholarly Criticism of the Koran and Islam, with Some Autobiographical Remarks," *Journal of Higher Criticism* 3 (Spring 1996): 73–109,
3 Cf. Herbert Berg, "The Implications of and Opposition to, the Methods of John Wansbrough," in Ibn Warraq, ed., *The Quest for the Historical Muhammad* (Amherst, NY: Prometheus Books, 2000), pp. 489–509. See also R. B. Serjeant's notorious review of John Wansbrough's *Quranic Studies* in *Journal of the Royal Asiatic Society* (1978): 76–78.
4 Claude Gilliot, "Une Reconstruction Critique du Coran ou comment en finir avec les merveilles de la lampe d'Aladin," in Manfred Kropp, ed., *Results of Contemporary Research on the Qur'ān: The Question of a Historical-Critical Text of the Qur'ān* (Beirut, 2007), p. 92 n. 385.
5 Jan M. F. van Reeth, "Le vignoble du Paradis et le Chemin qui y mène. La thèse de C. Luxenberg et les sources du Coran," *Arabica* 53, (2006): 511–12.
6 Personal communication from Christoph Luxenberg.
7 For example, Jan M. F. Van Reeth, "Le Coran et les Scribes," in C. Cannuyer, ed., *Les scribes et la transmission du savoir* (XLIIe Journées Armand Abel-Aristide Téodoridès, Université de Liège, 19–20 mars 2004) (Bruxelles, 2006); Jan M. F. Van Reeth, "Who Is the 'Other' Paraclete?" in Carlos A. Segovia and Basil Lourié, ed., *The Coming of the Comforter: When, Where, and to Whom? Studies on the Rise of Islam and Various Other Topics in Memory of John Wansbrough* (Piscataway, NJ: Gorgias Press, 2012).
8 Jan M. F. van Reeth, "Le vignoble du paradis et le chemin qui y mène. La thèse de C. Luxenberg et les sources du Coran," *Arabica* 53 (2006): 511–24.
9 Van Reeth, "Who Is the 'Other' Paraclete?" pp. 451–52 n. 148.
10 C. Luxenberg, "A New Interpretation of the Arabic Inscription in Jerusalem's Dome of the Rock," in Karl-Heinz Ohlig and Gerd-R. Puin, eds., *The Hidden Origins of Islam* (Amherst, NY: Prometheus Books, 2010), p. 141.
11 Ibid.
12 Christoph Burgmer, ed., *Streit um den Koran* (Berlin: Verlag Hans Schiler, 2004), p. 32.
13 Christoph Luxenberg, "Kein 'Mekka' (Makka) und kein 'Bakka' im Koran: Zu Sure 48:24 und 3:96: Eine philologische Analyse," *Imprimatur* 7 (October 2012).
14 Christoph Luxenberg, "Keine Schlacht von Badr: Zu Syrischen Buchstaben in frühen Koranmanuskripten," in Markus Gross and Karl-Heinz Ohlig, eds., *Vom Koran zum Islam,* Inârah: Schriften zur frühen Islamgeschichte und zum Koran, vol. 4 (Berlin: Schiler Verlag, 2008), pp. 642–76.
15 Christoph Luxenberg, talk at conference in Helsinki, September 2013. To be published soon.
16 Forthcoming.
17 Claude Gilliot, "Langue et Coran: une Lecture Syro-araméene du Coran," *Arabica* 50 (2003): 381–93; Gilliot, "L'Embarras d'un Exégète Musulman face à un Palimpseste: Māturīdī et la sourate de l'Abondance (al-Kawthar, sourate 108), avec

une note savante sur commentaire coranique d'Ibn al-Naqīb (died 698/1298)," in R. Arnzen and J. Thielman, eds., *Words, Texts and Concepts Cruising the Mediterranean Sea: Studies on the Sources, Contents and Influences of Islamic Civilization and Arabic Philosophy and Science*, dedicated to Gerhard Endress on his sixty-fifth birthday (Leuven/Paris: Peeters, 2004), pp. 33–69; Gilliot, "Une Reconstruction Critique du Coran ou Comment en Finir avec les Merveilles de la Lampe d'Aladin?" in Manfred Kropp, ed., *Results of Contemporary Research on the Qur'ān: The question of a Historico-critical Text of the Qur'ān* (Beirut: Ergon Verlag Würzburg, 2007).

18 Claude Gilliot and Pierre Larcher, "Language and Style of the Qur'ān," *Encyclopaedia of the Qur'ān*, vol. 3 (Leiden: E. J. Brill, 2003), pp. 109–35.

19 Ibid., pp. 130–32.

20 Claude Gilliot, "The 'Collections' of the Meccan Arabic Lectionary," in Nicolet Boekhoff-van der Voort, Kees Versteegh and Joas Wagemakers, eds., *The Transmission and Dynamics of the Textual Sources of Islam: Essays in Honour of Harald Motzki* (Leiden: E. J. Brill, 2011), p. 108.

21 For example, F. Corriente, "From Old Arabic to Classical Arabic through the Pre-Islamic Koiné: Some Notes on the Native Grammarians' Sources, Attitudes and Goals," *Journal of Semitic Studies* 21 (1976): 62–98.

22 Federico Corriente, "On a proposal for a 'Syro-Aramaic' reading of the Qur'ān," *Collectanea Christiana Orientalia* 1 (2003): 305–314.

23 Ibid., p. 314.

24 Crone wrote, "All [such] suggestions should be dismissed out of hand. . . . That places explicitly identified as southeast Arabian should have been misconstrued as Qurashī domains says much about the intoxicating effect of Mecca on the source-critical faculties of otherwise sober scholars. So does the identification of Ptolemy's *Macoraba* with Mecca, which has gained almost universal acceptance. It was first made on the ground that the names were vaguely similar and the location vaguely right, Macoraba being assumed to reproduce a name such as Makka-Rabba, 'Great Mecca.' But this is a most implausible construction, which has since been replaced by *makrab* or *mikrāb*, meaning temple. But in the first place the root *krb* does not denote holiness in Arabic, as opposed to South Arabian, so that once again the language reflected would not be the one expected. In the second place, a name composed of the consonants *mkk* cannot be derived from the root *krb*. It follows that Ptolemy would be referring to a sanctuary town which was not called Mecca. Why then identify the two? Rescue attempts such as *mikrāb* Makka, 'the sanctuary of Mecca,' are no better than Makka-Rabba, for all that we clearly need some sort of addition to account for the feminine form reflected in the Greek. The plain truth is that the name of *Macoraba* has nothing to do with that of Mecca, and that location indicated by Ptolemy for *Macoraba* in no way dictates identification of the two." Patricia Crone, *Meccan Trade and the Rise of Islam* (Oxford: Basil Blackwell, 1987), pp.135–36.

25 Jonathan Owens, *A Linguistic History of Arabic* (Oxford: Oxford University Press, 2006), p. 121.

26 Martin F. J. Baasten, "Review of Christoph Luxenberg (ps.), *Die syro-aramäische Lesart des Koran: Ein Beitrag zur Entschlüsselung der Koransprache* (Berlin: Das Arabische Buch, 2000), " *Aramaic Studies* 2, no. 2 (2004): 268–72.

27 Christoph Luxenberg, *The Syro-Aramaic Reading of the Koran: A Contribution to the Decoding of the Language of the Koran* (Berlin: Verlag Hans Schiler, 2007), p. 44.

28 Y. Tzvi Langermann (Professor of Arabic at Bar Ilan University, Ramat Gan, Israel) in *American Journal of Islamic Social Sciences* 25, no. 3 (Summer 2008): 122.

29 Ibid., p. 123.

30 Johannes J. G. Jansen, in *Bibliotheca Orientalis* 60, nos. 3–4 (May–August 2003), columns 477–80.

31 On Jansen's website, Arabistjansen.nl, http://www.arabistjansen.nl/rawwahnaahum .pdf (accessed April 24, 2014).

32 Enno Littmann, "Thamud und Safa," *Abhandlungen für die Kunde des Morgenlandes* 25, no. 1 (1940), Kraus reprint, Nendeln (Liechtenstein) 1966. [See index at p. 161 sub רוח, rwḥ].

33 W. G. Oxtoby, *Some Inscriptions of the Safaitic Bedouin* (New Haven, 1968), pp. 52–53.

34 *C: Corpus Inscriptionum Semiticarum: Pars Quinta Inscriptiones Saracenicas Continens,* inscription 4956: p. 607; C 2718: p. 355 (Paris, 1950).

34 Daniel King, "A Christian Qur'ān? A Study in the Syrian Background to the Language of the Qur'an as Presented in the Work of Christoph Luxenberg," *Journal for Late Antique Religion and Culture* 3, 44–71 (2009): 1.

35 Available at Dumbarton Oaks Research Library and Collection, http://www.doaks .org/research/byzantine/resources/syriac/lexica (accessed April 23, 2014).

36 Guillaume Dye, "Traces of Bilingualism/Multilingualism in the Qur'ānic Text," in Ahmad al-Jallad, ed., *Arabic in Context*, Papers of Congress, 2–3, November 2013, Leiden University. Forthcoming.

38 Guillaume Dye, "La Nuit du Destin et la Nuit de la Nativité," in Guillaume Dye and Fabien Nobilio, eds., *Figures Bibliques en Islam* (Brussels: E. M. E. and Inter-Communications, 2011), pp. 107–169.

39 Tor Andrae, "Der Ursprung des Islams und das Christentum," *in Kyrkohistorisk Årsskrift* [Sweden], year 23 (1923), pp. 149–206; year 24 (1924), pp. 213–292; year 25 (1921[5]), pp. 45–112; translated by Jean Roche as Tor Andrae, *Les Origines de l'Islam et le Christianisme* (Paris : Adrien-Maisonneuve, 1955).

40 Ibid., pp. 9–10.

41 Gerhard Uhlhorn, "Ebioniten," in *Realencyklopädie für protestantische Theologie und Kirche* (RE), 3rd ed., vol. 5 (Leipzig: Hinrichs, 1898), pp. 125–28.

42 Hugo Johannes Bestmann, *Die Anfänge des katholischen Christentums und des Islams* (Nördlingen, 1884).

43 Henry Preserved Smith, *The Bible and Islam* (New York, 1897).

44 Édouard Sayous, *Jésus-Christ d'après Mahomet, ou les Notions et les Doctrines Musulmanes sur le Christianisme* (Paris: E. Leroux et Otto Schulze, 1880).

45 Ibid., pp. 23–24.

46 Susannah Heschel, *Abraham Geiger and the Jewish Jesus*, Chicago Studies in the History of Judaism (Chicago: University of Chicago Press, 1998), p. 58.

47 Andrae, *Origines de l'Islam et le Christianisme*, p. 21.

48 Tor Andrae, *Mohammed: The Man and His Faith*, trans. by Theophil Menzel (Mineola, NY: Dover Publications, 2000); English translation first published in 1936, from of *Mohammed, Sein Leben und Sein Glaube* (Göttingen: Vandenhoeck and Ruprecht, 1932).

49 Ibid., pp. 87–88.

50 Ibid., p. 90.

51 Ibid., p. 96.

52 Ibid., p. 109.

53 Sidney Griffith, "Syriacisms in the Arabic Qur'an," in M. Bar Asher, et al., eds., *A Word Fitly Spoken* (Jerusalem, 2007), pp. 83 ff.; part 2, chapter 2 in present volume.

54 Personal communication from Professor Sebastian Brock.

55 Ibid.

56 Giulio Basetti-Sani, O. F. M., *The Koran in the Light of Christ: Islam, in the Plan of History of Salvation* (Chicago, IL: Franciscan Herald Press, 1977), translation of *Il Corano Nella Lice di Cristo* (Rome, 1972), pp. 153–55.

57 Hirschfeld was born in Prussia, received his Dr. phil. from the University of Strassburg for his study "Jüdische Elemente im Koran: ein Beitrag zur Korānforschung," and eventually became professor of Semitic languages at University College, London.

58 Luxenberg, *Syro-Aramaic Reading of the Koran*, p. 303.

59 Hartwig Hirschfeld, *New Researches into the Composition and Exegesis of the Qoran* (London: Royal Asiatic Society, 1902), p. 19.

60 Ibid., pp. 22–24.

61 Frère Bruno Bonnet-Eymard, *Le Coran: Traduction et Commentaire Systématique*, vol. 3 (Saint-Parres-lès-Vaudes: La Contre-Réforme Catholique, 1997), p. 270.

Christmas and the Eucharist in Early Islam? Remarks about Assumptions and Methodology

Markus Gross

In several of Christoph Luxenberg's articles, Christian liturgical practices are claimed to be the source of Koranic texts, above all the Eucharist and Christmas. His views have been contradicted vehemently, not only on apologetic Muslim websites, but also in scholarly publications. Therefore it seems fair to take the arguments against his new interpretation of Koranic texts seriously. The present article will present some of the arguments of one of his critics, Nicolai Sinai,[1] but also some of the findings of another scholar, Stephen Shoemaker,[2] who found a material source in the form of a church for the Koranic narrative of Jesus' birth. This should be understood rather as the invitation to further discussion than as a final judgment.

In the following, the articles of both Sinai and Shoemaker are first summarized in as objective a way as possible. Only after that are their arguments assessed and if possible either confirmed or refuted.

1. Luxenberg's Hypotheses

Before assessing the above-mentioned articles, we should have a short look at Luxenberg's reinterpretations to be found in the present anthology. He reinterprets Surah 97 as follows: "The Destiny (of the Star of Nativity)"

1. We sent him down (Infant Jesus) during the Night of Destiny (of the Star of Nativity).
2. What do you know what the Night of Destiny is?
3. The Night (Nocturnal Office) of Destiny (of the Star of Nativity) is more beneficial than a thousand vigils?
4. The Angels (accompanied by) the Spirit, send down with the permission of their Lord, all sorts of hymns.
5. Peace there is until the break of day.

The birth story in the Mary Surah (Q 19:22–27) is also reinterpreted by Luxenberg (see his article "*Christmas and the Eucharist in the Qur'ān*" in the present volume). Pickthall translated the story as follows:

22. And she, conceived him, and she withdrew with him to a place.
23. And the pangs of childbirth drove her unto the trunk of the palm tree. She said: Oh, would that I had died ere this and had become a thing of naught, forgotten!

24. Then (one) cried unto her from below her, saying: Grieve not! Thy Lord hath placed a rivulet beneath thee,
25. And shake the trunk of the palm tree toward thee, thou wilt cause ripe dates to fall upon thee.
26. So eat and drink and be consoled. And if thou meetest any mortal, say: Lo! I have vowed a fast unto the Beneficent, and may not speak this day to any mortal.
27. Then she brought him to her own folk, carrying him. They said: O Mary! Thou hast come with an amazing thing.

By interpreting the alleged word meaning "rivulet" – سريا (*sry'*) as the Syro-Aramaic form ܫܪܝܐ (šaryā) he comes to the following rendering of verse 24:

> Then he called to her immediately after her delivery: "Do not be sad, your Lord has made your delivery legitimate."

One of his main arguments for this reinterpretation lies in the plot of the story. Mary's concern is not food and drink, but the expected reactions of "her folk" to her illegitimate child. So although eventually she does eat and drink, she does so rather out of relief after having been assured of Jesus' legitimacy.

2. Nicolai Sinai's Criticism of Luxenberg

2.1. A Short Summary of Sinai's Argumentation

In his article in the prestigious periodical *Der Islam*, Nicolai Sinai presents his view about Surah 97, Luxenberg's reinterpretation, and the idea of Christmas being mentioned in the Koran. The article was written in German, its title in English would be "*Christmas in the Koran or the Night of Destination: An Interpretation of Surah 97.*"

His main points of criticism referring to Luxenberg's theory can be summarized as follows:

(1) Luxenberg judges certain Koranic passages, e.g., those dealing with the Virgins of Paradise, as dark because of their alleged "moral turpitude" ("moralische Anstößigkeit") and because they differ from Christian views of Paradise, not—as Luxenberg purports—because of their "ambiguity" ("Unklarheit," or "lack of clarity").

(2) Luxenberg does not mention that the identification of Surah 97 with Christmas is an old topos of Christian anti-Islamic polemic.

(3) Luxenberg violates a general philological rule: when the use of a word or phrase in a specific part of a larger text is investigated, then the use of the same word or phrase in other parts of the text must be taken into consideration. In the Islamic exegesis this is called *tafsīr al-qur'ān bi-l-qur'ān*. Luxenberg refers the verb *anzala* – "to send down" (as in

verse 1: *anzalnā-hu*) to the infant Jesus, while this verb is never used referring to persons in the rest of the Koran, but exclusively to things, typically to revelations (as scripture/*kitāb* or admonitions/*taḏkira*), e.g., 44:2-3: *wa-l-kitābi l-mubīn / ʾinnā ʾanzalnāhu fī lailatin mubārakatin ʾinnā kunnā munḏirīn* (2. By the Scripture that maketh plain 3. Lo! We revealed it on a blessed night. Lo! We are ever warning).
In verse 4 Luxenberg changes the reading *tanazzalu* into *tunazzilu*, thus it is not God who sends down, unlike in the rest of the Koran.

(4) Luxenberg interprets *qadr* as the equivalent of Syriac *ḥelqā*, meaning "destiny." As *helqā* is also a synonym of *bēṯ yaldā* ("birth/horoscope at birth"), he equates *lailat al-qadr* with Christmas. Luxenberg's new interpretation is explained in a much-too-compressed way (one sentence) and the steps of his argumentation are not convincing. If he could adduce an attested Syriac expression like *lelyā ḏ-ḥelqā* instead of the common *bet-yalda*, his theory might be taken seriously, but instead he only comes up with dictionary entries without quotations in real texts to prove his point.

(5) Luxenberg's interpretation of *šahr* in verse 5 as *šahrā* (vigil) is probably due to the fact that he assumes an earlier writing with *sīn* instead of *šīn*, thus interpreting the underlying root as *sahar/sahira* – "to guard, watch over (remaining awake)." There is, however, a similar text in the Psalms, known for a long time, 90:4: "For a thousand years in Your sight Are like yesterday when it passes by, Or as a watch in the night." This clearly indicates that the designation "night" here points to a much longer space of time.

(6) Equating the Koranic *ʾamr* with the Syriac *memrā* ("hymn") is an adhoc explanation and not corroborated by other passages.

Already at the beginning of his article, Sinai summarizes his assessment of Luxenberg's methods, calling them "seriously flawed" and "circular" and his results "a methodically arbitrary play with associations." However, his devastating criticism is coupled with an important reservation: Sinai does not entirely dismiss Luxenberg's "hunch" that this Koranic texts is somehow connected with Christmas, an idea he then develops in the second half of his article. At the very beginning of his argumentation, he clearly states that he assumes the traditional scenario ("[das] traditionelle Szenario") of Koranic exegesis, which he characterizes with the following basic features: proclamation ("Verkündigung") by a charismatic founder at the beginning of the seventh century in the West Arabian cities of Mecca and Medina. Moreover, he explicitly adheres to Theodor Nöldeke's subdivision of Surahs into four chronological layers (Early Meccan, Middle Meccan, Late Meccan, and Medinan). Interestingly, he assumes later changes and additions to the

Koranic text and opines that the dating of the "night of destiny" in the month of Ramaḍān is secondary and late.

He begins his further investigation with a lengthy discussion of the Arabic root *q-d-r* and comes to the conclusion that the *lailat al-qadr* was a "feast of the pre-Koranic Meccan cult which . . . was newly filled according to revelation theology" (p. 20). According to Sinai this was done by selectively reinterpreting Christian motives and replacing baby Jesus with the Koran, thus creating a "counter-Christmas" ("Gegen-Weihnachten").

He then dedicates a few pages to the interesting question of relative chronology, in other words: when was this Surah composed relative to other Koranic texts. As reasons for an early dating he mentions the brevity of the verses and the use of the particle *ʾinna*, although he does not consider this evidence conclusive. As the above-mentioned verses 44:2–3 (a "Middle Meccan" text) obviously refer to our text, they are almost certainly later. Although Sinai considers Surah 97 an Early Meccan text, he still does not count it among the oldest text fragments of the Koran. His main reason is its eschatological content, which is not found in Surahs Q 105 and Q 106, which display a rather positive attitude to the community of Mecca. According to Sinai, a break can be discerned between the latter Surahs and Q 99 or Q 101, which demonstrate a "fundamental disturbance and crisis in the relationship God–man and threaten the listeners with an individual eschatological reckoning."

Among the "non-eschatological" Surahs he enumerates Q 93, 94, and 108, which all use the second person. Sinai calls them "comfort surahs" ("Trostsuren").

Sinai's conclusion is that Surah 97 should be considered an ex post authorization of earlier Koranic texts, attributing them to an act of revelation during the *lailat al-qadr*.

In the following chapter, "Considerations Concerning Literary Criticism" ("Literarkritische Überlegungen"), Sinai comes up with a number of interesting ideas concerning the history of the text itself. His observation that verse 4 is longer than the other verses coincides with another observation regarding its contents: "*tanazzalu l-malāʾikatu wa-r-rūḥu fīhā* <u>*bi-ʾidni rabbihim min kulli ʾamrin*</u> – The angels and the Spirit descend therein, <u>by the permission of their Lord, with all decrees</u> (Pickthall)." If the underlined part is omitted, then the length of all verses is roughly the same, but then the angels are active agents able to take decisions. The addition, on the contrary, makes it clear that God alone has a free will. Sinai adds that the phrase "*bi-ʾiḏni* . . ." is not attested in other early texts.

Another peculiarity of verse 4 is the mentioning of the "spirit" (*al-rūḥ*), which, according to Nöldeke, is rather typical of Middle and Late Meccan texts. In one Medinan verse (Q 2:97) it then is identified with Gabriel. Sinai finally concludes that not only the second half, but the whole of verse 4 must be a later addition.

The next chapter deals with Surah 97 and the nativity. Sinai mentions an "intertext" found on the website of the project Corpus Coranicum[3] and discovered by his colleague Yousef Kouriyhe. It is one of Ephrem the Syrian's hymns[4] on nativity and uses the verb *naḥḥet*, which is the exact equivalent of Arabic *anzala* – "to send down." Sinai remarks (p. 26):

> In any case we cannot exclude that the original Koranic semantics of the verb *ʾanzala* in verse 1 and *tanazzala* in verse 4 respectively might have been partially influenced by such Christian references.

Sinai finds another parallel in verse 5: *"salāmun hiya ḥattā maṭlaʿi l-fağr* – (That night is) Peace until the rising of the dawn," which had already been seen in connection with Christmas by Richard Bell. Sinai himself sees it in connection to Luke 2:14: "Glory to God in the highest, And on earth peace among men with whom He is pleased."

In spite of his own arguments, however, Sinai does not think that Surah 97 is directly referring to the nativity. He rather assumes a "reinterpretation" ("Umwertung") of an Old Arabian night of destiny, by selectively adopting Christian motives and the construction of a kind of "counter-Christmas" ("Gegen-Weihnacht"). He concludes (p. 28): "The text could fulfill this function only if the Koranic listeners understood the Christian allusions as such."

In the following chapter, which deals with the interpretation of the inserted verse 4, he mentions a parallel verse in Gen 28:11–19. In verse 12 we read about angels who "ascend and descend:"

> He had a dream, and behold, a ladder was set on the earth with its top reaching to heaven; and behold, the angels of God were ascending and descending on it.

According to Sinai, the semantics of the word *rūḥ* is influenced by the Syriac *rūḥa d-qūdšā* or *ruḥā qaddīšā*, which designates the "holy spirit," an angelic being that "speaks through the prophets," according to the Nicene-Constantinopolitan creed:

> And we believe in the Holy Spirit, the Lord, and Giver of Life, Who proceeds from the Father, Who with the Father and the Son together is worshipped and glorified, Who spoke by the Prophets.

Sinai opines that here the descending angels do not—as in the Gospel of Luke—accompany the birth of Christ, but the transmission of the Koranic revelations, but he acknowledges the purposeful use of Christian motives in order to authorize the Koranic text and thus to "overwrite" Christmas with a feast of Koranic revelation. His last sentence is a German play on words:

> Gegen Korandeutungen im Stile *Luxenbergs* ist dabei auf den wesentlichen Unterschied zwischen *Über*schreiben und *Ab*schreiben zu insistieren. [In contrast to interpretations of the Koran in the style of *Luxenberg* we have to insist on the fundamental difference between *overwriting* and *copying*.]

2.2. Assessment of Sinai's Arguments

At first glance Sinai's article purports to be a clear refutation of Luxenberg's reinterpretation of Surah 97, more so of his whole method, as can be seen in formulations like "seriously flawed," "circular," "a methodically arbitrary play with associations." The very general rejection of Luxenberg, also to be felt in other publications of Sinai, is in some contrast to his otherwise scholarly and unemotional, even open-minded style. In how far he succeeds in refuting Luxenberg, or rather what remains of Luxenberg's theory and in how far Sinai manages to save the "classical" view, is a question to be answered in the present chapter.

Sinai's first point of criticism concerning Luxenberg's method is the reproach that he reinterprets linguistically clear passages because of their "moral turpitude" or because they differ from the Christian view, probably referring primarily to the Virgins of Paradise. This reproach was first made in a panel discussion in Germany by Stefan Wild, and it has meanwhile appeared in several German press articles. In Luxenberg's original books and articles he never adduced moral reasons for a reinterpretation, but rather pointed out the inconsistency of the notion of Virgins of Paradise on the one hand and Koranic verses that indicate that the believers will meet their wives in paradise, on the other, for example Q 36:56–57: "They and their wives, in pleasant shade, on thrones reclining; Theirs the fruit (of their good deeds) and theirs (all) that they ask."

Moreover, the linguistic form allegedly designating the Virgins of Paradise as pronounced today: *ḥūr ʿīn* – "white (ones), eyed (ones)" is far from clear, as can easily be demonstrated by the fact that in all later works of Arabic literature they are called *ḥurīya*. So the motives here assumed for Luxenberg's work are definitely wrong.

Sinai's second reproach refers to Luxenberg's style: he leaves out too much, does not check properly, and renounces on explaining in detail. In the present case, Luxenberg did not mention that the identification of Surah 97 with Christmas is an old topos of Christian anti-Islamic polemic, he does not consider the use of the verb *anzala* – "to send down" in other passages of the Koran and above all he explains his hypotheses by squeezing all his reasoning into one subordinate clause.

Here in fact Sinai broaches a subject that cannot easily be dismissed. Luxenberg's books are definitely not easy to digest, and they presuppose a reasonable command of several languages, including Syriac and Hebrew, apart from a fair knowledge of the Bible. His style is often very elliptic and complicated, and each of his articles could easily be expanded to twice its size by simply adducing all relevant secondary literature or parallel texts and by explaining his argumentation in more detail.

However, the fact that an idea has been used in polemic or apologetic works centuries ago does not necessarily mean that the idea is wrong. On the contrary, it might reflect an early counterargument in a debate. As Luxenberg's article was a mere *philological* analysis dealing with the *composition* of the text of Surah 97, he probably considered the much later discussion about the already *finished* and *interpreted* text as irrelevant.

But Sinai also reproaches Luxenberg for violating a general philological rule: the use of a verb *anzala*, if reinterpreted with a new meaning, would have had to be compared to its use in other passages of the Koran. Here in fact Sinai's criticism is not unfounded. In the Koran, the verb *anzala* is indeed mostly used with things that are "sent down" by God (primarily revelations), not with persons.

At this point we should have a look at other words based on the same root. In the Koran we find the word *manāzil*, plural of *manzil* ("mansion, station") and especially *munzil* ("a receiver of guests, one who causes to descend"),[5] for example in Q 23:29:

> *wa-qul rabbi 'anzilnī munzalan mubārakan wa-'anta ḫayru l-munzilīna* – And say: My Lord! Cause me to land at a blessed landing place, for Thou art best of all who bring to land.

In this verse the verb *anzil-nī* ("cause me to land/descend") obviously refers to a person, so Sinai is not right when he claims that the verb is never used with persons. The original meaning of the root *n-z-l* in the Koran seems to be "to descend, to come down from a higher position to a lower position," for example from a camel. That is why the one who makes you descend from your camel is a "receiver of guests (*munzil*)" and the place where you descend is a "station (*manzil*)." The root is certainly not limited to things, let alone to divine messages. Had Luxenberg done his homework here, it would only have corroborated his theory!

Another point of criticism is Luxenberg's interpretation of the word *qadr*, which he sees as the equivalent of Syriac *ḥelqā* ("destiny"), which itself is a synonym of *bēṯ yaldā* ("birth/horoscope at birth"). For Sinai, it is farfetched to infer from these equations that *qadr* actually can refer to the birth of Christ, although he does not question the equations as such. In fact, the evidence adduced is far from conclusive and suggests little more than a vague possibility. In the standard Syriac dictionary of Payne Smith[6] we find the following meanings of the underlying verbal root *ḥlaq*: "to allot, to determine by lot or fate, to destine," and for the noun *ḥelqā*: "lot, portion; fate, destiny." Moreover he quotes a sentence: "*npaq ḥelqā men alāhā* – the lot went forth from God." Given the importance assigned to astronomy at that time it is understandable how this word became a synonym of "birth." Moreover, in Brockelmann's dictionary the Syriac root is seen as the etymological equivalent of the Arabic root *ḫalaqa* – "to create." If we then consider that Christians to this day consider the birth of Christ to be a decisive moment for mankind, which in fact did change the "destiny" of humanity, then we have to agree that Luxenberg's reasoning is not compelling, though his explanation is at least possible.

Luxenberg interpreted the word *šahr* in verse 5 as *šahr-ā* (vigil), thus "The Night of Power is better than a thousand months" becomes "The Night (Nocturnal Office) of Destiny (of the Star of Nativity) is more beneficial than a thousand vigils?" Against this interpretation Sinai adduces a verse from the Psalms; that is, Ps 90:4:

> כִּי אֶלֶף שָׁנִים בְּעֵינֶיךָ כְּיוֹם אֶתְמוֹל כִּי יַעֲבֹר וְאַשְׁמוּרָה בַלָּיְלָה׃
>
> *kī äläp šānīm bə-ʿēnäy-ḵā kə-yōm äṯmōl kī yaʿᵃḇor wə-ašmūrāh ḇa-lāylāh*
>
> For a thousand years in Your sight Are like yesterday when it passes by, Or as a watch in the night.

With this verse he wants to prove that a "night" points to a much longer space of time. However, in the Hebrew Bible, as much as in modern literature, a very long period of time is hardly ever designated with a phrase containing the word "month," but typically with the word "year." A phrase like "a thousand years" appears in the lyrics of numerous songs, "a thousand months" virtually never. So Sinai's argument here is more than weak.

Finally, Sinai criticizes Luxenberg's equation of *ʾamr* with the Syriac *memrā* ("hymn") in the prase: *bi-ʾiḏni rabbihim min kulli ʾamrin* – Pickthall: "by the permission of their Lord, with all decrees." Semantically, the classical interpretation does not make very much sense. A permission is not given "with all decrees," but rather with one decree. Moreover, the equation of *ʾamr* with *memrā*, meaning the "logos, demiurge," is not only mentioned in Paret's commentary to his standard German translation of the Koran, but also in footnote 46 of Sinai's own article. So if *ʾamr* as the equivalent of *memrā,* meaning "logos," in general is accepted, why should it be so farfetched to assume it also as its equivalent when the latter means "hymn"?

As we have seen, Sinai's criticism of Luxenberg is not totally unfounded, but it is far from compelling.

But now we will have a look at his own alternative explanation. First of all, he explicitly states that he bases his research on the traditional scenario (proclamation by a charismatic prophet at the beginning of the seventh century in the West Arabian cities of Mecca and Medina) and assumes at least four layers of Surahs (Early Meccan, Middle Meccan, Late Meccan, and Medinan).

Then we have to consider his assumptions and conclusions in the second half of his article:

(1) The dating of the "night of destiny" in the month of Ramaḍān is secondary and late.

(2) In Surah 97, Christian motives were intentionally replaced with a new view—not the birth of a savior, but the sending down of the Koran took place—thus a "counter-Christmas" was created.

(3) Unlike most of the Koran, the earliest Surahs did not have eschatological content. The disturbance and crisis in the relationship God–man and the subsequent threats with hell-fire came later.

(4) One method of dating Surahs is the choice of words, for example the use of the particle *ʾinna*.

(5) Surah 97 should be considered an *ex post* authorization of earlier Koranic texts.

(6) Whole verses, in other cases whole phrases, were added later, in the present case verse 4, or at least the second half of it.

(7) The "spirit" (*al-rūḥ*) does not appear often in the earliest layer, is typical for the Middle and Late Meccan texts, and is reinterpreted as the archangel Gabriel in a Medinan Surah.

(8) The problem of free will is seen as a problem, therefore verse 4 was added.

(9) There is a parallel text in Ephrem's hymns, a text collection assumed by Luxenberg as a model also for other Surahs.

(10) There is a Biblical parallel text where angels ascend and descend in Gen 28:11–19.

(11) The semantics of the word *rūḥ* is influenced by the Syriac *rūḥa d-qūdšā* or *ruḥā qaddīšā*, which designates the "holy spirit."

If he should be right with these assumptions and conclusions, two things become clear:

(1) Although Sinai and other (former or current) staff members of the Corpus Coranicum try to give the impression that they defend the classical view of Early Islam, and thus their findings will not contradict the orthodox Islamic doctrines, this is definitely not the case. His view is incompatible with Islamic tradition. Especially the following points would certainly be rejected by pious Muslims:

- He assumes that the Koran as we know it today had sources or models, e.g., Ephrem the Syrian and the Bible.

- The layers in the Koran represent very different religious ideas (e.g., regarding the "spirit," eternal punishment, free will, etc.), different styles, and different wording. This is hardly compatible with the idea of one single charismatic founder and one original Koran in heaven.
- There are obviously no real polytheists in Sinai's explanation, but numerous allusions to the Old and New Testament.
- The dating of the Islamic calendar (e.g., regarding the dating of feasts) is secondary.
- If a "counter-Christmas" is created, the original Christmas must have been known to the target group of the Koran, thus they must have been familiar with Christianity.

(2) At least in his interpretation of Surah 97, he is not very far away from Luxenberg. Like Luxenberg, he assumes strong influence from both the Syriac language and the literature written in it. And like him he assumes that the decisive incident for mankind was reinterpreted: the birth of the savior is replaced by the sending down of the Koran. The difference is rather that for Luxenberg, Surah 97 still refers to the former, for Sinai already to the latter.

So we come to the following conclusion: Sinai's article at first glance looks like a refutation of Luxenberg, but on closer inspection it is at least a partial confirmation. To save the orthodox Islamic view, *both* Luxenberg *and* Sinai would have to be wrong!

3. Shoemaker's Kathisma Church

3.1. A Short Summary of His Article

In his above-mentioned article, "Christmas in the Koran: The Koranic Account of Jesus' Nativity and Palestinian Local Tradition," Stephen Shoemaker tries to demonstrate that the story of Jesus' birth in the Koran (Q 19:22–27) goes back to a liturgical tradition attached to the Kathisma church situated between Jerusalem and Bethlehem.

This church was discovered in 1997 on the outskirts of Jerusalem. It displays striking resemblences to the Dome of the Rock. It seems to point to a reinterpretation of the birth story under a palm tree, which provided nourishment for Mary—the story we also find in the Koran—leading to the new notion of a stopover, a rest on the flight to Egypt, after Bethlehem had become the undeniable birthplace of Jesus. Shoemaker writes:

> This church was originally associated with the Nativity of Christ, but eventually came to be linked with the commemoration of Mary's death and, more

> importantly, with certain events from the Holy Family's legendary flight to Egypt, as described in several early Christian apocrypha . . . it is (to my knowledge) the only place where these two early Christian traditions meet, outside of the Qur'ānic account of Jesus' Nativity.

That the palm tree is strongly linked to the "Flight to Egypt" is common knowledge among scholars dealing with Christian apocryphal literature, but here it seems that early Christians had used this church to commemorate the birth of Jesus, and when this was no longer possible, they reinterpreted the reason for building the church as the holy family's resting on their flight, i.e., exactly the story we find in the Koran.

The church was converted into a mosque in the eighth century, but the depiction of the Nativity of Jesus on the mosaics in the church was preserved. The significance of the church for the composition of the Koran is described by Shoemaker as follows:

> If we assume that the Christian traditions present in the Qur'ān derive from earlier Christian sources, rather than being revealed or composed *ex nihilo*, then the Kathisma church and its related traditions present the only known precedent for the Qur'ānic account of Jesus' Nativity.

He then explicitly mentions "revisionist" scholars of Islam:

> The probability that the Qur'ānic account of the Nativity developed under the influence of specific local Palestinian Christian traditions confirms the recognitions of Wansbrough and others that the content of the Qur'ānic text almost certainly continued to develop well after the death of Muḥammad.

Shoemaker surmises that in this case the

> text of the Qur'ān is not Muḥammad's, but rather a later product of his followers who drew on prior Christian traditions in composing the Qur'ānic account of Jesus' birth. . . . Similarly, the Qur'ān's dependence on these local, Jerusalemite traditions adds additional weight to revisionist arguments against the origin of Islam in the Ḥijāz. . . . In addition, the archaeological record of southern Palestine fits more with the traditions of early Islam than does the Ḥijāz.

Surprisingly, what now follows in Shoemaker's text is a lengthy apology, or rather justification, that one would have expected either at the very beginning or not at all:

> Furthermore, as should be quite obvious, this article is a work, in the words of Crone and Cook, "by infidels for infidels . . . which any Muslim whose faith is as a grain of mustard seed should find no difficulty in rejecting."

Further down he continues:

> Finally, I also wish to add that I am not at all insensitive to the concerns about "Orientalism" that have recently become an important focus of modern academic discourse. . . . Out of such concerns, many scholars from both the Islamic world and the West have argued that we must respect Islamic truth claims regarding Islam's most authoritative traditions, the Qur'ān and the sunna, and refrain from challenging them with historical criticism. To do so, many would maintain, is to commit an act of intellectual colonialism. Although I deeply sympathize with the intent of this position, it is simply not an acceptable option in my view, at least from the vantage of the academic discipline of Religious Studies. . . . It is therefore not intellectually defensible in my opinion to study the early histories of Judaism, Christianity, Buddhism, etc., both critically and skeptically, and then for some reason to exempt early Islam alone from this type of analysis.

Shoemaker then widens his perspective and mentions two texts that might contain motives that survived in the Koranic version of the Nativity story, the "*Latin Gospel of Pseudo-Matthew* and, to a lesser extent, the traditions of the *Protevangelium of James*." What can be found both in the Protevangelium and the Koran is the tradition of Jesus' birth in a remote place. According to the Protevangelium it took place in a cave halfway between Jerusalem and Bethlehem. The Koran is not very specific on this point, as Shoemaker notes:

> The stream and date palm seem to imply (but certainly do not demand) a rural location, and there is no indication in the text of the Qur'ān that this birth takes place in Bethlehem or any other city: this information is presumably supplied from the Christian tradition by later interpreters.

The second source mentioned by Shoemaker is more revealing:

> Modern scholars of the Qur'ān have long acknowledged that the Qur'ānic account of Jesus' birth is based largely on the reworking of a relatively obscure, apocryphal Christian tale, which is now known in several versions. . . . According to these traditions, while Mary and Joseph were travelling to Egypt with thir newborn son, the Holy Family came into a remote, desolate area. In the midst of this desert, Mary expresses her hunger to Joseph, and in response, her infant son causes a tall date palm to bend and offer her its fruit. Then, in some versions of the story, Mary also drinks from a spring that her son miraculously provides. The parallels between this legend and Mary's feeding from the date palm and stream in the Qur'ānic Nativity account are obvious. . . . The story of Mary and the Palm is never, to my knowledge, directly associated with the events of the Nativity in the Christian tradition. Thus we are left with a need to explain why, if in fact the Qur'ān has borrowed this earlier Christian legend,

> the Qur'ān has altered the legend's original setting, thereby transforming it into a Nativity tradition.

The second book mentioned by Shoemaker, the Gospel of Pseudo-Matthew,

> is primarily a reworking of the Protevangelium of James, to which Pseudo-Matthew adds some "unique" material, including in particular the story of Mary's encounter with the date palm during the flight into Egypt. . . . In view of Pseudo-Matthew's combination of these early Christian apocryphal traditions, it might at first glance be tempting to identify this apocryphon as the primary source of the Qur'ān's borrowed Christian traditions: most of the traditions that appear in the Qur'ān are found in some form or another in Ps.-Matthew. Unfortunately, however, the solution is not so simple.

The main argument against the Gospel of Ps.-Matthew as the direct source of the Koran is the fact that it stems from the West and was written in Latin. However, this text should not be prematurely dismissed, as

> Ps.-Matthew relies on earlier sources for many of its traditions, including the story of Mary and the palm in particular. . . . Recent efforts by the present writer have shown that the story of Mary and the date palm circulated in the Christian Near East perhaps as early as the third century, and beyond doubt by the early fifth century. The earliest extant version of this legend is found among the ancient traditions of the Virgin Mary's Dormition and Assumption, a collection of narratives that describe the events of Mary's departure from this life.

Shoemaker summarizes the Dormition narrative as follows:

> As the narrative opens, Christ, who is also identified as a "Great Angel," appears to his mother to announce her impending death. When Mary expresses some uncertainty at her interlocutor's identity, the Christ-Angel reassures his mother by reminding her of their journey through the desert into Egypt, when he miraculously fed her from the date palm. He then recapitulates for her the story of Mary and the date palm.

But hunger and thirst are not the only grief of the young couple:

> I first revealed it to you at the spring, where I led Joseph. He was crying, the child who is glorified because he is greater than everything, and Joseph was angry with you, saying, "Give your breast to your child." At once you gave it to him, as you went forth to the Mount of Olives, fleeing from Herod. And when you came to some trees you said to Joseph, "My lord, we are hungry, and what do we have to eat in this desert place?" Then he rebuked you, saying, "What can I do for you? Is it not enough for you that I became a stranger to my

> family on your account; why didn't you guard your virginity, so that you would [not] be found in this. . . . I [i.e., Jesus] say this to you Mary: know who I am and what power is upon me.

But Joseph refuses to eat, still angry:

> And I am afflicted because I did not know the child that you have; I only know that he is not from me. But I have thought in my heart, perhaps I had intercourse with you while drunk.

But then Joseph starts to calculate and finds out that he cannot be the father:

> And behold, now it has been made known that I was not negligent, because there were [only] five months when I received you in [my] custody. And behold, this child is more than five months; for you embraced him with your hand. Truly, he was not from your seed but from the Holy Spirit.

Then Jesus tells his father to climb the date-palm and bring it to her, then tells the date-palm to incline its head with its fruit. Jesus asks:

> And who made it incline? Is it not because I have power, which was because of me? And you and Joseph were satisfied, because the date-palm's branches were placed as a wave of the ocean on the shore.

At the end of the chapter, Shoemaker wonders (p. 21):

> But how are we to explain the very different setting of Mary's encounter with the date palm and spring in the Qur'ān?

His answer makes us return to the archeological site of the beginning of his article:

> With the discovery of the ancient Kathisma church near Jerusalem, we have almost certainly found the source of this transformation, not in a specific literary source, but in the local liturgical traditions and holy sites of the Jerusalem Christians.

Further down (p. 31 ff.) Shoemaker offers some interesting information about the Kathisma church itself:

> It was long thought that the Kathisma chuch had been discovered by archaeologists in the 1950s, during the excavations of Ramat Rahel, just to the south of Jerusalem. When the archaeologists excavating at Ramat Rahel discovered a large basilical church (13.5m x 20m) and monastery from the fifth-century, they quickly determined that they had uncovered remains of the long lost Kathisma church and monastery.

For almost fifty years, this church was considered to be the Kathisma church when

> in 1992, efforts to widen the Jerusalem–Bethlehem highway led to a salvage excavation in which the foundations of a large, octagonal church (43m x 52m) were uncovered, approximately 350 meters north of the monastery of Mar Elias.

In the center of the newly found church, a rock of about 2 x 4 meters was found. The excavators drew the conclusion that

> this new church was in fact the church of the Kathisma, rather than the church at Ramat Rahel, just few hundred meters to the north. This identification is supported, they argue, by the large rock at the center of this church, which, as we have already noted, certain accounts identify as an important feature of the Kathisma traditions.

Shoemaker thinks that

> there is strong indication that there were two such churches: an "Old Kathisma," a church and monastic community constructed sometime before 450, and a "New Kathisma," built sometime around 450. On the basis of both the literary evidence and the archaeology, I have argued that the smaller church and monastic community at Ramat Rahel were likely the Old Kathisma.

In this latter, bigger church a striking feature can be observed: Its floor is decorated with mosaics, one of them depicting "a large date palm, flanked by two smaller palms, all of which are laden with fruit." The mosaics stem from the time after the church had been converted into a mosque "near the beginning of the eighth century," which Shoemaker takes as a sign of this tradition's endurance. He is nevertheless undecided as to when the merging of the two early Christian traditions had taken place:

> It seems rather likely that the two early Christian traditions had already been merged by the Islamic tradition into the single Nativity tradition known from the Qur'ān.

Futher down he states:

> The dependence of this Qur'ānic tradition on the two earlier Christian traditions is, from a historical point of view, undeniable.

But then he adds:

> It is admittedly possible that the Qur'ānic story of Jesus' Nativity had already formed in its present state before the invading Arabs had ever seen or heard of the Kathisma church.

Another point worth mentioning is the influence of the New Kathisma Church on the Dome of the Rock:

> Experts on early Islamic art and architecture have long maintained that the Dome of the Rock is an architecturally unique edifice. . . . Numerous Byzantine churches, including several in Palestine, for instance, were constructed as concentric octagons, but "all of these buildings were planned according to standard ratios (Grabar, *Shape of the Holy*, p. 110)." . . . Oleg Grabar explains, "the plan of the Dome of the Rock is distinguishable from the plans of most comparable buildings by its inordinate size and by the perfection of its symmetries around multiple axes without visible focus or direction. (ibid., pp. 108–9) . . . With the recent discovery of the Kathisma chuch, however, the Dome of the Rock's uniqueness has suddenly come into serious question, . . . that this fifth-century church served as the primary architectural model for Abd al-Malik's construction of the Dome of the Rock . . . , about an hour's walk from the Temple Mount, it is architecturally almost identical with the Dome of the Rock, right down to the enormous, sacred rock at its center. Approximately the same size as the Dome of the Rock, the Kathisma consists of two concentric octagons, centered on a large rock which is enclosed by a third octagon. . . . Moreover, Avner has also shown that the mosaic floors of the Kathisma mosque are particularly unusual, with the only known parallels being found in the wall mosaics of the Dome of the Rock. More specifically, the Kathisma's palm mosaic . . . is identical to a mosaic from the Dome of Rock.

Shoemaker concludes:

> All of this suggests that the Dome of the Rock is not the unique building that it once was thought to be.

The question of why a church had to reinterpret the nativity tradition and instead to identify with the "tradition of Mary and the palm tree from the legend of the Holy Family's flight into Egypt," is also answered by Shoemaker:

> Once the basilica of the Nativity in the city of Bethlehem had emerged as the dominant Nativity shrine, with the authoritative support of the canonical gospels, new significance had to be found for the church of the Kathisma that would supplant this dissonant, and yet ancient, Nativity tradition.

At the end of his article, Shoemaker again returns to his purported apologies and justifications:

> Nevertheless, if one continues to adhere to the traditional model of the Qur'ān's composition and formation, then most of what we have proposed in this article will likely seem almost completely preposterous.

Still, he is adamant in his statement:

> Given the growing body of evidence that the Qur'ānic text, or at the very least, significant parts of it, developed only after the Arab conquests of the Near East, the influence of the Kathisma church and its traditions on the Qur'ān seems not only possible, but likely.

The burden of proof is consequently assigned to defenders of the traditional view:

> While many scholars who remain loyal to the traditional narrative of the Qur'ān's formation may reject our proposal, we would ask them to present equivalent evidence demonstrating the likelihood, or even possibility, that Muḥammad would have encountered the combination of these two traditions in the Ḥijāz.

3.2. Assessment of Shoemaker's Arguments

Shoemaker's article offers material evidence of far-reaching importance. First of all, he demonstrates that the story of Jesus' birth in the Koran is based on a liturgical tradition attached to the New Kathisma church situated between Jerusalem and Bethlehem, or at least religious ideas in connection with it. Two literary sources, the *Latin Gospel of Pseudo-Matthew* and the traditions of the *Protevangelium of James* probably played a major role in the development of the Koranic version of Jesus' birth.

Luxenberg's reinterpretation of the alleged "rivulet" is confirmed by the depiction of Joseph's anger and suspicions. For Mary the problem was legitimacy, not water. So Luxenberg's new rendering: "Do not be sad, your Lord has made your delivery legitimate" fits much better into the context than a rivulet between her legs.

After the excavation of the New Kathisma church, the Dome of the Rock resembles more and more a *church*, not a *mosque* in the modern sense. Moreover, it followed a model, even one that could be reached after a short walk from the Dome of the Rock.

The Arabic conquerors adopted the "message" of the church so easily that it is very likely that they were aware that their own traditions were linked to this church.

Shoemaker's article is also mentioned by Angelika Neuwirth in her essay "Imagining Mary: Disputing Jesus Reading Sūrat Maryam and Related Meccan Texts within the Koranic Communication Process."[7] In the "postscript" (p. 414) she writes:

> On the basis of these observations, the church seems to represent a materialized merger of the two traditions reflected also in the Koran, that prominently feature a palm tree nourishing the virgin in the situation of her delivery, with a

> stream of water nearby. The fact that this church with its double liturgical purpose—to recall both Mary's resting on the flight to Egypt and her delivery—was turned into a mosque by the early Muslims, serves Shoemaker as evidence for an assumption that the Koran should have been composed "not by Muḥammad but only after the conquests."

She tries to defend the traditional account on the next page and points out that if Shoemaker were right, then

> the Kathisma Church should hardly be the only case in point, but there should be existing analogous "Qur'anic" borrowings from other monuments such as studied from Klaus Bieberstein, Amiqam Elad, and Andreas Kaplony.

Absence of proof is not proof of absence, but in this case the point she makes seems to be: *Absence of <u>further</u> proof is proof of absence.*

At the end of our assessment, I have to come back with a personal remark about Shoemaker's "apologies" at the beginning and the end of his article.

The fact that the findings of researchers might contradict the teachings of major religions is not surprising. What does leave me nonplussed is the need he obviously feels to stress that he is "not at all insensitive to the concerns about 'Orientalism,'" that he "deeply sympathize[s] with the intent of this position" and that "most of what we have proposed in this article will likely seem almost completely preposterous." The fact, however, that he considers it "not intellectually defensible" to study the early histories of religions critically and skeptically, and then for some reason "exempt early Islam alone" from this type of analysis demonstrates his scholarly integrity. So why these initial statements?

Excavations of dinosaur bones and their subsequent dating by paleontologists clearly contradict the teachings of creationists, but representatives of this discipline never apologize in their publications for hurting the feelings of those who believe that the earth was created around 6000 BCE.

And historians who investigate the history of the Spanish Inquisition never apologize to the Catholic Church for findings that the latter might not like.

And finally, physicists who publish about the probability amplitude in quantum physics never apologize to Buddhists because their theory clearly contradicts the Buddhist doctrine of cause and effect.

The truth claims of the religions of the world are for the most part mutually exclusive, and they never apologize to each other, so in academia we should follow scientifically sound methods in an unbiased way and not worry about religious or ideological doctrines.

Notes

1 Nicolai Sinai, "'Weihnachten im Koran' oder 'Nacht der Bestimmung'?: Eine Interpretation von Sure 97," *Der Islam* 88 (2002): 11–32.
2 Stephen J. Shoemaker, "Christmas in the Qur'ān: The Qur'ānic Account of Jesus' Nativity and Palestinian Local Tradition," Jerusalem Studies in Arabic and Islam 23 (2003): 13–39.
3 See Corpus Coranicum, http://www.corpuscoranicum.de/kontexte/index?sure=97&vers=1&anzeigen= Anzeigen (accessed May 23, 2014).
4 Text edition with a translation to be found in Edmund Beck, ed., *Des heiligen Ephrem des Syrers Hymnen de Nativitate*, Corpus Scriptorum Christianorum Orientalium 186, Scriptores Syri 82 (Louvain, 1959), pp. 10–11.
5 Meanings according to John Penrice, *A Dictionary and Glossary of the Koran* (1873; reprint Delhi, 1990), p. 145.
6 The dictionaries used here are: Carl Brockelmann, *Lexicon Syriacum*, 2nd ed. (Halle, 1928) and J. Payne Smith, *Syriac Dictionary*, founded upon the Thesaurus Syriacus of R. Payne Smith (Oxford, 1903).
7 Angelika Neuwirth, "Imagining Mary: Disputing Jesus Reading Sūrat Maryam and Related Meccan Texts within the Qur'ānic Communication Process," in Benjamin Jokisch, Ulrich Rebstock, and Lawrence I. Conrad, eds., *Fremde, Feinde und Kurioses (Berlin: De Gruyter, 2009),* pp. 383–416.

Christmas and the Eucharist in the Qur'ān

Christoph Luxenberg

In the following article, several shorter texts by Christoph Luxenberg have been merged and revised by the author himself. The last part had previously been published in three different versions, the first two of which are in German: (1) the German periodical published in Trier, Imprimatur *1 (2003): 13–17; (2) Christoph Burgmer, ed.,* Streit um den Qur'ān: Die Luxenberg Debatte—Standpunkte und Hintergründe *[Controversy about the Qur'ān: The Luxenberg Debate—Viewpoints and Background], 2nd ed. (Berlin, 2007), pp. 62–68. The third version was an enlarged French translation: "Noël dans le Coran," in A. M. Delcambre and J. Bosshard, eds.,* Enquêtes sur l'islam *(Paris, 2004), pp. 117–38.*

1. Language of the Koran

In an earlier study entitled, *A Syro-Aramaic Reading of the Koran. A Contribution to the Deciphering of the Language of the Koran*, the author put before the public some results of his research on the language of the Qur'ān. Taking for his point of departure the linguistic situation that prevailed historically at the time the time the Qur'ān was edited (according to Islamic tradition 7th Century CE), the *lingua franca* and the literary language of the whole of the Near East was not Arabic, but Syriac, a variant of Aramaic. On this basis he succeeded in elucidating great many passages considered obscure and recognized as such not only by Western orientalists but also by Arab commentators themselves. This fact led him to show that the language of the Qur'ān, which constitues the essential foundations of written Arabic, is so intimately linked to Syriac that one can speak of a *mixed Arabo-Syriac* language.

From this finding it logically follows that without taking into consideration Syriac the intended meaning of the Qur'ān and Qur'ānic Arabic cannot be understood. Thus, ignoring Syriac, the Arab exegetes have interpreted Qur'ānic expressions as being, for example, Houris or Virgins of Paradise *(ḥūr 'īn)* whereas in their Syriac sense they designate white raisin or vine, eschatological components of the Christian Paradise, an allusion to the wine of the Last Supper. The same goes for the young boys or ephebes of Paradise *(wildān)* which the Arab commentators have imagined, when in reality the term is just another Syriac loan words designating the same raisins. By using these expressions, the Qur'ān compars the whiteness of these heavenly raisins to the limpidness of crystal and immaculate pearls.

2. St. Peter: Persevere in Your Prayers: Surah 108 (*al-Kawṯar* – (the) Abundance)

The author moreover has shown that it is not just on the level of simple isolated words but also at the level of syntax that the Arab commentators have misunderstood the Qur'ānic text, to the extent of misinterpreting entire surahs. Thus the Arab exegetes saw in the title of Surah 108 (*al-Kawṯar – Abundance*), among others, the name of a river in Paradise reserved exclusively for the Prophet or—according to another interpretation—for faithful Muslims, and in the following verse the reprobation of an opponent of the Prophet who must have despised the latter for having been deprived of children. However, the Syriac reading of this Surah recalls to mind the First Epistle of St Peter, Chapter 5 verses 8–95, according to which—and in accordance with the introduction to the compline of the Roman service—the faithful are exhorted to persevere in their prayers by which their adversary, Satan, is routed. Let us now examine this sura in philological detail.

The following summary of the views of traditional Qur'ān exegesis concerning this short Surah stems from Josef Horovitz's article from the *Encyclopaedia of Islam* 1st ed. (vol. 2, Leiden, Leipzig, 1927) and may serve as an introduction:

> KAWṮAR, a word used in Sūra 108:1 after which this Sura is called *Surat al-Kawṯar*. Kawṯar is a *faw'al* form from *ka<u>th</u>ara*, of which other examples occur in Arabic (e.g. *nawfal*; further examples in Brockelmann, *Grundriss der vergleichenden Grammatik*, I 344 [An Outline of a Comparative Grammar]). The word, which also occurs in the old poetry (e.g. the examples in Ibn Hi<u>sh</u>ām, ed. Wüstenfeld, p. 261, and Nöldeke-Schwally, *Geschichte des Qorāns*, I 92), means "abundance" and a whole series of Muslim authorities therefore explain al-Kawṯar in Sūra 108:1 as *al-<u>Kh</u>air al-ka<u>th</u>īr* (see Ibn Hi<u>sh</u>ām, *op. cit.*.; al-Ṭabarī, *Tafsīr*, XXX 180 f.). But this quite correct explanation has not been able to prevail in the *Tafsīr*. It has been thrust into the background by traditions according to which the Prophet himself explained Kawṯar to be a river in Paradise (see already Ibn Hi<u>sh</u>ām, p. 261 below, and notably al-Ṭabarī, *Tafsīr*, XXX 179), or Muḥammad says that it was a pool intended for him personally and shown to him on his ascension to Paradise (see al-Ṭabarī, *Tafsīr*, XXX 180), which latter view al-Ṭabarī considers the most authentic. Even the earliest Sūras (77:41; 88:12 etc.) know of rivers that flow through Paradise, but it is not till the Medīna period that they are more minutely described, notably in, Sūra 47:15: "there are rivers of water which does not smell foul: rivers of milk the taste whereof does not change; and rivers of wine, a pleasure

for those that drink, and rivers of clarified honey." These rivers correspond to the rivers of oil, milk, wine and honey, which had already been placed in Paradise by Jewish and Christian eschatology; the only difference is that Muḥammad replaced oil by water; in Arabia pure water was not to be taken for granted and besides it was necessary to mix with the wine of Paradise (see Horovitz, *Das Qur'ānische Paradies*, p. 9). When, after the Prophet's death, eschatological explanations of the "abundance" of Sūra 108:1 began to be made, al-Kawṯar was identified as one of the rivers of Paradise and when we find in one of the versions quoted in al-Ṭabarī's *Tafsīr* that "its water is whiter than snow and sweeter than honey" or "and its water is wine," etc. we have obviously an echo of Sūra 47:15. But they did not stop at simply transferring these Qur'ānic descriptions to the Kawṯar but the imagination of later writers gave the river of Paradise a bed of pearls and rubies and golden banks and all sorts of similar embellishments. According to a later view (see *Aḥwāl al-Qiyāma*, ed. Wolff, p. 107) all the rivers of Paradise flow into the *Ḥawḍ al-Kawṯar* which is also called *Nahr Muḥammed*, because, as we have seen above, it is the Prophet's own.

Before going into the philological analysis of this Surah, which has been made into a legend in the Islamic tradition, it would be good first of all to give the Qur'ānic text and its understanding on the basis of the Arabic exegesis with the traditional reading.

انا اعطينك الكوثر / فصل لربك وانحر / ان شانئك هو الابتر
innā a'ṭaynāka l-kawṯar / fa-ṣalli li-rabbika wa-nḥar /
inna šāni'aka huwa l-abtar

These three verses are rendered according to the Arabic understanding as follows:

Bell II 681[1] 1. Verily, We have given thee the abundance;[2] 2. So pray to thy Lord, and sacrifice. 3. Verily, it is he who hateth thee who is the docked one.[3]

Paret 519: 1: Wir haben dir die Fülle gegeben. 2: Bete darum (*fa-ṣalli*) zu deinem Herrn und opfere! 3: (Ja) dein Hasser ist es, der gestutzt [Note: D.h. ohne Anhang (*? abtar*). Oder: schwanzlos, d.h. ohne Nachkommen (?)] ist. [Note: Oder (als Verwünschung): Wer dich haßt, soll gestutzt (oder: schwanzlos) sein!]. *[1 : We have given you the abundance. 2 : Therefore pray to your Lord and sacrifice ! 3: (Yes) it is your hater who will be pruned (i.e., without attachment [?abtar]), or : will be without a tail, [i.e., without offspring (?) ; or : (as a curse) Whoever hates you, shall be pruned (or : be without a tail) !].*

> *Blachère* 668: 1 En vérité, Nous t'avons donné l'Abondance.[4] 2 Prie donc en l'honneur de ton Seigneur et sacrifie ! 3 En vérité, celui qui te hait se trouve être le Déshérité! [Verily, We have given you the abundance. So pray to honour your Lord, and sacrifice. Verily, he hates who hates you finds himself disinherited]

The explanation of this short Surah has caused Qur'ān scholars in the East and the West a great deal of trouble. Even a summary of the nearly eleven pages of attempted interpretations in *Ṭabarī* (XXX 320–330) would be taking things too far. In any case, this would only serve as an example of how falsely the Qur'ān text has been in part interpreted by the Arab exegetes. Nevertheless Paret devotes just under two pages to it in his *Kommentar* [*Commentary*] pp. 525–527). As an introduction (525) he remarks on the subject:

> Harris Birkeland has published an extensive interpretation of this short, but difficult Surah (Harris Birkeland. *The Lord Guideth: Studies on Primitive Islam*, Oslo 1956, pp. 56–99).

The following explanation of the individual words will show that all of the previous efforts were love's labor's lost.

1. The expression selected as the title of the Surah الكوثر (*al-kawṯar*) is the transliteration of the Syro-Aramaic ܟܘܬܪܐ / *kuttāra*, which is the nominal form of the second stem ܟܬܪ / *kattar* (*to persevere*). This verbal root (**kṯar*) is found in both languages, the Arabic root كثر / *kaṯura* (*to be much, many*) referring to quantity, while the Syro-Aramaic counterpart ܟܬܪ / *kṯar* (*to remain, to last*) merely refers to quantity of time, i.e., duration. In the Qur'ān this Syro-Aramaic meaning occurs only occasionally, e.g., in Surah 20:33, 34: كي نسبحك كثيرا / ونذكرك كثيرا / *kay nusabbiḥaka kaṯīrā / wa-naḏkuraka kaṯīrā* "that we may *constantly* glorify Thee and make *constantly* remembrance of Thee."[5] The medial و / *waw* in كوثر (*kawṯar*) is *mater lectionis* for short *u*, as is normal according to Syro-Aramaic spelling. The word should therefore be interpreted as *kuttār* as in Classical Syriac ܟܘܬܪܐ / *kuttārā* or Western Syriac *kūṯārā*[6] (*constancy, persistence, steadfastness*). The fricative *ṯ* (pronounced as *th* in English "*thing*") of the canonical Qur'ānic reading (*kawṯar*) reflects the Western Syriac pronunciation after the gemination of consonants was generally dropped. Since such a *mater lectionis* is uncommon in the Qur'ān, the Arabic philologists interpreted this *mater lectionis* as the non-syllabic part of the diphthong *aw*, thus reading the form as *kawṯar* (= *faw'al*). The corresponding Arabic form of the Syro-Aramaic *kuttārā* would be تكثير (*takṯīr*).[7]

   This uncommon form *kawṯar* ought to have aroused the scepticism of the commentators. It is also no accident that the word has never made its way into Arabic in the meaning of *abundance*. This is also, as it is often the case, why it is regarded as the name of a river in Paradise and, among other things, is still used today as a woman's name (with the actually Syro-Aramaic meaning of *Constantia*).

2. The same meaning is expressed by the borrowing from Syro-Aramaic صل / *ṣalli* (*pray*). On the other hand, the word that has been understood in Arabic as "slaughter," وانحر / *wa-nḥar*, has been misread. What is meant here in connection with "to pray" is the Syro-Aramaic root ܢܓܪ / *ngar* (*to wait, to hold out, to persist*).[8] The only meaning from this root that has entered into the Arabic borrowed form نجر / *najara* is the meaning "to plane." In the Qur'ān, however, it is the first meaning that is meant. Therefore, Arabic وانجر / *wa-nğar* (*and persist – in prayer*) should be read here. The Qur'ān employs in this connection among other things the synonymous root صبر / *ṣabara* (< ܣܝܒܪ / *saybar*). Parallels are offered here by Surah 19:65: فاعبده واصطبر لعبادته (*so worship him and wait in his worship*) and Surah 20:132: وامر اهلك بالصلوة واصطبر عليها (*command your family to pray and persist therein*). Furthermore, with the lexically equivalent Arabic verb دام على / *dāma ʿalā* (in modern Arabic داوم على / *dāwama ʿalā*) (*to persist in something, to do something constantly*), it is said in Surah 70:23 of those who pray: الذين هم على صلاتهم دائمون (*who say their prayers constantly*).
3. As a further adapted transcription of Syro-Aramaic ܣܢܐܟ / (*sānāḵ*)[9] (*your hater = enemy, adversary*) in Arabic, the Qur'ānic شانئك (*šāni'aka*) has been understood correctly as "your hater." In the Christian Syriac terminology, Satan is referred to, among other things, as a *"misanthrope"* —hence an "adversary"—in contrast to God, who is referred to as (*raḥmānā* > Arabic رحمن / *raḥmān*) "one who loves mankind" (philanthropist).
4. Finally, the root بتر (*batara*) (*to break off, to amputate*), based on the Arabic elative الابتر (*al-abtar*), is a metathesis of the Syro-Aramaic ܬܒܪ (*tḇar*), for which *Mannā* (829a) gives us the following Arabic meanings: (2) انكسر. انسحق (*to be broken, defeated, destroyed*), (3) فرّ. انهزم (*to make a dash for freedom, to be put to flight*).

3. Excursus: On the Etymology of the Arabic Root أعطى / aʿṭā

The result of the philological analysis of the individual expressions is that, except for the form, *scarcely one word in this Surah is of Arabic origin*. In the end, the only verb considered to be genuinely Arabic, أعطى / *aʿṭā* (*to give*), will prove to be, etymologically (by the shifting of the *hamza* to *ʿayn* and the resultant emphasizing of the ܬ/*t*), a secondary dialectal formation of Syro-Aramaic ܐܝܬܝ / *aytī* (*to summon, to bring*). This is already clear from the Qur-

'ānic use of these two roots. In other words, while the Arabic root عطى / *'aṭā* occurs a total of 13 times in the Qur'ān, the instances of the root borrowed from the Syro-Aramaic ܐܬܐ /*eṯā* > Arabic اتى /*atā* (*to come*), with all its derivatives, are countless. The Arabic form أعطى /*a'ṭā*(*to give*) corresponds to the Syro-Aramaic *Af'el* ܐܝܬܝ / *aytī* (*to summon, to bring*). The equivalent Arabic form of أتى / *'atā* would be > *أأتى >*'a'tā*, a form which would violate the phonotactical rule in Arabic, which does not allow two consecutive *hamza*, especially when the second one is *vowelless*.[10] To circumvent this rule, the second hamza was replaced by the acoustically most similar phoneme *'ayn*. As the place of articulation of the *'ayn* is pharyngeal, the following consonant was consequently pharyngealized, i.e., it became emphatic "*ṭ*." These phonetic replacements thus resulted in the secondary Arabic verb أعطى /*a'ṭā*(*to give*), the radicals of which, however, have no counterparts in any other Semitic language. C. Brockelmann, *Lexicon Syriacum*, gives the etymological correlatives of the Syro-Aramaic verbal ܛܥܐ / *'ṭā* (520a) (1. *delevit, evertit* / *to efface, to cancel, to exterminate*) as follows: Hebrew עטה (*'aṭā*) *velavit* (*to veil*), Arabic غطا (*ġaṭā*) *texit* (*to cover*), Accadean *e,ū obscurum esse* (*to be obscure*). These etymological correlations make clear that the Arabic verb أعطى /*a'ṭā*, in the sense of "to give," is not genuine Arabic, but a secondary derivation from the Syro-Aramaic verbal root ܐܬܐ (*eṯā*) > Arabic أتى (*atā*) > IVth stem *أأتى (*'a'tā*) > أعطى (*'a'ṭā*).

The last sceptics may be convinced by the following evidence quoted in A. Jeffery, *Materials for the History of the Text of the Qur'ān*, 146 (codex of Ubai b. Ka'b), Surah 20:36, where the canonical reading أوتيت (*'ūtīta*) (in the context—literally: "*you are given*" *your request* = *your request is granted*) is transmitted in this old codex as أعطيت (*'u'ṭīta*). Hence: أوتيت (*'ūtīta* < *'*u'tīta*) = أعطيت (*'u'ṭīta*).[11]

From the preceding discussion the following reading and understanding has now resulted for Surah 108 according to the Syro-Aramaic reading:

> انا اعطينك الكوثر / فصل لربك وانجر / ان سانيك هو الابتر
> (*inna a'ṭaynāka l-kawṯar* or *al-kuttār* /*fa-ṣalli li-rabbik wa-nǧar* /
> *in sānīka huwa l-abtar*)
> 1. We have given you the (virtue of) <u>constancy</u>;
> 2. so pray to your Lord and <u>persevere</u> (in prayer);
> 3. your <u>adversary</u> (the devil) is (then) the <u>loser</u>.

4. Christian Epistolary Literature in the Qur'ān (Surah 108)

This brief Surah is based on the Christian Syriac liturgy. From it arises a clear reminiscence of the well-known passage, also used in the *compline* of the Roman Catholic canonical hours of prayer, from the First Epistle General of Peter, Chapter 5, Verses 8–9 (according to the *Pšiṭṭā*):

> 8 Wake up (Brothers) and be vigilant, because your *adversary* the *devil*, as a roaring lion, walketh about, seeking whom he may devour:
> 9 Whom *resist steadfast* in the faith."

From this first evidence of Christian epistolary literature in the Qur'ān it now becomes clear that it has previously been a mistake to connect the text of Surah 108 with any of the enemies of the Prophet Muḥammad, not to mention with the expressions the Qur'ān has been accused of using in this regard, expressions which are unworthy of it. This text is without a doubt pre-Qur-'ānic. As such it is a part of that *matrix out of which the Qur'ān was originally constituted as a Christian liturgical book* (*Qəryānā*), and which as a whole has been designated in Western Qur'ān studies as the *first Meccan period*.[12] The address in the second person in this as in other Surahs is moreover not necessarily directed at the Prophet himself. Rather, as is customary in liturgical books, each believer is addressed in the second person.

As in the Roman Catholic *compline*, one can easily imagine these three verses as an introduction to an earlier Syro-Aramaic hour of prayer. Bell's suspicion that it is a fragment from Surah 74 cannot be ruled out, since this Surah as well as Surah 73 with their call to bedtime prayer, i.e., to the *vigils*, read in part like a *monastic rule*.[13] Whence there too the hitherto unrecognized Syro-Aramaisms, the explanation of which is being reserved for a future work.

5. The Eucharist: Surah 96: al-ʿAlaq – "the Clot"

In the same way the Arab exegetes had seen in Surah 96 (al-ʿAlaq – "the Clot") the start of the revelation announced to the prophet by the angel Gabriel. However the lexicological and syntactical analysis of this Surah, examined under its Syriac connection, has revealed—contrary to the confusion which has reigned in its Arabic reading up to now—a clear and coherent composition in which the faithful is entreated to pray and participate in the liturgical service that the Qur'ān designates as The Eucharist (corresponding to *iqtarib* taken from the Syriac liturgical term ܐܬܩܪܒ *eṯqarraḇ*, Arabic term *ta-qarrab* which signifies "take part in a liturgical service" as well as "to receive the Eucharist."

Islamic tradition sees in this Surah [Surah 96] the beginning of the Revelation, because the initial word *iqra' (iqrā)* ("read") has been interpreted as being the first word the angel Gabriel addressed to the Prophet inviting him to read the Qur'ān. However, the Arabic verb *qara'a*, derived from the Syriac *qrā*, has only retained the meaning "to read," whereas in Syriac it has at least twelve meanings and further nuances, the most appropriate in this context is "to invoke, to call." Verse 1 : "*Iqra' bi-smi rabbi-ka. . .*" corresponds to the

Syriac locution *qra b-šem maryā* meaning "Invoke the name of the Lord," a formula which introduces a prayer or a liturgical office. It concerns just such an office in this case, it is the last term used in verse 19 which we will now define. The verb *iqtarib* (Arabic meaning "draw closer") is in fact Arabic only in form and corresponds in reality to the liturgical Syriac term "ܐܬܩܪܒ *eṯqarraḇ*" meaning "to take part in the Offering (Eucharistic)" as well as "to receive the Eucharist."

With this term the Qur'ān reveals a detail hitherto unsuspected making an allusion to a Pre-Islamic Christian liturgy and we discover at the same time another term also not well-known until now.

Let us now look more closely at Surah 96, "al-ʿAlaq." In the Islamic tradition this is held to be the beginning of the prophetic revelation. Serving as the title is a keyword selected from the text, العلق (*al-ʿalaq*), which until now has been falsely translated by "clotted blood" (Bell), "der Embryo" (Paret), and "l'Adhérence" (Blachère). For purposes of comparison the following very literal rendering of Paret's translation[14] (513 f.) ought to be sufficient.

Surah 96:1-19: العلق / "al-ʿAlaq"

1: Recite in the name of your Lord who has created,

2: has created man out of an embryo!

3: Recite! Your Lord is noble like nobody in the world [Note: literally, the noblest (one) (al-akramu)],

4: (He) who [Note: (Or) Your Lord, noble like nobody in the world, is the one who] taught the use of the calamus-pen [Or who taught by means of the calamus-pen],

5: taught man what (beforehand) he did not know.

6: No! Man is truly rebellious (*yaṭġā*),

7: (for) that he considers himself his own master (*an raʾāhu staġnā*).

8: (Yet) to your Lord all things return (some day) [literally: To your Lord is the return].

9: What do you think, indeed, of him who

10: forbids a slave [Or: a servant (of God)] when he is saying his prayers (*ṣallā*)?

11: What do you think if he (i.e., the one?) is rightly guided 12: or commands one to be God-fearing? 13: What do you think if he (i.e., the other?) declares (the truth of the divine message) to be a lie and turns away (from it)? (That the latter is in the wrong should be clear.) 14: (For) Does he not know that God sees (what he does?) 15: No! If he does not stop (doing what he is doing) we will surely seize (him on Judgment Day) by the forelock, 16:a lying, sinful forelock. 17: May he then call his clique (nādī)! 18: We shall (for our part) call the henchmen (of Hell) (? *az-zabāniya*). 19: No! Prostrate yourself (rather in worship) and approach (your Lord in humility)!

The discussion of the underlined expressions will first of all be carried out verse by verse:

5.1 Verse 1:

Borrowed from the Syro-Aramaic ܩܪܐ (*qrā*), the Arabic verb قرأ (*qara'a*, although originally probably *qarā* like *banā* and *ramā*), has for the most part taken over the meaning "to read" from Syro-Aramaic. Elsewhere, the Qur'ān furnishes evidence of the meaning "to teach" once in Surah 87:6, سنقرئك فلا تنسى (*sa-nuqri'uka fa-lā tansā*, which should actually be read *sa-nuqrīka*), which is rendered as follows by Paret (507): "We will cause you to recite (revelatory texts). You will now forget nothing (thereof)." Under ܐܩܪܝ (*aqrī*) *Mannā* (698b) gives the meaning "to teach" in Arabic with علّم (*'allama*). Accordingly, what is meant by this verse is: "We will teach you (in a way) that you will not forget."[15]

The correct interpretation of the expression اقرا باسم ربك (*iqra'* [actually *iqrā*] *bi-smi rabbika*) is of crucial importance for the historical appraisal of this Surah, which Islamic tradition has declared to be the beginning of the prophetic revelation. In this regard, Nöldeke refers (*op. cit.* 81) to Hartwig Hirschfeld, who, in pointing to the frequent occurrence in the Bible of the Hebrew expression *qrā ḇ-šem YHWH*, had translated the Qur'ānic expression correctly with "proclaim the name of thy Lord!" The explanation given by the Arab grammarian Abū 'Ubaida—that قرأ (*qara'a*) means as much as ذكر (*ḏakara*) "to call (upon)" here—proves to be equally correct, despite the fact that it is rejected by Nöldeke with the comment: "But قرأ never has this meaning." For that, he refers to M. J. de Goeje in the glossary to *Ṭabarī* where قرأ بشئ is said to mean "he read in something."

Thus, Nöldeke took as his model for the explanation of this early Qur'ānic expression its later misunderstood use in Arabic, instead of tracing it back to its Syro-Aramaic (or Hebrew) origin. The fact is that the equivalent Syro-Aramaic expression taken from Biblical usage ܩܪܐ ܒܫܡ ܡܪܝܐ (*qrā ḇ-šem māryā*; with and without ܒ / *b*) has in general become a *technical term* for "*to pray, to hold divine service.*"[16] But as for how the preposition ܒ / *b-* is to be explained, it is simply to be understood here as follows: "Call: In the name of the Lord!" One does this particularly at the beginning of a prayer or a divine service, and indeed it was this that was also replaced later on in the recitation of the Qur'ān by the parallel formula بسم الله الرحمن الرحيم (*bi-smi l-lāhi r-raḥmāni r-raḥīm*) (*In the name of God, the compassionate, the merciful*).

Nöldeke has also not noticed that this expression, though not with the borrowed verb قرا (< ܩܪܐ / *qrā*), but with the lexically equivalent Arabic verb دعا (*da'ā*) (*to call, to invoke*), is documented in connection with the preposition بِ / *bi-* in this meaning in a verse[17] attributed to *Waraqa ibn Nawfal*

(ورقة بن نوفل ; cousin of *Ḫadīǧa*, the first wife of the Prophet),[18] which runs as follows:

أقول إذا صليت في كل بيعة تباركت قد أكثرت <u>باسمك</u> <u>داعيا</u>

> I say whenever I pray in a church.[19] "Be you praised, full oft *I call* [<u>with</u>] *your name*!"

There can accordingly be no doubt that the introductory formula اقرا باسم ربك (*iqra' bi-smi rabbika*) has the equivalent Syro-Aramaic sense and is to be understood as a call to prayer. Indeed, the subsequent context of the entire Surah argues for this as well. To understand from this a call to *read in a book* is simply without any objective foundation. The previous interpretation rests solely on the later Arabic exegesis's misunderstanding of the use of this *Syriacism*.

The logical conclusion is that the view held by the Arabic tradition, according to which the angel Gabriel had with this *formula* called upon the Prophet to read, even though the Prophet could not read, is a later pious legend growing out of this very same misunderstanding. The Surah is, as a whole, a thematically presented call to worship, as the other misunderstood expressions will show.

5.2 Verse 2

About the expression علق (*ʿalaq*) Blachère (657) remarks correctly that it seems originally to have been a noun derived from the verb *ʿalaqa*, "to stick, to cling." To that extent, he is doubting the interpretation "clots of blood" of the Arab exegetes, which Paret, in turn, interprets as "embryo." With the corresponding translation, "adhérence" (adhesion), however, he is nonetheless not able to explain the actual meaning of this metaphorical expression. This is because here, too, the *tertium comparationis* can only be determined by way of the Syro-Aramaic. Add to this that the *Thes.* (II 2902) cites for us under ܥܠܘܩܐ (*ʿālōqā*) (for which it gives the loan word in Arabic علقة / *ʿalaqa* "leech") the following commentary from the Syrian lexicographers, who, besides the *leech* named after this property, also explain the following with this *nomen agentis* "clinger:"

> ܐܘ ܛܝܢܐ ܘܠܝܫܐ ܕܕܒܩܝܢ ܒܐܝܕܐ ܘܥܣܩܝܢ ܠܡܬܬܫܝܓܘ
> *aw ṭīnā w-layšā d-dāḇqīn b-īḏā w-ʿasqīn l-mettšīgū*

The expression "clinger" designates either a "leech" "or the <u>clay</u> or <u>dough</u> that sticks to one's hand and is difficult to wash off."[20]

With that, the expression علق (*ʿalaq*) would be explained, since the property "sticky" is indeed used by the Qur'ān in connection with "clay," in one instance, in Surah 37:11: انا خلقنهم من <u>طين</u> <u>لازب</u> "we have created you out of <u>*sticky*</u>[21] <u>*clay*</u>." Adapted to the rhyme, the Qur'ān is here using the synonymous

Syro-Aramaic expression familiar to it. With من علق (*min ʿalaq*) what is meant in Arabic is من طين عالق = لازب (out of something *sticky* = *sticky clay*).

5.3 Verse 3

For the Arabic elative (absolute superlative) referring to God, الاكرم (*al-akram*), the meaning also common in modern Arabic, "honorable, admirable," is actually adequate, especially since it is here precisely a question of the worship of God in the church service.

5.4 Verse 4

Because God has taught man بالقلم (*bi-l-qalam*) "with the calamus reed-pen," surely the most plausible explanation is the *knowledge revealed through the scripture.*

5.5 Verse 6

There begins at this point in the Surah, with كلا (*kallā*),[22] which has been misread in Arabic and misunderstood abruptly in the context as "*No!*", a series of three adverbs, all of which mean the Syro-Aramaic ܟܠܗ (*kullā*) and which are, depending on the context, to be understood positively in the sense of "everything," but negatively in the meaning of "not at all." In this verse the كلا (Syro-Aramaic *kullā* in the sense of Arabic كليًا *kullīya*^{n}) belongs with the preceding ما لم يعلم (*mā lam yaʿlam*), because in the Qurʾān the sentence does not necessarily end with the rhyme. Hence this كلا is to be drawn into Verse 5, so that this verse will then be: "he taught man what he did <u>not</u> know <u>at all</u>."[23]

Secondly, Paret translates the verb طغى (*ṭaġā*) with "aufsässig sein [to be rebellious];" (Blachère: "L'homme … est <u>rebelle</u>;" Bell: "man <u>acts presumptuously.</u>") Except for the secondary غ / *ġ* there is, in itself, nothing Arabic about this verbal root.

6. Excursus: On the Etymology of the Verbal Root طغى (ṭaġā)

This verb is unusual in any Arabic dialect. Its use in modern Arabic is due exclusively to this misread Qurʾānic word. The etymological Arabic equivalent is in fact the verbal root ضاع / *ḍāʿa* (generated by sonorization of the Syro-Aramaic emphatic ܛ / *ṭ* > ض /*ḍ* with simultaneous sound-shifting). The Arabic ع / *ʿayn* in ضاع / *ḍāʿa* makes clear that the diacritical point in طغى / *ṭaġā* has not any justification and that the original spelling طعى / *ṭaʿā* renders truly the Syro-Aramaic verbal root ܛܥܐ /*ṭʿā*.

The etymology is covered by the original meaning of both verbal roots (cf. C. Brockelmann, *Lexicon Syriacum* 282a, ܛܥܐ / *ṭʿā* 1. *erravit* [*to go astray*]) =

Arabic ضاع /*ḍāʿa* (*to get lost*). According to the classical correspondence table of the Semitic sounds in C. Brockelmann's *Syrische Grammatik*[24] (p.15), the Arabic ض /*ḍ* can only correspond with a Syriac ܥ /*ʿayn*. A classical example is Syriac ܐܪܥܐ /*arʿā* = Arabic ارض /*arḍ* (*earth*). This is the classical rule. But that in the multiplicity of the Arabic (or common Aramaic) dialects a Syro-Aramaic emphatic *ṭ* can become occasionally an Arabic *ḍ* by sonorization, this phenomenon has hitherto not been considered in the Semitic philology. A first example we had with Syro-Aramaic ܛܪܦ (Eastern Aramaic *ṭrap̄*) > Arabic ضرب (*ḍaraba* [*to strike, to hit*]), from which there are three variants that illustrate the transition from Syro-Aramaic ܛ /*ṭ* into the Arabic ض / *ḍ:* a) طرف (*ṭarafa* < Western Syro-Aramaic ܛܪܦ / *ṭrap̄* = *ṭraf*) (*to hit, to touch the eye with something*) (*Lisān* IX 213b, 11f.); b) طرب (*ṭariba* < Eastern Syro-Aramaic ܛܪܦ / *ṭrap̄* – with sonorization of the *p* > *b*) (to be *touched* emotionally = *to be moved, to be delighted*); c) finally with sonorization of the emphatic ط /*ṭ* > ض /*ḍ* = ضرب (*ḍaraba* – "to strike").

The Qur'ān offers a further example of a sonorized Syro-Aramaic emphatic ܛ /*ṭ* with the secondary Arabic verbal root ضرّ (*ḍarra*) (*to harm, damage*) < Syro-Aramaic ܛܪܐ (*ṭrā*) (*to strike, to push*—7 further variants in C. Brockelmann), that C. Brockelmann, *Lexicon Syriacum* 287a, compares with the actually from Syro-Aramaic truly borrowed Arabic Verb طرأ (*ṭara'a*), the *tertiae hamza* of which is nothing but a fictitious pronunciation imagined by the Arab philologists. Not only the apparent restriction of this verb to the first stem and its semantics field to one general meaning (*to break in, overtake, befall*) shows that it is borrowed, but also the fact that the Arab lexicographers did not observe that its VIIIth stem إضطرّ (*iṭṭarra /uṭṭurra*) (*to be forced, compelled*), according to its original meaning, does not fall under the root ضرّ (*ḍarra*) (*to damage*), but under طرأ (*ṭara'a* = *ṭarā*), according to the meaning of Syro-Aramaic ܛܪܐ (*ṭrā*) (*to push away, to repel*) and its reflexive stem ܐܬܛܪܝ (*eṭṭrī*). That the secondary Arabic form ضرّ (*ḍarra*) is derived from the Syro-Aramaic ܛܪܐ (*ṭrā*), shows C. Brockelmann (*op. cit.*) by the same specific meaning quoted under 6.: *offendit* (*to harm*).

The second element that shows the perplexity of the Arab Qur'ān readers is the variable reading of the alternative writing of the nominal form of the verbal root ضرّ (*ḍarra*), depending on its spelling with or without the Syro-Aramaic emphatic ending *ā* of the *status emphaticus*. Apart from the reading *ḍarr* (*harm, damage*) as antonym of نفع (*nafaʿa*) (*use, benefit*), the Qur'ānic spelling ضرّ (without the emphatic end-*ā*) is read *ḍurr(u/i/a)* (derived from the IInd Syro-Aramaic intensive stem ܛܪܝ / *ṭarrī*, verbal noun ܛܘܪܝܐ / *ṭurrāyā*; 19 times in the Qur'ān in the sense of *distress, adversity*). When, on the other hand, the same word is written with the Syro-Aramaic emphatic end-*ā* ضرّا (properly: *ḍurrā*—with dropping of the unaccented *y* of the Syro-Aramaic word before the end-*ā*—as in قران < Syro-Aramaic ܩܪܝܢܐ / *qəryān(ā)* > Arabic *qurān* / *qur'ān*) or with the Arabic article الضرّا (etymologically: *aḍ-ḍurrā* < ܛܘܪܝܐ / *ṭurrāyā*; both spellings 9 times), this spelling is read with an added *hamza* after the end-*ā* as الضراء (*aḍ-ḍarrāʾu*), as though this spelling were etymologically different.

7. On the Origin of the Arabic Final Hamza

In his *Grundriß der vergleichenden Grammatik der semitischen Sprachen* [*Compendium of the Comparative Grammar of the Semitic Languages*] (I 593, C.a.), Carl Brockelmann supposes a verbal class *tertiae hamza*, according to the classical Arabic grammar, when he says: (add Kienast)

> Als 3. Radikal war ʾ schon im altarab. Dialekt des Ḥijāz nach *i* und *u* zu *ĭ* und *ŭ* geworden…[As 3rd radical, the ʾ (= *hamza*) had become already in the old Arabic dialect of Ḥijāz *ĭ* and *ŭ* after *i* and *u*. . .].

But in fact, what C. Brockelmann says about the Hebrew (*op. cit.* 594 b.), Syriac and Assyrian (594 c.) as to the "dropping" of the III ʾ (*tertiae hamza*), is likewise to apply on the so-called (post-Qurʾānic) *Old Arabic*. For the Qurʾānic orthography has no graphical sign for a final *hamza*. Spellings as اتوكوا (*atawakkaw* [*I lean*]—same spelling in both codices of Samarqand and British Library Or. 2165—traditional reading: *atawakkaʾu*; Surah 20:18) [makes one] suspect a hypercorrect late emendation according to the classical Arabic grammar. As to the supposed III ʾ (*tertiae hamza*), the end-*alif* in the Qurʾānic spelling has been erroneously regarded as a *hamza*-bearer. From Syro-Aramaic borrowed verbs, as e.g., قرا (*to read*) and برا (*to create*), are not to be read *qaraʾa* and *baraʾa*, but—according to the Syro-Aramaic pronunciation: *qarā* and *barā*. Except some onomatopoetic verbs in Arabic, as تأتأ / *taʾtaʾa* (*to stammer*), طأطأ /*ṭaʾṭaʾa* (*to bow one's head*) and the glottal stop in spoken Arabic in لأ / *laʾ*, *laʾa* = *lā* (*no*), perhaps also in the case of a softened ع /*ʿayn* as in بدأ / *badaʾa* < بدع / *badaʿa* < methatesis of Syro-Aramaic ܥܒܕ /*ʿḇaḏ* (*to create*),[25] it can be said that with regard to the Qurʾānic orthography the Qurʾān does not know a III ʾ (*tertiae hamza*).

Much graver is however the addition of the by no means justified *hamza* after an end-*alif*, as far as such an *alif* in Syro-Aramaic can designate at least three different categories:

a) The ending of a *status emphaticus* masculine (be it a noun or an adjective), as e.g., شفاء (traditional reading: *šifāʾun*—Surahs 10:57; 16:69; 17:82; 41:44) < Syro-Aramaic ܫܦܝܐ / *šep̄yā* or *šp̄āyā* (*clearness, purity*); the same Syro-Aramaic form ܗܕܝܐ / *heḏyā* or *hḏāyā* = Arabic هدى / *hudan* or هداية / *hidāya* (*leading, guidance*) shows how arbitrary the traditional different reading of the alternative spelling of these both words in Surah 41:44 (هدى وشفاء) as *hudan wa-šifāʾan* is, since both words, according to the same

Syro-Aramaic origin, are to read likewise as *hudā wa-šifā* (after dropping of the unaccented Syro-Aramaic *y* before the emphatic end-*ā*).

The superfluous end-*hamza* can also distort a genuine Arabic adverb, as in Surah 12:16, where it is said of Joseph's brothers: وجاو اباهم عشاء يبكون (Bell I 219: *They came to their father* [wa-ǧā'ū abā-hum] *in the evening* ['īšā'an], *weeping* [yabkūn]), whereas the adverb "in the evening" occurring four times in the Qur'ān (Surahs 19:11,62; 30:18; 40:46) as عشيا (*'ašīyan*) and not عشاء (*'išā'an*), should have called] the attention of the Arab readers to the fact, that the latter original spelling, without the end-*hamza*, [was to be read as] غشا يبكون (*ġiššan yabkūn*) "false tears."

b) All cases of the Arabic feminine elative with an end-*alif* reflect truly the ending of the Syro-Aramaic *status absolutus* feminine with an end-*ā* and are consequently to read without the superfluous end-*hamza*, as, e.g., صفرا (*yellow*) in Surah 2:69, that is to read adequately *ṣafrā* (as in spoken Arabic) and not صفراء (traditional reading: *ṣafrā'u*). The early Arab grammarians were obviously aware of this morphology, in so far as they declared such an ending as ممنوع من الصرف / *mamnū' min aṣ-ṣarf* (*banned as to the inflection* = *indeclinable*). Later grammarians may have interpreted this rule as *partially declinable* (rendered in the Western Arabic grammars by the term *diptotic*) and added to this purpose the fictitious end-*hamza*. This concerns as well the following plural endings.

c) The end-hamza in the the Arabic plurals of the types: فعلاء / *fu'alā'* and افعلاء / *af'ilā'*, are likewise superfluous. All these unjustified additions are an invention of the Arab philologists subsequent to the creation of the classical Arabic grammar in the second half of the eighth century and later. As far as such forms occur in Arabic poetry, this linguistic-historical criterion would provide a *terminus post quem* (= *a quo*) as to the origin of the corresponding poetical works. Further morphological formations of the classical Arabic grammar, borrowed from Syro-Aramaic, will be demonstrated with some examples from the early Arabic poetry in a forthcoming study.

8. Continuation of Surah 96:6

Since it became now clear that طغى (*ṭaġā* = *ṭa'ā*; with all other Qur'ānic derivations) is a borrowing from the Syro-Aramaic ܛܥܐ (*ṭ'ā*), its meaning can consequently be found among the equivalent semantic field appropriate to this context. It follows from the context that the meaning to be retained is the one cited in *Mannā* (289b f.) under (6) نسى (*nasiya* – "to forget"). Accordingly, this verse does not say "man is *rebellious*," but "man *forgets*."

8.1 Verse 6

First of all, the result of the above misunderstood ليطغى (*la-yaṭġā*) was that the particle following it, ان, was misread as *ʾan* (*that*) instead of *ʾin* (*when*). The personal suffix for the verb رءاه (*raʾ-hu*—properly: *rā-hu*) has been correctly understood reflexively from the context. This usage happens by chance, of course, not to be Arabic, but Syro-Aramaic.[26]

Secondly, however, in the case of the next verb استغنى (*istaġnā*), it is not "considers himself his own master" that is correct, but rather the alternative that Bell proposes (II 667) in note 4: "*he* has become rich."
The verses 6–7 are accordingly:

> In truth, man forgets when he sees that he has become rich.

8.2 Verse 7

In the first place, it should now be clear that this understanding yields a conjunction أنّ (*anna* – "that") introducing a dependent clause. The hitherto misunderstood context, however, has caused the syntactical unity of this sentence construction to be so torn apart that one made this dependent clause into an independent main clause introduced by the intensifying particle إنّ (*inna*).

Secondly, from this misunderstanding the need arose to interpret the Arabic verbal noun الرجعى (*ar-ruǧʿā*—rather *ar-raǧʿā*) in no other way than the general sense of "return to your Lord." If one considers the new understanding, however, then this "return," referring to the "man who has become rich," is to be understood as the "return" or "repatriation" of this circumstance unto God, which man "forgets" to the extent that he, in accordance with a familiar human experience, no longer thinks about praying. Verses 6–8 are thus directly concerned with the subject of this Surah and should be understood as follows:

> 6. In truth, man forgets, 7. when he sees that he has become rich, 8. that (this) is to be returned *unto* your Lord.

Whereas until now it was a question of a man become wanton who fails to pray out of personal conviction, in the sequence which now follows the Qurʾān addresses the external influence of an unbeliever who wants to stop a devout man (a *servant of God*) from praying. In the process, the verses 9–14 consist syntactically of two previously completely overlooked conditional clauses, the first formulated as a question and the second as a counter-question. From Paret's translation, the previous confused understanding is evident. Nevertheless, first of all, as an introduction to the syntactic structure, the individual elements will be analyzed.

8.3 Verse 9

From the perspective of the Arabic understanding, the particle أ *'a* prefixed to the verb ارءيت (*a̱-ra'ayta*—properly: *a-rayta*) in Verses 9 and 11 cannot be understood otherwise than as an interrogative particle. This understanding excludes a subsequent conditional clause, but exposes at the same time the disharmony of the syntactic period.

8.4 Excursus: (a) On the Meaning of the Particle أ /'a

This problem cannot be overcome without the help of Syro-Aramaic. For only the Syro-Aramaic can give us information about the genesis of the Arabic interrogative particle أ / *'a*, which until now has been considered *classical.* In his study on the subject Bergsträsser[27] naturally starts from the classical assumption and contents himself with a descriptive reproduction of the opinions of the Arabic grammarians. Nobody seems to have realized till now, however, that, on the basis of the Qur'ānic usage, the Arabic interrogative particle أ / *'a* has only grown secondarily out of the Syro-Aramaic particle ܐܘ (*aw*) through the omission of the ܘ *w*. Evidence for this is provided by the Qur'ānic usage itself. For example, it can be determined that the original particle او / *aw* occurs as an interrogative particle in conjunction with the negative particle لا (اولا *awa-lā*) three times and with لم (اولم *awa-lam*) 33 times, whereas, with 78 occurrences, the usage with the monophthongized particle أ / *'a*, for instance, ألم (*a-lam*), clearly predominates.

The *Lisān* (XIV 55b) cites *al-Farrā'*, who explains the و / *w* of the Qur'ānic interrogative particle أولم (*awa-lam*) as an "*isolated* wāw" to which the interrogative particle أ / *'a* was added (إنها واو مفردة دخلت عليها ألف الاستفهام). Hence the awareness that this interrogative particle is not of Arabic origin is lacking among all of the Arabic philologists. The other uses of the particle او / *aw* in the Qur'ān also coincide to a large extent with that of the homonymous Syro-Aramaic ܐܘ / *aw*.[28]

Thus, for example, the Qur'ānic use of the monophthongized particle أ / *'a* has found its place in Arabic as a conjunction introducing an apodosis expressing uncertainty or doubt, especially after corresponding negative verbs, as in لا أدرى أ (*lā adrī 'a*) or لا أعلم أ (*lā a'lamu 'a* – "I do not know whether. . .") (cf., e.g., Surah 72:10,25). As a rule this is felt to be an indirect interrogative particle. Anyone with a feeling for the language, however, would not be able to recognize this function as soon as he encountered the Syro-Aramaic particle ܐܘ / *aw* instead of the Arabically naturalized particle أ / *'a*. An example of this is provided by Surah 3:128:

ليس لك من الامر شئ او يتوب عليهم او يعذبهم فانهم ظلمون

Paret (55) renders this verse as follows:

3:128 —it is not for you (to decide) the matter—<u>or</u> to turn again to them (mercifully) <u>or</u> (else) to punish them. They are (indeed) wrongdoers.

The *Lisān* (XIV 55a) explains the particle أو / *aw* here in the sense of "*<u>until</u>* he takes pity on them" or "*<u>unless</u>* God takes pity on them" (حتى يتوب عليهم و إلى أن يتوب عليهم). However, according to the Syro-Aramaic understanding of the conjunction ܐܘ / *aw* the verse says:

3:128 It should be *a matter of indifference* to you <u>whether</u> (God) takes pity on them *<u>or</u>* dooms them to death (by fire): they are (in any case) wrongdoers.

8.5 (b) On the Usage of the Particle أ /ca in the Sense of إن /in (if)

The list that the *Thes.* (I 48) supplies, by way of the East Syrian lexicographers, on the usage of the Syro-Aramaic conjunction ܐܘ (*aw*) is interesting in this regard. Under the eight occasionally occurring functions *Bar Bahlūl* gives the meaning ܐܢ (*'ēn*) (*if*). This in turn coincides with the explanation provided by *Kisā'ī* (953–1002), cited in the *Lisān* (XIV 55a), that أو (*aw*) also occurs *conditionally* (قال الكسائي وحده : وتكون شرطا – "only Kisā'ī said: it also occurs conditionally").

8.6 The Solution of Verses 9 to 14

On the basis of this excursus, the following new interpretation emerges for these verses:

9–10. The first ارءيت is to be understood in the sense of إن رأيت (*in ra'ayta* – "*<u>if</u>* you see"). Accordingly, the double verse runs:

<u>If</u> you see one who (wants) to stop a worshipper (of God) (from praying) when he is praying. . . .

11–12. The second ارءيت is to be understood as a question in the sense of "to think": "do you (*then*) think *<u>that</u>*...." Accordingly, the falsely read إن (*in*) must be read as أن (*an*). As a result, this double verse reads as an *apodosis*:

do you (*then*) think *<u>that</u>* he is on the right path or *<u>is thinking</u> pious thoughts*?

13–14. Parallel to Verse 9, the repeated ارءيت is in turn to be read إن رأيت (*in ra'ayta* – "*<u>if</u>* you think"), followed once more by أن (*an*) (*<u>that</u>*) instead of إن (*in* – "if"), and understood as a counter-question with a protasis and apodosis:

> *If* (on the other hand) you think *that* he is denying (God) and turning away (from Him), *then* does he not know that God sees *everything*?

15. What is meant by the second كلا is again Syro-Aramaic ܟܠܐ (*kullā*) (in the sense of كل شئ / *kulla šay'* – "everything"); as an object it belongs to the preceding verb.

The particle لئن (falsely *la-'ēn*, actually to be read *l- n*) consists of the intensifying Arabic particle لـ / *la-* and the Syro-Aramaic conjunction ܐܢ (*'ēn*).[29] This form occurs 61 times in the Qur'ān. Older Qur'ānic manuscripts should provide evidence of the full spelling لاين (= *l-'n*). The *little peak* considered as a يـ / *y carrier* was, contrary to the Qur'ānic (i.e., Syro-Aramaic) pronunciation, subsequently occupied by a *hamza*. In the canonical version of the Qur'ān, this orthography (أفإين / *af-ēn* < ܐܦ ܐܢ / *āp̄ēn*) is documented twice (Surahs 3:144 and 21: 34).

The Arabic verb لنسفعا (*la-nasfa'an*) certainly does not mean "to seize." In the *Lisān* (VIII 157b f.) the meaning is given correctly as لطم (*laṭama*) and ضرب (*ḍaraba*) (*to strike*). On the other hand, the explanation that follows, وسفع بناصيته: جذب وأخذ وقبض ("to seize" by the "forelock"), is based on the false understanding of "*forelock.*" What is meant by "*to strike*," however, is "*to punish*" in a figurative sense (in modern Arabic usage, as well). According to Mandaean Orthography the final ا /*-ā* can also expeass the final ن /*-n.*[30] The terminations *-'n* and *-yn* are expressed by a simple alif without distinction. We often find the two orthographies in the same manuscript. The Koran applies the same rule by analogy to express the Arabic *energicus,* which is not to be confused with cases of *nunation.* A parallel to this is provided by Surah 12:32 (وليكونا / *wa-l-yakūna^n*).[31]

It is astounding that, of our Qur'ān translators, not one has objected to the expression "forelock" (Paret "Schopf," Blachère "toupet"). Yet, what is meant here by the spelling ناصية (except for the secondarily inserted ا / *ā*) is Syro-Aramaic ܢܨܝܐ (*naṣṣāyā*). For this, the *Thes.* (II 2435) first gives the meaning: *contentiosus, rixosus* (*contentious, quarrelsome*) (said of a woman, as in Prov. 21:9,19; 25:24). From the Syrian lexicographers it then cites, in addition to further Syro-Aramaic synonyms, the following Arabic renderings: مخاصم . مقاوم (*opponent, adversary*).

But more amazing than this is the discovery that, over and over again, even the *Lisān* (XV 327) explains the root نصا (*naṣā*), documented in earlier Arabic, as a denominative of ناصية (*nāṣiya*), presumably misunderstood in Arabic as "forelock, shock of hair," even though the *ḥadīṯ* of *'Ā'iša* that it cites actually makes the Syro-

Aramaic meaning clear. Namely, therein *'Ā'iša* is recorded as saying: لم تكن واحدة من نساء النبي تناصيني غير زينب (*none of the wives of the Prophet quarreled with me except for Zaynab*). Although the *Lisān* then explains this as: أي تنازعني وتباريني (i.e., "she quarreled with me, she opposed me"), it traces this explanation back to the circumstance that in doing so the two women, so to speak, "got into each other's hair" (وهو أن يأخذ كل واحد من المتنازعين بناصية الآخر), or more exactly, "seized each other by the scruff of the neck." It can be seen from this how little the later Arab philologists have understood the earlier Syriacisms and Aramaisms.

The following understanding therefore results for Verse 15:

> If he does not stop, we will (severely) punish the adversary.

In the same way as for ناصية (*nāṣiya*, but actually *naṣṣāyā*), the apparent feminine ending for كذبة (*kāḏiba*, actually *kaddābā*) and خاطية (*ḥāṭi'a*, actually *ḥaṭṭāyā*) is nothing other than the phonetic rendering of the Syro-Aramaic *emphatic* ending. Therefore, Verse 16, modeled on Verse 15, is to be understood as follows:

> The denying, sinful adversary.

17. The expression ناديه (*nādiyahu*), which occurs here, must be redefined. The "clique," as Paret translates the expression in the modern Arabic sense of "club, association," (Bell: "council;" Blachère: "clan"), is out of the question. Inasmuch as the facultative medial ا / *alif* in ناديه, according to the Eastern Syro-Aramean orthographical tradition, can occasionally designate a short *a*, the spelling yields the Syro-Aramaic ܢܕܝܗ (*naḏyeh* or *naddāyeh*). As a *nomen agentis* this form leads us to the intensive stem ܢܕܝ (*naddī*), whose primary meaning the *Thes.* (II 2291) gives as "commovit, concussit, terrefecit" (to agitate, to shake, to scare off). Applied to the *idols* that are probably meant here, this would result in the meaning "of the one who arouses fear" (i.e., whom one *fears* as a god). The *Thes.*, however, then refers to a further form: "Partic. ܡܢܕܝܐ (*mnaddā*) vide infra." The expression that is found further down (2292) ܫܒܝܪܬܐ ܘܡܢܕܝܬܐ (*šḇirtā wa-mnaddaytā* – something or someone] "disgusting and repulsive") brings us closer to the sense we are seeking. The Arabic meanings that are cited by *Mannā* (431b) under ܐܢܕ (*aneḏ*) are informative: (2) ابغض . مقت (*to hate, to detest*), (3) رذل. نبذ (*to reject, to disown*), (6) نجّس. قذّر (*to make dirty, to besmirch*), (7) ارعب. افزع (*to scare away, to frighten*). All these meanings lead namely to the "unclean spirit"

or "idols" designated with synonymous expressions in Syro-Aramaic (cf., e.g., *Thes.* I 1490, under ܛܢܦܐ *ṭanpā* "impurus, immundus;" *Ρκάθαρτος* de daemonibus, Matt. 10:1,...; further under ܛܢܦܘܬܐ / *ṭanpūṯā: pollutio, res quae polluit = idolum*, Exod. 8:26, Deut. 7:26, Jer. 32:34; de *idolatriis*, Deut. 20:18...; in connection with this, the following expression [1491], documented in the Qur'ān with انداد [*andād*],[32] ܢܕܝܕܘܬܐ [*nḏīḏūṯā*] [*impurity*] also becomes a designation for ܦܬܟܪܐ [*pṯakrā*] [*idols*], etc.).

Thus, with the *tertium comparationis* discovered via Syro-Aramaic, Verse 17 is to be understood as follows:

> May he then call upon his *idols* [literally: *impure ones*]!

18. The expression الزبانية (until now pronounced *az-zabāniya*)[33] is still considered a puzzle. The misreading of the preceding verbal form in the first person plural سندع (*sa-nad'u*) is of course responsible for one's seeing in this incomprehensible expression in Arabic the "henchmen" (of hell) that God will allegedly *call in*. However, if we transcribe the original spelling (without the secondary ا / *ā*) into Syro-Aramaic, the result is the reading ܙܒܢܝܐ (*zaḇnāyā*). As the adjective from ܙܒܢܐ (*zaḇnā*) (*time*), this simply gives us, according to the *Thes.* (I 1079) under ܙܒܢܝܐ (*zaḇnāyā*), the meaning: *temporalis, temporarius, haud aeternus* (*temporal, transitory, not eternal*). This designation is a perfect match for the (*transitory*) "idols" of the (God-) *denying adversary*. It is to this extent only logical that the verbal form سيدع is to be read in the third person (*sa-yad'u*). This results in the following understanding for Verse 18: ". . .he will (only) *call upon* a[34] *transitory* (*god*)!"
19. Although the third and last كلا can be read in Arabic as *kallā* (*no*) in connection with, and as intensifying, the negative imperative that follows it, in Syro-Aramaic (*kullā*) it has the meaning of "(not) at all."

In addition to the actual Syro-Aramaic meaning of "to bow" (as an external sign of respect), one should also assume for the Arabic borrowed verb سجد (*sağada*) (< ܣܓܕ / *sgeḏ*) the metaphorical meaning of "to worship God" (*Thes.* II 2522, "metaph. *adoravit* Deum").

The Arabic borrowed verb اقترب (*iqtaraba*) has in this context a quite particular content that the general Arabic meaning "approach" (without object or reference) is not able to provide. As a translation of Syro-Aramaic ܐܬܩܪܒ (*eṯqarraḇ*) the *Thes.* (II 3724) gives us (in particular as a *reflexive* or *intransitive* verb) the specific meaning that fits here, as follows: "spec. *celebrata est liturgia* (*to celebrate* the *liturgy*); it. *Eucharistiam accepit* (*to receive* the *Eu-*

charist). The latter meaning is logically to be assumed provided that one as a believer takes part in the *celebration of the Eucharist.* The term points in any case without a doubt to the participation in the "sacrifice of the mass," in the "celebration of the Eucharist" or in the "communion liturgy."

Those that this unambiguous explanation shocks are invited to refer to the Arabic dissertation written by Salwā Bā l-Ḥāǧǧ mentioned in the foreword of my book *The Syro-Aramaic Reading of the Koran* (Berlin, 2007), p. 11, note 6.[35]

In sum, the result of this philological discussion is the following reading and understanding for Surah 96 according to the Syro-Aramaic reading:

العلق

(*al-ʿalaq*) The Clay (Literally: the "*sticking*")

اقرا باسم ربك الذى خلق

1. *iqrā b-ism^i rabbik^a l-laḏī ḫalaq*
   <u>*Call*</u> the name of your lord who has created,
   خلق الانسن من علق
2. *ḫalaq^a l-insān^a min ʿalaq*
   (who) has created man from <u>*sticky*</u> (*clay*);
   اقرا وربك الاكرم
3. *iqrā wa-rabbak^a l-akram*
   <u>*call*</u> (indeed)[36] your <u>*most venerable*</u> Lord,
   الذى علم بالقلم
4. *al-laḏī ʿallam^a bi-l-qalam*
   who has taught by the reed pen (i.e., the *scripture*),
   علم الانسن ما لم يعلم كلا
5. *allam^a l-insān^a mā lam yaʿlam kullā*
   has taught man what he did <u>*not*</u> know <u>*at all*</u>.
   ان الانسن ليطعى
6. *in(na)* or *n : al-insān^u la-yaṭʿā*
   Verily, man <u>*forgets*</u>,
   إن راه استغنى
7. *ʾin* or *n rā-hu staġnā (Syriac ʾen > ʾin)*
   <u>*when*</u> he sees that he has <u>*become rich*</u>,
   أن الى ربك الرجعى
8. *an(n^a) ilā rabbik^a r-raǧʿā*
   <u>*that*</u> (this) is <u>*to be returned*</u> <u>*to*</u> your Lord.
   اريت الذى ينهى
9. *a-rayt^a l-laḏī yanhā*
   <u>*If*</u> you <u>*see*</u> one who (wants) to stop[37]
   عبدا اذا صلى

10. *ʿabd^{an} iḏā ṣallā*
a worshipper (of God) (from praying) when he is praying,
اريت أن كان على الهدى
11. *a-rayt^{a} an kān^{a} ʿalā l-hudā*
do you think (perhaps) <u>that</u> he is on the right path,
او امر بالتقوى
12. *aw amar^{a} bi-t-taqwā*
or is even[38] thinking pious thoughts?[39]
اريت أن كذب وتولى
13. *a-rayt^{a} an kaḏḏab^{a} wa-tawallā*
<u>If</u> you (on the contrary) <u>think</u> <u>that</u> he <u>is denying</u> (God) and turning away (from Him),
الم يعلم بان الله يرى كلا
14. *a-lam yaʿlam bi-an(n^{a}) llāh^{a} yarā kullā*
(then) does he not know that God sees <u>everything</u>?
لين لم ينته لنسفعا بالناصيه
15. *la-ʾin (< la-ʾēn > lēn) lam yantahi la-nasfaʿan bi-n-nāṣiya* (in Syriac: *naṣṣāyā*)
If he does not stop (doing that), (one day) we shall punish the <u>adversary</u> (severely),
ناصيه كذبه خاطيه
16. *nāṣiya kāḏiba ḫāṭiya* or *naṣṣāyā kaddāḇā ḥaṭṭāyā*
the <u>denying</u>, wicked <u>adversary</u>!
فليدع ناديه
17. *fa-l-yadʿu nādiya-hu* or *nadya-hu*
May he call (then) on his (whoever) <u>idol</u>—
سيدع الزبانيه
18. *sa-yadʿu z-zabāniya* or *zabāniy*
(in doing so) he will call on <u>transitory</u> (god)!
كلا لا تطعه
kullā lā tuṭiʿhu
واسجد واقترب
19. *wa-sǧud wa-qtarib*
You ought <u>not</u> to heed him <u>at all</u>,
perform (instead) (your) divine service[40]
and take part in the liturgy of Eucharist.

According to this understanding, Surah 96 proves to be a unified composition having as its overall content a call to take part in the divine service. As such it has the character of a ܦܪܘܡܝܘܢ (<προοίμιον proóimion [Greek]/ *prooemium*) introducing the Christian Syriac liturgy, which was replaced in the later Islamic tradition by the فاتحة (*fātiḥa*) (< Syro-Aramaic ܦܬܚܐ / *pṯāḥā*) (*introductory prayer*). That this liturgy is *Communion* is indicated by the final Syro-

Aramaic term. An important task in the history of religion would be to find out which pre-Islamic Christian Syrian (or possibly Judaeo-Christian) community this was.

The term *fātiḥa* is confined to the Koran. Only in later Islamic tradition it has been used to designate the first Surah of the Koran. As its Syro-Arabic literal meaning ("the opening one," i.e., the one that "introduces") seemed perfectly clear, it comes as no surprise that it was considered superfluous to question its origin. The importance of this question for the history of religions, however, is undeniable. The Koran mentions several religious groups in three passages (Q 2:62, Q 5:69, Q 22:17): the *Jews*, the *Nazarenes* (or Christians) and the *Sabaeans* (*al-Ṣābi'ūn*) or *Mandaeans*, which indicates that the Koran emerged in Mesopotamia and not in the Mecca region. Among the Mandaeans, the *pṯāḥā* is the term for the *breadbreaking* liturgy, as explained in the Mandaean dictionary of Drower/Macuch:[41]

> **ptaha** (rt. **PTH**): (*a*) opening, beginning, (*b*) a name given to the ritual meal, sacred "Breaking of Bread," communal meal (= **laupa**), ritual meal for the dead. (p. 227b):
>
> **laupa** (rt. **LUP** = **LPP**): uniting, union, communion, name of a ritual meal eaten for the dead, the communion of living and dead. . . **laupa ḏ-hiia** (*often*) the communion of life; (p. 366a): **laupa ḏ-patura:** the communion of the (ritual) platter (= *al-mā'ida*, actually: *mayda*).

The information in the last two lines confirms the conclusion that Surah 96:19 (*al-ʿalaq*) and 5:112–115 (*al-mā'ida* /*al-mayda*) both refer to the liturgy of the *Eucharist* or the Breadbreaking liturgy, which was only abolished in later Islam.

Now, if the Arabic tradition considers this to be the oldest Surah, one must concede that it is right to the extent that this Surah is, in any case, part of that *nucleus of the Qur'ān*, the *Christian Syrian origins* of which cannot be ignored. Whether this is also the first that was revealed to the Prophet is probably based on a later legend grown out of the misinterpretation of the opening verse. Arguing in favor of its being very probably pre-Qur'ānic, i.e., much more pre-Islamic, is its language, hitherto perceived as mysterious and puzzling. For it is precisely this language with its unadulterated expressions that reveals to us its venerable origins.

One such expression is the Arabic اقترب (*iqtaraba*) borrowed from the Syro-Aramaic verb ܐܬܩܪܒ (*eṯqarraḇ*). As a *technical term* of the Christian Syrian liturgy it gives us a valuable, hitherto unexpected insight into the origins, not only of the oldest parts of the Qur'ān in terms of the history of religion. For only this expression opens our eyes to a parallel occurring in what is held to be the last Surah revealed, Surah 5 (*The Table*), a parallel whose actual importance in terms of the history of religion has in a similar way been ignored until now. Between this *term* and the "table" that Jesus, the son of Mary, requests of God in Surah 5:114, تكون لنا عيدا لاولنا واخرنا "that it may become ours as *liturgy*,[42] for the first and the last of us," and which, in Verse 115, God sends down from heaven, threatening any "who would *deny* it" (فمن يكفر *fa-man yakfur*) with the severest of all punishments (فاني اعذبه عذابا لا اعذبه احدا من العلمين) (*him I shall punish in such a way as I shall punish no man*), there exists a connection insofar as both clearly allude to the *liturgy of Communion*, whose importance was misjudged in later Islam and has since been totally forgotten. This central item in the Christian components of the Qur'ān is, in any case, of eminent importance in terms of the history of religion.

If any should doubt, however, the importance of the Christian Syriac liturgical term اقترب (*iqtaraba* < ܐܬܩܪܒ / *etqarrab* – "to take part in the liturgy of Communion, to receive the Eucharist"), they may refer to the Arabic dissertation mentioned in the Foreword (p. iii, note 4) where the author (89), in the fourth chapter of the first part of her work *Religious Customs and Rites of Christian Arabs Before Islam*" refers to the Arabic compilation الأغاني (*al-Aġānī*) (vol. II 107) of *Abū l-Faraǧ al-Isfahānī* (d. 356 H./967 CE), who reports of عدي بن زيد (*'Adī ibn Zayd*) (d. circa 590 CE) and هند بنت النعمان (*Hind bint an-Nu'mān*) (d. after 602 CE) how they went on Maundy Thursday into the church of *al-Ḥira* (located southwest of the Euphrates in modern-day Iraq) " ليتقربا (*li-yataqarrabā*) – "to take part in the celebration of the Eucharist" (or "to receive the Eucharist").

In the corresponding passage in the كتاب الأغاني (*Kitāb al-aġānī*)[43] (*Book of Songs*) *Abū l-Faraǧ al-Iṣfahānī* (d. 967) cites the traditional account of the pre-Islamic Christian Arab poet *'Adī ibn Zayd* living in *al-Ḥīra* according to which he had gone on Maundy Thursday into the church of *al-Ḥīra* ليتقرّب (*li-yataqarrab*) "to take part in the celebration of the Eucharist" (or *to receive the Eucharist*). On this occasion, he wanted to see *Hind*, the daughter of the last of the Laḫmids' kings of *al-Ḥīra*, النعمان / *an-Nu'mān III* (580-602), who had gone to the aforementioned church تتقرّب (*tata-qarrab*) "to take part in the celebration of the Eucharist."[44] The term *taqarrab* is still used today by the Arabic-speaking Christians.

Thus, this *liturgical term* is already historically documented in the 6th century even from the Arab side as a Syro-Aramaic ecclesiastical term of the Christian Arabs of Syria and Mesopotamia.

9. Surah 5: al-Mā'ida – "the Table": The Last Supper in the Qur'ān

In Surah 5 (*al-Mā'ida*, "the Table"), considered by Islamic Tradition to be the last one revealed, Jesus, in response to the Apostles' demand (verse 112), prays to God in these terms (verse 114 , R. Blachère 15, p.150):

> Q 5:114 My God ! My Lord ! . . . send a table down from the sky which will be a celebration for the first and last among us.

Paret's commentary and concordance:

> Q 5:112–115: obviously allusion to the Last Supper; but could as well be influenced by St. Peters vision as recounted in the Acts of the Apostles 10,10 ff.; see Rudolph, W.: *Die Abhāngigkeit des Qorans von Judentum und Christentum*, Stuttgart 1922, p. 81f. [The Dependence of the Qur'ān on Judaism and Christianity]
> Q 5:114: "li-awwalina wa-akhirina" should be related to the succession of generations, see Q 56:48–50.

Bell translates as follows:

> Q5:114: O Allah our Lord, send down to us a table from the heaven, to be us a festival, to the first and to the last of us.

Bell's footnote to the whole scene (Q 5:112–115):

> This section, which is continuous with the preceding, is apparently based, not on any knowledge of the New Testament, but on some hearsay information about the Christian sacrament.

Paret's German translation is quite similar to Bell's:

> Du unser Gott und Herr (allahumma rabbana)! Sende uns vom Himmel einen Tisch herab, der (mit seinem Mahl) [=with the meal on it] fūr uns von jetzt an bis in alle Zukunft (?) eine Feier (id.) und ein Zeichen von dir sein wird!

Paret's footnote to "bis in alle Zukunft" [not important]: "W. (= literally): für den ersten und den letzten von uns—for the first and the last of us."

R.Blachère, who translates "table" (Q 5:112) by "table laid out "(with food), comments on this point:

> [Carl Friedrich] Gerock [*Versuch einer Darstellung der Christologie des Qur'ān* (1839)] followed by W Rudolph [*Die Abhangigkeit des Qur'āns von Judentum und Christentum*, 1922], thought that it concerned a reminiscence of the Last Supper, being St.Peter's vision as recounted in the Acts of the Apostles, X.10-13.

Blachère excludes, in the same footnote, the idea of the Last Supper, the death of Jesus not being admitted by the Qur'ān (see Surah 4:156). However the latter verse in Surah 4 according to which someone else would have been crucified in place of Jesus, is one of the erroneous historical interpretations of Islamic exegesis that Western scholars themselves have taken up totally uncritically. In fact, the intrinsic paradox that three Qur'ānic verses raise (19:33; 3:55; 5:117), where the Qur'ān clearly speaks of the death of Jesus before his Resurrection or his Ascension, should have been enough to cast doubt on such an interpretation. But as for the Houris or Virgins of Paradise, a forthcoming well-founded philological analysis will put an end to this obvious exegetical contradiction and give back to the Qur'ān its original harmony on this point. For the moment, this remark should be enough to allow the idea of the Last Supper suggested by Gerock and Rudolph.

It is in fact only by putting the words Last Supper in place of the paraphrase "laid out table" that this term will recover all its theological dimension in connection with the word which follows. The Arabic word *'īd*, borrowed from the Syriac, has been, in conformity with its Arabic meaning, correctly translated by "celebration." The table being laid out, one could have thought, in fact, that it was talking about "having a celebration." However, the same writing or script transcribed in Syriac as *'yd'*, pronounced *'yāḏā*, gives the meaning " liturgy." Thus one must understand this verse as follows :

> Lord our God, send us down from the sky a Last Supper which would be a liturgy for the first and last of us.

In his reply, God says (according to R. Blachère, op.cit., verse 115)

> I am going to send it down to you. Whoever is then impious among you will receive from me a torment the like of which I will not inflict on anyone else in the world.

Nothing to verse Q 5:115 in Paret's *Kommentar und Konkordanz.* Bell's translation is as follows:

> Q 5:115: Verily I am going to send it down to you; so if any of you afterwards disbelieve, I shall assuredly punish them as I punish no one else of (all) the worlds.

Paret's version of Q 5:114 is very similar to Bell's:

> Ich will ihn euch (nunmehr) hinabsenden. Und wenn einer von euch nachträglich nicht glaubt, werde ich ihn (dereinst) auf eine Weise bestrafen, wie (sonst) niemand in der Welt (al-'ālamūn)—[I want it sent down to you (now). And if any of you do not believe afterwards, I will punish him (one day) in such a manner as no one else in the world has been].

Here we are concerned with the word translated as "impious." It is true that the Arabic verb *kafara*, borrowed from Syriac, has this meaning. But more than the latter meaning, the Syriac verb ܟܦܪ *kp̄r* also means "to deny, to renounce." By this verb, according to Syriac syntax, referring back to the "liturgy," is clearly meant the latter sense here, to deny this liturgy. Thus the previous verse (Q 5:115) should be understood as:

> I will send it down to you. Whoever among you henceforth dismisses it, I will punish him as I would never punish any other humans.

Islam was not impressed by this divine injunction with its threats of the most severe punishments, not having grasped its significance. If the Muslim exegetes had understood these passages as the Qur'ān intended it, there would have been a liturgy of the Last Supper in Islam.

This linguistic aspect of the Qur'ān being confirmed historically as of Syriac origin leads the author henceforth to conclude that not only the form but the substance of the Qur'ān is of Syro-Christian origin, or at least the latter constitutes the foundation. The latter more so because the word "Qur'ān" itself is nothing other than a phonetic Arabic distortion of the Syriac term *Qəryān*, designating a Syriac liturgical book corresponding to the Lectionary (Lectionarium) of the Roman liturgy, from which the Readings, constituting extracts of the Old and New Testament, are read in the Christian liturgical service. It is thus not surprising that Jesus (*ʿĪsā*) is cited twenty five times in the Qur'ān and that he is there referred to as the Messiah (*al-Masīḥ*) eleven times. Thus it is only logical to see other Syro-Christian passages being a part of this foundation which constitutes the origin of the Qur'ān and that the author intends to elucidate in a forthcoming work.

10. Surah 19: Mary

In his first work the author tackled briefly Surah 19, *Mary*, verse 24, of which he gave a detailed philological analysis. The reproach of an illegitimate conception made indirectly to Mary, according to verses 24 and 28, pushes Mary to wish for her own death before giving birth. Her son, newly born, addresses her in verse 24 his first words to comfort her. The Arabic reading of this verse had led the commentators to the following understanding (passages in need of revision are underlined):

> "Don't be sad!," he cries from underneath her, "your Lord has placed below you a stream!"

Régis Blachère tries to soften this rather unlikely interpretation by translating Q 19:24 as follows:

> [But] the child who was at her feet spoke to her: "Don't be sad! Your Lord has placed at your feet a stream."

Paret's commentary and concordance:

> To Q 19:24: the subject of the verb "(fa-)nadaha" is Jesus, either still in his mother's womb or newly born. Muhammad seems to be influenced by a scene

in the so-called "Pseudo-Matthāus," chapter 20, where the story of the flight of the Holy Family to Egypt is told: tunc infantulus Jesus laeto vultu in sinu matris suae residens ait ad palmam: flectere, arbor, et de fructibus tuis refice matrem meam. . . aperi autem ex radicibus tuis venam, quae absconsa est in terra, et fluant ex ea aquae ad satietatem nostram. (Paret cites this text as commentary to verses 23–26); Translation of the Latin text: "Thereupon spoke the Infant Jesus, of joyful countenance sitting in his mother's lap, to the palm tree: Bend over, tree, and refresh my mother from your fruits. . . further open out of your roots a vein that lies hidden in the earth, and let waters stream out upon us to quench our thirst," p. 137.

Bell's version of Q 19:24:

> Then he called her from beneath her: "Grieve not; thy Lord hath placed beneath thee a streamlet;"

Bell's footnote to "he:" "Probably 'the child.'"
Paret [quite similar to Bell] renders it in German as follows:

> Da rief er ihr von unten her zu: "Sei nicht traurig! Dein Herr hat unter dir ein Rinnsal (*sari*) (voll Wasser) gemacht."

Paret's footnote to "er [he]:" [similar to Bell's interpretation]: "D. h. der Jesusknabe. [i.e., the boy Jesus]". His to "unter dir": "D. h. zu deinen Fūßen (?). [i.e., at your feet]."

However it is not by tinkering with the style that we are going to succeed in elucidating such an enigma, but only by an Arabo-Syriac reading, which leads the author to this meaning of Q 19:24:

> "Don't be sad!," he says to her as soon as he was born, "Your Lord has rendered your childbirth legitimate!" (op. cit., pp. 102–121).

There is no agreement among the Arab commentators on the Qur'ān about the real meaning of the expression occurring in two variants تحت (*taḥta*) as well as of سريا (*sarīyā*) in the following verse of the Mary Surah:

> Surah 19:24
> فناداها من تحتها الا تحزني قد جعل ربك تحتك سريا

In keeping with the majority of the Arab commentators, the Western Qur'ān translators render this verse as follows:

> *Bell* I 286:24. Then he (probably 'the child') called to her from beneath her: 'Grieve not; thy Lord hath placed beneath thee a streamlet';
>
> *Paret* 249:24: Da rief er (d.h. der Jesusknabe) ihr von unten her zu: "Sei nicht traurig! Dein Herr hat unter dir (d.h. zu deinen Füßen?) ein Rinnsal (*sarī*) (voll Wasser) gemacht."

Blachère 331:24 [Mais] l'enfant qui était à ses pieds lui parla: "Ne t'attriste pas! Ton Seigneur a mis à tes pieds un ruisseau."

For Arabic تحت (*taḥta*), which is understood as the preposition *under* by all of the commentators cited in *Ṭabarī*, Jeffery in *The Foreign Vocabulary* (32 f.) makes a reference to as-Suyūṭī (1445-1505), who reports that Abū l-Qāsim in his work *Luġāt al-Qurʾān* [(*Foreign*) *Expressions in the Qurʾān*] and al-Kirmānī in his *al-ʿAǧāʾib* [*The Miracles*] had both thought that this was a Nabatean (i.e., an Aramaic) word and meant as much as بطن (*baṭn*), (which Jeffery renders in English, on the basis of the Arabic understanding, as *womb*, although here, based on the Syro-Aramaic ܒܛܢܐ (*baṭnā*), *foetus*[45] is more likely what should be understood), a view that is not held by anyone in *Ṭabarī*. But Jeffery rejects the notion, saying that there is nothing in Nabataean that would confirm this assumption since, even in Aramaic, Hebrew, Syriac and Ethiopic, the homophonic expressions have exactly the same meaning as the Arabic expression تحت (*taḥta*) (namely *under*).

Yet had Jeffery considered that in the Semitic languages precisely the triliteral prepositions and adverbs were originally nouns and could at times even appear as subjects and objects,[46] he would have perhaps come to another conclusion. The above-mentioned tradition, according to which تحت (*taḥta*) was in this case to be understood as a noun, confirms the supposition that the Arabic tradition has occasionally preserved a memory of the original Aramaic form. Namely, the lack of a verbal root in Arabic suggests a borrowing from Syro-Aramaic ܢܚܬ (*nḥet*), of which the preposition ܬܚܬ (*taḥt*) (> Arabic تحت / *taḥta*) / ܬܚܝܬ (*tḥēṯ*) is only a secondary form. Let's first of all examine this clue in a little more detail.

Although the corresponding Syro-Aramaic nominal form ܢܚܬܐ (*nḥāṯā*) (as well as ܢܘܚܚܬܐ *nuḥḥāṯā*, ܢܚܬܘܬܐ *naḥtūṯā*, ܡܚܬܬܐ *maḥattā* and further derivatives) does not exactly mean *foetus*, it does have something to do with it insofar as, among other meanings, by way of the meaning *descent, origin*, what is meant here is *delivery*.[47] Therefore, the meaning of تحتها (*min*) *taḥtihā* would not be "under her," but "her delivery."

This Syro-Aramaic reading, however, first has the coherence of the context in its favor to the extent that we have interpreted the preposition من (*min*) before تحتها (*taḥtihā*) not *locally* (*from* beneath *her*), but *temporally* in the Syro-Aramaic sense of "from (that point in time), i.e.: instantly, immediately after her delivery."[48] This temporal use of من (*min*), though not attested in Classical Arabic,[49] is nonetheless quite common in modern Arabic dialects of the Near East as a Syro-Aramaic substratum, for example, in: حال وصولي قلت له = من وصولي قلت له (*instantly, immediately after my arrival I said to him*).

The memory of an earlier nominal use of تحت (*taḥt*) has, moreover, been retained by the *Lisān* (II 17b f.): تحت: تكون مرة ظرفا ، ومرة اسما (*taḥt sometimes occurs as an adverb, sometimes as a noun*). Even the adjectival use : قوم تحوت أرذال سفلة (*qawmun tuḥūtun: lowly people*) (*Lisān*, *op. cit.*) can be traced back to Syro-Aramaic ܬܚܬܝ̈ (*taḥtāy—Thes.* II 4425: *infimi hominum*).

Now that the *Lisān* has confirmed the nominal usage of تحت (*taḥtu*), there would be nothing to criticize about the traditional Qur'ānic reading were it not that the reading من نحتها (*min naḥtihā* or *nuḥātihā*) based on Syro-Aramaic ܢܚܬܐ / *nḥāṭā* or ܢܘܚܚܬܐ/ *nuḥḥāṭā* is better. Namely, under the root نحت / *naḥata* the *Lisān* gives a series of phases indicating the Syro-Aramaic origin of this root. For example, among others, it gives the following verse by the poet الخرنق / *al-Ḫirniq*, the sister of the Old Arabic poet طرفة / *Ṭarafa* (c. 538-564 CE):

> الخالطين <u>نحيتهم</u> بنضارهم
>
> who brought the <u>lowly</u> among them together with their nobles
>
> وذوي الغنى منهم بذي الفقر
>
> and the wealthy among them with the needy.

As a conjecture the *Lisān* explains the expression نحيت (*naḥīt*) as دخيل (*daḫīl*) (*stranger*). Yet the opposites of *lowly*[50] and *noble*, *poor* and *rich* in both parts of the verse clearly refer to members of one and the same community. The ignorance of Aramaic prompts the Arab lexicographers to guess the meaning of borrowed expressions from the context. That the error rate in the process is relatively high is evidenced by the countless unrecognized Aramaic roots in the *Lisān*, the encyclopedic dictionary of the Classical Arabic language. In our case, نحيت (*naḥīt*) is a clear borrowing from Syro-Aramaic ܢܚܝܬ (*naḥīṯ* or *naḥḥīṯ*), documented by the Thesaurus with ܢܚܝܬ ܓܢܣܐ (*naḥīṯ /naḥḥīṯ gensā*) *vir infimus, e plebe oriundus*: (*a man*) *of lowly origin*, and, citing the Syrian lexicographers, with the corresponding Arabic translation: لئيم الحسب والنسب والجنس , *ignobilis, humilis genere et conditione,* قليل . وطيّ الاصل . وضيع الحسب والنسب as well as further ܢܚܝܬ (*naḥīṯ*): *descendens,* نازل هابط (*Thes.* II 2345). As in opposition to نحيت (*naḥīt*) is also how the *Lisān* explains النضار (*an-nuḍār—*actually النصار / *an-nuṣār*): الخالص النسب[51] (*al-ḫāliṣu n-nasab*) (*a man*) *of noble descent*, which clearly confirms the antonymous Syro-Aramaic meaning of نحيت (*naḥīt*).

The situation is similar for the other expressions connected with this root, all of which the *Lisān* tries to explain through popular etymology, but whose real meaning is to be determined through Syro-Aramaic. Rich pickings are guaranteed to anyone willing to devote himself or herself to the deserving task of studying the Aramaisms in the *Lisān*. Such would reveal the extent of the Aramaic influence on the Arabic language[52] and smooth the way for a yet non-existent etymological dictionary of Classical Arabic.

Still, the above-mentioned evidence merely confirms the Syro-Aramaic meaning "to be low(ly)." For the meaning "to be hereditary, innate," the *Lisān* cites والنحيتة : الطبيعة التي نحت عليها الانسان أي قطع (*wa-n-naḥīta: aṭ-ṭabīʿatu l-latī nuḥita ʿalayhā l-insānu, ay quṭiʿa*—"an-*naḥīta* is the nature that is hereditary to a person = that is innate to him"). In the definition of the loan term from Syro-Aramaic *naḥīta* (possibly in Syro-Aramaic *nḥāṯā*), the *Lisān* uses the loan verb from Syro-Aramaic *nuḥita* (in the passive voice – "to be descended from, to come away from, to be delivered of" in the sense of "to be born"), which it takes to be the possibly homonymous root نحت (*naḥata*), but which was probably first borrowed from Syro-Aramaic and only understood in later Arabic in the sense of *to chisel* (actually *to knock off, to chop off, to knock down*), and correspondingly explains it as (the nature according to which one) "was hewn, cut, cut to fit," i.e., in its sense as "shaped." There is then a citation from *al-Liḥyānī*, which somewhat correctly explains the expression in question: هي الطبيعة والأصل (*hiya ṭ-ṭabīʿatu wa-l-aṣl* – "it is nature and origin, i.e., the innate").

The other examples in the *Lisān*, الكرم من نحته (*noble-mindedness is innate to him*), إنه لكريم الطبيعة والنحيتة (*he is of a noble-minded nature and birth*), وقد نحت على الكرم وطبع عليه (*noble-mindedness is his by birth and nature*),[53] furnish evidence of the earlier use of the root نحت (*naḥata*) (or *naḥita*) in Arabic as a borrowing from Syro-Aramaic ܢܚܬ (*nḥeṯ*) in the meaning "to come down from, to give birth to, to be descended from."

Now, whether one were to read من تحتها *(min taḥtihā),* من نحتها *(naḥtihā),* or *(*on the basis of the customary defective spelling in the Qur'ān) *nuḥātihā*,[54] would, to be sure, change nothing in terms of the sense, in any event what does speak for the last reading is the fact that both in Syro-Aramaic and in the *Lisān* this root corresponds more closely to the meaning "delivery," which the *Lisān* also documents with further derivatives. Since the Qur'ān elsewhere uses the root ولد (*walada*) for the general sense of *to give birth* and *to procreate*, but specifically uses the root وضع (*waḍaʿa* – "to lay, to lay down;" cf. Surahs 3:36; 22:2; 35:11; 41:47; 46:15; and 65:4,6) for "to be delivered of, to give birth to," the latter appears to correspond lexically to the Syro-Aramaic ܢܚܬ[55] (*naḥḥeṯ*). Accordingly, من نحتها (*min nuḥḥātihā*), expressed otherwise in Qur'ānic Arabic, would be من وضعها (*min waḍʿihā*) in the sense of حال وضعها (*ḥāla waḍʿihā*), which in turn could be rendered in modern Arabic as حال توليدها (*ḥāla tawlīdihā*) or حال ولادتها (*ḥāla wilādatihā* – "*immediately* upon her giving birth").

The fact that the Qur'ān here uses as a *hapax legomenon* borrowed from Syro-Aramaic this verbal root نحت (*naḥḥata*) (in the sense of نزل /*nazzala*, أنزل /*anzala: to make descend, to bring down = to give birth*), instead of the otherwise customary Arabic root وضع (*waḍaʿa* – "to lay, to lay down, to give birth to"), raises the question, relevant both theologically and in terms of the history of religions, as to whether the Qur'ān does not want deliberately, by this unusual expression, to connect and emphasize in a special way the extraordinary *delivery* of Mary with the supernatural *descent* of her son. This question imposes itself all the more since the basic stem ܢܚܬ (*nḥeṯ*) "to come down" (said, for example, of Christ, who came down from heaven) and the causative stems ܢܚܬ (*naḥḥeṯ*) / ܐܚܬ (*aḥḥeṯ*) "to cause to descend, to send down" (said, for example, of God, who sent down his son) have in fact been documented in this sense in Syro-Aramaic, though not in the specific meaning of "to give birth, to be born" in the sense of a natural birth.

The search for an equivalent usage in Aramaic finds its confirmation in a synonymous expression that Gesenius[56] gives under the Aramaic root נפל *n-p-l* "to fall" in the meaning of "to be born" and explains as "actually an extra term for a birth standing in opposition to regular natural processes." This usage, attested nowhere else in Arabic, of نحت (*naḥata*) or (*naḥḥata*) < Syro-Aramaic ܢܚܬ (*nḥeṯ* or *naḥḥeṯ*) in the meaning of "to give birth, to be born" (actually "*to cause to descend [from above]*")[57] would imply, at least in the case of this segment of the Mary Surah, an earlier period in the editing of the Qur'ān than the second Meccan period estimated by Nöldeke-Schwally.[58] In it one can recognize with certainty a central element of the Christian components of the Qur'ān.

According to the Syro-Aramaic reading, the first verse segment of Surah 19:24 should therefore be understood as follows:

> Then he called to her *immediately after her giving birth*: Be not sad!

Based on this understanding, the concerns expressed by Paret in his Qur'ān commentary to this passage (324) as to whether the caller is *the new-born infant Jesus or the infant Jesus still located in the womb*, as well as the reference to the text from Pseudo-Matthew cited below, are unnecessary.

It follows from the preceding remarks that in the second part of the verse قد جعل ربك تحتك سريا (according to the previous understanding) "Your lord has made a rivulet beneath you," the repeatedly occurring تحتك (*taḥtaki*) does not mean "beneath you," but "your giving birth." Still to be explained, however, is the expression سريا (*sarīya*), misinterpreted as "rivulet," with which we would have an example of case (c) (see page 24).

Ṭabarī (XVI 69 ff.) prefaces the explanation of the word سري (*sarī*) with the stereotypical remark that the commentators are of different opinions about its meaning. The majority (over nineteen traditionary chains) favor the meaning *river, little river, a river named Sarī, designation of the ʿĪsā river* (= *Jesus river*), *stream, rivulet*. In particular, *Muǧāhid* and *aḍ-Ḍaḥḥāk* believe it is *river* or *stream* in Syriac, whereas *Saʿīd b. Ǧubayr* is of the opinion that it is a *stream, rivulet* in Nabatean. On the other hand, two traditionists object and advocate the view that Jesus himself is meant by the designation *sarī*. Probably on the basis of the conjectured Persian meaning *noble, honorable,*[59] *Ibn Zayd* asks:

> But who, after all, could be أسرى منه (*asrā minhu*) *nobler* than Jesus!" Concerning the erroneous opinions of those who see a river in this term, he makes use of his good common sense and argues: "If this is a river, then it ought to be *beside her* and not, of all places, *beneath her*![60]

But *Ṭabarī* does not follow him. Like an arbitrator, on democratic principles he agrees with the majority that sees in it a stream, from which—in his opinion—God has, according to Surah 19:26, expressly ordered Mary to drink: فكلي واشربي "*So eat and drink.*"

Among our selected Western translators of the Qur'ān, only Paret (by placing *sarī* in parentheses) suggests that the meaning of this expression is unclear. Blachère and Bell seem for the most part to approve of the explanation *Ṭabarī* gives. Blachère only observes concerning من تحتها (*min taḥtihā*) that in accordance with Qur'ānic usage this expression means "at her feet," and not, as so often translated, "from beneath her."[61] Bell, on the other hand, refers to *Ṭabarī* (XVI 67 f.) and the controversial issue among the Arab commentators as to whether it was the Angel Gabriel or the Infant Jesus that called to Mary "from beneath her," concerning which he rightly supposes: "probably 'the child.'" [62] As to the word *sarī*, in his commentary (I 504 f., v. 24) he considers "stream" to be the most likely meaning, but points to the opinion held by several commentators that it could also mean "chief, head" (referring to Jesus) in accordance with the (probably Persian) meaning "to be manly, noble," which is listed in the *Lisān* (XIV 377b) under سرا (*srw*) and with a reference to سيبويه / *Sībawayh* and اللحياني / *al-Liḥyānī.*

In examining the corresponding passage more closely, Paret refers in his Qur'ān commentary (323, on Surah 19:23-26) to W. Rudolph,[63] who says about the *attendant circumstances* of the birth of Jesus described therein:

> The most likely explanation is that Muhammed is here influenced by a scene the so-called Pseudo-Matthew reports of the flight to Egypt in chapter 20 and transfers this to the birth:
> "*tunc infantulus Jesus laeto vultu in sinu matris suae residens ait ad palmam: flectere, arbor, et de fructibus tuis refice matrem meam ... aperi autem ex radicibus tuis venam, quae absconsa est in terra, et fluant ex ea aquae ad satietatem nostram.*" [Translation of the Latin text]:
> "Thereupon spoke the Infant Jesus, of joyful countenance sitting in his mother's lap, to the palm tree: Bend over, tree, and refresh my mother from your fruits. . . further open out of your roots a vein that lies hidden in the earth, and let waters stream out upon us to quench our thirst."

Blachère, too, sees a parallel to our Qur'ānic verse and an explanation for *the stream at Mary's feet* in this description from Pseudo-Matthew.[64] Bell argues along similar lines in his commentary (*loc. cit.*). By citing the quoted passage from Pseudo-Matthew the Western Qur'ān scholars had their proof that in the case of the expression سري (*sarī*) it must indeed be a question of a *watercourse, a stream*, just as the Arab exegetes had also finally assumed after all.

The commentators in the East and the West will be shown, however, that in the interpretation of this Qur'ān passage they have succumbed in the first case to a linguistic error and in the second to fallacious reasoning.

Careful attention to the Qur'ānic context is the fundamental prerequisite for a linguistically coherent understanding. That the Qur'ān transferred the scene depicted by Pseudo-Matthew of the flight to Egypt to the birth of Christ is in no way proven by the passage cited above. The sole parallel is the palm that is spoken of in both passages. The other circumstances, however, are completely different.

Namely, when according to Pseudo-Matthew the infant Jesus directs the palm to cause water to flow forth, the logical reason may lie in the fact that for mother and son there was otherwise no water in the surrounding desert. Hence the command that water bubble forth to slake their thirst.

Not so in the Qur'ān. Namely, when Mary according to Surah 19:23 calls out in despair, يليتني مت قبل هذا وكنت نسيا منسيا "If only I had died beforehand (i.e., before the birth) and been totally forgotten!" it is clearly not because she was *dying of thirst*! What depressed her so much was much more the outrageous insinuations of her family that she was *illegitimately* pregnant, something which is clearly implied by the scolding she receives in Verse 28: يأخت هرون ما كان ابوك امرأ سوء وما كانت أمك بغيا "Sister of Aaron, your father was after all no miscreant and your mother no strumpet!" (Paret: "Sister of Aaron! Your father was after all not a bad guy [note: man] and your mother not a prostitute!"). Most likely for the same reason it is also said, after she became pregnant, in Verse 22, فانتبذت به مكانا قصيا "whereupon she <u>*was cast out*</u> with him to a remote place" (Paret: "And she <u>withdrew</u> with him to a distant place").

What is crucial here is the Arabic verb فانتبذت (*fa-ntabaḏat*), which our Qur'ān translators have incorrectly rendered with "she withdrew" (Bell), "sie zog sich zurück" (Paret), and "elle se retira" (Blachère). Despite the original meaning of Arabic نبذ (*nabaḏa*), namely, "to send back, to reject, to cast out," this expression is actually explained in *Ṭabarī* with فاعتزلت (*fa-'tazalat*) and وتنحت (*wa-tanaḥḥat* – "she withdrew").[65] The reflexive eighth Arabic verbal stem may have also led the Qur'ān translators to make this grammatically equivalent, but nonetheless nonsensical assumption. When one considers, namely, that the Qur'ān, following Syro-Aramaic usage, also uses reflexive stems with a passive meaning,[66] the result is the better fitting sense for this verse, "*she was cast out*," which indeed also represents a continuation of the introductory statement of Verse 16:

واذكر في الكتب مريم اذ انتبذت من اهلها مكانا شرقيا

> Make mention further in the scripture of Mary when she was cast out by her family to an empty (= a *waste*)[67] place." (Paret: "Und gedenke in der Schrift der Maria (Maryam)! (Damals) als sie sich vor ihren Angehörigen an einen östlichen Ort zurückzog! ["And make mention in the scripture of Mary (Maryam)! (that time) when she withdrew from her family to a place in the East"]).

The passive usage is additionally confirmed here by the preposition من (*min*) (*by*), which again corresponds to Syro-Aramaic practice,[68] but is totally impossible according to Arabic grammar. There is namely no reason for the Qur'ān to submit, as classical Arabic grammar would have it, to the prohibition imposed by later Arabic (or Persian) grammarians against naming the active subject in a passive sentence by means of the preposition من *min* (*by*).[69] Therefore, seen in this light, the classical Arabic grammar proves rather to be a hindrance in determining the proper understanding of particular passages in the Qur'ān, while attention to Syro-Aramaic grammar assists in opening up insights into heretofore unimagined aspects of the Qur'ānic language. This basic Syro-Aramaic structure of the Qur'ānic language must be gone into in more detail.

Thus Verse 22—correctly understood—indicates that Mary is cast out by her family because she is suspected of illegitimate conception, especially considering that the Qur'ān does not place any fiancé or *sham husband* at her side to protect her from malicious tongues. As a result it is understandable that Mary in Verse 23, immediately before giving birth, longs desperately for her own death. The initial words of consolation from her newborn child would naturally need to be directed first of all to removing the reason for her desperation. But this could surely not occur by attempting to console her with the simple reference to a *stream* allegedly located beneath her. The idea assumed by *Ṭabarī* that God according to Verse 26 had commanded Mary to drink from it (فكلي واشربي / *so eat and drink*), therefore misses the mark. For it is not, say, the lack of food and drink that keeps Mary from eating and drinking, but much more her depressive mental state. That is why the consoling words of her child had to have such a content, so that she would no longer have any reason to be depressed and would therefore regain her desire to eat and drink.

The Western Qur'ān scholars' reference to the above-mentioned passage from Pseudo-Matthew is also wrong because the expression سريا falsely read *sarīyā*—in today's Qur'ān, and was traditionally interpreted as a *watercourse*.

But this unphilological and conjectural reading and interpretation, unfortunately, was taken to be definitive, and thereby sealed off further research.

Namely, in the case of this spelling سريا it is not a question of an Arabic, but of a Syro-Aramaic root. The problem is also already solved if it is presented in its original Syro-Aramaic form as ܫܪܝܐ (*šaryā*). For what one expects in the Qur'ānic context is a countering expression to the reproach of her illegitimate pregnancy that would suffice to free her of this stigma. Now if one understands *unmarried* in the sense of *unlawful, illegitimate*, then its countering expression *married* would accordingly be *lawful, legitimate.* And so it is in modern Arabic usage that an *illegitimate son* (especially as a swearword) is إبن حرام (*ibn ḥarām*), which is countered by its opposite إبن حلال (*ibn ḥalāl* – "a legitimate, legally born = an upright, honest person").

In this context the Syro-Aramaic expression ܫܪܝܐ (*šaryā*) has exactly this meaning, however, here it is not to be understood as a substantive (*stream, rivulet*), but as a verbal adjective in the sense of "legitimate."[70]

The twenty-fourth verse of the Mary Surah, which has previously been misunderstood as follows by all of the Qur'ān commentators we know of,

> Then he (probably "the child") called to her from beneath her: "Grieve not; thy Lord hath placed beneath thee a streamlet." (Bell)

is now, after this elucidation of its original meaning, to be understood as summarized in the following way:

> Then he called to her *immediately after her delivery*: "Do not be sad, your Lord has made your *delivery legitimate*."

Only after the infant Jesus has consoled this hitherto despairing mother with the *acknowledgment of his legitimacy* does he direct to her the encouraging words (from Verse 26) that she is therefore (and not because she is dying of thirst) "to eat and drink and be happy."[71] Just as logically does Mary (according to Verse 27) then take heart and return with her newborn child to her family. Confronted with the family's initial indignation (Verse 28), she follows the instructions of her newborn and allows her child to respond (Verses 30–33) and in so doing to reveal his miraculous birth.

Thus, in contrast to the hitherto distortedly rendered Arabic reading of this passage, the Qur'ānic presentation of the birth of Christ now for the first time acquires its original meaning through the bringing in of Syro-Aramaic.

11. Christmas in the Qur'ān—Surah 97: al-Qadr – "the Destiny"

11.1 Problems of the Traditional Understanding

If then the birth of Christ is mentioned it is only logical to pose the question as to other possible passages in the Qur'ān which could have been originally connected to a liturgy of Christmas. The author believes he has recognized just such a connection in the text, considered engimatic up to now, of Surah 97, entitled al-Qadr / Destiny. Here is how Régis Blachère translates this Surah agreeing with Arab commentators :

> Surah 97. The Destiny (Al-Qadar).
> 1. We made it come down during the Night of Destiny
> 2. Who will teach you what the Night of Destiny is ?
> 3. The night of Destiny is worth more than a thousand months .
> 4. The Angels and the Spirit descend with your Lord's permission, with all orders
> 5. Peace . It is until the break of dawn.

Bell:

> Surat al-Qadr – "Chapter of Power" [different to Blachère!]
> 1. Lo, We have sent it down on the Night of Power.
> 2. What has let thee know what is the Night of Power?
> 3. The Night of Power is better than a thousand months;
> 4. In it the angels and the spirit let themselves down, by the permission of their Lord, with regard to every affair.
> 5. It is peace until the rising of the dawn.

Paret's commentary und concordance:

> To the whole Surah see K. Wagtendonk: Fasting in the Qur'ān. Leiden 1968, p. 82–122. Wagtendonk examines the question whether or not and how close the fasting of the Ramadan and the revelation of the Qur'ān are related to each other, and what the Laylat al-Qadr is. He comes to the following conclusion *(Paret cites him as follows:)* "The date on which Surah 97 was revealed can now be determined. Mohammed must have indicated the night of the 27th Radjab as the night of his (first) revelation, after he abolished the 'Ashura' and before the battle of Badr took place (p.113)."
> To v. 1 "inna ansalnahu fi laylati l-qadri": see 44:2f; 2:185
> To v.2 "wa-ma adraka…": see 82: 14–18; 77:13f.; 101:1–3; 69:1–3; 74:26f.; 104:4f.; 101:9f.; 83:7f. and 18f.; 86:1f.; 90:11f.; 97:1f.; (33:63; 42:17; 80:3).
> To v.4: see 16:2; 40:15; 42:52; 17:85; 97:4; 26:192–194; 16:102;
> "amr": see 10:3; 13:2; 32:5; 10:31; (65:12; 7:54; 41:12); "amr" in these passages seems to mean a being of cosmological kind, in (as Paret says in his commentary to 2:109 to where he refers) the sense of the Greek 'logos' or the Syro-Aramaic *memra* 'min kulli amrin': various interpretations are possible; e.g., Wagtendonk (Fasting in the Qur'ān, p. 83f., annotation 5 and p. 86, anno-

tation 3) gives several interpretations and translates it (as follows, cited by Paret): "by virtue of every decree."

But Paret prefers his own interpretation and. 44:4 has a similar wording: *kullu amrin ḥakīmin* but probably another meaning. He proceeds:

To v. 5: see H. Ringgren: *Islam, aslama and muslim.* Uppsala 1949, p. 10

In his introduction to the Surah, Bell writes:

The origin of the idea of the Night of Power is unexplained. The only other passage in the Quran which has any bearing on it is 44:2a, 3. In some ways what is here said of it suggests that some account of the Eve of the Nativity may have given rise to it.

Bell's footnote to "it" in verse 1:

"It" must refer to something in the original context now lost, usually assumed to be the Qur'an.

Bell's footnote to "Night of Power" in verse 1:

The common translation of the prase has been retained; 'Night of Decree' would perhaps correspond better to the sense.

Bell's footnote to the whole verse 4:

The exact construction and sense of this phrase are uncertain. It is usually taken with the verb "let themselves down," not with "permission."

Paret's German version:

Die Bestimmung [This word is a very clever choice: In German, it can mean "destiny" as well as "power" as well as "decree"!]

1. Wir haben ihn in der Nacht der Bestimmung herabgesandt.
2. Aber wie kannst du wissen, was die Nacht der Bestimmung ist?
3. Die Nacht der Bestimmung ist besser als tausend Monate.
4. Die Engel und der Geist kommen in ihr mit der Erlaubnis ihres Herrn herab, lauter Logos(wesen) (*min kulli amrin*).

[Paret interprets the last part of the phrase in a totally different way: He thinks that *min kulli amrin* refers to "die Engel und der Geist" = "the angels and the spirit" and means "beings of logos"]

5. Sie ist (voller) Heil (und Segen), bis die Morgenröte sichtbar wird. [Heil = the "salut" of Blachère].

Paret's footnote to „ihn:"

[=it, see Bell's footnote] in verse 1: "D. h. den Qur'ān. [i.e., the Qur'ān]"

Paret's footnote to "sichtbar wird" ["becomes visible"] in verse 5:

[not important]: „W. (=literally): aufgeht. [“rises”]

Henning’s prestigious German translation from the 19th century:

Die Macht [=power, like Bell]

1. Siehe, wir haben ihn in der Nacht El-Qadr geoffenbart.
   [El-Qadr: Another clever solution: He translates the Arabic term ‘al-qadr’ in the title, but in the text itself he leaves it in Arabic, as a proper name!]
   [author’s note: *geoffenbart* means “revealed,” so the term is more specific than Paret’s “*herabgesandt*” which only means “sent down.”]
2. Und was lehrt dich wissen, was die Nacht El-Qadr ist?
3. Die Nacht El-Qadr ist besser als tausend Monate.
4. Hinab steigen die Engel und der Geist in ihr mit ihres Herrn Erlaubnis zu jeglichem Geheiß. [this is again like Bell’s and Blachères interpretation].
5. Frieden [=peace, like Bell] ist sie bis zum Aufgang der Morgenröte.

Rudolph’s footnote to „ihn“ [=it] in verse 1:

Der Qur’ān (so die Muslime) oder der Engel bzw. Geist der Offenbarung.“ [=“It“ refers either to the Quran, like the Muslims think, or to the angel or spirit of revelation]

Rudolph’s footnote to “Nacht El-Qadr” in verse 1:

D. h. die “Nacht der (göttlichen) Bestimmung” [this is exactly the word Paret choose] oder “Zumessung” [=allotment, apportion] (lailat al-qadr). In ihr soll Gabriel den Qur’ān aus dem siebenten Himmel zu Mohammed hernieder gebracht haben. Vgl. 2:181! Die Herkunft und ursprüngliche Bedeutung des Ausdruckes ist noch ungeklärt (Name der altarabischen Neujahrsnacht?). Vermutlich hat ihn Mohammed rückblickend auf sein Berufungserlebnis, das in einer Nacht stattfand. . ., geprägt. [=It is said that in this night the angel Gabriel brought the Qur’ān from the seventh heaven down to Muḥammad, see Surah 2, verse 181. The origin and exact meaning of the word are not yet clear, might be the name of the New Year’s night of the ancient Arabs, for example. Muhammad seems to have chosen it, looking back, for the night when he received his first revelation.]

Rudolph’s footnote to “zu jeglichem Geheiß” [to whatever behest] in verse 4:

Unsicher. Eher: “wegen jeder Ordnung (amr),” oder “aus jedem Logos.“ Vgl. 10,3; 16,2; 32,4; 42,52. [Rudolph doesn’t agree with Henning and proposes “because of every order”—which doesn’t make sense, does it? —or “from/of every logos” which is more like Paret’s interpretation.]

Islamic tradition sees in this brief Surah, entitled the Night of Destiny, an allusion to the revelation of the Qur'ān on this very night. It is for this reason that towards the end of Ramadan, the month of fasting, that vigils take place. However with regard to the history of religions this fact is all the more remarkable since Islam does not have a nocturnal liturgy (apart from the *tarāwīḥ*, prayers offered during the nights of Ramadan). There is thus every reason to think that these vigils corresponded originally to a Christian liturgical practice connected to the birth of Jesus Christ, and which was later adopted by Islam, but re-interpreted by Islamic theology to mean the descent of the Qur'ān. Islamic tradition meanwhile finds it difficult to explain to itself this new interpretation. It is enough to consult the great commentary on the Qur'ān of al-Ṭabarī (828–923) to confirm the confusion that Arab commentators manifest in their attempts to justify such an interpretation. The contradictory contents of the Islamic tradition, recorded by Ṭabarī, could be summed in the following way:

a) The Qur'ān descended in one go during the Night of Qadr, in the month of Ramadan, into the lower sky, at the site of the stars;
b) According to his decision, God made parts of it come down successively on earth until the Qur'ān was complete;
c) Between the beginning and the end of the revelation there was an interval of twenty years ;
d) Only the beginning of the Qur'ān came down during this night.

This perplexity of the Arab commentators could nevertheless find a simple solution in the deciphering of this Surah with the aid of Syriac. Three terms well-understood upto the present undoubtedly incited Richard Bell, in his introduction to this Surah, to suspect there an allusion to the liturgy of Christmas Eve, namely : i) *night* ii*) angels* iii) *peace*. But the key Arabic word *al-qadar*, which serves as an introduction to this Surah has remained unexplained upto now. The only laconic explanation that Ṭabarī reports of the Arab commentators is that God decided this night the events that were [destined] to take place during the year. However, the third comparison to which in reality this destiny relates can only be discovered by translating this word into Syriac, which gives us the Syriac word *ḥelqa* that the Thesaurus (I,1294) explains first of all by "fatum, sors" —destiny, and fate, *qadar* which uses here the *qdr* and *qda* in citing the corresponding Arabic words in the Qur'ān. But it then combines the word with its synonym "*ḥelqa w-bēṯ yalda* – 'fate and horoscope.'" The latter is, in Syriac, a composite word (*bēṯ yalda*) and has three meanings, designating i) *the birth* (meaning the moment of birth), ii) *the star under which one is born* and which determines the fate of the newly born, iii) *The Nativity* or *Christmas*. Thus defined, the term *al-qadar*, "destiny" is related to the star of birth, that the Qur'ānic *al qadr* implies, and in the context of this Surah, to the Star of Christmas. As a result, a connection is found to be established with Matthew 2:2:

> Saying, Where is he that is born King of the Jews? For we have seen his star in the East and are come to worship him.

These words are attributed to the Wise Men of whom it is said that they were astrologers come from the East, that is to say Babylon, considered the cradle of astrology, and whose cultural impact remains alive and well in our daily horoscope. It is with this very tradition that the Qur'ān joins hands with this term *al-qadar*, destiny, which, in this case, it substitutes in place of star of birth, that of the Nativity. This enigmatic word thus elucidated henceforth leads us to philologically analyze Surah 97, in its Arabo-Syriac reading, in this way:

11.2 Towards a New Interpretation of the Surah

The Destiny (of the Star of the Nativity)

Verse 1:

"We made it come down in the night of destiny"; that is to say the star of birth or horoscope which determines the destiny of the new-born—here to be taken in the sense of the Star of Nativity or Christmas. The Arabic verb anzala, "to send dow" corresponds perfectly with the Syriac noun *nuḥḥāṯ*, cited twice in verse 24 of Surah 19 (Mary), and means literally "send down," speaking of the childbirth of Mary, a term exclusively used in this passage and by which the Qur'ān wishes to point to the supernatural character of the birth of Jesus, whom, besides, they make speak right from the moment of his birth (op. cit. p.102–112).

Verse 2

In posing the question which follows verse 2,

> What do you know of what the night of destiny is?,

the Qur'ān wants to underline the special significance of this night considered as the night or the eve of Christmas. In fact, the Syriac word ܠܠܝܐ *lelyā*, night, is at the same time a liturgical term, a shortened form of ܨܠܘܬܐ ܕܠܠܝܐ *ṣlōṯā ḏ-lelyā* ("office of the night"), corresponding to the nocturns of the Catholic office. By night the Qur'ān thus does not mean here simply the natural phenomenon but more precisely this Syriac liturgical term.

The Qur'ānic word شهر *šahr*—normally understood as "month" —is in fact a transliteration of the Syriac ܫܗܪܐ *šahrā* which signifies first, "evening" but which is, like *lēlyā*, also a liturgical term in Syriac corresponding to "vigils" of the office, and which should be read in Arabic as *sahar* (*s* in Arabic usually corresponds to *š* in Syriac), i.e., without the three diacritical dots on the first letter.

These two terms thus being confirmed as synonyms of the Syriac liturgy, the Qur'ānic comparison becomes more logical. On the other hand, it is astonishing that no commentator, in the East or the West, has raised the slightest doubt as to the incoherence of the comparison between "night" and "month."

Verse 3

This leads us then to the Arabo-Syriac reading of verse 3:

> The night [taken here in the sense of nocturnal office] of Destiny [linked to the star of birth, i.e., of the Nativity] is more beneficial than a thousand vigils.

Verse 4

In place of the actual Qur'ānic reading ("tanazzalu l-malā'ikatu wa-r-rūḥu fīhā") of the verb *tanazallu* (intransitive) one must read *tunazzilu* (transitive) which gives us the following reading:

> The Angels, accompanied by the Spirit, send down

literally,

> The Angels, the Spirit (being) in them, among them

The Arabic particle does not here have the function of the conjunction "and" expressing the binding together, but introduces a so-called *ḥāl*-sentence, i.e., a sentence describing an accompanying circumstance. When translating such a sentence into English, the conjunctions "while," "whereas," "although" should be used, but rarely ever "and," the *wa* indicating simultaneity (cf. Surah 16:2, where the particle *wa* was replaced by *bi,* which has the same meaning as "accompanied with"). To understand, "the Angels and [particle] the Spirit" would be theologically untenable, "with the permission of their Lord " excluding the fact that the Lord is also that of the Spirit. To come back then to the verse:

> the Angels (accompanied by) the Spirit, send down with the permission (*amr*) of their Lord, all sorts of hymns.

The Arabic noun borrowed from the Syriac, could not have the meaning of the Arabic of order such as rendered by Régis Blachère agreeing with the Arab commentators. Moreover it is for this reason the latter have understood that God decided (ordered), this night, what was going to happen during the year. *Amr* is rather to be taken here in the sense of the Syriac noun ܡܐܡܪܐ *memrā* which means, among other things, speech in verse, "hymn." Ephrem the Syrian (306-373 C.E.) is known moreover for his *Memre* verses, some of which are still used in the Syriac liturgical office. Besides the following verse is going to show us that it really does concern the hymn chanted by the Angels.

Verse 5

With the word *"salām* – سلام – peace," this verse gives us the leitmotiv of these hymns and sends us back to the hymn of the Angels cited by Luke 2:14:

> Glory to God in the highest and on earth peace, good will toward men.

This chant of the Angels has always constituted the principal theme of the Syriac vigils of the Nativity which lasts into Christmas night, with all sorts of hymns, more than all the other vigils. According to the Qur'ān, the vigils went on *ḥattā maṭla' al-faǧr*–"until daybreak," confirming thus, once more, the tradition of the Syrian Church, according to which the Mass of the Nativity is celebrated not at midnight but at dawn. Whence the theme of these vigils of Christmas that the Qur'ān specifies for us:

> Peace (on earth) until daybreak.

Conclusions about the Surah

The fact that this Surah goes back very probably to a Syro-Christian or Arabo-Christian tradition is attested by the encyclopedic lexicon, *Lisān al-'Arab* (Ibn Manẓūr [1233–1312 C.E.] *The Language of the Arabs*, completed 1290 C.E., encompassing Arabic lexicography from the 9th century onwards). Making a reference to the celebrated Arab philologist al-Aṣma'ī (c.740–828) originally from Baṣra (Southern Iraq), the *Lisān al-'Arab* makes under the word *Tamām* (indicating the longest night of the winter) the following observation:

> The night of *at-Timām* is, in winter, the longest one. This night lasts so long that all the stars appear during it. It is also the night of the birth of Jesus—on our Prophet and on him blessing and well-being, and the Christians honour it and hold vigils during it.

This astonishing testimony of an Arab is of the utmost importance for the historical understanding of the Surah in question. It should have in fact earned its place in the Qur'ānic Commentary of al-Ṭabarī, who however seems never to have heard of it. It also explains to a large extent the actual Islamic Tradition according to which during the night of *al-Qadar* some vigils are held. But the blurred historical memory, as to the origins of this tradition, has resulted in the fact the Muslims of today are no longer aware that the night that they celebrate and honour with so much fervour is in reality the night of Christmas.

Furthermore, that that, in all probability, was really the case before the coming of Islam, is signaled to us more precisely by another *ḥadīt* of Aisha, the youngest wife of the Prophet, recorded in the *Lisān al-ʿArab* under the same word *at Tamām* in these terms :

> The Messenger of God—may the blessings of God and peace be upon him—had the habit of spending the night of at-Timām in vigil. He recited at that time the Surahs *The Cow, the Family ʿImran* and *the Women.* While doing this, he did not fail to implore God at each verse.

Regarding this *ḥadīt*, it is appropriate to note first of all the following:

The order of the Surahs cited is a later addition, for

a) according to Islamic tradition, the Qurʾān was not yet established in writing during the lifetime of the Prophet;
b) the actual order of the Surahs, according to the same tradition, goes back to the third caliph ʿUṯmān (644–656) or earlier;
c) the names of the Surahs as well as the division of the text into verses were introduced even later .

The only authentic kernel which remains of this *ḥadīt* would be then that the Prophet kept vigil the night of *at-Timām.* The latter being, according to the testimony of al-Aṣmaʿī, *laylat al-qadar* ليلة القدر identical to the night of the Nativity, which the Qurʾān qualifies as the night of Destiny, it is legitimate to deduce that the Prophet, followed before Islam the tradition, well-established among the Syrians or Arab Christians, of vigils of Christmas. Thus elucidated, *Surah al-Qadr* constitutes a precious document for the history of religions, in so far as it brings to light a pre-Islamic Christian liturgy of Christmas.

The already cited *ḥadīt* of ʿĀʾiša finds confirmation in another detail noted by Ibn Hišām in the Sīra, the biography of the Prophet, where it is reported that the Prophet before his mission used to spend one month a year in the cave of Ḥīra, near Mecca where he devoted himself to *taḥannuṯ* – تحنّث , an enigmatic word which he explains as being a synonym of *taḥannuf,* which designates the religious practice of a *ḥanīf,* someone who professes the pure faith, whereas the Qurʾān, identifying Abraham as a *ḥanīf,* means by this word, borrowed from the Syriac, the "pagan." God had in effect recognized Abraham's faith while he was still a *pagan (ḥanīf,* Syriac: *ḥanpā)* which has nothing in common with *taḥannuṯ* but neither with "idolator." On the other hand, the preceding word is the Arabic form of a Syriac liturgical term ܬܚܢܢܬܐ *taḥnantā* which means "supplication." In so far as Ibn Hišām vouches for the fact this religious service was practised by the Qurayš at Mecca before Islam, we have with this detail a further confirmation that the Prophet before his mission, had truly lived in an Arabo-Christian or Syro-

Christian tradition. This confirmation renders so much the more plausible the Syro-Christian understanding of *Surah al-Qadr*.

It is no doubt not only ignorance of the language of the Qur'ān but also and above all the political evolution of the Arab Empire which led to the estrangement of Islam from the origins of its founding text. The mounting political tensions between the Muslims and the Christians were doubled in the East, right from the beginning of the 8th century, taking the form of a religious polemic of an ideological character. It is under such circumstances that we have to imagine the new interpretation of this Surah and of its theological implications in the sense of Islamic theology. It is not *in Christ* that the Word of God is incarnated, but *in the Qur'ān*. In other words, to the Christian theological concept of the *Incarnation of Logos (al-Kalima) in Christ*, Islamic theology opposes the word of God incarnated in the Qur'ān. As a consequence, it is not the Infant Jesus who is born this night, but the Qur'ān which descends the same night.

The philological analysis of Surah 97 leads us to understand it henceforth, in its Arabo-Syriac reading, as:

Surah 97: The Destiny (of the Star of Nativity)

1. We sent him down (Infant Jesus) during the Night of Destiny (of the Star of Nativity).
2. What do you know what the Night of Destiny is?
3. The Night (Nocturnal Office) of Destiny (of the Star of Nativity) is more beneficial than a thousand vigils?
4. The Angels (accompanied by) the Spirit, send down with the permission of their Lord, all sorts of hymns.
5. Peace there is until the break of day.

Surah 97 could have served as an introduction to a liturgy of the Nativity of the Christian Arabs before Islam. Its linguistic understanding in its historical setting reveals its link to a Syro-Christian liturgical tradition. This account is a contribution to the history of religions in so far as it shows the initial closeness of Christianity and Islam.

12. The Difference Between the Methods of Lüling and Luxenberg

The author has been criticised many times for not having referred to the work of Günter Lüling, *Über den Ur-Quran* 34. The author however had clearly stated in his preface that he had no intention of taking into account all that had been written upto the present on this subject, these works hardly contributing anything to the new method purely philological that he intended to propose.

As for Günter Lüling, the precise difference between his method and that of the author seems to have escaped the scrupulous scrutiny of the critics. Lüling expresses first of all the thesis that a part of the Qur'ān is made up of Pre-Islamic Christian hymns, in this he was certainly not wrong. However, it is appropriate to note that he was not the first to discover this point. It is enough to glance at the introduction of the Swedish theologian and Islamologue Tor Andrae to realise that more than a generation of Orientalists had already worked on the question, beginning with the Austrian Alois Sprenger. While Lüling cites a number of others in his "Literaturverzeichnis," he omits nonetheless to cite the work though remarkable of Wilhelm Rudolph. The merit of Lüling has been nonetheless to relaunch the debate on this crucial question fallen into oblivion, but above all to state clearly that the Qur'ān contained Pre-Islamic Christian hymns. There we have the first constituent of his thesis and his point of departure.

In the second, Lüling intends to elucidate the Qur'ānic passages said to be obscure by modifying the diacritical points of Arabic writing, which in the early Qur'ānic manuscripts were lacking but which are of course essential in distinguishing the 22 phonemes of the actual Arabic alphabet comprising 28 signs. It is precisely on this point that the criticism has some weight as to the omission by the author of any reference to the person the critics consider to have been his predecessor. And it is also precisely there the critics misunderstand the essential difference between the two methods seemingly similar. However this method is not in itself entirely new. Ignaz Goldziher had already drawn attention to the haphazard way the diacritical points were introduced rather late into the Qur'ānic text. In this work, Goldziher describes the early efforts of Islamic exegesis in search of a Qur'ānic reading whose defective writing was far from creating a consensus. This debate generated moreover all a literature of variants (see R.B. ...) which incited Western orientalists to pursue research in this field. In this way the first attempt aiming to modify the diacritical points with a view to a more plausible reading of the Qur'ān was undertaken by Jacob Barth in *Studien zur Kritik und Exegese des Qorans*. In this essay, Barth, starting with Arabic, succeeded in displacing the points correctly in just four cases. But this first timid attempt did not have the expected impact since the number of words thus modified was limited.

Günter Lüling, more half a century later, thus was not the first to apply this technique, which, on its own, does not yet constitute a method. For the essence of the method is the linguistic base on which is founded this technique, and it would be too easy to reduce it to a simple deplacement of diacritical points. Anyone who has read the basics of the method of the author which Rémi Brague has so magisterially summarized in his review, could have judged the complexity. This method is not limited to an etymological explanation of simple words, it extends also to linguistic phenomena such as morphology, syntax and phraseology. It demands thus a very careful reading of the Qur'ān in a double Arabo-Syriac perspective with all the hazards such a reading entails. That is what critics do not seem to have clearly distinguished between the two methods.

The point of departure of Lüling is a Christian Arabic literary language, Pre-Islamic and Pre-Classical, a sort of *koiné*, but essentially Arabic. For the author, on the other hand, it is a matter of a mixed Arabo-Syriac language, such as must have prevailed at the time of the editing of the Qur'ān. There you have all the difference between the two methods. Surah 96 that Lüling has interpreted according to his method well illustrates moreover the gulf that separates it from the Syro-Syriac reading of the author. It is true that Lüling refers quite rightly to Gustav Weil and Hartwig Hirschfeld in rendering *iqra'* (verses 1,3) by "invoke," instead of the traditional reading "read," and that he interprets *'alaq* (verse 2) correctly as a metaphor for "clay," but apart from these two words, all the rest is far from being convincing, including and above all the syntax. And even where Lüling occasionally suspects a Syriac word, such as for *zabaniya* (verse 18) which he reads *rabbaniya* (that he takes for *Archangels*, instead of *zab̲nāyā*, an adjective signifying temporary, passing, in connection with the idol, to the mortal god of the adversary), he misses the point.

Another detail is worth noting: Lüling first presents his thesis and claims to prove it linguistically. In reality, he bases himself on essentially theological arguments that he projects into the text and that he tries to demonstrate in so doing, if necessary, without respecting the principles that should be applied when reading a *lectio difficilior*. His Arabic understanding of certain passages, that one can only understand, in my view, by means of Arabo-Syriac, pushes him to modify, even eliminate not only words but also entire verses that he judges to be misplaced or superfluous for not having revealed the true meaning. It is undoubtedly for this reason that he has not managed to be convincing. Although, he is certainly correct regarding the Christian origins of the Qur'ān, especially the strophic hymns.

The author proceeds in an inverse sense: he first submits the text to a rigorous philological analysis, with references always in support, and then reaches a double conclusion:

a) that the founding texts of the Qur'ān were originally in part Syro-Christian liturgical texts;
b) that the language of the Qur'ān is a mixed Arabo-Syriac.

The latter observation is the key which gives us access to an adequate understanding of the language of the Qur'ān. The author was thus justified in setting aside everything that was written, from a linguistic point of view, upto now on the subject of the language of the Qur'ān, since the previous scholars were not aware of the mixed Arabo-Aramaic character of its language.

In consequence, it is not at all for lack of intellectual probity that he, in his first study, passed over in silence that of Günter Lüling. He remains indebted nonetheless to criticism for having incited him to clearly discern the difference and to articulate it with precision.

Notes:

1 Bell's introductory remarks: "SURAH CVIII: This looks like a fragment, but it is difficult to find a suitable context for it. The rhyme might indicate a position in LXXIV—after v. 39 (?). That, however, necessitates a fairly early date, and the reference to sacrifice is difficult to explain, unless we are prepared to assume that Muhammad continued to take part in heathen rites in Mecca. Otherwise it seems necessary to assume that the Surah is Medinan. It is, in any case, an encouragement to the prophet under insult."

2 Bell's note 1: "Al-kauthar, from the root meaning 'many,' is interpreted as meaning much wealth, or by others as referring to the number of his followers; others again take the word as the proper name of a river or pool in Paradise."

3 Bell's note 2: "'Mutilated,' 'having the tail cut off,' probably in the sense of having no son. The word has presumably been applied to Muhammad by an enemy."

4 Blachère's note 1: "al-Kawṯar 'l'Abondance.' Ce thème, d'un emploi rare, est une épithète substantivée. Ce sens est ressenti par tous les commt., mais la tradition (cf. Buhl) prétend que ce terme désigne un des fleuves du Paradis." [This stem, of rare usage, is an attributive adjective that has been nominalised. This sense is felt by all the commentators, but the [Islamic] tradition claims that this term designates one of the rivers of Paradise.]

5 Although Bell here translates the adverb كثيرا (kaṯīrā) according to modern Arabic usage as "often," the Syro-Aramaic semantics and the context suggest the meaning "constantly." Another example of the Syro-Aramaic meaning can be found in Surah 56:32,33, wherein the believers are promised وفكهة كثيرة لا مقطوعة ولا ممنوعة (*wa-fākiha kaṯīra, lā maqṭū'a wa-lā mamnū'a*) "And fruit profuse, Not cut off and not forbidden" (Bell). The Arabic verb منع / *mana'a* (to forbid) is, however, only one possible equivalent of the Syro-Aramaic verb ܟܠܐ / *klā* (see Mannā 337b), the more common meaning being "to cease, to come to an end " (Mannā: 5. توقف / *tawaqqafa*, 6. انتهى / *intahā*). Moreover, قطع / *qata'a* here does not mean (as in modern Arabic) "to cut off," but according to the wider Syro-Aramaic semantics "to cease, to come to an end, to be used up." A preferable translation of the whole verse would therefore be: "and constant(ly available) fruit, never ending nor running out." The latter meaning is furthermore attested in Sura 38:54: ان هذا لرزقنا ما له من نفاد (*inna hāḏā la-rizqunā mā lahu min nafād*) "this is our provision, of it is no failing " (Bell).

6 Cf. *Thes.* I 1859 f., ܟܘܬܪܐ (*kuttārā*) (1) mora, expectatio, στηριγμός, duratio, fixitas. Further, in Mannā 360b, ܟܘܬܪܐ (*kuttārā*), ܟܬܪ (*kattar*) (2):. دام . استمر. ثبت . بقي / *dāma, istamarra, ṯabata, baqiya* (to last, to continue, to persist, to remain).

7 The و / waw in the irregular form *kawṯar* could also be justified as an element serving to dissolve the following gemination. However, for such a reading there is no evidence. A parallel case of Syro-Aramaic nominal forms of the second stem

can be found in Surah 78:28: وكذبوا بايتنا كذابا (*wa-kaḏḏabū bi-ʾāyātinā kiḏḏābā*) (Bell: And they counted Our signs false utterly), and 78:35: لا يسمعون فيها لغوا ولا كذابا (*lā yasmaʿūna fīhā laġwan wa-lā kiḏḏābā*) (Bell: In which they will hear neither babble nor accusation of falsehood). The form *kiḏḏābā* is an erroneous reading and reflects Syro-Aramaic ܟܘܕܒܐ /*kuddāḇā*, in this case, however, without mater lectionis for the short vowel *u*. The equivalent truly Arabic nominal form of the second stem كذّب /*kaḏḏaba* is تكذيب /*takḏīb*, as in Sura 85:19: بل الذين كفروا في تكذيب (*bali l-laḏīna kafarū fī takḏīb*) (Bell: Ney, those who have disbelieved are engaged in counting false). A similar same case is attested of the Syro-Aramaic second stem verb ܢܚܬ / *naḥḥeṯ*, of which the correct nominal form would be ܢܘܚܚܬܐ /*nuḥḥāṭā*. In Sura 19:24 the form occurs twice, in the first case as the false Arabic reading من تحتها / *min taḥtihā* (Bell: from beneath her), which should be read as Syro-Aramaic *min nuḥḥātihā*, i.e., "right after her accouchement," and in the second case as the erroneous Arabic reading تحتك /*taḥtaki* (Bell: beneath you) for Syro-Aramaic *nuḥḥātaki* – "your accouchement." See above, p. 127 ff., for the discussion of the passage from Surah 19:24. A remnant of this Syro-Aramaic form in today's Arabic is found in the specific (and abnormal) word كتّاب / *kuttāb* (Koran school or elementary school—plural: كتاتيب / *katātīb*), that morphologically could be taken for the plural of the Arabic singular كاتب / *kātib* (writer, author). But actually, it is the Syro-Aramaic infinitive of the second stem كتّب / *kattaba* (to make write = to teach the art of writing), corresponding to the Arabic infinitive تكتيب / *taktīb*.

8 Cf. *Thes.* II 2284 ff.: ܢܓܪ /*ngar* (1) longus fuit, productus, extensus est (to continue, to go on and on); (2) patiens, longanimis fuit (to be patient, to have patience), اصطبر. صبر. تمهّل .

9 Cf. *Thes.* II 2668 ff; actually Arabic *šāniyaka*.

10 The *Lisān* (XII 24b f.) quotes as sole exception the plural of إمام ('imām) = أئمة (*'a'imma*) (where the second *hamza*, however, is not vowelless) and explains nevertheless that this form with two *hamza*, according to the philologists of Kufa, is an exception and not a norm (شاذ لا يقاس عليه), since the most Koran readers read أيمة (*'ayimma*). Hence he concludes that "two successive radical *hamza* never occurred" in Arabic:

فلهذا لم يأت في الكلام لفظة توالت فيها همزتان أصلا البتة !

11 This is not the unique secondary Arabic formation from a Syro-Aramaic verbal root. The Koran offers us two further secondary derivations from the Syro-Aramaic verbal root ܐܬܐ /*eṯā*: 1. From the 2nd intensive stem ܐܬܝ / *attī* (to bring) (by secondary sonorization of the t > d) > Arabic أدّى / *addā* (in the Koran in the meaning "to bring, to give back" in the following passages: Surahs 2:283; 3:75 [2x]; 4:58; in the vernacular Egyptian Arabic ادّيني / *əddīnī* means means = اعطني /*aʿṭinī* [give me]); 2. from the most used Syro-Aramaic Afʿel stem ܐܝܬܝ / *aytī* in the sense of "to bring," the Qurʾān forms by monophthongization of the diphthong *ay* > *ā* the 4th Arabic stem آتى /*'ātā* (formally equal to the 3rd stem), as it is attested in numerous passages with the same meaning. A further secondary derivation is to be found in the today's spoken Arabic of Irak, where for example the imperative form انطيني /*anṭīnī* (give me) shows its derivation from the Syro-Aramaic intenx-sive stem ܐܬܝ / *attī* (imperative ܐܬܝܢܝ / *attī-n[ī]*) after the dissolution of the

gemination of the medial radical by insertion of a preceding ـنـ / *n*, as it can be observed in a number of Arabic verbs borrowed from the Eastern (Mesopotamian) vernacular Aramaic, as it is relatively frequent e.g., in Mandaic (cf. Th. Nöldeke, *MG*, § 68).

This phenomenon can help to clarify the etymology of the Hebrew (and Old Aramaic) verbal root נתן / *n-t-n* (to give) as a secondary formation from Eastern Aramaic with a secondary first and third radical from the second intensive stem אתא / *attā* > *antā* + the enclitic object suffix of the first person singular *–n(ī)* or plural *–n* = *אנתני or *אנתן / *antān(ī)* / *antān*, thereby accent-shifting on the last syllable and consequently dropping of the unaccented initial radical (א)נתן / *(a)ntān* > נתן / *natān* > *ntān* (hence no spirantization of the originally geminated ת / *t* after the vocalized secondary נ / *n*).

The end- ܠ / *l* in the parallel Syriac variant ܢܬܠ / *n-t-l* is the enclitic preposition ܠ / *l* marking the dative (or indirect object), by analogy with the verb ܝܗܒ ܠ/ *ya(h)ḇ l-* (to give "to" someone). This formation has been nearly recognized by Stade (according to Th. Nöldeke, *MG* 52, note 6: in *Lit. Centralbl.* 1873 Nr. 45, p. 1418), who, however, sees in this end-*l* (as well as Nöldeke) an assimilation of the end-*n* of the previous form, that Nöldeke regards as a former original one. But in reality, both variants are parallel secondary formations depending on the use of the original verb: a) *attā* as ruling the accusative (or direct object), b) *attī* as ruling the dative by means of the preposition ܠ / *l.*

While C. Brockelmann does not quote this irregular form in his *Lexicon Syriacum*, Mannā and the *Thesaurus* adduce it in alphabetical order under ܢ /*n*. Mannā (470b) explains the fictitious verbal root *ܢܬܠ / *ntal* as (ممات / *mumāt*) (died out); the Thes. (II 2480) explains it as verbum defectivum and compares it to Hebrew נתן / *natan* and Eastern Aramaic נתן / *ntan* beside נתל / *ntal* (without further etymological explanation). In his *Syrische Grammatik* [Syriac Grammar], p. 128, Th. Nöldeke refers only to נתן / *n-t-n* as root of the Syro-Aramaic infinitive ܡܬܠ / *mettal*, without further explanation.

12 Cf. Nöldeke-Schwally, *GdQ* I 74–17.

13 Cf. Tor Andrae, *Der Ursprung des Islams und das Christentum* [Christianity and the Origin of Islam] (Uppsala, 1926) 139: "The eschatological piety of the Qur'ān is thus very closely related to the religious viewpoint predominant in the Syrian churches before and at the time of Muhammed. This Syrian piety is actually a monastic religion. . . ."

14 Pickthall translates as follows: "1. Read: In the name of thy Lord who createth, 2. createth man from a clot. 3. Read: And thy Lord is the Most Bounteous, 4. Who teacheth by the pen, 5. Teacheth man that which be knew not. 6. Nay, but verily man is rebellious 7. That he thinketh himself independent! 8. Lo! unto thy Lord is the return. 9. Hast thou seen him who dissuadeth 10. A slave when he prayeth? 11. Hast thou seen if he (relieth) on the guidance (of Allah) 12. Or enjoineth piety? 13. Hast thou seen if he denieth (Allah's guidance) and is froward? 14. Is he then unaware that Allah seeth? 15. Nay, but if he cease not. We will seize him by the forelock 16. The lying, sinful forelock 17. Then let him call upon his henchmen! 18. We will call the guards of hell. 19. Nay! Obey not thou him. But prostrate thyself, and draw near (unto Allah)."

15 The phrase that is cited in Nöldeke-Schwally, *GdQ* I 33, قرأ على فلان السلام and قرأ فلانا السلام (to greet someone) can certainly be traced back to the Syro-Aramaic

expression ܩܪܐ ܫܠܡܐ (*qrā šlāmā*), as given in the Thes. (II 3713) and explained with salutavit. The same is in Mannā 698: ܩܪܐ ܫܠܡܐ ܥܠ (*qrā šlāmā ʿal*): سلّم . قرأ سلاما على . The *Lisān* (XV 174a ff.) lists under the root قرا (*qarā*) (with the variants قرو / *q-r-w* and قرى / *q-r-y*) a whole series of no longer common expressions in modern Arabic that can only be explained on the basis of their Syro-Aramaic origin. One of them is, for example, قرى الضيف (*qarā ḍ-ḍayf*), which the *Lisān* (179b) conjecturally explains with "to honor a guest," but which in Syro-Aramaic means "to call = to invite" a guest. Also interesting are the further forms such as إنه لمقرى للضيف ومقراء as well as إنه لقرىّ وإنها لقريّة للأضياف , whose form already betrays their Syro-Aramaic origin.

16 Cf. *Thes.* II 3713: ...ܩܪܐ ܒܫܡ (*qrā b-šem*) proclamavit nomen ejus; vocavit, invocavit Deum. Furthermore in Mannā 698: ܩܪܐ ܒܫܡ ܡܪܝܐ (*qrā b-šem māryā*) نوّه باسم الرب . صلّى . سجد. عبد الرب (to invoke God's name, to pray, to worship, to worship God). G. Lüling, *Über den Ur-Qur'ān* [About the Original Qur'ān], p. 30; A Challenge to Islam for Reformation, p. 32, was right in confirming this understanding by Gustav Weil and Hartwig Hirschfeld.

17 Avānī III 16, cited from: Jawād ʿAlī, *al-Mufaṣṣal fī tārīḫ al-ʿArab qabl al- Islām* (Exhaustive History of the Arabs Before Islam), vol. 6, Beirut, [3]1980, p. 651.

18 In the article WARAQA b. Nawfal b. Asad al-Qurašī in the *Shorter Encyclopaedia of Islam* (Leiden, 1934, 631) it is reported that Waraqa "encouraged and possibly influenced the Prophet in the first years of his mission" (in Mecca). As a Christian "he was abstemious, knew Hebrew, studied the Bible, and had written down" (i.e., translated) "the Gospels" (probably one Gospel) allegedly in the Hebrew alphabet. It was he "who found Muḥammad as a child when he strayed from his nurse." He is also the one who "warmly approved" of the first marriage of the Prophet to Waraqa's cousin Ḫadīja. The (Islamic) tradition admits that Waraqa was nonetheless never converted (to Islam).

19 Arabic بيعة (*bīʿa*) has already been recognized by S. Fraenkel, *Aram. Fremdwörter* [Aramaic Foreign Words] 274, as a borrowing from Syro-Aramaic ܒܝܥܬܐ (bīʿtā) (egg, dome = church); the plural بيع (*biyaʿ*) occurs in the Qur'ān in Sura 22:40. The expression is still common today among Arabic-speaking Christians in the Mesopotamian region.

20 As a Syro-Aramaic substratum *al-Munǧid fī l-luġa wa-l-aʿlām*, Beirut 1987, 526b, has recorded the expression العلق (*al-ʿalaq*) in the meaning الطين الذي يعلق باليد (*aṭ-ṭīn al-laḏī yaʿlaq bi-l-yad*) (the clay that sticks to one's hand). This meaning is missing in the *Lisān*.

21 Even though the meaning of the Arabic لازب (*lāzib*) "sticky, clinging" is actually clear, Paret (368) translates "of pliant [literally, consistent] clay," ["aus geschmeidigem (W: konsistentem) Lehm"], Blachère (475) "of solidified clay," ["d'argile solidifiée"]; and Bell (II, 443), approximately, "of clay cohering."

22 Paret begins the sentence with "Nein!"; Blachère sees in it a warning: "Prenez garde!" Like Paret, Bell understands "Nay."

23 The same sense has the Syro-Aramaic adverbial expression ܠܓܡܪ / la-ǧmār (Mannā 112b: ابدا. قطّ. بتّة / abadan, qaṭṭ, batta; C. Brockelmann, *Lexicon Syriacum* 121b: absolute, omnino [absolutely, completely, ever / never]).

24 Carl Brockelmann, *Syrische Grammatik* (Leipzig, 1938), p. 15; a more modern reference book is Burkhart Kienast, *Historische Semitische Sprachwissenschaft* (Wiesbaden, 2001).

25 This sense is attested in the Qur'ān in Sura 2:117 and 6:101: بديع السموت والارض / *badīʿ as-samāwāt wa-l-arḍ* = Syro-Aramaic ܥܒܕ ܫܡܝܐ ܘܐܪܥܐ / *ʿābeḏ šmayyā w-arʿā* (Creator of the heaven and the earth). The secondary Arabic verb بدأ / *bada'a*, with the secondary common meaning "to begin," has in the Qur'ān partially the original meaning of "to create," as it arises e.g., from Sura 7:29: كما بداكم تعودون / *kamā badākum or bada'akum taʿūdūn* (As He created you, you will turn again) (Bell I 139 translates: "As He began you, ye will come again").

26 Cf. Th. Nöldeke, *Syrische Grammatik* [Syriac Grammar] § 223: "The personal pronouns must also express the reflexive wherever this function is not already performed by the verbal form… . That is, very often one uses ܢܦܫܐ (nap̄šā) "soul," and less frequently ܩܢܘܡܐ (qnōmā) "person" with the personal suffixes for the exact expression of the reflexive relationship. . . ." In Arabic the only way to express the reflexive is by means of the equivalent expressions نفس (*nafs*) and حال (*ḥāl*). Accordingly, إن رءاه (*in ra'ā-hu*—properly: *rā-hu*) in Arabic should have properly been إن رأى نفسه (*in ra'ā nafsahu*).

27 Gotthelf Bergsträsser, *Verneinungs- und Fragepartikeln und Verwandtes im Kur'ān. Ein Beitrag zur historischen Grammatik des Arabischen* [Negative, Interrogative and Related Particles in the Qur'ān: A Study of the Historical Grammar of Arabic] (Leipzig, 1914) 89–100. Concerning ارايت (3-91) he says laconically: "Subordinate clauses are occasionally inserted after *a*, but then the *a* is usually repeated. The text causes more difficulties here than elsewhere. . . ."

28 Cf. Thes. I 47, particula (1) distinctiva; (48) (2) interrogativa, num, an, ne. The Hebrew particle הַ (ha) that Brockelmann associates with the Arabic interrogative particle ا ('a) in *Arabische Grammatik* [Arabic Grammar] § 86, note (a), would suggest a sound shift from *ha* to *'a*. But the parallel use of أو (*'aw*) and أ (*'a*) as an interrogative particle in the Qur'ān would seem to verify the creation of the latter through the monophthongization of the Syro-Aramaic particle ܐܘ (*aw*). This, however, does not rule out the possibility that the former was also first created through a sound shift of the demonstrative particle ܗܘ (*haw*) to ܐܘ (*'aw*).

29 The Thes. (I 249) gives the spelling ܐܝܢ ('yn), in addition to ܐܢ ('n), as Chaldean; the first spelling also appears at times in Christian Palestinian (250): ܐܢ ܀ For this: "Est ubi scriptum est ܢ . . ."

30 See Theodor Nöldeke, *Mandäische Grammatik* (Darmstadt, 1964), p. 162.

31 Cf. W. Diem, "Untersuchungen zur frühen Geschichte der arabischen Orthographie III. Endungen und Endschreibungen" [Studies in the Early History of Arabic Orthography III: Endings and Their Spellings], in *Orientalia*, vol. 50, 1981, § 193, 378. But actually, this orthography goes back to an Eastern Syro-Aramean (Babylonian) tradition.

32 The translation of the Qur'ānic plural انداد (*andād*) by (gods) "of his own kind," as our Qur'ān translators render it, trusting in the Arabic commentators (e.g., Paret at Sura 2:22), is therefore false.

33 In Jeffery, *Foreign Vocabulary* 148: "The guardians of Hell."

34 This would be justified as an appellative by the word determined by the Arabic article ال / al. The Qur'ān, however, does not always orient itself according to the

Arabic norm, and so it often happens that the Qur'ān also leaves out an article required by Arabic, as in Sura 95:5, ثم رددنه اسفل سفلين , where what is seen in Arabic as an indeterminate (and therefore as a false) genitive of the status constructus is considered as determinate (and as correct) in Syro-Aramaic. Variations in both directions are to be observed in the Qur'ān, so that criteria of Arabic as well as of Syro-Aramaic grammar must be taken into account depending on the context. Cf. for example the variants in the old codices edited by Arthur Jeffery, *Materials for the History of the Text of the Qur'ān*, Leiden 1937, p. 178 (Codex of Ubai b. Ka'b), Surah 95:5, where سفلين (*sāfilīn*) is transmitted with the article ال / al : السافلين (*as-sāfilīn*), "as Ibn Mas'ūd." The same occurs in the following Surah 96:16 : "He read الناصية الكاذبة الخاطئة *(an-nāṣiya al-kāḏiba al-ḫāṭi'a)*. So Abū Ḥaṣīn."

35 Salwa Bā l-Ḥağğ Ṣāliḥ al-'Āyub, *Al-masīḥīya al-'arabīya wa taṭawwurātuhā min naš'atihā ilā l-qarn ar-rābi' al-hiğrī/ al-'āsir al-milādī* [Arab Christianity and its Development from its Origins to the Fourth Century of the Hegira/Tenth Century of the Christian Era] (Beirut, 2007), part I, chapter 4, p. 89.

36 Namely, in Arabic the conjunction و /wa also has an explicative function, including that of a more detailed explanation.

37 Syro-Aramaic ܟܠܐ (*klā*) is the supposed lexical equivalent for Arabic نهى (*nahā*). For this, Mannā (337b) cites in Arabic, besides نهى. نفى (*nahā, nafā*) (to forbid), also صدّ. عاق (*ṣadda, 'āqa*) (to hinder, to hold back).

38 Among the eight different aspects (ܦܪܨܘܦܐ /parṣōpā) of the Syro-Aramaic conjunction ܐܘ (*aw*) that Bar Bahlūl names, the Thes. (I 48) cites the "intensifying" meaning designated with ܝܬܝܪ (*yattīr*). This conjunction is also used with such a meaning in the Qur'ān, in Sura 37:147, where it is said of Jonas وارسلنه الى مائة الف او يزيدون "and we dispatched him to one hundred thousand or (even) more." The Arab philologists have noticed this nuance (see *Lisān* XIV 54b).

39 The single meaning of the Arabic borrowed verb أمر (*amara*) "to command" does not do justice to the present context. It is not a question of "commanding," but rather of the "beliefs" or "convictions" upon which the action is based. To that extent the meaning given by Mannā (26a) in Arabic under (4) for the Syro-Aramaic ܐܡܪ (emar) ارتأى (*irta'ā*) (to think, to consider, to ponder) is appropriate.

40 Literally: Bow (instead) (to honor God). As a terminus technicus, سجد (*sağada*) here means "to hold divine service."

41 Ethel Stefana Drower and Rudolf Macuch, *A Mandaic Dictionary* (Oxford: Clarendon Press, 1963), p. 383b.

42 The true meaning of the term عيد (*'īd*), which occurs as a *hapax legomenon* in the Qur'ān, has until now been overlooked. Brockelmann, *Lexicon Syriacum* (515b), explains the derivation of Arabic عيد (*'īd*) in the meaning "feast" as the phonetic rendering of the common Aramaic pronunciation of ܥܐܕܐ ('ēḏā >'īḏā). As a faithful rendering of the Syro-Aramaic ܥܝܕܐ (*'yāḏā*), however, the Qur'ānic term has accordingly, in addition to the original meaning of "practice, custom," the meaning of "liturgy," which is clear here from the Qur'ānic context. Cf. also the Thes. II 2827: Valet etiam ܥܝܕܐ (*'yāḏā*) ritus, caeremonia (rite, ceremony).

43 Vol. II, 1st edition (Cairo, 1928) 129.
44 This term is still used among the Arabic speaking Christians of the Near and Middle East.
45 Cf. Thes I 514: Improprie de foetu, ܒܛܢܗ (*baṭnāh*): id quod conceperat.
46 Cf., e.g., C. Brockelmann, *Arabische Grammatik* [Arabic Grammar] § 85; *Syrische Grammatik* [Syriac Grammar] § 201.
47 Cf. Thes. II on ܢܚܬ (*nḥeṭ*) 2344, (γ) ortus est, genus duxit; further in C. Brockelmann, *Lexicon Syriacum* 424a, under 10: oriundus fuit (to spring from, to be descended from, to be born).
48 Cf. Thes. II 2155: Valet etiam ܡܢ ܕ (*men d-*): postquam (after). Mannā, 407a: ܡܢ ܕܩܪܝܗ (*men da-qrāy*) : حالما دعاه (as soon as he called him).
49 Not to be confused with the temporal من in the sense of مذ ، منذ (cf., e.g., *Lisān* XIII 421 b): من سنة = مذ سنة (min sana^{tin} : for a year).
50 Discovered with the help of Syro-Aramaic.
51 *Lisān* II 98a. The reading النصار / *an-nuṣār* results from the lexical equivalent of Syro-Aramaic ܢܨܝܚܐ / *naṣīḥā*, the meanings of which Mannā (461b) gives as follows: (4) مظفر. قاهر. فائز (successful, victorious, triumphant), and under (7) شريف. جليل. نبيل. فاضل (noble, honorable, highborn, illustrious). The Arabic expression النصار /*an-nuṣār* renders the Syriac meaning under (4), presupposing that the semantic nuance under (7) is included. Thus here النصار /*an-nuṣār* means الأشراف / *al-ašrāf* (the notables).
52 Theodor Nöldeke writes about this influence in a work that he labels a "sketch:" *Die semitischen Sprachen* [The Semitic Languages] (Leipzig, 21899) 52:

> During the entire dominance of Aramaic this language had at least a great influence on the vocabulary of Arabic. The more meticulous one's examination, the more one recognizes how many Arabic words signifying concepts or objects of a certain culture have been borrowed from the Arameans [Reference to the aforementioned work by Siegmund Fraenkel, Die aramāischen Fremdwīrter (Aramaic Foreign Words)]. The northern cultural influence expressed in these borrowings contributed considerably to preparing the Arabs for their powerful intervention in world history.

Nöldeke correctly traces the richness of the Arabic vocabulary partially to the arbitrarily devised expressions of Arabic poetry and partially to words that were common only to individual tribes. His concluding opinion on the subject (58) is all the more surprising:

> But still the abundance of words is exceedingly large, and the Arabic dictionary will always remain the principal aid in the search for instruction on obscure expressions in other Semitic languages [where just the opposite seems to be the case, though he then adds the qualifier]: only if this occurs with the requisite amount of level-headedness; then it's quite all right.

53 *Lisān* II 98b; through the conjectural explanation of Arabic نحت (*naḥata*) (97b) — النحت (*an-naḥt*) with النشر والقشر (an-našru wa-l-qašr): "to saw, to peel" —the *Lisān* testifies to its ignorance of the original meaning of this root originally borrowed from Aramaic, when, for example, it explains النحاتة / *an-nuḥātā* with ما نحت من الخشب (*mā nuḥita min al-ḫašab* – "what has been planed from wood"). At the same time, this nominal form already exhibits a direct borrowing from Syro-Aramaic ܢܚܬܐ (*nḥāṭā*) or ܢܘܚܬܐ (*nūḥḥāṭā*) with the correspondent meaning here,

"what has fallen off." Also, نحت الجبل (*naḥata l-ǧabal*) does not actually mean قطعه (*qaṭaʿahu*) "to cut," but according to the original Syro-Aramaic meaning "to chop off, to strike down" (the mountain); the same is true for النحائت (*an-naḥāʾit*) (98a): آبار معروفة (*ābār maʿrūfa* – "well-known wells"), whose original meaning the *Lisān* again derives from "to cut." The figurative sense "to degrade," on the other hand, derives from the following expressions (98b): نحته بلسانه : لامه وشتمه (*naḥatahū bi-lisānihi: lāmahu wa-šatamahū*) (to "degrade" somebody with the tongue: to rebuke, revile him); النحيت (*an-naḥīt*) (< Syro-Aramaic ܢܚܝܬ / *naḥīṯ*) means primarily that which is inferior, bad, reprehensible; نحته بالعصا : ضربه بها (*naḥatahū bi-l-ʿaṣā : ḍarabahu bi-hā*— "to hit somebody with a stick," actually in this way "to degrade" him, "to knock" him "down" with it); the same is true when one is said نحت المرأة : نكحها (*naḥata l-marʾa: nakaḥahā* – to "degrade = to dishonor" a woman: to lie with her).

On the other hand, in his *Lexicon Syriacum* 424b, C. Brockelmann categorizes the Syro-Aramaic ܢܚܬ (*nḥeṯ*) etymologically with the Arabic حتّ (*ḥatta*), and that its first radical ܢ / ن (*nūn*) has fallen off suggests, in turn, according to the expressions cited in the *Lisān* (II 22a ff.), a borrowing from this very Syro-Aramaic root with the original meaning "to fall off." That this root was unknown to the Arabs is shown not least by its reduction in colloquial modern Arabic to a verbal form with the meaning "to rub off, to scratch off" (see, for example, Hans Wehr) as well as "to become worn through use" (said of pieces of clothing and carpets, actually "to be worn out, run down").

54 Cf. *Lisān* II 98a where النحاتة (*an-nuḥāta*) is explained with the help of البراية (*al-burāya* – "shavings"). For this unidentified Syro-Aramaic root in the *Lisān* the derivation of the Arabic نحاتة (*nuḥāta*) from Syro-Aramaic ܢܚܬܐ (*nḥāṯā*) or ܢܘܚܬܐ (*nuḥḥāṯā*) would nevertheless be obvious, whereby the Arabic feminine ending is to be viewed occasionally as a purely phonetic rendering of the Syro-Aramaic emphatic ending of the masculine nominal form. This, however, does not rule out the possibility that an Arabic feminine ending may be derived from such an ending in Syro-Aramaic. Concerning this nominal form Nöldeke writes in his *Beiträge zur semitischen Sprachwissenschaft* [Essays on Semitic Linguistics] (Strasbourg, 1904) 30, under Nomina of the Form Fuʿāl : "In Arabic, then, the femininum فعالة (*fuʿāla*) is still quite alive as the form of refuse, of shavings. This is shown, among other things, by the fact that it can even be formed from recently borrowed words."

That Nöldeke, in the case of the examples named here نشارة (*nušāra*) (wood shavings) and كناسة (*kunāsa*) (sweepings), does not already recognize a borrowing from the Syro-Aramaic equivalents that he has also cited, ܢܣܪܬܐ (*nsārtā*) and ܟܢܫܬܐ (*knāštā*), may be because he views his presentation from the sole perspective of a neutral study in comparative Semitistics. The same applies for the Arabic form فعال (*fuʿāl*), which Nöldeke would like to see as separate from the preceding form, but which seems merely to be the Arabic pausal form or the reproduction of the status absolutus of the Syro-Aramaic nominal form ܦܥܠܐ (*pʿālā*), as several of the examples he cites also attest. Thus سعال (*suʿāl*) (coughing) can most likely be derived from ܫܥܠܐ (*šʿālā*), عطاس (*ʿuṭās*) (sneezing) from

ܛܫܫܐ (*ṭāšā*), خناق (*ḫunāq*) (angina) from ܚܢܩܐ (*ḥnāqā*). Other forms derived from Arabic roots would be merely analogous formations. From a purely philological perspective, comparative Semitics may be useful, but it leads one all too easily to blur the reciprocal influences, relevant to cultural history, of its individual languages.

55 Although not specifically in the meaning "to be delivered of, to give birth to," but in the general meaning "to send down, to drop, to lower," the Eastern Syrian lexicographers include among the various derivations the following Arabic equivalents: أنزل (*anzala*), أخفض (*aḫfaḍa*), حط (*ḥaṭṭa*), واضع (*wāḍaʿa*). (Cf. Thes. II 2344 f.; Mannā 442b f.). Since the Thes. does not provide any examples for ܢܚܬ (*naḥḥeṯ*) in the meaning "to be delivered of, to give birth to," it would be interesting to document this usage in other Aramaic dialects.

56 Wilhelm Gesenius, *Hebräisches und aramäisches Handwörterbuch* [Concise Dictionary of Hebrew and Aramaic], 1915, unrev. reprint (Berlin, Göttingen, Stuttgart, 171959) 512b, under (b).

57 What is striking here is that, regarding the "sent-down Scriptures" in the sense of revelations, the Qur'ān usually employs the Arabic انزل (*anzala* – "to have come down, to send down") in addition to آتى (*ātā* < Syro-Aramaic ܐܝܬܝ / *aytī* – "to have come, to bring, to deliver").

58 Cf. *GdQ* I 117–143; but on page 130 (line 3) it is conceded: "The Surah is the oldest, or at least one of the oldest, in which holy persons from the New Testament such as Mary, Zachary, John the Baptist and Jesus are mentioned."

59 Cf. *Lisān* XIV 377b: السرو : المروءة والشرف (*as-sarwa: al-murūʾa wa-š-šaraf* – "manfulness, noblemindedness"); 378a: additional remarks on سريّ (*sarī*) in the meaning of شريف (*šarīf*) (noble, nobleminded).

60 The compiler of the *Lisān* nevertheless saw no reason not to include the unrecognized Syro-Aramaic expression سري (*sarī*) in the supposed meaning of نهر (*nahr*) (river) and جدول (*ǧadwal*) (brook) and to cite in connection with it the corresponding misinterpretation by the Qur'ān commentators: النهر الصغير كالجدول يجري إلى النخل ("a small or a stream-like river that flows to the palms") (*Lisān* XIV 380a). As we shall see, this is not an isolated case of misread and misunderstood Qur'ānic expressions that have been accepted into the Arabic lexicography without being contested up to the present day. But also other expressions cited by the *Lisān* under the root شري (*šariya*) and سري (*sariya*) and explained by means of folk etymology provide ample proof of their Aramaic origins. To point these out here, however, would be to exceed the scope of this study. It would therefore be of eminent importance not only from the standpoint of cultural history, but also from that of philology, to scrutinize the Arabic lexicon for the countless Aramaisms that have until now been overlooked or falsely taken to be "Old Arabic."

61 Blachère, loc. cit. 331, notes 23–32.

62 Bell, loc. cit. I 286, note 2.

63 Wilhelm Rudolph, *Die Abhängigkeit des Qorans von Judentum und Christentum* [The Dependence of the Qur'ān on Judaism and Christianity] (Stuttgart, 1922) 79.

64 Blachère 331, notes 23–32.

65 Ṭabarī XVI 63.

66 Cf. C. Brockelmann, *Syrische Grammatik* [Syriac Grammar] § 167.

67 The Qur'ānic spelling سرقيا is to be read *sarqīyā* according to Syro-Aramaic

/sarqāyā (empty = waste) and not as Arabic شرقيا / šarqīyā (to a place,) "eastward" (Bell). The Syro-Aramaic reading is logically confirmed by the parallel verse 22, where it is said that Mary, after having become pregnant, was expelled with her child to a place "far away " (makānan qaṣīyā): فحملته فانتبذت به مكانا قصيا

68 Cf., e.g., Lk. 2:18: ܘܟܠܗܘܢ ܕܫܡܥܘ: ܐܬܕܡܪܘ ܥܠ ܐܝܠܝܢ ܕܐܬܡܠܠ ܠܗܘܢ ܡܢ ܪܥܘܬܐ (w-ḵullhōn da-šma‘ū eddammarū ‘al aylēn d-eṯmallalī l-hōn men rā‘awwāṯā) "And all they that heard (it) wondered at those (things) which were told them by the shepherds" (from the Syriac Bible 63DC, United Bible Societies [London, 1979] 77a). The Qur'ān, moreover, has the same passive construction in Sura 21:43, where it is said of the idols: لا يستطيعون نصر انفسهم ولا هم منا يصحبون "they are not (even) capable of helping themselves nor are they (as idols) accompanied by us (as helpers)" (i.e., nor are we put with them as god).

This construction, which is indefensible from the point of view of Arabic syntax, also confuses our Qur'ān translators. Paret, for instance, translates (265): "(– Götter) die weder sich selber Hilfe zu leisten vermögen noch (irgendwo) gegen uns Beistand finden [(– gods) who neither are capable of rendering themselves assistance nor find assistance against us (anywhere)] (?*wa-lā hum minnā yuṣḥabūna*)." Similarly Blachère (351): "et il ne leur est pas donné de compagnon contre nous [and they are not given a companion against us]" Only Bell translates correctly in terms of the meaning (I 308b 44): "and from Us they will have no company."

69 Cf. C. Brockelmann, *Arabische Grammatik* [Arabic Grammar] § 96.

70 See Thes. II 4308: ܫܪܐ (*šārā*) absolvens; solvit, liberavit. Further, Mannā 816b (among the 27 different meanings of ܫܪܐ šrā) (21): اذن . حلّل . ضد حرّم (to allow, to declare legitimate; opposite of to forbid, to declare illegitimate), and under ܫܪܝܐ šaryā (7): حلال. مباح. خلاف ممنوع ومحرّم (legitimate, allowed, opposite of forbidden and illegitimate). C. Brockelmann, *Lexicon Syriacum* [Syriac Lexicon] 804a: 6. ܫܪܝܐ (*šaryā*): licet (it is allowed, legitimate).

71 For the Qur'ānic expression وقري عينا (*wa-qarrī =aynaⁿ*), Mannā gives (698a) as the Syro-Aramaic equivalent ܩܘܪܪܬ ܥܝܢܐ *qurraṯ ‘aynā*), ܩܘܪܪܬ ܠܒܐ ܪܘܚܐ *qurraṯ lebbā, rūḥā*): قرّة العين . فرح . تعزية (*qurratᵘ l-‘ayn, faraḥ, ta‘ziya*) (cheerfulness, joy, consolation); see also Thes. II 3711: ܩܘܪܪܬ ܪܘܚܐ (*qurraṯ rūḥā*): consolatio (consolation).

No Battle of "Badr"

Christoph Luxenberg

The following article was first published in German as "Keine Schlacht von 'Badr': Zu Syrischen Buchstaben in Frühen Koranmanuskripten," in Markus Gross and Karl-Heinz Ohlig, eds., Vom Koran zum Islam, *Inârah: Schriften zur frühen Islamgeschichte und zum Koran, vol. 4 (Berlin, 2009), pp. 642–76. This English version will appear both in the present anthology and in the English translation of the original collection of essays.*

1. Introductory remarks

Our first monograph, *Die syro-aramäische Lesart des Koran* [*The Syro-Aramaic Reading of the Koran*], in which our procedure was introduced,[1] listed the main methodological results of an initial, tentative investigation of the Qur'anic text. We observed then that, in the case of individual words, a plausible reading could be deciphered only by assuming an underlying Syriac script (the so-called *Garshuni/Karshuni* script),[2] yet this first suspicion gradually became a certainty only when in-depth philological analysis had made evident a whole series of such erroneous transcriptions. Our initial findings in this regard were set forth in the essay, "Relikte syro-aramäischer Buchstaben in frühen Korankodizes im *ḥiǧāzī-* und *kūfī*-Duktus" ["Remains of Syro-Aramaic letters in early Koran codices in *ḥiǧāzī-* and *kūfī* script"] in the anthology *Der frühe Islam*[3] [*Early Islam*]. We will now note further examples, along with other erroneous readings in the canonical version of the Qur'ān.

2. Proof of a Syriac letter in the *kūfī*-codex of Samarqand

For many critics who consider such philological results to be a mere hypothesis, because they cannot pass judgment on it, this thesis would not be proved unless evidence of a Qur'ān manuscript composed in Syriac (*Garshuni*) script could be produced. There is little or no chance of fulfilling this expectation, however, since Ṭabarī (died 923) reports in the introduction to his commentary on the Qur'ān that the third Caliph 'Uṯmān/Osman (644-656), who had the version of the Qur'ān which today is considered canonical copied from "folios" [Arabic: *ṣuḥuf*] that were allegedly in the possession of the Prophet's widow Ḥafṣa, ordered after her death that these "folios," as well as all privately owned texts of the Qur'ān, be *destroyed* or *burnt*, and allowed from then on only one reading (to the exclusion of the six others), so as to preserve the unity of the young Islamic faith community. Hence there is no trace left of the six variant versions.[4] It is thought, however, that not everyone complied with this order. To this fact we owe the tradition of a large Qur'ānic corpus of writings which discuss variant readings [*qirā'āt*]. It includes the Qur'ān version of Ubai ibn Kaʿb, which attests, for example, to a variant Arabic name for Friday: whereas in Surah 62:9 Friday is usually called يوم الجمعة (*yawm al-ǧumʿa*) or "congregation day," in Ubai we find the expression يوم العروبة الكبرى (*yawm al-ʿarūba l-kubrā*), "Great Friday = Good Friday," as Good Friday was called in pre-Islamic Christian Arabic.[5]

Certainly this detail alone is not yet proof that the Arabic Qur'ān had been written in Syriac script. But perhaps another detail, a remnant ["*Relikt*"] from the famous *kūfī*-manuscript of Samarqand, can give us more conclusive evidence as to the way in which pre-Arabic Qur'ān was written down.

The following copy is taken from a facsimile, published in 1905, of Samarqand's Qur'ān manuscript.[6]

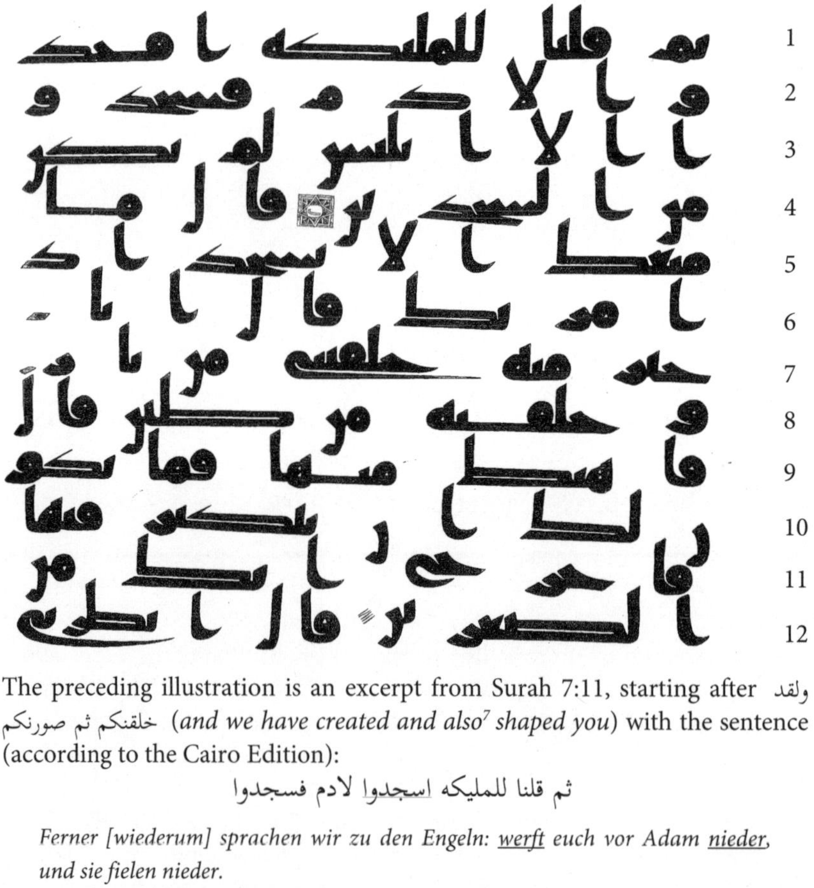

The preceding illustration is an excerpt from Surah 7:11, starting after ولقد خلقنكم ثم صورنكم (*and we have created and also[7] shaped you*) with the sentence (according to the Cairo Edition):

ثم قلنا للمليكه اسجدوا لادم فسجدوا

Ferner [wiederum] sprachen wir zu den Engeln: werft euch vor Adam nieder, und sie fielen nieder.

> After this [again] we spoke to the angels: cast yourselves down before Adam, and they fell down.

In the Cairo Edition the selfsame verb سجد / *sağada* ("to fall down, to cast oneself down") is repeated. In the Samarqand Manuscript, however, at the underlined first verb اسجدوا / *usğudū* (cast yourselves down) we find another word that could not be identified, either from the script or from the sense. Considered in isolation, the basic drawing or shape[*rasm*]looks like this:

This word does not agree with the Cairo Edition, a fact that had already been noticed by the pseudonymous Brother Mark.[8] Concerning the second and third letters that he circled in the Samarqand rasm, he remarks:

> In line #1 in the "original" of Q7:11 there is a *sad* [=صـ /*ṣād*] whereas there is a *sin* [=سـ /*sīn*] in the modern versions.

Here the author took 1) the first Syriac letter ܩ / q (= Arabic ق / q) for an Arabic صـ / *ṣād*, and 2) the following Syriac letter ܥ / *ʿayn* for an Arabic جـ / *ğ* (without a point beneath it). The latter character (حـ) in fact is distinguished in both *kūfī* and *ḥiğāzī* script from the Syriac ܥ / *ʿayn* by the fact that the upper stroke leaning to the left (in middle position) extends for almost the same length beneath the line (originally an imitation of the Syriac ܓ / *g*). Compare this with the word on the Samarqand page reprinted above in facsimile, line 2, to the left, the ح in middle position in the rasm فسجدوا (read: *fā-sağadū*) (and they fell down), and also in lines 4 and 5, whereas the initial حـ remains over the line, as in line 7: خلقتنى (read: *ḫalaqtanī*) (you created me), and line 8: خلقته (read: *ḫalaqtahu*) (you created him). In the latter instance you see that the initial Arabic حـ (*ğ* / *ḥ* / *ḫ*) is almost no different from the Syriac ܥ. / *ʿayn*. Moreover scribes turned the originally unambiguous Syriac ܓ / *g* into a sign for three different phonemes in the Arabic alphabet, which later were further specified by *diacritical* markings (جـ /*ğ* , حـ /*ḥ* , خـ /*ḫ*).

3. Deciphering the Samarqand *rasm*

The middle letter separately:

The preceding explanation truly clarifies the Samarqand riddle. Reading from right to left:

1. The first letter is a Syriac ܩ / *q*; it is easy to see that the Arabic ق / *q* is an imitation of it.
2. The real riddle lay in the following letter, until now not recognized as the Syriac ܥ. / *ʿayn*, which in combination with the following *kūfī* د / *d* results in the reading (Syro-Aramaic) ܩܥܕ / *qʿaḏ* = (Arabic) قعد / *qaʿada*.

But since this verb in Arabic means "to sit down," while the following سجد / *saǧada* means "to cast oneself down, to fall down," the early redactors of the Qurʾān could not imagine that God would have commanded the angels "to sit down," whereas in reality they were supposed to "cast themselves down," as the Qurʾān, too, attests in four other parallel passages (Surah 2:34; 17:61; 18:50; 20:116). Therefore this (for an Arabic reader) obviously nonsensical "misspelling" was emended simply replacing it with اسجدوا / *usǧudū* (cast yourselves down), in keeping with the following verb. This reading is found also in Ṭabari (VIII, 126), which suggests that this emendation had been carried out before him (d. 923).

The Syro-Aramaic spelling ܩܥܕ/ *qʿaḏ*, however, corresponds—as so often elsewhere in the Qurʾān—to Syro-Aramaic semantics. Thus Mannā (689a/b) interprets Syro-Aramaic ܩܥܕ / *qʿaḏ* or Arabic قعد / *qaʿada* = جثا *ǧaṯā* (to prostrate oneself), as ركع / *rakaʿa* (to kneel down). Thus it becomes apparent that the Samarqand reading اقـعـدوا = (Arabic) اقعدوا / *iqʿadū* is nothing other than a Syro-Aramaic synonym for the following Arabic verb (which was likewise borrowed from Syro-Aramaic), سجد / *saǧada* (to cast oneself down). Explained in this way, the Samarqand variant should be read in Arabic and understood (in Syro-Aramaic fashion) as follows:

ثم قلنا للمليكه اقعدوا لادم فسجدوا

(*ṯumma qulnā li-l-malāʾika* [actually: *la-l-malāykē*] *iqʿadū li-Ādam* [actually: *la-Ādam*] *fa-saǧadū*)

(After this we said to the angels, "Cast yourselves down," and they prostrated themselves).

Now if this proves *empirically* for the first time that a *Syriac* letter appears in one of the earliest known Qurʾān codices in the *kūfī* script, it would not be surprising if the same *Syriac* letter ܥ. / *ʿayn* should be detected in a Qurʾān codex in the *ḥiǧāzī* script that is considered to be even older. This proof will be offered in the following section.

4. On the battle of "Badr" (Surah 3:123)

Depending on the Internet search engine, the English-language results for the "battle of Badr" range from around 250,000 to 858,000 hits, although all of them may not pertain to the battle itself. From this, nevertheless, we can see the importance that is attributed to this "battle" even today and to the "historical" victory that is thus connected with the beginning of the Islamic conquests. By way of introduction we cite the following notes on the topic from Wikipedia, the free Internet encyclopedia:

> The Battle of Badr (Arabic: غزوة بدر), fought on Saturday, 13 March 624 CE (17 Ramadan, 2 AH in the Islamic calendar) in the Hejaz region of western Arabia (present-day Saudi Arabia), was a key battle in the early days of Islam and a turning point in Muhammad's struggle with his opponents among the Quraish in Mecca. The battle has been passed down in Islamic history as a decisive victory attributable to divine intervention, or by secular sources to the strategic genius of Muhammad. It is one of the few battles *specifically mentioned in the Quran*. Most contemporary knowledge of the battle at Badr comes from *traditional Islamic accounts*, both *hadiths and biographies* of Muhammad, recorded in written form *some time after the battle.* (my emphasis)

We are concerned here, not with the *historicity* of the *"Battle of Badr,"* but rather with the passage from the Qur'ān which is cited by Arabic-Islamic historiography. For this purpose the Qur'ānic context will be investigated hermeneutically with reference to its Syro-Aramaic background.

In order to understand the context, the preceding passages (verses 118-120) must be examined also. To summarize: The faithful are exhorted (118) not to befriend anyone who believes differently, since such people would not be well-disposed to them and would hate them. (119) In speaking with believers they would profess the faith, but behind their backs they would declare their rage against them. So may they die in their rage, for God knows what is concealed in the hearts of men. (120) If good things happen to believers, then the others will begrudge them their good fortune; if bad things befall them, then those who believe differently will rejoice in their misfortune. This mistrust, however, will not be able to harm believers, insofar as they are patient and fear God, for God knows what the envious are up to.

It is evident from the introductory sentence of verse 3:119 that the other persons referred to are the *People of the Book*. For syntactic reasons, among others, they are the ones being considered here. The sentence reads:

هانتم اولا تحبونهم ولا يحبونكم وتومنون بالكتب كله

The substance of this sentence is relatively simple; the translations that we consulted interpret it syntactically as follows:

> *Paret* (pages 54 f. [translated from German]):
> There, now [*Da ... nun*]: you love them, while they do not love you, and [you] believe [unlike them] in the whole Scripture. (Da liebt ihr sie nun, während sie euch nicht lieben, und glaubt (im Gegensatz zu ihnen) an die ganze Schrift.)
>
> *Blachère* (page 92 [translated from French]): 115/119
> You are like this [*Vous êtes tels que voici*]: you love [those people] while they do not love you; you believe in Scripture in its entirety.... (Vous êtes tels que voici : vous aimez [ces gens] alors qu'ils ne vous aiment pas ; vous croyez à l'Écriture tout entière)
>
> *Bell* (vol. I, p. 56): 115. There ye are! Ye love them but they love not you; ye believe in the Book, all of it....

All three prominent Arabists failed to recognize that this seemingly simple sentence is syntactically a *conditional sentence*, because *classical Arabic* has no such sentence construction. Understood according to Arabic rules of syntax, therefore, they could see in the word هـ / *ha* preceding the personal pronoun انتم / *antum* (you-plural) only a *demonstrative/indicative particle* (*da / voici /* there). In Aramaic, however, this Qur'ānic *ha* is just a reduction of the originally *interjectional* Old-Aramaic *conditional particle* הין /*hayn*, which by degrees

a) was reduced from the diphthong *ay* to the monophthong *hēn*, and then
b) by dropping the final *nūn* became הי /*hē*,

of which the Qur'ān has preserved for us only the defective spelling with a simple هـ / *h*, as in the text cited above. We owe the preservation of the unique full spelling with هيـ / *hy* (= *hē*) as an *interjection* to the Qur'ān likewise, where this particle occurs in Surah 12:23 as a proclitic (just as the Qur'ān combines the exclamatory particle يا / *yā* with the following word) in the hitherto puzzling word هيت (*hay-ta*), which Ṭabari (XII, 178 ff.), despite various opinions as to its origins (Ḥauranic, Coptic, Syriac, Arabic), ends up understanding correctly from the context, as do Paret ("Come here") and Bell ("Come on"), whereas Blachère with his translation *"Me voici à toi"* ["Here I am by/for you"] follows an alternative interpretation given by Ṭabari. In this passage the personal pronoun لك / *la-ka* (literally: to/for you) following هيت (*hay-ta*) and connected with the preposition لـ / *la-* should not be understood as an Arabic dative, but rather—as is common in Syro-Aramaic (and modern Arabic dialects)—as a reflexive *dativus ethicus*.[9] The Qur'ānic expression هيت لك (pronounced: *hē! ta la-ka!*) thus faithfully renders the Syro-Aramaic idiomatic phrase ܗܝ ܬܐ ܠܟ (*hē! tā lāḵ!*) and means literally: *"Hey! Come here!"*

This should refute the conviction that this expression is *genuine Arabic*, as Arthur Jeffrey supposed that he was correctly arguing in his standard work, *The Foreign Vocabulary of the Qur'ān*, while citing other authorities as follows (page 33):

> In xii,23, we read that Joseph's mistress says to him هيت لك. The word occurs only in this passage in the Qur'ān and is a rare expression even outside the Qur'ān, though, as has been pointed out by Barth,[10] there *can be no question* that it is *genuine Arabic*. It was so rare and unusual a word, however, that it was early taken by the exegetes as foreign[11] and explained as Coptic,[12] doubtless on the ground that the Egyptian lady would have spoken to her slave in the Egyptian tongue, and as the only Egyptian language known to the Muslim philologers was Coptic, this rare word was taken to be of Coptic origin.

Now if this originally *interjectional* Aramaic particle הין /*hayn* > *hēn* > *hē* has, in the aforementioned Qur'ānic expression, the meaning of an *exclamation*, as is customary in modern colloquial Arabic (like the English *hey!*), then the *tertiary* form, reduced to the mere letter ه / *h* in the sentence from Surah 3:119 cited above, has the same conditional meaning as the conjunction إن / *'in* (in reality in spoken Arabic the pronunciation is *'ən* = if,), which is considered *Arabic*. For this word, too, is the result of a four-step shift in pronunciation, starting from the Old-Aramaic הין /*hayn* and proceeding as follows: 1. הין / *hayn* > 2. *hēn* > 3. Syro-Aramaic ܐܢ / *'ēn* > 4. (by vowel reduction) New East Aramaic = Arabic إن /*'ən* (> *classical* Arabic: *'in*).

In order to be able to analyze syntactically the sentence from Surah 3:119 under consideration, we must understand the individual elements in Syro-Aramaic fashion thus:

1. The proclitic ه / *h* in the Qur'ānic spelling هانتم should not be read as the Arabic demonstrative/indicative particle *hā* (there), but rather as the Aramaic conditional particle *hē* (< *hēn* / if).
2. The demonstrative pronoun اولا should not be read in "*classical Arabic*" fashion as *'ulā'i*, but rather in Aramaic fashion (as in many Arabic dialects in the Near East) as *'ōlē* (< Syro-Aramaic ܗܠܝܢ /*hālēn* > West Syriac *hōlēn* > Syro-Arabic *hōlē* >*'ōlē*). This demonstrative pronoun refers not to the subject انتم / *antum* (you / plural), as the above-cited translators misread it, but rather to the object, which appears as a personal suffix in the 3rd person plural at the end of the verb تحبونهم / *tu-ḥibbūna-hum* and is to be understood reflexively (literally: "If you-(plural) these [you / plural] love them" = "If you [plural] love these [people]").

3. If the meaning of the particle هـ / *hē*, as explained above, makes clear that it introduces a *conditional clause*, then consequently it becomes clear that the conjunction *wa* (before ولا / *wa-lā*), in the following clause is not to be understood as "and" but rather as an introducing particle of the apodosis—as this function is often demonstrated in the Qur'ān.
4. The second conjunction و / *wa*, which introduces the third clause, has in this context an *adversative* or a *concessive* meaning (whereas, while, whereby however, although).

According to this philological examination, the verse excerpt from Surah 3:119 should be read and understood in Syro-Aramaic (and Arabic) fashion as follows:

هانتم اولا تحبونهم ولا يحبونكم وتومنون بالكتب كله

[*hē antum hōlē tu-ḥibbūna-hum, wa-lā yu-ḥibbūna-kum – wa-tūminūn(a) bi-l-kitāb(i) kullih(i)]*
If you (now) love these (people), they, on the other hand (on the contrary), do not love you—even though you believe in the whole Scripture!

A comparable sentence structure is imaginable only in Syro-Aramaic (as well as in modern Arabic dialects of the Near East). In terms of classical Arabic, however, such a syntactical construction is *bewildering*, as the translations of the seasoned Arabists cited above demonstrate.

The same sentence construction occurs in three other passages of the Qur'ān (Surah 3:66; 4:109; 47:38), all of which are categorized as the so-called Surahs of the Medinan period. These, too, should be discussed briefly. In order to understand Surah 3:66 we should take into consideration the preceding and following verses (65 and 67) as follows:

ياهل الكتب لم تحاجون في ابرهيم وما انزلت التورية (= اليورية) والانجيل الا من بعده افلا تعقلون / هانتم هولا حججتم فيما لكم به علم فلم تحاجون فيما ليس لكم به علم والله يعلم وانتم لا تعلمون / ما كان ابرهيم يهوديا ولا نصرانيا ولكن كان حنيفا مسلما وما كان من المشركين

The three Qur'ān translators that we have consulted render these three verses as follows:

Paret (p. 49 [translated from German]):

65 (58): You People of the Book! Why do you dispute about Abraham, whereas the Torah and the Gospel were not sent down until after him? Have you then no understanding? 66 (59): You have disputed there about something concerning which you (per se) have knowledge. Why do you dispute now about something concerning which you have no knowledge? God knows all about it, but you don't. 67 (60): Abraham was neither a Jew nor a Christian. He was instead a devoted (*i.e.*, to God) Hanīf *(ḥanifan*

musliman), and not a pagan. [Note 60: Literally: and he was not one of those who associate (other gods with the one God).] (Ihr Leute der Schrift! Warum streitet ihr über Abraham, wo doch die Thora und das Evangelium erst nach ihm herabgesandt worden sind? Habt ihr denn keinen Verstand? 66 (59): Ihr habt da über etwas gestritten, worüber ihr (an sich) Wissen habt. Warum streitet ihr nun über etwas , worüber ihr kein Wissen habt? Gott weiß Bescheid, ihr aber nicht. 67 (60): Abraham war weder Jude noch Christ. Er war vielmehr ein (Gott) ergebener Ḥanīf *(ḥanifan musliman)*, und kein Heide [Anm. 60: W: und er war keiner von denen, die (den einen Gott andere Götter) beigesellen.])

Blachère (p. 84 [translated from French]):

58/65 O Holders of the Book, why do you argue about Abraham, when the Torah and the Gospel were not brought down until after him? Well, what! Will you not reason [be reasonable]?

59/66 Here is what you are: you argue about things concerning which you have knowledge. Why do you argue [also] about things concerning which you have no knowledge? Allah knows, whereas you do not know.

60/67 Abraham was neither a Jew nor a Christian, but was *hanîf* and subject (*muslim*) [to Allah]; by no means was he among the Associators.

(O Détenteurs de l'Écriture !, pourquoi argumentez-vous au sujet d'Abraham, alors qu'on n'a fait descendre la Thora et l'Évangile qu'après lui ? Eh quoi ! ne raisonnerez-vous pas ?

59/66 Voici ce que vous êtes : vous argumentez sur ce dont vous avez connaissance. Pourquoi argumentez-vous [*aussi*] sur ce dont vous n'avez pas connaissance ?—Allah sait, alors que, vous, vous ne savez pas.

60/67 Abraham ne fut ni juif ni chrétien, mais fut *hanîf* et soumis (*muslim*) [*à Allah*] ; il ne fut point parmi les Associateurs.)

Bell (vol. I, p. 51):

58 O People of the Book, why do ye dispute about Abraham, seeing that the Torah and the Evangel were not sent down till after his time? Have ye no sense?

59. There ye are! Ye have disputed about a thing of which ye have (revealed) knowledge; why then will ye dispute about things of which ye have no knowledge? Allah knoweth, but ye do not know.

60. Abraham was not a Jew, nor was he a Christian, but he was a Ḥanīf, a Moslem, and he was not one of the Polytheists.

Lexical and grammatical explication:

At verse 65:

1. As for the conjecture of the traditional reading تورية (because of incorrect pointing: *Tawrāt*—to be read: يورية / *Yōrayya* /

Yawriyya), see the discussion in *Die syro-aramäische Lesart des Koran*, 1st ed., 68 ff.; 2nd ed., 99 ff.; 3rd ed., 101 ff.; English edition, 85 ff.

2. The Qur'ānic spelling افلا is composed of the Syro-Aramaic conjunction ܐܦ / *āp̄* (=*āf*) (then, consequently) and the negative particle لا / *lā* which is the same in Syro-Aramaic and Arabic, so that the compound should be read افلا / *āf-lā*, and not (in Arabic fashion) as *'a-fa-lā*.

On verse 66:

The Arabic conjunction *fa* (in فلم / *fa-li-mā*), which introduces the apodosis makes clear that the *h* at the beginning again introduces the conditional sentence: هانتم هولا (to be read as: *hē antum hōlē*).

On verse 67:

1. For the meaning of *Ḥanīf* see the discussion in *Die syro-aramäische Lesart des Koran*, 1st ed., 39 f.; 2nd ed., 65 f.; 3rd ed., 65 ff.; English edition, 55 f.; on the formal difference between the Qur'ānic *ḥanīf* and the Syro-Aramaic *ḥanpā*, see *ibid.* [3rd German edition], 102, note 134; see also *Zur Morphologie von syro-aramäisch* (*sāṭānā* = Satan) and Qur'ānic-Arabic شيطن (*šayṭān*) in Christoph Burgmer, ed., *Streit um den Koran*, 77.
2. In order to interpret the adjective مسلم (until now read: *muslim*) with reference to Abraham, who was actually a *heathen* to begin with and yet not a *polytheist* or *idolater*, the usual interpretation "devoted (to God)" or even "a Muslim" must be revised. For if *ḥanīf* is a loan-word from Aramaic, then this suggests that the descriptive adjective should likewise be understood in *Aramaic* fashion. Morphologically مسلم / *mslm* corresponds to the Syro-Aramaic ܡܫܠܡܐ / *mšlm* = *m-šalləmā*. The corresponding Arabic feminine form مسلمة / *mu-sallama* occurs in Surah 2:71 and refers to the cow that Moses required from the Israelites as a sacrifice. In response to the question, what sort of cow it should be, Moses answers finally that it should be مسلمة / *mu-sallama* = "intact, uninjured" and لا شية = لا شبه فيها / *lā šubha fīhā* [not as according to the canonical reading: *lā šiyata fīhā*], "without blemish, spotless" (concerning the latter conjecture, see the above-mentioned English edition, 232 f.). The reading *mu-sallama* is interpreted correctly in that passage and thus corresponds morphologically and semantically to the Syro-Aramaic participial form ܡܫܠܡܐ/ *m-šalləmā* (sound, intact). Of course there is no comparison between the cow and Abraham, but the term referring to the physical *soundness* of the cow refers in the case of Abraham to *moral integrity*. Just as in the case of the cow the word was not interpreted as *muslima* ("devoted" to God or even "a Muslim woman"), but correctly as

musallama (intact), so too the corresponding masculine form, referring to Abraham, should be read *musallam* (upright, honest), and not *muslim*.

This discussion results in the following and partially new understanding of Surah 3:65-67:

> 65. You People of the Book, why do you dispute about Abraham, since the Torah and the Gospel were not sent down until after him—can't you think, then?
> 66. If you (now) argue with these (people) about something concerning which you have knowledge, how could you argue about something (literally: how is it that you argue about something) about which you have no knowledge? For God knows, but you don't.
> 67. Abraham was neither a Jew nor a Christian. He was, rather, an *upright* ("integral," honest) *heathen*, and yet was not an idolater (literally: and he did not belong = but nevertheless did not belong to the idolaters)."

A third example of a conditional clause introduced by the Aramaic conjunction هـ / *hē* (if) occurs in Surah 4:109, where we read:

هانتم هولا جدلتم عنهم في الحيوة الدنيا فمن يجدل الله عنهم يوم القيمة

(*hē antum hōlē ğādaltum 'anhum fī l-haywa d-danyā* [the traditional reading is: al-ḥayāt ad- dunyā], *fa-man yuğādil 'anhum yawm al-qiyāma*)

This sentence, too, is understood syntactically by our Qur'ān translators as follows:

Paret (78):

109: You there have argued in the life of this world in their defense. But on the day of resurrection, who will argue with God in their defense...?" (Ihr habt da im diesseitigen Leben zu ihrer Verteidigung gestritten. Aber wer wird am Tag der Auferstehung mit Gott zu ihrer Verteidigung streiten...?)

Blachère (122):

109. Here is what you are: you argue in favor of [these traitors] in this life. Who, then, will argue in their favor on the Day of Resurrection?" (Voici ce que vous êtes : vous discutez en faveur de [ces traîtres] en la Vie immédiate. Qui donc discutera en leur faveur, au Jour de la Résurrection)

Bell (I, 83):

109. There ye are! Ye have disputed in defence of them in this life, but who will dispute with Allah in their defence on the day of resurrection, ...?"

Philological notes:

1. هانتم هولا should again be read as <u>*hē*</u> *antum* <u>*hōlē*</u>. Here too the demonstrative pronoun هولا / *hōlē* (these) refers not to the subject انتم / *antum* (you pl.), but rather to عنهم / *'anhum*, specifically to "<u>those whom</u> you defend." Translated into *classical* Arabic, it would have to read: إن أنتم جادلتم عن هؤلاء / *'in 'antum ğādaltum ʿan hā'ulā'i* instead of هؤلاء جادلتم عنهم / *hā'ulā'i ğādaltum ʿanhum.*
2. The fact that this, too, is a conditional *clause* is shown not only by the verb جدلتم / *ğādaltum*, which in keeping with the laws of Arabic grammar is formally in the perfect tense, although it is to be understood in the present, but also by the conjunction *fa* (in فمن / *faman*), which according to those same rules introduces the second clause (apodosis) of such a conditional sentence.
3. In the intermediate/middle-position و / *w* of the Qur'ānic spelling of حيوة the Arabic readers of the Qur'ān saw an indication (albeit an unusual one) of the long vowel *ā*, although the Arabic letter ا / *alif* is otherwise available to stand for that. It is astonishing, though, that the Arabic readers in this case (as also with صلوة / *ṣalwa* [prayer], زكوة / *zakwa* [alms, donation], منوة / *Manwa* [the goddess *Manāt*], ربوا < Syro-Aramaic ܪܒܘ / *rebbō* > *rebbū* [usurious interest]) took the current *colloquial speech* as their basis, but not in the case of ܗܠܝ / *hōlē*, for which they devised a supposedly *classical* expression *hā'ulā'i*, which however cannot be authenticated anywhere in the Arabic-speaking world.

In Syro-Aramaic, meanwhile, the *status absolutus* (*i.e.*, what Arabic grammar calls the *pausal form*) of ܚܝܘܬܐ / *ḥayūṯā* (life) is ܚܝܘ / *ḥayū*, from ܚܝܘܐ / *ḥaywā*. The latter form is derived from the pausal form in Imperial Aramaic; it has been preserved in Arabic in words like فتوى / *fatwā* (expert religious opinion), نجوى / *nağwā* (dialogue), بلوى / *balwā* (difficult trial), etc. Parallel to this in Arabic, secondary forms such as فتى / *fatā* (young man, youth) and فتاة / *fatāt* (young woman), نجاة / *nağāt* (rescue), بلاء / *balā'* (with the same meaning as بلوى / *balwā* with an invented final *hamza*), etc. arose through vowel reduction, especially with a rising [*steigendem*] diphthong (*wa, ya*). This explains the fact that in each case the secondary *vulgar Arabic* pronunciation *ḥayāt, ṣalāt, zakāt, Manāt, ribā* was transposed onto the aforementioned Qur'ānic-Aramaic spellings. The little or dagger *alif* ا / *ā* added by the later Arabic redactors of the Qur'ān after the و / *w* in each of these words, which misled generations of renowned Arabists and Qur'ān scholars in East and West, is therefore etymologically *wrong*. The hypothesis that in other written traditions, for instance the South Arabian, the *w/u* was used for a long *ā*, cannot be examined here. In any case this hypothesis has nothing to do with the Qur'ānic-

Aramaic written tradition. Instead, the Qur'ānic spellings just discussed are confirmed by their Aramaic etymology.[13]

4. Following the word الحيوة / *al-ḥaywa* is the descriptive adjective الدنيا / *dunyā* (literally: the "nearby" = the life "of this world," "this" life); here again we are dealing morphologically (and etymologically) with a Syro-Aramaic spelling. The traditional reading *dunyā*, with its secondary middle vowel *u*, approximately renders the centralized dialect pronunciation of the originally Aramaic *a* (from ܕܢܝܐ / *danyā*), which is uttered in dialect as the neutral vowel *ə* (*dənyā* /*dənyē*). Pronounced in this way, this participial noun in modern Arabic means the "world," "this life" [as opposed to the "hereafter"]. This *Arabic* form is actually a Syro-Aramaic passive participle, as is shown by its derivation from the corresponding Syro-Aramaic paradigm in [*i.e.*, exhibiting the forms] *p'el* (< *pə'el*) (masculine) and *pa'lā* (feminine), corresponding to the Syro-Aramaic ܕܢܝܐ / *danyā* = Qur'ānic Arabic دنيا / *danyā* (not *dunyā*) (compare the Arabic دني / *danīy*, feminine دنية / *danīya* [near, low]). By the spelling with a final ا / *alif* the Qur'ān renders the Syro-Aramaic feminine ending of the predicative participle, as we find in the feminine form فعلا / *fa'lā* of the Arabic *elative,* with a terminal *alif*, not a *tā marbūṭa* (as in the designations for colors, such as صفرا / *ṣafrā* [yellow], حمرا / *ḥamrā* [red], etc.). The so-called Arabic *elative* is in reality a secondary formation from the Syro-Aramaic *status absolutus* shows; this is demonstrated by, among other things, this feminine ending in ا / *alif* (besides the variant in ى / *ā*), to which, however, a supposedly *classical* final *hamza* was added arbitrarily by the Arab grammarians, so that they would after all be able to inflect (albeit *diptotically*, by means of diphthongs) this ending, which in Aramaic cannot be inflected (like the Arabic دنيا / *danyā* / *dunyā*). How they arrived at the formation of the masculine form, however, with the *prosthetic alif* ending in أفعل / *af'al*, we can determine phonologically from the dropping of the vowel of the first radical of the masculine form of the Syro-Aramaic participle **pa'al* as follows: **pa'al* < *pə'al* < *p'al* < (and then to resolve the resulting initial double-consonant, the addition of the Arabo-Aramaic *alif prostheticum*) = Arabic أفعل / *af'al*. The key to explaining the *classical Arabic elative* is thus provided to us precisely by the predicative feminine form ending with فعلا / *fa'lā* (< **pa'alā* / *fa'alā*) which is faithfully preserved in Arabic from the Syro-Aramaic; this feminine form needs no *alif prosthe-*

ticum because it preserves the first vowel and thus there is no double consonant.

After this philological excursus, the hitherto unnoticed *conditional sentence* from Surah 4:109 that we have just discussed should be read as follows:

> If you (now) argue about these (people) in this life, who will argue with God about them on the day of resurrection?

A similar sentence structure can be found, finally, in Surah 47:38, which reads:

هانتم هولا تدعون لتنفقوا في سبيل الله فمنكم من يبخل ومن يبخل فانما يبخل

عن نفسه والله الغني وانتم الفقرا

The translations that we have consulted render this sentence syntactically as follows:

Paret (426):

38 (40): You there are called for God's sake [note 27: Literally, on the way of God] to give alms. Now among you there are those who are avaricious. But anyone who is avaricious is so to his own detriment. God is the one who is rich [note 28: Or: dependent (*ġanī*) on no one]. You, though, are the poor ones. (Ihr werdet da aufgerufen, um Gottes willen [Anm. 27: W: auf dem Weg Gottes] Spenden zu geben. Nun gibt es unter euch welche, die geizig sind. Wer aber geizig ist, ist es zu seinem eigenen Nachteil. Gott ist derjenige, der reich [Anm. 28: Oder: auf niemand angewiesen *(ġanī)*] ist. Ihr aber seid die Armen.)

Blachère (541):

40/38 Here is what you are. You are called to make expenditures along the way of Allah, [but] among you there are some who prove to be avaricious. Now someone who proves to be avaricious only proves to be avaricious at his own expense, [for] Allah is the Self-Sufficient whereas you are the Needy. (Voici ce que vous êtes. Vous êtes appelés à faire dépense dans le chemin d'Allah, [*mais*] parmi vous, il en est qui se montrent avares. Or celui qui se montre avare ne se montre avare qu'à ses dépens, [*car*] Allah est le Suffisant à Soi-même alors que vous, vous êtes les Besogneux.)

Bell (II, 518):

40 There ye are! Ye are called to contribute freely in the cause of Allah, and some of you are niggardly; but any who are niggardly, are only niggardly to themselves; Allah is the Rich, and ye are the poor...."

Grammatical and lexical notes:

In terms of its content, this sentence is relatively easy to understand. Lexically the frequently occurring Qur'ānic expression في سبيل الله / *fī sabīl Allāh* (literally: on the way of God) reproduces the Syro-Aramaic idiomatic expression: ܒܐܘܪܚܐ ܕܐܠܗܐ / *b-urḥā d-Allāhā* (on the way of God), which the *Thesaurus syriacus* (I, 375) explains as follows under subheading 3) [*consuetudo, agendi ratio, institutum*]: "*in via Dei*, hoc est, in eo agendi modo qui Deo placet [in a manner pleasing to God]."

Syntactically the above-cited translators were unable, from an Arabic perspective, to recognize a *conditional sentence*, the initial clause of which, as in the three preceding examples, is introduced by the Aramaic conjunction هـ / *hē*, while its second clause (apodosis) begins with the Arabic conjunction *fa* (before فمنكم / *fa-minkum*). After هانتم / *hē antum* (If you) comes the Arabo-Aramaic demonstrative pronoun هولا / *hōlē* (these); in this context, in contrast to the three preceding parallel passages, the pronoun has a correlative function in the sense of "those who" and thus refers to the subject انتم / *antum* (you, plural). This is conceivable, however, only if one has in mind the corresponding Syro-Aramaic usage of this determinative (demonstrative) pronoun as Theodor Nöldeke explains it in his previously cited *Syrische Grammatik* [Syriac grammar] under the heading *"Das Relativpronomen"* (p. 175), §236, as follows:

> A. Very commonly, however, a correlative appears with no preceding noun. So it is with demonstratives (*e.g.*) ܗܠܝܢ ܕ/ *hālēn d-* (West Syriac *hōlēn* < *hōlē* / these = the ones).

According to this, the introductory Qur'ānic words هانتم هولا (*hē antum hōlē*), translated into Arabic, should be read إن أنتم الذين (*'in antum al-laḏīna*) = إن أنتم هم الذين (*'in antum hum al-laḏīna*) (if you are those who). That results in the following reading for the above-cited sentence from Surah 47:38:

> If you (now) [are] those [who] are called upon to donate to a cause that is pleasing to God, then there are among you some who are stingy; but anyone who is stingy is stingy with himself; for God is (in Himself) rich, but you are (ultimately) the poor ones.

5. Concerning the traditional reading ببدر / *bi-badr* (Surah 3:123)

Although the passages examined above mention differences with the People of the Book and also animosities toward unspecified hypocrites and envious individuals, it cannot be gathered from them that there were any sorts of conflicts, much less hostilities, with the godless or pagan inhabitants of Mecca, to which the following verses supposedly refer according to the biography of the Prophet and the Qur'ānic commentators. The philological analysis of the following sequence—Surah 3, verses 121 to 126—will attempt to explain their connection contextually. For purposes of comparison with the reading commonly accepted until now, the translations by Rudi Paret, Régis Blachère, and Richard Bell will be cited first after each verse from the Qur'ān. Then comes the philological discussion of the underlined passages (if any) and the suggested new translation. Surah 3:121–126:

واذ عدوت من اهلك تبوي المومنين مقعد للقتال والله سميع عليم

Paret (55):
3, 121: And (then) in the early morning when you went away from your family so as to direct the believers to their positions for battle (against the unbelieving Meccans)! God hears and knows (everything). (Und (damals) als du in der Frühe von deiner Familie weggingst, um die Gläubigen in die Stellungen zum Kampf (gegen die ungläubigen Mekkaner) einzuweisen! Gott hört und weiß (alles).)

Lexical notes:

1. The Qur'ānic *rasm* عدوت originally had no point over the ع / *'ayn* and was therefore supposed to be read *'adawta* (to run, hurry on foot), and not *ġadawta* (to do something in the morning). The *Lisān* (XV, 32a) suggests this reading when it comments on العديّ / *al-'adī*: جماعة القوم يعدون لقتال ونحوه (a military unit hurrying to a battle or the like) من يحمل من الرّجّالة ، وذلك لأنهم يسرعون العدو (it also means: the first infantry soldiers to attack, because in doing so they run swiftly). The fact that the Prophet set out *on foot* is confirmed by Ṭabarī (IV, 69) also. The commentators, however, do not agree about the battle that is referred to in this verse. Ṭabarī ends up favoring the majority opinion that it was a question of *Uḥud* rather than of *al-Aḥzāb*.
2. Ṭabarī (IV, 71) explains التبوئة / *at-tabwi'a* to mean اتخاذ الموضع (take up a position). As an alternative to تبوي / *tubawwi'* the alternative reading تثوي / *taṯwī* is suggested, from the Syro-Aramaic ܬܘܐ / *twā* according to Mannā (830b) (3): حثّ . رغّب (spur on, incite). This reading would have its parallels in Surah 8:65, which reads:

يايها النبي حرض المومنين على القتال

(O Prophet, spur the believers on to battle!)

3. The believers in the same verse are supposed to be صبرون / *ṣābirūn* (steadfast), a synonym for the *rasm* مقعد / *maq'ad*, which should be read as an infinitive; this should give us the meaning of the lexically equivalent Syro-Aramaic infinitive ܡܬܒ/ *meṯaḇ*, for which Mannā (319a, at [4]) indicates in Arabic ثبت . استقرّ (to be steadfast, constant), whereby the believers are admonished to *constancy*.

Hence for this verse the following translation is recommended:

3,121: Since you were now setting out and leaving your relatives, in order to incite the believers to constancy—whereby God hears (their prayers) and knows (everything)"

اذ همت طايفتان منكم ان تفشلا والله وليهما وعلى الله فليتوكل المومنون

Paret 122:
And (then) when two groups of you would have preferred to give up (lacking the courage to put up any resistance or to fight on) [Note 109a: Literally: when two groups of you had it in mind … to give up], even though God was your friend. [Note 110: Or: is]. The believers should (always) trust in God." (Und (damals) als zwei Gruppen von euch am liebsten (mutlos jeden Widerstand und weiteren Kampf) aufgegeben hätten [Anm. 109a: W: als zwei Gruppen von euch im Sinn hatten ... aufzugeben], wo doch Gott ihr Freund war [Anm. 110: Oder: ist]. Auf Gott sollen die Gläubigen (immer) vertrauen.)

Lexical notes:
1. Actually the verb هم / *hamma* is fittingly translated here with the definition noted by H. Wehr *et al.*: "to be worried, concerned," which is still current in modern Arabic.
2. Although ولي / *walī* is used in the Qur'ān in the sense of "friend" also, the meaning "helper" not only follows from this context but is also confirmed by other passages in the Qur'ān, where ولي / *walī* and نصير / *naṣīr* (helper) are used side by side as synonyms. In this respect ولي / *walī* came about as a loan-word based on the Syro-Aramaic ܥܝܠܐ / *ʿīyālā*, for which Mannā (16b) lists the Arabic equivalents معين / *muʿīn*, مساعد /*musāʿid*, نصير /*naṣīr* (helper).

This results in the following reading for verse 122:

whereas two groups of you were worried about failing, even though God was at your side (as your helper)—indeed, the believers should trust in God…

اذ همت طايفتان منكم ان تفشلا والله وليهما وعلى الله فليتوكل المومنون

Paret 123:
God helped you nevertheless (in due course) in Badr to attain victory, while you (for your part) were a modest, insignificant band. Therefore fear God! Perhaps you will be grateful. (Gott hat euch doch (seinerzeit) in Badr zum Sieg verholfen, während ihr (eurerseits) ein bescheidener, unscheinbarer Haufe waret. Darum fürchtet Gott ! Vielleicht werdet ihr dankbar sein.)

Philological analysis:

1. In this context the Arabic word نصر / *naṣara* does not mean "help to win the victory" (since there can be no question here of a "battle of Badr"), but rather "help, stand by."

2. Beneath the rasm ببدر, the second point (or dot) from the right, which led to the misreading Badr, is placed incorrectly. The original reading (copied below from the facsimile of the *ḥiǧāzī* codex of the Qur'ān BNF 328a, folio 5b, line 16, second word from the right) looks like this:

Separately:  the first two letters: 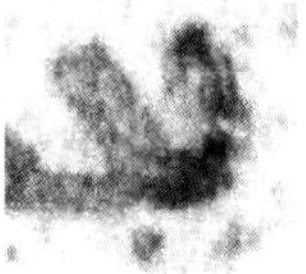

The *rasm* shows clearly that the two prong-shaped peaks are not the same. Whereas the first prong is vertical, the pen stroke of the second leans to the left. That proves that this written character—as in the case of the word in the earlier illustration اقـܥ دوا = (in Arabic) اقعدوا / *iq'adū* (cast yourselves down) from the *kūfī* Qur'ān codex of Samarqand—is a Syriac ܥ / *'ayn*. Since the two points beneath the written character are obviously later additions, we need only imagine the second point gone, which results in the reading: (Syriac) ܥ = (Arabic) بعذر / *bi-'iḏr*.

3. The meaning of the Syro-Aramaic word ܥܕܪܐ / *'eḏrā*. For this word the *Thesaurus syriacus* (II, 2814) gives the following definition: *"auxilium, adjumentum"* (help, aid, support; auxiliary troop, armed forces); Ap. lexx. (according to the East Syrian lexicographer, Bar Ali, in Arabic): معونة /*ma'ūna*, عون /*'awn*, نصرة /*naṣra*. The fact that the alleged "Badr" is in reality an "auxiliary troop" (from heaven) made up of "three thousand angels" will be demonstrated in the next verse.

   Nor is it any accident that Ṭabarī (IV, 74 f.) mentions the contradictory opinions of the Qur'ānic commentators as to the real origin of the name "Badr." In this regard he lists three opinions: a) *Badr* is the name of a man, after whom the *well* in question was named; b) others contradict this, saying that it is instead the name of the whole region, just as other lands are called by their respective names; c) *Badr*, finally, was a *well* to the right of the road from Mecca to Medina.

4. Ṭabarī (IV, 75) correctly understands the adjective اذلة / *aḏilla* (plural of ذليل /*ḏalīl* < Syro-Aramaic ܕܠܝܠܐ / *dlīlā*) to mean "few, small in number."

This philological discussion and the conjecture about the canonical misreading بـبـدر / *bi-badr* > بـعـذر / *bi-ʿidr* results in the following new interpretation of Surah 3:123:

(123) then God supported you with a (heavenly) help (= auxiliary troop)—so fear God, so that you might be grateful (to him)!

اذ تقول للمومنين الن يكفيكم ان يمددكم ربكم بثلثة الف من المليكه منزلين

Paret 124:
(Then) when you said to the believers, "Will it not be enough for you (then) that your Lord supports you with three thousand angels (that are) sent down (for that purpose from heaven)?" (Damals) als du zu den Gläubigen sagtest: "Wird es euch (denn) nicht genügen, daß euer Herr euch mit dreitausend Engeln unterstützt, (die dazu vom Himmel) herabgesandt (werden)?")

Philological and syntactical note[s]:

1. The Cairo Edition of the Qur'ān reads the particle introducing the direct discourse as a negative interrogative particle / *'a-lan* (< Aramaic interrogative particle *hā* > *'a* + negation *lā* > proclitic *la-* + demonstrative particle *hayn* > *hān* > *ān* > enclitic *an* = *'a-l-an* / *'alan*), which refers to the future. The same defective spelling, pronounced *al-'ān* (consisting of two Aramaic demonstrative particles: *hal* > *'al* + *hayn* > *hān* > *'ān* = *al-'ān*), means "now" and occurs seven times in the Qur'ān (once in plene writing الآن). In this context, however, the defective spelling should be read as الن = *al-'ān* (now). (The future الن / *'a-lan* occurs in two other places in the Qur'ān.)
2. The final clause of the sentence makes it clear that the misreading *"badr"* is in fact a *heavenly legion* consisting of three thousand angels, sent as reinforcement seeing that they were a small number (*aḏilla*).

Hence this verse should be understood as follows:

(124) when you said to the believers, "now it is enough for you that your Lord is supporting you with three thousand angels sent down (from heaven)."

بلى ان تصبروا وتتقوا وياتوكم من فورهم

هذا يمددكم ربكم بخمسة الف من المليكه مسومين

Paret 125:
Yes! If you are patient and God-fearing, and (if) they [Note 112: *i.e.*, the enemies] now immediately(?) [Note 113: Or: in a compact attack(?)] come

against [Note 114: Literally: to] you, your Lord supports you (even) with five thousand angels, which hurry onward(?) (in an attack against the enemy) [Note 115: Literally: which make (their horses) hurry onward(?) (against the foe), or: which are equipped with emblems (? *musauwimīna*). The meaning of the expression is uncertain.] (Ja! Wenn ihr geduldig und gottesfürchtig seid, und (wenn) sie [Anm. 112: D.h. die Feinde] jetzt sofort(?) [Anm. 113: Oder: in geschlossenem Angriff(?)] gegen [Anm. 114: W: zu] euch (daher)kommen, unterstützt euch euer Herr (sogar) mit fünf tausend Engeln, die (im Sturm gegen den Feind) vorpreschen(?) [Anm. 115: W: die (ihre Pferde gegen den Feind) vorpreschen lassen(?), oder: die mit Kennzeichen versehen sind (? *musauwimīna*). Die Deutung des Ausdrucks ist unsicher.])

Philological notes:

1. The Qur'ānic particle بلى / *balā* / *balē*, a contraction composed of the Aramaic particles *bal* + *hayn*, like the Syro-Aramaic particle ܐܝܢ / *'ēn*, has two functions: a) as an affirmative particle, "yes, indeed," b) as an adversative conjunction "however, but;" the latter function seems to have been overlooked in Arabic studies and Qur'ānic research to date.
2. To this day the expression من فورهم / *min fawrihim* has not been explained. Yet the verbal root *fwr* / *fār*, which is common to Arabic and Syro-Aramaic, is rather well known, not only in its basic meaning (to overcook, to bubble up or gush forth), but also in its extended meaning (to lose one's temper, to be angry). Thus Mannā (580b) defines the Syro-Aramaic ܦܪ *pār* / *fār* in Arabic (2) as إغتاظ . غضب (to be angry). Since the Qur'ān speaks in Surah 3:118-119 about the "fury" of the opponents against the believers, the relevance is clear. The sense therefore is:
   "If these opponents من فورهم / *min fawrihim* 'out of their fury = driven by their fury = infuriated' should turn against the believers, then...."
3. Following من فورهم / *min fawrihim* comes the even more puzzling هذا / *hāḏā*, which was taken for an Arabic *demonstrative pronoun* that logically had to refer to a very particular *fury*. Yet aside from the fact that هذا / *hāḏā*, too, is a secondary loan-word from Aramaic, in this passage it is nevertheless not a demonstrative but rather an *adverb* (albeit an unusual one); its reduction parallels that of the Syro-Aramaic ܗܝܕܝܢ / *hāy-dēn* (from **hayn-d-hayn*) as follows: Old Aramaic **hayn-d-hayn* > *hāy-d-hān* > *hā-d-hā* > *hā-ḏā* = هذا / *hāḏā*, which in this context has the same meaning as the Qur'ānic-Arabic حينئذ / *ḥīna'iḏen* (thereupon).
4. Finally, it is less problematic to explain the equally puzzling participle مسومين / *musawwimīn* referring to the five thousand angels—a term which causes Qur'ān translators unnecessary headaches. For we simply need to look up in Mannā (775b f.) the Syro-Aramaic verbal root ܫܡ / *šām*, in order to find the corresponding participial form ܡܫܝܡܢܐ /*m-šīmānā*, which indicates for us the Arabic meaning of the Qur'ānic expression as

follows: شائم . متعس . مؤذ . مؤلم الخ . (disastrous, causing pain or damage, etc.).

This philological discussion results in the following reading for Surah 3:125:

(125) But if you are steadfast and God-fearing and they (the unbelievers), infuriated (literally: out of their fury), should importune you, then your Lord will support you with five thousand powerful (literally: tormenting) angels.

Verse 126, finally, summarizes and repeatedly confirms that all help comes from God:

وما جعله الله الا بشرى لكم ولتطمين قلوبكم به

وما النصر الا من عند الله العزيز الحكيم

Paret 126:
God made it [Note 116: *i.e.*, the declaration that he will support you in this way] for this purpose only: to let you have a good tiding, so that you should feel quite secure [Note 117: Literally: so that your heart might be calmed thereby]. The victory comes from God alone, the Mighty and Wise. (Gott machte es [Anm. 116: D.h. die Ankündigung, euch auf diese Weise zu unterstützen] nur zu dem Zweck, euch eine frohe Botschaft zukommen zu lassen, und dass ihr euch ganz sicher fühlen solltet [Anm. 117: W: damit euer Herz sich dadurch beruhige]. Der Sieg kommt von Gott allein, dem Mächtigen und Weisen.)

Verse 126 presents no particular difficulty apart from the word victory, which in Arabic also means "aid, support," which is more appropriate in this context. Thus the passage about "Badr" concludes:

God intended it only as a good tiding for you, so as to calm your hearts thereby, for help (comes) from God alone, the Mighty, the Wise.

6. Comments on individual written characters of the *ḥiǧāzī*- and *kūfī* script

The Syriac letter ܥ. / *'ayn*, detected in the Qur'ān codex of Samarqand, is imitated in the *kūfī* and *ḥiǧāzī*- script, inasmuch as the corresponding letter consists of an additional *counterstroke* leaning to the right, which gives this written character approximately the appearance of a (spread-out) Latin "v." See also in the illustration above, line 4, the third written character (reading from right to left) in the *rasm* مىعك / *(mā) mana'aka* (what prevented you). Later in cursive script the two prongs were connected in a triangle, because that made it possible to write the character in one stroke. So developed the current but greatly simplified form of the medial Arabic ـعـ / *ʿayn*, in which the original form is scarcely recognizable. The similarly-shaped final ع / *ʿayn* concludes with a bow-shaped, elongating line extending downward, which was retained in modern Arabic script.

In the case of initial عـ / *ʿayn* the *ḥiǧāzī*- and *kūfī*- scripts show their dependence on the Syriac ܥ. / *ʿayn* in that the starting stroke of the ܥ. was rounded off to about a quarter circle, so as to avoid confusion with the very similar-looking initial حـ (*ǧ* / *ḥ* / *ḫ*). See also in Illustration 0342 of the Samarqand Manuscript, verses 7 and 8, the way the initial عـ / *ʿayn* is written in the preposition عن / *ʿan* (from, out of, away from, etc.). Later the rounded starting stroke was further emphasized and was drawn as a half circle open toward the right (عـ / *ʿayn*), as is usual in modern Arabic. The same rasm shows a final *nūn* extending under the line, which apparently is an adaptation of the Aramaic נ / *n*, which in modern Arabic script, however, developed into a half circle ن / *n*.

This final *nūn* is remarkable, however, in that both the *ḥiǧāzī*- and the *kūfī*- scripts occasionally use the Syriac final ܢ / ܢ , which leads to a confusion with the Arabic retroflexive (retrograde) final *yā*, as was already demonstrated in the article *Relikte syro-aramäischer Buchstaben in frühen Korankodizes*[14] ["Relics of Syro-Aramaic letters in early Qur'ān codices"]. We find a further example of this sort of hitherto unrecognized Syriac final *nūn* in Surah 40:81, which according to the Cairo Edition reads:

ويريكم ايته فاي ايت الله تنكرون

Ostensibly there is no other way for an Arabist to interpret this verse than the way in which Paret translates it (395):

> And God [Note 56: Literally: he] allows you to see his signs. <u>Which one</u> of God's signs do you now wish to refuse?

The problem here is with the underlined interrogative pronoun اي / *ayya* (which, masc. fem.), which as a secondary formation is borrowed from Syro-Aramaic,[15] although there can be no doubt as to its use in Arabic.

We are indebted to the Samarqand Qur'ān, nevertheless, for having preserved for us in the written character ا‍ܢ the unaltered way of writing the Syriac final *nūn* (ܢ); in the canonical edition of the Qur'ān it was mistakenly misread and transcribed as an Arabic final *yā*, and for centuries all traces of it were blurred. This written character, in fact, corresponds to the Syro-Aramaic defective spelling of ܐܢ / *ēn* (originally ܐܝܢ / *ayn* > ܐܢ / *ēn*). Both ways of writing/spelling it occur in the Qur'ān. The particle in question was originally *interjectional*; depending on the situation it could acquire various semantic nuances, which will be examined in detail in a future study.[16] We limit ourselves for the moment to this passage in the Qur'ān, where the written

character ܐܢ should not be read in Arabic fashion as *"ayya"* but rather in Syro-Aramaic fashion as *"ēn."* In the context of the above-cited verse from the Qur'ān, *"ēn"* has the meaning of an *interrogative particle* and as such corresponds to the Arabic هل / *hal*, which for its part is a defective spelling, consisting of two Syro-Aramaic particles: the interjection ܗܐ/ *hā* and the negative particle ܠܐ / *lā* = *hā-lā* (*"hā"* not? = perhaps not?) or in reverse order: ܗܐ+ܠܐ[17] / *lā* + *hā* (surely not?).
Now the Samarqand spelling looks like this:

T

The Syriac final *nūn* (ܢ) separately:

If we read the second letter as a Syriac final *nūn*, the word should be written in Arabic (defectively) ان and pronounced in Syro-Aramaic fashion (*plene*) as *"ēn."* If we add that the traditional Qur'ānic word آية / āya, as already explained,[18] has been misread a total of 384 times in the Qur'ān (albeit without a change of meaning), then this results in the following emendation and new reading for verse 81 from Surah 40:

ويريكم اثته فان (= فهل) اثت الله تنكرون

wa-yurīkum āṯātahu[19] *fa-'ēn (= fa-hal) āṯāt(a)*[13] *Allāh(i) tu-nkirūn ?*

> and he (God) shows you his (wondrous) signs—would you then deny the (wondrous) signs of God ?

The Qur'ān moreover gives examples of the *defective* as well as the *full spelling* (*plene*) of the Syro-Aramaic interrogative particle ܐܢ / ܐܝܢ = اين / ان (*ēn*) in the following almost identical verses from Surah 7:113 and Surah 26:41:

وجا السحره فرعون قالوا ان لنا لاجرا ان كنا نحن الغلبين

فلما جا السحره قالوا لفرعون اين (أئنّ!) لنا لاجرا ان كنا نحن الغلبين

Although the question emerges clearly from the context, Paret sees in the two Syro-Aramaic interrogative particles the Arabic intensifying particle إنّ / *inna* and even أئنّ / *a-inna* (*sic!*) (both pronounced *"ēn"*) and translates:

Paret: (Q 7:113): And the magicians came to Pharaoh. They said:[20] "We will (certainly) receive a reward [won't we], if *we* are the victors?"
(Q 26:41): Now when the magicians had come, they said to Pharaoh, "We will (certainly) receive a reward, if we are the victors?"

Sure 7:113 should be understood thus:

Now the magicians came to Pharaoh (and) said (= asked): "Does a reward[21] belong to us if we are the victors?"

Syntactical notes:

1. Concerning the combination of two verbs in sequence *without a conjunction*, because they essentially amount to one main action, see Theodor Nöldeke, *Kurzgefasste syrische Grammatik*,[22] § 337.A.
2. The final ا /*ā* in اجرا /*aǧrā* / *aǧrā* does not indicate here the *Arabic accusative*, since the rule (arbitrarily) laid down by the Arab grammarians—that after an introductory إنّ / *inna* the following subject should be in the *accusative* (ending in *a* / *ā*) while the predicate should be in the *nominative* (ending in *u*), does not take effect here, since ان / *ēn* in this sentence is an interrogative particle which, as everyone knows, is *neutral with regard to inflection.* Hence with the spelling اجرا / *aǧrā* the Qur'ān faithfully reproduces the Syro-Aramaic word ܐܓܪܐ / *agrā* in the *status emphaticus.* The Arab grammarians later saw in this Syro-Aramaic spelling the indication of the Arabic *accusative* in its various aspects. This phenomenon occurs rather frequently in the Qur'ān.
3. To the word لاجرا / *la-aǧrā* is prefixed لـ / *la-*, which here has no intensifying function, as is frequently the case in the Qur'ān when it appears in combination with the intensifying particle إنّ / *inna* (< Syro-Aramaic ܐܢ / *ēn*, "yes, indeed!") or before an oath; instead it expresses an uncertainty that underlies the interrogative particle ان < ܐܢ / *ēn*, which naturally lends to it a *dubitative* nuance.

   Further examples of this sort of semantic use of ان < *ēn* (combined with a personal pronoun) and ل / *la-* are provided by the Qur'ān in Surah 12:90. When Joseph reveals his identity indirectly to his unsuspecting brothers, they ask him:

انك لانت يوسف

The Cairo Edition, which sees from the context that this is a question but is unable to recognize an interrogative particle in the spelling انك / *ēn-ka*, interpolates after the *alif* a *hamza* (invented by the Arab grammarians), whereby the *alif* becomes an (Arabic) *interrogative particle* and the following *'inna* becomes an (Arabic) *intensifying particle*, especially since the latter seems to confirm this function through the following prefixed ل / *la-*, and the edition reads:

أءنّك لانت يوسف ؟ /*a-'inna-ka la-anta Yūsuf?*

Paret (198) accordingly translates this correctly: "Are you, *then*, Joseph?" By rendering the prefixed ل / *la-* as "then," Paret may have sensed an *intensifying* nuance in the question. Here, however, this ل / *la-* is intended to emphasize precisely the *dubitative* character of the question, which means that this question should best be translated as: "Are you *perhaps* Joseph?"

We find another textbook example in Surah 79:10-11, which reads:

يقولون انا لمردودون في الحافرة / اذا كنا عظما نخره

Here, too, the Cairo Edition misses the interrogative particle in انا (Arabic: *'innā*) and once again interpolates a *hamza* after the *alif*, reading: اءنا / *a-'innā*. This, however, is superfluous, since the underlying element is not the Arabic explanatory particle إنّ / *inna* which introduces a declarative sentence, but rather the Syro-Aramaic interrogative particle *"ēn,"* and it is connected with the suffix of the first person plural نا / *-nā*, resulting in the doubling of the middle/medial *nūn*. Hence the original Qur'ānic *rasm* should be read انا / *ēn-nā* (and not: *a-'innā*). This interrogative particle is followed, as above, by the prefixed *dubitative* ل / *la-(mardūdūn)*.

In the following verse the *hamza* interpolated at the conjunction اذا / *iḏā* (when) is not only superfluous but also *wrong*, because in this temporal clause there should be no repetition of the interrogative particle. Exasperated by the Cairo reading, Paret (498) translates the two connected verses as follows:

> 10. They say, "Shall we perhaps be brought back (again to life) on the spot(?)? [Note 3: Or: Shall we perhaps be brought back to our former condition(?)? Or: Shall we (who lie?) in the earth's bosom be brought back (again to life)? The meaning of the expression *fī l-ḥāfirati* is quite uncertain.] 11. (Shall that perhaps happen) after [Note 4: Literally: when] we are (*i.e.*, have become) decaying bones?" (Sie sagen: ‚Sollen wir etwa auf der Stelle (?) (wieder ins Leben) zurückgebracht werden? [Anm. 3: Oder: Sollen wir etwa in den früheren Zustand(?) zurückgebracht werden? Oder: Sollen wir (die wir) in der Erde Schoß (liegen)(?) (wieder ins Leben) zurückgebracht werden? Die Deutung des Ausdrucks *fī l-ḥāfirati* ist ganz unsicher.] 11. (Soll das etwa geschehen) nachdem [Anm. 4: W: wenn] wir (zu) morsche(n) Knochen (geworden) sind?)

Blachère, too, cannot quite cope with the double verse and translates (635):

> 10. [The unbelievers] ask: In truth, will we be certainly sent back to earth 11 when we shall be fleshless bones? [Note 11: Instead of the variant handed down here, the Vulgate has: *'a'iḏâ* = "is it when," but this reading compels us to suppose that there is a missing sentence.] ([Les infidèles] demandent :

> « En vérité, serons-nous certes renvoyés sur la terre 11 quand nous serons ossements décharnés ? [Note 11: Au lieu de la var. reçue ici, la Vulg. porte : *ʾaʾiḏâ* « est-ce que lorsque », mais cette leçon contraint à supposer une phrase en suspens.])

Bell (II, 633) sees no particular difficulty in these two sentences, except for the real meaning of انا = *ēn-nā* with a following ل /*la*-, which he renders with "verily:"

> 10. Saying: "Are we verily bought back as we were before? [Note 4: The meaning is uncertain; but the word is usually said to mean "original state."]
> 11. When we are bones decayed?"

According to the following philological analysis, however, this verse should be interpreted thus:

> They say (= they ask), "Will we *perhaps* in the *grave* (*i.e.*, while we are lying *in the grave*) be brought back (to *new life*), *when* [23] we are *decayed* [24] bones?

Unlike Paret and Blachère, Bell gives a translation of this two-part sentence that is semantically and syntactically almost fitting. Granted, he does not enter into a discussion of the word حافرة / *ḥāfira*, which Paret considers suspect. Ṭabarī (XXX, 33 f.) offers three explanations for it: 1. *return to earth* or *to life*, 2. *grave, pit*, 3. *the fire [of hell]*. The second meaning is correct. Morphologically, too, الحافرة / *al-ḥāfira* is correctly explained to mean الأرض المحفورة التي حفرت فيها قبورهم (the earth dug up to make graves) and interpreted as a passive participle like the Arabic محفورة / *ma-ḥfūra* (dug, hollowed out). This corresponds to the Syro-Aramaic passive participle ending in *paʿlā*, as we find in the form ܣܥܛܐ / *saʿṭā* (rejected), ܣܥܛܢܐ /*saʿṭānā* (reprehensible, abominable) > ܣܛܢܐ /*sāṭānā* (the abominable, detestable one) = "Satan."[25] After this the medial *alif* in حافرة as *mater lectionis*, stands not for a long *ā*, but for a short *a* (*ḥafra* > dialect form *ḥəfra* = pit, hollow). Now if such a Syro-Aramaic form is carried over into Arabic, as a rule the emphatic *ā* ending is dropped. Through the resulting vowel shift, the Syro-Aramaic form *paʿlā* then gives rise to the Arabic forms *faʿl*, *faʿal* and *faʿil*, which the Arabic philologists (as the *Lisān* frequently attests) usually took for noun forms with adjectival meaning. One example (among many others) is the Qurʾānic word صمد / *ṣamad* (Surah 112:2), which remains a riddle in Islamic exegesis. For more about this theological term see the above-cited essay in the anthology by Christoph Burgmer, ed., *Streit um den Koran*, page 76, note 1. According to that essay, Sure 112 should be interpreted thus:
(To the question, who is God the One, you should reply):

> 1. Say: God the One, 2. (that is) God the *"United/Allied"* (*Ṣamad*) (into a unity) (= the *"Triune"*[26]), 3. (who) has not begotten and was not begotten 4. And who has no equal."[27]

The fact that God is One is stated in Surah 72:3 also. It is astonishing that the word حد / *ḥad* (someone) (< Syro-Aramaic ܚܕ / *ḥaḏ*) (one), which occurs in that Surah and is used extensively in many modern Arabic dialects, was altered with a superfluous and meaningless point beneath it, which distorted the agreement in the sentence. The verse reads:

وانه تعلى جد ربنا ما اتخذ صحبه ولا ولدا

For the dubious word جد / ğadd the translators have a choice in Arabic between grandfather, seriousness, eagerness and happiness. Paret translates (485):

> 3. And (I was inspired to know that the jinn said): "Our Lord, the epitome of happiness (and blessing), is exalted. [Note 1: Literally: The happiness (*ğadd*) of our Lord is exalted.] He has found for himself neither a female companion nor a child [Note 2: Or (in the plural): children]." (Und (mir ist eingegeben worden, daß die Dschinn sagten): "Unser Herr, der Inbegriff von Glück (und Segen), ist erhaben." [Anm. 1 W: Das Glück (*ğadd)* unseres Herrn ist erhaben.] Er hat sich weder eine Gefährtin noch ein Kind [Anm. 2: Oder (Mehrzahl): Kinder] zugelegt.)

Blachère (619) offers an elegant solution for this verse:

> 3. Our Lord (may His greatness be exalted!) took neither female companion nor child." (Notre Seigneur (que Sa grandeur soit exaltée !) n'a pas pris de compagne ou d'enfant.)

Bell (II, 610) agrees with him and translates:

> 3. And that He—exalted be the majesty of our Lord—hath taken for Himself neither wife [Note. 1. Literally: "female companion"] nor offspring; ..."

It is just as astonishing that it did not occur to these translators of the Qur'ān to eliminate the point under جد / *ğadd* and to read حد / *ḥad* (one). This results in the following reading:

> And the Most High[28] (is) One: Our Lord neither took a female companion nor (adopted) a child.

7. On the erroneous reading of صاحبه / *ṣāḥiba* (female companion)

The Qur'ānic defective spelling of صحبه admits two readings. The Cairo Edition of the Qur'ān reads صاحبه / *ṣāḥiba* and makes it out to mean (God's) "female companion," whereas the reading صحابه / *ṣaḥāba* (plural) results in the meaning "companions" (*e.g.*, the comrades or associates of the Prophet),[29] which is more in keeping with Qur'ānic theology. In other passages the Qur'ān uses as a synonym for this the term شريك / *šarīk* (in the singular) and (in the plural) شركا / *šurakā* (participants). This misreading of the *rasm* صحبه occurs a second time in the Qur'ān in Surah 6:101 as follows:

بديع السموت والارض انى (= أين) يكون له ولد ولم تكن (= يكن) له صحبه

(صاحبه = صحابه) وخلق كل شي وهو بكل شي عليم

Paret (114) translates:

> 101. (He is) the Creator of heaven and earth. How could he acquire children, when he had, after all, no female companion (who could have brought them into the world for him) and (on his own) created everything (in the world)? He knows about everything." ((Er ist) der Schöpfer von Himmel und Erde. Wie soll er zu Kindern kommen, wo er doch keine Gefährtin hatte (die sie ihm hätte zur Welt bringen können) und (von sich aus) alles geschaffen hat (was in der Welt ist)? Er weiß über alles Bescheid.)

Blachère (164) and Bell (I, 125) understand the term accordingly (*compagne/ female companion*). According to the recommended emendation, however, this verse should be interpreted thus:

> (He, who is) the Creator of heaven and earth, how[30] could he have a child? After all, he had no companions, since he created everything and knows about everything (or: *is able to do* everything)!"[31]

The twofold misreading of the Qur'ānic defective spelling صحبه and its erroneous interpretation as صاحبه / *ṣāḥiba* (female companion) instead of صحابه / *ṣaḥāba* (companions)[32] is confirmed by two parallel passages in the Qur'ān. Surah 17:111 reads:

وقل الحمد لله الذي لم يتخذ ولدا ولم يكن له شريك في الملك

> And say: Praise be to God, who took for himself no (adopted) child and had no one participating in his sovereignty…."

The same idea is found in Surah 25:2:

الذي له ملك السموت والارض ولم يتخذ ولدا ولم يكن له شريك في الملك

> . . . to whom (*i.e.*, God) (belongs) sovereignty over heaven and earth, (who) did not adopt a child and had no one participating in his sovereignty. . . .

The notion that God would have needed a *female companion* in order to *acquire a child*, as Paret understood the passages under discussion, thus becomes baseless. Instead, the last-cited passages make clear the fundamental Monarchic idea of Qur'ānic theology. This [second- and third-century Christian heresy] rejects not only the theology of *Divine Sonship* (alluded to in Surah 112:3), but also that of *Adoptianism* (which held that God adopted a human being as his Son). The latter polemic is presumably directed against the theology of the East Syrian Nestorians. An *adoptive son* who allegedly participated in the divine lordship is rejected just like any other form of participation. Hence God has neither an *adoptive son* nor other sorts of *participants* (and not a "*female companion*").

8. Typical erroneous transcriptions of similar-looking Syriac letters

The erroneous copying of Syro-Aramaic letters into the more recent Arabic system of writing during the redaction ["*Erstellung*"] of the Arabic Qur'ān has already been pointed out by means of the concrete, philologically and contextually reasoned examples above. At what historical point in time this transcription took place cannot be determined at the present state of Qur'ānic scholarship. Nor is that the purpose of this essay. Instead it intends to contribute to a more plausible interpretation of the Qur'ānic text through the examination of further examples. This essay limits itself first of all to the confusion of the following similar-looking letters of the Syriac alphabet.

ܠܥܝܢܝܗܘܢ *l-ʿēnay-hōn*. The first three letters enlarged: ܠܥܢ *l-ʿ-n*

These three letters taken from the Rabbula Gospel Book (586 A.D.)[33] (from right to left: ܠ / *L*, ܥ / *ʿayn*, ܢ / *N*), as even the layman can see, were mistaken for each other even within the Syriac system of writing, depending on the diligence or carelessness of the copyist in question. No wonder such typical mistakes occurred also in transcriptions into the more recent Arabic system of writing, which was not yet entirely familiar to the Arabic or Arabo-Aramaic copyists. The (fateful) difference, though, is that, whereas the Syriac reader could recognize such copyist's mistakes within the Syriac language relatively easily from the context, this was no longer possible for the educated Arab reader, since the corresponding Arabic letters are so different from each other in form that it was practically impossible to mistake one for another.

The Syriac-Arabic correspondence of the three Syriac letters illustrated above is as follows (from right to left):

Syriac ܠ = Arabic ﻟ /*L* ;
Syriac ܥ = Arabic ﻋ /*ʿayn* ;
Syriac ܢ = Arabic ﻧ /*N*

The erroneous transcription of the Syriac ܥ / *ʿayn* as an Arabic ﻟ / *L* was first noticed in the essay "Neudeutung der arabischen Inschrift im Felsendom zu Jerusalem"[34] ["New interpretation of the Arabic inscription in the Dome of the Rock in Jerusalem"]. It was demonstrated there that the Arabic ل / *L* in the rasm لبدا (read: *libadan*—meaning unclear), which occurs in Surah 72:19, should be read as a Syriac ܥ/ *ʿayn*. In context the Cairo Edition of the Qurʾān reads:

وانه لما قام عبد الله يدعوه كادوا يكونون عليه لبدا

Following the interpretation of the Arabic commentators, Paret (486) translates: [the invisible *spirits* go on to say:]

> 19. And "As the servant of God [Note 12: *i.e.*, Muhammad] stood up, so as to call on him [Note 13: Or: to pray to him], they might almost have crushed / overwhelmed him (*kādū yakūnūna ʿalaihi libadan*). [Note 14: The interpretation of the verse is quite uncertain.]" (Und: ‚Als der Diener Gottes [Anm. 12: D.h. Mohammed] sich aufstellte, um ihn anzurufen [Anm. 13: Oder: zu ihm zu beten], hätten sie ihn (vor lauter Zudringlichkeit?) beinahe erdrückt *(kādū yakūnūna ʿalaihi libadan)*' [Anm. 14: Die Deutung des Verses ist ganz unsicher].")

Reading in Arabic عبدا / *ʿibādan* instead of لبدا / *libadan* produces the following interpretation:

> 19. [The invisible *spirits* say] further: "When the *Servant of God* (namely *Jesus, son of Mary*) had *arisen* (and) continued to call on him (= God) (*i.e.*, continued to worship the one God), they (= people) might almost have *worshipped* him (as God). 20: [The *Servant of God* resisted this and] said: "Indeed I am invoking my Lord (*i.e.*, I, however, am worshipping only the one God) and associate no other with him!"[35]

Further examples of confusing Syriac letters in this way followed in the essay, "Relikte syro-aramäischer Buchstaben in frühen Korankodizes im *ḥiǧāzī*- und *kūfī*-Duktus."[36]

On the subject of the erroneous transcription of the three Syriac letters in the illustration above, another publication is in the works, which will present, together with philological and contextual arguments, further examples from the canonical version of the Qurʾān as we have it in the Cairo Edition.

Notes:

1 Christoph Luxenberg, *Die syro-aramäische Lesart des Koran: Ein Beitrag zur Entschlüsselung der Koransprache* (Berlin, 20001), 8–15; revised and expanded edition (Berlin 20042), 23–29; (Berlin, 20073), 23–30; English edition: *The Syro-Aramaic Reading of the Koran: A Contribution to the Decoding of the Language of the Koran* (Berlin, 2007), 22–28.

2 The first case cited as an example was the Arabic spelling of [يلحدون] (traditional reading: *yu-lḥidūna*), which in the context makes no sense but supposedly means "allude to" (Suras 7:180; 16:103; 41:40); the meaning finally becomes clear, however, from the Syriac (Garshuni) spelling, transcribed phonetically into Arabic as يلغزون (yu-lġizūna), which the *Lisān* (V, 405b) also corroborates: ألغز الكلام وألغز فيه: عمّى مراده وأضمره على خلاف ما أظهره (with reference to speech, *alġaza* means "to obscure what is meant and not to express it clearly").

3 In: Karl-Heinz Ohlig, ed., *Der frühe Islam: Eine historisch-kritische Rekonstruktion anhand zeitgenossischer* Quellen (Berlin, 2007[1]), 377–414.

4 Ṭabarī (Commentary on the Qur'an), I, 26 ff. It is reported there that the Syrians quoted the reading by Ubai b. Ka'b, whereas the Iraqis cited the one by Ibn Mas'ūd.

5 For a more detailed discussion, see Christoph Luxenberg, "Die syrische Liturgie und die 'geheimnisvollen Buchstaben' im Koran: Eine liturgievergleichende Studie," ["The Syriac liturgy and the 'mysterious letters' in the Qur'an: A study in comparative liturgy,"] in: Markus Gross and Karl-Heinz Ohlig, eds., *Schlaglichter: Die beiden ersten islamischen Jahrhunderte, Inarah 3* (Berlin, 20081), 435 ff; the English translation of the article is in the present anthology.

6 Handwritten edition in Russian and French: САМАРКАНДСКІЙ КУФИЧЕСКІЙ КОРАНЬ / *Coran coufique de Samarcand—écrit d'après la tradition de la propre main du troisième calife Osman (644–656) qui se trouve dans la bibliothèque IMPÉRIALE publique de St Petersbourg : Édition faite avec l'autorisation de l'Institut Archéologique de St Petersbourg—(facsimile)—par S. Pissaref* (St Petersbourg, 1905).

7 Syro-aramaic ܬܘܒ /tūḇ > Mandaean (= East Aramaic-Babylonian) תום /tūm > Arabic ثم /ṯum(ma) [Old Aramaic תוב /*ṯūḇ > Hebrew שוב /šūḇ] does not actually mean "after that," as Paret (123) translates it ("And indeed we created you [men]. After that we gave you a [harmonious] form"), but rather: "again, furthermore, both-and"; see Mannā (831b), article ܬܘܒ/tūḇ : ايضاً. ثانية , (furthermore, also, again), 2) بعدُ. ما عدا ذلك (in addition, besides); see also C. Brockelmann, *Lexicon Syriacum* (817b), who notes examples illustrating 7 nuances, among them #7. ܠܐ ܬܘܒ (lā tūḇ) *nondum* (not again = not yet), according to the *Thesaurus* (II, 4400), however, (or else in addition), at the article ܬܘܒ ܠܐ (tūḇ lā): *non amplius* (not again = no longer); corresponding to this is the Qur'anic-Arabic ثم لا (ṯumma lā), as in Surah 11:113 (ثم لا تنصرون), rendered by Paret (189) as follows: "(And some day) you will not be helped," with the note (107): "Literally: after that." Yet it should be understood (in Syro-Aramaic fashion) to mean: "And you will no longer be helped." So too in various passages of the Qur'an, where the connecting

words ثم لا /ṯum(ma) lā don't mean "after that not," but as a rule, "again not = not again = no longer."

8 Brother Mark, *A 'Perfect' Qur'an* (New York: International Bible Society, 2000), Appendix A: Samarqand MSS VS 1924 Egyptian Edition, p. XIX, line 1, at page 338.

9 See Th. Noldeke, *Kurzgefasste syrische Grammatik*, p. 169, § 224.

10 *Sprachwissenschaftliche Untersuchungen*, i, 22, with reference to Ibn Yaʿīš, I, 499, line 7. Cf. also Reckendorf, *Die syntaktischen Verhältnisse des Arabischen* (Leiden, 1898), 325; Wright, *Arabic Grammar*, 1:294 d.

11 Siddiqi, *Studien*, 13.

12 Itq, 325. Others thought it Aramaic (Mutaw, 54) or Ḥauranic (Muzhir, I, 130), or Hebrew (Itq, 325).

13 On this subject see Anton Spitaler, "Die Schreibung des Typus صلوة im Koran: Ein Beitrag zur Erklärung der koranischen Orthographie," *Wiener Zeitschrift fur die Kunde des Morgenlandes*, vol. 56, Festschrift Herbert W. Duda (Vienna, 1960).

14 In: Karl-Heinz Ohlig, ed., *Der frühe Islam: Eine historisch-kritische Rekonstruktion anhand zeitgenössischer Quellen* (Berlin, 2007[1]), pp. 393–412.

15 From the Syro-Aramaic ܐܝܢܐ /*aynā*, composed of the interjectional particle ܐܝܢ/ *ayn* < *ܗܝܢ / *hayn*) and the enclitic demonstrative/indicative particle [*Deutepartikel*] ܗܐ /*hā*, which by sound-shift becomes > ܐܝܢܐ (*aynā*) by the assimilation of the *nūn* and the resultant doubling of the *yā* by way of substitution, we get the Arabic form أيّ (pronounced: *ayyā* / *ayy*). N.B.: The inflection according to nominative, genitive and accusative (*ayyu, ayyi, ayya*) prescribed by classical Arabic grammar is fictitious, since etymologically this interrogative pronoun should be treated no differently from the demonstrative pronoun هذا / *hāḏā* (this), which is also borrowed from Aramaic and which Arabic grammar –rightly this time—considers indeclinable. The original Syro-Aramaic form ܐܝܢܐ (*aynā*) (pronounced *ayna* and *ēna*) is still alive today in several Arabic dialects of Syria and Mesopotamia. Contrary to the analysis of the *Thesaurus* (I, 158), which explains the Syriac ܐܝܢܐ (*aynā*) as a combination of [1] the secondary particle ܐܝ / *ay* (which comes about only when the final nūn is dropped) (from *ܗܝܢ / *hayn* > ܐܝܢ /*ayn* > ܐܝ /*ay*), in which it sees an independent interrogatory particle (*particula interrogativa*), and [2] ܗܢܐ /*hānā* (which again arises secondarily from a contracted *ܗܝܢ /*hayn* > ܗܢ / *hān* + ܗܐ / *hā*), modern Arabic dialects of the Near East employ surviving variants of "here" such as *hēn, hān* > (West Syriac) *hōn, hena* / *həna* and *hnā*, which are all contracted forms from the Syro-Aramaic *ܗܝܢ / *hayn* > ܗܢ / *hēn* / *hān* > *hōn* (isolated + enclitic ܗܐ / *hā*), from which comes, last but not least, the classical Arabic هنا / *hunā* (in which the *u*, if not fictitious, could be explained only by West Syriac pronunciation). The Chaldaic (= East Syriac-Babylonian) variants mentioned in the *Thesaurus* can be explained in a similar way; their plural forms הנון /*hənnōn* > אנון /*ənnōn* are composed of the demonstrative **hayn* > *hēn* > *hən* > *ən* and the enclitic plural personal pronoun *hōn*, whereby the assimilation of the enclitic *h* results in the doubling of the medial *n*.

16 On the particular meanings of Syro-Aramaic ܐܝܢ (*ēn*) see Mannā (16b): نعم. بلى (yes, indeed); (2) يا. أيا للنداء (Oh as an exclamation); (3) هل للاستفهام (interrogative particle); (4) لكن. إلا. غير أنّ (but, nevertheless, however).

17 Mannā (165a) : ܠܐ ܗܐ (*lā hā* ?) أليس . أو ما (is it not ...?); moreover the *Thesaurus* (II, 1869) notes: ܠܐ (*lā*), particula negativa et privativa,... 3) interrogativa, nonne; Valet: ∗) annon ? nonne ? Jud. 10:11, Matt. 7:22, 10:29...; ita ܠܐ ܗܐ (*lā hā* ?), Matt. 5:46–47, 6:26, Hebr. 1:14 ; ita ܠܐ ܗܘܐ (*lā (h)wā* ?), Heb. הלא (*hā-lā* /*hā-lō* [perhaps contracted > *hallā*] ?), Exod. 4:4, 1 Cor. 10:16, James 2:5, 21, 25...

18 Christoph Luxenberg, "Die syrische Liturgie und die 'geheimnisvollen Buchstaben' im Koran" ["The Syrian liturgy and the 'mysterious letters' in the Koran"], in: Markus Gross and Karl-Heinz Ohlig, eds., *Schlaglichter*, 426–435.

19 The fact that the final inflection of the regular feminine plural (ات / *āt*) is *i* and not *a*, is an arbitrary determination of the later founders of classical Arabic grammar, which finds no application in the language of the Qur'an, especially since the Syriac singular (ܐܬܐ/ *āṯā*) ends in *ā*, just like the plural form (ܐܬܘܬܐ/ *āṯwāṯā*) of this Qur'ānic loan-word.

20 Concerning the combination of two verbs in sequence without a conjunction, because they essentially amount to one main action, see Theodor Nöldeke, *Kurzgefasste syrische Grammatik*, § 337.A.

21 a) To the word لاجرا / *la-aǧrā* is prefixed ل / *l-*, which here has no intensifying function, as is frequently the case in the Qur'an when it appears in combination with the intensifying particle إنّ / *inna* (or before an oath); instead it expresses an uncertainty that underlies the interrogative particle ان < ܐܢ / *ēn*, which naturally lends to it a dubitative nuance.

22 Theodor Nöldeke, *Kurzgefasste syrische Grammatik*, second revised edition (Leipzig, 1898); reprinted with an appendix edited by Anton Schall (Darmstadt, 1977), 263.

23 Depending on the context, the Qur'anic forms اذ / *id* and اذا / *idā* correspond semantically to the Syro-Aramaic ܟܕ / *kaḏ* (when, while, as), in rare cases even in a concessive sense (although), as in Sura 7:12, where God asks Iblīs: ما منعك الا تسجد اذ امرتك (What kept you from casting yourself down, although I commanded you to do so?).

24 Like حافرة / *ḥāfira* (actually: *ḥafra*), نخرة / *naḫira* (= *naḫra*) is morphologically a Syro-Aramaic passive participle ending in *paʿlā* (= Arabic محفورة / *maḥfūra* [dug, hollowed out], منخورة / *manḫūra* [perforated, punctured]).

25 On this subject see Christoph Luxenberg, *The Syro-Aramaic Reading of the Koran*, 100-104: "On the Morphology and Etymology of Syro-Aramaic ܣܛܢܐ (*sāṭānā*) and Koranic شيطن (*šayṭān*)"; a more extensive discussion can be found in: Christoph Burgmer, ed., Streit um den Koran: Die Luxenberg-Debatte: Standpunkte und Hintergrunde, third expanded edition (Berlin, 2007), 69–82: "Zur Morphologie und Etymologie von syro-aramäisch ܣܛܢܐ (*sāṭānā* = Satan) und koranisch-arabisch شيطن (*šayṭān*)."

26 This interpretation can be corroborated in the Qur'ān. Surah 17:85 reads:
ويسلونك عن الروح قل الروح من امر ربي وما اوتيتم من العلم الا قليلا
"If they ask you about the Spirit, then answer: The Spirit (is = proceeds) from the Logos of my Lord" (cf. the Creed of Nicaea-Constantinople: *"et in Spiritum Sanctum qui ex Patre Filioque procedit"*). The rejection of this doctrine in Sura 5:73 لقد كفر الذين قالوا ان الله ثالث ثلثة ("They are heretics who say that God is the

third of three") shows that the author of this anathema overlooked or did not comprehend the theological statement in Sura 17:85. The conclusion of this verse reads: وما اوتيتم من العلم الا قليلا "Of course you have little notion of theology!" (literally: "and no 'knowledge' [= divine knowledge / theology] has been conveyed to you, except a little").

27 The Arabic كفى / *kafā* (to suffice) corresponds lexically (and consequently semantically as well) to the Syro-Aramaic ܣܦܩ/ *sfaq*, for which Mannā (508a) notes the following Arabic meanings: (1) كفى . كان كافيا (to suffice, be enough); (4) فهم . أدرك (to understand, comprehend); (5) ساوى . كان أهلا جديرا (to be equal, of equal rank). The traditional Qur'anic reading for كفوا is (erroneously) *kufuwan*, a hypothetical noun form, whose final *alif* (according to the rule of classical Arabic grammar) was regarded as a sign of the accusative as the predicate of the verb كان / *kāna* (to be). The Aramaic spelling, however, points instead to the reading *kafū hin* (in classical Arabic كفوء / *kafū'*), which morphologically also corresponds to a *nomen agentis* [name of an acting person or thing] and harmonizes better syntactically with the sentence. We find a comparable form in Surah 4:99, which reads وكان الله عفوا غفورا / *wakāna llāh(u) 'afūwa(n) ġafūrā* (literally: for God is [a] Lenient, Forgiving [One]). Alternatively one could interpret the last sentence of Sura 112 in Syro-Aramaic fashion thus: "and no one can comprehend him." This theologically tenable interpretation (for instance with regard to the mystery of the "Doctrine of the Trinity") would have to be examined, however, in terms of the history of religions.

28 Granted, تعالى / *ta 'ālā* means "he is/may he be exalted," but this commendation is used as a verbal name for God and is still customary today.

29 The *Lisān* (I, 519b f.) lists the following plural forms of صاحب /*ṣāḥib* : أصحاب / *aṣḥāb*, أصاحيب / *aṣāḥīb*, صحبان/ *ṣuḥbān*, صحاب / *ṣiḥāb*, صحب / *ṣaḥb*, صحابة / *ṣaḥāba*, *ṣiḥāba* (and also a *ḥadīṯ* referring to the Prophet with the comment): ولم يجمع فاعل على فعالة إلا هذا (this is the only case in which the form *fā'il* is pluralized as *fa'āla*); concerning the final *–h* (which in Arabic indicates the feminine singular ending) adopted by Arabic to indicate the Aramaic plural ending in *–ē*, the *Lisān* explains: تزاد الهاء لتأنيث الجمع (the *h* is added in order to make a "feminine" out of the plural).

30 Concerning the erroneous transcription انى / *annā* instead of اين / *ayna* (28 times in the Qur'an) through a confusion of the Syriac final *nūn* with the Arabic final *yā*, see Christoph Luxenberg, "Neudeutung der arabischen Inschrift im Felsendom zu Jerusalem," in: Karl-Heinz Ohlig and Gerd-R. Puin, eds., *Die dunklen Anfänge: Neue Forschungen zur Entstehung und frühen Geschichte des Islam* (Berlin, 20051), 136, note 18.

31 In this context the latter meaning should preferably be taken into consideration, inasmuch as the Arabic علم / *'alima* is borrowed from the Syro-Aramaic ܥܠܡ / *'lem, 'lam*, and this verbal root is in turn a secondary construction from the Syro-Aramaic ܚܠܡ / *ḥlam* through the vocalization of the guttural sound ܚ / *ḥ* as ܥ / *'ayn* (basic meaning: to be strong). Arabic borrowed only the extended meaning, "knowledge" (as intellectual strength). As a result of the pronunciation of the guttural sound *ḥ* as *ḫ* (kh / ch) in East Syriac-Babylonian, in Arabic the *ḫ* was again vocalized as (tertiary) *ġ*, producing the word غلام / *ġulām* (a growing boy, a youth who is gaining strength < Syro-Aramaic ܚܠܡܐ/ *ḥalmā*, ܚܠܝܡܐ /*ḥlīmā* > ܥܠܝܡܐ / *'laymā*) and the corresponding verbal root غلم / *ġalima*.

32 According to the *Lisān* (I, 520a) this may also be intended as an infinitive or a verbal noun (مصدر / *maṣdar*) (perhaps "participation, membership").

33 *The Rabbula Gospels, Facsimile Edition of the Miniatures of the Syriac Manuscript Plut. I, 56 in the Medicaean-Laurentian Library*, edited and commented by Carlo Cecchelli, Giuseppe Furlani and Mario Salmi (Olten and Lausanne: URS Graf-Verlag, publishers, 1959), f. 159a, column b, line 11.

34 In: Karl-Heinz Ohlig and Gerd-R. Puin, eds., *Die dunklen Anfänge: Neue Forschungen zur Entstehung und frühen Geschichte des Islam* (Berlin, 20051), 131 ff.

35 *Cf.* Surah 19:36.

36 In: Karl-Heinz Ohlig, *Der frühe Islam: Eine historisch-kritische Rekonstruktion anhand zeitgenössischer Quellen* (Berlin, 20071), pp. 377–414. [See note 3 above.]

Syriac Liturgy and the "Mysterious Letters" in the Qur'ān: A Comparative Liturgical Study

Christoph Luxenberg

The present article was first published in German in Markus Gross and Karl-Heinz-Ohlig, eds., Schlaglichter: Die Beiden Ersten Islamischen Jahrhunderte *[Flashlights: The First Two Centuries of Islam] (Berlin, 2008). Because of its outstanding importance, this English version will appear simultaneously both in the present anthology and in the English translation of the original collection of essays. Unlike all other theories and views brought forward by Islamological "revisionists," Luxenberg's explanation of the mysterious letters in the Koran has no "traditional" alternative. If asked about the life of the prophet, the edition of the Koran and the meaning of most Koranic verses, Islamic scholars will adduce quotations from the Islamic traditional literature and agree at least about the main points. Not so about the mysterious letters: there is consensus neither among Islamic nor Islamological scholars about their meaning and origin. If any of Luxenberg's theories should have a chance to be accepted or at least discussed in the Islamic world, it's those expounded in the following article.*

1. Introduction

The meaning of the letters that appear before twenty-nine Qur'ānic Surahs has perplexed scholars in both East and West since the beginning of the Qur'ānic exegetical tradition. For example, Ṭabarī (d. 923), considered in Islamic tradition as the most important and most prolific Qur'ānic commentator, discussed this enigma in an effort to explain the first set of letters الم / *alm*, found at the beginning of Surah 2 ("al-Baqara" ["The Cow"]).[1] After his stereotypical remarks by way of introduction—"there are different opinions among the Qur'ānic commentators concerning God's word الم / *alm*"—he lists fourteen interpretations, generally supported by lists of transmitters. These meanings can be summarized thus:

1) The letters denote one of the names of the Qur'ān;
2) They are "<u>introductory</u>" letters (فواتح / *fawātiḥ*), with which God "<u>introduces</u>, <u>opens</u>" the Qur'ān (from this meaning comes the traditional Islamic term فواتح السور ["the introductory {letters} of the Surahs"]);
3) They denote the <u>names</u> of the Surahs;
4) They denote the <u>names</u> of the exalted <u>God</u>;

5) They denote oath-formulae, with which God swears and which allude to his name;
6) They are individual letters representing nouns and verbs, so that each letter has a different meaning;
7) They are specific letters of the alphabet (without further explanation);
8) They are letters, of which each one may have its own distinct meaning (as in 6 above);
9) They are letters that represent an entire sentence;
10) Every book contains a secret, and the secret of the Qur'ān is its introductory letters (hence the name "mysterious letters");
11) A few Arabic philologists defend the position that they are letters which take the place of the twenty-eight letters (of the Arabic alphabet);
12) The Surahs begin with these letters in order to open the hearing (in order to focus attention upon the Surahs) of the *mušrikīn* ("the associators" = those who associate other gods with the one God);
13) They are letters with which God introduces his word;
14) If one inquires after the meaning of these letters, one learns that the Prophet supposedly interpreted these letters as representing numbers (following the Syro-Aramaic number-system of the alphabet). (If this is true, then the letters الم / *alm (='lm)*[2] would stand for the number 71 [*a* = 1; *l* = 30; *m* = 40; 1+30+40=71]. It is interesting in this regard that the Prophet asked his hearers whether they knew that the time of a prophet's activity and the duration of his community supposedly lasts 71 years. The Prophet used ascending number-values to follow this number-symbolism, by means of the following groups of letters: المص / *almṣ* [*a* = 1; *l* = 30; *m* = 40; *ṣ* = 90] = 161 years; الر / *alr* [*a* = 1; *l* = 30; *r* = 200] = 231 years; المر / *almr* [*a* = 1; *l* = 30; *m* = 40; *r* = 200] = 271 years. Indeed, the sums agree with the respective roots, but the progressive order of the letters does not correspond to the degressive Aramaic number system, where the letter with the highest value appears first. Nonetheless, the hint at the possibility that specific letters represent numbers is not without interest, as the interpretation of the individual letters will attest. The Qur'ānic number-mysticism that developed in later Islam—possibly connected with Jewish traditions—can be traced back to these number-letters that were originally Aramaic but were taken over by the Arabs.)

Ṭabarī considers each of the Qur'ānic commentators' various interpretive attempts, and he expends a great deal of effort assigning authority to each one. He concludes by defending the point of view that the letters in question do not represent words that are to be taken together, but rather should be seen as divided letters (hence the term حروف مقطعة / *ḥurūf muqaṭṭa'a*) that can have different meanings. With this conclusion he justifies the opinions of the

Qur'ānic commentators that he describes, without committing himself to firm decisions. Ṭabarī is not unjustified in taking this tentative line, because these letters (and letter-combinations), as we will see, can in fact mean different things. Further, such a position leaves room for the later Islamic tradition to offer further attempts at explanation, as the literature shows, ample as it is even into our own day. We will not focus here on this later literature, as it rests entirely on speculations that would not bring us any closer to the solving of the mystery. Rather, we will first discuss briefly the Western Qur'ānic scholarship that has dealt with the question of the "mysterious letters."

2. The Current State of Western Qur'ānic Scholarship

In his collection of essays entitled *Der Koran*, Rudi Paret lists in section VI (pp. 330–385) the most important contributions to Western scholarship concerning the "mysterious letters." He provides this information "because the phenomenon has been only partially explained" and in order to spare someone who "wants to *continue to speculate*" a time-consuming search.[3] In his introduction he discusses his sixth section on the mysterious letters with these words:

> As I have already noted above, in section VI I attempt to gather together as fully as possible the new publications concerning the enigmatic letters that precede a few Surahs and should be understood as *sigla*, that is, signs (German: "*Siglen*"). However, I have omitted Arthur Jeffery's contribution in *The Moslem World* 14 (1924), pp. 247–260, because it only refers to the work of others, without offering anything original. I have also left out (for reasons of space and the age of the items in question) the works of Loth (*Zeitschrift der Deutschen Morgenländischen Gesellschaft* 35 [1881], pp. 603–610) and Hartwig Hirschfeld (*New Researches into the Composition and Exegesis of the Qoran* [London, 1902], pp. 141–143), although these works are important in their own right. I should also mention another recently-published treatment, namely, James A. Bellamy's 'The Mysterious Letters of the Koran: Old Abbreviations of the Basmalah' from the *Journal of the American Oriental Society* 93 (1973), pp. 267–285, although Bellamy also fails to offer a convincing solution to the problem.[4] In my opinion, the foundational work on this topic remains the results of Hans Bauer's investigations (published in 1921). According to Bauer the sigla appear to be very old and to function as pointers to collections of Surahs that already existed at the time of the production of 'Uṯmān's edition of the Qur'ān and that were, just like the edition itself, ordered according to the principle of declining length. Bauer also offers perceptive thoughts concerning the meaning of the individual letters and the combinations of letters.

However, he did not succeed in coming to a full explanation of this difficult complex of questions.[5]

In these observations we see Paret's correct understanding that the problem of the mysterious letters has not been solved despite their *acute insights.* A short review of the works mentioned by Paret will show us why their efforts could not lead to a conclusive result.

a) *Hans Bauer, "Über die Anordnung der Suren und über die geheimnisvollen Buchstaben im Qoran" (1921)*[6] [*Concerning the Order of the Surahs and the Mysterious Letters of the Qur'an*]

Bauer's point of departure is his acceptance of the idea that "in four (or five) cases" the letters *ys* (Q[7] 36), *ṣ* (Q38), *q* (Q 50), *ṭh* (Q 20), and (possibly) *n* (Q 68) played the same function as the titles by which we now know the Surahs, but this thesis contradicts the historical constitution of the Qur'anic text, in so far as Bauer overlooks the fact that the earliest Qur'ānic manuscripts of which we are aware bear no Surah titles at all. Rather, these were added by later Qur'ānic editors, largely according to arbitrary criteria. In the course of this editorial work, the letters we are considering here were made into titles, from which one can deduce that they stood at the heads of the Surahs in question from the very beginning. However, we should not exclude his suggestion that these sigla could have belonged to other texts. Bauer ends his treatment with a brief consideration of this last problem; his conclusion is as follows: "The explanation of these questions demands further investigations dedicated to individual aspects of the matter."[8] He is surely mistaken, however, in accepting that "the meaning of the abbreviations is to be gained directly from the Surahs they precede" or that one can find "definite *internal or external relationships between these Surahs*" and the letters that precede them.[9]

b) *Eduard Goossens, "Ursprung und Bedeutung der koranischen Siglen" (1923)*[10] *[Origin and Meaning of the Koranic Signs]*

Goossens' contribution is more extensive and is designed in the form of a doctoral thesis. Here he recognizes that these letters represent abbreviations that to some degree are of a *technical sort* and were once generally understood; however, he does not even approximately succeed in delineating their individual meanings. Nonetheless, he does conclude with the general statement that these "abbreviations" are "in these 29 Surahs to be set in parallel with the extant titles of the Surahs." One would not be unjustified, he says, in assuming "that the mysterious letters and groups of letters represent nothing other than *old titles.*" In his introduction,[11] Goossens reproduces the following table of the data concerning these sigla, derived from Schwally's list:[12]

Root	Surah(s)
'lr	10, 11, 12, 14, 15
'lm	2, 3, 29, 30, 31, 32
'lmr	13
'lmṣ	7
ḥm	40, 41, 43, 44, 45, 46
ḥm'sq	42
ṣ	38
ṭs	27
ṭsm	26, 28
ṭh	20
q	50
khy'ṣ	19
n	68
ys	36

In section III (p. 344 in Paret's edition) Goossens attempts to interpret the individual signs. However, despite the effort he expends, his interpretations are based upon assumptions that do not lead to any plausible result because he does not recognize the actual function of these sigla.

c) Morris S. Seale, "The Mysterious Letters in the Qur'ān" (1957/59)[13]

In this essay Seale points rather interestingly to "one example of *memoria technica* from the Talmud" (*Y'ALKGM*). Also, his suggestion concerning the explanation of the letter-group *KHY'Ṣ* at the beginning of the "Surah Maryam" (Q 19) is thought-provoking. However, in this as in his other suggestions, he does not distinguish himself from his erring predecessors Bauer and Goossens, in that he (like they) sees in the individual letters the roots of names or expressions, which he then seeks in the corresponding Surahs.

d) Alan Jones, "The Mystical Letters of the Qur'ān" (1962)[14]

Jones sees a purely mystical meaning in the Qur'ānic sigla. His closing remarks are as follows:

> My own feeling is that the letters are intentionally mysterious and have no specific meaning.

He also appropriates an early opinion of Nöldeke (one that Nöldeke himself later abandoned), whom he then cites as follows:

> The prophet himself can hardly have attached any particular meaning to these symbols; they served their purpose if they conveyed an impression of solemnity and enigmatical obscurity.[15]

e) James A. Bellamy, "Again the Mysterious Letters" (see above, n. 3)
In the afore-mentioned article by Bellamy, he again discusses our theme and strengthens his position that these unexplained letters actually concern other ways of writing an ancient *basmalah* (the shortened form of *bi-smi llāh ar-raḥmān ar-raḥīm* / "in the name of God, the Gracious One, the Merciful One"). He traces the bold emendations that he suggests in order to justify his thesis back to mistakes made by copyists. He summarizes his argument with the following conclusion:

> I am more than ever convinced that the *fawātiḥ* are indeed old abbreviations of the *basmalah* that suffered corruption at the hands of later copyists. And after all, what can more properly stand before a Surah than the *basmalah*?

Even if Bellamy was thinking at least partially in the right direction, it is not possible that all the abbreviations, attested multiple times in the early Qur'ānic manuscripts, can be traced back to earlier mis-transcriptions.

These various attempts by western scholars to explain the problem of the "mysterious letters" in the Qur'ān are hardly distinct from the solutions proposed by the Qur'ānic commentators. They all fail to consider the Qur'ānic text in its context of the history of religions, a problem of historico-cultural relevance. Since these works were published, it has become a widely-accepted fact that the Qur'ān arose in a Syro-Aramaic context. The discussions that follow will seek to demonstrate consistently these historico-cultural connections and to make plausible the thesis that the so-called "mysterious letters" of the Qur'ān originally dealt with a tradition closely related to the Syrian (Syriac) Christian liturgy.

3. Terms Constituting the Framework of the Qur'ān

It seems important here to remind the reader that the three terms concerning the Qur'ān (*Qur'ān*, *Sūra*, and *Āya*) were all borrowed from the Syro-Aramaic language. I will now briefly discuss their etymology.

3.1 قران / *Qur'ān* < ܩܪܝܢܐ / *Qeryān*

Western Qur'ānic scholars since Theodor Nöldeke (1836–1930) have recognized that قران / *Qur'ān*, as the name of the holy book of Islam, was taken over from the Syro-Aramaic ecclesiastical term ܩܪܝܢܐ / *Qeryān* ("lectionary, reading").[16] The author has expounded upon this topic more fully in his study *Die syro-aramäische Lesart des Koran*.[17] There the author argued that the loan-word *Qur'ān* / *Koran* (actually *Qeryān*) provides the key for understanding the Qur'ānic language. But two other expressions also arise in this discussion of the Qur'ānic text: the first of them, Surah (سورة / *sūra* ["Surah" = "chapter"]), indicates the individual chapters, and the second term, aya,(اية /

āya ["sign"]) refers to each individual "letter" of this text (and by extension, the written word of God), and not "verses" of the Koran as it was later falsely interpreted.

3.2 سورة / *sūra* < ܨܘܪܬܐ / *ṣūrtā*

The term "Surah" as a title above the individual chapters of the Qur'ān is clearly a later addition, because it does not appear in the earliest Qur'ānic manuscripts. There are ten Qur'ānic verses in which this word appears (Surahs 2:23; 9:64, 86, 124, 127; 10:38; 11:13; 24:1; 47:20 [2x]; nine of these occurences are in the singular, one in the plural); from these texts it has been concluded that the Qur'ān refers by this word to the individual textual units, which were not at that time defined more distinctly. This understanding was justified by the introductory verse to Surah 24, and from this point the term was taken over into the later Islamic tradition with regard to all the Qur'ānic chapters, in connection with the names for the Surahs which were later derived from the individual texts themselves.

3.2.1 Concerning the Etymology of سورة / *sūra*

Before the term *sūra* ("Surah") became a technical term indicating the individual chapters of the Qur'ān, well-known Arab philologists (and later western Qur'ānic scholars) had attempted to explain its etymology. While Ṭabarī supposed that this word was generally familiar, *Lisān al-'Arab* (IV:386a f.) cited the lexicographer al-Ǧawharī (d. 1005), who explained its basic meaning as كل منزلة من البناء ("any portion of a building"); with regard to the Qur'ān, then, it said that سورة / *sūra* means "partition, section" because it divides the textual portions of the Qur'ān from one another. This explanation gives *Lisān* an advantage over the other philologists' explanations that are derived from folk etymologies.

In Paret's commentary on Surah 24:1 (p. 358), he reproduces the important results of western Qur'ānic scholarship concerning the etymology of *sūra*:

> The etymology of the word *sūra* is controversial. Nöldeke considers it a likely derivation from the Hebrew *šūrā* ("row"), while Bell thinks it comes from the Syriac *surtā* (*ṣūrtā, sūrtā*) ("writing, written text"). Cf. Nöldeke, *Neue Beiträge*, 26; *Geschichte des Qorans*, I:30 f; Horovitz, *Proper Names*, 211f.; Bell, *Origin of Islam*, 52; *footnote and introduction*, 51f., 131; Jeffery, *Foreign Vocabulary*, 180–182."[18]

Among the authorities cited only Bell came close to the truth with his thesis that *sūra* could be a loan-word from the Syriac ܨܘܪܬܐ / *ṣūrtā*, not from ܣܘܪܛܐ / *surṭā*, as Jeffery had conjectured:

> The most probable solution is that it is from the Syr. ܣܘܪܛܐ, a "writing" (n. 2 here: Bell, *Origin*, 52; the suggestion of derivation from ܣܒܪܬܐ, "preaching," made by Margoliouth, *ERE*, x, 539, is not so near. Cf. Horovitz, *JPN*, 212, a word which occurs in a sense very like our English *lines* (*PSm*, 2738), and thus is closely parallel to Muḥammad's use of قرآن and كتاب, both of which are likewise of Syriac origin.[19]

One could superficially consider the two Syriac written forms ܣܘܪܛܐ / *surṭā* and ܨܘܪܬܐ / *ṣūrtā* to be merely emphatic variants, but in reality they are distinct from one another both in their forms and in their verbal roots. The masculine form ܣܘܪܛܐ / *surṭā* is based on the root ܣܪܛ / *srṭ*, which corresponds to both the Arabic form with metathesis سطر / *saṭara* ("to draw, write, mark a line") and the Syriac variant ܬܪܨ / *traṣ* ("to be straight, to make straight").[20] The feminine form ܨܘܪܬܐ / *ṣūrtā*, however, derives from the verbal root ܨܘܪ / *ṣwar* (variants ܨܝܪ / *ṣyar* and ܨܪ / *ṣār*) ("to present, to depict, to draw, to note") and leads to the Arabic forms صوّر / *ṣawwar* ("to present, to depict, to draw"), صيّر / *ṣayyar* ("to make, to do"), and صار / *ṣār* ("to become"). Consequently, the Syriac form has the meaning of "record" (literally: "drawing"); such a meaning is widely attested in the well-known expression ܨܘܪܬ ܟܬܒܐ / *ṣūrāṯ kṯāḇ* ("the "drawing" = writing of the book" = "the text of the Bible").[21]

In the Qur'ān one finds the root *ṣwr* once in the nominal form (still current today) صورة / *ṣūra* ("picture, design") (Q 82:8) and four times in the second verbal stem with the meaning "to form" (= "to make") (Surahs 3:6; 7:11; 40:64; 64:3); in the latter two cases, the repetition of the Syro-Aramaic infinitive (or verbal substantive) ܨܘܘܪܐ / *ṣuwwārā* has been considered an Arabic plural form because of the Qurānic defective written form (صوركم / *ṣwr-km*) and because this particular form of the infinitive is foreign to Arabic grammar. As a result, in both places the canonical text reads as follows: وصوركم فاحسن صوركم / *wa-ṣawwara-kum fa-aḥsana* <u>*ṣuwara-kum*</u> ("He has formed you and made <u>your images</u> beautiful"); the second form should be *ṣuwwāra-kum*, according to the way the Syro-Aramaic builds its infinitives of the intensive stem *Pa'el*. According to Arabic verbal paradigms, the infinitive form should read وصوركم فاحسن تصويركم / *wa-ṣawwara-kum fa-aḥsana* <u>*ta-ṣwīra-kum*</u> (literally: "He has formed you and made your <u>forming</u> [that is, the way in which he has formed you] beautiful"). This way of building infinitives in Syro-Aramaic is preserved in a few Arabic substantives, but the Arab philologists did not recognize this morphological phenomenon. Among such terms is the common word كتاب / *kuttāb* ("school," especially a "Qur'anic school "); one would normally consider this form an Arabic plural of كاتب / *kātib* ("writer, author"), but it has actually preserved faithfully the Syro-Aramaic verbal noun *katteḇ* (= Arabic *kattaba*), which corresponds in Arabic to the form تكتيب / *ta-ktīb* (= "to cause to write"). Understood from an

Aramaic point of view, *kuttāb* then means a school in which one learns not only reading but especially writing.

The Qur'ān offers a similar form in Q 108:1 titled al-Kawṯar ; here the readers of the Qur'ān have not been able to recognize in the spelling الكوثر an Aramaic nominal form from the intensive stem ܟܬܪ / *kattar* ("to await, to persist"). For this reason they also misread the medial و/ *w*, which in Aramaic orthography can serve as a *mater lectionis* for a short *u* in a closed syllable (ܟܘܬܪܐ / *kuttārā*), as the diphthong *aw* (*kawṯar*). If the morphologically identical form كتٰب / *kuttāb* (written defectively) had indeed had a و / *w* as a *mater lectionis* for short *u* (كوتب), then the Arab readers would not have been able to read this strange written form other than as *kawtab* (instead of *kuttāb*) (and then also *kawṯar* instead of *kuttār*).[22]

3.2.2 Excursus

Returning to the Qur'ānic usage of the Syro-Aramaic root *ṣwr* / *ṣyr*, we would no longer deprive the curious reader of the remarkable mis-reading and mis-interpretation of a Syro-Aramaic form in the Qur'ān that belongs to this root.

In terms of its topic, the term concerns the famous "satanic verses" (Q 53:19–20) that name the three goddesses *al-Lāt*, *al-'Uzzā*, and *Manāt* (actually *Manwa*). In the canonical edition of the Qur'ān, the worshipers of these divinities are initially asked (v. 21) whether it is appropriate to attribute female natures to God when they themselves desire male children. The text continues in v. 22 thus:

تلك اذا قسمة ضيزى

(Canonical reading: *tilka iḏan qismatun ḍīzā*)

Paret (p. 53) translates the clause thus:

> That would be an *unjust* division. [Das ware eine *ungerechte* Verteilung.]

Here Paret does not even question the underlined adjective in the way that he normally does with doubtful expressions; he and the other Qur'ānic scholars do not recognize that the phrase in question is in fact problematic. Indeed, Blachère and Bell cast no doubt upon this unusual word and translate it in same manner:

> *Blachère*, p. 561: This, then, would be an *unrighteous* division! [Cela, alors, serait un partage inique!]
>
> *Bell*, II:541: In that case it is a division *unfair*.

With such translations the most authoritative Western translators of the Qur'ān are following uncritically the philologically untenable explanations of the Arab commentators and lexicographers. It would be unnecessary to discuss the root *ḍa'aza* / *ḍayaza*, which does not even exist in Arabic, as

Ṭabarī (XXVII:60f.) does so doggedly in his efforts to explain this incomprehensible reading, calling as he does on the authorities of classical Arabic. A verse from (post-Qur'ānic) poetry becomes an incontrovertible argument for him; in the verse in question, the Qur'ānic word (in fact, misread word) appears in the presumed participial form مضئوز / *maḍ'ūz* (without further explanation), as Ṭabarī says at third-hand, reportedly from al-Aḫfaš.[23]

The various readings from some "Arabs" that Ṭabarī wants to have examined are just as arbitrary as the meanings contrived for them. The putative "Arabs" disagree even as they approach the vocalization of this peculiar word; some apparently spoke the Qur'ānic word as *ḍayzā*, others as *ḍa'zā*, and still others as *ḍū'zā*. Because the Qur'ānic readers seem not to have known these "dialectal" variants, Ṭabarī prefers the traditional reading *ḍīzā*, which he considers morphologically to be a secondary form of the feminine adjective *ḍūzā*. The famous philologist al-Farrā' (from Kūfā, d. 822) opposed this explanation, as Ṭabarī notes; according to the former, a feminine adjectival form could be *ḍayzā* or *ḍūzā*, and the pronunciation *ḍīzā* is possible only for noun forms. Of course, al-Farrā' did not recognize that this form corresponds to the Syro-Aramaic passive participle of the form *p'īl* / *p'īlā*.

Ṭabarī then considers the meaning of this formally controversial word in the Qur'ānic expression *qismatun ḍīzā*, and he lists the following four definitions (supported by chains of tradition): 1) a twisted division; 2) an unjust division; 3) a faulty division; and 4) a disputed division. For the final meaning he cites Ibn Wahb, who has Ibn Zayd saying that *aḍ-ḍīzā* "in the spoken usage of the Arabs" means "opposition." However, it should be noted that Ṭabarī introduces all the meanings listed here by assigning them to the "Arabs."

Western Qur'ānic scholars seem to have come to a consensus on the definition "unfair division" (German: *ungerechte Teilung*; French: *partage inique*). Because no Western scholar had ever doubted the truthfulness of this conclusion, Hans Wehr believed in all earnestness that the expression in question, considered to be "classical," could not be left out of his famous dictionary [*Arabisches Wörterbuch für die Schriftsprache der Gegenwart / A Dictionary of Modern Written Arabic*]; he was clearly unaware of the fact that this Qur'ānic *hapax legomenon*, mis-read and mis-understood from the very beginning, never became established in the "spoken usage of the Arabs." As a result, under the presumed (but not named) root *ḍyz*, he includes the expression قسمة ضيزى / *qisma ḍīzā* ("unjust division"), as though it had become a "winged word." But it surprises every Arabic speaker to hear the word *ḍīzā*, as it does not sound Arabic at all; perhaps it merely elicits a shake of the head or a restrained smile because of the association that this word bears in connection with a similar term ("*ṭīz* – buttocks, derrière") that sounds bawdy to contemporary Arabs.

Just like countless other mis-readings in the Qur'ān, this phrase reduces the traditional legend of an "oral tradition" of the Qur'ānic text (which functions as a dogma for some scholars of Arabic or Islamic studies) *ad absurdum*. Even the "variant readings" literature, (*qirā'āt*) documented in the Islamic tradition, is no argument for an oral transmission of the text, as some Qur'ān scholars tend to think, but rather a testimony to redactional diversity.

3.2.3 Deciphering the Enigmatic Term ضيزى / *ḍīzā*

With this example the *Syro-Aramaic Reading of the Koran* will prove its efficiency in solving such problems. We must simply erase in our minds the two diacritical points above the term ضيزى, as these were added at a later date by an incompetent scribe and led to this mis-reading. When the term has been purified in this way, we are left with the written form صيرى; if we preserve the Qur'ānic vocalization, we have the term *ṣīrā*. In reality, the reading *ṣīrā* might sound no less strange to an Arab than *ḍīzā*, and rightly so. The reason is that at first glance he would not recognize the otherwise familiar verbal root *ṣwr* ("to depict, to draw"), because the orthography of صيرى would appear entirely unusual to him.

In actual fact, this orthography can only be explained with the aid of the Syro-Aramaic verbal paradigm. According to the latter, verbs with a medial *w* / *y* (just like the other triliteral verbs) build their passive participles on the first stem following the pattern *p'īl*.[24] The written form in the Qur'ān suggests that the Syro-Aramaic root ܨܘܪ / *ṣwar* > ܨܪ / *ṣār* ("to depict, to draw") is the one in question; this root corresponds to the Arabic صور / *ṣwr*. However, because in Arabic the first verbal stem of this root is still current only in the contracted secondary form صار / *ṣāra* (basic meaning: "to become"), we cannot conclude with certainty that the root صور / *ṣwr* (basic meaning: "to depict") is meant, especially because this root is only current in the second and fifth Arabic verbal stems (*ṣawwara* / *ta-ṣawwara* ["to depict, to draw" / "to visualize, to imagine"]).

Syro-Aramaic grammar turns out to be an indispensable key for deciphering this unusual Arabic spelling صيرى / *ṣīrā*.[25] Under the Syro-Aramaic participial form ܨܝܪܐ / *ṣīrā* (in the *status emphaticus*), the *Thesaurus* (II:3384) gives as an Arabic correspondence the form مصوّر / *mu-ṣawwar*. For the semantics of the verb ܨܪ / *ṣār*, Mannā (632b, under [4]) gives the Arabic meanings تصوّر / *ta-ṣawwara*), تخيّل /*ta-ḫayyala* ("to visualize, to imagine").

Conclusion:

In understanding the term ضيزى / *ḍīzā*, a Qur'ānic expression (Q 53:22) that has not even yet been recognized as problematic and that has nonetheless been mis-read and mis-understood, the Syro-Aramaic language has proven to be an unavoidable prerequisite for explaining both its morphology and its semantics. This new understanding gives the following result:

Mis-transcribed Arabic: تلك اذا قسمة ضيزى
Canonical reading: *tilka iḏan qismatun ḍīzā*
Resulting meaning: "That would be an unjust division"

Corrected Syro-Arabic: تلك اذا قسمة صيرى
New reading: *tilka iḏan qismatun ṣīrā*[26]
New meaning: "This is therefore a fictional attribution."[27]

If we were to bring this statement into contemporary Arabic, it would read thus:

تلك اذا قسمة مصوّرة = مخيّلة = خيالية
(*tilka iḏan qismatun mu-ṣawwara = mu-ḫayyala = ḫayālīya*)

3.2.4 On the Qur'ānic Spelling سورة / *sūra*

Our discussion of the semantic field of the root صور / *ṣwr* concludes with some comments on the Qur'ānic spelling سورة / *sūra* (with ـسـ / *s*), over against the Syro-Aramaic spelling ܨܘܪܬܐ / *ṣūrtā* (with the emphatic ص / *ṣ*). The interchangeability of the voiceless sibilant س / *s* and the emphatic ص / *ṣ* is hardly rare in Semitic languages. As just one example, one might think of the Syro-Aramaic ܣܝܒܪ / *saybar* ("to undergo, to endure") and the Arabic صبر / *ṣabara* ("to be patient, to persevere"); the two ways of writing the Qur'ānic form صراط / *ṣirāṭ* ("line, way") with ص /*ṣ* or with س /*s* as سراط / *sirāṭ*, are also well-known (even though here there is no phonetic difference due to the emphatic ط / *ṭ*). In the case of *sūra*, *Lisān* (IV:387a) provides an interesting note concerning the inhabitants of Baṣra (in what is now southern Iraq), who apparently built the plurals of سورة / *sūra* and صورة / *ṣūra* in precisely the same way; unfortunately, the text does not give any other information regarding a possible difference in meaning.

It is likely no accident, however, that we find the decisive evidence for writing *sūra* with س / *s* rather than with ص / *ṣ* in southern Babylonia, namely, in Mandaean. The Mandaean lexicon offers us the following testimony:

> *Surah 2* for *ṣura*? in *surḫ udmutḫ ḏ-gabra* Gy 391:6 the image (?) and likeness of a man.[28]

The question marks are unnecessary, for the Qur'ān provides further evidence that the word *sūra* could be written in Mesopotamia either with س / *s* or with ص / *ṣ*. This surprising testimony from Mandaean adds another detail in favor of the thesis that the Qur'ānic text emerged in the region of Eastern Syria/Mesopotamia.

Finally, from the perspective of the history of religions, we must ask how the Qur'ān came to describe its own text with the term *sūra*. I have already anticipated the answer above (n. 20):

> unde ܨܘܪܬܐ (*ṣūrtā*) etiam sine ܟܬܒ (*kṯāḇ*) valet *textus Scripturarum*, B.O. iii. i. 87, 97, 153, 166, 174, 261; ܨܘܪܬܐ (*ṣūrtā*) "*Vetus et Novum Testamentum,*" Ass. C.B.V. iii. 280 ult."

Following this evidence, in the Syrian Christian tradition, the word ܨܘܪܬܐ / *ṣūrtā* (> Arabic صورة / *ṣūra* = سورة / *sūra* = "transcription") meant the entire text of the Old and New Testaments, just as "Scripture" meant "Bible." By using the term *sūra*, then, as it repeatedly expressed, the Qur'ān understood itself originally as a partial reproduction of the Syriac ܨܘܪܬܐ / *ṣūrtā*, that is, "Scripture" = the "Bible." However, that the Qur'ān used the term to indicate its own individual chapters does not change its fundamental self-understanding, according to which it wanted to see itself as a part of the entire text of the Bible.

3.3 اية / *āya* < ܐܬܐ / *āṯā*

As the third and final term in this series of words concerning textual units, the word اية / *āya* means the smallest element of the Qur'ānic *sūra* (= "transcription, text, wording"), that is, the individual letters. When God speaks in the Qur'ān of his ايات / *āyāt* (in the plural), he means by this term the contents of the written signs that make up his recorded, transcribed words. As a result, the word *āya* (a word that in Syriac also meant "wondrous sign") became a synonym for كلمة الله / *kalimat Allāh*, the "Word of God." This is why one encounters repeatedly the phrase ايات الله / *āyāt Allāh* ("the written signs of God") in the Qur'ān.[29]

An innovation here is the use of اية / *āya* in the sense of "verse," that is, to indicate units from the division of the Qur'ānic Surahs into individual sentences (or units thereof), a process that was introduced in the later Islamic tradition, following the example of the Bible. When the Qur'ān speaks of ايت محكمت / *āyāt muḥkamāt* and واخر متشبهت / *wa-uḫar mutašābihāt* in Q 3:7, however, it does not mean "distinct and ambiguous verses" in the modern sense, as Paret translates it (44), but rather "precise, faithful," or (following Syro-Aramaic understanding) "well-known sections of the mother-text (i.e., corresponding to the Bible) and other (non-canonical sections) comparable (to these canonical parts, in content)."[30]

3.3.1 On the Etymology of اية / *āya*

Arthur Jeffery, following Alphonse Mingana, considered it more likely that the Arabs took this strange word over from Syriac-speaking Christians than from the Hebrew word אות / *ōṯ*.[31] However, Mingana (himself an Eastern

Syrian) seems not to have recognized that the Syriac word ܐܬܐ / *āṯā*, as a Qur'ānic *rasm*, must have read as اثة / *āṯa* rather than as اية / *āya* (following traditional pronunciation).[32] But he could not have doubted his conclusion, because the Qur'ānic mis-reading had been taken over into Christian Arabic long ago in the past, namely, in the Arabic translation of the Bible. It is therefore no surprise that even famous German scholars of Semitics—men such as Theodor Nöldeke, Carl Brockelmann, Wilhelm Gesenius, as well as the *Thesaurus* (to name only a few) —saw no reason, in the case of the Qur'ānic mis-reading اية / *āya*, to suspect anything other than the etymologically adequate, classical Arabic expression corresponding to the Syro-Aramaic (or Hebrew) one.[33] However, the absence of this expression in the Arabic dialects makes its presence in the Qur'ān quite glaring, as an unmediated loan-word from Syro-Aramaic, as Jeffrey rightly noted.[34] But concerning what Jeffrey mentions in conclusion, namely, its appearance in the so-called "Old Arabic" poetry, we must conclude that either this poetry was post-Qur'ānic, or the word was just as mis-read when it was written down in the ninth or tenth century as it was in the Qur'ān; either possibility would contradict the theory of oral transmission.[35]

In fact, the Qur'ān itself provides testimony for the pronunciation اثة / *āṯa*. Qur'ānic scholars in both East and West up to the present day have overlooked the fact that the Qur'ān has preserved the etymologically-correct written form of the plural (following Syro-Aramaic pronunciation) in Surah 19:74. There the text reads (following the canonical reading):

وكم اهلكنا قبلهم من قرن هم احسن اثثا وريا

(wa-kam ahlaknā qablahum min qarnin hum aḥsanu aṯāṯan wa-ri'ya)

Paret, 252: But how many generations have we allowed to perish before them —generations who were better endowed and presented themselves better (than they)! [Aber wie viele Generationen haben wir vor ihnen zugrunde gehen lassen, die *besser ausgestattet* waren und *mehr vorstellten* (als sie)!]

The two expressions اثثا / *aṯāṯan* and ريا / *ri'yā* (read as *ru'yā* in contemporary and classical Arabic) are synonyms that explain one another. While اثثا / *aṯāṯan* reproduces the Syro-Aramaic plural form ܐܬܘܬܐ / *āṯwāṯā* (after the disappearance of the unstressed medial semi-vowel *w* before the stressed, long *ā* > *āṯāṯā*) in its contracted form[36], ريا / *ri'yā* (*ru'yā*) is a loan-translation from the Syro-Aramaic ܚܙܬܐ / *ḥzāṯā*. Mannā gives the following Arabic correspondences for the two expressions: a) (46a) ܐܬܐ / *āṯā* (8): عبرة / *'ibra* ("example, model"); b) (230b) ܚܙܬܐ / *ḥzāṯā* (4, besides the basic meaning of "seeing, sight, appearance"): قدوة. مثال. عبرة / *qudwa, miṯāl, 'ibra* ("example, model").

Ṭabarī (XVI:117ff.) cites fourteen chains of transmission concerning these two Arabic expressions, and he then gives the explanations of the traditional commentators as follows: he says a) that اثاث / *aṯāṯ* means "possession" or "furnishing" (hence the meaning of "furniture" in modern Arabic); and b) that ريا / *ri'yā* (*ru'yā*) means "appearance." He reports that the Arab philologists do not agree with one another as to whether اثاث / *aṯāṯ* actually represents a singular or plural form. For example, while al-Aḥmar defends the position that it is a plural whose singular is اثاثة / *aṯāṯa*, al-Farrā' saw it as a type of collective noun, so that there would be no corresponding singular form; the latter goes on to say that, if one were to build a plural form from اثاث / *aṯāṯ*, it would be either آثة / *āṯṯa* or أثث / *uṯuṯ*.

Due to the Qur'ān's authority, the *Lisān* (II:110f.) could not help seeing in this difficult word the verbal root أثث / *aṯaṯa* (which does not actually exist in Arabic). It sets this root with its homophone that bears the basic meaning of "to be plentiful" and then adduces expressions that have nothing whatsoever to do, phraseologically speaking, with this Qur'ānic loan-word.[37]

Based on the conjectural and inconclusive explanations of the Arab commentators and philologists, Paret (as opposed to Blachère and Bell) recognized that the two expressions in question from Surah 19:74 are enigmatic.

Following Ṭabarī, the two latter translators give the verse under discussion as follows:

> *Blachère*, 335: [Yet] how many generations before them have We destroyed—generations that were more impressive in goods and appearance? [Combien (pourtant), avant eux, avons-Nous fait périr de générations qui en *impo-saient* advantage par les *biens* et *l'apparence*?)
>
> *Bell*, I:290, 75: But how many a generation have We destroyed before them, better both in goods and in repute?

The preceding philological analysis has shown that these two enigmatic expressions can be explained in two different steps, thanks to the methodology demonstrated in *The Syro-Aramaic Reading of the Koran*: a) اثاث / *āṯāṯ* can be explained morphologically as a secondary Aramaic plural form and semantically with the meaning "examples;" b) by means of back-translation into Syro-Aramaic, the meaning of the Arabic word ريا / *ri'yā* / *ru'yā* in its Qur'ānic context can be unlocked, showing the lexically corresponding Syro-Aramaic word to be a synonym of the preceding Qur'ānic word. Based on these conclusions, then, we should now read and understand Surah 19:74 in the following way:

> وكم اهلكنا قبلهم من قرن هم احسن اثثا وريا
>
> *wa-kam ahlaknā qablahum min qarnin hum aḥsanu āṯāṯā wa-ru'yā*
>
> How many generations before them have we allowed to perish, who (in comparison) were better examples and (quite) exemplary (lit. 'example')!"

3.3.2 Correction of اية / *āya* into اثة / *āṯa*

At first glance it may appear too daring to make the Syro-Aramaic *hapax legomenon* اثثا / *āṯāṯā* (< ܐܬܘ̈ܬܐ / *āṯwāṯā*), transmitted correctly in the Qur'ān at Q 19:74, the justification for changing the reading اية / *āya* to اثة / *āṯa*, especially since the former appears in at least 382 places in the Qur'ān (in the singular and the plural, with and without a personal suffix) and has become standard over the centuries, even beyond the Islamic world. Nevertheless, the fact that this word has no real Arabic root, just like the many other Qur'ānic mis-readings that I have demonstrated (among them real Arabic words), should not exclude the possibility of a later, incompetent setting of diacritical points to this foreign (Syriac) word. Still, we should not proceed too hastily to conclude that we have here a mis-reading before we have carefully analyzed the Syro-Aramaic semantic field.

If we assume that the Qur'ānic plural form اثثا / *āṯāṯā* (< ܐܬܘ̈ܬܐ / *āṯwāṯā*) is the correct reading, then the corresponding Syro-Aramaic singular form would be ܐܬܐ / *āṯā*, which would equal the Arabic اثة / *āṯa*, not اية / *āya*. Someone might suggest that the plural form اثثا / *āṯāṯā* is a mis-reading, but we can exclude this possibility on morphological grounds, because *external* (i.e., regular) feminine plurals in Arabic cannot take a final-*alif* (*ā*). Or, if one wanted to see here an Arabic *accusative of specification (tamyīz)* in the Qur'ānic written form اثثا (reading it as اياتا / *āyātan* instead of *āṯāṯā*), then the final-*ā* would not be permissible. In other words, the Qur'ānic orthography faithfully reproduces the Syro-Aramaic plural form with its final-*ā*.

If we adduce other Syro-Aramaic variants that derive from the verb underlying our term (ܗܘܐ / *hwā* ["to be"]), then we find the following primary nominal constructions (*Thesaurus*, I:987f.): ܗܘܝܐ / *hwāyā* ("existence, birth, generation, creation"); ܗܘܝܘܬܐ / *hwāyūṯā*, ܗܘܝܢܘܬܐ / *hawyānūṯā* ("creation, bringing into existence"). The form ܗܘܝܬܐ / *hwāytā* ("creation, formation"), known from Neo-Aramaic, leads us to posit a related (but unattested) form *ܗܘܝܬܐ / *hwīṯā* (> Arabic هوية / *huwīya*, or dialectically, *hawīya* ["nature, identity"]). From this Syriac form, and by means of sound-shift, comes the expression of existence ܐܝܬ / *īṯ* (*ܗܘܝܬܐ / *hwīṯā* > *ܐܝܬܐ / *īṯā* > ܐܝܬ / *īṯ*) and another secondary form, ܝܬܐ / *yāṯā* ("essence, existence, nature"). The Syriac forms with postponed definite article ܐܝܬܝܐ / *īṯyā* and *ܐܝܬܐ / *īṯā* must go back to an Imperial Aramaic form, which in the *status absolutus* must have been **īyā*. This form entered Arabic as إيا / *īyā* and was used alone as a particle in connection with the personal suffix as a sign of the accusative (mostly), e.g., in Q 1:5: اياك نعبد واياك نستعين / *īyāka naʿbudu wa-īyāka nastaʿīn* ("It is <u>you</u> we worship and <u>your</u> <u>assistance</u> we request").[38] In the dialects إيا / *īyā* is also used in connection with the personal suffix, but prepositionally (after the conjunction و / *w*), in the sense of "and" or "with," e.g., أنا وإيّاك / *anā w-īyā-k*

("I and 'your being'" = "I and you" or "I with you"). However, the substantive آية / *āya* cannot be derived from this particle إيا / *īyā*.

A remnant of the Syriac secondary form ܝܬܐ / *yāṯā* ("essence, existence, being, presence") (> Arabic *yāt*) still exists today in the contemporary colloquial Arabic of the Middle East, in connection with *kull* / *kəll* ("entirety" = "all"), as follows: *kull* + *yāt* + *nā* = *kullyātnā* (literally, "the entirety of our being" = "we all"), *kull* + *yāt* + *kon* = *kullyātkon* ("you all"), *kull* + *yāt* + *(h)on* = *kullyāt(h)on* ("they all"). In north Mesopotamian dialects the forms are contracted: *kəllətnā* ("we all"), *kəllətkən* ("you all"), *kəllətən* ("they all"). However, there is no trace whatsoever of this form *yāt* in Arabic literature. Consequently, it is hard to accept that the hypothetical Qur'ānic reading آية / *āya* could have been derived from the Syriac secondary form ܝܬܐ / *yāṯā*, or even from the dialectal Arabo-Aramaic *yāt*.

These considerations have allowed us to conclude that the diacritical points placed underneath the word آية / *āya* are incorrect in 382 places in the Qur'ān. In addition, though, an examination of the Qur'ānic usage of آية / *āya* shows that the various semantic nuances that appear (depending on the context) are exactly the same as those of the Syro-Aramaic ܐܬܐ / *āṯā*.[39] So, for example, we see Q 3:41, where Zechariah asks God for a "sign" (آية / *āya*) of what God has announced to him, namely, the birth of John; there God announces to him as a "sign" that he will communicate with other people for three days by means of sign-language alone (رمزا / *ramzan* < Syro-Aramaic ܪܡܙܐ / *rmāzā*, *remzā* [Luke 1:22]). In the Peshitta (the Syriac version of the Bible), the angel gives the shepherds a "sign" (ܐܬܐ / *āṯā*) as well, namely, that they will find a child wrapped in swaddling cloths and lying in a manger (Luke 2:12).

We also find a typical loan-translation in Q 17:12, with the expressions اية الليل / *āyat al-layl* and اية النهار / *āyat an-nahār*, which Paret (228) translates literally as "sign of the night" and "sign of the day" [Bell, Surah 17:13, translates in the same manner]. Although the sense of both expressions is clear, in themselves they remain foreign to the Arabic language. In the Syro-Aramaic language, however, ܐܬܘܬܐ / *āṯwāṯā* ("sign") means, among other things, the heavenly bodies (cf. the English expression "signs of the zodiac"), including the "sun" and the "moon."[40]

Such loan-translations provide especially clear evidence that the Qur'ān transcribed the Syro-Aramaic orthography ܐܬܐ / *āṯā* to mean the Arabic word اثة / *āṯa* rather than the (at a later date) mis-read and mis-pointed اية / *āya*, especially as this word is not known in any Arabic dialect with this pronunciation. As a result, we can say that the correction of اية / *āya* into اثة / *āṯa* is well-founded from the perspectives of philology and historical linguistics. The plural here, then, should no longer read آيات / *āyāt* but rather

آثات / *āṯāt* or آثاث / *āṯāṯ* (following the Aramaic spirantizing of the final-*t*, and corresponding to the correctly-transmitted form found in Surah 19:74).

We may adduce here two other Qur'ānic texts, where written forms have been mis-read in the same way. In Surah 44:36 we read:

فاتوا بابئنا ان كنتم صدقين

(*fa-'tū bi-ābā'inā in kuntum ṣādiqīn*)

This verse has been understood by the modern Qur'ānic translators just as Ṭabarī (XXV:128) explained it:

> *Paret*, 414: But produce our (dead) fathers (again), if you speak the truth! [Bringt doch unsere (*verstorbenen*) *Väter* (*wieder*) herbei, wenn (anders) ihr die Wahrheit sagt!]
>
> *Blachère*, 527: Bring our fathers back, if you are truthful! [*Faites revenir* nos *pères*, si vous êtes véridiques!]
>
> *Bell*, II:500, 35: Produce our fathers, if ye speak the truth.

The Qur'ānic context concerns people who doubt, those who demand for themselves proofs concerning the resurrection at the last day; they do not ask for the immediate return of their dead fathers, for there is no discussion of "fathers" here at all. The mis-read written form بابائنا / *bi-ābā'inā* could be read باياتنا / *bi-āyātinā* according to the current mis-reading, but it should now be read as باثاتنا / *bi-āṯātinā* (or, following the Aramaic, باثاثنا / *bi-āṯāṯinā*) and understood thus:

> Then bring the proofs (that convince) us (lit.: "our proofs"), if you speak the truth![41]

In a similar way, we should correct the written form found in Surah 45:25 that has been equally mis-pointed:

و اذ تتلى عليهم اثـتـنا بينت ما كان حجتهم الا ان قالوا
ايتوا باثـتـنا ان كنتم صدقين

(*wa-iḏ tu-tlā 'alayhim āṯātunā bayyināt(in) mā kāna ḥujjatuhum illā an qālū aytū bi-āṯātinā in kuntum ṣādiqīn*[42])

It has been traditionally understood thus:

> *Paret (417)*: And when our verses (lit.: "signs") are read out to them as clear proofs (*baiyināt*), they have no other argument (to introduce) than to say, "Produce our (dead) fathers (again), if you speak the truth!" [Und wenn ihnen unsere Verse (w.: Zeichen) als *klare Beweise* (baiyināt) verlesen warden, haben sie keinen anderen Beweisgrund (anzuführen), als daß sie sagen: "Bringt unsere (*verstorbenen*) *Väter* (*wieder*) *herbei*, wenn (anders) ihr die Wahrheit sagt!"]
>
> *Blachère (531):* When our clear *aya* are communicated to them, they have no other argument than to object: "Bring our fathers back, if you are truthful!"

> [Quand Nos claires *aya* leur sont communiquées, ils n'ont d'autre argument que d'objecter: "*Ramenez*-nous nos *pères*, si vous êtes véridiques!"]
>
> *Bell, II:505, 24:* And when Our signs are recited to them as Evidences, their only argument is: "Produce our fathers, if ye speak the truth."

New understanding:

> And when our written signs (i.e., our transcribed words) are recited to them (so that they are self-)evident [43], they have no other objection than to say, "Then bring the proofs (lit.: signs) (that convince) us (lit.: "bring our signs"), if you speak the truth!"

If we include these two emendations (Surahs 44:36; 45:25), then the total number of textual locations rises to 384 in which one single written form has been mis-read (in its plene and defective forms). However, because the Qur'ān, in the verse-numbering of the canonical Cairo edition, has approximately 6,236 verses, all of which are called by the mis-read word "*āya*," one can easily imagine how difficult it would be for the new reading of "*āṯā*" to carry the day. If one takes this reality into account, then one will have to decide to live with the traditional mis-reading, all the while clarifying it as a historico-linguistic error. In a similar fashion, all historical linguists have resigned themselves to accept the arbitrary reading of the loan-word *Qur'ān* which should have been read as the original Syro-Aramaic word *Qeryān*. Once again, both misreadings are further proof against the "dogma" of the oral transmission of the Koran.

4. The Christian-Syriac Origin of Friday as Islam's Weekly Day of Prayer and Rest

4.1 Introductory Remarks

Even if we have already sufficiently shown the Syro-Aramaic origin of the three basic terms of the Qur'ān as an originally Christian-Syriac liturgical book, there still remains the question, relevant for the history of religions, of whether a Christian-Syriac background (in liturgical perspective) could lie behind Friday as the weekly day of prayer and rest in Islam. An easy conjecture is this: at its beginning Islam attempted to establish Friday as the weekly day of prayer and rest in order to distinguish itself from the Jews' Sabbath and the Christians' Sunday, and in order to underscore the growing self-confidence of a national religion that was expanding along with the political power of the newly-founded (Arabian) theocracy. Such a conjecture could seem at first glance to illuminate the situation, but it is not entirely satisfactory. A search for other reasons in the history of religions leads to the subsequent question as to why such desires in early Islam did not lead to the choice of Monday, as that day would have made more chronological sense, as following on the Christians' Sunday, which in its turn followed on the Jews' Sabbath. In other words, why did they choose Friday, as this choice seems, so to speak, to go anti-clockwise? We shall now attempt to explain this religio-historical question, which hitherto was not even posed.

4.2 A Qur'ānic Hint

In the canonical edition of the Qur'ān, there is one single text in which Friday is mentioned, but without any context that gives more specific information. In Surah 62, which was later named the "Friday Surah" (سورة الجمعة), verse 9 reads thus:

ياايها الذين امنوا اذا نودي للصلوة من يوم الجمعة
فاسعوا الى ذكر اللـه وذروا البيع ذلكم خير لكم ان كنتم تعلمون

Paret: O you who believe: when there is a call to prayer on Friday (lit.: "*community day*"), then hurry to the prayer (lit.: think of God), and let your business (lit.: "*selling*") be, for the former (brings) you better things if you only knew. [O ihr, die ihr glaubt, wenn am Freitag (wörtlich: *Gemeindetag*) zum Gebet aufgerufen wird, so begebt euch zum Gottesgedenken und lasst das Geschäft (wörtlich: das *Verkaufen*) sein, denn dies (bringt) euch Besseres (ein), wenn ihr wüsstet.]

Pickthall: O ye who believe! When the call is heard for the prayer of the *day of congregation*, haste unto remembrance of Allah and leave your *trading*. That is better for you if ye did but know.

Scholars have not drawn consistent conclusions concerning this late Surah, which is ascribed to the Medinan period. For his part, Ṭabarī (XXVIII:99ff.) does not mention the institution of Friday as the weekly day of prayer at all; of course, by his time (ninth/tenth century) Friday had long been the customary "congregation day" in Islam. One wishes that he had said something about the actual liturgical practices on this day that is so important for Islam.

Lisān is much more illuminating, for there, under the entry الجمعة / *al-ğum'a* (VIII:58b f.) (lit.: "[day of] assembly, congregation day" = "Friday"),[44] we learn that *al-jum'a* (Friday) has only been called *al-ğum'a* since the advent of Islam, and that earlier this day went by the name of يوم العروبة / *yawm al-'arūba* (< Syro-Aramaic ܝܘܡ ܥܪܘܒܬܐ / *yawm 'rub̲tā* = "day of the sunset"). Under the word عروبة / *'arūba*, *Lisān* (I:593) gives a similar explanation: عروبة / *'arūba* and العروبة / *al-'arūba* both mean الجمعة / *al-ğum'a* (Friday). After giving a *ḥadīṯ* (a statement of the Prophet) concerning Friday, it states:

كانت (الجمعة) تسمى عَروبةً ، هو اسم قديم لها ، وكأنه ليس بعربي . يقال : يوم
عروبة ، ويوم العروبة ، والأفسح أن لا يدخلها الألف واللام

> "Earlier Friday was called *'arūba*, a name which does not appear to be Arabic. This expression was current as *yawm 'arūba* or *yawm al-'arūba*, but the form *'arūba*, without the prefixed article *al-*, is more literary (i.e., more classical)."

The form *yawm 'arūba* (i.e., without the Arabic article *al-*) corresponds exactly to the Syro-Aramaic form ܝܘܡ ܥܪܘܒܬܐ / *yawm 'rubtā*, which means "day of the sunset," or "Saturday Eve."[45] This word originally meant the evening before the Sabbath, which Syrian Christians used as a name for Friday after taking it over from the Jewish tradition and re-interpreting it in the light of Christianity. According to this re-interpretation, the setting of the sun on Good Friday, that is, the darkening of the sun that occurred after Jesus' crucifixion (Mt. 27:45; Mk. 15:33; Lk. 23:44-45), symbolizes the end of the Old Covenant and the beginning of the New.[46] As a result, among Syrian Christians Friday is called ܥܪܘܒܬܐ / *'rubtā* ("setting of the sun" = "Friday").

There still remains open the interesting question of whether the pre-Islamic Arabs learned this Syro-Aramaic name for Friday (*'arūba*) from Jews or Christians. The fact that Jewish-Aramaic tradition gives the name ערובתה / *'robtā* (*status emphaticus*) or ערובה / *'rōbā* (*status absolutus*) not only to the evening before the Sabbath but also to the evening before other high holidays speaks in favor of a Christian origin.[47] In Christian Syrian tradition, though, Friday alone is called ܥܪܘܒܬܐ / *'rubtā*, while the evening before other holidays is called ܪܡܫܐ / *ramšā* ("evening[time]" = "vespers"). Incidentally, Heinrich Lewy long ago showed the etymology of the name "Europe" as deriving from the Aramaic ערובה / *'rōbā* ("setting of the sun" = "Occident" = "West").[48]

There is an apparently legendary report in *Lisān* (I:593a f.), according to which Ka'b b. Lu'ayy / لؤي (actually لوي = lwy = Levi), who was the purported grandfather of the Prophet, was the first one to re-name the (Aramaic name) يوم العروبة / *yawm al-'arūba* ("day of the sunset") as الجمعة / *al-ǧum'a* ("assembly-, congregation-day"). If one were to believe this story as true, then it would be ensured that Friday was called *al-ǧum'ā* only after the advent of Islam; on the other hand, we could then not exclude a Jewish-Aramaic origin for the name.[49]

However, it is in a testimony transmitted in the Arabic tradition that we find the explanation that truly settles the question in terms of the history of religions, specifically in the Qur'ānic "readings literature." This particular text concerns the famous work كتاب المصاحف / *Kitāb al-maṣāḥif* ("The Book of the Qur'ānic Codices"), written by the Qur'ānic scholar as-Siǧistanī (d. 316 AH / 941 CE) and edited by Arthur Jeffery (1892–1959).[50] The readings transmitted in this work supposedly trace back to written witnesses that are older than the canonical Qur'ānic edition of 'Uṯmān (Osman) that is known to us. Jeffery makes the following statement in the section entitled "The Old Codices":

> The Kitāb al-maṣāḥif of ibn abī Dāwūd together with a collection of the variant readings from the codices of ibn Mas'ūd, Ubai, 'Alī, ibn 'Abbās, Anas, abū Mūsā and other early Qur'ānic authorities which present a type of text anterior to that of the canonical text of 'Uthmān.

Jeffery seems to overlook an extremely important reading on Surah 62:9 from the codex of Ubai b. Ka'b; alternatively, he may simply not have grasped its wide-ranging importance for the history of religions. In the Qur'ānic text in question, where the Cairo edition has يوم الجمعة / *yawm al-ǧum'a* ("assembly-, congregation-day") for "Friday," the Ubai codex (p. 170, Q 62:9) has the variant يوم العروبة الكبرى / *yawm al-'arūba l-kubrā.* This corresponds to the Syro-Aramaic expression ܝܘܡ ܥܪܘܒܬܐ ܪܒܬܐ / *yawm 'rubtā rabbtā* ("day of the great setting of the sun" = "day of the great Friday").[51] This in turn corresponds to the expression in contemporary Christian Arabic يوم الجمعة العظيمة / *yawm al-ǧum'a l-'aẓīma* ("day of the great Friday" = "Good Friday").

This authentic testimony provides us clear proof that the Syro-Aramaic Good Friday was the direct predecessor to the Islamic Friday. If one is aware that the Syriac liturgical office for every Friday commemorates Good Friday, then one will be able to understand why this day's soteriological meaning causes it to receive more honor than the day of the Resurrection in some Christian congregations (and especially in the piety of the common people). This perspective casts an entirely new light on the emergence of Islam and on the pre-Islamic Arabo-Christian community whose trace seems to have become entirely blurred due to an understanding of history distorted by the lens of Islam. The meaning of the Dome of the Rock in Jerusalem, as a testimony to this pre-Islamic, Syro-Arabian Christianity, henceforward achieves a new liturgical confirmation of its importance as the grave of Christ (Arabic قبة الصخرة / *qubbat aṣ-ṣaḫra* = "stone grave") and as a pilgrimage site of the Christian Arabs under the caliph 'Abd al-Malik b. Marwān (685-705).[52] We should here remember the only Qur'ānic text that concerns the crucifixion of Christ (Q 4:157), a text that has been completely misunderstood and misinterpreted by the Qur'ānic commentators; this text must be interpreted anew in concert with the other Qur'ānic texts that speak of the death and resurrection of Christ (Surahs 3:55; 5:117; 19:33; 72:19).[53]

Now that we have shown the Christian Syrian origin of the basic terms of the Qur'ān as an originally Christian Syrian lectionary, this unexpected hint of a pre-Islamic, Christian Syrian liturgy leads us logically to the original topic of this essay: the mysterious letters in the Qur'ān. In what follows I will demonstrate how these "mysterious" abbreviations are connected to a Christian Syrian liturgy.

5. Concerning the Meaning of the Abbreviations in the Syriac Daily Office

The breviary for the liturgical year in the West Syrian (Antiochene) church's liturgical tradition exists in seven volumes; one of these volumes, the one concerning the Advent and Christmas seasons, serves as the foundation for this presentation of the Syriac daily office.[54] The abbreviations in the Syriac breviary belong to the rubrics that contain specific information for each portion of the office. There is a technical term for these abbreviations that consist of one, two, or three letters, with a line above them: the word is either ܝܕܥܐ / *yaḏʿā* (lit., "recognized") or ܝܕܝܥܐ / *yaddīʿā* (lit., "making known"), essentially meaning "clue" or "hint."[55]

These ܝ̈ܕܥܐ / *yadʿē* ("hint-signs"), which generally occur at the beginning of a liturgical text or section, serve to indicate the first words of a hymn that is to follow, as W. Wright surmised: "the word ܝܕܥܐ (*yaḏʿā*) seems to denote the first words, or catch-words of well-known hymns."[56] In fact, depending on the abbreviation, they can indicate much more:

a) Because the liturgy typically begins with a psalm, indicated by the abbreviation ܡܙܡ / *mzm* (=ܡܙܡܘܪܐ / *mazmōrā*), up to three letters can indicate the number of the psalm in question in the Psalter; these letters run from ܐ / *a* (= Ps. 1) to ܩܢ / *qn* (= Ps. 150).

b) The letter ܩ / *q* stands for ܩܠܐ / *qālā* ("musical key, melody, tune") and indicates the tone of the following chant (from the eight tones in Syrian hymnody); then follow the introductory words of the exemplary hymn (e.g., "to the tune of 'Praise the Lord'").

c) The letters ܦܬ / *pt* mean ܦܬܓܡܐ / *peṯgāmā* ("responsorial") and are followed by the corresponding responsorial lyrics.

d) The abbreviations ܦܘ / *pu* (=ܦܘܢܝܐ / *punnāyā*) and ܥܘ / *ʿu* (=ܥܘܢܝܐ / *ʿunnāyā*) both mean "antiphon" and are followed by the corresponding lyric.

e) Occasionally one finds before a Gospel reading a chapter with the letters ܩܦ / *qf* (= ܩܦܠܐܘܢ < κεφαλαῖον)

f) The letters ܘܫܪ / *wšr* (=ܘܫܪܟܐ / *w-šarkā*) mean "etc."

g) Between the individual hymns one regularly finds the letters ܫܘ / *šu* (=ܫܘܒܚܐ / *šuḇḥā*), representing the doxology "Gloria Patri" ("Glory be to the Father…"), sung by the priest; after this, one finds the word ܡܢ / *men* ("from [now and unto ages of ages]"), which the choir or congregation answers as the beginning of the stanza that follows. One sometimes sees a ܗ / *h*, which stands for *hallelujah*; in the dictionaries and other texts, one sees for the ܗ / *h* the meaning ܗܢܘ /

hānaw ("that is, i.e."). There are also a number of other abbreviations in the Syriac literature.

The following selections from the Syriac breviary cited above are intended to serve as visual illustrations of a few of the abbreviations I have mentioned. These examples include a few pointers to individual psalms. On the scans they can easily be found as the only letters with a horizontal stroke above.

5.2 Individual Examples

Example 1

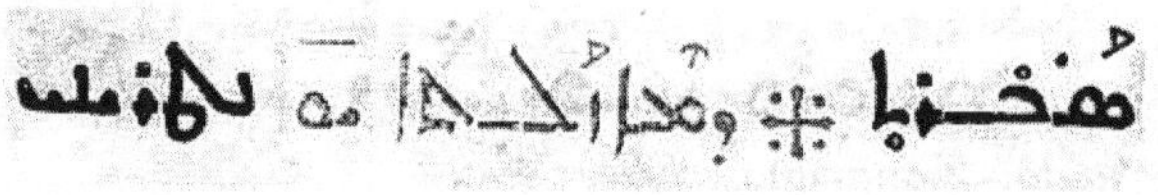

(p. 52) After the division marker in the middle of the line, we see *d-mezaltā YW naṭarayn(i)*. The first word means "(Advent Sunday) of the Visitation," referring to Mary's visit to her cousin Elizabeth. "*YW*" is a number marker, referring to Psalm 16. The following word *naṭarayn(i)* provides the beginning of the corresponding Psalm: "Protect me (Lord)!"

Example 2

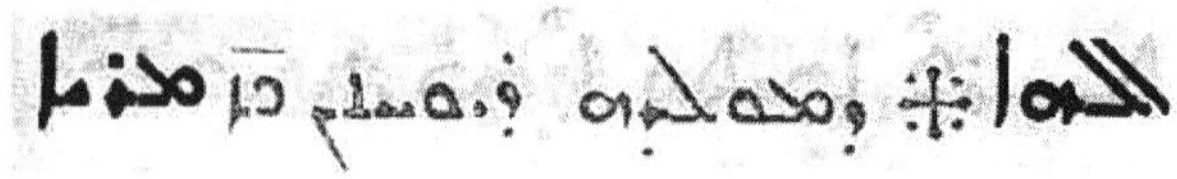

(p. 52) *d-mawlāḏeh d-Yoḥannān* = "(Advent Sunday) of the Birth of John"
KZ = Psalm 27
Māryā = the beginning of the Psalm: "The Lord (is my light)"

Example 3

(p. 52) *d-Yawsep̄* = "(Advent Sunday) of Joseph's Dream(-Vision)"
KW = Psalm 26
dunayn^{y} = the beginning of the Psalm: "Vindicate me (Lord)"

Example 4

(p. 52) *da-qḏām yaldā* = "(Advent Sunday) before the Nativity"
LG = Psalm 33
šabbaḥ[w] = the beginning of the Psalm: "Praise (the Lord, O you righteous ones)"

Example 5

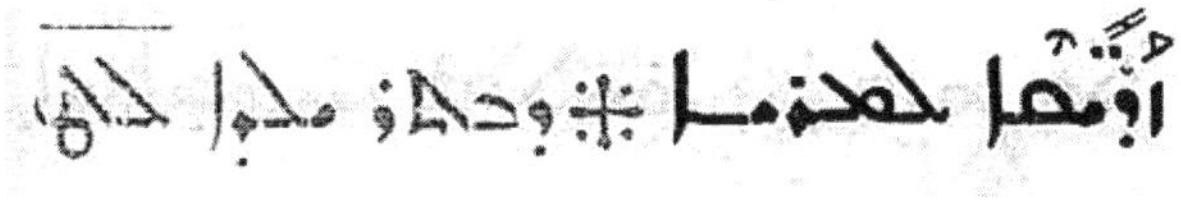

(p. 52) *d-ḇāṯar yaldā* = "(Sunday) after the Nativity"
LṬ = Psalm 39

Example 6

(p. 52) After the division marker: *kurrāḵā* = "response"
BQ = *b-qālā*, meaning "according to the tune;" *qām Māran* are the first words of the tune: "Our Lord is risen"

Example 7

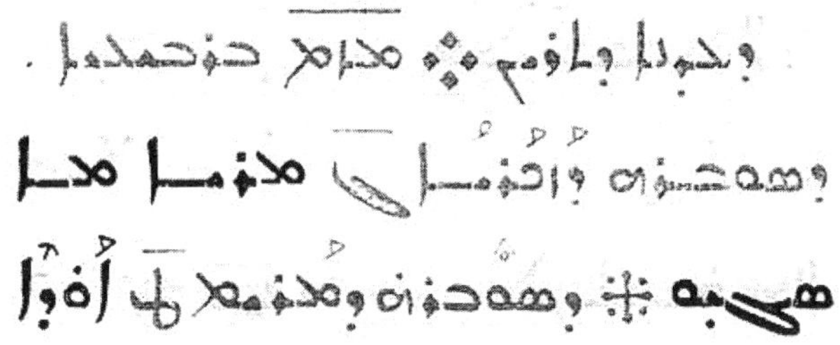

1st line: (p. 53) After the upper division marker: *MZM* = *mazmōrā* = "Psalm" *ba-rḇīʿāyā* = in the fourth tone

2nd line: *d-subbāreh da-Zḵaryā* = "(Sunday) of the Annunciation to Zechariah" – *G* = Psalm 3; *Māryā mā sgīw* = the beginning of the Psalm: "Lord, how numerous are (my foes)"

3rd line: After the lower division marker: *d-subbārāh d-Maryam* = "(Sunday) of the Annunciation to Mary" – *Ṭ* = Psalm 9 – *awdē* = the beginning of the Psalm: "I will praise (the Lord with all my heart)"

Example 8

(Q 61) Before the division marker: *ŠW* = *šuḇḥā lāḵ* = "Praise be to you"
After the division marker: *šuḇḥā leh l-ḥaḏ ba-ṯlāṯā* = "Praise be to the One in Three (the Trinity)"

Example 9

The division marker in this Syriac edition consists of four points arranged in the form of a cross; it serves to divide stanzas, textual sections, and primary sentences. The marker by itself looks like this:

Compare the division marker for verses that one finds in a Qur'ānic manuscript:

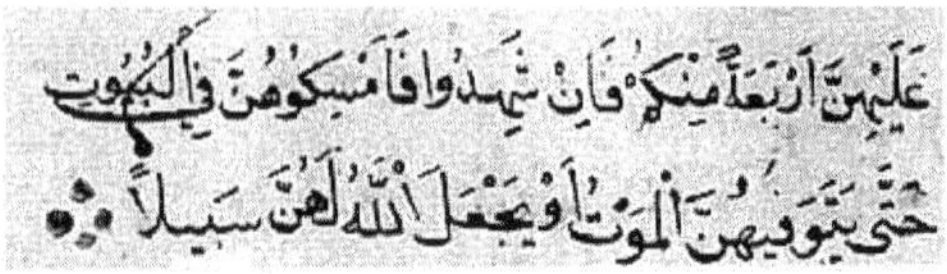

(detail:)

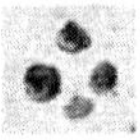

5.3 Summary

This analysis of the normal abbreviations found in the Syriac daily office edition has demonstrated their use to indicate the following categories: doxologies; psalms; responsorial texts, antiphons, and responses; tunes, melodies, and modes; and biblical readings. These results are certainly connected with the etymological analysis of the three Qur'ānic expressions of literary scope, of whose Syro-Aramaic origin there is now no doubt. But the results are also confirmed liturgically through the explanation of the Christian Syriac Good Friday as the precursor to the Islamic Friday, as I have shown above. The reconstruction of these facts, relevant as they are to the history of religions, allow us to consider it well-founded to attempt to place the so-called "mysterious letters in the Qur'ān" in their religio-historical setting and thus to interpret them anew in connection with the liturgical traditions of Syrian Christianity.

6. The "Mysterious Letters" in the Qur'ān

6.1 Introductory Remarks

In order to forestall overly optimistic expectations, I must initially note that the Qur'ān—despite the Syro-Aramaic origin of its name—should only be considered as partially connected with a Christian Syrian liturgy, in that this liturgy originally formed the foundation of the Qur'ān. We must leave it to future studies to show that this liturgy is to be found in the oldest portions of the so-called "Meccan" Surahs; such work will also show that there is far more Christian Syrian liturgy to be found in these earliest sections of the Qur'ān than scholars have thus far seen. However, this liturgy is not the same as those Eastern and Western Syrian liturgies with which scholars are familiar and whose roots stretch back into early Christianity. It is certain that the Qur'ānic liturgy is older in some parts than Islam; indeed, as we already know, it goes back to a pre-Nicene Christianity and is similar to an early Christian Syrian liturgy. However, its predecessors seem to have vanished in the mists of history; we have no written evidence for it whatsoever before the Qur'ān. If one adds to this recognition the confused circumstances under which laypeople apparently collected, edited, and sometimes misunderstood the Qur'ānic materials at a later date, one can begin to understand the scholarly discomfort with the efforts to disentangle and historically reconstruct this text.

Theodor Nöldeke's *Geschichte des Qorans* ([History of the Qur'ān]1909–38; ed. Schwally, Bergsträßer, Pretzl) provided western Qur'ānic scholarship with a crucial recognition, namely, that the Islamic exegetes' rough division of the Qur'ānic text into earlier Meccan and later Medinan Surahs must be chronologically sub-divided into a greater number of time periods. Analysis of the sigla (or "mysterious letters") has led us to the further understanding that these letters are exclusively associated with the beginnings of Meccan Surahs (with the exception of Surahs 2 and 3, although their beginnings should in fact be assigned to the Meccan period). On the basis of this knowledge, and in interpreting the sigla, we will need to distinguish between the first and second Meccan periods. Naturally, the liturgical portions of the Qur'ān belong to the first period; there we will find sigla that have a relationship to the liturgy. We can assign the beginning of a sermon (cf. Q 75:17–19) to the second period; in that group are preserved portions whose beginning invokes the revealed "written text" (*kitāb*), of which the Qur'ān understands itself to be a part. Some scholars have already noted that some sigla stand at the beginning of such Surahs, a recognition that will make the meaning of a whole set of sigla comprehensible. Because these latter sigla are, generally speaking, not identical with those of the Syrian liturgy, and because the pre-Qur'ānic liturgical tradition was apparently irreparably lost by this point in time, it is possible that we have only interpretive proposals to make based on comparisons with liturgical texts; our hope, though, is that these will best allow for the unique ways in which the Qur'ānic text was edited.

With all of this said, we can now proceed to the explanation of the individual sigla.

6.2 Concerning the Meaning of the Individual Sigla

Given that the Qur'ān is a liturgical book (*qəryānā* ["lectionary"]), and corresponding to the tradition of the Syrian daily office, some Surahs begin with a Psalm verse. This is the case with Surahs 57, 59, 61, 62, and 64 (and possibly also Surahs 67 and 87). So, for example, in Surah 62:1, we read: *yusabbiḥ l(i)-Allāh mā fī s-samāwāt wa mā fī-l-'arḍ* ("Let all that is in heaven and on earth praise God"). The Hebrew reads: יְהַלְלוּהוּ שָׁמַיִם וָאָרֶץ יַמִּים וְכָל־רֹמֵשׂ בָּם *yəhal^ə lū-hū šāmayim wā-ʾārāṣ yammīm wə-kāl [=kɔl] romēś* (Ps. 69:34: "Let heaven and earth praise him!").

Sigla 1–3: ص / Ṣ, ق / Q, ن / N (Surahs 38:1; 50:1; 68:1)

We should view the fact that the Qur'ān mentions the Psalms on nine occasions as a pointer to the Psalter, which was a part of the pre-Qur'ānic liturgy just as it was of the Syrian liturgy. Consequently, as in the Syrian daily office, individual letters in the Qur'ān can serve as numbers, pointing to particular Psalms in the Psalter. Of course, the use of these Psalms disappeared in the later Islamic tradition. As a result, the following three letters in the Qur'ān can possibly indicate three Psalms: 1) ص / Ṣ (Q 38:1) would refer to Psalm 90; 2) ق / Q (Q 50:1) would refer to Psalm 100; and 3) ن / N (Q 68:1) would refer to Psalm 50.[57] One could also interpret the ص / Ṣ as ܨܒܐܘܬ / *ṣḇaōṯ* or صباوت / *ṣaba'ūt* ("Lord of Hosts" = "the Powerful, the Almighty"), the ق / Q as ܩܕܝܫ / *qaddīš* or قدوس / *quddūs* ("holy [is/be he]"). In fact, both expressions appear in the "Trisagion": "Holy (are you, God), (holy are you,) Strong...."

Siglum 4: يس / YS = بس / BS

At the beginning of Q 36, there are letters that are traditionally read as يس / *ys*, from which the Islamic tradition has developed a personal name (*Yāsīn*). However, reading the letters as بس / *bs* (because the diacritical points originally did not exist) appears to make more sense, as an abbreviation for the *basmala*, as a normal formula at the beginning of that liturgy. The Syro-Aramaic would have read ܒܫܡ / *b-šem*, which would correspond to the Arabic بسم / *b-ism* = بسم الله الرحمن الرحيم / *b-ismi llāh ar-raḥmān ar-raḥīm* ("in the name of the gracious and merciful God"). This siglum, then, would correspond to the Syriac abbreviation ܫܘ / *šu* (=ܫܘܒܚܐ / *šuḇḥā*) as the doxology "Gloria Patri."

A further group of sigla that can refer to individual Psalm verses and have as their content the praise of God are the following:

Siglum 5: طه / *ṬH (Q 20:1)*

This abbreviation has also been made in the later Islamic tradition into a personal name: *Ṭāhā*. However, it seems to make much more sense to read in it the Syro-Aramaic ܛܒ ܗܘ / *ṭāḇ hū*, which would correspond to the Arabic طيب هو / *ṭayyib(un) huwa* ("he [the Lord] is good"). This also fits well with the following two sigla.

Siglum 6: طسم / *ṬSM (Surahs 26:1; 28:1)*

This abbreviation represents the Syro-Aramaic ܛܫܡ / *ṬŠM* = ܛܒ ܫܡ ܡܪܝܐ / *ṭāḇ šem Māryā*, which would correspond to the Arabic طيب هو اسم الرب / *ṭayyib(un) huwa (i)sm(u) r-Rabb* ("the name of the Lord is good").

Siglum 7: طس / *ṬS (Q 27:1)*

This abbreviation represents the Syro-Aramaic ܛܫ / *ṬŠ* = ܛܒ ܫܡܗ / *ṭāḇ šmeh*, which would correspond to the Arabic طيب هو اسمه / *ṭayyib(un) huwa (i)sm(u)-(hu)* ("[his] name is good").

Siglum 8: حم / *ḤM (Surahs 40:1; 41:1; 42:1; 43:1; 44:1; 45:1; 46:1)*

The seven Surahs that start with the abbreviation حم / *ḥm* also all begin with a text of revelation. As such, this abbreviation has as its content a well-known formula that should be understood as both a praise of God and also an intensifying oath-formula (functioning to emphasize the following text's character as revelatory). Here we should see a correspondence with the fifth proposal of some commentators that Ṭabarī mentioned, according to which some scholars thought that some of these abbreviations did indeed concern oath-formulas that belong to the name of God without stating it explicitly.[58] This conjecture, which has been ignored by Western Qur'ānic scholars, will now be confirmed and concretized with the following analysis.

The Qur'ānic abbreviation حم / *ḥm* corresponds to the Syro-Aramaic ܚܡ / *ḥm*, which is short for ܚܝܘ ܡܪܝܐ / *ḥayy(h)ū Māryā*, which in turn corresponds to the Arabic حي هر الرب / *ḥayy(un) huwa r-Rabb* ("The Lord is alive!" or "As the Lord lives!").[59] Mannā (235b) reproduces this formula in Arabic, but as following the Syro-Aramaic written form, as follows: حي هو الرب / *ḥayy(un) huwa r-Rabb* ("The Lord is alive!"), والله / *wa-llāh* ("in God['s name]!"). The Qur'ānic abbreviation حم / *ḥm*, then, is a formulaic intensification of the divine origin of the text that follows it.

Siglum 9: عسق / *'SQ* = ܥܫܩ / *'ŠQ*

In Q 42:2, the siglum عسق / *'šq* follows logically upon the abbreviation حم / *ḥm*. If we transcribe it into Syro-Aramaic, we have the abbreviation ܥܫܩ / *'šq*, which stands for ܥܠܐ ܫܡܗ ܩܕܝܫܐ / *'lā šme-h qaddīšā*. This phrase, brought over into Arabic, is علا اسمه القدوس / *'alā (i)smu-hu l-quddūs* ("High [= praised] be his holy name!"). In this case we can combine this abbreviation with the previous one into a coherent sentence, reading as follows in Syro-Aramaic and Arabic:

> ܚܝܘ ܡܪܝܐ ܥܠܐ ܫܡܗ ܩܕܝܫܐ / *ḥayy(h)ū Māryā 'lā šme-h qaddīšā*
> حي هو الرب علا اسمه القدوس / *ḥayy(un) huwa r-Rabb 'alā (i)smu-hu l-quddūs*
> "As the Lord lives—praised be his holy name!"

Just as this formula emphasizes the divine origin of the revelatory text it precedes, so do the Surahs ascribed to the second Meccan period use the following four sigla for the same purpose: الم / *ALM*; الر / *ALR*; المر / *ALMR*; المص / *ALMṢ*.

Siglum 10: الم / *ALM (Surahs 2:1; 3:1; 29:1; 30:1; 31:1; 32:1)*

Abū Mūsā al-Ḥarīrī, in his 1979 study in Arabic entitled قس ونبي / *Qass wa-nabī* ("A Priest and a Prophet"), conjectured that this abbreviation, which appears six times in the Qur'ān, represents the Syro-Aramaic letters ܐܠܡ / *ALM*, standing for the Syro-Aramaic sentence ܐܡܪ ܠܝ ܡܪܝܐ / *emar lī Māryā* (= Arabic قال لي الرب / *qāla lī ar-Rabb* ["The Lord spoke to me"]).[60] This stereotypical sentence appears often in the Old Testament with regard to the prophets. This reading and explanation will be confirmed by the analysis of the next abbreviation.

Siglum 11: الـر / *ALR (Surahs 10:1; 11:1; 12:1; 14:1; 15:1)*

As the afore-mentioned author rightly surmised, these letters, which appear five times in the Qur'ān, correspond to the Syro-Aramaic letters ܐܠܪ / *ALR*. Consequently, we should read these letters as an acronym for the following Syro-Aramaic words: ܐܡܪ ܠܝ ܪܒܐ / *emar lī Rabbā*, which would correspond (as above) to the Arabic قال لي الرب / *qāla lī ar-Rabb* ("The Great One [the Lord] spoke to me").[61] This interpretation has recently been assigned in Internet forums to the writers who go under the pseudonyms Haï Bar-Zeev and Hanna Zakarias (alias Gabriel Théry).[62] The interpretation I have cited from Abū Mūsā al-Ḥarīrī has in its favor the plausibility of the Qur'ānic context.

The wavy horizontal line that appears over the abbreviation الم / *ALM* (as above the other sigla) means (as is the case in the Syriac scribal tradition, see the Syriac scans above) that the letters are an abbreviation. We can see this in the following selection (in the second line, on the right side), along with the detail:

This wavy line has been interpreted in the Islamic tradition as a *madda* [i.e., a sign for a long ā in the Arabic alphabet], but in the case of Koranic recitation it is considered as a sign of prolongation of each individual letter while reciting (as follows: *aliiif…laaam…miiim…*).

Siglum 12: المر */ ALMR (Q 13:1)*

This siglum appears but one time and is a combination of the two previously mentioned. Thus, it should be read as follows: Syro-Aramaic ܐܡܪ ܠܝ ܡܪܝܐ ܪܒܐ / *emar lī Māryā rabbā*, corresponding to the Arabic قال لي الرب العظيم / *qāla lī ar-Rabb al-ʿaẓīm*, meaning "The great (almighty) Lord spoke to me."

Siglum 13: المص */ ALMṢ (Q 7:1)*

This siglum also appears once and should be read as follows: Syro-Aramaic ܐܡܪ ܠܝ ܡܪܝܐ ܨ̱ܒܐܘܬ = ܐܠܡܨ̱ / *emar lī Māryā ṣḇaōṯ*, corresponding to the Arabic قال لي الرب الصبأوت / *qāla lī ar-Rabb aṣ-ṣaba'ūt*, meaning "The strong (almighty) Lord spoke to me."

Siglum 14: كهيعص */ KHYʿṢ (Surah 19:1)*

We should first note that, unlike the other previously mentioned Surahs, whose sigla indicate a revealed text, the Surah Maryam begins with a liturgical text that one can ascribe to the Advent season of the Christian Syrian liturgy. The first Sunday of Advent in the Syrian daily office has as its theme, just as we find in the Qur'ān, the announcement to Zechariah of the birth of John the Baptist. This theme corresponds to the Gospel pericope Luke 1:5–23; the Qur'ān summarizes this story in verses 2–11 in a free and succinct form.[63] In the Syrian liturgical tradition, the second Sunday of Advent is devoted to the annunciation to Mary (Luke 1:27–38). The Qur'ān reproduces this report also, in verses 16–21, with a version that summarizes the story (albeit from a Qur'ānic perspective). The report of the birth of Christ found in verses 22–33, however, diverges quite a bit from Luke 2:1–20 and suggests a non-canonical Qur'ānic *Vorlage* [model or original].

What is important for our purposes, however, is that the two "annunciation sequences" that precede the Christmas story in the Qur'ān agree exactly with the corresponding Advent Sundays in the Syrian liturgical year. This is relevant for historical studies of liturgy because in this way the Qur'ān follows a West Syrian tradition that can be traced back at least as far as the early sixth century, while the Eastern Syrians had four Advent Sundays (or "Sundays of Annunciation") long before the middle of the seventh century.[64] By means of its structure, in concert as it is with the Gospel of Luke, the Surah Maryam testifies to a pre-Islamic, Christian Syrian tradition with two Advent Sundays before the Christmas celebration, for which Surah 97, as a "Christmas Surah," has preserved a historical memory.[65]

Because we can now say that Surah 19 belongs to the liturgical texts in the Qur'ān, the siglum that introduces it must naturally have as its content the praise of God, in a way corresponding to the Syrian liturgy. This is also an indicator that the Surah Maryam does <u>not</u> belong to the second Meccan period, which distinguishes itself by texts that present a sermon supported by revelation; rather, it is a liturgical text (at least up to verse 33) that belongs to that earlier portion of the Qur'ān that serves as its foundation as originally a <u>lectionary</u>, that is, as a liturgical book.

This longest siglum in the Qur'ān can therefore be decoded according to the Syrian liturgy and in the following way: كهيعص / *KHY'Ṣ* represents the Syro-Aramaic letters ܟܗܝܥܨ. These latter stand for the words

> " ܟܒܝܪ ܗܘ ܝܗ ܥܠܝܐ ܨܒܐܘܬ / *kabbīr hū Yah 'ellāyā ṣḇaōṯ*, which corresponds to the Arabic كبير هو الرب العلي الصبأوت / *kabīr(un) huwa r-Rabb al-'alī aṣ-ṣaba'ūt*, meaning "Great is [= Praise be] the Lord (*Yah*), the Exalted, the Sabaoth (= 'the Powerful')."[66]

7. Summary and Prospects

At first glance the most important result of this essay may appear to be the solution to the question of the so-called "mysterious letters." This question, which has functioned as the "Gordian knot" of the Qur'ān for approximately 1300 years, serves merely to indicate the deficiencies in eastern and western Qur'ānic scholarship, having failed to place the Qur'ān in its cultural and historical contexts. All attempts up to this point to solve this problem could not have succeeded because they proceeded from a faulty starting point. The preceding analysis, therefore, has attempted to explain methodologically the origins of some basic expressions of the Qur'ān from the perspectives of the histories of linguistics and cultures. It was only by means of these small, logical steps, which actually employ nothing other than the historico-critical method, that we could hope to come closer to an objective solution of this problem.

To the critical observer, the problem will by no means appear to be solved, in that the concrete proofs for the suggestions I have made here could not be provided. Unfortunately, given the state of affairs concerning the Qur'ānic documentary materials, we can at the moment hardly meet this justified desire, which ultimately results in the demand to produce the "*Ur-Qur'ān*." Nonetheless, even if one were to discover the sought-after *Ur-Qur'ān* by means of an unexpected happenstance, we would still have this same problem of the "mysterious letters," because the creators of the Qur'ānic sigla were well-schooled in the tradition and have once and for all exited this world. This, of course, explains the perplexity of the Qur'ānic exegetes and most clearly illustrates the absence of the "unbroken" oral transmission of the text that has been claimed by Islamic tradition. Therefore, it would be unnecessary to speculate as to whether one or another of the letters in question could be interpreted in another way. Unfortunately, we cannot expect final certainty, given the conditions I have indicated. Therefore, the most important contribution of this analysis must remain a closer definition of the function that these sigla had in their Qur'ānic contexts.

Concerning the Christian Syrian tradition, however, we are in a quite fortunate position, in that this tradition has continued unbroken into our own day, with the result that we can learn what these sigla mean individually. It might appear that adducing this tradition only serves as a makeshift aid when we attempt to solve the problem of the Qur'ānic sigla; however, this attempt has never yet been made. After all, as we have shown, all the Qur'ānic sigla were to be read originally as Aramaic. We must continue to wait to see if this approach and its results (including the expressions which constitute the framework of the Qur'ān, which all point, from the beginning, to a written Syro-Aramaic cultural tradition) will prove convincing.

A further problem that this study has made quite clear is the absolute necessity of the knowledge of Aramaic (alongside Arabic, of course), not only for understanding the language of the Qur'ān, but especially for the historico-linguistic reconstruction of a text that has been mis-read and mis-interpreted in innumerable places (despite the legend of an oral transmission). Without this prerequisite of understanding Aramaic, all efforts to overcome the manifold problems of the Qur'ānic text will fall flat. The realization of ambitious and desirable projects, such as the *Corpus coranicum*, will not help to solve these problems alone.

8. Bibliography

Azzi, Joseph, *Le Prêtre et le Prophète: aux sources du Coran* (Paris: Maisonneuve and Larose, 2001); *The Priest and the Prophet* (Los Angeles: Pen Publishers, 2005).

Abū Mūsā al-Ḥarīrī (alias), *Qass wa-nabī, baḥṯ fī naš'at al-islām*, 13th ed., (Lubnān (Lebanon): Diyār ʿaql (metaphorical place-name), 1991).

Baumstark, Anton, *Festbrevier und Kirchenjahr der syrischen Jakobiten: Eine liturgiegeschichtliche Vorarbeit* (Paderborn: F. Schöningh, 1910).

Breviarium iuxta ritum Ecclesiae Antiochenae Syrorum: Pars autumnalis: Volumen secundum (Mausili: Typis Fratrum Praedicatorum, 1886).

Bell, Richard, *The Qur'ān: Translated, with a critical re-arrangement of the Surahs*, 2 vols., (Edinburgh: Clark, 1937–39).

Biblia Hebraica, Edited by Rudolf Kittel. 11th ed., (Stuttgart: Privileg. Württ. Bibelanstalt, 1937).

Blachère, Régis, *Le Coran, traduit de l'arabe* (Paris: Librairie orientale et américaine, 1957).

Brockelmann, Carl, *Lexicon syriacum*, 2nd ed. (Halle: M. Niemeyer, 1928).

Id., *Syrische Grammatik*, 8th ed. (Leipzig: Verlag Enzyklopädie, 1960).

Burgmer, Christoph, ed., *Streit um den Koran: Die Luxenberg-Debatte: Standpunkte und Hintergründe*, 3rd rev. ed. (Berlin: Hans Schiler, 2007).

Gesenius, Wilhelm, *Hebräisches und aramäisches Handwörterbuch*, 17th ed. (Berlin, Göttingen, and Heidelberg: Springer, 1959).

Ibn Warraq, ed., *What the Koran Really Says: Language, Text, and Commentary* (Amherst, NY: Prometheus Books, 2002).

Jeffery, Arthur, *The Foreign Vocabulary of the Qur'ān* (Baroda: Oriental Institute, 1938).

Id., ed., *Materials for the History of the Text of the Qur'ān* (Leiden: Brill, 1937); Arabic portion: كتاب المصاحف ، للحافظ أبي بكر عبد الله بن أبي داود سليمان بن الأشعث السجستاني / *Kitāb al-maṣāḥif li-l-ḥāfiẓ abī Bakr ʿAbdallāh b. abī Dāwūd Sulaymān b. al-Ašʿaṯ as-Siǧistanī* (Cairo, 1936).

Luxenberg, Christoph, *Die syro-aramäische Lesart des Koran: Ein Beitrag zur Entschlüsselung der Koransprache* (Berlin: Das arabische Buch, 2001 [1st ed.]; Hans Schiler, 2004 [2nd ed.], 2007 [3rd ed.]).

Id., *The Syro-Aramaic Reading of the Koran: A Contribution to the Decoding of the Language of the Koran* (Berlin: Hans Schiler, 2007).

Macuch, R., and E. S. Drower, *A Mandaic Dictionary* (Oxford: Clarendon Press, 1963).

b. Manẓūr, Abū l-Faḍl Jamāl ad-Dīn Muḥammad b. Mukarram al-Ifrīqī al-Miṣrī, *Lisān al-ʿarab* ("Tongue of the Arabs"), 15 vols. (Beirut: 1955–56).

Mannā, Jacques Eugène, *Vocabulaire Chaldéen-Arabe* (Mossoul: Impr. des Pères Dominicains, 1900). Reprint edition, with a new appendix by Raphael J. Bidawid: Beirut: Babel Center Publications, 1975.

Mingana, Alfons, "Syriac Influence on the Style of the Koran," *Bulletin of the John Rylands Library* 11 (1927): 77–98; also in Ibn Warraq, *What the Koran Really Says* (Amherst, NY: Prometheus Books, 2002), pp. 171–220.

Nöldeke, Theodor, *Geschichte des Qorâns* (Göttingen: Verlag der Dieterichschen Buchhandlung, 1860).

Id., *Beiträge zur semitischen Sprachwissenschaft* (Strassburg: K.J. Trübner, 1904).

Id., and Friedrich Schwally, *Geschichte des Qorāns*, vol. 1, *Über den Ursprung des Qorāns*, 2nd ed. (Leipzig: T. Weicher, 1909), vol. 2, *Die Sammlung des Qorāns*, 2nd ed. (Leipzig: Dieterich, 1919), vol. 3 (ed. Bergsträßer-Pretzl), *Die Geschichte des Qorāntextes*, 2nd ed. (Leipzig: Dieterich, 1938); reprint edition: Hildesheim: Olms, 1961.

Ohlig, Karl-Heinz, and Gerd-R. Puin, eds., *Die dunklen Anfänge: Neue Forschungen zur Entstehung und frühen Geschichte des Islam*, 3rd ed. (Berlin: Hans Schiler, 2007).

Paret, Rudi, *Der Koran: Kommentar und Konkordanz* (Stuttgart: W. Kohlhammer, 1971).

Id., ed. *Der Koran*. Wege der Forschung, no. 326 (Darmstadt: Wissenschaftliche Buchgesellschaft, 1975.

Id., *Der Koran: Übersetzung*, 2nd ed. (Stuttgart, Berlin, Cologne, and Mainz: W. Kohlhammer, 1982).

Praetorius, Franz, "Über einige Pluralformen des Semitischen," *Zeitschrift der deutschen morgenländischen Gesellschaft* 56 (1902): 685–696.

Qur'ān karīm (Cairo, 1972).

Sokoloff, Michael, *A Dictionary of Jewish Palestinian Aramaic of the Byzantine Period*, 2nd printing (Ramat-Gan: Bar-Ilan University Press, 1992).

Smith, R. Payne, ed., *Thesaurus syriacus*, 2 vols. (Oxford: Clarendon Press, 1879, 1901).

Syriac Bible (63DC), London: United Bible Societies, 1979.

aṭ-Ṭabarī, Abū Ja'far Muḥammad b. Jarīr, *Jāmi' al bayān 'an ta'wīl āy al-Qur'ān*, 30 parts in 12 vols. 3rd ed. (Cairo: Shirkat Maktaba, 1968).

Wehr, Hans, *Arabisches Wörterbuch für die Schriftsprache der Gegenwart*, 5th ed. (Wiesbaden: Harrassowitz, 1985).

Zakarias, Hanna (alias Gabriel Théry), *De Moïse à Mohammed*, 2 vols. (Cahors: privately published, 1955–56).

Internet source: http://www.unbound.biola.edu (biblical text in Hebrew, with numerous translations)

Notes

1 aṭ-Ṭabarī, Abū Ǧaʿfar Muḥammad b. Jarīr, *Jāmiʿ al bayān ʿan taʾwīl āy al-Qurʾān* (Qurʾānic commentary), 30 parts in 12 vols., 3rd ed. (Cairo: Shirkat Maktaba, 1968), I:86–96.

2 For better readability, the "ʾ" will be replaced by the letter "a" for "a(lif)" in the following.

3 Rudi Paret, ed., *Der Koran, Wege der Forschung*, no. 326 (Darmstadt: Wissenschaftliche Buchgesellschaft, 1975), xiii.

4 NB: Bellamy has also produced a more recent article: "Some Proposed Emendations to the Text of the Koran," *Journal of the American Oriental Society* 113 (1993), 562–573; cf. especially section 12, which bears the title "Again the Mysterious Letters." This article has been reproduced in Ibn Warraq, ed. (with translations), *What the Koran Really Says: Language, Text, and Commentary* (Amherst, NY: Prometheus Books, 2002), pp. 508–510.

5 Paret, *Koran*, xxi f.

6 *Zeitschrift der deutschen morgenländischen Gesellschaft* 75 (1921), pp. 1–20; discussed in Paret, *Koran*, pp. 330–335.

7 Surahs will be indicated by the letter Q (for Qurʾān).

8 Paret, *Koran*, 335.

9 Paret, *Koran*, 333.

10 *Der Islam: Zeitschrift für Geschichte und Kultur des islamischen Orients* 13 (1923), pp. 191–226; discussed in Paret, *Koran*, pp. 336–373.

11 Paret, *Koran*, p. 336.

12 Theodor Nöldeke, *Geschichte des Korans*, 2nd ed., vol. 2, edited by F. Schwally (Berlin, 1919), 68f.

13 *Akten des 24. internationalen Orientalisten-Kongresses* (München, 28. August— 4. September 1957), ed. Herbert Franke (Wiesbaden: Franz Steiner Verlag in Komm., 1959), pp. 276–279; discussed in Paret, *Koran*, pp. 374–378.

14 *Studia Islamica* 16 (1962), 5–11; discussed in Paret, *Koran*, pp. 379–385.

15 *Encyclopedia Britannica*, 9th ed., s.v. "Koran."

16 Cf. on this topic Arthur Jeffery, *The Foreign Vocabulary of the Qurʾān* (Baroda: Oriental Institute, 1938), p. 233f.

17 Christoph Luxenberg, *Die syro-aramäische Lesart des Koran: Ein Beitrag zur Entschlüsselung der Koransprache* (Berlin): 1st ed. (Das Arabische Buch, 2001), pp. 54ff.; 2nd ed. (Hans Schiler, 2004), pp. 81ff.; 3rd ed. (Hans Schiler, 2007), pp. 83ff.

18 Paret, *Koran*, p. 358.

19 Jeffery, *Foreign Vocabulary*, p. 182.

20 Cf. the English form "trace" as well as the German forms *Trasse (roadway, trail)* and *Trassee*, all of which come from the French word *tracer* ("to draw a line"), apparently from a vulgar Latin form, which itself derived from the classical Latin tractum. The aural similarity between the French tracer and the Syriac traṣ (with the same semantic contents) must be as much a coincidence as that between the Syro-Aramaic metathesis ܣܪܛܐ / *srāṭā* ("line") > the Qurānic صراط / *ṣirāṭ* and سراط / *sirāṭ* and the Latin form strata. Cf. here the new etymological interpretation by the author in his English edition *The Syro-Aramaic Reading of the Koran: A*

Contribution to the Decoding of the Language of the Koran (Berlin: Hans Schiler, 2007), pp. 226ff. Cf. also Jeffery, *Foreign Vocabulary*, pp. 195f.

21 Mannā, 633b; *Thesaurus Syriacus* (Thes.), II:3386, penult., Spec. ܨܘܪܬ ܟܬܒ (ṣūraṯ kṯāḇ) textus, ܒܨܘܪܬ ܟܬܒ (b-ṣūraṯ kṯāḇ), Eus. *Hist. Eccl.* iii.37(38); (3387) ܟܠܗ ܨܘܪܬ ܟܬܒ ܕܥܬܝܩܬܐ ܘܕܚܕܬܬܐ (kullāh ṣūraṯ kṯāḇ d-ʿattiqtā w-ḏaḥḏattā), totus textus Veteris et Novi Test. ("the whole text of the Old and the New Testament"), Chr. Eccl. § ii.215; ib. 481...; unde ܨܘܪܬܐ (ṣūrtā) etiam sine ܟܬܒ (kṯāḇ) valet textus Scripturarum, B.O. iii. i. 87, 97, 153, 166, 174, 261; ܨܘܪܬܐ (ṣūrtā) "Vetus et Novum Testamentum," Ass. C.B.V. iii. 280 ult.; ܨܘܪܬܐ ܕܐܘܢܓܠܣܛܐ (ṣūrtā ḏ-ewangelisṭē) textus evangeliorum [the text of the Evangelists], Syn. ii. Eph. 149. 2.

22 Cf. on this form *The Syro-Aramaic Reading of the Koran*, pp. 295f., especially n. 353.

23 Three different famous Arab philologists are known by this name; the earliest died in 793, the second in 830, and the most recent in 920.

24 The form فعيل / faʿīl, attested by many Arabic adjectives and substantives, arose at an earlier period in a region in which Aramaic was spoken. We know this because the form belongs to the Aramaic verbal paradigm rather than the Arabic one. As is well-known, Arabic builds its passive participles on the first stem with an m-prefix according to the form مفعول / *ma-fʿūl.* Nonetheless, the Arab philologists occasionally recognized the corresponding meaning of the form فعيل / faʿīl, but this recognition depended upon context. So, for example, *Lisān* often explains this form with فعيل بمعنى مفعول ("*faʿīl* in the sense of *ma-fʿūl*").

25 Cf. Carl Brockelmann, *Syrische Grammatik*, 8th ed. (Leipzig: Verlag Enzyklopädie, 1960), 142, for the paradigms of the verbs with medial w / y, especially their passive participles.

26 If al-Farrā' wanted to think that such a form must be restricted to nouns, he may have had in mind an Arabic substantive like ميزة / mīza ("distinction, quality"). If this was the case, he did not recognize that this word as well is a substantivized passive participle according to the Syro-Aramaic verbal paradigms and that, consequently, it is not morphologically different from the Qur'ānic participial adjective صيرى / ṣīrā.

27 This understanding is proven by the following verse 23, which seems to be a commentary on vv. 19–22. The text there should be understood thus: "These are nothing but names that you and your fathers named, and concerning which God has sent down no authority at all (by means of a revealed writing). (In this) They (the people addressed) follow exclusively (their) speculation (الظن / *aẓ-ẓann*) and whatever their souls (i.e., each one according to his own perception or sense) devise. In this they have preserved from their Lord the correct guidance (the correct teaching)" (literally: "In this the correct guidance has come to them"). The expression ما تهوى الانفس / *mā tahwā l-anfus* comes from Aramaic and traces back to the Syro-Aramaic terms ܐܗܘܝ / *ahwī* ("to create, to invent") and ܢܦܫܐ / *napšā* ("soul"), with the meaning "that which one desires" = "desire, wish" (cf. Mannā, 460a, under ܢܦܫܐ / *napšā*, (5): شهوة. رغبة / *šahwa, raġba*). Following this meaning, the anonymous commentator (in verse 23) read and understood correctly the Syro-Aramaic word (*ṣīrā*) that was present in Q 53:22 at that time (in place of the later word ضيزى / *ḍīzā*, as it was mis-read in the canonical edition of the Qur'ān), but Ṭabarī and the other "authorities" to which he appealed overlooked this fact.

28 E. S. Drower and R. Macuch, eds., *A Mandaic Dictionary* (Oxford: Clarendon Press, 1963), 323b.

29 A. Jeffery, *Foreign Vocabulary*, 73, n. 1, cites a biblical text (Daniel 3:33) for the use of the biblical Aramaic word אָת / *āṯ* in the sense of "a sign wrought by God," but he is wrong. The double expression *āṯōhī w-ṯimhōhī* (Peshitta: *āṯwāṯeh w-ṯeḏmrāṯeh* ["his signs and his wonders"]) makes clear that, in the biblical context, the meaning of אָת / *āṯ* is in the sense of "wondrous signs")

30 For more on this topic, cf. *The Syro-Aramaic Reading of the Koran*, pp. 106ff.

31 *Foreign Vocabulary*, pp. 72f.

32 A more recent diminutive form of ܐܬܐ / *āṯa* appears to be ܐܬܘܬܐ / *āṯūṯā* ("letter, symbol"); cf. here Nöldeke's *Kurzgefasste syrische Grammatik*, 78, Diminutiva, §134: "Cf. also §112, as well as the diminutives at §122 formed by the repetition of the third radical." ܐܬܘܬܐ / *āṯūṯā* would be an appropriate addition to the examples that Nöldeke offers; however, we should not exclude the possibility that this word is rather a more recent secondary form of the plural form ܐܬܘ̈ܬܐ / *āṯwāṯā*.

33 The references, respectively, are to *Mandäische Grammatik*, 110; *Lexicon Syriacum*, 53b; *Hebräisches und aramäisches Handwörterbuch*, 19b; and *Thesaurus Syriacus*, I:412.

34 *Foreign Vocabulary*, 72: "The struggles of the early Muslim philologers to explain the word are interestingly set forth in LA, xviii, 66ff. The word has no root in Arabic, and is obviously, as von Kremer noted [n. 6: Ideen, 226 n.; see also Sprenger, *Leben*, ii, 419 n.; Cheikho, *Naṣrānīya*, 181; and Margoliouth, *ERE*, x, 539], a borrowing from Syr(iac) or Aram(aic)."

35 Ibid., 73: "The word occurs in the old poetry, e.g., in Imrū'ul-Qais, lxv, 1 (Ahlwardt, Divans, 160), and so was in use before the time of Muḥammad."

36 Franz Praetorius, *Zeitschrift der deutschen morgenländischen Gesellschaft* 56 (1902), 688f., has already given attention to plural forms like these in the Aramaic dialects, which arise from the contraction of "rising" diphthongs, as we see them in Arabic. This correct observation received negative criticism at the time from Nöldeke, who expressed the following opinion in his *Beiträge zur semitischen Sprachwissenschaft* (Strassburg: K. J. Trübner, 1904), 55 (under "II"): "Praetorius will find little agreement concerning his identification of the (classical Arabic) رعاة (*ru'āt*), أساة (*'usāt*), سقاة (*suqāt*) with the (Syro-Aramaic) ܪ̈ܥܘܬܐ (*rā'awwāṯā*), ܐܣܘ̈ܬܐ (*āsawwāṯā*), ܫܩܘ̈ܬܐ (*šāqawwāṯā*) ('shepherd,' 'healer/physician,' 'giving,' respectively)...." With this critique Nöldeke demonstrates that he did not recognize this sound-shift through contraction, as the argumentation which follows also shows. However, he is correct to surmise a middle-stage between classical Syriac and the Arabic form, a stage that must have been the direct predecessor to the Arabic form. If one begins from the classical Syriac form, one can well imagine the three-stage sound-shift as follows (using the example of رعاة [*ru'āt*]: a) Syriac **rā'awwāṯā* > b) vernacular Aramaic *rā'wāṯā* > Arabic *ru'āt*. The change from the Syro-Aramaic ܐܬܘ̈ܬܐ / *āṯwāṯā* ("symbols, letters") to the Qur'ānic-Arabic form (in pause) اثات / *āṯāṯ* (therefore: *āṯwāṯ* > *āṯāṯ*) also corresponds quite regularly to this last schema.

37 The verbal root أثث / *aṯaṯa*, which sounds odd in Arabic, apparently traces back to the Syro-Aramaic variant ܝܬܬ / *yatteṯ* (Mannā, 319a: كوّن. اوجد. ابدع / *kawwana, awǧada, abda'a* ["to build, to make, to produce"]). This term in turn seems to be a

secondary denominative construction from the "expression of being" ܐܝܬ / īṯ or ܝܬ / yāṯ; an entry in *Lisān* (II:110b) speaks in favor of this possibility concerning "luxuriant, thick" vegetation, as a verse from Imru' al-Qays testifies (أثيث / aṯīṯ), which would correspond exactly to the Syro-Aramaic adjective ܝܬܝܬܐ / *yattīṯā* or *yaṯīṯā* ("luxuriant") as cited in Mannā (319a). The further examples that *Lisān* cites confirm the origin of this root as from Syro-Aramaic and testify once more that the so-called "Old Arabic" stood much closer to Aramaic than some contemporary scholars of Arabic want to allow.

38 *Lisān* (XIV:61b f.) cites Abū Manṣūr, who says the following on the topic: "Regarding the meaning and origin of إيا / *īyā*, I have heard nothing." Regarding an attempted definition based on folk etymology, the same source says, "In reality this word is cryptic (مبهم / *mubham*); it serves to indicate the accusative (يكنى به عن المنصوب)." This word corresponds to the Hebrew particle את / *eṯ*, which seems to be a contracted secondary form of the Aramaic אית / *īṯ* (cf. W. Gesenius, *Hebräisches und aramäisches Handwörterbuch*, 17th ed. [Berlin, Göttingen, and Heidelberg: Springer, 1959], 76a, "1. Zeichen des determinierten acc." [sign of the determinated accusative]).

39 Even *Lisān* (XIV:62a f.) recognizes the meaning of the mis-read آية / *āya* – "signal," "example," "model," or "wondrous sign," depending on the Qur'ānic context—without explaining its origin. Here *Lisān*'s anonymous citation is interesting, in that it claims that آية / *āya* is named "*āya*" because it means a "sum of the letters [or individual words] of the Qur'ān" (لأنها جماعة من حروف القرآن).

40 *Thesaurus*, I:413, meaning 4: constellatio, ܐܬܘܬܐ ܕܫܡܝܐ (*āṯwāṯā ḏa-šmayyā*) constellationes coeli, Jer. X.2, Did. Ap. 87.16. It. signa quibus sol, luna, et planetae ab astronomis designantur, quae omnia descripta inveniantur ap. Laud. cxxiii. 245 v.[Signs, designated by astronomers as sun, moon, and planets, as described at Laud . cxxiii.245 v.]

41 Concerning this meaning of the Syriac ܐܬܐ / *āṯā*, cf. *Thesaurus*, I:413, under β: indicium, argumentum, ܐܬܐ ܕܩܝܡܬܐ / *āṯā ḏa-qyāmā* ("sign" = "proof of the resurrection"), Gen. ix. 12, 2 Cor. xii. 12. With this note, the *Thesaurus* gives us at one time the proof for the correct understanding of the mis-readings at Surahs 44:36 and 45:25.

42 The Qur'ānic written form ايتوا here reproduces clearly the Syro-Aramaic Afel form (ܐܝܬܘ / *aytaw*), unlike the written form فاتوا / fa-'tū (first Arabic verbal stem) in the parallel text at Q 44:36; as a result, the former should be read in Arabic as aytū. However, the Cairo edition of the Qur'ān neutralizes the prefixed *Alif* of the Afel form by means of a *waṣla*, places an inadmissible *hamza* over the following y-carrier, and reads the verb as though it belongs in the first Arabic verbal stem: (qālū)'tū. The Arabic grammarians call such a mis-assignment of written forms by the name تصحيف / *taṣḥīf*; there are many examples cited in *Lisān*, because this phenomenon can also be found in post-Qur'ānic Arabic. So, for example, "to bring" is represented in classical Arabic by اتى بـ / *atā bi-* (in the first verbal stem), but in Syro-Aramaic one uses the Afel form (which corresponds to the fourth Arabic verbal stem; cf. Mannā, 45b: ܐܝܬܝ / *aytī*: اتى بـ / *atā bi-*). Apart from the fact that the Arabic اتى / *atā* is a loan from Syro-Aramaic, the imperative of the fourth verbal stem in the second person plural would be اوتوا / *ūtū* (or *u'tū*), which is not the case here. The Qur'ānic written form therefore faithfully reproduces the

Syro-Aramaic Afel form. Such vacillations between the Arabic and Syro-Aramaic verbal systems are by no means rare in the Qur'ān; a close investigation of Qur'ānic orthography would bring more of them to light.

43 The Arabic بيّن / *bayyana*, as a loan-word from the Syro-Aramaic ܒܝܢ / *bayyen*, has similar semantic nuances, as Mannā (56a) indicates: "to explain, to make clear, to make comprehensible, to teach."

44 The Arabic expressions الجمعة / *al-ğum'a* ("Friday") and جامع / *ğāmi'* ("mosque") both appear to be loan-translations from the Syro-Aramaic ܟܢܫܐ / *kenšā*, ܟܢܘܫܝܐ / *knušyā* ("assembly, gathering of the community") or ܒܝܬ ܟܢܘܫܝܐ / *bēṯ knušyā*, ܒܝܬ ܟܢܘܫܬܐ / *bēṯ knuštā* ("house of assembly, community house"); cf. on this topic Mannā, 345a, and the Arabic expressions it gives as correspondences.

45 The original German gives another equivalent name, the German "Sonnabend," which is one German name for "Saturday." The suffix "-abend" means "evening," so that the word itself literally means "Sunday Eve" (to use the parallel English structure from days like "Christmas Eve"), or "Saturday."

46 Cf. *Thesaurus*, II:2984, 29: "ܥܪܘܒܬܐ sic vocatur propterea quod propter Christum in ea crucifixum ܥܪܒܬ ܫܡܫܐ ܘܐܚܫܟ ܝܘܡܐ ('*rubṯā* is called by this name because on the day on which Christ was crucified, the sun set and darkness reigned)."

47 Cf. Michael Sokoloff, *A Dictionary of Jewish Palestinian Aramaic of the Byzantine Period*, 2nd printing (Ramat-Gan: Bar-Ilan University, 1992), pp. 418b f.

48 See the note in Gesenius, *Hebräisches und aramäisches Handwörterbuch*, 615b, under IV: ערב, l. 9: Heinrich Lewy, *Die semitischen Fremdwörter im Griechischen* (Berlin: 1895; reprint: Hildesheim [Olms], 2004).

49 This legendary report goes on to say that the Qurayš gathered on this day (for prayer), and that this particular Lu'ayy (= Levi) typically gave a sermon before them, in which he announced to the Qurayš the coming prophetic mission of his grandson and expressed the desire (in the cited verse) that he could enjoy this experience just once.

50 Arthur Jeffery, *Materials for the History of the Text of the Qur'ān* (Leiden: Brill, 1937) (362 pages); Arabic portion: Kitāb al-maṣāḥif li-l-ḥāfiẓ abī Bakr 'Abdallāh b. abī Dāwūd Sulaymān b. al-Aš'aṯ as-Siğistanī (Cairo, 1936) (223 pages).

51 *Thesaurus*, II:2984, under ܥܪܘܒܬܐ / *'rubṯā*, l. 23: ܥܪܘܒܬܐ ܪܒܬܐ / *'rubṯā rabbṯā* (along with other expressions for "Good Friday").

52 On this topic cf. the new interpretation contained in the present author's contribution to the volume edited by Karl-Heinz Ohlig and Gerd-R. Puin, *The Hidden Origins of Islam: New Research into Its Early History* (Amherst, NY: Prometheus Books, 2008), especially the section on the Christian symbolism of the Dome of the Rock. In addition to the argument presented there, we should add that there is actually a crypt under the stones themselves, a discovery that provides archaeological support for the idea of the Dome of the Rock (= "stone grave") as the burial site of Christ. Further, there are two traditions that have survived from the prior, Christian period into contemporary Islam. First, the Dome of the Rock is the pilgrimage site recommended for Muslims, and this pilgrimage only "counts" as complete if one visits the crypt (parallel to the Christian visit to the grave in Jerusalem's Church of the Holy Sepulchre). Second, there is a custom in which it is mainly Muslim women who give themselves to prayer in the Dome of the Rock; this may connect with the tradition attested in the Gospels, according to which the visitors to the grave of Christ on the morning of the Sunday of the

Resurrection were women (Mt. 28:1; Mk. 16:1; Lk. 24:1; Jn. 20:1)—not, of course, that we should thereby exclude other traditions.

53 Again, see the essay in Ohlig and Puin, *The Hidden Origins of Islam*.

54 The edition in use is *Breviarium iuxta ritum Ecclesiae Antiochenae Syrorum*. Pars autumnalis. Volumen secundum (Mausili: Typis Fratrum Praedicatorum, 1886).

55 C. Brockelmann, *Lexicon Syriacum*, 2nd ed. (Halle: M. Niemeyer, 1928), 296b, ܝܕܥܐ (*yaḏʿā*): "1. indicium ("index, specification"), 2. signum ("label"), 3. custos (in libro) ("mark"), 4. notitia ("notice"), 5. signum vocalis aut accentus ("vowel- or accent-mark").

56 *Thesaurus* (I:1559).

57 Following the Peshitta, the three Psalms begin as follows: "A Prayer of Moses: 'Lord, you have been for us a refuge for all eternity'" (Ps. 90); "Praise the Lord, all the earth; serve the Lord with joy!" (Ps. 100); "The Lord, the God of all gods, has spoken and summoned the earth from the rising of the sun unto its setting" (Ps. 50).

58 Ṭabarī (XXIV:39) also cites another tradition concerning this abbreviation that is closer to the truth and that supposedly traces back to Ibn ʿAbbās, as the second of the four opinions he gives at the beginning of his commentary on Q 40.

59 Biblical testimonies to the phrase ܚܝܘ ܡܪܝܐ / ḥayy(h)ū Māryā: 1 Sam. 25:26 ("And now, my Lord, as YHWH lives and your soul lives") (וְעַתָּה אֲדֹנִי חַי־יְהוָה וְחֵי־נַפְשְׁךָ); 1 Sam. 26:16 ("This thing is not good that you have done, as Yahweh lives"); 1 Kings 18:10 ("As Yahweh, your God, lives"); Jer. 44:26 ("But hear the word of YHWH, all you Jews that live in the land of Egypt: 'See, I have sworn by my great name,' says YHWH, 'that no one from Judah living anywhere in Egypt will ever again invoke my name, in saying "As surely as the Lord YHWH lives!") (לָכֵן שִׁמְעוּ דְבַר־יְהוָה כָּל־יְהוּדָה הַיֹּשְׁבִים בְּאֶרֶץ מִצְרָיִם הִנְנִי נִשְׁבַּעְתִּי בִּשְׁמִי הַגָּדוֹל אָמַר יְהוָה אִם־יִהְיֶה עוֹד שְׁמִי נִקְרָא בְּפִי כָּל־אִישׁ יְהוּדָה אֹמֵר חַי־אֲדֹנָי יְהוִה בְּכָל־אֶרֶץ מִצְרָיִם).

60 A French translation of this work appeared under the title *Le Prêtre et le Prophète: aux sources du Coran* (Paris: Maisonneuve and Larose, 2001) and the author's real name, Joseph Azzi. An English translation entitled *The Priest and the Prophet* appeared in 2005 from The Pen Publishers in Los Angeles.

61 On this topic Abū Mūsā al-Ḥarīrī notes (p. 26, n. 75):

" الر" ، و " الم " وغيرها من الحروف السرية الواردة في أوائل السور ... يقول فيها المفسرون : " الله أعلم بمراده " . " الر " ترد هكذا خمس مرات و " الم " ست مرات وتبتدئ الآيات بعدها بأمر الهي في أهمية الكتاب ووحيه الالهي مثل : " الر . تلك آيات الكتاب " ، و " الر . كتاب أحكمت آيته " ، و " الم . تنزيل الكتاب " ... وقد تعني ما كان يرد عادة على لسان الأنبياء : " قال لي الرب" ، وفي الارامية : أمر لي مرهو" (sic) (= مريم) : (أ . ل . م .) وذلك للدلالة على مصدر الكتاب الالهي.

"Concerning the (abbreviations) 'ALR' and 'ALM,' as well as the other mysterious letters that stand at the beginning of Suras, the commentators have this to say: 'What he means by them, God himself knows best.' 'ALR' appears five times, and 'ALM' appears six times. After these abbreviations we find verses with a divine statement regarding the meaning of the text and its divine revelation, e.g., 'ALR; these are the written signs of the book,' and 'ALR; a book whose written signs were taught,' and 'ALM; the sending-down of the book' ... These could correspond to the statement commonly on the prophets' lips: 'The Lord spoke to me,' or in

Aramaic, ʿEmar lī Mōryō (= Māryā) (ALM), and thus serve as a pointer to the divine origin of the book."

62 Haï Bar-Zeev, *Une lecture juive du Coran* (Paris: Editeurs Berg International, 2005), but he refers here to our other author, Hanna Zakarias, *De Moïse à Mohammed*, 2 vols (Cahors: privately published, 1955–56), who in turn points to Kurt Hruby's work.

63 One notices here the agreement of Q 3:41 and the Peshitta version of Luke 1:22; the former uses the term *ramzan* (meaning "by sign" = "sign-language"), while the latter reads *w-hū mermaz rāmez (h)wā l-hōn* ("but he made signs to them," that is, "he made his intentions known to them by sign language").

64 Cf. Anton Baumstark, *Festbrevier und Kirchenjahr der syrischen Jakobiten* (Paderborn: F. Schöningh, 1910), 169: "Between our Sunday for the dedication of churches and the Christmas feast, there developed completely what we might call the 'Advent' of the Jacobite liturgical year. We know that Antioch already had a season of preparation before the feast of Christ's birth at the time of Severus [bishop from 512 to 518].... Correspondingly, the liturgical year of the Jacobites originally had two Sundays in preparation for Christmas, for both of which the Gospel pericope was taken from λ [Luke]; more specifically, the first celebrated the annunciation of the birth of John the Baptist, and the second that to Mary. The lectionary of the ninth century, in agreement with three of the earliest extant choral books, restricts itself in its pre-Christmas services to this "double annunciation" celebration...." Concerning the Nestorian liturgical year, cf. 170.

65 Cf. the new interpretation of Q 97 by the present author in the essay "Christmas in the Qurʾān" in the present anthology, a translation of "Weihnachten im Koran," in Christoph Burgmer, ed., *Streit um den Koran: Die Luxenberg-Debatte: Standpunkte und Hintergründe* [Quarrel about the Koran: The Luxenberg Debate: Points of View and Backgrounds], 3rd rev. ed. (Berlin: Hans Schiler, 2007), pp. 62–68.

66 Concerning "Yah," cf. Ex. XV.2; Thes. I:1563, ܝܗ / Yah: nomen Dei; possibly a Status absolutus from ܝܬ / yaṯ ("essence"); Thes. I:1840. Cf. also Mannā, 306a: "(Yah): الرب الأزلي ("the eternal God"). Concerning the possible translation of "to be greatly praised," and the transitive usage of the Qur'ānic كبر / kabbara in the sense of the Latin meaning magnifico ("to praise greatly, to exalt"), cf. Surahs 2:185; 17:111; 22:37; 74:3.

Relics of Syro-Aramaic Letters in Early Qur'ānic Codices of the *ḥiǧāzī* and *kūfī* Style

Christoph Luxenberg

The following article was first published in German as "Relikte syro-aramäischer Buchstaben in frühen Korankodizes im ḥiǧāzī- *und* kūfī-*Duktus," in Karl-Heinz Ohlig, ed.,* Der Frühe Islam, *Inârah: Schriften zur frühen Islamgeschichte und zum Koran, vol. 2 (Berlin, 2007), pp. 377–419. This English version will appear both in the present anthology and in the English translation of the original collection of essays.*

1. Introductory Remarks

The present essay builds upon one first published in the volume *Die dunklen Anfänge: Neue Forschungen zur Entstehung und frühen Geschichte des Islam*, where I discussed a text from the current Cairo edition of the Qur'ān.[1] There I argued that it is clear that there exists at least one faulty transcription into the younger Arabic writing system, from a Qur'ānic *Vorlage* written (earlier) in Syriac script (not in Syriac language). In this essay I explained the basis for the confusion regarding the similarly-formed Syriac letters ܠ / *L* and ܥ / *'ayn*, which resulted in the latter's being incorrectly transcribed as an Arabic ـل / *L*. I will briefly summarize my findings here.

The ـل / *L* in the Arabic word لبدا / *LBDA* (S. 72:19) incorrectly represents the Syriac letter ܥ / *'ayn*; this mistake resulted in the reading *libadan*, which makes no sense in its context, instead of عبدا / *'ibādan* (which should actually be *'ābidē* < original *'ābidayn* > *'ābidēn* > *'ābidīn*), which corresponds to the Syro-Aramaic ܥܒܕ̈ܐ / *'ābdē* (< *'ābdayn* > *'ābdēn* > *'ābdīn*). The doubts expressed by Western scholars as to the real meaning of this expression in their translation bring into relief the possibility of a faulty transcription. This is evident from the following context of Surah 72:18–20:

وان المسجد للــه فلا تدعوا مع اللــه احدا

وانه لما قام عبد اللــه يدعوه كادوا يكومون عليه لبدا

قل انما ادعوا ربي ولا اشرك به احدا

Paret: (18) And, "The cultic places (*masāǧid*) are (exclusively) there for God. Consequently, do not call upon anyone (else) besides God!" (19) And, "When the servant of God (n.: "i.e., Muhammad") raised himself up in order to call upon him (n.: or, "to pray to him"), they would have nearly crushed him (for blatant meddling?) (*? Kādū yakūnūna 'alaihi libadan*)" (n.: "The meaning of this verse is very unclear."). (20) Say: "I will call upon my Lord (alone) (n.: or, "I will pray to my Lord alone"), and I will associate no one with him."[2]

Blachère: (18) The [sacred] mosque is for Allah. Therefore do not pray to any person besides Allah! (n. 18: "*The [sacred] mosque*: cf. Q 9:17)" (19) When the Servant of Allah got up, praying, [the infidels] failed to be against him in masses (?). (n. 19: *The Servant of God* = Muhammad; concerning *Kâdû yakûnûna 'alay-hi libadâ* (var. *lubada* and *lubbâda*), "the infidels, etc.," the subject is uncertain – the commentators say that they are the *jinn*, but this is hardly probable.) (20) Say: "I will not pray to anyone but my Lord, and I will not associate anyone with Him."[3]

Bell: (18) And that, the places of worship belong to Allah; so along with Allah call not ye upon anyone; (19) And that, when a servant of Allah stood calling upon Him, they were upon him almost in swarms. (n. 3: The meaning is uncertain. The "servant of Allah" is usually taken to be Muhammad, and "they" to refer to jinn, which is possible if angels now speak.) (20) Say: "I call simply upon my Lord, and I associate not with Him any one."[4]

My philological analysis of Q 72:18–20, three verses which hang together in terms of their meaning, resulted in the following interpretation:

(The Jinn, the invisible beings, spirits, claim:)

18. And that worship (belongs) to God (alone), and so you should call upon no other besides God;
19. And that, when the servant of God was resurrected and called (once again) upon him (that is, "worshiped him"), they (the people) would nearly have worshiped him (as God);
20. (Upon which, when the Servant of God was defending himself,) he said (NB: *not* "say!"), 'No! I call upon my Lord, and I associate no other with him!"

The original discovery of individual Syro-Aramaic letters in the Qur'ān is not due to any particular Qur'ānic manuscripts; rather, it resulted step-by-step from the contextualized philological analyses of the canonical Qur'ānic text using the method presented in my study *Die syro-aramäische Lesart des Koran.*[5] The manuscript material that has since come to light has contributed to the clarification of the sources of the mistakes in transcribing from the older Syriac into the younger Arabic writing system, and also to the recognition of an especially striking Syriac letter, which I will discuss at the end of this essay. Methodologically speaking, this has resulted in an expansion of the methods used up to this time, which consisted primarily of seven parts. In the past scholars have typically seen the main problem in the Qur'ānic text as the lack of diacritical points in the early Qur'ānic manuscripts (even though the actual problem is of a philological nature, in which the diacritical points play only a subordinate role); henceforth, however, research methods in Qur'ānic textual analysis must take into consideration the possibility of confusion regarding a group of Syro-Aramaic letters. In what follows I will discuss these letters and the new Qur'ānic readings that result from their confusion, in the cases of words that were mis-written and mis-read.

My research thus far has shown that several letters from the Syriac alphabet have led to mis-transcriptions or mis-readings, because they are formed similarly either to one another or to Arabic letters:

1) There are not a few cases of mis-transcription due to confusion regarding the identically shaped Syriac *serṭā /serṭō* letters ܕ / *d* and ܪ / *r*, the only letters in the Syriac alphabet that are distinguished by means of a point placed above or below the letters. It must have been inexperienced copyists who were the causes of mis-transcriptions of these letters, not only into the Arabic د / *d* (or ذ / *ḏ*) and ر / *r* (or ز / *z*), but even into an Arabic و / *w*, due to the similarity of its basic form to the two Syriac letters.]
2) Less common is confusion regarding the two similarly-formed Syriac letters ܠ / *l* and ܥ / *'ayn*; the latter was sometimes transcribed as an Arabic ـلـ / *l*, while the former was transcribed as an Arabic ـعـ / *'ayn* less often (due to its more distinct form).
3) The confusion that appears most often by far concerns the final forms of the Arabic letters ن / *n* and ى / y / *ī* or *ā*. That such exchanges took place within the Arabic writing system, due to similarities between the hand-written final forms of these letters, has already been proposed, but below I will provide the graphic proof for this conjecture by means of the early *ḥijāzī* and *kūfī* fragments of the Qur'ān, in that the confusion actually goes back to unchanged (and therefore faithful) transcriptions of the Syriac final ܢ / ـبـ / *n*. This identification is the discovery that gives us concrete proof that the Qur'ānic *Vorlage* was originally, at least partially, composed in the Syriac script (a phenomenon known as "Garshuni" or "Karshuni").
4) Finally, a few cases have been found thus far in which a Syriac ܣ / *s* was falsely transcribed as an Arabic ـهـ / *h*, due to the similarities between the two letters. This will be shown in a later study.

2. Concrete Examples

2.1 The Mis-transcription of the Syriac ܥ / ‘ayn as an Arabic ـلـ / l

The example I explained at the beginning of this essay concerns such a mis-transcription in the canonical Qur’ānic text. The present section contains further examples of this phenomenon; in all cases I have underlined the falsely transcribed ـلـ / *l*.

Example 2: Surah 104:1

و يل لكل همزه لـمزه

Paret, 517, translates this text as follows, indicating his dependence upon the Qur’ānic commentators: “Woe to every taunter and grumbler.”[6]

Introductory comments

The Cairo edition reads: *waylun li-kulli humazatin lumazatin*. Several emendations are required here. First, the introductory vowel *u* in the last two words (*humaza* and *lumaza*) is arbitrary and has no grammatical justification. The Arab readers of the Qur’ān did not recognize that these two forms represent a Syro-Aramaic *nomen agentis* that came into Arabic as a *fa“al* and must have been familiar to the Arab grammarians. Consequently, it must have been inexperienced readers who read here *hu* and *lu* instead of *ha* and *la*. Second, in the *fa“āl* form the middle consonant is doubled, and the vowel that immediately follows is to be pronounced as a long *ā*. Third, the Arab readers apparently did not recognize that the final *h* indicates the Aramaic *status emphaticus* masculine ending with *ā*, which has nothing to do with the Arabic feminine ending or with a mark of intensification, as *Lisān* (V:407) explains. The two diacritical marks above the final *h* are therefore false, as is the inflection to *in*, because the Aramaic final *h* (= *ā*) is uninflectable. Because the entirety of Surah 104 is based on a rhyme with the *a*-sound, verse 1 should be read (without final vowels) thus: *wayl la-kull* (not *li-kull*) *hammāza lammāza*.

Philological Analysis

The word ويل / *wayl* is a combination of the interjection وي / *way* (< Syro-Aramaic ܘܝ / *wāy*) (“woe!”) and the preposition ـلـ / *la* (< a reduction from على / *‘alā* by the disappearance of the introductory syllable *‘a*), which takes the dative case. This preposition was added enclitically to the exclamatory particle وي / *way* (“woe!”) to form the substantive ويل / *wayl* (similar to the folk etymologically explained construction of مال / *māl* as ما / *mā* + ـلـ / *l* = “what belongs to [someone]" = "property, assets"). The latter etymology was accepted upto now by Arabists. But meanwhile, the author has recognised it as "folk" etymology, in so far as the Arabs understood by this word مال / *māl,* according to the *Lisān*, in the first instance, their possessions in the form of camels, which makes it clear that the word مال / *māl* is an abbreviation of the word (ḥi)māl (beast of burden) or (ğı)māl (camels).

Before personal suffixes وي / *way*, with the following preposition لـ / *la-*, appears sometimes proclitically as an exclamatory particle, as in ويلكم / *way-lakum* ("woe to you" [S. 20:61]) (= Syro-Aramaic ܘܝ ܠܟܘܢ / *wāy l-ḵōn*), and sometimes substantively (placed before and after), as in ولكم الويل / *wa-lakum al-wayl* (lit.: "To you the woe" [S. 21:18]).

2.2 Concerning the Mis-Transcription of the لـ / l̲ in لـمزه (traditional reading: l̲u̲mazat̲i̲n̲)

The Arabic لـ / *l* here is a mis-transcription of a Syriac ܥ / *ʿayn*. The original form in the Syriac script was ܥܡܙܗ, which corresponds to the Arabic عمزه / *ʿammāza*. The عـ / *ʿayn*, if it is viewed with a diacritical point, results in the Arabic reading غمزه / *ġammāza*.

Lexically, the verbal root لمز / *lamaza* cannot be shown to be in use in any Arabic dialect. Everything that appears in the lexica can be traced back to this Qur'ānic mis-transcription and actually belongs under the root غمز / *ġamaza*. *Lisān* (V:406b) does not note that لمز / *lamaza* actually concerns a falsely-transcribed غمز / *ġamaza* (without a diacritical point); about لمز / *lamaza* it simply says وأصله الإشارة بالعين ("originally this meant winking, or make a sign with an eye"). This note simply reproduces the definition *Lisān* (V:388b) gives concerning غمز / *ġamaza*: والغمز : الإشارة بالعين والحاجب والجفن (*al-ġamz* = "to give a sign with the eye, the eyebrow, and the eyelid").

Because there is no verb لمز / *lamaza* in Arabic, the Arab lexicographers and commentators on the Qur'ān attempted to speculate on some meaning for the word from the Qur'ānic context. So, for example, in *Ṭabarī* (XXX:291ff.) and in *Lisān* (V:406b f.), a *lumaza* (= *lammāza*) is one who "disdains" or "slanders" someone else.

However, the Qur'ān makes the actual meaning of the term quite clear for us by self-reference, provided that the mis-reading I suggest in a different place is correctly transcribed and read. The Qur'ānic commentators would not have noticed this, because they did not see the connection between the two texts. Surah 83:29–30 reads:

ان الذين اجرموا كانوا من الذين امنوا يضحكون

واذامروابهم يتغامزون

traditional reading: ʾinna llaḏīna ʾağramū kānū mina llaḏīna ʾāmanū yaḍḥakūna wa-ʾiḏā marrū bihim yataġāmazūna

Paret (?): The sinners make fun of the faithful (in this world) / and when they pass by them, they wink at one another (in a mocking way).

Pickthall: 29. Lo! the guilty used to laugh at those who believed, 30. And wink one to another when they passed them.

Paret (504) did not catch this last nuance, for he translated the text

> . . .they wink at one another (in a strained way/ verkniffen) (*yataġāmazūna*).

Indeed, winking can have a variety of motivations. However, the Qur'ānic context makes the mocking intention of the verb ("to laugh, make fun of") in v. 29 quite clear. For this reason, the Qur'ān intends the *nomen agentis* غمزه / *ġammāza* to mean "one who mocks." In the context of Q 104, this meaning would describe someone who makes fun of the after-life and sees his happiness in the prosperity he enjoys in the present life, and thus someone to whom the punishments of hell are promised. This leitmotif—the unbelievers who mock in this life, and the faithful who laugh in the after-life—appears multiple times in the Qur'ān with such synonymous expressions as سخر / *saḫira* ("to mock"), ضحك / *ḍaḥika* ("to laugh"), استهزأ / *istahzaʾa* ("to make fun of"), لعب / *laʿiba* ("to amuse oneself, enjoy oneself"), etc.

Concerning the allophone همزه / *hammāza*, which appears in Q 104:1 before the word we have just been considering (and whose mis-reading *humaza* was chosen for the name of the Surah), *Lisān* (V:425b) makes the root همز / *hamaza* synonymous with غمز / *ġamaza*. It also (426a) lists the present participle هامز / *hāmiz* alongside the *nomen agentis* همّاز / *hammāz* and همزة / *humaza* (= *hammāza*); these forms it explains as الغيّاب / *al-ġayyāb* ("the slanderer"). With this information, همزه / *hammāza* would be understood as an intensifying expression that is parallel to غمزه / *ġammāz* (which is possible according to Mandaean i.e., eastern vernacular Aramaic phonetics). The traditional understanding recognizes the possibility that the root همزه / *hamaza* may actually be a phonetic variant of همس / *hamasa*, which *Lisān* (V:426b) connects with the devil, who makes suggestions in the hearts of human beings. According to Mannā (176a), however, the Syro-Aramaic root ܗܡܣ / *hmas* means, among other things (def. 4), شك ارتاب / *šakka, irtāba* ("to doubt, entertain suspicion"). Because the Qur'ān puts "doubt" together with "unbelievers"—e.g., in Q 34:21, where God allows humans to be tested by the devil, to learn who believes in the after-life, and who doubts—then همزه / *hammāza* = همسه / *hammāsa* ("one who doubts") would fit well with غمزه / *ġammāza* ("one who mocks"), as one who doubts the after-life and therefore makes fun of it. In the eschatological context of Q 104, this is why such a person is threatened with the punishments of hell.

As a result of the corresponding Syro-Aramaic morphology and orthography, the traditional reading of Q 104:1 (*waylun li-kulli humazatin lumazatin*) should be adjusted to read *wayl(un) l(a)-kull(i) hammāza ġammāza*. The traditional understanding of this text—"Woe to every taunter and grumbler!" —should be amended semantically and syntactically as follows:

"Woe to every mocking doubter!"

These first two examples derive from Meccan Surahs. I will now present three further examples from Medinan Surahs that exhibit the same mis-transcription.

Example 3: Surah 49:11

و لا تِلمزوا انفسكم ولا تنابزوا بالالقب

Pickthall: Neither defame one another, nor insult one another by nicknames.

Paret (431) translates this text thus:

> And do not criticize (each other), and do not give each other derogatory names!" ("Und *bekrittelt* euch nicht (gegenseitig) und *gebt euch* keine Schimpfnamen!")

This section of the Medinan text begins with a warning to the faithful not to make fun of one another (لا يسخر قوم من قوم / *lā yasḫar qawmun min qawm*); the verselet in question follows thereafter. The clarity of the former statement makes obvious the synonymous meaning of the latter, which contains the mis-transcribed verb و لا تِلمزوا / *wa-lā talmizū*. As was the case above, Ṭabarī (XXVI:131) speculates as to the meaning of this expression that was unknown to him, giving it the sense of "to slander." Here again we see that the medial ـلـ / *l* in تِلمزوا (*ta*l*mizū*) is a mis-transcription of the Syriac ܥ / *ʿayn* (without a diacritical point). If we replace the ـلـ / *l* with an Arabic medial *ʿayn* (with a diacritical point), we have the reading ولا تِغمزوا انفسكم / *wa-lā taġmizū anfusakum* ("and do not wink at one another [mockingly, with the eyes] = do not mock one another").

The reconstructed verb غمز / *ġamaza* ("to wink") is widely current in Arabic, but the verb-form that follows, ولا تنابزوا / *wa-lā ta(ta)-nābazū*, is not. Consequently, Ṭabarī (XXVI:132) thought it was a denominative form based on an assumed substantive نبز / *nabz*, whose plural would be انباز / *anbāz*; he also assumed that it was a synonym of the word that follows, لقب / *laqab* ("epithet, nickname"), which is an authentic Arabic word with the identically-constructed plural ألقاب / *alqāb*. *Lisān* (V:413a) also accepted this linguistically unfounded explanation, apparently without question, and following him, Hans Wehr (*Arabisches Wörterbuch*). As a result, Wehr explained this questionable expression as "to give an insulting or derogatory name;" he defined the assumed substantive *nabaz/anbāz* as "nickname." It was from a similar understanding that Paret (431-2) neglected to translate the unfamiliar verb and paraphrased the expression thus:

> . . .and do not give each other derogatory names.

In this case the Syro-Aramaic language can bring us closer to a solution to the problem. Mannā (427a) defines the root ܢܒܙ / *nḇaz* as a dialectical form of ܢܘܙ / *nwaz* (435b). But actually, the root ܢܒܙ / *nḇaz* is, from the point of view of phonetical historical evolution, the original form. One also finds there (435b) under (3) the Arabic parallels خاصم. شاجر / *ḫāṣama, šājara* ("to argue, bicker"). If we place this Syro-Aramaic meaning at the foundation of our reading, then the second portion of the Qur'ānic sentence, ولا تنابزوا بالالقب / *wa-lā ta(ta)-nābazū bi-l-alqāb*, would (literally) mean, "do not argue amongst yourselves with (pejorative) nicknames;" the sense would be literally: "do not pelt each other with (pejorative) nicknames." The latter translation actually lies closer to the original Syro-Aramaic meaning than "to argue"; on closer examination, the Syro-Aramaic root ܢܒܙ / *nḇaz* turns out to be the etymological correspondence to the Arabic نبذ / *nabaḏa* ("to cast out, toss, throw away"). As a result, the speculation that the Arabic letter ز / *z* is a mis-transcription of the Syriac ܕ / *d*, which is only distinguished from ܪ / *r* by a diacritical point, lends credence to the *lectio difficilior*. If we transfer the letter as an Arabic د / *d* (with the additional point above: ذ / *ḏ*), this Arabic correction results in the following reading: ولا تنابذوا بالالقب / *wa-lā ta(ta)-nābaḏū bi-l-alqāb* ("and do not pelt each other with (pejorative) nicknames"). This reading is even more plausible because the root نبز / *nabaza* is unknown in Arabic, while the root نبذ / *nabaḏa* is rather common and appears in the Qur'ān twelve times. With this new reading, the number grows to thirteen.

As a result of this orthographic and semantic review, and over against the translation of Paret quoted above, the section of Q 49:11 under consideration should now be translated thus:

> . . .and do not wink (mockingly, with the eyes) at one another (i.e., do not mock one another), and do not pelt each other with (pejorative) nicknames.

Example 4: Surah 9:58

ومنهم من يلمزك في الصدقت

فان اعطوا منها رضوا وان لم يعطوا منها اذا هم يسخطو

Pickthall: And of them is he who defameth thee in the matter of the alms. If they are given thereof they are content, and if they are not given thereof, behold! they are enraged.

Paret (157) translates this text thus:

> And among you there are some who criticize you because of your alms-giving (*ṣadaqāt*). When they then (?) receive some of this, they are satisfied, but when they do not receive any, they are immediately upset.

The context of this passage excludes the possibility of understanding the falsely-transcribed term as above, so that يلمزك / (traditional reading:) *yalmizuka* would be يغمزك / *yaġmizuka* ("to wink mockingly with the eyes"). "To criticize," as Paret translates the term, also makes little sense, for a supplicant can only hope to receive alms from some kind of corresponding behavior. Ṭabarī (X:156) defends the opinion in this context that this expression is intended to mean "to seek (to receive something)" or "to request;" consequently, the "winking" mentioned here can have meant only a gesture of solicitation (perhaps with an outstretched hand) whose goal was to dispose the addressee favorably toward the speaker. This meaning is confirmed by *Lisān* (V:388b), under غمز / *ġamaza*. According to Ibn al-Aṯīr, الغمز / *al-ġamz* ("winking"), like الرمز / *ar-ramz* ("sign"), should be understood in a few hadith (*ḥadīṯe*) to mean "a sign with the eye, the eyebrow, and the hand" (فسر الغمز في بعض الأحاديث بالإشارة كالرمز بالعين والحاجب واليد).

Consequently, this verse can be understood as follows:

> Among you there are some who (making a friendly request) wink at you regarding alms (i.e., "turn to you with a gesture of solicitation"). If something is granted to these, they are satisfied; if something is not granted to them, they become indignant.

Example 5: Surah 9:79

الذين يلمزون المطوعين من المومنين في الصدقت و الذين لا يجدون

الا جهدهم فيسخرون منهم سخر اللـــه منهم ولهم عذاب اليم

Pickthall: Those who point at such of the believers as give the alms willingly and such as can find naught to give but their endeavours, and deride them Allah (Himself) derideth them. Theirs will be a painful doom.

Paret (159) translates the text thus:

> Those (grumblers) who (on the one hand) criticize those believers who are ready to give voluntary services (and donations) because of the gifts of alms (*ṣadaqāt*) (given by them over and above their duty) [*note 86: Or:* "Those (grumblers) who, on the one hand, criticize those believers who are ready to give voluntary services as they give alms"] and who (on the other hand) (criticize) those who (from a lack of means) can produce nothing but their zeal (?) [*note 87: Or:* ". . .who can bring anything (at all) only with great difficulty" (*? allaḏīna lā yajidūna illā juhdahum*)] and scoff at them—God will also scoff at them someday (when they come to the judgment), and they can expect a painful punishment.

This complex translation by Paret indicates clearly that the Qur'ānic sentence is difficult to understand on lexical, phraseological, and syntactic grounds.

Philological Analysis

First, orthographically, we should reconstruct the falsely-transcribed word يلمزون / *yalmizūn*, as يغمزون / *yaġmizūn*, in accordance with our discussion above. Semantically, the accompanying, synonymous verb سخر / *saḫira* makes the derogatory intention of this instance of "winking" so clear that one can acceptably translate the word that literally means "to wink" as "to mock."

Example 6: Mis-Transcription of the Syriac ܠ / l̠ as an Arabic ـعـ / 'ayn)

Second, as luck would have it, in the same verse (Surah 9: 79) just after our falsely-transcribed Arabic ـلـ / *l* (from the Syro-Aramaic ܓ / *ayn*, in يلمون / *yalmizūn* = بغمزون / *yaġmizūn*), a word appears that presents the opposite phenomenon, namely, that a Syro-Aramaic ܠ / *l* is transcribed as an Arabic ـعـ / *'ayn*. Because we recognize this mis-transcription, we can reconstruct the falsely-transcribed word المطوعين / (traditional reading:) *al-muṭṭawwi'īna* as المطولين / *al-muṭṭawwilīn*.

Philological and Lexical Rationale

The Arabic verbal root طوع > طاع / *ṭawa'a* > *ṭā'a* has the basic meaning of "to obey, comply." The fifth verbal stem تطوع / *taṭawwa'a* is understood in modern Arabic in the sense of "to volunteer for military service." This idea corresponds to the explanation given in *Lisān* (VIII:243b) for المطوعة / *al-muṭṭawwi'a*: الذين يتطوّعون بالجهاد / *al-laḏīna yataṭawwa'ūna bi-l-ğihād* ("they are those who voluntarily fight in the (holy) war"). *Lisān* (VIII:243b) explains the verbal noun تطوّع / *taṭawwu'* as follows: ما تبرّع به

من ذات نفسه مما لا يلزمه فرضه ("it is that which one does voluntarily [actually *tabarra'a* means ". . .an action by which one distinguishes oneself"- [cf. Arabic, *bāri'* = brilliant, illustrious]), what is not imposed upon one as a duty." In reality, however, تطوع / *taṭawwa'a* means "to behave obediently, to comply obediently with a duty."

The meaning of "to volunteer for military service" has taken hold in modern literary Arabic, but the basis of this expression as a "voluntary offering" has remained foreign to spoken usage. This is true even if one wants to understand the Qur'ānic expression من تطوّع خيرا / *man taṭawwaʿa ḫayran* (S. 2:158, 184) as Paret translated it (23, 26): "when someone does a good deed voluntarily." In the Qur'ānic context, however, the fifth reflexive stem تطوع / *taṭawwaʿa* seems to have the meaning of the tenth reflexive stem استطاع / *istaṭāʿa* ("can, to be able, to be capable"), and this is the meaning of the synonymous verb اطاق / *aṭāqa* in Q 2:184: وعلى الذين يطيقونه فدية طعام مسكين ("...and those who are able to do so (should make) a (corresponding) gift of food to a poor person." The addendum that follows then reads: فمن تطوع خيرا فهو خير له ("and who is able to do more [i.e., "still more"[7]], this will be for that person's benefit); Paret translated the clause, "...and if someone does a good work voluntarily, that is better for that person."

If this explanation eliminates the reading المطوعين / *al-muṭṭawwiʿīn* as meaning "the voluntary (donors)," because the word "donors" is missing, then the next step is to examine whether the reading المطولين / *al-muṭṭawwilīn* gives this meaning.

The Arabic verbal root طول > طال / *ṭawala* > *ṭāla* is easy to understand on its own; it has a foundational meaning of "to be long." However, three Qur'ānic texts lead one to decide on a meaning that semantically has nothing to do with this fundamental Arabic definition. These texts are:

1) S. 4:25: concerning the wedding-gift mentioned in the introductory sentence و من لم يستطع منكم طولا, Ṭabarī (V:15f.) understood the word طول (traditional reading: *ṭawl*; but actually *ṭūl*, meaning "length" in Arabic) more or less correctly from its context: "whoever among you is not able to produce a (wedding-)gift";
2) S. 9:86: again, Ṭabarī (X:207) used the context to correctly understand the expression اولوا الطول (traditional reading: *'ūlū ṭ-ṭawli*) as meaning "the wealthy, the affluent;"
3) S. 40:3: once again, Ṭabarī (XXIV:41) correctly understood from its context the divine attribute ذي الطول / *ḏī ṭ-ṭawli* / *ḏī ṭ-ṭūli*) in the list غافر الذنب وقابل التوب شديد العقاب ذي الطول ("he who forgives sins, who accepts contrition, who punishes harshly and possesses abundant mercy"); Paret (388) translates this text indecisively: "and (also) possesses sufficient means (*ḏī ṭauli*) (to help the faithful?)."

Clearly, then, the common Arabic word طول (*ṭūl*) should not be interpreted based on its foundational meaning ("length") in these Qur'ānic texts. For this reason, the early Arabic readers devised a fictive reading for the *rasm* (*ṭawl* instead of *ṭūl*), in order to justify an uncommon understanding in each text's context.

In reality, in this case we are encountering a phenomenon which is not terribly rare in the Qur'ān, namely, a lexical "loan-translation," or calque, from Syro-Aramaic. As a result, according to our reliable methods, we must simply translate the word back into Syro-Aramaic in order to ascertain the corresponding semantic meaning. To this end, we have two verbal roots from which to choose:

1) ܐܪܟ / *erak̲* ("to be long"); and

2) ܦܫܛ / *pšaṭ* ("to stretch, stretch out, reach out").

Mannā provides Arabic meanings that speak to the terms' semantics. For the first, on 40a, it gives

> طال. سبغ / *ṭāla, sabaġa* (< Syro-Aramaic ܣܒܥ / *sb̲aʿ*) ("to be long, abundant"); under ܐܘܪܟ / *awrek̲*, it gives أطال / *aṭāla* ("to make long, elongate"), and in connection with ܛܝܒܘܬܐ / *ṭaybūṯā* ("grace"), it gives اسبغ نعمة / *asbaġa niʿma* ("to show gracious action richly").

For the second, on 618b, it gives

> بسط. نشر / *basaṭa, našara* ("to stretch out, extend, elongate"); the third entry here is قدّم. أعطى / *qaddama, aʿṭā* ("to grant, to give").

The semantics of these two synonymous verbs suffices to explain the Qur'ānic expression طول / *ṭūl* (in Arabic, "length") with the meaning "richly gracious action, riches, wealth, gift, present" as a lexical calque from the corresponding Syro-Aramaic expression.[8]

Even if this meaning for طول / *ṭūl* had not become accepted in modern Arabic, *Lisān* testifies that the Arabic expression was still in use in the ninth century (presumably in Mesopotamia) with the Syro-Aramaic semantics that I have indicated; this testimony takes the form of the *Ḥadīṯe* that are cited there. *Lisān* (XI:414) points to two of the three Qur'ānic texts mentioned above (SS. 4:25; 40:3) and explains الطول / *aṭ-ṭūl* (which it mis-reads as *aṭ-ṭawl*) with the following expressions: القدرة / *al-qudra* ("power, wealth"), الغنى / *al-ġinā* ("riches"), الفضل / *al-faḍl* ("gracious action, benefaction"). It offers an idiomatic expression in which the last of these is a synonym to طول / *ṭūl*, which can also mean المنّ / *al-mann* ("favor, benefaction, gift"). In addition, it clarifies the fifth verbal stem تطوّل / *ta-ṭawwala* with the meaning of امتنّ / *imtanna* (< Syro-Aramaic ܡܢܐ / *mnā*) ("to make/do a benefaction, gracious action, favor; to grant something graciously; to give as a gift"). As illustrations of this meaning, then, the text offers the following *ḥadīṯe* (with the verb تطوّل / *ta-ṭawwala*): تطاول عليهم الرب بفضله أي تطوّل ("The Lord showed his grace to them"); قال لأزواجه أوّلكنّ لحوقا بي أطولكنّ يدا ("He said to his wives, 'The first one of you who are closest to me is that one that has the "longest hand"); and أراد أمدّكنّ يدا بالعطاء ("With this statement he meant those who reach farthest with the hand in giving"), with the commentary وكانت زينب تعمل بيدها وتتصدّق ("at that time Zaynab made it a habit to give from the work of her own hands").

Concerning the nominal form تطوّل / *a-ṭawwul* ("donation"), the text attributes to Abū Manṣūr the following statement: عند العرب محمود يوضع و التطوّل موضع المحاسن ("*at-taṭawwul* [= 'donation'] is highly respected by Arabs and is considered a praiseworthy deed"). There are still more explanations in *Lisān* (XI:414) that testify to the earlier Arabic use of تطوّل / *taṭawwul* in the sense of "donation."

Even if this semantic content, foreign to the understanding in modern Arabic, may point back less to the "spoken usage of the Arabs" than to a calque from Syro-Aramaic, still the fifth verbal stem, تطوّل / *ta-ṭawwala*, attested multiple times in *Lisān*, substantiates the derivation of a masculine singular active participle متطوّل (*mu-ta-ṭawwil* ["the one granting, the giver"]), whose plural form, in the reconstructed written text المطولين, turns out in the Qur'ān to be a *hapax legomenon* that is to be read (as transmitted in the Qur'ān) with a "haplological syllabic ellipse" (from المتطولين / *al-mu-ta-ṭawwilīn*) as *al-mu-ṭṭawwilīn* (corresponding to the Syro-Aramaic [or Garshuni] ܐܠܡܛܘܠܝܢ = the Arabic المطولين). In addition, analysis of the *ḥijāzī* Qur'ānic manuscript BNF 328a shows that there as well (f. 41b, l. 14) the ـعـ / *'ayn* in the written text المطوعين / *al-muṭṭawwi'īn* had already been mis-transcribed, which shows that this manuscript too is secondary.

The analysis of this unique Qur'ānic expression has given two primary results:

1) this text represents the first discovery of a mis-transcription in the Qur'ān of a Syro-Aramaic ܠ / *l* as an Arabic ـعـ / *'ayn*; and
2) the discovery of the mis-transcription would not have been possible without the assistance of philology.

The method I have used in this section has shown that one could only have come to a conclusive result by means of a combination of two linguistic components, namely, a) the Qur'ānic-Arabic and historico-linguistic usage of the expression in question, and b) also the semantics of the Syro-Aramaic expression to which it corresponds lexically. I will employ the same degree of empirical exactness in depicting other Arabic mis-transcriptions from a Qur'ānic *Vorlage* composed in the Syro-Aramaic script ("Garshuni/ Karshuni").

Phraseologically, Paret's footnote 87 (mentioned above) points up the sentence that is difficult to understand and that he places in parentheses: "(? *allaḏīna lā yajidūna illā ǧuhdahum*)." Such an emphasis is quite appropriate, for the idiomatic expression وجد جهدا (*waǧada ǧuhdan*, lit. "to find an effort") is not to be found in any Arabic dictionary and yet is a word-for-word representation of the Syro-Aramaic idiomatic expressions ܡܨܐ ܚܝܠܐ (*mṣā ḥaylā*) and ܐܫܟܚ ܚܝܠܐ (*eškaḥ ḥaylā*), which literally mean "to have power" = "to have the power available" = "can, be able, be in a position to do something." In the latter of the two Syro-Aramaic formulations, the word ܐܫܟܚ / *eškaḥ* has two meanings:

1) "can, be able" and
2) "find."

The Qur'ān represents the latter of these two by using the Arabic word وجد / *wajada* ("to find") rather than استطاع / *istaṭā'a* ("can"). In another text the Qur'ān reproduces the same Syro-Aramaic expression by means of the Arabic استطاع حيله / *istaṭā'a ḥaylā* (mis-read as حيلة / *ḥīlatan*); the text in question is Q 4:98: لا يستطيعون حيلة / *lā yastaṭī'ūna ḥīlatan* (literally understood in Arabic as "to have no cunning," when the Syro-Aramaic means "to have no power" = "not to be in a position to do something"). As a result, sometimes وجد / *wajada* ("to find") should be understood in the Qur'ān as a semantic mis-translation from the Syro-Aramaic ܐܫܟܚ / *eškaḥ* (2nd definition: "to be able, to be in a position") in the Arabic sense of استطاع / *istaṭā'a* ("can, to be in a position"), e.g., in Q 58:4, where فمن لم يجد / *fa-man lam yajid* (lit., "who does not find") is rightly clarified in the following clause with the Arabic فمن لم يستطع / *fa-man lam yastaṭī'* ("who is not a position to…"). This explanation makes clear the usage of وجد / *wajada* ("to find") as a calque from the Syro-Aramaic ܐܫܟܚ / *eškaḥ* ("can, is able") when the context would suggest the Arabic استطاع / *istaṭā'a* (cf. also Surahs 2:196; 4:92; 4:121; 5:89; 18:53; 24:33; 58:4, 12). Current written Arabic uses the expression جهد جهدا / *jahada juhdan* ("to do his best, to do what is most possible, to act to the best of his abilities") to correspond to the Qur'ānic expression وجد جهدا / *wajada juhdan*, itself borrowed from Syro-Aramaic.

Syntactically, Paret relates the second الذين / *allaḏīna* ("those who, they") to the first one, a demonstrative pronoun that indicates the subject of the clause; he does not see that the second introduces a relative clause that relates to the "faithful" who were mentioned later in the first clause.

After this wide-ranging philological analysis, the afore-mentioned verse from Q 9:79 should be understood thus, in terms of its semantics, phrasing, and syntax: "Those who mock the donors among the faithful because of (their) gifts of alms, in which they (perform this service) only according to what lies in their possession, but they (nonetheless)[9] mock them—God will mock these people and (cause) them (to take part in) a severe punishment."

Example 7: Surah 17:78

اقم الصلوة لدلوك الشمس الى غسق اليل

وقران الفجر ان قران الفجر كان مشهودا

Pickthall: Establish worship at the going down of the sun until the dark of night, and (the recital of) the Qur'an at dawn. Lo! (the recital of) the Qur'an at dawn is ever witnessed.

Paret (234): Perform the prayer (*ṣalāt*) when the sun bends (toward the horizon), until the night darkens! And the recitation of the early morning (*wa-qur'āna l-fajri*)! People should (generally) be present for this (*? inna qur'āna l-fajri kāna mahšūdan*).

First, the word in question here is دلوك (traditional reading: *dulūk*). In that it relates to the sun, Paret attempts to come closer to an understanding by saying, "when the sun bends (toward the horizon)." Although some of the authorities cited in Ṭabarī (XV:134ff.) understand the term to refer to the "setting of the sun" (Ibn Mas'ūd, Ibn 'Abbās, et al.), Ṭabarī decides in favor of the majority of interpreters, who see in this phrase the meaning "noon-time." In Paret's commentary (p. 305), he suggests rightly that the expression originally referred "quite generally to the time of the evening prayer"; however, this suggestion only becomes certain when one replaces the falsely-transcribed Arabic ـل / *l* with the original Syro-Aramaic ܥ / *'ayn*. Read in the Syro-Aramaic Garshuni/Karshuni ܕܥܘܟ (= Arabic دعوك / *du'ūk*), the Syro-Aramaic verbal root ܕܥܟ / *d'eḵ* bears the following meaning according to Mannā (155b): 1) طفى / *ṭafi'a* ("to extinguish"); 4) غاب. غرب / *ġaba, ġaruba* ("to disappear"). Consequently, the Qur'ānic *hapax legomenon* دعوك / *du'ūk*, understood as a Syro-Aramaic loan-word, clearly means "the setting of the sun."

Second, the Arabic passive participle مشهودا / *mašhūdā* should not be understood in the Arabic sense of "to be present." Rather, it should read in the Syro-Aramaic sense of "commanded, prescribed" (cf. Mannā, 480a, under ܐܣܗܕ / *ashed*: 3) نبّه. حذّر / *nabbaha, ḥaddara*). In the same source, the nominal form ܣܗܕܘܬܐ / *sāhdūṯā* which derives therefrom bears the meaning (3) شريعة. ناموس. وصية / *šarī'a, nāmūs, waṣīya* ("rule, law, command").

Third, and syntactically, the Arabic conjunction و / *wa-* before وقران / *wa-qur'ān* begins a new, nominal protasis, whose apodosis is introduced by the intensifying conjunction ان / *inna*.

The Qur'ānic verse cited above, therefore, should be understood semantically and syntactically thus: "Perform the prayer from the setting of the sun until dusk. However, (concerning) the Qur'ānic recitation at dawn, this is commanded!"

3. Graphic Analysis of the Early Qur'ānic Codices in the *ḥiǧāzī* and *kūfī* Traditions (BNF 328a, British Library Or. 2165, Samarqand, San'ā')

The first edition of the book *Die syro-aramäische Lesart des Koran* (Berlin, 2000) bears on its cover a reproduction of folio 3b of the Qur'ānic manuscript BNF 328a. In line 14 of this folio, the name "John" appears (second word from the right, from Q 3:39) with the expression يحںے *ygnn* following (without the prefixed preposition بـ / *bi-*). This expression is re-written in the Cairo edition of the Qur'ān as يحيى and read as *Yaḥyā*. With this reading, the originally retroflex ending (that is, one that bends sharply back against the grain of the writing), used in early Arabic script as a variant alongside the final-ى which is current today, was replaced by that final-ى, with the result that the original graphic text was lost.

3.1 The Graphemic Meaning, Overlooked until Now, of the Arabic Retroflex Final-ى (ے)

Qur'ānic scholars up to the present day have known that both forms of the final-ى are attested without distinction in the Qur'ānic manuscripts (as *ī* and *ā*). Indeed, both forms can appear with the same word seemingly at random.[10] Consequently, there is no cause at all for the least suggestion that these two final forms could represent distinct phonemes. However, the Arabic reading يحيى / *Yaḥyā*, which diverges from the Syro-Aramaic ܝܘܚܢܢ / *Yoḥannān* (or *Yuḥannān*), forces such a suggestion upon us, not least because there is no trace of this name whatsoever in the early Arabic literature or in the pre-Islamic period.[11]

Alphonse Mingana was the first to point attention to a mis-reading by the Arabic *Qurrā'*, but in this he began from the graphic text current today (يحى, read as يحيى), whose final-ـى could also be interpreted as the modern final-ـں. In this connection he says,

> I believe, with Margoliouth (*Moslem World*, 1925, p. 343), that the name (*Yaḥya*) is almost certainly the Syriac *Yoḥannan*. In the early and undotted Kur'āns the word stood as يحى, which could be read *Yoḥanna*, *Yoḥannan*, or *Yaḥya*, and the Muslim *kurrā'* who knew no other language besides Arabic adopted the erroneous form *Yaḥya*. I am absolutely unable to agree with Lidzbarski (*Johannesbuch*, ii., 73: cf. also Nöldeke in *Z. A.*, xxx, 158 sq.) that this curious name is an old Arabic one.[12]

We can conclude from these comments that, for Mingana, who critically considered the original *rasm* from the standpoint of the final-ى that has one form and is standard in the current Cairo edition, the unpointed ـى could actually be read as a secondary final-*ā* or final-*n* (ن).

Although he was familiar with the earlier Qur'ānic manuscripts, Mingana apparently did not realize the difference between the final-ى that is current today and the retroflex one (ے) often used in the earlier Qur'ānic codices. But if we recognize that the Arabic retroflex final-ے (ى) (*ī/ā*) should not be formally distinguished from the Syro-Aramaic final-ے (*-n*) (at least in terms of the manuscripts), and if we proceed from this recognition, then the spelling (*rasm*) يحى cannot bear the alternative readings *Yaḥyā* or *Yoḥannā* (with final-*ā*). The Arabic reflexive final-ے (=ى) in this spelling, read as the Syro-Aramaic final-ے (*-n*) (يحى = يحنن), gives a clear pointer to the Syro-Aramaic reading ܝܘܚܢܢ / *Yoḥannān*. This verbal name was rightly perceived to be an imperfect form, which accounts for the Qur'ān's failure to reproduce the *mater lectionis* ܘ / (*o*) of the Syriac spelling. In such a form, the vowel of the first open syllable is realized in Arabic as a short vowel, analogous to the prefix of the third person of Arabic imperfect of the expanded verbal stems II-IV.[13] This example corresponds to the transcription of Syro-Aramaic loan-words, in which the *mater lectionis* was regularly left out in favor of the short *u* of the Qur'ān.[14]

If this discovery is correct—if the Arabic retroflex final-ى (ے) appears as a representation of the Syro-Aramaic grapheme for a final-*Nūn* not only in the name *Yoḥannān* as an exceptional case—then further examples from the Qur'ān will likely prove its accuracy. In what follows I will provide the proof from further spellings that have been mis-read by scholars up to now.

3.2 Exhibit A: ساى (ساے)

This expression, usually written in the Paris manuscript BNF 328a with the retroflex final-ى (i.e., ساے, read as either *šaʾī* or *šāy*) has been considered as an archaic spelling of the Arabic word شيء / *šayʾ*, current today with the meaning of "thing, object, something." In this understanding of the spelling ساى, scholars have taken the middle *Alif* (ـا) as a possible "*Hamza* carrier" which should actually follow the ى (Diem, see below). Because in the case of شيء, however, a final *Hamza* is written according to modern orthographic rules without a "carrier," the medial *Alif* (ـا) has simply been left out of the Cairo editions as superfluous or false and replaced with the final, carrier-less *Hamza*. Consequently, the modern spelling شيء has been recognized once and for all by the editors of the Cairo edition as an orthographic correction of the presumably archaic form ساى; as a further result, it has been accepted by Qur'ānic scholars in both East and West with no questions asked.

In his article "Untersuchungen zur frühen Geschichte der arabischen Orthographie, II: Die Schreibung der Konsonanten"[Studies on the Early History of Arabic Orthography, II: The Orthography of Consonants] (*Orientalia* 49 [1980] 67–106), W. Diem attempted to explain this supposedly archaic form on a historical basis. Included in his comments were the following:

> §127 (l. 7): With regard to شاى, we must note that this spelling must have been more common than its one Qur'ānic occurence (S. 18:23: لِشَاْىْءٍ) suggests. According to a report in ad-Dānī (n. 92: *Muqni*ʿ 45 above; cf. also *GdQ* III 49, n. 4), Ibn Masʿūd's text contained merely شاي. Also, Lewis's palimpsests reflect the simpler form شاي in all locations but one (n. 93: cf. *GdQ* III 56 above). This form also appears in the codex of Samarqand (n. 94: cf. Jeffery-Mendelson: "Samarqand Qur'ān Codex," 187, etc.), and it is still present in early Islamic witnesses (cf. n. 95). As far as phonetics is concerned, there can be no further doubt that the spellings شاي and شى were intended to represent an phonetic form *šayy* < *šay'*...
>
> §128: My analyses allow me to conclude that the spellings ... شاي corresponded to the pronunciation ... *šayy* .... As a result, we may dispose of a reason for writing the word with *alif*; according to the *Hijāzi* pronunciation of the words. It appears that the older forms ... *šay'* ... contained a *hamza* that must have been written with an *alif* in the early orthography. The spelling *شيا .... is thus to be admitted as the oldest one, but in the Qur'ān this spelling appears as ... شاي . Nonetheless, we cannot exclude a historical connection between these two spellings. So, each time in the Qur'ānic text that an *alif* that has no longer a phonetical function it is combined with the letters *yā' / wāw* in representation of the current pronunciation, the order *alif-yā' / alif-wāw* is preserved, ... in other words, the *alif* is kept, and it always appears behind the *yā'* or *wāw*, never in front of it [i.e., . . .] The spelling... *شيا ... contradicted this order *alif-yā'* by writing the letters with the order *yā'-alif*, but otherwise scribes would have understood them in exactly the same way, since here as well an *alif* was nonfunctional, and the *yā'* expressed the sound in question. In other words one can imagine that the scribes, without knowledge of the etymology (indeed, knowledge that they could not have had at all), might have changed the letter-combination *yā'-alif* of the spellings ... *شيا into the normal order *alif-yā'*, resulting in the attested forms ... شاي ... (cf. n. 98: ... Rabin: *Ancient West-Arabian*, 140, regards شاى as the result of an orthographic analogy...). In such a case as this, one becomes seriously aware of the total absence of *ḥijāzī*-Arabian witnesses for the long period of time from the latest Nabataean-*ḥijāzī* inscriptions and graffiti to the appearance of the Qur'ānic corpus.

In the attempt to solve this orthographic riddle, there is in fact an explanation that is less complicated than these rambling and ultimately fruitless speculations, if one simply reads the Arabic retroflex final-ى as the Syro-Aramaic final-*Nūn* (ܢ). According to this reconstruction, the spelling سا‍ܢ should be read neither as *ša'ī* (or *šāy*) nor *šayy* < *šay'*, but rather as شان (*šān* / *ša'n*). Therefore, God has على كل شان over every affair [according to current

Arabic, but according to Syro-Aramaic]footnote: every situation, every circumstance, rather than على كل شيء قدير, over every thing and every object (cf. e.g., in BNF 328a, Surah 2:282, 284 (f. 1b, ll. 7, 14); Surah 3:5, 26, 28, 29, 92, 128, 154 (2x), 165, 189 (f. 2a, l. 6; f. 3a, ll. 6, 11, 15; f. 4a, l. 16; f. 6a, l. 1; f. 7a, ll. 12, 14; f. 7b, last line; f. 9a, l. 10); Surah 4:4, 32, 33, 59, 85, 86, 113, 126, 176 (f. 10a, l. 5; f. 12a, l. 21; f. 12b, l. 2; f. 14a, l. 4; f. 15b, ll. 5, 7; f. 17a, l. 21; f. 18a., l. 4; f. 20b, l. 12); Surah 5:17, 19 (f. 22a, ll. 9, 16); etc.

Naturally, a full synopsis of the orthography of the oldest extant Qur'ānic manuscripts would shine more light on the original structure of the language of the Qur'ān. In the meantime, in the next few pages, I shall present testimonies to the alternating full and defective forms of سا and سـ (*ša'n / šān*) as they appear in the (admittedly fragmentary) manuscripts that are available to us:

1) BNF 328a (written in a calligraphed script of the *ḥiǧāzī* tradition, consisting of ca. one-quarter of the Cairo edition of the Qur'ān);
2) Samarqand (written in the *kūfī* tradition, consisting of ca. one-half of the Cairo edition); and
3) Sanaa (written in the simple *ḥiǧāzī* tradition, excluding the final folios which were a later addition, and containing more than one-fourth of the Cairo edition).

1) BNF 328a

a) BNF 328a has the full form with the retroflex final-ـ (سا) in the following 52 Qur'ānic verses (the verse-numbering follows the Cairo edition):
SS. 2:282, 284; 3:5, 26, 28, 29, 92, 128, 154 (2x), 165, 189; 4:4, 32, 33, 59, 85, 86, 113, 126, 176; 5:19; 6:38, 44, 52 (2x), 69, 80, 91, 93, 99, 101 (2x), 102, 111, 148; 7:145 (2x), 156, 185; 9:115; 12:111; 13:8, 14, 16; 14:18, 38; 15:19, 21; 35:18.

b) BNF 328 has the full form with the Arabic final-ى (ساى) in the following three verses: Surahs 5:17; 6:102 (2nd occurrence); 14:21.
A comparison of the orthography of the شان found in BNF 328a in Q 5:17 (fol. 22a, l. 9—with the *ḥiǧāzī* final-ى moved down and bent to the left: ساى) and in Q 5:19 (fol. 22a, l. 16—with the retroflex final-ى: سا) shows that the later copyist no longer understood the originally graphic distinction between the Syro-Aramaic final-*Nūn* (ـ) and the Arabic retroflex final-ى in all three of the above-mentioned locations. This phenomenon becomes especially clear in the case of the two different and alternating forms that appear in Q 6:102:

ذلكم الله ربكم لا اله الا هو خلق كل سا‍ـ و هو على كل ساى و كيل

In the latter case (ساى), the Sanaa codex (fol. 16a, penultimate line) has سا‍ـ (*šān* / *ša'n*), and in the former (سا‍ـ) it has the defective form س‍ـ (*šān*); further, Samarqand has the defective form س‍ـ in both places. This does not necessarily mean that the copyist of BNF 328a undertook this change on his own; he could have copied it equally well (and faithfully!) from an earlier document. This possibility raises the question of the dating of this Qur'ānic manuscript, which surface evidence suggests can not belong to the first generation of Qur'ānic texts transmitted in writing. The criteria that are necessary for an earlier dating will dictate a rejection of this manuscript in favor of those that do not exhibit an alteration such as this one.

c) BNF 328a has the defective form with the Arabic final-ى (سى) in the following two verses: Surahs 6:154; 7:89.

It is clear that, in both of these textual locations, we have a faulty interpretation of the Syro-Aramaic final-*Nūn* (ـ) that was altered into an Arabic final-ى by a later hand; we can conclude this in both cases based on the Samarqand manuscript (fol. 327, l. 9, and fol. 377, l. 4), where the same word in both of these cases concludes with the retroflex final-ى, that is, with the Syro-Aramaic final-*Nūn* (ـ). In addition, both contexts (6:154: وتفصيلا لكل شـ; 7:89: وسع ربنا كل شـ علما) suggest that the reading شـ / *šān* ("situation") makes more sense than شيء / *šay'* ("thing"), because the Arabic word شأن (*ša'n*) has a more wide-ranging set of meanings than شيء (*šay'*).

Conclusion

If we assume in these latter two cases an originally defective spelling شأن (*šān* / *ša'n*), and then use the texts from the Samarqand manuscript to show that the full form [*scriptio plena*] ساى in the three cases from BNF 328a is actually a later re-writing of an original form سا‍ـ (*šān*), then the result is that BNF 328a has 55 occurrences of the full form شأن (*ša'n* / *šān*) and 2 occurrences of the defective form [*scriptio defectiva*] شن (*šān*), so that we should read شأن (*ša'n* / *šān*) in all 57 cases. All 57 of these cases have been altered to شيء (*šay'*) in the Cairo edition, mainly through improper intrusions into the original structure of the text.

This conclusion leads to two further findings:

a) the Syro-Aramaic final-*Nūn* in this current Arabic word, was not recognized as such by later Arab copyists and was instead considered to be an Arabic retroflex final-*Yā'*; and
b) Such confusion regarding these two elementary Arabic words, as well as the number of their occurrences, contradicts the traditional

Islamic thesis of an oral transmission of the Qur'ānic text that was unbroken from its very beginnings.

2) The Samarqand Codex (in *kūfī* ductus)

a) The Samarqand codex, written in the *kūfī* style, has the full form (سا‍ؠ) (*ša'n / šān*) with the retroflex final-ؠ (ى = ن) in the following twelve verses: Surahs 4:32; 6:38, 91, 93; 11:57, 101; 16:35, 75, 89; 18:23, 70; 20:50.

The Qur'ānic text from the Cairo edition that was cited by W. Diem (18:23: لِشَاْىْءٍ) is thus explained by means of the corresponding spelling in the Samarqand codex with the retroflex final-ؠ and spoken as a final-ن (لسا‍ؠ [*li-ša'n / li-šān*]).

b) In one location (S. 15:21) the Samarqand codex has the full form and an Arabic final-ى. As I have explained above, in this location BNF 328a also has the full form, but with the retroflex final-ؠ (سا‍ؠ / *šān*). Once again, this evidence suggests an incorrect alteration made by a later hand. As a result, the Samarqand cannot belong to the first generation of the Qur'ānic manuscripts.

c) The Samarqand codex has the defective form (سـؠ / *šān*) in the following 56 verses: Surahs 2:113 (2x), 148, 231, 259, 282, 284; 3:128, 165, 189; 4:33, 86, 113, 126; 5:97, 117, 120; 6:44, 52 (2x), 69, 80, 99, 101 (2x), 102 (2x), 111, 148, 154, 159, 164; 7:89; 11:72; 15:19; 16:35, 40, 48, 76, 77; 17:12, 44; 18:45, 54, 76, 84; 20:98; 27:16; 36:12, 15, 83; 38:5, 6; 40:7; 41:21; 42:36.

d) In one location (S. 5:94) the Samarqand codex has the defective form (سـى) with an Arabic final-ى. This text is absent in both BNF 328a and the Sanaa manuscript, and so there is no basis of comparison here. In the context ليبلونكم الله بشى من الصيد (God wants to test you about something regarding the hunt, that you undergo a specific test), it is permissible to read the *rasm* as بشيء (*bi-šay'*). The Arabic final-ى, then, is correct in this location and makes especially clear the distinction between the retroflex final-ؠ that in most often to be read in instances of this word as the Syro-Aramaic grapheme *Nūn*.

Conclusion

In contrast to the situation in BNF 328a, the Samarqand codex's usage of the defective form (سـؠ / *šān*), with 56 textual locations (plus one correct location for شـيء / *šay'*), clearly dominates that of the full form (سا‍ؠ = *ša'n / šān*), with 12 locations (and additionally the incorrect spelling سـاى).

3) The Sanaa manuscript (which has not yet been given a more specific name)

a) The Sanaa manuscript has the full form (ساے) (*ša'n* / *šān*) with the retroflex final-ے (ى = ن) in the following 24 verses: SS 2:155, 178; 5:68, 97, 117; 6:17, 19, 52 (2nd occurrence), 91, 93, 102 (2nd occurrence); 8:72; 16:75, 76, 77, 89; 51:42, 49; 57:29; 58:6; 66:8; 67:1, 9; 72:28.
b) In one other location with the full form (S. 8:60), the expected retroflex final-ے has been replaced by an Arabic final-ى. The Sanaa manuscript itself shows that this alteration has been made by a later, incompetent hand, in that a parallel location in the same codex (S. 34:39) has the final-ے (although it is written in the defective script سے / *šān*).
c) In the Sanaa manuscript, the full form ساے (*ša'n* / *šān*) with its 24 (or 25) locations is outnumbered by the defective form سے (*šān*), which is present in the following 55 locations: Surahs 2:20, 29, 106, 109, 113 (2x), 148; 5:120; 6:38, 44, 52, 69, 80, 99, 101 (2x), 102, 111, 148; 8:41 (2x), 75; 13:8, 14, 16; 14:18, 21, 38; 20:98; 21:30, 81; 22:17; 23:88; 33:54, 55; 34:16, 21, 39, 47; 35:1, 18, 44; 36:12, 15, 83; 38:5, 6; 48:21, 26; 50:2; 57:2, 3; 65:12; 67:19; 80:18.
d) The second occurrence of سى in Q 65:12 is written with the current Arabic final-ى. This spelling is also a case of a later mis-interpretation of the prior final- ے (سے / *šān*), as the context of the verse demonstrates, a context which produces the following reading:

لتعلموا ان الله على كل شے قدير

وان الله قد احاط بكل شي علما

. . .so that you (plural) know that God has power over every circumstance, and that God knows about every circumstance.

The latter spelling shows once again that this manuscript (or at least the folio in question) does not belong to the early generation of Qur'ānic manuscripts.

e) There are certain folios that are apparently less ancient than the original manuscript and were incorporated into the codex at a later date; these contain the following eight locations that have the current final-ى (سى): Surahs 15:19, 21; 16:35 (2x), 40, 48; 20:50; 49:16. In some of these cases, the reading شي (*šay'*) is justified, in the sense of "thing, object" (S. 15:19, 21) or in the Syro-Aramaic sense of "someone" (S. 16:35 [2x]); in the other cases, it is clear that شن (=شان) (*šān* / *ša'n*) is intended.

Summary

It is now clear that, in the early Qur'ānic manuscripts of both the *ḥiǧāzī* and *kūfī* styles, the Arabic final-ى appears in both forms that I have described and with the same graphemic meaning. The new information that this analysis has produced is that the Arabic retroflex final-ى also appears in the early Qur'ānic manuscripts, sometimes representing the Syro-Aramaic grapheme for a final-*Nūn*. Accordingly, the following should be kept in mind:

1) Following the results drawn from the three manuscripts in question, the full form ساے (with a medial *Alif* and a retroflex final-*Nūn*) should consistently be read as شـان (*šān* / *šaʼn*).
2) The defective form سـے (with the retroflex final-ى) can mean two different things:
   a) In a majority of cases, a comparison with parallel textual locations and/or an analysis of the corresponding context give the reading شـان (*šān* / *šaʼn*). One example occurs in the Samarqand manuscript (ff. 454-55), in Q 16:75, where one finds one occurrence of the full form ساے (=شـان) in the text لا يقدر على شي, while the following sentence (in the following verse [76]) contains the defective script سـے (=شـن) in precisely the same context and with the same meaning.
   b) But the reading شـيء (*šay'*) can also emerge from the context; I will discuss this topic more in what follows.
   c) In cases where the accusative ending is present, it is more difficult to distinguish between the readings شـيا (*šayya*^{n} = *šay'a*^{n}) ("something") and شـنا (*šāna*^{n} = *šaʼna*^{n}) ("issue, affair"); this spelling appears 77 times in the Qur'ān, in all cases in the defective form. In cases where the sense of the term does not clearly emerge from the context, parallel texts can be consulted to arrive at the correct understanding. In favor of the reading شـيا (*šayya*^{n} = *šay'a*^{n}) ("something," in the sense of "someone," and following the Syro-Aramaic ܡܕܡ / *meddem*, which, according to Brockelmann's *Lexicon Syriacum*, can mean both *aliquid* ["something"] and also *quidem* ["someone"]), we find the usage أشرك بالله شـيا ("to associate something i.e. anyone with God) (cf. Surahs 4:36; 6:151; 22:26; 24:55; 40:74 – لم نكن ندعوا من قبل شـيا "Formerly we worshiped nothing [else]"; 60:12). The Qur'ān confirms the Syro-Aramaic meaning of شـيء, in the sense of أحد ("someone"), with the usage أشـرك بالله أحدا "to associate someone, another [being] with God") in the following parallel texts: Surahs 18:38, 42, 110; 72:2; 72:18 – فلا تدعوا مع الله أحدا "You should not invoke anyone else besides God" (as a parallel to the aforementioned Q 40:74); and 72:20. A. Mingana, in his *Syriac Influence*, 92, has already and correctly pointed scholars' attention to this meaning of شيء in Q

60:11: وان فاتكم شيء من ازواجكم الى الكفار "And if any of your wives escape from you to the unbelievers...." Two readings from the Samarqand codex's text of Q 16:35 (ff. 440-41) are interesting in this regard: there is one instance of the defective script سے in the context ما عبدنا من دونه من شي ("we would not have worshiped anyone else besides him"), which should be read as شيء ("thing," in the sense of "someone") as indicated above; but there is also one instance of سا = شان (in the sense of "issue, affair"): ولا حرمنا من دونه من شے ("nor would we have declared any affair or circumstance as forbidden without him").

In the Cairo edition, the reading شيء (*šay'*) appears 202 times, and that of شيا 77 times, while the reading شان (*šān / ša'n*) only three times, along with one occurrence of شأنهم. In this last case, the orthography of Q 10:61 agrees with that of BNF 328a, f. 48a, l. 8 (with the *ḥiǧāzī* final-ن). From this we can conclude that the Cairo edition's شيء (*šay'*) is usually false, even though this does not affect the sense of the texts in question. This is also true for the texts in which the Sanaa codex regularly has شي (without the medial *alif*) with the retroflex final-ى (سے), as for example in Surahs 2:20, 29, 106, 109, 113 (2x) (Sanaa, f. 1b, ll. 2–25; f. 4b, ll. 21, 27; f. 5a, ll. 5–6); in these cases the defective form شا (=شان) (*šān / ša'n*) is to be accepted. The example of Q 2:113 makes this conclusion clear. There the text partially repeats itself:

وقالت اليهود ليست النصرى على شي

وقالت النصرى ليست اليهود على شي

(Cairo edition)

Pickthall: And the Jews say the Christians' follow nothing (true), and the Christians say the Jews follow nothing (true);

Given the context, Paret (18) has paraphrased this passage quite appropriately:

> The Jews say, "The Christians dispense with the foundation (in their religious opinions)." And the Christians say, "The Jews dispense with the foundation (in their religious opinions."

But one only comes to this understanding if one reads the term in question not as شيء but rather as شان (*ša'n*; in Qur'ānic Arabic, actually *šān*), following the Syro-Aramaic expression ܫܪܒܐ (*šarbā*) that corresponds to it lexically and semantically. Mannā (819a) gives Arabic equivalents for this term as (3) أمر. شأن ("matter, affair") and (4) علة . سبب ("reason, cause"); the *Thesaurus* (II:4323) offers us the following evidentiary examples:

ܥܠ ܫܪܒܐ ܕܗܝܡܢܘܬܐ (*'al šarbā ḏ-haymānūṯā*: de re fidei); ܒܫܪܒ ܬܘܕܝܬܐ (ba-šreb tawdīṯā: causa fidei).

In the context in question, the Qur'ānic text means "the matter (of faith)," and it has the word "faith" lying under the surface. In other words, in order to arrive at the correct understanding of the Qur'ānic expression شـان in its various contexts, we must always inquire after the semantic content of the Syro-Aramaic expression that corresponds to it lexically.

The Sanaa codex gives us another example that shows how the spelling شـ can be the defective form of شـان; this text occurs at f. 11b, l. 1 of the codex, in Q 5:120. Here the stereotypical sentence (following the Cairo edition) على كل شـي قدير appears in BNF 328a as the full form على كل شـا (شـان) قدير (cf., e.g., the texts presented above from BNF 328a on Surahs 2:284; 3:26, 29, 165, 189; 5:17, 19; etc.). Even if this reading does not change the sense at all, nonetheless it brings in another nuance to the inquiry, because the expression شـان ("matter, affair, circumstance") is more wide-ranging in meaning than the expression شيء ("object, thing").

Even if there is no substantive distinction of meaning between the readings شـيء (*šay'*) and شـأن (*ša'n*), three conclusions emerge from this analysis quite clearly:

1) there was no authentic oral transmission at the time of the establishment of the Qur'ānic text;
2) Syriac scribes participated in an unmediated way in the first redaction of the Qur'ān;
3) there was a considerable chronological distance between the establishment of the text and an earlier tradition of Qur'ānic orthography, the closer investigation of which will offer us an entrée into an understanding of the Qur'ānic text that is based in historical linguistics.

Precisely in light of this question, and in order to prevent premature and faulty conclusions, we should attempt to locate further examples of unusual Qur'ānic spellings and then investigate their orthography. We should also inquire as to the possibility of other orthographic traditions in the area in which Aramaic was the *lingua franca* at the time of the appearance of the Qur'ān, so that their assistance may help us determine whether Qur'ānic orthography of this kind may need to be re-evaluated.

The reasons for this search can be found in the peculiar orthography of a written form that appears twice in Q 6:95 in BNF 328a (f. 26a, ll. 16–17), namely, الحاى (*al-ḥāy*, with a medial *alif*), while the two other parallel texts (SS. 3:27 [f. 3a, l. 8] and 10:31 [f. 46b, ll. 16–17, the latter bearing the retroflex final-ى]) appear as the defective and correct form الحي (*al-ḥayy*). Although the former two forms were written with the retroflex final-ى, their reading is secured by means of the unambiguous parallel locations, especially the opposition of الحى (*al-ḥayy*: "the living") and الميت (*al-mayyit*: "the dead"). As a result, we can exclude a different interpretation of the retroflex final-ى in this example. But how, then, are we to explain the presence of the medial *alif* in the two written forms in Q 6:95?

One possible explanation would be that the copyist (or an earlier scribe), influenced by the familiar (to him) Syro-Aramaic pronunciation of the identically-sounding ܚܝ (>حي), whose short *a*-vowel was spoken long (*ḥāy*) according to west Syrian tradition (as in most single-syllable words[15]), brought this long *ā* with the medial *Alif* into Arabic. In the Qur'ānic orthography with which scholars are familiar, we have not yet observed the *Alif* as a letter representing the short-*a* vowel. However, we see this function in the scribal traditions of the Mandaeans who lived in southern Mesopotamia. Nöldeke explained in his Mandaean grammar this use of the medial *Alif* as a *mater lectionis* for both short and long *a*:

> א represents medial- and final *a* and *ā*: מאַלכא = מלכא (*m*a̲*lkā*); מאַן = מן (*mān*) . . .Similarly, מהאַיא stands for מהאַייא ܡܚܝܐ (*m-ḥayyē*) ("to bring to life, to make alive").[16]

The latter example, the active participle of ܚܝܐ / *ḥyā* (=حيى), corresponds exactly with our Qur'ānic text, which concerns the use of the medial *Alif* as a letter representing a vowel. However, because in west Syrian pronunciation the doubling of the *y* is eliminated by the compensatory lengthening of the preceding *ā* (resulting in the form *m-ḥāyē*), the latter pronunciation (*al-ḥāy*) could be meant by the medial *Alif* of the Qur'ānic spelling الحاى. But the Mandaean spelling probably indicates the phonetically secondary long *ā*, while the Syriac form, with the same pronunciation, was written defectively. The Qur'ān generally follows this orthography, so that in the repeated form found in BNF 328a's text of Q 6:95 (الحاى / *al-ḥāy*), we see an exceptional instance of the full form, which certainly reproduces the Syro-Aramaic pronunciation (and most likely also that of the Mandaeans) and follows Mandaean orthography.

One also finds such a medial *Alif*—as an indicator of a short *a*—occasionally in Syriac, as Nöldeke noted in his *Syrische Grammatik*:

> Additionally, one often finds ܐ as an apparently superfluous letter—where it should not appear at all—in words like ܡܣܐܒ for ܡܣܒ (*ma-ssab̲* / *ma-ssāb̲*, "to take/receive"), etc.[17]

What Nöldeke surmised concerning the use of the medial *Alif* as representing a vowel, that it was "apparently superfluous" in comparison with "normal" Syriac orthography, probably in reality went back to an earlier Mesopotamian scribal tradition overlooked until now. Rudolf Meyer's comments in his *Hebräische Grammatik* are illuminating:

> Linear vocalization in Hebrew developed quite remarkably in the Hellenistic period, probably under influence from both Aramaic and Greek. People still restricted themselves at this time to the traditional letters *aleph*, *he*, *waw*, and *yod*; however, they also put forth considerable effort in establishing more exactly their phonetic values, and they used the letters to represent not only long, but also short vowels. Because the text of Holy Scripture had not yet been normatively established, this new form of vocalization, which remained as optional as before, infiltrated the Hebrew Bible text in some places quite strongly; this new principle asserted itself even in those places that tended to vary only occasionally from the earlier, sparing usage of letters representing vowels. As a result, we have the following situation in the second century CE: *Aleph* usually represents *a*, less often *e* in medial and final positions in a word; [the letter] *he* indicates the final, long vowels *ā* and *ē*, but no longer *ō*; *waw* stands for *o* and *u*; and *yod* represents *i* and *e* in both medial and final positions. When *aleph*, *waw*, and *yod* are used in medial position, they can indicate either long or short vowel sounds.[18]

The following observations concerning Qur'ānic orthography result from Meyer's comments:

1) We must revise the conclusion that has been accepted until now, namely, that the use of *Alif* as a *mater lectionis* for a medial long *ā* sound was a later and genuinely Arabic development.[19]

The fluctuation in the early Qur'ānic manuscripts' practice of writing a medial *Alif* for a long *ā*, as indicated in *GdQ* I:31f., is confirmed by Meyer's testimony concerning the optional usage of the same in the Hebrew of the second century CE; Meyer rightly traced this back to earlier Aramaic influence. In fact, Segert confirmed this theory in his *Altaramäische Grammatik* [Old Aramaic Grammar]. In chapter 2.4.4 ("Vowel-Letters in Medial Position"), section 3 ("The Use of *Alef* for Long -*ā*-"), he explains:

> This usage of א for long *ā* in medial position, so widespread in later Aramaic texts, actually goes back to a Persian pattern. However, examples of this practice were already present in the archaic inscriptions from Ja'udi in the eighth century BCE, e.g., ואגם P 5.[20] The reader will also find interesting chapter 2.4.7 ("The Use of Vowel-Letters in Medial Position in Imperial Aramaic and Biblical Aramaic") (p. 65).

This is an important observation [*Festellung*] for future Qur'ānic research. The idea of a later reform of Qur'ānic orthography, as part of which the *Alif* began to be used for a medial long *ā*, has been generally accepted by scholars including the present author[21]: concerning the Arabic orthography that is still current today, we must modify this thesis to say that this written practice was imposed upon it at a later time.[22] Concerning Qur'ānic orthography, however, we must accept that this written practice existed from the very beginning, even if it was irregular; the early Qur'ānic manuscripts that are available to us illustrate this thesis in their vacillations on the matter. The problem is even more difficult for later additions of the *Alif* by incompetent copyists, additions that led to mis-readings; close text-critical analyses of Qur'ānic texts are required to detect these mis-readings.

2) We have not observed the use of *Alif* in the Qur'ān as a *mater lectionis* for short *a* (as was common practice in Mandaean) in the manuscript material that has been available to us thus far, even though the Cairo edition does have a few examples of this phenomenon.

It is doubtful, therefore, that the spelling الحاى with a medial *Alif* offers a first witness thereunto, because as I have shown above, this *Alif* can represent the West Syriac (or Mandaean) pronunciation that uses a long *ā* (*al-ḥāy*). If الحاى were a first proof of the use of the medial *Alif* for short *a*, then the entire explanation of the spelling شاے as شـان (*šān* / *šaʼn*) that I have offered here would be invalid, and one would not be able seriously to object to the reading of the text as *šay* (or *šay'*), as is common today. The reading of the spelling يحيے as يحنن (*Yoḥannān*) instead of يحيى (*Yaḥyā*) would then hardly be convincing as the only witness for the reading of the retroflex Arabic final-*y* as the Syriac final-*n*; in such a situation, it would not be convincing to bring forward further examples from the Qur'ān as confirmation of this orthography. The following texts, however, are intended to provide just this confirmation.

3.3 Exhibit B (S. 10:53): اے وربي (*'ēn wa-rabbī*)

The particle that introduces this text is written in the Cairo edition with the final-ى that is normal in current Arabic, and it is read as إِي (*'ī*); in BNF 328a (f. 47b, l. 16), however, it is written with the retroflex final-ے (اے) and corresponds to the defective Syro-Aramaic spelling ܐܝ = ܐܝܢ (*'ēn* or *'īn*: "yes!"). In fact, this expression, widespread in the current Arabic dialects as a general Aramaic substrate, has lost its final-*n* and is thus spoken as *'ē* or *'ī*; for the Qur'ān, however, this vulgar Arabic pronunciation is not to be admitted. This conclusion is even more obvious because this Aramaic particle appears multiple times in the Qur'ān in both the defective and full forms (ܐܝ or ܐܝܢ = *'ēn*); the present author has already brought attention to the 61 occurrences in the Cairo edition of the Qur'ān of the spelling لين (*l-ēn*) (a combination of the defective form of the Aramaic particle ܠܐ [*lā*] and the full form of the conditional particle ܐܢ [*'ēn*]), as well as the two occurrences of the spelling افاين (< ܐܦ ܐܢ / *āp̄-ēn* = "now if, if thus."[23] The thesis there, that the full form لاين (*lā-'ēn* > *l-ēn*) would likely be demonstrated by the early Qur'ānic manuscripts, is confirmed by the *ḥiǧāzī* codex of Sanaa, where this full form لاين (*lā-'ēn* > *l-ēn*) occurs twice (SS. 6:109 [f. 16b, l. 10]; 13:37 [f. 31a, l. 10]). As Segert has indicated, this combined text in a defective, early Aramaic form (להן / *lā-hēn*) has already been discovered in early Aramaic:

> In early Aramaic the negative particle ל- was written together with the word immediately following. ... The conjunction להן (*lā-hēn*: "if not") arose from the combination of the negative particle *lā* with the hypothetical conjunction *hēn*.[24]

In other words, the Qur'ānic spelling لين (*l-ēn*) follows early Aramaic writing traditions but reproduces the later, Syro-Aramaic pronunciation (להן / *lā-hēn* > לין / *l-ēn*).

3.4 Excursus: On the Origins of the Particle لـ (la-)

In connection with this question, further study reveals the prefixed particle لـ (*la-*), up to now considered an intensifying particle peculiar to classical Arabic,[25] to be a borrowing from early Aramaic. In early Aramaic the particle must originally have functioned as an *interjection*; from this function developed semantic aspects that varied from the perspective of historical linguistics, including the well-known function of negation, but also the intensifying meaning found in the Qur'ān (as well as in later classical Arabic and in current Arabic dialects[26]).

Two things become clear from these comments. First, the "energetic" prefixed particle لـ / *la-*, just like the one that introduces the apodosis of a unreal conditional sentence, is nothing else than the defective form of the word لا / *lā*, whose close connection with the following word, as testified in Arabic dialects of today, led to the reduction of the originally long vowel *ā*. Second, as a logical consequence, and just as in the case of لاين, the Qur'ān sometimes uses the full form لا, as the introduction to the oath-formula لا اقسم [27], eight times in the following Surahs: Surahs 56:75; 69:38; 70:40; 75:1, 2; 81:15; 84:16; 90:1. In all these cases, the modern Qur'ānic translators are not particularly conclusive.

Paret translates thus: "*But no! I swear...*"

Blachère has French "*No! I swear it...*"

And *Bell* even sees in these texts a formal negation: "*I swear not...*"[28]

It is quite clear in these cases that the originally Aramaic particle לא (*lā*) is meant, and that the Qur'ān uses the term alternatively with the full or defective form. Despite this double usage, the defective form is the one that survived into later classical Arabic, albeit as a heretofore unrecognized relic of Aramaic.

Another such relic is present in the expressions ليس (*laysa*, but actually *lays*) and ليت (*layta*, actually *layt*), which both reproduce variants of the same Aramaic expression in Arabic script. In Arabic, however, these have become independent semantically and thus bear two different meanings. In the first case, ليس (*laysa*) ("not to be") is the combination of the defectively-written, prefixed Aramaic particle ל- (= לא) (*lā*), here with the meaning "not," and the Aramaic particle of existence יש (*ys* / *īs* / *yš* / *īš*), meaning "to be." In this form the Arabic sibilant س (*s*) goes back to the Aramaic ת (*ṯ*), which was originally aspirated, so that the Arabic ليس (*laysa*) is nothing other than a dialectical variant of the Aramaic לא (*lā*) in combination with the expression of existence אית (*īṯ*), whose spirantization again points to an original separation between these two components at an earlier stage of the language.

The Arabic ليت (*layta*) points to a more recent Aramaic development, however; this form corresponds precisely, both in form and phonetics, to the Syro-Aramaic ܠܝܬ (*layt*), insofar as Syro-Aramaic did not aspirate after a diphthong. But if the two forms were morphologically identical, they were different semantically. In the Syro-Aramaic form ܠܝܬ (*layt*), the prefixed ܠ (*lā*) indicated a negation ("not to be"), but in the Arabic form ليت (*layta*) it meant a wish ("that it would be"). I will explain لات (traditionally read *lāta*: Q 38:3) in another publication.

3.5 Exhibit C: هيى / يهيى

The Cairo edition reads these spellings, which appear in verses 10 and 16 of Surah 18, as *hayyi'* and *yu-hayyi'*. I should note at the outset of this section the following:

a) originally, the Qur'ānic ى never had the function of a "*Hamza*-carrier";
b) Qur'ānic orthography prohibits a و and ي that immediately follow one another (cf. here, e.g., Q 2:28, where the Cairo edition—conforming to modern orthography—reads يحييكم, while the Sanaa codex we have considered [f. 1b, l. 23] has يحيكم quite clearly; this means that the spellings هيى and يهيى are mis-readings).

Our foundational knowledge about Qur'ānic orthography is sufficient to accept the thesis that in these examples the originally retroflex final-ى (ے / -*n*) was later interpreted as a final-ي (*y*). The original orthographic tradition leads necessarily to the acknowledgement that we should read here a final-ں; in other words, instead of هيى / *hayyi'* and يهيى / *yu-hayyi'*, we should read هيّن / *hayyin* and يهيّن / *yu-hayyin* ("to lighten, relieve"). In order to prove this reading, it would be desirable (but not absolutely necessary) to have texts from the early Qur'ānic manuscripts; in their absence, parallel texts and other criteria from the Qur'ān itself should suffice for this purpose. First, then, we should note that the verb هيّأ never appears anywhere else in the Qur'ān in order to communicate the meaning "to prepare;" rather, the Qur'ān regularly (twenty times) uses the verbal root أعدّ. Second, we can confirm our supposed reading from parallel texts, when we provide the context of Q 18:10, 16 (according to the Cairo edition):

ربنا اتنا من لدنك رحمة وهيّء لنا من أمرنا رشدا

ينشر لكم ربكم من رحمته ويهيّء لكم من أمركم مرفقا

> *Pickthall* (18:10): Our Lord! Give us mercy from Thy presence and shape for us right conduct in our plight.
> (18:16): Your Lord will spread for you of His mercy and will prepare for you a pillow in your plight.

Paret (238) translates these two verselets thus:

> (18:10) Lord, give us mercy from you, and prepare (*rašadan*) a correct path for us in our affairs.
> (18:16) Then your Lord will grant you (something) from his mercy and provide relief *(yuhaiyi' lakum min amrikum mirfaqan)* for you in your affairs.

A parallel text from Q 20:26 shows that the verb in question should be read هيّن (*hayyin*) and not هيئ (*hayyi'*); there we find the synonym يسّر / *yassara* (=هيّن ["to lighten, relieve"]) immediately in connection with أمر / *amr* ("affair"). There the text reads:

رب اشرح لي صدري / ويسّر لي أمري

> *Pickthall:* My Lord! Relieve my mind. And ease my task for me.

Paret (255) has it thus:

> Lord, widen my chest (26) and make it easy for me. (Actually, "make my affair [what concerns me] easy for me.)

In conclusion, we should not hesitate to mention another criterion that will confirm our reading, namely, that the verbal root هيّن / *hayyana* appears twice as an adjective in the "Mary" Surah (S. 19:9, 21): هو علي هيّن / *huwa 'alayya hayyin* ("this is easy for me"). With these two new readings, there is now a total of four texts. Consequently, the two verses from Surah 18 should be read thus:

ربنا اتنا من لدنك رحمة وهيّن لنا من أمرنا رشدا

ينشر لكم ربكم من رحمته ويهيّن لكم من أمركم مرفقا

As a result, they should be understood thus:

> (18:10) O our Lord, grant us mercy from you, and make the correct path easier for us in the things that concern us (lit., "with regard to our affair").
> (18:16) Thus will your Lord give you from his grace[29] and make what you must undergo[30] easier for you in your affairs (that is, in what concerns you). (That is, *God will help you through his grace to endure with patience the test that is before you.*)

The early Qur'ānic fragments that we have considered in this essay do not have these verses. However, one would expect that other manuscript materials would attest the retroflex written form of the final-ى in the expressions هيى (=هين) and يهيى (=يهين). A facsimile of the British Library's codex Or. 2165 (ff. 1-61) has recently become available and shows that the manuscript has a final-*Alif* in both locations: at 18:10 (f. 43a, l. 21) it reads وهيا, and at 18:16 (f. 43b, l. 9) it has ويهيا. According to east Aramaic-Babylonian orthography, the final-*Alif* can represent a final-*Nūn* (which has nothing to do with the Arabic phenomenon of "Nunation"), as is the case in the Qur'ān with the spellings of the "energetic" وليكونا (*wa-la-yakūnan*) in Q 12:32 and also of لنسفعا (*la-nasfa'an*) in Q 96:15. In the future, I will demonstrate other examples from the Qur'ān and also explain the reasons for this defective form of a final-*Nūn* that is foreign to Arabic orthography.

According to the Koranic context, the form مرفقا – *mrfq* should be read as the the Syriac *mep̄raq* (with metathesis), the infinitive of the Syro-Aramaic verb *p-r-q* – "to save." Accordingly, the verse quoted above is to be understood as follows:

> 18:16 "Thus will your Lord give you from his grace and will liberate you from your plight."

3.6 Revision of the Spellings هيى and يهيى on Comparison with the Spellings وهيا, and ويهيا.

The spellings وهيا (a Syro-Aramaic imperative: *bring about*) and ويهيا (a Syro-Aramaic conjunctive: *may he bring about*) reproduce the Syro-Aramaic orthography of the verb *hwā* (to be) in the second stem form *hawwī* (lit.: *to cause to be = to create, to bring about something*). This observation makes clear that the spellings هيى *and* يهيى are just a variant writing of the same Syro-Aramaic verb which are both to be pronounced as *hayyē* which is an alternative form of *hawwē* (*bring about*) (cf. the words *Ḥawwā* [Eve] and Arabic *ḥayya* [serpent]). This explains that the Arabic adjective / adverb هيّن (*hayyin*) is derived from this Syro-Aramaic verb with an Aramaic suffix (*ān* /

nā) whose original emphatic form was **hawī-nā* >*hwī* –*nā* which resulted in the contracted Arabic form *hayyin* (in some contemporary Arabic dialects still pronounced *hwayyin* > *hayyin*). This adverb means in modern Arabic "easy," but the original Syro-Aramaic meaning is: "feasible." This observation renders the primary conjecture of the author as to the Syro-Aramaic final nun in the Koranic spelling هيى (=هين) and يهيى (=يهين) invalid.

4. Conclusion

With this provisional analysis of Qur'ānic orthography, one has provided the first empirical proof of a Qur'ānic *Vorlage* originally written in Syro-Aramaic script. As unexpected as this discovery may be at first glance, it will only surprise those who previously had an incorrect conception of the cultural, linguistic, and religio-historical environment in which the Qur'ān appeared. Even if the Qur'ān was the first book written in the Arabic *language*, this does not necessarily mean that it was composed in the Arabic *alphabet* so well known today. Further, if those who initiated the written and literary form of Arabic had training in the practice of writing, then it stands to reason that they would have acquired this training before the appearance of the Qur'ān and in the world of Syro-Aramaic culture.

It is obvious that the Syro-Aramaic script belonged to this Syro-Aramaic culture. Also, many instances in the history of cultures can be named in which a newly-emerging culture took over the writing system of an older one, before it developed its own under its own circumstances. The situation of the Qur'ān is no exception; the copyists of the Qur'ān were in all probability either Syro-Aramaeans or Arabs trained in Syro-Aramaic.

The tradition, according to which Arabic was written in Syro-Aramaic script, was a Christian Syrian one and still exists today in the liturgical books of the churches of the Near East that use the Syro-Aramaic language. This Syro-Aramaic/Arabic script goes by the name of "Garshuni" or "Karshuni," that is to say, Arabic language written in Syriac script. An extensive Christian-Arabic literature, mostly consisting of theological texts, was written in this script; many such manuscripts exist in the manuscript stocks of the European libraries (among other places). The results of the foregoing analysis make it clear that the *Ur*-Qur'ān was written in this script; more wide-ranging studies in the future will strengthen this partial result.

However, it has also become clear that probably all of the Qur'ānic manuscripts known to us and written in the Arabic script are secondary. This result suggests again that the Qur'ānic text, although written in the Syro-Aramaic script, was redacted at a historical point earlier than the manuscripts we possess. It will be no easy task for the historians of culture and religion to define more closely the time in which the (according to Islamic tradition) earlier Meccan and later Medinan Surahs came to be.

There is a rumor at present, that there is a Qur'ān written in Garshuni script preserved in the University al-Azhar in Cairo (or in another Arabic library). This would not be surprising despite the Islamic tradition that the caliph Uthman had destroyed the Qur'ānic *Vorlage* belonging to Ḥafṣa, the widow of Muhammad, after the canonical version was established. One can certainly imagine that this *Vorlage* was written in Garshuni; this possibility would also explain the cautious respect that Muslims traditionally display to the Syro-Aramaic language (called السريانية [*as-suryānīya*] in Arabic).

It was not possible in this short essay to consider all the letters in the current edition of the Qur'ān that were falsely-transcribed from the Syro-Aramaic script. A more complete presentation remains for a future publication.

Notes

1 Christoph Luxenberg, "Neudeutung der arabischen Inschrift im Felsendom zu Jerusalem," in Karl-Heinz Ohlig and Gerd-R. Puin, eds., *Die dunklen Anfänge: Neue Forschungen zur Entstehung und frühen Geschichte des Islam* (Berlin, 2005), 124–147; translated as *The Hidden Origins of Islam* (Amherst, NY, 2010) 125–151; see especially the section entitled "Verwechslung syro-aramäischer Buchstaben," pp. 134ff; (English edition: "Confusion of Syro-Aramaic letters," p.134ff).

2 Rudi Paret, *Der Koran: Übersetzung*, 2nd ed. (Stuttgart, Berlin, Cologne, and Mainz, 1982), p. 486. The original German is as follows: "(18) Und: 'Die Kultstätten sind (ausschließlich für Gott da. Daher ruft neben Gott niemand (anders) an!' (19) Und: 'Als der Diener Gottes [Anm.: d.h. Mohammed] sich aufstellte, um ihm anzurufen [Anm.: Oder: zu ihm to beten], hätten sie ihn (vor lauter Zudringlichkeit?) beinahe erdrückt (? Kâdû yakûnûna 'alaihi libadan)' [Anm.: Die Deutung des Verses ist ganz unsicher.] (20) Sag: Meinen Herrn (allein) rufe ich an [Anm.: Oder: Ich bete allein zu meinem Herrn] und geselle ihm niemand bei."

3 Régis Blachère, *Introduction au Coran* (Paris, 1947), 620. The original French is as follows: "(18) La Mosquée [sacrée] est à Allah. Ne priez donce personne à côté d'Allah! (n.: "La mosquée [sacrée]. V. sourate IX, 17.") (19) Quand le Serviteur d'Allah s'est levé, priant, [les Infidèles] ont failli être contre lui des masses (?). (n.: "Le serviteur d'Allah = Mahomet. // Kâdû yakûnûna 'alay-hi libadâ (var. lubada and lubbâda), 'les Infidèles etc.' Le sujet est incertain. Les commt. disent que c'est djinns, mais c'est peu probable.") (20) Dis: 'Je ne prie que mon Seigneur et ne Lui associe personne.'"

4 Richard Bell, *The Qur'ān: Translated with a Critical Re-arrangement of the Surahs*, 2 vols. (Edinburgh, 1937–39).

5 1st ed., Berlin, 2000; 2nd ed., Berlin 2004; 3rd ed., Berlin 2006.

6 The original German reads: "Wehe jedem Stichler und Nörgler."

7 It is well-known that the Arabic words خير / ḫayr ("something good; better; something better") and شر / šarr ("something bad; worse; something worse") are

used substantively and elatively. Classical Arabic grammar explains the latter usage as "diptotic," and a final Alif is to be eliminated in the accusative along with this construction; this rule, however, does not apply for the Qur'ān. In my study *Die syro-aramaischen Lesart des Koran* (1st ed., 2000: pp. 166ff., n. 211; 2nd ed, 2004: pp. 199ff., n. 242; 3rd ed., 2006: pp. 298ff., n. 248), I have pointed to a similar situation at Q 18:71, where the spelling امرا was mis-read as *imran*, because the Arabic readers were not able to recognize an elative because of the final Alif; the text should have been read as amarra.

8 By a calque from Syro-Aramaic, the Qur'ān uses another Arabic synonym, مد / madda ("to stretch, reach out") in the sense of "to give." This word is understood in contemporary Arabic as meaning "to furnish, support." This understanding arises from the following Qur'ānic texts: Surahs 3:124, 125; 17:6, 20; 23:55; 26:132, 133; 27:36; 52:22. To reproduce in modern Arabic the Qur'ānic expression from Q 74:12, مالا ممدودا / *malan mamdūdā* (literally, "elongated property," that is, "sizeable, extensive property"), one would say أموالا طائلة / *amwālan ṭā'ila* (literally, "property that is stretched long, wide-ranging, extensive"). Note that this expression in turn connects back with the Qur'ānic expression طول / ṭūl (literally, "length" = "property" = "richly, abundantly").

9 The Arabic conjunction ـفـ / fa (< the Old Aramaic פ, פא / pā = fa), which normally expresses a result or conclusion in declarative sentences, should be understood in this context as adversative.

10 Cf., e.g., BNF 328a, f. 3a, l. 14: ويعلم ما فى السموت وما فى الارض, where the first فى concludes with the form current today, and the second with the retroflex final-ى (فے). We see the same phenomenon, but in the opposite order, in the same MS., f. 12b, ll. 2-3: الرجال قومون على النسا بما فضل الله بعضهم على بعض.

11 Cf. for the former, A. Jeffrey, *Foreign Vocabulary* (Baroda, 1938), pp. 290ff; for the latter, see Josef Horovitz, *Koranische Untersuchungen* (Berlin and Leipzig, 1926), p. 151).

12 *Syriac Influence*, 84.

13 One also sees this phenomenon in that, in current Christian street-Arabic, the open and unstressed first syllable yu has completely disappeared; the result is that the name, with its final-Nūn also absent because the final syllable is unstressed, is simply حنا / Ḥannā.

14 Cf. Luxenberg, *Die syro-aramäische Lesart*, 1st ed., 193, n. 228; 2nd ed., 226, n. 260; 3rd ed., 227, n. 267.

15 E.g., ܡܢ: a) *man* (= Arabic مَن / *man* ["who"]), spoken as *mān*; b) *men* (= Arabic مِن / min ["from"]), spoken as mēn; etc. In his *Syrische Grammatik* [Syriac Grammar](2nd ed., Leipzig, 1898; reprint: Darmstadt, 1977), Nöldeke did not explicitly discuss this characteristic of the Western Syrians; the only mention of the phenomenon came in the explanation of ܟܠ (*kull* / *kūl* = Arabic كل *kull* / "entirety, everything) (§48, third paragraph): "Can it be long: kōl?"

16 Theodor Nöldeke, *Mandäische Grammatik* [Mandean Grammar] (Halle an der Saale, 1875; reprint: Darmstadt, 1964), §3.1, final lines; and §9, l. 5. Nöldeke places the Mandaean texts he discusses between the years 650 and 900 CE, but some may reach as far back as the Sassanid period (cf. his "Einleitung," p. xxii).

---

17 Nöldeke, *Syrische Grammatik*, §35, l. 4.

18 Rudolf Meyer, *Hebräische Grammatik*, vol. 1, Einleitung, Schrift- und Lautlehre, 3rd rev. ed. (Berlin, 1966), 50. After the text I have quoted, Meyer provides examples from the Dead Sea Scrolls text 1QIsaa, a vulgar text written ca. 100 BCE.

19 A. Spitaler, "Die Schreibung des Typus صلوة im Koran," *Wiener Zeitschrift für die Kunde des Morgenlandes* 56 (1960), 215, n. 8: "The use of alif to indicate an ā in the middle of a word is a purely Arabic development. Cf. also J. Cantineau, *Le Nabatéen* I, 47: 'Its transcription by means of א is an Arabic phenomenon – quite a bit later, for the inscription of en-Nemâra was unaware of it.' At the time when the Qur'ānic text was written down, this development was by no means closed off, cf. the presentation in GdK III:31f. In a few cases, as is well known, the defective writing of ā has endured into the present day."

20 S. Segert, *Altaramäische Grammatik*, 4th ed. (Leipzig, 1990), p. 64.

21 Luxenberg, *Die syro-aramäische Lesart*, 1st ed. (Berlin, 2000), p. 16.

22 Ibid., 2nd ed. (Berlin, 2004), 3rd ed. (Berlin, 2006), 31ff.

23 Luxenberg, Ibid., 1st ed., 288, 15.2, n. 204; 2nd ed., 323, n. 337; 3rd ed., 324, n. 345.

24 Segert, *Altaramäische Grammatik*, p. 232 (ch. 5.5.6.1.4.f.), p. 358 (cf. 6.5.3.3.2.a). The latter was originally an exclamatory particle that, from the perspective of historical linguistics, took on a variety of nuances. Depending on the context, the combination *lā-hēn* can mean "not this" or – understanding the proclitic lā- as an intensifier – "now if."

25 Cf. Luxenberg, *Die syro-aramäische Lesart*, 1st ed., p. 288, 15.2.

26 E.g., in Syrian dialects, before verbs to express various kinds of emotional agitation, including elation, defiance, frustration, etc., e.g., لفرجيه (la-[a]farǧīh): "I'll show him!"

27 This construction may correspond to Syro-Aramaic usage. The *Thesaurus* (II:1809) considers the particle ܠܐ (lā) before certain (if rare) oath-formulae as a negation ("formula est negandi cum jurejurando"), although the examples I provide here confirm its intensifying function as an oath-particle: ܠܐ ܚܝܝܗ̇ ܕܫܢܝܘܬܟ (lā ḥayyē-h d-šanyūṯā-ḵ): "by your life, O madman!;" and ܠܐ ܚܝܝܟܘܢ ܘܠܐ ܚܝܘܗܝ (lā ḥayyay-kōn w-lā ḥayya-w[hī]): "by your lives, and by his life!" Mannā (364b) also begins from a conception of a negative oath (المنفي للقسم), despite the two parallel examples it cites (entirely under the influence of the لا, understood as Arabic). Naturally, depending on the context, it is possible that a negation is in view.

28 Paret's original German is "Nein doch! Ich schwöre..."; Blachère's French is "Non! J'en jure...."

29 The Arabic نشر (našara) represents the Syro-Aramaic ܦܫܛ (pšaṭ), for which Mannā (618b) gives under (3) the Arabic قدّم. أعطى (qaddama, aʿṭā / "to give, to grant").

30 Ṭabarī (XV:208f.) explains مرفق (mirfaq / marfiq) laconically as ما تر تفقون به من شيء (and seems to mean "that through which kindness is given to you"). Paret translates this phrase as "to provide relief" (clearly following *Lisān* [X:118b], where it reads: والرفق والمرفق: ما استعين به [ar-rifq, al-mirfaq, al-marfiq, al-marfaq: "that which one uses as an aid"]); Blachère has it as "a softening" (un adoucissement); and Bell reads "a kindly arrangement," both of which represent the current Arabic meaning of رفق (rifq) as "kindness." Mannā (751a) explains the identically-sounding Syro-Aramaic root ܪܦܩ (rpaq), which may be the source of

the Arabic term (with a small shift of meaning), with the Arabic terms رفق. حلم. لطف. صبر (rafaqa, ḥaluma, laṭafa, ṣabara / "to be mild, kind, friendly, patient"); it defines the nominal form ܪܦܩܐ (rp̄āqā) even more precisely with احتمال. صبرعظيم (iḥtimāl, ṣabrun'azīm / "forbearance, great patience"). The Thesaurus, however, relates this substantive to the name "Rebecca" (cf. II:3966, under ܪܦܩܐ ["Rebecca"]: "nom. uxoris Isaaci, ... Ap. lexx. valet patientia magna, الصبر ܡܣܝܒܪܢܘܬܐ ܣܓܝܬܐ (*m-saybrānūṯā saggīṯā*), صبر شديد (*šabrun šadīd* ["great patience"]). We should not therefore exclude the possibility that this expression was current in east Syrian as a denominative; the explanation in Mannā also speaks for this possibility. At any rate, this understanding lies closer to the Qur'ānic context than the quests for meaning in modern Arabic that have occurred up to now. Moreover, the Qur'ānic nominal form مرفقا (*mirfaqan*) corresponds to the Syro-Aramaic infinitive ܡܪܦܩ (*me-rpaq*) with the *m*-prefix (a verbal noun, named in Arabic مصدر ميمي / *maṣdar mīmī*; cf. Brockelmann, *Syrische Grammatik*, §174; Nöldeke, *Syrische Grammatik*, §126).

Part 6

Aramaic, Syriac, and Hebrew into Arabic

Notes on Islam and on Arabic Christianity and Judaeo-Christianity

Shlomo Pines

Originally published in Jerusalem Studies in Arabic and Islam *4 (1984): 135–52.*

I

In what follows an attempt will be made to show that significant inferences may plausibly be drawn from some of the references in the Qur'ān to the relations between the *Banū Isrā'īl* and Jesus, to the intestine conflict in which factions of the *Banū Isrā'īl* were engaged, to the differences between the *Yahūd* (or *Hūd*) and the *Naṣārā* and cognate topics. We shall start with the following verse:[1]

> (Q 61:14) O you who believe: Be the helpers of Allah, as when Jesus, the son of Mary, said to the Apostles: 'Who are my helpers with regard to Allah?' The Apostles said: 'We are the helpers of Allah.' Hereupon a faction (*ṭā'ifa*) from among Banū Isrā'īl believed (*āmanat*), and a faction disbelieved. And we helped those who believed against their enemies, and they were victorious.

Thus according to this verse the Children of Israel were divided into two conflicting factions, one of which believed in Jesus and one that did not. The text makes it clear that the former was in the right.

These two antagonistic groups are familiar to readers of the New Testament and other Christian texts. The following passages may be quoted in this context: First, the Acts of the Apostles 14:1–2:

> Now at Iconium they (Paul and Barnabas) entered together into the Jewish Synagogue and so spoke, that a great company believed (*pisteusai*, [in Syriac *deyhaimnun*]), both of Jews and Greeks. But the unbelieving (*apeithēsantes*, in Syriac *de-la methṭpisin*) Jews stirred up the Gentiles.
> Acts 21:20: And they said unto him (Paul), Thou seest, brother, how many thousands there are among the Jews who have believed. (*pepisteukotōn*, in Syriac *aylen de-heymen*).

The following passage occurs in the pseudo-Clementine *Recognitiones*[2] (I, 43, 1–2). In this text Peter, who in a previous passage[3] refers to his Hebrew origin, makes the following statement:

> They often sent to us (messengers) asking us to tell them about Jesus: (namely) whether he was the prophet who was foretold by Moses and who is the eternal Christ. For it is only on this point that there seems to be a difference[4] between us who believe in Jesus and the unbelieving Jews.[5]

In the Syriac version of the *Recognitiones* the fact that both groups, those who believe and those who disbelieve in Jesus, are Jewish comes out even more clearly. Instead of "the unbelieving Jews," *non credentes Iudaeos*, this version has: "Those among our people who do not believe," *henon de-1ā meheimenīn men bnei ʿaman.*[6] It is conceivable that the expression "our people" occurred in this context in the original text of the Recognitiones and was changed in the Latin translation or in some adaptations of this work into "Jews." The transformation of "Jews" into "our people" is most unlikely.

In another passage of the *Recognitiones* (I, 53, 1, p. 38) Peter refers to *infideles quique ex Iudaeis* "all unbelievers among the Jews." The expression implies that there were also Jewish believers. Origen (*Contra Celsum*, II, 1) states that "one should consider what he says against those among the Jews who believe" (*pros tous apo Ioudaiōn pisteuontas*).

Eusebius (*Historia Ecclesiastica*, IV, 5, 2) mentions that from the Apostles till the siege during the reign of Hadrian "the whole church (of Jerusalem) consisted of faithful Hebrews" (*ex Hebraiōn pistōn*). The *Didascalia Apostolorum* refers (in its translation)[7] in speaking of the date of Easter, to the *computatio Hebraeorum fidelium*.

In the third century Origen (*Contra Celsum*, II, 1) states that those Jews who believe (*pisteuantes*) in Jesus did not abandon the Law of their fathers (*ton patrion nomon*).[8] The Jewish Christians regarded themselves as being both Jews and Christians, whereas their opponents denied them either quality. Jerome, for instance, speaking of a sect found in the Synagogues of the East, who are called Minae (the Hebrew *minim*) and also Nazareni[9] asserts that

> while they wish to be both Jews and Christians, they are in fact neither.[10]

Let us now go back to the Qur'ān, LXI, 14. It is obviously an easy task to interpret this verse by recourse to Christian and Judaeo-Christian terminology, for the two factions of the *Banū Isrā'īl*, those who believed and the unbelievers, correspond to the "believing" and the "unbelieving" Jews (or Hebrews) of the Greek, Latin and Syriac authors.[11] Moreover, it may be maintained that the Qur'ānic verse has characteristic Judaeo-Christian overtones, for the "believers," who are favoured by the author and are said to have been victorious, form a section of the Children of Israel; they have no lesser a claim to this appellation than their opponents. The clash of opinions between the followers and the adversaries of Jesus appears to be regarded as a purely intestine Israelite conflict. There is no reference in this context to people other than the Children of Israel, those who have embraced Christianity and the unbelievers.

Possibly, the (Meccan) 43rd *sūrah* also contains an allusion to the conflict between these two groups, but this is by no means certain. In this *sūrah* Jesus (*ʿĪsā*), who is said (v. 59) to have been made an example for the Children of Israel, is reported as having said "after having come with evident proofs" (*bayyināt* v. 63).

> I came to you with wisdom, and I shall explain to you some (of the things) about which you differ (*taḫtalifūna*); trust God and obey (v. 64). For God is my and your Lord, therefore worship him; for this is a straight way (v. 65). Thereupon the factions among them disagreed (*fa-iḫtalafa al-aḥzāb min baynihim*); woe to those that were unjust because of the punishment of a day of torment.

The first quotation and possibly also the second seem to show that the *Banū Isrāʾīl* included at least at a certain time both "believers" and "unbelievers," [12] i.e., both people who rejected Jesus and Judaeo-Christians who, as the context of the quotation shows, were people of "Israelite" stock and not members of the community of *Verus Israel* (i.e., Gentiles converted to Christianity). It is also made clear that the author of the first passage favors the believers.'

Unbelievers among the Children of Israel are also mentioned in Qur'ān, 5:110. In this verse, God speaking to Jesus bids him remember (the time) when the latter made out of clay something in the shape of a bird, which upon his blowing upon it, turned with God's permission into living birds. When he cured a dumb man and a leper and made the dead come forth (from their graves), when (God) made the Children of Israel turn away from him when he came with evident proofs: for those among them who disbelieved (*kafarū*) said: this is nothing but obvious sorcery.[13]

The charge of sorcery made against Jesus by the unbelievers among the *Banū Isrāʾīl* has a long history; it seems to be a reformulation of a similar accusation put forward from the early centuries of Christianity onward by Jews against Jesus. This appears to have been already done by the Jews whose polemics against Christ Celsus in the second century purports to quote.[14]

The fact that the predominantly Christian or Judaeo-Christian terms *kafara, āmana* and cognate words are sometimes used in the Qur'ān in stories concerning Moses[15] suggests the possibility that the Old Testament lore found in that book may have originated from Judaeo-Christian rather than Jewish sources. However, it is equally possible that it was the author of the

Qur'ān who had chosen without any outside influence to use in the context of the story of Moses terms known to him in connection with Jesus. The terms are also used to characterise differing attitudes towards Muḥammad.

Mīṯāq (compact, testament) seems to be another Qur'ānic term which may have a Christian or a Judaeo-Christian origin. In Qur'ān V, 15 the *mīṯāq* of the *Banū Isrā'īl* is referred to, whereas in V, 17 another *mīthāq*, the one that permits to those "who say: 'We are Naṣārā'" is mentioned. It seems to me probable that *mīṯāq* is a rendering of the Greek or the Syriac term for the Old and the New Testament: *diathēkē* (compact) in Greek, *diyathēkē* in Syriac. In this the phonetic similarity may have been a factor. It may be conjectured that it is by a process of extension that *mīṯāq* is used in the Qur'ān not only in connection with the *Banū Isrā'īl* and the *Naṣārā* but also in relation to other communities.

A correspondence can be discovered between the main traits of the Christology of the Qur'ān and doctrines held by the Judaeo-Christians, or some of them. As far as we know, all of them deny, as does the Qur'ān, the divine nature of Jesus; they regard him as a human being.

On the present evidence at least some of Judaeo-Christians believed that he was a prophet,[16] which is of course the doctrine of the Qur'ān. According to this doctrine, the birth of Jesus was supernatural; this belief may be compared with that of the majority of the Ebionites who, according to Origen[17] accepted the virgin birth.

The principal text of the Qur'ān dealing with the death of Jesus occurs in the 4th sūra (156). It is directed against the People of the Book and maybe rendered as follows:

> ...Because of their saying: we have killed the Messiah (*al-masīḥ*) Jesus the son of Maryam, the Messenger of God: they did not kill him, nor did they crucify him; but (the matter) was made to seem so to them.[18] In truth, those who disagree with regard to him are in doubt with regard to him. They have no knowledge about him, rather do they follow suppositions; they did not kill him in (all) certainty, but God raised him [19] to Himself.

The denial of the crucifixion of Jesus was fairly widespread.[20] One of the relevant texts may have a bearing on the subject of our enquiry. It occurs in 'Abd al-Ǧabbar's *Taṯbīt Dalā'il al-Nubuwwa*,[21] a work whose section on Christianity contains, as I have attempted to show,[22] Judaeo-Christian materials. The text may be rendered as follows:

> (P. 143) (It is written) in the Gospel (*Inǧīl*), Christ (*al-maṣīḥ*) was standing on (one) side in the place of crucifixion, and Maryam, the mother of Christ, come to the place. (Thereupon he who was) crucified (*al-maṣlūb*) looked at her and

> said to her, while he was (suspended) on the piece of wood: "This is your son." And he said to Christ: "And this is your mother." (Hereupon) Maryam took his hand (the hand of Christ) and went away from the crowd. [23]

This text is possibly a falsification of the Gospel according to John 19:26–27.[24] But admitting this, the falsification may go back to the pre-Islamic period.

The Qur'ān refers to Jesus's attitude towards the Mosaic commandments in 3:144, which purports to quote Jesus addressing the Children of Israel: He describes himself as

> affirming the truth of whatever in the Torah is in my hands[25] (and as having been sent) in order to declare permitted some (of the things) that were forbidden to you.

Some other passages of the Qur'ān may be relevant in this context:

3:87: Before the Torah was sent down, every (kind of) food was permitted to the Children of Israel except those which Israel (considered as) prohibited for himself. Say:[26] Bring the Torah and read it, if you are truthful.

4:158: Because those who adhered to Judaism (*allaḏīna hādū*) did wrong, we forbade them goodly (things) which had been permitted to them; (this was) because they strayed in many (respects)[27] from the Way of God.

6:147 and 148. In the first of these verses, certain kinds of foods are declared prohibited (for the Muslims). In the second verse the reason is given for the prohibition, imposed upon the Jews, of some other kinds of food: this prohibition was a "reward" for their rebellion (*baġy*).

Some of the concepts referred to in the foregoing verses may be compared with a doctrine set forth in the *Didascalia Apostolorum*, a work that may have been composed in the third or the beginning of the fourth century. According to this doctrine,[28] laws which were not good were imposed upon the Children of Israel when they had angered God[29] by adoring the golden calf. These laws include *inter alia* (the commandments) that establish a distinction between various kinds of food and differentiate between pure and impure animals (p. 352). Jesus abrogated the laws in question, which served as chains for the people. His message on this point was addressed not to the Gentiles but "to us, who were his disciples from among the Hebrews" (p. 356).[30]

The similarity between the doctrine of some of the Qur'ānic verses quoted above and that of the *Didascalia* is patent. Both the former and the latter consider that some of the Judaic commandments were promulgated because of the sins of the people. However the Qur'ān mentions in this context only some of the elementary prohibitions whereas the *Didascalia* refers in this connection to all these prohibitions and also various other laws. There is also another important difference. The Qur'ān, contrary to the *Didascalia*, does not set forth the view that the sin for which the Children of Israel were punished in the manner described above was the worship of the golden calf.[31]

In the pseudo-Clementine *homilies*, Peter, who figures as the spokesman of sectarian Judaeo-Christians, cites in the course of a disputation with Simon Magus (who in this work in some passages represents the apostle Paul[32] and the post-Pauline orthodox church) the following phrase (16:7, 9): *heis estin ho theos kai plēn autou ouk estin theos*[33] "God is one, and there is no God except Him."

This phrase, like similar Qur'ānic statements such as *lā ilāh illā huwa*, "there is no God except Him" and the less frequent *lā ilāh illā Allāh*, "there is no God except Allah," probably is derived in the last analysis from Isaiah, 44:6, 44:8 and 44:21. There is however a certain parallelism between the context in which the Greek phrase is used in the *Homilies* and that in which *lā ilāh illā huwa* occurs at least in two passages of the Qur'ān: 6:101–102; 27: 8 (cf. 6). In these passages the phrase in question forms a part of or follows a rebuttal of the belief that Allah has a son or a female companion.[34]

The parallel Greek formula of the *Homilies* is likewise—and this is a very significant fact—employed in the service of a unitarian theology, although admittedly the Christology of the pseudo-Clementine text is different from that of the Qur'ān. In the course of the disputation in which this formula is cited, Simon quotes Genesis, 1:26: "Let us make man in our image, after our likeness." He argues that the plural employed in this verse (which is one of the most frequently invoked by the proponents of Trinitarian doctrines) proves that these are more than creators; a contention opposed by Peter (17:11, 1–12, 1; pp. 223–224).

Further on in the disputation, Peter asserts that our Lord (i.e., Jesus) denied that there were gods other than the Creator of all things or that he himself was a god; he did, however, approve of the person who said that he was a Son of God. Asked by Simon whether he did not believe that "He who is from God is God,"[35] Peter points to the essential difference between the ungenerated Father and the generated Son (XVII, 15-16, p. 225).

The difference between the Christology of the *Homilies* and that of the Qur'ān is evident. Nevertheless in these two texts the phrase *lā ilāh illā huwa* and the parallel Greek formula are used to buttress a unitarian theology. It may be added that the Christology of the Qur'ān conforms to that of the Judaeo-Christian sects according to whom Jesus was a mere man (*psilos anthrōpos*).[36]

A passage in the Qur'ān cited above—it is the only one of its kind—distinguishes between the *mīṯāq* of the *Banū Isrā'īl* and that of the *Naṣārā*, i.e., the Christians. This differentiation does not seem to tally with the distinction—referred to in several passages—between the *Naṣārā* the Jews (*al-Yahūd, al-Hūd, allaḏīn hādū*). It may be noted that when some sort of value judgement is expressed, the texts are contradictory with respect to the former; they are either praised or disparaged. The characterizations of the Jews on the other hand are (when not neutral) negative. There is no question of the author of the Qur'ān adhering to either of the two communities; instead the formation of a third one is envisaged in several verses. This should be "a middle community"(*ummatan wasaṭan*; 2:137); a theological justification for its creation appears to have been provided by the assumption implied in the rhetorical question in 2:134, that Abraham, Ishmael, Isaac, Jacob and the ancestors of the twelve tribes were neither Jews nor Christians. Or, as 2:60 puts it, Abraham was neither Jew nor Christian, he was a *ḥanīf*, a Muslim. In fact it is the religion of Abraham (*millat Ibrāhīm*) that in a divine revelation Muḥammad was bidden to follow (16:124; see also 4:124). In other words, the third community, which was to be the community of Islam, was to have as its model the example and the religion of Abraham. In this context it may be significant that Tertullian seems to address himself to people[37] (of whom apparently he does not altogether approve) who wished to model their conduct upon that of Abraham. They were possibly of Gentile origin; for in the *De Monogamia*[38] he poses the rhetorical question whether, in order to follow the example of Abraham, they propose to become not only bigamous but also circumcised. His advice seems to be to imitate (if they are so inclined) the monogamous and uncircumcised Abraham as he was at an earlier period in his life.[39]

A summing up

Several scholars, such as S.D. Goitein, Tor Andrae and H. J. Schoeps, have propounded the hypothesis that Judaeo-Christianity may have been one of the main formative influences on Islam. Several points of resemblance were adduced in order to support this hypothesis. The points mentioned in this connection include, *inter alia*, the doctrine concerning the falsification *(taḥrīf)* of the Scriptures by the Jews, the commandments concerning ritual ablutions, the direction of the first *qibla*. Reference has also been made to similarities between the views of certain Moslem sects or schools of thought (as distinct from the teaching of the Qur'ān) and the Ebionite belief in the "true prophet" (*alēthēs prophētēs*).

As far as I know, at least some of the points raised in the present study have not been discussed previously. The points discussed concerning *inter alia*:

(1) The probably Christian origin of the Qur'ānic terms *mu'min* and *kāfir* and the fact that believing Children of Israel are alluded to in the Qur'ān. This portion of the Jewish nation is referred to in the New Testament and in the patristic literature, but in the seventh century Christendom at large was probably oblivious of its existence.[40] The reference to it in the Qur'ān may denote Judaeo-Christian influence.

(2) The Christology of the Qur'ān: it is possible to derive all its traits from Judaeo-Christian doctrines; as far as I can see, the conception that Jesus was (despite his supernatural birth) a mere man can be found prior to the seventh century in Christianity only in the tenets of the so-called Judaeo-Christian sects.

(3) Jesus's attitude to the Mosaic commandments; the Qur'ānic view of the matter is to some extent reminiscent of that of the *Didascalia*, a work that may have been composed by "believing" Jews.

(4) The Qur'ānic formula *lā ilāh illā huwa*, a counterpart of which occurs in the pseudo-Clementine *Homilies*, a work with considerable Judaeo-Christian elements.

(5) The Qur'ānic references to the religion and example of Abraham; according to Tertullian, these were people who wished to model themselves after this Patriarch. There is, however, no indication that these people were Judaeo-Christians.

(6) The Qur'ānic term *mīṯāq*. It probably reflects the Christian *diathēkē*. Applied to the scriptures of the Children of Israel and of the Christians, it was by extension used in connection with other communities.

The unavoidable conclusion resulting from points 1 to 4, as well as from the studies of the scholars referred to above, is that Judaeo-Christian terminology and beliefs[41] appear to have had a very considerable impact on the Qur'ān. I may add that the Jewish lore (including its midrashic component) contained in the Qur'ān may well have been transmitted to its author by Jewish Christians rather than by "Talmudic" Jews. The former could have been as versed as the latter in this type of learning.

II

The existence in Jerusalem during the reign of Mu'āwiya of a community of Jews who believed in Jesus is affirmed in a story occurring in the *De Locis Sanctis*,[42] a work written by Adomnan,[43] who was Abbot of Iona from 679 to 704. According to Wilkinson (op. cit., p. 10) the work in question appears to have been composed by Adomnan between 679 and 688. As the Venerable Bede puts it,[44] this book. . .

> had as its source the things told and dictated by Arculf, a bishop of Gaul, who went to Jerusalem to visit the holy places. He travelled all over the Promised Land, and then went to Damascus, Constantinople, Alexandria and many islands. On his return to his native land he was carried by a storm onto the Western shores of Britain. After many experiences he reached Adomnan... He was very happy to provide him with hospitality, and happier still to listen to him. So much so, indeed that whenever Arculf described one of the important things he had seen in the Holy Land, Adomnan took care to write it all down as quickly and completely as possible.

According to Wilkinson (op. cit., p. 10), Arculf's journey must have taken place some time between 679 and 688. If we take at its face value a reference (see below) to the Caliph Muʿāwiya, who died in 680 "the latest date for his visit to Adomnan is 683."

The following text seems to have a bearing on the subject of the present enquiry. Wilkinson's translation (*op. cit.*, p. 98) has been used:

> We know from holy Arculf's report about a sacred cloth (sudarium) of the Lord's, which was placed over his head in the tomb. Arculf saw it with his own eyes... Holy Arculf learned it in this version from what was told by the Christian residents of Jerusalem (*plurimorum... testimonio fidelium Hierosolimitanorum*)... several times they told it to him in the following manner:
> About three years ago every one came to hear about the sacred linen cloth (*linteolum*) which was rediscovered after many years. Immediately after the Lord's resurrection a certain Jew who was a true believer (*satis idoneus credulus Iudaeus*) stole it away from the Sepulchre and hid it for many days in his home. . . .This blessed and Christian (*fidelis*) thief came to the time when he was about to die and he called his two sons to him so that he could tell them the truth about this cloth of the Lord's.

The cloth is given to the second son. . .

> from this thrice-blessed ancestor the cloth of the Lord was handed on from father to son, and from one Christian to another (*fideles fidelibus*) until the fifth generation. But many years had gone by, and after the fifth generation there were no more Christian heirs (*hereditariis fidelibus*) in that family so the holy cloth was handed on to some Jews who were not Christians (*in manibus aliquorum infidelium... Iudaeorum*)... But when the believing Jews (*Iudaei... credentes*) heard among their people the true story about the Lord's cloth, they

> began a violent dispute over it with the non-Christian Jews (*cum infidelibus Iudaeis*) seeking with all their might to get it into their hands. This contention... divided the people of Jerusalem into two factions, one the Christian believers (*fideles credulos*), and the other the non-Christian infidels (*infideles incredulos*). Both parties appealed to Muʿāwiya (Mauias), King of the Saracens, and he adjudicated between them. In the presence of the Christian Jews (*coram praesentibus Iudaeis Christianis*) he addressed the unbelieving Jews (*incredulos Iudaeis*)... in these words, "Put your holy cloth in my hand!" They obeyed the King... With great reverence the King took it, and commanded that a bonfire be made in the courtyard in the presence of all the people. When it was fully alight he rose... and said to the two parties to the quarrel, "May Christ, the Saviour of the world, who suffered for mankind, whose head, when he was entombed, was covered by this cloth... now judge by fire between you, since you are disputing about the cloth. Thus let us know which of these contentious mobs is the one to which he desires to entrust this great gift!" With these words he threw the Holy Cloth of the Lord into the flames.
>
> The fire could in no way touch it. It rose undamaged and unharmed above the fire, and began flying like a bird in the air... Then, guided by God, it began its descent. Already the Christian faction (*partem Christianorum*) had been praying for the judgement of Christ, and it came in their direction and landed among them... One day our brother Arculf saw it. He was one of the crowd present when it was lifted out of its box, and with the rest he also venerated it. It measured about eight feet in length.

The evident legendary elements in this story include not only the miracle or near-miracle, but also such a flight of fancy as the invocation of Christ that Muʿāwiya is supposed to have made in terms befitting a Christian ruler. However, the legend also presupposes certain facts that must have been well known at the time of its creation. These facts are: 1) the existence of the Holy Cloth and 2) the existence in Jerusalem of two Jewish communities, one comprising the Christian, and the other the unbelieving (*infideles, increduli*) Jews.[45] The Christian Jews (*Iudaei Christiani*) are also called the "believing Jews" (*credentes Iudaei*) or "believers" (*fideles*); one of them is designated as credulus Iudaeus. These terms may have been chosen by Arculf or Adomnan either because they were known to them from New Testament, patristic and other Latin texts or because they rendered the appellations in use in Jerusalem; or for both reasons. Whatever the correct answer may be, it seems undeniable that at the time of Muʿwāiya some of the inhabitants of Jerusalem were "believing" Jews, who, as far as their definition is concerned, do not seem to have been essentially different from the "believing" Children of Israel alluded to in Qurʾān (61:14).

III

In an incidental remark, J. Wansbrough[46] called attention to some points of similarity between the prohibitions of the so-called Apostolic Council of Jerusalem reported in Acts, ch. 15, and the account given by Ibn Hišām[47] of an interview of Ǧaʿfar b. Abī Ṭālib and a ruler (*naǧāšī*) of Ethiopia, a country to which some of the Moslems converted by Muḥammad in the earliest phase of his mission emigrated. This episode is sometimes designated as *al-hiǧra al-ūlā*. According to Acts 15:19–20 James

> the Lord's brother proposed at the council (v. 19) that we should not trouble those of the Gentiles who turn to God (v. 20) but should write to them to abstain from pollutions of idols and from unchastity and from what is strangled and from blood.[48]

These proposals having been adopted messengers are sent to the converted Gentiles in Antioch, Syria and Cilicia in order to inform them that no greater burden shall be laid upon them than these necessary things: (v. 29) that you abstain from what has been sacrificed to idols, and from blood and from what is strangled and from unchastity.[49]

In the interview with the Abyssinian ruler, Ǧaʿfar describes as follows his own state and that of his companions before their conversion (Wansbrough's translation, p. 38): "We were a people, folk in ignorance

(1) worshipping idols (*naʿbud al-aṣnām*)
(2) and eating carrion (*wa-naʾkul al-mayyita*)
(3) frequenting prostitutes (*wa-naʾtī al-fawāḥiš*)"

Three other reprehensible habits of these ignorant people are mentioned. There is a clear parallelism between points 1, 2 and 3 listed above and the prohibitions of the Apostolic Council of Jerusalem. The deviation in point 2 is rectified in what Wansbrough calls (p. 39) "the counterpoint," i.e., the list of the obligations (set forth in a different order) that the members of the community assumed upon being converted. There the prohibition that apparently corresponds to point 2 does not refer to the eating of carrion; as in the ordinances of the Apostolic Council it bids the members of the community to abstain from blood (*al-dimāʾ*).

These points of similarity appear to lead to the conclusion that there is some relation between Ǧaʿfar's exposé of the rules of conduct followed by his people before and after their conversion and the ordinance in question. In my opinion, the hypothetical influence of the text of the Acts cannot fully account for this resemblance.

Unless we deny Ǧaʿfar's exposé[50] all historical value, it must be regarded as reflecting efforts to model Islam in its first stages upon some community in which these ordinances of early Christianity (including the one referring to abstinence from certain kinds of food) were still considered as binding.

IV

An early Arabic refutation of Christianity written by the Zaidite author al-Qāsim b. Ibrāhīm (d. 860), edited and translated by I. Di Matteo, was published in *Rivista degli Studi Orientali*, IX (1921), pp. 301–374. The treatise, which bears the title *Kitāb al-Radd ʿalā ʾl-Naṣārā*, contains *inter alia* several quotations from the Gospels or perhaps, if one follows the editor, who invariably refers to Matthew as the source of these quotations, from one Gospel only. A translation of the Sermon on the Mount (Matt. IV:24–72), which is included in the treatise, shows some omissions and many deviations from the Vulgate text.

The following deviation reflects perhaps a sectarian doctrine. In two verses the words *Hyioi Theou*, Sons of God (applied in v. 5:9 to the peacemakers and in vv. 5:44–45 to those who pray for their persecutors), are replaced in the Arabic translation p. 326 and p. 327 by the expression *aṣfiyāʾ Allāh* "those chosen by God."

Another deviation has a greater bearing on the subject of our enquiry. The second half of v. 5:22 is translated into Arabic as follows (p. 327):

> *wa-man qāla li-aḫīhi li-yuʿayyirahu innaka la-aġral*[51] *lam taḫtatin fa-qad istawǧaba fi ʾl-āḫira nār ǧahannam* Whoever says to his brother in order to shame him: "You are uncircumcised, you have not been circumcised," deserves in the other world the fire of hell.[52]

The Greek text reads:

> *hos d'an eipē,*[53] *Mōre,*[54] *enokhos estai eis tēn geenan tou pyros.*—And whoever says (to his brother), "You fool," shall be liable to the hell of fire.

"Uncircumcised" was a derogatory term and employed as such by the Arabs who were generally circumcised already in the pre-Islamic period.[55] This fact by itself does not however account for the replacement of the Greek word *mōros*, "fool," by an expression carrying an altogether different meaning,[56] for obviously other offensive terms had as wide a currency.

A possible explanation might be that Judaeo-Christians had inserted in pre- or post-Islamic times the expression in question into the Sermon on the Mount in order to prove to the uncircumcised Christians that there existed a scriptural sanction for considering the word "uncircumcised" as a term of abuse.

V

Patricia Crone and Michael Cook, at the beginning of *Hagarism, The Making of the Islamic World*[57] (Cambridge 1977, pp. 3–4), quote a passage from the *Doctrina Iacobi*,[58] a tract "cast in the form of dialogue between Jews set in Carthage in the year 634, it was probably written in Palestine within a few years of that date." It ostensibly records the effort of Iacobus, a baptized Jew, to convince of the truth of Christianity other Jews, who were forcibly christened in execution of an edict of the Emperor Heraclius. A part of the passage that is quoted reads as follows[59]:

> A false prophet has appeared among the Saracens.... They say that the prophet has appeared coming with the Saracens, and is proclaiming the advent of the Anointed One, the Messiah who is to come (*tou erkhomenou Eleemmenou kai Khristou*). I Abraham, went off to Sykaminu and referred the matter to an old man very well versed in the Scriptures. I asked him: "What is your view, master and teacher, of the prophet who has appeared among the Saracens." He replied, groaning mightily: "he is an impostor. Do the prophets come with sword and chariot."

This quotation is juxtaposed in *Hagarism* (p. 40 with a passage from a Hebrew mid-eighth century apocalypse, *The Secrets of Rabbi Simon ben Yohay*, in which Muḥammad is called a prophet. Here I propose to call attention to a historical phenomenon, which seems likewise relevant to the quotation from *Doctrina Jacobi*, particularly to the statement that the Saracen prophet "is proclaiming the advent of the Anointed One, the Messiah who is to come."

Abū ʿĪsā al-Isfahānī,[60] a leader of a Jewish sect, headed an uprising against the Caliphate. According to one report he battled with the forces of the Caliph ʿAbd al-Malik b. Marwān. According to another source, his rebellion occurred later, in the reign of the last Umayyad caliph. Abū ʿĪsā considered that both Jesus and Muḥammad were true prophets. Muḥammad was held by him to have been sent to his own people. As to Jesus there are two conflicting reports. According to one author he, like Jesus, was sent to a community of his own, while another heresiographer states that, according to Abū ʿĪsā, Jesus was a prophet of the Children of Israel. If the latter report is correct, Abū ʿĪsā was in many respects or for all intents and purposes a Judaeo-Christian.

Al-Shahrastānī states[61] that

> Abū ʿĪsā believed that he was a prophet (*nabī*) and a messenger (*rasūl*), the *masīḥ* who is expected (to come; *al-muntaẓar*). He believed that the *masīḥ* had five messengers who come before him one after another.

The *masīḥ* was charged by God to deliver the Children of Israel from the rebellious nations. Al-Bīrūnī[62] also mentions that both Abū ʿĪsā and another Jewish sectarian designated as al-Rāʿī believed that they were messengers of the *Masīḥ*. Bīrūnī applies the term *mutanabbī* (pretender to prophethood) to both of them.

We learn from these reports that Abū ʿĪsā regarded himself as a prophet and messenger of the Messiah and that he waged war. In other words, he enacted a role similar to that of Muḥammad as described in the above quotation from *Doctrina Jacobi*. This resemblance appears to indicate that Abū ʿĪsā's conception of his function may have derived from doctrines concerning the mission of the prophet that were current among Jews (and perhaps non-Jews) at the time of Muḥammad and may have influenced, as far as certain groups were concerned, the attitude adopted towards this *nabī ummī* – *prophētēs ethnikos*. These groups must have been in the main Judaeo-Christian if, as seems likely, Abū ʿĪsā inherited his teaching from them. For, as already mentioned, the prophethood of Jesus is part of this teaching. A further question may be asked, namely, whether the views held on the evidence of the *Doctrina Jacobi* at the time of the advent of Islam may be regarded as a form of reaction to this event or may have antedated it[63] and perhaps at some stage helped to shape the beliefs of the followers of the new religion. In our present state of knowledge, no conclusive answer to this complex of questions is possible.

The foregoing disparate studies were put together within the framework of one article because they have a common unifying theme. They are meant to illustrate the presence of Judaeo-Christianity[64] in the pre-Islamic and Islamic milieu of the seventh, eighth and ninth centuries. In many cases, the discovery of this presence is rendered difficult by the equivocal character of the terms that were current. In certain cases the adjective "Jewish" and the adjective "Christian" may mean Judaeo-Christian.

Notes

1 The *sūrah* in which they occur is supposed to have been revealed in Medina. The present edition conforms to Flügel's edition of the Qur'ān, as far as the numbering of the *sūrahs* and the verses is concerned.

2 Ed. B. Rehm, Berlin, 1965, p. 31. The so-called pseudo-Clementines were composed in the early centuries of the Christian era. The hypotheses as to the date of their writing differ widely.

3 I, 32, 1, p. 26: "Vicesima prima generatione extitit vir quidam sapiens... nomine Abraham, a quo nostrum Hebraeorum deducitur genus."

4 Or: disagreement.

5 "Frequenter mittentes ad nos rogabant, ut eis de Jesu dissereremus, si ipse esset propheta, quem Moyses praedixit, qui est Christus aeternus; de hoc enim solo nobis qui credimus in Jesum, adversum non credentes Iudaeos videtur esse differentia."

The last sentence may be compared with the following statements made by Epiphanius (*Kata Haireseōn*, 1, 29, 7) concerning the members of a Judaeo-Christian sect called by him the Nazōraioi: "They do not think anything (that is) other than (what is) preached by the Law, but wholly accept everything except indeed as regards their belief (*pepisteukenai*) in Christ... In this alone they differ (*diapherontai*) from the Jews and from the Christians. They do not agree with the Jews because of their belief (*pepisteukenai*) in Christ; and they are not in accord with the Christians because of their still being bound by the Law (as regards) circumcision, the Sabbath and the rest."

6 See P. A. Lagarde, *Clementis Romani Recognitiones Syriace* (Leipzig-London, 1861), p. 2.

7 See *Didascalia et Constitutiones Apostolorum*, ed. F. X. Funk, Paderborn, 1905, p. 286.

8 According to the lengthy statement made in *Contra Celsum* II, 3, some Jews who believed in Jesus appear to have ceased to observe the commandments, while other believing Jews continued to keep them. The Jews who believe in Jesus are also mentioned in *Contra Celsum*, II, 58.

9 A designation used, according to Jerome, by the Pharisees.

10 *Epistula CXII ad Augustinum, Migne, Patrologia Latina* XXII, Col. 924. Cf. Augustinus, *Epistula LXXXII ad Hieronymus*, Patrologia Latina XXII, Col. 942: "Haeretici, qui dum uolunt et Iudaei esse et Christiani, nec Iudaei nec Christiani esse potuerunt." See N. de Lange, *Origen and the Jews*, Cambridge 1976, pp. 35 and 164.

11 *Al-mu'minūn al-kāfirūn* and other derivatives from the two roots in question very often refer in the Qur'ān in the first place to the attitude taken up by a person or a group of persons to one of the prophets and only in the second place to belief or disbelief in God, the Day of Judgment and so forth.

Similarly, the Greek terms *pistos* and *apistos*, as well as cognate words, appear in Christian writings to refer first and foremost to the attitude towards Jesus. It is more than probable that the Christian usage accounts for the Qur'ānic one.

12 The fact that in some Qur'ānic passages the *Banū Isrā'īl* are depicted as rejecting the claims of Jesus need not of course imply that none of the Children of Israel were believers.
13 Cf. Qur'ān, LXI, 6.
14 See Origenes, *Contra Celsum*, II, 51–53. It seems most unlikely that the references made in the Qur'ān (apparently already in Sūrah 74, v. 24) considered as being the earliest of the sections of this book—to accusations of sorcery brought forward against Muḥammad are due merely to an analogy having been drawn between Jesus and the Prophet of the Arabs. The corresponding hypothesis does not appear too probable with regard to the similar accusations reported to have been made against Moses (cf. Qur'ān, XXVIII, 36).
15 Cf., for instance, II, 83, 85, 87; VII, 120, 123, 140; XXVIII, 48.
16 Cf. the *Pseudo-Clementine Recognitiones*, I, 43; I, 58 f.
17 In Matt. XVI, 12; see *Origen and the Jews*, N. De Lange, Cambridge 1976, p. 36; cf. W. Bauer, *Das Leben Jesu im Zeitalter des Neutestamentlichen Apokryphen* (Darmstadt, 1967), p. 30 ff.
18 Or: he was replaced with a view to them by (someone) similar.
19 Rafa'ahu.
20 Cf. E. Hennecke and W. Schneemelcher, *Neutestamentliche Apokryphen* (Tübingen, 1964), II, p.157; W. Bauer, *Das Leben Jesu*, pp.35, 238 ff.
21 Ed. ʻAbd al-Karim ʻUthman (Beirut, 1966).
22 See S. Pines, "The Jewish Christians of the Early Centuries of Christianity According to a New Source," *The Israel Academy of Sciences and Humanities, Proceedings* Vol. 11, (Jerusalem, 1966). A further study concerning the subject will be shortly published in Jerusalem Studies in Arabic and Islam.
23 Ğamāʻa; literally: company.
24 "When Jesus saw his mother, and the disciple whom he loved standing near, he said to his mother, 'Woman, behold, your son!' Then he said to the disciple, 'Behold, your mother.' And from that hour the disciple took his own home (*eis to idia*)." In this passage Jesus is represented as speaking from the cross.
25 Cf. Qur'ān, LXI, 6.
26 To the Children of Israel.
27 Or: often.
28 See *Didascalia et Constitutiones Apostolorum*, ed. F. X. Funk, I (Paderborn, 1905), p. 352 ff.
29 According to the tenth-century Qaraite author Yaʻqūb al-Qirqisānī, "modern Christian philosophers" spoke of commandments of the Torah given "in wrath" (*ʻalā saḫṭ*); see S. Pines, "Some Traits of Christian Theological Writing in Relation to Moslem Kalām and to Jewish Thought," *Proceedings of the Israel Academy of Sciences and Humanities*, Vol. V, no. 4 (1973), p. 108, n. 14.
30 Cf. p. 360: "Therefore, beloved brethren, who are believers originating in the nation (literally: who have believed from the nation) remove the chains with which you wished to bind yourselves." The believers to whom this injunction is addressed are clearly of Jewish origin.

31 The similarity between the views set forth in the *Didascalia* and the position of the Qur'ān with regard to some of the points indicated in the text is remarked upon by H. J. Schoeps, *Theologie and Geschichte des Judenchristentums*, pp. 340–341, and others.

32 In other passages he appears to represent Marcion.

33 Die Pseudoklementinen, I, Hamilien, ed. B. Rehm / J. Irmscher, F. Pascke, *Die Griechischen Christlichen Schriftsteller der ersten Jahrhunderte* (Berlin, 1969), p. 222.

34 IX, 31, in which the formula *lā ilāh illā huwa* also occurs the Christians are blamed for considering their *ruhbān* as well as Christ as *arbāb* (Lords) and the Jews for giving this title to their *aḥbār*.

35 *Ton apo theou theon einai*; an orthodox formula.

36 H. J. Schoeps (op. cit., p. 339) remarks on the similarity between the Moslem *Šahāda* and the following formula occurring in the pseudo-Clementine Homilies (7, 8): *Thrēskeia estin hautē, to monon auton sebein kai tōi tēs aletheias monōi pisteuein prophētēi*: "Religion is this: to worship Him alone and to believe (or: trust) only the Prophet of Truth."

37 Who probably lived in the 2nd century.

38 See VI, 1, 3; Corpus Christianorum, series latina H, Terttulliani Opera, pars 11, pp. 1235–1236: "Ad Abraham denique prouocant, prohibiti patrem alium praeter Deum agnoscere... Aut si posteriorem Abraham patrem sequeris, id est digamum, recipe et circumcisum... Adeo autem monogami Abrahae filius es, sicut et praeputiati, ut, si circumdaris iam non sis filius, quia non eris ex fide, sed ex signaculo fidei in praeputatione iustificatae... Nam etsi postea pater multarum nationum nuncupatur sed earum quae ex fide digamiam praecedente filii habebant deputari Abrahae. "

39 See the preceding note. Cf. also Tertullian, *Adversus Iudaeos*, III, 1; Corpus Christianorum, II, p. 1344: "Sed Abraham" inquies, "circumcisus est, sed ante Deo placuit quam circumcideretur. Nectamen sabbatazauit." The wish to contrast Abraham who did not keep the Sabbath with the Jews who attach great importance to its observance may account for the juxtaposition of Qur'ān 16:124 and 125; v. 124 (Cairo edition: 123): *ṯumma 'awḥaynā 'ilayka 'ani ttabiʿ millata 'ibrāhīma ḥanīfan wa-mā kāna mina l-mušrikīn*[a]*; a. v. 125: 'innamā ğuʿila s-sabtu ʿalā llaḏīna ḫtalafū fīhi wa-'inna rabbaka la-yaḥkumu baynahum yawma l-qiyāmati fī-mā kānū fīhi yaḫtalifūn*[a]. Cf. 4:47: *nalʿanahum ka-mā laʿannā 'aṣḥāba s-sabti.*

40 Though, as we shall see, there is some evidence of the presence of Jewish Christian in Jerusalem during the Caliphate of Muʿāwiya.

41 *Largo sensu*; the compartmentation, propounded by the heresiographers who sometimes contradict each other, of the various Judaeo-Christian sects may have been to some extent artificial.

42 Adomnán, *De Locis Sanctis*, ed. D. Meehan, Scriptores Latini Hiberniae, Vol. III, Dublin 1958.

43 According to J. Wilkinson, *Jerusalem Pilgrims before the Crusades* (Jerusalem, 1977), p. 9, this, rather than the usual Adamnan, is the correct form of the name.

44 Wilkinson, op. cit., p. 9.

45 It is noteworthy that "unbelieving" Jews are supposed to have inherited the Holy Cloth from "believers." There must have been a family connection.

46 See his *Quranic Studies* (Oxford, 1977), p. 39 [Reprint: Prometheus Books: Amherst, NY, 2004, ed. Andrew Rippin].

47 Ibn Hišām, *Sīra*, ed. F. Wüstenfeld, Göttingen 1858, I, p. 219.

48 V. 20 reads in Greek: *alla episteilai autois tou apekhesthai tōn alisgēmatōn tōn eidōlōn kaiṣ tēs porneias kai tou pniktou kai tou haimatos.*

49 *Apekhesthai eidōlothytōn kat haimatos kai pniktou kai porneias.*

50 Cf. also Wansbrough's remarks (op. cit., p. 40 f) on the relation between this exposé and the Qur'ān: "Now the exact relationship between this very concise catechism and the canonical text of the Quranic revelation is not very clear. Acceptance of the historicity of Ja'far's interview with the Najāshi must lead one to suppose either that the injunctions here expressed had been the subject of revelations before the emigration to Ethiopia, or that they represent prophetical logia later confirmed by or incorporated into the text of scripture. On the other hand, the structure of the report suggests a careful rhetorical formulation of Quranic material generally supposed to have been revealed after the date of the event." Cf. Qur'ān, 2:168; 5:4; 6:146; 16:116.

51 The printed text has *la-ar'al*; which hardly makes sense. The emendation clearly fits into the context

52 The Italian translation of the half-verse reads: "E chi dice a suo fratello per vituperarlo: to sei matto, non ti sei circonciso, merita nell'altra vita il fuoco dell'inferno" (p. 360).

53 The sense requires the addition of the words *toi adelphoi autou*, which occur in the first half of the verse.

54 A term, which, in the context, may appear as something of an anticlimax.

55 Cf. E. Schürer, *The History of the Jewish People in the Age of Jesus Christ*, a new English version revised and edited by G. Vermes and F. Millar (Edinburgh, 1973), p. 538 f.

56 It could be argued that the original text of the Sermon on the Mount had "uncircumcised," and that the replacement of the term in the Vulgate version was due to censorship exercised by the Church whose members were uncircumcised, being predominantly of Gentile origin. But this hypothesis seems farfetched.

57 The title of the work has tended to obscure whatever merit (the merit may be considerable) the theses put forward in the first part of the work may have, and has given rise to a good deal of facile and captious criticism. In my opinion, the title is not apposite because it diverts attention from the most significant of these theses, namely the contention that the Arab wars of conquest at the beginning of Islam were supposed to be "an exodus" (as the authors of *Hagarism* render the Arabic term) toward Palestine. This view is borne out to some extent (see *Hagarism*, p. 8 f and elsewhere) by the appellation *mhaggrāye (muhāǧirīn)*, which is used in relatively early Syriac texts to designate the Moslems. The use of the designation *Hagarenes* by various chroniclers and theologians may have been suggested by its phonetic similarity to the incomprehensible term *mhaggrāye*. This designation

had the obvious advantage of reminding the Arabs of their lowly origin: they were the descendants of a slave.

58 Ed. N. Bonwetzsch, "Doctrina Jacobi Nuper Baptizati," in *Abhandlungen des Koniglichen Gesellschaft der Wissenschaften zu Göttingen*, Philologisch-historische Kp. Vol. XII, 1910; see p. 86.

59 I quote the translation given in *Hagarism* except for one slight modification.

60 See S. Pines, "al-ʿĪsāwiyya," in the 2nd edition of the *Encyclopaedia of Islam.*

61 *K. al-Milal wa l-Niḥal*, ed. A. Fahmī Muḥammad, Cairo, 1941, 11, p. 24.

62 *Al-Āṯār al-Bāqiya*, ed. C.E. Sachau, Leipzig 1878, p. 15.

63 The *ʿĪsāwiyya* claimed to be an ancient sect; they contended that they were already in existence at the time of the Second Temple.

64 Perhaps also of other early forms of Christianity.

The Version of the Gospels Used in Medina Circa 700 AD

Alfred Guillaume

Originally published in Al-Andalus *15 (1950): 289–96.*

Muslims have always maintained that the apostleship of Muḥammad was foretold in the Scriptures, both in the Old and in the New Testament. With stories about individuals who claimed to see in the Arabian prophet the promised deliverer we are not concerned. They have been discussed by most Orientalists and there is little or nothing new to be said about them. But in the earliest prose work in the Arabic language that has come down to us, the *Sīra Nabawīya* of Ibn Isḥāq, there is a citation from the Gospel of St. John in support of this claim—a citation of quite unusual interest because it tells us what text of the New Testament was known in Medina in the early 8th century A.D. That it is a translation, and not, as might at first sight seem possible, a defective quotation from memory will become certain as we proceed.

Since it will prove difficult, if not impossible, to show how and whence and by whom this copy of the Gospels became known in Medina it is worth while to set down in the barest outline the facts we know about the author. Muḥammad ibn Isḥāq was the grandson of a man—probably a Christian who was captured in a church at ʿAyn Tamr in ʿIrāq, and brought to Medina. Ibn Isḥāq was born *c.* 85/704 and at an early age devoted himself to the study of tradition—not from the point of view of a lawyer or theologian, but primarily as a historian. He went to Egypt in search of information, returning to Medina in 115/733. There he completed his work, gathering his material from the citizens of the town. Mālik ibn Anas detested him, probably because he regarded him as a trespasser on his preserves, and in the controversy that arose Ibn Isḥāq scored some telling points against his enemy. However he found it wise to quit his native city and after enjoying the patronage of the early Abbasid caliphs he died in Baghdad *c.* 150/767.

The following extract from the *Sīra*,[1] therefore, may be said to represent a text of the New Testament to which the author had access sometime in the second quarter of the 8th century A.D.

قَالَ ٱبْنُ إِسْحَاقَ:

وَقَدْ كَانَ فِيمَا بَلَغَنِي عَمَّا كَانَ وَضَعَ عِيسَى بْنُ مَرْيَمَ فِيمَا جَاءَهُ مِنَ ٱللهِ فِي ٱلْإِنْجِيلِ لِأَهْلِ ٱلْإِنْجِيلِ فِي صِفَةِ رَسُولِ ٱللهِ صَلَّى ٱللهُ عَلَيْهِ وَسَلَّمَ، مِمَّا أَثْبَتَ يُحَنِّسُ ٱلْحَوَارِيُّ لَهُمْ حِينَ نَسَخَ لَهُمُ ٱلْإِنْجِيلَ عَنْ عَهْدِ عِيسَى بْنِ مَرْيَمَ عَلَيْهِ ٱلسَّلَامُ فِي رَسُولِ ٱللهِ صَلَّى ٱللهُ عَلَيْهِ وَسَلَّمَ إِلَيْهِمْ، أَنَّهُ قَالَ: «مَنْ أَبْغَضَنِي فَقَدْ أَبْغَضَ ٱلرَّبَّ. وَلَوْلَا أَنِّي صَنَعْتُ بِحَضْرَتِهِمْ صَنَائِعَ لَمْ يَصْنَعْهَا أَحَدٌ قَبْلِي مَا كَانَتْ لَهُمْ خَطِيئَةٌ. وَلٰكِنْ مِنَ ٱلْآنَ بَطِرُوا وَظَنُّوا أَنَّهُمْ يَعُزُّونَنِي، وَأَيْضًا لِلرَّبِّ. وَلٰكِنْ لَا بُدَّ مِنْ أَنْ تَتِمَّ ٱلْكَلِمَةُ ٱلَّتِي فِي ٱلنَّامُوسِ: أَنَّهُمْ أَبْغَضُونِي مَجَّانًا — أَيْ بَاطِلًا فَلَوْ قَدْ جَاءَ ٱلْمُنْحَمَنَّا هٰذَا ٱلَّذِي يُرْسِلُهُ ٱللهُ إِلَيْكُمْ مِنْ عِنْدِ ٱلرَّبِّ وَرُوحِ ٱلْقِسْطِ، هٰذَا ٱلَّذِي مِنْ عِنْدِ ٱلرَّبِّ خَرَجَ، فَهُوَ شَهِيدٌ عَلَيَّ وَأَنْتُمْ أَيْضًا، لِأَنَّكُمْ قَدِيمًا كُنْتُمْ مَعِي. فِي هٰذَا قُلْتُ لَكُمْ لِكَيْمَا لَا تَشُكُّوا».

وَٱلْمُنْحَمَنَّا بِٱلسُّرْيَانِيَّةِ: مُحَمَّدٌ؛ وَهُوَ بِٱلرُّومِيَّةِ ٱلْبَرْقَلِيطُسُ، صَلَّى ٱللهُ عَلَيْهِ وَعَلَى آلِهِ وَسَلَّمَ.

I venture to translate this passage because the very familiarity of the words may well cause us to overlook the different meaning which they would inevitably convey to the ordinary Arab reader:

> Among the things which have reached me about what Jesus son of Mary stated in the Gospel which he received from God for the followers of the Gospel, in applying a term to describe the apostle of God (God bless and preserve him!), is the following; it is an extract[2] from what John the Apostle set down for them when he wrote the Gospel for them from the Testament of Jesus son of Mary (Peace be upon him!): "He that hateth me hateth the Lord. And if I had not done in their presence works which none other before me did they had not had sin: but from now they are puffed up with pride and think that they will overcome me and also the Lord. But the word that concerns the Nāmūs must be fulfilled 'They hated me without a cause,' i.e., without a reason. But when

> the Comforter has come whom God will send to you from the Lord's, and the spirit of truth which will have gone forth from the Lord's presence, he (shall bear) witness of me, and ye also because ye have been with me from the beginning. I have spoken to you about this that ye should not be in doubt." The *Menaḥḥemānā* (God bless and preserve him!) in Syriac is *Muḥammad*; in Greek he is the *Paraclete*. (editor's emphasis)

In order to show the relation of this text to the Textus Receptus I set out below the Latin Version which differs hardly at all from the Syriac Peshitta Version:

> 23. Qui me odit et Patrum meum odit. 24. Si opera non fecissem in eis quae nemo alius fecit, peccatum non haberent: nunc autem et viderunt et oderunt et me et Patrem meum 25. Sed ut impleatur sermo qui in lege eorum scriptus est quia odio me habuerunt gratis. Cum autem venerit Paracletus quem ego mittam vobis a Patre, Spiritum veritatis qui a Patre procedit, ille testimonium perhibebit de me; 27. Et vos testimonium perhibetis, quia ab initio mecum estis. XVI, 1. Haec locutus sum vobis ut non scandalizemini.

It will be apparent to the reader that Ibn Isḥāq is quoting from some Semitic version of the Gospels, otherwise the significant word *menaḥḥemānā* could not have found a place there. This word is not to be found in the Peshitta version, and in the Eastern patristic literature as will appear below it is applied to our Lord Himself. Furthermore the Peshitta, Old Syriac, and Philoxenian versions all write the name John in the form *Yuḥanan,* not in the Greek form *Yuḥannis* found in the Arabic text. Accordingly to find a text of the Gospels from which Ibn Isḥāq could have drawn his quotation we must look for a version which differs from all others in displaying these characteristics. Such a text is the Palestinian Syriac Lectionary of the Gospels[3] which will conclusively prove that the Arabic writer had a Syriac text before him which he, or his informant, skilfully manipulated to provide the reading we have in the *Sīra.*

In the following notes the peculiar readings of the Lectionary will be discussed first, and a discussion of the Islamic turn which has been most skilfully given to the text will follow, together with a few observations on the "Syrian" character of the Arabic. Apart from the spelling of the name *Johannes,* noted above, the renderings of *Paracletus* and *Spiritus veritatis* are crucial. It has long been recognized that the Palestinian Syriac Lectionary has been strongly influenced by Jewish Aramaic and nowhere is this more perceptible than in their rendering of Paraclete which the Syriac Versions and the Vulgate simply transliterate, preserving the original Greek-term as does the English Bible in some places. The word Paraclete has been "naturalized" in Talmudic Literature and therefore it is strange that the Syriac translators of the Lectionary should have gone out of their way to introduce an entirely new rendering, which, given its Hebrew meaning has, by a strange coincidence, the meaning "Comforter" of the English Bible. (However if the Lectionary was intended for Jewish converts the word is not ill-chosen, for the verb in Isaiah 40[4] *naḥamu* is translated *parakaleite* by the LXX and *consolamini* by the Vulgate). But in ordinary Syriac no such meaning is known. There *menaḥḥemānā* means "life-giver" and especially one who raises from the dead, while *nuḥāmā* stands for "resurrection" in John 11:24, 25. Obviously this cannot be the meaning of our Lord's words in the passage before us. What is meant is one who consoles *and* comforts people for the loss of one dear to them, their advocate and strengthener, a meaning that is attested by numerous citations in Talmudic and Targumic dictionaries.

Secondly for *spiritus veritatis* the best MSS of Ibn Isḥāq have *rūḥu l-qisṭ* which later writers have gratuitously-altered to *rūḥu l-quds.* But *qisṭ* is not "truth," but rather "equity" or "justice." Whence, then, came the word? There is no authority for it in the Old Syriac or Peshitta, which read correctly *sherārā.* Again the answer is to be found in the Lectionary which has *rūḥa d-quštā,* the correct meaning in Jewish Aramaic.

Turning now to what we may call internal differences in the Arabic text certain alterations in the interest of Islamic orthodoxy leap to the eye:

a) *abā,* father, (which can mean "my father" in Syriac and Jewish Aramaic[5]) *becomes rabb.* Undoubtedly the alteration is intentional because, owing to the carnal association of fatherhood in Islam, father is blasphemous term to use in reference to God and bears the stigma of trinitarianism. *Rabb* is similar in sound, and not entirely devoid of the same connotation, for the verb which denotes lordship and mastery can be applied also to the bringing up of children and thus in a sense a *rabb* can be an *abb.* The use of *rabb* here seems to point to a desire on the part of the translator to keep as near as possible to the original text of the Gospel.

b) In 24 the Arabic text is corrupt. The rare word *baṭirū* is an obvious error for *naẓarū,* "they have seen" which all versions presuppose. *Waẓannū* looks like another shot at the meaning from a mutilated fragment of an original *naẓarū.*

c) *Yaʿuzzūnanī* I cannot account for. Palestinian Syriac has *senau* and the Arabic translator has twice rendered *senā* correctly by *abġaḍa* in the preceding verse.

d) 25. By omitting *da keṯībā—qui... scriptus est* and the pronoun in *namūšūn—in lege eorum* the translation given above results and instead of the Received Text of Christendom we have a mysterious prophecy about the Nāmūs which early Muslim commentators identified with Gabriel who is the Holy Spirit. One cannot escape the conclusion that the alteration is deliberate.

e) 26. By altering *"whom I will send to you from the Father"* to *"whom God will send to you from the Lord"* an impossible sentence results. As the words stand they can only mean that God will send a Comforter from Himself, but the language in which the statement is expressed is tortuous and unnatural and can only be the result of a violent alteration of the original text.

f) 16,[6] All but Syrian Arabs would understand *šakk* to mean "doubt," but all versions agree in the rendering *scandalizemini* and this, too, is what Pal. Syr. has here. In classical Arabic *šakk* can mean to "limp, be lame;" but to limp is not necessarily to stumble (*ʿaṯara*). In the dialect of the Lebanon *šakk* still means to fall headlong,[7] and the Syrian Arabs knew the meaning "scandalized."[8] Thus it would seem that the translator was himself a Syrian Arab.

Trustworthy information about the Christians of Arabia before and immediately after the rise of Islam is so scanty that it has seemed worth while to draw attention to this citation from the New Testament in such an early work as the *Sīra*, in the hope that some scholar may be able to pursue the enquiry further. How far did this version of the Malkite Church penetrate competing as it must with the far more popular Peshitta and the probably still existing Old Syriac version? It would seem unlikely that it would have moved far outside its original Syrian orbit for the obvious reason that its strongly marked Jewish Aramaic would make it unintelligible in places to those unfamilar with that dialect.

Nothing more than a probability can be hazarded; and it may well be that Ibn Isḥāq obtained his information from some Syrian Christian. Ayla where there was a bishop fell to the Muslims before the prophet's death and it was not so far away in St. Catherine's Monastery on Sinai that the two MSS of the Lectionary were discovered within the last generation. Somewhere in this area would seem to be the most likely provenance of the text and one can feel reasonably certain that his informant was a Syrian Christian from the use of the word *šakk* instead of *ʿaṯar.*[9]

Generally when Ibn Isḥāq speaks of Jewish prophecies or expectations of a Messiah he gives the names of his informants or some hint as to whence he got his information—but in our passage he uses the vaguest possible term *balaġanī,* "it has reached me." Thus we may perhaps infer that his informant was a Christian. Had he been a Muslim Ibn Isḥāq would have given his name. Possibly he asked a Christian whether Christ had promised that someone should follow him. He would be told of the promise of the descent of the Holy Spirit (which he would interpret to mean Gabriel coming to Muḥammad) and he would ask the Christian to translate the passage for him. He himself would edit the text and the result lies before us.

P S.—Professor Gibb has drawn my attention to the notes on this passage in the Encyclopaedia of Islam (art. Indjil, p. 502). If my study is sound, the paragraph there will need correction. As we have seen the citation cannot belong to the "Vorislamisches Arabisch-christliches Schriftthum" as Sprenger, Das Leben... des Mohammad, i, 131, thought in 1861.

Notes:

1 F. Wüstenfeld, ed., *Das Leben Muhammeds nach Muhammed Ibn Ishāk*, herausgegeben von Dr. Ferdinand Wüstenfeld, Göttingen, 1858, p. 149 f.

2 John 15:23 f.

3 *Evangeliarium Hierosolymitanum*, ex codice Vaticano Palaestino deprompsit edidit Latine vertit, prolegomenis ac glossario adornavit ed. Comes Franciscus Miniscalchi Erizzo (Verona: Apud Vicentini et Franchini, 1861), p. 347.
Margaret Dunlop Gibson, *The Palestinian Syriac lectionary of the Gospels*; re-edited from two Sinai MSS. and from P. de Lagarde's edition of the "Evangeliarium Hierosolymitanum;" Lewis, Agnes Smith, [1843–1926] (London: Kegan Paul, Trench, Trübner and Co. Ltd., 1899), p. 187.

4 The word maǧǧān in 25 is Syriac and has to be glossed by the Arab author, but for our purpose it is neutral, as it is a good Syriac word often to be found in the Peshitta. Another indication of a Jewish dialect is *mešallah* in 26 where the Peshitta reads *mesbaddar* for *mittam.*

5 F. Crawford Burkitt, ed., *Evangelion da-Mepharreshe*: *the Curetonian Version of the Four Gospels, with the Readings of the Sinai Palimpsest and the Early Syriac Patristic Evidence* (Cambridge: Cambridge University Press, 1904), Vol.II, p. 47.

6 Burkitt, *Evangelion da Mepharreshe*, II, p. 47.

7 I owe this information to my colleague Dr. Mājid Fakhrī.

8 Similarly in the Sūdān today, my colleague Dr. El-Tayyib tells me.

9 V. s. under (f.). This version seems to have been made with an eye to the many Palestinian Jews who joined the Byzantine State Church under pressure from the emperor Justinian (527–565). Later it was used in the diocese of Antioch and was also known in Damascus and Egypt. Fr. Schulthess, *Grammatik des christlich-palästinischen Aramäisch* (Tübingen, 1924), p. 1, states that the earliest MSS of the Lectionary are not older than the beginning of the 9th century. If that be so then Ibn Isḥāq's citation is a century older than any known text.

The "*Amr* of God" in the Koran

J. M. S. Baljon

Originally published in Acta Orientalia *23 (1959): 7–18.*

In 1892 H. Grimme stated:

> Der Koranische *Amr*, wörtlich Befehl, entspricht dem *Memra* der Targume ... Mohammed stellt ihn dar als einen Ausfluss von Gott, ursprünglich als Wort des göttlichen Mundes gedacht und als solches von rein geistiger Natur. Dieses hat Gott von Anfang an in die Schöpfung hineingesprochen. 41, 11. Darauf schied er sieben Himmel und bedeutete jeder Himmelszone ihren *Amr*. So entsteht für Gott ein weites Organ, vermittelst dessen er die Räume des Himmels in stetiger Verbindung an sich selbst setzt.
> [The *Amr* of the Koran, literally "order, command," corresponds to the *Memra* of the Targumim. . . Mohammed depicts it as an emanation of God, originally as word from the divine mouth and as such of purely spiritual nature. It was spoken into creation by God in the very beginning. 41, 11. After that, he separated the seven heavens and alloted each celestial zone their own amr. Thus, a vast organ emerges to God, through which he continuously connects the spaces of heaven to himself.] *(Mohammed,* II, 51).

For a long time this view was a received opinion:[1] Rudolph calls the *amr* "das hypostatierte Wort" ["the word having become a hypostasis"], comparable with the *memrā* and the *logos* of Philo and the New Testament, Eichler styles it a "göttliche Hypostase" ("divine hypostasis") and Tor Andrae renders *amr* in 16:2 without more ado by "*Wort*" ("words").[2]

In the last two decades, however, one couches it in more guarded terms, and particularly the Anglo-Saxons discern the hypothetical character of this view. MacDonald declares that *amr* "inclines towards a memra or logos doctrine," Jeffery states cautiously: "it would seem," Sweetman writes: "might point," while Tritton speaks of "a suggestion of hypostases." O'Shaughnessy avoids altogether the use of the *logos*-idea in this connection, and prefers to limit its function to an "intermediary force between God and the world."[3] Through a close semasiological[4] examination of this Koranic notion we intend to raise still more doubts concerning Grimme's theory.

In the Koran *amr* occurs 152 times in the singular, 13 times in the plural (*umūr*). Mostly—nearly a hundred times—it is used in connection with Allāh, less often it is applied to men, and once to the heavens (XLI, 11).

When *amr* is attributed to or effected by men, it can signify:

1) *Command*: 22:65 of the Pharao *c. s.;* 20:92 of Aaron; 20:94 of Moses; 21:81 of Solomon; 3:145 of Muḥammad.
2) *Affair*: E. g. 18:15 "He will favour your affair," i. e. of the people of the Cave.
3) *Intentions*: 10:72 "Collect your intentions and your idols (i.e. make up your mind with respect to your idolatry) and do not longer conceal your (malicious) intentions (towards me Noah)."
4) *Deeds, conduct*: 59:15; 45:9: People, citizens, who taste the evil results of their conduct.
5) *Religion, rites*: 23:55 "And they have become divided as to their religion among themselves into sects." See also 22:66.

In the passage, where *amr* has become an attribute of the heavens (41:11), it points to the destiny and task, indicated to them by the Creator.

Amr^u^ *-llāh* is usually translated by "command" or "bidding of God." And indeed, sometimes this expression says nothing more than that *amr* is a quality of leading individuals like Moses or Solomon. So, for instance, in 18:48, where it is said that Iblīs withdraws from God's command. But generally *Amr*^u^ *-llāh* has a more pregnant sense.

In 10:3 is described how God after the creation of the world ascends His throne to "arrange the *amr*" (*yudabbiru l-amra*). According to 7:52, this relates to the course of the celestial bodies, the change of day and night. It is also due to God's *amr* that heaven and earth endure (30:24), that man receives his food and life on earth continues (10:32). In these passages *amr* refers to the preservation of the universe which is represented in Semitic thought [5] as a sequel to the creation. 7:52: "His is the creation *(ḫalq)* and the *creatio continua (amr).*" World-order is not held up by secondary causes of which God is the First Cause, but by a series of separate well-considered divine dispensations which are one by one creative acts.

From His throne the Almighty plans His government. To this end the *amr, i.* e. the design to-be-prepared for the *Gubernatio Dei,* "descends" (*yatanazzalu*) between the seven heavens and the earth (65:12). Thus "He arranges the *amr* from the heaven to the earth; then it (i. e. the *amr*-design when completed) ascends *(yaʿruğu)* to Him" (32:4). Now, after this preceding inquiry of the state of affairs in the world, God "determines" *(yaqḍiya)* the *amr,* and then it is "ripe for execution" *(maf ʿūlan;* see VIII, 46). The design has become a dispensation.

When *amr* is settled in this way, providential rule can be exercised. This proves to have a two-sided effect: for the good and for the bad, accordingly as men deserve to be favoured or to be punished. In the first case *amr* is synonymous with God's guidance and grace, in the second case with God's judgment and damnation.

In 21:73 Isaac and Jacob are charged to guide people with God's *amr, i.* e. guidance, since it consists of appeals to good works, prayer and alms-giving. In 45:16 it is said that God gave first the Israelites *bayyinātin mina 'l-amri,* concrete directions in regard to the *amr,* which again must have the sense of "divine guidance" *(cf.* its alternative reading in 2:181: *bayyinātin mina l-hudā wa l-furqāni,* concrete directions in regard to the divine guidance and help,[6] this time as a present to the Muslims), In the next verse of Surah 45 Muḥammad is encouraged as follows:

> Then We granted you a clear way *(sharī'a)* in regard to the divine guidance *(amr).* (In a direct line of this meaning of *amr* lies the fifth noticed use of *amr* when attributed to men, *viz.* "rites," divine guidance in an instituted form!).

Occasionally this providental *amr*-rule manifests itself even as divine favour. For when in 22:64 is mentioned that the ships "range the sea through His *amr*" (*tağrī fīl-baḥri bi-amrihi),* then in a parallel passage (31:30) *amr* is explained as "favour of God" *(tağrī fīl-baḥri bi-ni'mati 'llāhi).* Another instance of this gives 11:76, where *amr Ullāh* is specified as "God's mercy and blessings," inasmuch as it will be realised in the birth of a son for Abraham and his wife.

More frequently, however, the heavenly dispensations are inauspicious and sinister:

> 10:25: Till ... Our *amr* comes to it (the earth) by night or by day, then We make it a stubble-field, as if there had been grown nothing the day before;
> 54:50: And Our *amr* is but a single (cry),[7] like the twinkling of an eye.

If the *amr*^{u} *-llāh* is coming, one should not wish to hasten it (16:1). And Lot is told of the *amr* concerning the Sodomites "that their roots would be cut off towards the morning" (15:66). At the moment Noah is said to embark it comes (11:41 f.), and when it has been executed, the water of the Flood abates (11:46). *Amr* is the doomsday which the Israelites accelerate through their worship of the golden calf (7:149). But for the God-fearing the *amr* is "easy," since for him it consists of pardon of sins and excellent reward (65:4f.; see also 18:87).[8]

With respect to the executive part of His *amr, i.* e. His plans and purposes for the world, God is assisted by a host of faithful angels. 19:65 "We"—as they state themselves[9]— "descend only with an *amr* of your Lord." They are employed for the drawing up of the *amr* when still a design (*cf.* 79:5 *fa l-mudabbirāti amr*^{an}), as well as for the carrying out of the *amr* when ripened into a dispensation (*cf.* LI, 4 *fa l-muqassimāti amr*^{an}). In the first case, *amr* is presumably related to the account of human deeds which is made for the coming divine Judgment. Everybody on earth has guardian angels around him as a kind of secret service "to observe him in view of the *amr*" (13:12), and his deeds are accurately recorded by them (*cf.* 82:10 ff.); it is their account which is read on the resurrection day! (*cf.* 17:14f.).[10]

An interesting example of *amr* as divine dispensation communicated by angels gives 97:4:

> The angels and the spirit descend therein (i. e. the night of *qadr)* (to the earth), by the permission of their Lord, in view of every *amr.*

As Wensinck has shown,[11] elements of the New Years night are mixed up with the night of *qadr,* that is to say the belief that God decrees in it everything for the coming year. This agrees well with our idea of *amr* as dispensations to be executed, for which purpose the angels, after God's deciding of fates, descend to the earth in the same night.[12]

The spirit (*rūḥ*), mentioned in 97:4, occurs more times in connection with *amr.* Then it is qualified as *min amri rabbī, min amrihi, min amrinā* (17:87; 16:2; 40:15; 42:55). Usually one resorts here again to a hypostasis-hypothesis, and declares that *rūḥ* is a second emanation, subsequent to *amr* (Grimme, II, 51f.; Rudolph, p. 41; Horovitz, *Hebrew Union College Annual,* II, 189). *Min* is understood as denoting a separation.

In 17:87 we are told that Muḥammad is questioned about the spirit, and that he is instructed to answer: *al- rūḥu min amri rabbī* – "The spirit belongs to *(min partitivus!)* the *amr* of my Lord." Could it not be that Muḥammad at this moment is thinking of the earlier revelation (97:4) in which is stated, as we have seen above, that the angels and the spirit descend from heaven on account of every *amr?* If this supposition is right, the *rūḥ* at this place must be, as in Ezekiel, an angelic being[13] who in particular is entrusted with the execution of *amr*-dispensations. In 16:2 and 40:15 he re-enters on the scene, and is sent down to warn servants of God's choice to fear their Lord. It is a kind of final notice in view of the impending doomsday. In 42:52 *rūḥ* is undefined and the object of the verb *waḥā* IV – "to reveal something to (*ilā*) someone." The most plausible inference, therefore, is to take here *rūḥ* for a divine revelation, message or communication,[14] and to render:

> And thus We acquainted you (Muḥammad) with a communication from Our guidance (*amr*) —you did not know, ere this, what the Book was, or what the faith—but We made it a light whereby We guide the servants of Our choice.

Looking for possible "sources" of the Koranic *amr,* it appears useful to turn one's eye to the Ancient Arabian Poetry. Although its relation to the Koran poses a lot of unsettled questions, it offers at least parallels dating from the time before and during Muḥammad's appearance as a prophet. And one has a fair chance that such a parallel exerted an influence on the idiom and thought of the Holy Book.

A use of *amr,* analogous to the Koran, is especially made by the so-called *homines religiosi* among the Arab poets, people with a strong inclination to monotheistic belief and with interest in religious matters which is rarely found among their fellows.

First, we cite a few parallels of *amr,* attributed to men or heavenly bodies. Umayya b. Abī l-Ṣalt XXXI, 5 (ed. Schulthess) *ağma'a 1-qawmu amrahum*—"They (the Sodomites) made up their mind;" par. to X, 72 *fa-ağmi'ū amrakum. Amr* in the sense of intention, plan also in Labīd XLI, 4 (ed. Brockelmann) in *kāna yaqsimu amrahu*—"If he (man) makes his plans." Umayya. XXIV, 1 and 5 *lam yuḫlaq al-samā'u wa l-nuğāmu. . . illā li-amrin sha'nuhu 'aẓīmu*—"The heavens and stars are only created. . . for a lofty destiny;" compare with XLI, 11—"He (God) indicated to every heaven its destiny (or task)."

Next, some examples are given of poetic views of the *amr*[u] *-llāh* with a striking resemblance to the Koranic notions of it.

Umayya LV (after a description of the King of Heaven on His throne follows an eulogy of the angels who are drawn up in front of Him:)

10 They who are elected for His *amr,* are excellent servants! ...

16 And in the depth of the air and under the compact masses of water, they ascend and descend;

17 And between the layers of earth's innermost parts angels move to and fro with the *amr.*"

This is *amr* in its first stage: the outlines of the proposed world-government are being marked, and to this end angels traverse the universe in all directions, carrying the *amr*-designs which are to be drawn.

Labīd III, 1 ff. (ed. al-Ḫālidī, p. 10f.):

Innamā yaḥfaẓu l-tuqā l-abrārū	*wa-ilā llāhu yastaqirru l-qarāru*
Wa-ilā 'illāhi tarğa'ūna	*wa-'inda llāhi wirdu l-umūri wa l-iṣdāru*
Kulla shai'in aḥṣā kitāban	*wa-ladaihi tağallati l-asrāru wa-'ilman*
Verily, the pious walk in the fear of the Lord	and in God constancy is established
To God you are returned	and with God is the coming in and dispatch of the *umūr*
Everything He determines and bears in mind	and to Him the secrets are disclosed.

This is *amr* in its second stage: in the heavenly council-hall the *amr*-designs are brought in (by the angels, as may be understood), and dispatched as amr-

dispensations when every communicated act of the creatures has been recorded.
Zaid b.ʿAmr b. Nufail says in one of his poems: *(Kitāb al-Aġānī* III, 16)

... rabban adīnu iḏā tuqussimati l-umūru
a-lam taʿlam bi-anna llāhi afnā riğālan kāna sha'nuhum
wa-abqā aḫarīna bi-birri ul-fuğūru qawmin;
. . . a Lord (i.e. no idols) I profess. When the *umūr* are alotted
Do you not know that (then)
God wrecks the impious
And saves the others because of their piety?

The last stage of the *amr*-process: the divine decrees are being executed. The pious will enter upon the joys of Paradise, the wicked will go to Hell.

It is on the ground of this faith the devout Ḥassān b. Ṯabīt dares to wish in one of his poems (CXXXIII, 7 f. ed. Hirschfeld):

That the *amr* of God may descend upon us hastily
this very night or to-morrow,
Then we shall stand in the Hour and participate in the pure good.

Whereas on the other hand the same poet attributes an ominous sense to *amr,* when referring to the enemies killed in the battle of Badr he states (XV, 15b):

wa-amru lāhi ya'ḫuḏu bi-1-qulūbi
And the *amr* of God clutched the hearts.

Finally, we wish to call attention to a remarkable parallel of *amr* with an idea in the Old Testament, namely *ʿeṣā*-counsel.[15] Though it is there far from being such a dominant notion as *amr* in the Koran, it is nevertheless a like characteristic term for the divine Providence, and it bears as such interesting corresponding connotations.

Applied to men, *ʿeṣā* means often "plan, intentions" (e. g. in Ezra 4:5; Psalm 20:5), sometimes, like in Surah 10:72, implying malicious by-motives: Psalm 33:101. "The Lord foils the plans of the peoples *(ʿaṣat-goyim)*. . . The purpose of the Lord *(ʿaṣat Yahwè)* stands for ever." (*Cf.* Sara XII, 21 "And God is well able to execute His purpose (*amr*)," *i.* e. in spite of the evil intentions of his brethren, in Egypt things were going well with Joseph on account of God's protection.)

Used as an attribute of God, it refers first of all to His purposes in the world-order. When in Isaiah 28:29 it is stated that Yahwe's עֵצָה *ʿēṣā ("counsel")* is wonderful, it is a conclusion made after an exposé on the wise providential rule which procures everything at the right moment *(cf.* also Job 38: 2ff.). In Is. 46:11 God declares that He "designs" as well as "executes" His *ʿēṣā*. The executed *ʿēṣā*-dispensations are, equally as in the Koran, for good or ill.

In Is. 46:10f. it appears to be divine favour, expressed in the intention to liberate Israel from the Babylonian captivity through the rise of Cyrus. For Babylon, however, God's *ʿēṣā* effects dismay and ruin (Jeremiah 50:45; see also 19:17 and Micha 4:12). And just as the disbelieving Meccans in Sūrah 6:58, the wicked warned in Is. 5:181. defy the impendent doom, saying:

> Let the *ʿeṣā* of the Holy One of Israel approach and come, that we may get to know it.

But also the sense of divine guidance is appropriate to *ʿeṣā*. The poet of Ps. 73 confesses that God will guide him by His *ʿeṣā*, i. e. His guiding wisdom (vs. 24; see also Ps. 106:13; 107:11).

If we want to draw some conclusions on the ground of what we have found, it can be stated:

a) Only in a few cases the *amr* of God is what a translation of "command" or "bidding" would justify. For, instead of representing incidental or arbitrary actions of a divine will, *amr refers usually to different stages of* a *carefully prepared and well-thought out world-order.* And instead of depicting the activity of a more or less despotic ruler of the universe, it relates to the discretion of a wise and righteous governor of the world. Consequently it is advisable, either to leave it untranslated or to render it differently, as the context requires, by "providential rule," "dispensation," "guidance," "mercy," "divine judgment," "punishment," "doom(sday)," and such like.

b) It appears that one can do without a hypostasis-hypothesis when elucidating the expression *amr*[u] *llāh.* And if Koranic ideas can be made clear from within, i. e. from the context and parallel passages, it is to prefer to explanations with the help of non-Islamic notions. Moreover, it is very unlikely that Muḥammad would have operated with a *logos*-doctrine. It is far from the Koran with its extreme and overheated monotheism to ascribe to God hypostases! Divine attributes are the utmost. Not even the more appropriate term for a logos, *kalima,* gives occasion for such an assumption, as Th. O'Shaughnessy demonstrates in his monograph *"The Koranic Concept of the Word of God"* (1948). And he quite rightly observes: "'Word' or 'Verbum' as a proper name is a Christian idea, not Muḥammad's idea (p. 59)."

But also—supposing the hypothesis were right that *amr* in the Koran is related to the *memrā* of the Targumim—one is not entitled to infer a logos-doctrine from *amr.* For, Strack and Billerbeck have found in their penetrating study of this concept that *memrā* is merely a somewhat vague designation of God ("eine umschreibende Gottesbezeichnung"), in substitution for the name *Yahwè*. It has the same function as the known appelative *Adonai*. Its theological import is very limited and it has certainly no bearing on a divine hypostasis.[16]

c) Surprising parallels of the Koranic *amr^u llāh,* as we have seen, are met in the religious parts of the Ancient Arabian Poetry. There, for instance, the angels are equally busy with their intermediary functions, while assisting in the make-up and execution of the dispensations. It appears that by means of some selected examples the whole process of the *amr* of God in the Koran could be reproduced. But details may vary. In Umayya LV, 16f. the *amr* is carried throughout the universe by angels, whereas in Sūrah 65:12 the *amr* seems to traverse the world on its own (Yet, I presume, that at this place the angels as carriers are to be understood, as Blachère supposes that in 32:4 the word *yaʿruğu* indicates "non seulement le décret divin mais aussi 1'Archange chargé de le transmettre sur terre" ["not only the devine secret, but also the archangel in charge of transmitting it on earth"]. The application of *amr* in the Koran is also more elaborate.

d) It is noteworthy that, while the parallels in the Arab poems relate especially to the equipment and entourage of the *amr,* the analogies of *ʿeṣā* in the Old Testament are more of a semasiological nature. The whole apparatus of the angelic service is missing, but on the other hand nearly all the Koranic connotations of the *amr^u llāh* are found again. Or, to put it otherwise: the amplification which Muḥammad gives to the *amr* of the poets appears to be for the greater part exactly that which the Koranic *amr* has in common with *ʿeṣā.* If we wished to indicate this schematically, we would get: the *amr^u llāh* of the poets + the *ʿeṣā* of the OT = the Koranic *amr^u llāh.* Thus the tempting conclusion seems obvious that Muḥammad combined ingeniously the *amr*-conception of the poets with the connotations of *ʿeṣā.* Yet, this is reconstruction made up in a study, and a bit over-simplified and conjectural.

Besides, we have to bear in mind

1) the connection between Arab Poetry and the Koran is still obscure;
2) it is generally regarded a very precarious procedure to assume *direct* Koranic borrowings from the OT;
3) one would like to have more similar instances of Arab Poetry + Old Testament = Koran. One example does not allow far-reaching conclusions;
4) a possible factor always to be reckoned with is a common Semitic stock to which such similarities can be reduced.

However this may be, whether the discovered analogies are "accidental" or represent an historical connection, they illustrate the *amr*-idea of the Koran and bring it out in relief.

Notes

1 With one exception, however! In the third "stelling" of his thesis "Mohammed en de Joden to Medina" (1908), A. J. Wensinck combats Grimme's point of view. Unfortunately, W. has never mentioned later on in any of his writings his grounds for this attack. He makes merely an oblique reference to it in his "La Pensee de Ghazzālī" (1940): "il est cependant douteux si, dans la terminologie de ce livre (Koran), *amr* ait une relation quelconque avec le *logos* chrétien ou philonien" (p. 83).

2 W. Rudolph, *Die Abhängigkeit des Qorans von Judenium and Christentum* (1922), p. 40 f.; P. A. Eichler, *Die Dschinn, Teufel und Engel im Koran* (1928), p. 125; Tor Andrae, *Der Ursprung des Islams und das Christentum* (1926), p. 168.

3 D. B. MacDonald in *Muslim World* XXII (1932), p. 28; A. Jeffery, art. on *amr* in *The Foreign Vocabulary of the Qur'ān* (1938); J. W. Sweetman, *Islam and Christian Theology* (1947), I, 2, 143; A. S. Tritton, *Muslim Theology* (1947), p. 9; Th, O'Shaughnessy, *The Development of the Meaning of Spirit in the Koran* (1953), p. 39.

4 [OED: That branch of philology which deals with the meaning of words, sense-development, and the like].

5 For the Old Testament, see W. Eichrodt, *Theologie des Alten Testaments* (1939), II, 78.

6 For this translation of *furqān*, see Ch. G. Torrey, *The Jewish Foundation of Islam* (1933), p. 48.

7 Dropped off is here *zaǧra* (cf. 37:19; 79:13) or *ṣayḥa* (cf. 54:31; 38:14; 36:28, 49:53) or ṣaʿiqa (cf. 51:44). Zamaḫsharī supposes that *kalima* (word) should be added, and that it refers to the creative command of God "kun" (2:423). But it is more likely that this passage points at the Last Judgment, for it forms part of a long penitential sermon. Moreover, the only place where the expression *ka-lamḥin bi l-baṣari* (like the twinkling of an eye) also occurs is 16:79 which deals with the Lord's Day.

8 For other places where *amr* is the divine judgment and doom, see 82:19; 54:3; 36:28; 19:40; 18:87; 16:35; 79; 11:61, 69, 78, 84, 103; 40:78; 7:75; 46:24; 6:8, 58; 2:103, 106; 47:23; 57:13; 9:24, 107; 5:57.

9 Cf. B. Bell, *Introduction to the Qur'an* (1953), p. 61: "there is one passage which everyone acknowledges to be spoken by angels, namely XIX, 65 f."

10 See also Baiḍāwī at XIX, 40 *'iḏ quḍiya'l-amru*: "The reckoning (ḥisāb) is finished and the two groups go to Paradise and Hell." And compare 65:4 "God will make for him (the God-fearing) His *amr* easy" with 84:8 "And he shall be reckoned with by an easy reckoning."

11 A. J. Wensinck, *Arabic New Year and the Feast of Tabernacles* (1925), p. 3.

12 See also Ṭabarī at XGVII, 4 "The night of qadr, i. e. the night of Decision (*ḥukm*), in which God fixes the destinies (*qaḍā*) of the (coming) year."

13 The other possibilities, suggested by the Muslim commentators, are that with *rūḥ* a divine revelation or the soul of man is meant.

14 Also Ṭabarī interprets *rūḥ*^{an} here by "revelation"(*waḥy*^{an}).

15 For a detailed analysis of it see the thought-provoking article of P. A. H de Boer "The Counsellor in Wisdom in Ancient Israel," in *Wisdom in Israel and the Middle East*, presented to Harold Henry Rowley, by the Society for Old Testament Study in Association with the Editorial Board of *Vetus Testamentum*, in Celebration of His 65th Birthday, 24 March 1955. Supplements to *Vetus Testamentum*, volume III. Edd., Noth, M. and Thomas, D. Winton, E. J. Brill: Leiden, 1955.

16 H. L. Strack u. P. Billerbeck, *Kommentar zum N. T. aus Talmud und Midrasch* (1924) II, 302–314. Similar conclusion: Treittel in "Judaica," *Festschrift H. Cohen* (1912), p. 179 II

The Origin of the Term *'Īsā al-Masīḥ* (Jesus Christ) in the Koran

Michel Hayek

Originally published as "L'origine des termes Isa al-Masih dans le Coran," in L'Orient Syrien *7 (1962): 223–54, 365–82; translated by Ibn Warraq.*

All that relates to Jesus in the Sacred Book of Islam engenders a host of historical, philological and theological problems, which seem to be inextricable, and which, in fact, ought to be, in the majority of cases, studied once and for all as such. It is as much to claim, faced with the complexity of the problem of the Koranic Christology, that the discussion will remain always open between Christians and Muslims, as long as the latter accept to enter into it on a serious, scientific basis. However, upto now unfortunately, the dialogue, undertaken in apologetic and polemical terms, has only been a sterile encounter of the deaf.

For the researcher, who wishes to remain simply scientific, the complexity of the Koranic Christology obliges him to confess the impossibility wherever appropriate, after all those who have dealt with it before him, of any solution which would be, if not defintive, at least absolutely satisfying. It seems consequently that he must inevitably content himself with enumerating previous solutions to discuss them, in weighing up the chance and probability of success, and, at the very most, retain the criticisms/analysis that could be applied to them. It is in the final analysis to this result that our study seems to end in, despite a personal stand for a particular hypothesis in favour of which we shall obviously advance some justificatory evidence.

1. The Term *'Īsā* (Jesus)

The initial problem addressed in this first paragraph concerns the origin of the term *'Īsā* by which the Koran designates Jesus. It goes without saying that this term has no equivalent in the Canonical Books and the Apocrypha of the New Testament. The Greek, Latin, Syriac, Ethiopian, Armenian, Arabic languages in which these books have come down to us, never present the name of Jesus under this bizarre and disconcerting form. It is without doubt however that it must depend on one or the other languages spoken around the birthplace of the Arabian Prophet. However, it is precisely the question here to know what this original language is. If it is Christian, then which Christian dialect are we talking of? If it is Jewish, then how did the Jews come to thus deform the name of Jesus? If this form *'Īsā* is entirely a creation of Muḥammad, it must have been from a root that one must determine. Unless one supposes that it came down to the Prophet in that form, already deformed by the Jews or the Christians. But then only an enquiry into literary and epigraphic documents of Pre-Islamic Arabia could confirm or refute such a supposition. One cannot exclude any of these possibilties *a priori.* What's more, they have given rise to various opinions expressed as much by the lexicographers and Muslim exegetes as by the orientalists. The hesitant, even contradictory, results to which this laborious research had led, are of the kind to provoke embarrassment, if not an almost total skepticism. These different opinions, none of which was able to rally, upto now, total approval, indicate to us the approaches, underline probablities, some of which, it must be admitted, offer a greater chance of being true than others obviously less convincing. And after all is said and done, to whatever opinion one rallies, it remains true, in Jeffery's expression, that "the name is still a puzzle to scholarship."[1]

1.1 The Muslim Authors

While waiting for science to unravel, if possible, this "riddle," Muslims continue to invoke Jesus under the term that their Scripture has transmitted to them. Even those who know the Arabic form, actually in use among the Eastern Christians, remain faithful to the Koranic appellation.[2] Being for Muslims an infallible book, the exact reproduction of the celestial archetype guarded by angels[3], the Koran, contrary to the Jewish and Christian Scriptures,[4] is supposed not to have undergone any alteration or manipulation; it remains thus the supreme criterion of complete truth for all Muslims. Determined in advance by the theological postulate, moreover elaborated late, of the eternal and uncreated character of the Koran, the Muslim authors extend this dogma over questions of a philological nature, like the one which is the object of this study. This basic position, that science by its very nature cannot allow, confines the questions to categories established in advance as definitive. For them, to undertake any research on the "sources" of the Koran smacks of impiety, given that the only "source" of the Koran is the "Preserved Tablet."[5]

It is certain however that the first circle of exegetes of Early Islam openly recognized and admitted the existence of at least foreign terminology in the Koran.[6] It is later, when the dogma of the eternal and uncreated Koran was elaborated and imposed by force by the Mutazilites that this privilege of apostolic times must have been rejected with vehemence by the majority of authors, in such a way that it became a sin against God. To shore up this dogma, scriptural arguments were found. Doesn't the Book of God say that it is an "Arabic Koran" (*qur'ānan ʿarabīyan*), inspired in "Arabic language" (*lisānan ʿarabīyan*)?[7] And didn't the Prophet reply to those who reproached him for seeking information from "foreigners" (*aʿǧamī*) that he understood only the Arabic language?[8]

Some other arguments were to be invoked against the existence of foreign terms in the Koran; this time they turned to linguistic chauvinism which follows in a straight line from its basic theological position: the Koran being the most perfect divine revelation, God chose the most perfect of languages, Arabic, in which to transmit it. How could He have need to recourse to Syriac, to Hebrew, to Persian, to Nabatean, in order to borrow from these languages the vocabulary of which He is the master?[9] That He should be so needy! And besides isn't the Arabic language the most beautiful, the richest of all! That cannot be. If then there are sometimes coincidences of terms and meaning between the Koran and other languages, it is because these languages themselves have borrowed from the Arabic the terminology in question, and not the other way round.[10]

This position is obviously untenable, though it has often been sustained. Suyūṭī expounds another which safeguards the dogma of the exclusively divine origin of the Koran and at the same time meets the demands of the most obvious exegesis [les exigences de l'éxègèse la plus obvie]. For Suyūṭī, if the Koran is the definitive and universal revelation, it must recapitulate and contain all the earlier revelations. And, to reconcile the two extreme positions, he decided that *de jure* or rightfully certain terms are of foreign origin, but since they had been arabized, they had become, *de facto*, Arabic.[11]

This position is prudent and conciliatory. But we are far from being able to go from there to a concrete application to the case in hand. For the passage of a word from its original linguistic milieu to the arabized state is thrown back to the Pre-Islamic period; it is supposed to have taken place before the advent of the Prophet. The latter in any case could not, himself, have borrowed directly from a foreign language a terminology which was not Arabic or already perfectly arabized.[12] For the linguistic phenomenon of arabization (*taʿrīb*) only interests the Muslim authors obliquely. It belongs in fact to the abhorred age of Ǧāhiliyya or Ignorance or Barbarism. The Muslim exegetes describe the process only exceptionally, and only recognize it reluctantly, not without first having tried to extract an explanation from specifically Arabic linguistic resources, the only one that seemed to satisfy them completely.

We must then rely upon finding an application of this traditional method on the present case. Instinctively, the Muslim authors, lexicographers or exegetes, are going to try to find an Arabic root for the name *ʿĪsā*. Now Arabic etymology here provides four roots whose meanings seem rather far from the word in question, but to which the latter has been brought back, since, on principle, at all costs, a foreign word must be arabized before being admitted into the Koran, and so that it can be derived from some Arabic root. *ʿĪsā* would thus be derived from either *ʿayas*, the reddish white colour[13] characteristic of the camel family; or from *ʿays*, sperm of the same animals; or from *ʿawas*, good management of one's belongings;[14] or from *ʿaws*, to prowl at night. Thus several authors such as Zağğāğ, Azharī, Sībawayh, Ibn Sīdah, though sometimes recognizing its foreign origin, think that it has been transmuted (*maʿdūl*) for it to be arabized (*muʿarrab*).[15] Others are content to say that it is foreign (*aʿğamī*), without feeling the need to assign it a precise Arabic root. On the whole, preference is for a Hebrew or Syriac origin, as with Ğawharī and Layṯ[16]. Baydāwī and Zamaḫšarī, in recognizing the Hebrew-Syriac origin, deemed to be *ʾIšūʿ*, or *ʾIsūʿ* mock those who persist in vain in their wish to derive it from Arabic; Zamaḫšarī compares them to a man "who writes on water."[17] But what the latter authors understand by Hebrew or Syriac remains something extremely confused and vague in their mind; it signifies an ancient origin, venerable, without any greater precision.[18]

Let us retain from our authors that the Koranic *ʿĪsā* is an arabization of the word, not Hebrew,[19] but Syriac *ʾIšūʿ*, and not *ʾIsūʿ*. And since this arabization is supposed to have been accomplished before Muḥammad, one must look into Pre-Islamic Arabic documents. But these have not preserved any trace of it. A similar form, *Yasūʿ*, that Arabic-speaking Christians currently use, is confirmed by the texts of Christian literature. Already in the 14th century, it is present in the *Apocryphal Gospel of John*,[20] which is a translation from the Syriac. One comes across it once again in the writings of Abū Qurrah († c. 823), in an epistle that the Bishop of Harrān would have addressed to a convert from Jacobitism.[21] But such documents, since they are post-Islamic, can only be interesting as witnesses of a certain antiquity of the appellation. Could one arrive at a date Pre-Islamic?

In fact, one comes across a verse by the poet Nābiġa († 604), himself a Christian or with a smattering of Christianity, the term *Sūʿ* that the lexicon *Tāğ al-ʿArūs* registers with a variant *Yasūʿ*.[22] This incertitude is quite significant in itself; combined with what we know of the manipulation undergone by the Pre-Islamic literature and of the rarity of the term in this literature, it loses all possibilty of being momentous. Even if we assume that the verse was authentic, we still cannot rely on one single case to draw sure, scientific conclusions. We have said "unique case," although Pre-Islamic Arabic onomastics reveals the existence of people having the name *ʿAbd Yasūʿ*.[23] But these people are suspect and should be considered Post-Koranic.[24] In conclusion, one can say with all likelihood that Pre-Islam could not have known the form *Yasūʿ* to allow us to look in this direction for the origin near or far of the Koranic *ʿĪsā*.

One can say as much of the passages in the Arabic literature of the time of Muḥammad, or just a little before him, where the term *ʿĪsā* itself appears. The texts reveal three passages which refer to those mysterious figures called *ḥanīf*. The first concerns the famous *Quss ibn Sāʿida* († 600), presented as the bishop of the Najrān tribe, and "preacher of the Arabs" (*ḫaṭīb al-ʿArab*). He met both St. Peter and Muḥammad since he had lived for 600 or 700 years. Muḥammad would have heard him preach at the fair in ʿUkāz. In one of his sermons, he would have referred to Jesus as *ʿĪsā*:

> Glory to Allah who has not created in vain, who has not created men needlessly after Jesus" (*al-ḥamdu lil-Lāh al-laḏī lam yaḫluq al-ḫalq ʿabaṯ wa-lam yaḫluq an-nās suda min baʿd ʿĪsā).*[25]

Regardless of the historicity of the person[26], the text mentioned here does not seem to be from him; it obviously depends on the Koran where one finds the same idea expressed in the same terms:[27] God did not create in vain (*suda, ʿabaṯ*). One must set it aside as inauthentic. Similarly, one must consider as apocryphal the account in the *Kitāb al-Aġānī* on the monotheism of Ḫadīǧa's cousin, Waraqa ibn Nawfal who supposedly worshipped the one God according to the law of Moses and the "great message of Jesus" (*nāmūs* ʿĪsā *al-akbar).*[28] That this *ḥanīf* had really existed and that he had been in effect a monotheist, one could, if pushed, allow; but it is impossible to know if he had known Jesus under the appellation *ʿĪsā*. Already the image itself of the person has been overwhelmed by legendary accretions.

The third text is a verse of the celebrated *Umayya ibn Abī-ṣ-Ṣalt*:

> In your credo, he is a sign of Mary's Lord announcing the servant Jesus son of Mary.[29]

This epithet "servant" (*ʿabd*) applied to Jesus, as well as ʿĪsā *ibn Mariam*, evokes Koranic terminology.[30] Horovitz is right in declaring this verse apocryphal.[31] Besides, the authenticity of all the religious poetry of this author is generally doubted by all the orientalists.[32]

On could say that in the present state of research nothing allows us to seriously conclude the existence of the term *ʿĪsā* in the Pre-Islamic literary documents, or those contemporaneous with Muḥammad. More than that, everything seems to indicate the contrary.

1.2 Epigraphic Evidence

If the literary remains of Pre-Islamic Arabia, transmitted from memory, then written down during the Islamic centuries, are suspect, it is a domain where the activity of forgers could operate freely and effectively. Because of this fact, it is epigraphy that offers the surest guarantee for the reconstruction of the religious ideas of *Arabia Sacra*. What do we find there?

I wanted to refer to an inscription from southern Arabia, more precisely Sabean; it dates from a period before Islam, and presents the form *hys*ʿ. I thought I would find there the origin of the Koranic *ʿĪsā*. Ryckmans reminds us of the uncertain character of the inscription whose reading is not sure,[33] and because of this could not be considered decisive.

Winett,[34] in examining the inscriptions in southern and northern Arabia, believed to have discovered a mention of the name of Jesus under the name of a deity called *Yt*ʿ which recalls the Koranic term. For Winett, these epigraphic texts must emanate from the syncretic Christian milieus where *Yt*ʿ which is, according to him, Jesus, was considered the Moon God next to his consort Rūda. But once more it is Ryckmans, one of the greatest contemporary experts on Arabic epigraphy, who was to destroy one by one the arguments put forward by Winett in support of his thesis. *Yt*ʿ is only a pagan deity which has nothing to do with Jesus, since its existence is vouched for in Arabia long before the Christian era.[35] One could obviously suppose that the Christians had adopted, as they did often in different parts of Arabia and Persia, a pre-existing pagan form in order to attribute to it more easily the contents and values of their faith. But one readily understands that one cannot lean on suppositions of this kind to arrive at a firm conclusion.

Among the Thamudic inscriptions of North Arabia copies and photographs of which were sent to Enno Littmann by M.G. Lankaster Harding, Chief Curator of Antiquities of the Hashimite Kingdom of Jordan, the one numbered 476 merits particular attention.[36] This unique document is composed of a cross surrounding a circle, and below the foot of the cross there are five letters clearly visible and a part of a sixth one, forming thus from right to left and left to right twice the word *Yš*ʿ, Jesus. The symbol itself inscribed in the circle is equally read in a way that represents magically four times the same word *Yš*ʿ, Jesus. This document, thus interpreted by Littmann, puts us in the presence of the oldest Christian text from North Arabia bearing the name of Jesus. Thus it is of the utmost importance. But it cannot be shielded from all criticism, and Van den Branden did not fail to raise doubts on Littmann's manner of interpreting it.[37] Even though he recognizes the existence in Thamudic texts of magical elements, Van den Branden points out that the usual method used in Thamudic inscriptions is a centrifugal reading [i.e., moving away from the centre],[38] and not a centripetal [i.e., moving towards the centre] one, as Littmann would have it, thus creating a unique example, apparently without precedent. Taking into account the examples and usual methods of centrifugal magical inscriptions, Van den Branden would rather read not *Yš*ʿ-ʿ*Šy*, twice the name of Jesus, but twice the name *ʾAyūb* (Job): *Buyaʾ-ʾAyub*.

Furthermore, from the bars of the cross inscribed in the circle with the quasi-triangular forks to each of their intersections with the circle, Littmann still read the word *Yš*ʿ four times, top to bottom, left to right. On the other hand, the meticulous examination that Van den Branden carried out led him to discover four times the word *Ḥyt* (life). Thus it is perfectly appropriate to ask onself if what we have here is a Christian symbol. Without excluding the possibility "of interpreting in a Christian sense the idea of 'life' in relation to the cross," Van den Branden meanwhile reminds us by examples that "the word *Ḥyt* (life) is also a part of the religious polytheist vocabulary of the Thamudians," life being an attribute of their deity. And, according to him, even the cross is not necessarily a Christian symbol; the example that he gives shows that the cross is well-known as *waṣm* ("seal, ring") in Thamudic. And he concludes by saying that he "does not think that one can attribute a Christian character to these texts."[39]

It seems that these objections raised by Van den Branden seriously compromise the reading put forward by Littmann. In fact they are not decisive. The unusualness of a case of an inscription with a centripetal reading would only be suspect if one assumed that we had exhausted our knowledge of all the resources of Arabic epigraphy. Moreover, anticipating the objection of the Arabists who expected to read *Ys*ʿ or not *Yš*ʿ (a *sīn* instead of *šīn*), Littmann took care to warn us that the *šīn* must have subsisted in Thamudic as in Christian Syriac. This is possible. And if in addition he fails to read the letter f= A (?) which is found above the symbol, this lacuna changes nothing of the inscription proper; if it belongs to the text itself, it contributes rather to clarifying it further, for one would thus have the meaning of the dedication or prayer: to *Yš*ʿ, to *Jesus*. As to the other objection concerning the vertical bar that crosses the symbol, as opposed to the horizontal bar which remains inscribed, it could easily be explained by the author's wish to form a base for the symbol, and not leave it suspended in empty space.

On the other hand, to justify his interpretation, Van den Branden is obliged to make a certain number of assumptions too ingenious to be well-founded: he tries to find a way to

> distinguish on the photograph faint traces [almost rubbed out] of the horizontal prolongation" in the inscription proper,[40] to see. . . the remains of a *b* whose back has been cut by the photograph. . ., to add the letters *y* and *b* that the photograph no longer gives?"

In the middle of the symbol itself, he suspects a *yod* that he thinks was added for a reason that escapes him.[41] Added to all that is the uncertainty in which he himself leaves us as to the accuracy of his reading of the inscription and the firmness of his interpretation. He lays down a conditional. [42]

For all that, should we see it as a Christian inscription? If we cannot reasonably exclude this hypothesis, one cannot however settle the debate categorically in its favor. At this point it is well to remember, and take note of quite a significant convergence, the manner of writing the name of Jesus among the Mandaeans. The latter transcribe *'Sw*[43] where the final *wāw* serves as a *y.*[44] The Thamudic *Yš'* read in the opposite direction (it is perhaps this reading which is primary) gives exactly the Mandaean *'Sy*, the *Šīn* being maintained in the first case just as one noted above. There is there a precious epigraphic clue that we must not lose sight of, while waiting for its confirmation or falsification by subsequent discoveries.

Since no source convincingly indicates the presence of the form *'Īsā* in the Pre-Islamic period, it is to be presumed that it is an invention, pure and simple, of Muḥammad himself. This final hypothesis is becoming a basic premise of the orientalists who have tried to solve the problem. The Prophet must have picked up from his entourage or on some caravan route a word X which designates Jesus. He only remembered it vaguely when he undertook his apostolic role; a hole in his memory must have led him to this deformity; or more precisely, it would have been he who consciously arranged the original word to make it rhyme with *Mūsā* (Moses). Loewenthal is convinced of it, who after having insisted on the taste of the Arabs for the

> purity of symmetry and proportion, line answering to line, cupola to cupola, minaret to minaret, ornament to ornament,

declared that Muḥammad had invented the form *'Īsā* in order to make it rhyme with *Mūsā.*[45] Besides it is common to insist on this tendency of the Koran to polish the terminations of names in order to present them by pairs with consonantal endings; thus we find apart from *'Īsā-Mūsa*, pairs such as *Ibrāhim-Ismā'il, Harūt-Mārūt, Jālūt-Ṭālūt, Yāğūğ-Māğūğ.*[46] Bittner, Nestle, Lammens, Ahrens and others reveal this characteristic, which does not in any way solve the problem; for before that we need to know the source from which Muḥammad derived the Koranic form. In addition we must remember that at its first appearance in the Koran, in the second Meccan period,[47] the word *'Īsā* is not to be found accompanied by *Mūsā* but mentioned either alone, as in Surah 43:63, or under the title of "Son of Mary," as in verse 57 of the same surah. Similarly, it is as *Ibn Maryam* that he is linked to *Mūsā*, as in Surah 23: 91. And besides we are there confronted with a part of the question, which is of secondary importance. The essential is less the origin of the symmetry than locating the term X, this basic evidence that one must discover and from which the "consonantenpermutation" was carried out, if permutation there is, which is contested by Bittner.[48]

1.3 Scholars Seeking Jewish Origins for the Form *'Īsā*

Faced with these problems, the scholars became divided into two clans, some opting for a Jewish origin, and the others for a Christian one. The first who had tried to take *'Īsā* back to a Jewish origin, was the celebrated mystic from

Andalusia, Ibn ʿArabī (†1240). After having cited authors who traced it back to a Hebrew or Syriac source, such as Layṯ and Ǧawharī, he gives his own personal opinion:

> For us, this deformation was the work of Jews who introduced it among the Arabs, out of hatred for Christians. Thus they call Jesus (*Yasūʿ*) by the name of *ʿĪsā* or *ʿIsū* (Esau) who is the brother of Jacob ... . They switched around the name *Yasūʿ*, transferring the final *ʿayn* to the beginning, putting the tail in place of the head. No one claims that *ʿĪsā* was originally *ʿIwsā*; the *wāw* being transmuted into *yā'*, the word becomes *ʿĪsā*.[49]

This explanation passed into the West. A number of orientalists gave it a legal status based on well-developed scientific considerations; it continues to enjoy a certain credibility. The first[50] who seems to have adopted it and whom all the others must have followed was Marracci in his *Refutatio Alcorani*:

> Vocat Alcoranus Salvatorem nostrum corrupte..., ʿĪsā, pro... Jasuh seu Jesus, litteris penis retrogradis, ac praepostere collocatis, contra omnem Scriptorum tam sacrorum quam profanorum consuetudinem. Judaei scelestissimi fuerunt in hoc Mahumeto magistri, Judaeis vero Diabolus. Etenim sanctissimum hoc nomen scriptum ... (ʿĪsā), prout scribit Mahumetus et Mahumetani, est id ac... (Esaü), permutata litera ultima *wāw* in *yā*, prout tam apud Hebraeos quam apud Arabes solet permutari. Est autem...Esau, cujus animam scelestissimi as spuricissimi Juadaicae faecis Magistelli, in corpus Jesu transisse confingunt, eo quod etiam nomen Hebraicum...Esau aliquatenus cum nomine...(Jasuh) convenire videatur.[51] [The Koran names Our Savior in a distorted way ... , *ʿĪsā*, instead of *Jasuh (transl.: meaning: Yasūʿ)* or *Jesus*, by putting the letters in the wrong order, against all habits of both Sacred and profane Scriptures. Mahumet's *(transl.: Muḥammad)* teachers were the most nefarious Jews, the teacher of the Jews (themselves), however, the Devil. That is why this most sacred name appears as ... (ʿĪsā), as written by Mahomet and the Mohammedans, and is the same as ... (Esaü), by changing the last *wāw* to *yā*, as it is commonly done amongst both the Hebrews and the Arabs. It is, however, Esau, whose soul the Jews, most mischievous and bedaubed by the faeces of a sorcerer, have imagined to have entered the body of Jesus, so that also the Hebrew name Esau somehow seems to match the name (Jasuh).]

The Koran distorts our Saviour into ᶜĪsā for Yasūᶜ or Jesus, setting back scholarship, and placing an absurdity..., contradicting all writings, whether profane or sacred. (part of a quotation?)

Henceforth the tone was established, and a tradition was created to which the great scholars gave their blessings. Thus Nöldeke was inclined to adopt this opinion according to which Muḥammad would have welcomed innocently this appellation that the Jews would have "out of bitter derision" applied to Jesus.[52] Landauer,[53] Roediger,[54] Kampffmeyer,[55] Pautz,[56] and Zwemer[57] defended the same point of view:

> the Koranic name 'Isa...represents the Hebrew Esau, the brother of Jacob, and since the descendants of Esau were hostile to the people of the Covenant, the later Jews caricatured the name of Jesus by calling Him Esau. Mahomed [sic] doubtless took this form of the name from the Jews without being conscious of the evil significance connected with it.

The Jews would therefore have given this nickname to Jesus out of hatred, thinking that the damned soul of Esau had passed into him; Muḥammad adopting the same appellation, without being aware of the perverse allusions that it evoked, must have adapted and modified it to make it rhyme with *Mūsā.*[58] Lammens was won over to this thesis which he expressed with clarity. He was convinced that one could "prove with difficulty the Christian provenance"[59] of the Koranic *'Īsā.* He ascertained that this doubtful orthography that one did not encounter in the oldest surahs, at a time when the Prophet must have been subject to Christian influence, should be sought on the Jewish side. He recalls[60], as did Nöldeke, the widespread Jewish custom of applying names with little to recommend them to their enemies. It was in this manner that their historians used to call Rome (Christianity) Edom, and the Christians *Banū l-Aṣfar,*[61] which is a precise allusion to Esau-Jesus. They must have propagated this name among the Arabs who knew well the country of the Edomites or Idumea, formerly called Mount Seir.[62] It was among the Jews of Mecca or Medina that Muḥammad must have picked up this appellation that he modified into *'Īsā* to obtain a resemblance with *Mūsā.* From *'Esū* to *'Īsā* the path was easy and verifies itself as much by the rules of Hebrew grammar itself[63] as by the rules of Arabic grammar both tending to substitute the final *wāw* for an *alif.*

Such is the position of those holding the Judaizing theory. However, despite the historical and philological arguments that one invokes to shore it up, it does not fail to expose itself to serious criticism. Although the arguments in its favour are simple, solid and satisfying, we can easily subscribe to Horovitz's assessment who pronounced it "wenig wahrscheinlich" ("unlikely").[64] The reasons to deny its truth are principally of a psychological kind.

First of all, it is important to recall here that right from the moment of its appearance in the Koran,[65] during the second Meccan period, Jesus is mentioned either as *Ibn Maryam* (son of Maryam) or under the isolated term *'Īsā.* It is later that one finds it combined with *Mūsā* by a rapprochement which remains in all rather infrequent in the Koran.[66] This simple observation already raises doubts about the reliability of the explanation according to which the Prophet must have looked for a consonance with *Mūsā.* Moreover, from its first appearance in surah 43:57-64, during a contentious discussion with the polytheists, *'Īsā* is presented as an "example," a "model for the Sons of Israel" as much as for the polytheists themselves (verses 57, 59). Muḥammad has faith in his miracles and in the "wisdom" that he brought; for Muḥammad Jesus is certainly only a "servant," but it is a servant on whom, as almost in the prophecy of Deutero-Isaiah, God has "lavished His grace;" he will return at the end of times, as "knowledge of the Hour" (verses 61, 63). The polytheists turn away from him, and do not accept the argument of Muḥammad in his favour, not because of the infamy attached to his name, but only because they cannot bear to see him compared to their deities (verses 57-58) If the Jews had been there they too would not have tolerated the sympathy with which Muḥammad pleaded for him and they would have had a bone to pick with him, as would be the case in Medina. For nothing leaves one to suppose that quarrels of that kind would not have failed to occur, if the Jewish community had been sufficiently represented and sufficiently representative in Mecca. Before his *hiǧra*, Muḥammad had been rather in contact with Christians, who even would have had his primary sympathies. These were the sentiments of friendship that would push him, at this period when he endured the cruelty and insults of his fellow citizens, to send his first followers to the Negus of Abyssinia, to help them escape the persecution to which their young faith had exposed them. The tradition[67] contents itself in underlining the warmth of the welcome which was reserved for the Emigrants from the Negus. Ǧa'far ibn Abī Ṭālib, head of the Emigrants, would have recited at the Negus' request, parts of the new revelation, more precisely the passages of Surah 19, which is Marial. The Negus was reduced to tears by it and, taking a rod would have said to the guests:

> Between what you recited and what is in the Gospels there is no more than the thickness of this rod.[68]

Whatever the authenticity of the words of discourse exchanged in Axum, it seems that there took place, if not two, at least one *hiǧra* to Abyssinia.[69] But that is already quite indicative of the good intentions of the Prophet towards Jesus and the Christians. It would be astonishing for him to borrow from the Jews a word whose intentional alteration would not have failed to set the Christians against him. We know him to be too subtle a statesman and too informed a diplomat to admit that he could have committed such a fault, at a time when he was looking to enter into the good graces of the Christians. In any case, nowhere has it been said that the Christians reacted against the word. We have not come across any trace of such a reaction, neither in the Koran, nor in the *Sirā* [biography of Muḥammad]. The sources are absolutely silent on this subject. Unless one supposes that neither Muḥammad, nor his followers, nor the Christians suspected any insulting intention or allusion behind this term. In this case, one must further suppose that the word had already been in use for a such a long time that no one could have thought any longer of the spiteful insinuations that it possessed. But one can suppose anything!

More directly this time, it seems rather unlikely that the Jews had applied to Jesus the nickname of Esau, despite and even because of the behaviour invoked to this effect. Nöldeke[70] had indeed put forward several examples of nicknames used by the Jews to designate their enemies. For all these names cited as examples never served, among the Jews, to indicate individuals, but groups, communities or nations, thus *Rome* for *Christians, Ismail* for *Muslims.*[71] It would be surprising had they in a special case, particularly important, deformed the name of Jesus into Esau, without one encountering traces of this appellation, elsewhere, in their writings.

1.4 Scholars Seeking Christian Origins for the Form *ʿĪsā*

It remains to envisage the possibility of a Christian provenance for *ʿĪsā*. One knows that Christianity was present in a diffused state in this Arabia that Eusebius describes as a "cocktail of heresies," *haeresium ferax*. Multiple sects and sub-sects had chosen for themselves the desert to take cover from the defenders of the Chalcedonian orthodoxy, these Byzantine emperors who were not known for their gentleness. More precisely, Christianity was represented in Mecca as much by the Abyssinians, who made up the military contingent of *aḥābiš* in charge of the defending the mercantile city, as by the Syrians, merchants temporarily installed or passing through in this commercial metropole of the Ḥiǧāz. The Nothern tribe of the Ghassanids, and that of the North-East, the Lakhmids, kept a watch on the edge of the desert on behalf of Byzantium and Persia, respectively. In the South, the Najrānites formed the only organized Christian community of Arabia. The liturgical language of these Christians was Syriac of which we find so many echoes in the Koran. Tor Andrae had remarkably brought out the influence of Nestorian Christians of Naǧrān and of Ḥīra on the eschatological piety of the Prophet.[72] Above all, the political and military influence of the Jacobites of Ghassān on Mecca is not to be despised, not more than their monachism often of nomads and gyrovagues (monk-errants).[73] The latter pronounced *Yéšū*, while the Nestorians said *ʾIšōʿ*. It is on the latter form that the word *ʿĪsā* seems to depend. How and by whom was this deformation of *ʾIšōʿ* into *ʿĪsā* accomplished?

Certain authors think that it was due to Muḥammad himself, by an operation in two phases: the first deformation which carried over the final *ʿayn* to the beginning was provoked by bad hearing; thus the Prophet would have heard instead of *ʾIšō* an *ʾIšō* or *ʿIšō*. The second alteration, deliberate this time, would be due to his desire to create a consonantal symmetry with *Mūsā*. This Nestorian origin of the term arranged

> mit Angleichung an die Namen Musa, Jahja [to align with the name Musa, Yahya] (Yaḥyā, John the Baptist)

is the one adopted by Ahrens[74]. Fraenkel[75] had suggested the same thing that Nestle had equally expressed: he explains the last syllable in an open vowel

> to get an assonance with Musa… and not to identify the name with Esau. This was more easy because the Nestorians pronounced the Name 'Isho' not Yeshu' like the Jacobites.[76]

Jeffery,[77] while waiting for new information more enlightening, is satisfied to say that this form permuted for the consonance is due to Muḥammad himself, who could have been influenced, as Horovitz[78] thinks, by the Nestorian pronunciation.

Sell and Margoliouth wished to be in agreement with everyone: not excluding the possibility of an application to Jesus of the name of Esau, they think that it is more probable that this formation was due either to bad hearing or an intentional alteration. And to end, they note:

> It is however equally likely that the alteration was due to Muḥammad's informant, who may have been moved by some superstitious consideration.[79]

Here is something new! Then, it must have been Muḥammad's teacher who would have altered the term in this way, and not the Prophet himself. One cannot obviously pose here the entangled problem of Muḥammad's mentor. Let us be content to say that if this person had existed, and there is a strong chance that he did, he must have been a foreigner, an *'a'ǧamī,* by the Koran's[80] own admission: a non-Arab Christian, or an Arab speaking a non-Meccan dialect and who was betrayed by his accent. An Abyssinian? Or rather a Syrian from Mesopotamia, such as Ṣuhayb ar-Rūmī, or this Diḥya ibn Ḫalīfa, merchant of Byzantine lime oil whose secret talks with Muḥammad and the elegant manners would have made him to be taken for Archangel Gabriel by the Companions of the Prophet? Or these two slaves of 'Ayn al-Tamar, Ǧabr and Yasār, who used to read the Torah and the Gospel, and whom Muḥammad used to enjoy listening to? Or again the celebrated Kalbi of Dūmat-al-Ǧandal where Christian influence had made many disciples, one Zayd ibn Ḥāriṯa, whose son, an African black, Usāma was called ḥibb ibn ḥibb Rasūl Allah ("beloved son of the beloved of the Messenger of God")? The influence of the latter on Muḥammad was from early on considerable. One of these people, whose identity has not been revealed, but whose maternal dialect was surely not Qurayshite, must have transliterated, as best as he could, the Syriac name of Jesus into Arabic.

Fraenkel[81] had equally suggested that the term *ʿĪsā* could have been formed by the Christian Arabs themselves before Muḥammad, starting from the word *Yéšūʿ*, which is the Jacobite pronunciation. One would then explain the falling off of the final *ʿayn* by its absence in the form *Yéšū* of the Manichaean and Ancient Jewish documents, among which one finds *Yéšū* for *Yéšūʿ*. And conversely, the presence of the *ʿayn* at the beginning is explained by the fact that Arabic frequently uses the initial *ʿayn* in Arabized words borrowed from Aramaic. Vollers provides numerous examples that allow one to support this opinion.[82]

For Derenbourg,

> in Galilee where the guttural letters become confused and were disregarded, *Yéšūʿ* easily became *Yéšū*. The Arabs do not much like to end words by a silent *wāw* and readily replace this letter by a *yōd*; if one assumes that they had made this change, that they besides propped up the *yōd* by an *alif*, one obtains *ʾĪsā*, and then *ʿĪsā*, by the ease with which such an *alif* swaps with *ʿayin*. Examples of such a change are abundant in Aramaic and it is from that side that the Christian legend had come to Muḥammad… Perhaps *Yéšūʿ*, read in the Western manner, produced ʿĪsā.[83]

***

Let us sum up: the explanations proposed by the Muslim authors are not, apart from the one by Ibn ʿArabī, of any help in finding a solution to the problem. Besides the epigraphic documents which could have been of decisive importance were revealed, by their meagreness and uncertainty, to be, in fact, unhelpful in bringing the debate to a close, while the masterpieces of Pre-Islamic Arabic literature, already discredited by science, only present a few rare examples whose fraudulent nature is easy to unmask, at the very least in the form they have been presented. On the other hand, the Jewish origin of the term, which has had quite a success among the orientalists, does not have much chance of being true. However seductive it may be in many respects, it cannot withstand a rigorous historical and psychological critique of the Prophet. The objections which it raises are too serious for us to be able to support it firmly.

Only the resort to the popular Christian Syriac tradition can in all likelihood dissolve the difficulty. It is either from the Nestorian pronunciation or that of the Jacobites, that one can still be on the track to a probable solution. The *ʾIšōʿ* of the Nestorian form must have at first lost its final *ʿayn* to become *Išō*; then the final *wāw* became an *alif* to form *ʾIšā*. It is this *ʾIšā* which enriches itself with an initial *ʿayn*, the very one that it had been unburdened with en route. Thus we have *ʿIšā-ʿĪsā*.[84]

The deformation starting with the Jacobite pronunciation following the same linguistic process described above, leads from *Yéšūʿ* to *Yéšū*, then Yéšā and finally *ʿIšā-ʿĪsā*. One must note that these successive passages of one form into another do not constitute exceptional cases artificially invented for the needs of the cause. The rules of grammar explain them and numerous examples bear witness to them. There is no need to have recourse then to this question of consonance with *Mūsā* on which one has insisted so much and which is totally superfluous. This is likewise to say that we do not subscribe to the opinion according to which the term *ʿĪsā* had been invented by Muḥammad himself. Even if the Pre-Islamic documents do not reveal any absolutely probative evidence on this subject, it highly likely that there was a Christian or rather Christians at the foundation of this deformation; however it is in fact impossible to decide to which denomination these Christians belonged.

Meanwhile let us note, for the precious parallelism that it allows to establish, the Mandean manner of writing the name of Jesus: *ʿSw*, which was discussed above. For one can notice that another inscription found at Ḥarrān gives *Yḥw* for John the Baptist[85], who the Koran calls *Yaḥyā*. From *ʿSw* to *ʿĪsā* and from *Yḥw* to *Yaḥyā*, the parallelism is striking, as much for the original transcription as for the deformation at which we arrived. The term *Yaḥyā* had already been discovered on a Pre-Islamic graffito dating from 306, at al-ʿUla, among the Nabataean Christians[86]. Would this *Yaḥyā* have, still at this level, a mission of the Precursor [or Forerunner of the Lord]? Then all hope of finding the name of his cousin, a Pre-Islamic *ʿĪsā*, is not lost. The Thamudic inscription that Littmann has already described to us gives us at least an early warning sign, if, in reality, it has not already given it to us, as we are personally inclined to think.

***

The particular problem of the origin of the name of Jesus fits into a much larger context, which is the entirety of the religious terminology of the Koran. Between the latter and the Pre-Islamic Arabic literature, "light and impious," according to Renan, there has to be a solution of continuity. It looks like spontaneous generation. The Muslim authors, resolving the problems before having posed them scientifically, have recourse to a solution of a dictated inspiration. They meanwhile suggest the importance of Ḥanifites among whom the ideas and religious vocabulary of Judaeo-Christianity had been welcomed, in order to be "adapted to Arab taste."

The terrain thus was already prepared in a certain manner that the Muslims exploited in the sense of a *praeparatio islamica*, parallel to the *praeparatio evangelica*. The organisational genius of Muḥammad had succeeded in this fusion of heterogeneous and disparate elements collected together by his predecessors or contemporaries and resulted in, through tentative procedures, of inquiries and corrections, the creation of an original religion, Islam.

For the solution of the present problem, the Christians on their side had always had recourse to an informer X, placed next to the Prophet "to give him the details of the Prophetic writings, night and day," as the Koran itself puts it; and with these writings the expressions themselves were passed into a halting and clumsy Arabic. There again we re-encounter the genius of Muḥammad who had known how to give an authentically Arab stamp to these writings and terms.

Nevertheless there is already an impression that clearly disentangles itself from this ensemble, and which has become more precise since *Der Ursprung des Islams und das Christentums* [The Origins of Islam and Christianity] (1926) of Tor Andrae, and in proportion as the Syriac Patrology gave up something of its mystery. Muḥammad seems dependent, as much in his religious conceptions as in his technical vocabulary, on diffused, sporadic Christianity, taken to Arabia by "humble people," to whom he owed his first sympathies, wine and oil merchants from Syria, slaves, mercenaries, installer of airvents from Abyssinia, transplanted from their localities of origin, near the bourgeois of Mecca. They had been the vehicles of their naïve religiosity, in this Arabia whose language they had learnt so badly, creating a vernacular which resembled more of a pidgin language. To names already deformed of their Biblical characters, they must have added this monstrous deformation, the Koranic name of "the most beautiful of the children of men," to the most disfigured face of all, *ʿĪsā*, Jesus.

2. The Term *al-Masīḥ* (Christ)

With *ʿĪsā* whose origin we previously discussed in Part I above,[87] the Koran mentions *al-Masīḥ,* the term which Arabic-speaking Christians had always used to designate Christ. Although its precise provenance is almost as uncertain as that of *ʿĪsā,* this term nevertheless presents an aspect less complex. Sure and numerous facts allow us to confirm that it was not a complete fabrication of the Prophet, but rather that he must have received it as such.

Al-Masīḥ appears late in the Koran, always accompanied by the definite article *al.* At Mecca where however a certain Christology had developed, no literal mention is ever made of *Al-Masīḥ.* It is only in Medina that the term appears for the first time, at a date which would be difficult to state precisely, but which could not have been later than Muḥammad's rupture with the Jews, that is to say before the seventeenth or eighteenth month of the Hiǧra.[88] During the Medinan period which was spread over about ten years, *al-Masīḥ* is cited twelve times. It is used three times on its own.[89] On five other occasions, it is cited as *Al-Masīḥ ibn Maryam.*[90] It was finally attached to *ʿĪsā ibn Maryam* to form, in three places quite close in date and inspiration,[91] a complete title.

The question of the origin of the term arises here as with *ʿĪsā*, and the same enquiry asserts itself across the same fields of investigations. For, let us say it straightaway, the means for the solution are here more efficacious, and the results to which they lead us seem, at least in part, more substantial.

2.1 Pre-Islamic Sources

In fact the epigraphic documents are less silent on this point. Glaser, the celebrated explorer of southern Arabia, provides us the proof with a Christian inscription entirely trinitarian, dated to 542, where it is a question of

> the power, the grace and compassion of He who has pity for all, and His Messiah and the Holy Spirit.

Here is the transcription and translation reconstituted by Glaser:

> *bhīl wdʾ wrḥmt Rḥm kl w-Mšḥhw w-Rḥ ds*: in der Kraft und der (Gn)nade und der Barmherzigkeit des Allbarnherz(gen) und seines Massias un der heiligen Geistes.[92]

This epigraphic clue gives hope of other evidence more direct in favor of a Pre-Islamic Christian origin of the term *Al-Masīḥ*. In fact, the Arabic poetry of the Ğāhiliyya confirms it. What is the exact situation?

Let us first of all put to one side the two eschatological verses attributed to the famous and unavoidable *Umayya ibn abī ṣ-Ṣalt*. There he alludes to a time when Christians met Christ of the Parousia [the Second Coming]: *aiyāma yalqā naṣārāhum Masīḥahumū.*[93] The other, of which the lexicon *Lisān al-ʿArab* only gives a hemistich without mentioning the author, also makes an allusion to Christ of the Parousia killing the False-Messiah: *iḏ yaqtulu-l-Masīḥu-l-Masīḥā.*[94] The discredit which weighs on the presumed author of the first verse, like the uncertitude of the second, leave one skeptical about the authenticity of these two texts, which moreover, have the odor of the rhyming forger in light of the apocalyptical preoccupations of later Islam. One must also consider as apocryphal the verse in which the Jewish poet as-Samawʾal (middle of the 6th century) also speaks of the "end of times when our Messiah has come…": *wafī āḫiri l-ayyāmi ğāʾa Masīḥunā…*[95]. If there is nothing to make us doubt the Jewish faith of this poet, it seems on the other hand certain that all the pieces that "allow us to conclude most definitely the Judaism of their author," must be taken to be inauthentic.[96]

More authentic, despite our uncertainty in being able to identify the author, is a verse attributed at one and the same time to ʿAmr ibn ʿAbd al-Ḥaqq, to ʿAmr ibn ʿAbd al-Ğinn,[97] to Aḫṭal, and to Aʿšā:

Wamā sabbaḥa-r-ruhbānu fī kulli bi'atin [98]
Abīla-l-abīlīna-l-Masīḥa-bna Maryama.[99]
As long as the monks will sing the praises, in all churches, of the monk par excellence, Christ son of Mary.

The first two authors can certainly not claim paternity of this verse. Moreover, concerning the two called *'Amr ibn 'Abd*, there must have been confusion between *Ḥaqq* and *Ǧinn*. The literary ownership should rather be disputed between the two others. There is meanwhile every chance that it is not Aḫṭal, because of what we know of his attachment to his religion: he could not have at the Umayyad court, in front of Muslims, have preached a sermon in the name of pagan deities, 'Uzzā et Nasr,[100] who are mentioned in the verse immediately preceding this one. The presence here of these deities and the fact that Ibn al-Kalbi in his *Kitāb al-Aṣnām* claims not to know of a poem mentioning the god Nasr, had pushed Wellhausen to reject the authenticity of the verse.[101] Horovitz, for the same reasons, feels he has at least to doubt it.[102] We find there on the contrary the principal reason for its authenticity and particularly of its attribution to A'šā. In fact this verse is typical of the religiosity of this attractive poet seduced as much by the "bottle" as by the prayerful atmosphere of the monks. Often he evokes in the same verse

the clear cup like the eye of the cock that he swallows early in the morning, at the hour when one sounds the wooden clacks [Simandres].[103]

Elsewhere, he describes the Last Supper in a Bacchic context and speaks of this

red wine that the monk carries in procession. . . in a glass that he places in front of him, full of desire, and over which he prays.[104]

He often alludes to these monks whom he designates as here by the term *abīlīn*,[105] and whom he must have encountered during his travels

in search of fortune, between Oman, Emessa, Jerusalem, the court of Negus, the land of the Nabataeans and those of the Persians.[106]

One must note that this term *abīl*, which is of Syriac origin and which means "mourning monk" [weeping monk], would be taken up by the later tradition of Islam to designate Jesus and his the gift of tears" (*charisma tōn dakyrōn*; *French: charisme de larmes*)[107]

There is another verse of Ḥassān ibn Ṯābit, the poet who sang Muḥammad's praise and wrote satires against his detractors. This verse is to be found in a poem on the Christian Ghassanids:

Ṣalawātu-l-Masīḥi fī ḏālika-d-dayri du'ā'u-l-qissīsi war-ruhbānī[108]
The prayers of Christ in this monastery, invocations of priests and monks.

This verse is probably inauthentic. For a start, it is missing from the poet's diwān, and ought to be considered a later interpolation.[109]

Pre-Islamic onomastics is less disappointing than the poetry. A number of proper names composed of *ʿAbd al-Masīḥ* are borne by a number of people but they are not all certain. Ibn al-Aṯīr, Ibn Ḫaldūn, Abū-l-Fidā mention a ʿAbd al-Maṣīḥ, as the sixth king of Mecca, of the Second Jurhumites.[110] There was another *ʿAbd al-Masīḥ* ibn ʿAmr ibn Baqīla who is mentioned among the *Muʿammirīn* by Siğistānī[111] and to whom Yāqūt[112] attributes the foundation of a monastery on the outskirts of Ḥīra; he must have refused to convert to Islam at the time of the conquest of Sawād (Iraq) by General Ḫālid; very old at that time, he met the latter and negotiated the conditions of the surrender.[113] The Murra tribe must have had among its poets a *ʿAbd al-Masīḥ ibn ʿAsala*[114] who however does not seem to have composed the three poems attributed to him by the Mufaḍḍalīyāt.[115] There is still another *ʿAbd al-Masīḥ*, one of the leading citizens of Nağrān, against whom Aʿšā pushed his camel:

> *Nazūru Yazīdan wa-*ʿAbd al-Masīḥi
> *Wa-Qaysan, wahum ḫayru arbābihā.*[116]

Ibn Saʿd makes him out to be a Kindite.[117]

The father of the poet Mutalammis would have borne the name *ʿAbd al-Masīḥ.*[118]

The distribution of these names in the different Christians tribes, the best known being those of Ḥīra, Ghassān, Nağrān, Kinda, invites on the other hand caution; or one would be tempted to see behind these names, not the face of particular people, but of types representative of Arab Christianity in the various corners of Arabia where it had exercised its influence before Islam. Moreover, the uncertitude that surrounds the precise allocation of places eventually casts doubt on the persons themselves. However, we are not justified for all that to reject entirely their historicity. Nothing speaks, for example, against the verse of al-Aʿšā who, one knows, moreover frequented the court of the Lakhmids and the city of Nağrān; he recounts consequently names which he must have known personally and which must have been borne by Christian Arabs, in the same manner that their co-religionists of the Syriac language were called *ʿAbd Yéšūʿ.* Without being able to say precisely from which corner of Arabia the word *al-Masīḥ* came to the ears of the Prophet, we are on the other hand largely justified in thinking it of Christian origin.

Is there a question of an Ethiopian intermediary, since the word is current in Ethiopian?

Horovitz has come round to this opinion,[119] or at least not to exclude it. If an Ethiopian origin can be explained by the emigration of the first Muslim believers to Abyssinia, it woud no longer explain then the late appearance of the term in Medina, in approximately 624; this date also eliminates the possibility of making *Masīḥ* an import due to the Emigrants, since the latter are not supposed to have returned to Medina before 628. Unless one thinks that this mention has no connection to the emigration, but that it was due to some encounter with the Abyssinians settled in Medina, which is possible.

We should prefer to come back to a Syriac origin which is, besides, the root of the Ethiopian word, as much as of the Armenian, of the Manichean,[120] of the Pahlavi.[121] We think that the word *Mšīḥā* or *Mšīḥo* in Syriac has been arabized into *Mašīḥ* and was taken as the baptism name by the Arab Christians before Islam, and that it is from this quarter that Muḥammad picked it up.

Certain authors have, however, wished to trace it back to a Jewish source. Such was the opinion of Hirschfeld[122] who supposes an Aramaic intermediary, *Mšīḥā* commonly used by Jews as a title of the awaited savior. Wensinck[123] inclines rather to a Hebrew origin which seems to him more probable. For Pautz[124] also, and even more firmly for Sayous,

> the form Macih (sic) comes directly from the Hebrew.[125]

In the two cases, whether it is a question of Hebrew or of Aramaic, it would have been Jewish influence that would have prevailed. Muḥammad would have picked it up from the Jews of Medina. The proof would be the appearance of the word in this town. If in addition one takes into account the fact that the term appears precisely at the time of the difficulties with the Jews, one assumes that Muḥammad had wanted to taunt his enemies, while recognizing thus against them, along with the Christians, the Messianic character of Jesus.

It would be difficult to accept this argument. Let us note first of all that the silence of the Meccan period does not necessarily indicate ignorance. Moreover, one notices that nowhere in the Koran is there a question of polemics with the Jews on the subject of the Messianism of Jesus; polemic would rather concern the fact of the Crucifixion that the Prophet denied as against the Jews who prided themselves on it.[126] He does not seem to be able to choose neatly between the Jews and Christians, there was disagreement on this precise point which brought into play the whole meaning of the Scriptures. He knows for certain that the Jews loved to live the longest time possible, around a thousand years[127]; and, without suspecting that there was behind this wish an intense Messianic desire, he attributes it rather to their love of life of the world. When he himself uses the term, he considers it more as a *kunya* than as a proper name. For, although he recognizes in Jesus the Messenger of God to the Israelites, for him *al-Mašīḥ* seems to have more the sense of "Christ" than of "Messiah,"[128] as the commentators and mystics would explain it later on. Besides it seems unlikely that the Jews of Medina would have applied the title of Messiah, except out of derision, to Jesus, with which they had, according to the Koran 4:156, calumniated the mother, and they prided themselves of having put him on the cross.

It is much simpler to think that the word whose Syriac origin is not in doubt[129] had spread among the Arabs before Muḥammad. The *Mšīḥā* or *Mšīḥo* of the Nestorians and Jacobites had been translated into Arabic by *Mašīḥ* to which the definite article *al* was added each time in Arabic where the title, applied to a man, ended by supplanting the name itself of the individual in question, thus al-Aʿšā (the Blind), al-Muhalhil, al-Mutanabbī, et al. According to the poetry and Pre-Islamic Arab onomastic, this *al-Mašīḥ* had been borne by Christian Arabs; now, the latter had been evangelized by the Syrians. In the North and South of Arabia[130] where they were widely prevalent, the ancient ʿAbd al-ʿUzzā had become through baptism ʿAbd al-Mašīḥ, as was the case of the poet Mutalammis who was called *Ibn ʿAbd al-Mašīḥ ibnʿAbd al-ʿUzzā.*

2.2 The Islamic Documents

It remains to be seen as to what origin Islam has given this term, and in what manner it has understood it. Faithful to their doctrine and their methods of exegesis which we discussed above, the Muslim authors should have encountered fewer difficulties here than on the question of *ʿĪsā* to bring round *al-Mašīḥ* to a really Arabic origin. Certain among them, it is true, recognized the foreign origin of the word. Thus Abū ʿUbayd thinks that it derives from the Syriac *Mašīḥā.*[131] Others more numerous, such as Ibrāhīm an-Naḫaʿī, al-Aṣmaʿī, Ibn al-Aʿrābī, Ibn Sīdah, Ibn al-Hayṯam, derive it from the Hebrew *Mašīḥā* (as in Syriac) which they explain either by "just" (*ṣiddīq*),[132] or by "blessed" (*mubārak*).[133] It is thus supposed to have been "arabized by the Arabs" (*ʿarrabathu l-ʿArab*), becoming in this way authentic Arabic patrimony, in order for the Koran to owe nothing to earlier revelations. It is therefore in referring to the resources of their language that our authors looked to find a sense for the term *al-Mašīḥ*. An entire literature was to come out of it, resulting in all at once the possibilities of Arabic philology as well as ascetic and mystical considerations resulting from the contacts of Islam with Christian monachism of ancient Syria.

In bringing round *al-Mašīḥ* to an Arabic root, the lexicographers and Muslim commentators ended in multiple interpretations, sometimes contradictory. For the related words or words derived from the same root are numerous; it would be interesting to draw up an inventory, as exhaustive as possible.

Murtaḍā[134] gets us on the way when he claims to have assembled fifty different opinions concerning the derivation of *Mašīḥ,* in his

"Commentary"[135] of a work by Ṣaġātī.[136] He adds that Ibn Diḥyah[137] remained on this side of this impressive figure, in only transmitting twenty three opinions, but as for al-Muṣannif,[138] he beat all records in discovering fifty six different interpretations.

It would be obviously tedious to lay out these points of view according to the divisions adopted by our authors. One could rather group them by starting with the two principal roots which have helped in their derivation. Let us first eliminate the least customary interpretations as not being representative enough of the traditional exegesis:

1. Munḍirī derives *Mašīḥ* from the verb *masaḥa* and explains the latter word as meaning "to create" (*ḫalaqa*). He rejects all other possible senses and declares that if Jesus is called *Mašīḥ* it is because God "created him from a beautiful and blessed creation, like he created the Antichrist from an ugly and cursed creation."[139]
2. Ibn ʿAbbas, and Ibn as-Sayyid in his *Farq*, lean towards the sense of *mašīḥat* which signifies "piece of silver" to indicate that Jesus was called *Mašīḥ* because of the beauty of his face which was as pure as a piece of silver.[140]
3. It is said (*qīla*) that he was so called because his feet were without toes (*amsaḥ ar-riǧl*).[141] This interpretation is not without link to the feat frequently reported that makes Jesus walk on water.
4. It is this link that ʿAynī in his *Tafsīr* established between the term *Mašīḥ* and the walk on the water.[142]
5. Passing from feet to the head, Rāġib, as well as Azhari and Abū ʿUbayd, translate *Mašīḥ* by "one-eyed," and specifying that it concerned the right eye, in contrast to the False Messiah (*Daǧǧāl*) who will be one-eyed but of the left one (*amsah al-ʿayn al-yusrā*). These details have a hortatory intent for the usage of the believers so that they know how to distinguish, at the end of times, the True (*Ṣiddīq*) Messiah from the False (*Kaḏḏāb Daǧǧāl*). For there are two Messiahs, the one which guides (*hudā*), and the other which leads astray (*ḍalālat*).[143] This explanation, which perhaps translates the preoccupations of the Prophet himself, and more certainly those of later Islam, take up very large parts in the collection of the ḥadiths.[144]
6. Another (*ġayruhu*) says that the term *mašīḥ* signifies "sweat" (*ʿaraq*),[145] probably because the Christ was represented as a pilgrim constantly travelling, as we shall see below.
7. Another [146]says that it signifies "donkey-driver" (*mukārī*), without further details. Could there be here some recollection of Christ of Palms[147] entering Jerusalem on the back of a donkey?[148] He would be more likely to think of the sense of "dyer" (*makara* signifying *ṣabaġa*), in remembrance of the tale to which the Muslim story-

tellers come back constantly: Jesus, still a child, apprenticed to a professional dyer, puts all the clothes to be dyed various colors in a liquid of a single color; in taking them out, each item of clothing had already received the tint desired by its owner.[149]

8. Al-Muṣannif[150] starts from the sense of *mašīḥat* that we have translated by piece of silver and which signifies here "the equilibrium of forces" (*quwā ğaïyda*). Jesus would thus have been called *Mašīḥ* because of "his force, his vigor, his equilibrium and his average height" (hence balanced). There would be there once again a reminiscence of the Muslim Christ of the Parousia who the Prophet would have described as being *marbūʻ*, "neither big, nor small, stocky, average."[151]
9. And finally, someone[152] said that *al-Mašīḥ* signified "the King" (al-Malik). This interpretation, little found among the Muslim authors, comes back to the fundamental meaning in the Old Testament; here it concerns a title making an allusion to Royal Unction that should have been applied to the Expected Messiah and whose signboard on the Cross carried the fulfilment: "Jesus of Nazareth, King of the Jews," anointed by his own blood.[153]
10. Rāģib in his *Mufradāt* links *Mašīḥ* to the verb *masaḥa* whose meaning is "to clean," "to wipe," "to scrape." Thus Jesus is *mašīḥ* because he has been "purified of blameworthy qualities, such as ignorance, gluttony, avarice and all other reproachable habits, in the same manner that the False Messiah has been depurated of praiseworthy habits."[154] It is in this way that Islam has represented Jesus: a model of poverty, of renunciation, of asceticism, he had achieved true knowldege, the gnosis in the manner of the mystics.

This last interpretation of the word leads to the most common meanings given by the Muslim authors for the word *al-Masīḥ*. One will find the systematic exposé of their points of view, either in the commentaries to Koran 3:45, when they are exegetes, or, when they are lexicographers, in the great dictionaries under the root *masaḥa* and *sāḥa* (*sayaḥa*). Thus one will have two groups of interpretations whose starting point is purely Arabic, and which were not without determining, at least in part, the representation of the career of Christ, in Late Islam.

A first group refers to the sense of the verb *sāḥa* which means "to peregrinate," "travel." One would thus say that Jesus was named *Al-Masīḥ* because he was a pilgrim, always travelling with his longing for God, to the extent that he had become the prototype, the "Chief of the Wanderers" (*Imām as-Sā'iḥīn*). Thus Ṭabarī, Bayḍāwi, Rāzī, Zamaḫšarī, Murtaḍā, Ibn Manẓur[155] and others gather, some from Ibn as-Saïyd, some from Ibn Sīdah, some from Aḥmad ibn Yaḥya, some from Ibn ʿAbbās himself et al…, that Jesus travelled incessantly, was the wanderer par excellence, which merited him this title. The authors of "Lives of the Prophets," like those of the great mystical treatises, would insist on this characteristic which was, according to them, the charism proper to Jesus. Already since his childhood, he was traveling with his mother (allusion to the Flight to Egypt); and it was during the course of these travels that the Prophetologists situate a group of marvels reproduced, most of the time from Apocryphal Infancy Gospels. We have published elsewhere all the texts of these stories.[156]

When he had grown up, Jesus still travelled across the solitudes of the deserts. We find him wandering alone, sometimes accompanied by his cousin John the Baptist with whom he competed for asceticism, often with his disciples to whom he related minutely lessons of poverty and renunciation. Satan came sometimes to tempt him, and God did not cease to speak to him, by a mysterious voice heard in the bottom of his heart. And everywhere he went, he sowed marvels, those that the Koran has mentioned and those that the popular and mystical tradition has multiplied indefinitely. In summary one can say with Huğwīrī[157] and Ibn ʿArabī[158] that, for the mystics, the special feature of Jesus was to wander incessantly, as that of Abraham was hospitality, and so forth, each Prophet being in possession of his own charism.

Another group of explanations refers to the verb *masaḥa* from which *Masīḥ* is said to have been derived. *Masaḥa* which we have already seen, could mean "to wipe," "to forget the past," or "to graze or skim the ground, space," (*masāḥat*), "to survey (land)." It is in this sense that Jesus had been called *Masīḥ*, that is to say a wandering pilgrim, as we explained earlier. However *masaḥa* means equally "to anoint," and it is to this last sense that the Muslim authors still accord an obvious preference, drawing on besides the venerable authorities of the apostolic age. The form *masīḥ* can perhaps be interpreted in the passive or active sense, as a present participle or a past participle. Our authors do not hesitate to exploit this double possibility. *Masīḥ* could be at the same time someone who is anointed and someone who anoints.

In the passive sense, Jesus is *al-Masīḥ* for several reasons:

1. Either because he was, like all men anointed by Allah who passed his hand over the loins of Adam to summon his descendants. Since Allah does not put Jesus back into the loins of a common father, according to the Primordial Pact,[159] but keeps him outside the generations, "to throw" him, at the designated time, directly into the womb of Mary, this exception marks him out as the Anointed par excellence.[160]
2. Or because he was anointed by consecrated oil with which only Prophets were anointed.[161]

3. Or because he was born anointed, or was anointed as soon as he was born.[162]
4. Or, more precisely, because at his birth he was "grazed" (*masaḥaḥu*) by the wing of the Angel Gabriel, who thus protected him against the bite of Satan who "nipped all first-born in the cradle."[163]
5. Or because Zachariah, Mary's guardian in the temple, had anointed him at his birth which is a point of view discarded by Abū Manṣūr.[164]
6. Or because he was "purified" (*musiḥat ʿanhu*) of the bad forces, to be anointed for the blessings, all the grace and all the honors.[165]

As a subject of unction, in the active sense of the term *masīḥ*, we see Jesus administring to others this rite of anointing of which he himself was favored:

1. Because he had never anointed, by passing a hand over, a sick person, without the latter being healed instantly. Examples of this kind of miracles abound in his career as a thaumaturge or wonder-worker.
2. More precisely he passed his hand over people born blind and on lepers to heal them. Already the Koran mentions the wonders worked in favor of this double category of the sick.[166]
3. Because he anointed the head of orphans thus consecrating them to Allah.[167]
4. Finally it is remarked that Jesus, during his parousia, encountered a group of final believers having taken refuge in Jerusalem under the terror of the Antichrist; he "wiped from their faces" (*yamsaḥu ʿan wuǧūhihim*) the sweat of fear or the dust of the flight.[168]

The sources of these interpretations are too obvious for it to be necessary to dwell on it for too long. In referring, on the one hand, to the Koranic text as well as the evangelical rudiments found in the Apocrypha, the Muslim authors commandeered all these elements in the service of their philology. On the other hand, determined by the basic presuppositions according to which the Koran contains only Arabic or arabized words, they start from the two verbs *masaḥa* and *sāḥa* to find confirmation of that which they already know of the life of Christ; if necessary they make up stories to serve their arguments in favor of their philological principles. In re-uniting them, the two philological schemes or procedures could only be in agreement to reinforce each other. But this agreement turns out to be more forced than re-inforced and, from this fact, it establishes between it and rigorous science a fundamental discord.

However to be just one should note the difference which exists between the Commentators, Lexicographers, and Authors of Lives of Prophets, and even between the Commentators themselves. The latter on the whole realize that the term *al-Masīḥ* is of foreign origin, but the only way they can express it is by saying "Syriac" and "Hebrew." Some among them such as Baḍāwī[169] and Zamaḫšarī[170] ridicule those of their predecessors or contemporaries who want at all cost to attempt the impossible in looking to derive *Masīḥ* from an Arabic root, without any other reference. The solution adopted by Rāzī as being that of the majority of the Commentators is that which conforms the most to historical truth: *Masīḥ,* it claims, is of Hebrew origin—we would say straightaway Syriac; the word was adopted by the Arabs who arabized it, before Islam, we would add.

It is obvious that none of these authors would dream of telling us from whom the Prophet picked up this term, nor how he himself understood it. What he understood by *Masīḥ* is nowhere explicitly explained in the Koran and remains unexplained in the exegetical tradition of Islam after him.

3. Bibliography

NB. Only those works which have been cited more than once during the course of this study will appear in this list. For the others, as well as the articles from journals, the bibliographical details will be provided *in loco.*

Due to a lack of the required typographical conditions, it was not possible to reproduce the Arabic, Hebrew or Syriac words in their proper characters. For the Koran, we have used the Cairo edition of 1358 AH.

Abū Nu'aym, *Ḥilyat al-Awliyā*, 10 vols. (Cairo, 1932–1938).

Aġānī, *Kitāb al-Aġānī*, 1st ed., Būlāq, 1285; 20 vols., with a vol. of index by R. E. Brünnow (Leiden, 1305/1888).

K. Ahrens, "Christliches im Qoran," *ZDMG*, LXXXXIV, 1930, 15–68, 148–190.

Tor Andrae, "Der Ursprung des Islams und das Christentum," *Kyrkhistorisk årsskrift* 23, 1923, 149–206; 24, 1924, 213–25; 25, 1925, 45–112. (Uppsala and Stockholm); *Les origines de l'islam et le christianisme,* trans. J. Roche. (Paris: Adrien-Maisonneuve, 1955).

Balāḏurī, *Futūḥ al-Buldān*, ed. Raḍwān (Cairo, 1959).

Bayḍāwī, *Anwār al-Tanzīl wa-Asrār al-Ta'wīl*, 2 vols. (Cairo, 1355 AH).

R. Blachère, *Le Coran*, 3 vols., (Paris: Maisonneuve, 1947–1951).

Buḫārī, *Al-Jāmi' aṣ-Ṣaḥīḥ*, 8 vols. (Būlāq, 1296 AH).

L. Caetani, *Annali dell'Islam*, 10 vols. (Milan, 1905–1926).

L. Cheikho, *An-Naṣrānīya wa-'āḏābuhā qabl-al-Islām* (Beyrouth, 1912–1923); cited as "Le Christianisme."

Id. – *Šu'arā an-Naṣrānīya qabl-al-Islām*, 6 part., Beyrouth, 1890–1891.

Dvorak, R., *Uber die Fremdwörter im Qur'ān*, Munich, 1884, cited as "Fremdwörter."

Fraenkel, S., *De vocabulis in antiquis Arabum carminibus et in Corano peregris*. Leiden, 1880.
Id., *Die aramäischen Fremdwörter in Arabischen* (Leiden, 1886).
Ġazālī, *Iḥyā 'Ulūm ad-Dīn*, 4 vols. (Cairo, 1312 AH).
Ǧawaharī, *As-Siḥāḥ*, 2 vols. (Cairo, 1296 AH).
Ḫafāǧī, *Šifā al-ġalīl fī mā fī kalām al-ʿArab min-as-daḫil* (Cairo, 1325 AH), cited as "Šifā."
Ḥalabī, *As-Sīra al-ḥalabīya*, 2 vols. (Cairo, 1349 AH).
M. Hayek, *Le Christ de l'Islam* (Paris, 1959).
Id., *Al-Masīḥ fīl-Islām*, 2nd edn. (Beyrouth, 1961).
H. Hirschfeld, *Beiträge zur Erklärung des Qur'āns* (Leipzig, 1886).
J. Horovitz, *Qur'ānische Untersuchungen* (Berlin and Leipzig, 1926).
Ibn ʿArabī, *Muḥādrat al-Abrār wa-musāmarat al-Aḫyār. . .*, 2 vols. (Cairo, 1305 AH).
Ibn Aṯīr, *Al-Kāmil fi-t-Tārīḫ*, ed. C. J. Tornberg, 14 vols., (Leiden, 1851–76); corrected repr. 13 vols., (Beirut 1385–7/1965–7).
Ibn Ḥanbal, *Musnad*, 6 vols., (Cairo, 1313 AH).
Ibn Hišām, *Das Leben Muḥammad's nach Muḥammad Ibn Ishaq bearbeitet von A.-M. Ibn Hischam*, 2. vols., ed. F. Wüstenfeld (Göttingen, 1858–1860).
Ibn Ḫallikān, *Wafayāt al-aʿyān wa-anbā' al-zamān*, ed. F.Wüstenfeld, 4 vols. (Göttingen 1835–50).
Ibn Manẓūr, *Lisān al-ʿArab*, 20 vols. (Cairo, 1299–1308 AH).
Ibn an-Nadīm, *Kitāb al-Fihrist*, ed. G. Flügel (Leipzig, 1874).
Ibn Sa'd, *Kitāb at-Ṭabaqāt al-kabīr*, ed. H. Sachau et al. (Leiden, 1905–40).
Antonin Jaussen and Raphaël Savignac, *Mission archéologique en Arabie*, 3 vols. (Paris: Leroux/Geuthner, 1909–1922).
A. Jeffery, *The Foreign Vocabulary of the Qur'ān* (Baroda, 1938).
P. de Largarde, *Übersicht über die Bildung der Nomina* (Göttingen, 1889).
H. Lammens, *L'Arabie occidentale à la veille de l'hégire* (Beyrouth, 1928).
Makkī, *Qūt al-Qulūb fī muʿāmalat al-Maḥbūb*, 2 vols. (Cairo, 1932/1351 AH).
L. Marraccius, *Prodromus ad refutationem Alcorani; Refutatio Alcorani*; 4 vols. (Rome and Padua, 1691, 1698).
A. Mingana, "Syriac Influence on the Style of the Ku'ran," *Bulletin of the John Rylands Library* 11 (1927): 77–98, also in Ibn Warraq, ed., *What the Koran Really Says: Language, Text, and Commentary* (Amherst, NY: Prometheus Books, 2002), pp. 171–192.
Murtaḍā, *Tāǧ al-ʿArūs*, 10 vols. (Cairo, 1307 AH), cited as "Tāǧ."
Muslim, *As-Saḥīḥ*, 2 vols. (Cairo, 1290).
C. A. Nallino, *Chrestomathia Qorani arabica* (Leipzig, 1892).

Nawawī, *Tahḏīb al-asmā'*, ed. F. Wüstenfeld (Göttingen, 1842–1847), cited as "Tahḏīb."
T. Nöldeke, *Mandaïsche Grammatik* (Halle, 1875).
Id., *Neue Beiträge zur semitischen Sprachwissenschaft* (Strasbourg, 1910).
O. Pautz, *Muhammeds Lehre von den Offenbarung* (Leipzig, 1898), cited as "Offenbarung."
Rāġib al-Iṣfahānī, *Al-Mufradāt fī ġarīb al-Qur'ān* (Cairo, 1324), cited as "Mufradāt."
Rāzī, *Mafātīḥ al-Ghayb*, 6 vols. (1862/1278 AH).
C. Conti Rossini, *Chrestomathia arabica meridionalis epigraphica*, with *Glossarium* (Rome, 1931), cited as "Glossarium."
G. Ryckmans, *Les Noms Propres sud-sémitiques*, I–III (Louvain, 1934–1935).
Suyūṭī, *Al-Itqān fī 'Ulum al-Qur'ān*, 2 vols. (Cairo, 1368 AH), cited as "Itqān."
E. Sayous, *Jésus-Christ d'après Mahomet* (Paris, 1880).
Sha'rānī, *Muḫtaṣar taḏkirat al-Imām al-Qurtubī* (Cairo, 1300 AH), cited as "Taḏkirat."
A. Sprenger, *Das Leben und die Lehre des Mohammad*, 3 vols. (Berlin, 1861–1865).
S. Sycz, *Ursprung und Wiedergabe der biblischen Eigennamen im Qoran* (Frankfurt, 1903), cited as "Biblischen Eigennamen."
Ṭabarī, *Ta'rīḫ al-rusul wa l-mulūk* (*Annales quos scripsit. . .aṭ-Ṭabarī.*), ed. M. J. de Goeje et al., 15 vols. (Leiden, 1879–1901).
Id., *Ǧāmi' al-bayān fī tafsīr al-Qur'ān*, 30 vols. (Cairo, 1323–1329 AH), quoted as "Tafsīr."
Ṯa'labī, *Qiṣaṣ al-Anbiyā* (Cairo, 1951/1370).
J. Wellhausen, *Reste arabischen Heidentums*, 2nd edn. (Berlin, 1897), cited as "Reste."
A. J. Wensinck, *Handbook of Early Mohammedan Tradition* (Leiden, 1927).
Yāqūt, *Mu'ǧam al-Buldān*, ed. F. Wüstenfeld, 6 vols. (Leipzig, 1866–1873).
Zabīdī, *Itḥāf as-Sādat al-Muttaqīn*,10 vols. (Cairo, 1311 AH), cited as "Itḥaf."
Zamaḫšarī, *Al-Kaššāf*, 2 vols. (Cairo, 1354 AH/1935).

Abbreviations of Names of Periodicals:

EI	Encyclopedia of Islam
MIDEO	Mélanges de l'Institut Dominicain d'Etudes Orientales du Caire
MW	The Moslem World
OED	Oxford English Dictionary
REJ	Revue des Etudes Juives
RSO	Revista degli Studi Orientali
WZKM	Wiener Zeitschrift für die Kunde des Morgenlandes
ZDMG	Zietschrift der Deutschen Morgenländischen Gesellschaft
ZDPV	Zeitschrift des Deutschen Palastinavereins

Notes

1 A. Jeffery, *Foreign Vocabulary of the Qur'an* (Baroda, 1938), p. 219.
2 Since 1942 [upto 1962, the date of Hayek's article], eight works by Muslim authors, of which seven are Egyptian, have appeared on Christ. See the reviews of four of them, by G. Anawati, in *MIDEO* [Mélanges de l'Institut dominicaine d'études orientales du Caire], vol. 2, 1955, p. 71 ff.; H. Teissier in *Cahiers religieux d'Afrique du Nord*, no. 10, Jan.–March 1959, p. 28 ff.; and especially, J. Jomier, in *MIDEO*, vol. 5, 1958, p. 367ff. All these authors use the form *'Īsā* for Jesus, and never use the Christian form *Yasū'*; with the exception of M. K. Hussayn, in his remarkable narrative *Qarya Zālima* (Cairo, 1954) (Eng. trans. by K. Cragg, *City of Wrong: A Friday in Jerusalem* [Amsterdam, 1959]), which avoids both terms by using only *al-Masīḥ*, "Christ:" this could only be intentional.
3 Koran 85: 22; cf. 3: 7 ; 13:39; 43:4.
4 Koran 4:46; 5:13, 41; cf. 2:75; the accusation of *taḥrīf*, alteration, levelled initially only at the Jews of Arabia did not concern the Biblical text strictly speaking, but its interpretation; it was abusively extended by later Islam to all Scriptures, Old and New Testament.
5 Suyūṭī, *Itqān*, pp. 136–137; see also similar assessments by a jurist such as Šāfi'ī, commentator such asṬabarī, a theologian such as Bāqillānī, et al.
6 See some examples in Ibn al-Nadīm, *Fihrist*, p. 53, 54; Ibn Ḫallikān, *Wafayāt*, III, p. 388; Nawawī, *Tahdīb*, p. 748; Anbāri, *Ṭabaqāt*, p. 137; Jawālīqī, *Mu'arrab*, p. 4; Ḫafāğī, *Šifā*, p. 3 relates that Ibn 'Abbās himself, who was the Prophet's cousin, known as an "ocean" of knowledge, "Rabbi of the Community," "Interpreter" of the Koran par execellence, as well as his disciples Muğāhid and 'Ikrima and many others affirmed that "several words in the Koran were foreign to the Arabic language."
7 Koran 12:2; 16:105; 26:195; 41:2, 44; 42:5; 43:2; 46:2.
8 Koran 16:105; 25:5; 44:13; see Dvorak, *Fremdwörter im Koran*, p. 5.
9 They explain then the fact that the first exegetes had recognized the existence of foreign words in the Koran by resorting to the incalculable richness of Arabic of which no human being was reputed to have known all the varieties; thus what they had recognized as foreign was in fact Arabic, but which was beyond the competence of these exegetes, Suyūṭī, *Itqān*, p. 137.
10 Ṭabarī is almost of this opinion, in his *Tafsīr*, I, p. 6–9; Suyūṭī typifies this position which ends with these extreme consequences; see *Itqān*, p. 137.
11 Suyūṭī, *Itqān*, p.138; "*inna hāḏihi-l-ḥurūf qad iḫtalaṭat bikalām-l-'Arab; fa-man qāla innahā 'arabīyat fahwa ṣādiq, waman qāla innahā a'ğamiyat fa-ṣādiq;*" that is exactly what is explained in Ğawālīqī, *Mu'arrab*, p. 5.
12 On all these questions see Jeffery, *Foreign Vocabulary*, Introduction. Note that his references to Suyūṭī are not exact.
13 This etymology has probably determined the description that the *ḥadīṯ* gives of Christ of the Parousia; he would be recognisable by his "reddish white color" (ilā-l-ḥumrat wal-bayāḍ); see Hayek, *Le Christ de l'Islam*, p. 248; id., *Al-Masīḥ fī-l-Islām*, p. 256, and the references.

14 Christ appears precisely in the writings of the Muslim authors of the Middle Ages as someone detached from all belongings, wandering in solitude; see Hayek, *Le Christ de l'Islam*, ch, VI; id., *Al-Masiḥ fī-l-Islām*, ch. VII. What is the link between this root *'awas* and the following *'aws*, and this representation of a wandering Christ? See rather below, Part II; to be noted equally is that the word *'ys* is the proper noun of a battle of the year 6 AH.

15 Ibn Manẓūr, *Lisān*, VIII, pp. 30–31; Rāġib, *Mufradāt*, 359; Murtaḍā, *Tāǧ*, IV, 199–200.

16 Ibn Manẓūr, ibid.; Murtaḍā, ibid.; Jawāliqī, *Mu'arrab*, p. 105; Ḫafājī, *Šifā*, p. 134; Jawharī, *Ṣiḥaḥ*, s.v.

17 Bayḍāwī, *Anwār*, I, p. 75; Zamaḫšari, *Kaššāf*, on Koran 3:40: *ka-l-rāqim fī-l-mā'*; Rāzī, *Mafātīḥ*, on Koran 3:40: *Lā yakūn lahu ištqāq*.

18 Goldziher, in *ZDMG*, XXVI, p. 774, citing Ibn 'Abd Rabbihi who said about a bad copyist: "When he had copied the same work twice it became Syriac": *kāna idā nasaḫa-l-kitāba marrataynī 'ada suryānīyan.*

19 The Hebrew gives *Yéšūa'*.

20 This apocryphal work was discovered by J. Galbiati, *Johannis Evangelium apocryphum arabice* (Milan, 1957).

21 Mayāmir Theodoros Abī Qorra, ed. C. Bacha (Beyrouth, 1904), pp. 104, 105; it should be noted that none of the other epistles name Yasū'; in the latter, it appears twice; were it inauthenic, it would be even more evident because of the style which differs from the others. Among the Muslims, only, as far as we know, Ibn 'Arabī († 1240) correctly cites Yasū', in *Muhādrat al-Abrār*, II, p. 50.

22 Murtaḍā, *Tāǧ*, V, p.390; Cheikho, *Christianisme*, p. 464.

23 Aġānī, XX, p. 128, a certain Sa'dān ibn 'Abd Yasū', and Qatāmī. XXVI, 4, cites a person of the Christian tribe of Taġlib called Abd Yasū'.

24 See the discussion in Horovitz, *Koranische Untersuchungen*, p. 129.

25 Related by Ibn 'Arabī, *Muḥādrat*, II, p. 50.

26 Excellent account by Lammens in EI, II, p.1228 who rejects in an exaggerated manner the historicity of this person; see Sprenger, *Das Leben* I, p. 102, ff.

27 85:36; 23:115; comp. 3:191; 38:27 (*bāṭilan*: in vain).

28 Aġānī, III, p.13; cf. Ibn Hišām, *Sīra*, pp. 143–144, 153–154, 205.

29 *Kitāb al-Bad'* (ed. C.Huart), III, p. 123.

30 4:172; 43:58; 2: 87, 253; 3:45; 4:157, 171; 5:46, 78, 110, 112, etc.

31 *Koranische Untersuchungen*, p. 128.

32 See Tor Andrae, *Les Origines de l'Islam*, p. 55.

33 G. Ryckmans. "Les inscriptions monothéistes sabéenes," in *Miscellanea historica in honorem Alberti de Meyer* (Recueil de travaux d'histoire et de philosophie de l'Université de Louvain, 3rd series, 22nd fascicule) (Louvain, 1946), p. 201.

34 F. V. Winett, "References to Jesus in Pre-Islamic Arabic Inscriptions," in *M. W.* XXXI (1941), pp. 341–353.

35 G. Ryckmans, *La mention de Jésus dans les inscriptions arabes préislamiques*, ap. Mélanges Paul Peeters, Analecta Bollandiana, LXVII (1949), pp. 63–73.

36 See [Enno Littman, "Jesus in a Pre-Islamic Arabic Inscription," in *Muslim World*, (January 1950, vol. 40, Issue 1, pp. 16–18]
"Mr. G. Lankaster Harding, Chief Curator of Antiquities Hashimite Kingdom of Jordan, kindly sent me copies of a little more than five hundred Thamudic

inscriptions. [...] It is the inscription [Harding No. 476] that interests us here. [...] Below the circle there are four letters: *a y, a sh, a c*, and again a *y*."

37 A. Van den Branden, "Une inscription thamoudéene (pseudo-chrétienne?"; in *Le Muséon*, LXIII (1950), pp. 47–51.

38 Ibid., p. 48

39 Ibid., pp. 50–51.

40 Ibid., p. 48

41 Ibid., pp. 49–50

42 Ibid., pp. 49, 51.

43 Horovitz, *Koranische Untersuchungen*, p. 129.

44 See Nöldeke, *Mandäische Grammatik*, XXIX, and p. 55.

45 I. Loewenthal, in *Muslim World*, I (1911), pp. 267–282.

46 See Koran, for example, 2:125, 133, 136, 140; 3:84; 4:163; 28:76; 29:39; 40:24; 28:34; 37:114, 120; 2: 247, 249; 18:94; 21:96.

47 See Blachère, *Le Coran*, II, 265; notice that the name *ʿIsā* appears 25 times in the Koran, either on its own: 3:55, 58, 62, 63; 4:163; 6:85 (five times); or with his full title, "Jesus Christ, son of Mary," 3:45; 4:157, 171 (three times), or as "Jesus son of Mary," 2:87, 253; 3:45; 5:46, 78, 110, 112, 114, 116; 19:34; 57:27; 61:6, 14 (13 times); only four times is it found combined with Mūsā, 2:136; 3:84; 33:7; 42:13.

48 See Biitmer, in *WZKM*, XV, p. 395: "Kann nicht Consonantenpermuatation vorliegen."

49 Ibn ʿArabī, *Muḥādarat*, II, p. 50; cf. Cheikho, *Le Christanisme*, p. 186.

50 Marracci, Prodromus…, Refutatio Alcorani, p. 30.

51 Already Christian Reineccus [died 1752, published revised edition of L. Marracci's translation of the Koran]: "Nomen Jesu in Alcorano convertitur in nomen (Isā)… quod pessimam redolet Juadaeorum perversionem, qui nomen… Esavi substituerunt pro nomine… Jesu, a Esavi animam criminantur transmigrasse in Jesum. Cumque Muhammed usus sit praeceptoribus juadaeis, hanc perversam nominis Jesus scriptionem procul dubio ab iis habuit, qui ejus tamen scriptionis perversam rationem ipsi forte non exposuerunt," cited in Adriaan Reland, *De religione mohammedica*, trans, by David Durand, *La religion des Mahometans* (The Hague, 1721), p. 83. In the two Latin quotations, the Hebrew and Arabic words, since the right fonts were lacking, were replaced by suspension points.

52 Nöldeke, in *ZDMG*, XLI (1887), p. 720, n.2.

53 Landauer, see Nöldeke, ibid.

54 Cf. Fraenkel, in *WZKM*, IV (1890), p. 340, n.2 : „Die Form. . . ist aber jüdisch. Mein Freund Landauer erklärt sie mir schlagend aus Esau; so nannten jenen die Juden in bitterm Spott, und Muhammad oder seine Vorgänger nahmen das bona fide hin, wie die gehässige Bezeichnung Rom's als Edom ja auch Christen und Muslime zu der Annahme geführt hat, die Römer stammten von Isaac ab."

55 Kampffmeyer, in *ZDPV*, XV, p. 107.

56 Pautz, *Offenbarung*, p. 191.

57 Zwemer, in *MW*, I (1911), p. 266.

58 Ibid., Mahomet "borrowed and adpated from Judaism"; see Loewenthal, Lammens, et al.

59 Lammens, *L'Arabie occidentale*, p. 4, n. 3
60 Lammens in *al-Machriq*, I (1898), p. 334.
61 The word "Edom" means in Hebrew "red-pale-yellow," nickname for Esau in the Bible, Genesis 25:30; 36:1, whence the malevolent allusion of the appellation Banū-l-Aṣfar (the Sons of Yellow).
62 Cf. Genesis 32:3; 36:8, etc.
63 Thus Šlū becomes Šlā; there are plenty of examples in Arabic. Similarly all verbs in *ā* whose muḍari' [imperfect tense] is a *ū*, such as *danā, samā, ǧalā*, etc.
64 Horovitz, *Koranische Untersuchungen*, p. 129.
65 Koran 43:57 and 63; already he was discussed at length, even though he was not named in the passage concerning the Annunciation and Christmas, 19:16–33.
66 For the first time in 42:13 of which part b is, according to Bell, Barth and Blachère, a Medinan addition; see Blachère, *Le Coran*, III, p. 548, n. 11; the three other times where we find the doublet 'Isā-Mūsā are undeniably of the Medinan period: 2:136; 3:84; 33:7.
67 For the passages of the Sīra, see Caetani, *Annali dell'Islam*, in the Index to Vol. II/II, and above all at the year 6 AH, §45–55; for the Ḥadīṯ, see under the word Nadjāshī in Wensinck, *Handbook of Early Muhammadan Tradition*.
68 See for example, Ḥalabī, *Sira Ḥalabīya*, I, p. 325; the same in Ibn Hišām, Ṭabarī, et al.
69 See V.Vacca, "Le ambascerie di Maometto ai sovrani secondo Ibn Ishaq e al-Waqidi," in *RSO*, 10 (1923–25), pp. 87–109; this emigration is found to be related a group of legendary traditions which were later grafted onto it.
70 See *ZDMG*, XLI, p. 720. n. 2.
71 Dérenbourg, "Le nom de Jésus," in *REJ*, XVIII (1889), p. 127.
72 Tor Andrae, *Der Ursprung des Islams und das Christentum* (Uppsala, 1926).
73 [O.E.D. gyrovague (Hist. rare.)]
One of those monks who were in the habit of wandering from monastery to monastery. 1801 A. Ranken Hist. France I. i. ii. 224 "The Gyrovagues, or Vagabonds, who strolled about from one monastery to another, gratifying too freely their inclinations and appetites."]
74 Ahrens, *Christliches im Qorān*, pp. 24–25.
75 Fraenkel, "Miscellen," in *WZKM*, IV, p. 336; cf. Equally Sycz, *Biblischen Eigennamen*, p. 62.
76 Nestle, in *Dictionary of Christ and the Gospel*, I, (1906), p. 861.
77 Jeffery, *Foreign Vocabulary*, p. 220.
78 Horovitz, *Koranische Untersuchungen*, p. 128.
79 Sell and Margoliouth, in *Dictionary of Christ and the Gospels*, II (1908), p. 882, note.
80 Koran 16:105; 25:5; 44:13.
81 Fraenkel, Miscellen, in *WZKM*, IV (1890), pp. 334–335.
82 Vollers, "Ueber die lautliche Steigerung bei Lehnwörtern im Arabischen," *ZDMG*, XLV (1891), pp. 353–355.
83 Dérenbourg. Ibid., in *REJ*, XVIII (1889), p.128; in the text, the different forms of the name are in Hebrew-Aramaic characters.
84 The changing of *šīn* into *sīn* does not pose any difficulty; it is done each time the Koran arabizes a word of Syriac origin, such as *Mūsā*, for *Mūšé* (Moses), *Sulaymān* for *Šlémūn* (Salomon), etc.

85 W. H. Waddington, *Inscriptions grecques et latines de la Syrie* (Paris, 1870), 2464.
86 Jaussen and Savignac, *Mission Archéologique*, II, p. 228 ; Horovitz, op. cit., p. 151; the country of the Nabataens and Thamudians must have formed the *Provincia Arabia*, which would be the center and field of action of Jacobitism.
87 Originally in *L'Orient Syrien*, vol. VII, fasc. 2, 1962; pp. 227–254; Part II originally in *L'Orient Syrien*, 7 , 1962, pp. 365–382.
88 Blachère, *Le Coran*, III, p. 864. "Nothing prevents them (these verses) from being placed before or at the moment of the rupture with the Medinan Jews."
89 Koran, 4:172; 5:72; 9:30.
90 Koran 5:17 (twice); 5:72: 5: 75; 9:31.
91 Koran, 3: 45; 4:157; 4:171.
92 Inschrift Glaser 618, II, p. 31; in *Mitteilungen der Vorderasiatischen Gesellschaft*, Berlin, 1897; the translation cited here is on p. 42; for the dating of the text, see ibid., p.68.
93 Cited in Cheikho, *Le Christianisme*, p. 187.
94 *Lisān al-ʿArab*, III, p. 431.
95 *Diwān*, (ed. L. Cheikho, Beyrouth, 1920), p. 32.
96 Paret, article, "Al-Samaw'al" in *EI*, IV, p. 138.
97 Cheikho, *Le Christianisme*, p. 186, 190, corrects this name such as it is given by *Lisān al-ʿArab*, s.v. abīl, by the first.
98 A double variant: in place of *sabbaḥa, qaddasa*, and in place of *bīʿalin, haykalin*.
99 Yāqūt, *Muʿǧam al-Buldān*, IV, 781; cited in Cheikho, *Le Christiansime*, p. 186, in Horovitz, *Koranische Untersuchungen*, p. 129, etc.
100 Other Christian poets, but not he, of Pre-Islamic times, such as ʿAdī ibn Zayd, swore by Rabbi Makkata was-Ṣalībi, see Cheikho, Šuʿarā, IV, p. 451.
101 Wellhausen, *Reste Arabische Heidentums*, p. 23.
102 Horovitz, *Koranische Untersuchungen*, p. 129.
103 Cheikho, *Šuʿarā*, III, p. 381.
104 Id., *Le Christianisme*, p. 210.
105 Id., *Šu'arā*, III, p. 392; cf. frequents mentions of the term abīl in Ibn Hišām, *Sīra*; Yāqūt, *Muʿǧam al-Buldān*; Aġānī, s.v.
106 Cheikho, *Šuʿarā*,III, p. 378.
107 [O.E.D. charism, charisma (ˈkærɪz(ə)m, kəˈrɪzmə) Pl. charismata (kəˈrɪzmətə), charisms. [a. Gr. χάρισμα pl. -ατα, (esp. in N.T.) favour given, gift of grace, f. χαρίζ-εσθαι to show favour, f. χάρις grace, favour. In the pl., the Greek form charismata has been in use since the word's introduction; in the sing., the Anglicized charism was for long the usual form, but has been supplanted by the reborrowed charisma (the only form used in sense b).]
a. Theol. A free gift or favour specially vouchsafed by God; a grace, a talent.
"The Gift of tears, a religious experience by which a person is moved to a profound sense of sorrow for sin, repentance, adoration, or gratitude before God. … [The] religious significance of [these tears] goes far beyond the the merely physical." Richard McBrien, *Catholicism*.
"Many have emphasized the importance of the 'gift of tears'; there is a set of

prayers in the Roman Missal whose petition is to obtain this favor." New Catholic Encyclopedia].

108 Aġānī, XIII, p. 170

109 Horovitz, *Koranische Untersuchungen*, p. 129.

110 Cheikho, *Le Christianisme*, p. 116; A. P. Caussin de Perceval, *Essai sur l'histoire des Arab avant l'Islamisme*, pendant l'époque de Mahomet, et jusqu'à la réduction de toutes les tribus sous la loi musulmane (Paris : H. Welter, 1902), I, p. 199.

111 Abū Ḥātim al-Siğistānī [died 869], *Kitāb al-Muʿammarīn*, ed. I. Goldziher, *Abhandlungen zur arabischen Philologie*, ii (Leiden, 1899), p. 38.

112 *Muʿğam al-Buldān*, II, p. 677; Cheikho, *Le Christianisme*, p. 242.

113 Balāḏurī, *Futūḥ al-Buldān*, p. 244; Ṭabarī, *Annales*, I, p. 981 ff.; Cheikho, *Le Christianisme*, cites yet another ʿAbd al-Masīḥ ibn al-Mu'ahhib, whose verses Buḥturī preserved in his *Ḥamāsa* (ed. L.Cheikho), p. 196.

114 *Al-Mufaḍḍaliyāt* ed. C. J. Lyall, i, Arabic text, Oxford, 1921, LXXXII, LXXIII, LXXXIII; Cheikho, *Šuʿarā*, III, pp. 254–255.

115 If these poems are not by him, Horovitz, *Koranische Unter.*, p. 129, the poet himself must surely have existed towards the end of the 6th Century.

116 Yāqūt, *Muʿğam al-Buldān*, IV, p. 756.

117 Ibn Saʿd, *Ṭabaqāt*, IB, p. 84.

118 Ibn Durayd, *Kitāb al-Ištiqāq*, ed. F. Wüstenfeld (Göttingen, 1854), p. 191; Cheikho, *Šuʿarā*, III, p. 330.

119 Horovitz, *Koranische Unter.*, p. 129.

120 [Manichean Script:, a right-to-left Semitic script, used mainly to write Middle Iranian languages and Uighur (Old Turkish). It is closely related to the Palmyrene script of Aramaic and the Estrangelo script of Syriac; some of its orthographical conventions are also to be found in the Mandaean script (see Naveh, 1982, pp. 151–52. The Manichean script was used by adherents of Manicheism to write texts in (Manichean) Middle Persian, Parthian, Sogdian, Early New Persian, Bactrian, and Uighur; these texts were found in Central Asia…"
Encyclopedia Iranica: http://en.wikipedia.org/wiki/Manichaean_alphabet.]

121 Jeffery, *Foreign Vocabulary*, p. 265.

122 Hartwig Hirschfeld, *Beiträge zur Erklärung des Korans* (Leipzig, 1886), p. 89.

123 Article: "Al-Masīḥ," in *EI*, III, p. 444.

124 Pautz, *Offenbarung*, p. 193, n. 3.

125 Sayous, *Jésus-Christ d'après Mahomet*, p. 21, n. 1.

126 Koran, 4:156

127 Koran, 2:96.

128 G. Graf, "Wie ist das Worth al-Masīḥ zu übersetzen," in *ZDMG* (1954), p. 119 ff.

129 Ahrens, *Christliches im Qoran*, p. 24; Fraenkel, *De Vocabulis*, p. 24; Lagarde, *Bildung der Nomina*, p. 94; Mingana, *Syriac Influence*, p. 85; Cheikho, *Le Christianisme*, p. 186, etc.

130 See also Ryckmans, *Noms Propres*, I, p. 19; Rossini, *Glossarium*, p. 179.

131 Ibn Manẓur, *Lisān al-ʿArab*, IV, pp. 431–432; Murtaḍā, Tāğ, II, p. 224.

132 Ibid.

133 Bayḍāwī, *Anwār at-Tanzīl* I, p. 75.

134 Tāğ, II, p. 224.

135 Titled, he says, *Šawāriq al-asrār al-ʿalīya*.

136 *Mašariq al-anwār an-nabawīya*.

137 *Maǧmaʿ al-Baḥrayn.*
138 *Baṣā'ir dawī-t-tamīz fī laṭā'if kitāb Allah al-ʿazīz.*
139 Ibn Manẓur, *Lisān al-ʿArab*, III, p. 432 : *masaḥahu ay ḫalaqahu ḫalqan mubārakan ḥasanan wa-masaḥahu ay ḫalaqahu ḫalqan qabīḥan malʿūnan.*
140 Murtaḍā, *Tāǧ*, II, pp. 224, 226.
141 Ibn Manẓur, *Lisān al-ʿArab*, III, p. 431.
142 Murtaḍā, *Tāǧ*, II, p. 226
143 Ibn Manẓur, *Lisān al-ʿArab*, III, pp. 431, 432; Ragib, *Mufradāt*, p. 484.
144 Buḫari, Ṣaḥīḥ, VII, 54; VIII, p. 96; Muslim, *Ṣaḥīḥ*, II, pp. 374, 375; Ibn Ḥanbal, *Musnad*, I, p. 195; II, p. 135; III, pp. 79, 103, etc.; see Hayek, *Al-Masīḥ fil-Islām*, p. 250 ff.
145 Ibn Manẓur, *Lisān al-ʿArab*, III, p. 435.
146 Murtaḍā, *Tāǧ*, II, p. 226.
147 Palm Sunday celebrates Jesus' entry into Jerusalem on the back of a donkey when the people strewed branches of palms in front of him.
148 Matt. 21: 2, 7; Mark, 9: 2–7; Luke, 19: 30–35; John, 12:14.
149 See the accounts the different Muslim authors and their sources in the Apocryphal Gospels, in Hayek, *Al-Masīḥ fil Islām*, pp. 102–103.
150 In his Baṣā'ir, see Ibn Manẓur, *Lisān al-ʿArab*, II, p. 226.
151 See the description by the Muslim traditionists, in Hayek, *Le Christ de L'Islam*, p. 251 ff.; Id. *Al-Masīḥ fil Islām*, p. 250 ff.
152 Murtaḍā, *Tāǧ*, II, p. 226.
153 Numerous passages in the Old Testament, for example, I Sam. 9:16; 24:7; Ezekiel, 37:21 ff; Psalms, 17:21 ff; title applied to the Prophets, I King, 19:116; to the priest, Exodus, 28:41; to Cyrus, Isaiah, 45:1; to Jesus in the New Testament: Mark 14:61; Luke, 22:67 ff; Mark, 15:2; 8:27; Matt, 27:37; John, 19:19, 21.
154 Raġib, *Mufradāt*, p. 484; Murtaḍā, *Tāǧ*, II, p. 224.
155 Ṭabarī, *Tafsīr*, III, p. 169; Bayḍāwī, *Anwār al-tanzīl*, I, p. 75; Rāzī, *Mafātīḥ al-ġayb*, s.v. III, 45; Zamaḫšari, *Kaššāf* I, p. 190; Murtaḍā, *Tāǧ*, II, p. 225; Ibn Manẓur, *Lisān al-ʿArab*, III, p. 431.
156 See *Le Christ de l'Islam*, p. 97 ff; and *Al-Masīḥ fil Islām*, p. 250 ff.
157 Al-Huǧwīrī, *Kašf al-Maḥǧūb*, trans. R. A. Nicholson, (Leiden and London, 1911), p. 39: *wa-'amma-s-siyāḥalu fali-ʿIsā.*
158 Ibn ʿArabi, *Al-Futūḥāt al-Makkīyat,* 4 vols. (Cairo, 1269–1274), II, p. 56: *ʿwa-kānat lahu-s-siyāḥat*; in Ġazālī, Makkī and many others, one finds similar clichés or equivalent ones, such as *wa-kāna sā'iḥan lā yastaqirru, sā'iḥun dawman*, etc.
159 Koran 7: 172,
160 See J.-M. Abd-el-Jalil, *Marie et L'Islam* (Paris, 1950), p. 59, which retains, in all, six senses according to the Commentary of al-Alūsī.
161 Rāzī, *Mafātīḥ al-ġayb*, s.v. III, 45.
162 Murtaḍā, *Tāǧ*, II, pp. 225. Ibn Manẓur, *Lisān al-ʿArab*, III, p. 431.
163 Rāzī, ibid., and almost all the other commentators; cf. Koran III, 36 and the celebrated account of the Nativity, in Ṭabarī, *Annales*, I/III, pp. 727–728; Ibn Aṯīr, *Kāmil*, I, 221–222; al-Ṯaʿlabī, *Qiṣāṣ al-Anbiyā*, pp. 384–385; and the famous

ḥadīṯ on the "bite" of Satan, Muslim, *Ṣaḥīḥ*, II, p. 224; Ibn Ḥanbal, *Musnad*, II, p. 233; Buḫārī, *Ṣaḥīḥ*, III, p. 366 etc.

164 Recorded by Ibn Manẓur, *Lisān al-ʿArab*, III, p. 432.

165 Raġib, *Mufradāt*, p. 484; Rāzī, *Mafātīḥ al-ġayb*, s.v. III, 45; Murtaḍā, *Tāǧ*, II, p. 224.

166 Koran, 3:49; 5:110; see these marvels in Ṯaʿlabī, *Qiṣāṣ al-Anbiyā*, p. 387 ff.

167 Rāzī, ibid.: *li'annahu kāna yamsaḥu ra'sa-l-yatāmā lil-Lāhi taʿālā.*

168 Muslim, *Ṣaḥīḥ*, II, p. 376 etc.

169 Bayḍāwī, *Anwār al-tanzīl*, I, p. 75: *wa-štiqāquhu mina-l-misḥi takallufun la ṭā'īla ṭaḥtahu.*

170 Zamaḫšari, *Kaššāf*, s.v. III, 45: *muštaqquhuma min-al-misḥi and wa-l- ʿisi karrāqimi fī-l-mā*: "to beat the water with a rod," you said it!

The Debt of Islam to Monophysite Syrian Christianity

John Bowman

Originally published in Nederlands Theologisch Tijdschrift *19 (1964/ 1965) 177–201; later anthologized in E. C. B. MacLaurin,* Essays in Honour of Griffithes Wheeler Thatcher 1863–1950 *(Sydney: University of Sydney Press, 1967). We thank the* Nederlands Theologisch Tijdschrift *for their kind permission.*

In Muslim Arabic sources, the paganism of the pre-Islamic Arabs has been overemphasized presumably to mark the more clearly the contrast made, reminding one of "the testimony" of the recent convert. But there is clear evidence in both Arabic and Syriac sources that both Judaism and Christianity were indeed to be found in various parts of pre-Islamic Arabia. Some European scholars since last century have stressed the great indebtedness of Islam to Judaism. Few have emphasized the debt to Christianity. While it was not denied that Muhammad knew something of Christianity, he used to be seen as reacting against as, for example, Sir William Muir could say in *The Coran*[1] "the imperfect and garbled form" of Christianity known in Arabia. Syrian Christianity, Nestorian and Monophysite condemned by the fifth-century Councils of Ephesus and Chalcedon respectively has been regarded as heretical ever since. It is not surprising then that with notable exceptions like Bell, Tor Andrae and Guillaume little or no credit has been given to the influence Syrian Christianity had on Muḥammad the Reformer (as he used to be seen in the Protestant West).

For his part, Muḥammad claimed to be bringing no new message but recalling men to the God and the religion of Abraham, the friend of God, and to be confirming the Law and the Evangel. Muḥammad did not think he was calling God a new name in calling Him in Arabic Allah, the God. Allah is also the Syriac word for God.

The Koran refers to personages of both Old Testament and New Testament and teaches the Virgin Birth and Ascension of Jesus the Messiah. It is obvious then that his knowledge was not derived entirely from Jewish sources. There are, however, problems of the Biblical historiography of the Koran which makes the Mother of Jesus, Aaron's sister Miriam. In this article we will seek to show that Muḥammad's Biblical historiography and his view of the Old Testament is entirely derived from the Syrian Church interpretation of the Old Testament seen through the eyes of the New Testament. We shall also attempt to show that Muḥammad's monotheism is derived from a Monophysite Syriac Christianity protesting against Orthodoxy. We believe that we can give Koranic evidence of lexical indebtedness to early Syriac religious texts.

One could describe Arabia as the large peninsula at the southwest extremity of Asia, bounded on the west by the Red Sea and the south-east by the Gulf of Bab-el-Mandeb and the Indian Ocean, and on the north-east by the Persian Gulf. At the northern end, Arabia's limits were indefinite and could include the whole of the desert country between Egypt and Syria on the northwestern and northern side, and the banks of the Euphrates on the north-eastern. Professor A. Guillaume goes further and says,

> By Arabia its people understand the land enclosed on the north by the mountains of Asia Minor, on the south by the Indian Ocean, on the east by the mountains of Persia, and on the west by the Mediterranean and the Red Sea.[2]

It is worthwhile pausing to define the geographical extent of Arabia, because since Islam was first preached in Mecca in the Hedjaz (Ḥiğāz) in Arabia, and the Koran was revealed in Arabic, there has been too great a tendency to identify Arabia and Islam. However, Christianity was preached in Arabia by Paul the Apostle (cf. Gal. I:17) who was afterwards to be the Apostle to the Gentiles.

Origen (196–253/4) (cf. Eusebius[3] *H.E.* VI, ch. 19:36) was sent from Egypt to go to Arabia and dispute with an Arabian Christian sect who denied the immortality of the soul and claimed that it died with the body and would be resuscitated along with it by the power of God. In the time of Origen too, there was Beryllus Bishop of Bostra in Arabia whom Eusebius (*H.E.* VI, ch. 19) mentions as an author of some distinction. Eusebius cites a letter of Dionysius of Alexandria relating to the persecution by Decius (249–251) in which he mentions the Church of Arabia. Again, Eusebius (*H.E.* VIII, ch. 12) speaking of the persecution in the time of Diocletian (284–305) says:

> Why need we mention the rest by name, or number the multitude of the men or picture the various sufferings of the admirable martyrs of Christ. Some of them were slain with the axe as in Arabia.

Socrates' *Ecclesiastical History*[4] Book III, ch. 25, mentions Theotimus of the Arabs among the bishops who in Jovian's time accepted the Nicene Creed. All such references would apply to Christians in north Arabia, i.e., in the Roman Province Arabia Petraea, which, however, included the north-west part of the Hedjaz. However, Philostorges[5] (*H.E.* Book I, ch. 3) states that a monk named Theophilus who was an Indian bishop was sent by the Emperor Constance in 342 to the Himyarite king of Yaman, and obtained permission to build three churches, one at Zafar, another at Aden and a third at Hurmuz on the Persian Gulf. It would appear then that over two hundred years before the birth of

Muḥammad, Christianity was represented in widely distant parts of Arabia, north, south, east and west.

So far we have spoken of Arabian Christianity in general, now we must turn to specifically Syrian Christianity. Syrian Christian churches claim St. Thomas and not St. Peter as the fount of their Apostolic Tradition. Whether we accept or not the tradition that St. Thomas sent Addai as apostle to Edessa, a city of northern Mesopotamia, there was a Church with a bishop there by the second part of the second century. The Edessan Church, situated as it was in Edessa an important entrepot for eastern trade with the Roman Empire, became the Mother Church of many Churches in Persia, central Asia, India, and by A.D. 600 if not before, in China. After Nestorius Bishop of Constantinople was anathematized in 436 at Ephesus on rejecting the innovation "Theotokos," "Mother of God" instead of "Christotokos," "Mother of Christ" as title of the B.V.M.[6], the Edessan Church which followed his teaching was excommunicated. The "Theotokos" issue was more than a question of an honorific title for the B.V.M. It is connected with the basic question, "What think ye of the Christ, whose son is He?" (cf. Matt. 24:42) which is posited by the Gospels. The answer to this basic question the Creed of Nicea had sought carefully to define as a result of the controversies which came to a head in the third century.

The Church from the beginning had preached that there is one God, the God of the Old Testament who sent Jesus the Messiah. But what was the relation of Jesus to God? The Four Gospels in their several ways indicated answers. In Mark, He had received the Spirit, and Divine recognition of Sonship at the Baptism. Matthew and Luke gave their stories of the Virgin Birth. Mary's child was conceived of the Spirit. John had no Virgin Birth story but identified Jesus with the Word of God that was with God from all Eternity.

In the Gospels as indeed in all the Apostolic and Sub-Apostolic writings there is the conviction that Jesus and His message and work both confirm and fulfil the Old Testament. Apart from Gnostic heretics the Early Church held fast to the Old Testament and claimed it as her Bible. She did not stop at that but claimed she was the real Israel. The Church preached the One God of the Prophets but claimed Jesus was His Son, and that Jesus' message was the message of the Old Testament, as *properly* understood.

To preach and maintain belief in *one* God was the constant aim of the Church. But what was the relation of Jesus to God? There were basically two lines of approach which alike sought to protect the Unity of God:

(a) *Adoptionist*, i.e., that Jesus was a prophet and God gave Him His Spirit at the Baptism, e.g., cf. the doctrine of Paul of Samosata;

(b) *Modalist*, i.e., that God showed Himself to the Jews as Father, to the Apostles as Son, and to the Gentiles as Holy Spirit (cf. e.g., the views of Sabellius).

These attempts to explain the problem, when so expressed, were regarded as heretical. Arius at the beginning of the fourth century brought the issue to a head by teaching that God created the Son or pre-existent Christ before the *general* creation, but the Son was not consubstantial with the Father. The Nicene Creed formulated to correct this error, specifically stressed the coeternity of God the Father and God the Son and of their being of one and the same Nature. True, it says that He was born of the Virgin Mary. But Nestorius felt that to call her "Theotokos" undermined the structure of the Nicene Creed by saying she bore God. For Nestorius, following his teacher Theodore of Mopsuestia, looked back to St. John's Gospel where Jesus says of His body, "Destroy this temple, and in three days I will raise it." So God the Son was in the human Jesus from the womb and throughout His ministry as God in the Temple; i.e., Jesus Christ, Son of God was made up of two natures, Divine and human, *not* united, but forming one person. Though Nestorius and Nestorians were anathematized, it highlighted the fact that further definition in precise terms of the nature of the Incarnation was required. The Council of Chalcedon, less than a generation later defined the relation of the Divine and human natures in Christ, and it was at this Council that most of the Syrians who had not left the Orthodox Church with Nestorius were anathematized. These were the Monophysites. Here follows the Monophysite Confession of Faith as given by Philoxenus (Mar Aksenaia) Bishop of Mabbug (fifth century).

> We confess three divine Hypostases, one God (Allah). The Father is God (Allah), the Son is God (Allah), the Holy Spirit is God (Allah) but there are not three Gods (Allahs). The Father is (Divine) Nature, and the Son is the son of (the Divine) Nature (i.e., consubstantial) and the Holy Spirit is of the (Divine) Nature, but there are not three Natures. The Father is Essence, and the Son is the Son of the Essence, and the Holy Spirit is of the Essence, but there are not three Essences: Nature equal which is not divided, the Essence which is confessed in the Hypostases, one Nature in three Hypostases which are equal and in complete accord. Here is our God (Allah) whom we adore, and in whom we believe.

The Eastern Roman Empire and the Sassanid Persian Empire maintained the same attitude one to the other as the earlier Roman Empire and the Parthians. Both had Arab mercenary forces. The Persian Arab forces were mainly Nestorian, the Roman Arab forces mainly Monophysite. The Eastern Roman Empire was Orthodox: Monophysitism was a heresy. The tension between the Arabs and their Eastern Roman overlords was increased because of religious differences on the questions of the Trinity and Incarnation. In the sixth century the Arab chief Ḥāriṯ, a Monophysite, went to Constantinople to ask the Greek Orthodox Emperor Justinian I that his people be given a bishop but a Monophysite bishop. Justinian agreed; after all the Arab tribes were his mercenaries employed in fighting the Persian forces, also Arab, but Nestorian. In 563 Ḥāriṯ, conscious of how much the Emperor was indebted for his services against the Persians, brought a document to Constantinople which he tried to get accepted. It said:

> *The Trinity is One God, One Nature, One Essence*; those who do not accept this doctrine are to be anathematized.

On two bishops refusing to sign, Ḥāriṯ said:

> Now I know you are heretics. We and our armies accept this doctrine as do the Orientals.

As Professor Guillaume who cites this incident says,

> Here plainly is a claim to a native Arab Christianity stripped of the subtle refinements of the Greek theologians, and an explicit claim to the right to defend that faith by the sword.[7]

Ḥāriṯ's statement is pure Monophysitism.

Monophysitism certainly conserved the Unity of God and the Divinity of the Son, but was related to heresies like that of Eutyches or that of Julian of Halicarnassus where Christ is denied a human nature. On the other hand there was the Arabian Tritheist heresy springing in reaction from Monophysitism; it held that since it is certain that the (Divine) Nature belongs to each one of the Hypostases in particular, and that it is God, then there are Three Natures, and Three Gods, as well as Three Hypostases.

According to Philosterges (*H.E. op. cit.)* Christianity came to Nağrān in the Yemen in the fifth century. It was Syriac Monophysite Christianity, and in 514 the great Monophysite Theologian Jacob of Sarug wrote to the Arab Christians of Nağrān of whose number so many (20,000, so Muir, *Life of Mahomet,* Introduction) had then fallen martyrs to the faith in death by fire, in the persecution of Ḏū l-Nuwās Himyarite Arab King who had adopted Judaism. This had its repercussions, as one survivor with a half-burnt Gospel reached Constantinople and demanded retribution. At Justinian's request the Abyssinians in 525 sent an armada and destroyed Ḏū l-Nuwās .

It is usually held that the Koran Sura 85, The Sura of the Zodiacal Signs (a Meccan Sura), alludes to this persecution.

> And the fire with its kindling, When they sat over it, And witnessed the while what they were doing with those who believed (i.e., with the Monophysite

> Christians). And took not vengeance on them save for their belief in God, The Mighty, the praiseworthy, Whose is the Kingdom of the heavens and the earth; For God is witness over all.

The Egyptian Copts and the Abyssinians became Monophysites. Not so long before Muḥammad was born in 571, a huge Christian church was built at Ṣan'ā' in the Yemen. It was the wonder of the age. The Arabs of the Yemen were ordered by the ruler of Abyssinia to perform a pilgrimage to this new church instead of the Ka'ba at Mecca. This edict was resisted and traditionally gave rise to the "War of the Elephant" when Abrahah, the Viceroy of Egypt, took an oath that he would destroy the Meccan Shrine and marched at the head of an army of Abyssinians mounted on an elephant. The "War of the Elephant" marks the period of Muḥammad's birth. There is the Surah of the Elephant in the Koran referring to Divine intervention against the Abyssinians.

Professor Guillaume points out that

> the Monophysites were extraordinarily active in converting the Arabs, and shortly before the birth of Muḥammad large numbers had been baptised. A priest and deacon were appointed to each tribe. Churches were founded, alms-giving and fasting were regularly practised. Monasteries were open day and night to travellers, who were given food and drink before they were sent on their way. Women were veiled when out of doors.[84]

Professor Guillaume goes on to point out that the Nestorians were equally active; that they established schools in many towns. Whereas in the fifth century they had a monastery at Ḥīra from where Christianity went to Bahrain, by the time Muḥammad was a young man, King Nu'man of Ḥīra was converted to Christianity. Now in 597 the Persians conquered the country. The Persians after the lengthy persecution in the fourth century in the reign of Šāpur II, favoured the Nestorians; their Arabs were mainly Nestorian. So though Monophysites and Nestorians were regarded alike as heretics by the Eastern Roman Empire, they did not see eye to eye. The Nestorians were very missionary. It is they who went to central Asia, India and China. We can be sure that they, conscious of the sympathy of the Persian government, sought to spread Nestorianism in Arabia at the expense of Monophysitism. After all, the Monophysite Arabs had fought for Rome. That is not to say that the Monophysite Arabs loved Rome, who regarded them as heretics, as not belonging to the true Israel, the Orthodox Church. Hitherto scholars have not paid enough attention to the importance of the divisions both theological and political between Monophysite and Nestorian Arabs. This had great significance as providing an opportunity for the emergence of Muḥammad as Prophet of Islam which owed much to what was common in each, but solved their mutual differences on Trinity and Incarnation (the very points on which the Eastern Roman Empire had anathematized them both) by abandoning such positions: cf. Koran Surah Nisā' 166:

> O ye people of the Book! do not exceed in your religion, nor say against God aught save the truth. The Messiah, Jesus son of Mary, is but the apostle of God and His Word, which He cast into Mary and a spirit from Him; believe then in God and His apostles, and say not "Three." Have done, it were better for you. God is only one God.

The Ka'ba, the Holy Place of Mecca, according to Professor Guillaume had pictures of Biblical personages surrounding its inside walls in the time of Muḥammad. Muḥammad after Islam was triumphant removed all except that of the Virgin and Child. The Virgin Mary has long been held in honour by Arabs. There was the sect of Collyridians in Arabia in the fourth century who worshipped St. Mary as a goddess, and thought she ought to be honoured and appeased with libations, sacrifices and offerings of cakes (*κολλυριδες*, cf. Mosheim, Bk. II, p. 414). The immaculate conception of the B.V.M. was taught in Medieval Islam: only last century did it become a dogma in the Roman Catholic Church.

Professor Guillaume, in a lecture he gave in Leeds University in 1958, held that it was from the paintings, arranged in no apparent historical sequence, inside the Ka'ba that Muḥammad derived his peculiar notion of Biblical history with Mary Mother of the Lord apparently Aaron's sister. Professor Guillaume pointed out that the paintings had been done by a Copt. He demonstrated that the order was most probably a reproduction of the same order as that inside an ancient Coptic Church in Upper Egypt. But he did not go on to explain why that order would arise in the first place. The present writer feels that the paintings done by a Coptic monk or even an ordinary Copt would reflect this Monophysite Christian's concept of Biblical history. Tor Andrae points outs[9] that tradition tells that Muḥammad heard Kuss ibn Sa'd, said to have been Bishop of Nağrān, preaching in the market at Okatz (cf. Kitāb al-Aġanī XIV, pp. 41ff.; Mas'ūdi, i. p. 33). So it was Christian Missionary Sermons which provided him not only with his knowledge of the Bible, but basic Christian doctrines. Tor Andrae[10] sees three possible heads in such a sermon:

(1) God's Providence,
(2) Man's duty to God in return,
(3) Judgement for those who do not fulfil this duty.

Whereas it could be that the Copt's pictures in the Ka'ba could be better explained as representing Biblical history derived from a sermon, even this stops short. The sermon's attitude to Biblical history as illustrating God's Providence would be conditioned by a theological attitude to the Old Testament.

We should note here that we have a tradition which claimed that Muḥammad actually received instruction in Christianity from learned Christians Ǧubrā and Yasārā, and that on this account Qurayš said:

> It is only some mortal that teaches him. Cf. Baiḍāwī on Surah 16:105.

The Syrians saw the Old Testament as fulfilled in the New Testament. In this they were not so different from the first writers of the New Testament who depicted the life of Christ to a great extent in the light of the Testimonia which they believed they found relating to Him in the Old Testament. The incident on the way to Emmaus, Luke 24:27,

> And beginning from Moses and from all the prophets, he interpreted to them in the scriptures the things concerning himself

gives a pointer to this. The infant Church had had to justify its very existence theologically *vis-a-vis* the parent body Judaism. Judaism had the Law, the Torah, and the Jews claimed a "once-for-allness" for the Revelation of the Law at Sinai. They claimed that through it they were God's Chosen People. St. Paul went behind the Law to Abraham and claimed that God had covenanted with Abraham long before the Law was given, that in his seed which Paul, using Rabbinic Exegetical methods,[11] takes not as the Rabbis took as referring to the Jewish Community, but to Jesus, all nations would be blessed. Paul saw the Law as an interlude and not only so, but occasioned by sin. Cf. Galatians 3:19 – "What then is the Law? It was added because of transgressions." With Christ the promised Seed come, it was done away with. The great Syrian Father Theodore of Mopsuestia, taught that Jesus was the true Son of God, old Israel were only sons by adoption; but in and by what the Godman Christ had done, those who believed in Him could become sons of God by adoption; the Church under the leadership of Christ was the new true Israel, the continuation and fulfilment of the Israel of the Old Testament. But this was basic to the theology of the Church Catholic since Paul. The Syrian Fathers perhaps went further than the Greek and Latin Fathers in the stress they put on this, to wit, that in fact it is Christ the Word as Second Person of the Trinity who speaks to man of Himself in the Old Testament. Therefore the Syrian Christian writers like Aphraates, early fourth century, Ephraem, fourth century, Jacob of Sarūg, fifth to sixth century, in the homilies on New Testament themes quote the Old Testament more than the New Testament. The early Christians in general and Syrians in particular regarded the Jews as heretics and as completely wrongly interpreting the Old Testament.

The Syrian Christians supplied Muḥammad with a ready-made argument against the Jews. It is often alleged that he said that they had falsified the *Taurat*. But evidence is clearer that he alleged that they *hid* the proper (in his eyes) meaning, cf. Surah 6:92. This was the usual Christian polemic against the Jews. In Surah 2.:141 Muḥammad seems to use the same argument against the Christians as well as the Jews.

Muḥammad called his revelation: The Koran. Professor Guillaume, speaking of the Nestorians (but the same would apply to the Monophysites), writes:

> In their monasteries monks could be heard chanting their offices, so that the Arabs became accustomed to seeing the monks at prayer day and night, prostrating themselves with their faces to the ground. In prayer, the Christians turned to the east. Such men were a familiar sight on all caravan routes of Arabia. [12]

As Tor Andrae points out, the word used in the Syrian Church for the Scripture reading in Divine Service is *qeryānā.*[13] It seems that Tor Andrae is correct in suggesting that Muḥammad, familiar with readings by the monks of their revealed books, took this name for his Revelation, both each revelation and as descriptive of the whole. When he received the first revelation, he was commanded to *read*, not silently, but aloud to proclaim, cf. Surah 96:1f., which would be just as the monks did. However, the Syrian monks' sacred books were in Syriac and their *qeryānā,* their readings, were in Syriac, a tongue similar to Arabic but a foreign tongue to the Arabs of Qurayš, Muḥammad's tribe in the Hedjaz. It is doubtless with pride that Muḥammad claimed his was an Arabic Koran (cf. Surah 12:1).

The Scripture readings of the Syrian Fathers would be from the Old Testament and New Testament. Muḥammad, while referring frequently to the earlier revelations as *Taurat* (Pentateuch), and the Inğīl. (the Gospel) *never* uses the terms Old Testament and New Testament. The Zubur, the Psalms of David are twice mentioned. Moses, the Koran tells us, brought the Taurat, the Jews fell away from it. Prophets came and warned them, but they killed them, then Jesus was sent with the Inğīl, the Gospel. This was not a new Revelation, but confirmed the truth of the first. Note Muḥammad does not say there were Four Gospels. If by Gospel he meant Four Gospels, he would have shown the discrepancies between them. He does *not* say the Christians corrupted the Gospel. He blames the monks for adding the doctrine of the Trinity and tells the Christians to get back to their Scripture, i.e., the Inğīl.

In the Koran, there is mention of more Old Testament personages than New Testament figures; as a result it has been understood that Muḥammad was influenced more by Jews and Judaism than by Christians. It is true that at Medina after the Hiğra he did hope to gain the Jews who were numerous and prominent there. While in Medinan Surahs knowledge of Rabbinic Midrashic traditions can be seen supplementing the Old Testament story, and in Surah Nisā' (Women), the Mishnaic Tractate Sanhedrin is once quoted, yet

Muḥammad's whole attitude to the Old Testament even at this period is that which is derived from Syrian Christianity: the Old Testament is confirmed in the New Testament which gives the original sense of the Old Testament before it was corrupted. What then is the Gospel which Muḥammad heard? In Surah (19) Maryam (Mary), the annunciation to Zacharias of the birth of John the Baptist is virtually in the words of Luke's Gospel, whereas in the Surah (61) of the Ranks there is a reference, Muslims believe, to the promise of the Paraclete in John's Gospel. Now in the mid-second century when it was already generally agreed that the Four Gospels, and *they only* were acceptable to the Catholic Church, Tatian of Edessa made a harmony of the Four called the Diatessaron. It is not agreed whether the Diatessaron was originally in Greek or Syriac. The Syriac Fathers, Aphraates and Ephraem, of the fourth century quote the Diatessaron as the Gospel. It seems that the text of the Four separate Gospels existing in Syriac before the Diatessaron was that used in its compilation. The Diatessaron displaced them. However, about 400, Rabula, Bishop of Edessa, it is said destroyed all copies of the Diatessaron and had the Syriac "Vulgate" Peshitta Gospels produced in a Syriac text close to the readings of the Greek Gospels. Rabula was Orthodox, and the Diatessaron was still used by Monophysites and Nestorians after they were declared heretics. In the ninth century Išoʻdad of Merw was still quoting the Diatessaron in his Commentary of John's Gospel. The only early complete text of the Diatessaron is that of the Arabic Diatessaron translated from a Syriac MS. in the ninth century.

The present writer has for several years sought an answer to the problem of why it is that the Old Testament personages in the Koran are of the patriarchal period with few exceptions; allied with them as if of the same generation are Zacharias, Mary, Jesus and John. I believe the answer is that Muḥammad gained his knowledge of the Old Testament from the Diatessaron, the Harmonized Gospel. I do not know of this solution having been put forward before.

In the first place the Diatessaron cuts out the Matthean and Lucan genealogies of Jesus. The groundwork of the Diatessaron is John's Gospel, 96 per cent of which is reproduced: 76.5 per cent of Matthew is used, 66 per cent of Luke, 50 per cent of Mark.[14] The beginning of the Diatessaron is John: 1-5 with the emphasis on the Word, in Arabic Kalām, which in the Koran Surah Nisā' 166 is applied to Jesus in the phrase "which He cast into Mary." The promise of the son to Zacharias, Luke 1:5ff. follows next. Now in Luke 1:5 it is said that Zacharias' wife was of the daughters of Aaron. Mary (Miryam in Syriac and Arabic (Maryam) as well as in Hebrew) is her kinswoman – Luke 1:36. Surely it is plain how Muḥammad could confuse Mary the B.V.M. and Miryam, since Mary is a kinswoman of one of the daughters of Aaron, especially as *no* genealogy of Jesus is given in the Diatessaron, the Inǧīl of the Syrian Churches in Arabia.

It is worthwhile pausing to see how many Old Testament figures are mentioned in the Diatessaron: The Gospel, and see if they at all compare with those in the Koran. Adam, Abel, Noah, Abraham, Lot, Isaac, Jacob, Moses, David, Elijah, Elisha, Jonah are mentioned in the Diatessaron and in the Koran. I insert here a table showing the complete identity of the spelling of some of these names in the Arabic of both Koran and Diatessaron and even of the Syriac Gospel. Even where the spelling is not identical, close relationship can be noted.

The following Old Testament personages appear in the Koran and the Diatessaron (i.e., the harmony of the Four Gospels). Where the name is differently spelt in Peshitta, Koran and Arabic Diatessaron, I indicate this.

ADAM	*Peshitta, Koran, Arabic Diatessaron*
ABEL	HĀBEL *Pesh; Koran* and *Ar. Diatessaron* HĀBĪL
NOAH	NŪH *Pesh; Koran* and Ar. *Diatessaron* NŪH
ABRAHAM	ABRAHAM *Pesh; Koran* and Ar. *Diatessaron* IBRĀHĪM
LOT	LŪT *Pesh; Koran* and *Ar. Diatessaron*
ISAAC	ISHAQ *Pesh; Koran* and *Ar. Diatessaron*
JACOB	YA'QŪB *Pesh; Koran* and *Ar. Diatessaron*
JOSEPH	YAUSEF *Pesh; Koran* and *Diatessaron* YŪSUF
MOSES	MŪSHEH *Pesh; Koran* and *Ar. Diatessaron* MUSA
AARON	AHRŪN *Pesh; Koran* and *Ar. Diatessaron* HARŪN.
MIRYAM	*Pesh, Koran* and *Ar. Diatessaron MIRYAM* (MARY)
JOSHUA	(In LXX and in Greek N.T. Jesus) YESHU ' *Pesh; 'ISĀ Koran; 'ISU' Ar. Diatessaron* (Jesus ancestor of St. Joseph, Luke 3:29 YŪSI *Pesh.)*
JONAH	YAUNAN *Pesh; Koran* and Ar. *Diatessaron* YŪNUS
DAVID	DAVĪD *Pesh; Koran* and *Ar. Diatessaron* DĀ'ŪD
SOLOMON	SHLEIMŪN *Pesh; Koran* and *Ar. Diatessaron* SULAĪMAN
ELIJAH	ELYA or ILYĀ *Pesh; ILYĀ Koran* and *Ar. Diatessaron*
ELISHA	ELISHA *Pesh;* ALYASA' *Koran; ALĪSHA': Ar. Diatessaron*
ISRAEL	YISRAEL (but cf. Rev. 7:4, 2 Cor. I.1:2 ISRAELITE; ISRAELAYA) *Pesh;* ISRA'IL *Koran* and *Ar. Diatessaron*
ZACHARIAS	ZKARYĀ *Pesh; Koran* and *Ar. Diatessaron*
JOHN	YAUHANĀN *Pesh; Koran* YAHYA; *Ar. Diatessaron* YUHANA
GABRIEL	GABRIEL *Pesh; Koran* and *Ar. Diatessaron* GIBRIL

The following are Old Testament personages mentioned in the Koran and in the New Testament outside the Gospels.

CAIN	QAYEN *Pesh; Koran* QĀBĪL
ENOCH	HNOK *Pesh; Koran* IDRĪS
GOG	GŪG *Pesh; Koran* YĀGŪG
MAGOG	MAGŪG *Pesh; Koran* MĀGUG
PHARAOH	FERŪN *Pesh; Koran* FIRŪN
SAUL	SHĀUL *Pesh; Koran* TĀLŪT
MICHAEL	MIKAIL *Pesh; Koran* and *Ar. Diatessaron* MIKĀ'IL

It may be too much to assume a written translation of the Diatessaron from Syriac into Arabic in the time of Muḥammad. The Syrian Churches have not encouraged the replacing of the public reading of the Gospel in Syriac by the Vernacular. On the other hand the Syrian Churches encouraged the young to learn and understand Syriac, not merely to read it. The names of Biblical characters would be arabicized. It is interesting that Surah 7:39 uses the Gospel phrase "a camel pass through the eye of a needle." The Arabic Diatessaron in translating Matthew 19:24 uses exactly the same Arabic words. Since the Arabic Diatessaron does not use a Syriac root like *slm* to translate Syriac *šlm* in a good sense because of Muslim overtones, it is striking that the Arabic Diatessaron which has come down to us uses forms of names and expressions and turns of phrase found in the Koran; this surely shows it does not regard such as primarily Muslim.

The Koran also mentions Cain, Ishmael, Joseph, Amran, Miryam, Pharaoh, Korah, Job, Ezra. Of these, since Miryam is confused with Mary the B.V.M., Joseph may well be confused with St. Joseph. The Koran does not mention his name in connection with Mary, but gives the story of the Patriarch Joseph, stressing his chastity. Cain, Job and Pharaoh are mentioned in the New Testament outside the Gospels. The spelling of Job and Pharaoh in Syriac is exactly the same as in Arabic. Pharaoh in Syriac New Testament and Arabic Koran is *Fir'awn*: in Hebrew Old Testament it is פַּרְעֹה *P̱ar'ōh.* Muḥammad presumably heard the story of Pharaoh in a Syrian missionary sermon. The other Old Testament personages mentioned in the Koran but not in the Diatessaron or New Testament, he may quite probably have heard mentioned in Syrian missionary sermons which like the old style Scots sermon found the Gospel in the Old Testament. As to the angels, Gabriel is mentioned in both Diatessaron and Koran. Michael is mentioned in the Koran and in the New Testament (Jude 9; Rev. 12:7).

But did Muḥammad merely hear these names in Syriac sermons? If so, it is most odd that the orthographical forms of the names in Arabic are identical or remarkably similar to the form in the Syriac Bible.

'Abdu l-Ḥaqq, commentator on the Miškāt, says that Wāraqa the cousin of Lady Ḫadīğa the first wife of the Prophet, had embraced Christianity and had translated the Gospels into Arabic. There is the tradition in Ṣaḥiḥ al-

Buḫarī that when Muḥammad told Wāraqa what he had seen on Mt. Ḥīra, at the first revelation, Wāraqa exclaimed:

> It is the Nāmūs that appeared from God to Moses.

Nāmūs is not the usual word used in the Syriac New Testament for the Law. It occurs only in I Corinthians 9:21 and once in the Diatessaron paragraph 3 and John 1:17, Arabic and Syriac Nāmūs, where it is said:

> For the Law/Nāmūs was given through the mediation of Moses, but truth and grace were through Jesus Christ.

Later Nāmūs was thought to be an angel, but Wāraqa's exclamation may indeed point to his knowing the text of the Diatessaron: the Inǧīl. Wāraqa was a *ḥanīf*.

In Surahs 2:129; 3:60 in the Koran, Muḥammad says Abraham was neither a Jew nor a Christian, but a *ḥanīf*, and not of the idolaters. Ibn Isḥāq cited by Tor Andrae[15] says four men separated themselves at a sacrificial feast of the Qurayš given in honour of one of their idols. Wāraqa b. Naufal was one of the four: he became a Christian and acquired much knowledge from the Christians and out of their books. ʿUṯmān b. Ḥuwairiṯ, another cousin of Lady Ḫadīǧa, went to Byzantium and became a Christian, and occupied an honourable position at court. Zaid ibn Amr, another of the four, became neither Jew nor Christian, nor Muslim.

> "My God," he is reported to have said, "if I knew what form of worship is most pleasing to Thee I would choose it, but I know it not."

He had had much contact with Syrian Christians. Only one of the four, ʿUbaydallāh b. Ǧaḥš, became a Muslim and then a Christian, telling his former co-religionists

> We see clearly, but you are still blinking like newly-born puppies.

Certainly in the Koran Meccan Surahs, *ḥanīf* means a monotheist, though in Syriac *ḥanpā* means "heathen" or Apostate. (Tor Andrae cites as example *Yulyana ḥanpā* – Julian the Apostate, in Syriac.)[16] Tor Andrae wants to identify *ḥanpā* with Manichee, and then give *ḥanīf* in the Koran that meaning. This is narrowing too much the connotation of *ḥanpā* in Syriac. This suggested connotation of *ḥanīf* by Tor Andrae, is tied up with his view that Muḥammad besides being influenced by Syrian missionary sermons was influenced by Manichaeism. He sees the drive in Muḥammad to be prophet of the Arabs with a Revelation in Arabic, as deriving from Manichaean influence. But there is no need for this. With regard to the *ḥanīfs* they may have taken the name given them and others by Christian missionaries, and felt convicted that they were heathen, but could not as yet accept Christianity in the form offered. The slur became the slogan.

Muḥammad calls himself *al-nabī al-'ummī.* The expression occurs twice in the Surah 7:157, 158. This was usually taken to mean the illiterate prophet. *Ummī* in Arabic can mean "national, Gentile," and then as a result of the meaning "Gentile," "illiterate" (cf. how the Greeks regarded other nations as "barbarous"). It has been understood that by claiming himself to be an illiterate prophet Muḥammad was stressing the miracle of such bringing the Koran. It is *the* sign, indeed all its verses, i.e., *āyāt,* are signs also. Could it be that John 7:15 (in the Diatessaron) "How doth this man know writing seeing he hath not learned," said of Jesus, is thought of in relation to *al-nabī al-'ummī.* This is the sign he shares with Jesus, who in Muslim eyes also brought a book. Like Jesus Muḥammad was expected to show a sign. On the other hand Surah 7:157 says of this *nabī 'ummī* that "they find him written down with them in the Law and the Gospel." This could refer to the Prophet (cf. John 7:40, also Acts 3:22, 7:37) all referring to the Mosaic promise of Deuteronomy 18:18, of the prophet like unto Moses. But he was to be an Israelite prophet from among your brethren, i.e., fellow Israelites. *'Uma* in Hebrew is not so common as *'am* but has the same meaning: "people." However, it may be significant in Genesis 25:16 it is used in connection with Arabian tribes. In Syriac *'umṭā* (the *t* is not a radical but only a feminine ending) means a nation and the adjective *'umṭaya* Gentile. It could be that the meaning which best suits *al-nabī al-'ummī* is the Prophet of the Gentiles. The Syrian Christians as well as other early Christians had been very concerned to show that a man in Christ was not a Gentile, but one of the new Israel. The word *'ammī* in Syriac means Gentile, and *'Amme* the Gentiles is in Bar Hebraeus *Eccles. Hist.* applied to the Arabs.[17] This is not a late usage because it occurs early in the title of George Bishop of the Arabs.[18] In Arabic the adjective form *'Ammī* exists as does *'am,* people, instead of *'Ummī* and *'Umma* and have similar meanings. Above we have seen how *ḥanpā,* heathen, could be turned from a slight into a proud title. One ventures to suggest the same has been done with *'ummī.* He is the Gentile prophet, the prophet of the Gentiles in either the Old Testament or New Testament sense, and for the Gentile Arabs he is the national prophet, the prophet from among themselves. He can use that verse because his people who follow his message are no more Gentiles but the true people of God. Just as the Christians took over the promises to Abraham, he, Muḥammad, believing he is recalling men to the religion of Abraham, the first Muslim, feels that he and his followers are the heirs of the promises. He had learned well from Paul the first Apostle to the Gentiles whose teaching the Syrian Fathers had developed fortheir own benefit. Surah 2:135

> They say "Be ye Jews *or* Christians,so shall ye be guided." Say, "Not so, but the faith of Abraham, the *Ḥanīf,* he was not of the idolaters." (cf. also Surah

> 2:120). The Jews will not be satisfied with thee, nor yet the Christians, until thou followest their creed, say, God's guidance is the guidance.

The present writer ventures to suggest that Muḥammad was not illiterate; that he delivered his revelations, the Surahs or part Surahs of the Koran *vice voce,* the way a Nabī of the Old Testament would have done as well as how a monk or priest would read his scriptures. One cannot see any quotations from or reminiscence of Pauline phraseology in the Koran, though in the Syrian Churches the Apostle meant Paul; one can see more the influence of John's Gospel which was an integral part of the Diatessaron. However, Deissmann[19] saw John's Gospel as an attempt to make a synthesis of the Synoptic Gospel and the Pauline Christ. If so, there is indirectly considerable Pauline influence in the Diatessaron of which John is the largest single element.

The word Nabī is used also in the Diatessaron as well as in the Old Testament. John the Baptist was a prophet; Elijah is mentioned beside him in the Diatessaron (cf. John 1:21). As far as Muḥammad was concerned they were therefore contemporaries. In John's Gospel Jesus speaks much of being sent, or of "Him who sent me." This note comes through very much in the Koran where Muḥammad speaks too of himself as the Apostle of God. "Witness" is another keyword in the Johannine structure of the Diatessaron, likewise of the Koran. Muḥammad in words reminiscent of the Johannine Christ stresses that he needs the witness of no man, God is his witness.

Gabriel looms large in the Koran. Gabriel in fact takes the place of the Holy Spirit of Christianity. In the first section of the Diatessaron Gabriel figures in the annunciation to Mary and in the second section (derived from Matthew). Joseph finds her with child of the Holy Spirit. This may have led to the Koranic identification. In the Surah of the Ranks (61:6), a Meccan Surah, we have the famous passage where Muḥammad cites Jesus as saying:

> O children of Israel, verily, I am the *apostle* of God to you (Muḥammad's name for himself too) verifying the Law that was before me and giving you glad tidings of an apostle who shall come after me, whose name shall be Aḥmad.

This is understood to be an allusion to the Paraclete in John 16:17, Muslims declaring that the word *παράκλητος* had been substituted in the Greek for περικλυτός, praised, laudable, which is also the meaning of Aḥmad. In Arabic the word for paraclete is *Fārqalīṭ* and is exactly the same as the Syriac *P̱ārqalīṭ* even to the hard final *ṭ*. *P̱ārqalīṭ* in Syriac just like *παράκλητος* in Greek can mean "advocate" (cf. I John 2: i) as well as "comforter," but does not lend itself to a translation "praiseworthy," "laudable," nor is the root *ḥmd* used in Syriac. Here it may seem that some reference has been made to the Greek, not necessarily to the Gospel of John by itself, but to the Greek Diatessaron, which of course includes the promise of the Paraclete. Actually this is not absolutely necessary for παράκλητος was taken as a proper name, and the consonants transliterated in the Syriac. However, Tor Andrae[20] has demonstrated that the sensuous pictures of Paradise in the Koran were inspired by the great Syrian Church hymnologist Ephraem Syrus of Nisibis (fourth century) in his hymns of Paradise. According to Ephraem for those who have abstained from wine on earth for him the vines of Paradise yearn. For the man who lived in chastity there will be in Paradise females to receive him to pure bosoms. These features remind one of Koranic Paradise. If Muḥammad were influenced by one Syrian Father, it is possible that he could be influenced by another, e.g., Jacob of Saroug, who had had contacts with the Monophysite Christians in Nağrān. This writer in his famous *Liber Graduum*,[21] an important theological work on the training required to acquire the beatific vision, has much to say on the Paraclete as if he were still to come. Syriac Literature of the fourth and fifth and sixth centuries is not extensive. Ephraem's hymns would be known to every Syrian Christian in Arabia, and Jacob of Sarūg's mystical treatises to every Monophysite monk, of whom there were many in Muḥammad's time.

However, from St. John's Gospel in the Diatessaron Jesus' words

> for if I go not away, the Paraclete will not come unto you: but if I go away I will send him unto you. And when he cometh, he will reprove the world for sin, and for righteousness, and for judgement:

could be taken as referring to a successor. Muḥammad did feel that he was sent, and the phrase

> reproving the world for sin, and for righteousness, and for judgement

could be used to describe his mission. In John 15:25

> But when the Paraclete is come, whom I will send unto you from my Father,

if a break is made here in the sentence and we have a new beginning with

> The spirit of truth, which goeth forth from my Father, he shall bear witness of me,

the Paraclete and the Spirit of Truth need not be taken as one and the same. One means, it could have been possible for Muḥammad to have identified himself with the Paraclete and seen the Spirit of Truth as Gabriel (cf. above Muḥammad's identification of Gabriel and the Holy Spirit). Muḥammad could claim that he had indeed witnessed to Jesus the son of Mary and the truth of His revelation. The difficulty in deriving the name *Aḥmad* from Paraclete is *not* primary. Muḥammad had accepted the Christian interpretation of the Old Testament which took the latter over as fulfilled in itself the

New Testament. Muḥammad admits that Moses foretold Jesus' coming. He knew Jesus promised to send the Paraclete. He, Muḥammad, was anxious that he was sent. He was not the first to think he was the Paraclete; there was Montanus and the Montanists nearly 400 years before, who misled even Tertullian. The squaring of the name was secondary; when it squared so easily it would strengthen his certainty in himself. The system that the Christians had drawn up to take over the promises of the Old Testament from the Jews was his. The Christians saw themselves in the tradition of true Abrahamic religion: that was now his: it was for him in his function as the Paraclete to take over from the Christians their heritage and reprove them of sin and warn them of judgement. In Abraham all *'ammē,* the nations, would be blessed. Yes, the Arabs whom the Christians called *'ammē*, Gentiles, would be blessed, and he was their prophet.

It is undisputed that Muḥammad's basic message is to warn of impending judgement. This eschatological note is *not* typical of Rabbinic Judaism in the sixth century. Whereas Day of Judgement is a Jewish Eschatological term, the *Sā'a* "the hour" is not. It is specifically Christian and is found in St. John's Gospel and therefore in the Diatessaron. Gehinnom and the Fire, also common terms for the judgement that awaits sinners, are not only Gospel terms but stressed in Syrian Eschatology.

Jesus in Arabic is *'Īsā.* The form *Ishōʿ* is the normal Syriac. Jesus is often referred to in the Koran as Jesus the Messiah. *Ishōʿ Mašīʿ* is the corresponding form in Syriac. The Koranic term for Christian is *Naṣāra.* This is the word used in the Syriac Gospel for Jesus the Nazarene (Matt. 2:23), whereas *Naṣāra* is not used in Syriac outside the Gospels for "Christian." The name *Naṣāra* for a Christian in Arabic seems clearly derived from the Syriac Diatessaron which includes Matthew 2:2 3. Perhaps we should note here that the Arabic word *mu'minūn* occurs much more frequently in the Koran as the apparent name for the followers of the religion proclaimed by Muḥammad than *Muslimūn.* I am indebted to Dr. A. K. Kazi, Senior Lecturer (Islamic Studies) in the Department of Semitic Studies, for pointing this out. Dr. Kazi suggests that in the Koran *Mu'min* seems to point to a deeper religious experience than the term *Muslim.* We know that Umar did not call himself *Amīru l-Muslimīn* but *Amīru l-Mu'minīn.* So, apparently even in the time of the second Caliph, Muslim was not the name the followers of Muḥammad called themselves. The emphasis on belief is one of the features of St. John's Gospel and therefore of the Diatessaron. The word in Syriac for believer is *mhaimen.* The Nicene Creed in Syriac starts off with *'ana mhaimen* 'I believe.' *Mhaimnīn* is already used in the Syriac New Testament as the term for Christians. Payne Smith (*Thesaurus*) points out that that was specifically the term the Monophysites adopted to describe themselves. Could it be that

Muḥammad while stressing belief in the One God like the Christians, as the test of the true Muslim used the term *Mu'minīn* in the hope of bringing in the *Mhaimnīn,* the Christian Arab Monophysites? Later, when the advance had not been accepted and the new religious community was strong it would then drop the term *Mu'minīn* for *Muslimīn.* In the Syriac New Testament the root *šlm* is used in the Gospels in the sense of "being betrayed, being delivered up, being perfected, fulfilled, accomplished" in both active and passive sense. In the Gospel story there is a Divine irony, Judas Iscariot by betraying Jesus helps on the fulfilment of His Mission. This is brought out by the way the Gospel plays on the root *šlm.* However, the Syrian Christians later, cf. Arabic Diatessaron, use the root *šlm* (Arabic *slm)* of the betrayal affected by Judas, and when speaking of Judas Iscariot as *al-Muslim,* the betrayer. (Cf. Diatessaron ch. XLVIII [Matt. 26:49]. While this is a literal translation of the Syriac *Mašlmāna,* it makes Judas, as it were, the first Muslim.) For the other uses of the Syriac root *šlm*, the cognate Arabic root *slm* is not used, but the root *tmm,* to fulfil, and *kml,* to accomplish, perfect. It seems that Syrian Christianity did not want to use the root *šlm* in the sense of "fulfilment, completion," because Islam and the Muslims were claiming that Islam was the fulfilment of Christianity, and that Muslims in becoming Muslims had delivered themselves up fully to God in a way that Jesus and Christianity as well had not, being outside Islam.

In the reference to John the Baptist in the Koran the term *saba'* is used. This root means "to dye or dip." It has been said that Muḥammad did not understand that it meant baptism. However, the same root appears in Syriac, meaning to baptize. In Surah 2:132 it is said:

> The dye/baptism of God! and who is better than God at baptizing/dying?" (The root *sb'* is used here) and we are worshippers of Him.

It looks as if Muḥammad here is disposing of baptism as a sacrament dispensed by priests. The Koranic Arabic word for priest, *Qissīs,* is the same word as in Syriac. The term used for the "person" of God three times in the Koran is *wağh,* i.e., face. This reminds one of the Syriac theological term "Prosofa." In Syriac Incarnation Theology *Prosofa* is applied to Jesus (two natures, i.e., divine and human—one *prosofa,* one person). Muḥammad, by applying this term to God, is probably stressing Divine Unity. There is only one person in the Godhead, not three.

Muḥammad's criticism of the Trinity being three Gods was justified in so far as there had been the Arabian Tritheistic heresy (see p. 196 above) but is probably polemic against Monophysitism from which this heresy had sprung in reaction.

Muḥammad did not hold a Docetic view of Jesus, though he denies His death on the cross (Surah 4:154 f.). It was someone else who was crucified. This goes beyond Nestorianism, which said that only Jesus the Messiah died:

God the Son returned to God. In Monophysitism, Jesus being One nature Divine and human conjoined, the Divine suffered with the human on the Cross. With Muḥammad's view neither suffers, and thus he solves the argument between Nestorianism and Monophysitism.

Jesus is only an apostle—Rasūl (Surah 5:79)—and was a real man. Muḥammad's argument to prove this is that both Jesus and His Mother ate food. Jesus wrought miracles (Surah 5:110 ff.). The same Surah ends with an obvious adaptation of the Feeding of the Multitude in the story of the sending down of the Table from heaven. In the Diatessaron this miracle gets much space (in fact both the feeding of the five thousand and of the four thousand are given). To the reader of the Diatessaron the Feedings of the Multitudes are as it were the centres of the Gospel: all the more so as the Johannine sacramental discourse following the feeding of the Five Thousand is given in full, after a complete narrative based on Matthew, Mark, Luke and John. It may be that Muḥammad has deliberately taken this miracle, followed as it is in the Diatessaron with the Sacramental discourse on the bread of heaven to underline as he does in this Sum of the Table that God is the Giver. This was but a sign of God's providence manifested by Jesus. It is all the more noteworthy that in the Surah Jesus disclaims that He told men to take Him and His Mother as Gods, and to say that He was only a witness of God. Muḥammad is also here clearly disposing of the Sacrament of Holy Communion just as he had disposed of baptism. Jesus' message of Sum 5:117 is "Worship God, my Lord and your Lord." Jesus of Himself can provide nothing, even His miracles were given Him by God as signs. He, like Muḥammad, or Muḥammad like Him are recalling other men to God.

Bell in *The Origin of Islam in its Christian Environment,*[22] while seeking to show development in both Muḥammad's knowledge of Christianity and his attitude to Christians does admit two significant facts. First, that words like "*ṣalāt* - prayer," "*sabbiḥ* - to ascribe glory to," "*tazakka* - to seek purity" - by giving alms, "*ʿabd* - a worshipper," "*qara'a* - to read," and even the word *Koran* and *Sūrah* (cf. Syriac *šūrtā* - a writing, a portion of scripture), were to hand.[23] Bell speaks rightly of "an atmosphere of Jewish and Christian ideas pervading Arabia at all time."[24] The present writer would suggest that *Bismi llāhi r-Raḥmāni r-Raḥīm* may derive from the Syriac *Bešma Raḥmānā Raḥīmā* which would give the meaning "In the name of God, the Merciful, the Beloved (better surely than the tautological 'The Compassionate')."

Bell to back his claim that Christian ideas were part of the heritage of Arabia points to Imru l-Qais of the pre-Islamic period likening a troop of game to "monks at a festival with fringed robes."[25] Imru l-Qais in his *Muʿallaqa* (line 40) could say too:

> Years have passed over it (the camp of a loved one) since I knew it, it has become like the writing of the Psalms *(zubur)* in the books *(masāḥif)* leaves of the monks.

One recalls the term *musḥaf* used later of the Koran. St. Simeon Stylites, famed for his long session on his pillar, was an Arab by race. Though he witnessed at Antioch, as Bell points out,[26] we are told crowds of desert Arabs flocked to see him and to hear him proclaim the Gospel from his lofty perch. The second thing that Bell admits is that the Muḥammad of Mecca was not so different from the Muḥammad of Medina. Bell writes:

> He was a very practical character. In Medina that side of his character is most painfully evident ... Even in Mecca the practical direction of his thought is very marked. He had the mystic quality of a seeker after truth, but that did not destroy his practical bent.[27]

In short, there is a danger of overemphasizing the eschatological stress in Muḥammad's preaching even in the Meccan period. It is there throughout, but so is his stress on God's goodness in creation and His generous Providence. For both of which, like in the Anglican General Thanksgiving, we owe Him gratitude. It is because men have forgotten and still forget that they must be warned. This reminds us of Tor Andrae's Missionary Sermon. When the Faithful Little Flock grew, there would not be so much need to stress the dread warning of the End. One is not so certain that Bell can have it both ways, i.e., see in the Muḥammad of Mecca the Muḥammad of Medina and *vice versa* and also stress that Islam and the Koran is virtually the creation of the Medinan period.

We have only the Koran's witness for both periods, and while one is willing to admit Bell's evidence that Muḥammad did obtain gobbets of more detailed knowledge about the Old Testament and New Testament from Jews and Christians in the Medinan period, one feels that Bell makes such new scraps of knowledge responsible for producing too much in a relatively short time. After all Muḥammad was not a young man when he received his call and intimates of his knew of Christianity and its doctrines.

It is surely significant, as Bell points out but does not unfortunately draw the right conclusions, that only after the Hiğra did Muḥammad realize that the Christian Inğīl and the Taurat are separate books. This in itself points to Christian influence on Muḥammad from the beginning. Just as the Gospel claimed to fulfil the Law, so he claimed his Koran fulfilled both. But just as the Church never jettisoned the Law and the idea of the Chosen People and the promises thereto, but took them over for herself, so did Muḥammad who saw himself after the battle of Badr as a second Moses even as he had seen himself as *Fārqalīṭ/Aḥmad* successor of Jesus.

In Surah 3:43 Jesus is made to say

> I will confirm what is before you of the Law and will surely make lawful for you some of that which was prohibited from you.

In Surah. 6:147 Muḥammad teaches that God says (through him):

> To those who were Jews did we prohibit everything that hath a solid hoof; and of oxen and sheep did we prohibit to them the fat, save what the backs of both do bear, or the inward or what is mixed with bone; with that did we recompense them for their rebellion, for verily, we are true.

This last reminds one strongly of the Pauline argument about why the Law was given. Whereas Surah 3 is a Medinan Surah, it is that special restrictive legislation was put in the Law because of the rebellion of the people (presumably in the Golden Calf incident, cf. Surah 2:51, 2:87, 7:146 ff.). (In fact in Surah 7 [a Meccan. Surah] v. 157, Muḥammad sees himself as "setting down for them their burdens and the yokes" which were upon them.)

Very important is Surah 16 (Meccan) vv. 115–25 showing as it does that not only the restrictive food legislation and the Sabbath are criticized, but the people are encouraged to follow the faith of Abraham—v. 124.

In Syriac salvation is *purqānā.* The Day of the battle of Badr was called in the Koran, the Day of *Furqān. Furqān* should not be rendered "decision," but "salvation." Now Jesus in the Koran is son of Miryam, Moses' sister. The word for Joshua in Syriac is the same as that for Jesus. Joshua is mentioned twice in the New Testament (Acts 7:44 and Heb. 4:18). In Surah 3:45 we read:

> And when 'Īsa perceived unbelief on their part (that of the Jews) he said, "Who are my helpers for God's sake?" The Apostles replied: "We are God's helpers; we have believed and we testify that we are Muslims."

Also in Surah 61:14:

> O ye who have believed be helpers of God: as 'Īsā son of Maryam said to the Apostles, "Who are my helpers for God's sake?" And the Apostles said, "We are God's helpers. So part of the Banū Isrā'īl believed and part disbelieved. So we assisted those who believed, against their enemies, and they appeared as conquerors."

This last reminds one of Moses quelling the worshippers of the Calf—Exodus 32:26 (an incident referred to several times in the Koran) or Joshua going to fight against Amalek—Exodus 17:7 "Choose us out men."

Elsewhere in the Koran, cf. Surah 2:215, we have the call to the Jihad or Holy War. But it seems that it is implicit here. If Jesus equals Joshua and he led his people to the promised land (after all the Christian Greeks did possess it), his successor Muḥammad would do likewise. The Apostles were the helpers of God, the *Anṣāru llāh*, i.e., the *Naṣāra* the Christians had been the helpers of God. The Muslims of Medina who helped Muḥammad were to be his *Anṣār*. Muḥammad with their help would take his holy land Mecca and afterwards extend the *Dāru l-Islām*. Even the Jihad had its origins in the Judaeo-Christian tradition.

Surah 2:209 says: "Men were *one nation ('Umma wāḥida)* once." Islam, conscious that it now is heir of the promises to Abraham, from the beginning felt that it was incumbent on all Muslims to bring all men back to God and to be one through Him One can see where they derived this example. There is neither Jew nor Greek, bond nor free, but all are one in Jesus Christ. Remembering the equation Jesus = Joshua, the Jihad was the answer.

Heraclius, the Eastern Roman Emperor a decade earlier than the Arab conquest of Palestine in 636, had driven the Persians out of Palestine and Mesopotamia. This weakened his and the Persian Empire and made it the easier prey to the Muslim armies.

Heraclius' massacre of the Jews in Jerusalem in 629 and his treatment of the Monophysites in Mesopotamia further prepared the way for the armies of Islam. The Jews welcomed the Arabs to Palestine, as did the Monophysites of Syria and Mesopotamia. Abel-Farağ (Bar Hebraeus) the Syrian historian could write after Jew and Christian have lived under Muslim rule for three-quarters of a millennium:

> When our people complained to Heraclius, he gave no answer. Therefore the God of Vengeance delivered us out of the hands of Romans by means of the Arabs.[28]

The Copts of Egypt had been alienated by the Patriarch Cyrus (Heraclius' nominee). The Persian governor of Ḥīra in Iraq, a Christian called 'Abdu l-Masīḥ, agreed to a treaty with Ḫālid b. al-Walīd the Muslim leader to be of help to the Muslims against the Persians, provided their Churches were not destroyed.[29]

It was not just that Islam was an Arab religious movement, but because it provided the downtrodden Jews and Arab Christians with a means of hitting back at their Greek and Persian oppressors that such help was given. Not that Jews and Arab Christians could accept the claims of Islam, but on the whole they fared better under Islamic rule than under Greek Orthodox Emperor and Sassanid Shah; both Jew and Christian in Islam were to make their contribution to Islamic civilization and culture. The Syrians with their translations they had made into Syriac of Greek scientific, and medical and philosophical works, and which in the time of Caliph Ma'mūn were to be translated by the Syrian priest Ḥunain b. Isḥāq into Arabic, in culture just as in religion were the middlemen.

Notes

1 Sir William Muir, *The Corān: Its Composition and Teaching, and the Testimony It Bears to the Holy Scriptures* (London: S.P.C.K., 1878).
2 Alfred Guillaume, *Islam* (Harmondsworth, UK: Pelican Books, 1954), p. 1.
3 [Eusebius c. AD 260/265–339/340 (also called Eusebius of Caesarea and Eusebius Pamphili). *Historia Ecclesiastica* (H.E) (Church History) first seven books ca. 300, eighth and ninth book ca. 313, tenth book ca. 315, epilogue ca. 325.]
4 [Socrates of Constantinople, also known as Socrates Scholasticus, born at Constantinople c. 380: the date of his death is unknown. Little is known of his life except what can be gathered from his *Historia Ecclesiastica* ("Church History"), which unlike Eusebius' work, emphasized the place of the emperor in church affairs and in giving secular as well as church history.]
5 [Philostorgius (Greek: Φιλοστόργιος; 368–ca. 439), an Anomoean Church historian. Anomoeans or Eunomians formed a heretical sect that denied that Jesus was the same nature as God the Father.]
6 [B.V.M.: Beata Virgo Maria, or Blessed Virgin Mary]
7 A. Guillaume, *Islam* (Harmondsworth, UK: Pelican Books, 1954), p. 17.
8 Guillaume, op. cit., pp. 14–15.
9 Tor Andrae, *Mohammed: The Man and his Faith* (London, 1936), pp. 126–7.
10 Ibid., p. 126.
11 Cf. Joseph Klauser, *From Jesus to Paul* (London, 1944), op. cit.
12 A. Guillaume, op. cit., p. 15
13 Tor Andrae, op. cit., p. 153
14 For these percentages cf. G. F. Moore, *Journal of Bibl. Lit.*, vol. IX, 1890, p. 201 ff.
15 Tor Andrae, op. cit., p. 154.
16 Ibid., p. 152.
17 In connection with *al-nabī al-'ummī* it should be noted that in Koran Surah 3:19 the word 'Ummiyīn, plural of 'Ummiyu, applied twice to the prophet in Surah 7:157, 158, here seems clearly to refer to the Pagan Arabs in contradistinction to Jesus and Christians.
18 Cf. R. Payne Smith, *Thesaurus Syriacus* (Oxford, 1879).
19 Gustav Adolf Deissmann, *The Religion of Jesus and the Faith of Paul: The Selly Oak Lectures*, 1923 on the communion of Jesus with God and the communion of Paul with Christ, W. E. Wilson, trans. (London, 1923).
20 Tor Andrae, op.cit., pp. 119–121.
21 Cf. Patrologia Syriaca, Vol. III.
22 Richard Bell, *The Origin of Islam in Its Christian Environment: Gunning Lectures* 1925 (London, 1926), op. cit.
23 R. Bell, op. cit., pp. 51, 52.
24 Ibid., p. 53.
25 Ibid., p. 44.
26 Ibid., p. 19.
27 Ibid., p. 71.
28 Cited by Bell, op. cit., p. 166.
29 Cf. ibid., p. 173.

The Nestorian Antecedents of the Šahāda

Philippe Gignoux

Originally published as "Les antecedents nestoriens de la Chahada," in Acta Iranica *28 (1988): 403–406; translated by Ibn Warraq.*

To Professor Jes P. Asmussen, who has always shown to me, as to many others, such kindness and friendship, I should like to offer this modest note on the history of comparative religions, a domain which has often interested and occupied him, apart from his works of Iranology, and especially the important publications that he has carried out for our knowledge of Manichaeism.

It is only a few contacts between the Nestorians and Islam that I wish to put in evidence here, concerning the formula of the *Šahāda*.[1]

In a small article, still unnoticed, forming a part of a collective work,[2] I tried to show that the Arabic *bismillāh*[3] could have been a calque on the well-known Mazdean formula, "in the name of the gods," modified into a singular, as it must be for a religion strictly monotheist. Besides, the formula in the singular seems to appear in Pehlevi or Pahlavi[4] only from the Islamic period onwards. One finds a good example of it on a bilingual weight, that I have published with Raoul Curiel,[5] where the *bismillāh* is translated into Pahlavi by *PWN ŠM Y yzdt', pad nām ī yazd*, and the citation of a verse from the Koran as well as the mention of the weight have been equally rendered into Pahlavi on the other side of the object. The inscription is interesting because the weight is datable to the Umayyad period, to the end of the seventh century, as Curiel demonstrated.[6]

Today we know of quite a number of objects inscribed in Arabic and Pahlavi at the same time, a witness to the slow disappearance of Iranian to the benefit of Arabic, as R. Gyselen has shown.[7] Among these objects, it seems to me interesting to draw attention to a coin in the collection of M. Foroughi, published by M. I. Mochiri,[8] and which provides us with a translation of the Shahada in Pahlavi:

yzdt' Y BR' 'LH 'ḤRN yzdt' L'YT
yazd ī be ōy any yazd nēst

that is to say: "a God besides this one, another God there is not," an almost literal translation of Arabic formulas, as we shall see, but where the order of the terms has been inverted.[9]

If the arguments that I have developed in favour of an Iranian origin of the *Bismillāh* remain still inadequate, it is not the same concerning the *Šahāda* whose Greek and Syriac origins seem obvious.

In a recent study, the distinguished comparatist of Jerusalem, Shlomo Pines[10] has drawn attention to the Greek version of the Arabic formula that he found in the Homilies of the Pseudo-Clementines, which one can date to the 4th century C.E.[11] The Greek says [Homily XVI, Chapters7, 9:

> *heis estin ho theos kai plēn autou ouk estin theos* – "God is one, and there is no God except Him."

This phrase is clearly the equivalent to the one we read in the Koran, under two closely related forms:

> *Lā ilāh illā huwa* – "there is no God except him"
> *Lā ilāh illā Allāh* – "there is no God except Allah,"[12]

the second one being less frequent, and undoubtedly derived from Isaiah, 44:6, 44:8 and 45:21, as Pines points out.[13]

In these two texts, of the Pseudo-Clementines and of the Koran, the formula has the goal of supporting a unitary theology, and the Christology of the Koran conforms to those of the Judaeo-Christian sects according to which Jesus was simply a man; or more precisely the Pseudo-Clementines are strongly impregnated with Judaeo-Christian elements.[14]

In a text even more ancient, the Gnostic "The Apocryphon of John,"[15] that M.Tardieu had dated to the end of the second century CE,[16] I found the following passage:

> ...For he said, "I am God and there is no other God beside me," for he is ignorant of his strength, the place from which he had come.[17]

This affirmation of an exclusive monotheism has its source, as the editor reminds us[18] in Isaiah, 45:5–6, and 46:9.[19]

Among the formulas of the Shahāda that epigraphy reveals to us, and notably the inscriptions on seals and bulla, one can note some variants:

on a clay bulla which must be very old:	*illā ilāh illā Allāh* [20]
or on a lead bulla: the complete formula:	*lā ilāh illā Allāh*
	muḥammad rasūl Allāh.[21]

In some formulations slightly different, but quite parallel, the Acts of the Persian Martyrs[22] provide us with quite a few examples of the Pre-Islamic formula, undoubtedly the origin of the *Šahāda*, in some passages that one can date to 5th–6th centuries,[23] which, as far as I know has never been noted before. Without pretending to be exhaustive, I cite the following examples:

> *w'lh 'ḥryn lbr mnh lyt ln*[24] – "and there is for us no other God beside Him"

dḥd hw 'lh' wlyt 'ḥrn' lbr mnh[25] – "that God is one and there is no other beside Him."

This formula is almost an exact translation of the Greek of the Pseudo-Clementines.

wtd' dhwyw wlyt 'ḥryn lbr mnh[26] – "and you know that He exists and that there is no other beside Him"
wlyt 'lh lbr mnh[27] – "and there is no God beside Him."
wlyt 'lh 'ḥryn lbr mnk[28] – "and there is no God beside You"
'nt 'nt 'lh' šryr wlyt 'ḥryn lbr mnk[29] – "You are the true God and there is no other beside You."
wlyt 'lh 'ḥryn lbr mnh[30] – "and there is no other God beside Him."

The very monotheist affirmation of the Nestorians, attested to in these formulas, is easily explained vis-à-vis Mazdeism which in contrast flaunted openly its polytheism, for which the Christian martyrs reproached it.

One must above all note that the formula most used in the Koran "there is no God beside Him" is exactly the one attested to, in the Pseudo-Clementines in Greek and in the Acts of the Martyrs in Syriac, while the second formula of the Koran, in which the God of Islam is named, does not have its equivalence in Syriac. One cannot evade the conclusion which imposes itself, that is to say that the *Šahāda* has its origin in the Judaeo-Christian circles, but it was also very well-known among the Nestorian community in the middle and at the end of the Sassanian period.

It is not for me to give a history of the Islamic formula, whose popularity is evident, and which has even furnished a modern author like Jamalzade the title of one of his works, published in 1960, "*Qayr az Ḫodā hič kas na būd,*" though in an adapted form.

Notes

1 First of the five pillars of Islam, Šahāda, bearing witness that there is no deity but God.
2 "Pour une origine iranniene du bi'smillah," Pad nām ī yazdān, *Etudes d'epigraphie, de numismatique et d'histoire de l'Iran ancien* (Paris, 1979), pp. 159–163.
3 Literally, "In the name of God." An ejaculation frequently used at the commencement of any undertaking.
4 The Middle Persian language, esp. as used in classical Zoroastrian and Manichean literature.
5 "Un poids arabo-sasanide," in: *Studia Iranica* 5, 1976, pp. 165–169.
6 Ibid., p. 169.
7 "La transition de l'Iran sassanide à l'empire des Califes, d'après les monnaies," in:

Comptes Rendus de l'Académie des Inscriptions et Belles-Lettres de l'année, 1984, pp. 692–701.

8 "A Pahlavi Forerunner of the Umayyad Reformed Coinage," *JRAS* 1981, pp. 168–172.

9 Corresponding to the second formula cited below; the inversion is rendered necessary by the place of the verb at the end of the phrase in Pahlavi.

10 "Notes on Islam and on Arabic Christianity and Judaeo-Christianity," *Jerusalem Studies in Arabic and Islam* 4 1984, pp. 135–152. See above all pp. 141–142. [Reprinted in Shlomo Pines, *Collected Works of Shlomo Pines*, Volume, IV, Studies in the History of Religion, edited by Guy G. Stroumsa (Jerusalem: The Magnes Press, The Hebrew University, 1996), pp. 316–33, also in the present volume, pp. 587–605.

11 Cf. B. Altaner, *Précis de Patrologie*, ed. Salvator (Mulhouse, 1961), pp. 148–149.

12 The accumulation of the liquid "l" in this formula which is merely a fact of the Arabic, must have conferred on it a new status, and lent itself, in any case, to declamation and repetition which are the characteristics of Muslim prayer.

13 Pines, op. cit., p. 142. [Isaiah 44:6, "Thus saith the Lord the king of Israel, and his redeemer the Lord of hosts; I am the first, and I am the last; and beside me there is no God" King James Version. Isaiah 44: 8, "Is there a God beside me? Yea, there is no God; I know not any." KJV. Isaiah. 45: 21–22: "21. …and there is no God else beside me; a just God and a Saviour; there is none beside me. 22. Look unto me, and be ye saved, all the ends of the earth: for I am God, and there is none else." KJV].

14 Pines, op. cit., p. 144.

15 [Also known in English as *The Secret Book of John* or *The Secret Revelation of John*, and in French as *Livre des secrets de Jean* or *Livre secret de Jean*, *Apocryphe de Jean*, or still *Apocryphon de Jean*. There are four copies extant: one in the Berlin Codex, and the others in the Library of Nag Hammadi, where it is found in two versions: one long and one short. It is a work of mythological Gnosticism. See also Rodolphe Kasser, "Le Livre secret de Jean dans ses différentes formes textuelles coptes," *Le Muséon* 77 (1964), also Michael Waldstein and Frederik Wisse, *The Apocryphon of John: Synopsis of Nag Hammadi Codices* II, 1; III, 1; and IV, 1 with BG 8502, 2 *Nag Hammadi and Manichaean Studies* Vol. 33, Coptic Gnostic Library (E. J. Brill, 1995)].

16 *Codex de Berlin, Sources gnostiques et manichéennes* I, Paris, éd. du Cerf, 1984, pp. 43–46. Other scholars, before him, have dated the same work to the beginning of the second century: cf. M. Tardieu et J.-D. Dubois, *Introduction à la littérature gnostique* I, Collections retrouvées avant 1945 (Paris. Ed. du Cerf/Ed. du C.N.R.S.: 1986), pp. 122–123.

17 Tardieu, *Codex de Berlin*, III § 32. [My English translation is by Dr. Wisse, who prepared it for the Nag Hammadi Library in English, and used all four manuscripts to produce a single text. Found at: http://www.gnosis.org/naghamm/apocjn.html]

18 Tardieu, *Codex de Berlin*, 294, where he comments on § 38 off text, 117, where the demiurge declares that he is a jealous god and that "there is no other God besides me."

19 Isaiah 45:5–6, "I am the Lord, and there is none else, there is no God beside me: I girded thee, though thou hast not known me: That they may know from the rising

of the sun, and from the west, that there is none beside me. I am the Lord, and there is none else": 46:9, "Remember the former things of old: for I am God, and there is none else; I am God, and there is none like me."

20 Cf. Ludvik Kalus, *Catalogue des cachets, bulles et talismans islamiques*, Paris, Bibliothèque Nationale, 1981, 59 no. 1.2 A.

21 Kalus, op. cit., 63 no. 2.9 A et B.

22 ["Acts of the Persian Martyrs , a collection of the acts of martyrdom under Šāpūr II (309–79 AD). They were made known by S. E. Assemani on the basis of Ms. Vat. Syr. 160 (Acta sanctorum martyrum I, Rome, 1748). New and better manuscripts emerged, which made possible a new edition by P. Bedjan (Acta martyrum et sanctorum II, Leipzig, 1891), based on the Ms. Dijarb. 96, Ms. B.M. Add. 14,645 and Ms. Berlin Sach. 222. Other sources have also emerged; however, only the acts of Šemʿōn have been critically edited, by M. Kmosko (Patrologia Syriaca I/2 Paris, 1907, col. 715–960).... According to the internal evidence, the collector must have done his work during the period of troubles prior to Yazdegerd (399–420). Thus we are dealing with a very ancient source." From *Encyclopaedia Iranica*, vol. I, fasc. 4, pp. 430–43.]

23 See the problerns of dating, especially the work of G. Wiessner, *Untersuchungen zur syrischen Literarurgeschichte* I, *Zur Märtyrerüberlieferung aus der Christenverfolgung Schapurs II* (Göttingen, 1967).

24 P. Bedjan, *Acta martyrum et sanctorum* 7 vols, Paris 1890–1897. This passage is in vol. II, pp. 346–347.

25 Op, cit., II, p. 375.

26 Op. cit., II, p. 384.

27 Op. cit., II, pp. 406 and 410.

28 Op. cit., II, p. 425.

29 Op. cit., II, p. 447.

30 Op. cit., II, p. 458.

The Creed of Abū ʻĀmir

Moshe Gil

Originally published in Israel Oriental Studies *12 (1992): 9–57.*

1. The Ideological Background

1.1 Ḥanīf

Since the opposition in Medina was centered around a *ḥanīf*, the meaning of this term must be reexamined. Clearly enough, the old and true *ḥanīfiyya* which Abū ʻĀmir claimed to represent, eventually declined and disappeared after Muḥammad prevailed, and its leader died a lonely fugitive in Byzantine territory. The Muslim sources are therefore far from unanimous in defining the word *ḥanīf*, although the prevalent view assimilates it with Islam itself.

This study is centered around matters of an apparently theological nature. Having been engaged for several years in historical rather than theological studies, I only dare approach these matters since I believe to have put to use some sources of a real historical nature wherein true persons are seen engaged in a struggle in which theological matters are just an external aspect, perhaps even a secondary one.

In my article "The Medinan Opposition to the Prophet," published in the *Jerusalem Studies in Arabic and Islam* (Vol. X, pp. 65–96, 1987), I believe that I have shown convincingly who were the main opponents to the Prophet; also, that the two main events in which the ideological incentives of these opponents were brought to light were the Tabūk expedition and the building of the dissenters' mosque, *Masǧid al-Ḍirar*. The reader is also referred to that article in order to see that these dissenters were in fact *ḥanīfs*—followers of Abū ʻĀmir, leader of the 'true *ḥanīfs*', the deadliest enemy, of Muḥammad. Further references to this *JSAI* article will be given by the initials MO with page no., in brackets, in the main text.

This real struggle that went on in Medina toward the end of the Prophet's lifetime sheds light on the meaning of terms such as *ḥanīf*, and may serve to improve our understanding of the roots of Islam as they developed in the social and political realities of the tribal society of Medina.

I first became involved with this subject while preparing a series of lectures on the history of the Jews of Arabia, in the department of Jewish History of Tel Aviv University. At that time I came across the conversation between Muḥammad b. Maslama and the Banū Naḍīr as recorded by Wāqidī (MO, p. 91). There Abū ʿĀmir, the leader of the conservative *ḥanīfs* is mentioned. It is around this personality that I focused my search for sources and was able, at a later stage, to see the manifold implications of his feud with Muḥammad. I also found relevant connections with two topics I was acquainted with from my earlier studies, the Enoch texts, and Mazdak.

This article underwent some important changes and had several passages added after I was given the unique opportunity to present it before the International Seminar "From Ǧāhiliyya to Islam," directed by Prof. M. J. Kister, at the Institute for Advanced Studies of the Hebrew University, Jerusalem. I am very much indebted to Prof. Kister and to the many other participants at the seminar, who scrutinized the various parts of my study with much zeal and, during two meetings of the seminar, expressed their mercilessly critical remarks on them. My gratitude also goes to my friend and colleague, Prof. J. Kraemer of Tel Aviv University, who read this work very carefully and contributed very valuable remarks and suggestions. It goes without saying that all responsibility for whatever is said in the following pages belongs to myself, not to any of these who are my teachers and friends.

Does *ḥanīf* mean "Christian" or "Jew"? Clearly not, as shown by the famous Quranic phrase:

> *mā kāna -brāhīmu yahūdiyyan wa-lā naṣrāniyyan wa-lākin kāna ḥanīfan musliman wa- mā kāna min al- mušrikīn.* [Abraham was not a Jew, nor was he a Christian; he was rather (that kind of a) *ḥanīf* who is monotheistic, not of (hose *ḥanīfs*) who are polytheists].

See the interpretation of *muslim* as "monotheist" in D. Z. H. Baneth, "What Did Muḥammad Mean," etc., Israel Oriental Studies, 1:183, 1971.) *Ḥanīf* will be shown to have meant originally "Manichaean." It emerges that the closest challengers of the Prophet were the old-fashioned Manichaeans of Medina; these were guilty of not being monotheistic and, of course, of not recognizing who the true prophet was.

In the Quran the term *ḥanīf* sometimes designates the adherent of the *fiṭra*, the natural religion. In poetry, the two terms, *muslim* and *ḥanīf*, are often paired; and *ḥanīf* often substitutes for *muslim*, especially in antithesis to *naṣārā*, for instance in reference to wine-drinking. By virtue of this identification some features characteristic of Muslims were transferred to the *ḥanīfs*, among them circumcision, monotheism, and performing the pilgrimage. In fact, the word *muslim* is considered to be the "modern" equivalent of the archaism *ḥanīf*. Umayya b. Abī Ṣalt (whose name was ʿAbdallāh) b. Abī Rabīʿa b. ʿAwf al-Ṯaqafi was a *ḥanīf*; he had knowledge of books and read them; out of piety he used to wear haircloth (*musūḥ*); he used to invoke Ibrāhīm and Ismāʿīl and forbade wine-drinking and idolatry. In the Prophet's words, he was virtually a Muslim.[1]

Arab lexicographers have made great efforts to find the Arabic etymology of *ḥanīf*. There are attempts at lexicographical explanations of the word also in *sīra* collections and other books of traditions. Thus, for instance, Ibn Hišām tries to explain the root *ḥ-n-f* as derived from *ḥ-n-ṯ*, and he gives other examples of occurrences of this shift. There is also the explanation of *ḥnf* as designating an irregularity or deviation of the legs or of walking; therefore also as meaning "inclination," or (*ḥanafa ʿan*) "to recoil," of course from vanity to truth.[2] These explanations are of little use in trying to understand and identify the *ḥanīfiyya*.

The meaning of *ḥanīfiyya* as the religion of the *fiṭra*, the natural one, is explained in simple words and conclusively by Ṭayālisī, in a tradition attributed to the Prophet, who allegedly said it in a *ḫuṭba*: God created human beings to be all *ḥanīfs*: but once the *šayāṭīn* made them sin, God forbade things which had been permitted at first.[3]

Another way of indicating that the *ḥanīfiyya* was originally the religion of the righteous was to call it the religion of Abraham. A legion of Arab figures antedating Islam are described by the sources as *ḥanīfs*, followers of the religion of Abraham, as in the Quran, and in conformity to its description of Abraham these individuals are said to have been neither Jews nor Christians. A tradition preserved in Wāḥidī calls the Prophet's uncle Abū Talib "the head of the *ḥanīfiyya, millat al-ašyāḫ,*" the religion of the good old times. Abū ʿĀmir was not the only *ḥanīf* who declined to accept Muḥammad; at least one additional leader of the *ḥanīfs*, also a Medinan, Abū Qays Ṣayfi b. al-Aslat, was opposed to Muḥammad as well. He was apparently the leader of the Ǧaʿādira, a group of clans of ʿAws, and a poet; he died nine months after the *hiǧra*. There is much significance in his famous verses on the *ḥanīfs*, quoted by Ibn Isḥāq, in which he praises God for not having made him and his people Jews or Christians, but *ḥanīfs*.[4]

The Kaʿba is said to have been at first a *ḥanīfī* place of worship. ʿAmru b. Luḥayy was the one who first introduced idols there by bringing with him the idol called Hubal.[5] The non-idolatric character of the Kaʿba sanctuary is also confirmed by another tradition preserved by Ibn Isḥāq; people from Qurayš found in the foundation of the sanctuary a text written in Syriac which a Jew read to them. It turned out to be a dedication formula blessing the sanctuary. It mentions seven *amlāk ḥunafāʾ* whom God placed around heaven, earth, the sun, and the moon (or perhaps around Mecca). These *ḥanīfī* angels are theologically significant and will be referred to below in connection with an explanation of the *ḥanīfiyya*.

There was also another version about what was written there saying that

> whoever sows goodness will reap happiness, but those who sow evil will reap regret; you cannot be rewarded with good things for doing bad ones, just as no grapes can be picked from thorns;

this is obviously reminiscent of Matthew 7:15–20. We shall see below among which circles this passage enjoyed popularity.[6]

1.2 Sabians

From what has been shown to this point it seems clear that the *ḥanīfiyya* was not an invention of Islam, but was rather a very lively and active movement among Arab tribes in the *ǧāhiliyya*. There are good reasons for concluding that it was also known as the religion of the *ṣābi'ūn*, and there is evidence that the two terms were identical. *Ṣābi'* is also used as a synonym of *muslim*, just like *ḥanīf*. About to visit the Prophet, Umar says he is going to visit "Muḥammad, this *ṣābi'*;" after accepting Islam,'Umar is described as *qad ṣaba'a*.[7]

In a tradition recorded by Ibn Ḥazm, Abraham is said to have been sent by God to the Sabians to make their shortcomings right by *al-ḥanīfiyya al-samḥa*; in those times they were called *ḥanīfs*; there is a remainder of them "today" in Ḥarrān, but they are very few. In other words, the tradition recorded by Ibn Ḥazm says precisely what we assumed above, that *ṣābi'* and *ḥanīf* were the same.[8]

We are concerned here with understanding these terms as they were understood in ancient Arabia and at the time of the Prophet. There are sources concerning various kinds of people calling themselves Sabians in later times, mainly in Ḥarrān and in the Sawal of Iraq. We shall not go into detail concerning the differences between them which are the object of study and discussion of several eminent scholars. Let us just state that even in later times the Sabians (and Ḥarrānians) are still credited with views and beliefs which bear the marks of Manichaeism. That these are the characteristics of the ancient *ḥanīfiyya* as well will be shown in what follows. It is also noteworthy that even in later times, these sects were known to hold in esteem the books of fit (Seth) and Idrīs (Enoch) and make pilgrimages to what they believed were the tombs of these two prophets.[9]

In portraying these *ḥanīfs*—*ṣābi'ūn* the sources stress the dualistic nature of their beliefs. Ṭiḥāwī understands *ḥanafa* to mean "to incline," namely one's inclination to what he was created, since at the moment of man's creation it is decided who shall be happy and who unhappy; the unhappy ones are ruled by the devils, the happy by their opposite (i.e., good angels). Bīrūnī traces the origin of the *ṣābi'ūn* to a false prophet, Būḏasf, thus showing their Persian origin; they absolve God of all that is evil and call him by beautiful names, attributing the leadership of the world to heaven and its bodies. They have prophets, whom Bīrūnī names, such as Hermes the Egyptian whom they identify with Idrīs, who is Iḫnūḫ (Enoch) of the *tawrāh*.[10]

1.3 Ḥanpē

The word *ḥanīf* is related to Syriac Aramaic *ḥanpā*. Here we come across the question of how it was that what had a negative connotation in Christian Syriac parlance became meritorious in Muslim sources. The most reasonable answer is that the Arabs became acquainted with the people and beliefs represented by this term through non-Christian contacts, mainly through direct relations with *ḥanīfs*. In using this term the Syriac sources primarily condemned idolatry. This use of the term infiltrated even early Arab sources, which used materials taken from ancient Syriac writers. Yaʿqūbī calls the Philistines, the Greek kings and the Roman emperors *ḥanīfs* as well as *ṣābiʾūn*, as does also Masʿūdī. This same use of *ḥanpā* is found in the Syriac version of the Bible and Syriac ecclesiastical literature. Jeroboam, for instance, was a *ḥanpā* who went in the way of his father Solomon's *ḥanpūtā*. The use of *ḥanpā* corresponds also to Greek Ἕλλην ("Hellēn") and ἔθνικος ("éthnikos"). Andrae assumed that Muḥammad adopted the use of the term to mean "monotheistic," since in Syriac it was in use also to designate Mani and Manichaeism, namely monotheistic, without being either Jewish or Christian.[11]

1.4 Manichaeans

As is well known, historical data on Manichaeism is rather meager. It was a religion opposed to worldly rulers and to the great religions of the time. It never achieved any enduring political entity of its own, and never attained any stable worldly power. Most of our knowledge of Manichaeism therefore comes from the writings of its adversaries. However, these writings suffice to convey the impression that its beliefs were widely disseminated in various parts of the world, and that beginning in the second half of the third century A.D., it represented a serious threat to the ruling religions of the period. Moreover, it found a way to the hearts and minds of masses of people, perhaps mainly because of its eclectic nature, its ability to adapt itself to local convictions and superstitions. It had a considerable influence on masses of Christian believers, thanks mainly perhaps to an ability to disguise itself. More than once it has been quite difficult for us to decide whether some ancient source refers to either Manichaeism or Christianity; but Manichaeism succeeded, it seems, also by means of its social aspirations and striving for reforms. We have considerable evidence showing its dissemination in the Arabian peninsula and in the areas bordering it among the Arab tribes. Manichaeans were a main target of Christian propaganda. Cyril of Scythopolis tells us the story of Euthymius and of the monastery he founded south of Hebron: Many desert people who were formerly adherents of the Ravia, i.e., of the Manichaeans, cursed Mani (as required by the law of the Church) and went over to the καθολικὴ καὶ ἀποστοικὴ πίστις (the universal and apostolic faith).[12]

When Mar Saba's pupil Agapet was given authority over the new *laura* (A.D. 514–519), he found four monks there who belonged to the heresy of Origenes. The most remarkable among them was a Palestinian named Nonnos, who pretended to be a Christian, but in fact adhered to the beliefs of the godless Hellenes, Jews, and Manichaeans, mainly the belief in πρυπάρξις (pre-existence of souls).[13] Here we can see how paganism, or Hellenism, came to be identified with Manichaeism just as the two merged in Syriac *ḥanpē*, as will be seen presently.

Payne-Smith in his *Thesaurus* collected the various occurrences of *ḥanpā*, among them *ḥanpūtā dĕ-Mānī.* [14] Many occurrences of the word have been regularly translated by modern scholars as "pagan," whereas "Manichaean" would fit better. In the book of Ḥimyarites, e.g., where the Jews are said to co-operate with the *ḥanpē*, why should the assumption be that idolaters are meant? Manichaeans could have been meant as well.[15] The *fihrist* speaks of Mani as of *aḥnaf al-riǧāl*, "the most *ḥanīf* of men."[16]

In one of his epistles Išōʿyhab tells us of the Maronites, who tried their luck in making propaganda in his district, Rādhān. Speaking of this region, he mentions that *ḥanpūtā* was more widespread there than Christianity and the Maronite propaganda failed completely, neither the Christians nor even the *ḥanpē* paying attention to it. He wonders how it was that in the Persian district, to which he is writing (to Simon, bishop of Revardagir), the Maronites gained the attention of the *ḥanpē*, while the Christians looked on in silence. It stands to reason that here also the reference is to Manichaeans, whom the writer expected to make common cause with the Christians (i.e., of course, the Nestorians).[17]

Bar-Hebraeus, *sub anno* 896, refers to Abū al-Ḥasan Ṭābit (Ibn Qurra), who was one of the Ḥarrānian *ḥanpē*. Among other details he mentions sixteen Syriac books he wrote, including one on the laws of the *ḥanpē*. He also notes his division of the days of the week according to the seven planets, his writings on Hermes' laws and on the prayers of the *ḥanpē*. Obviously, the subject is the Manichaean creeds, not pagan ones as assumed by Budge in his translation.[18]

A Syriac text mentions the book of Bābā the Ḥarrānian, read devotedly by the *ḥanpē*, here too obviously referring to Manichaeans.[19]

The Syriac law-books in one place speak of the claim, made by Jews and *ḥanpē*, that there is no Christian law. Here again, *ḥanpē* seems to mean the Manichaeans.[20]

As for the matter of Manichaean infiltration among Arabs, we have information on Scythianus, who disseminated Manichaean teachings in the areas populated by Arab tribes, on the Euphrates, in Syria, and in the south of Palestine. He is said to have died in Judaea, or on his way there. He was a Saracen himself. These writings were brought to the region of the Jordan by an army veretan called Akouas, of Mesopotamian extraction, who settled in Eleutheropolis (Bet Guvrin), which had a large Manichaean population. Epiphanius, who was himself a native of Eleutheropolis, even says that the Manichaeans are called ʾΑκουανῖται ("Akuanîtai") after him.[21]

Mark the Deacon, in his biography of Porphyry of Gaza (early fifth century), after describing the Manichaeans' eclecticism, mentions Julia, a woman from Antioch (described as a centre of Manichaean propaganda) who was on a mission in southern Palestine to spread Manichaeism there, whose mouth was shut and "tongue cleaved to the roof of her mouth," through the curse of Porphyry.[22]

Epiphanius, whose reports on the innumerable heretical sects should be treated with a grain of salt, could not however have invented the information that Arabs coming to Jerusalem belonged to various sects, such as Antidicomarianites or Collyridians. Yaʿqūbī was also aware of the fact that some Arabs who relinquished paganism became Manichaeans, just as others became Jews or Christians.[23]

We have seen thus far that Manichaeism was particularly active in the areas bordering the Arabian Peninsula, that it spread among the Arabs, and that there is good reason to believe that Syriac ḥanpē sometimes denotes the Manichaeans. This evidence forms the background to what will be discussed further.

1.5 Jewish Manichaeans

Bīrūnī conveys information deserving more attention than it previously received. He claims that the real *ṣābiʾūn*, in contrast to those who merely pretend to be such but are in fact idolaters, are descendants of the Jews who remained in Iraq after having been deported there by Buḫt Nasr (Nebuchadnezzar). In many respects they follow Judaism. They are split into various sects, since they differ on essential religious matters.[24] The existence of Jewish Manichaeans should be taken into account in considering the so-called Jewish messianic sects, like the followers of Abū ʿĪsā (*al-ʿīsāwiyya*), or of Severus- Sereni, of the eighth century.[25] In addition, in light of what is said here of Syriac *ḥanpē*, and in connection with this information on the Jewish Manichaeans – *ṣābiʾūn* in Bīrūnī, it is important to notice a parallel term in Jewish sources. There are, in fact, third century Jewish sources in which the term is clearly explained, as meaning *mīnīm* (a common designation for heretics in Talmudic literature; the possibility of its etymological connection with the name Mani cannot be excluded). Thus Rabbi Jonathan (b. Eleazar, third century), a Babylonian living in Palestine and often quoted for his sayings against the heretics, explained that every *ḥănuppā* (that is any word derived from the root *ḥnp*) in the Bible refers to *mīnīm*, the main passage (*binyan āv*) being 'the sinners in Zion are afraid; fearfulness hath surprised the *ḥănēfim*' (Is. 23:14). One senses an allusion here to the persecutions which these *mīnīm* underwent. The term *ḥānēf* is also used concerning Enoch. It is said that Enoch was a *ḥānēf*, sometimes righteous (*ṣaddīq*), sometimes wicked. There is also a discussion between *mīnīm* and Rabbi Abbāhū, one of the leading sages of the period (ca. A.D. 300), who lived in Caesarea. The latter proves to his opponents that Gen. 5:24 did not mean that Enoch was immortal. Enoch (probably meaning the Enoch of the book named after him, to be discussed below) is inscribed in the register of the wicked, not in that of the righteous.[26] The *ḥănēfim* are also mentioned as a kind of people that should be brought before the public and cautioned, or the public should be cautioned about them (*mĕfarsĕmīn*); perhaps there is here a hint that they used to act under false colours. The purpose of this warning is to make their iniquity subject to a sentence of death, according to Ezek. 3:19–21:

> Yet if thou warn the wicked, and he turn not from his wickedness, nor from his wicked way, he shall die in his iniquity, etc.

This tradition is found in three Talmudic sources, the Tosefta, the Babylonian Talmud, and in the tractate Kallā. It is of special interest to notice the form *ḥănāfin*, found in a Geniza fragment quoted by Abramson.[27]

1.6 Anathēma (?)

The reading *ḥanāf* with *ā* in the second syllable instead of *ī* (*ḥanīf*) or *ē* (*ḥānēf*), is obviously an interesting *lectio difficilior*; it suggests the possibility of a Greek etymology of the term. Let us consider first the fact that the term has a pejorative meaning in Syriac, a mainly honorific sense in Arabic, whereas a Jewish source (*Bĕrēšīt rabbā*) is rather equivocal, though tending toward the pejorative (as do some additional Jewish sources). There is a corresponding ambivalence in the Greek terms *anathema* and *anathēma*, the first meaning mainly "curse" or "ban," the latter meaning "vow" or "offering," both taboo and holy. It is possible that *anathēma* was used by the Manichaeans themselves when speaking about their monks, or elect, who devoted themselves to a holy life (see below). It is noteworthy that in patristic literature, too, this term is used several times to designate the vow, or offering, made by a person who was dedicated to monastic or ascetic life. There may have been a contamination first among Aramaic-speaking Jews, between Biblical *ḥānēf* and *anathēma*. In post-classical Greek the *ēta* was pronounced *ī*, and the word rendered as *anathīma*. The two other shifts, of the *spiritus lenis* into *ḥ* and of θ into φ, are well-known. The first occurs in Aramaic, as for instance ἄκρα *ḥaqrā*. The latter was quite common among Greek speakers themselves. Thus *anathēma* was apparently thought of as a plural by the Aramaic speaking population, and what was pronounced in spoken Greek *anaphīma* became *ḥanāfim*, as we have just seen above. Of course, it is quite impossible to retrace the stages of the further penetration of the term, into Syriac Aramaic on one hand and into Arabic on the other. What seems very plausible, however, in the light of the situation obtaining is that all three groups of sources, the Jewish Aramaic, Syriac Aramaic, and the Arabic—evidently used this term, *ḥanāf*, *ḥanpā*, *ḥanīf*, to mean a Manichaean. Naturally, the Arab *ḥanīfs* called themselves by this term as meaning "holy." This can be seen in the expression *amlāk ḥunafāʾ* of the Kaʿba inscription mentioned above, which actually meant "holy angels," like the Ethiopic *qədusān malāʾəkt* in the book of Enoch, 93:2.[28]

1.7 Eastern Influences

So far we have dealt with Manichaean ideas spreading among the tribes and into the Arab Peninsula mainly from the Byzantine area; but Manichaeism was alive and sometimes even more active, in the Persian realm. There were tribes on the Euphrates, centred around Ḥīra, that came under direct Manichaean influence, although Christian influence is better known and documented.

As early as the second half of the third century A.D. there is information in Coptic Manichaean texts on Amarō, "King of the Arabs," who was the protector of the Manichaeans against the Sassanid king Narses (ca. 290). Schaeder first proposed that this Arab king was identical with ʿAmru b. ʿAdī king of Ḥīra (ca. 272–300). The fact of ʿAmru's vassalage to Narses was preserved by the latter in the Paikuli inscription. His son Imru al-Qays is mentioned in the Namāra funeral inscription, where he is called "king of all Arabs and of the Asadites." The date in the inscription corresponds to 7 December 328. It is said that during his lifetime he appointed his sons rulers of the tribes (*šuʿūb*) and recognized representatives of Persia and Byzantium. In fact Imru al-Qays is known to have been on good terms with the Byzantines as well.[29]

The influence of these contacts, of whose ancient roots we have only such vague hints, was felt as far as Mecca in the days of the Prophet. The sources mention the *zindīqs* (*zanādiqa*) of Qurayš, implying that their beliefs were of Persian extraction. This may be referring, of course, to Mazdak (on whom see the discussion below), but the essentially Persian colouring of Manichaeism was felt even before his era; Eusebius, for instance, states that Mani, after having rekindled some heretic beliefs which had ceased before his time, was the one who spread "the Persian venom," One of the *zindīqs* of Qurayš was Abū Sufyān himself, but seven other notables of Mecca as well are named among them. Some of them were executed by the Prophet (i.e., on his order) after the taking of Mecca. Indeed, some of these people seem to have been among the fiercest adversaries of Muḥammad and fought the Muslims at Badr and Uḥud, where some of them were killed.

One of them was Walīd b. Muġīra, who complained that the Quran was revealed to Muḥammad and not to some respectable man, preferably of Ṭaqīf, like Kināna b. ʿAbd Yālīl (Abū ʿĀmir's friend). Another one was Naḍr b. Ḥāriṯ al-ʿAbdari, of Qurayš, of the stock of ʿAbd Manāf; he was known also as Abū Fā'id and was one of the main adversaries of Muḥammad. He was a man of great knowledge in the traditions and books of the Persians and maintained close relations with Christians and Jews. It is perhaps the way these *zindīqs* – Manichaeans prayed which is described in a statement of the Prophet concerning the late *ʿaṣr* prayer, to which he was opposed. Such a *munāfiq*, he says, sits and observes the sun entering between Satan's horns, then he mutters something hastily, and there is very little mention of God. It should be noted that the term *zindīq* came into use in Arabic only in the Muslim period, not in the *ǧāhiliyya* or in the Prophet's lifetime. One should ask oneself what were the Manichaeans called in those earlier days. In the light of the sources discussed here, it seems quite obvious that they were called *ṣābi'* or *ḥanīf*. Both terms were used in the Prophet's time also in the meaning of Muslim (above p. 10), and this supports the view emerging from this study, that Islam's first appearance was as a non-conformist off-shoot of Manichaeism.[30]

1.8 Mazdak

The obvious growth of Manichaean influence in Arabia and among Arab tribes outside it was, one may say with certitude, a result of the events of the Mazdakite revolution. Joshua Stylites speaks of a kind of upheaval among the Arabs, mainly of the B. Ṭayy. In general, it seems that the whole of what is today the Middle East was ablaze. In Palestine the Samaritans were up in arms, proclaimed Justus their king and began fighting the Christians. Theophanes describes 499 / 500 and 503/ 504 as years when the Arabs under Agaros (that is, Ḥuğr) and Badikharimos (Maʿddikarb), the sons of Ḥāriṯ, waged war against the Byzantines.[31] More complete and coherent are the Arab reports, which put the tribe of Kinda and its chief Ḥāriṯ in the centre of the events and connect the events among the Arabs with the Mazdakite revolution.

Mazdak's personal background and details are rather obscure and there are conflicting reports on them in the sources.[32] His period of rule, apparently in conjunction with the king Qubāḏ, was one of far-reaching social changes.

Sources hostile to him greatly exaggerated in this respect, depicting his rule as a period of general anarchy, abolition of private property, dissolution of family life, etc. Later sources generally put greater stress on the theological aspects of the movement. According to the Siyosat-Name he was the first to introduce atheistic doctrines, striving to abolish all faiths, Zoroastrian, Jewish, Christian, and idolatrous.[33]

However, there are many indications of the precise nature of Mazdak's movement. It was Manichaean in every respect. Thus, for instance, we find a strong pacifistic orientation and a prohibition against eating meat, out of opposition to bloodshed of any kind. This is characteristic of Manichaeans.[34] A very convincing proof of the movement's Manichaean nature is the fact that in describing the events in Persia the Byzantine writers do not even mention the name Mazdak but speak about Manichaeans. It is while describing the Persian events at the end of the fifth century A.D. that Malalas puts the story of Bundos, who toward the end of the third century preached Manichaeism of a radically dualistic nature and then came to Iran where he spread his faith; of the Daristhenoi, the believers in the good God; it is from them that Mazdakism sprang.[35]

Malaṭī (d. 377/987) explicitly states that the *mazdakiyya* belonged to the *mānawiyya*, those who believe in two Gods and two creators, the one who created Good and the other who created Evil. The *mazdakiyya*, he further explains, were *zanādiqa*, their main belief being that since there was only one Adam, all his descendants were equal.

The most complete description of Mazdak's ideology is found in Šahrastānī's book. His report is taken from the well informed Abū 'Īsā al-Warrāq, of the first half of the ninth century A.D., who certainly had more ancient sources at his disposal.[36] (See the text and translation of Šahrastānī's fragment in the appendix below.)

This report clearly states the Manichaean nature of the Mazdakites first of all in what concerns "the two beings and the two principles" (*al-kawnayn wa-l-aṣlayn*). It is hard to say what degree of dualism both Manichaeism and Mazdakism arrived at, whether it was the kind of absolute separation in human beings between what is material, earthly, and irrational from what is spiritual and divine, as in Philo and in apocalyptic literature like Enoch and some of the Judaean Desert writings, or a total division of the world into Good and Evil.[37]

Another aspect is the principle of free will as far as Light is concerned, whereas "Darkness acts at random and arbitrarily." This was probably linked with the social aims of the movement, involving a call upon personal responsibility of every individual. The mixture between Light and Darkness, as well as their separation from each other, occurs at random, without any free will.

Therefore Mazdak forbade people to hate and fight each other. The idea of the mixture is peculiar to Manichaeism, which taught that every soul had two elements in it, some being so strongly impregnated by Darkness that it could no longer be separated from them; but the real purpose of man is precisely the separation between Light and Darkness in his own soul.[38]

Mazdak saw death as a way of solving the problem of separation from Evil. It is not absolutely clear from the text that he meant suicide. He seems rather to call for radical asceticism, a kind of becoming "reduced to skeletons, with a hungry look from want of food, prey of disease, in training for dying," as Philo has put it.[39]

Most instructive is Šahrastānī's report about the cosmological views of Mazdak, which certainly reflect accepted Manichaean concepts. The organization of the world is described as that of a kingdom, with "the object of worship (*maʿbūḏu*)" at the summit like a Ḫusraw. The other layers of the hierarchy also parallel human government; among them there are the four spirits, the twelve spirits, and the seven angels-viziers, whose names are known.[40]

It is perhaps of significance that the source does not speak of God explicitly, but of a heavenly king, symbolized by a human being. One can hardly avoid the impression that we have before us the idea of the Son of Man governing the worlds, as in the New Testament and in Enoch literature. This ruler of the worlds uses the intermediate powers as his servants for performing such concrete tasks as are inappropriate to himself.[41] Moreover, we find the idea that the wise man is free. As the text puts it, whoever has in himself the twenty-three powers acting together, becomes *rabbānī* (clearly an Aramaic word, meaning "master" or "free"), free from *taklīf* (servitude).[42]

There is also the idea of the hidden name of the supreme ruler, who rules with the help of the letters forming his name. To know even a few of these letters is the greatest of revelations.[43]

To this should be added what Ibn al-Aṯīr says about Mazdak, that he wanted to call for the way of Abraham, "the friend." Unless written under the influence of later Muslim ideas, this offers us an additional link between Manichaeism, as represented by Mazdak, and the *ḥanīfiyya*, "the Creed of Ibrāhīm."[44]

To sum up the description of this creed attributed to Mazdak, let us list the main points. (Several marginal ideas, or terms, will be pointed out further on, in comparing them with those related to the *ḥanīfiyya*.)

1. Dualism.
2. Free will on the side of the Good, or Light.
3. The "Mixture," an expression of the dialectic essence of the world as a combination of the two principles.
4. Asceticism, aiming to free the spiritual from the material.
5. Exact knowledge of how things work in the upper world as the exclusive attribute of wise men.

6. Freedom in wisdom.
7. An all-powerful technique of influencing the great mechanisms of the world, such as by the letters of the hidden name.

It should be borne in mind that during the period including the end of the fifth and the first quarter of the sixth centuries Manichaeans ruled Persia. It is noteworthy that in the same period they seem to have been quite influential in Byzantium as well, as Cedrenus tells us about the reign of Anastasius (491–518):

> Under his rule Manichaeans and Arians flourished; the Manichaeans, because the emperor's mother was a fervent adherent and friend of theirs[45]

1.9 Mazdak and the Arabs

In view of the strong Persian influence among the Arab tribes, some of which lived on the very border of the Persian Kingdom, on the Euphrates, concentrated around Ḥīra, it is not surprising that Mazdakite influence spread among them. There is no way of knowing whether Mazdakite propaganda reached them in written form or whether they knew Mazdak's own book, mentioned in the *fihrist*.[46]

However this may be the main link of the Arabs with Mazdakism was through the tribe of Kinda. Tradition has it that their chief, Ḥāriṯ b. ʿAmru, who was in a continual state of war with the kings of Ḥīra (i.e., of Laḫm), managed to penetrate deep into Babylonian territory. When upon the death of the Laḫmid king Imru al-Qays b. Munḏir, his son Munḏir succeeded him, Ḥāriṯ attacked and gained control of the kingdom, the tribes swearing allegiance to him. He managed to achieve this since at that time Qubāḏ, the *zindīq*, was king of Persia and demanded that Munḏir become a *zindīq* as well, which he refused to do. (The term *zindīq*, which the sources use, is clearly anachronistic.) Thus Ḥāriṯ, who agreed to become a *zindīq*, thereafter enjoying Qubāḏ's support, remained in power until the Mazdakites were crushed by Kisra Anfigirwan. Ḥāriṯ divided the control of the tribes among his sons, Ḥuǧr, Šuraḥbīl, Salima, and Maʿdikarb. The B. Asad, however, killed their king, Ḥuǧr b. Ḥāriṯ (the father of Imru al-Qays the poet), whereupon the power of the other sons vanished too, and as Kinda rule was destroyed, they migrated to Ḥaḍramawt.

Ṭabarī describes Qubāḏ as a sworn pacifist, in so far as he was a *zindīq*. He would negotiate with his enemies, being opposed to bloodshed. He also observes that events were affected by another factor, namely Ḥimyar. It emerges that the father of Ḥāriṯ, ʿAmru b. Ḥuǧr, was a kind of vassal of the *tubbaʿ* of Ḥimyar, whose name was ʿAmru as well. ʿAmru the Ḥimyarite became *tubbaʿ* after killing his brother Ḥassān, and gave the daughter of his murdered brother in marriage to ʿAmru b. Ḥuǧr of Kinda. In this way he intended to diminish the status of Ḥassān's offspring (since Kinda were considered of lower station). Ḥāriṯ, born of this marriage, was thus a descendant of the kings of Ḥimyar. Later the son of Ḥassān regained the throne of Ḥimyar and sent his cousin, Ḥāriṯ, to raid the region of the Euphrates. He later joined the expedition himself, after being informed what kind of strange ruler Qubāḏ was; he initiated the digging of a channel, known as *nahr al-Ḥīra*. He also sent his nephew, Šamir, to penetrate deep into Persia, where he fought Qubāḏ and killed him in Rayy. This last piece of information, conveyed by Ṭabarī, that Qubāḏ was killed in Rayy, is certainly untrue. In general, there is a persistent internal contradiction in the sources, which, on the one hand, make Ḥāriṯ an adherent of Mazdak and therefore a recipient of the support of his fellow Mazdakite, King Qubāḏ, and, on the other, describe Kinda and Ḥimyar as waging war inside the Persian kingdom. However, this contradiction is a result of the eclectic nature of the historical annals written by Arab authors, who collected information from various earlier sources, both tribal traditions and Syriac chronicles; thus, neither of the two versions should be excluded. In other words, there was, no doubt, a period of war and one of cooperation between Mazdakite Persia and the tribes.[47]

The missing link, from the point of view of our discussion, namely evidence on the diffusion of Mazdakite views into the Arabian Peninsula as a result of the conversion of Kinda, is supplied by a source indicated by Kister. This is Ibn Saʿīd's *Našwat al-ṭarab*, which aside from providing the details found in the previous sources, tells of missionary activity and even the forced conversion of Naǧd and Tihāma carried out by Ḥāriṯ on Qubāḏ's orders. Some people in Mecca also converted to the new faith ("*tazandaqa*"). The same idea, namely, that the Manichaeans of Qurayš (see what was said on them above) took their ideas from Ḥīra, is found also in Ibn Rusteh: *wa-kānat al-zandaqa fī qurayš aḫaḏūhā min al-Ḥīra.*[48]

That the influence of Mazdak and Qubāḏ probably reached Medina too can be inferred from a tradition preserved by Siǧistānī, saying that the original name of Qubāʾ, the centre of B. ʿAmru b. ʿAwf at the entrance of Medina, was Qubāḏ, as preserved by the Jews.[49]

1.10 More on the Kinda

Ḥāriṯ was known as a descendant of Ḥuǧr b. ʿAmru, his grandfather, leader of the Kinda, also known as *ākil al-murār*. Their ancient base was at a place called Šaraf, in the centre of Naǧd, near another centre, Šurayf.[50] Affiliation with *ākil al-murār*'s tribe was a source of pride for the Kinda people. Arab traditions generally explain this nickname as "the eater of *murār*," a kind of plant which the sources do not further define. However, there is no doubt that the title meant that he held a position of a kind of suzerain over the B.

Murra, a tribe connected with B. Ġaṭafān, whose connections with the Kinda are known. Suzerains of that kind were more often referred to by the title of *ḏawū al-ākāl*, which apparently involved recognition by the Persian king and perhaps by Ḥimyar as well, and authority over the vassal tribe, mainly the prerogative of gathering some kind of tax.[51]

Surprisingly enough, Hind, the daughter of Ḥāriṯ, seems to have been a good Christian, perhaps due to her marriage with the Laḫmid Munḏir.[52] Yāqūt has evidence about a convent named after her in Ḥīra (*dayr Hind*) and quotes the text of an inscription found there:

> This shrine was built by Hind, daughter of Ḥāriṯ b. ʿAmru b. Ḥuğr, a queen, daughter of kings, mother of King ʿAmru b. Munḏir, maid of Christ, mother of His servant, daughter of His servants; under the rule of the King of Kings, Ḫusraw Anūširwān, Mār Ephraim being bishop, etc.[53]

1.11 The Kinda and Qurayš

Ibn Isḥāq has preserved the conversation between the Kinda delegation headed by Ašʿaṯ b. Qays and the Prophet. Apparently, the Kinda were not overly enthusiastic about Islam (Ašʿaṯ later took part in the *ridda* war, after the Prophet's death). The delegation was dressed in expensive clothes, garnished with silk. Ašʿaṯ tried to win the sympathy of the Prophet by pointing out that the latter was the offspring of *ākil al-murār* just like Ašʿaṯ and his own people. The Prophet then explained to the audience that his uncle, ʿAbbās, and the latter's nephew, Rabīʿa b. Ḥāriṯ, who used to travel about in their trading business, would boast of their being the offspring of *ākil al-murār*, who was of a family of kings. He, however, did not accept this familial link, insisting that he was the descendant of Naḍr b. Kināna. Was Ašʿaṯ only trying to stress a family relationship? Ibn Isḥāq's version of the meeting with the Kinda as preserved by Ḥalabī and Daḥlān has an important addition. To prove to Ašʿaṯ and his people that he was the true prophet, Muḥammad recited to them *sūrat al-ṣāffāt* (37) until he reached verse 5 (of *rabb al-mašāriq*), when he started weeping, which he explained by fear of "the one who has sent him."[54] One may infer from this story that by mentioning the *ākil al-murār* Ašʿaṯ intended to indicate more than family relationship, namely the Manichaean background of the chiefs of Kinda. In other words, he tried to speak to Muḥammad as to a fellow *ḥanīf*. Muḥammad partly rejected this attempt, but the recitation of *sūrat al-ṣāffāt* might have been intended to show what the new *ḥanīfiyya* was. The plural form *mašāriq* (which made the Prophet weep), found three times in the Quran, seems to be of some relevance in this respect. To express "east" by the plural is peculiar to Greek. Muslim traditionalists have occasionally attempted to explain this Quranic plural as referring, for instance, to the 360 sunrises during the year. It is almost self-evident, however, that it reached the Qur'ān from Greek apocalyptic writings through either Ethiopic or Aramaic (Jewish or Syriac) translations. In fact, this plural form is found in Ethiopic: *məsrāqāt*, in Biblical texts translated of course from Greek; and in the Aramaic text of Enoch, found in Qumran: *wĕ-āzĕlīn lĕ-midnĕḥē šĕmayyā*. It seems that what the first part of *sūrat al-ṣāffāt* contained, along with the expression *mašāriq*, were formulae and images familiar to the Kinda people through their Manichaean background, like "We have adorned the lower heaven with the adornment of stars and to preserve against any rebel Satan; they listen not to the High Council." These images are clearly reminiscent of the book of Enoch.

However, it is precisely these images and ideas that the new *ḥanīfiyya* abolished. Indeed, the most relevant Qur'ānic expression of the rupture between the old *ḥanīfiyya* and that of Muḥammad seems to be contained in the *sūras* 37 and 72 (*al-ṣāffāt* and *al-ǧinn*). The idea here is that since the mission of Muḥammad, the spirits—companions of Satan—were forbidden to mix amongst the divine creatures and inform their nearest of kin—the humans—of any mysteries which they overheard in the heavenly councils.[55]

2. Enoch's Journey into Islam

We have seen above that Bīrūnī mentions Hermes-Idrīs as one of the prophets of the *ṣābi'ūn*. Muslim collections of traditions, almost without exception, contain traditions on Idrīs, who is always presented as identical with Ḫanūḫ, or Iḫnūḫ, i.e., Enoch. As we shall presently see, Enoch entered into these traditions through the contacts which, several generations before Islam, were established between the tribes and the Manichaean sects.

In order to better identify the nature and directions of these streams of ideas and religious symbols, let us review very briefly the main characteristics of the book of Enoch, dealing here mainly with 1 Enoch, which contains the bulk of traditions and sermons woven around this Biblical personality. Discernible in the book are four main topics, which are dispersed throughout in a disorderly manner.

(1) A description of the world of Evil; here we find references to the original sin, the union with the wicked angels, Satan and evil powers of all kinds, inclusive of kings and the rich.
(2) A description of the world of Good, at the centre of which we find the Ancient of Days, the Lord of the Spirits, the Son of Man, Moses and Elijah (implied), the angels, the elect; the prayers. This world is a world of Light, white in colour.
(3) A vision of the Last Day, the Day of Judgment; the Kingdom of Heaven; the Resurrection; the New Temple.

(4) A cosmology, describing the mechanisms of the world put in motion by angels; in connection with which we find some very peculiar principles of the calendar.[56]

As of some sixty years ago, when Alfaric published his book on Manichaean literature, evidence has been coming to light concerning Enoch's position therein. There is today enough evidence to enable us to speak of the Manichaean nature of this book. On the other hand, there is a very deeply rooted conviction among scholars that it is Jewish in nature. There is also a prevailing view fixing the date of its composition at a very early time, generally under Hasmonean rule, thus making it a source of Jewish history for that period. These views assume that there must have been a transitional stage, represented, among others, by the book of Enoch, between Judaism (considered to be of a lower nature) and Christianity (which is superior, purified of materialistic elements, and mainly spiritual).[57]

A comparison between the Aramaic Qumran fragments of Enoch and the correspondent parts in Ethiopic and Greek proves that its language of composition was Greek.[58]

The Manichaean nature of Enoch can be recognized by the following characteristics: The frequency of seven (chs. 18, 21, 23, 67, 77, 89): seven hills, seven stars, seven islands, seven saints, seven rivers, seven heavenly men, seven windows of heaven; the struggle against Evil and evil spirits (chs. 10, 15, 18, 21, 67, 69, 80); the personification of Wisdom, generally as a woman (chs. 42, 49, 69, 82, 92, 94, 105); the Son of Man called (ch. 62:5) Son of a Woman, reminiscent of the Manichaean Mother of all Life. Behind all this there seems to flow a developed myth of the "Primal Man" (also: "the Hidden Man"), as well as an intense dualistic trend, and a great preoccupation with names, their meanings and the combinations of their letters. Nor are mythological monsters lacking (mainly in ch. 60). We find also a stress on Light (and white) as a sign of righteousness.

Light as a token of the righteousness of the Manichaeans is derided by their Christian adversaries. The Manichaeans called themselves "Sons of Light," whereas Christian propaganda called them "Sons of Darkness." Aphraates, in the first half of the fourth century, calls God's wrath upon the pupils of Mani, Sons of Darkness, those serpents that imitate Chaldaean worship and multiply their fasting days, but whose fasting is not accepted. St. Augustine in his reply to the Manichaean epistle also attacks the Manichaean Light belief, on "the Father" who is the Ruler of Light, and the Light that is composed of twelve elements. Manichaean texts speak of the Apostle of Light, and discuss the form (morphe) of Light.[59]

This pervasive presence of the myth of Light reminds us of the book of Enoch, where Light is presented as the special recompense of the righteous elect, who are the Sons ("*arnowalda; tawalda*") of Light (108:11). The colour of their clothes is white, as is the colour of the angels, contrary to the embellishments and purple patches of the rich (87:2; 90:22, 32; 98:2).[60]

The central position held by Enoch in Manichaean theology is now proven also by direct evidence. There is the Persian Manichaean fragment edited by Henning, which mentions Enoch as one of the first prophets; Henning also quoted another manuscript, where Mani himself is said to have read Enoch texts and recommended them to his pupils.[61]

Henning has called our attention to the many parallels between the Book of Enoch and the Manichaean "Book of the Giants," which confirm that the Enoch texts were part of the Manichaean literature. This connection has recently been clarified by Milik's publication of Jewish-Aramaic Qumran fragments of the Book of the Giants.[62]

Widengren, Puech, Böhlig and Labib have also shown various parallels between Manichaean literature and the book of Enoch, such as the description of the paradise, the garden of life, and the inclusion of Enoch among the central prophetic figures. These are clearly Manichaean elements, even if some prefer to call them "gnostic," apparently in order to stress their early dating.[63] Such parallels and connections have also been detected by Henrichs and others among Manichaean texts and other writings in the same category as Enoch, such as the Manual of Discipline and the Damascus Covenant.[64]

We also have the explicit evidence of Timotheus of Constantinople (early seventh century A.D.) who counts among the forged Biblical books of the Manichaeans books on Moses, Enoch, Adam, Isaiah, David, Elijah, and the three patriarchs.[65]

It almost goes without saying that in all these parallels and correspondence between Manichaean (sometimes called "gnostic") and Enoch texts, the latter are considered to be the antecedents, allegedly adopted and taken over by the Manichaeans. Since Enoch fragments were found in Qumran, the usual line of thought is that they are Essene, and of course Jewish, written first in Hebrew or at least in Aramaic, and consequently ancient, composed before the Christian era or at the very latest in the first century A.D.[66] However, the Enoch literature has nothing specifically Jewish in it; and Essenes are never mentioned therein. The fact that such texts were preserved in Jewish Aramaic proves nothing but that there existed Jewish Manichaeans as well as non-Jewish and that they strove to spread their views among Jews, as is proven mainly by the Jewish-Aramaic fragments of the Book of the Giants, a manifestly Manichaean text. We saw that Arab sources mentioned such Jewish Manichaeans. Those who seem to have been the Jewish contemporaries of the writers of these texts were well aware of their true character. It would seem that these writers are alluded to by the following statement:

> The *ḥănēfē tōrā* (*ḥănēfīm* of the *tōrā*) are thought by all to be teachers of the Bible, but they are not; or teachers of the Mishna, but they are not; (although) they are wrapped in their cloaks and have *tĕfillīn* on their heads.[67]

It is hard to say exactly how the Enoch traditions entered into Islam. As said above, Enoch is identified with Idrīs, whom the Quran describes as a man of faith (*ṣiddīq*) who was raised to heaven (19: 57–58 and 21:85–86). Quite a few etymologies have been proposed for the name Idrīs, such as from Iblis, Ezra (Greek Esdras), Andreas, and Poimandres (which according to Albright was a pagan-gnostic designation of Enoch).[68] Besides, there are Muslim traditions deriving it from the root *d-r-s* "to teach." It seems, however, that the clue to the name is given by the many Muslim traditions themselves, identifying Enoch with Hermes Trismegistos. Thus Idrīs may very well be an alteration of Hirmīs, dating from the pre-Islamic period. However, there is much significance in the remarks of N. Wieder on a passage from the Damascus Covenant

> and the star (*kōḵāḇ*) is the interpreter (dōrēš) of the Torah, who came to Damascus, as it is written (Nu xxiv: 17): there shall come a star out of Jacob, etc.

Wieder points out the identity *kōḵāḇ* (11) – Hermes (the first meaning the planet Mercury-Hermes in Hebrew); then he shows the relation, which is common in gnostic texts, Hermes-Hermaneia (interpretation), which comes back to the *dōrēš* of that passage. That would supply us with an additional argument to show that Idrīs (root *d-r-s*) stems from Hermes-Enoch, the interpreter.

What is remarkable in the extensive Idrīs-Enoch traditions is that these Muslim traditions never attribute the stories of Enoch to Judaism, and that there is a very obvious trend connecting Enoch with the region of Ḥīra, which accords very well with the historical data on Ḥīra as a centre of Mazdakism (i.e., Manichaeism) under Ḥāriṯ b. ʿAmru, as described above.

Idrīs is described as a tall person, with a fat belly, not very hairy on the body but with much hair on his head, with dissimilar ears, having a white spot on his body, but no scars. His voice and way of speaking were soft and he took small steps when walking. He was called Idrīs since he taught God's book, which God revealed on thirty tablets (*ṣaḥīfa*) to him. He was the first to write with a pen and to weave and to sew with thread, whereas before him man used to wear animal skins. After God raised him to heaven dissent broke out among his followers, lasting up to the time of Noah.[69]

There is also a certain amount of confusion between Enoch and Elijah. *Ilyās* is said to be *Idrīs*, the forefather of Nūḥ, son of Lāmik, son of Matūšalaḥ, son of Iḫnūḫ who is Idrīs.[70] Some traditions attribute to him knowledge of stars and constellations; the *ṣābi'ūn* who are his believers, says Bīrūnī, attribute the management (*tadbīr*) of the world to the sky and its bodies (*ağrām*; which of course goes back to the book of Enoch).[71] There is a controversy among the learned about whether he was the second of the prophets, after Šīṯ, or the first. According to Abū 'Īsā ibn al-Munağğim in his lost book on world history written in the ninth century A.D., Šīṯ and Idrīs were the founders of the religion of the *ṣābi'ūn*; he also describes a book attributed to Šīṯ, containing the description of virtues and that of vices.[72]

Another lost book, of Mas'ūdī, written a few generations later, also contained some special traditions on Idrīs, besides the usual ones. Accordingly, he used to talk with the angels and clouds. He was also called "the threefold" (*al-muṯallaṯ*, after Hermes Trismegistos, the "triply great") since he had three attributes: of prophet, king, and sage. The *kitāb sirr al-malakūt*, the book of the secret angelology, first taught to Adam by the angel Zarā'īl (clearly Raziel is meant), was revealed to him.[73]

Of very special value are reports on Enoch texts written in the early Islamic period. Michael the Syrian has such a report on Kyriakos of Siğistān who wrote the apocalypse of Enoch, toward the middle of the eighth century A.D., under Marwān II, together with Bar Salṭā of Reyš 'Aynā. The book included prophecies foretelling a long rule for Marwān (the last Umayyad) and his son after him. This made him very happy, "like a child," and he asked Kyriakos to write a commentary on the book.[74] Then there is the story of a book entitled *Sunan Idrīs*, which was found in the *waqf* of the mosque (*mašhad*) of al-Ṭāhir in Kūfa. It was translated from Syriac by the son of Hilāl al-Ṣābī, Ibrāhīm, and copied by a certain 'Īsā.[75]

Also very meaningful are traditions showing the region of Ḥīra-Kūfa as a centre of the Idrīs-Enoch cult. A Kūfan mosque called al-Sahla was believed to have been built on the spot where Idrīs used to sew clothes and from which he was raised to heaven. In the early Muslim period it was still considered a very suitable place for prayer, through that connection with Idrīs; in the middle of it was a green rock on which there were pictures of the prophets. Quoting Ibn Ṭāwūṣ' *Maṣābīḥ al-zā'ir*, Buraqi has the tradition that the best time for prayer there would be between sunset and evening, on Wednesday, a point which is meaningful in itself.[76]

There is some evidence that during his bitter struggle for power 'Ali ibn Abī Ṭālib adopted the Manichaean traditions of the Kūfa region, which was his main base. He might, however, have held them even earlier. In a tradition preserved by Ibn A'ṯam a man asking 'Ali ibn Abī Ṭālib whether he should go to Jerusalem (*bayt al-maqdis*) or stay (and pray) at the *masğid* of Kufa (apparently al-Sahla), is told to stay, as "this is the fourth *masğid* (i.e., after Mecca, Medina, and Jerusalem) and the place where Idrīs and Nah used to pray."[77]

It was also not by mere chance that the *šīʿa* so enthusiastically embraced the genuine Manichaean idea (discussed above) of the divine light, and projected it onto Muḥammad and ʿAli, and onto both their forefathers and offspring, the *nūr allah*.[78]

3. Manichaeism and Islam

As a general idea, Manichaean influence upon Islam has been proposed by Clemen and by Andrae, who saw it as a logical consequence of the enormous Manichaean influence on various populations in the pre-Islamic period.[79] We have noted, in addition, the Manichaean background of the *ḥanīfiyya*, as well as the Mazdakite revolution at the turn of the fifth century which created a strong centre of Manichaean influence among Arab tribes. Enoch-Idrīs in particular as a manifestation of Manichaean influence on early Islam has also been indicated.

In fact there are still other instances of this influence. Perhaps the most essential idea behind Muḥammad's claim to prophecy, that of the successive incarnation, or revelation, seems to have been taken over from the Manichaeans. Muḥammad believed in the essential identity of his own mission and revelation with that of the former prophets. The basic idea is that the history of mankind is divided into periods, and that mankind itself is divided, in accordance with God's will, into various groups. In each period God chooses one of these groups, from which he singles out an individual to invest with prophetic power and make a messenger of divine revelation. Now, as the end of the world is approaching, the time of the last group, the Arabs, has come, and Muḥammad was chosen as the last of the prophets, their so-called seal. Friedländer has shown the Neoplatonic nature of this idea, but exactly the same claim was made by Mani.[80]

North-African Manichaeans, contemporaries of Mazdak, while pretending to be Christians, worshipped Hermes Trismegistos and believed in the imminent saviour, of whose incarnations Jesus was the last or seal.[81] This last, or farthest, end of the prophetic chain of revelations was apparently depicted by Manichaean theologists as a spiritual creation of the "congregation which is at the edge." Such Manichaean claims were derided by St. Nilus at about the same time (beginning of the fifth century A.D.); he accused the Manichaeans of fabricating fairy tales ἐπὶ τῆς ἐκκλησίας τῆς ἐν τῇ ἐσχατιᾷ. It is most probably this *ekklēsia* "of the edge" which in Islam became the *masǧid al-aqṣā*, originally a purely theological concept, whatever its ulterior geographical interpretations may be.

The idea of *šarḥ al-ṣadr* also seems to have sprung from a Manichaean source; in the *Evangelium Veritatis* we find 'unveiling of the breast' as the way in which God the Father reveals the Holy Ghost. The most genuine expression in this respect, in the Quran, is to be found in one of the earliest *sūrahs* (94:1), here it is the bosom of the Prophet which was unveiled, or rather enlarged.[82]

The number twelve is of course a very frequently used typical number, as e.g., in the tribes of Israel. However, the appointing of exactly twelve *nuqabā'* over the earliest Muslim organization by the Prophet is reminiscent of the twelve leaders appointed to head Manichaean ecclesiastical organizations.[83]

Above (p. 13 and p. 21) I have already dealt with the seven *amlāk ḥunafā'* of the Kaʿba inscription and briefly indicated their background. In view of the early meaning of *ḥanīf*, Manichaean, it is clear that these seven holy angels also represent an expression of Manichaean beliefs. I have already mentioned the position of the seven angels in the Manichaean cosmology (above, p. 25) as attributed to Mazdak. A Chinese Manichaean text also contains the explicit idea of the seven central powers, progenitures of God himself. The Manichaeans of Ḥarrān identified them with the seven planets.[84] As to the other version of the inscription, reminiscent of Matthew ch. 7, it is of obvious interest to consider here the special Manichaean predilection for this passage in Matthew, as mentioned in the sources.[85] The presence of Christian elements in Manichaeism is evidently due to the latter's eclectic nature in the first place, though it might well be that, according to what al-Ǧaṣṣāṣ has preserved for us in one of his traditions, there were Manichaean populations which were forced to accept Christianity by the Byzantine rulers and continued to pretend to be Christians under Muslim rule as well in order not to be considered idolaters.[86]

Some Muslim traditions on Jesus, of an especially strange character, seem to have been taken from the Manichaeans. One of these is the tradition first giving a physical description of Jesus' person, prophesying that he would return and destroy all pigs; at that time the many religions in existence would be destroyed as well and everybody would accept Islam. Also, God would then kill the false Christ and an era of peace would follow, lion and camel would pasture together (and there follows a description reminiscent of Is. ch. 11). Such a tradition, attributed to Muǧammiʿ, about Jesus killing the *daǧǧāl* which was noted (MO, p. 85), seems to be Manichaean in origin.[87]

According to traditions attributed to ʿĀ'iša and and repeated by many others, Waraqa ibn Nawfal, one of the leading *ḥanīfs* of Mecca, used to read the gospel, and in Hebrew.[88] Both Yaʿqūbī and Bīrūnī explicitly mention Manichaean gospels.The first tells us that Mani himself wrote twelve gospels, each of them designated by a letter. Bīrūnī mentions that the Manichaeans had their own gospel, which was different from that of the Christians, and was known as "the gospel of the seventy," its composition being attributed to Balāmis (Ptolemaeus?).[89]

There is considerable evidence from non-Muslim sources as well confirming the existence of Manichaean gospels. Scythianus, the Manichaean missionary among the Arabs, is said to have composed a gospel, notes Cyril of Jerusalem. The gospels of Thomas and of Philipp, as well as "the living gospel," have also been attributed to Manichaeans.[90]

Koenen and Henrichs edited fragments of Mani's gospel, in Greek. That Manichaean-gnostic sects had various gospels of their own is known from many sources; such were the gospels of Simon Magus, the gospel "of the twelve," and others. In view of all this, more than one element, apparently reminiscent of Christianity, should be reconsidered in dealing with Muslim tradition, and the possibility of its being of Manichaean nature taken into account.[91]

Then there is the issue of fasting, already pointed out as being a feature of Manichaeism according to Aphraates. Some sources say the Manichaeans had no less than fifty annual fast days. According to Ibn al-Nadīm the Manichaeans used to fast until sunset for thirty days beginning at Aquarius, i.e., March, from the eighth day; quite significantly, 1 Ramaḍān of the first *hiǧra* year fell on 9 March (623). To be sure, this datum merits consideration. In dealing with the issue of fasting in Islam, Manichaean influence should thus undoubtedly be taken into account, at least in the same measure in which Jewish and Christian fasting rules are considered. Furthermore, Manichaean prohibition against wine should likewise be kept in mind when the Islamic prohibition is considered.[92]

The Docetic view of Jesus, namely the denial of his crucifixion, found in the Qur'ān, 4:156, was also the view of the Manichaeans. This view is first attributed to Basilides (middle of the second century A.D.) and his followers, by Irenaeus and Epiphanius. As to the Manichaeans, they are said even to have believed that there were two Jesuses, the crucified one, and the true one. The Manichaeans sometimes called the false Jesus "the devil" and sometimes "son of the widow," used by God as a replacement of Himself. Polotsky has detected this belief in the abjuration formula of Manichaeans returning to Christianity.[93]

Such beliefs have been attributed also to the Monophysite radical wing whose founder and leader was Julian of Halicarnassus. Its members called themselves *aphtartodokētai* (*aphtarsia* meaning non-destruction) and were very influential in Naǧrān and in Ethiopia; and there is the evidence of Anastasius on the Manichaean beliefs of these Monophysites.

Another point which should be added is the myth of the giants. As Widengren has rightly pointed out, the term *kavi* in the Iranian fragments of the Book of the Giants is the correspondent of Syriac *gabbārā* (Heb. *gibbōr*,

Greek γίγας). The same is found indeed in the Aramaic Qumran fragments of that book: *gabbārāyē*. Here we have the *ǧabābira* of the Muslim traditions.[94]

4. The Medinan Opposition Again

I have reviewed some general trends in Islam which can be thought of as being taken from the Manichaeans. Manichaeism was still alive and active in Arabia and among the tribes outside it. There was a common Arab designation for people of this creed, namely, *ḥanīf*. What the Prophet did was to hammer out his own way of *ḥanīfiyya*, different from that of the extant ones, such as that of Abū ʿĀmir, for instance. He had previously received some instruction in matters of the *ḥanīfiyya* by various mentors, of whom two are outstanding, Waraqa b. Nawfal and Quss b. Sāʿida al-Iyādī. He met the latter, who is mentioned less in the sources, in ʿUkkāẓ. Quss is said to have been one of those who forbade drinking wine in the *ǧāhiliyya* times. The episodes connected with the Medinan opposition shed light on several images and terms connected with the rupture between the two factions.[95]

Charity: As I have shown (MO, p. 71), the declared purpose of the dissenters' mosque was to serve as a shelter for the poor and those who were in misery. This fits very much what we know about Manichaean cloisters, known to have been a kind of combination of schools and hospices. Alms and charity had a central position in Manichaean views; the believers were required to give alms, which were collected in their churches.[96]

The elect. The importance and weight attached to the concept of the elect in the book of Enoch, which we have seen was of utmost importance in Manichaean literature, shows clearly how central this concept was in Manichaean theology. The elect are of course part and parcel of the world of light. Enoch promised them peace and favour, eternal life together with the Son of Man who is one of them. They avoid wearing costly clothes, live in austerity, hard work, and suffering.

As convincingly shown by Vööbus, the Manichaean example had a wide-reaching impact on the spread of monasticism in Christianity. The Manichaeans were preaching sexual abstinence, and avoidance of meat and wine. Their monks held a central position in Manichaean communities. Their elect were required to fast 50 days a year; the monks even more than that.[97]

Abū ʿĀmir appears to have been such an elect among his numerous supporters. Significantly enough, as we have seen (MO, p. 90), he became a *rāhib* and started to behave in daily life as the bearer of such a title should. *Rāhib* has come in Arabic to have the meaning of "monk," and later compilers of traditions were understandably inclined to describe such a man as a Christian, Manichaeism having been long forgotten. The central part monks played among Manichaeans, however, is abundantly clear at present. At the same time, a fifth century Manichaean manuscript shows definitely the importance attached to the "elect" among them. Thus the basic ancient meaning of *rāhib* seems to have been precisely that, an elect. Apparently, the various expressions of austerity and asceticism, such as the prohibition of wine or of meat, and the recommendation to stay away from marriage and intercourse with women were aimed in the main at the elect, the *rāhib*.[98] Abū ʿĀmir, we have seen, evidently became a *rāhib* at a rather late stage of his life, as before this happened he had a family (MO, p. 89).

Al-ḥanīfiyya al-samḥa. As noted above (p. 692), Ibn Ḥazm reports a tradition that Abraham was sent to the Sabians to teach them *al-ḥanīfiyya al-samḥa*. This term often specifies the *ḥanīfiyya* preached by Muḥammad in contrast to that of Abū ʿĀmir. A tradition told in the name of ʿĀʾiša quotes the words of the Prophet regarding *al-ḥanīfiyya al-samḥa*, which he described as the belief which God likes and prefers to any other. As a first case in point there seems to be the story of ʿUṯmān b. Maẓʿūn al-Ǧumaḥī, one of the first Muslims in Mecca, a very rich man, who was among the participants in the *hiǧra* to Ethiopia. He was a very pious man who practised asceticism and even wanted to castrate himself; the Prophet rebuked him and said that he was sent by God to propagate the *ḥanīfiyya al-samḥa*, not *rahbāniyya*. The meaning of the word *samḥa* was not self-evident to traditionalists and commentators, and they usually added to it an explanation, saying that it meant "easiness, moderation;" there is moderation in our religion, the Prophet would point out. In other words, as against the rigours demanded of the *rāhib*, here is something which suits the commoner.[99]

Turning now to earlier *ḥanīf*s, the Manichaeans, we find that there was some heterogeneity among them. The main division was between *eklektoi*, the elect (further divided into *didaskaloi* [teachers], *episkopoi* [overseers], *presbyteroi* [elders]), and the commoners, the *katekhoumenoi*, who were the mass of the believers. According to St. Augustine these were called the *auditores* (hearers) and unlike the elect, they ate meat, cultivated land, and married if they wished to, whereas the elect refrained from these things. Although Epiphanius relates those among the Manichaeans who call themselves *Akouanitai* to the army veteran called Akouas who came from Mesopotamia and settled in Eleutheropolis (see p. 18 above), it seems that their name originally had the same meaning, namely "hearers," as the Greek root of the name shows. And then we also have the Arabic correspondent of the term, describing the common mass of Mani's followers as the *sammāʿūn*.[100]

It is almost self-evident that it is this kind of *ḥanīfiyya* which the Prophet wanted, the moderate one, which does not impose too drastic restrictions on its followers. That this was indeed the general attitude of the Prophet is well known. It appears therefore that by *al-samḥa* the *ḥanīfiyya* of the hearers was meant. This was apparently one of the main points at issue in the feud between Muḥammad and Abū ʿĀmir, the *rāhib*, (MO, p. 90 and the references there).

Pacifism: Finally, the explicit reason given by the leaders of the opponents of the Tabūk expedition, the *muḫallafūn*, was that they did not want the bloodshed of war against the Byzantines (MO, p. 91). In this respect also, it seems that these people were inspired by the aversion to war characteristic of the Manichaeans, as shown by their attempt to overcome the major differences between religions by means of eclectic dogmas. This aversion is confirmed also by the evidence of Mazdak's revolution, when Qubāḏ, king of Persia, who was a follower of Mazdak, strove to follow a policy of peace (above p. 27). How far these people were always consistent with the pacifism they displayed on this occurrence is a different matter. Some of them might have been involved in bloodshed during earlier Muslim expeditions, or were apparently prepared to shed blood in their fight against their Medinan opponents, the Muslims, even with the help of the Byzantines. However, this relativism can be detected among pacifists in various historical periods and milieus.[101]

5. Conclusion

In my paper on the Medinan opposition to the Prophet I summed up a series of events, of a very peculiar nature, which happened at a time when the Prophet of Islam was approaching the end of his life; these events bring to light internal dissent in the young Muslim community. Through an examination of the available information on the individuals in the dissenters' movement we have been able to see that this opposition was not a fortuitous manifestation in the early history of Islam, but that it had deep roots in the past, if one considers the matters chronologically. That opposition was also relatively far-flung, involving groups from both of the two larger and most important tribes of Medina, the ʿAws and the Ḫazraǧ.

The movement also had a leader, in exile, it is true, but still a tremendous menace to Muslim unity. Though much effaced by later generations, the sources still contain considerable indications of the sharpness and harshness of Muslim polemics with the dissidents, who were finally silenced because of their numerical inferiority.

Thanks to information which has come to light in our generation on the history and beliefs of the Manichaeans, we are in a position to see, on the one hand, the influence these had on Islam itself and to recognize this influence in several beliefs and terms of the period. On the other hand, we can now see the movement headed by the *rāhib* Abū ʿĀmir, styled *ḥanīf*, as representing the older Manichaean tradition against the innovations of the new *ḥanīfī*, movement, the Muslims. It is more than gratifying to find this idea expressed by a Muslim scholar, perhaps eleven centuries ago:

> The Sabians were the oldest religion in the world and were ruling the world, until they brought into (their religion) innovations and changed its laws, as we explained above. Then God the Almighty sent His friend Abraham to them with the religion of Islam, the same which is nowadays ours, to make good what they had spoiled, by (preaching to them) the *ḥanīfiyya al-samḥa*, the same which Muḥammad was sent with by God the Almighty. As written in the Qurʾān, he explained to them how unjust their innovations were, namely their adoration and worship of idols. In those days, and also after that, they (the Sabians) used to be called *ḥanīfs*. (Ibn Ḥazm, I, p. 35, probably taken from Abū ʿĪsā ibn al-Munağğim.)

The outbreak in the ninth year of the *hiğra* centred around the dissenters' disapproval of waging war against the Byzantines, in line with their pacifist beliefs, and around their attempt to establish a regular meeting place in which to expound their teachings and fulfil the commandments of offerings, charity, and alms prescribed by Manichaeism.

By having preserved, in quite an authentic and trustworthy way, the memory of the links between actual events and ideological statements expressed in the Qurʾān, Muslim tradition has given us sufficient clues to understand the nature of the continuous arguments of the Prophet with his Medinan opponents. Quite clearly, the disagreements were not sporadic incidents, but the expression of a far-reaching confrontation between two beliefs.

6. Appendix

Šahrastānī's Report on Mazdak
(pp. 192–194 in Cureton's edition)

حكي الوراق ان قول المزدكية كقول كثير من المانوية في الكونين والاصلين الا ان مزدك كان يقول ان النور يفعل بالقصد والاختيار والظلمة يفعل علي الخبط والاتّفاق والنور عالم حسّاس والظلم جاهل اعمي وان المزاج كان علي الاتّفاق والخبط لا بالقصد والاختيار وكذلك الخلاص انما يقع باتّفاق دون الاختيار وكان مزدك ينهي الناس عن المخالفة والمباغضة والقتال ولما كان اكثر ذلك انما يقع بسبب النساء والاموال فاحلّ النساء واباح الاموال وجعل الناس شركة فيها كاشتراكهم في الماء والنار والكلاء وحكي عنه انه امر بقتل الانفس ليخلّصها من الشر ومزاج الظلمة ومذهبه في الاصول والاركان انها ثلثة الماء والنار والارض ولما اختلطت حدث عنها مدبّر الخير ومدبر الشر فما كان من صفوها فهو مدبّر الخير وما كان من كدرها فهو مدبر الشر وروي عنه ان معبوده قاعد على كرسيه في العالم الاعلي علي هيئة قعود خسرو في العالم الاسفل وبين يديه اربع قوي قوة التمييز والفهم والحفظ والسرور كما بين يدي خسرو اربعة اشخاص موبدان موبد والهربد الاكبر والاصبهبد والرامشكر وتلك الاربع يدبرون امر العالمين بسبعة من وزرائهم سالار وبيشكار وبالون وبروان وكاردان ودستور وكودك وهذه السبعة تدور في اثني عشر روحانين خواننده دهنده ستاننده برنده خورنده درنده خيزنده كشنده زننده كننده آينده شونده پاينده وكل انسان اجتمعت له هذه القوى الاربع والسبعة والاثنى عشر صار ربانياً فى العالم السفلي وارتفع عنه التكليف قال وان خسرو بالعالم الاعلي انما يدبر بالحروف التي مجموعها الاسم الاعظم ومن تصوّر من تلك الحروف شيئا انفتح له السر الاكبر ومن حرم ذلك بقي في عمي الجهل والنسيان والبلادة والغم في مقابلة القوي الاربع الروحانية.

Translation

Al-Warraq relates that the view of the Mazdakites is the same as that of most of the Manichaeans concerning the two beings and the two principles; except that Mazdak was wont to say that Light acts with purpose and choice, whereas Darkness acts at random and accidentally; Light is knowing and sensitive, whereas Darkness is ignorant and blind; the mixture (between Light and Darkness) occurred at random and accidentally, not by intention and choice; likewise the separation (between the two) rather occurs at random, without any choice. Mazdak forbade people to engage in conflict, hatred and warfare; since these always happen because of women and property, he abolished restrictions concerning women, liquidated property, and made people partners in these as they are partners in sharing water, fire, and pasture. It is related that he recommended suicide as a way of separation from evil and from intermingling with Darkness. His doctrine concerning the principles and elements was that they were three: Water, fire, and Earth; as they mixed together two rulers were produced from them: The ruler of Good and the ruler of Evil; the one produced of the clear part (of the mixture) is the ruler of Good; whereas the one produced from the turbid one is the ruler of Evil. It is also told concerning him that the object of his worship is sitting on his throne in the upper world, just as Ḫusraw is sitting in the lower one; in front of him there are four powers: The powers of discrimination, understanding, memory, and joy; just as Ḫusraw has before him four individuals: The Mūbāḏān Mūbāḏ, the grand Harbad, the Aṣpahbad and the Rāmišgar; these four conduct the affairs of both worlds through seven of their *wazīr*s: Sālār, Bīškār, Bālūn, Barwān, Kārdān, Dastūr, and Kūdak; these seven operate through twelve spirits: Ḫwānande, Dihande, Satānande, Borande, Ḫwarande, Dawande, Ḫīzande, Kašande, Zanande, Āyande, Šawande, Pāyande. Every man in whom these four, and seven, and twelve powers have combined, becomes a free man (still being) in the lower world, and is relieved from servitude. He said: Ḫusraw (who sits on the throne) in the upper world, rules by means of the letters which form together the most mighty name. Whoever conceives any of these letters has revealed to him the greatest mystery, whereas anyone who is deprived of this privilege remains in blind ignorance, oblivion, stupidity, and distress—regarding the four spiritual powers.

7. Index of Authors

(The numbers in italics indicate the notes)

Aphraatis Sapientis Persae, *Demonstrationes*, Patrologia Syriaca I (Paris, 1894), *59, 92.*

S. Augustinus, *Epistulae*, *MPL* 36, *42, 59, 100.*

ʿAzizi, ʿAlī b. Aḥmad, *Al-sirāǧ al-munīr* (Cairo, 1957), *2, 99.*

Baġawī, Ḥusayn b. Masʿūd, Ibn al-Farrāʾ, *Miškāt al-maṣābīḥ* (Damascus, 1380), *99.*

Bakrī, ʿAbdallāh b. ʿAbd al-ʿAzīz, *Muʿǧam ma-staʿǧam* (Cairo, 1945 ff.), *47.*

Balāḏurī, Aḥmad b. Yaḥyā, *Ansāb al-ašrāf* I, ed. M. Hamidullah (Cairo, 1959), *30.*

Bar Hebraeus, *The Chronicle in Syriac*, ed. P. J. Bruns and E. W. Kirsch (Leipzig, 1789), ed. Bedjan (Paris, 1890); English translation: E. A. W. Budge (Oxford, 1932), *18, 31, 73.*

Bar Hebraeus, *Chronicon ecclesiasticum*, ed. J. B. Abbeloos (Louvain, 1872), *76.*

Barbier de Meynard, A. C. "Surnoms et sobriquets arabes," *JA*, 10th series, vol. 9: 172, 1907, *51.*

Bardy, G., "Manichéisme," *DThC* IX: 1841, *59, 83, 90, 92, 100, 101.*

Beck, E., "Abraham in der Entwicklung Muhammeds," *Le Muséon* 65:73, 1952, *6.*

Benveniste, E., "Le témoignage de Théodore bar Konay sur le Zoroastrisme," *Le Monde oriental* 26–27: 170, 1932/3, *61.*

Bezold, C., *Die Schatzhoehle* (Leipzig, 1888), *11.*

Bīrūnī, Muḥammad b. Aḥmad, *Al-āṯār al-bāqiya*, ed. E. Sachau (Leipzig, 1927), *10, 24, 34, 69, 71, 76, 80, 89.*

Boehlig, A. and P. Labib, *Die koptisch-gnostische Schrift. . .aus Nag Hammadi,* Deutsche Akad. d. Wiss. Veroeffentlichungen, No. 58 (Berlin, 1962), *59, 63.*

Brockelmann, C., *Geschichte d. arab. Literatur* (Leipzig, 1937–49), *75.*

Brown, P., "The Diffusion of Manichaeism in the Roman Empire," *JRS* 59: 92, 1969, *12, 97.*

Buhl, F., *Das Leben Muhammeds* (Heidelberg, 1954), *1, 80, 92.*

Buḫārī, Muḥammad b. Ismāʿīl, *Ṣaḥīḥ* (quoted by chapter), *99.*

Burāqī, Ḥusayn b. Aḥmad, *Taʾrīḫ al-Kūfa* (Naǧaf, 1968), *76.*

Cedrenus, Georgius, *Historiarum compendium*, *MPG* 122; ed. I. Bekker (Bonn 1838–39), *45.*

Cerfaux, L., "Le vrai prophète des clémentines," *Recherches de science religieuse* 18:143, 1928, *6.*

Chabot, J. B., *Synodicon orientale* (Paris, 1902), *17.*

Chavannes, E. and P. Pelliot, "Un traité manichéen retrouvé en Chine," *JA*, 10th series, vol. 18: 499, 1911, *84, 93.*

Christensen, A., *L'Iran sous les Sassanides* (Copenhague, 1944), *35.*

Christensen, A., *Le règne du roi Kawadh I et le communisme mazdakite* (Copenhague, 1925), *32, 34, 35, 40, 42.*

Christides, V., "Saracens' *Prodosia* in the Byzantine Sources," *Byzantion* 40: 5, 1970, *31.*

Chronicon paschale, ed. L. Dindorf (CSHB I) (Bonn, 1832), *34.*

Chwolsohn, D., *Die Ssabier und der Ssabismus* (Petersburg, 1856), *9, 72.*
Clemen, C., "Muhammeds Abhaengigkeit von der Gnosis," *A. von Harnack-Ehrung* (Leipzig, 1921), *79, 92, 93.*
Colpe, C., "Anpassung des Manichaismus an den Islam," *ZDMG* 109:82, 1959, *8.*
Couret, A., *La Palestine sous les empereurs grecs* (Grenoble, 1869), *23.*
Cyprianus of Carthage, De Pascha computus, *MPL* 4, *76.*
Cyrilli Hierosolymitani, *Catechesis, MPG* 33, *21, 90.*
Daḥlān, Aḥmad b. Zaynī, *Al-sīra al-nabawiyya* (Cairo, 1320), *50, 54.*
Dib, P., *History of the Maronite Church* (Washington, 1971), *17.*
Dimašqī, Muḥammad b. Abī Ṭālib, *Nuḫbat al-dahr*, transl. A. F. Mehren (Copenhagen, 1874), *10.*
Ḏahabī, Muḥammad b. Aḥmad, *Siyar aʿlām al-nubalāʾ* (Cairo, 1962), *1.*
Ḏahabī, Muḥammad b. Aḥmad, *Taʾrīḫ al-Islām* (Cairo, 1367 ff.), *1, 4.*
Ḏū al-Rimma, *Dīwān* (Damascus, 1973), 1.
Enoch, Ethiopic Book of (1 Enoch), ed. R.H. Charles (Oxford, 1906); ed. M.A. Knibb (Oxford, 1978), *41, 43, 55, 56, 97.*
Enoch, Hebrew Book of (3 Enoch), ed. H. Odeberg (Cambridge, 1928), *41, 43.*
Enoch, Slavonic Book of (2 Enoch), A. Vaillant (Paris, 1952), *41.*
Epiphanius, *Adv. Haeres., MPG* 42, *21, 23.*
Epiphanius, *Panarion*, ed. K. Holl, *MPG* 41 (Leipzig, 1915–1931), *93, 100.*
Eusebius of Caesarea, *Historia Ecclesiastica*, *30.*
Evangelium Veritatis (M. Malinine et alii eds.) (Zürich, 1956), 82.
Faris, N. A. and H. W. Glidden, "The Development of the Meaning of Koranic Ḥanīf," *JPOS* 19: 1, 1939; Arabic version in: *Abḥāṯ*, 13: 25, 1960 1, *11.*
Festugière, see Kyrillos Skythopolitanus.
Fluegel, G., *Mani* (Leipzig, 1862), *9, 100.*
Frend, W. H. C., "The Gnostic- Manichaean Tradition in Roman North Africa," *JEH* 4: 13, 1953, *81, 93, 96, 98.*
Friedlaender, I., "Jewish- Arabic Studies," *JQR*, N.S. 3: 235, 1912/13, *80.*
Fück, J., "Die Originalitat des arabischen Propheten," *ZDMG* 90: 509, 1936, *95.*
Geiger, A., *Was hat Mohammed aus dem Judenthum aufgenommen* (Leipzig, 1902), *42.*
Gĕʾōnē Mizrāḥ u – maʿărāv, ed. J. Mueller, reprint (Jerusalem, 1958/9), *27.*
Gil, M., "Enoch in the Land of Eternal Life," (in Hebrew), *Tarbiz* 38: 322, 1968/ 9, *55, 58.*
Gil, M., "If a Man Sold a Courtyard" (in Hebrew), *Tarbiz* 46: 17, 1976/7, *28.*
Gil, M., "The Rādhānite Merchants and the Land of Rādhān," *JESHO* 17: 299, 1974, *16, 42.*
Goldziher, I., "Der *Dīwān* des Ġarwal," *ZDMG* 46: 173, 471, 1892 1.
Goldziher, I., *Muhammadanische Studien* (Halle, 1889–90), *30.*

Graetz, H., *History of the Jews* (Hebrew transl. by S.P. Rabinovitch) (Warsaw, 1894), *25.*

Grant, R. M., "Manichees and Christians in the Third and Early Fourth Centuries," *G. Widengren Pres. Vol.* I : 430 (Leiden, 1972), *21.*

Greenfield, J. C., רטין מגושא, *J. Finkel Festschr.* NY 1974: 63, *30.*

Greenlees, D., *Gospel of the Prophet Mani* (Adyar, 1956), *91.*

Gregoire, M. H., "Mahomet et le monophysisme," *Mel. Ch. Diehl* I (Paris, 1930: 107), *94.*

Gruenbaum, M. "Miscellen," *ZDMG* 42:45, 1888, *11.*

Ğarīr, *Naqā'iḍ*, ed., A. A. Bevan (Leiden, 1908/9), *1.*

Ğaṣṣāṣs, Aḥmad b. ʿAlī, *Aḥkam al-qur'ān* (Cairo, 1347), *9, 86.*

Ġāyat al-ḥakīm (ed. H. Ritter), Leipzig 1933 = *Picatrix* (Arabic part; eds. H. Ritter and M. Plessner) (London, 1962), *10.*

Ġayṭī, Muḥammad b. Aḥmad, *Qiṣṣat al-isrā'* (Cairo, 1295), *69.*

Al-Ḥaddād, Y., "*Al-naṣrāniyya fī diyār al-ʿarab qabla al-baʿṯa al-nabawiyya,*" *Masarra* 45: 455, 607, 1959, *4.*

Ḥalabī, Nūr al-Dīn b. ʿAlī, *Insān al-ʿUyūn* (Cairo, 1320), *54.*

Halperin, D. J. and G. D. Newby, "Two Castrated Bulls," etc., *JAOS* 102: 631, 1982, *68.*

Ḥamza b. Ḥasan al Iṣfahānī, *Ta'rīḫ sinī mulūk al-arḍ*, ed. I. M. E. Gottwaldt (Leipzig, 1844), 47.

Harkavi, A. E., see H. Graetz.

Hegemonius, *Acta Archelai*, ed. C. H. Beeson (Leipzig, 1906), *21, 85.*

Henning, W. B., "The Book of the Giants," *BSOAS* 11: 52, 1943, *62.*

Henning, W., "Ein manichaeisches Henochbuch," *Sitzungsberichte, Preuss. Akad. d. Wiss., phil.-hist. Kl.*, 1934: 27, *61.*

Henrichs, A., "Mani and the Babylonian Baptists: A Historical Confrontation," *Harvard Studies in Classical Philology* 77: 23, 1973, *80.*

Henrichs, A. et alii, "Ein griechischer Mani-Codex," *Zeitschr. f Papyrol. u. Epigraphik* 5: 97, 1970, *64, 91, 97.*

Herodianus, apud Photium, Bibliotheca, *MPG* 10, *90.*

Herzfeld, E., *Paikuli* (Berlin, 1924), *29.*

Hieronymus, In Daniele, *MPL* 25, *41.*

Higger, M. (ed.), *The Treatises Derek Erez* (NY, 1935), *27.*

Honigmann, E., *Évêques et évêchés monophysites* (Louvain, 1951), *94.*

Horovitz, J., *Koranische Untersuchungen* (Berlin, 1926), *1(2), 9.*

Houdous, E. J., "The Gospel of the Epiphany," *CBQ* 6: 69, 1944, *55.*

Ḫaffāğī, Aḥmad b. Muḥammad, *Nasīm al-riyāḍ* (Istanbul, 1312–15), *4, 69.*

Ḫalīfa ibn Ḫayyāṭ al-Aṣfūrī, *Ta'rīḫ* (Nağaf, 1967), *54.*

al-Ḫāzin, ʿAlī b. Muḥammad, *Lubāb al-ta'wīl* (Cairo, 1910), *2, 55.*

Ibn ʿAbd al-Barr, Yūsuf b. ʿAli, *Al-durar fī iḫtiṣār al-maġāzī wa-l-siyar* (Cairo, 1966), *4, 54.*

Ibn ʿAbd al-Barr, Yūsuf b. ʿAli, *Al-istīʿāb fī maʿrifat al-aṣḥāb* (Cairo, 1957), *4, 99.*

Ibn ʿAbd Rabbihi, Aḥmad b. Muḥammad, *Al-ʿiqd al farīd* (Cairo, 1953 ff.), *1, 47 (2).*
Ibn Abī Uṣaybiʿa, Aḥmad b. Qāsim, *ʿUyūn al-anbāʾ fī ṭabaqāt al-aṭibbāʾ* (Beirut, 1965), *71.*
Ibn ʿAsākir, ʿAli b. Ḥasan, *Taʾrīḫ madīnat dimašq*, ed. Badran (Damascus 1331 ff.); ed. Damascus 1951 ff., *4.*
Ibn Aʿṭam, Aḥmad al-Kūfī, *K. al-futūḥ* (Hyderabad, 1968 ff.), *77.*
Ibn al-Aṯīr ʿAlī b. Muḥammad, *Al-Kāmil fī al-taʾrīḫ* (Beirut, 1965), *34, 44, 47.*
Ibn al-Aṯīr, ʿAlī b. Muḥammad, Usd al-ġāba (Cairo, 1384–87), *4 (2), 99.*
Ibn al-Aṯīr, Mubārak b. Muḥammad, *Ǧāmiʿ al-uṣūl* (Cairo, 1949 ff.), *4, 30.*
Ibn al-Aṯīr, Mubārak b. Muḥammad, *Al-nihāya fī ġarīb al-ḥadīṯ wa-l-aṯar* (Cairo, 1311), *42.*
Ibn Bābawayh, Muḥammad b. ʿAlī al-Qummī, *ʿIlal al-šarāʾiʿ* (Naǧaf, 1966), *69.*
Ibn Bābawayh, Muḥammad b. ʿAlī al-Qummī, *Maʿānī-al-aḫbār* (Teheran, 1379), *55.*
Ibn Ḥabīb, Muḥammad, *K. al-muḥabbar* (Beirut n. d.), *4, 30, 47, 51, 54, 95.*
Ibn Ḥanbal, Aḥmad, *Musnad* (Cairo, 1896), (reprint, Beirut 1969), *42, 99 (2).*
Ibn Ḥazm,ʿAlī b. Aḥmad, *Al-fiṣal fī al-milal* (Cairo, 1317–20), *8, 72.*
Ibn Hišām,ʿAbd al-Malik, *Sīrat rasūl allāh*, ed. F. Wüstenfeld, Göttingen 1858; English translation by A. Guillaume, London 1955, *1, 2, 4(2), 5, 6, 7, 50, 51, 54(2).*
Ibn Iyas, Muḥammad b. Aḥmad, *Badāʾiʿ al-zuhūr* (Cairo n. d.), *69.*
Ibn al-Ǧawzī, ʿAbd al-Raḥmān b. ʿAlī, Zād al-masīr (Cairo, 1964), *1, 2, 55.*
Ibn al-Kalbī, Hišām b. Muḥammad, *Ǧamharat al-nasab*, ed. W. Caskel (Leiden, 1966), *4.*
Ibn Kaṯīr, Abū al-Fidāʾ Ismāʿīl, *Šamāʾil al-rasūl* (Cairo, 1967), *69.*
Ibn Kaṯīr, Ismāʿīl b. ʿUmar, *Al-bidāya wa-l-nihāya* (Beirut, 1966), *4, 50, 54.*
Ibn Manẓūr, Muḥammad b. Mukarram, *Lisān al-ʿArab* (Beirut, 1955–56), *1, 2, 99.*
Ibn al-Nadīm, Muḥammad b. Isḥāq, *Fihrist*, ed. G. Flügel (Leipzig, 1871); English translation: B. Dodge, Columbia Univ. Pr. 1970, *9,16, 38, 46, 59, 92, 100.*
Ibn Qifṭī, ʿAlī b. Yūsuf, *Taʾrīḫ al-ḥukamāʾ* (Leipzig, 1903), *71.*
Ibn Qudāma al-Maqdisī, ʿAbdallāh b. Aḥmad, *Al-istibṣār fī nasab al-ṣaḥaba min al-anṣār* (Beirut, 1972), *4.*
Ibn Qutayba, ʿAbdallāh b. Muslim, *Al-maʿārif* (Cairo, 1969), *47, 69.*
Ibn Qutayba, ʿAbdallāh b. Muslim, *Al-šiʿr wa-l- šuʿarāʾ*, ed. M. J. De Goeje (Leiden, 1902), *1.*
Ibn Qutayba, ʿAbdallāh b. Muslim, *Tafsīr ġarīb al-qurʾān* (Cairo, 1958), *2.*
Ibn Qutayba, ʿAbdallāh b. Muslim, *ʿUyūn al-aḫbār* (Cairo, 1925 et. sqq.), *1.*
Ibn Rusteh, Aḥmad b. ʿUmar, *Al-aʿlāq al-nafīsa (BGA* VII) (Leiden, 1891), *30, 48.*
Ibn Saʿd, Muḥammad, *Ṭabaqāt* (Leiden, 1905 ff.), *4(2), 95, 99(2).*

Ibn Sayyid al-Nās, Muḥammad b. Muḥammad, *'Uyūn al-aṯar* (Cairo, 1356), *1, 4, 54, 69.*

Ibn Šahrāšūb, Muḥammad b. 'Alī, *Manāqib āl Abī Ṭālib* (Naǧaf, 1956), *69.*

Ibn Sīda, 'Alī b. Ismā'īl, *K. al-muḫaṣṣas* (Tunis, 1956), *99.*

Ibn Ṭāwūs, 'Alī b. Mūsā, *Sa'd al-su'ūd* (Naǧaf, 1369), *75.*

Ibn Ẓafar, Muḥammad b. 'Alī al-Ṣaqalī, *Ḫayr al-bišar* (Cairo, 1280), *1.*

Irenaeus, *Adv. haereses*, ed. W.W. Harvey (Cambridge, 1857), *93.*

Iṣbahānī, Abū al-Faraǧ 'Alī b. Ḥusayn, *K. al-aġānī* (Cairo, 1285*), 1, 47 (2), 51(2).*

Išō'yahb Patriarchae III, *Liber epistularum*, ed. R. Duval (Leipzig, 1905), (CSCO – Syri, ser. 2, t. 64*), 17.*

Jaubert, A., "Le calendrier des Jubilees," *VT*, 3:250, 1953, *76.*

John of Ephesus, *Lives of the Eastern Saints*, ed. Brooks, PO XVII (1), 1.

Joshua the Stylite, *The Chronicle*, ed. W. Wright (Cambridge, 1882), 31.

Kawar, I. "Byzantium und Kinda, Procopius und Kinda," *BZ*, 53: 57, 1960, *31.*

Kindi, 'Abd al-Masīḥ, *Risāla*, ed. A. Tien (London, 1880), *1.*

Kister, M. J., "Ḥaddithū 'an b. Isrā'īla," *IOS* 2: 215, 1972, *75.*

Kister, M. J., "Al-Ḥīra," *Arabica* 15: 143, 1968, *48, 51.*

Kister, M. J., "Al-taḥannuth," *BSOAS* 31: 223, 1968, *2.*

Kister, M. J. and M. Plessner, "Notes on Caskel's Ǧamharat an-nasab," *Oriens* 25–26: 48, 1976, *54.*

Klima, O., *Mazdak* (Prague, 1957), *32, 34, 43.*

Knibb, M.A., see *Enoch, Ethiopic Book of.*

Kosegarten, J. G. L. ed., *Carmina Hudsailitarum* (London, 1854), *1.*

Krauss, S., *Griechische und lateinische Lehnwoerter* (Berlin, 1898), *28.*

Kulaynī, Muḥammad b. Ya'qūb, *K. al-kāfī* (Teheran, 1381), *76.*

Kyrillos Skythopolitanus, *Opera*, ed. Ed. Schwartz (Leipzig, 1939), (TUGAL 49–2); translated in: Festugière, A. J., *Les moines d'Orient* III (Paris, 1962), *12, 13.*

Lammens, H., "Les Chrétiens à la Mecque à la veille de l'hégire," *BIFAO* 15: 191, 1918, *6.*

Lammens, H., *Études sur le règne du calife omaiyade Mo'awia* I (Paris, 1908), *98.*

Lampe, G. W. H., *A Patristic Greek Lexicon* (Oxford, 196–68), *28.*

Leontius Byzantinus, *De sectis, MPG* 86, *90.*

Liddell, H. G. and R. Scott, *A Greek English Lexicon* (Oxford, 1966), *28.*

Lidzbarski, M., *Ephemeris* II (Giessen, 1908), *29.*

Lisān al-'Arab, see Ibn Manẓūr.

Lyall, C. J., "The Words Ḥanīf and Muslim," *JRAS*, 1903: 771, *1.*

Maǧlisī, Muḥammad Bāqir, *Biḥār al-anwār*, new edition (Qumm n.d.), *69, 75, 76.*

Mahlow, G., *Neue Wege durch die griechische Sprache* (Berlin, 1926), *28.*

Malalas, Ioannes, *Chronographia, MPG* 97; cf. ed. Dindorf (Bonn, 1831), *35.*

Malaṭī, Muḥammad b. Aḥmad, *Al-tanbīh wa-l-radd 'alā ahl al-ahwā' wa-l-bida'* (Baghdad, 1968), *6, 36.*

Mansi, G. D., *Sacrorum conciliorum nova et amplissima collectio* (Paris, 1927), *59.*

Maqdisī, Muṭahhar b. Ṭāhir, *Al-bad' wa-l-ta'rīḫ*, ed. C. Huart (Paris, 1899), *47, 69.*

Maqrīzī, Aḥmad b. ʿAlī, *Ḫiṭaṭ* (Beirut n. d.), *71.*

Marcus Diaconus, *Vita S. Porphyrii Gazensis, MPG* 65, *22, 28.*

Margoliouth, D. S., "On the Origin and Import of the Names Muslim and Ḥanīf," *JRAS* 1903 : 467, *1.*

Marquart, J., *Ērānšahr* (Berlin, 1901), (= *Abhandlungen*, Göttingen, Koenigl. Ges. d. Wiss., phil.-hist. Kl. n. F. 111–3), *17.*

Marquet, Y., "Sabéens et Iḫwān al-Ṣafā'," *SI* 24: 35, 1966; 25: 27, 1967, *72.*

Mas'ūdī, ʿAlī b. Ḥusayn, *Murūǧ al-ḏahab*, ed. C. Barbier de Meynard (Paris, 1861 ff.), *5, 11, 35, 69.*

Mas'ūdī, ʿAlī b. Ḥusayn, *Al-tanbīh wa-l-išrāf* (*BGA* VIII) (Leiden, 1894), *11.*

Māwardī, ʿAlī b. Muḥammad, *Aʿlām al-nubuwwa* (Cairo n. d.), *72.*

Mawṣilī, Ismāʿīl Hibatallāh b. Abi al-Riḍā, *Ġāyat al-wasā'il*, MS. Cambridge Or. Oq 33 5, *72.*

Mawṣilī, Mu'āfā b. Ismāʿīl, *Nihāyat al-bayān*, MS. BM Or. 2981, *2, 4.*

Methodius, *De iis qui abnegarunt, MPG* 100, *28.*

Methodius, *Symposion, MPG* 100, *28.*

Michael the Syrian, *Chronicle*, ed. J. B. Chabot, Paris 1905–1910, *74, 76, 90.*

Milik, J. T., *The Books of Enoch* (Oxford, 1976), *55, 62, 94.*

Milikowsky, C., "Gehenna and 'Sinners of Israel,' in the Light of Seder *'Olam,*" (Hebrew), *Tarbiz* 55: 311, 1985/6, *27.*

Mingana, A., "Syriac Influence on the Style of the Kur'an," *BJRL* 11: 77, 1927, *6.*

Moberg, A., *The Book of the Himyarites* (Lund, 1924), *15.*

Monnot, G., "Sabéens et idolatres," *MIDEO* 12: 13, 1974, *9.*

Mueller, W., "Mazdak and the Alphabet Mysticism of the East," *History of Religions* 3 (1): 72, 1963, *43.*

Nemoy, L., "Al-Qirqisānī's Account of the Jewish Sects and Christianity," *HUCA* 7: 317, 1930, *25.*

Nilus, *Epistulae, MPG* 79, *82.*

Niẓām al-Mulk, *Siyāsat-nāme*, ed. H. Darke (Teheran, 1962), *33.*

Nöldeke, T., *Geschichte der Perser u. Araber z. Zeit d. Sasaniden* (Ṭabarī) (Leiden, 1879), *32, 36, 47, 51, 53.*

Nöldeke, T., *Die von Guidi herausgegebene syrische Chronik, Abhandlungen*, Akad. d. Wiss., philos.-hist. Kl., Vienna, 128 (IX), 1893, *17.*

Nöldeke, T., *Neue Beiträge zur semitischen Sprachwissenschaft* (Strassburg, 1910), *11.*

Olinder, G., *The Kings of Kinda*, Lunds Univers. Arsskrift N.F. Avd. I vol. 23–6, *47(2).*

Origenes, *Contra Celsum, MPG* 11, *28.*

Payne-Smith, R., *Thesaurus Syriacus* (Oxford, 1879), *14.*

Pedersen, J., "The Sābians," *E. G. Browne Pres. Vol.* (Cambridge, 1922: 383), *9, 24, 93.*
Pellat, C., "'Amr b. 'Adī," *EI*[2] 1:450, *29.*
Philippi, F., see n. 57.
Philo, *De confusione linguarum*, Opera omnia (London, 1929 ff.) (Loeb), IV, *37.*
Philo, *De Mutatione nominum*, Opera omnia (London, 1929 ff.) (Loeb), V, *43.*
Philo, *De plantatione*, Opera omnia (London, 1929 ff.) (Loeb) III, *39.*
Philo, *De posteritate Caini*, Opera omnia (London, 1929 ff.) (Loeb), II, *42.*
Philo, *De specialibus legibus,* Opera omnia (London, 1929 ff.) (Loeb), VII, *42.*
Philo, *Quod deterius*, Opera omnia (London, 1929 ff.) (Loeb) II, *37, 39.*
Philonenko, M., "Une citation manichéenne du livre d'Hénoch," *RHPR* 52: 337, 1972, *62, 66.*
Philonenko, M., "Une tradition essénienne dans le Coran,"*RHR* 170:143, 1966, *66.*
Pines, S., "The Iranian Name for Christians and the 'God-Fearers,'" *Proceedings*, Israel Academy of Sciences and Humanities, 2 (no. 7): 143, 1967, *42.*
Plato, Phaedo (Loeb ed. of his works, 1914 ff., I), *39.*
Plessner, M., "Hermes Trismegistos and Arab Science," *SI* 2: 46, 1954, *71.*
Plotinus, *Enneads* (Loeb ed. of his works, 1966 ff.), *39.*
Polotsky, H. J., "Manichäismus," *PW* Suppl. VI: 240, *80, 91, 93, 100.*
Polotsky, H. J. and A. Böhlig, *Kephalaia* I (Stuttgart, 1940), *61, 85, 96.*
Poznanski, S., "Ibn Ḥazm ueber juedische Sekten," *JQR* 16: 765, 1904, *25.*
Puech, H.C., *Le Manichéisme* (Paris, 1949), *63.*
Pugliese Carratelli, G., "La Persia dei Sasanidi nella storiografia romana da Ammiano a Procopio," in: *La Persia nel medioevo* (Roma, 1971: 597), *35.*
Qaramānī, Aḥmad b. Yūsuf, *Aḫbār al-duwal* (Baghdad, 1282), *73.*
Qiṣaṣ al-anbiyā' (anonymous; attributed to al-'Askarī, MS. BM Or. 1510 (Suppl. Rieu No. 466), *69.*
Al-Qurašī, 'Abdallāh b. Wahb, *Al-Ǧāmi' fī al-ḥadīṯ*, MS. Chester Beatty, 3497, *99.*
Qurṭubī, Muḥammad b. Aḥmad, *(Tafsīr) al-ǧāmi' li-aḥkām al-qur'ān* (Cairo, 1933), *1, 6.*
Rabin, C., *Qumran Studies* (Oxford, 1957), 42.
Rāġib al-Iṣfahānī b. Muḥammad, *Al-mufradāt fī ġarīb al-qur'ān* (Cairo, 1324), *2.*
Rahmani, I. A., *Studia Syriaca*, I (Charfé, 1904), *19.*
Rāwandī, Sa'īd b. Hibatallāh, *Al-ḫarā'iǧ wa-l-ǧarā'iḥ* (Bombay, 1301), *70.*
Reckendorf, H., "Al-Ash'ath," *EI*[2] I: 696, *54.*
Recognitiones Clementinae, *MPG* 1, *28.*
Répertoire chronologique d'épigraphie arabe (Cairo: IFAO, 1931 ff.), *29.*
Riedel, W. and W.E. Crum, *The Canons of Athanasius of Alexandria* (London, 1904), *11.*
Rosenthal, F., *Knowledge Triumphant* (Leiden, 1970), *78.*
Rosenthal, F., "Nineteen," *Analecta Biblica* 12: 304, 1959, *84.*

Rosenthal, F., “The Prophecies of Bābā the Ḥarrānian,” *S. H. Taqizadeh Pres. Vol.* (London, 1962), *19.*

Rothstein, G., *Die Dynastie d. Laḫmiden in al-Ḥīra* (Berlin, 1899), *31, 47(2).*

Rubin, U., “Pre-existence and Light,” *IOS* 5: 62, 1975, *78.*

Rudolph, K., *Die Mandäer* (Göttingen, 1960), 9.

Ruska, J., “Thabit b. Kurra,” *EI*[1], p. 733, *18.*

Ry 506 = G. Ryckmans, “Inscriptions sud-arabes” (published in continuations), *Le Muséon* 66: 267, 1963, *47.*

Sachau, E., *Syrische Rechtsbuecher* III (Berlin, 1914), *20.*

Sa’īd Ibn Biṭrīq *Ta’rīḫ*, ed. L. Cheikho (Leipzig, 1906), 1909 (CSCO, Arabici, ser. III, vols. VI, VII); Latin translation: Pococke, *MPG* 111, *34, 100.*

Saḫāwī, Muḥammad b. ʿAbd al-Raḥmān, *Al-maqāṣid al-ḥasana* (Cairo, 1375), *99.*

Ṣāliḥī, Muḥammad b. Yūsuf, *Subul al-hudā wa-l-rišād* (Cairo, 1962), *69.*

Samhūdī, ʿAlī b. ʿAbdallah, *Wafā’ al-wafā’ bi-aḫbār dār al-muṣṭafā* (Cairo, 1908), *49.*

Schader, H. H., *Iranische Beiträge* I (Halle, 1930), *30.*

Schader, H. H., Review of: Schmidt-Polotsky, *Mani-Fund, Gnomon* 9: 337, 1933, *29.*

Scher, A. (ed.), *Histoire nestorienne* (Chronique de Séert) II, PO 7, fasc. 2 (Paris, 1990), *33.*

Schmidt, C. and H. J. Polotsky, “Ein Mani-Fund in Aegypten,” *Sitzungsberichte*, Preuss. Akad, d. Wiss., phil-hist. Kl., 1933: 4, *59, 91.*

Schmidt, J., “Zwei arianische a-Laute,” etc., *Zeitschrift fuer vergleichende Sprachforschung* 25: 1, 1881, *28.*

Schreiner, M., “Zur Geschichte der Polemik zwischen Juden und Muhammedanern,” *ZDMG* 42: 591, 1888, *25.*

Segal, J. B., “Pagan Syriac Monuments in the Vilayet of Urfa,” *Anatolian Studies* 3: 97, 1953, *10.*

Segal, J. B., “Some Syriac Inscriptions of the 2nd–3rd Cent. A.D.,” *BSOAS* 16:13, 1954, *84.*

Seston, W., “Le roi sassanide Narses, les Arabes et le Manichéisme,” *Mel. R. Dussaud* (Paris, 1939: 227), *29.*

Sezgin, F., *Geschichte des arabischen Schrifttums* (Leiden, 1967 ff.), *72.*

Shaban, M. A., *Islamic History* (Cambridge, 1971), *54.*

Sibṭ Ibn al-Ǧawzī, Yūsuf b. Qazā’uġlī, *Mir’āt al-zamān*, MS. BM Or 4215, *72.*

Siǧistānī, Abū Bakr Muḥammad, *Tafsīr ġarīb al-qur’ān*, MS. India Office 3794 (Cat. Storey 1175), *1, 2, 42.*

Siǧistānī, Abū Ḥātim Sahl B. Muḥammad, *Mu’ammarīn*, ed. I. Goldziher (Leiden, 1899), *49.*

Siyāsat-nāme, see Niẓām al-Mulk.

Starr, J., "Le mouvement messianique au début du VIIIe siècle," *REJ* 102:81, 1937, *25.*

Stern, S. M., "Abū 'Īsā al-Warrāq," *EI*[2] I: 130, *36.*

Stern, S. M., "Quotations from Apocryphal Gospels in 'Abd al-Jabbār," *Journal of Theological Studies* 18: 34, 1967; 19: 128, 1968, *9, 11.*

Suyūṭī, 'Abd al-Raḥmān b. Abī Bakr, *Al-durr al-manṭūr* (Cairo, 1314), *55, 99.*

Suyūṭī, 'Abd al-Raḥmān b. Abī Bakr, *Itqān fī 'ulūm al-qur'ān* (Cairo, 1967), *42.*

Suyūṭī, 'Abd al-Raḥmān b. Abī Bakr, *Mu'tarak al-aqrān* (Cairo, 1969), *1, 2, 69.*

Šahrastānī, Muḥammad b. 'Abd al-Karīm, *Al-milal wa-l-niḥal*, ed. W. Cureton, London 1842; German translation: Th. Haarbruecker (Halle, 1850), *8, 36, 42, 80.*

Šiblī, Muḥammad b. 'Abdallāh, *Maḥāsin al-wasā'il*, MS. BM Or 1530 (Suppl. Rieu p. 394), *69.*

Ṭabarī, Muḥibb al-Dīn Aḥmad b. 'Abdallah, *Al-riyāḍ al-naḍra* (Cairo, 1327), *4.*

Ṭabarī, Muḥammad b. Ǧarīr, *Aḫbār (ta'rīḫ) al-rusul wa-l-mulūk*, ed. De Goeje, reprint (Leiden, 1964); ed. Cairo, Dār al-ma'ārif, 1969, *47(2), 54(3), 68, 69.*

Ṭayālisī, Sulaymān b. Da'ūd, *Musnad* (Hyderabad, 1321), *3, 87, 88.*

Theophanes Confessor, *Chronographia*, ed. C. De Boor (Leipzig, 1883), *31.*

Ṭiḥāwī, Aḥmad b. Muḥammad al-Ḥanafī, *Mu'taṣar* (Hyderabad, 1362), *2, 10, 70.*

Timotheus Constantinopolitanus presbyter, *De receptione haereticorum*, *MPG 86, 65, 68, 90.*

Ṯa'ālibī, 'Abd al-Malik b. Muḥammad, *Laṭā'if al-ma'ārif* (Cairo, 1960), *30, 71.*

Vadet, J. C., "Les *Ḥanīfs*," *REJ* 130:165, 1971, *6.*

Vajda, G., "Idrīs," *EI*[2] III: 1030, *68.*

Vollers, K., "Das Religionsgespraech von Jerusalem," *Zeitschr. f. Kirchengesch.* 29: 29, 1908, *1.*

Vööbus, A., *History of Asceticism* (*CSCO* 184, 197, Subsidia 14, 17) (Louvain, 1958–60), *97.*

Vööbus, A., "Manichaeism and Christianity in Persia under the Sasanids," *Yearbook of the Estonian Learned Society* 1: 7, 1951–53, *97.*

Wāḥidī, 'Alī b. Aḥmad, *Asbāb al-nuzūl* (Cairo, 1968), *4.*

Waldschmidt, E. and W. Lentz, "Die Stellung Jesu im Manichaismus," *Abhandlungen*, Preuss. Akad. d. Wiss., phil.-hist. K1., 1926(3), *91.*

Watt, W. M., "*Ḥanīf*," *EI*[2] III: 165, *1.*

Watt, W. M., "Two Interesting Christian-Arabic Usages," *JSS* 2: 360, 1957, *11.*

Wellhausen, J., *Lieder d. Hudhailiten* (*Skizzen u. Vorarb.* 1–2) (Berlin, 1884), *1.*

Wellhausen, J., *Reste des arab. Heidentums* (Berlin, 1897), *7, 9, 55.*

Wensinck, A. J., "Muhammed und die Propheten," *Acta Orientalia* (Copenhagen) 2: 168, 1924, *11.*

West, E. W., ed., *Pahlavi Texts* (Oxford, 1880–82), *33.*

Widengren, G. *Mesopotamian Elements in Manichaeism* (Uppsala, 1946), (Universitets Arsskrift no. 3), *59, 61, 62.*

Widengren, G., *Mani und der Manichäismus* (Stuttgart, 1961), *38, 61, 91, 94.*

Wieder, N., "The 'Law-Interpreter' of the Sect of the Dead Sea Scrolls: The Second Moses," *JJS* 4: 158, 1953, *69.*

Yaʿqūbī, Ibn Wāḍiḥ, *Taʾrīḫ* (Leiden, 1883), *11, 23, 89.*

Yāqūt b. ʿAbdallāh al-Ḥamawī al-Rūmī, *Muʿǧam al-buldān*, ed. F. Wüstenfeld (Leipzig, 1866–70), *47, 50, 53.*

Zamaḫšarī, Maḥmūd b. ʿUmar, *K. al-amkina wa-l-miyāh wa-l-ǧibāl* (Baghdad, 1968), *50.*

Notes

---

1 See the article "Ḥanīf," *EI*[2], III, pp. 165 f. (W.M. Watt); a few quotations showing the proximity between *muslim* and *ḥanīf*, in Margoliouth, *JRAS*, 1903, pp. 483 f.; the Christian monk resolutely denies, in a fictitious religious dispute written under Muslim rule, the argument that Jesus was a *ḥanīf-muslim* since, he says, Jesus strongly criticized the *ḥanīfs* (and Samaritans), see the text in Vollers, *Zeitschr. f. Kirchengesch.* 29 (1908), p. 45; see other quotations, mainly from Arab poetry, and the discussion on *fiṭra* in Horovitz, *Koran. Unters.*, pp. 57 ff., who strongly defends the view that *ḥanīf*, and *muslim* were identical; on pp. 121 f. he discards the view that *ḥanīf*, and *ṣābiʾ* were identical; see also Buhl, p. 68. The matter of the *fiṭra* can be seen in a somewhat new light, as meaning originally "worship of nature," if one considers a passage in John of Ephesus' Lives, p. 236: "What kind of *ḥanpa* or any other (of those) who worship creation would suspend for such a long time their honouring the object of their worship" (in addressing Christians who neglected their church). [I am grateful to Prof. J.B. Segal for this reference.] Quotations, both from the Qurʾān and from poetry, can be found in Faris and Glidden, *JPOS*, 19:1, 1939, who followed the references listed by Horovitz, *l.c.* See also Wellhausen, *Hudhailiten*, p. 63 (*wa-rabba kulli muslimin ḥanīfin*; Kosegarten, *Huzailis*, p. 45 (no. 18; ... *naṣārā yusāqawna lāqaw ḥanīfan*); Abū Ḏuʿayb,14 (no. 9, 1.3); Goldziher, *Gharwal, ZDMG*, 46 (1892), p. 479 (*muslimu taḥallā. . . ḥanīfu*; *Lisān al-ʿArab*, V, p. 211b (Abū al-Aḫzar al-Ḥammānī ...*naṣrānatun lam taḥannafi* ; cf. Ibn Qutayba, *Šiʿr*, ed. De Goeje, p. 338); ibid., IX, p. 57; *al-ḥanīf, al-muslim*, who has the inclination to the right belief; see there also more quotations; see Ǧarīr, *Naqāʾiḍ* II, p. 595: The religion of the one who *taḥannafa* is the opposite of Christianity; Faris and Glidden, p. 27, n. 11, criticize Horovitz, *Kor. Unters.*, p. 58, for having understood it the other way around, namely that the verse refers to a Christian monk; but Horovitz was led to understand it that way by the text as printed by Bevan. See also Abū ʿUbayda, I, p. 58, who quotes Ḏū al-Rimma's verses containing the antithesis *ḥanīf-muslim* vs. Christian, cf. Ḏū al-Rimma, *Dīwān*, pp. 632f.; Qurṭubī, *Tafsīr*, II, p. 128; Ibn Hišām, p. 995, who cites verses the poetess Umāma recited after Sālim b. ʿUmayr killed the poet Abū ʿAfak, the enemy of the Prophet, in which she said "a *ḥanīf* (i.e., *muslim*) hit you...;" Ibn Qutayba, *ʿUyūn*, I, p. 34, where *ḥanīf* means *muslim* in the mouth of ʿUmar, as opposed to Jews or Christians; Siǧistānī, *Ġarīb*, fol. 52b (Ibrāhīm was a *ḥanīf* since he desisted from worshipping idols; this being an interpretation of the root *ḥnf*; *wa-l-ḥanīfu-l-yawma al-muslimu*); Ibn ʿAbd Rabbihi, *ʿIqd*, p. 411 (wine of Gurgan, untouched by any *ḥanīf*); Anbārī, *Aḍdād*, pp. 116f.; on Umayya b. Abī al-Ṣalt see Iṣbahānī, *Aġānī*, III, p. 187; Alūsī, II, p. 253; cf. Lyall, *JRAS*,

1903, p. 773; see also Ibn Ẓafar, p. 13: God foretold to Jesus the appearance of Muḥammad, whose faith will be the *ḥanīfiyya*; Ibn al-Ǧawzī, *Zād al-masīr*, I, p. 150; Ibn Sayyid al-Nās, *'Uyūn*, I p. 266, contains verses in which the Muslims are called *ḥanīfiyyan* and the battle of Badr is presented as the beginning of the fall of the Persians and Byzantines (Kisrā and Qayṣar); Ḏahabī, *Ta'rīḫ*, III, p. 100: A Christian hired labourer who accepted Islam says *taḥannaftu* (same expression, see idem, *Siyar*, III, p. 324): Suyūṭī, *Muʿtarak*, II, p. 63. A Christian source, Abū Ṣāliḥ al-Armanī, p. 101, confirms it while referring to the Muslim conquest of Egypt: . . . *ẓaharat al-umma al-ḥanīfiyya*.

2 Ibn Hišām, I, p. 152; cf. Kister, *BSOAS*, 31 (1968), pp. 228f.; Siǧistānī, *Ġarīb*, fol. 52b (ed. Cairo, p. 18); Ibn Qutayba, *Ġarīb*, p. 64; Ṭiḥāwī, II, p. 337; Rāġib, p. 190; Ibn al-Ǧawzī, *Zād al-masīr*, I, p. 150; Mawṣilī, *Nihāya*, fol. 93a; Ḫāzin, I, p. 94; Suyūṭī, *Muʿtarak*, II, p. 63; Abū al-Suʿūd, I, p. 267; ʿAzīzī, I, p. 54; *Lisān al-ʿArab*, IX, p. 57.

3 Ṭayālisī, p. 145.

4 Cf. al-Ḥaddād, *Masarra*, 45 (1959), pp. 460, 607, who describes these people as forerunners of Islam, and considers the *ḥanīfiyya* to be a blend of monotheism and old Arabian customs. See Wāḥidī, p. 178; Ibn Hišām, pp. 143f., on the four people who abandoned idolatry and on Zayd b.ʿAmru b. Nufayl, the true *ḥanīf*; cf. Ibn Saʿd, III (1), p. 276 and Ibn al-Aṯīr, *Usd*, II, pp. 236f., who has details on Zayd's view of the people of Ḫaybar (i.e., the Jews) who in his opinion were idolaters. See on Zayd b. ʿAmru also Ḫaffāǧī, III, p. 296; al-Ṭabarī al-Muḥibb, II, p. 203. In the traditions on Salmān al-Fārisī and his search for the true religion it is also said that he was looking for the religion of Abraham; one explains to him that this religion was out of fashion "today," see e.g., Ibn Sayyid al-Nās, *'Uyūn*, I, p. 65, who also has the traditions on Zayd b. ʿAmru, on pp. 66f., taken from Ibn Isḥāq. Zayd b. ʿAmru b. Nufayl was a cousin of ʿUmar b. al-Ḫaṭṭāb:

Nufayl
/ \
al-Ḫaṭṭāb ʿAmru
/ \ \
Zayd ʿUmar Zayd

See also Ibn Kaṯīr, *Bidāya*, II, p. 237. See the description of Abū Qays Ṣayfi b. al-Aslat, the pre-Islamic *ḥanīf* of Medina, in Ibn Saʿd, IV (2), pp. 94f., and the stress on the fact that he came to *ḥanīfiyya* after having examined Judaism and Christianity thoroughly; cf. on him Ibn al-Kalbī-Caskel, I, table 184; Ibn Hišām, p. 293, quotes his verses and describes his doubts regarding Muḥammad's prophecy; Ibn Ḥabīb, *Muḥabbar*, p. 420; Ibn Qudāma, p. 271; Ibn ʿAbd al-Barr, *Durar*, p. 73; *Istīʿāb*, IV, pp. 1734 f., cf. Ibn al-Aṯīr, *Usd*, V, pp. 278f.; Ibn ʿAsākir, VI, pp. 454ff., and the verses on the *ḥanīfs* ibid., p. 456; see the Prophet's prayer, in Ibn al-Aṯīr, *Ǧāmiʿ*, V, p. 69, where he says that he observes "the religion of our father Abraham." See more on "the religion of Abraham" in Anbārī, *Aḍdād*, p. 116: *al-ḥanīfiyyatu-l-tadayyunu bi-dīni-brāhīma*; Mawṣilī, *Nihāya*, fol. 93; Ḏahabī, *Ta'rīḫ*, I, pp. 52 f.

5 Ibn Hišām, pp. 50f.; Mawṣilī, *Wasā'il*, fol. 74. Masʿūdī, *Murūǧ*, IV, p. 44, has a tradition, according to which in the *ǧāhiliyya* period some people of Mecca considered the Kaʿba to be the house of *zaḥl* (the planet Saturn); since *zaḥl* was the one who took care of life, stability, and survival, that was a guarantee in their view that this temple would last forever.

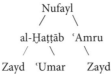

6 Ibn Hišām, p. 124; cf. Wüstenfeld's note, in vol. II, p. 40. *Amlāk* means angels here, as understood also by Guillaume in his translation, not kings as understood by Vadet, *REJ* 130 (1971), p. 172. See also Qurṭubī, *Tafsīr*, II, p. 113, where the version is *malāk*. That *amlāk* here means angels is supported by a tradition attributed to Wahb b. Munabbih about four *amlāk* who carry God's throne (*ʿarš*), cf. Malaṭī, *Tanbīh*, p. 102. These traditions are so contradictory to accepted views on the transition of the Arabs from paganism to monotheism, that Lammens, *BIFAO*, 15 (1918), pp. 195f., was induced to proclaim *ḥanīfs* a non-historical fiction, just a term used in the Quran to mean a monotheist and a righteous man, like Abraham, and translated *ḥanīf* as "monotheist." Mingana, *BJRL*, 11 (1927), pp. 97f., points out the fact that *ḥanpā*, the Syriac equivalent of *ḥanīf*, had a rather negative meaning, of idolater; in his view, Muḥammad took over the point that Abraham had been a *ḥanpā*, which he was indeed before becoming a monotheist; then, by virtue of its being attached to Abraham, the term received a positive meaning in the Quran and in the traditions of Islam. This is of course pure speculation. Beck, *Le* Muséèon 65 (1952), pp. 86f. rightly shows that there was a link between Muḥammad's new message and the image of Abraham even before the Medinan period and the Prophet's contacts with the Jews. He also points out that there is an ancient Christian parallel to Muḥammad's description of Abraham as being neither a Jew nor a Christian, namely that of Eusebius in his *Demonstratio Evangelica:* Abraham was not a Jew, he was a Christian. However, the difference should rather be insisted upon; whereas Eusebius transferred Abraham directly in his own realm, the Prophet of Islam first made him pass through the *ḥanīfiyya*, and for good reasons, as will be seen further. On Abraham in the Clementines see Cerfaux, *RSR*, 18 (1928), pp. 160ff.; he is considered to be the prototype of the true prophet. From what will be said further it will emerge even more that the image of Abraham as archetype of a prophet was well known in the ambience in which Muḥammad began his activities.

7 Ibn Hišām, pp. 225, 229; also, p. 997; *ṣabawta*, "you became a Muslim," p. 300; *al-ṣubbāʾ* "the Muslims;" p. 835; *ṣabaʾnā*, *ṣabaʾnā*, "we became Muslims!"; p. 841: B. Hawāzin call the Muslims at Ḥunayn: *al-ṣubbāʾ*, cf. Wellhausen, *Reste*, pp. 236 ff.

8 Ibn Ḥazm, *Milal* I, p. 35; Šahrastānī, pp. 203 f., did not follow Ibn Ḥazm's path, but differentiated between Sabians, whose name comes from *ṣabaʾa*, meaning "to deviate (from the truth)," and *ḥanīfs*. The former follow the spiritual path, whereas the latter are after the flesh. This interpretation seems to be pure imagination; cf. Colpe, *ZDMG* 109 (1959): 82 and his survey on Šahrastānī's source, Abū ʿĪsā Muḥammad b. Harūn al-Warrāq. On the meaning of *samḥa* see p. 713 below.

9 See D. Chwolsohn, *Ssabier and der Ssabismus*, mainly for its industrious gathering of sources. Wellhausen, *Reste*, pp. 236 ff. shows a good insight into the nature of ancient Sabians and views Islam as a development from them; Horovitz, *Kor. Unters.*, pp. 58 f., on the other hand, challenged his views, as well as those of Sprenger and Pedersen, on the connection between these three terms (and beliefs); on pp. 121f. he denied the possibility of identifying Islam with Sabians. See Pedersen's article in *E G. Browne Pres. Vol.*, especially pp. 386–389. See also Flügel, *Mani*, p. 133 on the Sabians of southern Iraq, the *Muġtasila* which would correspond to the original Aramaic etymology of *ṣābiʾūn*, baptists. See also Stern, *JTS*, 19 (1968), p. 161 on Ḥarrānians and

Sabians; see some sources on Sabians and Ḥarrānians in al-Ǧaṣṣāṣ, II, pp. 401f.; Ibn al-Nadīm, pp. 318ff.; ʿAbd al-Ǧabbār, *Muġnī*, V, pp. 152f.; cf. Monnot, *MIDEO*, 12 (1974), pp. 14ff.; Abū al-Fidāʾ I, pp. 81f. On the link between *ḥanīf-ṣābiʾ-muslim* see also Andrae, *Mohammed*, p. 150. Of a special interest is the matter of the connection between Sabians and Mandaeans. In Kurt Rudolph's opinion, it is impossible to decide which of the two religions, Mandaean and Manichaean, gave birth to the other or whether they both stem from a common source; see his *Mandäer*, pp. 176ff. See also what he says on the relationship between the Sabians of the Quran and the Mandaeans, on p. 37. One reaches the conclusion that in spite of the numerous similarities between the three, Manichaeans, Sabians, and Mandaeans, we are still not able to say whether they were identical, or whether and how they emerged from each other. This, one should add, as far as those who were called Sabians in later generations are concerned. In the Prophet's lifetime, I believe Arabic *ṣābiʾ* meant Manichaean, just as was the case with *ḥanīf*.

10 Ṭiḥāwī, II, p. 337; Bīrūnī, pp. 209 ff.; he also has a peculiar explanation of the term *ṣābiʾ* as being derived from the name of a son of Methuselah. On Enoch, see p. 704 below. Concerning the worship of celestial bodies by the Ḥarrānians see Segal, *Anatolian Studies* 3 (1953), pp. 110ff. In the ruins of the temples he investigated in Sumatar (some 100 km. S.E. of Urfa, 40–50 km. N.E. of Ḥarrān, see ibid., p. 97) and the inscriptions found there he sees proof of the worship of the seven planets. He dates the findings in the second century A.D. on the assumption that the dates are based on the Seleucid era, though that is by no means certain. A quite correct view of the ancient Sabians seems to be expressed by Dimašqī in his *Nuḫbat al-Dahr* (ed. A.F. Mehren), pp. 41–51. After describing some gruesome yet questionable details about their human sacrifices, he points out that their views were held by various Arab tribes. The main point in their beliefs was that there were intermediaries between God and the Universe, represented by the various luminaries, which they worshipped. This same view, people worshipping the luminaries, who are known by the two identical designations of Sabians or *ḥanīfs*, with their main centre in Ḥarrān, is found also in *Ġāyat al-ḥakīm*, pp. 205, 216 f., 224.

11 Yaʿqūbī, 1, pp. 51f., 166; Masʿūdī, *Tanbīh*, pp. 6, 122f. ; idem, *Murūǧ*, 11, p. 323. See Bezold, *Schatzhöhle*, pp. 183f.; the Arabic version translates the term *ḥanpā* by *ḥanīf*; cf. Faris and Glidden, *Abḥāṯ*, 13 (1960), pp. 29f., who also cite more similar sources; see Andrae, *Mohammed*, pp. 152 f.; Stern, *JTS*, 19 (1968), pp. 145, 161 f. (the use of *ḥanīf* in the meaning of idolater in Arabic sources is not as frequent as he asserts). Noldeke, *Neue Beitr.*, p. 35 notes the use of the term *hanfa* in Ethiopic in the meaning of idolater and assumes it was taken from Arabic, but it is more likely that it was derived directly from Syriac. Grünbaum, *ZDMG* 42 (1888), p. 45, compares Biblical *ḥānēf* with Syriac *ḥanpā*, which is irrelevant, for there is, in fact, no similarity in the way the two words are used. The Arabic translation made in the eleventh century of a fourth century Coptic Christian text has *ḥunafāʾ* where the original had *ethnikoi*, meaning non-Christians, used in the context of a complaint against the diacre's aid (*hypodiakonos*) for neglecting the church by letting dogs and *ethnikoi* in; see Riedel and Crum, *Canons of Athanasius*, pp. 87 (Coptic), 18 (Arabic). Wensinck, *Acta Orientalia* 2 (1923/ 4), p. 191 based his explanation of Qurʾānic *ummī* as *ḥanīf* on the similar use of *ḥanpā* in Syriac texts as a translation of *ethnikos*; but it is quite obvious by now that the semantics of Arabic *ḥanīf* and Syriac *ḥanpā* are not necessarily the same; on the contrary, as shown above, they are rather opposed to each other. Watt

noticed the use of *ḥanīf* in Christian Arabic sources, in the meaning of 'pagan'; in *JSS*, 2 (1957), pp. 360ff., he shows that this stems from pre-Islamic times. He quotes ʿAbd al-Masīḥ al-Kindī's *Risāla* p. 42 where it is said that Abraham was a *ḥanīf*, i.e., a pagan, who later relinquished paganism. In the same article, p. 360, 1. 4, Watt enumerates more Christian Arab writers who used *ḥanīf* in that meaning, like Syriac *ḥanpā*. However, he raises the possibility that *ḥanīf* might have been the designation of a creed which parted from idolatry, while remaining different from Islam. This is not too far from my own conclusions in the present paper.

12 Kyrillos Skythop., p. 22; cf. Festugière, III (1), p. 76 and n. 45 on puns related to Mani (like mania). See also Brown, *JRS* 59 (1969), pp. 92 ff., on the ubiquity of the Manichaeans of the lateRoman empire, and on the witch-hunt against them.

13 Kyrillos Skythop., p. 124; cf. Festugière, III (2), p.50

14 Payne-Smith, *Thes.*, I, p.1322.

15 Moberg, pp. 21b, 42a, of the Syriac text.

16 Ibn al-Nadīm, p. 328; the author certainly took it from a Syriac source. Flügel translated it: "limped," preferring the version *aḥnafa al-rağulu*. Dodge translated: "He, moreover, had a deformed foot." The name of his country of origin, ibid., which Flügel printed without diacritical marks, is not Ḥūḥī but Ğūḫā, which is identical with the region of Rāḏān, east of the Tigris; see my remarks in *JESHO* 17 (1974), pp. 317f.

17 Išōʿyhab, *Epist.*, 251 (cf. pp. 181f.) Cf. the translation, which has Mazunaei, but the writer most probably refers to Maronites, and this should be considered a source for the history of Maronism as well. The text everywhere has *marōnāyē*, which Duval consistently corrected, following Marquart, *Ērānšahr*, pp. 43f., who explains Mazōn as the Persian name of ʿUmān, which was the seat of an east-Syrian bishop. Cf. Nö ldeke, *Syr. Chronik*, 33, n. 6; in describing Yezdigard's flight the text has Marōnāyē, which Nöldeke corrected into Marwazī, from Marw; in fact the chronicle probably refers also to the land of the Maronites. See also Chabot, *Synodicon,* in the Index, p. 677, where he also corrected the text, Marōnāyē (referring in fact to Stephen, bishop of the Maronites) into Mazōn, a groundless correction; cf. also Dib, *Maronite Church*, pp. 9f., 12ff., who tries hard to show that in the sixth and seventh centuries the Maronites were devoted to the Chalkedonians (i.e., the mainstream, the orthodox one, of the Church) and not to the Monophysites. The text of Išōʿyhab, read correctly, shows the opposite; it makes much more sense that in speaking of Maronites he meant Monophysites.

18 Bar Hebraeus, *Chron. Syr.*, pp. 168f.; cf. Faris and Glidden, *Abḥāṯ*, 13 (1960), p. 30. See the article "Thābit b. Ḳurra" (by J. Ruska), in *EI*[1], IV, p. 733

19 Rahmani, *Studia Syriaca*, I, no. XI; editor's translation, p. 47: *Ethnici*; cf. Rosenthal, *Takizadeh Pres. Vol.*, pp. 228–231, who translates a fragment of that text, using "pagans," although he calls Bābā's views gnosticism.

20 Sachau, *Syr. Rechtsb.*, III, p. 20; editor's translation, p. 22, *Heiden*.

21 Epiphanius, Adv. Haer., *MPG* 42, col. 29; cf. Alfaric, I, p. 57; II, p. 7, where he assumes that Scythianus was Mani's contemporary. Grant, *Widengren Pres. Vol.*, I. pp. 432f., writes about the information found in Epiphanius, and attempts various explanations for the term Akouanites. But he disregarded the most plausible one, emerging from the meaning of the Greek root of that term; which was Latin *auditores* (see below). See

also *Acta Archelai*, pp. 90 f., which adds that Scythianus' wife was a captive from Upper Egypt and convinced him to prefer life in Egypt to that in the deserts. Mention is made also of another pupil of Scythianus, Therebinthus, who wrote four books for him: The book of mysteries, the book of the chapters, a gospel, and a *thesaurus*. See the same in Cyril of Jerusalem, Catechesis vi: 22, *MPG* 33, cols. 576 f.

22 Marcus Diaconus, *Vita S. Porphyrii Gazensis*, *MPG* 65, cols. 1247ff., cf. Alfaric, I, p. 58.

23 Epiphanius, Haer. 78, 79, *MPG* 42, cols. 700–756; cf. Couret, *La Palestine*, p. 78; Yaʿqūbī, *Ta'rīḫ* I, p. 298.

24 Bīrūnī, pp. 206, 318–321; he does not seem to be very well informed on these Jewish Manichaean sects; he attributes to them the addition of the word *hilāl* (new moon) before the names of the months, e.g., *hilāl tišrīn*; they begin the day at sunrise, and not from sunset; they practice the intercalation of months; they have their own festivals, which Bīrūnī lists, which do not seem to be at all Jewish, e.g., the Venus feast (*al-zahra*). Cf. Pedersen, *E.G. Browne Pres. Vol.*, p. 389.

25 This intricate matter of the early medieval Jewish sects has been widely discussed; see, e.g., Grätz, *History* III, pp. 428–433, 453–459 and the appendix written by A.E. Harkavy ibid., pp. 493–503; Schreiner, *ZDMG* 42 (1888), pp. 659f.; Poznanski, *JQR* 16 (1904), pp. 765 ff.; Nemoy, *HUCA* 7 (1930), p. 328; Starr, *REJ* 102 (1937), pp. 81 ff.

26 *Bĕrēšīt rabbā*, v:24; x1:5 (ed. Theodor and Albeck, pp. 238, 480).

27 See Tosefta, *Yōm ha-kippūrīm*, v:12 (Zuckerm. 191); B.T., *Yōmā* 86b; tractate *Kallā* (found at the end of Nĕzīqīn in printed editions of the Babylonian Talmud), ch. iii; see also B.T., *Sōṭā* 42a, where the *kat ḥănēfim* is mentioned among the four groups of people who are excluded from salvation ("will not take part at the reception of the *šĕḵīnā*"); see the same in Higger's *Treatises Derek Erez*, p. 281; see the Geniza fragment from the E.N. Adler Collection of the Jewish Theological Seminary, New York (ENA 2750, f. 4r), quoted by Abramson, *Lĕšonénu*, 39 (1974/5), p. 160. Abramson attributes the quotation to the tractate *Kallā* because of the additional word *bĕ-šabbāt* (on Saturdays, i.e., one warns against or denounces the *ḥănēfim* even on Saturdays). According to him, this addition found in the Geniza fragment is extant only in the version of the proscription in tractate *Kallā* (and not in the B.T. or the Tosefta); there is however a Gaonic version, apparently quoting B.T *Yōmā*, which has this addition, see *Gĕ'ōnē mizrāḥ u-maʿărāv* (ed. J. Muller), fol. 18a (no. 71). Milikovsky, *Tarbiz*, 55 (1985/6), p. 334, noticed that *ḥănēfim* has a meaning in Talmudic literature which is different from the Biblical one; but he did not realize its true nature and background, as described here.

28 See, for instance, Origenes, *Contra Celsum* vii i:1 7, *MPG* 11, col. 1544: God prefers offerings (ἀναθήματα) that are not statues or material things, but things that He created himself (meaning the man himself); Methodius, Symposion, v: I , *MPG* 18, col. 97A: To dedicate one's virginity is the best *anathēma*; Liddell and Scott have under *anathēma* an example of a slave becoming *anathēma poleōs*, i.e., donated to the temple by the *polis*. On the other hand, see Recognitiones Clementinae, *MPG*1, col. 1465, where there is a text of an *anathēma* which a Manichaean has to pronounce while abjuring his religion to become a Christian (he curses those who bow in innumerable prayers in all directions instead of the direction of the true God, which is to the east). See more examples in Lampe, 102f.; in Mark the Deacon's *Vita Porphyrii*, *MPG* 65, col. 1321, there is an *anathēma* against Mani, against his *vivens evangeliurn*, against anybody who worships the sun, the moon, and the stars; see Methodius, De iis qui abnegarunt (ca. 830), *MPG* 100, p. 1321. On the shift θ > φ see in Greek grammar

books; cf. Schmidt, *Zeitschr. f. vergleichende Sprachforschung* 25 (1881), p. 174; Marlow, *Neue Wege*, p. 497. On the shift of the *spiritus lenis* into ḥ see Krauss, *Lehnwörter*, p. 61; cf. αὔλισμα > *ḥulsīm* B.T. *Bāvā batrā* 67a and my article in *Tarbiz*, 44 (1977), pp. 25f. and n. 29.

29 See the Namāra inscription as reprinted by Lidzbarski, *Ephemeris*, II, p. 34; cf. *Répert. chronol.* I, p. 3 (no. 1); Herzfeld, *Paikuli* I, pp. 136f.; Schaeder, *Gnomon* 9 (1933), pp. 344f.; Seston, *Mél. R. Dussaud*, pp. 229f.; see the article on ʿAmr b. ʿAdī by Ch. Pellat, where there is also a list of references to Arab sources, *EI*², I, p. 450.

30 Eusebius, *Hist. Eccl.*, vii, 3; Ibn Ḥabīb, *Muḥabbar*, p. 161; Ibn Rusteh, p. 217; Ṯaʿālibī, *Laṭāʾif*, p. 102; Balāḏurī, *Ansāb*, I, pp. 134, 139; Ibn al-Aṯīr, VI, p. 183 (the prayer); here the root *nqr* is used, "to rattle." The way Zoroastrians (and Manichaeans) pray is usually designated as *raṭana*, or *zamzama*, see Goldziher, *Muh.St.*, I, pp. 170f., n. 3; Greenfield, **רטין מגושא**, *Finkel Festschr.*, N.Y. 1974:63, with more sources on this topic. On the term *zindīq* see Schader, *Ir. Beitr.*, I, pp. 274–279. It was detected in Armenian texts in the meaning of Manichaean not earlier than the fifth century

31 Joshua, *Chronicle*, XXII; Theophanes, pp. 141ff.; cf. Rothstein, p. 88 (whose chronology is incorrect); Theophanes calls the leader of the Arabs Arethas son of Thalaban (Ḥāriṯ b. Ṯaʿlaba), whereas the hero of Muslim tradition is Ḥāriṯ b. ʿAmru; it is impossible to say with certainty, whether the two are identical. See also Bar Hebraeus, *Chronicon*, ed. Bruns-Kirsch, p. 79 text, pp. 76f. transl.; ed. Bedjan, pp. 741.; see the English translation of Budge, pp. 70f. See also Kawar, *BZ*, 53:57, 1960, and Christides, *Byzantion*, 40:5, 1970, on the Byzantine aspects of the events.

32 Full details and discussions on these matters can be found in Noldeke, *Geschichte* (based on Ṭabarī); Christensen, *Le règne*; Klima, *Mazdak*

33 *Siyāsat-Nāme*, p. 239 of the text, p. 195 of the translation. West, *Pahlavi Texts* (Bahman Yašt), pp. 193, 201. See the *Histoire nestorienne* edited by Scher, p. 55: "The Persian king became a believer of the doctrine of Mani, claiming that there were two primary Gods, of Good and of Evil. He therefore abolished the doctrine of the Zoroastrians."

34 See Christensen, *Le règne*, p. 102; cf. *Chronicon Paschale* (ed. Bonn), p. 444, on the Manichaeans τὰς σάρκας ἀποβαλλόμενοι. Cf. Klima, p. 197; Ibn al-Aṯīr, *Kāmil*, I, p. 413; Bīrūnī, p. 109; Saʿīd ibn Biṭriq, pp. 146f. (those Manichaeans who are called *ṣiddīqūn* refrain from meat and eat fish instead; referring to ca. A.D. 380; see on these *ṣiddīqūn* pp. 42f., 44 n. 100 below).

35 Malalas, Chronogr., *MPG*, 97, col. 465 (=ed. Bonn, p. 309); cf. Christensen, *Le règne*, p. 97; *L'Iran*, pp. 337 ff. Mazdak the *zindīq*, see for instance Masʿūdī, *Murūǧ*, II, p. 195. Malalas (Bonn), p. 444, has a description of the suppression of the Manichaeans in Persia "at that time," roughly the first quarter of the sixth century (though it deals with matters belonging to Emperor Justinian it also has there the account of the war in Ḥimyar, i.e., before 525). This refers evidently to the Mazdakites. Pugliese Carratelli, *La Persia*, p. 600, discusses the Byzantine sources and the information there on the Persian king joining the rebels.

36 See Malaṭī, *Tanbīh*, p. 92; Šahrastānī, p. 192. On Abū ʿĪsā al-Warrāq see the article in *EI*¹, I, p. 130 (by S.M. Stern). Cf. on the identification of Mazdakism with Manichaeism in Byzantine and Arab sources also Nöldeke, *Gesch.*, pp. 462 f.

37 Philo, *Quod deterius*, 91 (Loeb ed., II, p. 262); *De Confus. ling.*, 176–178 (IV, p. 106).

38 See the evidence on the "land of light" and the "God of light" in Ibn al-Nadīm, *fihrist*; p. 332. See also Widengren, *Mani*, p. 71

39 Μελετῶντες ποθνήσκειν see Philo, *Quod deterius*, 34 (II, p. 224); *De plantatione*, 111 (III, p. 268); cf. Plato, *Phaedo* 67 E (Loeb ed. I, p. 234); the idea was adopted by Neoplatonics, cf. Plotinus, *Ennead* I, 4 (Loeb ed. 1, pp. 171–211).

40 The king, Ḫusraw, a generic name for Persian kings, like Kisrā, which is common in Arabic, used in this case by a source later than Mazdak himself, most probably in the Muslim period, from which Šahrastānī copied it; there is no basis, therefore, for the conjectures of Altheim and Stiehl, *La nouvelle Clio*, 5 (1953), p. 360. On Manichaean parallels, cf. Christensen, *Le règne*, p. 81.

41 See, for instance, the Ethiopic book of Enoch, chs. 42, 48, 52, 59, 60, 61, 71; cf. the *angeloi kyriotētēs, exousiai, arkhai*, of the N.T. The Biblical precedent is found in Dan. iv:10, ʿīrīm, which in Hieronymus' words *significat angelos quod server vigilent et ad Dei imperium sint parati*, *MPL*, 25, col. 538. See also the Slavonic book of Enoch, chs. 16, 20. The idea penetrated into Jewish late midrashic literature in the Muslim period, see, e.g., 3 Enoch (Odeberg edition), p. 23, where we even find *rĕhāṭī'ēl*, corresponding exactly to دونده of Šahrastānī's list, "the runner," who is in charge of the constellations. (Odeberg's early dating of the book is pure conjecture.)

42 The translation of this passage in Haarbrücker, 1, p. 292, is erroneous, as are the improved ones of Christensen, *Le règne*, p. 81, and of Altheim and Stiehl, *La nouvelle Clio*, 5 (1953), p. 364. See Philo, *De posteritate Caini*, 139 (II, p. 408): "The highest of truths is that only the wise man is free and a master (ἄρχων), albeit he may have ten thousand masters of his body"; cf. what he says in *De spec. leg.* ii, 69 (VII, p. 350), "no man is a slave by nature." That *rabbānī* was not genuine Arabic was already felt by Suyūṭī, *Itqān* I, p. 138, who assumed it to be Hebrew or Aramaic. Muḥammad b. al-Ḥanafiyya, after his death, was called "the *rabbānī* of this *umma*" by Ibn ʿAbbās, see Siğistānī, *Ġarīb*, fol. 63b. As one might expect from a Syriac loanword it sometimes showed an inserted *h* after the initial *r*, see Quran lvii:27, *rahbāniyyatan* (besides the form *rabbāniyyūn*, see iii: 73, v: 48, 68); also, in the *ḥadīṯ* relating the Prophet's words: *ʿalayka bi-l-ğihādi fa-innahu rahbāniyyatu al-islāmi*, often quoted, sec, e.g., Ibn Ḥanbal, III, p. 82; lbn al-Aṯīr, *Nihāya*, II, p. 113. Both forms, *rabbāniyya* and *rahbāniyya*, are therefore Syriac-Aramaic loanwords. See however a different view in Rabin, *Qumran St.*, p. 128, n. 2 (there is a slight misunderstanding in his reference there to Geiger, who did not propose to derive *rāhib* from Syriac *rabba* or *rabbāna*, see his *Was hat Mohammed* etc., p. 52). One should also take account of the view that *rāhib* meant "fearer of God" or "of Heaven," which shows a similarity or is in line with the *metuentes*, influenced by Judaism, as described by Pines, *Proceedings of the Israel Acad. of Sciences and Humanities*, 2 (no. 7), 1967, p. 144. Cf. my remarks on similar occurrences of the inserted *h*, like Rāḏān> Rāhḏān, *JESHO*, 17 (1974), p. 306. What seems certain is that there was an interplay between Syriac *rabbānī* and Arabic *rāhib*, *rahbāniyya*, connoting the figure of the spiritual leader, the sage, the righteous man, and not just a monk.

43 Cf. Philo, *De mutatione nominum*, 13ff. (V, p. 1149); the most mighty name of the Son of Man, Phillipp. ii:9; Hebr. i:4; 1 Enoch, ch. 69, the hidden name *səma ḥabu'a*, whose revelation is a high achievement for the elect and righteous; 3 Enoch (Odeberg), p. 34. Klima, pp. 191, 221 has some unfounded conjectures on the origin of these ideas; they certainly do not stem from "Jewish doctors." See also the discussion (somewhat

incomplete) on Mazdakite dualism, cosmology and angelology, in Müller, *History of Religions*, 3 (1963), pp. 74–77.

44 Ibn al-Aṯīr *Kāmil*, I, p. 413.

45 Cedrenus, *MPG*, 121, col. 681 (=ed. Bonn, I, p. 626).

46 Ibn al-Nadim, *fihrist*, p. 118, in the article on ʿAbdallāh Ibn al-Muqaffaʿ, who translated this book into Arabic (beginning of the ʿAbbāsid period).

47 Ibn Ḥabīb, *Muḥabbar*, p. 369; Ibn Qutayba, *Maʿārif*, p. 634; Ṭabarī, *Taʾrīḫ*, I, pp. 888ff.; Nöldeke, *Gesch*., pp. 1491.,170f.; Nöldeke doubted the story of Shamir's incursion into Persia; but it is confirmed by the report of Joshua Stylites, above, n. 31; Ibn ʿAbd Rabbihi, *ʿIqd*, V, p. 222; Iṣbahānī, *Aġānī*, VIII, p. 63, who calls Munḏir not the king but the governor (*ʿāmil*) of Ḥīra; the tribes slaughtered a great number of the family of Ḥāriṯ after Mazdak's defeat, forty-eight of them being killed by the B. Taġlib; Ḥamza al-Iṣfahānī p.140, has a short account of the events, pointing out that Ḥāriṯ agreed to Qubāḏ's request that he become a *zindīq*; the same is told in Maqdisī, *Badʾ* III, pp. 168, 199; see also Bakrī, *Muʿǧam*, p. 1363; Yāqūt, *Buldān*, IV, p. 294; Ibn al-Aṯīr, *Kāmil*, I, pp. 410ff., has copied the report of Ṭabarī, but expresses disbelief concerning the story of the Ḥimyarite expedition into Persia: Who could believe that Yaman and Ḥaḍramawt would put together such armies! (ibid., p. 421). Rothstein, *Laḫmiden*, p. 90, doubts that Qubāḏ preferred Ḥāriṯ because of his Mazdakite inclinations, and assumes that Ḥāriṯ succeeded in his takeover of Ḥīra and the tribes due to the situation in Persia, namely the decline which followed the Mazdakite upheaval. Cf. Olinder, *Kinda*, pp. 63ff., who rightly points out that Munḏir and Laḫm must have regained power before 524, when the Syriac sources on the war in Ḥimyar have Munḏir ruling Ḥīra and receiving messengers from Ḏū Nuwās and Byzantium. Iṣbahānī, *Aġānī*, XI, p. 64, has Ḥāriṯ becoming chief of B. Bakr b. Wāʾil; Munḏir the Laḫmid is said there to have accepted Ḥāriṯ as his suzerain of his own free will, in view of Qubāḏ's weakness and shortcomings in granting him protection; he also became the son-in-law of Ḥāriṯ by marrying his daughter Hind. Some sources make Hind the wife of Ḥāriṯ's ancestor, Ḥuǧr *ākil al-murār*; see Ibn ʿAbd Rabbihi, *ʿIqd*, I, p. 271. Another family connection between the Laḫmids and the Kinda was through the marriage of Ḥāriṯ's sister, Umm al-Mulk bint ʿAmru b. Ḥuǧr, to Munḏir b. Munḏir; their son was Nuʿmān II, nicknamed al-Aswad; see Ṭabarī, *Taʾrīḫ*, I, p. 900, cf. Rothstein, Laḫmiden, p. 73; Olinder, *Kinda*, p. 11, where non-Arab sources on the Kinda are listed; ibid., p. 22, on the general view of the south-Arabian sources (preserved through Ibn al-Kalbī) about the Kinda. He rightly adduced an additional proof (p. 33), and a very authentic one at that, concerning the strong ties between Kinda and Ḥimyar, namely the mention of *kdt* in the Ḥimyarite inscriptions. (See also Ry 506, in *Muséon* 66 [1953], p. 278,1.4.) Altheim and Stiehl, *Die Araber* V, pp. 370f., sum up the matter of the Kinda based on Rothstein and Olinder, but they seem to ignore the remark that Ḥāriṯ could not have ruled Ḥīra after 524, as well as the Mazdakite aspects of his career.

48 See Kister, *Arabica*, 15 (1968), pp. 144f. and his reference to the Tübingen MS. in n. 5 on p. 144; Ibn Rusteh, p. 217.

49 Siğistānī, *Muʿammarīn*, p. 80. Samhūdī, II, p. 358, says that the name Qubāʾ was after a well called Hubār, or Qubār, or Qutār; but Siğistānī's version seems to be the more reliable one.

50 Zamaḫšarī, *Amkina*, p. 132, and many of the sources quoted in n. 47; Ibn Hišām, p. 953; Daḥlān, III, p. 28; Yāqūt, *Buldān*, III, p. 277; Ibn Kaṯīr, *Bidāya*, II, p. 218.

51 See the *ḏawū al-ākāl* described by Ibn Ḥabīb, *Muḥabbar*, p. 253; cf. Kister, *Arabica*, 15 (1968), p. 150; see Ibn Hišām, pp. 953f.; Iṣbahānī, *Aġānī*, XIX, p. 127 who has information on the authority of Ḥuğr *ākil al-murār* over some of the B. Ṭayy. Nöldeke, *Gesch.*, p. 168, n. 3, referring to *ākil al-murār* "murār ist ein bitteres Kraut;" he confesses that the expression is incomprehensible to him; cf. Iṣbahānī, *Aġānī*, VIII, p. 63, "he used to eat a very bitter plant." Cf. Barbier de Meynard, *JA*, 1907, pp. 218f., who tries to define the plant (=ear): Centaurea calcitropa, which of course, makes no sense.

52 Hind was married to Munḏir, see above, n. 47.

53 Yāqūt, *Buldān*, II, p. 709; cf. Nöldeke, *Gesch.*, p. 172, n. 1.

54 Ibn Hišām, p. 953; Ṭabarī, *Taʾrīḫ* I, p. 1739; cf. Kister and Plessner, *Oriens*, 25–26 (1976), pp. 58f. on the background of this statement. Naḍr b. Kināna was considered the forefather of Qurayš, see Ibn Hišām, p. 60; Ṭabarī, *Taʾrīḫ* I, p. 1104; Ḥalabī, III, p. 256; Daḥlān, III, p. 27. It is certainly of significance that Ašʿaṯ later took part in the *ridda*; also, that the majority of the Kinda seems to have been on the side of ʿAlī at Ṣiffīn, see Ḫalīfa b. Ḫayyāṭ, I, pp. 221ff.; mainly Ḥuğr b. ʿAdī b. al-Adbar, see Ṭabarī, *Taʾrīḫ* II, p. 136; cf. Shaban, *Isl. Hist.*, p. 72; "al-Ashʿath" (by H. Reckendorf), in *EI*[2], I, pp. 696f. (re-edited). There have been strong ties between Kinda and Qurayš for many generations. Qurayš used to travel to Rābiya in Ḥaḍramawt where a yearly fair was held. There the traders of Qurayš enjoyed the protection of the *banī ākil al-murār*, who respected Qurayš and preferred them over all other peoples; see Ibn Ḥabīb, *Muḥabbar*, pp. 266f.; see the story of the Kinda delegation also in Ibn ʿAbd al-Barr, *Durar*, p. 273; Ibn Sayyid al-Nās, *ʿUyūn*, II, p. 242, where some more details on Ašʿaṯ's involvement in later events are reviewed; Ibn Kaṯīr, *Bidāya*, V, p. 72.

55 Ibn Bābawayh, *Maʿānī*, p. 221; Ibn al-Ğawzi, *Zād al-masīr* VII, p. 45; Ḫāzin, IV, p. 15; Suyūṭī, *Durr*, V, p. 271. *Anatolē* (sing.) means "rising" in Greek; *anatolai* only (pl.) is used to mean "east," cf. Houdous, *CBQ*, 6 (1944), pp. 81f. See the plural *midnĕḥē*, which is unusual in Aramaic and is obviously the result of a literal translation from Greek, in Milik, *Enoch*, p. 289 (1. 6); Knibb, *Enoch*, p. 180; cf. Gil, *Tarbiz*, 38 (1969), p. 329. See also Ibn Hišām, 132; cf. Wellhausen, *Reste*, 137.

56 For the purposes of this study it is sufficient to consult the edition of R. H. Charles' 1 Enoch (Oxford 1912), especially his references to patristic and other sources (pp. lxxxi-xcv) and the Index II, containing an excellent analysis of the contents of the book. The recently published edition by M.A. Knibb (Oxford, 1978) is highly recommended, mainly for its conveniently arranged parallels and discussion on the Greek and Aramaic fragments, although the lack of a detailed index detracts.

57 F. Philippi, *Das Buch Henoch* (Stuttgart, 1868), put forward the view about a relatively late, Christian composition of the book.

58 I believe to have proven this in my paper in *Tarbiz*, 38:322, 1969.

59 On the symbolism of seven, which was connected with the seven planets, in Manichaeism, see Mansi, *Ampl. Coll.*, II, p. 1057 (a preface to the Nicaean council, compiled from Arab manuscripts): *Secta Manichaeorum...solem, lunam ac septem planetas colunt.* See also Ibn al-Nadīm, p. 336, on Mani's chapter about the seven spirits; cf. Alfaric, II, p. 15. See also below, p. 39, more evidence for the symbolism of seven in

Manichaeism. The story of the *daǧǧāl* (MO, p. 85) apparently also belongs to a Manichaean source describing the apocalyptic struggle against evil. See Aphraatis Sapientis Persae Demonstrationes, *Patrologia Syriaca* I, p. 116; cf. Adam, *Texte*, p. 58 (no. 37). St. Augustinus, Contra epistulam Manichaei, *MPL*, 42, p. 182; cf. Bardy, *DTHC*, IX, pp. 1872 f. See Schmidt and Polotsky, *Mani-Fund*, pp. 65f. Relevant here is also the description of "the Man of Light" (even though it is called "gnostic") in the Coptic MS. of Nag Hammadi, edited by Böhlig and Labib, *Koptisch-gnostische Schrift*, pp. 58–61. Of course, the term "Mother of life"stems from Gen. iii:20, see the discussion on this term by Widengren, *Mesopot. Elements*, pp. 15 ff; also ibid., pp. 124 f., on the description of Mani as "the tree of life."

60 The Babylonian Talmud, *Megilla* 24b, probably refers to Manichaeism when stating the reason why whoever refused to lead prayers in coloured clothes and insists on wearing white should not be allowed to lead prayers at all (as said in the Mishna): "We fear that he may be infested by *mīnūt*."

61 Henning, *Sitzungsberichte*, Preuss. Akad. d. Wiss., Phil.-hist. Kl., 1934, pp. 27 f.; cf. Benveniste, *Le Monde oriental*, 26–27 (1932/3), p. 175; Polotsky and Bohlig, *Kephalaia* I, pp. 72f.; Widengren, *Mesopot. Elements*, pp. 16f.; idem, *Mani*, p. 81.

62 Henning, *BSOAS*, 11 (1943), p. 53; see also his numerous quotations from Enoch in his annotations to texts he edited there; cf. Philonenko, *RHPR* 52 (1972), pp. 339f.; and see now Milik, *Enoch*, pp. 298–339, and also the numerous parallels from the Book of Giants accompanying the Enoch fragments published in his book.

63 Widengren, *Mesopot. Elements*, pp. 19–26; Puech, *Manichaeism*, pp. 144 f. (a. 241); Böhlig and Labib, *Kopt.-gnost. Schrift*, p. 65.

64 Henrichs et alii, *ZPE*, 5 (1970), p. 143.

65 Timotheus, De receptione haereticorum, *MPG*, 86, col. 24

66 This general pattern of thinking may be illustrated by Philonenko's articles on an Essene tradition in the Quran, *RHR*, 170 (1966) and on a Manichaean passage in the Book of Enoch, *RHPR*, 52 (1972). In an alleged parallel between the so-called 151st Psalm and two Quranic verses he finds sufficient grounds to suggest Essenes who escaped Titus' persecutions and settled first in Qumran and then in Medina! A passage of a Manichaean MS. whose parallel he found in Enoch brings him to the discovery of a Jewish author of the Greek original of the Slavonic Enoch, who, he says, wrote in the first century A.D.

67 See *Qōhelet rabbā* to Eccl. 4:1 ("So I returned, and considered all the oppressions that are done under the sun"); see the Vilna edition, fol. 12b.

68 See the article "Idrīs," in *EI*², III, pp. 1030f. (by G. Vajda), where an extensive bibliography is listed. The life story of an apostle Andreas is mentioned in patristic sources of the middle of the fourth century A.D. among Manichaean writings, see Timotheus Constantinop., De Receptione haereticorum, *MPG* 86, col. 21; cf. Alfaric, I, pp, 61, 67. Albright, *JPOS* (1922), pp. 197 f.; *JAOS* 60 (1940), p. 287, n. 14. A parallelism between Enoch and a tradition attributed to Kaʿb al-Aḫbār, but denied by Ibn ʿAbbās, is pointed out by Halperin and Newby, *JAOS* 102 (1982), pp. 631ff. See that tradition, on the 'two castrated bulls' (being the sun and the moon) and the whole story in Ṭabarī , *Taʾrīḫ* I, pp. 62ff., where on p. 74 *ḥadīṯ al-ʿahd* certainly does not mean as understood by the two above-mentioned authors, "the report of the

covenant," but "recent," referring to the "new book" quoted allegedly by Ibn ʿAbbās. Probably that book was *bi-l-raḥmān*, about God, or else something was skipped and the text is corrupt, as assumed by the authors of the article.

69 Ibn Qutayba, *Maʿārif*, pp. 21f., 552; Ṭabarī, *Taʾrīḫ* I, p. 174 notes that in Idrīs' day the king was Bīwarāsb, that every wish of his was fulfilled at once, he only had to blow a golden horn (*qaṣaba*); whence the Jewish custom of blowing the *šabūrāt*, a detail added in the Cairo edition of Ṭabarī's *Taʾrīḫ* I, p. 171; Masʿūdī, *Murūğ* I, p. 73, besides the usual traditions, says that Hirmīs is the name of a planet; also, that before the thirty tablets revealed to Idrīs, twenty-one were revealed to Adam and twenty-nine to Šīṯ. See also Ibn Bābawayh, *ʿIlal*, pp. 27f.; *Qiṣaṣ al-anbiyāʾ* attributed to ʿAskarī, fols. 24b–25a (where there is a discussion about which heaven Idrīs was raised to, the fourth, the sixth, or even the seventh); cf. Ġayṭī, *Qiṣṣat al-isrāʾ*, pp. 102, 107 f.; Ibn Kaṯīr, *Šamāʾil* p. 550 (he is in the fourth heaven, Muḥammad met him there during his *isrāʾ*); Ḫaffāğī, II, p. 259 (Idrīs, whose Hebrew name is Iḫnūḫ, the "triply great" in wisdom, of stars, of writing, of teaching; called "the righteous" [*al-ṣāliḥ*] by Muḥammad when they met in the fourth heaven). See also Mağlisī, *Biḥār* XI, p. 270; Bīrūnī, p. 206 (the *ṣābiʾūn* call Idrīs, who is Iḫnūḫ of the Tawrāh, Hirmīs); Quḍāʿī, *Taʾrīḫ*, fol. 7a; Maqdisī, *Badʾ*, III, p. 11; Ibn Šahrāšūb III, p. 37; Ibn Sayyid al-Nās,*ʿUyūn*, I, p. 144; Šiblī, *Maḥāsin*, fol. 45; Suyūṭī, *Muʿtarak*, I, pp. 519f.; Ṣāliḥī, *Subul*, pp. 377f. (who denies the possibility of Idrīs being identical with Ilyās); Ibn Iyās, *Badāʾiʿ*, pp. 48f. See Wieder, *JJS*, 4 (1953), pp. 165f.

70 Ṭiḥāwī, II, p. 366; Rāwandī, *Ḫarāʾiğ*, p. 154, attributes to Idrīs the Biblical story about Elisha and the widow (2 Ki ch. iv), paraphrased.

71 Ṯaʿalibī, *Laṭāʾif*, p. 6; Bīrūnī, p. 205. Maqrīzī, *Ḫiṭaṭ* I, pp. 209f., states the identity between Idrīs and Hirmīs the First, who built the pyramids and sphinxes; he foretold the deluge thanks to his knowledge of the stars. See also Plessner in *SI* 2 (1954): 46, who has an English translation of the Hermes-Idrīs fragments written by Abū Maʿšar al-Balḫi (d. 886) as preserved by Ibn Abī Uṣaybiʿa, *ʿUyūn* (see the Beirut edition, pp. 31f.), where three personages named Hirmīs are described, the first of whom was identical with Enoch-Idrīs; Ibn al-Qifṭī, pp. 346–50, puts the description of Enoch (Hermes I) in the middle, pp. 348f.

72 Māwardī, *Aʿlām*, p. 30 (who also says that he was the first to make laws, and the first to bear arms and fight *fī sabīli-llāhi*; he fought the offspring of Cain-Qabīl; he was the first to introduce weights and measures); cf. Mawṣilī, *Wasāʾil*, fol. 72b; see also Sibṭ Ibn al-Ğawzī, MS. BM Or. 4215, fol. 37; see Ibn al-Munağğim's book quoted by Abū al-Fidāʾ, *Muḫtaṣar* I, pp. 81f. (where the printed text has Abū ʿĪsā al-Maġribī; but it is almost certainly Abū ʿĪsā ibn al-Munağğim, from whom the other excerpts on ancient nations and religions in Abū al- Fidā's book were copied. Ibn Ḥazm, *Milal* I, pp. 34f., apparently also wrote under the influence of Ibn al-Munağğim's account. Ibn al-Munağğim's book: *K. Al-bayān ʿan taʾrīḫ sinī zamān al-ʿālam ʿalā sabīl al-ḥuğğa wa-l-burhān*, see Abū al- Fidāʾ, ibid., p. 3, and Sezgin, I, p. 322. The passage is taken from the chapter on the Syrians and the Sabians). See also the discussion on Idrīs-Hermes in Chwolsohn, *Ssabier* I, pp. 787–792. Marquet, in his article on the Sabians and the *Iḫwān al-ṣafāʾ*, assumes that the Ḥarrānians were those who transferred the Greek Hermes tradition into the Enoch texts; he quotes the traditions concerning Hirmīs-Idrīs of the *Iḫwān* (similar to those found in so many Arab sources); see *SI* 24 (1966), pp. 58ff. In the other parts of this article he discusses very interesting points, but they

are beyond the scope of this study, being a comparison between the views attributed to the Sabians and those of the *Iḫwān al-ṣafāʾ*.

73 Masʿūdī's *ʿAǧāʾib al-dunyā*, quoted by Qaramānī, *Aḫbār* I, p. 31. Bar Hebraeus, *Chronicle*, ed. Bedjan, p. 5 (see Budge, p. 5), besides the usual traditions on Enoch-Hermes, makes him a builder of cities, 180 in number, the smallest of which was Urhī (Urfa, Edessa). He was the first to spread the knowledge of stars and constellations, he ordered people to worship God, to fast, pray, give alms, vows and tithes. He forbade unclean food and drunkenness. He also ordered to celebrate the entrance of the sun into each one of the constellations (another possible explanation for *maṣāriq*, see above, p. 24), the new moon, the rising and setting of every star.

74 Michael the Syrian, II, p. 507 (text 13. 465); Abel, *SI* 2 (1959), p. 28.

75 Ibn Ṭāwūs, *Saʿd al-suʿūd*, pp. 32–40, and Maǧlisī, *Biḥār* XI, pp. 283f., cite some quotations from this book, mainly regarding prayer and fasting; cf. Kister, *IOS* 2 (1972), p. 231 and n. 127. On Ibrāhīm b.Hilāl al-Ṣābī (d. 384/994), sec Brockelmann, *GAL*, G 195, S I 153, where his *sunan Idrīs* should be added.

76 See Burāqī, pp. 49ff., 53, 81f., 153. The idea of Wednesday as the central day of the week probably caught the imagination of the Manichacans. In the Qumran calendar as well the year always begins on Wednesday, cf. Jaubert, *VT* 3(1953), pp. 251ff. See Cyprianus of Carthage, De Pascha computus, *MPL*, 4, col. 1027, asserting that Wednesday should properly be the first day of calendar computation, since God created the luminaries on that day. This special status of Wednesday recalls the information of Dionysios of Tell Maḥrē, copied by Michael the Syrian, p. 517 (see its translation in vol. III, p. 65), and by Bar-Hebraeus, *Chronicon eccl.* (ed. Abbeloos) I, p. 366 describing the sect of the ʿAnānāyē as observing Wednesday instead of Saturday (Jewish Manichaeans?). Bīrūnī, p. 284, seems to be more precise on this matter, quoting Abū ʿĪsā al-Warrāq; he informs us that the Jewish sect of the *Maġāriba* (sic; should be *Maġāriyya*) maintain that New Year's day should always fall on a Wednesday, the day on which the luminaries were created. Passover also has to fall on a Wednesday. Quite obviously, this recalls the Qumran calendar. On *masǧid al-Sahla* as the former site of "the house of Idrīs" see also Maǧlisī, *Biḥār* XI, pp. 280, 284; Kulaynī, *Kāfi* III pp. 490,494.

77 Ibn Aʿṯam, *Futūḥ* I, p. 287.

78 See the extensive discussion of this concept in the paper of Rubin, *IOS* 5:62, 1975. On the concept of "light" in the Quran see F. Rosenthal's *Knowledge*, pp.156f.

79 Clemen, *Harnack-Ehrung*, pp. 258–262; Andrae, *Mohammed*, pp. 104f.

80 Buhl, pp. 212f.; Andrae, *Mohammed*, p. 98. Friedländer, *JQR* N.S., 3 (1912/3), pp. 246–254. On Mani's claim to be "the seal" see Bīrūnī, p. 207. Šahrastanī, p. 192, has "improved" the picture, making Mani a herald of Muhammad as the seal of the prophets. See also Polotsky, *PW*, Suppl. VI, cols. 266f. it is worthwhile noticing, with Henrichs, *Harvard Studies in Classical Philology* 77 (1973), pp. 47 f., that the term *nāmūs*, which in early Muslim tradition means revelation, and has long since been identified as Greek νόμος, was the term preferred by the Manichaeans as designating their creed.

81 Frend, *JEH* 4 (1953), p. 2.

82 See Nilus' epistle (to Philo the elder), in *MPG* 79, col. 357. See the "unveiling of the breast" in *Evangelium Veritatis*, pp. 24, 96; the conjecture of the editors is that it was a "gnostic" work, written before A.D. 180. In the N.T. the Son is said to be in the bosom of the Father (John i:18). However different the setting, the image and terminology still seem to have entered Islam through Manichaeism.

83 Bardy, *DThC* IX, p. 1885.

84 See Chavannes and Pelliot, JA, 1911, p. 545; Segal, *BSOAS* 16 (1954), p. 15. In connection with this, one should also note Rosenthal, *Analecta Biblica* 12 (1959), pp. 315–318, where he relates the occurrence of the number nineteen in the Quran (lxxxiv:30–31) to gnostic influence; we saw however (above, p. 25) that these nineteen are present in the description of the Mazdakite creed as well, the seven *wazīrs* and the twelve spirits. See more parallels in: Ahrens, *Mohammed*, pp. 30f.

85 See *Acta Archelai* XV (XIII):6, p. 24; cf. Alfaric, I, p. 49, n.3, who has more references. See Polotsky and Böhlig, *Kephalaia* I, pp. 17ff., the allegory on the good tree whose fruits are good, and the bad one, with the bad fruits.

86 See Adam, *Manichäismus*, pp. I 3ff.; al-Ǧaṣṣāṣ, II, pp. 4011, who quotes Abū Ḥanīfa: "they pretend to be Christians and read the *inǧīl*; some Muslim jurists demand that they be forced to accept Islam or else be killed and that no poll tax (*ǧizya*, which grants protection) be accepted from them."

87 Ṭayālisī, pp. 303, 305.

88 For instance, Ṭayālisī, p. 206.

89 Ya'qūbī, *Ta'rīḫ*, I, p. 181; Bīrūnī, pp. 23, 208.

90 Cyrilli Hierosol., Catechesis, V1:22, *MPG*, 33, cols. 675f.; Herodianus bishop of Chalkedon, apud Photium, Biblioth. cod. 95, in *MPG*, 10, cols. 14251.; Timotheus Constant inop., De receptione hacreticorum, in *MPG*, 86, col. 22; Leontius Byzantinus, De sectis, *MPG*, 56, col. 1213; cf. Bardy, *DThC*, IX, p. 1845 and his references to patristic sources. See on the Manichaean gospel also Michael the Syrian, I, text, p. 117; transl., p. 198.

91 Henrichs et alii, *ZPE* 5 (1970), pp. 189–202; Alfaric, I, pp. 5, 1214 see Waldschmidt and Lentz, *Abhandlungen*, Preuss. Akad. d. Wiss.,phil.-hist.Kl., 1926 (3), pp. 23, 64, on hymns to the gospel of the Manichaeans; Polotsky, *PW* Suppl. VI, p. 244; Schmidt and Polotsky, in *Sitzungsberichte*, Preuss. Akad. d. Wiss., phil-hist. K1. 1933, p. 35; Adam, *Texte*, pp. 1, 80; Widengren, Mani, p. 79. A Gospel of the Prophet Mani was edited by D. Greenlees (Adyar, Madras 1956), based on fragments collected from various sources.

92 Aphraates, see above, p. 32 and n. 59; cf. Bardy, *DThC* IX, pp. 1851, 1879. See Ibn al-Nadīm, *Fihrist*, pp. 333f.; cf. Clemen, *Harnack-Ehrung*, p. 260; and more references in: Buhl, p. 227, n. 70.

93 Irenaeus, *Adv. Haer.* (ed. Harvey) I, p. 200; Epiphanius, *Panarion* (ed. Holl) I, 23:3 (p. 260); cf. *MPG* 41, col. 312; cf. Chavannes and Pelliot, *JA*, 1911, p. 566, n. 3; Clemen, *Harnack-Ehrung*, p. 259; Pedersen, *Browne Pres. Vol.*, p. 391; Andrae, *Mohammed*, pp. 144, 156f; see the abjuration formula, *MPG* 1, col. 1464 D; cf. Polotsky, *PW* Suppl. VI, col. 269; see also Frend, *JEH* 4 (1953), p. 21.

94 See Grégoire, *Mél. Ch. Diehl* I, pp. 113f.; 116f.; Honigmann, *Evêques*, pp. 125 f.; Anastasius Sinaita (patriarch of Antioch, second half of the sixth century A.D.), Viae dux, *MPG* 89, col. 102; cf. Alfaric, I, p. 58. See Widengren, *Mani*, p. 81; Milik, *Enoch*, p. 313 (*gabbārāyē*).

95 See on Quss b. Sāʿida: Ibn Ḥabīb, *Muḥabbar*, pp. 136 (he was one of the *ḥukkām*), 238; Ibn Saʿd, I(2), p. 55; cf. Fück, *ZDMG* 90 (1936), p. 519; in that article see also his general view of Muḥammad as a *ḥanīf*; he assumed there that the *ḥanīfī* movement had connections with centres found outside the Arab world. Such terms as *ṣuḥaf Ibrāhīm wa-Mūsā* in the Quran (1xxxviii:19) were, in Fück's opinion, typically *ḥanīfī*. The Prophet applies the term *munāfiqūn*, generally explained as "hypocrites," to those who refuse to accept the new *ḥanīfiyya*.

96 See Polotsky and Böhlig, *Kephalaia* I, pp. 217 ff., cf. Adam, *Texte*, p. 37. See also Frend, *JEH* 4 (1953), p. 24.

97 1 Enoch, passim, esp. 1:1,8; 46:8; 58:3; 62:5; 98:2; 103:4. Vööbus, *Hist. of Asc.* I, pp. 109–137; II, p. 66; idem, *Yearb. of the Estonian Learned Society* 1 (1951–53), p. 7. The monastic and ascetic character of Manichaeism is also stressed by Brown, *JRS* 59 (1969), p. 102. See on Mani's extremist views on alimentary restrictions: Henrichs et alii, *ZPE* 5 (1970), pp. 146f.

98 Lammens, *Muʿāwiya*, p. 423, saw the problem behind the title *rāhib* attached to Abū ʿĀmir; he thought it was bestowed on him as a token of admiration for the austere and respectable life of a *ḥanīf*. On the position of monks among Manichaeans see Alfaric, I, p. 60. See Frend, *JEH* 4 (1953), p. 22 on the "elect" in a fifth century MS.

99 Ibn Ḥanbal, I, p. 236; V, p. 622; VI, pp. 116, 233; Buḫārī, *Ṣaḥīḥ, īmān, bāb al-dīn yusrun*. Baġawī, II, p. 361 (no. 384a, quoting Ibn Ḥanbal); Saḫāwī, *Maqāṣid*, p. 109; Ibn Sīda, *Muḫaṣṣaṣ* XIII, p. 106; Suyūṭī, *Durr* I, p. 140; ʿAzīzī, *Sirāǧ* I, pp. 54, 260; *Lisān al-ʿArab* IX p. 58; ʿAǧlūnī, *Kašf* I, pp. 51, 217. See the story of ʿUṯmān b. Maẓʿūn in lbn Saʿd, III(1), pp. 286f.; Ibn Ḥanbal, I, pp. 175,183; Ibn ʿAbd al-Barr, *Istīʿāb* III, pp. I053f.; Ibn al-Aṯīr, *Usd* III, p. 386. ʿUṯmān b. Maẓʿūn's sister's daughter, Ḥafṣa b. Zaynab, was the wife of ʿUmar b. al-Ḫaṭṭāb, see Ibn Saʿd, VIII, p. 56. According to Ibn Wahb al-Qurašī, in MS. Chester Beatty 3497, fol. 37b, the Prophet recommended to him fasting instead of castration. Fasting is *maġfara* (a means to diminish sexual desire), he said. [I am grateful to Prof. M.J. Kister for this reference.] Concerning this matter of the elect note also the story of Baḥīrā (=elect in Syriac), whose name was, according to some, Sergius. See the article "Baḥīra" (by A. Abel), in *EI*[2], I, pp. 922f., and the references there.

100 Polotsky, *PW* Suppl. VI, cols. 259, 262f.; St. Augustine, Epistulae, *MPL* 36, col. 1033; cf. Bardy, *DThC* IX, p. 1882, Epiphanius, Adv. Haer., *MPG* 42, col. 29; *sammāʿūn*, see Ibn Nadīm, p. 333; also in Flügel, *Mani*, p. 64; see also his translation on p. 95, and note 216 on pp. 286–289, where he quotes several patristic parallels. Saʿīd Ibn Biṭrīq, p. 148, also knows of the ancient division of the Manichaeans into two categories; the elect he calls *ṣiddīqūn*, whereas the others are *sammāʿūn* (miswritten: *sammākūn*, and so transcribed in Pococke's translation, *MPG* 111, col. 1023; *Sammacun, id esi piscarii*; since they eat fish instead of meat, which is forbidden to them; cf. Alfaric, I, p. 60, where the reference to *MPG* should be corrected.

101 Cf. on the Manichaean prohibition of war Bardy, *DThC* IX, p. 1880.

Charging Steeds or Maidens Doing Good Deeds?

A Reinterpretation of Qur'ān 100 (*al-ʿĀdiyāt*)[1]

Munther Younes

Originally published in Arabica *55, no. 3 (2008): 362–86.*

1. Introduction

Among the parts of the Qur'ān that have defied Muslim interpreters and modern scholars alike are the introductory verses of some early Makkan *sūra*s which take the form of "oath clusters."[2] The introductory oaths of Q 37, 51, 77, 79, and 100 are particularly enigmatic.[3]

Some scholars have taken the enigmatic nature of these verses as evidence of the superior nature of the language of the Qur'ān. For example, Hajjaji-Jarrah declares that,

> *sūrat al-ʿādiyāt* (Q 100) offers an excellent example of how the Qur'ānic *ʿarabiyya* brings forth a dazzling assembly of word meaning and sound defying the conventions of both the Arabian *sağʿ* and the literary rules of classical Arabic literature. It represents the persuasive, arresting construction, pervasive rhythm, and important message of the Qur'ānic *ʿarabiyya* which has selected and expressed these materials in just this way.[4]

I have examined the first five verses of Q 100 to find out if other reasons may lie behind the difficulty in understanding them. Such an examination was prompted by the work of two scholars who do not accept the traditional Muslim interpretation of certain parts of the Qur'ān, Günter Lüling[5] and Christoph Luxenberg.[6] Lüling argues that about one-third of the Qur'ān is based on ancient Christian Arabic hymns[7] that were reworked by the editors of the Qur'ān after the Prophet's death and given a new meaning. On the one hand, this meaning masks the Christian origins of the hymns, and, on the other, it gives them a new Islamic character.[8] In his view, these editors, starting with the unpointed text of the ʿUṯmānic *muṣḥaf*, [9] imposed a new reading on the old text. For example, the word *zabāniya* (Q 96:18), traditionally understood as "guardians of hell," was originally *rabbāniyya* "High Angelship" before it was reworked by the editors. This was possible because in the ʿUṯmānic *muṣḥaf*, both words were written the same: رىاىىه[10]

Restricting his study to selected Qur'ānic passages that the Qur'ān commentators found particularly difficult and admitted their inability to understand, Luxenberg offers alternative interpretations that result "in a more reasonable reading" or "a decidedly more logical sense" than what is found in the standard accounts. In addition to examining alternative interpretations found in the Arabic exegetical (*tafsīr*) literature itself, he explores different ways of reinterpreting these passages by changing the dotting on some of their letters or by examining Aramaic, and in particular, Syriac, cognates.[11]

2. Traditional Interpretation of Q 100:1–5

Before discussing the problems of Q 100:1–5, I will present their traditional interpretation, starting with Pickthall's English translation, which is based on the Muslim tradition.

1	والعاديات ضبحا	*wa-l-ʿādiyāti ḍabḥā*	By the snorting coursers
2	فالموريات قدحا	*fa-l-mūriyāti qadḥā*	Striking sparks of fire
3	فالمغيرات صبحا	*fa-l-muġīrāti ṣubḥā*	And scouring to the raid at dawn,
4	فأثرن به نقعا	*fa-aṯarna bihi naqʿā*	Then, therewith, with their trail of dust
5	فوسطن به جمعا	*fa-wasaṭna bihi ǧamʿā*	Cleaving, as one, the center (of the foe)

In an effort to recover the original Muslim understanding of Q 100:1–5, I consulted the earliest published accounts that I was able to find. These include the *tafsīrs* of Muǧāhid b. Ǧabr (d. 104/719),[12] al-Ḍaḥḥāk b. Muzāḥim (d. 105/723),[13] Muqātil b. Sulaymān (d. 150/767),[14] Sufyān al-Ṯawri (d. 161/777),[15] Sufyān b. ʿUyayna (d. 196/811),[16] Abū Zakariyyā Yaḥyā b. Ziyād al-Farrā'(d. 207/822),[17] Abū ʿUbayda Maʿmar b. al-Muṯannā (d. 210/825),[18] and ʿAbd al-Razzāq al-Ṣanʿānī (d. 211/827).[19]

Since none of these *tafsīrs* is comprehensive, I have concluded my examination with the interpretation given by Ṭabarī (d. 310/923), the earliest comprehensive and systematic *tafsīr* available.[20]

Al-Ṯawrī and Ibn ʿUyayna do not say anything about Q 100; the other six commentators, who preceded Ṭabarī, offer brief comments.

Muqātil and al-Farrā' cite as the occasion of the revelation of the introductory verses of Q 100 the delay in receiving news of a detachment led by al-Munḏir b. ʿAmr. Earlier, the Prophet had sent the detachment on a military mission to Ḥunayn, Tihāma,[21] or Kināna,[22] When no news came for sometime, God informed the Prophet about the detachment by revealing the first verse, which refers to "the horses." Another account of the occasion of the revelation states that

> when no news came, the Jews and the hypocrites, upon seeing a Muslim, whispered among themselves to make him think that someone close to him had died.[23]

Muqātil continues:

> It is said that the Muslims attacked and God defeated them [the enemy], and they started hitting one another until there was a glow (*wahağ*) which rose from the hooves of the horses. God defeated the unbelievers and killed them, and then informed him [the Prophet] of the horses, the dust, and what he did to them [the unbelievers]. The Prophet said: "O, Gabriel, when was this?" He [Gabriel] replied: "Today." So the Prophet went to the Muslims and read the *sūra* to them, and they were happy for the good news, and God shamed the Jews and the hypocrites.[24]

In the following, I will present the different interpretations of each verse, starting with Muğāhid, who is the earliest, and ending with Ṭabarī.

2.1 Q 100:1 *wa-l-ʿādiyāti ḍabḥā*

Muğāhid: the horses barking (*al-ḫayl taḍbaḥ*).[25]
Al-Ḍaḥḥāk: [the reference is to] the horses.[26]
Muqātil: the horses went out in the morning on the raid until they barked, [i.e.] they blew the breath out of their mouths, so they produced a barking like that of the fox.[27]
Al-Farrāʾ: Ibn ʿAbbās said it is [a reference to] the horses, and *ḍabīḥ* is the sound of their breathing when they run.[28]
Abū ʿUbayda: *al-ʿādiyāt* [refers to] the horses; *ḍabḥā* means *ḍabʿā*. Both *ḍabaḥat* and *ḍabaʿat* mean the same thing. Some [interpreters] said: *taḍbaḥ* means "they neigh" (*tanḥam*), those who say this imply that there is a pronoun [in the verb].[29]
ʿAbd al-Razzāq: [the reference is to] the horses running until they bark.[30]
Ṭabarī: Summarizing the opinions of previous authorities, Ṭabarī explains that *al-ʿādiyāt* refers to horses and *ḍabḥā* to their neighing. According to him, the interpretation is supported by reports going back to ʿAbd Allāh b. ʿAbbās, one of the Companions of the Prophet and a major *ḥadīṯ* authority. The word *ḍabḥ* signifies the barking of dogs. Ṭabarī points out that *ʿādiyāt* may also refer to camels. In this case *ḍabḥ* means "breathing." He adds that ʿAbd Allāh b. ʿAbbās changed his view about the meaning of *ḍabḥ* after ʿAlī b. Abī Ṭālib told him that the word refers to camels. He

concludes by stating that for those commentators who hold that the word refers to camels, the context is the scene of the pilgrimage and the movement of the camels with their riders from one place to another, rather than the detachment led by al-Munḏir b. ʿAmr, but his own opinion is that the word refers to horses, because horses, not camels, bark (*taḍbaḥ*).[31]

2.2 Q 100:2 *fa-l-mūriyāti qadḥā*

Muǧāhid: This means the malice of men.[32]

Al-Ḍaḥḥāk: they (i.e. the horses) light the stones with their hooves.[33]

Muqātil: They (i.e. the horses) spark fire with their hooves and the stones, like the fire of Ḥubāḥib,[34] an old man from Muḍar during the Ǧāhiliyya who had a small light which was lit once and extinguished once so that no guest would pass by him.[35]

Al-Farrāʾ: They made fire with their hooves, which is like the fire of Ḥubāḥib, one of the most miserly people. He was so miserly that he lit fires only at night. If someone wanted to borrow some of it, he would extinguish it. So the fire that the horses light is of no use, just as Ḥubāḥib's fire is of no use.[36] Abū ʿUbayda: they light the fire with the [hard] sides of their hooves.[37]

ʿAbd al-Razzāq: [It refers to] man's malice.[38]

Ṭabarī keeps the door open to many interpretations. The phrase may refer to horses kindling fire with their hooves, people kindling fire with drills or flints, the tongue making fire with logic, men making fire with their malice, or horses provoking war among their riders when they meet in battle. He concludes that God did not specify which meaning is intended.[39]

2.3 Q 100:3 *fa-l-muġīrāti ṣubḥā*

Muǧāhid: it [refers to] the horses in the fight. He also quotes Ibn Masʿūd, who said [that it refers to the camels] during the pilgrimage.[40]

Al-Ḍaḥḥāk: no mention of v. 3.

Muqātil: the horses raided the enemy in the morning.[41]

Al-Farrāʾ: the horses raided in the morning. He reports that ʿAlī b. Abī Ṭālib said [the reference is to] the camels.[42]

Abū ʿUbayda: They raid in the morning.[43]

ʿAbd al-Razzāq: They (i.e. the horses) raided in the morning.[44]

Ṭabarī offers two interpretations: in one, the reference is to horses raiding the enemy in the morning, in the other to camels taking their riders from Ǧamʿ to Minā on the Day of Sacrifice. He concludes that God made an oath by those who raid in the morning, without specifying one raider or another, and adds that Zayd b. Aslam treated this verse simply as an oath that does not require an interpretation.[45]

2.4 Q 100:4 *fa-aṯarna bihi naqʿā*

Muǧāhid: No mention.
Al-Ḍaḥḥāk: No mention.
Muqātil: they stirred up *naqʿā* in the dirt with their running or with their hooves. The meaning of *naqʿā* is not clear (*fa-aṯarna bi-ǧaryihinna yaʿnī bi-ḥawāfirihinna naqʿan fi l-turāb*).[46]
Al-Farrāʾ: al-naqʿ is dust or dirt. By saying *bihi naqʿā*, He (Allāh) means "in the valley." He did not mention it [viz., the valley] before that, which is permitted, because dust is stirred up only in a place, even if it is not mentioned. If the name of the thing is known, it can be referred to even if it is not mentioned.[47]
Abū ʿUbayda: They raised dust in it. *Naqʿā* means dust.[48]
ʿAbd al-Razzāq: [*Naqʿā* refers to] dust.[49]
Ṭabarī: Using the same reasoning as al-Farrāʾ, Ṭabarī explains that the third person singular pronoun *h* of *bihi* refer to *the valley*. He suggests that the pronoun could also refer to *the hooves* [of the horses]. Finally, a report attributed to ʿAlī b. Abī Ṭālib on the authority of Ibn ʿAbbās states that he (ʿAlī) told him that the verse refers to the runners going from ʿArafa to Muzdalifa and from Muzdalifa to Mina. The pronoun refers to the hooves of the horses and camels (*aḫfāfihā wa-ḥawāfirihā*).[50]

2.5 Q 100:5 *fa-wasaṭna bihi ǧamʿā*

Muǧāhid: [*Ǧamʿā*] refers to those and those.[51]
Al-Ḍaḥḥāk: Al-ǧamʿ (the gathering) [refers to] the brigade (*katība*).[52]
Muqātil: [*Wasaṭna* refers to] their running, when the horses run [into] the crowd, i.e. the enemy.[53]
Al-Farrāʾ: al-Farrāʾ says only that the commentators were in agreement on pronouncing one *sīn* in *fa-wasaṭna* even though *wassaṭna* is also correct since the Arabs use *wasaṭa* (Form I), *wassaṭa* (Form II), and *tawassaṭa* (Form V) with the same meaning.[54]
Abū ʿUbayda: no mention.
ʿAbd al-Razzāq: Ǧamʿ refers to the gathering (crowd) of the enemy. ʿAmr b. Dīnār is quoted as saying that ʿUbayd b. ʿUmayr said [it, i.e. *ǧamʿ* the gathering] refers to the camels. ʿAbd al-Razzāq quotes Ibn ʿUyayna on the authority of Ismāʿīl from Abū Ṣāliḥ that ʿAlī (b. Abī Ṭālib) used to say that it refers to the camels. ʿIkrima said to him: "Ibn ʿAbbās used to say, ʿIt

is the horses'" to which Abū Ṣāliḥ responded, 'My master is more knowledgeable than your master.'[55]

Ṭabarī offers three possibilities: (a) the verse is simply an oath with no specific meaning, (b) they (i.e. the horses) went into the middle of the crowd of people (or the crowd of unbelievers, the crowd of the enemy, or the brigade) with their riders, or (c) the pronoun in *bihi* refers to Muzdalifa.[56]

3. Problems with Q 100:1–5

One wonders why five verses, with a total of 12 words, should require so much interpretation, with conflicting views and no satisfactory answers to some key questions: (a) to what does *al-ʿādiyāt* refer? What do the words *al-ʿādiyāt* and *naqʿā* mean? In vv. 4–5, to what does the pronoun *hi* in *bihi* refer?

Reflecting the commentators' difficulty in understanding these verses, Pickthall states in a footnote to his translation of Q 100:

> The meaning of the first five verses is by no means clear. The above is a probable rendering.

In my view, no amount of interpretation will produce a meaningful and coherent set of verses, because the original structure was destroyed and linguistic elements which fit with one another at some point were replaced with others that do not. The first step in support of my thesis will be a detailed examination of the linguistic problems that characterize these verses.

The problems are of two types: syntactic and lexical. The first category includes one phenomenon and the second three lexical items.

3.1 Syntactic Problem: The Reference of the Pronoun in v. 4

The traditional interpretation of this verse does not provide a reasonable explanation for the referent of the third person masculine singular pronoun *h* in *bihi*. The standard explanation is that suggested by al-Farrā', which was followed by later authorities, including Ṭabarī and al-Zaǧǧāǧ.[57]

Some commentators[58] suggest that the pronoun refers to the hooves of the horses. This proposal is problematic, however, since the pronoun must have a masculine singular reference while hooves (*ḥawāfir*) requires a feminine singular reference. Al-Qurṭubī agrees with those commentators who understand the pronoun as referring to a place that is not mentioned, but adds that it can also refer to the running (*ʿadw*),

> The pronoun in *bihi* goes back to the place or location in which the raid occurred. If the meaning is understood, it is permitted to refer to what has not

> been mentioned explicitly. . . It is also said *fa-aṯarna bihi*, i.e. in the running (i.e. the pronoun refers to the *running*).[59]

Ibn Kaṯīr suggests "the place where the horses fight,"[60] while al-Maḥallī and al-Suyūṭī explain that the pronoun refers to "the place of their [horses] running or [to] that time."[61]

All these explanations involve a great deal of speculation, and none of them addresses the syntactic difficulty in a convincing manner.

3.2 Lexical Problems

Of the twelve words in the five verses under discussion, six are *hapax legomena: al-ʿādiyāt, ḍabḥā, qadḥā, al-muġīrāt, naqʿā*, and *wasaṭna*, a disproportionately high number. In at least one case, i.e. *naqʿā*, a word is used with a meaning not found in the language outside of this *sūra*. In other cases, a clear attempt is made by the commentators to force a meaning to fit the context of the *sūra*. In the following paragraphs, I will focus on those words that I believe are particularly problematic.

3.2.1 ḍabḥā

The peculiar usage of this word in Q 100 has generated a great deal of controversy among the Qur'ān commentators, as exemplified by al-Qurṭubī's account, summarized below.

> Qatāda said, "They (i.e. the horses) bark, when they run, i.e they neigh (*taḍbaḥ idā ʿadat ay tuḥamḥim*). Al-Farrā' said *ḍabḥ* is the sound of the horses when they run. Ibn ʿAbbās [said]: no beast *taḍbaḥ* except the horse, the dog, and the fox. It is said: they [the horses] were muzzled so that they would not neigh, lest the enemy become aware of their presence, so they breathed heavily ... The linguists said: The words *ḍabḥ* and *ḍubāḥ* are used for foxes, and the usage was extended to horses. It is used by the Arabs, as in "[the fire] changed its color" (*ḍabaḥathu l-nār*), but not by much ... and *inḍabaḥa lawnuh* if its color changed slightly to black ... Animals *taḍbaḥ* if their condition changes from fright, fatigue, or greed ... *ḍabḥ* also means ashes ... Abū ʿUbayda said: *ḍabaḥat al-ḫaylu ḍabḥā* is like *ḍabaʿat*, which is *going*, and Abū ʿUbayda added *ḍabḥ* and *ḍabʿ* mean "running" and "going." Al-Mubarrad said: *ḍabaḥa* means "to extend the *aḍbāʿ* (later explained as 'necks') in the movement". . .
>
> Among those who said that the intended meaning of *al-ʿādiyāt* is horses are Ibn ʿAbbās, Anas [b. Mālik], al-Ḥasan [al-Basrī], and Muǧāhid. . . Another account says that it refers to *camels*. Muslim said, "I had a disagreement about it with ʿIkrima, who said, Ibn ʿAbbās said 'horses,' and I said that ʿAlī said

> 'camels at the time of the pilgrimage,' and my master is more knowledgeable than your master. . ."
>
> Whoever said that it is the camels, when he says *ḍabḥā* means *ḍabʿā*, where the *ḥāʾ* is converted from *ʿayn*, because it is said *ḍabaʿat al-ibil*, i.e. they extend their necks while walking ... *ḍabḥ* is used with horses and *ḍabʿ* with camels ... Abū Sāliḥ [said] *ḍabḥ* with the horses is *neighing* and with the camels *breathing.*[62]

Behind the various interpretations and conflicting views on the word *ḍabḥā*, one can discern a clear attempt to link the verb *ḍabḥa*, meaning "to bark," to the running horses. This attempt reaches absurd levels when the other meaning of *ḍabaḥa* (to change color as a result of burning) is used to impose an alternative interpretation where a comparison is made between the change in the color of a burned object and the change in the condition [presumably of horses] from fright, fatigue, and greed. Rāġib al-Iṣfahānī (d. 1108) makes a similar attempt to accommodate the peculiar Qur'ānic usage of the word. He writes:

> The word *ḍabḥ* refers to the sound of the breath of the horse, which is similar to the sound of the fox. It is said that it is the hissing produced by the act of running [itself]. It might also be said of the running. It is also said that *ḍabḥ* is like *ḍabʿ*, which is "to extend the neck while running." It is said that its origin goes back to the burning of a stick, and the running was compared to the fire in its speed.[63]

Finally, it should be noted that if one considers the way Arabs and Muslims have traditionally viewed horses, on the one hand, and dogs and foxes, on the other, one would expect the analogy to go in the opposite direction. Comparing the sound made by horses going into battle for the cause of Islam to that of dogs or foxes or even rabbits is demeaning and insulting to those noble animals.

3.2.2 qadḥā

Most exegetes interpret this word as the sparks produced by the running horses. This interpretation is particularly problematic when one takes into account the alternative interpretation that runners, *ʿādiyāt*, refers to camels, not horses.[64] No one would argue that the hooves of camels produce sparks.

3.2.3 naqʿā

As was pointed out above, the usage of *naqʿ* in the sense of *dust* is peculiar to Q 100.[65] While there is general agreement among the Qur'ān commentators that *naqʿ* means "dust," al-Rāzī, sensitive to the peculiar usage of the word, tries to relate "dust" to other meanings of the root, such as "to raise the voice or "to soak in water." He states:

> It is said that it is from soaking in water, as if the one associated with the dust plunged into it, like the man who plunges into the water (*wa-qīla huwa min al-naqʿ fī l-māʾ, fa-kaʾanna ṣāḥib al-ġubār ġāṣa fīhi, kamā yaġūṣu l-rağulu fī l-māʾ*).[66]

He adds, describing women wailing after a raid, "they provoked in those who have been raided the shouts of wailing women, whose voices were raised (*ay fa-hayyağna fī l-muġār ʿalayhim ṣiyāḥ al-nawāʾiḥ, wa-rtafaʿat aṣwātuhunn*)."[67]

Again, there is a clear attempt to force a meaning on a word that it does not have outside of the verse in question.

To sum up, the claims that *ḍabḥā* is a sound made by horses or camels, that *qadḥā* is a spark produced by running horses or even camels, and that *naqʿā* refers to dust have no foundation in the Arabic language. These claims are used to provide an explanation where one founded on sound linguistic principles is not possible.

4. An Alternative Account

As noted, there was a period when the written text of the Qurʾān was represented by a consonantal skeleton in which most vowels and *hamza* (glottal stop) were not represented and letters with similar shapes, which later came to be distinguished by dots, were written the same, e.g., *rāʾ* and *zāy; sīn* and *šīn*; and *bāʾ*, *tāʾ*, *tāʾ*, *nūn*, and *yāʾ*, particularly in the middle of a word. According to some accounts, dots were introduced into the writing system more than half a century after the stabilization of the ʿUṯmānic text, i.e. around 700 CE.[68] Others claim that the first copies of the Qurʾān did have dots but that they were removed by the Prophet's Companions after his death. Dots were reintroduced towards the end of the first century AH. Their reintroduction met with resistance, and the Qurʾān continued to be written without dots for a long time, which resulted in erroneous readings.[69]

If this was the case, then there was a period of time when a letter symbol could have been read in a number of different ways, as in رىاىىه above. In this environment, it is possible that when the text of the Qurʾān took its final written shape, mistakes were made in the dotting of some of its letters, e.g., a ت (*tāʾ*) was written instead of a ث (*ṯāʾ*) or a ب (*bāʾ*).

In the following, I will attempt to reconstruct what might have been an older version of Q 100:1–5 by changing the traditional placement of dots in three words and the replacement of a *hamza* by a *madda*.

4.1 Q 100:1

Adding a dot in the first word and removing one in the second produces *wa-l-ġādiyāti ṣubḥā*:

والعاديات ضبحا ← والغاديات صبحا

The basic and most common meaning of the verb *ġadā* is "to go out or to perform an act in the morning, especially in the early morning."[70] The basic and most common meaning of the noun *ṣubḥ* is "morning," or "early morning."[71] Syntactically, the word *ṣubḥā* in the phrase *wa-l-ġādiyāti ṣubḥā* is unambiguously an adverb of time. Semantically, the two words fit together perfectly: "They (f.) are going out in the morning." This perfect fit is clearly absent in the traditional interpretation of Q 100:1.

In his *Kitāb Aḫbār al-Muṣaḥḥifīn*, the tenth century Muslim scholar al-ʿAskarī wrote about the famous narrator and transmitter of Arabic poetry Ḥammād al-Rāwiya:

> I heard those who tell that Ḥammād al-Rāwiya one day read *wa-l-ʿādiyāti ṣubḥā*, and that Baššār the Blind took him to ʿUqba b. Salm [and told him that] he is able to narrate all the poetry of the Arabs but he knows only the first *sūra* of the Qurʾān. ʿUqba examined him by having him read some of the Qurʾān, so he distorted a number of verses[72]

Al-ʿAskarī lists sixteen verses from different *sūra*s which Ḥammād "distorted" (*ṣaḥḥaf*). A close look at his "distorted" reading shows that it in fact makes more sense than the traditional reading and may have been the correct one. His reading of the second word of Q 100:1 as صبحا was probably closer to the original form.[73]

It is interesting to note that in Muqātil's interpretation of Q 100:1, the verb *ġadā* is used to describe the horses going out to the raid in the morning. He writes: *wa-l-ʿādiyāti ḍabḥā, yaqūl: ġadat al-ḫayl ilā l -ġazw ḥattā aḍbaḥat* (with respect to *wa-l-ʿādiyāti ḍabḥā*, he says, "the horses went out to the raid in the morning until they barked. . .").[74]

4.2 Q 100:4

Changing the *hamza* to a *madda* in the first word and removing a dot from the *qāf* of the third produces the phrase *fa-āṯarna bihi nafʿā*:

فأثرن بـه نـقعا ← فآثـرن بـه نـفعا

Again, syntactically and semantically, *fa-āṯarna bihi nafʿā* is a well-formed phrase:

> And they (f.) chose/preferred/favored by (doing) it (to perform/render) a good deed.[75]

The verb *āṯara* "to prefer" occurs five times in the Qur'ān (Q 12:91; 20:72; 59:9; 79:38; 87:16) while *aṯāra* "to stir up" occurs twice in the same phrase *tuṯīru saḥāban* (it, i.e. the wind, stirs up clouds) (Q 30:48; 35:9). However, while the root *n-q-ʿ* occurs only once, in Q 100, as was pointed out above, the root *n-f-ʿ* occurs fifty times.[76]

4.3 Foreign Borrowings

A comparison of the meanings of several words in the verses under discussion with their cognates in Hebrew and Syriac offers some clues as to what might have been the original meaning of these verses. In particular, I will consider the meanings of two words, *qadḥā* and *fa-wasaṭna*.

It is well-known that the Qur'ān contains many loan words from foreign languages. According to Jeffery,

> Closer examination of the question [of foreign vocabulary in the Qur'ān] reveals even further and more detailed correspondences than those which appear on the surface, and forces on one the conviction that not only the greater part of the religious vocabulary, but also most of the cultural vocabulary of the Qur'ān is of non-Arabic origin.[77]

This position was fully accepted by the early Muslim exegetes; it was only later that the influence of other languages on the language of the Qur'ān was minimized or even denied.[78]

Syriac, followed by Hebrew, accounts for the highest number of borrowings,[79] although borrowings from Greek, Persian, and Ethiopic are also attested.

In his widely quoted *Kitāb al-Maṣāḥif*, which treats the history of the collection of the Qur'ān, the tenth century Muslim scholar Abū Bakr b. Abī Dawūd al-Siǧistānī (d. 928) writes:

> ʿAbd Allāh related to us saying ʿĪsā b. ʿAffān b. ʿĪsā had narrated: my uncle Yahyā b. ʿĪsā related, on the authority of al-Aʿmaš, from Ṯābit, on the authority of ʿUbayd, on the authority of Zayd b. Ṯābit, who said, the Prophet (peace be upon him) said, Books come to me that I do not want every one to read. Can you learn the Hebrew script? (Or he said: Syriac). I said: Yes. So I learned it in seventeen days.[80]

In a slightly different version, the Prophet asked Zayd b. Ṯābit if he knew Syriac, to which he answered in the negative. The Prophet asked him to learn it and he learned it in nineteen days.[81]

It is clear from these reports that the Prophet borrowed materials from Syriac and/or Hebrew. This statement becomes even more significant when we take into consideration the fact that Zayd b. Ṯābit, who may have been a convert from Judaism,[82] was the Prophet's secretary who later was placed in charge of the collection and codification of the Qur'ān.

The morphological similarity between Syriac and Hebrew, on the one hand, and Arabic on the other, may explain the fact that borrowings from the former languages into the latter can be assimilated easily, even seamlessly, without leaving a trace.

In his short article "The Buddha Comes to China," Michael Schub (2002, p. 391) argues that a verb (*yuḥbarūn*) was borrowed from Hebrew into the Qur'ān and came to be treated as an Arabic verb. According to him,

> Its [*yuḥbarūn*] coincidence with the possibly indigenous Arabic root *ḥ-b-r* ... and its similarity in form and intended meaning to the two other Arabic roots [*ḥ-d-r, ḥ-š-r*] catalyzed its infiltration into the Arabic system.[83]

The three languages share many roots with overlapping sets of meanings. Compare, for example, the meanings of the root *q-d-ḥ*,

Arabic

1) a cup, 2) to strike fire, 3) to influence, affect, 4) to manage or look into a matter, 5) a disease that destroys trees and teeth, 6) slander, 7) to scoop, to ladle food from a pot, 8) a ladle, 9) an arrow, 10) to remove spoiled water, 11) the flower before it opens, 12) the tender tips of plant leaves.[84]

Biblical Hebrew

1) to be kindled, glow, 2) feverish heat, 3) glowing precious stone, ruby, 4) to bore.[85]

Syriac

1) to tear the hair, shave the head as a sign of grief, 2) to catch fire, blaze up, to rekindle, revive (of error or fever), 3) to set light, a lighted fire, 4) to bore, pierce.[86]

Now, I will examine the two potential borrowings from Syriac or Hebrew.

4.4 Two Potential Borrowings from Syriac or Hebrew

4.4.1 *qadḥā*

As used in the *sūra*, this word is typically glossed as "a spark produced by the hooves of running horses." In both Biblical Hebrew and Syriac, one of the main meanings of the root *q-d-ḥ* is "fire," or "kindling a fire," as shown above. A "lighted fire" in Syriac is *ywrā d-qdḥā*.[87] Compare this phrase with *fa-l-mūriyāti qadḥā*, where the two languages share the same roots for the two words in the phrase.

4.4.2 *fa-wasaṭna*

This word is traditionally glossed as "going into the middle (of the foe)." While this meaning follows from the standard interpretation of vv. 1–4, it is unique to this verse. An alternative interpretation attributed to Ibn Masʿūd by al-Qurṭubī, refers to "the act of going into the middle of the crowd of pilgrims at al-Muzdalifa."[88]

An examination of cognate forms in Biblical Hebrew and Syriac suggests another meaning that fits well with the alternative interpretation to be offered below. The cognate of the Arabic root *w-s-ṭ* is *y-š-t* in Biblical Hebrew and Syriac. In Biblical Hebrew it means "to extend" or "hold out,"[89] and in Syriac it means "to hold out, stretch out," "to be offered, presented, to advance," and "to reach forward, stretch forward, offer, grow up, make progress, succeed, be advanced, especially in dignity."[90] These meanings will be proposed as alternatives to the Arabic meaning assigned to this root in the interpretation of Q 100:5.

The language of the Qurʾān itself offers a certain degree of support for an alternative interpretation of the root *w-s-ṭ* in Q 100:5. Besides its occurrence in Q 100:5, this root occurs four times in the Qurʾān: in Q 2:143, 238; 5:89, and 68:28.[91] None of these four occurrences is a verb and none can be related to the theme of battle. In Q 2:143 (*wa-ka-ḏālika ǧaʿalnākum ummatan wasaṭan li-takūnū šuhadāʾ ʿalā l-nās*), *wasaṭ* is interpreted by Ṭabarī as either *best, more just, honest* (*ʿadl*), or *not extreme* (*tawassuṭ wa-ʿtidāl*).[92] In Q 2:238 (*ḥāfiẓū ʿalā l-ṣalawāti wa-l-ṣalāti al-wusṭā*), there is a wide range of opinions among the interpreters as to which prayer is referred to by *al-wusṭā*, with each of the five daily prayers offered as possible candidates.[93] For *awsaṭ* in Q 5:89 (*fa-kaffāratuhu iṭʿāmu ʿašrati masākīna min awsaṭi mā tuṭʿimūna ahlīkum*), Ṭabarī gives a similar interpretation to that given for Q 2:143, namely either *best*, or *not extreme.*[94] Finally, in Q 68:28 (*qāla awsaṭuhum, a-lam aqul lakum lawlā tusabbiḥūn*), only one definition of *awsaṭ* is given, *aʿdal* (best, most honest, most just, upright).[95]

If the word *wusṭā* in *al-ṣalāti al-wusṭā* of Q 2:238 is excluded because of the complete lack of agreement over its interpretation, then the three other occurrences of the root *w-s-ṭ* (Q 2:143; 5:89, and 68:28) discussed above strongly suggest the meaning of *best, favored, preferred*, or *chosen*. In fact, an interpretation of Q 2:143 and 5:89 based on this meaning makes more sense than one based on *middle: we made you a favored nation* (Q 2:143), *feeding ten needy people from the best (food) that you feed your people* (Q 5:89).

4.5 Foreign Borrowing, or Old Arabic Forms?

While it is possible that the words *qadḥā* and *wasaṭna* were borrowed into the Qur'ān from Syriac or Hebrew, it is also possible that these words entered the Arabic lexicon at an earlier stage but had lost their original meanings by the time the Qur'ān exegetes recorded their commentaries. One piece of evidence in favor of this hypothesis is the verb *wasaṭa* in Q 100:5. If this verb had been borrowed directly from Hebrew or Syiac, it would have a *yā'* as its first consonant, since *wāw*-initial roots in Arabic regularly correspond to *yā'*-initial roots in Hebrew and Syriac. The initial *wāw* of *wasaṭ* confirms its Arabic identity.

Regardless of which view is adopted, what is relevant for the purposes of this essay is that certain meanings attested for these words in Hebrew and Syriac, but not reported in the traditional Muslim interpretation of the *sūra*, may be the ones that had existed in an earlier form of it.

4.6 Q 100:3: *fa-l-muġīrāti ṣubḥā*

The third verse of the *sūra* is a good candidate for what Lüling calls a second-sense Qur'ān text, a verse that was added by the Qur'ān editors to obscure the original text and give it a new meaning.[96] Once the theme of "charging steeds" was established at the beginning of the *sūra*, it was possible to continue with the same imagery. The addition of this verse reinforces the theme of the charging steeds at the expense of another older meaning: a Christian Arabic hymn, as will be suggested below.

Unlike the other verses, Q 100:3 does not require a great deal of interpretation. The only point that requires clarification is whether *al-muġīrāt* refers to horses or camels, which is a problem in v. 1. The reader may recall Ṭabarī's statement that Zayd b. Aslam treated this verse as a simple oath that does not require further explanation. This is an indication that the verse was added at a later stage.

The difference between the syllable structure of Q 100:3 and that of 100:1 and 2 supports my hypothesis that this verse is an addition to the *sūra*. The syllable structure of the three verses is shown below, where C=consonant, V=short vowel, VV=long vowel, and a dot indicates syllable division.

wa-l.- ʿā.di.yā.ti. ḍab.ḥā	CVC.CVV.CV.CVV.CV.CVC.CVV
fa-l.-mū.ri.yā.ti. qad. ḥā	CVC.CVV.CV.CVV.CV.CVC.CVV
fa-l.-mu.ġī.rā.ti. ṣub.ḥā	CVC.CV.CVV.CVV.CV.CVC.CVV

Vv. 1 and 2 share an identical syllable sequence that is not shared by v. 3.
Vv. 4 and 5 also show an identical prosodic structure. This is clear in the traditional form of these verses, as shown below.

fa-aṭarna bihi naqʿā	CV.CV.CVC.CV.CV.CV.CVC.CVV
fa-wasaṭna bihi ǧamʿā	CV.CV.CVC.CV.CV.CV.CVC.CVV

The version of these two verses proposed in this essay appears to violate this prosodic identity, since *fa-aṭarna* differs in its syllable structure from *fa-wasaṭna,*

fa-āṭarna	CV.CVV.CVC.CV
fa-wasaṭna	CV.CV.CVC.CV

However, a case can be made on the basis of variant Qurʾānic readings for *fa-wassaṭna* as the correct form of this word. Among those who read *fa-wassaṭna* are ʿAlī b. Abī Ṭālib and ʿAbd Allāh b. Masʿūd.[97] Since in Arabic prosody the two syllable types CVC and CVV have the same weight, vv. 4 and 5 turn out to have similar prosodic structures.

fa-āṭarna bihi nafʿā	CV.CVV.CVC.CV.CV.CV.CVC.CVV
fa-wassaṭna bihi ǧamʿā	CV.CVC.CVC.CV.CV.CV.CVC.CVV

5. Reconstructing Q 100:1–5

On the basis of the above discussion, I propose making the following four changes in the first five verses of Q 100:

(1) redot the three words *al-ʿādiyāt, ḍabḥā* and *naqʿā*;

(2) replace one diacritic by another (*hamza* by *madda*) in *aṭarna*;

(3) substitute the traditional understanding of the two words *qadḥā* and *wasaṭna* (or *wassaṭna*) with meanings in the two closely related languages of Biblical Hebrew and Syriac or from older Arabic meanings; and

(4) remove the verse that may have been added at a later stage (*fa-l-muġīrāti ṣubḥā*).

If all of these changes are incorporated, the reconstructed introductory part of Q 100 will be as follows:

والغاديات صبحا	*wa-al-ġādiyāti ṣubḥā*	And those (f.) going out in the (early) morning
فالموريات قدحا	*fa-l-mūriyāti qadḥā*	And [those (f.)] kindling a flame[98]

فآثرن به نفعا	*fa-āṯarna bihi nafʿā*	By which they (f.) chose to render a good deed
فوسطن به جمعا	*fa-wassaṭna bihi ǧamʿā*	And [they (f.)] extend it to the multitudes

In this version of Q 100:1–5, all the syntactic and lexical problems discussed above as well as the enigmatic nature of these verses are addressed and answered in a meaningful manner. What we have is a short hymn glorifying women who go out in the morning and kindle a flame by which they mean to do good and extend it to the multitudes. The theme, tone, and words of a religious hymn permeate the passage and give it a coherent structure. The syntactic problem of the unexplainable reference of the pronoun *hā'* of *bihi* in vv. 4 and 5 is resolved: in the proposed version the pronoun refers unambiguously to *qadḥā*, the light or candle in v. 2. As for the lexical problems, the number of *hapax legomena* in the version proposed decreases from six to two: *qadḥā* and *wassaṭna*, the two borrowings or old Arabic forms. The alternative forms proposed here (*ġadā, ṣubḥā, āṯara, nafʿ*) occur in the Qur'ān with reasonable frequency. Apart from the need to explain the two older Arabic, or Hebrew or Syriac, words, the meaning of these verses is straightforward.[99]

6. Innocent Mistakes or Deliberate Manipulation?

If my reconstruction of Q 100:1–5 is correct, then how could the original forms have been replaced by those that became part of the Qur'ān as we know it? Two possibilities present themselves.

The first is that there were errors in the transmission of the text of the Qur'ān:[100] for والغاديات صبحا the transmitter substituted والعاديات ضبحا. This would have been possible since the two phrases would have been identical when written in the defective Arabic script, which had no dots. This assumption implies that the Qur'ān started as a written document as opposed to an oral recitation, or that there was a time when the written text was not clearly supported by an oral tradition;[101] as a result, there was room for reading errors. The proliferation of Qur'ānic readings, which were restricted to seven in the first quarter of the fourth century AH, can be taken as evidence of misreadings of the same written text, since one of the main criteria employed by Ibn Muǧāhid (d. 324/935)[102] in determining the acceptability of the seven canonical readings was conformity to the ʿUṯmānic *muṣḥaf*, which, as noted, lacked dots. Indeed much of the variation among the seven readers revolves around differences in dots among homographs.[103]

The second possibility is that the text was deliberately changed by the Qur'ān editors after the death of the Prophet, as argued by Lüling. Support for this claim is found in the Muslim tradition.[104]

6.1 The Fire of Malice and Deceit (*nār al-makr wa-l-ḫadīʿa*)

As an example of a possible manipulation of the meaning of the text, I would like to cite al-Farrā''s and al-Qurṭubī's interpretation of Q 100:2. Al-Farrā' goes out of his way to disassociate this verse from the idea of doing good, which would have been the original meaning of the verses if my reconstruction is correct. He states,

They, i.e. the horses, ignited a fire by their hooves. It is the fire of Ḥubāḥib. Al-Kalbī said on his own *isnād* (chain of transmission) that Ḥubāḥib was an Arab man who was among the stingiest of people. He was so stingy that he made his fire only at night. If someone noticed it [and wanted to] borrow some of it, he would extinguish it. And the same is true of the fire made by the horses; it is of no use, in the same way as Ḥubāḥib's fire is of no use.[105]

I am inclined to think that such a story belies al-Farrā''s conscious attempt to impose a new interpretation on the verse. The parallel is so far-fetched as to suggest motives unrelated to the language of the verse. Al-Qurṭubī adds a new twist to the interpretation. He states,

> It is said that [the word] *qadḥā* [refers to] the thoughts of men which ignite the fire of malice and deceit (*wa-qīla hiya afkār al-riǧāl tūrī nār al-makr wa-l-ḫadīʿa*).[106]

6.2 Erasing the Book of God ([*ʿUṯmān*] *maḥā kitāb Allāh*)

As related in *Kitāb al-Maṣāḥif*,[107] one of the grievances the people of Miṣr al-Ǧaḥfa against ʿUṯmān, was that *he erased the Book of God* (*maḥā kitāb Allāh*). Addressing them after hearing their grievance, ʿUṯmān stated,

> As for the Qur'ān, it is from God, and I have forbidden you, because I feared disagreement among you, so read it in the manner you desire (*ammā l-qur'ān fa-min ʿind Allāh, innamā nahaytukum li-annī ḫiftu ʿalaykum min al-iḫtilāf, fa-qra'ū ʿalā ayyi ḥarfin ši'tum*).

The meaning of *nahaytukum*, translated here as "I have forbidden you" is not clear. Be that as it may, ʿUtmān does not deny the claim that he *erased the book of God*.

The word *maḥā* signifies "to erase, remove the trace of (*maḥā l-šay'a yamḥūhu wa-yamḥāhu maḥwan wa-maḥyan: aḏhaba aṯarahu*)."[108] Naturally, one cannot conclude that ʿUṯmān erased the Qur'ān without leaving a trace; the likely interpretation is that he removed a feature from the Qur'ān, thereby angering the people of Miṣr al-Ǧaḥfa. ʿUṯmān's justification—he was afraid of disagreements and divisions and that his action would enable the Muslims to read the holy book in any manner they desired—fits the standard explanation in the Muslim tradition for the absence of dots and diacritics in the ʿUṯmānic *muṣḥaf.* What is significant here is the fact that ʿUṯmān is said to have changed the Qur'ān to make possible its different readings.

A number of authorities quote the Companion and well-known Qur'ān authority ʿAbd Allāh b. Masʿūd as saying *ǧarridū l-Qur'ān* (literally, strip off the Qur'ān). This statement is understood as meaning one of two things: either (a) remove the dots, diacritics (short vowel symbols), and other signs from the holy book, or (b) do not confuse it with other books because anyone who follows other Divine revelations follows the Jews and Christians, who cannot be trusted with these revelations.[109]

Ibn al-Ǧazarī (d. 832/1429), who understood the phrase in the first sense, elaborated on its rationale:

When the Companions [of the Prophet], may God be pleased with them, wrote these *muṣḥaf*s [during ʿUṯmān's time] they stripped from them the points and diacritics so that the script bears what was not in the final edition, according to what was attributed to the Prophet, peace be on him. They removed the points and diacritics from the *muṣḥafs* so that one orthographic symbol may refer to two pronunciations that were heard, transmitted, and recited, similar to the way in which one linguistic form may have two plausible and potentially understandable meanings.[110]

The evidence of papyri and inscriptions demonstrates that dots were used by the Arabs as early as the year 22 AH, and that the Prophet himself told Muʿāwiya, one of his scribes, to use dots to distinguish certain letters.[111] As noted, al-Munaǧǧid claims[112] that the first copies of the Qur'ān had dots which were removed deliberately by the Prophet's Companions after his death. Their reintroduction at the end of the first century AH encountered a great deal of resistance, and the Qur'ān continued to be read without dots, which resulted in erroneous readings.[113] Ibn Rawandi[114] and Lüling[115] claim that during the first century AH, diacritical points (including dots) were forbidden.

The strong evidence points to the possibility that dots were deliberately removed from the written text of the Qur'ān, and that for a period of several decades certain pairs or groups of letters were written the same. Presumably, this policy was adopted in order to accommodate Arabic dialectal variation. However, an examination of such variation demonstrates the weakness of this assumption. Arabic dialects do not differ in ways that reflect different dot assignments.

According to the 20th century Arabic linguist Ibrahim Anis, the differences among the Arabic tribal dialects in the early Islamic period can be summarized as follows:

(1) *imāla*, the pronunciation of the low vowel *a* (and its long counterpart *ā*) as front (between *ā* and *ī*);
(2) *idġām*, assimilation of adjacent consonants such as *ʿayn* to *ḥāʾ*, *tāʾ* to *dāl*, and *ṣād* to *zāy*;
(3) the presence or absence of *hamza* (the glottal stop);
(4) cases and moods;
(5) *wāw/yāʾ* (*ṣawwām/ṣayyām*);
(6) vowel harmony (*baʿīr/biʿīr*);
(7) *tāʾ/ṯāʾ*, which was restricted to the Jews of Ḫaybar;
(8) *zāʾ/sin/tāʾ* alternations;
(9) *ḍād/ẓāʾ*;
(10) *ǧim/gā*;
(11) *kāf/sīn, šīn*;
(12) *ǧīm/yāʾ*.[116]

No single Arabic dialect differs with another in the pronunciation of triplets like *ǧīm*, *ḥāʾ*, and *ḫāʾ*, where *ḥāʾ* of one dialect corresponds to *ḫāʾ* or *ǧim* in another, or doublets like *rāʾ* and *zāy*. A stronger case can be made for the use of dots to distinguish letters that show variation between Arabic, on the one hand, and Syriac and Biblical Hebrew on the other. Consider, for example, the following table of correspondences, in which, ArL represents the Arabic letter used in the comparison, ArS the Arabic sound represented by that letter, BH represents the Biblical Hebrew cognate, and Syr the Syriac cognate.[117]

ArL	ArS	BH	Syr		ArL	ArS	BH	Syr
ت	t	t	t		ش	š	s'	s
ث	ṯ	š	t		ص	ṣ	ṣ	ṣ
ح	ḥ	ḥ	ḥ		ض	ḍ	ṣ	ʿ
خ	ḫ	ḥ	ḥ		ط	ṭ	ṭ	ṭ
د	d	d	d		ظ	ẓ	ṣ	ṭ
ذ	ḏ	z	d		ع	ʿ	ʿ	ʿ
س	s	s	s		غ	ġ	ʿ	ʿ

Removing the dots from the pairs or triplets of letters would accommodate the Arabic sounds and their Biblical Hebrew and/or Syriac cognates. For example a word like ارص can be read as Arabic *arḍ* or Hebrew *ereṣ* "earth," and a word like حطىا can be read *inter alia* as Arabic *ḫaṭāyā* "sins" or Syriac *ḥaṭṭāyā* "sinner."

This suggests another motivation for an unpointed text: to make possible more than one reading in order to accommodate variations like *ʿādiyāt/ġādiyāt*, *ḍabḥā/ṣubḥā*, and *naqʿā/nafʿā*.

7. Conclusion

I understand that my reconstruction of Q 100:1–5 might seem random to some and that alternative interpretations or reconstructions are possible. I also understand that the exact character of these verses in their original forms may never be known. However, the strongest argument I can put forth in support of my reconstruction is that, as they stand now, these verses are highly problematic, and all the interpretations and commentaries that have been proposed, which have grown longer over time and are often contradictory and speculative, have failed to address their problems. I believe that the account given in this essay brings us closer to an understanding of the structure, meaning, and character of these verses.

Notes

---

1 I would like to express my gratitude to my colleague David Powers for his careful reading of several drafts of this essay and for making many insightful suggestions and comments. I am also grateful to the editorial committee of Arabica for their comments on an earlier form of the essay.

2 Angelika Neuwirth, "Images and metaphors in the introductory sections of the Makkan sūras," in *The Koran: Critical Concepts in Islamic Studies*, ed. Colin Turner, London and New York, III (Style and Structure), 2004, pp. 244–73, at 245.

3 Ibid., p. 246.

4 Soraya M. Hajjaji-Jarrah, "The enchantment of reading: sound, meaning, and expression in sūrat al-ʿādiyāt," in *The Koran: Critical Concepts in Islamic Studies*, pp. 359–80, at 360.

5 Günter Lüling, *A challenge to Islam for reformation: the rediscovery and reliable reconstruction of a comprehensive pre-Islamic Christian hymnal hidden in the Koran under earliest Islamic reinterpretations* (Delhi, Motilal Banarsidass Publishers, 2003), translated from the 2nd German edition of 1993 of the author's book *Über den Ur-Koran*, 1st edition 1974.

6 Christoph Luxenberg, *The Syro-Aramaic Reading of the Koran* (Berlin: Verlag Hans Schiler, 2007).

7 Lüling, *Challenge*, p. 1.

8 Ibid., xiii.

9   According to Muslim tradition, the first complete collection of the Qur'ān took place during the reign of the third caliph 'Uṯmān (23–35/644–656). This version of the Qur'ān became the authoritative one, and all others were destroyed. Copies were sent to the main centers of the Muslim state at the time. The text consisted of an unpointed consonantal skeleton.

10 Lüling, *Challenge*, pp. 71–2.

11 Christoph Luxenberg, *Syro-Aramaic Reading*, pp. 23–4.

12 Abū l-Ḥağğāğ Muğāhid b. Ğabr al-Qurašī l-Maḫzūmī, *Tafsīr Muğāhid*, ed. Abū Muḥammad al-Asyūṭī, Beirut, 2005.

13 Al-Ḍaḥḥāk b. Muzāḥim, *Tafsīr al-Ḍaḥḥāk*, ed. Muḥammad Šukri Aḥmad al-Zāwītī, Cairo, 1999.

14 Muqātil b. Sulaymān, *Tafsīr Muqātil b. Sulaymān*, ed. 'Abd Allāh Šiḥāta, Cairo, 1988.

15 Abū 'Abd Allāh Sufyān b. Sa'īd b. Masrūq al-Ṯawrī l-Kūfī, *Tafsīr al-Ṯawrī*, riwāyat Abī Ğa'far Muḥammad 'an Abī ḥuḍayfa l-Nahdī, ed. committee of scholars under the supervision of the publisher, 1983.

16 Sufyān b. 'Uyayna, *Tafsīr Ibn 'Uyayna*, ed. Aḥmad Ṣāliḥ Maḥāyirī (Beirut-Damascus-Riyadh, 1983).

17 Abū Zakariyyā Yaḥyā b. Ziyād al-Farrā', *Ma'ānī l-Qur'ān*, ed. 'Abd al-Fattāḥ Šalabī (Cairo, 2002).

18 Abū 'Ubayda Ma'mar b. al-Muṯannā l-Taymī, *Mağāz al-Qur'ān*, ed. Muḥammad Fu'ād Sizgīn (Cairo, 1962).

19 'Abd al-Razzāq b. Hammām al-Ṣan'ānī, *Tafsīr 'Abd al-Razzāq*, ed. Maḥmūd Muḥammad 'Abduh (Beirut, 1999).

20 Abū Ğa'far Muḥammad b. Ğarīr al-Ṭabarī, *Tafsīr al-Ṭabarī l-musammā Ğāmi' al-Bayān fī ta'wīl al-Qur'ān* (Beirut, 2005).

21 Muqātil, *Tafsīr*, IV, p. 801.

22 Al-Farrā', *Ma'ānī l-Qur'ān*, III, p. 284.

23 Muqātil, *Tafsīr*, IV, p. 801.

24 Ibid., pp. 802–3.

25 Muğāhid, *Tafsīr*, p. 776.

26 Al-Ḍaḥḥāk, *Tafsīr*, II, p. 982.

27 Muqātil, *Tafsīr*, IV, p. 801.

28 Al-Farrā', *Ma'ānī l-Qur'ān*, III, p. 284.

29 Abū 'Ubayda, *Mağāz al- Qur'ān*, II, p. 307.

30 'Abd al-Razzāq, *Tafsīr*, III, p. 451.

31 Ṭabarī, *Ğāmi'*, XII, pp. 665–7.

32 Muğāhid, *Tafsīr*, p. 776.

33 Al-Ḍaḥḥāk, *Tafsīr*, II, p. 982.

34 I would like to thank an anonymous reviewer who pointed out that the correct form of the name is Ḥubāḥib, not Abū l-Ḥubāḥib, as it appears in Muqātil.

35 Muqātil, *Tafsīr*, IV, pp. 801–2.

36 Al-Farrā', *Ma'ānī l-Qur'ān*, III, p. 284.

37 Abū 'Ubayda, *Mağāz al-Qur'ān*, II, p. 307

38 'Abd al-Razzāq, *Tafsīr*, III, p. 451.

39 Ṭabarī, *Ǧāmiʿ*, XII, pp. 667–8.
40 Muǧāhid, *Tafsīr*, p. 776.
41 Muqātil, *Tafsīr*, IV, p. 802.
42 Al-Farrāʾ, *Maʿānī l-Qurʾān*, III, p. 284.
43 Abū ʿUbayda, *Maǧāz al-Qurʾān*, II, p. 307.
44 ʿAbd al-Razzāq, *Tafsīr*, III, p. 452.
45 Ṭabarī, *Ǧāmiʿ*, XII, pp. 669.
46 Muqātil, *Tafsir*, IV, p. 802.
47 Al-Farrāʾ, *Maʿānī l-Qurʾān*, III, pp. 284–5
48 Abū ʿUbayda, *Maǧāz al-Qurʾān*, II, p. 307.
49 ʿAbd al-Razzāq, *Tafsīr*, III, p. 452.
50 Ṭabarī, *Ǧāmiʿ*, XII, p.670.
51 Muǧāhid, *Tafsir*, p. 776.
52 Al-Ḍaḥḥāk, *Tafsir*, II, p. 982.
53 Muqātil, *Tafsir*, IV, p. 802.
54 Al-Farrāʾ, *Maʿānī l-Qurʾān*, III, p. 285
55 ʿAbd al-Razzāq, *Tafsīr*, III, pp. 451–2
56 Ṭabarī, *Ǧāmiʿ*, XII, pp. 670–1.
57 Abū Isḥāq Ibrāhīm b. al-Sarī l-Zaǧǧāǧ, *Iʿrāb al-Qurʾān*, ed. Ibrāhīm al-Ibyārī, Cairo, 1965, III, p. 925.
58 Muqātil, *Tafsīr*, IV, p. 802; Ṭabarī, *Ǧāmiʿ*, XII, p. 670; Ḥāmid Muḥammad b. Muḥammadal-Ġazālī, *Iḥyāʾ ʿulūm al-dīn* (Cairo, 2003), I, p. 344; Abū Ṭālib Muḥammad b. ʿAlī l-Makkī, *Kitāb Qūt al-qulūb*, ed. ʿAbd al-Munʿim al-ḥifnī (Cairo, 1991), I, p. 117.
59 Muḥammad b. Ahmad al-Qurṭubī, *al-Ǧāmiʿ li-Aḥkām al-Qurʾān* (Cairo, 1950), XX, pp. 158–9.
60 Ismāʿīl b. ʿUmar b. Kaṯīr, *Tafsīr al-Qurʾān al-ʿaẓīm*, ed. Sāmī b. Muḥammad al-Salāma (Riyadh, 1997), VIII, p. 465.
61 Ǧalāl al-Dīn al-Maḥallī and Ǧalāl al-Dīn al-Suyūṭī, *Tafsīr al-Ǧalālayn*, ed. Abū Fāris al-Daḥdāḥ (Beirut, 2000), p. 818.
62 Qurṭubī, *al-Ǧāmiʿ* XX, pp. 153–6.
63 Al-Ḥusayn b. Muḥammad al-maʿrūf bi-l-Rāġib al-Iṣfahānī, *al-Mufradāt fī Ġarīb al-Qurʾān*, ed. Muḥammad Aḥmad Ḫalaf Allāh (Cairo, 1970), II, p. 433.
64 See al-Ḥusayn b. Aḥmad b. Ḫālawayh, *Iʿrāb al-Qirāʾāt al-sabʿ wa ʿilaluhā*, ed. ʿAbd al-Rahmān b. Sulaymān al-ʿUṯaymīn (Cairo, 1992), p. 518; Maḥmūd b. ʿUmar al-Zamaḫšarī, *al-Kaššāf ʿan Ḥaqāʾiq ġawāmid al-tanzīl wa-ʿuyūn al-aqwāl fī wuǧūh al-taʾwīl*, ed. ʿĀdil Aḥmad ʿAbd al-Mawǧūd and ʿAlī Muḥammad Muʿawwaḍ (Riyadh, 1998), p. 419
65 Ibn Manẓūr, *Lisān al-ʿArab*, ed. ʿAbd Allāh al-Kabīr, Muḥammad Ḥasab Allāh and Hāšim al-Šāḏili (Cairo, n.d.), XI, pp. 4525–8.
66 Faḫr al-Dīn Muḥammad ibn ʿUmar al-Rāzī, *al-Tafsīr al-Kabīr* (Tehran, 1980), XXXII, p. 66.
67 Ibid.
68 See Youssef Mahmoud, *The Arabic Writing System and the Sociolinguistics of Orthographic Reform*, Ph.D. Dissertation (Georgetown University, 1979), p. 8.
69 Ṣalāḥ al-Dīn al-Munaǧǧid, *Dirāsāt fī Tārīḫ al-ḫaṭṭ al-ʿarabī munḏu bidāyatihī ilā nihāyat al-ʿaṣr al-umawī* (Beirut, 1972), pp. 126–7.
70 Ibn Manẓūr, *Lisān*, pp. 3220–1

71 Ibid., pp. 2388–91.
72 Al-Ḥasan b. ʿAbd Allāh al-ʿAskarī, *Kitāb Aḫbār al-Muṣaḥḥifīn*, ed. Ibrāhīm Ṣāliḥ, 1995, p. 72.
73 Ibid., p. 72. See in particular his reading of Q 7, 56 ; 16, 68 ; 19, 74 ; 28, 8 and 31, 32.
74 Muqātil, *Tafsīr*, p. 801.
75 It seems that there was some uncertainty surrounding the correct form of the word أثرن (*aṯarna*). It was read as أثّرن (*aṯṯarna*) with a šadda. See al-Ḥusayn b. Aḥmad b. Ḫālawayh, *al-Muḫtaṣar fī Šawāḏḏ-Qurʾān min Kitāb al-Badīʿ li-bn Ḫālawayh*, ed. by G. Bergstrasser (Baghdad, 1968), p. 178; ʿAbd Allāh b. al-Ḥusayn al-ʿUkbarī, *Iʿrāb al-Qirāʾāt al-šawwāḏ*, ed. by Muḥammad al-Sayyid Aḥmad ʿAzzūz (Beirut, 1996), p. 735; Muḥammad b. Abī Naṣr al-Kirmānī, *Šawāḏḏ al-Qirāʾāt*, ed. Šamrān al-ʿIǧli (Beirut, 2001), p. 521.
76 Muḥammad Fuʾād ʿAbd al-Bāqī, *al-Muʿǧam al-mufahras li-alfāẓ al-Qurʾān al-karīm* (Cairo, 1958), pp. 714–5.
77 Arthur Jeffery, *The Foreign Vocabulary of the Qurʾān* (Lahore, 1977), p. 2, first published by the Oriental Institute (Baroda, 1938).
78 For example, in his *al-Mufradāt fī Ġarīb al-Qurʾān*, the lexicographer al-Rāġib al-Isbahānī (d. 1108) writes as follows about the well-known Greek borrowing sirāṭ "path" from Greek strata. "Sirāṭ is the road that is thought to be easy. Its origin is from saraṭṭu al-ṭaʿām wa zaradtuhu, i.e., "I swallowed it," Some say *sirāṭ* is a metaphor, that the one walking on it swallows it, or it swallows the one walking on it." (al-sirāṭ: al-ṭarīq al-mustashal. aṣluhu min saraṭṭu al-ṭaʿām wa zaradtuhu-ibtalaʿtuhu. fa-qīla sirāṭ taṣawwuran annahu yabtaliʿuhu sālikuhu aw yabtaliʿu sālikahu). *Al-Mufradāt fī Ġarīb al-Qurʾān*, I, p. 337.
79 Jeffery, *The Foreign Vocabulary*, pp. 19–26. See also Alphonse Mingana, "Syriac Influence on the Style of the Koran," in *What the Koran Really Says*, ed. Ibn Warraq (Amherst, NY, 2002), pp. 171–92, at 173–4, first published in *Bulletin of the John Rylands Library*, 11 (1927), pp. 77–98.
80 Abū Bakr b. Abī Dawūd al-Siǧistānī (ʿAbd Allāh b. Sulaymān al-Ašʿaṯ), *Kitāb al-Maṣāḥif*, ed. Muḥammad b. ʿAbduh, Cairo, 2002, pp. 34–6.
81 Ibid.
82 See Michael Lecker, "Zayd b. Ṯābit, a Jew with Two Sidelocks: Judaism and Literacy in Pre-Islamic Medina (Yatrib)," in *Journal of Near Eastern Studies*, LVI/4 (1997), pp. 259–73.
83 Michael Schub, "The Buddha Comes to China," in *What the Koran Really Says*, pp. 391–393, at 392, first published in *Journal of Arabic Linguistics*, 29 (1995), pp. 77–8.
84 Ibn Manẓūr, *Lisān*, pp. 3541–2.
85 Matityahu Clark, E*tymological Dictionary of Biblical Hebrew: based on the commentaries of Rabbi Samson Raphael Hirsch* (Jerusalem, New York, 1999), p. 224. See also Francis Brown, S. R. Driver and Charles A. Briggs, *The Brown, Driver, Briggs Hebrew and English lexicon* (Peabody, 1999), p. 869.

86 Robert Payne-Smith, *A Compendious Syriac Dictionary founded upon the Thesaurus Syriacus of R. Payne-Smith*, ed. J. Payne-Smith (Winona Lake, 1998), p. 489, first published by Oxford University Press, 1902.
87 Payne-Smith, *Syriac Dictionary*, p. 489.
88 Qurṭubī, *al-Ǧāmiʿ* XX, p. 160.
89 Clark, *Etymological Dictionary*, p. 112; Brown et al., Lexicon, p. 445.
90 Payne-Smith, *Syriac Dictionary*, p. 198.
91 ʿAbd al-Bāqī, *al-Muʿǧam*, p. 750.
92 Ṭabarī, *Tafsīr*, II, pp. 8–10. When quoting his sources, Ṭabarī uses the word *ʿadl*, but in his own narrative he uses the verb *faḍḍala* "to prefer, choose": *yaʿnī ǧalla ṯanāʾuhu/ka-ḏālika ḫaṣaṣnākum fa-faḍḍalnākum ʿalā ġayrikum min ahl al-adyān* (May He be exalted means: Thus we singled you out and preferred you to people of other religions.)
93 Ṭabarī, *Tafsīr*, II, pp. 569–76
94 Ṭabarī, *Tafsīr*, V, pp. 17–22.
95 Ṭabarī, *Tafsīr*, XII, p. 193.
96 Lüling, *Challenge*, p. 11.
97 The following eight readers read *fa-wassatna*: Abū Ḥaywa, Ibn Abī ʿAbla, ʿAlī b. Abī Ṭālib, Zayd b. ʿAlī, Qatāda, Ibn Abī Laylā, ʿAbd Allah b. Masʿūd, and Abū Raǧāʾ. See Aḥmad Muḫtār ʿUmar and ʿAbd al-ʿĀl Sālim Mukarram, *Muʿǧam al-Qirāʾāt al-qurʾāniyya* (Cairo, 1997), V, p. 455.
98 In his interpretation of Q 100, Muqātil, *Tafsīr*, p. 802, comes close to the meaning suggested here. His use of the word *wahaǧ* (glow) is significant in light of the fact that the horses are not likely to produce a glow, but a fire lit by maidens is.
99 The word *awrā* "to light a fire" might need to be explained to the modern Arabic reader. There are many such words in the Qurʾān that would need to be explained as a result of historical development. This is different from cases in which the earliest generations of Qurʾānic scholars had difficulty understanding certain words or their peculiar usage. A case could be made that the lengthy interpretations of certain verses in the Qurʾān generally revolve around familiar words which have a Qurʾānic usage that is at odds with normal usage. In such cases, the work of the interpreters is more of a justification for an invented meaning than an interpretation. It would be much easier for the interpreter to explain that a certain form is an old Arabic form or a borrowing from another language with a certain meaning. In the context of Q 100, the use of *ḍabḥ* and *qadḥ* to describe running horses or even camels, and naqʿ, on which the meaning "dust" is imposed, are harder to explain than stating that the word *qadḥ* is an old Arabic or Syriac word with the meaning of light or fire.
100 Scribal errors in the Qurʾān were acknowledged by the earliest Qurʾānic authorities. When ʿĀʾiša was asked about the wrong case assignment in the phrase *inna hāḏāni la-sāḥirān* in Q 20:63, she replied: "Son, this was an error by the scribe" (*ya-bna aḫī hāḏā kāna ḫaṭaʾ min al-kātib*), al-Farrāʾ, *Maʿānī l-Qurʾān*, I, p. 106. A similar account is given in Siǧistānī, *Kitāb al-Maṣāḥif*, p. 129.
101 Focusing on the seven occurrences of the word furqān in the Qurʾān, Donner argues, against the standard Muslim account, that the Qurʾān commentators were working with a written text that was not clearly supported by an oral

tradition (Fred M. Donner, "Quranic Furqān," *Journal of Semitic Studies*, LII/2 (2007), pp. 279–300

102 Aḥmad b. Mūsā Ibn Muǧāhid (d. 935), *Kitāb al-Sabʿa fī l-qirāʾāt*, ed. by Šawqī (Dayf, Cairo: Dār al-Maʿārif, 1972).

103 An important question which, to my knowledge, has never been addressed is: how could an alphabetic writing system function in which up to five phonemes (bāʾ, tāʾ, ṯāʾ, nūn, yāʾ) are represented by one symbol?

104 A third possibility is that the Prophet himself deliberately manipulated the language of these texts for a certain effect. Sprenger, quoted in Nöldeke (Theodor Nöldeke, "The Koran," in *The Origins of the Koran*, ed. Ibn Warraq (New York, 1998), pp. 36–63, at p. 48, originally published in the Encyclopaedia Britannica, 9th ed., vol. 16 (1891), p. 597 ff.), claims that the Prophet used foreign words and peculiarly constructed expressions, some of which he invented. He elaborates "Muhammad makes a certain parade of these foreign terms ... in this he followed a favorite practice of contemporary poets. It is the tendency of the imperfectly educated mind to delight in out-of-the-way expressions, and on such minds they readily produce a remarkably solemn and mysterious impression" (ibid.).

105 Al-Farrāʾ, *Maʿānī l-Qurʾān*, III, p. 284.

106 Qurṭubī, *al-Ǧāmiʿ*, XX, p. 157.

107 Siǧistānī, *Kitāb al-Maṣāḥif*, p.137.

108 Ibn Manẓūr, *Lisān*, pp. 4150–1.

109 Ǧalāl al-Dīn ʿAbd al-Raḥmān al-Suyūṭī, *al-Itqān fī ʿulūm al-Qurʾān* (Bombay, 1978), p. 219; Abū ʿUbayd al-Qāsim b. Sallām, *Ġarīb al-Ḥadīṯ* (Haydarabad, 1964), IV, pp. 47–8.

110 Muḥammad b. Muḥammad b. al-Ǧazarī, *al-Našr fī l-Qirāʾāt al-ʿašr*, ed. by ʿAlī Muḥammad al-Dabbāʿ (Beirut, n.d.), I, p. 33.

111 Al-Munaǧǧid, *Dirāsāt*, p. 126.

112 Ibid.

113 Ibid., p.127.

114 Ibn Rawandi, "On pre-Islamic Christian strophic poetical texts in the Koran: A critical look at the work of Günter Lüling," in *What the Koran Really Says*, p. 656.

115 Lüling, *Challenge*, p. 3.

116 Ibrāhīm Anīs, *Fī l-Lahǧāt al-ʿarabiyya* (Cairo, 1973), pp. 60–131.

117 Sabatino Moscati (and others), *An Introduction to the Comparative Grammar of the Semitic languages: phonology and morphology*, 1980, pp. 43–4.

Ungrateful or Honorable? A Re-Examination of the Word Kanūd in Qur'ān 100 (al-ʿĀdiyāt)

Munther Younes

Originally published in Arabica *56, no. 2 (2009): 274–85.*

1. Introduction

A brief examination of the *tafsīr* literature shows that the Muslim interpreters of the Qur'ān were by no means certain of their understanding of much of its material. Different and often conflicting interpretations of the same word or phrase and statements like *wa-llāhu aʿlam* "God only knows!" are quite common. Consider, for example, the different views these interpreters held with respect to the reference of the word *al-nāziʿāt* in the opening verse of Q 79, which ranged from *angels*, to *death*, to *stars*, to *bows*, to the *soul*.[1]

This uncertainty was compounded by the defective Arabic script, which allowed for different readings of the same form. So, for example, the word *fa-tabayyanū* "seek a clarification" (Q 4:94), was read by most *Kūfī* readers as *fa-taṯabbatū* "make sure,"[2] since both readings share the same consonantal skeleton. Examples of such multiple readings abound in the *tafsīr* literature.

Not only did the defective script result in multiple readings, but it was also behind instances that may arguably be described as misreadings. An example of such a misreading discussed by Luxenberg is the word *ināh* in Q 33:53, traditionally understood to mean its, i.e., the food's, completion.[3] An examination of its written form إنىه (*alif*, followed by two vertical strokes, typical of the letters *b*, *t*, *ṯ*, *n*, and *y*, followed by *h*), the context in which it is used, and the active participle *nāẓirīn* immediately preceding it, which is typically understood to mean "looking" rather than "waiting," clearly demonstrate that the word should be, as Luxenberg argues, *ināṯahu* "his wives," and not *ināh*.[4]

In a recent study, I argued that the first five verses of Q 100 (*wa-l-ʿādiyāt*) were misread and misunderstood by the Qur'ān interpreters, and proposed an alternative reading, as follows.[5]

Standard Form		**Reconstructed Form**	
wa-l-ʿādiyāti ḍabḥā	والعاديات ضبحا	*wa-l-ġādiyāti ṣubḥā*	والغاديات صبحا
fa-l-mūriyāti qadḥā	فالموريات قدحا	*fa-l-mūriyāti qadḥā*	فالموريات قدحا
fa-l-muġīrāti ṣubḥā	فالمغيرات صبحا	Addition	
fa-ʾaṯarna bihinaqʿā	فأثرن به نقعا	*fa-ʾāṯarna bihinafʿā*	فآثرن به نفعا
fa-wasaṭna bihiǧamʿā	فوسطن به جمعا	*fa-wasaṭna bihiǧamʿā*	فوسطن به جمعا
By the runners snorting,		(And) those going out early in the morning,	
And lighting a spark,		And kindling a flame,	
And raiding in the morning,		----------------------------	
And they stirred up dust in it,		By which they chose to do a good deed,	
And they went with it into the middle of a gathering.		Which they extended to the multitudes.	

My goal in this essay is to examine the second half of Q 100 and propose an alternative reading to the traditional one. In particular, I will focus on a re-reading of the word *kanūd* and a new understanding of the word *ḫayr*.

2. *Kanūd*

This word is a *hapax legomenon* in the Qurʾān. The earliest commentators interpreted it as *kafūr* "a denier or an ungrateful person."[6] As time went on, the interpretations became longer, with new elements being added, such as one who eats alone, beats his slave, and withholds giving;[7] a person who blames his Lord, counts misfortunes, and forgets blessings;[8] land that doesn't grow anything;[9] one who remembers misfortunes, and forgets blessings, disobedient" (in the dialect of Kinda and Ḥadramawt), one who cuts (such as cutting a rope), a woman who denies intimacy to men, one who appreciates the gift but not the giver, a person who is terrified in times of misfortune and is miserly in times of fortune, a malicious and envious person, and a person who is ignorant of his own worth.[10]

The lexicographers' accounts of *kanūd* echoed those of the interpreters in both its meanings and their number. Under the root *k-n-d*, al-Ḫalīl (d. 791) lists only the word *kanūd* with the meaning "ungrateful to a blessing" and in

Q 100:6 "it is interpreted as one who eats alone, beats his slave, and withholds giving."[11]

Ibn Sīda (d. 1066) lists six derivatives of the root *k-n-d* along with *kanūd*:

> 1) *kanada-yaknudu* "to deny a blessing;" 2) *kannād* (and *kanūd*) "ungrateful" or one who eats alone, does not give others, and beats his slave, 3) *kund* (and *kanūd*) (said of a woman) one who denies intimacy to men, when referring to soil, *kanūd* means barren; 4) Kinda is an Arab tribe, 5) *Kannād, Kunāda,* (and *Kanūd*) are proper names.[12]

Ibn Manẓūr (d. 1311), who took much of his material from Ibn Sīda, reproduces the latter's list but adds two verses (*šawāhid*) by two contemporaries of the Prophet, al-Namir b. Tawlab and al-Aʿšā, in which the words *kanūd* and *kannād* are used.[13]

With the exception of the proper name *Kinda*, the meanings associated with *kanūd* by both the interpreters and lexicographers all revolve around the meaning *kafūr*, an ingrate, given by the earliest authorities.

Ibn Sīda adds to his definition of *kanūd*:

> *wa-lā aʿrifu lahu fī l-luġa aṣlan, wa-lā yasūġu ayḍan maʿa qawlihi "li-rabbihi"*[14] (I do not know of a foundation for it in the language, and it is also not appropriate with the word *li-rabbihi* "to his Lord").

There are strong indications that the word *kanūd* does not have an independent existence in Arabic outside of this Qur'ānic verse and may have been introduced into the language for the first time through it. The first piece of evidence in support of this hypothesis is Ibn Sīda's comment quoted above. Second, Arabic appears to be the only Semitic language in which the root *k-n-d* exists; it is not found in Ge'ez, Epigraphic South Arabian, Syriac, Aramaic, Hebrew, Phoenician, Ugaritic, or Akkadian.[15] Third, the context in which the word *kanūd* is found makes the occurrence of a word with such a strongly negative meaning unlikely, as will be shown below.[16]

The possibility that *kanūd* was most likely used in Arabic for the first time in Q 100:6 raises the question of a misreading of the word in its consonantal skeletal form as it would have been found in the earliest copies of the Qur'ān. If it was misread, what is the correct form likely to have been? The answer to this question lies in the context in which the word is found.

3. Positive vs. Negative Interpretations: A Close Look at the Word *Ḫayr*

My proposed reconstruction of Q 100:1–5 replaces the image of horses charging into battle with one in which women are going out to do good deeds to benefit others.[17] One feature of Q 100 that is shocking to the discerning ear is the abrupt transition from *inna l-insān li-rabbihi la-kanūd* in v. 6 "man is an ingrate to his Lord," a strongly negative attribute, to *wa-innahu li-ḥubb al-ḫayr la-šadīd* in v. 8, whose apparent meaning is "his love of good is intense," a clearly positive attribute.

The word *ḫayr*, or a form of it, e.g., *aḫyār*, *ḫayrāt*, occurs 188 times in the Qur'ān.[18] In 185 of these occurrences, the meaning revolves around *good, good deed(s), better, favorite (people), or preferred*, all positive and desirable characteristics. In two cases (Q 2:180 and Q 33:19), it is interpreted as "wealth" or "inheritance." Only in Q 100:8, and in combination with the word *šadīd*, is it given a decidedly negative interpretation as miserly (*baḫīl*).[19]

Ibn Manẓūr lists the following meanings for *ḫayr*:

> 1) to be, become good, (opposite of bad or evil), 2) better, best, 3) to prefer, be preferred, 4) of noble birth, 5) wealth in Q 2:180, 6) to choose, 7) to seek, pray for goodness, 8) to ask for compassion, 9) cucumbers (not of Arabic origin), 10) name of a tribe.[20]

For *šadīd*, he lists the following:

> 1) to be, become, or make hard, 2) strength, 3) to struggle, 4) to be tough, 5) a hard consonant, 6) famine, 7) hard time, 8) miserly (as in Q 100:8: *innahu li-ḥubb al-ḫayr la-šadīd*), 9) to hurry, run, 10) courage, 11) to attack (an enemy), 12) maturity (in people), 13) patience, 14) to reach a high point (day), 15) to tie up.[21]

Neither of Ibn Manẓūr's predecessors, al-Ḫalīl and Ibn Sīda, list "wealth" as a meaning of *ḫayr*,[22] and only Ibn Sīda lists "miserly" as a meaning of *šadīd*.[23]

The three-word combination *ḥubb al-ḫayr la-šadīd* is clearly assigned a meaning in Q 100:8 that is not warranted by the individual meanings of the words as typically used in Arabic. If the typical meanings of the three words *ḥubb*, *ḫayr*, and *šadīd* used in the language as a whole and in the overwhelming majority of instances in the Qur'ān are used in this verse, then it would translate as: *And he (man) is intense/strong in his love of good* or *goodness.*

Such a positive reading of Q 100:8 strongly suggests a positive reading of Q 100:6:

> Man is (positive attribute) to his Lord, AND he greatly loves to do good.

Such a reading would be much less shocking than one in which man is portrayed as an ingrate, and he loves goodness or good deeds.

4. *Kabūd*

The language itself does not provide a positive reading of the word *kanūd*. However, such a reading is possible if, first, one starts with the undotted form of the word, as the first Qur'ān editors did, and applied another dotting scheme and, second, if the investigation is expanded to closely related Semitic languages from which comparative information can help understand older, now obsolete, meanings of Arabic cognates.

Placing a dot under the second letter rather than above it results in the word **kabūd*. This word is not attested in Arabic in this form, but a related one is found in the Qur'ān. Q 90:4 reads "*la-qad ḫalaqnā l-insān fī kabad*," which Bell translates "Verily, We created man in trouble (subject to trouble or by a troublesome process)"[24] and Pickthall translates "We verily have created man in an atmosphere or in affliction."[25]

These two translations partially reflect the Arabic interpretive tradition, as shown, for example, in Ṭabarī,[26] who starts by declaring that the interpreters (*ahl al-ta'wīl*) differed in its interpretation; one group said that "We (Allah) created Adam in hardship and with difficulty and fatigue and for a struggle in this life and in the Afterlife;" another group said, "man was created like no other creature."[27]

Other interpreters cited by Ṭabarī glossed the word as "upright in stature" or "upright on two legs."[28] Still others said that it means "man was created in the heavens."[29]

According to Ibn Manẓūr, the meanings associated with the root *k-n-d* in Arabic are 1) liver, 2) to hit the liver, 3) a disease that affects the liver, 4) the inside of the body, 5) a legume used as a cure for liver pain, 6) middle or midpoint, 7) the name of a mountain, 8) large in the middle, 9) rough piece of ground, 10) curdled milk, 11) (in the Qur'ān) erect and upright, or toiling in this life and the afterlife, or in toil and hardship.[30]

There is evidence that *kabad* should have a positive interpretation, along the lines of *upright*, rather than a negative one such as in *trouble*, *affliction*, or *for suffering*. An examination of Q 95:4 supports this interpretation.

5. Q 95:4: *la-qad ḫalaqnā l-insān fī aḥsan taqwīm*

Q 95:4 reads "*la-qad ḫalaqnā l-insān fī aḥsan taqwīm*," which Ṭabarī interprets as either "in the most perfect creation and in the best image," "as a strong, patient, youth," or "unlike animals, its face is not directed at the ground." The third interpretation is identical to that of *fī kabad* as "upright."[31]

The identity of the phrase *la-qad ḫalaqnā l-insān* in both Q 90 and Q 95 and the identity of one interpretive opinion in the meanings of *fī kabad* in Q 90 and *fī aḥsan taqwīm* in Q 95, strongly point to a positive meaning of *kabad* as "upright," or "unlike animals." In Biblical Hebrew, the word *kaḇōd*, from the root *k-b-d* signifies *abundance, honor*, and *glory*.[32] Adopting this meaning for the word **kabūd* not only serves to resolve the mystery surrounding the word *kanūd*, but also makes the text of Q 100:6–8 more coherent. Does it not make more sense that God, who created the whole world and who created man in the best image, also created man in honor and glory rather than in toil and hardship, affliction, disease of the heart and rottenness of the inside, or in "an atmosphere"?

Replacing *kanūd* by **kabūd*, with the meaning of "honored" or "glorified," and replacing the traditional negative interpretations of *ḫayr* and *šadīd* by the commonly used meanings of these two words results in a more meaningful and more coherent reading of Q 100, as follows.[33]

Standard Form		**Reconstructed Form**	
By the runners snorting,	والعاديات ضبحا	Those going out early in the morning,	والغاديات صبحا
And lighting a spark,	فالموريات قدحا	And kindling a flame,	فالموريات قدحا
And raiding in the morning,	فالمغيرات صبحا	Addition	
And they stirred up dust in it,	فأثرن به نقعا	By which they chose to render a good deed,	فَآثرن به نفعا
And they went with it into the middle of a gathering.	فوسطن به جمعا	Which they extended to the multitudes.	فوسطن به جمعا
Truly man is an ingrate to his Lord,	إنّ ألانسان لربّه لكنود	Truly man honors/ is honored by/ glorifies his Lord,	إنّ ألانسان لربّه لكبود
And truly he (He) is a witness to that;	وإنه على ذلك لشهيد	And he is a witness to that,	وإنه على ذلك لشهيد
And truly he is violent in his love of wealth	وإنّه لحبّ الخير لشديد	And he is intense in his love of good deeds,	وإنه لحب الخير لشديد
Does he not know when what is in the graves has been scattered,	أفلا يعلم إذا بُعثر ما في القبور	Does he not know when what is in the graves has been scattered,	أفلا يعلم إذا بعثر ما في القبور

And what is in the breasts is made known	وحُصّل ما فى الصدور	And what is in the breasts is made known	وحصّل ما فى الصدور
Truly on that day their Lord will be perfectly informed of them.	إنّ ربّهم بهم يومئذ لخبير	That on that day their Lord will be perfectly informed of them?	أنّ ربّهم بهم يومئذ لخبير؟

6. Foreign Borrowings or Older Arabic Forms?

It is well-known that the Qur'ān contains many borrowings from foreign languages, particularly from the closely related languages of Syriac and Hebrew.[34] Whether **kabūd* was originally an Arabic word which was not known to the Qur'ān commentators or whether it was directly borrowed from Hebrew is not relevant for the purposes of this essay. What is relevant is that the word was misunderstood and misinterpreted by the Qur'ān exegetes.

7. The Qur'ān as Written Text, Not Oral Recitation

If my reconstruction of Q100 is correct, then it raises a number of fundamental questions about the history of the Qur'ān. One of these questions is the implication that parts of it were misread, which in turn implies the absence of an oral tradition to eliminate the possibility of a misreading. The traditional Muslim account of the early history of the Qur'ān asserts that it started as an oral recitation, and that it was committed to writing at a later stage. The Prophet received the revelations, recited them to his scribes who memorized them and then wrote them down. The authoritative version, which was finalized during 'Uṯmān's rule, some twenty years after the Prophet's death, came into existence in this environment, where the written text was directly supported by an oral tradition. The implication is clear: no written text predated the oral recitation. However, evidence exists that points to a text in which parts were misread, which in turn points to the absence of an oral tradition that would have provided an accurate reading. Arguing for a misreading of two Syriac words [*pūrqānā* and *pūqdānā*] on which the Qur'ānic word *furqān* is based, Donner writes:

> The implication [of the derivation of the word *furqān* from two Syriac sources] is that some passages of the Qur'ān text must have been transmitted, at some point, only in written form without the benefit of a secure tradition of oral recitation, otherwise, the misreading of Syriac *pūqdānā* as *furqān* could not have occurred.[35]

A similar conclusion is reached by Luxenberg about the early history of the Qur'ān, who states:

> The findings of this first study, however, force one to conclude that the previous thesis of a reliable oral transmission of the text of the Koran stemmed from a mere legend. According to the examples presented here, if the Arab philologists and commentators have misread genuinely Arabic expressions, the only possible conclusion regarding the oral transmission of the Koran is obvious. If such a tradition existed at all, it must be assumed that it was interrupted fairly early on.[36]

The literature on the variant readings of the Qur'ān offers additional evidence in support of the claim that at least parts of the Qur'ān were read in the absence of an oral recitation supporting them. Hundreds of examples are given in Ibn Muǧāhid in which variants differed in their dotting schemes. One example is *fa-tabayyanū* (Q 4:94), which was read as *fa-taṯabbatū* by most Kūfī readers, as was pointed out above. As long as words shared the same consonantal skeleton, alternative readings were accepted as canonical, as in *yaʿmalūn* "they do"/*taʿmalūn* "you, m.pl., do" (Q 2:74, 85:144),[37] *kabīr* "big"/*kaṯīr* "plentiful" (Q 2:219),[38] and *nanšuruhā* "we spread them" / *nunšizuhā* "we bring them to life" (Q 2:259).[39] A robust and continuous tradition of oral recitation would have eliminated such variation.

Finally, in his *Kitāb al-Maṣāḥif* on the history of the collection of the Qur'ān, the tenth century Muslim scholar al-Siǧistānī writes:

> ʿAbd Allāh and ʿĪsā b. ʿUṯmān b. ʿĪsā, said, my uncle Yaḥyā b. ʿĪsā from al-Aʿmaš from Ṯābit b. ʿUbayd, from Zayd b. Ṯābit, who said, "the Prophet (peace be upon him) said, books come to me that I do not want every one to read. Can you learn Hebrew writing? Or he said: Syriac." I said: "Yes." So I learned it in 17 days.[40]

This *ḥadīṯ* is described as authentic (*saḥīḥ*).[41] If these reports are reliable, and if we consider the fact that Zayd b. Ṯābit was put in charge of producing the authoritative copy of the Qur'ān by ʿUṯmān, then it is clear that some parts of the Qur'ān were read before they were recited.

8. Conclusion

A major problem with Q 100 is lack of theme unity. The first five verses introduce a theme of horses charging into battle (or camels running during the pilgrimage)[42] and the last six speak of man's ingratitude to his Lord, the All-knowing, two clearly unrelated themes. The reconstruction presented in this essay provides a more logical link between the two parts of the *sūra*: the first speaking of women going out to do good deeds and benefit the world (in the service of religion) and the second confirming that man is respectful of, glorifies, (or is honored by) his Lord. Both sub-themes can be related as two parts of the same hymn. Such a reconstruction is in line with Lüling's conclusion that about one-third of the Qur'ānic text is based on ancient Christian Arabic hymns that were reworked by the Arab grammarians and Qur'ān interpreters, after the Prophet's death, and given a new meaning.[43]

Notes

1 Abū Ǧaʿfar Muḥammad b. Ǧarīr al-Ṭabarī, *Ǧāmiʿ al-Bayān fī taʾwīl al-Qurʾān*, Beirut, 2005, XI, pp.420-1.

2 Ṭabarī, IV, p.227.

3 *Yā ayyuhā llaḏīna āmanū lā tadḫulū buyūt al-nabī illā an yuʾḏana lakum ilā ṭaʿām ġayr nāẓrīn ināh, wa-lākin iḏā duʿītum fa-dḫulū, fa-iḏā ṭaʿimtum, fa-ntaširū wa-lā mustaʾnisīn li-ḥadīṯ inna ḏālikum yuʾḏī al-nabī fa-yastaḥī minkum, wa-llāh lā yastaḥī min al-ḥaqq. Wa-iḏā saʾaltumūhunna matāʿan fa-sʾalūhunna min warāʾ ḥiǧāb, ḏālikum aṭhar li-qulūbikum wa-qulūbihinna, wa-mā kāna lakum an tuʾḏū rasūl Allāh wa-lā an tankiḥū azwāǧahu min baʿdihi abadan, inna ḏālikum kāna ʿinda llāh ʿaẓīmā.*

O Ye who believe! Enter not the dwellings of the Prophet for a meal without waiting for the proper time, unless permission be granted you. But if ye are invited, enter, and, when your meal is ended, then disperse. Linger not for conversation. Lo! that would cause annoyance to the Prophet, and he would be shy of (asking) you (to go); but Allah is not shy of the truth. And when ye ask of them (the wives of the Prophet) anything, ask it of them from behind a curtain. That is purer for your hearts and for their hearts. And it is not for you to cause annoyance to the messenger of Allah, nor that ye should ever marry his wives after him. Lo! that in Allah's sight would be an enormity. (Marmaduke Pickthall, *The Glorious Koran: a Bi-lingual Edition with English Translation, Introduction, and Notes* (Albany, 1976), pp. 557–8).

4 Ch. Luxenberg, *The Syro-Aramaic Reading of the Koran* (Berlin, 2007), p. 246. Richard Bell (in *The Qurʾān*, translated, with a critical re-arrangement of the Sūrahs, Edinburgh, 1939, I, p. 417) writes the following about the word *ināhu*: "As it stands in the text, this is usually taken as referring to the meal. But the grammatical construction of the phrase is difficult as is also that of the phrase which follows."

5 M. Younes, "Charging Steeds or Maidens Doing Good Deeds? A Reinterpretation of Qur'ān 100 (al-ʿĀdiyāt)," *Arabica*, 55/3 (2008); in the present volume pp. 743–767.

6 Muǧāhid, Abū l-Haǧǧāǧ b. Ǧabr al-Qurašī, *Tafsīr Muǧāhid*, ed. Abū Muammad al-Asyūṭī (Beirut, 2005), p. 350; al-Daḥḥāk b. Muzāḥim, *Tafsīr al-Ḍaḥḥāk*, ed. Muḥammad Šukrī Aḥmad al-Zawītī (Cairo, 1999), p. 983; Muqātil b. Sulaymān, *Tafsīr Muqātil b. Sulaymān*, ed. ʿAbd Allāh Šiḥāta (Cairo, 1987), p. 803.

7 Muqātil, *Tafsīr*, p. 803

8 Abū Zakariyyā Yaḥyā b. Ziyād al-Farrāʾ, *Maʿānī l-Qurʾān*, ed. ʿAbd al-Fattāḥ Šalabi, Cairo, 2002, II, p. 283.

9 Abū ʿUbayda Maʿmar b. al-Muṯannā l-Taymī, *Maǧāz al-Qurʾān*, ed. Muḥammad Fuʾād Sazgīn (Cairo, 1962), I, p. 307.

10 Muḥammad b. Aḥmad al-Qurṭubī, *al-Ǧāmiʿ li-aḥkām al-Qurʾān* (Cairo, 1950), XX, pp. 158–159.

11 Al-Ḫalīl b. Aḥmad al-Farāhīdī, *Kitāb al-ʿAyn*, ed. Dāwūd Sallūm, Dāwūd al-ʿAnbakī, and Inʿām Sallūm (Beirut, 2004), p. 730.

12 ʿAlī b.Ismāʿīl b. Sīda, *al-Muḥkam wa-l-muḥīṭ al-aʿẓam* (12 parts in 2 volumes), ed. ʿAbd al-Fattāḥ al-Sayyid Salīm and Fayṣal al-Ḥafyān (Cairo, 2003), I (Part 6), p. 471.

13 Muḥammad b. Mukarram b. Manẓūr, *Lisān al-ʿArab*, ed. ʿAbd Allāh al-Kabīr, Muḥammad Ḥasab Allāh, and Hāšim al-Šāḏilī, Cairo, n.d., V, p. 3936.

14 Ibn Sīda, *al-Muḥkam wa-l-muḥiṭ al-aʿẓam*, I (Part 6), p. 471.

15 Martin A. Zammit, *A Comparative Lexical Study of Qurʾānic Arabic* (Leiden-Boston: Brill, 2002), pp. 351–352.

16 The evidence from pre-Islamic and early Islamic Arabic poetry cannot be taken as conclusive one way or the other. On the one hand, outside of the tribe name Kinda, the root *k-n-d* is not found in the poetry of six major pre-Islamic poets (Imruʾ al-Qays, Zuhayr b. Abī Sulmā, Ṭarafa b. al-ʿAbd, ʿAlqama b. ʿAbada l-Faḥl, ʿAntara b. Šaddād, and al-Nābiġa l-Ḏubyānī) and some of the poetry of four minor ones (Badr b. Hiḏār al-Māzinī, al-Tawʾam al-Yaškurī, al-Rabīʿ b. Abī l-Huqayq, and Kaʿb b. Zuhayr), Albert Arazi and Salman Masalha, *al-ʿIqd al-ṯamin fī dawāwīn al-šuʿarāʾ al-sitta l-ǧāhiliyyīn* (Jerusalem, 1999), p. 961. On the other, the word *kanūd* is said to exist in the poetry of at least two poets, who were contemporaries of the Prophet, al-Namr b. Tawlab and al-Aʿšā (Ibn Manẓūr, *Lisān*, V, p. 3936). Finally, serious doubt has been cast on the authenticity of this poetry. For example, the well-known Egyptian scholar and literary figure, Ṭahā Ḥusayn, who was quoted above, argues in his book *Fī l-Šiʿr al-ǧāhilī* (On pre-Islamic Poetry) that most of what is described as pre-Islamic poetry is not pre-Islamic at all but was created in the second and third hiǧra centuries and falsely attributed to the pre-Islamic era. He writes:

> Another type of investigation which I believe is more indicative and more convincing than previous investigations, which is the technical and linguistic. This investigation will lead us to [the conclusion] that this poetry which is attributed to Imruʾ al-Qays or to al-Aʿšā or to the other pre-Islamic poets cannot from the linguistic and technical points of view possibly be their poetry or that it was recited and had spread before the appearance of the Qurʾān. This investigation will lead us to an unexpected conclusion, that this poetry should not be used as evidence for the interpretation of the Qurʾān and ḥadiṯ, but that the Qurʾān and ḥadiṯ should be taken to interpret this poetry ... This poetry does not prove or show anything and should not be used as it has been in [interpreting] the Qurʾān and ḥadiṯ. It was invented so that the scholars will use it as evidence in proving what they wanted to prove (Ṭāhā Ḥusayn, *Fī l-Šiʿr al-ǧāhilī*, ed. ʿAbd al-Munʿim Tulayma (Cairo, 1995), p. 20).

17 Younes, "Charging Steeds."

18 Muḥammad Fuʾād ʿAbd al-Bāqī, *al-Muʿǧam al-mufahras li-alfāẓ al-Qurʾān al-Karīm* (Cairo, 1958), p. 249–51.

19 Al-Farrāʾ, *Maʿānī*, II, p. 285; Abū ʿUbayda, *Maǧāz*, I, p. 307; Ṭabarī, *Ǧāmiʿ*, XI, p. 673.

20 Ibn Manẓūr, *Lisān*, I, p. 1298–1300.

21 Ibn Manẓūr, *Lisān*, IV, p. 2214–2216; *sadīd* "correct, right" offers a strong alternative to *šadīd*. Note its occurrence in the phrase: *allāhumma saddidnā li-l-ḫayr, ay waffiqnā lahu* "O, Allah, put us on the right path of goodness," Ibn Manẓūr, *Lisān*, II, p. 1970.

22 Al-Ḫalīl, *Kitāb al-ʿAyn*, p. 232; Ibn Sīda, *al-Muḥkam*, V, p. 155–6.

23 Al-Ḫalīl, *Kitāb al-ʿAyn*, p. 402; Ibn Sīda, *al-Muḥkam*, VI, p. 419.

24 Bell, *Qurʾān*, I, p. 657.

25 Pickthall, *Glorious Koran*, p. 807.

26 Ṭabarī, *Ǧāmiʿ*, XI, p. 587–9.

27 ʿAbd al-Razzāq, *Tafsīr*, p. 428.

28 Al-Farrāʾ, *Maʿānī* , II, p. 264.

29 Ṭabarī, *Ǧāmiʿ*, XI, p. 589.

30 Ibn Manẓūr, *Lisān*, p. 3806–7.

31 Ṭabarī, *Ǧāmiʿ*, XI, p. 635–7.

32 F Brown, S.R. Driver and Ch. A. Briggs, *The Brown, Driver, Briggs Hebrew and English Lexicon* (Peabody, Mass.: Hendrickson, 1999), p. 458.

33 An even more coherent reading can be accomplished if the traditional reading of inna "verily" of the last verse is replaced by the variant reading anna "that" attributed to Ibn Masʿūd, Abū l-Sammāl and al-Haǧǧāǧ, ʿUmar, Aḥmad Muḫtār and ʿAbd al-ʿĀl Sālim Mukarram, *Muʿǧam al-Qirāʾāt al-qurʾāniyya* (Cairo, 1997), V, p. 457.

34 See, for example A. Jeffery, *The Foreign Vocabulary of the Qurʾān* (Lahore, al-Biruni, 1977), p. 2 and Alphonse Mingana, "Syriac Influence on the Style of the Koran," in Ibn Warraq, ed., *What the Koran Really Says* (New York, 2002), p. 171–192 (First published in Bulletin of the John Rylands, XI (1927), pp. 77–98, at p. 173–174).

35 F. Donner, "Qurʾānic Furqān," *Journal of Semitic Studies*, LI/2 (2007), pp. 279–300 at p. 279.

36 Luxenberg, *The Syro-Aramaic Reading*, p. 332.

37 Aḥmad b. Mūsā b. Muǧāhid, *Kitāb al-Sabʿa fī l-qirāʾāt*, ed. Šawqī Ḍayf (Cairo, 1972), p. 160.

38 Ibid., p. 182.

39 Ibid., p. 189.

40 Abū Bakr b. Abī Dawūd al-Siǧistānī (ʿAbd Allāh b. Sulaymān al-Ašʿaṯ), *Kitāb al-Maṣāḥif*, ed. Muḥammad b. ʿAbduh (Cairo, 2002), p. 34–6.

41 Ibid., p. 34.

42 Younes, "Charging Steeds."

43 G. Lüling, *A challenge to Islam for reformation: the rediscovery and reliable reconstruction of a comprehensive pre-Islamic Christian hymnal hidden in the Koran under earliest Islamic reinterpretations* (Delhi, 2003), translated from the 2nd German edition of 1993 of the author's book *Über den Ur-Koran*, 1st edition 1974).

Makka, Bakka, and the the Problem of Linguistic Evidence

Ibn Warraq and Markus Gross*

1. Introductory Remarks

Not only Muslims, but Westerners alike will claim to know that Islam originated in Mecca, the holy city of Islam. But is this really so? In the Koran, there is but one attestation of the alleged name *Makka* and one of an alleged variant: *Bakka*. On closer inspection, however, it turns out that in neither of the two passages does the text tell us something about a city, let alone a holy one.

That the holy city of Mecca and home to the prophet should have been mentioned only twice in the Koran, and even then in two variants in unspecific sentences, is of course quite strange, especially if we consider the redundant character of this text: The story of Noah is told in numerous Surahs, albeit rather in the form of allusions than as a real story, but the holy city seems to be totally unimportant to the author(s) of Koranic texts.

Thus it comes as no surprise that several scholars have dedicated publications to these place names.

2. *Makka* in the Koran

The form *Makka* appears only once in the Koran: 48:24–25

وَهُوَ الَّذِي كَفَّ أَيْدِيَهُمْ عَنكُمْ وَأَيْدِيَكُمْ عَنْهُم بِبَطْنِ مَكَّةَ مِن بَعْدِ أَنْ
أَظْفَرَكُمْ عَلَيْهِمْ ۚ وَكَانَ اللَّهُ بِمَا تَعْمَلُونَ بَصِيرًا

wa-huwa llaḏī kaffa ʾaydiyahum ʿankum wa-ʾaydiyakum ʿanhum bi-baṭni makkata min baʿdi ʾan ʾaẓfarakum ʿalayhim wa-kāna llahu bi-mā taʿmalūna baṣīra[n]

Pickthall[1] *translates this as:* "And it is He Who has restrained their hands from you and your hands from them in the midst of Makka, after that He gave you the victory over them. And Allah sees well all that ye do."

Paret: "Und er ist es, der im Talgrund von (in the valley of) Mekka ihre Hand von euch und eure Hand von ihnen zurückgehalten hat (so dass es nicht zum Kampf kam), nachdem er euch (früher?) über sie hatte siegen lassen. Gott durchschaut wohl, was ihr tut."

As we can see, the expression *bi-baṭni makkata* ("in the 'belly' of *makka*") is not unproblematic for our translators. What in fact do we learn about this *makka*? Hands are restrained from someone and some kind of victory happened. As battles normally did not take place in towns, but rather on open fields in those days, this verse does not really match as the designation of a town. In fact, anything could be meant; it is not even clear that a place is talked about.

3. *Bakka* in the Koran

This form also appears only once, in Surah 3:96:

إِنَّ أَوَّلَ بَيْتٍ وُضِعَ لِلنَّاسِ لَلَّذِي بِبَكَّةَ مُبَارَكًا وَهُدًى لِّلْعَالَمِينَ

inna ʾawwala baytin wuḍiʿa li-n-nāsi la-llaḏī bi-bakkata mubārakan wa-hudan li-l-ʿālamīn[a]

Pickthall: "The first House (of worship) appointed for men[2] was that at Bakka: Full of blessing and of guidance for all kinds of beings."

Paret: "Das erste (Gottes) haus, das den Menschen aufgestellt worden ist, ist dasjenige in Bakka (d.h. Mekka), (aufgestellt) zum Segen und zur Rechtleitung für die Menschen in aller Welt."

Apart from the fact that *Bakka* is not the same as *Makka*, as little as a "bill" is the same as a "mill," this verse is not clearly about a town either. The preposition used before the alleged place name is *bi* and not *fī* as we would expect.

Of course one might object that in Aramaic and Hebrew the particle *b-* is actually used before place names, but then again this argument would only be acceptable if a strong Syro-Aramaic influence on the language of the Koran is assumed. As we will see, the undotted consonant skeleton (Arabic: *rasm*) would allow totally different readings, for example, *yabkā-hu*.

The reason why the preceding verse was interpreted as referring to Mecca is the following verse (3:97):

فِيهِ آيَاتٌ بَيِّنَاتٌ مَّقَامُ إِبْرَاهِيمَ ۖ وَمَن دَخَلَهُ كَانَ آمِنًا ۗ وَلِلَّهِ عَلَى النَّاسِ حِجُّ الْبَيْتِ مَنِ اسْتَطَاعَ إِلَيْهِ سَبِيلًا ۚ وَمَن كَفَرَ فَإِنَّ اللَّهَ غَنِيٌّ عَنِ الْعَالَمِينَ

fīhi ʾāyātun bayyinātun maqāmu ʾibrāhīma wa-man daḫalahū kāna ʾāminan wa-li-llāhi ʿalā n-nāsi hiǧǧu l-bayti mani staṭāʿa ʾilayhi sabīlan wa-man kafara fa-ʾinna llāha ġaniyyun ʿani l-ʿālamīn[a]

Pickthall: "In it are Signs Manifest; (for example), the Station of Abraham; whoever enters it attains security; Pilgrimage thereto is a duty men owe to Allah, – those who can afford the journey; but if any deny faith, Allah stands not in need of any of His creatures."

Paret: "In ihm liegen klare Zeichen vor. (Es ist) der (heilige) Platz Abrahams. Wer ihn betritt, ist in Sicherheit. Und die Menschen sind Gott gegenüber verpflichtet, die Wallfahrt nach dem Haus zu machen – soweit sie dazu eine Möglichkeit finden. Wer jedoch ungläubig ist (ist es zu seinem eigenen Schaden). Gott ist auf niemand in der Welt angewiesen."

From the perspective of modern Islam, this seems to be an unambiguous reference to Mecca. Again, on closer inspection, nothing is clear: The form *maqāmu 'ibrāhīma* – "the Station of Abraham" does not fit the sentence very well and could have been inserted later, as can be seen in Pickthall's insertion in brackets: "for example."

The verbal form *kāna* is a bit surprising, too. It is true that the perfect tense is often used in rules; still, the imperfect *yakūnu* would seem more appropriate here.

The alleged word designating the "pilgrimage" is not *ḥaǧǧ*, as in standard Arabic, but *ḥiǧǧ*. Of course the rasm (undotted consonant skeleton) is the same, but why would generations of reciters have retained the vowel *i* in this word if it were clear that it refers to the pilgrimage. Moreover, in Hebrew, the corresponding word *ḥāg* means "feast, holiday," not "pilgrimage."

And finally, we all know that in order to perform the pilgrimage to Mecca, one has to be able to afford it, the basis for this rule being this very verse. But the wording is—to say the least—odd: *istaṭāʿa* means "to be able to," not "to afford," as Pickthall rendered it, and *sabīl* does not mean "journey" or "pilgrimage," but "way, path." The word appears frequently in the Koran as *sabīl Allāh* or "the path of Allāh," thus designating a "way of life" but not a journey.

To sum up, it does not seem too farfetched to assume at least the possibility that this traditional understanding of the verse is secondary.

4. *Masǧidu l-ḥarām* – "the Sacred Mosque"

Another expression often to be found in the Koran and interpreted as meaning "Mecca" is *Masǧidu l-ḥarām,* for example in Surah 48:25:

هُمُ الَّذِينَ كَفَرُوا وَصَدُّوكُمْ عَنِ الْمَسْجِدِ الْحَرَامِ وَالْهَدْيَ مَعْكُوفًا أَن
يَبْلُغَ مَحِلَّهُ ۚ وَلَوْلَا رِجَالٌ مُّؤْمِنُونَ وَنِسَاءٌ مُّؤْمِنَاتٌ لَّمْ تَعْلَمُوهُمْ أَن تَطَئُوهُمْ
فَتُصِيبَكُم مِّنْهُم مَّعَرَّةٌ بِغَيْرِ عِلْمٍ ۖ لِّيُدْخِلَ اللَّهُ فِي رَحْمَتِهِ مَن يَشَاءُ ۚ لَوْ
تَزَيَّلُوا لَعَذَّبْنَا الَّذِينَ كَفَرُوا مِنْهُمْ عَذَابًا أَلِيمًا

*humu llaḏīna kafarū wa-ṣaddūkum ʿani l-masǧidi l-ḥarāmi wa-l-hadya maʿkūfan ʾan yabluġa maḥillahū wa-law-lā riǧālun muʾminūna wa-nisāʾun muʾminātun lam taʿlamūhum ʾan taṭʾūhum fa-tuṣībakum minhum maʿarratun bi-ġayri ʿilmin li-yudḫila llāhu fī raḥmatihī man yašāʾu law tazayyalū la-ʾaḏḏabnā llaḏīna kafarū minhum ʿaḏāban ʾalīma*ⁿ

Pickthall: "These it was who disbelieved and debarred you from the Inviolable Place of Worship, and debarred the offering from reaching its goal. And if it had not been for believing men and believing women, whom ye know not lest ye should tread them under foot and thus incur guilt for them unknowingly; that Allah might bring into His mercy whom He will. If (the believers and the disbelievers) had been clearly separated We verily had punished those of them who disbelieved with painful punishment."

Paret: "Sie sind es, die ungläubig sind (oder: nicht geglaubt haben) und euch von der heiligen Kultstätte abgehalten haben, (euch) und die Opfertiere, so dass sie verhindert waren, ihre Schlachtstätte zu erreichen. Und wenn ihr nicht (im Falle einer kriegerischen Auseinandersetzung) gläubige Männer und Frauen, die es (in Mekka) gab, von denen ihr aber nichts wußtet, zu Schaden gebracht (w. niedergetreten) hättet, so daß ihr euch unwissentlich an ihnen versündigt hättet (w. so daß euch von ihnen her Schuld(?) getroffen hätte) – Gott läßt eben in seine Barmherzigkeit eingehen, wen er will (und hat so auch jene Männer und Frauen in Mekka für den wahren Glauben vorgesehen) – (wenn sie nicht gewesen wären, hätte das Unternehmen anders geendet). Wenn sie sich (von den übrigen, heidnisch gebliebenen Mekkanern vorher) getrennt hätten (und so nicht in Mitleidenschaft gezogen worden wären), hätten wir den Ungläubigen unter ihnen (d.h. unter den Mekkanern) eine schmerzhafte Strafe zukommen lassen."

Again, the fact that Pickthall translated *Masǧidu l-ḥarām* as "inviolable place of worship" shows a certain uncertainty as to what it means: certainly not a town, but maybe the Kaʿba? If we did not know anything about modern Islam and only had this text at our disposition, we would never arrive at this conclusion!

5. The Traditional Explanation

In the *Encyclopedia of Islam*[3] we find the following explanation:

> Pre-Islamic Mecca—Mecca had been a sacred site from very ancient times. It was apparently known to Ptolemy as Macoraba. The Ḳurʾān has the name Makka in XLVIII, 24, and the alternative name Bakka in III, 96/90. It also (II, 125–7/119–21) speaks of the building of the Kaʿba by Abraham and Ishmael, but this is generally not accepted by occidental scholars, since it cannot be connected with what is otherwise known of Abraham.

What then follows is an uncritical renarration of the Traditional Report. So here the form *Bakka* is considered to be a phonetic variant of *Makka*.

A different explanation can be found in Ibn Isḥāq's biography of the prophet[4]:

> Now in the time of paganism Mecca did not tolerate injustice and wrong within its borders and if anyone did wrong therein it expelled him; therefore it was called "the Scorcher" [note: al-Nāssa], and any king who came to profane its sanctity died on the spot. It is said that it was called Bakka because it used to break [note: From the verb *bakka*, he broke] the necks of tyrants when they introduced innovations therein.

This explanation is totally different. *Bakka* is explained as a nominal form of a root *b-k-k*. Apart from the semantic gymnastics performed to make this popular etymology work, the form is also very unlikely on morphological grounds.

Both explanations apparently have survived until today, as the article "Bakkah" in *Wikipedia*[5] shows. It should be mentioned that the article starts with an exclamation mark and the warning "This article has been nominated to be checked for its neutrality. (October 2012)" followed by "The neutrality of this article is disputed. (October 2012)." We are informed as follows:

> One meaning ascribed to it [Bakkah] is "narrow," seen as descriptive of the area in which the valley of the holy places and the city of Mecca are located, pressed in upon as they are by mountains.[3] Widely believed to be a synonym for Mecca, it is said to be more specifically the early name for the valley located therein, while Muslim scholars generally use it to refer to the sacred area of the city that immediately surrounds and includes the Kaaba.

So here a geographical distinction is made between the town and and area within it. Further down, we read:

> The form Bakkah is used for the name Mecca in the Quran in 3:96, while the form Mecca is used in 48:24.[8][11] In South Arabic, the language in use in the southern portion of the Arabian Peninsula at the time of Muhammad, the *b* and *m* were interchangeable.[11][6]

Interestingly, the verse in the Psalms discussed below in the present article is also mentioned at the end of the main text, albeit with a warning:

> This section possibly contains previously unpublished synthesis of published material that conveys ideas not attributable to the original sources. Relevant discussion may be found on the *talk page*. (October 2012)

As we will see, the real source of this discovery is in fact not on the website. The discussion on the "talk page" is vivid, as can be inferred from the following statement:

> This article has been repeatedly vandalized with the net effect of censoring the Psalms 84 passage that it references, to exclude the actual location of the temple that the pilgrimage of the Psalms passage references, as being "IN ZION."

As we can see, the topic is indeed both "sensitive" and "disputed." But as will become clear, there are more explanations for both *Makka* and *Bakka*.

6. Alternative Explanations

6.1. A. Regnier

In his article "Some Literary Enigmas of Koranic Inspiration,"[7] published in 1939, Regnier explains a number of enigmatic passages of the Koran, among them the verse with the form *bakka*. For the Koranic verse[8]

> *"inna ʾawwala baytin wuḍiʿa li-n-nāsi la-llaḏī bi-bakkata mubārakan wa-hudan li-l-ʿālamīn*[a]
> The first House (of worship) appointed for men was that at Bakka: Full of blessing and of guidance for all kinds of beings,

he found a parallel in the Psalms (Ps. 84:6–7). The Hebrew, Greek, English, and German wordings are as follows.

> עֹבְרֵי ׀ בְּעֵמֶק הַבָּכָא מַעְיָן יְשִׁיתוּהוּ גַּם־בְּרָכוֹת יַעְטֶה מוֹרֶה׃
> *ʿōḇirê bi-ʿemeq ha-bbāḵāʾ maʿyān yišîṯû-hû gam-birāḵôt yaʿiṭeh môreh. . . .*
> *Septuagint:* ἐν τῇ κοιλάδι τοῦ κλαυθμῶνος εἰς τόπον ὃν ἔθετο καὶ γὰρ εὐλογίας δώσει ὁ νομοθετῶν. . . .
> Passing through the valley of Baca they make it a spring; The early rain also covers it with blessings. . . .
> die durch das Jammertal (the valley of wailing) gehen und machen daselbst Brunnen; und die Lehrer werden mit viel Segen geschmückt. . . .

Here the Syro-Aramaic version of the Pešiṭṭa might be added, which uses a similar expression[9]:

ʿbrw	b-ʿwmqʾ	d-bktʾ	w-ʿbdw-hy	byt	mʿmrw
they pass	*in depth*	*of BKTʾ*	*and make it*	*house*	*of dwellers (???)*

The words corresponding to the Hebrew *bi-ʿemeq ha-bbāḵāʾ* are the etymologically corresponding ones: *bə-ʿumqā də-ḇaḵṭā*. Whether this term means a "valley of Baca"—thus a place name—or a "valley of weeping" (as in the

Greek "ἐν τῇ <u>*κοιλάδι*</u> τοῦ κλαυθμῶνος") is obviously not clear to the translators of this passage.

In the relevant verses in both the Koran and the Psalms we are dealing with a "blessed" place of worship, not a town:

> *Koran:* The first House (of worship) appointed for men was that at Bakka: Full of <u>blessing</u> and of guidance for all kinds of beings.
>
> *Bible:* Passing through the valley of Baca they make it a spring; The early rain also covers it with <u>blessings</u>.

The corresponding words in Hebrew and Arabic are both from the same root: *b-r-k*:

Koran/Arabic: mubārakan
Bible/Hebrew: birāḵôṯ

As in Hebrew and Arabic, the corresponding Syro-Aramaic root *b-k-ʾ* also means "to cry, to weep":

bḵā – weep
bēt bāḵē – place of those that weep, lamentation, mourning

So it seems to be a well-justified assumption to translate "Bakka" and the "valley of Baca" not as a place name, but as the "valley of tears" in both cases. The Koranic passage would thus be a clear reminiscence of the psalm.

Regnier also mentions the traditional Muslim view that equates Makka/Mecca and Bakka:

> The commentary of the Jalālayn, which represents current opinion, gives as the motive for this alteration the symbolic attachment to the root **bakka*, to crush, "Because Mecca crushes (or breaks) the neck of the proud"! Some philologists believe *Bakka* is a dialect pronunciation that confuses the two labials *b* and *m*. So be it, but it is strange that the other place where Mecca is mentioned in the Koran (sura XLVIII, 24), it takes the form Makka (in a passage concerning the conquest of the city).

Regnier adds another parallel of the Koranic passage and the psalm:

> It so happens that our *Bakka*, which one finds a single time in the Koran, in a context relating to the site of worship and pilgrimage, corresponds to a Biblical word *Baca*, which one finds a single time in the Bible, in Psalms 84:6–7, precisely in a song of pilgrimage! If we look more closely, we find this: "Happy are those whose strength is in you, in whose heart are the highways to Zion. As they go through the valley of Baca, they make it a place of springs; the early rain also covers it with pools." Thus the pilgrims arrive in the courts of Zion.

6.2. Christoph Luxenberg

As we have seen, Regnier explains the form *bakka* but has no alternative rendering for the second form *makka*. Christoph Luxenberg, on the contrary, has come up with no less than two new possible explanations for *bakka* and two for *makka*.

In the first edition of his book, he opined that the word *makka* might be the Aramaic root meaning "valley; low."

> *maḵ, māk, mḵeḵ* – "lie down flat, prostrate oneself; be laid low, be spread or strewn flat"; e.g. in the combination: *rāmēh w-māḵē* – "high and low" (followed by: "kings and paupers").[10]

Although the interpretation of *bi-baṭni makka* as "in the middle of the valley" would certainly make sense in the Koranic verse, he later dismissed this view, instead favoring another explanation[11]: He begins his reasoning with an observation made by Edouard-Marie Gallez.[12] In the Koranic verse 48:24–25 the topic is God's interference in a hand-to-hand fight between two groups:

> And it is He Who has restrained their hands from you and your hands from them in the midst of Makka, after that He gave you the victory over them. And Allah sees well all that ye do.

The verb used in *wa-huwa llaḏī kaffa ʾaydiyahum* "He Who has restrained their hands" is *kaffa*, according to Luxenberg a secondary derivation of *ʾakafa* – "to turn away." As we are dealing with a brawl in this passage, Luxenberg explains the form *makka* as going back to an original form *maʿka*, which itself goes back to the Aramaic root *mʿak* – "to press, harass," which is still common in the modern Arabic colloquial of Syria, for example, in the verb *tamāʿakū* – "they quarreled." Thus the new interpretation would be:

> And it is He Who has restrained their hands from you and your hands from them <u>in the midst of a row</u>, after that He gave you the victory over them.

Luxenberg then goes on to explain the term *bakka*. He first mentions and dismisses the idea that this term refers to a "valley of tears." His point of departure is the Arabic script of the term *bi-bakka*:

بِبَكَّةَ

If we take away all the vowel signs and diacritical dots, the undotted rasm consists of four consonant characters: *BBkH*.

The capital letters represent so-called *archigraphemes*; that is, entities that can stand for more than one grapheme or letter. In this case, *B* can be read as a *y*, *n*, *t*, *ṯ*, or *b*. The *H* at the end of the word can represent the feminine ending -*ah* or the personal pronoun -*hu*, referring to the preceding word "bayt." All characters except the first and the last can also represent double consonants. As already briefly anticipated in his first book,[13] Luxenberg reads this form as follows: *tayyaka-hu* – "he fenced in, enclosed." The whole sentence then would be:

> *inna ʾawwala baytin wuḍiʿa li-n-nāsi la-llaḏī tayyaka-hu mubārakan wa-hudan li-l-ʿālamīna*
> This first (holy) house, which was built for mankind, is the one that he fenced in as a blessed (sanctuary) (and) for the guidance of the world.

What is meant here is the temple district. This understanding is corroborated by Surah 17:1:

> Glorified be He Who carried His servant by night from the Inviolable Place of Worship to the Far Distant Place of Worship the neighbourhood whereof We have blessed (*allaḏī bāraknā ḥawlahu*), that We might show him of Our tokens!

The form *tayyaka-hu*, however, is not Classical Arabic but rather the Syro-Aramaic verb *tayyeḵ* – "to rail or fence in" from the root *t-w-k* – "to be contained, enclosed." In Arabic, a similar root with an emphatic *ṭ* and a *q* exists, the corresponding form of which is *ṭawwaqa* – "to encircle."

In the second part of the same article, Luxenberg then offers a second possibility: instead of reading *tayyaka-hu*, the same consonant skeleton (rasm) could also be read as *bannaka-hu* – "(which) he founded." This form is not attested in Classical Arabic either, but in Syriac. In his Syriac-Arabic dictionary, J. E. Manna[14] translates this verb in Arabic as "ta-bannaka" and explains it as "to be at a certain place; to strike root; to become consolidated." Luxenberg considers the emendation

> *allaḏī bannaka-hu* (instead of: *bi-bakkata*) *mubārakan wa-hudan li-l-ʿālamīna*
> – which he founded of blessing and of guidance for all kinds of beings

as more plausible, especially when seen in context with the preceding text: "*inna ʾawwala baytin wuḍiʿa li-n-nāsi* – "the first House (of worship) appointed for men." The verb *wuḍiʿa* (passive of *waḍaʿa*) corresponds to the Syriac *sām*, for which Manna (483b) gives, among others, the Arabic equivalents: *assasa* (to found), and *šayyada*, *banā* (to build, to found).

7. Assessing the Alternatives

When diverging explanations for a given phenomenon have to be assessed and weighed against each other, the first step should always be to draw up a checklist of probabilities for different relevant criteria. The explanation with the highest score is then the most likely to be the correct one, or at least the one that comes closest to the truth. What would the criteria be in our case?

First, we have to be concerned about the origin of primary sources, for example manuscripts, inscriptions, coins, and so on. How old and how well attested are they? Is it possible that modifications occurred in the process of transmission?

Then, in case we are dealing with linguistic material, we have to question its philological value and/or probability. How ambiguous is the writing system, the grammar; how ambiguous are the word forms? Are other interpretations possible? Does the language of the source match the postulated era it allegedly stems from, for example regarding sound changes, semantics, morphology, letter forms, and so forth.

Then, in case we are dealing with longer texts, their context has to be scrutinized. Do all parts of the text match, or is it possible that interpolations or later corrections have been made?

And finally, does the explanation match the historical context as we know it from material evidence.

In the following, the attempt shall be made to assess the diverging and mutually exclusive explanations, with this checklist in the back of our minds, and to come to a preliminary conclusion. The question whether Islam emerged in a town called Mecca or whether Mecca is the same town as Ptolemy's Macoraba[15] will be left out of the discussion on purpose, as the topic of this article is only the attestation of the forms *makka* and *bakka* in the Koran.

7.1. The Traditional View

As we have seen, the traditional view is unclear, as there are two different explanations that exclude each other. The first one assumes that *bakka* and *makka* are in fact variants of the same word. Here the question arises whether such a variation is probable.

First of all it is an oversimplification to talk about a "b" and an "m." The phonemes /b/ and /m/ in Arabic have only got two realizations (so-called *allophones*), namely [b] and [m], whereas in Aramaic (and Hebrew) in many positions the phoneme /b/ was pronounced as a [v] or possibly as a [β] (bilabial voiced fricative, in transliteration: *ḇ*). Fricatives are continuants (like the nasals [m] and [n]), not plosives (like [b] and [p]), so it is not impossible that in some positions an original [β] alternates with [m]. A phonetician would say that they are both bilabial continuants, the first sound a fricative, the second a nasal. A classic example is the word for "time," which in Classical Syriac is *zaḇnā* and in Arabic *zamān*, a form also attested for older forms of Aramaic. So it is not surprising that in the above mentioned South Arabic forms /m/ and /b/ alternate. A similar phenomenon has been described for alleged ancient Arabic dialects.[16] Such alternations due to position are also known in Old Irish, the dot above the letter *ṁ* indicating that the [m] in other forms of the word has to be pronounced as a nasalized [β] in this position.[17]

The well-known Indian city presently called *Mumbai* and formerly *Bombay* is another example that might be adduced. Some Modern Indo-Aryan languages have the name in a form with *m* (Marathi, Konkani, Gujarati, Kannada), others in a form with *b* (Hindi and Urdu).

Still, the statement from *Wikipedia*, "In South Arabic, the language in use in the southern portion of the Arabian Peninsula at the time of Muhammad, the *b* and *m* were interchangeable," is not to be taken as a satisfactory explanation for the forms *bakka* and *makka*, and this for a number of reasons: First of all, it is not irrelevant whether the sounds in question are to be found in the middle of a word or in initial position. The phonemes /b d g/ in Spanish for example are plosives in initial position: [b d g] but fricatives in most other cases: [β ð ɣ], much like in Syriac or Biblical Hebrew. In the world's languages a sound change like [b] > [β] or [v] between vowels is very common, the sound change [b] > [m] in the same position is much less common, though it occurs, but the same changes in initial position before a stressed vowel like in *bakka* and *makka* is extremely rare. In Classical Arabic as well as in Syriac it does not occur at all.

Here we have to ask ourselves what sound changes actually are and how they function in human speech. What we can state is that they do not happen randomly. They follow rules, and from the Neogrammarians[18] of the nineteenth century we know that sound changes (in specific positions) do not allow exceptions. So if Latin *ca* becomes Old French *cha* [ʧa], later [ʃa] (e.g., carolus > Charles; cantare > chanter; carus > cher; calidus > chaud), it should be found in *all* words. And if there are exceptions—there are quite a few—then they must be explained! The word c*ampagne* at first glance looks like an exception, but it could be a dialect word from the South of France or a word borrowed directly from Latin, which would explain the anomaly. And on closer inspection we find the form we would expect: "Champagne," as the name of a region of France.

A German example would be the sound change t > z (cf. *English*: ten – *German*: zehn, two – zwei, toe – Zehe). An exception would be English *tits* vs. German *Titten*. What we expect, according to the rule, is the form *Zitzen* for German. This word does in fact exist and it means "teats" (the "tits of a cow"), and it was borrowed from Northern German. So here—like in the case of French—the explanation for the exception is a loanword from a neighboring dialect.

Another point is the fact that "sacred" terms are usually more conservative in the preservation of sounds. The "holy spirit" is called "espirit*u* santo" in Spanish. The ending we would expect here, like in the adjective *san-*

to, is *-o*. The expected form "espírito" actually does exist in the closely related Portuguese. The reason for the anomaly is the fact that in the Latin word *spiritus*, *-ūs* belongs to the so-called *u*-declination, which normally merged with the more common *o*-declination, except in this "sacred" word.

A similar case is the word *Qurʾān* in modern Arabic dialects. Many of them, for example Egyptian[19] and Lebanese Arabic, have lost the former phoneme /q/ and replaced it by a glottal stop (ʾ, [ʔ]), the only exception being sacred words from Classical Arabic, like *Qurʾān*, not *ʾurʾān* as would have to be expected.

The sound change q > k is also attested in both Modern Arabic and ancient dialects,[20] so the real name might as well be *Baqqah*. According to the geographer Yāqūt al-Hamawī a town of the Lakhmids "at the Euphrates between Hīt and al-Anbār." Interestingly, one of the other two attested Kaabas of the Orient—the one in Sindād—was located there.

At this point another place name might be considered: Baalbek, Arabic Baʿlabakk, which might be interpreted as "Lord (*baʿl*) of *Bakkah*."

A last point to consider is the fact that sound changes are a diachronical phenomenon: they normally appear in two different layers of a language, for example between Old English and Middle English. In the case of *Qurʾān*, however, we have the two forms in the same layer.

To sum up, it would be very surprising if *makka* and *bakka* were really two pronunciations of the same name.

The old Arab grammarians and commentators of the Koran must have indeed felt uncomfortable with these two forms, otherwise the explanation of *bakka* as a separate name, derived from a verb *bakka* – "to break" ("breaker of the necks of tyrants") would not have been invented. This explanation is about as likely as Isidorus of Seville's etymology of the Latin word for "dog" – *canis*. The word *canis*, he thought, was derived from the verb *canere* – "to sing," because "a dog does *not* sing."[21]

7.2. Regnier's Explanation

Regnier only explains the form *bakka*, and does so with a parallel from the Psalms. Biblical motives can be found in many passages of the Koran, but in this case we are dealing with a similar wording, which is rather uncommon. The fact, however, that the parallel Biblical text is from the Psalms is decisive. No other Biblical book is explicitly mentioned in the Koran, but the Psalms are referred to in many places, for example, in Surah 17:55:

وَلَقَدْ فَضَّلْنَا بَعْضَ النَّبِيِّينَ عَلَى بَعْضٍ وَآتَيْنَا دَاوُودَ زَبُورًا

. . . wa-la-qad faḍḍalnā baʿḍa n-nabiyyīna ʿalā baʿḍin wa-ʾātaynā dāwūda zabūr^an^

> . . . And we preferred some of the Prophets above others, and unto David We gave the Psalms.

Phonetically the Hebrew and Arabic forms are unproblematic, as they both go back to the same root consonants, and even semantically the interpretation as "valley of tears" is plausible. What makes this explanation most likely, however, is the fact that a "blessing" is talked about in the following clause, the corresponding forms in Hebrew and Arabic going back to the same Semitic root.

Moreover it should be added that the root *b-k-ʾ* – "to weep" has indeed got a religious meaning in Islam, as can be seen from the term *bakkāʾ* in the *Encyclopedia of Islam*:

> BAKKĀʾ, pl. *bakkāʾun, bukkāʾ*, "weepers," ascetics who during their devotional exercises shed many tears. Older Islamic asceticism and mysticism are characterised by a strong consciousness of sin, by austere penance, humility, contrition and mourning. Laughter was denounced. An outward sign of this attitude is the act of weeping. The Ḳurʾān (Sūra xvii, 109: "and they fall down on their chins, weeping," and Sūra xix, 58: "when the signs of! the Merciful were recited before them, they fell down, prostrating themselves, weeping"), and then, above all, the ḥadith acknowledge and commend the shedding of tears during devotional exercises. The Prophet Muḥammad is said to have wept audibly at times in the course of the ritual prayers. A similar behaviour is reported of the first Caliphs Abu Bakr and ʿUmar.

7.3. Luxenberg's Explanation

The explanations offered by Christoph Luxenberg are in several ways remarkable. As we have seen, he has offered two possible explanations for both *makka* and *bakka*. This inevitably means that at least two of his explanations must be wrong, a clear indication that he can hardly be blamed for being apodictic. The first explanation for *makka*, the Syriac verb *maḵ, māk, mḵeḵ* – "be laid low, be spread or strewn flat" would be phonetically unproblematic, and it yields an acceptable meaning, *makka* simply being a place designated as "low and flat," thus *bi-baṭni makka* meaning "in the middle of the valley." *Makka* is not attested as the normal word for "valley," but it is quite possible that a place name might go back to a root meaning "low" or "flat." This rather etymological explanation could even be accepted within the framework of mainstream Islamic Studies.

Although there is no strong argument against this interpretation, Luxenberg dismissed it rather early.

His alternative explanation for the form, *makka* going back to *maʿka*, meaning "hand-to-hand fight," has several weak spots. The phonetic problem remains why in the word *kaʿba* the old Arabs apparently had no problems to pronounce an *ʿayin* [ʕ] before a consonant, while in the case of *maʿka* they dropped this sound and instead doubled the following consonant, especially if we consider the adduced dialect form *tamāʿakū* – "they quarreled." Moreover, the root *mʿak* is only found in one of the standard dictionaries (Brockelmann); the copious *Thesaurus Syriacus* does not know this root. Even there, it is only represented by one form, no nominal forms or derived stems are attested, and the meaning "perturbavit [to press, harass]" does not match the postulated meaning in the Koran very well. There is an Arabic root *maʿaka* – "to rub," but here as well the meaning does not really fit the context. It must, however, be admitted that his new interpretation of *makka* as a "row," a "hand-to-hand fight," fits the context better than any of the other explanations.

Luxenberg's first alternative reading for *bi-bakka* does in fact make sense semantically: *tayyaka-hu* – "he fenced in, enclosed" is not attested in Arabic but could well be a borrowing going back to Syro-Aramaic *tayyeḵ* – "to rail or fence in." That a fence is built around a sanctuary is certainly not unusual. But here again, Luxenberg prefers another explanation, although his first choice is not really problematic.

As in the case of *mʿak*, the second alternative reading *bannaka-hu* – "(which) he founded" is hardly attested in Syriac. None of the standard dictionaries has got it; the only one mentioning it is Manna's Syriac-Arabic lexicon. So the word is far from being common, although it is precisely Manna's dictionary that proves that the root actually did have an equivalent in at least one variant of Arabic, although its use must have been very limited. Here again, Luxenberg's reason for favoring his second alternative is certainly semantic. It makes more sense to "build" or "found" a sanctuary than to "fence" it.

8. Preliminary Conclusion

Of the above-mentioned alternative explanations for the terms *makka* and *bakka* the traditional ones are probably the weakest, at least the popular etymology of *bakka*. The explanation that both forms are phonetic variants of the same etymon is possible but rather improbable due to linguistic reasons.

Luxenberg's favored solutions would match the context of the Koranic passages better than any of the other explanations, but they go back to hardly attested Syriac roots. The two dismissed alternative interpretations are certainly preferable from a linguistic point of view.

Regnier's hypothesis seems to be the least problematic, both from a phonetic and a semantic perspective. If it should turn out to be the correct explanation it would mean that the author of the Koranic verse in question knew the Psalms very well, which on the other hand would not be too surprising considering the frequency with which this Biblical book, in Arabic *zabūr*, is mentioned in the Koran.

A last point that might corroborate Regnier's view ironically comes from Christoph Luxenberg himself. In his article about the "Mysterious Letters," which can be found in the present anthology, he explains these enigmatic characters as a kind of shorthand logograms that indicate that certain passages from the Psalms are to be recited or sung in liturgy. What distinguishes this article from so many other publications about the Koran is the fact that it is the only conclusive and plausible explanation of these letters ever written. Not even Islamic tradition managed to cook up a convincing story allowing us to make heads or tails of these symbols.

In general terms, we can state a rule for the assessment of differing views: For a theory A to be considered superior to theory B it must be able to explain everything theory B can plus something more.

In the case of the "Mysterious Letters," Luxenberg's view ("theory A") can explain the whole phenomenon in a satisfactory way—but there is no theory B, at least not so far.

So if he should be right, he would have proved the enormous role the Psalms played in the emergence of the Koran, which would make it very likely that *bakka* is in fact the "valley of tears."

Notes:

* *We thank Gerd-R. Puin for many interesting ideas, valuable pieces of information, important references, and for proofreading the present article.*

---

1 The translations used are the English one of Marmaduke Pickthall, *The Meaning of the Glorious Koran: An Explanatory Translation* (London, 1930), in digital form available at http://al-quran.info, and the literal rendering of the scholarly German translation of Rudi Paret, *Der Koran: Übersetzung*, 1st ed. 1966, 9th ed. (Stuttgart, 2004); the transliteration of Koranic passages is from Hans Zirker's version, which is downloadable at http://www.eslam.de/begriffe/t/transliteration_des_quran.htm.

2 The particle *li-* can also indicate the agent in a passive sentence, so "built by men" would be an alternative translation.

3 P. Bearman, T. Bianquis, C. E. Bosworth, E. van Donzel and W. P. Heinrichs, eds., *Encyclopaedia of Islam*, 2nd ed. (Leiden: Brill, 1954–), vol. 6 (1991), p. 144 ff.

4 A. Guillaume, trans., *The Life of Muhammad: A Translation of Isḥāq's "Sīrat Rasūl Allāh*, with introduction and notes by A. Guillaume (Oxford: Oxford University Press, 1955), p. 47.

5 "Bakkah," *Wikipedia*, http://en.wikipedia.org/wiki/Bakkah (accessed May 4, 2014).

6 The references adduced at the bottom of the page are: [11] Philip Khûri Hitti (1973). *Capital Cities of Arab Islam* (Illustrated ed.). University of Minnesota Press. p. 6; [8] Kees Versteegh (2008). C. H. M. Versteegh and Kees Versteegh, ed.

Encyclopedia of Arabic Language and Linguistics, volume 4 (Illustrated ed.). Brill. p. 513.

7 Originally published as A. Regnier, "Quelques Enigmes Littéraires de L'inspiration Coranique," *Le Muséon* 52 (1939): 145–62; a translation by Susan Boyd-Bowmann appeared as "Some Literary Enigmas of Koranic Inspiration" in Ibn Warraq, ed., *Koranic Allusions* (Amherst, NY: Prometheus Books, 2013), pp. 251–64; here p. 253.

8 The following quotations from the Koran and the Bible were not taken from Regnier's article.

9 Syriac Bible (United Bible Societies, 1979).

10 Cf. J. Payne Smith, ed., *A Compendious Syriac Dictionary, a Syriac Dictionary Founded upon the Thesaurus Syriacus of R. Payne Smith* (Oxford, 1903).

11 The other three explanantions were published in Trier in the German magazine *Imprimatur* in two parts. The periodical's focus is more theological than linguistic, therefore he renounces on original scripts and scientific transliterations. The article is available online at http://www.imprimatur-trier.de/2012 /imp120406.html#fnB4 (first part, October 2012) and http://www.imprimatur-trier.de/2012/imp120706.html (second part, December 2012; both accessed May 6, 2014).

12 Edouard-Marie Gallez, *Le messie et son prophète: Aux origines de l'Islam*, vol. 2, *Du Muhammad des Califes au Muhammad de l'histoire* (Versailles: Éditions de Paris, 2005), pp. 311 ff.

13 Christoph Luxenberg, *Die Syro-Aramäische Lesart des Koran: Ein Beitrag zur Entschlüsselung der Koransprache*, 2nd ed. (Berlin: Verlag Hans Schiler, 2004), p. 336 n. 352.

14 J. E. Manna, *Chaldean-Arabic Dictionary* (Beirut 1975), 70a.

15 Patricia Crone has argued convincingly that it is highly unlikely that Macoraba is Mecca. See Patricia Crone, *Meccan Trade and the Rise of Islam* (Oxford: Basil Blackwell, 1987), pp.135–36.

16 Allegedly a sound change to be found in the dialect of the kommt es bei den Tayy, a small Christian tribe, in whose dialect *sīn* and *ṣād* and *ʿayn* and *hamza* (glottal stop) were also confused—all changes unknown in Classical Arabic; see Chaim Rabin, *Ancient West-Arabian* (London, 1951), p. 201.

17 R. P. M. and W. P. Lehmann, *An Introduction to Old Irish* (New York, 1975), p. 16. The phenomenon of alternating consonants according to preceding words is generally called "mutation" in Celtic languages; in this case the mutation is "lenition."

18 This group of linguists was called "Junggrammatiker" in German. Some of its representants were luminaries of their disciplines like August Leskien (1840–1916), Karl Brugmann (1849–1919), Hermann Osthoff (1847–1909), Otto Behaghel (1854–1936), Karl Venner (1846–1896). Most of their findings were not published in separate general monographs but rather in specialized publications dealing with Indoeuropean comparative linguistics or Slavic studies, with the exception of Hermann Paul (1846–1921), *Prinzipien der Sprachgeschichte* (Halle: Max Niemeyer, 1880); English edition, *Principles of the History of Language* (College Park, MD: McGroth Publishing, 1891).

19 Cf. Kurt Munzel, *Ägyptisch-Arabischer Sprachführer* (Wiesbaden, 1958), p. 9.

20 About the sound change q > k see August Haffner, *Texte zur Arabischen Lexikographie* (Leipzig: Harrassowitz, 1905), concerning Ibn al-Sikkīt, *Kitāb al-Qalb wa-l-ibdāl*, p. 37 f.; about *Baqqah* see Ibn al-Kalbī, *Kitāb al-Asnām* (The Book about Idols), ed. Ahmad Zakî, p. 45.

21 *Canis a non canendo*—"dog from not singing; [it is called] dog, because it does not sing]," cf. Isidorus of Seville, *Etymologiae* 1, 29, 3. Other examples are: *bellum a nulla re bella*— "war [bellum] because there are no beautiful thing [re bella] in it," and *lupus a non lupendo*— "wolf because he does not mourn."

Appendixes

1. Charts of Arabic, Hebrew, and Aramaic

SYRIAC						NAME		TRANSCRIPTION	HEBREW	ARABIC
SERTO OR JACOBITE				NESTORIAN OR CHALDAEAN	ESTRANGHELO	SYRIAC	HEBREW			
ALONE	FINAL	INITIAL	MEDIAL							
ܐ	ܐ			ܐ	ܐ	ʾālap	ʾālep	ʾ	א	أ
ܒ	ܒ	ܒ	ܒ	ܒ	ܒ	Bēṯ	Bēṯ	b	בּ ב	ب
ܓ	ܓ	ܓ	ܓ	ܓ	ܓ	Gāmal	Gimel	g	גּ ג	ج غ
ܕ	ܕ			ܕ	ܕ	Dālaṯ	Dāleṯ	d	דּ ד	د ذ
ܗ	ܗ			ܗ	ܗ	Hē	Hē	h	ה	ه
ܘ	ܘ			ܘ	ܘ	Waw	Wāw	w	ו	و
ܙ	ܙ			ܙ	ܙ	Zayn	Zayin	z	ז	ز
ܚ	ܚ	ܚ	ܚ	ܚ	ܚ	Ḥēṯ	Ḥēṯ	ḥ	ח	ح
ܛ	ܛ	ܛ	ܛ	ܛ	ܛ	Ṭēṯ	Ṭēṯ	ṭ	ט	ط
ܝ	ܝ	ܝ	ܝ	ܝ	ܝ	Yōḏ	Yōḏ	y	י	ى
ܟ	ܟ	ܟ	ܟ	ܟ	ܟ	Kāp	Kāp	k	כּ כ ך	ك خ
ܠ	ܠ	ܠ	ܠ	ܠ	ܠ	Lāmaḏ	Lāmeḏ	l	ל	ل
ܡ	ܡ	ܡ	ܡ	ܡ	ܡ	Mīm	Mēm	m	מ	م
ܢ	ܢ	ܢ	ܢ	ܢ	ܢ	Nūn	Nūn	n	נ	ن
ܣ	ܣ	ܣ	ܣ	ܣ	ܣ	Semkaṯ	Sāmeḵ	s	ס	س
ܥ	ܥ	ܥ	ܥ	ܥ	ܥ	ʿē	ʿayin	ʿ	ע	ع
ܦ	ܦ	ܦ	ܦ	ܦ	ܦ	Pē	Pē	p	פּ	ف
ܨ	ܨ			ܨ	ܨ	Ṣāḏē	Ṣāḏē	ṣ	צ	ص
ܩ	ܩ	ܩ	ܩ	ܩ	ܩ	Qōp	Qōp	q	ק	ق
ܪ	ܪ			ܪ	ܪ	Rēš	Rēš	r	ר	ر
ܫ	ܫ	ܫ	ܫ	ܫ	ܫ	Šīn	Šīn / Śīn	š	שׁ	ش
ܬ	ܬ			ܬ	ܬ	Taw	Tāw	t	תּ	ت ث

2. Syriac Writing

TABLE OF THE SYRIAC WRIT

hebr.	phönik.	Sendschirli 800 v.Chr. Teima 500 v.Chr.	aram.Siegel &c. 8–400 Jahrh.v.Chr.	nabatäisch 1–100 n.Chr.	palmyren. ↑–270 n.Chr.	ägypt.aram. Papyruase 3–1.Jahr v.Chr.	palästin.–syr.Mss. XII(?)Jahre.n.Chr. (n.Wright &Land)	A.D.411 edessenisches Estrangelo Pal.Soc.I.Pl.XI.	A.D.509 Wright I Cat.syr Br.Mus.) Pl.IV	nach A.D.509 Wr.Pl.IV,Note

Nöldeke's Syriac Grammar. – English Edition

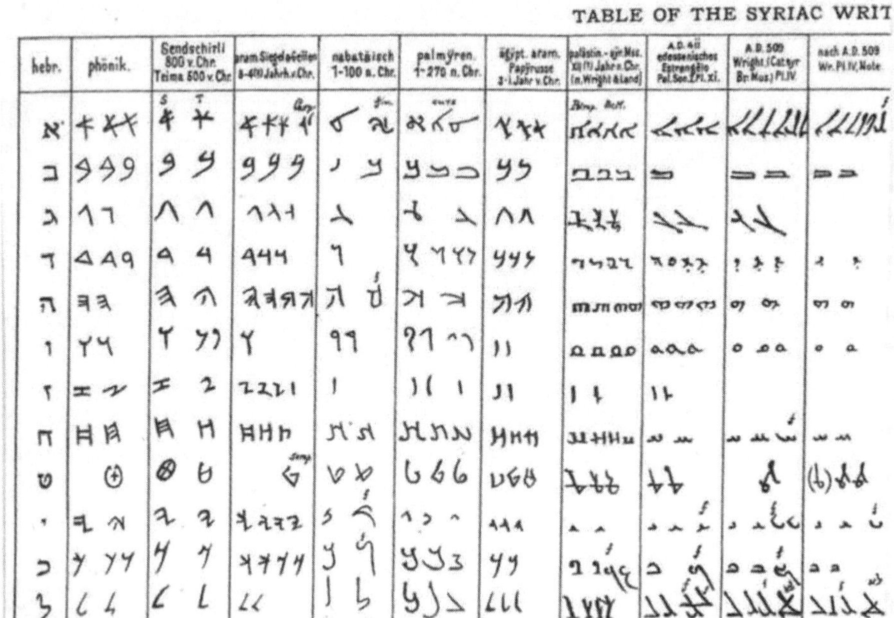

'TEN-CHARACTER. DRAWN BY J. EUTING.

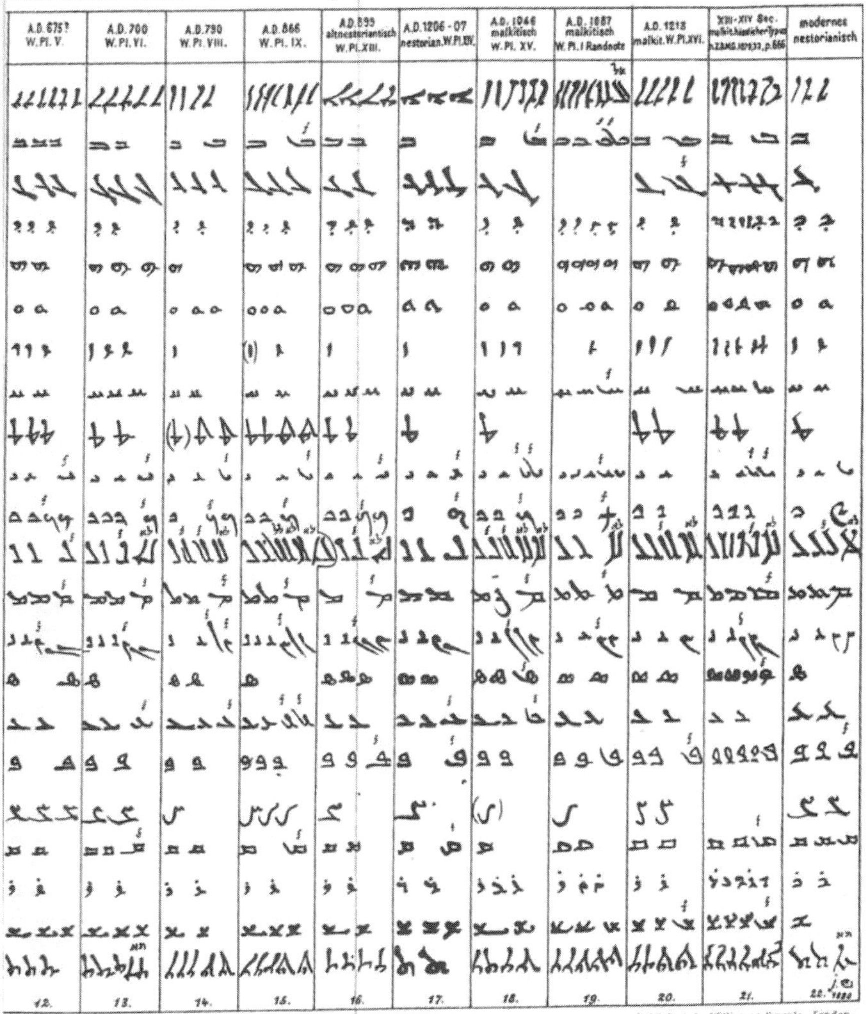

Published by Williams & Norgate, London.

3. List of Contributors

1. **J. M. S. Baljon** (1919–2001) studied theology and oriental languages at the universities of Leiden and Utrecht, obtaining a doctorate in 1949 for his thesis *The Reforms and Religious Ideas of Sir Sayyid Ahmad Khan*. He also wrote *Modern Muslim Koran Interpretation* (1961) and *Religion and Thought of Shah Wali Allah Dihlawi* (1986). Dr. Baljon taught for many years at Leiden University.

2. **Anton Baumstark** (1872–1948), a German philologist, liturgist, and orientalist, was seen as the founder of the study of the Christian Orient and of comparative liturgy. After receiving training in classical and oriental philology in Leipzig, he completed a doctorate with a thesis in Greek-Syriac translation literature, which was followed by a habilitation thesis on the Syriac-Arabic biographies of Aristotle at the University of Heidelberg. He founded and edited the journal *Oriens Christainus*, and his writings include *Die christlichen Literaturen des Orients* (2 vols., 1911) and *Geschichte der syrischen Literatur mit Ausschluss der christlich-palästinischen Texte* (1922).

3. **John Bowman** (1916–2006), a graduate of Glasgow University, received his PhD in 1951 from Oxford for his thesis *The Pharisees and Rabbinic Studies*. He taught Hebrew and Semitic studies at Glasgow and Leeds before taking up an appointment as professor and chairman of the Department of Middle Eastern Studies at Melbourne University in 1959. His writings include *Samaritan Documents Relating to Their History, Religion, and Life* (1977).

4. **Philippe Gignoux** (born 1931) is a scholar of Pre-Islamic Persia affiliated with the École pratique des hautes études, Paris. He received his doctorate from the University of Paris for his thesis *L'Anthroponymie de l'Iran sassanide à partir des sources épigraphiques*. Other writings include *Glossaire Des Inscriptions Pehlevies Et Parthes* (1972), *Sceaux sassanides de diverses collections privées* (1983), and *Incantations Magiques Syriaques* (1987).

5. **Moshe Gil** (born 1921) graduated from Tel Aviv University in 1966 and received a PhD in 1970 from the University of Pennsylvania for *The Institution of Charitable Foundations in the Light of the Cairo Geniza*. Gil is professor emeritus of the Chaim Rosenberg School of Jewish Studies at Tel Aviv University and holds the Joseph and Cecil Mazer Chair in the History of the Jews in Muslim Lands. His publications include *A History of Palestine, 634–1099* (1992); "The Medinan Opposition to the Prophet," in *Jerusalem Studies in Arabic and Islam* (1987); and "The Origin of the Jews of Yathrib," in *Jerusalem Studies in Arabic and Islam* (1984).

6. **Sidney Griffith** (born 1938) is a professor of Early Christian Studies at the Catholic University of America, specializing in Arabic Christianity, Syriac monasticism, medieval Christian-Muslim encounters, and ecumenical and interfaith dialogue. His publications include *The Church in the Shadow of the Mosque* (2007), *The Bible in Arabic* (2013), and *The Beginnings of Christian Theology in Arabic* (2002).

7. **Markus Gross**, linguist (esp. Phonetics and Phonology, Romance Studies, Indo-European Comparative Linguistics, Historical Linguistics, Oriental Studies); from the third anthology on co-editor of the *Inârah* series (together with K.-H. Ohlig).

8. **Alfred Guillaume** (1888–1965) received his DD from Oxford in 1934 for *The Scholasticism of Christianity and Islam*. He was a visiting professor at the American University of Beirut, and he was later elected a member of the Arab Academy of Damascus and the Royal Academy of Baghdad. He was the first foreign lecturer on Christian and Islamic Theology at Istanbul University. Guillaume was known for his translation of Ibn Ishaq's *Life of Muhammad* (1955). Other publications included *Traditions of Islam* (1924) and *Islam* (1954).

9. **Adolf von Harnack** (1851–1930) was a German Lutheran theologian and professor of Church History in Leipzig (1876), Giessen (1879), Marburg (1886), and Berlin (1888). A member of the Academy of Sciences, and devoted to the study of the New Testament and Early Church History, his most significant result was his *Lehrbuch der Dogmengeschichte* (3 vols. 1885–1889), which traced the influence of Hellenistic philosophy on early Christian writing. Harnack's questioning of tradition led him to doubt the authenticity of the Gospel of John, in favor of the Synoptic Gospels. He played an important role in the founding of Kaiser-Wilhelm-Gesellschaft.

10. **Fr. Michel Hayek** (1928–2005) was a Lebanese scholar devoted to the study of Maronite theology and liturgy, and to the defense of Oriental Christianity. Father Hayek's works include *Le Christ de l'Islam* (1959), his 1980 lecture "L'Eglise Maronite et la terre," and *Le Christ, le Liban et la Palestine* (1974).

11. **Robert M. Kerr** (born 1968) read Classics and Semitics at Tübingen and Leiden Universities. At the latter, he received his doctorate on the survival of Punic in Roman North Africa. Some of his published academic work can be found at www.academia.edu.

12. **Christoph Luxenberg** is the pseudonym for a scholar who has been engaged in research and teaching in Germany for many years, specializing in Semitic philology. His years of teaching Classical Arabic, as well as several vernaculars or dialects, and Syriac in German universities informed his comparative study of the two languages, giving him a deeper understanding that went beyond grammars and dictionaries. His works include *Die syro-aramäische Lesart des Koran: Ein Beitrag zur Entschlüsselung der Koransprache* as well as numerous journal articles.

13. **Albert F. H. Naccache** (born 1945) graduated from the Institut d'Etudes Politiques de Paris in 1969. He has a Master of Science in physiology from the American University of Beirut, 1972, and he earned his PhD for the thesis *The Long-Span History of the Mashriq and Its Structures* from the University of California at Berkeley, 1985. He taught in the Department of Arts and Archaeology, Lebanese University, Beirut (section I) from 1986 until 2009. His writings range from studies on the Mashriqian (Semitic) Languages, the archeology of Beirut, and the history of the Mashriq, to human and language evolution.

14. **Hans Joachim Schoeps** (1909–1980) was a conservative German-Jewish historian of religion. From 1950 onward Schoeps was Professor of Religious and Intellectual History at the University of Erlangen. He studied philosophy of religion, history, and literature at the universities of Berlin, Marburg, Heidelberg, and Leipzig and went on to author numerous scientific studies on the history of religion and philosophy of religion of Judaism; his collected works were published in sixteen volumes between 1990 and 2006. His works include *Jüdischer Glaube in dieser Zeit: Prolegomena zur Grundlegung einer systematischen Theologie des Judentums* (1932), *Geschichte der jüdischen Religionsphilosophie in der Neuzeit* (1935), *Jüdisch-christliches Religionsgespräch in neunzehn Jahrhunderten: Die Geschichte einer theologischen Auseinandersetzung* (1949), and *Theologie und Geschichte des Judenchristentums* (1949).

15. **Shlomo Pines** (1908–1990) studied at Heidelberg, Genève, and Berlin, where he received a doctorate in philosophy in 1936 with a thesis titled *Beiträge zur islamischen Atomenlehre*. From 1937 to 1939, Pines was lecturer in the history of science at the University of Paris. In 1952 he was appointed professor at the Hebrew University, Jerusalem. His publications include *An Arabic Version of the Testimonium Flavianum and Its Implications* (1971) and *The Collected Works* (1979–1986).

16. **Munther Younes** (born 1952) received a PhD in Arabic linguistics from the University of Texas at Austin in 1982. He worked as an assistant professor of English and linguistics in Saudi Arabia from 1982 to 1986 and then as an Arabic instructor at the Defense Language Institute in Monterey, California, from 1987 to 1990. Dr. Younes has been working as a senior lecturer in Arabic language and linguistics and director of the Arabic Program at Cornell University since 1990. He has published five textbooks for teaching Arabic as a foreign language as well as a number of articles on Arabic linguistics, Arabic pedagogy, and the language of the Koran.